OXFORD PAPERBACK REFERENCE

The Concise Oxford Companion to
Classical Literature

Margaret Howatson is a Fellow and Tutor in Classics at St Anne's College, Oxford. She is the editor of the second edition of *The Oxford Companion to Classical Literature*.

Ian Chilvers is a freelance writer and editor. He is the editor of *The Concise Oxford Dictionary of Art and Artists*.

Oxford Paperback Reference

The most authoritative and up-to-date reference books for both students and the general reader.

Abbreviations
ABC of Music
Accounting
Archaeology*
Architecture*
Art and Artists
Art Terms*
Astronomy
Bible
Biology
Botany
Business
Card Games
Chemistry
Christian Church
Classical Literature
Classical Mythology*
Colour Medical Dictionary
Colour Science Dictionary
Computing
Dance*
Dates
Earth Sciences
Ecology
Economics
Engineering*
English Etymology
English Grammar*
English Language*
English Literature
English Place-Names
Euphemisms
Film*
Finance
First Names
Food and Nutrition
Fowler's Modern English
   Usage
Geography
King's English
Law

Linguistics
Literary Terms
Mathematics
Medical Dictionary
Medicines*
Modern Quotations
Modern Slang
Music
Nursing
Opera
Operatic Characters*
Philosophy
Physics
Plant-Lore
Political Biography*
Politics
Popes
Proverbs
Psychology*
Quotations
Sailing Terms
Saints
Science
Shakespeare*
Ships and the Sea
Sociology
Superstitions
Theatre
Twentieth-Century Art*
Twentieth-Century Poetry
Twentieth-Century World
   History
Weather Facts
Women Writers
Word Games
World Mythology
Writers' Dictionary
Zoology

*forthcoming

The Concise
Oxford Companion to

Classical
Literature

Edited by
M. C. HOWATSON
and
IAN CHILVERS

Oxford   New York

OXFORD UNIVERSITY PRESS

Oxford University Press, Great Clarendon Street, Oxford OX2 6DP

Oxford New York
Athens Auckland Bangkok Bogota Bombay
Buenos Aires Calcutta Cape Town Dar es Salaam
Delhi Florence Hong Kong Istanbul Karachi
Kuala Lumpur Madras Madrid Melbourne
Mexico City Nairobi Paris Singapore
Taipei Tokyo Toronto Warsaw

and associated companies in
Berlin Ibadan

Oxford is a trade mark of Oxford University Press

British Library Cataloguing in Publication Data
Data available

Library of Congress Cataloging in Publication Data
Howatson, Ian Chivers.
p.   cm.—(Oxford reference.)
"Revised and condensed version of the Oxford companion to
classical literature, which was published in 1989."
1. Classical literature—Dictionaries.   2. Classical dictionaries. I. Chilvers, Ian.
II. Howatson, M. C.   Oxford companion to classical literature.
III. title.   IV. Title: Concise companion to classical literature. V. Series.
880.9'001'03—dc20   PA31.H69   1993   92-18585

ISBN 0-19-282708-1 pbk

10 9 8 7

Printed in Great Britain by
Biddles Ltd
Guildford and King's Lynn

PREFACE

The Concise Oxford Companion to Classical Literature is a revised and abridged version of *The Oxford Companion to Classical Literature*, which was published in 1989. It is approximately a third shorter than the parent work, but most of the entries that form the heart of the book—the biographies of authors, summaries of major works, and accounts of literary genres—are unchanged or only slightly amended. A few of the more obscure mythological figures have been omitted, but generally the entries in this area likewise stand more or less unchanged. The reduction in length has been achieved by dropping or radically shortening the long general entries that are not specifically literary—such as agriculture, architecture, and army—and by recasting in pithier form those on the historical, political, and topographical background. Thus the entries on major wars, for example, now give a much briefer outline of events (although the references within them to the ancient literary sources are unchanged), and the entries on cities and states are similarly condensed, serving more to place them for the reader and to point out their literary associations than to describe their development and institutions. There has also been some rearrangement (and occasional amplification) of material in the interests of accessibility; for example, Romulus, the legendary founder of Rome, now has his own entry rather than a cross-reference to the article on the history of the city.

The period covered by this book begins with the entry of the Greeks into Greece in about 2200 BC. Its stopping-point is not so easily identifiable. Readers will find that from the third century AD there are entries for Christian writers who were important from a classical viewpoint. From this time to the closing of the philosophy schools at Athens in AD 529 only the most significant people and events are selected for inclusion, but the fate of classical literature is traced in outline through the Dark Age to the Renaissance. The book is intended for any reader who is curious to find out about the classical world, rather than for the specialist, so I have tried to present the generally accepted view (or indicate the range of possibilities) in every case rather than be over-lavish in the use of 'possibly' and 'perhaps'. I may therefore on occasions sound more dogmatic than I feel, or achieve more consistency and coherence, especially in the matter of dates, than the evidence would warrant.

Some guidance is given in the headwords to their pronunciation in English: the stressed syllable is followed by the sign '; and long vowels are marked by the sign ‾. Classicists should note that in many cases the English stress accent or syllabic length does not coincide with the Greek or Latin original. All Greek is transliterated (v = y, χ = ch) and all Greek and Latin is translated. Proper nouns are spelt by and large in the Latinized form in which they have become familiar in English, but where these are headwords their transliterated Greek form is also given. Roman names generally appear under the *nomen* (second name, or middle name of three), e.g. Gaius *Marius*, Quintus *Fabius* Maximus; but in many cases where the subject is best known by his *cognomen* or third name the entry is under that headword, e.g. Marcus Tullius *Cicero*, Tiberius Sempronius *Gracchus*. Where there are several individuals with the same name, the entries appear in chronological order. Geographical names are given in classical form (except for those which are very commonly used in English even in a classical context, e.g. Athens, Adriatic Sea). Modern equivalents, where they are judged to be helpful or interesting, are also indicated. A discretionary policy of cross-referencing has been adopted. An asterisk before a word draws the reader's attention to its existence as a separate entry only where more information may be found of direct relevance to the subject.

I owe a considerable debt of gratitude to many people: to the Principal and Fellows of St Anne's College for leave of absence, and in particular to Margaret Hubbard, Gwynneth Matthews, Barbara Mitchell, Emily Kearns, and Mary Whitby for generously undertaking duties which were properly mine; to Catriona, Gabrielle, James, and Robert Howatson for their contribution of an entry apiece, and for warm encouragement; to Robert for pertinent if searing comment; to Mark Bostridge for constructive help; to Rachel Woodrow and Janet Randell for flawless typing; to the editors of the Press for their great patience and unobtrusive advice. Most of the work of revision for this concise edition has been carried out by Ian Chilvers, to whom I give warm thanks.

A debt is particularly owed to Sir Paul Harvey, compiler of the original *Oxford Companion to Classical Literature*, published in 1937. The new *Companion* is very different in detail, assumptions, and emphasis, reflecting the discoveries and reappraisals of half a century of scholarship and the fact that readers of today are in some respects more ignorant than those of fifty years ago but in others more sophisticated and demanding (though fewer people know the ancient languages, many more have visited the countries in which they were once spoken, and have read the guide-books, toured the museums, or watched television programmes). Nevertheless, the pattern and proportions of the *Companion* are closely based on Harvey's (the indispensable book summaries are still largely in his words), and anyone who attempts to revise and build on his work can feel nothing but admiration for the original conception and execution.

I am very deeply obliged to Alastair Howatson, my most dedicated reader and critic. I have striven to satisfy his exacting standards as well as his admiration for Cicero. My inadequacies and errors will, I know, be pointed out in customary trenchant fashion by the classical undergraduates past and present of St Anne's College.

St Anne's College, Oxford   M. C. H.

A

Abas, in Greek myth, son of *Lynceus (2) and Hypermnestra, father of *Acrisius and *Proetus.

Abdē'ra, Greek city on the coast of *Thrace, founded in the seventh century BC and refounded in the sixth by Ionians from Teos in Asia Minor, among them the Greek lyric poet *Anacreon. It was the birthplace of the sophist *Protagoras and the philosopher *Democritus, but was nevertheless proverbial for the stupidity of its inhabitants.

Absy'rtus, see APSYRTUS.

Abȳ'dus, Milesian colony on the Asiatic side of the Hellespont, at its narrowest point. Here *Xerxes crossed to Europe in 480 BC during the *Persian Wars, and here, in Greek myth, lived *Leander.

Acadē'mica (*Academics*), dialogue by *Cicero ((1) 5) discussing the philosophical views of the Greek New *Academy, particularly the Sceptic view of *Carneades on the impossibility of attaining certain knowledge. The work, written in 45 BC, was originally in two books, but while Cicero's 'publisher' *Atticus was having copies of it produced, Cicero remodelled it into four books. Both 'editions' went into circulation; of the first edition we possess the second book, *Lucullus*; of the second edition we possess part of the first book, known as *Academica posteriora*. In the latter, *Varro expounds the evolution of the doctrines of the Academy, from early dogmatism to the Scepticism of Arcesilaus and Carneades. In *Lucullus* that interlocutor attacks the position of the Sceptics. Cicero defends the Sceptic view and approves Carneades' doctrine of accepting what seems most probably true.

Acadē'mus, see ACADEMY.

Academy (Akadēmia or Akadēmeia; the earlier Greek name was Hekademeia), originally a shrine in olive groves sacred to the hero Akademos (or Hekademos) on the western side of Athens near the hill of Colonus. In classical times it was also the site of a gymnasium, surrounded by gardens and groves. Here, perhaps as early as the 380s BC, Plato established his school, consequently known as the Academy; it survived continuously until AD 529, when the Christian emperor Justinian closed the philosophy schools in Athens. Plato was buried nearby. Sulla cut down the trees during his siege of Athens in 87–86 BC, but they must have grown again, for Horace, who studied at Athens, refers to the 'woods of Academus' (*Epistles* II. 2. 45). Finds on the site in the twentieth century include schoolboys' slates, some with writing on them.

Although the Academy gave its name to a school of philosophy which, broadly speaking, continued to teach philosophy and science in accordance with Plato's own teaching (see PLATO 3), its doctrines naturally changed direction several times before it was closed. For this reason, and for convenience, ancient writers several centuries after Plato divided the history of the Academy into periods designated by numbers or, more usually, by the terms Old, Middle, and New; they did not always agree (nor do authorities today) on where the divisions occurred.

The *Old Academy* describes the period when the school was headed by Plato and his conservative successors Speusippus, Xenocrates, Polemon, Crantor, and Crates, down to 265 BC. The *Middle Academy* is the term often used for the period initiated by Arcesilaus (or Arcesilas) of Pitane (*c*.315–242 BC) who gave the school the *Sceptical approach which it kept with minor variations until the leadership of Antiochus of Ascalon in the first century BC. The *New Academy*, sometimes taken to include Arcesilaus, is more usually agreed to have started in the mid-second century BC under Carneades (d. 129), who developed Scepticism further.

The destruction of the Academy with

its library during the sack of Athens by the Roman general Sulla in 86 BC broke the direct link with Plato. Antiochus of Ascalon, head of the (Fifth) Academy from 86 to 68 BC, abandoned the Scepticism of his predecessor Philo of Larisa and aimed to return to what he thought was genuine Platonism by maintaining that there was essential agreement between the doctrines of the Old Academy, the Aristotelians (*Peripatetics), and the Stoics. Although not original he exerted great influence; his lecture audience included Cicero, to whom his eclecticism appealed and who later proclaimed himself an Academic (see ACADEMICA). For the development of Platonism after Antiochus see MIDDLE PLATONISM.

Little is known of the Academy in the following centuries until it appears in the fifth century AD as a centre of Neoplatonism, particularly under the leadership of *Proclus, who powerfully influenced the form in which the Greek philosophical inheritance was passed on to Renaissance Europe.

Aca'rnan, son of *Alcmaeon.

Aca'stus, son of *Pelias and Anaxibia, and brother of Alcestis. He sailed with the *Argonauts against his father's wishes; see also PELEUS.

acatalectic, metrical term; see METRE, GREEK 6.

Acca Lare'ntia or **Larentina,** an obscure Roman goddess who was worshipped at the Larentalia on 23 December. According to one of several conflicting legends she was the wife of the herdsman *Faustulus, mother of the original Fratres Arvales (see ARVAL PRIESTS) and the nurse of Romulus and Remus.

accents, Greek. The invention of accent marks as a guide to the pronunciation of classical Greek, denoting not stress but the pitch of the voice, has been attributed to the Alexandrian scholar *Aristophanes of Byzantium c.200 BC. It may have been prompted by the need to guide Greek speakers in the pronunciation of by then unfamiliar words (e.g. in Homeric epic) and to teach the language to foreigners. The low tones are left unaccented, except in a few cases where the grave accent is used, and the high and compound tones are indicated by the acute and circumflex accents.

A'ccius or **Attius Lucius** (170–c.86 BC), Latin poet and dramatist of Pisaurum in Umbria. He was a younger contemporary of *Pacuvius and the last great Roman tragedian. Cicero records that he heard him lecturing early in the 80s. Fragments of some 46 named tragedies are extant, most of those which are recognizable being free translations of Greek tragedies. He also wrote two *fabulae praetextae* on Decius Mus and Brutus the Liberator. Accius created for his tragedy a vigorous and dignified style much admired by later rhetoricians. He was an influential figure in his day, and of great importance for the development of Latin literature. Cicero quoted him often and Virgil imitated him. His *Atreus* contained the tyrant's phrase *oderint dum metuant* ('let them hate, so long as they fear'), said by Suetonius to have been frequently quoted by the emperor Caligula.

His other works show him as a scholar with a particular interest in spelling reform (e.g. using u and s, not y and z), and a collector and critic of the works of his predecessors. His books include the *Annales*, books of hexameter poetry on months and festivals, and the *Didascalica*, on the history of the Greek and Roman theatre and other literary matters, from Homer to Accius himself. The few surviving fragments suggest that it may have been written in a mixture of prose and verse, thus anticipating the Menippean satires of *Varro.

Ace'stes (Aigestēs, Aigestos), in Virgil's *Aeneid*, son of the river-god Crimisus and a Trojan woman, Egesta or Segesta; he entertains Aeneas and his comrades in Sicily. The city of Egesta (Segesta) was originally named Acesta after him by its founders, the Trojan followers of Aeneas who remained in Sicily.

Achae'a, Achae'ans (Achaioi). In historical times these denoted two regions and peoples, one in south-east Thessaly (Phthiotan Achaea), the other a narrow strip in the north of the Peloponnese between Elis and Sicyon, a territory comprising twelve small towns forming a loose confederacy. In Homer the names are used both in a restricted and in a general sense. They may denote the region and people in south Thessaly where Achilles lived, and also the people in the north-east Peloponnese (Argolis), the followers of Agamemnon who ruled Mycenae and the surrounding area. But they may also denote, by extension, Greece and the Greeks in general. Modern scholars sometimes use the name 'Achaeans' to refer to the Greeks of the *Mycenaean period. Peloponnesian Achaea plays little part in Greek history until the third and second centuries BC when the *Achaean Confederacy became the chief power in Greece. From 146 BC this area was attached to the Roman province of Macedonia, but in 27 BC the name Achaea was given to the senatorial province which included a large part of Greece.

Achaean Confederacy or **League,** a confederacy of ten Achaean cities, founded in 280 BC to resist the power of Macedon (it revived an older confederacy that had flourished in the fourth century BC). The Confederacy became the leading power in the Peloponnese, and defeated Sparta in 188. It frequently came into conflict with Rome, however, and in 167 Rome deported to Italy a thousand eminent Achaeans, including the historian *Polybius, for political investigation; they were released in 150. In 148 there was again trouble with Sparta. Rome intervened and imposed harsh terms on the Confederacy, which rebelled and declared war; but after a short struggle it was completely defeated by Mummius in 146 and dissolved.

Achaeme'nidae, the first royal house of Persia, so named from the legendary hero Achaemenes (Persian, Hakhāmanish), founder of the family. To this family belonged Cyrus, Cambysēs, and Darius. The line perished in 330 BC at the hands of Alexander the Great.

Acha'rnians (*Acharnēs*), Greek comedy by *Aristophanes, produced at the Lenaea in 425 BC by Callistratus, perhaps because the author was too young to produce it himself. It is his first surviving play, and won first prize in the dramatic competition.

The Athenians had for six years been suffering the horrors of the *Peloponnesian War, the devastation of their territory, plague in the overcrowded city, and shortage of food, but their spirit was unbroken. The Acharnians (inhabitants of an Attic deme lying north-west of Athens near the foot of Mount Parnes), of whom the chorus of the play is composed, had been among the chief sufferers, their territory having been repeatedly ravaged.

The play opens with Dikaiopolis, an Athenian farmer, sitting and waiting for the meeting of the assembly, sighing for the good times of peace. Amphitheos ('demigod') appears, sent by the gods to arrange peace with Sparta, but unfortunately lacking the necessary travelling-money. This Dikaiopolis provides, but the treaty with Sparta is to be a private one for himself alone. Amphitheos presently brings the treaty, narrowly escaping from the chorus of bellicose and infuriated Acharnians. Dikaiopolis celebrates with a procession consisting of his daughter and servants, and this leads to a dispute between Dikaiopolis and the chorus on the question of peace or war, in which *Lamachus, portrayed as a typical general, takes part. Dikaiopolis is allowed to make a speech before being executed as a traitor; and to render this more pathetic borrows from the tragedian Euripides some of the stage properties that make his tragedies so moving. As a result the chorus are won over to the pro-peace view of Dikaiopolis. After the *parabasis* (see COMEDY, GREEK 3), in which the poet defends his position, there is a succession of amusing scenes illustrating the benefits of peace. A Megarian comes to Dikaiopolis to buy food (Athens had been trying to starve out Megara by a blockade), offering in exchange his little daughters disguised as pigs in sacks. A Boeotian brings eels and other good things, and wants in return local produce of Attica; he is given an informer tied up in a sack. A farmer wants peace-salve for his eyes, which he has cried out over the loss of his oxen; and so on. Finally Lamachus has to march off through the snow against the Boeotians, and returns wounded by a vine-stake on which he has impaled himself, while Dikaiopolis celebrates the *Anthesteria with the priest of Dionysus.

This play has been interpreted as a serious plea for peace on the part of the poet.

Achā'tēs, in Virgil's *Aeneid*, the faithful friend and lieutenant of Aeneas, frequently referred to as *fidus Achates*, 'faithful Achates'. He is in the epic tradition of faithful friends, comparable with Patroclus, friend to Achilles, and Pirithous, to Theseus.

A'cheron, in Greek myth, one of the rivers of the Underworld (see HADES). The name was also that of an actual river in southern Epirus, which, issuing from a deep and gloomy gorge, passed through the lake Acherusia and after receiving the waters of the tributary Cocytus fell into the Thesprotian Gulf. In Hellenistic and Latin poetry the name denoted the Underworld itself.

Achillē'id (*Achillēis*), epic poem in hexameters by the Roman poet *Statius on the story of *Achilles, of which only the first book and part of the second exist, the work having been cut short by the poet's death. The poem describes how Thetis, anxious that her son Achilles shall not take part in the Trojan War (from which she knows he will not return), removes him from the care of the Centaur *Chiron to the island of Scyros. It relates his adventures there in the disguise of a girl, his discovery by Ulysses, and departure for Troy.

Achi'llēs (Akhilleus), in Greek myth, only son of the mortal *Peleus, king of Phthia in Thessaly, and Thetis, a seanymph, daughter of Nereus (see also PARIS, JUDGEMENT OF). In the Trojan War Achilles was the chief hero on the Greek side; Homer draws his portrait once and for all in the *Iliad*, the plot of which turns on Achilles' ungovernabl^ anger. He came to Troy with a contingent of fifty ships and many followers usually referred to as Myrmidons (for which name see AEACUS). When he sulked in his tent and refused to fight after his quarrel with Agamemnon, as related in the *Iliad*, the Greeks were driven back to their ships and almost overwhelmed. Then followed the intervention and death of his friend Patroclus in the battle at the hands of the Trojan hero Hector, and Achilles' terrible grief. After reconciliation with Agamemnon, he slew Hector, taking further vengeance for Patroclus' death by dragging the body behind his chariot. The *Iliad* ends with Achilles, purged of anger and grief, allowing Priam, Hector's father, to ransom the body.

The *Aethiopis* tells how Achilles killed Penthesilea, queen of the Amazons, who was fighting on the Trojan side. Mourning her for her beauty, he was mocked by *Thersites and killed him in a rage; subsequently he killed *Memnon. Soon afterwards he was himself killed, shot in the heel by Paris (or by Apollo); see below. Odysseus saw him in the Underworld (*Odyssey* 11), but it was said later that he lived immortal on an island in the Black Sea. After the fall of Troy his ghost claimed Polyxena, daughter of Priam, as his prize, and she was sacrificed on his tomb.

In these accounts Achilles has a passionate nature and seems more savage than the other Greeks. His treatment of Hector's body and his sacrifice of Trojan prisoners at Patroclus' funeral are both stigmatized as evil deeds. When roused to anger he spares no one and has no respect for a visible god, but he shows great devotion to his friend Patroclus. He is aware that his life is fated to be short, his death at Troy having been foretold.

The poets of the *Epic Cycle and later authors add to the story of Achilles. It was said that in infancy he was dipped in the river Styx by his mother Thetis (or anointed with *ambrosia by day and held in the fire at night) to make him invulnerable. She was interrupted by Peleus, and in anger abandoned her husband and the child, who remained vulnerable in the heel by which she had held him; it was in his heel that Achilles according to epic tradition received his death wound from an arrow shot by Paris. He had his education from the Centaur *Chiron. When the Greek contingents were gathering for Troy, Peleus or Thetis, seeking to save him from his fated death, hid him on the island of Scyros at the court of King

Lycomedes dressed as a girl and called, according to one source, Pyrrha. (Suetonius says that the emperor Tiberius liked to puzzle the scholars at his court with questions such as, 'What was the name of Achilles when he hid himself among the girls?') The king's daughter Deidameia bore him a son *Neoptolemus (sometimes called Pyrrhus). When the seer Calchas told the Greeks that Troy could not be captured without Achilles, Odysseus sought him out, after which he went willingly to Troy, by way of Mysia, where he wounded *Telephus, Aulis, where the incident concerning *Iphigeneia took place, and Tenedos, where he slew Tenes, king of the island and son of Apollo. There are also various stories of his exploits at Troy not related in the *Iliad*, notably the killing of *Cycnus (2) and *Troilus.

Achi'llēs Ta'tius, see NOVEL, GREEK.

Ācis, see GALATEA.

Aco'ntius, in Greek myth, youth from the Greek island of Ceos who being in love with an Athenian girl Cydippē threw her an apple on which he had written, 'I swear to Artemis to marry none but Acontius.' This she read aloud, as was usual in the ancient world, and being thus bound by the oath she had inadvertently made she fell ill whenever her parents tried to marry her elsewhere. In this way Acontius won her.

A'cragas (Lat. Agrigentum, modern Agrigento—until 1927 Girgenti), one of the richest and most famous of the Greek cities in Sicily, founded c.580 BC on the south-west coast by a colony from nearby Gela. It first came to power under the tyrant *Phalaris and continued to prosper under the tyrant *Theron. After Theron's death his son Thrasydaeus was overthrown and a democracy established in which the philosopher *Empedocles took part. The democracy continued until Acragas was sacked by the Carthaginians in 406. It revived to some extent in the time of Timoleon (d. c.334 BC) but suffered badly in the Punic Wars. In the time of the Roman governor Verres it was again wealthy, and with the rest of Sicily received full Roman citizenship after Julius Caesar's death in 44 BC.

Acri'sius, in Greek myth, son of Abas, king of Argos, and father of *Danae. His brother was Proetus.

Acro'polis ('upper town'), the citadel, standing on high ground, of a Greek town. The most famous is the Acropolis of Athens, a rocky plateau about 50 m. (165 ft.) high, the flat summit measuring about 300 m. east to west and 150 m. north to south, and inaccessible except by a steep slope on the west. It was the fortress and sanctuary of the city, and had been enclosed by a massive wall as early as the thirteenth century BC. All previous fortifications, buildings, and statues were destroyed in the Persian occupation of 480–479 BC (see PERSIAN WARS). The walls were rebuilt by *Themistocles and *Cimon and in celebration of the final defeat of the Persians a statue of Athena Promachos by *Pheidias was erected in the 450s. Pheidias was directed by *Pericles to superintend the latter's general scheme for the rebuilding of the Acropolis. First came the *Parthenon, then the *Propylaea, Temple of Athena Nikē, and *Erectheum, as well as many lesser sanctuaries such as that of *Artemis Brauronia.

acta, under the Roman empire, an emperor's enactments which magistrates and succeeding emperors swore to observe, unless they had been explicitly rescinded immediately after an emperor's death: *acta senatūs* ('enactments of the senate'), under the empire, the official record of proceedings in the senate; *acta diurna* ('daily events'), a gazette of social and political news published daily from 59 BC and read both in Rome and in the provinces.

Actae'on, in Greek myth, son of *Aristaeus and Autonoë, daughter of *Cadmus. For some offence, either because he boasted that he was a better hunter than Artemis or because he came upon her bathing, the goddess changed him into a stag, and he was torn to pieces by his own hounds.

A'ctium, promontory in the south of Epirus, off the west coast of Greece, where Octavian defeated the fleets of Antony and Cleopatra on 2 September 31 BC. This battle marked the end of the

Roman republic and introduced the empire.

Ade'lphoe or **Adelphi** ('brothers'), Roman comedy by *Terence adapted from Menander and Diphilus (see COMEDY, GREEK 6), produced in 160 BC.

Aeschinus and Ctesipho are the two sons of Demea. Ctesipho is brought up by his father in the country, but Aeschinus is entrusted to his uncle Micio and brought up in the town. The theme of the comedy is the contest between two methods of education. Demea makes himself hated and distrusted by his harshness and frugality; Micio makes himself loved and trusted by his indulgence and open-handedness. Aeschinus has seduced an Athenian girl Pamphila, living in modest circumstances, whom he loves and wishes to marry. Ctesipho, whom his father believes a model of virtue, has fallen in love with a music-girl. Aeschinus, to help his brother, carries off this girl from the slave-dealer to whom she belongs and brings her to Micio's house. He is therefore suspected of carrying on an affair with her just when his own girl-friend needs his support. The truth becomes known; Aeschinus is forgiven by Micio and his marriage arranged. Demea is mortified at the revelation of Ctesipho's behaviour. Finding that his boasted method of education has earned him only hatred, he suddenly changes his attitude and makes a display of geniality, forcing his old bachelor brother into a reluctant marriage with the bride's mother, endowing one of her relatives with a farm at his brother's expense, and obliging him to free his slave and give him a good start in life—showing that even geniality can be overdone.

The *Adelphoe* was played at the funeral games of Aemilius *Paullus.

ad Here'nnium, Rheto'rica, see RHETORICA.

Admē'tus, in Greek myth, son of Pheres and king of Pherae in Thessaly. When Zeus killed *Asclepius for restoring Hippolytus to life, Apollo, the father of Asclepius, furious at this treatment of his son, took vengeance on the *Cyclopes who had forged Zeus' thunderbolt, and slew them. To expiate this crime Zeus made him for a year the servant of Admetus, who treated him kindly. Apollo in gratitude helped him to win *Alcestis as his bride. At the bridal feast it was revealed that Admetus was fated to die imminently, but Apollo again intervened and by making the Fates drunk persuaded them to grant Admetus longer life, provided that at the appointed hour of his death he could persuade someone else to die for him. Admetus' father and mother having refused, his wife Alcestis consented, and accordingly died. Just after this, Heracles, on his way to one of his Labours, visited the palace of Admetus who, in obedience to the laws of hospitality, concealed his wife's death and welcomed the hero. Heracles presently discovered the truth, went out to intercept Death, set upon him, and took from him Alcestis, whom he then restored to her husband.

For Euripides' treatment of the story see ALCESTIS.

Adoniazū'sae, the title of Idyll 15 of *Theocritus.

adonean, see METRE, GREEK 8 (i).

Adō'nis, in Greek myth, a beautiful youth, son of *Cinyras, king of Cyprus, by his daughter Zmyrna or Myrrha. Their union was brought about by Aphroditē in revenge for Zmyrna's refusal to honour the goddess. When her father discovered the truth and was about to kill her the gods turned her into a myrrh tree. Adonis was born from this tree. He was very beautiful from birth, and Aphrodite fell in love with him. One story says that she placed him in a chest and gave him to Persephone to take care of, and Zeus decreed that for part of the year he should stay with her and for the remaining part with Aphrodite. Another story relates that Adonis, having been brought up by nymphs, was out hunting when Aphrodite met him and fell in love with him. He was killed by a wild boar, and from his blood sprang the rose, or from Aphrodite's tears the anemone.

The story of Adonis has been explained as a vegetation myth, in which the god dies every year and is restored to life with the growth of new crops. The name could be oriental in origin, from the

Semitic *Adon*, 'Lord'. Other explanations of this strange myth have been suggested. The cult of Adonis reached Athens probably from Cyprus in the fifth century BC; his festival was marked by women mourning and lamenting his death, and by the setting on the housetops of the 'Gardens of Adonis', seedlings in shallow soil which withered as soon as they sprang up.

Adra'stus, mythical king of Argos at the time of the conflict of Polyneices and Eteocles for the kingdom of Thebes (see OEDIPUS). He was the son of Talaus and Lysimachē. After a quarrel with another branch of the royal family he fled to Sicyon, where the king made him his heir. He became king of Sicyon, but then made his peace at Argos and returned there, giving his sister Eriphylē in marriage to Amphiaraus. To his court came the exiles *Tydeus and Polyneices. The latter married his daughter Argeia, the former her sister Dēipylē. Adrastus undertook to restore them to their kingdoms and began by leading an army, the *'Seven against Thebes', to set Polyneices on the throne of Thebes. When the expedition was defeated, Adrastus escaped, thanks to the swiftness of his horse Arīon, the offspring of Poseidon and Demeter. In his old age he successfully led the sons of the Seven, the *Epigonoi, against Thebes, but died on his way home from grief at the loss of his son, Aegialeus, who alone had fallen in the attack. His grandson Diomedes became king.

Adriatic Sea (Gk. Adrias, Lat. Mare (H)Adriaticum or (H)Adria), the gulf between Italy and the Balkan peninsula; in the south it meets the Ionian Sea (east of Sicily). Its name is derived from the Etruscan town of Atria (or Hatria; modern Adria), not very far from the mouth of the Po. The Adriatic is notoriously stormy.

Ae'a, in the story of the *Argonauts, the realm of *Aeētēs, later identified with Colchis.

Ae'acus, in Greek myth, son of Zeus and the nymph Aegina. He married Endeis and became the father of *Telamon (father of the Greater Ajax)

and of *Peleus (father of Achilles). He was a man of great piety. His prayers once ended a drought in Greece; on another occasion when the inhabitants of his island, Aegina, were destroyed by a plague, Zeus, to reward him, repeopled it by creating human beings out of ants (*myrmēkes*); they were therefore called Myrmidons, the name by which the subjects of Peleus and Achilles are known in Homer. After his death he became, with *Minos and *Rhadamanthys, a judge of the dead in the Underworld, imposing punishments for misdeeds in life.

Aeae'a (Aiaiē), in Homer's *Odyssey*, the island of *Circē, situated in the stream of Ocean (see OCEANUS).

aediles, at Rome, originally two plebeian magistrates, named from the *aedes* or temple of *Ceres, where they superintended the cult, one which was particularly important to the *plebs*. Their administration was soon extended to public buildings in general and especially to the archives. In 367 BC their number was increased to four by the addition of two *curule aediles elected from the patricians. The office of aedile was elective and annual, not an essential part of the *cursus honorum* but the lowliest office to permit its holder to enter the senate.

Aē'don, in Greek myth, daughter of Pandareōs and wife of Zēthus. Envying Amphion's wife *Niobē for her many children, she plotted to kill them. By mistake she slew her own child, Itylus (or Itys), and mourned for him so bitterly that the gods changed her into a nightingale, *aedon*. (Compare the story of Procne: see PHILOMELA.)

Ae'dui or **Haedui,** Gallic tribe which in Roman times occupied a region corresponding with modern Burgundy. Their chief town was Bibractē (Mont-Beuvray, near Autun). They became allies of Rome *c.* 121 BC, and gave support to Julius Caesar during most of the Gallic Wars, joining Vercingetorix (of the Arverni) somewhat reluctantly in his revolt of 52 BC; see COMMENTARIES I (book 7). Under the empire they were the first Gallic tribe to have members in the senate at Rome.

Aeë'tēs, in Greek myth, king of Colchis; he was the son of *Helios, brother of *Circē, and father of *Medea. See ATHAMAS and ARGONAUTS.

Aega'tēs I'nsulae, islands off Lilybaeum in Sicily, near which was fought in 241 BC the naval battle in which C. Lutatius Catulus, the Roman admiral, defeated the Carthaginian fleet, so terminating the First *Punic War.

Aegean Sea (Aigaios pontos), the part of the Mediterranean between Greece and Asia Minor. The origin of the name is uncertain but was connected by some with Greek *aigis*, 'storm' and by others with Aegeus, father of *Theseus.

Aegeus, see THESEUS.

Aegi'aleus, son of Adrastus and the only one of the *Epigonoi to be killed in the expedition against Thebes.

Aegi'mius, in Greek myth, the king of Doris in Greece who asked Heracles for help to expel the *Lapiths from his land. Heracles asked as his reward the right of his descendants to claim asylum in Doris. Later the *Heracleidae (from whom the Dorian kings claimed descent) were believed to have settled there, and thus were 'Dorians'. Aegimius' sons Dymas and Pamphylus together with Heracles' son Hyllus gave their names to the three Dorian tribes. See DORUS.

Aegī'na. 1. Nymph, daughter of the river-god Asopus, who was carried to the island (see below) by Zeus, to whom she bore *Aeacus.

2. Island of some 90 sq. km. (35 sq. miles) in the Saronic Gulf, about 20 km. (13 miles) south-west of Athens, famous in Greek myth, as the realm of *Aeacus, and in history. Around 1100 BC it was conquered by the Dorians who introduced the Dorian dialect and customs (see DORIAN INVASION). In the seventh century it became subject to the Argive tyrant *Pheidon. It soon developed great commercial importance and gradually built up a navy which by 500 BC had no rival in Greece. In 506 began the long feud with neighbouring Athens, whose navy was developed partly to combat the Aeginetan threat. In 457/6 Aegina was decisively defeated by Athens and com-

pelled to join the *Delian League. In 431, at the outbreak of the *Peloponnesian War, which the Aeginetans helped to foment, the Athenians expelled the whole population from the island and resettled it with Athenian *cleruchs. The exiles were restored by Lysander in 405, after which Aegina played a minor role in history.

aegis, attribute of the Greek gods Zeus and Athena, usually represented as a goat-skin or skin-covered shield, later having a fringe of snakes and a *Gorgon's head, used to frighten enemies and protect friends.

Aegi'sthus, see PELOPS.

Aegospo'tami (Aigospotamoi, 'goat's rivers'), small river in the Thracian Chersonese, with at one time a town of the same name on it. Off the mouth of the river Athens suffered her final naval defeat of the *Peloponnesian War in 405 BC. For the famous fall of a meteorite there see ANAXAGORAS.

Aegy'ptus. 1. See DANAUS. **2.** See EGYPT.

Ae'lian (Claudius Aeliānus) (AD c.170–235), a Greek rhetorician, a *Stoic, who taught at Rome. His writings were much drawn upon by later moralists. His extant works are: *On the Characteristics of Animals*, a collection of excerpts and anecdotes of a moralizing nature in seventeen books; and *Historical Miscellanies* (usually known as *Varia Historia*), a similar collection dealing with human life and history in fourteen books.

Ae'lius Aristei'des, see ARISTEIDES.

Ae'lius Lampri'dius, see HISTORIA AUGUSTA.

Ae'lius Spartia'nus, see HISTORIA AUGUSTA.

Aemi'lius Paullus, Lucius, see PAULLUS.

Aenē'as, in Greek and Roman myth, one of the Trojan leaders in the Trojan War, son of *Anchises and the goddess Aphroditē (at Rome, Venus), and the subject of Virgil's Latin epic, the *Aeneid*. In the account of the Trojan War given in Homer's *Iliad* he is not depicted as an outstanding hero, being descended from the younger branch of the Trojan royal house (Priam, king of Troy, was of the older branch), but the Greek god Poseidon prophesies of him that he and his descendants will rule over the Trojans. Hence there developed, after Homer, the legend of his flight from ruined Troy with his father, son *Ascanius, and the *penates (indicative of his pious and dutiful nature), and of his subsequent wanderings. (See TABULA ILIACA.) Hellanicus the Greek *logographer writing in the fifth century BC makes the first certain literary allusion to Aeneas crossing the Hellespont and coming to the West; he may even allude to his being in Italy. There is no evidence that the Romans at that time thought of him as their founder, although artistic evidence shows that Aeneas was known in Etruria by the late sixth century BC. The Greek historian *Timaeus a century or so after Hellanicus speaks of Lavinium as Aeneas' first foundation in Italy. These were Greek views of Italy, attributing to Greek heroes (or in this case a Trojan hero) the settlement of the known West. Perhaps at the same period *Alba Longa began to claim that Aeneas was the ancestor of her kings. Rome soon took over, however, and developed the legend of Aeneas as founder of the Romans, national pride leading her to connect her own history with that of the Greek world. When *Pyrrhus launched his attack against Rome in 281 BC he saw himself as the descendant of Achilles making war on a colony of Troy. The story of Rome's Trojan origin took full shape in the third century BC when it was synthesized with the chronologically difficult legend of the foundation of Rome by *Romulus (a descendant of Aeneas through his mother). Probably both the Roman historian *Fabius Pictor and the Roman poet *Ennius filled the gap between the supposed dates of the fall of Troy (1184) and Romulus' foundation of Rome (753) with a sojourn by Aeneas' descendants at Alba Longa. Certainly by the third century BC the story later known to Virgil was well-established and familiar. From the second century BC the Julian gens ('clan'), Julius Caesar above all, exploited their descent from Aeneas and Venus for political aggrandizement. Virgil, while celebrating in the Aeneid the

Trojan ancestry of Octavian, adopted son of Julius Caesar, also re-created Aeneas as a national hero.

Aeneas is portrayed by Virgil as *pius*, 'dutiful', conscious of his heavy destiny as founder of Rome, obedient to the will of the gods, a responsible leader to his followers, and a devoted father and son.

Aene'as Ta'cticus ('the tactician'), probably Aeneas of Stymphalus, an Arcadian general of the fourth century BC, named 'Tacticus' for his military treatises, one of which has survived, 'On the defence of fortified positions'. It is interesting for revealing social and political conditions in early fourth-century Greece, as well as for being a work outside the Attic literary tradition of its time.

Ae'nēid (*Aenēis*), Latin epic poem in twelve books of hexameters by *Virgil, composed during the last ten years of his life, 29–19 BC, after the battle of Actium (31 BC) had finally established the rule of Octavian (later the emperor Augustus). The poem is designed to celebrate the origin and growth of the Roman empire, the achievements both of Rome and of Augustus. The groundwork is the legend of Aeneas, the Trojan hero, who survived the fall of Troy and after long wanderings founded a Trojan settlement (Lavinium) in Latium in Italy, named after his Italian bride Lavinia, and became through his (Trojan) son Iulus the ancestor of the gens *Julia and founder of *Alba Longa (and ultimately of Rome). Virgil was still working on the poem when he died (it was edited after his death by his friends *Varius Rufus and Plotius Tucca), and indications of its incompleteness are some sixty half lines scattered throughout the poem which the poet would have expected to complete. It is unlikely that he intended to go beyond the present ending. There seems to have been pressure put on the poets of the day, perhaps by *Maecenas, to produce an epic on Augustus. Horace and Propertius both declined to do so, but from the introduction to the third book of the *Georgics* it seems clear that Virgil was promising such a work. In the event he produced an epic not simply on Augustus but on the origins of Rome. Even so Augustus eagerly awaited its completion, and in 23 BC had the poet read to the imperial family books 2, 4, and 6.

The poem is immensely complex. Its framework is Homeric epic, which entailed the presence of the gods and their interference in human action, as well as exploits of a heroic nature; individual episodes are indebted to Attic tragedy and to the *Argonautica* of *Apollonius Rhodius, as well as to the ancient Roman poets *Naevius and *Ennius, but it is permeated by Roman themes, Roman values, and Roman history. At a simple level the Roman people and their chief families are glorified by the representation of their ancestors in the heroic age; at the same time the triumphs of Roman history are shown prospectively, as leading up to the reign of Augustus. Not only Rome, but also Italy, is shown as part of the scheme of things. One striking feature of the poem is the conception of Italy as a single nation, and of Roman history as a continuous whole from the founding of the city to the promise of the empire. The religious beliefs underlying the poem are far more profound than the epic machinery of gods and goddesses of myth. Ancient beliefs and practices, treated with reverence, coexist with philosophical ideas taken from the Greeks and modified by Roman attitudes. The theology of book 6, and the moral issues of books 4 and 12, raise questions which defy a final answer. The love affair between Dido and Aeneas in book 4 in particular has been the subject of much debate, and the poet has been censured for giving such a shabby portrayal of Aeneas while so powerfully enlisting our sympathies for the Carthaginian Dido. But it is his great achievement, here and throughout the poem, to reveal not only Rome's divinely ordained destiny to rule, to pacify, and to civilize, but also the terrible suffering entailed, for conquerors and conquered alike, for the noble and the less noble, and for those caught up in the fates of others: Creusa, Turnus, Lausus, Pallas, and Mezentius. The events are as follows.

Book 1. Aeneas, who in the seven years since the fall of Troy has been making his way to Latium in Italy with the Trojan fleet, has just left Sicily. The goddess Juno, enemy of Troy and guardian of Carthage (which she knows is fated to be destroyed by a race of Trojan descent), has the wind-god Aeolus let loose a storm on the fleet. Some of the ships are wrecked, but the sea-god Neptune calms the storm; Aeneas and the remaining ships reach the Libyan coast. The Trojans are well received by Dido, queen of the newly founded Carthage; she has fled from Tyre, where her husband Sychaeus has been killed by his brother Pygmalion, the king. The goddess Venus, mother of Aeneas, fearful of both Juno and the Tyrians, arranges that Dido should fall in love with Aeneas.

Book 2. At Dido's request, Aeneas relates the fall of Troy and the subsequent events: the building of the Trojan Horse and the cunning of Sinon, the death of *Laocoon, the firing of the city, the desperate but unavailing resistance by the Trojans, Priam's death and Aeneas' own flight at the bidding of Venus; he tells how he carried his father Anchises on his shoulders and took his son Iulus (Ascanius) by the hand, how his wife Creusa, who followed, was lost, and his destiny revealed to him by her ghost.

Book 3. Aeneas continues his story. He and his companions build a fleet and set out. They land at Thrace, but leave after Aeneas finds there the grave of his murdered kinsman Polydorus, and hears his voice; they sail on to Delos. The Delian oracle tells them to seek the land that first bore the Trojan race. This they wrongly think means Crete, from which they are driven by a pestilence. Aeneas now learns that it means Italy. On their way there the Trojans land on the island of the *Harpies and attack them. The Harpy Celaeno prophesies that they shall found no city until hunger makes them 'eat their tables' (see book 7). At Buthrotum in Chaonia they find Helenus the seer (son of Priam) and Andromache. The seer tells Aeneas the route he must follow, visiting the Cumaean Sibyl and founding his city where by a secluded stream he shall find a white sow with a litter of thirty young. Going on his way, Aeneas visits the country of the *Cyclopes in Sicily; his father dies at Drepanum. From there he reaches Libya.

Book 4. Dido, though bound by a vow to her dead husband, confesses to her sister Anna her love for Aeneas. Juno and Venus arrange that the union of Dido and Aeneas should be sealed when a hunting expedition is interrupted by a storm and they take shelter in the same cave. The rumour of their love reaches Iarbas, a neighbouring king, who has been rejected by Dido and now in his anger appeals to Jupiter. The god commands that Aeneas should leave Carthage. When Dido realizes that the fleet is preparing to sail, she confronts Aeneas and pleads with him. He replies that he has no choice, and must go to Italy even against his will. Dido's fury does not stop the Trojan preparations, and even a last entreaty from her fails to weaken Aeneas' resolve. She prepares for death, and, having seen the Trojan fleet depart, takes her own life while cursing Aeneas and his descendants.

Book 5. The Trojans return to Sicily and are received there by their compatriot *Acestes. It is a year since Anchises died in the same place, and the anniversary is celebrated with sacrifices and games. The first event of the latter is a race between four ships. Gyas, captain of *Chimaera*, angrily pushes his helmsman overboard when he loses the lead to Cloanthus in *Scylla*; Sergestus in *Centaur* runs aground; Mnestheus in *Pristis* overtakes Gyas but just fails to catch Cloanthus. There follows a foot-race in which the leader, Nisus, having slipped and fallen, deliberately trips Salius so as to let his friend Euryalus win. In a boxing match between the Trojan Darēs and Entellus of Sicily, Aeneas stops the fight when Darēs is savagely attacked by the Sicilian. Next comes a competition with bows and arrows, and finally a display by thirty-six young horsemen led by Ascanius, an event which was later to become a tradition at Rome (see LUDUS TROIAE). Meanwhile the Trojan women, weary of their long wanderings, are incited by Juno to fire the ships; but only four are destroyed before a rain-storm quenches the flames in answer to Aeneas' prayer. Later the Trojans set sail again, some staying behind to found a new city under Acestes. The helmsman Palinurus falls asleep and is lost overboard.

Book 6. Aeneas visits the Cumaean *Sibyl and she foretells the trials he will face in Latium. At her bidding he plucks the *Golden Bough and descends with her through the cave of Avernus to the Underworld. Arriving at the river Styx they see the ghosts of the unburied dead unable to cross; among them is the helmsman Palinurus, who recounts his fate and begs for burial. On seeing the Golden Bough, Charon allows Aeneas and the priestess to cross the Styx; they send *Cerberus to sleep with a drugged cake. Beyond their cave they find various groups of the dead: infants, those unjustly condemned, those who have died of love (among them Dido, unmollified by the excuses Aeneas offers), and those killed in battle. They arrive at the entrance to Tartarus, where the worst sinners suffer torments, but go on until they reach Elysium, where the souls of the virtuous live in bliss. Here Aeneas greets his father Anchises, but tries in vain to embrace him. Aeneas sees ghosts drinking at the river *Lethē, and Anchises explains how they are the ones who will be reincarnated: over a long period they have been purged of all evil and now drink the waters so as to lose all memory. (This doctrine of rebirth may have been taken by Virgil from Plato or from Orphic–Pythagorean traditions: see MYSTERIES.) Anchises points out the souls of men who are destined to be illustrious in Roman history: Romulus, the early kings, the great generals, Augustus himself, and his nephew *Marcellus (to whose brief life Virgil makes touching allusion). After this Aeneas and the Sibyl leave the Underworld through the Ivory Gate, by which false visions are sent to mortals (the significance of this has been much debated). This book contains these lines (851–3) on the destiny of Rome which are central to the poem:

> *tu regere imperio populos, Romane,*
>   *memento;*
> *hae tibi erunt artes: pacisque imponere*
>   *morem,*
> *parcere subiectis, et debellare*
>   *superbos.*

(Roman, let your concern be to command the nations; your skills shall be these: to impose the rule of peace, to spare the submissive, and to crush the proud.)

Book 7. Aeneas and the Trojans reach the mouth of the Tiber and land in Latium. They fulfil the prophecy of the Harpy Celaeno (see book 3 above) by eating the bread cakes which they have used as platters during a meal. Lavinia, the daughter of Latinus, king of Latium, has many suitors of whom the most favoured is Turnus, king of the Rutulians; but Latinus has been told by his father's oracle that she must marry not a Latin but a stranger who will arrive. Ambassadors from the Trojans are welcomed by Latinus, who offers Aeneas alliance and his daughter in marriage. Juno sees the Trojans preparing to settle and summons the Fury Allecto, who stirs up mad hostility to the Trojans in queen Amata, Lavinia's mother, and in Turnus. When Ascanius is hunting, Allecto causes him to wound a stag which is kept as a royal pet, and a fight ensues. Latinus is powerless to stop the preparations for war, and the Italian tribes gather under their leaders; among these, apart from Turnus, are Mezentius, scorner of gods and a hated tyrant, Messapus, Virbius (son of *Hippolytus), and the Volscian warrior-maiden *Camilla.

Book 8. The god of the river Tiber encourages the anxious Aeneas, telling him to seek alliance with the Arcadians under Evander, who have founded a city on the Palatine hill (which will in the future be part of Rome). Rowing up the river, Aeneas sees on the bank a white sow with her litter, as had been prophesied. Evander promises his support. Vulcan, at the request of Venus, makes armour for Aeneas. Evander, who has shown Aeneas a number of places in his city which will eventually be famous sites in Rome, urges alliance with the Etruscans. Venus brings Aeneas his armour; it includes a shield on which are depicted various events in the future of Rome, down to the battle of Actium.

Book 9. Aeneas has told the Trojans to keep to their camp in his absence, and they refuse to join battle even when Turnus and his forces surround them. When Turnus tries to set fire to the Trojan ships, Neptune changes them into sea-nymphs. At night Nisus and Euryalus leave the camp in order to summon Aeneas. They kill a number of the enemy

in their drunken sleep, but are seen by a mounted column and surrounded; both are killed, after Nisus has bravely tried to save his friend. The Rutulians attack the Trojan camp, and Ascanius, in his first feat of battle, kills one who has been shouting taunts. Turnus is cut off inside the camp, and kills many Trojans before plunging into the river to escape.

Book 10. On Olympus the gods debate the conflict. Aeneas secures the alliance of Tarchon, king of the Etruscans, and sets out with him and with Pallas, Evander's son, to return to the Trojans. Turnus attacks them as their ships reach the shore. In the battle which follows Turnus kills Pallas. Juno contrives a phantom of Aeneas; Turnus pursues it on board a ship which bears him away. Aeneas wounds Mezentius and reluctantly kills the latter's son Lausus as he tries to protect his father; Mezentius mounts his faithful horse Rhaebus for a last attack on Aeneas before horse and rider are both killed.

Book 11. Aeneas celebrates the Trojan victory and laments the death of Pallas. The Latins send ambassadors and a truce is arranged. King Latinus and the Italian chiefs debate; Drances proposes that Turnus, being mainly responsible for the war, should settle it by meeting Aeneas in single combat. Turnus, scornful of Drances, accepts the challenge. The Latins now hear that the Trojans and Etruscans are advancing against them; Camilla and her Volscian cavalry confront the attackers. In the battle which follows Tarchon drags Venulus from his horse; Arruns seeks out and kills Camilla, who is avenged by Opis, messenger of the goddess Diana. The Volscians are defeated.

Book 12. The Latins are discouraged, and Turnus decides to fight Aeneas alone despite the efforts of Latinus and Amata to dissuade him. Preparations for the duel are made, but the Rutulians, already anxious about the outcome, are stirred up to intervene by Turnus' sister Juturna; the two armies join battle again. Aeneas is wounded by an arrow, but Venus heals him and he pursues Turnus; then Aeneas sees that the city of the Latins is unguarded and turns the Trojan army to attack it with fire. Amata, distraught, takes her own life. Turnus seeks out Aeneas and the armies draw back while the two leaders fight. Aeneas wounds Turnus with his spear and finally, enraged by the sight of his enemy wearing the spoils taken from Pallas, kills him with his sword.

Aeo'lic. 1. For the dialect see DIALECTS, GREEK. **2.** For the metre see METRE, GREEK 8 (i).

Ae'olis, the name given in classical times to the territory in the northern part of the west coast of Asia Minor, from the Troad to the river Hermus, which had been occupied by Aeolian Greeks (for the name see AEOLUS (2)). These Greeks, around the end of the second millenium BC, migrated from Boeotia and Thessaly and founded their first settlements in Lesbos; from there they spread northwards and along the coast.

Ae'olus. 1. Described in Homer's *Odyssey* as the son of Hippotēs, a mortal and a friend of the gods, to whom Zeus gave control of the winds. He was later thought of as the god of the winds. He lived on the floating island of Aeolia. He received Odysseus hospitably and gave him a leather bag in which he had secured those winds adverse to the latter's voyage. Virgil depicts him as keeping the winds imprisoned in a cave (*Aeneid* 1. 50–9). He is sometimes confused with (2).

2. Son of *Hellen and the legendary ancestor of the Aeolians; he was the father of *Sisyphus, *Athamas, *Salmoneus, *Alcyone, Calycē (mother of *Endymion), *Canacē, and other children.

Ae'pytus, SEE MEROPE.

aera'rium, the treasury of the Roman state, situated in the temple of Saturn below the Capitol, and containing also some state documents. The *aerarium sanctius* was a 'special reserve fund' drawn upon only in emergencies. The *aerarium militarē* was founded by the emperor Augustus in AD 6 to provide pensions for discharged soldiers.

Āë'ropē, wife of Atreus, seduced by Thyestes (see PELOPS).

Ae'schinēs, Athenian orator and great rival of *Demosthenes (2), born in Athens *c.*390 BC or earlier. Only three of his speeches survive. Of obscure family, he was (at least according to Demosthenes) first an assistant in his father's school, then a tragic actor, then a soldier, taking part in the battle of Mantinea in 362, then a clerk under *Eubulus, who controlled Athenian finances. By 348 he had embarked on a public career. Soon afterwards, he and Demosthenes were part of an embassy (led by *Philocrates) sent to negotiate peace terms with Philip II of Macedon. These were finally agreed in 346 but not until Philip had made further advances, thus bringing the Peace into disrepute. Demosthenes was now anxious to dissociate himself from the Peace, and became implacably hostile to Aeschines, who supported it, choosing to believe that he had been won over by Macedonian bribes. In 346/5 Demosthenes began a prosecution against him for his part in the peace negotiations, with the support of Timarchus. The latter was a man long active against Philip but notorious for his private life. Aeschines replied with a speech of counter-accusation, *Against Timarchus* (still extant), in which he invoked a law forbidding those of known misconduct from addressing the assembly. He was successful, but the mood of Athens was becoming more hostile to Macedon.

In 343 Demosthenes attacked again in a speech *On the False Embassy,* as if Aeschines had been solely responsible for the discredited Peace, and had supported it because he was bribed. Aeschines replied in a speech of the same title (which also survives) and was narrowly acquitted. He continued to be influential in the Assembly and provoked a *Sacred War at the very time when unity was essential to avoid furnishing Philip with an opportunity to intervene in Greek affairs. Philip's subsequent invasion ended with the defeat of Athens and Thebes at *Chaeronea in 338. Aeschines was a member of the embassy sent to negotiate with Philip after the battle. In 336 Demosthenes' friend Ctesiphon proposed that Demosthenes should be crowned in the theatre at the *Dionysia for his services to the city. Aeschines indicted Ctesiphon for the alleged illegality of the proposal but did not proceed with the indictment until 330 when Athens was in almost complete isolation, with no prospect of liberation from Macedon. In his speech *Against Ctesiphon* he attacked the whole career of Demosthenes as injurious to Athens. Demosthenes replied in his speech *On the Crown* with such devastating effect that Aeschines failed to obtain the necessary fifth of the jury's votes to save him from a fine. He retired from Athens to Rhodes, where he died in about 322. At Rhodes he gave declamations, and once delivered his speech *Against Ctesiphon*. When the islanders expressed amazement that it did not win he replied, 'You would not wonder if you had heard Demosthenes.'

Aeschines was not a professional rhetorician. A story tells that when the Rhodians asked him to teach rhetoric he replied that he was ignorant of it himself. He seems not to have written speeches for others, and it is probable that he received no rhetorical training, but he was thoroughly familiar with all the conventions. He was famous for his dignified presence and splendid voice. His speeches, of which only the three named above were known to ancient critics, are characterized by a fondness for the legalities of the case, an astute use of diversionary tactics, and vivid descriptions. In ancient as well as modern times he has suffered from comparison with Demosthenes. The general aim of his activities was to find a compromise between Athens and Macedon which would leave Athens independent and at peace, and inevitably he had to trust Macedon to some extent. This policy was not a noble one, nor was it possible to give it rhetorical expression. In consequence he avoided the deeper issues of policy, and in contrast with Demosthenes, who was for ever generalizing and broadening the issues, he seems lacking in a wider vision.

Ae'schylus (525–456 BC), the earliest Greek tragic poet whose work survives. Born at Eleusis, near Athens, of a noble family, he witnessed in his youth the end of tyranny at Athens, and in his maturity the growth of democracy. He took part in the Persian Wars, at the battle of Marathon in 490 (where his brother was killed) and probably at Salamis in 480

(which he describes in the *Persians). At some time in his life he was prosecuted, it was said, on the charge of divulging the Eleusinian *mysteries, but exculpated himself. He visited Syracuse at the invitation of the tyrant Hieron I more than once and died at Gela in Sicily; an anecdote relates that an eagle dropped a tortoise on his bald head and killed him. Soon after his death it was decreed as a unique honour that anyone who wished to produce his plays should be 'granted a chorus' (see TRAGEDY 1). He had a son, Euphorion, like himself a tragic poet.

Aeschylus wrote some eighty to ninety plays (including satyric dramas) and won his first victory in the dramatic competitions of 484. He won at least thirteen victories in his lifetime. In his early days he was the rival of Pratinas, Phrynichus, and Choerilus of Athens, and in later life of Sophocles, who defeated him in 468. Seven plays only have come down to us, six of which we know to have come from prize-winning tetralogies: the *Persians*, produced in 472, the **Seven Against Thebes* in 467, the *Oresteia trilogy, comprising the *Agamemnon*, the *Choephoroe*, and the *Eumenides*, in 458, and the *Suppliants; this last used commonly to be regarded as the earliest play because of certain archaic features, but a papyrus fragment published in 1952 containing a note on its production shows that it cannot have been produced before 468, and 463 is a likely date. The other surviving play, *Prometheus Bound, has several features not found elsewhere in the plays. Its date is uncertain, but it seems not to be an early work.

Aeschylus is generally regarded as the real founder of Greek tragedy: by increasing the number of actors to two and diminishing the part taken by the chorus he made true dialogue and dramatic action possible. Either he or Sophocles added a third actor, and three are used in his later plays. He also had a liking for spectacular effects and for mechanical devices. He displays a similar taste in his long and magnificent descriptions, e.g. of the battle of Salamis in the *Persians* and the fall of Troy in the *Agamemnon*. His language has a matching grandeur which to the succeeding generation seemed occasionally to border on the bathetic, to judge from the criticism in Aristophanes' comedy the *Frogs*. He coins long compound words and is lavish with epithets and bold metaphors, creating striking and memorable images which often gain in significance from repetition throughout a play or trilogy. His principal characters are drawn without complexity or elaboration; they are not so much individual as 'typical', governed by a single dominating idea. The choruses also show 'typical' characterization; they have a role to play and are intimately involved in the action. Their songs are relevant, often explaining the significance of events that preceded the action.

It has always been for many people the religious and moral ideas of Aeschylus that give his drama a lasting significance. The action of an Aeschylean tragedy, which is of the kind that Aristotle in the *Poetics* calls 'simple', flows inexorably on towards its end without any intervening surprise or complication, because the events that precipitated it have occurred long before. One effect of this form of plot is to suggest the slow but certain workings of divine justice. It is by suffering that men eventually learn that whatever happens is the will of a just Zeus. By his design the rival claims of men and of deities are eventually reconciled and made to work together to produce universal order. This is one moral that can be drawn from the *Oresteia* and also, as far as we can see, from the trilogies that contained the *Suppliants* and the *Prometheus Bound*. But this is not to say that Aeschylus relieves men of their ordinary human responsibility: 'the doer shall suffer'. Aeschylus accepts the moral presuppositions of his time: guilt is inherited; the guilty man, 'the doer', shall suffer but it may be in the person of his son. Guilt may even produce fresh guilt, as in the case of Orestes. Another presupposition is that great prosperity deludes men into committing acts of insolence that lead to destruction, and once set upon that path there is no turning back. To Aeschylus these were the lessons not only of history but of the events of his own time.

Aescula'pius, the Latin form of the name of the Greek god of healing, *Asclepius. His cult was brought to Rome from the famous temple at Epidaurus in Argos in 293 BC, after the Romans had consulted the Sibylline books (see SIBYL) because of a severe pestilence. The temple, with a sanatorium, stood on the island of the river Tiber.

Aeson, see ARGONAUTS.

Aesop (Aisōpos), the traditional composer of Greek *fables. The story of his life, which was already known to Herodotus in the fifth century BC, has been overlaid by many fictions, but it seems likely that he came from Thrace and lived as a slave on the island of Samos in the early sixth century. See also RHODOPE.

Aesō'pus, Claudius, celebrated Roman tragic actor in the first century BC. Horace rates him as the equal of his contemporary *Roscius, the great comic actor. He was a friend of Cicero, and during the latter's exile helped to move popular feeling in his favour by allusions to him on the stage. Cicero says that he had great power of facial expression and gesture.

aether (aither), the rarified and pure atmosphere in which the Greeks imagined the gods to live, commonly called the 'upper air'; often by extension the sky generally. In Greek myth, Aither (Sky) is an elemental deity, father of *Tartarus.

Aethio'pia, see ETHIOPIA.

Aethio'pica, novel by Heliodorus; see NOVEL, GREEK.

Ae'thiopis, lost poem of the *Epic Cycle, ascribed to Arctinus of Miletus, a sequel to the *Iliad*.

Aethra, in Greek myth, daughter of Pittheus, king of Troezen, and mother of *Theseus.

Aetna. 1. Europe's highest active volcano, in Sicily. Eruptions were attributed in literature to the mythical monster *Typhon or the Giant Enceladus (see GIANTS) imprisoned by Zeus beneath the mountain; occasionally it was described as the workshop of *Vulcan.

Various notable eruptions are recorded in antiquity (see PINDAR (Pythian 1)).

2. The name given to the city of Catana (Gk. Katanē, modern Catania) at the foot of Mount Aetna by Hieron I, tyrant of Syracuse, when he refounded the city in 475 BC, removing the former inhabitants and re-peopling it with Dorian mercenaries. In 461 these were expelled and the old name restored. The name Aetna was then transferred with the mercenaries to the nearby city of Inessa.

Aetna, Latin didactic poem in 645 hexameters of unknown authorship. It is attributed by its manuscripts and doubtfully by *Donatus (1) to Virgil, but is almost certainly not by him. The authorship and date have been the subject of much speculation with no agreement reached, but the style seems to point to the first century AD. The author rejects mythological explanations and attributes eruptions to the action of wind at high pressure in cavities of the earth on subterranean fires (substantially the same explanation as that of Lucretius, 6. 680). The poem is enlivened by digressions and closes with a story to illustrate justice in natural events: on the occasion of a sudden eruption the inhabitants of Catana hastily fled, each carrying the property he thought most precious; they were overwhelmed, but a certain Amphinomus and his brother, who carried away nothing but their aged father and mother and their household gods, were spared.

Aeto'lia, Aetolian Confederacy or **League.** Aetolia was a country of central Greece, bounded on the west by Acarnania and on the south by the Corinthian Gulf. Its most famous town, near the coast, was Calydon. Since its only coast was marshy and lacked a harbour, Aetolia's history was that of a landpower. In the fifth century BC she was undeveloped and organized not in cities but in tribes (Thucydides reports that one tribe was said to speak an almost unintelligible dialect and to eat raw meat). She grew in power after the founding of the Aetolian League—a confederacy of tribes—in about 370 BC. From about 290 the League occupied Delphi, and gradually extended its territory until by 220 it

controlled the whole of central Greece outside Attica, and became Macedonia's chief rival in the peninsula and Rome's first ally in Greece. Later, the League's hostility to Rome and co-operation with Antiochus III in his war with Rome (see SELEUCIDS) brought about its downfall, and after Antiochus' defeat in 189 the Aetolians were forced to become Roman subject-allies.

Afrā'nius, Lucius (active *c*.160–120 BC), writer of Roman comedies (*fabulae *togatae*), of which only scanty fragments and forty-two titles survive. He may also have been an advocate in the law-courts. His plays depicted Italian life and characters; Horace says (*Epistles* II. 1. 57) that admirers compared him with the Greek writer of comedy *Menander. Afranius acknowledges his indebtedness to Menander, but the extent of it is unknown. The popularity of his plays continued under the empire; the emperor Nero staged a realistic and costly performance of 'The Fire', allowing the actors to keep what furniture they could rescue from a house which was actually set on fire.

Africa. The Greeks called the African continent, or the part of it they knew, Libya. The name Africa was given by the Carthaginians to the territory around Carthage, and was applied subsequently to all of the known continent; it was retained by the Romans when they made the Carthaginian territory a Roman province after the Third Punic War (146 BC). The province was gradually expanded with the planting of new Roman colonies until under the empire it stretched along the north coast from Cyrenaica (which remained Greek-speaking; see CYRENE) to the Atlantic. The area was heavily urbanized; during the second century AD African senators at Rome (who included the orator Fronto) comprised the largest group from the western provinces. The wealth of Roman Africa was proverbial, and was derived chiefly from the export of vast quantities of corn. In the third century Christianity spread rapidly in the province; Cyprian, Tertullian, and Augustine were all African by birth. For the later history see CARTHAGE. See also EGYPT.

afterlife. In Greece and Rome there was no generally accepted religious dogma on an afterlife. An unequivocal acceptance of human mortality pervades Greek literature. Yet a belief in some sort of survival after death was general and many often contradictory ideas existed side by side. The most primitive and long-lasting belief was that the dead lived on in their tombs, where offerings were regularly made to them by their families (see ANTHESTERIA). From earliest times Greek religious beliefs were a strong influence in Italy, and the Graeco-Roman world was essentially one in its religious and philosophic views of the afterlife. For specifically Italian beliefs see MANES and LEMURES.

The most general belief of antiquity, given its essential form by Homer, was that all the dead dwell below the earth in the realm of *Hadēs and *Persephonē, good and bad alike, leading a shadowy and cheerless existence. From the sixth century BC onwards ideas of happiness after death for those who have deserved well in this life are expressed, together with ideas of punishment in the Underworld or *Tartarus for the wicked, and of reincarnation and even transmigration of souls. These ideas are particularly associated with the names of *Orpheus and *Pythagoras, and with the Eleusinian mysteries (see MYSTERIES), where both righteousness and initiation in this life are the prerequisites for happiness in the next.

Plato argued that the soul is immortal, and Aristotle allowed immortality of a non-personal kind to part of a man's soul. The Epicureans (see EPICURUS) believed that the soul was made of atoms as the body is, and so dies with the body. To the Stoics death was no evil, but they made no dogmatic pronouncements on an afterlife. It was partly these philosophic speculations on the soul that lent strength to the teachings of the mystery religions which offered as their highest promise a happy afterlife, however it was thought of, and thus helped to foster the feeling, which was a feature of the religious beliefs of late antiquity, that the soul survived death.

Agamē'dēs, see TROPHONIUS.

Agame'mnon, in Greek myth, son of *Atreus, brother of *Menelaus, husband of *Clytemnestra, king of Mycenae, or Argos, and leader of the Greek forces in the Trojan War. He is represented in Homer's *Iliad* as a valiant fighter, a proud and passionate man, but vacillating in purpose and easily discouraged. His quarrel with *Achilles is the mainspring of the poem's action. The *Odyssey* tells how, on his return from Troy, he was feasted in the palace of his wife's lover, and there murdered by them both, together with his captive *Cassandra. This story is retold by later authors, with minor variants (see especially ORESTEIA). All accounts include a son *Orestes among his children, who avenged his father's murder, usually with the help of his sister *Electra. The *Cypria* is the earliest witness to the story that Agamemnon was required to sacrifice his daughter Iphigeneia to atone for an offence against Artemis, who in anger was keeping the Greek fleet wind-bound at Aulis.

Agamemnon. 1. Greek tragedy by *Aeschylus; for the plot see ORESTEIA.

2. Roman tragedy by Seneca the Younger (see SENECA (2) 4). The play shows variation in details from the *Agamemnon* of Aeschylus. The ghost of Thyestes is introduced urging Aegisthus to the crime, and Aegisthus strengthens a weaker Clytemnestra's resolve. Cassandra is not murdered with Agamemnon but later. Electra appears and contrives the escape of her brother Orestes.

Agani'ppē, spring sacred to the Muses on Mount *Helicon in Boeotia; compare HIPPOCRENE.

Agapē'nor, in Greek myth, leader of the Arcadian contingent against Troy in the Trojan War. On the way back he arrived at Cyprus where he founded the city of Paphos.

Aga'thias (AD c.531–c.580), Greek poet and lawyer who lived most of his life in Constantinople. He made a collection of epigrams written by his contemporaries, generally known as the *Cycle*, which partially survives in the Greek *Anthology. The Anthology also contains about a hundred of Agathias' own

Agathocles

18

poems, some highly artificial and mannered, others, particularly the love poems, warm and charming. Later he started a *History* which was to bring the narrative of *Procopius' *Wars* up to his own day, but he died when he had completed only five books, covering the years 553–9.

Aga'thoclēs, see SYRACUSE.

A'gathon (*c.*445–*c.*400 BC), Athenian tragic poet, perhaps the most important apart from the three great tragedians (see TRAGEDY 4) and celebrated for his good looks. Less than forty lines of his work survive. His first victory in the dramatic competitions was gained at the Lenaea in 416 BC when he was probably under 30. It is the banquet held at his house to celebrate this victory that forms the setting of Plato's *Symposium*. Agathon was an innovator: he was the first to construct a tragedy on an imaginary subject with imaginary characters rather than taking it from Greek myth; he made the songs of the chorus mere interludes (*embolima*, 'interpolations') without reference to the subject of the play, thus preparing the way for the division of the tragedy into acts; and he also introduced some changes in the character of the music. Aristophanes in the *Thesmophoriazusae* parodies Agathon's lyrics, hinting that they are voluptuous and effeminate and at one point describing them as like the walking of ants, and also makes fun of his effeminate appearance. When, towards the end of the Peloponnesian War, Agathon, like Euripides, withdrew to the court of Archelaus of Macedon, Aristophanes in the *Frogs* (84) regrets his abandonment of Athens. He died in Macedon.

Aga'vē (Agauē), in Greek myth, the mother of Pentheus (see BACCHAE). For the pantomime with this title see STATIUS.

Agdi'stis, the Phrygian name of *Cybelē; see also ATTIS.

Agē'nor, in Greek myth, king of Tyre, twin-brother of *Belus, and father of *Cadmus and *Europa.

ager pu'blicus, 'state land' or 'public land', land confiscated during the Roman conquest of Italy, from communities that put up a strong resistance or subsequently rebelled. Some of the land was assigned to individuals and much was allocated to colonies, but vast tracts especially in the south were held by rich investors who used it mostly for ranching, thus dispossessing small farmers. The question of *ager publicus* became an issue on several occasions afterwards as victorious generals like Sulla, Julius Caesar, and Octavian wanted land for their veterans. It was not until the time of the emperor Augustus that a pension scheme, as a means of support other than grants of land, was devised for discharged soldiers.

Agesilā'us (*c.*444–360 BC), king of Sparta from 399. He was lame, and his opponents drew attention to the warning of an ancient oracle against a 'lame reign' at Sparta. But he was a man of great efficiency and Spartan virtues. His successful campaigns against the Persians in 396–395 and his victory over the Boeotians and Athenians at Coronea in 394 are related by his friend the Athenian historian *Xenophon in his *Hellenica*. Spartan intervention in the affairs of autonomous states, which Agesilaus condoned, resulted in an alliance between Thebes and Athens which his invasions of Boeotia in 378 and 377 did not succeed in disrupting. His refusal in 371 to admit *Epaminondas' claim to represent all Boeotia at the peace congress in Sparta precipitated the battle of Leuctra at which Sparta lost the leadership of Greece. In the years of humiliation which followed he organized the defence of the city. Sparta needed money, and in order to earn a subsidy Agesilaus conducted an expedition in aid of an Egyptian prince against Persia in 361. In this he met his death. His Life was written by *Nepos and by Xenophon (see below).

Agesilā'us, one of the minor works of Xenophon, a biographical essay on his friend the Spartan king (see above). Xenophon relates in some detail the campaign of Agesilaus against the Persian satrap Tissaphernes in 395 BC and the march back to Greece through Macedonia and Thessaly, and gives a full description of the battle of *Coronea at which, according to Plutarch, Xenophon fought for his friend against his fellow-countrymen.

A'giads (Agiadai), the name of the senior royal house at *Sparta, derived from the name of a legendary Dorian king Agis, son of Eurysthenes (see HERACLEIDAE), who made the original inhabitants of Sparta subject to the Dorian invaders (see DORIAN INVASION). The junior branch was the Eurypontid.

agōn ('contest'). 1. In Greece and later at Rome, a public festival at which competitors contended for a prize, usually in chariot- and horse-races and athletics but occasionally in musical or dramatic competitions.
2. The 'debate' in Attic Old Comedy; see COMEDY, GREEK 3 (iii).

a'gora, in Greek literally 'assembly', especially of the people; then 'place of assembly', market place (Lat. *forum*), or city centre of a Greek city.

Agri'cola, Gnaeus Julius (AD 40–93), Roman general and governor of *Britain, on whose career his son-in-law the historian *Tacitus wrote *Agricola*, a laudatory monograph (see below). Agricola did his early military service in Britain as *tribunus militum* to the governor Suetonius Paulinus, in the troubled times which culminated in *Boudicca's rebellion. In AD 70–3 he was commander of the Twentieth Legion in Britain. After that he became governor of Aquitania and then consul for part of 77, and then returned to Britain late in 77 or in 78 as governor. In Britain his sympathy and justice towards the provincials enabled him to pacify the country, while his military skills, particularly his good eye for terrain, helped him to extend Roman occupation northward into Scotland. In 84 Agricola finally succeeded in bringing about a pitched battle with the highlanders at Mons Graupius (a much-sought battlefield, but the discovery of a large Roman camp near Inverurie in Aberdeenshire suggests that it may be the mountain now called Bennachie). Phrases from the speech attributed by Tacitus to the Caledonian leader Calgacus, exhorting his troops before the battle, have become famous: *omne ignotum pro magnifico est* ('what men know

nothing about they see as wonderful'), and *ubi solitudinem faciunt, pacem appellant* ('when they create a desolation they call it peace'). Agricola's victory in this battle was final for its generation. After it, in 84, he was recalled and given no further command. He lived long enough to see Rome abandon the system of forts with which he had blockaded the highlands and secured the northern frontier. Agricola was remembered by later Roman historians for his circumnavigation of Britain after his campaign in Scotland. His civil policy encouraged urbanization and he founded many small quasi-independent 'states' in southern Britain to fill the administrative gap caused by moving the legions north.

Agri'cola, monograph by Tacitus in praise of the Roman general Agricola, published AD 98. It includes an account of Britain and its tribes, the continual rain and cloud, and the long days and short nights of summer, but it is somewhat vague about the geography.

Agrige'ntum, see ACRAGAS.

Agri'ppa. 1. **Marcus Vipsā'nius Agrippa** (64–12 BC), the life-long friend and supporter of the emperor Augustus and the holder of important military and naval commands. He defeated Sextus *Pompeius in 36, and commanded the left wing at Actium in 31 BC to bring about the defeat of Mark *Antony. After this he helped to manage the affairs of Rome and in 23 BC Augustus, when he was seriously ill, probably intended that Agrippa should succeed him. He continued until his death to be Augustus' right-hand man in the government of the empire.

Agrippa was an honest and able administrator, whose personal tastes were simple. He devoted his life and his immense wealth (probably due to his first marriage; see below) to Rome and the empire, and left most of his property to Augustus at his death. Among his many public works were the building of the *Pantheon and the first great public baths at Rome, and the renewal of the water-supply and sewage systems. He also carried out many works in the provinces. He wrote an autobiography and a geographical commentary, both now lost. He married first the daughter, known as Attica, of Cicero's friend Titus Pomponius *Atticus; she bore him a daughter Agrippina who was to marry the emperor Tiberius. Secondly, he married Augustus' niece Marcella; thirdly, Augustus' daughter Julia, who bore him five children including Gaius and Lucius Caesar who were adopted by Augustus but died young (AD 2 and 4 respectively), and Agrippina, who married Germanicus.

2. Marcus Vipsanius Agrippa Po'stumus (12 BC–AD 14), son of Agrippa (1) and Julia, daughter of the emperor Augustus; he was born after his father's death, as his *cognomen* indicates. Along with Tiberius he was adopted by Augustus in AD 4, but was passed over by the emperor for the throne because of his boorish ways, and soon after Augustus died in 14 was put to death, possibly by order of Tiberius.

3. Marcus Julius Agrippa, see HEROD (2).

Agrippī'na. 1. Vipsānia Agrippina (d. AD 20), daughter of *Agrippa (1) and Attica, and first wife of the emperor Tiberius.

2. Agrippina the Elder (c.14 BC–AD 33), daughter of *Agrippa (1) and Julia, and wife of *Germanicus to whom she bore nine children. She was present at his death-bed in Syria and brought back his ashes to Rome. The hostility that she showed to Tiberius, whom she suspected (without evidence) of causing her husband's death, led to her arrest in 29 and banishment by the senate to the island of Pandataria (Ventotene). She starved herself to death in 33. She was the mother of the emperor Caligula (see GAIUS CAESAR).

3. Agrippina the Younger (AD 15–59), daughter of (2) above, married to Cn. Domitius *Ahenobarbus, to whom she bore one son, later the emperor Nero. She was exiled on suspicion of plotting against her brother the emperor Caligula in 39, and was recalled in 49 by Claudius, her uncle, who married her when she was widowed. She persuaded Claudius to adopt Nero, and when Claudius died in 54 she was generally believed to have poisoned him to make way for Nero. In the early years of the latter's reign she was almost co-regent with him, but eventually lost her influence through her imperious ways. In 59 Nero had her murdered.

Ahenoba'rbus later **Aenobarbus,** 'bronze-beard', the *cognomen* (see NAMES) of a distinguished branch of the Roman *gens*, the Domitii. Legend relates that the *Dioscuri had announced to an early member of the family the victory of Lake Regillus (496 BC), and to prove their supernatural powers had stroked his black beard, which immediately turned bronze-coloured. One Cn. Domitius Ahenobarbus, after fighting against Julius Caesar in 49 BC and being subsequently pardoned by him, was one of the republican leaders after Caesar's death, and commanded a fleet against the triumvirs. He was later reconciled to Mark *Antony, accompanied him in his expedition against the Parthians in 36, and was with him in Egypt. Abandoning Antony he joined the cause of Octavian before the battle of Actium in 31, and died soon afterwards. He figures in Shakespeare's *Antony and Cleopatra*.

Another Cn. Domitius Ahenobarbus, consul in AD 32, married *Agrippina (3), daughter of Germanicus, and was father of the emperor Nero. Suetonius described him as 'wholly despicable'. The timely death of the emperor Tiberius saved him from being charged with treason, adultery, and incest. According to Suetonius, the family possessed a streak of vicious cruelty. Of one member the orator Licinius *Crassus remarked, 'Should his bronze beard really surprise us? After all, he has a face of iron and a heart of lead.'

Aïdēs, Aïdō'neus, variant forms of *Hades.

Ai'gialeus, see AEGIALEUS.

Aisa, see FATE.

aither, see AETHER.

Ajax (Aias). **1.** In Greek myth, son of *Telamon, king of Salamis, and Eriboea or Periboea (called Telamonian Ajax or 'the Greater Ajax', to distinguish him from (2) below), leader of the Salaminians who were with the Greeks at the siege of Troy. He is represented by Homer in the *Iliad* as being of great size and of dogged courage, the 'bulwark' of the Achaeans, who repeatedly leads the Greek attack or covers the retreat. His characteristic attribute is the all-enveloping Mycenaean body-shield. In the *Odyssey* his death is mentioned in a version that has become famous through Sophocles' tragedy *Ajax* (see below) and was narrated in the *Little *Iliad*. After Achilles' death there was a dispute between Ajax and Odysseus over who should receive his armour as a mark of personal prowess, and by the votes of the Greek leaders the armour was adjudged to Odysseus; Ajax went mad with resentment and killed himself. In fact various stories of his death were told in antiquity.

2. In Greek myth, son of Oileus (or Ileus), 'the Lesser Ajax', the captain of the Locrian contingent on the Greek side at the siege of Troy and the fastest runner, brave but arrogant and hated by the gods, particularly Athena. He was killed by the sea-god Poseidon on the way home from Troy for boasting that he had escaped from ship-wreck without divine aid. At the fall of Troy he dragged king Priam's daughter Cassandra by her hair from the altar of Athena, together with the statue (*Palladium) which she was embracing (a story told in the *Iliupersis*). For this impiety the Locrians continued to make atonement (until the second century BC), by sending every year two maidens of noble birth to serve in the temple of Athena at Troy. The girls had to reach the temple unseen or be killed by the townspeople.

Ajax, Greek tragedy by *Sophocles, of uncertain date, perhaps his earliest and written before 441 BC.

Ajax son of Telamon (see (1) above), bitterly resentful that Achilles' arms had been awarded to Odysseus, planned a night attack on the Greek leaders but, having been driven mad by the goddess Athena, killed cattle and sheep instead. When the play opens he is still mad and gloating over his supposed captives, but he recovers and is stricken with shame, while his concubine Tecmessa and the chorus of Salaminian sailors try to soothe him. He calls for his son Eurysaces, gives

him his shield, and in his grief resolves upon suicide. After an interval Ajax speaks more calmly before going away to purify himself and to bury his sword. The chorus and Tecmessa are reassured, only to learn from his half-brother Teucer that the seer Calchas has declared calamity can be averted only if Ajax, who has angered the gods by his arrogance, is kept within his tent for that day. But it is too late; Ajax is found having fallen upon his sword. Menelaus forbids his burial, as an enemy to the Greeks; Agamemnon confirms the edict but is persuaded by Odysseus to relent, and Ajax is carried to his grave.

A'laric, the *Visigothic leader who after several defeats finally succeeded in entering Rome in August AD 410 and plundered it for three days. It was the first time the city had been occupied by a foreign enemy since the Gallic invasion of 390 BC, and the civilized world was profoundly shocked. Alaric died soon after.

Alba Longa, very ancient Latin city (see LATIUM) built on the northern slope of the Alban Mount near modern Castel Gandolfo some 20 km. (13 miles) southeast of Rome; it was traditionally founded c.1152 BC by Aeneas' son Ascanius, who moved his seat of government there from Lavinium. It appears once to have headed a league of Latin cities, but lost its primacy in Latium in about the seventh century BC, being destroyed allegedly by Rome in the reign of Tullus Hostilius. It was never rebuilt.

Albion, the ancient (Celtic or pre-Celtic) name for Britain, soon ousted by the Celtic 'Britannia'. The Romans connected it with *albus*, 'white', and referred it to the cliffs of Dover.

Albu'nea, the *Sibyl who lived at Tibur (Tivoli) in central Italy and had a cult there. Her oracular verses were deposited in the Capitol at Rome, with the Sibylline books.

Alcae'us. 1. Greek lyric poet (b. before 620 BC) from Mytilene, chief city of Lesbos. Until recent years his poetry survived only in quotations made by later authors, but since the decipherment in the twentieth century of certain Egyptian papyri (see PAPYROLOGY) much more of his poetry has come to light, though the tattered fragments have yielded very few complete poems. Many of the poems concern the politics of the time, in which Alcaeus was closely involved. After the overthrow of the ruling family, the Penthelidae, Mytilene was governed by a series of tyrants, Melanchrus (612–609), Myrsilus, and *Pittacus (590–580), all of whom were generally opposed by Alcaeus' family or party. There was a closing of ranks when the Lesbians, Alcaeus among them, fought under Pittacus against the Athenians, c.606 BC, for the possession of Sigeum, a key stronghold on the Hellespont. Athens held Sigeum and Alcaeus describes himself as abandoning his shield in the retreat, as the poet Archilochus did before him. At some stage when Pittacus was ruling, Alcaeus went away to Egypt and his brother Antimenidas became a mercenary of Nebuchadnezzar, king of Babylon. He was eventually reconciled with Pittacus before the latter laid down the tyranny in 580, and returned home. The date of his death is unknown.

His poetry consists of lyrical songs, mostly monodies (see LYRIC POETRY) in two- or four-lined stanzas, in a great variety of metres. Many of these were later adapted to Latin poetry by Horace (see METRE, LATIN 3 (iii)), who imitated and wrote variations upon Alcaic themes throughout the Odes. As well as writing of politics and personalities with passion and gusto, Alcaeus composed love-songs (not always in his own person), now almost totally lost, drinking-songs, and hymns to the gods, all with simple directness, economy, and little imagery. (In some of his political poems he writes allegorically, using the image of the ship of state tossed by storm to describe political strife.) His language was the Aeolic vernacular spoken in Lesbos at that time, with a few Homeric forms (see DIALECTS, GREEK 2).

2. Greek comic poet, writer of Old Comedy, known to be active at the beginning of the fourth century BC.

3. An epigrammatist of the third to second century BC who has some fifteen epigrams in the Greek *Anthology.

4. In Greek myth, a son of *Perseus and father of *Amphitryon; see also ALCIDES.

alca'ic, see METRE, GREEK 8 (i) and LATIN 3 (iii).

Alce'stis, in Greek myth, daughter of Pelias and Anaxibia, wife of *Admetus. Her father would let her marry only a suitor who could yoke a lion and a boar to a chariot and drive it, a condition fulfilled by Admetus with the help of the god Apollo. See also below.

Alce'stis, Greek drama by *Euripides produced in 438 BC in place of a satyr play (see SATYRIC DRAMA). The tetralogy of which it was the final play (and which included the famous *Telephus*) won second prize in the dramatic competition. It contains a certain burlesque element provided by the character of the genial, drunken Heracles, and a happy ending.

In the story, Heracles rescues Alcestis from Death and restores her to her husband *Admetus. The latter is represented at first as an ingenuous egoist, fond of his wife, deeply grieved to lose her, and indignant with his father for refusing to make the required sacrifice in her place. But he returns from his wife's burial sorrowfully, and with self-knowledge. Alcestis is a virtuous wife, accepting as natural the duty of dying for him, and concerned in a practical way for the future of her children. Heracles is an attractive character, relaxing between the Labours that form the main business of his life, to enjoy himself and do a good turn for a friend.

Alcibi'adēs (c.450–404 BC), Athenian politician and general of noble family, an Alcmaeonid (see ALCMAEONIDAE) on his mother's side. After his father was killed at Coronea in 446 he was educated by his guardian Pericles, and became a follower and friend of Socrates. A leading figure during the *Peloponnesian War against Sparta, he was elected *strategos in 420, probably at the earliest legal age, and at a time when he had already become a leader of the extreme democrats. His ambitious imperialism contributed most to the launching in 415 of the disastrous *Sicilian Expedition, of which he was appointed one of the three leaders. He was recalled soon after to answer charges of sacrilege, but he escaped to Sparta. In his absence Alcibiades was condemned to death and his property confiscated. He intrigued against Athens, but was mistrusted by the Spartans, and he returned to the Athenian side as a naval commander in 411. From then until 406 he directed their war operations with brilliant success, but defeat in the sea-battle at Notium (fought against his orders) in 406 lost him his prestige, and he was not elected *strategos* for 406/5. He retired to the Thracian Chersonese, and was assassinated in Phrygia in 404, perhaps through the influence of the Thirty Tyrants and Lysander.

The chief authority for the career of Alcibiades is Thucydides. Alcibiades figures in Plato's *Symposium* and the spurious Platonic dialogue that bears his name, and there are Lives of him by Nepos and Plutarch. He was an outstandingly able politician and military leader, with remarkable looks and great personal magnetism, but his unscrupulous personal ambition, his vanity, and his dissolute life aroused the distrust of the Athenians at times when his leadership might well have been a decisive factor in the Peloponnesian War. In Aristophanes' *Frogs* (produced in 405), when the tragic poets are required to give a sample of their political advice, it is their opinion of Alcibiades that is sought: Aeschylus thinks it 'wiser not to rear a lion's whelp, but if you do, you must accept its ways'. One of his most spectacular acts was to enter seven chariots for the Olympian games (perhaps those of 424 BC), in which he won first, second, and fourth places. He married Hipparetē, daughter of Hipponicus (son of *Callias) who was reputed to be the richest man in Greece. Alcibiades' career is referred to in two speeches of Lysias directed against his son, the younger Alcibiades, b. *c*.416, for whom Isocrates wrote one in support.

Alcibī'adēs, spurious dialogue attributed to *Plato.

Alci'damas (early fourth century BC), Greek *sophist and rhetorician from Elaea in Aeolis, pupil and follower of Gorgias, and opposed to the teaching of Isocrates. One genuine work of his survives, 'On the Sophists', in which the author argues in favour of extempore rather than prepared speeches.

Alcī'das, Spartan admiral in the early part of the Peloponnesian War.

Alcī'dēs (Alkeidēs), in Greek myth, a name meaning 'descendant of Alcaeus' used to designate Heracles, whose mortal father *Amphitryon was son of Alcaeus.

Alci'nŏus, in Homer's *Odyssey*, king of the Phaeacians in Scheria, father of *Nausicaa, who received Odysseus on his wanderings and sent him home to Ithaca on a magic ship.

A'lciphron (*c*. AD 200), Greek writer, author of fictitious letters (of which we have about a hundred) purporting to be by Athenians of various classes of society, depicting Athenian life in the fourth century BC.

Alcmae'on or **Alcmeon,** in Greek myth, son of *Amphiaraus. In accordance with his father's command he became leader of the expedition of the *Epigonoi which took Thebes. On his return, in further execution of his father's commands, he avenged him by slaying his own mother Eriphylē (or, in some sources, the matricide came before the expedition). For this murder he was (like Orestes) pursued from place to place by the Furies. At Psophis in Arcadia he received partial purification from Phegeus, whose daughter Arsinoë, or Alphesiboea, he married. To her he gave the necklace of Harmonia (see CADMUS (1)). But the crops of the country began to fail, and Alcmaeon set out again to discover a land on which the sun had not shone when he murdered his mother. This he found in an island newly thrown up at the mouth of the river Achelōus, between Acarnania and Aetolia in Greece. Here he married Callirrhoē, a daughter of Achelous. She in turn begged for the necklace of Harmonia, and Alcmaeon obtained it from Phegeus on a false pretence. But the brothers of Arsinoe waylaid and killed him, afterwards shutting their sister up in a chest because she protested, and selling her as a slave. Acarnan and Amphoteros, the sons of Alcmaeon and Callirhoe, avenged their father by killing Phegeus and his sons; the fatal necklace was dedicated to Apollo at Delphi. A later story tells that it was stolen by a Phocian when Phocis was at war with Philip of Macedon, and brought ill luck to the thief.

Alcmaeo'nidae (Alkmeōnidai), a noble (Eupatrid) Athenian *genos* prominent in politics. Its origins are obscure, but its name seems to derive from that Alcmaeon who commanded the Athenian forces in the First *Sacred War from *c.*595 BC onwards, and who in 592 won his family's and Athens' first victory at the Olympian games. The first notable member of this family was Alcmaeon's father *Megacles (1) who as archon in perhaps 632 incurred a hereditary pollution (see CYLON) which put all his descendants under sentence of banishment, a sentence that was periodically enforced upon them for political reasons. Banished at some time after 632 they were back in Athens under Solon. Alcmaeon's son Megacles (2) married the daughter of Cleisthenes, tyrant of Sicyon. Banished again during the tyranny of *Peisistratus (who was briefly and unsuccessfully married to a daughter of Megacles (2)) they returned once more to Athens before the archonship in 525 of Cleisthenes, son of Megacles (2), but the tyrant *Hippias expelled them yet again. They finally succeeded in overthrowing Hippias and returned in 510. In the fifth century the pollution was invoked at intervals by political enemies. *Pericles, like *Alcibiades an Alcmaeonid on his mother's side, was able to ignore the Spartan appeal to the pollution in 432; it does not appear to have been invoked against Alcibiades.

Alcman, Greek *lyric poet who lived in Sparta in the second half, perhaps the last quarter, of the seventh century BC. In antiquity it was a matter of dispute whether he was a Laconian or whether he came from Sardis in Lydia. His works contain no direct reference to contemporary history but seem to belong to a period of peace, and are mainly choral lyrics for the festivals. His poems were collected in six books, now all lost except for a few quotations and papyrus fragments. His *partheneia* ('maiden-songs') were especially celebrated but we hear also of

hymns and wedding songs. Most of the surviving fragments defy classification, but one or two are obviously from love-songs, of which he was said to be the inventor. The longest fragment of his poetry and the earliest piece of choral lyric we possess is from a *partheneion*. It was found on an Egyptian papyrus and shows the unaffected charm and freshness of his writing. His dialect is for the most part the Laconian vernacular with some Homerisms. His simple metres were markedly dactylic, with some iambo-trochaic and aeolic elements (see METRE, GREEK 8 (i) and (ii)). It is not certain whether his lyric was *triadic in structure or composed in stanzas.

Alcme'na (Alkmēnē), see AMPHITRYON.

A'lcmeon, see ALCMAEON.

Alcy'onē, in Greek myth, a daughter of *Aeolus (2) and wife of Cēyx, son of Eosphorus ('morning star'). They were changed into birds, she into the halcyon (kingfisher), he into the bird of his name (perhaps a tern or gannet), either because he was drowned at sea and her despair was so great that the gods reunited them, or because of their impiety (they called themselves Zeus and Hera). 'Halcyon days' were fourteen days of calm weather around the winter solstice, supposed to be sent by Aeolus when the halcyon bird was brooding.

Ale'cto, see FURIES.

Aleu'adae, one of the leading aristocratic families of Thessaly (the other was the Scopadae; see SIMONIDES). They sided with Persia and conspired with Xerxes during the Persian Wars, and vigorously opposed the tyrants of Pherae (see JASON and ALEXANDER (1)).

Alexander (Alexandros). **1. Alexander of Pherae** (in Thessaly), nephew and successor of *Jason, tyrant of Pherae 369–358 BC. He was opposed by most of the cities of Thessaly and allied himself with Athens to counteract Theban expansion. When the Theban general *Pelopidas visited him on one of his expeditions, he detained the general as a hostage until the latter was eventually rescued by a second Theban expedition in 367. As the result of a fresh appeal from Thessaly in

364, Pelopidas marched against him and defeated him at Cynoscephalae, but was himself killed. Later, a larger Theban army defeated Alexander and forced him to become the ally of the Thebans. In 362 he felt free to make piratical raids against Athens and raided the Piraeus. He was assassinated in 358 by his wife's brothers.

2. Alexander the Great, Alexander III of Macedon (356–323 BC), son of Philip II and Olympias of Epirus. He was educated by Aristotle and became king of Macedon in 336 upon the murder of his father. Before his death Philip had been about to lead an army against Persia in punishment for the wrongs inflicted on Greece in the Persian Wars 150 years earlier. Alexander aimed to continue this war, and in 334, after securing his position in Greece (rivals were put to death), he crossed the Hellespont into Asia to join the remnants of his father's advance army. He had a force of about 43,000 men and a fleet of the Greek allies with about fifty warships.

He routed the Persian king Darius III at Issus (333) and captured his family, treating them with notable chivalry. In the following year he occupied Phoenicia (where the capture of the city of Tyre is regarded as his most brilliant military feat), Palestine, and Egypt, and after crushing the Persians again at Arbela (331), he sacked Persepolis (330), the ritual centre of their empire. (Alexander is said to have been incited to this act of destruction by the Greek courtesan Thais and to have later regretted it.) When Darius was murdered in 330, Alexander regarded himself as the legitimate ruler of the Persian empire, and between 330 and 327 he subdued vast tracts of the outlying areas of the empire—Hyrcania, Areia, Drangiana, Bactria, and Sogdiana.

In 327 he invaded northern India, and in 326 he crossed the Indus and reached the river Hydaspes (Jhelum). Here he fought his last great pitched battle to defeat the local king Porus and his formidable elephants. This was the last battle too for *Bucephalas, Alexander's horse since childhood, which was wounded and died soon after the battle. Alexander advanced quite easily through the rest of the Punjab to the river Hyphasis (Sutlej) and contemplated proceeding across

India to the Ganges but his army, exhausted by the monsoon as much as by the campaigning, refused to go further. He turned back, and in 323, at Babylon he fell suddenly ill at a drinking party, perhaps through fever, perhaps through poison, and after ten days died, aged 32. His body was finally brought to rest in *Alexandria, where three centuries later his coffin was seen by the young emperor Augustus. It was probably destroyed in riots during the late third century AD.

Alexander is the greatest general of antiquity. This position he owes partly to the splendidly organized Macedonian army and its technically improved siege weapons, partly to his own versatile and intelligent strategy, but much more to qualities that were uniquely his: an unprecedented speed of movement, resolution in tackling the seemingly impossible, personal involvement in the dangers of battle and the rigours of campaigning, and a heroic sense of style in all that he did. To these qualities as well as to his generosity Alexander owed his ascendancy over the army. His most unusual characteristic was his double sympathy with the life styles of the Persians as well as the Greeks (his two wives—Roxana and Barsine—were Persian, and he encouraged his soldiers to follow his example). His desire to see Macedonians and Persians alike ruling his empire was not popular and may have been partly the cause of the various plots against his life.

Alexander clearly felt an intense concern for religion and showed scrupulous respect for local gods wherever he encountered them. In his lifetime he was widely acclaimed as divine, the son of Zeus, and he seems to have believed in his own divinity and to have been encouraged in this belief by his mother. Certainly he strove to emulate those other sons of gods, the Homeric heroes. His most lasting achievement was to extend the Greek language and institutions over the eastern world in such a way that he brought about an absolute break with the past. No region once conquered and settled by Alexander resumed its old ways uninfluenced by the conquest. The Greek city-states too never regained the independence that they lost with Philip.

The centre of the (*Hellenistic) Greek world shifted to Alexandria, and with that shift arose a new kind of Greek culture.

The principal extant authority for the history of Alexander's campaigns is the *Anabasis* of *Arrian, who used as sources the writings, now lost, of Alexander's officers Ptolemy (later King Ptolemy I Soter of Egypt), Aristobulus of Cassandreia, and the sea-captain Nearchus, all of whom were sympathetic to Alexander. He may also have used Alexander's lost journal (*Ephemerides*), but some scholars doubt the existence of an authentic journal. There is also a tradition, which may be seen in the fragmentary history of Quintus *Curtius, of writers hostile to Alexander, who represented him as a tyrant corrupted by power; most of them are of the *Peripatetic (Aristotelian) School, whose hostility was natural enough after *Callisthenes' death. Plutarch's Life is compiled from every kind of source, good and bad. The most influential tradition, however, stems from the narrative of Cleitarchus, written in the third century BC and known to us through the writings of *Diodorus Siculus; Cleitarchus introduced the fabulous, an element that was further developed in the various Eastern versions of Alexander's life. From Latin versions supposedly translated from Callisthenes the legends passed into French poetry of the eleventh and twelfth centuries, thus giving the twelve-syllabled alexandrine line its name. There are two Old English works of the eleventh century based on the Latin legend, but it is from the French poems that the Alexander legends passed into the Middle English metrical romances such as 'King Alisaunder'.

3. Alexander of Aphrodisias (flourished *c.* AD 200), the most important of the early commentators on Aristotle. Of his commentaries (in Greek) a few survive, and his works are widely quoted by later writers.

4. Alternative name for *Paris (1).

Alexandra, see LYCOPHRON (2).

Alexa'ndria, city on the north coast of Egypt, near the Canopic or western mouth of the Nile, founded by Alexander the Great in 331 BC on a virtually virgin site, occupied only by a village and fort called Rhacotis; it was the first of his many foundations, and the first city known to have been named after its founder rather than a god or mythological figure. According to the historian Arrian, Alexander himself established where the main points of the city, the agora and the temples, should be, and drew the line of the city walls with the meal which his soldiers were carrying, a good omen for the city's future prosperity. After Alexander's general Ptolemy had established his authority in Egypt, the seat of government was transferred from the ancient city of Memphis to Alexandria. The new city grew rapidly and soon became the first city of the Hellenistic world, a centre of learning as well as of commerce and industry. By 200 BC it was the largest city in the world, and in the Roman period it counted as the second city of the empire, after Rome itself. It did not decline until the Arab conquest in the seventh century caused Egypt to look towards Asia rather than towards Europe.

Alexandrianism, Latin, term used of the influence of the Alexandrian school of Greek poets of the third and second centuries BC (see HELLENISTIC AGE) on Roman poets of the first century BC, of whom Catullus is the only surviving representative. The chief features of the school were a development of new, miniature genres, especially epyllion, elegy, and epigram; a regard for form, which left a lasting impression on Latin literature; the cult of erudition; and the emergence of a subjective and personal way of writing. See NEOTERICS.

Alexandrian Library. The greatest library of antiquity, founded in Alexandria probably by Ptolemy I Soter (reigned 323–283 BC) and greatly augmented by his son Ptolemy II Philadelphus (see PTOLEMIES). At its head was placed a series of distinguished scholars, Zenodotus, Apollonius Rhodius, Eratosthenes, Aristophanes of Byzantium, Apollonius the Eidograph, Aristarchus; the poet Callimachus also worked there. It is variously said to have contained 100,000 to 700,000 volumes. It is also said that Ptolemy II purchased the library that

Aristotle had formed; and that Ptolemy III appropriated the official copies of the texts of Aeschylus, Sophocles, and Euripides (see LYCURGUS 3), forfeiting the large deposit he had paid when borrowing them from Athens. The library became the great centre of literature in the Hellenistic world and the practice of its copyists was probably decisive in the forms of book production. Callimachus made catalogues (*pinakēs*) of its contents. There was keen rivalry between the kings of Alexandria and *Pergamum in the enlargement of their respective libraries. According to Plutarch, in 47 BC when Julius Caesar was in Alexandria the main library was burnt, but more probably it was a storehouse of books accidentally destroyed. Later legend magnified this episode. The true destruction happened in the late third century AD, when parts of the city were laid waste after rebelling against Rome.

Alexandrian literature, see HELLEN-ISTIC AGE.

Alexandrian scholars, see HELLENISTIC AGE.

Alexandrian War, see *BELLUM ALEXANDRINUM*.

Alexipha'rmaca, see NICANDER.

Ale'xis (*c*.375–275 BC), Greek comic poet of Middle and New Comedy, who lived most of his life at Athens. He was a prolific writer. It is difficult to assess from his few remaining fragments the part he played in the transition from the older to the newer forms of comedy, but he seems to have used the kind of plot especially associated with New Comedy, concerning love affairs of an intricate kind, and to have had a pleasant wit. His fame continued to Roman times when his plays were adapted by Roman comedians. See also COMEDY, GREEK 5.

Alle'cto, see FURIES.

allegory. Allegory in literature is the presentation of a subject under the guise of another suggestively similar. It was rarely written deliberately by the Greeks (but see ALCAEUS (1)). As a device of literary interpretation its most flourishing period was in the late fifth century BC

when certain sophists found in the poets, particularly Homer and Hesiod, 'hidden meanings' of a cosmological or ethical nature. This kind of allegorizing was closely connected with etymology, at that time a pseudo-science which dealt in the 'true' meaning of words and names as revealed by assonances. Plato and the Alexandrian scholars rejected allegorical interpretation of literature. Its main proponents were the Stoic philosophers (third century BC onwards), who used it for the illustration and corroboration of their doctrines, and from them derive the surviving collections of allegorical interpretations of Homer.

The Romans, following the Greeks, found certain moral meanings implicit in Homer, and Horace took over Alcaeus' allegory of the 'ship of state', but they did not compose large-scale allegories. Instead they used numerous poetic conceits and personifications (such as calling the sea Neptune) often in a way that suggests rather the influence of symbolic painting. A Roman innovation was the allegorical representation of contemporary persons and events, as in Virgil's *Eclogues*, but perhaps this too had been done before by Theocritus (in Idyll 7), and scholars of both poets still dispute the degree of correspondence with real people. The profundity and ambiguity of much of the *Aeneid* led interpreters from the fourth century onward to find in it an allegory of ideas rather than of facts. Allegory entered Christian literature from Stoic sources. See also BUCOLIC.

A'llia, a small stream flowing into the Tiber about 18 km. (11 miles) north of Rome, near which the Romans suffered a notable defeat by the Gauls in 390 BC. The disaster occurred on the anniversary (18 July) of the ambush of the Fabii (see FABIA, GENS) by the Veientes in 479 BC.

alliteration, the literary device in which two or more words in close connection begin with the same letter (see ASSONANCE). It was not a common device of Greek poetry, but is a feature in Latin saturnian verse (see METRE, LATIN 1), and was adopted thence by later Roman poets including Ennius and Virgil, as when Ennius writes:

fraxinu' frangitur atque abies constern-
itur alta.
pinus proceras pervortunt.

('The ash tree is shattered and the lofty
fir laid low. They overturn the tall
pines.')

It is carried to grotesque excess by the
same poet in the line:

o Tite tute Tati tibi tanta tyranne tulisti.

('O Titus Tatius, such great things you
brought upon yourself, arrogant
ruler.')

A'lmagest, see PTOLEMY.

Alō'adae, Alōï'dae, see OTUS.

alphabet
1. *Greek*. The earliest examples of Greek
writing to survive are all inscribed on
Greek pottery from the second half of the
eighth century BC, and examples are
found almost simultaneously in all parts
of the Greek world, from Ischia off the
coast of south Italy in the West to Rhodes
in the East. In these examples the writing
runs from right to left in odd-numbered
lines and from left to right in even-
numbered lines, a form known as
boustrophēdon, 'as the ox turns'.

The standard Greek alphabet, still in
use today, is as follows:

Small letters	Capital letters	Greek names	English equivalents
α	A	alpha	a
β	B	bēta	b
γ	Γ	gamma	g
δ	Δ	delta	d
ε	E	epsīlon	ĕ
ζ	Z	zēta	z (pronounced sd)
η	H	ēta	ē
θ	Θ	thēta	th
ι	I	iōta	i
κ	K	kappa	hard c or k
λ	Λ	lam(b)da	l
μ	M	mū	m
ν	N	nū	n
ξ	Ξ	xī	x (pronounced ks)
ο	O	omīcron	ŏ
π	Π	pī	p
ϱ	P	rhō	r (or rh)
σ, ϛ†; or ϲ	Σ, ϲ	sigma	s
τ	T	tau	t
υ	Y	upsī'lon	u (usually transliterated y)
φ	Φ	phī	ph
χ	X	chī	kh (sometimes transliterated ch)
ψ	Ψ	psī	ps
ω	Ω	ōmega	ō

†ϛ is the form used at the end of a word; ϲ is
an alternative to either form.

A distinction between 'capital' and
'small' letters was not clearly made until
the ninth century AD; see BOOKS AND
WRITING 6. Small letters are used conven-
tionally in what follows.

The alphabet from alpha to tau was
taken over from a north Semitic alphabet
(probably a Phoenician script used in
Syria); its introduction to Greece is
perhaps reflected in the myth which tells
how *Cadmus, son of Agenor king of
Tyre, brought letters to *Thebes, the
city he had founded. The shapes of the
letters, their names and their order are
virtually the same in both alphabets but
they do not necessarily represent the
same sounds. The Semitic alphabet has
no characters for vowels, and the Greek
therefore used for its vowels Semitic
characters for consonants not in use in
Greece. Thus Semitic consonant characters were used for α, ε, o, and ι. The
character for upsilon was taken over from
a *cursive Phoenician script and added to
the alphabet after tau. In Greece local
variations lasted for centuries. Some
dialects had an extra letter, Ϝ, between
epsilon and zeta, pronounced like
English w and called first 'wau' by the
Greeks and later *digamma. It disappeared in pre-classical times from the
Attic–Ionic dialects and does not appear
in the standard alphabet given above.
Other letters were added after upsilon to
represent the sounds ph and kh. The
alphabet thus obtained, comprising the
first 22 letters of the 24 listed above, was
used by the Athenians down to the end of
the fifth century BC. The sounds represented have not changed, except that the
letter eta (η) up to that time stood for
the aspirate (h). Epsilon (ε) was written
to represent all forms of the e sound and
omicron (o) for all forms of the o sound.
In 403 BC, in the archonship of Eucleides,
Athens adopted the more developed East

Ionic (Milesian) alphabet which distinguished between short and long o sounds by using *o* and *ω* respectively, and between short and long e by using *η* for the latter, as well as admitting diphthongs in its spelling to express variations of these sounds. The letter *ψ* was also introduced for the sound ps. All Ionic dialects, however, lacked the aspirate, and when the East Ionic alphabet was adopted the aspirate (for which *η* was no longer available) was ignored in writing. In some scripts this deficiency was remedied by the sign ⱶ (the left half of capital eta). The Alexandrian scholar *Aristophanes of Byzantium subsequently introduced both ⱶ and ⱶ written above initial vowels to mark the presence or absence of the aspirate (known as 'rough breathing' and 'smooth breathing'). These are written in modern texts as ʽ and ʼ respectively.

2. *Latin*. The Latin alphabet seems to have come from an early form of Etruscan script which was itself derived from the (Euboean) Greek alphabet as used at Cumae (in Campania), a colony of Chalcis in Euboea. The early Latin alphabet was the same as its modern English derivative except that it lacked the letters G, J (for which I did duty), U, W (for which V also served), Y, and Z. The character X represented the sound ks (unlike the Greek X, which represented the sound kh). H represented the aspirate (for its varying significance in Greek see I above). Greek gamma was represented by the character C which was at first used for the G sound as well as for the K sound (compare the names Gaius and Gnaeus which when abbreviated were written in archaic fashion C. and Cn.); the character G was introduced in the third century BC. Originally the character K was written instead of C where the following letter was A, but it was later replaced by C and K became redundant (a relic of this old spelling is *Kalendae*, 'the Calends'). The letter Q (from Greek ϙ, koppa, found in some Greek alphabets after pi), originally written instead of C before O and U, was later used only before U (English q). Z was introduced to express the original ds sound in words borrowed from Greek, and was added at the end of the alphabet, its seventh place in the Greek alphabet (after digamma) having been occupied by G. The Latin f sound was most closely represented by the Greek digamma. V (a form of capital upsilon) represented both the vowel and the semivowel U. Y (the usual form of capital upsilon) was added in the late republic to transliterate Greek words containing upsilon.

See also BOOKS AND WRITING and EPIGRAPHY.

Alphesiboe'a, see ALCMAEON.

Alphē'us (Alpheios), one of the largest rivers in Greece, rising in Arcadia in the Peloponnese and, after receiving many tributaries (including the Erymanthus and the Ladon), flowing through Elis to the Ionian Sea. The plain of *Olympia is situated by the side of it. Its waters were fabled to pass unmixed through the sea and to be mingled with the fountain of *Arethusa in the island of Ortygia near Syracuse; perhaps the subterranean passage of the river in the upper part of its course gave rise to this myth.

Alps. There is no evidence that the early Greeks knew of the existence of these mountains; the Roman conquest of Cisalpine Gaul and Hannibal's invasion of Italy in the third century BC brought detailed information. The campaigns of Julius Caesar in Gaul opened up the Alps until by the second century AD a dozen passes were known and at least five paved roads built across them.

Althae'a, in Greek myth, mother of *Meleager.

Amalthē'a (Amaltheia), in Greek myth, the goat that suckled the infant *Zeus in Crete; or a nymph (according to one version the daughter of Melissus, king of Crete) who fed Zeus with the milk of a goat. Zeus gave her the horn of the goat; it had the power of producing whatever its possessor wished, and was known (in Latin) as the *cornu copiae*, 'horn of plenty'.

Amā'ta, in Virgil's *Aeneid*, the wife of *Latinus and mother of *Lavinia.

Amazons (Amāzonĕs), legendary nation of female warriors supposed by the Greeks to have lived in the time of the heroes. Their home is always situated on the bounds of the known world, usually in remote north-east Asia. They figure in the exploits of various Greek heroes down to Alexander the Great, who according to legend met their queen on the borders of India, and are very popular in art from at least the seventh century BC. Their name, supposedly meaning 'breastless', was said to derive from their custom of cutting off the right breast to facilitate the use of arms in battle. Their occupations are hunting and fighting, always from horseback. They propagate their kind by associating for a time with men from a neighbouring tribe and rearing only their daughters. They are mentioned in Homer's *Iliad* and appear as allies of the Trojans in the poems of the Epic Cycle; their queen Penthesilēa was killed by Achilles. They also play a part in the careers of Heracles (see HERACLES, LABOURS OF 9) and *Theseus.

Ambarvā'lia, 'the procession round the fields', at Rome, a solemn annual purification of the fields of the *ager Romanus* ('Roman territory'), at which sacrificial animals, pig, sheep, and ox (*suovetaurīlia*), were led around the old boundaries of Rome. Sacrifice was offered at particular points. This ceremony may be identical with the sacrifice to the Dea Dia performed by the *arval priests.

A'mbiorix, leader of the Gallic tribe of the Eburōnēs in their revolt against the Romans in 54–53 BC. He successfully evaded capture. See COMMENTARIES I (books 5 and 6).

Ambrose, Saint (Aurēlius, Ambrŏsius) (*c.* AD 340–97), bishop of Milan, born of a Christian family at Trier, his father being prefect of Narbonese Gaul. He was educated at Rome and entered on an official career, and at an early age was made governor of the region of Milan with the title of consul. On the death in 374 of Auxentius, the Arian bishop of Milan, Ambrose was chosen to replace him by popular acclamation, although he was a Christian only by belief, and unbaptized. He received baptism and the priesthood after his appointment. Famous as an upholder of orthodoxy, and as a preacher, Ambrose exercised mounting influence

over the Roman emperors, his aim being the establishment of an empire which excluded all errors of belief—paganism, Judaism, and Arianism. He used his knowledge of Greek to study philosophy and theology, and a knowledge of these sources is apparent in his commentaries and sermons (which were a great influence on *Augustine's conversion). His treatise on the duties of priests, *De officiis ministrorum*, is modelled on Cicero's *De officiis*. His letters, panegyrics, and sermons are a primary source for the history of his period. Of the hymns attributed to him, a few are certainly authentic, but he was not the author of the *Te Deum*, as tradition relates. The Ambrosian Library at Milan (founded in 1609) is named after him.

ambrosia and **nectar,** the mythical food and drink of the gods, associated with divine immortality. A mortal who took them became immortal; shed on a corpse they kept it from decay. Various things connected with the gods are described as ambrosial, sometimes with the connotation of 'sweet-smelling'.

Ammiā'nus Marcellī'nus (*c.* AD 330– 95), the last great Roman historian who wrote in Latin, although in fact he was a Greek born at Antioch. His history in 31 books was a continuation of the histories of Tacitus, covering the years AD 96–378, from the death of Domitian to the disastrous defeat of the Romans by the Goths at Adrianople in 378. Books 1–13 have been lost. The remaining books 14– 31 deal in extreme detail with the years 353–78, covering events in his own lifetime, many of which he witnessed himself and, it is believed, reported accurately. As a young man he joined the army and served on the eastern frontier, and in Gaul under *Julian (later emperor) whom he admired profoundly but not uncritically. He took part in Julian's fatal campaign in Persia and later visited Egypt and Greece. In 378 he settled in Rome, where he wrote his history; his friends included *Symmachus, the leading literary figure at the time. Ammianus' narrative is interesting and enlivened by digressions—on the Egyptian obelisks and their hieroglyphics, earthquakes, lions in Mesopotamia, the artillery of his time, and includes a famous description of the *Huns (31. 2). He writes largely without prejudice on the various nations dealt with, on the Christians, and on the emperors themselves. His style, which he was never fully in command of, was ornate and rhetorical, and partly based on Tacitus; it was much admired by later writers.

Ammon or **Amo(u)n,** Egyptian god represented sometimes as a ram, whose oracle at the oasis of Siwa in the Libyan desert became known to the Greeks probably through the north African Greek colony of Cyrene. Its fame rivalled that of Delphi and Dodona, and it was consulted on a notable occasion by *Alexander the Great. The poet Pindar wrote a hymn to the god, and his cult had arrived at Athens by the fourth century BC. Ammon was usually portrayed in the Greek world with the head of Zeus bearing a ram's curling horns. See also ANDROMEDA.

amoebe'an verse, literary form found mainly in bucolic poetry, for example in Theocritus and Virgil, consisting of couplets or 'stanzas' assigned alternately to two characters, usually in singing matches where the verses of one character are capped by the other.

Amō'res, fifty love-poems by the Roman poet *Ovid, written in the elegiac metre, some of them among his earliest works. There were two editions, the first in five books published perhaps in 20 BC, possibly under the title *Corinna.* This is lost; what we possess is the second edition in three books, published a little before 1 BC.

Most of the poems are studies or sketches of love in different moods, nearly always of sophisticated love, acted out in the city of Rome in the context of a pleasure-seeking, leisured society. They are polished, contrived, and amusing, the product of wit rather than of passion. 'Corinna' figures prominently in them, but it is doubtful whether she had any real existence. There are interesting illustrations of contemporary life—a scene at the circus, or a festival of Juno, for example. Poem III. 9 is a touching

lament for the death of the poet *Tibullus.

Amphiarā'us, in Greek myth, an Argive hero and seer, son of Oikles, who played an important part in the stories of the Greek *Epic Cycle which relate to a generation earlier than the heroes of the Trojan War. He married Eriphylē, whom Polyneices bribed, with the necklace of Harmonia (see CADMUS), to persuade Amphiaraus to take part in the expedition of the Seven against Thebes (see OEDIPUS), although the seer knew that none of the Seven except Adrastus would return from it alive. He set out reluctantly, but before starting commanded his children to avenge his death by killing their mother, and by making a second expedition against Thebes (see ALCMAEON). He attacked Thebes but was driven off, and as he fled was swallowed up in a cleft in the ground made by Zeus' thunderbolt. Thus originated the famous oracular shrine of Amphiaraus at Oropus, where oracles were given by the interpretation of dreams.

amphi'ctyony (amphiktyoneia), religious association or league of Greek communities who lived in the neighbourhood of, and had some responsibility for, the shrine of a god (from *amphictuones,* 'dwellers around'). The most important amphictyonic league was that of Delphi, whose sanctuaries were the temples of Apollo at Delphi and of Demeter at Thermopylae. Many of the principal peoples of Greece, including Thessalians, Dorians, and Ionians, belonged to it. *Sacred wars were occasionally proclaimed against violators of amphictyonic laws. The foundation of the amphictyony was attributed in antiquity to an eponymous Amphictyon, son of Deucalion and brother of Hellen (the ancestor of the Greeks).

Amphi'on and Zethus, see ANTIOPE.

Amphi'polis, city founded by a colony of Athenians in 437 BC, of great strategic and commercial importance, particularly in the Peloponnesian War. Situated near the coast on the east bank of the river Strymon, the boundary between Macedonia and Thrace, it commanded the only crossing-place on the southern reaches of that river and thus the route into Greece from the Hellespont. In 424 BC during the Peloponnesian War Amphipolis surrendered to the Spartans; the historian Thucydides was held responsible for the loss and exiled. In an unsuccessful attempt to recapture it in 422 the Athenian and Spartan commanders Cleon and Brasidas were both killed. Amphipolis was to have been restored to Athens by the Peace of Nicias in 421 but it remained practically independent, despite Athenian pressure, until it was annexed by Philip II of Macedon in 357 BC.

Amphitrī'tē, Nereid (see NEREUS), wife of the god *Poseidon.

Amphi'truo, Roman comedy by *Plautus (*c.*195 BC), perhaps an adaptation of a Greek comedy by Philemon, on the mythical subject of the cuckolding of Amphitryon (see below) by the Greek god Zeus (in Plautus' play, the Roman god Jupiter). Jupiter takes on the appearance of Amphitruo after the latter's departure for war, and seduces his virtuous wife Alcmena. Plautus calls the play a *tragico-comoedia* because of the unusual blend of contrasting elements, the morally virtuous but unwittingly unchaste wife, and the burlesque situation of the outraged husband. Foils are provided by the god Mercury and Sosia, the long-suffering but cheerful slave. The theme proved popular with later comic dramatists, Molière, John Dryden (with music by Henry Purcell), and in more recent times, Jean Giraudoux.

Amphi'tryon, in Greek myth, son of Alcaeus king of Tiryns, and Astydameia; grandson of *Perseus. His sister Anaxo married her uncle Electryon (brother of Alcaeus), king of Mycenae, and their daughter Alcmena was betrothed to Amphitryon. After the death of his sons in a feud Electryon handed over his kingdom to Amphitryon, but the latter, while helping to recover stolen cattle, unfortunately killed Electryon and so had to take refuge with Creon, king of Thebes. Alcmena wished Amphitryon to avenge her brothers before she would marry him, and this he did; but during his absence Zeus fell in love with her and just

before Amphitryon's return visited her in the guise of her husband. Alcmena gave birth to twin sons, Iphiclēs the child of Amphitryon and Heracles the child of Zeus.

Amȳmō'nē, in Greek myth, one of the fifty daughters of *Danaus, rescued from a satyr and seduced by the god Poseidon, who created the spring Amymone in commemoration.

Ana'băsis (*Kyrou anabasis*, 'Cyrus' expedition inland'), prose narrative in seven books by *Xenophon, describing the expedition of the younger Cyrus, son of king Darius II of Persia, against his elder brother Artaxerxes II, the then king. Xenophon published the first part under the pseudonym of Themistogenes of Syracuse, but in the second part he abandoned the pretence and magnified his own role in the expedition.

Cyrus, who was satrap of Lydia, was disappointed that he had not been chosen to succeed his father, as the favourite son. His resentment against his brother was increased, according to Xenophon, when he was arrested by Artaxerxes, soon after his accession, on a false charge of conspiracy. Cyrus prepared to attack Artaxerxes, and recruited an auxiliary force of 10,000 Greeks. Xenophon describes the long march of Cyrus' expedition, the 'Ten Thousand', which he accompanied at the invitation of his friend Proxenus, one of the Greek generals, from Sardis to the neighbourhood of Babylon in 401 BC. It was interrupted by the reluctance of some of the troops to proceed when they discovered the true object of the expedition, which had been concealed from them. The majority were persuaded to go on, and fought in the battle of Cunaxa, near Babylon; Cyrus himself was killed, and his Asiatic troops took flight.

This disaster dismayed the Greeks, but they resisted the attempts of Artaxerxes to induce them to surrender. Their dismay increased when the satrap *Tissaphernes, who had been conducting the negotiations on the Persian side, lured the Greek generals into his quarters to have them seized and beheaded. At this point Xenophon induced the remaining officers to reorganize the force and arrange a safe retreat. Cheirisophus commanded the van while Xenophon took the more dangerous command at the rear. His advice on the route and his courage and resourcefulness enabled the Greek army, after great hardships and severe fighting in the mountains of Armenia, to reach the Black Sea. Xenophon's account includes a famous description (IV. 7. 20–6) of the scene when the Greeks, climbing Mount Theches, at last saw the sea and cried *'thalassa, thalassa!'* (the sea, the sea!). They now reached comparative safety at Trapezus, a Greek colony on the Black Sea coast; but difficulties had still to be overcome, and there was dissension among the troops before they reached Byzantium. After spending a winter in the service of the treacherous Seuthes, a Thracian, Xenophon handed over the remnant of the Ten Thousand to the Spartan Thimbron, for the war against Persia. In his narrative Xenophon's piety is noticeable: he takes no important decision without sacrificing to the gods and being guided by the omens.

Anacha'rsis, according to Herodotus, a Scythian prince of the sixth century BC who travelled widely and acquired a high reputation for wisdom. On his return to Scythia he was put to death for trying to introduce the cult of Magna Mater (see CYBELE). Later writers made him the guest of Solon at Athens and include him among the Seven Sages. He was traditionally supposed to have despised all Greeks except the Spartans, and thus arose the picture of him as a 'noble savage' uttering *Cynic diatribes against a corrupt civilization. The sayings and letters attributed to him furnished a model for the French political philosopher Montesquieu and the Irish writer Oliver Goldsmith, writing in the eighteenth century.

Ana'creon (b. *c.*570 BC), Greek lyric poet, born in the Ionian city of Teos on the coast of Asia Minor, whence he migrated when the Persians threatened and joined other Teians in the foundation of Abdera in Thrace. Some time later he moved to the court of Polycrates, tyrant of Samos *c.*533–522, to whom he wrote many poems, though in the extant fragments Polycrates' name is nowhere

found. After the fall of Polycrates, Hipparchus, brother of the Athenian tyrant Hippias, brought him to Athens; it is probable that after Hipparchus' murder he went to Thessaly. The place of his death, at an advanced age, is unknown. He wrote in the Ionic Greek dialect perhaps five books of lyric, iambic, and elegiac poetry from which only a few complete poems survive, more often in the quotations of later grammarians and metricians than in fragments of papyrus (see PAPYROLOGY). Most of his surviving fragments are from poems composed in simple metres (especially anacreontics and glyconics; see METRE, GREEK 8 (i)), which speak most memorably of love and the convivial pleasures. His love poems are tender and delicately sensuous, often characterized by a self-deprecating humour and verbal wit that give a nice touch of ambiguousness to the tone of some of them. They are far removed from the mere 'prettiness' of later imitators (see below).

Anacreontēa, body of short poems mostly on amorous or convivial themes composed at various times in late antiquity. They were modelled not very accurately on the style and subject matter of Anacreon and often ascribed to him, so much so that his fame in Europe after the Renaissance depended very largely on these imitations. With their literary conceits and prettiness the best of them have a charm that disguises their slightness.

anacrū'sis, 'upbeat' in metric, an alternative term for *arsis.

anagnō'risis, 'recognition', see *POETICS.*

Analy'tica prio'ra and *posterio'ra,* treatises on logic by *Aristotle (4 (i)).

a'napaest, see METRE, GREEK I (iii).

Anatolia, 'the East', the late Greek name for that part of Asia which is roughly equivalent to modern Turkey. It is now used to denote that part of the world in ancient times.

Anaxa'goras (*c.*500–*c.*428 BC), of Clazomenae in Ionia, the first philosopher to reside in Athens, probably between 480 and 430 (the chronology of his life is disputed). He became the friend and mentor of Pericles. Later he was prosecuted for impiety (and perhaps for having Persian sympathies) by Cleon and so withdrew to Lampsacus, where he founded a school and was held in high esteem. He appears to have written only one book, *On Nature*, a prose work of which several extensive fragments are preserved by quotation. He belongs to the Ionian tradition of philosophy (see PHILOSOPHY I and PROSE I), and his interests were in cosmology and physics, but conflicting testimonies make it difficult to reconstruct his thought. His universe is composed of 'seeds' of every distinct substance, which take their quality from their prevailing component but contain at the same time infinitesimal particles of every other substance ('everything has a share of everything'). Changes in things therefore occur as a consequence of the regrouping of the constituent substances. The animating principle of plants and animals and the initiator of cosmic motion is Mind, *Nous*, which is 'the finest of all things and the purest', and is itself separate and unmixed, omnipresent and eternal. In this cosmology Mind starts a rotary motion which gradually spreads and separates the seeds, the dense, moist, cold, and dark going to the centre and their opposites to the circumference. To Anaxagoras the heavenly bodies were huge stones ('the sun is larger than the Peloponnese') torn from the earth and rendered incandescent by their motion. This view may have been influenced by the famous fall of a meteorite in the region of Aegospotami in 467. Anaxagoras believed that the earth was flat and floated on air, but he understood that the heavenly bodies rotated and that the moon received its light from the sun, and he therefore grasped the principle of eclipses. Doctrines such as his, destructive of the traditional and official pantheon, exerted great influence on late fifth-century thought.

Anaxima'nder (Anaximandros) (*c*.610–545 BC), Ionian philosopher of Miletus, the first Greek known to have written (*c*.546) a book in prose, a treatise on nature, now lost except for one quotation. It was said that he introduced into Greece the gnomon (the vertical rod whose shadow indicates the sun's direction), and to have constructed the first map of the earth and the first celestial globe (this last is improbable).

Anaximander is the first philosopher we know of who tried to explain rationally the origins of the world and of mankind. He declared that the origin of all things was the Unbounded (*to apeiron*), which is 'the divine' (*to theion*), being immortal and indestructible. This 'enfolded' and 'controlled' the *cosmos*, or indeed many *cosmoi* (whether successive or co-existent is not clear). The most important forces at work in the cosmos and the agents of physical change were pairs of opposites, chiefly the hot and the cold, the wet and the dry. Anaximander thought that the earth was shaped like a drum of a column, its people living on its upper surface. Of his many interesting ideas about details of our cosmos two are notable. Alone of the Presocratics he explained why the earth remains in the same place without postulating some material support, declaring that there was no reason why what was symmetrically placed in the middle, equidistant from the extremities, should move downwards rather than in any other direction. The second is his conjecture about the origins of animal and human life. He supposed that the first living creatures were produced by spontaneous generation from mud by the action of the sun, and this became a standard account. Further, he inferred from the helpless condition of men in infancy that they could not have survived in primitive conditions without protection, and so conjectured that in the beginning they were reared in fish-like creatures from which they burst out when they were able to nourish themselves.

Anaxi'menēs, of Miletus (flourished *c*.546 BC), Ionian philosopher and younger contemporary of Anaximander. His writings are lost and our knowledge of them depends on the statements of later writers. For Anaximenes the originative principle (*archē*) of the cosmos was air; when air was rarified as fire or condensed as water or earth these elements compounded together could make up the wide diversity of the natural world. Furthermore air was the actual breath of the cosmos and so its ever-living and therefore divine source. Anaximenes thought that the earth was flat and shallow—'table-like'—and supported by air. His theory of condensation and rarefaction as observable means of change from the basic form of matter to the diversity of natural substances was his important contribution to the thought of his time.

anceps ('ambivalent'), in *metre (see 1), a syllable that can be scanned either long or short.

Anchī'sēs, in Greek myth, a Trojan prince, great-grandson of Tros (see TROY) and a member of the younger branch of the Trojan royal house. The goddess Aphroditē fell in love with him, and the child of their union was *Aeneas. Anchises when drunk boasted of the goddess's favour and was struck blind, or paralysed, by the thunderbolt of Zeus. We are told in the *Aeneid* that he was carried from burning Troy on his son's shoulders, and accompanied him in his wanderings. Tradition gives many accounts of his death; Virgil places it at Drepanum in Sicily (see *Aeneid*, 3, 5, and 6).

ancī'lia. At Rome a shield (*ancīle*) was said to have fallen from heaven during the reign of *Numa (715–673 BC), and an oracle declared that the seat of empire would lie wherever that shield should be. Thereupon Numa caused eleven other shields to be made like it, so that, if a traitor should wish to remove it, the genuine shield could not be distinguished. These shields were of the ancient 'figure of eight' shape, known from Mycenaean art, and were preserved in the Temple of Mars (part of the old royal palace in the Forum) in the custody of the *Salii and carried round the city yearly in solemn procession in the month of March, the shield being supposed to have fallen on the first day of that month. On a declaration of war, the Roman general moved the shields, with the words 'Awake, Mars!'

Ancus Ma'rcius, one of the legendary *seven kings of Rome.

Ancȳrā'num Monumentum, see MONUMENTUM ANCYRANUM.

Ando'cidēs (*c*.440–*c*.390 BC), one of the earlier Attic orators and member of an ancient aristocratic Athenian family which traced its descent from the god Hermes. He was accused of sacrilege, notably in sharing in the mutilation of the *Hermae in 415, and in order to secure his own immunity and, he claimed, to save his father, who had been implicated, confessed to his involvement. Subsequently he repudiated the confession, but at the time his account was accepted by the Athenians. He retired from Athens and began to trade as a merchant when a decree was passed limiting his rights as a citizen. We possess three of his speeches, the first, 'On his Return', delivered in the *ecclesia*, probably in 410, when he unsuccessfully pleaded for the removal of the limitation on his rights. The second, 'On the Mysteries', was made in 399 when, having been restored to full public rights under the amnesty of 403, he successfully defended himself against a charge of still being subject to the former limitation (the sixth speech in the works of Lysias is apparently part of the prosecution); it is interesting as an eye-witness account of an intriguing event in Athenian history. His third speech, 'On the Peace', is a political discourse urging peace with Sparta in 390, the fourth year of the Corinthian War. The Athenians rejected the peace, and Andocides retired into exile and oblivion. He was not, like the other orators, a trained or professional rhetorician, but a man of ability and shrewdness, who excelled in a natural and persuasive eloquence.

A'ndria ('woman of Andros'), the first comedy of *Terence, produced in 166 BC. An anecdote, perhaps apocryphal, relates that Terence appeared before *Caecilius by order of the *aediles to read his first play to him when Caecilius was at dinner. The latter was so impressed that Terence was invited to share the meal.

Pamphilus, a young Athenian, has seduced Glycerium, supposed to be the sister of a courtesan from Andros, and is devoted to her. His father, Simo, has arranged a match for him with the daughter of his friend Chremēs. But

Chremes has heard of the relations between Pamphilus and Glycerium and withdraws his consent to the match. Simo conceals this and pretends to go on with preparations for an immediate marriage, hoping by this means to put an end to the affair. Pamphilus, learning from his cunning slave Davus that the intended marriage is a pretence, temporizes and offers no objection. Simo now persuades Chremes to withdraw his objection, so reducing Pamphilus to despair. At this stage Glycerium bears a son to Pamphilus, and Davus arranges to have this made known to Chremes, who now finally breaks off the match. At this point an acquaintance newly arrived from Andros reveals to Chremes that Glycerium as a child was shipwrecked there in circumstances which show that she is in fact his daughter. Chremes and Simo consent to the marriage of Pamphilus and Glycerium, and all ends happily.

The play contains the often-quoted phrases *hinc illae lacrimae*, 'hence those tears', and *amantium irae amoris integratiost*, 'the quarrels of lovers are the renewal of love'.

Androclus and the Lion, see GELLIUS, AULUS.

Andro'machē, in Greek myth, daughter of Ēĕtiōn king of Thēbē in Cilicia, and wife of *Hector. Her father and brothers were killed by Achilles, her mother taken prisoner and ransomed. Her son Astyanax was put to death by the Greeks after the fall of Troy (see *TROJAN WOMEN*) and she herself fell to the lot of Neoptolemus to whom she bore three sons, Molossus (eponym of the Molossians), Pielus, and Pergamus (named after the citadel of Troy). The conflict between her and Hermione, the jealous, childless wife of Neoptolemus, is the theme of Euripides' play *Andromache*. After Neoptolemus' death she married the Trojan seer Helenus, a son of Priam, and lived in Epirus. When Helenus died she was taken by her son Pergamus to Asia Minor, where he founded the city of Pergamum.

Andro'machē, Greek tragedy by *Euripides, probably produced *c*.426 BC,

in the early part of the Peloponnesian War.

The play deals with that period in the life of *Andromache when she was living as the concubine of Neoptolemus in Thessaly. She had borne him a son, Molossus. After ten years Neoptolemus had married Hermione, daughter of Menelaus; she remained childless and suspected that this was the doing of her hated rival Andromache. Helped by Menelaus, Hermione takes advantage of the absence of Neoptolemus on a journey to Delphi to draw Andromache, by the threat to kill Molossus, from the shrine of Thetis where she had taken refuge, in order to kill both mother and son. They are saved by the intervention of the aged Peleus, the grandfather of Neoptolemus. *Orestes, who has contrived the murder of Neoptolemus at Delphi and who arrives unexpectedly, carries off Hermione, to whom he had been betrothed before Neoptolemus had claimed her. The death of Neoptolemus is announced. Thetis appears and arranges matters. The odious character which the poet attributes to (the Spartan) Menelaus has been seen as according with the feeling against Sparta which prevailed at this time at Athens.

Andro'meda (Andromedē), in Greek myth, daughter of Cepheus king of the Ethiopians and his wife Cassiopeia. The latter had offended the Nereids (sea-nymphs) by boasting that her daughter was more beautiful than they. Thereupon they complained to the sea-god Poseidon, who sent a sea-monster to ravage the country. The oracle of *Ammon said it could be appeased only by the sacrifice of Andromeda, who was accordingly fastened to a rock on the sea-shore. Perseus changed the monster to stone by showing it the Gorgon's head, and married Andromeda, after first fighting and turning to stone her uncle Phineus, who had been betrothed to her and who now attacked him. Their children included Alcaeus and Electryon.

Androni'cus, Lucius Livius, see LIVIUS ANDRONICUS.

Andro'tion, Against, speech in a public

prosecution by Demosthenes. See DEMOS-
THENES (2) 4.

Ane'cdota, see PROCOPIUS.

anima'lium, Historia, treatise by
*Aristotle (4 (iii)).

Anna, sister of *Dido. According to the
poet Ovid, Anna came to Italy after
*Aeneas had established himself there,
and was entrusted by him to his wife
Lavinia. But Lavinia was jealous of her,
and Anna fled to the river Numicius and
was taken by the river-god into his care.
The story is not in Virgil's *Aeneid*.

Anna Pere'nna, ancient Roman goddess whose festival was celebrated on the
Ides (15th) of March. This was a feast at
what used to be the first full moon of the
year, since by the old reckoning March
was the first month. She is usually
explained as being a year-goddess but her
name and attributes are not clear, though
obviously connected with the year
(*annus*). She had no mythology. Ovid
(*Fasti* 3) gives several explanations of
her, perhaps of his own invention. He
also paints a vivid picture of the Roman
crowd celebrating the festival by picnick-
ing on the banks of the Tiber, returning
home drunkenly at night.

Annā'lēs. **1.** Of Ennius, see ENNIUS.
2. Of Tacitus, see below.

Annals (*Annales* or *Ab excessu divi
Augusti*, 'from the death of the late
emperor Augustus'), a history of the
reigns of the Julio-Claudian emperors
Tiberius, Caligula, Claudius, and Nero,
by Tacitus, written after his *Histories*.
There is evidence that Tacitus was still
writing it in AD 116. The surviving portions are books 1–4, a small piece of 5, 6,
part of 11, 12–15, and part of 16. The
work is notable for its style, concise to the
point of obscurity, its sustained dignity
and vividness, and its epigrammatic sayings, memorable for their irony or melancholy. The record is in the main gloomy
and depressing, and although Tacitus
bears occasional witness to the efficient
civil administration of the empire, the
emphasis seems to be rather on the
crimes, the sycophancy, the informing,
and the oppression that marked this
period at Rome. Tacitus claims to write

without partiality and prejudice, to aim at
saving worthy actions from oblivion while
recording evil deeds for posterity (3. 65),
but he has in fact a republican bias. It is
generally recognized that the impression
he gives of Tiberius is unduly dark, and
the life of debauchery imputed to him in
his last years at Capri inherently improbable. The most important matters
covered in the surviving books are as
follows.

Book 1 (AD 14–15). After a rapid
review of the reign of Augustus, the
author passes to that of Tiberius, relating
the suppression by Germanicus of the
mutiny of the legions in Pannonia and
Germany in 14, and his first two
campaigns (14–15) against the Germans.
There is a notable description of the visit
of the Roman army to the scene of the
disaster of Varus.

Book 2 (AD 16–19). The third campaign
of Germanicus (16), in which he defeats
Arminius. His expedition to the East with
Cn. Piso (17), and his death, suspected to
have been due to Piso.

Book 3 (AD 20–2). The return of Agrippina, the widow of Germanicus, to Italy,
and the trial (20) and suicide of Piso. The
growth of luxury and sycophancy at
Rome.

Book 4 (AD 23–8). The character and
career of Sejanus, who, in league with
Livia, the wife of Drusus (son of
Tiberius), has Drusus poisoned (23) and
plots against the children of Germanicus.
The proposal of his marriage to Livia is
set aside by Tiberius. In 26 Tiberius withdraws to Capri. The increase in the
activity of informers and in judicial
murders, such as that of Cremutius
Brutus, accused of having in a history
praised Brutus and Cassius.

Book 5 (AD 29). The death of Julia
Augusta or Livia (29), mother of
Tiberius. The story of the conspiracy and
fall of Sejanus in 31, which formed part of
this book, is lost.

Book 6 (AD 31–7). Tiberius at Capri;
his vicious life, anguish, and ferocity. The
death of Drusus (son of Germanicus) by
starvation in prison, and of Agrippina his
mother (33). The ceaseless bloodshed at
Rome, by executions and suicides. The
death of Tiberius in 37, and a summary of
his life.

Book 11 (AD 47–9). The seventh year of the reign of Claudius (47). The excesses of Messalina, her marriage with Silius, the dismay of the emperor, and the execution in 48 of Silius and Messalina at the urging of the freedman Narcissus.

Book 12 (AD 49–54). Claudius marries in 49 his niece Agrippina, daughter of Germanicus. Through her influence her son, the future emperor Nero, is adopted by Claudius, preferred to his own son Britannicus, and married to his daughter Octavia. Silanus, to whom Octavia had been betrothed, is brought to ruin and death in 49 by Agrippina. Seneca is recalled from exile to be Nero's tutor. The insurrection in Britain and the defeat (50) of Caratacus, king of the Silures, who is brought to Rome and pardoned. Claudius is poisoned by Agrippina, and Nero becomes emperor (54).

Book 13 (AD 55–8). The promising beginning to the reign of Nero, who is restrained by Seneca and Burrus, the prefect of the praetorians. Cn. Domitius Corbulo is sent to the East to resist Parthian aggression. Agrippina, whose influence is weakened, takes up the cause of Britannicus; Nero has him poisoned (55) and Agrippina removed from the palace. Nero in love with Poppaea Sabina.

Book 14 (AD 59–62). The attempt to remove Agrippina by scuttling her ship, followed by her brutal murder (61). The great rising of 61 in Britain under Boudicca, and its suppression (London is mentioned as much frequented by merchants and trading vessels). Armenia is recovered from the Parthians by the Romans under Corbulo. The death of Burrus in 62 and the retirement of Seneca. Nero marries Poppaea; his virtuous former wife Octavia is banished to Pandataria (Ventotene) and there murdered.

Book 15 (AD 62–5). The ignominious defeat of Caesennius Paetus in Armenia, followed by the reduction of the country by a Roman army under Corbulo to a dependency of the empire (63). The great fire of Rome, which devastates ten out of the city's fourteen districts, and its rebuilding on an improved plan. The persecution of the Christians, to whom Nero attributes the fire. The conspiracy of C.

Calpurnius Piso and the putting to death of Seneca and Lucan in 65.

Book 16 (AD 65–6). The extravagances of Nero, who appears in public as a singer; the death of Poppaea (65). The suicide of the Stoic Thrasea and the banishment of his son-in-law Helvidius in 66. In chapter 16 of this book, one of the last surviving, Tacitus laments the melancholy and monotonous record of bloodshed. The part relating to the last two years of Nero's reign is lost.

annals, annalists. From the beginning of Roman history to 400 BC scarcely any records were kept, but from c.300 BC regular records of magistrates and 'the most important records', the so-called *annales maximi*, were inscribed by the *pontifex maximus on the tabulae pontificum*, 'tables of the priests', displayed outside his official residence. These tables constituted the first annals, from which Ennius took the title of his historical epic, but for a long time the information they contained was minimal and mainly sacral (names of the magistrates for the year, and records of wars and eclipses, for instance). The first historians of Rome, the so-called senatorial historians, Fabius Pictor, Cincius Alimentus, Postumius Albinus, and C. Acilius, writing in Greek in the first half of the second century BC, owed very little to the annals and were really continuing the tradition of Hellenistic Greek historical writing (see HISTORIOGRAPHY, GREEK). Cato the Censor, writing his history of Rome, the *Origines*, at this time, was also continuing the Greek tradition but writing in Latin. Under his influence the first systematic reconstruction of Roman history based on Roman evidence was made by the 'old' annalists Cassius Hemina and Calpurnius Piso, writing in the second half of the second century BC. Then P. Mucius Scaevola (d. c.115 BC), *pontifex maximus* in 130, ended the annual display of the annals and authorized their publication, in eighty books, from the earliest times up to his own day, involving for the regal period legendary speculation and for the early republic a reconstruction of events in the light of tradition. The arrangement of this historical work determined the form adopted by all later Roman historians, including those who, like Valerius Antias and Claudius Quadrigarius, expanded the records in rhetorical style. A few historians, like Licinius Macer and Aelius Tubero, appear to have checked their material, but most annalistic historians like Livy accepted both the narrative form and the content of their sources. See HISTORIOGRAPHY, ROMAN.

Antae'us, in Greek myth, a giant, son of the god Poseidon and Gaia (Earth), who lived in Libya. Heracles wrestled with him while on his way to fetch the golden apples of the Hesperides (see HERACLES, LABOURS OF 11). Whenever Antaeus was thrown, he arose stronger than before from contact with his mother Earth. Heracles, perceiving this, lifted him in the air and crushed him to death.

Antei'a, see BELLEROPHON.

Antē'nor, one of the elders of Troy during the siege. He was in favour of restoring Helen to the Greeks, since she had been taken by treachery. It was said that the Greeks, recognizing his fairness, spared him and his family when the city was captured. Later legend made him out a traitor to the Trojans, telling the Greeks to steal the *Palladium and build the Wooden Horse. Several stories were told of what happened to him after the Trojan War. One legend known to Livy, which may be as old as Sophocles' lost tragedy *Antenoridae* ('sons of Antenor'), relates that Antenor led the Eneti, who had lost their king at Troy, from Paphlagonia to the head of the Adriatic Sea, where they settled in Venetia and founded the city of Patavium (Padua).

Anthestē'ria, at Athens, an important festival, lasting three days, of the god *Dionysus, which gave its name to the month Anthesterion (February–March), signifying the time of year when the flowers (*anthē*) begin to appear. It was the custom to garland with flowers children who were 3 years old, and children participated in the festival, perhaps because Dionysus was in some aspects the god of life and growth. As he was also god of wine, wine was much in evidence; the first day was the *pithoigia*, 'jar-opening', when the new wine was tasted and

offered at the shrine of Dionysus in the Marshes, *en limnais* (the marshes which were the home of the Frogs in Aristophanes' comedy of that name). The second day was called *khŏĕs*, 'wine-jugs', the *khous* being a type of pot with a wide curving belly, short neck, and trefoil mouth, numbers of which survive in miniature form, having evidently been given to children as presents. Much drinking took place, and there was a procession in which Dionysus (perhaps personified by a masked actor) was borne along on a ship mounted on wheels, and was supposed to 'marry' the wife of the *archon basileus* (see ARCHONS (i)). At the end of Aristophanes' *Acharnians* the hero Dikaiopolis prepares to celebrate the feast of the wine-jugs while the general Lamachus has to go off to war. The third day was called *khytroi*, 'pots', in which a mixture of all kinds of vegetables was boiled and offered to the god Hermes Chthonios, 'of the Underworld', on behalf of the dead, to placate their hostility. It was a day of ill-omen, when the spirits of the dead (*keres*) were thought to roam the city. At the end of the day they were banished with the cry, 'Be gone, keres, the Anthesteria are over!'

A'nthimus, Greek doctor who wrote soon after AD 511, in the form of a letter to Theodoric the Great (see GOTHS), a short Latin treatise 'on dietetics', *De observatione ciborum*, half medical text-book, half cookery book. The book is of great interest for the picture it gives of the eating and drinking habits of a Germanic people, and for the unclassical nature of the author's language which he had learnt entirely from the speech of the people (see LATIN 4).

anthology

1. *Greek.* The word *anthologia*, literally 'flower-gathering', has come to denote a collection of extracts from literary works, and particularly a collection of poems. Many collections of poems were made in Greece from the fourth century BC onwards. These have been lost as separate entities, but a vast collection of short poems, mostly in the elegiac metre, ranging in time from the seventh century BC to the tenth century AD, survives in what we

know as the Greek Anthology. The basis of this collection went back many centuries. The earliest source of which we know is the *Garland* compiled by *Meleager in the early years of the first century BC; it contains poems attributed to some fifty poets from *Archilochus to Meleager himself. Few were more than eight lines long. Another anthology of epigrams written after Meleager's time was compiled around AD 40 by Philip of Thessalonika. The next most notable collection was the *Syllogē* or *Cycle* made *c.* AD 560 by the Byzantine poet and scholar *Agathias from epigrams written by his contemporaries and himself. These three anthologies became the principal sources for an important and comprehensive anthology compiled *c.* AD 900 by the learned Constantine Cephalas, an official of the Imperial Palace at Byzantium, but perhaps never completed or published in the normal way. All these various collections have perished as such; the surviving Greek Anthology, a collection of sixteen books of epigrams, is derived from two Byzantine compilations which were based on Cephalas' work but with many additions. The first and larger is the Palatine Anthology, so-called because the unique tenth-century manuscript that contains it was found in the Count Palatine's Library at Heidelberg. The second is a collection made by the scholarly Byzantine monk Maximus Planudes in about 1300, and the only one known until the Palatine manuscript was discovered by the young French scholar Salmasius (Claude de Saumaise) in 1606. Those epigrams of Planudes which are not found in the Palatine manuscript are now published as book 16 of the Palatine Anthology.

The Greek Anthology contains a wide variety of poems, many of great charm. There are epitaphs (including the famous epitaphs attributed to Simonides), dedications, reflections on life and death and fate, poems on love, on family life, on great poets and artists and their works, and on the beauties of nature. A certain proportion are humorous or satirical, making fun of doctors, rhetoricians, athletes, etc., or of personal peculiarities, such as Nicon's long nose.

The dedicatory poems form perhaps the group that throws most light on ancient Greek life. There are dedications not only of arms, but of many kinds of implements and articles of daily use: a girl about to marry offers up her dolls and toys, a traveller his old hat, 'a small gift, but given in piety'.

2. *Latin*. The Anthologia Latina is the title given to a collection of some 380 short Latin poems made in Africa during the early sixth century AD and preserved in the famous Codex Salmasianus (named after its former owner Salmasius: see above) of the seventh or eighth century. The collection contains poems written by African poets during the Vandal occupation (fifth to early sixth century) and a few miscellaneous earlier pieces, including the *Pervigilium Veneris* and three epigrams of the philosopher Seneca. It played an influential part in the development of medieval Latin poetry.

Anticle'a (Antikleia), in Greek myth, the wife of Laertēs and mother of *Odysseus.

Antidosis, On the, see ISOCRATES.

Anti'gonē. In the version of the myth of *Oedipus most familiar to us from Greek literature, Antigone is one of the four children (two daughters and two sons) of Oedipus by his union with his mother Jocasta. Antigone's part in the myth seems to have originated largely in fifth-century Attica. She accompanied the blind Oedipus after his banishment from Thebes, and they eventually arrived at Colonus, near Athens. When Oedipus' sons Polyneices and Eteocles died by each other's hand as they fought for the kingdom of Thebes, Jocasta's brother Creon, now king of Thebes, forbade the burial of Polyneices as being the aggressor. Antigone refused to accept this decree, gave the body a token burial, was discovered, and by Creon's order walled up alive in a tomb although she was betrothed to his son Haemon. She hanged herself and Haemon stabbed himself beside her body. This is the version of Sophocles' *Antigone* (see below). Euripides in his (lost) play *Antigone* told a modified version.

Anti'gonē, Greek tragedy by *Sophocles, probably written in 441 BC.

Creon, king of Thebes, has forbidden

the burial of the body of Polyneices (see above). Antigone resolves to defy his decree, performs funeral rites for her brother, and is caught and brought before the king. She pleads that her act is in accordance with the overriding laws of the gods. Creon is unrelenting and condemns her to be immured alive in a cave. Her sister Ismenē, who has refused to share in Antigone's actions, now claims a share in her guilt and punishment, but the king regards her as demented. Creon's son Haemon, who is betrothed to Antigone, pleads with his father in vain; he leaves with a warning that he will die with her. The seer Teiresias threatens the king with the terrible consequences of his defying the divine laws, and Creon, at last moved, goes to the cave. He finds Haemon clasping the dead body of Antigone, who has hanged herself. Haemon lunges at Creon with his sword, but misses and then kills himself. Creon returns to his palace, to find that his wife Eurydicē, in despair, has taken her own life.

Anti'gonus and **Anti'gonids.** The first bearer of the name Antigonus of whom we know was one of the generals of Alexander the Great, the son of a noble Macedonian family, who was satrap of Phrygia at the time of Alexander's death in 323 BC and eventually aspired to rule all the empire. He was defeated and killed at the battle of Ipsus in 301. His grandson Antigonus II Gonatas, son of Demetrius Poliorcetes, established in Macedonia the Antigonid dynasty, which maintained a partial control over Greece. After Gonatas the most prominent of the Antigonids was his grandson *Philip V (238–179 BC) who by provoking Rome into the Macedonian Wars was largely responsible for bringing Greece under Roman domination. After the Macedonian army was practically annihilated by the Romans at the battle of Pydna in 168 BC the Antigonids were dethroned and the Macedonian realm broken up into four federal republics. In 146 BC it became a Roman province.

Anti'lochus, in Greek myth, son of Nestor, in Homer's *Iliad* a brave fighter for the Greeks in the Trojan War. The *Aethiopis* described how he was killed defending his father against Memnon.

Anti'machus, of Colophon (flourished c.400 BC), the first Greek 'scholar-poet' and as such a forerunner of the Hellenistic poets, anticipating them in their learned obscurities. He wrote an epic on Thebes, and in his long elegiac poem *Lydē* was the originator of narrative *elegy, a genre in which he had many imitators. Only scanty fragments of his works survive. The *Lyde* was much admired by some Hellenistic poets, but objected to by *Callimachus (see his *Answer to the Telchinēs*) on the grounds of excessive length and obscurity.

Anti'nŏus. 1. In Homer's *Odyssey*, the most arrogant of the suitors of Odysseus' wife Penelope, and the first of them to be killed by Odysseus.
  2. Bithynian youth of great beauty, a favourite of the emperor *Hadrian. He was drowned in the Nile in AD 130 and gossip surrounded his death with romantic legends. Hadrian founded the city of Antinŏopolis on the Nile and erected temples in his memory. Antinous was frequently represented in sculpture, and some of these representations survive.

A'ntioch (Antiocheia), on the river Orontēs, the capital of ancient Syria, founded by Seleucus I (see SELEUCIDS) about 300 BC, and named after his father. Antiochus I, the Great, king of Syria 223–187 BC, adorned it with works of art, a theatre, and a library. It became a centre of trade and a city of pleasure; the Greek poet Aratus of Soli lived for a time at the court of Antiochus I (281–261 BC) and the Greek poet Euphorion was appointed librarian of the public library. Antiochus IV Epiphanes (175–163 BC), an ardent lover of classical Greek culture, considerably beautified the city. Antioch was prominent in Christian life: it was here that Christians were first so called (Acts 11: 26), and the city ranked after Rome and Jerusalem as the third Patriarchal see. After the inauguration of Constantinople in AD 330 Antioch gradually ceased to be a principal city of the East. It was destroyed in the Persian invasion of AD 538 and never fully recovered. Many other cities founded by the Seleucids, besides the capital, bore the name Antioch.

Anti'ochus. 1. The name of several of the Seleucid kings of Asia; see above, and SELEUCIDS.

2. Of Ascalon, see ACADEMY.

Anti'opē. 1. In Greek myth, daughter of Nycteus, king of Boeotia. Her story has come down to us chiefly through Euripides' tragedy *Antiope*, now lost. Antiope was seduced by Zeus and became the mother of the twin brothers Amphion and Zethus. To avoid her father's anger she fled to Sicyon. Nycteus in despair killed himself, but first charged his brother, Lycus, who was king of Thebes during the minority of *Laius, to punish Antiope. Lycus captured Sicyon and imprisoned Antiope; her treatment was made more cruel by the jealousy of Dircē, the wife of Lycus. At last Antiope escaped and joined her sons, now grown to maturity. These revenged her by tying Dirce to the horns of a bull, so that she was dragged to death; and they killed or deposed Lycus. Amphion and Zethus now became rulers of Thebes and built its walls. (In Homer's *Odyssey* they are represented as the city's first founders.) Amphion was a harper of such skill that the stones were drawn into their places by his music. He married *Niobē, and Zethus married the nymph Thebē, whence the name of Thebes.

2. Another name for Hippolytē, queen of the Amazons.

Anti'pater (Antipatros). **1.** (397–319 BC), one of the most able generals of Philip II of Macedon and subsequently of his son Alexander (the Great). During Alexander's absence in the East he was the governor of Macedonia and the Greek states. After the death of Alexander he suffered an uprising from a league of Greek states but was eventually victorious; he drove the Athenian orator Demosthenes to suicide by demanding his surrender. He remained loyal to the Macedonian dynasty, and it was his death in 319 that precipitated the break-up of Alexander's empire. His son was *Cassander.

2. Of Sidon (flourished *c.*120 BC), Greek writer of short elegiac poems,

some of which are preserved in the Greek *Anthology.

Anti'phanes, Greek poet of Middle Comedy; see COMEDY, GREEK 5.

A'ntiphon (*c.*480–411 BC), Attic orator whose surviving speeches are the earliest we have. He gained a great reputation by writing speeches for others to deliver on their own behalf (litigants at Athens were required to plead in person), but he himself remained in the background until he revealed his ability by guiding the oligarchic revolution and establishing the rule of the *Four Hundred in Athens in 411. After their overthrow he was put to death by the restored democracy. The speech he delivered in his own defence was widely admired; a few fragments of it have been found on papyrus. His name is a common one in Attica and this fact together with his many-sided activity make it difficult to separate him from the sophist Antiphon, with whom he is often confused or identified; it does not, however, seem likely that the extreme right-wing views of Antiphon the orator and the sophist's proclamation of the equality of all men could co-exist in the same person. We possess three of the orator's speeches for murder trials, and twelve more that are rhetorical exercises on imaginary lawsuits.

Antiquita'tes rerum humana'rum et divina'rum, see VARRO.

Anti'sthenes, see CYNIC PHILOSOPHERS.

Antonines, a collective name for the Roman emperors Antoninus Pius, his adopted son Marcus Aurelius, and the latter's son Commodus, who reigned successively from AD 138 to 192. Antoninus' reign was proverbially peaceful and happy, and the age of the Antonines was part of the period, including also the reigns of Trajan (98–117) and Hadrian (117–38), when the Roman empire reached its greatest extent and its peak of prosperity.

Antonine Wall, see BRITAIN and ANTONINUS PIUS.

Antoni'nus Pius, Roman emperor AD 138–61, born in 86 at Lanuvium (Città Lavinia) and named Titus Aurelius Fulvus Boionius Antoninus. He won fame for his integrity as proconsul of Asia and joined the circle of advisers of the emperor Hadrian, who adopted him as successor not long before his death. Antoninus maintained good relations with the senate and his reign was peaceful and orderly, without striking incident. His policies were beneficent and mildly progressive, lacking extravagance; his reign is marked by a general sense of well-being, aptly expressed in Aristeides' oration 'To Rome'. He married *Faustina (1). It was in his reign, c.142, that the wall of turf known as the Antonine Wall was built in Britain between the Forth and Clyde estuaries by his lieutenant Lollius Urbicus.

Anto'nius, Marcus. 1. (143–87 BC), one of the greatest orators of his day, consul in 99, a member of the party of Sulla, and put to death by the supporters of Marius. He was grandfather of the famous Mark Antony (see next entry). He is one of the chief interlocutors in Cicero's *De Oratore*.

2. Mark Antony, see ANTONY, MARK below.

Antony, Mark (Marcus Antonius) (c.82–30 BC), Roman general and statesman, grandson of Marcus Antonius (above). He was an officer of Julius *Caesar in the wars in Gaul and against Pompey, and after Caesar's assassination in 44 his eloquence won over the people, so that he was in a favourable position to take over the leadership of the Caesarians. However, his leadership was threatened by Caesar's heir *Octavian, who sided with the senate in opposition to Antony. Civil war broke out between Caesarians and republicans. It was at this time that *Cicero ((1) 5) delivered his speeches against Antony known as the *Philippics*, and powerfully contributed to raising the republican opposition to him. Antony was defeated by the republican Decimus Brutus at the battle of Mutina in 43. At this time Octavian had joined forces with the senate, but after Mutina the differences between him and Antony were settled, and Octavian, Antony, and Lepidus were appointed as a triumvirate to rule for five years (this period was later extended for another five years). In 42 Antony, sharing the command with Octavian, defeated the republicans Marcus Brutus and Cassius at Philippi. Afterwards a division of the Roman world was made, in which the East was assigned to Antony, the West to Octavian (Lepidus having diminished in importance). But hostilities soon broke out between the two leaders, temporarily settled by the treaty of Brundisium in 40, and by the marriage of Antony to Octavian's sister Octavia (Antony's wife *Fulvia having died in 40). This marriage interrupted his liaison with *Cleopatra, queen of Egypt, which had begun when he met her at Tarsus in Cilicia in 41. Their association was resumed in 37 and they had three children. On the last day of 33 the agreement between Antony and Octavian came to an end, and in the following year he divorced Octavia. Having alienated the sympathy of Rome he gave Octavian the opportunity to declare a national war against Cleopatra. The result was decided by Octavian's victory in the sea-battle at Actium in 31. In 30 Octavian invaded Egypt; Alexandria capitulated, and Antony took his own life. Shakespeare's play *Antony and Cleopatra*, based on Plutarch's Life of Antony, in which he is presented as a man who lost the world for love, may give a romantic and distorted view of events.

Anū'bis, in Egyptian religion, the jackal-headed god who conducted the souls of the dead to the region of immortal life, identified by the Greeks with *Hermes.

A'nytē, Arcadian poetess of Tegea who lived in the early third century BC. Some eighteen of her epigrams survive in the Greek *Anthology. They have great charm and are among the first pastoral descriptions of wild nature in Greek literature, and also include the first epitaphs for animals.

A'nytus, one of the three accusers who brought Socrates to trial, a wealthy Athenian, a moderate in politics, represented by Plato in the *Meno* as an enemy of the *sophists. He may have thought that by attacking Socrates he was acting in the best interests of Athens.

Ao'nia. The Aonians were, according to legend, ancient inhabitants of Boeotia.

Aonia is the name sometimes used by learned poets to denote Boeotia; the Muses who frequented Mount Helicon in Boeotia are sometimes called Aonidēs.

Apatu'ria (Apatouria), see PHRATRIAI.

ape'lla, the assembly of the people at Sparta.

Ape'llēs, the most famous painter of antiquity, born at Colophon in Ionia in the first half of the fourth century BC. None of his works survives, but there are descriptions by several ancient authors. One of the most renowned was of Aphroditē Anadyomenē, 'Aphrodite rising from the sea', wringing the sea-water from her hair. Apelles was court painter to Philip of Macedon and his son Alexander the Great and is known to have painted several portraits of Alexander, sometimes in allegorical situations. His work was renowned for its gracefulness.

Aphai'a, see BRITOMARTIS.

A'phobus, Against, speeches by Demosthenes against his fraudulent guardian; see DEMOSTHENES (2) 2.

Aphrodī'tē, the Greek goddess of love, beauty, and fertility, identified by the Romans with *Venus. She has two alternative genealogies: according to Hesiod she sprang from the foam (*aphros*) of the sea that gathered about the severed genitals of the god Uranus when he was castrated by his son *Cronus. To Homer she is the child of Zeus and Dionē; Homer also calls her 'the Cyprian', and it was probably from Cyprus, in the Mycenaean age, that she first entered Greece. Many of her attributes indicate her partially oriental origin and her kinship with the Asian goddess Astarte. This is borne out by the legend that she first landed either at Paphos in Cyprus or at Cythera (an island off the Laconian coast), whence her title 'Cytherean'. Homer makes her the wife of Hephaestus. When her amorous intrigue with *Ares was discovered, the pair were caught in a net by Hephaestus and exposed to the ridicule of the assembled gods. Aeneas is her son by the Trojan *Anchises, and she always supported the Trojan cause against the Greeks (see TROJAN WAR). In later literature she is the mother of *Eros. For other legends about her see ADONIS and PARIS, JUDGEMENT OF. Although she was primarily a goddess of love, she was also a protector of sailors and a goddess of war. Two common titles of Aphrodite are Urania ('heavenly') and Pandemos ('popular'), cult names which Plato interpreted as symbolizing intellectual and sensual love. She had a famous sanctuary on Mount Eryx on the northwest coast of Sicily. This the Romans especially honoured, because Aphrodite, as the mother of Aeneas, passed for their ancestress. The title of Venus Erycina, who had a temple at Rome on the Capitol, outside the Colline Gate, was derived from the sanctuary on Mount Eryx.

Api'cius, Marcus Gavius, gourmet of the reign of Tiberius (AD 14–37). His recipes were written down; but the work on cookery which bears the name of Caelius Apicius is thought to be a compilation of a later period, perhaps the fourth century. It is sometimes entitled *De opsoniis et condimentis sive de re culinaria libri decem*, 'Ten books on catering and seasoning, or on cookery'.

Apis, see OSIRIS.

Apocolocynto'sis, title of a Menippean satire (see MENIPPUS) by *Seneca (2), formed from the words *apotheosis*, 'deification', and *colocynta*, 'pumpkin'. Manuscripts give the further title *Ludus de morte Claudii*, 'a joke about the death of Claudius'. It was written early in the reign of the emperor Nero in mockery of the deification of his predecessor Claudius; the pumpkin perhaps alludes to the latter's stupidity. It describes Claudius' arrival in heaven, the difficulty of finding out who he is because of his stammer, and the proposal of the deified emperor Augustus that he should be deported to the Underworld because of the murders he has committed. Here he meets his victims and is brought for trial before *Aeacus. Following Claudius' own system, Aeacus hears the case against him and pronounces sentence without listening to the defence. Claudius is finally made clerk to one of his own freedmen.

Apollina'ris Sido'nius, see SIDONIUS.

Apo'llō (Apollon)

1. *In Greek myth.* The god Apollo was the son of *Zeus and *Leto, and twin brother of Artemis. The most characteristically Greek of all the gods, he embodied youthful but mature male beauty and moral excellence, and was associated especially with the beneficent aspects of civilization, giving to Greek culture its ideal of the beautiful, athletic, virtuous, and cultivated young man. Apollo was the god of plague but also of healing, of music (especially the lyre), archery (but not war, nor hunting), and prophecy; the god also of light (whence his epithet Phoebus, 'the bright'), sometimes identified with the sun. He was also associated with the care of flocks and herds, whence the epithet Nomios, 'of the pastures'. There is no certain occurrence of his name in the *Linear B tablets.

Apollo's first feat was to seize *Delphi for his abode; in doing so he destroyed the dragon Python, its guardian deity who personified the dark forces of the Underworld, an act he had to expiate by exile and purification. His 'fusion' with this earlier deity explains his title Apollo Pythios, 'Pythian Apollo'. Of his many loves, the most famous was that for Coronis, mother of *Asclepius. Others loved by Apollo include Cassandra, the Cumaean Sibyl, Cyrenē, Daphne, Hyacinthus, and Marpessa (see individual entries).

Apollo was not worshipped at Delphi before the eighth century BC. His origins are uncertain, but it is believed that he came either from somewhere north of Greece or from Asia. One of his most common epithets is Lykeios, and Homer's *Iliad* connects him with Lycia. Moreover, in that epic he is an enemy of the Greeks. There are also many oracles of Apollo in Asia Minor. But his Asian origin remains unproved. How and why he became a prophetic god in Greece is not known, but he is so from our earliest records. Delphi was the most important of his oracular shrines but those in Ionia at Branchidae and Claros were notable, and he had a famous shrine on the holy island of Delos. All Greece worshipped him and respected him. Apart from favouring Troy in the *Iliad*, Apollo was usually impartial in politics. Notable departures from impartiality occurred when the Delphic Oracle began by supporting the Persians in the Persian Wars, and when it supported Sparta in the Peloponnesian War. The *Homeric Hymns to the Delian and the Pythian Apollo relate the story of his birth and of the founding of his Pythian temple. The *paean was traditionally sung to him.

2. *In Roman religion.* Apollo was introduced early into Italy, partly through Etruria and partly through the Greek settlements in Magna Graecia, but he was never properly identified with a Roman god. He was first introduced as a god of healing, but soon became prominent as a god of oracles and prophecy. In Virgil he figures in both these characters, but especially as the giver of oracles; the Cumaean Sibyl was his priestess. In Virgil's *Eclogues* Apollo appears also as the patron of poetry and music. The oldest temple to him in Rome was erected in 432 BC. His cult was further developed by the emperor Augustus, who took him as his special patron and erected to him a great temple on the Palatine.

Apollodō'rus, of Athens (flourished *c.*140 BC), the author of a long treatise in Greek prose 'On the gods', and of a 'Chronicle' (*Chronike syntaxis*), a chronological work of some importance, written in iambic trimeters, covering the period from the fall of Troy to 144 BC. Only fragments of these survive. He also wrote a *Bibliothekē*, a study of Greek heroic mythology, but the uncritical work that survives under this name was probably compiled in the first or second century AD.

Apollo'nius. 1. **Apollonius Rhō'dius** (*c.*295–215 BC), Hellenistic Greek poet from Alexandria who spent the later part of his life in Rhodes. He was tutor to Ptolemy III Euergetēs and at some point head of the Alexandrian Library. Apollonius' main work, which survives, is the *Argonautica*, an epic on the story of Jason and the *Argonauts, narrating in four books the voyage of the *Argo* to Colchis by way of the Propontis and the Black Sea (books 1–2), the winning with Medea's aid of the Golden Fleece (book

3), and the return (to Iolcus in Thessaly) by the Danube, Po, Rhone, Mediterranean, and North Africa (book 4). This was the only epic before Virgil's *Aeneid* that could be compared with Homer in subject and extent, and the first epic to give a prominent place to love—Medea's for Jason. For the effect this had in subsequent writing the *Argonautica* holds a significant place in the history of European literature. Apollonius in true Hellenistic literary style combines poetry with scholarship and erudition, but he also excels in delicate psychological portrayal, and in this lies the perennial charm of book 3. The structure of the work as a whole has frequently been criticized, perhaps undeservedly, but there are many individual scenes which are brilliantly contrived. A late and probably unreliable tradition tells of a quarrel between the poets Apollonius and *Callimachus which it represents as the consequence of a bitter controversy between writers of long traditional epics and writers of short and highly polished poems. Callimachus was said to have been victorious and Apollonius to have retired to Rhodes in consequence, but it was the long epic that continued in popularity. Apollonius was much admired in late antiquity and is one of the few Hellenistic poets whose work survived in medieval manuscripts.

2. Apollonius of Pergē in Pamphylia (active second half of the third century BC), mathematician, who founded the branch of geometry known as 'conics', the study of cones, and whose terminology and methods were accepted by all students of the subject. His work on conics largely survives (four books in Greek, three in Arabic, and one lost), though much on other topics has disappeared. *Hypatia wrote a (lost) commentary on the 'Conics'. In theoretical astronomy too Apollonius did work of fundamental importance, and among mathematicians in antiquity he ranks second only to Archimedēs.

3. Apollonius of Tya'na, in Cappadocia (b. *c*.4 BC), a wandering Pythagorean philosopher and mystic who attained so great a fame by his wonder-working powers that divine honours were paid to him. He wrote a life of Pythagoras and other works, of which hardly anything has survived. His own life was written by *Philostratus.

4. Apollonius Dy'scolus ('bad-tempered') (second century AD), the author of several treatises which first placed Greek grammar on a scientific basis. He lived in poverty at Alexandria and wrote numerous works, only four of which survive, on the pronoun, conjunction, adverb, and syntax. His writings were much used by *Priscian. He was father of Aelius *Herodianus, who wrote on Greek accents.

5. Apollonius of Tyre, see NOVEL 2.

Apology of Socrates (*Apologia Sokratous*, 'speech in defence of Socrates').

1. The speech, as related by *Plato, made by *Socrates in the Athenian law-courts in answer to the charge of impiety that was brought against him. How far it represents the words actually used by Socrates is unknown.

Socrates distinguishes between previous vague accusations (that he speculated about physical questions, and made the worse cause appear the better) and the specific charge of impiety now brought by Meletus. On the former, he explains that he is neither a *sophist nor a natural philosopher; his only wisdom consists in knowing that he knows nothing. Instigated by an oracle, he has sought constantly to find a wiser man than himself, but has found none. He has gone to those who had a reputation for wisdom, and finding they had none has tried to convince them of his; this has provoked their enmity and given rise to these accusations. Socrates turns next to Meletus and cross-examines him on his particular charge. He then addresses the judges and declares himself unrepentant: he will persist in the practices complained of, for he must continue, in obedience to the divine voice, to preach the necessity of virtue. If they kill him, they will be injuring themselves, for he is the gadfly sent by the gods to stir Athens to life.

Socrates is convicted and the death penalty is proposed. The speech assumes a loftier tone. Why should he propose an alternative punishment? As a benefactor of Athens he ought to be rewarded.

Imprisonment, exile, a fine, would certainly be evils, but as for death he does not know whether it is an evil or a good. Nevertheless he suggests a fine of thirty minas, which his friends will guarantee since he himself has no money. He is sentenced to death, and in his final words prophesies that many will arise after his death to condemn his judges. He comforts his friends with regard to his own fate, for death is either a dreamless sleep or a journey to a place of true justice, where he will be able to converse with Hesiod and Homer and the heroes. Nothing evil can happen to a good man; if he is to die, it must be better for him. He forgives his accusers and judges.

2. An account by *Xenophon of Socrates' defence in the same trial. At the time Xenophon was taking part in the expedition of Cyrus (see ANABASIS), and he relies on the authority of Hermogenēs, a friend of Socrates who is mentioned in Plato's *Phaedo as present at the execution. This account is intended to bring out especially that Socrates was willing to die, not for the spiritual reasons given by Plato, in (1) above, but in order to escape the disabilities of old age. His pleas are here stated with less elaboration than by Plato.

Appendix Virgilia'na, collection of short Latin poems mostly dating from *Virgil's lifetime or soon after, ascribed to Virgil in late antiquity but of very doubtful authenticity. The collection comprises the following:

Catalepton ('on a small scale'), fourteen epigrams, perhaps identical with the *Epigrammata* attributed to Virgil by Donatus and Servius; a few are possibly authentic. The title had been used earlier by *Aratus for a collection of short poems.

Ciris, an *epyllion of Alexandrian inspiration relating the story of Scylla, daughter of Nisus. Ciris is the mythical bird into which Scylla was changed. The poem contains Virgilian verses and phrases often inappropriately adapted to a new context. Not by Virgil.

Cōpa ('dancing girl'), a short elegiac poem containing phrases from Virgil and Propertius, describing with a lively vigour and charm a tavern girl who dances to castanets to entertain her customers. Not by Virgil.

Culex ('gnat'), a poem in hexameters telling the story of a shepherd who kills a gnat that has saved his life. The ghost of the gnat later appears to the shepherd, reproaches him, and describes the Underworld. Though this poem was widely believed in antiquity to be by Virgil it is a later pastiche of Virgilian phrases.

Dirae, transmitted as one hexameter poem in the manuscripts but usually edited as two: *Dirae*, 'furies', in which a farmer curses the soldiers who have dispossessed him of his farm, and *Lydia*, in which the poet laments in pastoral style his separation from his mistress. Neither is by Virgil.

Elegies on Maecenas, two elegies on *Maecenas' death, handed down in the manuscripts as one continuous poem.

Moretum, 'the salad', a realistic and only mildly mock-heroic poem in hexameters about a farmer's preparation of a meal, much in the spirit of the *Georgics*. It vividly describes the farmer rising early on a winter morning, lighting his fire, grinding his corn in a hand-mill, collecting from the garden the ingredients for his salad and preparing his meal; then starting for his day's work at the plough. Not by Virgil.

Priapea, three small poems ascribed to Virgil among a collection of eighty addressed to the god *Priapus, not by Virgil but made in the reign of Augustus.

Aetna, see the entry AETNA.

A'ppian (Appianos), of Alexandria (flourished *c.* AD 160). He practised as a lawyer in Rome and compiled narratives in Greek of the various Roman conquests from the earliest times to the accession of Vespasian, in twenty-four books. Of these, nine books survive complete and there are portions of others. The most valuable are books 13–17 which describe the civil wars between 146 and 70 BC.

Appian Way (Via Appia), Rome's principal road to south Italy, named after Appius *Claudius the Censor, who is said to have initiated its construction in 312 BC. Originally it stretched from Rome to Capua (132 miles), but by 244 it had been extended to Brundisium (another 234 miles).

A'ppius Claudius, consul in 451 BC; see CLAUDIUS (1).

A'ppius Claudius Caecus, famous Roman *censor (312–308 BC); see CLAUDIUS (2).

Apple of Discord, see ERIS.

Apsy'rtus, in Greek myth, brother of *Medea.

Apule'ius, Lucius (flourished *c.* AD 155), author of the only Latin novel that survives entire. He was born at Madaura in Africa, on the borders of Numidia and Gaetulia. On a journey to Alexandria, when a young man, he fell ill, was nursed by a rich widow named Aemilia Pudentilla, and married her. Her relatives brought an action against him on the charge of having won her by the use of magic. His *Apologia* or speech for the defence survives. From this we learn that he had inherited a considerable fortune but had wasted it, that he was deeply interested in natural science, and that the accusation of magic was founded on trivial grounds. That Apuleius was in fact much interested in magic appears from many passages of his novel, the *Metamorphoses* (see below). He was acquitted and subsequently settled at Carthage, from where he travelled among the African towns, lecturing in Latin on philosophy. We possess a collection, perhaps made by a later admirer, of excerpts from these lectures, under the name *Florida* ('anthology'). Two popularizations of Platonic philosophy are attributed to him, *De dogmate Platonis* ('On the beliefs of Plato') and *De deo Socratis* ('On the god of Socrates'), as well as a free translation (*De mundo*, 'On the world') of the *Peri kosmou* attributed falsely to Aristotle.

The work for which he is famous is his *Metamorphoses* or *Golden Ass*, a Latin romance in eleven books. A version of the same story also exists in Greek, *Loukios e onos*, 'Lucius or the Ass', doubtfully attributed to *Lucian; both works probably derive from the *Metamorphoses* of an unknown Lucius. This original was remodelled by Apuleius and enlarged by many incidental tales.

The romance takes the form of a narrative recounted in the first person by a young man named Lucius, a Greek, whose adventures begin with a visit to Thessaly, the reputed home of sorceries and enchantments. There, while being too curious about the black art, he is accidentally turned into an ass, falls into the hands of robbers, and becomes an unwilling and much-beaten partaker in their exploits. Some of the robber stories are excellent, but the most beautiful and famous of the stories embedded in the novel is the exquisite tale of Cupid and *Psyche. After many vicissitudes, in the course of which he serves one of the strange bands of wandering priests of *Cybele, and becomes a famous performing ass, Lucius is transformed back into human shape by the favour of the goddess *Isis, and appears to become Apuleius the author himself. The last portion of the work refers to his initiation into the mysteries of Isis and Osiris and bears witness to the interest shown in his day to oriental religions. The many realistic details that he gives vividly illuminate the popular life of his time. The style of the novel resembles the exuberantly Asianic style of oratory (see ORATORY 1), with vocabulary drawn from a variety of registers, archaic, poetic, Greek, and colloquial.

Apu'lia, region of south-east Italy, modern Puglia. Its dry but fertile soil was excellent for sheep-rearing and Apulian wool was famous. The region was extensively Hellenized. In the late fourth century BC it became subject to Rome and remained loyal against *Pyrrhus. In the *Punic and *Social Wars however many Apulians revolted and Apulia was much devastated in consequence. Wolves were common in the wilder parts.

aqueducts (Lat. *aquae*, 'waters'), one of Rome's greatest contributions to architecture and public amenity, the structures built to supply Rome and other cities of the Roman empire with water. Whereas Greek cities were usually supplied with water from their numerous natural springs, often elaborated into artificial fountains, early Rome had only the river Tiber and wells sunk in the city, and it was the unwholesomeness and inadequacy of these supplies that led to the development of aqueducts to bring large quantities of pure water from the distant hills. The water was carried as far as possible underground, in stone-built channels lined with a special cement. There were frequent inspection points, and the conduits had to be kept clear of deposits. Open channels on substructures of solid masonry or arches were for the most part used only on the approach to the city. The channels were built with a more or less uniform gentle gradient. Pipes were also used occasionally for parts of the route, allowing water to be carried across intervening low ground, as well as for the distribution system in the city; according to their situation and size they might be made of terracotta, lead, wood, or leather.

Our detailed knowledge of the aqueducts of Rome is derived from the book *De aquis urbis Romae* by *Frontinus, who was in charge of the Roman aqueducts in the late first century AD. 'With so many indispensable structures for so many aqueducts, compare, if you will, the idle pyramids or the useless, though famous, works of the Greeks' (*De aquis* 1. 6). In his day there were nine; when Rome fell to Alaric in AD 410 there were eleven. The aqueducts were vastly expensive to build and maintain, and the works were usually a liability to the community. The whole water-course through the aqueducts was public property; when the water arrived it was stored in reservoir buildings, *castella*, and piped thence to public fountains, baths, and private consumers, who paid a rent for the privilege.

A'quilo (Gk. Boreas), the north wind; see WINDS.

Arabia. The name Arabia was first applied to the desert region on the northern coast of the Arabian peninsula that lies east of the Nile delta and merges with Syria. Later it was extended to the whole peninsula. The Greeks and Romans were familiar with this area and with the eastern shore of the Arabian Gulf, and their knowledge was increased after the exploratory voyages of Alexander's admirals in the later part of the fourth century BC. The interior however always remained unknown. Arabia was regarded by the ancients as the land of spices and

proverbially rich. It had vast stretches of desert grass fragrant with aromatic herbs, which also provided pasturage for its famous horses, and the fruitful terraced districts near the west coast grew balsam, aloe, myrrh, and frankincense. But Arabia stood on many trade routes and many of her exports—spices and precious stones—came from India or lands further east. When Egypt came under Roman rule in the first century AD the Romans traded directly with southern Arabia and India, and the old 'incense route' to the north diminished in importance.

Ara'chnē ('spider'), in Greek myth, a woman of Lydia who challenged the goddess Athena to a contest in weaving. She depicted in her web the amours of the gods, and Athena, angered at her presumption and choice of subject, tore the web to pieces and beat the weaver. Arachne in despair hanged herself, but Athena turned her into a spider.

Ara Ma'xima ('greatest altar'), the altar of *Hercules at Rome, which stood in the *Forum Boarium. It was here that, as related by Virgil in the *Aeneid* (book 8), Aeneas found *Evander sacrificing. The spot was connected with the legend of Hercules and *Cacus. Tithes of booty and commercial profits, etc., were offered at the altar.

Ara Pācis ('altar of peace'), in the Campus Martius at Rome, constructed during the years 13–9 BC by order of the senate to commemorate the safe return of the emperor Augustus from Gaul in the former year.

Ara'tus. 1. A Greek perhaps from Soli in Cilicia (*c*.315–*c*.240 BC), who came to Athens and subsequently spent part of his life at the court of *Antigonus Gonatas, king of Macedon; there he wrote hymns for the king's marriage. His best known work, and the only one still extant, is a didactic poem, the *Phaenomena* ('astronomy'), in 1,154 hexameters, describing with elegant clarity and little mythological allusion the relative positions of the chief stars and constellations, and their risings and settings; it is based on a prose treatise of the same name by the mathematician and astronomer *Eudoxus of Cnidus. The last 400 lines of the poem, dealing with meteorology, were sometimes given the separate title *Diosemeia*, 'weather signs'. This part was derived from a similar work, perhaps by Theophrastus. The *Phaenomena* achieved immediate fame, which it enjoyed until the end of antiquity, and found many commentators. Its language is Homeric Greek but the thought is consistently Stoic. It was translated into Latin by Cicero in his youth, and the latter part of it also by *Germanicus and *Avienus. Cicero's translation is thought to have had considerable influence on the style of Lucretius. Other poems were ascribed to Aratus but have not survived. The apostle Paul, who also came from Cilicia, quotes from the *Phaenomena* when preaching to the Athenians (Acts 17: 28).

2. Of Sicyon, general of the *Achaean Confederacy.

Arbē'la, town in Assyria; near it was fought in 331 BC the battle of Gaugamela (sometimes called the battle of Arbela) in which Alexander the Great finally overthrew Darius.

Arca'dia, region of Greece in the centre of the Peloponnese, very mountainous, especially in the north. The most prosperous parts were the eastern plains of Orchomenus, Mantinea, and Tegea. Among its rivers were *Alpheus, *Stymphalus, and *Styx. It was a land of villages and so was of little direct importance in Greek politics, although *Mantinea and *Tegea were involved in Spartan expansion, particularly in the fifth century BC. Its chief strength lay in its manpower. Under *Epaminondas an Arcadian confederacy was formed in the fourth century BC against Sparta (see MEGALOPOLIS) and it later joined the *Achaean Confederacy. Arcadia's isolated geographical position is the reason for several of its distinctive features. The inhabitants regarded themselves as the most ancient people of Greece. Their dialect, which is not seen in extant literature and is known only from inscriptions, closely resembles that of Cyprus, an area similarly cut off from later Greek influences, and is consequently known as Arcado-Cypriot (see DIALECTS, GREEK). It seems to be closest

to Mycenaean Greek, a fact which suggests that Arcadia, with its mountainous and inaccessible countryside, remained largely unpenetrated by invading Dorians (see DORIAN INVASION). Arcadia also preserves remarkable myths and cults; the gods Hermes and Pan are particularly connected with the country. According to one tradition Zeus was born on Mount Lycaeus (see LYCAON). Through *Evander, who is said to have been an Arcadian, Arcadia is connected with the origins of Rome. A famous temple of Apollo was built at Bassae. The idealized picture of the pastoral life of Arcadia, the home of Pan, is due to the Roman poet Virgil, who made it the setting of *bucolic poetry (see ECLOGUES). The Latin tag familiar from seventeenth-century pastoral paintings, *et in Arcadia ego*, often translated as 'I too ⟨have lived⟩ in Arcadia', may more correctly mean 'I ⟨am found⟩ in Arcadia as well', and refer to death.

Arcesila'us or **Arce'silas. 1.** The name of many of the ruling dynasty of *Cyrene in North Africa, which ruled from the foundation of the colony (*c*.630 BC) for some 200 years.

2. Of Pitanē in Aeolis, see ACADEMY.

Archaic age, name given to one of the five periods of the Greek era (defined on the basis of pottery styles). It begins *c*.620 BC and ends in 480. Compare PROTO-GEOMETRIC, GEOMETRIC, ORIENTALIZING, and CLASSICAL. The term Archaic age is sometimes used more widely to describe the period from *c*.750 to 480 BC.

Archelā'us, king of Macedon *c*.413–399 BC. See MACEDONIA.

archetype, see TEXTUAL CRITICISM.

Archidamian war, see PELOPONNESIAN WAR.

Archidā'mus, see ISOCRATES.

Archi'lochus, Greek poet from the island of Paros, who lived probably around the mid-seventh century BC and wrote short poems in a variety of metres, elegiac, iambic, and trochaic. Little is known of his life; he took part in the colonization of Thasos and fought there, and was reputedly killed in a battle between

Paros and Naxos. His poetry survives only in the quotations of later writers and some papyrus fragments. Ancient tradition says that he fell in love with Neobulē, daughter of Lycambes, but her father forbade the marriage, and Archilochus avenged himself with such biting satires that father and daughter hanged themselves. Some lines of his verse seem to confirm the existence of Neobulē; one poem recovered from a papyrus vividly recounts the poet's seduction of her younger sister. Other fragments confirm his ancient reputation for being an innovator in metre, language, and subject matter. His *iambic poems in particular show a great variety of tone—mockery, enthusiasm, melancholy, and a mordant wit. The poems are remarkable for their strongly personal note. His self-consciously anti-heroic epigram on the shield he left behind in battle had a considerable literary following (see ALCAEUS (1) and HORACE; a fragment suggests that even Anacreon had a similar experience).

Archimē'dēs (*c*.287–212 BC), Greek scientist, the greatest mathematician of antiquity, an astronomer, physicist, and inventor. Born at Syracuse, the son of an astronomer, Pheidias, he probably studied at Alexandria and subsequently lived at the court of Hieron II, tyrant of Syracuse, where he was killed at the capture of the city by the Romans under Marcellus. Popular history (see Plutarch's Life of Marcellus) knew him as the inventor of marvellous machines which helped to postpone the fall of Syracuse, and other devices such as the screw for raising water and the compound pulley. It attributed to him the boast, 'Give me a place to stand, and I will move the earth', and the exclamation '*eureka*' ('I have found it') when he discovered how to test (by specific gravity) whether base metal had been introduced into Hieron's gold crown, after observing in his bath the displacement of water by his body.

Cicero, who was quaestor in Sicily in 75 BC, discovered the tomb of Archimedes near one of the gates of Syracuse, overgrown with brambles and forgotten. By Archimedes' own wish it was marked by a column depicting a cylinder circumscribing a sphere, which recalled his discovery that their volumes were in the ratio 3 : 2.

In his breadth and freedom of vision Archimedes ranks as one of the greatest mathematicians of all time. In his work called the *Sand-reckoner* he describes a system for expressing very large numbers verbally in Greek when the language stops at a myriad, 10,000 (10,000 × 10,000 becomes 'a second myriad' and so on). He showed that he understood the nature of a numerical system as no one else did in antiquity. A number of his treatises survive on various topics including the circle, the sphere, and the cylinder, and notably on hydrostatics, a science which Archimedes invented. Two more of his works survive only in Arabic.

architecture. Classical architecture is based on the 'order', a unit of design categorized mainly by the type of column used. Each order in its entirety consists of the column, plus its base, plinth, or pedestal (if any), its capital (the crowning feature of the shaft), and its entablature (the decorative horizontal member that surmounts the column, divided into three bands—architrave, frieze, and cornice). The Greeks had three orders, getting progressively slimmer and more richly decorated: Doric, Ionic, and Corinthian, named after regions of Greece in which they are said to have been first used. Doric, the style of the Parthenon, was the norm in mainland Greece, Sicily, and Magna Graecia. The Romans added two more orders—Tuscan, a starker form of Doric, and Composite, the richest of all, combining features of Ionic and Corinthian—but Corinthian was the great order of imperial Rome. The orders were discussed by *Vitruvius, and from the Renaissance their proportions and detailing were codified and illustrated in countless architectural treatises.

The most important literary source for Greek architecture is the detailed guidebook written by the traveller *Pausanius (2) in the second century AD.

archons (*archontēs*), name given in most Greek states including Athens to the holders of the highest office, who had wide judicial as well as executive duties.

Archy'tas, of Tarentum (flourished c.400 BC), Pythagorean philosopher and mathematician, interested in music and mechanics, and a friend of Plato. He was also a military commander and repeatedly led the forces of his city in successful campaigns. Among his inventions were the screw, the pulley, and the rattle, and he is said to have solved (by geometry) the problem of the proportion between the sides of two cubes having the volume ratio two. Some fragments of his mathematical works survive. He figures in an ode of Horace (1. 28), where he is addressed as a 'sand-reckoner' (compare ARCHIMEDES).

Arcti'nus, see AETHIOPIS, EPIC CYCLE, and ILIUPERSIS.

Arctu'rus, see BOOTES.

Areopagī 'ticus, see ISOCRATES.

Areo'pagus (Areios pagos), the 'hill of Arēs' at Athens, west of the Acropolis and separated from it by a depression; also the name of the ancient council that met on it. According to legend, it was so called because there Ares was tried by the gods and acquitted of the murder of Halirrhothios, Poseidon's son, who had raped Ares' daughter at that place. Again according to legend, as found in the *Eumenides* of Aeschylus (see ORESTEIA), it was there that Orestes was tried for the murder of his mother Clytemnestra, the goddess Athena having referred the case to a tribunal of Athenian citizens.

Ārēs, in Greek myth, the only son of *Zeus and his wife *Hera, the god of war or, rather, of warlike frenzy. He is of no great importance in mythology, although he is one of the twelve Olympian gods, and plays no very glorious part in the stories in which he appears. He is a stirrer of strife, unchivalrous, and does not always have the advantage in encounters with mortals (see for example OTUS AND EPHIALTES); nor does he ever develop into a god with a moral function, like Zeus or Apollo. He is frequently associated with the goddess *Aphroditē, wife of Hephaestus, and she bore him *Harmonia. Their amorous intrigue was the subject of a tale told at the Phaeacian court by the bard Demodocus in Homer's *Odyssey*. The Romans identified him with *Mars, a god of greater dignity and importance. See also AREOPAGUS.

Arē'tē, in Homer's *Odyssey*, the wife of Alcinous, king of the Phaeacians.

A'rethas, see BYZANTINE AGE and TEXTS, TRANSMISSION OF ANCIENT 3.

Arethū'sa (Arethousa). 1. One of the *Hesperides.

2. A spring on the island of Ortygia, in the harbour of Syracuse. According to legend the river-god *Alpheus fell in love with the nymph Arethusa when she bathed in his stream in Arcadia. She fled from him to Ortygia and was changed into a fountain (by Artemis, in one version); but Alpheus flowed under the sea to Ortygia to be united with the fountain. It was believed in antiquity that there was a real connection between the two and that a cup thrown into the river would be recovered from the spring.

Argēs, one of the *Cyclopēs.

Argīlē'tum, at Rome, district north-east of the Forum, between the Esquiline and the Quirinal hills. It was occupied by artisans and shop-keepers, including booksellers and shoemakers.

Arginu'sae (Arginousai), small islands south of Lesbos, off which in 406 BC the Athenian fleet heavily defeated that of Sparta, capturing or destroying seventy Spartan ships. The Athenians lost twenty-five ships whose crews were not rescued owing to bad weather. It was thought at Athens that insufficient efforts had been made to take up the dead and save the wounded and drowning, and the blame was laid on the eight generals who had been present. Two of them fled; the remaining six were condemned to death by the assembly in a wave of popular anger, sentence being pronounced on all the accused together instead of each being judged, as was constitutional, separately. These were executed, including Pericles, son of the great statesman, and Thrasyllus (see also THERAMENES and THRASYBULUS (2)). Socrates, one of the presidents of the assembly (*prytaneis*) at the time, bravely opposed the illegality of the proceedings.

Argonau'tica, see APOLLONIUS (1), VALERIUS FLACCUS, and VARRO ATACINUS.

A'rgonauts (Argonautai), in Greek myth, the heroes who sailed on the ship *Argo* with Jason to recover the Golden Fleece, and the subject of many stories. Jason was the son of Aeson (son of Cretheus and Tyro), who was the rightful king of Iolcus in Thessaly, but the throne had been usurped by Aeson's half-brother Pelias (son of the god Poseidon and of Tyro). Jason had been sent for safety and education to the centaur Chiron. Pelias had been warned that he would be killed by a descendant of Aeolus (see AEOLUS (2)) who would come to him wearing only one sandal. This prophecy was fulfilled when Jason, grown up, returned to Iolcus to claim his inheritance, having lost a sandal while carrying an old woman (the goddess Hera in disguise) across a river. Pelias promised to restore the throne to him if he would first recover the Golden Fleece. This was the fleece of the ram that had carried away Phrixus and Hellē (see ATHAMAS), and had been hung in the grove of Ares at Colchis, at the eastern end of the Black Sea, guarded by a dragon that never slept. Jason undertook the task, and embarked in the *Argo* at Pagasae with some fifty of the chief heroes of Greece. These must originally have come from Thessaly, the home of the *Minyans (as the Argonauts are often called), but later story-tellers added heroes from different times and traditions, such as Heracles. Heroes most generally said to have been on the expedition include Orpheus, Peleus, Telamon, the Dioscuri, Zetēs and Calais, Idas and Lynceus, Tiphys the helmsman, Argus, who built the ship, Admetus, Augeas, and Neleus' son Periclymenus. Acastus joined at the last moment. Many of the stories concern dangers which are overcome by the particular virtue of one hero or another (e.g. Polydeucēs by his boxing defeated Amycus, son of Poseidon). For other adventures see HYLAS, HYPSIPYLE, PHINEUS, and SYMPLEGADES).

The expedition eventually reached Colchis, where the king Aeētēs expressed willingness to surrender the fleece if Jason would perform certain apparently impossible tasks. These included yoking to a plough a pair of fire-breathing bulls with bronze hooves, and ploughing a field

and sowing it with teeth from *Cadmus' dragon; from these armed men would arise whose fury would be turned against Jason. With the help of the magic arts of *Medea, the king's daughter, who fell in love with Jason, the tasks were successfully accomplished, and Jason and Medea and the other Argonauts returned to Iolcus with the fleece. The account of the expedition now divides into several main variants describing adventures in many parts of the Mediterranean and Black Sea areas. Some stories have the Argonauts returning to Greece by sailing west along the stream of *Ocean, either to the north or the south, and entering the Mediterranean by the Pillars of Hercules. For the rest of Jason's story, see MEDEA. Jason was said to have died at Corinth, killed, according to one version, as he sat under the old *Argo* by a falling piece of her woodwork. For the subsequent adventures of Medea, see THESEUS.

The story of the Argonauts is one of the oldest Greek sagas, containing many elements from folk-tale including two of the most popular themes, that of sending a hero on a dangerous voyage to get rid of him, and that of confronting him with a series of difficult tasks, in which he is helped to success by an unexpected ally.

Argos, Greek city in the north-east Peloponnese 5 km. (3 miles) from the sea, on a site occupied since prehistoric and Mycenaean times. The name often signifies also the territory belonging to the city, sometimes called Argolis ('the Argolid'). In Homer the name is used to describe (i) the city, of which Diomedes was the king, (ii) the kingdom of Agamemnon, who was Diomedes' overlord, and (iii) by extension the whole of the Peloponnese, as opposed to Hellas, i.e. Greece north of the Isthmus of Corinth. Hence the name 'Argives' in Homer frequently means 'Greeks'. In the stories of the *Dorian Invasion, Argos became the stronghold of Temenus, the eldest of the *Heracleidae. It probably retained leadership of the Peloponnese until challenged by Sparta in the seventh century BC. Argos defeated Sparta at the battle of Hysiae in 669, perhaps under the leadership of its king *Pheidon, a legendary figure to whom no certain date can be ascribed. However, the wide power which Argos won under Pheidon did not survive his death, and thereafter, largely influenced by jealousy of Sparta, Argos played a secondary and not always very glorious role in the history of Greece.

The great Argive goddess was Hera, worshipped at the *Heraeum some 10 km. (6 miles) north of Argos. Argive sculptors were outstanding in the early classical period, notably *Polycleitus. For Argive myth see ADRASTUS.

Argus. 1. In Greek myth, the herdsman that Hera set to watch *Io, given the epithet Panoptēs because he had eyes all over his body; when Hermes killed him, Hera placed his eyes in the peacock's tail.

2. The craftsman who built the ship *Argo* (see ARGONAUTS).

3. In Homer's *Odyssey* (7. 292) the dog which recognizes its master Odysseus on his return and then dies.

Aria'dnē, in Greek myth, daughter of *Minos and Pasiphae. When *Theseus came to Crete she fell in love with him and gave him the thread by which he found his way out of the labyrinth after killing the Minotaur. He then fled, taking her with him, but abandoned her on the island of Dia (Naxos). There the god Dionysus found her, married her, and made her immortal.

Ari'cia, town in a hollow of the Alban hills about 25 km. (16 miles) south-east of Rome. In a grove near the town was the famous seat of worship of the goddess *Diana.

Arimaspians, legendary people of the far north who were one-eyed, and fought with griffins who guarded a hoard of gold. They were supposedly written about by the poet *Aristeas of Proconnesus.

Arī'on. 1. Greek lyric poet, perhaps of the seventh century BC, said to have been born at Methymna in Lesbos, but largely a figure of legend. He is said to have been a pupil of the lyric poet *Alcman and to have spent the greater part of his life at the court of *Periander, tyrant of Corinth. He visited Italy where he amassed much wealth. On his return he was thrown overboard by the sailors, who wanted his treasure, but a dolphin, charmed by the song he had been allowed

to sing before his death, carried him to land. To Arion was attributed the creation of the *dithyramb as a literary composition. He was also connected with the birth of tragedy, which perhaps means that his type of dithyramb helped eventually to produce tragedy. Nothing survives of his work.

2. Name of a legendary horse, the offspring of *Poseidon and Demeter. It belonged to the Argive hero *Adrastus and its speed enabled him to escape after the failure of his expedition against Thebes.

Ariovi'stus, chief of the Germanic Suebi, called into Gaul c.71 BC to assist a Gallic tribe in local warfare and then impossible to dislodge. The Roman senate acquiesced in his conquests but he was eventually routed by Julius Caesar in 58 BC and died soon after.

Aristae'us, in Greek myth, son of the god Apollo and the Thessalian nymph Cyrenē, whom Apollo carried off to the region in North Africa which bears her name. Aristaeus was a god of various kinds of husbandry, including bee-keeping, and of hunting. He fell in love with *Eurydicē who, trying to escape from him, trod on a serpent and died from its bite. The dryads avenged her by killing all his bees. According to Virgil (*Georgics* 4. 315), after this calamity Aristaeus, on his mother's advice, consulted the god Proteus, appeased the dryads and obtained new swarms from the carcasses of bulls. Aristaeus married Autonoē, daughter of Cadmus, and became the father of *Actaeon.

Arista'rchus. 1. Of Samos (b. c.320 BC), an astronomer who is famous for hypothesizing that the earth revolves about the sun, and that it rotates about its own axis. His only extant treatise, however, presupposes a geocentric universe.

2. Of Samothrace (c.215–c.143 BC), head of the *Alexandrian Library from c.180 to c.145 BC and the originator of professional scholarship. He produced commentaries on Greek classical authors and treatises on particular topics, especially Greek grammar, scraps of which still survive in the ancient notes on classical authors which are found in some manuscripts (see SCHOLIUM). His most notable contribution to scholarship was his critical edition of Homer, followed by his editions of, or commentaries on, Hesiod, Archilochus, Alcaeus, Pindar, the tragedians, and Aristophanes, and among prose writers, Herodotus. His editions were accompanied by a full apparatus of critical signs (see TEXTS, TRANSMISSION OF ANCIENT I).

Ari'steas, of Proconnesus (an island in the Propontis), an early Greek traveller of, probably, the seventh century BC, and supposedly the possessor of magical powers which enabled him to leave the body and return to it at will. He was a devoted follower of Apollo and introduced the cult of the god at Metapontum in south Italy. Inspired by Apollo he visited the peoples of the far north beyond the Black Sea, reaching the Issedonēs, beyond whom lay the Arimaspians. He wrote about his travels in an epic poem of three books, the *Arimaspeia*, which was subsequently regarded as a source of geographical and historical information. Scanty fragments survive which are purported to come from this poem.

Aristei'dēs. 1. (d. *c.*468 BC), Athenian statesman known as 'the Just', a cousin of *Callias, famous for his rectitude, patriotism, and moderation. He was one of the *strategoi* at the battle of Marathon in 490 (see PERSIAN WARS), and *archon in 489/8. He came into conflict with *Themistocles when the latter rose to power, and as a consequence was ostracized in 482. According to a story told by Plutarch, who wrote his Life, an illiterate citizen requested Aristeides to vote in favour of his ostracism; on being asked what harm Aristeides had ever done him, he replied, none, he did not even know the man, but he was sick of hearing him always called 'the Just'. Aristeides returned from exile in 480, in the general amnesty issued under the Persian threat; he held a command at Salamis, and led the Athenian contingent at Plataea (for an anecdote see NYMPHS). His greatest achievement was in the apportionment of tribute by the *Delian League, when he fixed each member's contribution, a task

entrusted to him on account of his justice and discretion. We have a Life of him by Nepos as well as that by Plutarch.

2. Of Miletus, see MILESIAN TALES.

3. Aelius Aristeides (AD 117–89), Greek rhetorician of the Second *Sophistic. Born in Mysia, he was educated at Pergamum and Athens, and spent much of his life giving demonstrations of his oratory in the chief cities of the Greek world. Fifty-five of his compositions are extant. The best known is his eloquent encomium of Rome, but these works are now read chiefly for the light they throw on the social history of Asia Minor in his day. When on a visit to Rome at the age of 26, he was struck down by an illness, perhaps psychological in origin, from which he suffered for the rest of his life. He sought a cure in the temple of *Asclepius at Pergamum, and left an account of the dreams he experienced there in a book called 'Sacred Teachings' (*hieroi logoi*), which is interesting as a record of the personal religious experiences of a pagan, and valuable as evidence for the practice of *incubation. He was known to the physician *Galen, who cited him as an example of one whose power of oratory had 'caused his whole body to waste away'.

Aristi'ppus, of Cyrene, a pupil of *Socrates. It was probably not he but his grandson who founded the Cyrenaic school of philosophy, and was the first to teach its characteristic doctrine, that immediate pleasure is the only end of action; knowledge is based on sensation, and the present moment is the only reality. His works are entirely lost.

aristocracy. The Greek word means 'rule of the best', and originally denoted government by the hereditary nobility. At Athens, before the rise of *democracy ('rule of the people') the land-owning nobles were the ruling class of the citystate, prominent by birth, wealth, and personal prowess (see EUPATRIDAE). They governed the state through a council (see AREOPAGUS) whose authority was unchallenged. After the eighth century BC society changed throughout Greece, and wealth, not birth, became the criterion for power. As a consequence the councils which governed city-states were gradually reconstituted to admit these people (for Athens, see SOLON and BOULE), and non-aristocrats rose to the same political levels as the nobles. Aristocracy in Greece often developed into *oligarchy, but for a long time aristocratic families dominated political life. Sparta and Thessaly remained strongly aristocratic throughout the classical period. The poems of *Theognis (of Megara) show the views of an aristocrat alarmed by the effect of wealth in disturbing the old social and political order, while the odes of the Theban poet *Pindar reflect some of the ideals of the aristocratic life. For aristocracy at Rome see REPUBLIC.

Aristo'crates, Against, speech in a public prosecution by *Demosthenes (2).

Aristodē'mus. 1. One of the *Heracleidae, father of Eurysthenēs and Proclēs.

2. The only one of *Leonidas' three hundred Spartans to return home after the battle of Thermopylae (480 BC), having missed the fighting through sickness. He was disfranchised, and according to Herodotus (7. 230), 'no man would give him a light for his fire or speak to him; he was called Aristodemus the coward.' At the battle of Plataea in the following year he redeemed himself by fighting recklessly to the death.

3. Legendary Messenian hero of the First Messenian War against Sparta. He killed his daughter in consequence of an oracle which said that the sacrifice of a maiden would ensure the preservation of Messenia. He became king and was at first victorious over the Lacedaemonians, but later, despairing of ultimate success, committed suicide over his daughter's grave.

Aristogei'ton, see HARMODIUS.

Aristo'menēs, legendary Messenian hero of the Second Messenian War against Sparta, who was eventually defeated.

Aristo'phanēs. 1. (c.445, or earlier, –c.385 BC), Athenian comic poet, writer of Old Attic Comedy (see COMEDY, GREEK

3). Virtually nothing is known of his life. He may have lived or owned property on Aegina. Eleven of his plays survive; we also have some 32 titles and many fragments. His plays may be dated as follows:

427 *Daitaleis* ('banqueters', people of an imaginary deme of that name), now lost. Fragments of two speeches survive. The play won second prize in the dramatic competitions.

426 *Babylonians*, produced at the Dionysia, now lost. Afterwards Aristophanes was apparently prosecuted by Cleon for his 'attacks on the magistrates' in the presence of the allies (who were bringing their tribute to Athens as members of the *Delian League). No penalty seems to have been imposed. The play may have won first prize.

425 *Acharnians*, produced at the Lenaea, the first of his surviving comedies; it won first prize.

(These three plays were not produced by Aristophanes, but by a certain Callistratus; the reason is not known for certain, but it may have been that Aristophanes was under the customary age.)

424 *Knights* (Lenaea, first prize).

423 *Clouds* (Dionysia), on the subject of Socrates and the new learning. It was perhaps too subtle for popular taste; it won third prize (i.e. came last). It was rewritten by Aristophanes in the form we now have; we know that he substituted two scenes showing hostility to the new school. This second edition was not produced at either of the great festivals.

422 *Wasps* (Lenaea, second prize).

421 *Peace* (Dionysia, second prize).

414 *Birds* (Dionysia, second prize).

411 *Lysistrata* (produced by Callistratus) and *Thesmophoriazusae* (probably at the Lenaea and Dionysia respectively).

405 *Frogs* (Lenaea, first prize).

392 (probably) *Ecclesiazusae*.

382 *Plutus*, the second play of this name.

After these, Aristophanes wrote two comedies which he gave to his son Araros to produce, but which are now lost. One of them, the *Kokalos*, we are told, started the type of New Comedy (see COMEDY, GREEK 6), introducing romantic features which are characteristic of the plays of Menander. Aristophanes' plays down to 421 show him as the chief representative of Old Comedy, but from the *Birds* onwards he introduced significant changes in the structure.

Aristophanes' language is colourful and imaginative, his lyric poetry subtle and varied in tone. His humour lies largely in exaggeration, parody, and satire, directed against new movements in thought or culture, and prominent men who are suitable for this treatment. No group or class is exempt, and as a result it is notoriously difficult to decide what moral or political lesson, if any, we are meant to derive from a play. The sympathetic characters are in the main people who wish to be left alone to enjoy their private lives in a traditional way, untroubled by wars and politicians and intellectuals, but they themselves are often narrowly self-seeking, and no final decision is made as to who, or which cause, is 'right'. Plato in his *Symposium* represents Aristophanes as an agreeable and convivial companion who gives an amusing turn to a serious discussion, and this is perhaps the light in which to regard much of his work. It does not appear in fact to have affected the course of events.

Aristophanes had a direct influence on English literature, notably on the comedies of Ben Jonson (1572/3–1637), Thomas Middleton (1580–1627), and Henry Fielding (1707–54).

2. Aristophanes of Byzantium, head of the *Alexandrian Library c.*200 BC. He was a scholar of wide learning, the teacher of *Aristarchus, who continued along the lines laid down by his master. Aristophanes made the first critical editions of several Greek poets, including Homer, Hesiod, Anacreon, Pindar, and Aristophanes (1). He is said to have invented or regularized Greek *accents; and he devised a set of critical signs to indicate passages in manuscripts suspec-ted of being interpolations or otherwise noteworthy; see TEXTS, TRANSMISSION OF ANCIENT I.

A'ristotle (Aristotelēs) (384–322 BC), Greek philosopher.

1. *Life.* Aristotle was born at Stageira in Chalcidice, the son of Nicomachus, physician to Amyntas II (father of Philip II), king of Macedon. In 367 he came to Athens, and for the next twenty years was a pupil of Plato, until the latter's death in 347. In that year he left Athens. It may be the case that when Plato was succeeded as head of the *Academy by Speusippus, Aristotle found the latter's mathematical kind of philosophy repugnant. Perhaps more probable is the theory that Aristotle left Athens for political reasons, because Demosthenes and his anti-Macedon party were in the ascendancy. However that may be, in the same year his home town of Stageira was destroyed by the then king of Macedon, Philip II, and Aristotle settled at Assos in the Troad, where there was a small colony of philosophers from the Academy. These were supported by Hermias, the enlightened tyrant of the neighbouring city of Atarneus, to whom Aristotle later wrote a poem of praise and whose niece, Pythias, he married. He remained there for three years, probably lecturing and writing, until the philosophers were driven out after the murder of Hermias. Aristotle retreated to Mytilene in Lesbos (where he met *Theophrastus), teaching there until 343/2. It was during his stay at Assos and Mytilene that he conducted many of his zoological researches. At the end of that time he was invited by Philip to be tutor to his 13-year-old son *Alexander (the Great). His teaching of Alexander was probably mainly in Homer and the dramatists (he was said to have prepared for his pupil an edition of the *Iliad*), but the need for some political education may have stimulated Aristotle's own interest in politics (a lost work is entitled 'Alexander, or On Colonization').

In 335, when Alexander had succeeded to the throne and started on his expedition to Asia, Aristotle returned to Athens and taught there in a *gymnasium built in a grove sacred to Apollo Lykeios and

..nown in consequence as the Lyceum. Here he was said to have lectured to his pupils in the morning and the general public in the evening. The kind of philosophy he taught came to be known as the Peripatetic, owing its name to the covered court (*peripatos*) where the students walked up and down. Scholarly research of all kinds was carried on, literary, scientific, and philosophical. Aristotle collected manuscripts and maps, and formed the first considerable library of antiquity as well as a museum of natural objects. At some time during this period Pythias died, and Aristotle lived afterwards with Herpyllis, by whom he had a son Nicomachus. He enjoyed the friendship and protection of Antipater, whom Alexander had made governor of Macedon and Greece. After the death of Alexander in 323 the anti-Macedonian party at Athens became dominant, and Aristotle, having obvious Macedonian connections, was charged with impiety on the grounds that his poem to Hermias befitted a god, not a man, an accusation probably political in origin. Rather than let the Athenians 'sin twice against philosophy' (the first time being the execution of Socrates) Aristotle left his school to Theophrastus and departed from Athens. He died the following year at Chalcis in Euboea, where in the last months of his life he lamented his isolation. His will, reproduced by *Diogenes Laertius, shows him to have been of a kindly and affectionate disposition.

2. *The general character of his work*. Aristotle left a vast number of works—some 400 were attributed to him—on a great variety of subjects, but only about a fifth has survived. The works we now possess belong mostly to the later period of his life and were never published in his lifetime. Those that were read in classical antiquity, by Cicero and his friends for example, were the published works of his early life and are now lost. Sometimes referred to as the 'exoteric works' (i.e. works for the 'outside' public), they were written in a fluent and polished style for the general reader, and were undoubtedly Platonic in their general assumptions (though the extent to which Aristotle in his early life adhered to the tenets of the Platonic Academy is still a matter of debate). At his death Aristotle bequeathed to Theophrastus, his successor as head of the Lyceum, not only his books but also his manuscripts. The manuscripts comprised his full lecture-notes, which had not been prepared for publication, sometimes called the 'acroastic works' (Gk. *akroasthai*, 'to attend a lecture'); it has come about by chance that the works of Aristotle which we now possess are in origin lecture-notes, reworked over a number of years and never intended to be read by the public. They may have been set in order after Aristotle's death by his colleague Eudemos of Rhodes and his son Nicomachus. What use was made of them in the third and second centuries BC is not clear, but they cannot have been entirely unknown: there were lists of the titles in circulation, made by or for the librarians of the Alexandrian Library, and some Stoic philosophers seem to have had some knowledge of Aristotle's logic. Eventually, in a crumbling condition, the manuscripts were sold and went to Athens, whence Sulla shipped them to Rome as part of his war-booty after the Mithridatic War (89–85 BC). There they were edited by the head of the Lyceum at Athens, Andronicus of Rhodes, and this edition is the basis of all our surviving manuscripts of Aristotle both in Greek and in other languages. It was circulated and closely studied and commented upon as being more profound and original than the published books; as a consequence the latter ceased to be read and were eventually lost.

3. The works of Aristotle may be divided into three classes:

(i) The early popular works of philosophy, mostly in dialogue form, published by Aristotle himself and now lost except for fragments preserved by quotation in later writers. These include the *Protrepticus* ('exhortation to philosophy') which served as a model for Cicero's *Hortensius* but is now lost. They were Platonic in tone.

(ii) Large collections of historical and scientific facts, made by Aristotle sometimes in co-operation with others and now mostly lost. They included lists of the victors at the Olympian and

Pythian games and the **didascaliae* (records of the dramatic performances at Athens), traces of which remain in our scholia to the extant Greek plays. The only work from this class to have survived almost entire is the *Athenaiōn politeia*, 'constitution of the Athenians', the first in a collection of 158 such accounts of the constitutions of the Greek states, recovered from an Egyptian papyrus in 1890.

(iii) Philosophical and scientific works, many of which are still extant.

There are very few indications by which one may date Aristotle's works or arrange them in order of composition (and by their nature most reached their present form after being reworked over a number of years: see 2 above). On the whole they seem to reflect a progressive withdrawal from Plato's influence, although some of the works that show opposition to Plato could date from Aristotle's early years at the Academy. He did not believe in the separate existence of unchanging Ideas (or Forms) nor did he accept them as sufficient explanation of the facts of change and motion—an explanation he was still seeking in his latest work. He did not feel, as Plato felt, that physical science was founded on mathematics; hence in his physical works he was sometimes led to argue from plausible but mistaken assumptions, in the absence of actual measurement. In astronomy, for example, he made many errors, and his influence on later thought was a retarding one. In biology, however, a science which he brought into existence, exact measurement is less crucial in its early development, and his combination of close observation and acute reasoning made an outstanding contribution to knowledge. Politics he viewed in similar fashion, as a study which depends on observation and whose function it is to discover general laws governing the rise and fall of political systems, always with a practical end in view. His thought is distinguished partly by an inspired common sense which makes him avoid extremist views. This does not mean that he accepts half-hearted compromise, rather that he always recognizes equally the parts played by the senses and the intellect, the

claims of mind and body; in this spirit he advocates the rule of the middle class as being the steadiest element in a state. His other striking characteristic is his love of order and system, and to this aspect of his mind we are greatly indebted for the classification of the sciences to which we still adhere, and for much of our philosophical terminology. Many of the terms that he first introduced—universal and particular, premiss and conclusion, subject and attribute, form and matter, potentiality and actuality—have become commonly used both in philosophy and outside it.

4. *Extant works*. The surviving treatises may be classified as follows.

(i) *On logic*, a group which much later came to be called the *Organon* ('tool' or 'instrument'), consisting of six treatises known as: **Categoriae* ('predicates'), *De interpretatione* ('on interpretation'), *Analytica priora* and *posteriora* ('prior' and 'posterior analytics'), *Topica* ('topics'), and *De sophisticis elenchis* ('refutations in the manner of the sophists'). In these Aristotle was the first to explore the science of reasoning, both formal (in the *Prior Analytics*) and scientific (in the *Posterior Analytics*), on the basis of the syllogism, which he discovered. His analysis, as far as it went, was admirable and still remains valid.

(ii) *On metaphysics*, a mixture of treatises or lecture notes from different periods, put together by Andronicus of Rhodes (see 2 above) and called by him *Metaphysica* because in his edition they came 'after the physics' (*meta ta physika*). From this the branch of philosophy now known as metaphysics takes its name, but Aristotle's name for the subject is *prōtē philosophia*, 'primary philosophy'. The fourteen books, known by letters of the Greek alphabet, cover a range of topics concerned with basic realities, including the 'being' of things (*to on*, compare English 'ontology'), matter, form, substance, and essence. The Aristotelian 'form', the intelligible nature of a thing, differs from the Platonic 'idea', at least as Aristotle conceived it, in being immanent in the thing and not existing apart from it. Aristotle concludes that the universe must have a single, unchanging, final cause (see (iii) *a* below), an 'unmoved mover' engaged in the eternal activity of pure thought or contemplation (*theōria*), giving supreme happiness. This 'unmoved mover', who may be called God, has no interest in the universe but the latter ultimately depends on him, since the eternal circular motion of the stars which brings about the change of seasons and the rhythm of birth, reproduction, and death, is in imitation of God's activity. People, through their possession of mind (*nous*), can imitate God by themselves engaging in pure thought (although only briefly and intermittently), and this is their highest activity.

(iii) *On natural science* (physics, biology, psychology). The treatises in this group are: (*a*) *Physica* ('physics'), an examination of the constituent elements of things that exist by 'nature' ('nature' being an 'innate compulsion to movement'), and a discussion of such notions as matter and form, time, space, and movement, with an exposition of the four causes, the material cause (that out of which a thing comes to be), the formal cause (the intelligible nature of a thing, that in virtue of which it is what it is), the motive (or efficient) cause (the immediate origin of a change), and the final cause (the end or aim of the change); (*b*) *De caelo* ('on the heavens'), on the movement of celestial and terrestrial bodies (Aristotle knew that the earth was spherical, but thought it was situated at the centre of the universe); (*c*) *De generatione et corruptione* ('on coming into being and passing away'); (*d*) *Meteorologica*, principally on weather phenomena; (*e*) a group of works on biology: the nine books of the *Historia animalium*, ('inquiry into animals'), a collection of facts on animal life, showing acute observation (Aristotle knew, for instance, that whales were mammals), and a series of treatises in which he deals with the classification of animals, their reproduction, and the adaptation and evolution of their organs; (*f*) *De anima* ('on the soul'), a treatise in three books on the proposition that soul and body are two aspects of a single living thing, in the relation of form to matter. Thus the soul, which is the life force, does not survive the death of the body, though Aristotle

seems also to say that the soul of man possesses a portion of 'active reason' which is immortal and eternal, and is perhaps akin to God; (*g*) several monographs known collectively as *Parva naturalia* ('short works on nature'), on the general physiological conditions of life.

(iv) *On ethics and politics*. Aristotle wrote two ethical treatises to which he gave the title *Ēthika*, 'matters to do with character', known as the *Nicomachean* and the *Eudemian Ethics*. These cover much the same ground, though with certain important differences of view. The relation between the two works is still a matter of debate; the former is the better known. It is in the main a study of the end to which conduct should be directed. Aristotle accepts 'happiness', *eudaimonia*, doing well, making a success of life, as the end of human action, and wants to instruct men how to achieve it. For a person to be happy he must do well those things which are distinctively human. Humans are distinguished from other animals by possessing intellect, 'the god within us'. The happiness that is distinctively human is therefore achieved by intellectual activity. Not all human virtue is intellectual; there is also moral virtue. Aristotle defines the latter as a disposition to choose a certain mean, as determined by 'a man of practical wisdom' (*phronimos*), between two opposite extremes of conduct; a mean, for instance, between ascesticism and yielding to uncontrolled impulses. Aristotle lays stress on the notion of moral intention, but virtue of character is also important.

Virtue cannot be practised by the solitary individual: 'a human being is by nature a political animal' (i.e. it is our nature to live in a city, *polis*). In the eight books of the *Politica* ('politics'), Aristotle discusses the science of politics from the point of view of the city-state, which he assumes to be that most conducive to the fullest life of the citizen. He thinks the state was developed naturally by the grouping of families in villages, and of villages in a state, for the purpose of securing for the citizens a good and self-sufficing life. Since the essential purpose of the state is to pursue this moral, and not a material, end, it is necessary that the power should rest, not with the wealthy or with the whole body of free citizens, but with the good. He discusses citizenship, the classification of actual constitutions, and the various types of these, their diseases and the remedies; he recognizes the advantages of democracy, but finds the highest type in the monarchy of the perfect ruler if such is available, and failing this in an aristocracy of men of virtue and enlightenment. But this, too, is difficult, and on the whole he regards a limited democracy as the constitution best suited to the practical conditions of Greece in his day. He regards slavery as a natural institution, so far as it is based on the inferiority of the nature of the slave rather than on right of conquest. But the master must not abuse his authority, and slaves must have the hope of emancipation.

As the work has come down to us it is neither uniform nor complete; the various parts may well have been composed at different times. Books 7 and 8, containing the discussion of the ideal state, seem to belong to an early text in which the purely constructive method of Plato is followed. Books 4–6, dealing with actual historical states and containing an allusion to the death of Philip II of Macedon (in 336), must have been written later, when Aristotle had at his disposal the collection of the 158 constitutions of which the *Athenaion politeia* is the only survivor (see 3 (ii) above). That traces the development of the Athenian constitution from the earliest times (the first chapters are missing) down to the fall of the Thirty Tyrants (404), and then describes the mature democracy of Aristotle's own day.

(v) *On rhetoric and poetry*. Aristotle's *Rhetoric* deals with methods of persuasion, divided into those by which the speaker produces on his audience a favourable view of his own character, those by which he produces emotion, and thirdly argument, whether by means of example or of enthymeme (Gk. *enthymema*, the rhetorical form of the syllogism, based on probability). It then discusses style (of which the leading characteristics should be clearness and

appropriateness) and arrangement. The object of this treatise is practical, how to compose a good speech (see RHETORIC).

See also POETICS for Aristotle's treatise of that name.

5. *The influence of Aristotle*. The influence that Aristotle exerted on later generations of philosophers and scientists was immense, by the stimulus he gave, by the instruments of investigation which he invented, and by his actual contributions to knowledge. In western Europe in the early Middle Ages, down to about AD 1200, it was mainly his writings on logic, and not all of these, that were known and studied and became such a rigorous influence upon the disputations of medieval Schoolmen. Aristotelian logic more than any other single influence formed the European mind. His writings on science and philosophy, however, followed a different path. From about AD 800 onwards they were translated and expounded by the Arabs, first in the East and then, as a result of the Arab conquest, in Spain. The Arab versions were then retranslated into Latin and these Latin texts made their way from Spain into the rest of Europe, where they had previously been unknown, at the beginning of the thirteenth century. At first the study of these new writings was prohibited, but in the hands of Albertus Magnus (1206–80) and Thomas Aquinas (c.1225–74) they soon became the basis of a Christian philosophy which was a fusion of theology and Aristotelianism.

When at the end of the thirteenth century the Latin translations from Arabic were superseded by more accurate translations made directly from the Greek, Aristotle's authority in virtually all aspects of learning was absolute. It was particularly unfortunate that astronomy, which with alchemy made up the entire scientific interest of the Middle Ages, was the one subject in which Aristotle went furthest astray in believing the earth to be a stationary sphere and the universe geocentric. When Galileo (1564–1642) disputed the truth of it, it was against a very Aristotelian Christianity that he was offending. Galileo's English contemporary Francis Bacon (1561–1626), though contemptuous of the ancient philosophers in general, adopts Aristotle's division of the four causes, and entitles part of his own work the *Novum Organum*. In the sphere of literature, Aristotle's *Poetics* was regarded as an authority from Elizabethan days onward.

Aristo'xenus (b. between 375 and 360 BC), philosopher and musical theorist, pupil of Aristotle, passed over by him for headship of the *Lyceum in favour of Theophrastus. He was famous in antiquity for his works on rhythm and on harmonics, parts of which have survived. His exposition of the theory of harmonics in particular was a strong influence for many centuries. He also had a deep interest in the ethical and educational value of music.

Arminius, see VARUS.

Arpi'num, town in Latium, the birthplace of Marius and Cicero.

arre'phoroi, see PANATHENAIA.

A'rria. 1. Wife of Caecina Paetus, who, when her husband was ordered to death under the emperor Claudius, 'taught her husband how to die', stabbing herself and handing him the dagger with the words *Paete, non dolet* ('It doesn't hurt, Paetus').

2. The daughter of the above and wife of *Thrasea, a Stoic philosopher put to death by Nero.

A'rrian (Flavius Arrianus), b. AD 85–90, a Greek of Nicomedia in Bithynia, a successful officer in the Roman army, who became *consul suffectus* (129 or 130) and legate (131–7) in Cappadocia. He retired to Athens, where he was archon in 145/6. He was author of various extant works in Greek: a valuable *Anabasis* ('expedition up-country') *of Alexander* (the Great), in seven books, narrating his campaigns, with an eighth book, *Indikē*, describing India and Indian customs and relating the voyage of Nearchus in the Persian Gulf; an *Encheiridion* or manual of the philosophy of his master *Epictetus, and *Diatribai*, a record of the same philosopher's lectures which he attended in Greece, four books of which survive from an original eight; *Periplous* ('circumnavigation') of the Black Sea; *Cynegeticus* ('on hunting') purporting to supplement

the treatise attributed to Xenophon; and other minor works.

Arsacids, the royal dynasty of Parthia *c.*250 BC–*c.* AD 230.

Ars amatō'ria, poem in three books of elegiacs by *Ovid, written not before 1 BC. Its title means 'treatise on love'; it is in fact a mock-didactic poem on the art of seduction, written for a cultivated and pleasure-loving society where love is a game to be played with style and good humour. The first two books consist of instructions to men, the third of instructions to women on how to entice men. There are intriguing glimpses of Roman life and manners—the circus, the theatre, the banquet. The work was very popular, and quotations from it have been found on the walls of Pompeii. With its frivolous attitude to sexual morality it seems to have been one reason why the emperor Augustus banished the poet.

Arsi'nŏē. 1. In Greek myth, daughter of Phegeus and first wife of *Alcmaeon.

2. The name of several princesses among the ruling *Ptolemies of Egypt (who were of Macedonian descent). The most important was Arsinoe II (*c.*316–270 BC), daughter of Ptolemy I and Berenice, who married first Lysimachus, one of the generals and successors of Alexander the Great, secondly her stepbrother Ptolemy Ceraunus, and thirdly her brother Ptolemy II Philadelphus, thus becoming queen of Egypt. Her influence contributed to the brilliance of court life and the great expansion of Ptolemaic power overseas, and she and her husband were both deified in their lifetime. Her death was lamented in an elegy by Callimachus.

3. Greek settlement founded by Ptolemy II in the Faiyum (an oasis some 80 km. (50 miles) south of Cairo in Egypt), of which extensive ruins survive. It was the first source in modern times of papyri of Greek texts (see PAPYROLOGY).

arsis, in metric, the up (or weak) beat. The metrical foot (see METRE, GREEK 1) was divided between *arsis* (sometimes known as *anacrusis*) and *thesis*, the down (strong) beat. The terms are often confused and used in the opposite of these (original) senses.

Ars poe'tica, title by which *Horace's poetic *Epistle to the Pisos* soon became known (see EPISTLES). The poem takes the form of a letter of advice on the pursuit of literature, addressed to a father and two sons whose identity is as uncertain as the date of composition, which is perhaps about 19 BC. It is in the same tradition as Aristotle's *Poetics* and perhaps owes something to earlier Latin didactic poems, but the purpose of the *Ars poetica* in the form Horace gave it has always puzzled critics. First, as a treatise it is far from systematic. Where Aristotle is analytical and descriptive Horace is impressionistic, personal, and allusive. Transitions from one subject to another are abrupt and the arrangement seems haphazard. Secondly, its concentration on epic and drama seems irrelevant to the contemporary Roman literary scene. An ancient commentator said that Horace selected his material from the similar treatise of Neoptolemus of Parium, a Hellenistic Greek writer of the third century BC, but the structure of the *Ars poetica* and Horace's practice elsewhere suggest rather that he used no one Greek source but selected from among several sources those precepts which agreed with his own views on poetic style and were suitable for imaginative poetic treatment.

The lively autobiographical approach of the *Ars poetica* and its expression of personal standards in literature make it unique as a work of criticism in the ancient world. Many of its apt phrases, the *ridiculus mus* ('ridiculous mouse') of bathos, *in medias res* ('in the middle of things'), of an abrupt beginning, the 'purple patch' (*purpureus pannus*) and the reference to 'Homer nodding' (*dormitat Homerus*), have passed into common literary parlance. It exercised a great influence in later ages on European literature, notably on French drama through Nicholas Boileau's *L'Art Poétique* (1674), written in imitation, and was translated into English (1640) by Ben Jonson.

Artaphe'rnēs. 1. Half-brother of Darius I, king of Persia. He took a leading part in suppressing the Ionian Revolt against Persia in 499 BC (see PERSIAN WARS).

2. Son of (1), who with Datis commanded the Persian expedition which was defeated at the battle of Marathon in 490 BC.

Artaxe'rxēs, name of several Persian kings.

Artemidō'rus, of Daldis in Lydia (late second century AD), author of an extant Greek treatise *Oneirocritica* ('interpretation of dreams'); see DIVINATION.

A'rtemis, in Greek myth, the daughter of Zeus and *Leto, and twin sister of Apollo; a goddess universally worshipped in Greece. The etymology of her name is still unclear, nor is there agreement on whether or not it occurs on *Linear B tablets, but she is closely connected with Asia Minor. For the myth of her birth see APOLLO. She is by origin a goddess of wildlife, but her worship is found in cities through her association with women. She brings fertility to mankind and to the beasts; she is the goddess who helps women in child-birth, but she is also the virgin huntress to whose arrows is ascribed their sudden death. She has a fairly slight mythology. Her principal adventure was the slaying of *Orion, and she is associated with *Hippolytus and the death of *Callisto. She plays an undignified part in the *Iliad* where she is beaten by Hera with her own bow and sent away weeping. *Brauron in Attica was the site of a famous cult of the goddess; and a festival, the Brauronia, at which little girls 'acted the bear' in her honour, was held there.

Artemis was often in ancient times confused with *Hecatē, whose functions were similar, and *Selenē, another goddess of women. She was also identified with foreign goddesses having similar functions, such as the Cretan goddess *Britomartis. The most notable identification was with the great goddess of *Ephesus ('Diana of the Ephesians'). From there the worship of this 'Artemis' spread to Massilia (Marseilles) and thence to Rome, where the temple of Diana on the Aventine had a statue modelled on the Ephesian type.

Artemi'sia. 1. (early fifth century BC) daughter of Lygdamis, ruler of a Carian kingdom which included Halicarnassus, and after his death regent of his kingdom. With five ships she accompanied Xerxes

on his invasion of Greece in 480 (see PER-
SIAN WARS), and is said by Herodotus
(himself from Halicarnassus) to have
shown bravery and resource at the battle
of Salamis.

2. Sister and wife of *Mausolus of
Caria in whose memory she built the
Mausoleum at Halicarnassus c.353 BC.
She instituted a literary competition in
which the most famous rhetoricians of the
age took part, including Isocrates and
Theopompus, who won the prize.

Artemi'sium, promontory on the north-
west coast of Euboea, where the Greek
fleet was stationed during Xerxes'
expedition against Greece in 480 BC, and
whence they were forced to withdraw
(see PERSIAN WARS).

arval priests or **brothers** (*fratres
arvales*), the most ancient college of
priests in Rome, already in existence under the early republic and restored by the
emperor Augustus. They were so called
from offering public sacrifices for the
fertility of the fields (*arvum*, a ploughed
field). For their mythical origin see ACCA
LARENTIA. Many of their records survive
in inscriptions. The college had twelve
members chosen for life from the most
distinguished senatorial families; from
imperial times they seem to have
included the reigning emperor. Their
most important ceremony took place in
May in honour of the agricultural goddess
Dea Dia, in a grove on the Via Campania
8 km. (5 miles) from Rome. The famous
song of the priests, the *carmen arvale*, has
been preserved on an inscription of AD
218; it dates originally from the sixth or
fifth century BC and is the oldest surviving
specimen of Latin poetry. Other surviving inscriptions recording vows and offerings they were required to make are
important for the history of Latin script in
Rome and also for the chronology of the
empire, since many events in the house
of the reigning emperor were commemorated by the priests. Compare
SALII.

Arverni, Gallic tribe which for a long
time fought the Aedui for the supremacy

of Gaul. In 52 BC Vercingetorix, the son
of a former Arvernian king, led the Gallic
revolt against Julius Caesar (see COMMEN-
TARIES I (book 7)).

arx ('citadel'), at Rome, the north-east
summit of the Capitoline hill, the citadel
proper. The temple of *Juno Moneta was
here.

Asca'laphus, in Greek myth, the son of
Acheron who revealed that Persephonē
while in the Underworld had eaten some
pomegranate seeds, obliging her to
remain there for part of each year.
According to Ovid, Persephone turned
him into an owl for his betrayal.

Asca'nius or **Iūlus,** in Roman legend,
son of Aeneas and, according to Virgil in
the *Aeneid*, the Trojan princess Creusa;
he accompanied his father to Italy after
the fall of Troy. The historian Livy mentions an alternative version in which his
mother was the Italian princess *Lavinia.
The *gens* *Julia at Rome claimed descent
from him.

asclē'piad, see METRE, GREEK 8 (i).

Asclēpi'adēs, of Samos (b. c.320 BC),
also called Sicelidas, one of the earliest
writers of the Greek literary *epigram,
and in particular of the love epigram, in
the Hellenistic age, a contemporary of
Philetas and Theocritus. Many of his
poems survive in the Greek *Anthology.
He gave his name to the 'asclepiad'
metres, used earlier by Sappho and
Alcaeus, because he revived them.

Asclē'pius (Lat. Aesculapius), the
Greek god of healing. Strictly speaking
he was a hero, the son of the god Apollo
(himself a healing god) by a mortal, Coronis, daughter of Phlegyas. Apollo killed
Coronis for being unfaithful to him.
(Regretting it afterwards, he turned the
crow which had told him of her infidelity
from a white bird into a black.) He saved
his unborn child Asclepius, and entrusted
him to the care of the centaur *Chiron.
From him Asclepius learned the art of
medicine. Answering the prayer of the
goddess Artemis he restored to life her
favourite Hippolytus, son of Theseus.

Zeus, angered at his interference, slew Asclepius with a thunderbolt; Apollo in his turn was angry at the death of his son, and in revenge killed the *Cyclopes who had made the thunderbolt. To expiate this murder Apollo became for a year the slave of *Admetus. Homer in the *Iliad* represents Asclepius as the father of Machaon and Podaleirius, the doctors of the Greek army at the siege of Troy.

There is still controversy as to whether Asclepius was originally a god or, more probably, a nearly-divine type of hero, but certainly by classical times he had overshadowed other healing gods and heroes and was worshipped as a god and the founder of medicine. The most famous seat of his cult was at Epidaurus. From there lesser shrines were founded in other places, notably at Athens in 420 and at Rome in 293 BC (see AESCULAPIUS). There is a tradition that the poet Sophocles played a prominent part in establishing the Athenian cult. Many inscriptions found at Epidaurus and at Athens describe successful cures, achieved perhaps sometimes through faith but also through normal medical treatment. In historical times the Asclepiadae were a clan (*genos*) which practised medicine as a hereditary skill, tracing their descent from Asclepius and perhaps deriving their science partly from the priestly cult. They seem to have admitted to membership doctors from other families (compare HOMERIDAE). Asclepius was closely associated with the snake, and in instituting new shrines a sacred snake was always taken from the temple at Epidaurus. In art he is often shown bearing a staff, which is usually entwined with a snake; he is sometimes accompanied by a dog. See also ARISTEIDES (3).

Asco'nius Pediā'nus, Quintus (9 BC– AD 76), the writer of a historical commentary on Cicero's speeches, of which a fragment survives.

Asia

1. *The continent*. The early Greek geographers until *c*.500 BC divided the land mass of the world into two roughly equal parts, Europe in the north and north-west, and Asia including Africa

(Libya) to the south and south-east. By the time of Herodotus in the fifth century BC they had separated Africa from Asia and set the boundaries of the latter at the Indian Ocean in the south and the river Tanais (Don) in the north. Herodotus saw Asia Minor as a peninsula jutting into the Mediterranean Sea. Asia extended east as far as India, beyond which the earth was desert and unknown, with the river Oxus apparently marking its northern boundary. Not until the expedition of Alexander the Great towards the end of the fourth century BC did the Greeks have any detailed knowledge of the eastern regions of the continent. The conquest by the Romans of Asia Minor and Syria and their wars with Mithridates and the Parthians in the first century BC greatly increased their knowledge not only of western Asia but more especially of the Caucasian north, a region of which the Greeks were almost totally ignorant. The Romans' taste for luxuries such as silk and spices led to their exploration of the ancient trade routes and even to contact with Chinese merchants.

2. *The Roman province*. When Attalus III of Pergamum died in 133 BC he bequeathed his kingdom to the Romans. It included all of Greek Asia Minor; its eastern boundary was a line from Bithynia in the north to Lycia in the south and it later included Phrygia. It was rich in natural resources and had flourishing agriculture, industry, and trade. As a consequence of the exactions of Roman governors and profiteers, it was ready to join Mithridates VI, king of Pontus, who, seeking to extend his territory, occupied most of Asia Minor in 88 BC. He was forced by the Roman general Sulla to make peace in 84 and to give up all his conquered territory. Sulla reorganized the province and its system of taxation, but it continued to suffer from periodic exactions. During the partition of the provinces between Augustus and the senate after 27 BC, Asia became a senatorial province to be governed by a proconsul. It was essentially made up of many city states, some of which remained nominally free under Roman rule. Their rivalries prevented any real sense of provincial unity

but individual city-states were often enriched by the pride of their citizens. During the first two centuries of the empire Asia enjoyed great prosperity. The coastal cities retained a sophisticated Greek society but those of the interior became Hellenized only gradually, and always retained something of their non-Greek background. In the fourth century when Constantinople became the capital of the eastern Roman empire, Asian traffic was inclined to stop there, no longer passing on to Greece and Italy as it had for centuries. Thus Asia was deprived of the western influences which over the centuries had helped to mould its complex character.

Asia Minor, the ancient name for the peninsula in the extreme west of Asia that is now called Anatolia and forms the greater part of Turkey. It is a largely fertile country which was inhabited from earliest times by a variety of tribes from Asia and Europe. In the second millennium BC it was the centre of the Hittite empire. Greek tradition said that as a consequence of the *Dorian Invasion into mainland Greece many of the dispossessed emigrated to the coast of Asia Minor and there planted the Greek language and customs (see AEOLIS, and IONIA). *Lydia and *Phrygia developed in the interior. Asia Minor was conquered by Cyrus II of Persia in 546 BC and by Alexander the Great in 333. The peninsula came under Roman rule in the second and first centuries BC and remained part of the Roman and Byzantine empires until the 11th century AD.

Asianism, name given to the artificially mannered style of Greek oratory which developed in the period after Demosthenes (d. 322 BC); see ORATORY 1.

Asina'ria ('she-ass'), farcical Roman comedy by *Plautus, adapted from the Greek comedy of the same name, *Onāgros* (or *Onagos*) of Demophilus.

Demaenetus, an indulgent father, wishes to help his son Argyrippus to save the prostitute Philaenium from an old procuress, but he is tyrannized by his wife Artemona, who keeps tight control of the purse-strings. By a trick of one of his slaves he gets possession of twenty minae which were to be paid to Artemona's steward for some asses which have been sold (whence the name of the play), and father and son spend the evening banqueting with Philaenium. But a rival for the girl's favours, furious at finding himself anticipated, warns Artemona; she descends on the party, and with dire threats removes her husband.

The saying *homo homini lupus* ('man is a wolf to man') is taken from the play (l. 495).

Asi'nius Po'llio, see POLLIO.

Aspā'sia, of Miletus, the mistress of the Athenian statesman *Pericles after he divorced his wife. She had the reputation of being a woman of intellect who conversed with Socrates. Naturally enough she was often attacked for supposedly influencing Pericles' political actions, and was a target for writers of comedy. She bore Pericles a son, also called Pericles, who was legitimated by decree after the death in the plague of 430 of his father's two sons by his lawful wife. After Pericles' death she was said to have married the democratic politician Lysicles and to have borne him a son.

Asphodel, Plain of, in Homer's *Odyssey*, the place in the Underworld (see HADES) where all the dead dwell, leading a shadowy continuance of their former life in the world. The asphodel (whence 'daffodil') is a flowering plant of the lily family; in Hesiod it is given as an example of the cheapest and plainest food.

Aspis ('shield'), Greek comedy by *Menander, a substantial part of which has been recovered on a papyrus.

One of three brothers has died, leaving a son and daughter. The son Cleostratus goes off to the wars, leaving his sister under the protection of their uncle Chaerestratus. Cleostratus is reported dead, leaving his property to his sister. By Greek law the closest male relative of an heiress (within the permitted degree) was entitled to marry her. Chaerestratus was already planning to marry the girl to his stepson, but now his brother Smicrines tries to marry her for her money. A plot is laid to trick Smicrines into offering marriage to Chaerestratus' daughter instead, but Cleostratus, alive after all, returns. The play probably ended with the marriages of the cousins and the discomfiture of Smicrines.

The play is enlivened by the character of the resourceful slave Daos who engineers the deception and must be typical of many such slaves in other of Menander's plays, but now known chiefly from Roman comedy.

assonance, the noticeable recurrence of a sound in successive words; compare ALLITERATION.

1. *Greek.* The Greeks occasionally employed assonance for the sake of its aesthetic effect but took no pains to avoid it when no effect was intended, even when the repetition of sound seems to us displeasing. To judge from a comic fragment, fault was found with Euripides for excessive use of the letter sigma, but his extant plays are not noticeably more sigmatic than the rest of Greek literature. Punning assonance sometimes occurs, but not always for humorous effect; many Greek thinkers believed that there was a significant connection between similar-sounding words. Hence phrases like *pathei mathos* ('through suffering comes knowledge') and *soma sema* ('the body is a tomb') acquired deeper meaning. There is little evidence for deliberate rhyming in epic or drama, though it seems occasionally to happen in the final lines of a scene, or in a proverbial phrase. Prose writers avoided rhyme, except for conscious and mannered stylists like Isocrates.

2. *Latin.* The kind of assonance known as alliteration, often obtrusively and artlessly employed, is a common feature of early Latin poetry. By the time of Virgil, however, it had come to be employed with great subtlety and with emotional effect. A similar development is seen in prose, Cicero using the device with more point and less obtrusiveness than his predecessors. Tacitus uses alliterative pairs of words with great effect. The Roman ear seems to have enjoyed the judicious repetition of similar terminations in the more impassioned parts of oratory, an aspect of assonance employed more subtly by the poets. This usage easily turns into a species of rhyme found occasionally in poetry of all periods, but used deliberately in the accentual hymns from the fifth century AD onwards and with great beauty in the secular medieval lyrics.

Aste'ria, in Greek myth, sister of *Leto and mother, by the Titan Persēs, of Hecatē. Being pursued by Zeus she turned into a quail, leapt into the sea and became Ortygia ('quail island'), afterwards known as Delos.

Astrae'a, 'starry maiden' (later applied as an epithet to Queen Elizabeth I of England), the constellation Virgo, identified with Justice (Gk. *Dikē*), the last god to leave the earth, by *Aratus. She was supposed to have lived among men in the *Golden Age, retired to the mountains in the Silver Age, and finally, during the wickedness of the Bronze Age, fled to heaven.

astrology. The study of the heavenly bodies as predicting the fate of individuals was ultimately due to the Babylonians. The belief underpinning astrology, common to educated people generally, was that the cosmos was a unity, and that whatever happened in the heavens was bound to affect or be reflected in events on earth. As it was possible to predict the recurrence of celestial phenomena by astronomy, so it might also be possible to predict terrestrial events by observation of the heavenly bodies (astrology), and it came to be generally believed that the fortunes of an individual depended upon the aspect of the sky at the moment of his birth, and that astrologers could give guidance accordingly.

Astrology does not seem to have exerted much influence on Greek life until after the third century BC, in the wake of Alexander the Great. By the next century astrology had spread to Rome, and a vogue for it began when a number of manuals began to circulate widely. Believers included Sulla, Posidonius, and Varro (but not Cicero). Vitruvius, Propertius, and Ovid all professed to believe, and Augustus published his horoscope. From the first century AD onwards virtually everyone,

Christians, pagans, and Jews alike, accepted the predictability of fate and the maleficent powers of the planets (see MANILIUS). A few held out against this tyranny, usually with the argument that while stars, by reason of the universal 'sympathy' pervading the cosmos, may indicate the future, they cannot *determine* it. Rome particularly was sensitive to the potential political dangers, and at times of national crisis banished all professional astrologers. However, no permanent ban was intended, and the emperors themselves frequently had recourse to horoscopes. It was not until the fourth century, with Augustine's emphatic denial of its validity, and with the advent of the Christian emperors, that the practice of astrology was officially banned. Neverthless for the ordinary man it retained an axiomatic validity until the seventeenth century and beyond. See also PTOLEMY.

Astrono'mica, didactic poem on astrology by *Manilius.

astronomy. The science of astronomy (to which Rome contributed nothing) developed comparatively late in Greece and, being for the Greeks essentially a system for predicting the positions of the heavenly bodies, it covered only a part of what we understand by the term. In the classical period interest was confined to observations of the solstice and equinox and of the rising and setting of the most obvious stars and constellations, for the practical ends of navigation and establishing a *calendar. The fifth-century Athenian astronomer *Meton tried to correlate the lunar year with the solar year in a 19-year cycle (c.435 BC), but it seems that his system was not incorporated into the Athenian calendar. By the fifth century BC it was known to some individuals that the earth is a sphere and that the moon receives its light from the sun, and *Anaxagoras understood the principles of eclipses. Not till the fourth century can we be sure that the Greeks identified the five planets known to the ancient world, Venus, Mercury, Mars, Jupiter, and Saturn (see EUDOXUS). In that century became crystallized the picture of the cosmos which was accepted by Aristotle (see 4 (iii)) and given final

shape in the second century AD by *Ptolemy, who was able to calculate the position of all the known heavenly bodies at a given moment, predict eclipses, and foretell the appearance and disappearances of the planets and fixed stars. At the centre of the cosmos was the earth, a globe suspended in space, whose weight had taken it to the centre. The earth was surrounded by a system of concentric spherical shells, rotating at various speeds and about various axes; on these were carried the moon, sun, planets, and fixed stars. The terrestrial atmosphere reached as far as the moon. The outermost sphere, that of the fixed stars, was composed of the rarest of all elements, the aether, and revolved daily about the earth. Ptolemy in his *Almagest* gave canonical form to this view of the cosmos, and his work remained uncorrected except in small details throughout all antiquity until Copernicus (1473–1543) and Galileo (1564–1642). For a heliocentric view of the universe see ARISTARCHUS (I). See further the names cited under MATHEMATICS.

Asty'anax, known also as Skamandrios, the son of Hector and *Andromachē, born during the siege of Troy and thrown from its battlements by *Neoptolemus or killed by Odysseus after the capture of the city.

Atala'nta (Atalantē), in Greek myth, daughter either of Iasos, an Arcadian, or of Schoeneus, a Boeotian; in either case her mother was *Clymenē. She was a huntress, averse to marriage, and loved by *Meleager with whom she took part in the Calydonian boar-hunt. She refused to marry any man who could not defeat her in a race, and any suitor whom she defeated was put to death. Hippomenēs (or Milanion) took up the challenge, and on the advice of Aphroditē carried with him three golden apples which she gave him. He dropped these at intervals and, as Atalanta could not resist the temptation to stop and pick them up, won the race. Their son was *Parthenopaeus in most accounts.

Ata'rgatis, often known simply as 'the Syrian goddess', worshipped as a fertility goddess at Hierapolis (Bambycē) where her temple was the greatest and holiest in Syria. Her consort was Hadad. In the second century BC her worship spread to a number of Hellenic cities, but appeared only sporadically in the West. *Lucian describes the cult, and *Apuleius the life of her Galli, wandering priests.

Ātē, in Greek myth, the personification of blind folly in the grip of which the victim cannot distinguish between right and wrong, advantageous and disadvantageous courses of action.

Ate'llan farces (*fābulae Atellānae*), named after the town of Atella in Campania, ancient dramatic performances apparently in the form of coarse comedies of low life. There were certain stock characters, Maccus the fool, Dossennus the hunchback, Mandūcus the glutton, Pappus the greybeard, etc., who were probably introduced in ridiculous situations. Some of the later titles suggest burlesques of mythology. Atellan plays became popular at Rome, probably in the third century BC, and were acted by amateurs. They were revived in more literary form, with the same stock characters but with a written plot in verse, by Pomponius of Bononia and Novius, who probably flourished early in the first century BC. These revivals were acted by professional comedians, were staged after the end of performances of tragedy, and seem often to have been tragic parodies. They continued intermittently until the end of the first century AD. Only fragments survive. See OSCAN.

A'thamas, in Greek myth, son of *Aeolus (2) and king of Thebes. The myth of his family is variously told, but in essentials is as follows. By his first wife Nephelē, a cloud-goddess, he had two children, Phrixus and Hellē. His second wife Ino, daughter of Cadmus, conceived a bitter hatred of her step-children, who escaped death on a winged and golden-fleeced ram which carried them away across the sea. Helle became giddy and fell into that part which is in consequence called the Hellespont. Phrixus arrived safely in Colchis, where Aeētēs the king received him hospitably. The ram was sacrificed to Zeus and its golden fleece hung up in Colchis and guarded by a dragon. For the rest of this myth see ARGONAUTS, and for the fate of Athamas, Ino, and her two sons see DIONYSUS.

Athē'na or **Athē'nē**, the patron goddess of Athens. In Homer she is generally called Athene, in tragedy Athenaia. The (abbreviated) form Athena became common in the fourth century BC. She was worshipped in the *Parthenon, her great temple on the Acropolis, and throughout Greece, the islands, and the colonies. Whether Athens is named after the goddess or the goddess after Athens is an ancient argument, but the latter is generally considered more probable. Her name is perhaps to be found on a *Linear B tablet from Cnossus, and she is probably a prehellenic deity. She is sometimes known as Pallas Athene for reasons which remain obscure; Pallas was sometimes understood to mean 'maiden', sometimes 'brandisher' (of weapons). Equally obscure is the meaning of her name Tritogeneia, 'Trito-born', for which a number of explanations was given in antiquity. In classical times she was pre-eminently the city goddess of Greece, and had temples not only on the Acropolis at Athens but also on the citadels of Argos, Sparta, and Larisa (in Thessaly). In Homer, despite the fact that she is the enemy of Troy, she is still the goddess of the Trojan citadel; see PALLADIUM. She was *par excellence* a war-goddess, and is most frequently represented in art as armed, but in addition she was the patroness of all urban arts and crafts, especially spinning and weaving, and so ultimately the personification of wisdom. She is also the inventor of the musical instrument the *aulos* (a flute). The principal myth concerning her relates to her birth. She was the daughter of Zeus and *Mētis. Zeus swallowed Metis for fear she should give birth to a son stronger than himself. In due time the god Hephaestus (or Prometheus, it was sometimes said) opened Zeus' head with an axe and Athena emerged, fully armed and uttering her war-cry. She is regularly regarded as virgin; Zeus gave Hephaestus leave to marry her, and from his unsuccessful attempt sprang the Athenian king *Erichthonius. She also strove with *Poseidon for possession of Attica, a contest in which she emerged victorious by producing the olive tree. (For another myth see ARACHNE.) She is generally represented as a goddess of severe beauty, in armour, with helmet, *aegis, spear, and shield (sometimes bearing the Gorgon's head); she often has an owl sitting on her shoulder, especially in fifth-century Athens, in reference to her stock epithet *glaukōpis* which appears to mean 'owl-faced' but could also be interpreted as 'bright-eyed'. Compare MINERVA.

Athenae'um, at Rome, the emperor Hadrian's famous institute for lectures and recitations by rhetors and other literary figures.

Athenae'us (flourished *c.* AD 200), of Naucratis, Greek author of the *Deipnosophistai* ('men learned in the arts of the banquet') in fifteen books. Twenty-three learned men (some having the names of real persons, such as Galen and Ulpian) are represented dining together at Rome on several occasions, and conversing on all aspects of food and on a wide range of other subjects. In reality Athenaeus was an industrious collector of excerpts and anecdotes, which he reproduces as conversation. The work is a fruitful source of information on the literature and usages of ancient Greece; it survives except for the first two books and part of the third, which we have only in a later epitome.

Athēnaiōn politeia. 1. A treatise by *Aristotle (see 3 (ii)). 2. A political pamphlet attributed to Xenophon (see *CONSTITUTION OF THE ATHENIANS* (2)).

Athens (Athenai, Lat. Athenae), the chief city of *Attica, in Greece. In classical times the city stood about 5 km. (3 miles) from the sea at its nearest point, in the central plain of Attica, surrounded by mountains on all sides except the south. The citadel of Athens, the *Acropolis, sometimes called simply *polis*, from being the original 'city', is a squareish rock rising steeply out of the plain. Immediately west of it is a second hill, the *Areopagus, and to the south-west a third, the *Pnyx. The Acropolis was continuously inhabited from Neolithic times (*c.* 5000 BC). In the *Mycenaean period a palace was built on it, and it was fortified by a wall in the second half of the thirteenth century BC. (This was during the imagined lifetime of Athens' national hero *Theseus; for other myths relating to this early period see ERECHTHEUS, ERECHTHONIUS, and CECROPS.) Archaeological evidence suggests that the city was occupied continuously during the *Dark Age, and after 900 BC it was perhaps the most prosperous community in Greece.

In early times Athens, like other Greek states, was ruled by kings. Traditionally the last king was *Codrus, who was succeeded by elected *archons, and Athens became an *aristocracy. Although the archonship was an elected office, the aristocrats, being rich and powerful, monopolized it. The attempt by *Cylon to overthrow them and become tyrant (*c.*632) failed. Despite the legislation of *Draco (621) their position was not weakened until the reforms of *Solon in 594 BC. These however could not prevent tyranny at Athens, and the popular leader Peisistratus seized power in the mid-sixth century. The period of the Peisistratid tyrants, lasting until 510 BC, saw a considerable increase in the city's material prosperity and cultural standing. After the expulsion of *Hippias, the reforms of *Cleisthenes established a true *democracy.

At the beginning of the fifth century BC Athens was a powerful state. But her intervention in the Ionian Revolt was unsuccessful and exposed her to the menace of Persia (see PERSIAN WARS). The Persian King Xerxes sacked the city in 490, but Athens emerged from the struggle with her fleet intact, her prestige increased, and her position as leader of all the Ionian Greeks acknowledged (see DELIAN LEAGUE). Under *Pericles—in effect ruler of the city from 461 to 430— Athens reached its cultural and political zenith. The *Parthenon and other celebrated buildings were constructed, Aeschylus, Euripides, and Sophocles were among the writers who flourished, and political offices were open to all— citizens were paid for undertaking their political duties, so that even the poorest could afford to exercise their rights. However, rivalry with Sparta led to the *Peloponnesian War (431–404), from which Athens emerged a dependant of

Sparta, impoverished, her population severely depleted, all her overseas possessions lost, and her fleet reduced to twelve ships. Sparta imposed an oligarchy on the city, and for eight months in 404–403 Athens was ruled by the *Thirty Tyrants. However, she soon regained her democracy and her freedom, and in 376 won back her supremacy at sea by a decisive naval victory over Sparta near Naxos.

The most prominent Athenian statesman of this period was *Callistratus, whose general policy was based on harmony with Sparta and a balance of power between that city and Thebes, which was now aspiring to the leadership of Greece. Athens, having supported the Thebans until their victory over the Spartans at Leuctra in 371, was more influenced by jealousy of neighbouring Thebes than by the old rivalry with Sparta. In the ensuing struggle between these two, Athens was in alliance with Sparta in 369, and an Athenian contingent fought on the Spartan side at Mantinea in 362. By this time *Macedon was rising in importance and threatening the Athenian position in the north Aegean. Athens had to choose between two policies: to attempt to recover the leadership of Greece, or to come to terms with Philip II of Macedonia, with some loss of independence. The 'peace' party included the statesman *Eubulus, the orator *Aeschinēs, the general *Phocion, and the statesman Philocratēs (see also ISOCRATES); the 'war' party was led by the orators *Demosthenes, *Lycurgus, and *Hypereides. The eloquence of Demosthenes prevailed, and a final battle between Athens and Thebes on the one side and Philip on the other was fought at Chaeronea in 338. Athens was defeated, and was obliged to accept Philip's moderate terms (the loss of the Hellespont) and join the Hellenic confederacy which he organized.

The death of Philip's son Alexander the Great in 323 appeared to give the Greeks an opportunity to recover their freedom, but in the so-called *Lamian War (323–322) Athens with the other Greek states was defeated at Crannon by *Antipater. Demosthenes took poison to avoid capture. The democrats were reinstated at Athens under the brief rule of Polyperchon (the immediate successor of Antipater as regent of Macedonia), but *Cassander, Antipater's son, restored in the main his father's constitution and appointed as his governor at Athens in 317 the distinguished Athenian citizen *Demetrius of Phalerum, a friend of the philosopher Aristotle. His ten years' governorship was a period of peace and prosperity for the city. Yet when *Demetrius Poliorcētēs, son of Antigonus, captured the city from Cassander in 307 he was looked upon by the Athenians as a liberator, and was granted divine honours.

The fourth century shows the last phase of the intellectual and cultural pre-eminence of Athens. The character of her intellectual activity had become less creative and more analytical and critical. It was the age of Plato and Aristotle, the great orators, and New Comedy. Art became more realistic, less infused with the old religious ideas, no longer centred on the interests of the city state.

The third century BC saw the end of the political importance of Athens and after the defeat of the *Achaean League by the Roman consul Mummius in 146 BC Greece became a Roman protectorate (not a province until the time of Augustus). Athens and Sparta did not have to pay taxes to Rome, however, and there was a revival of material prosperity. This prosperous period came to an end with the Mithridatic War of 89–85, when Athens, which had sided with *Mithridates, was sacked and in part destroyed by the Roman general *Sulla. Greece suffered severely, both from Sulla and from the barbarian allies of Mithridates, who sacked Delphi. Even greater ruin followed from the Roman civil wars of the first century BC, and endured until the emperor Augustus made Greece a Roman province in 27 BC.

In spite of her political decline Athens retained much of her intellectual prestige and remained pre-eminent for the study of philosophy. She was patronized in the second century BC by the *Attalids of Pergamum, who adorned the city with colonnades and sculptures. It became fashionable for Romans to go to the philosophical schools of Athens as to a university. *Atticus lived there for many years; Cicero and his son and Horace were among those who studied in the city. Horace, and in a later age Lucian, appreciated the peaceful charm of Athens compared with the turmoil of Rome. Athens enjoyed some revival of her former glories in the second century AD under the emperor Hadrian and the Antonines, and in the fourth century Julian the Apostate was a lover of the city. The end of her period of intellectual eminence came in AD 529, when the Christian emperor Justinian ordered the closing of her schools of philosophy.

Athens, Constitution of, see CONSTITUTION OF THE ATHENIANS.

Athos, headland on the most easterly of the promontories of Chalcidice, with a mountain some 2,000 m. (6,600 ft.) high rising sheer from the sea, sacred to Zeus. To avoid the sea passage around Mount Athos when he was invading Greece, the Persian king Xerxes cut a canal through the isthmus (483–481 BC). Athos is now the site of several monasteries.

Ath. Pol., i.e. *Athēnaiōn politeia*, see CONSTITUTION OF THE ATHENIANS.

Atla'ntis, huge mythical island thought of as situated off the Straits of Gibraltar, first mentioned in literature in Plato's dialogues *Timaeus* and *Critias*. The name is derived from Atlas (see below). Its empire supposedly came into contact with the Athenians in prehistoric times and was defeated, the island being afterwards swallowed up in great earthquakes and floods. There has been frequent speculation as to whether the myth embodied folk memories of, for example, the Minoan civilization of Crete or the eruption at Thera (Santorini).

Atlas, in Greek myth, a Titan, son of *Iapetus and Clymenē; he married the *Oceanid Pleionē. His name probably means 'he who carries' or 'he who endures'. In Homer he is the father of Calypso but usually his daughters are the *Pleiades, and sometimes the *Hyades and the *Hesperides too. He is the guardian of the pillars of heaven (which hold up the sky), and later as punishment for his part in the revolt of the Titans he had to hold the sky up himself. He

became identified with the western part of the Atlas mountains in north-west Africa, and sometimes with the southern Pillar of Hercules. A later tale said that *Perseus had turned him into stone with the Gorgon's head. When Heracles was seeking the apples of the Hesperides (see HERACLES, LABOURS OF 11) Atlas offered to fetch them if Heracles would hold up the sky; he then refused to take back his burden until tricked into doing so by the hero.

atomists, see DEMOCRITUS.

Ato'ssa, wife of *Darius I, king of Persia, and mother of Xerxes.

A'treus, in Greek myth, one of the sons of *Pelops; he was king of Mycenae, husband of Aerope, and father of Agamemnon and Menelaus. After Pelops was cursed by the dying Myrtilus, each generation of the family came to disaster. Pelops' brother Thyestes seduced Aerope and aimed at the kingship of Mycenae. Atreus banished him, but later pretended to be reconciled and invited him to a banquet at which he served up to Thyestes the flesh of his own children. Thyestes fled, then later married his own daughter Pelopia and became the father of Aegisthus, who was to be a further agent of the curse. The details of this story are variously told.

A'tropos, 'irresistible', one of the three *Fates. Her function, according to the poets, was to cut off the thread of life.

Atta, Titus Quintus (d. 77 BC), Latin poet, composer of comedies of the kind called *fabulae *togatae*, of which very few fragments survive. He is said to have excelled in female character portrayal.

A'ttalids, the ruling dynasty of Pergamum in the third and second centuries BC; three of its members were called Attalus. The dynasty was founded c.282 when Philetaerus became ruler of Pergamum under *Seleucid suzerainty, and it ended in 133 with the death of Attalus III, who bequeathed his dominions to Rome; they became the Roman province of Asia Minor. The Attalids ruled over what was constitutionally a Greek city-state, but they had wide powers of interference and ruled directly over the native population of the surrounding country. This country possessed natural resources including silver mines but its wealth, for which the Attalids were proverbial, lay in its agricultural produce and the dependent industries of wool and parchment (a word derived from Pergamum). The Attalids were devoted patrons of art and literature, and under their influence Pergamum became one of the most beautiful of all Greek cities, famous for its library and school of architecture.

Atthis (i.e. *Atthis historia*, 'history of Attica'), name given to a type of chronicle dealing with the history of Athens and Attica, popular from *c.*350 to 250 BC out of nostalgia for the past glories of Athens. The pattern seems to have been set by *Hellanicus' history published soon after 404 BC. The contents of *Atthides* were traditional and concentrated on mythology, origins of cults, and descriptions of political institutions. The writers are referred to as 'atthidographers'. Only fragments of their work survive.

Attic (adj.), see ATTICA below.

A'ttica, the country around *Athens (its chief city), a mountainous and largely arid area forming the south-east promontory of central Greece, about 2,500 sq. km. (1,000 sq. miles) in extent. Attica is dominated by its four mountain systems, Aegaleus, Hymettus, Pentelicus, and Laurium, which divide the land into three plains, to the west the Thriasian plain with its chief town Eleusis, in the centre the Attic plain, and to the east the Mesogeia. The main rivers of Attica, which are full only in winter or after heavy rains, are the Cephi(s)sus and the Ili(s)sus. Of natural resources, Attica was famous for its dazzling white Pentelic marble, and the grey, blue, and black marble from Hymettus. Its potters' clay was excellent, and there were silver and lead at Laurium. Attica originally consisted of many separate communities, traditionally twelve in the time of the king *Cecrops, which were later fused into a single Athenian state, an achievement attributed to *Theseus but in fact a gradual process probably lasting into the

seventh century BC. Athens became the capital city, although local loyalties remained and even during the sixth century aristocratic families still lived independent lives in the countryside. It was the tyranny of *Peisistratus and even more the reforms of *Cleisthenes which finally broke local ties and brought the whole of Attica under a centralized government at Athens.

A'ttica, Pompō'nia, see AGRIPPA (1).

Attic dialect, see DIALECTS.

Attic drama, see DRAMA, COMEDY, TRAGEDY.

A'tticism, see SOPHISTIC, SECOND.

Attic Nights, see GELLIUS.

A'tticus, Titus Pompō'nius (110–32 BC), intimate friend of *Cicero ((1) 1), born at Rome of an equestrian family. In 85 he left the turbulence and bloodshed of Rome for Athens, where he lived for many years (whence his *cognomen* Atticus, i.e. 'of Attica'). He adopted the *Epicurean philosophy and took no active part in the politics of the ensuing troubled period, but maintained an attitude of neutrality and friendship with all parties. He helped Marians and Pompeians; he protected Cicero's wife Terentia when Cicero went into exile, and Antony's wife Fulvia and his lieutenant Volumnius at the time of *Mutina (43 BC). In consequence he was spared by Antony in the proscriptions. He became the friend of the emperor Augustus, and his daughter Attica married *Agrippa. (Their daughter Vipsania married Tiberius and was mother of the younger Drusus.) His sister Pomponia married Cicero's brother Quintus. The series of Cicero's letters to Atticus begins in 68, and their friendship, which started when they were students together, continued until Cicero's death. In both public and private life Cicero constantly turned to him for sympathy and advice. Atticus had inherited a considerable fortune, with which he bought land in Epirus, and which he gradually increased by judicious investment until he became very wealthy. He had strong literary tastes; he kept a large staff of slaves trained in copying and binding manuscripts, and he helped in the circulation of Cicero's writings. His own works, which have not survived, included a *Liber annālis* ('annals'), an epitome of Roman history in one book dealing with laws, wars, and political events from the earliest times down to his own day; and a genealogical treatise on certain Roman families and the magistracies they had held. He also helped to establish 753 BC as the date of the founding of Rome. He committed suicide in 32 BC when suffering from an incurable illness. We have a Life of him by *Nepos.

A'ttila, king of the Huns AD 434–53 (known as Etzel in medieval German saga); he ruled an empire stretching from the Alps to the Caspian Sea. In 452 he invaded Italy and sacked several cities, but was persuaded to withdraw without entering Rome. While preparing to invade the eastern empire again, having ravaged it in the 440s, he died suddenly on his wedding night. See FALL OF ROME.

Attis, in mythology, the youthful consort of the Phrygian goddess *Cybelē (also known as Agdistis in Phrygia). The Phrygian version of his myth relates that he was the son of Nana, daughter of the river god Sangarius (a river in Asia Minor). She conceived him after gathering the blossom of an almond-tree sprung from the severed male organs of Agdistis/Cybele who, born both male and female, had been castrated by the gods. When Attis wished to marry, Cybele, who loved him and was jealous, drove him mad so that he castrated himself and died. There are many variants of this myth, which, among other things, purports to explain why Cybele's priests, *Galli, are eunuchs. Attis appears only rarely in Greece, but with Cybele became an accepted deity at Rome under the emperor Claudius. For a poem on the subject of Attis see CATULLUS.

A'ttius, Lucius, see ACCIUS.

Augē, in Greek myth, the mother by Heracles of *Telephus.

Auge'as (Augeiās), king of Elis whose stables Heracles was required to clean as one of his Labours (see HERACLES, LABOURS OF 6). *Trophonius and Agamedes, the legendary architects, are said to have built his treasury.

augury and **auspices,** divination by observing the habits of birds. The terms 'auguries' and 'auspices' were used interchangeably. Augury was as common for the Greeks as for the Romans, but it was the latter who made it a complete system governed by fixed rules and practised by a college of augurs (elected for life) who alone were authorized to 'take the auspices', that is, read the signs. The function of augury was not to reveal the future but to tell whether or not a proposed course of action had the approval of the gods. Signs might be offered unsolicited, but often were deliberately sought; of the latter the best-known example is the observation by the Romans of sacred chickens, carried by armies in the field. Food was given to these birds and if they ate it greedily so as to drop some from their mouths it was a good sign. When, before the sea-battle of Drepanum between Rome and Carthage in 249 BC, they refused to eat, the Roman admiral threw them overboard, saying, 'Then let them drink'; the Romans were, of course, defeated. If wild birds were to be observed, the augur indicated with a wand the part of the sky to be observed (the *templum*, the word also used for an area of ground consecrated for the augur's use), dividing it into left and right, front and back regions. He would stand facing south or east; the significance of a bird's flight or cry varied according to the direction from which it came. The auspices were taken before any important military or public event (and in early times before many private events too), but the officer responsible had the power to reject the advice of the augurs if he so pleased: see above. Another notable occasion was the morning of the battle of Lake Trasimene in 217 BC, during the Second Punic War, when the consul C. Flaminius ignored the auguries with disastrous results. Cicero, although an augur himself, wrote *De divinatione* ('on divination') to disprove the possibility of divination. The emperor Augustus seems to have believed in the auspices. See also DIVINATION and HARUSPICES.

Augusta, see AUGUSTUS, THE.

Augustan age of Latin literature, a term applied to the period following the *Ciceronian age, of which the empire of Augustus was the formative influence. It spans roughly the time from the assassination of Julius Caesar in 44 BC to the death of Ovid in AD 17 (Augustus died in AD 14); its great authors were Virgil, Horace, Tibullus, Propertius, Ovid, and Livy. It started with the turmoil, destructions, and slaughter of the civil war, saw the death of republican government after the battle of Actium in 31 BC, and ended after the restoration of tranquillity and order following nearly a century of revolution. Political activity as it existed under the republic came to an end with the institution of the empire (see AUGUSTUS); Augustus' ambition was to restore something of the spirit of the republic in its heyday, and to imbue the Italian people with the old Roman traditions and virtues. To some extent freedom of political and historical inquiry and expression were limited; hence perhaps the eclipse of oratory and prose literature in general. The support given to Augustus' policy by the poets and historians of the time gives to their literature its unique flavour. This support was deliberately enlisted by the emperor himself and by other patrons in high official positions, men such as *Maecenas and *Messalla. Their writings are serious and mature; their themes, often drawn from the moralizing tradition, come alive because the authors are themselves inspired by love of Italy and the traditional Roman values. Even Ovid and Propertius, who appear often to ignore contemporary politics, show the pleasure they feel in the Italian scene. The poetry in particular is characterized by an increasing technical refinement and, what is less obvious, by a subtle and enriching blend of Greek and Roman themes, which requires from its readers a more intellectual appreciation.

Augu'stine (Aurēlius Augustīnus, AD 354–430), St Augustine of Hippo, born in Roman Africa at Thagastē (Souk Ahras, in Algeria). He was the son of a pagan father and a Catholic mother, Monica, who brought up her son as a Christian and was a dominant influence on his early life. Both parents were determined to give Augustine a good classical education, but though he revelled in the Latin poets he failed to learn Greek, the only Latin-speaking philosopher in antiquity to be virtually ignorant of that language. At 19 he read Cicero's *Hortensius (now lost), an exhortation to the study of philosophy, and was fired with a passionate desire to acquire wisdom. This he sought in the heretical Christian sect of the Manichaeans who expounded a *Gnostic form of Christianity based on a supposed conflict between light and darkness, where Christ was represented as the principle of wisdom and goodness in eternal opposition to a principle of evil. Attracted by their claim to offer reason where the church appealed only to authority, Augustine remained a Manichaean for nine years, during which time he taught rhetoric at Carthage, Thagaste, and Rome, and was finally chosen by *Symmachus to be professor of rhetoric at Milan. His mother arranged for him an advantageous marriage (which never came about) with an heiress, and he had to send back to Africa, with a pang, his concubine with whom he had lived for fifteen years and who had borne him a son. However, under the influence of *Ambrose, whose intellect he respected, and the Neoplatonic writings of *Plotinus and *Porphyry, read in a Latin translation, Augustine was converted to Neoplatonism and Catholicism almost at the same time, and did not discard Platonism for many years. In 387 after a long inward struggle he was baptized and renounced the secular life; in the same year his mother died while they were both on the return journey to Africa. He arrived in Africa in 388 and never left it again. During a visit to the sea port of Hippo in 391 he was seized by the people and ordained priest somewhat against his will, and in 395 he was consecrated coadjutor bishop of Hippo. The rest of his life was spent in his see, where he died on 28 August 430 while the Vandals were besieging the town.

Augustine's Christianity was based on his central preoccupation as a bishop, biblical exegesis. During his episcopate he had to combat the heresies of Manichaeism, Donatism, and Pelagianism; through these struggles his own theology was formulated. His teaching about the Fall of Adam and original sin, from which mankind can be saved only by the grace of God, showed that Augustine believed in predestination, and this side of his teaching exercised a great influence on subsequent Western theologians, especially John Calvin. His early works, written before and immediately after his baptism, were criticisms of ancient philosophies from the Christian standpoint, but after his appointment to the bishopric his writings became more polemical and doctrinal. The *De doctrina Christiana* ('on Christian learning', begun 396–7), on a scheme of Christian education, outlines a literary culture that was to be subordinated to the Bible. *De Trinitate* ('on the Trinity', 399–419) gives a philosophical account of the doctrine of the Trinity. His autobiography, the *Confessions* (*c*.397–400), is a highly selective account of his life to the time of his conversion, in which he analyses the heart's restless search to return to its Maker. The title is to be taken in its biblical sense of 'praising'; it is Augustine's thanksgiving for his conversion. The composition of *De civitate Dei* ('the city of God') in 413–26 arose out of the *Fall of Rome to *Alaric in 410, an event which had dismayed the civilized world. 'A great and arduous work', as Augustine called it, this is a monumental demolition of paganism and defence of Christianity.

Augustine wrote some ninety-three books as well as letters and sermons; his ancient biographer felt that no man could ever read them all. These works moulded the thought of Western theology down to the thirteenth century, when, with the rediscovery of *Aristotle (see 5), Christian philosophers such as Thomas Aquinas built up their systems on an Aristotelian basis, and there was a reaction against Augustinianism.

Augustus (63 BC–AD 14), the first of the Roman emperors. He was born Gaius Octavius, his parents being Atia (daughter of Julius *Caesar's sister Julia) and the wealthy equestrian C. Octavius. After 44 BC he was named C. Julius Caesar Octaviānus (Octavian; see NAMES 2), and after 27 BC was known by his title Augustus. When Caesar was murdered in 44, his will revealed that he had adopted Octavian and named him as his heir. With Mark *Antony and M. *Lepidus he set up a *triumvirate in 43 and together they ruled Rome and the empire, Octavian obtaining Africa, Sicily, and Sardinia as his provinces. When (the dead) Julius Caesar was deified in 42 Octavian became *divi filius*, 'son of god', and hence acquired a divine aura. Differences between the triumvirs were reconciled by the treaty of Brundisium in 40, and Antony married Octavian's sister Octavia, an event which some people think occasioned Virgil's fourth *Eclogue. Octavian married *Livia to whom he remained devoted throughout his life although she did not bear him children. In 36 Octavian compelled Lepidus to retire from the triumvirate and after he defeated Antony and *Cleopatra at Actium in 31 he controlled the whole empire. In 27 Octavian laid down his *de facto* dictatorship and handed back the government of the state to the senate, thereby formally restoring the republic. However, he retained immense power and received the title of Augustus (Gk. *sebastos*, 'reverend') which set him above the entire state. By this title Octavian was thereafter known, and together with the designation *Imperator* ('general', the origin of the English 'emperor'), it subsequently became part of the formal title of the Roman emperors (see following entry). In 23 he resigned the consulship but instead received for life the tribunician authority, which in effect gave him complete control. During subsequent years he organized the provinces and make religious and moral reforms aimed at restoring the old Roman virtues of simplicity, hard work, and faithful and prolific marriages. In this aim he was widely supported by the influential literary figures of the age (see AUGUSTAN AGE). The premature deaths of promising young men in his family thwarted plans for his successor (his first choice was *Marcellus) and he was compelled to accept *Tiberius, son of Livia by a previous marriage. After his death Augustus was deified.

Augustus, the (Gk. *sebastos*, 'reverend'), title held exclusively by all the Roman emperors except Vitellius. When the emperor *Diocletian established a tetrarchy by dividing the empire among four rulers in AD 293, he established two nominally joint emperors who shared the title of Augustus to rule the eastern and western halves of the empire, each with a subordinate ruler, designated a Caesar, who might expect to succeed to the higher rank. By personal authority the senior Augustus could hope to remain in effect sole emperor. Although the system failed as a means of establishing the succession, the titles and their general application survived. The title 'Augusta' was bequeathed by the emperor Augustus to his wife Livia, and after Domitian was held by the wife of the reigning emperor.

Aulis, town of Boeotia in central Greece, celebrated as the place where the Greek fleet assembled for the expedition against Troy and where Agamemnon sacrificed his daughter *Iphigeneia to Artemis to allay the contrary winds.

Aululā'ria ('pot of gold'), Roman comedy by *Plautus, probably adapted from a Greek comedy by *Menander. The prologue is spoken by the *lar familiaris* (see LARES).

Euclio, an old miser, has found a pot full of treasure buried in his house. He hides it and continues to pretend poverty, for fear that the treasure will be taken from him. His daughter Phaedria has been seduced, at a feast of Ceres, by Lyconides, a young man who is now repentant and wishes to marry her. But meanwhile his uncle Megadorus approaches Euclio with a view to marrying her himself. Euclio, thinking that Megadorus has designs on the treasure, takes it away from his house and hides it in one place after another. He is seen by a slave of Lyconides, who removes it. Euclio is in despair at its loss. (The end of the play is lost, but it may be supposed that Lyconides restores the treasure to Euclio, who in gratitude agrees to his marriage to Phaedria).

The play is especially noteworthy for the character of the old miser, on whom Molière's character Harpagon in *L'Avare*

(1669) is closely modelled. It includes the famous incident in which Euclio kills a cock which is scraping the earth near his treasure, because it is evidently bent on theft.

Aulus Ge'llius, see GELLIUS.

Aure'lian (Lucius Domitius Aurelianus) (*c.* AD 215–75), Roman emperor 270–5, a brilliant soldier who was successful against Gothic invasions, and a man of humble origin made emperor by the army. His most famous campaign was against *Zenobia, queen of Palmyra.

Aurē'lius, Marcus (AD 121–80), Roman emperor from 161 to his death. He was born M. Annius Verus, of consular family; his father and grandfather had the same name. He received a careful education from the best tutors, including *Fronto (in Latin) and *Herodes Atticus (in Greek). While still young he won the favour of the emperor Hadrian (who punningly and aptly called him *Verissimus*, 'most true'). When Hadrian adopted *Antoninus Pius as his successor in 138, the latter adopted Marcus. In 145 he married Faustina, Antoninus' daughter (and his own cousin). He became emperor in 161, and shared the throne with Lucius Verus (who had also been adopted by Antoninus) until Lucius' death in 169. His reign was dominated by warfare against invaders on all the important frontiers. His twelve books of 'Meditations' (*ta eis heauton*) were written, in Greek, during the last ten years of his reign while he was on campaign. They were not published until after his death; by whose agency is not known. As a young man he had adopted *Stoicism through the influence of one of his tutors, Apollonius of Chalcedon, and was the last great proponent of that philosophy. Except for the first book, in which he pays his debts of gratitude, the 'Meditations' are arranged in no systematic order but appear just as he wrote them, as a series of entries in personal diaries, and record his thoughts about the meaning of world-order and the relationship of man to it. Hence they have an immediacy and intensity that impart a strongly personal feeling to traditional Stoic moralizing. They show him to be disillusioned and despondent, seeking fortitude against the fear of death, the cares of this world, and the misdeeds and injustices of others. Thus he is more intimately known than any other Roman statesman or emperor since Cicero. Part of the correspondence between him and his tutor Fronto has survived. He was succeeded as emperor by his son Commodus.

Aurō'ra, see EOS.

Ausō'nia, Ausō'nes, poetic names for Italy and Italians, in Latin and Greek; Ausonia was derived from *Ausones*, an ancient, perhaps Greek, name for the inhabitants of middle and south Italy, who have been variously identified.

Ausō'nius, Decimus Magnus (*c.* AD 310–*c.*393), Latin poet, the son of physician of Burdigala (Bordeaux), educated there and at Tolosa (Toulouse). After teaching rhetoric at Burdigala for thirty years he was appointed tutor to Gratian, son of the emperor Valentinian I. With his pupil he accompanied Valentinian's expedition against the Germans in 368–9. When Gratian succeeded his father Ausonius received rapid official advancement, becoming prefect of the Gallic provinces, and later of others, and finally consul in 379. After the murder of Gratian he returned to his family estate at Burdigala, where he appears to have spent most of the remainder of his life. He was nominally at least a Christian, but without any depth of religious feeling: he tried to dissuade his pupil Paulinus (later St Paulinus of Nola) from abandoning the world for a life of religion.

Ausonius wrote a great deal of verse in a variety of metres, showing great technical ability. There are over a hundred epigrams, some of which are in Greek. He seems to have written on any theme that presented itself, such as the names of the days and months, or the properties of the number three. He particularly delighted in verse catalogues: the professors of Burdigala, the famous cities of the world, the Twelve Caesars, the Seven Sages. He delighted also in such feats of skill as the composition of a prayer in forty-two *rhopalic hexameters beginning *spes deus aeternae stationis conciliator* ('God, | our

hope | of haven | safe for ever, | uniter of all'). His more important and interesting poems are the *Ephēmeris* ('a day's events'), a description of a normal day in his life (when and where are not clear), his awakening, talking with his various servants, and so on; and the *Mosella*, a long hexameter poem describing in considerable detail the beauties of the river Moselle and the life that goes on around it. His prose writing includes a long *Grātiarum actio*, or thanksgiving for his consulship, addressed to Gratian.

auspices, see AUGURY.

auster, the south wind (Gk. *notos*). See WINDS.

Auto'lycus, in Greek myth, a son of the god *Hermes and a master of trickery and thieving. He received from his father the gift of making himself and his stolen goods invisible, or of changing the appearance of the latter so as to escape detection, but he was outwitted by *Sisyphus. He was the father of Anticlea, mother of Odysseus.

Auto'medon, in Homer's *Iliad*, the charioteer of Achilles.

Auto'noē, in Greek myth, daughter of Cadmus, mother of *Actaeon.

A'ventine, the most southerly of the seven hills of Rome. It remained outside the *pomerium* or city boundary for religious reasons until AD 49. It was the scene of the story of Hercules and *Cacus, whose cave Evander showed to Aeneas (Virgil, *Aeneid* 8. 184). It was a quarter occupied by the plebeians; a temple of Diana stood on the summit.

Ave'rnus, lake near Cumae and Naples. Close to it was the cave by which Aeneas descended to the Underworld (Virgil, *Aeneid* 6). The name was sometimes used for the Underworld itself. It was supposed to be derived from the Greek *aōrnos*, 'without birds', and the lake was in consequence thought to have no bird life.

Avēs, see BIRDS.

B

Ba'brius, Greek writer of fables who lived probably in the second century AD but about whom nothing is known. The fables exist today in two books, of which the second is incomplete. They are written in verse in the choliambic metre (see METRE, GREEK 5 (iii)) in the ordinary language of the period and are based on the fables of *Aesop with some apparently original additions. They remained very popular in later centuries and were frequently paraphrased in Greek prose and verse.

Bacchae ('women of Bacchus', i.e. female celebrants of the rites of Bacchus or Dionysus), Greek tragedy by *Euripides probably written during the poet's stay in Macedonia and found after his death in 406 BC. It was subsequently produced at Athens (probably in 405) by the poet's son (or nephew) also named Euripides, together with *Iphigeneia at Aulis* and *Alcmaeon in Corinth* (the latter now lost).

*Dionysus, divine son of Zeus and the Theban Semelē, travelling through the world to make himself known to men as a god, comes to Thebes, where his divinity has been denied even by Semele's sister Agavē, mother of Pentheus, king of Thebes. Dionysus has driven the women of Thebes mad and compelled them to celebrate his rites on Mount Cithaeron. Pentheus is implacably hostile to the new religion in spite of the remonstrances of his grandfather Cadmus and of the seer Teiresias, and imprisons Dionysus (who claims to be not the god himself but a votary). Dionysus proves his power over material things by causing Pentheus to bind a bull in his stead and by making an earthquake destroy the palace. A messenger arrives and describes the behaviour of the Theban women on the mountains. Dionysus induces Pentheus to disguise himself as a woman in order to see for himself, and then engineers Pentheus' discovery by the women, who tear him to pieces. Agave, in her frenzy, bears his head triumphantly to Thebes. It is only when she recovers that she finds she has killed her son. The family of Cadmus is doomed to banishment from Thebes and the play ends with their departure.

The *Bacchae* is about a supposed historical event, the introduction into Greece of a new religion which by Euripides' time had long been accepted as part of Greek life. Worship of Dionysus offered a different religious experience from that expressed in the cult of the traditional Olympian gods, and this play shows the power of Dionysus, a power beyond good and evil, and the fate of those who resist him.

Bacchanā'lia, Latin name for the fundamentally Greek religious rites (*orgia*) of the god *Dionysus, derived from his alternative name of Bacchus. They are chiefly known from the description by Livy in his history of Rome of the wild excesses and criminal acts committed by the devotees under the cloak of religion, after the rites had been introduced to Rome from Etruria and south Italy. As a consequence the senate in a celebrated decree of 186 BC banned the Bacchanalia from Rome and Italy. See also MYSTERIES.

Bacchants (Bacchantēs, Bacchanals, Maenads), women inspired to ecstasy by the Greek god *Dionysus (sometimes called Bacchus), as described by Euripides in the *Bacchae*. They are depicted wearing the skins of fawns or panthers and wreaths of ivy, oak, or fir and carrying a thyrsus (a wand wreathed in ivy and vine leaves, topped with a pine cone). Freed from the conventions of normal behaviour they roamed the mountains with music and dancing and inspired by the god performed supernatural feats of strength, uprooting trees, catching and tearing apart wild animals, and sometimes eating the flesh raw.

bacchī'ac, in Greek metre the sequence ⏑ – –. (See METRE, GREEK 1 (ix).)

Bacchī'adae, royal clan in *Corinth who claimed descent ultimately from Heracles (see HERACLEIDAE) but more immediately from Bacchis, king of Corinth perhaps *c*.900 BC. The monarchy was overthrown in 747 (the traditional date) and thereafter the city was governed by a Bacchiad oligarchy until 657 BC when they too were destroyed by *Cypselus who made himself tyrant. The Bacchiadae supposedly laid the foundation for Corinth's greatness in colonization, maritime affairs, trade, and in particular pottery.

Ba'cchidēs ('girls called Bacchis'), Roman comedy by *Plautus, adapted from the Greek comedy of *Menander *Dis exapatōn* ('the double deceiver').

The opening of the play is missing, but the situation is clear. A young man Pistoclerus is searching in Athens on behalf of an absent friend Mnesilochus for a courtesan Bacchis of Samos. He finds that she has visited her sister, also called Bacchis, and succumbs himself to the sister's charms. When Mnesilochus arrives he is horrified to learn that his friend is making love to 'Bacchis'. The confusion about the supposed disloyalty is soon cleared up, but by then the young men's fathers have been informed. Finally, the sisters beguile the fathers into forgiveness and all ends happily.

Bacchus, alternative name (probably Lydian in origin) for the Greek god *Dionysus, and his usual name in Latin.

Bacchy'lides, Greek lyric poet and nephew of the poet *Simonides, born at the end of the sixth century BC in the island of Ceos, and dying probably in the middle of the fifth century. His poetry survived only in quotations until, at the end of the nineteenth century, the British Museum acquired the remains of two papyrus rolls containing fifteen epinician odes (see EPINIKION) and six *dithyrambs. A few small fragments have turned up since. Bacchylides seems to have been employed by the same patrons who employed his uncle Simonides and also *Pindar, whose great rival ancient scholars believed him to be. Pindar and Bacchylides both composed odes for at least two victories won in the great Games by Hieron tyrant of Syracuse: thus Bacchylides' Ode 5 and Pindar's *O*. 1 both commemorate the horse-race at the Olympian games of 476 BC, and Ode 4 and *P*. 1 the chariot-race at Delphi in 470. The epinician odes of Bacchylides contain the same elements as Pindar's odes contain—central mythical narrative, passages praising the victor, his country, and the gods, passages of moralizing—but he lacks Pindar's profundity and brilliant imaginative gifts. His strength lies in his moving and dramatic narratives, as is also apparent in the dithyrambs. Ode 18, a dithyramb, is unique in surviving choral lyric in being wholly a dialogue, between the leader of the chorus representing Aegeus, king of Athens, and, presumably, the remainder of the chorus who represent his followers. Aegeus has heard the news of the imminent arrival of a young hero and in reply to questions elaborates on the deeds of the young man whom he does not yet know to be his son Theseus. Perhaps the form of the poem was influenced by contemporary drama, but it is tempting to see in this dithyramb's unparalleled dramatic style a survival of an older form of dithyramb which Aristotle believed to be the precursor of *tragedy (see 1). Bacchylides also wrote *hymns, *paeans, maiden-songs (see PARTHENEION), *hyporchemata, and *encomia, very little of which survives.

Baiae, small place near Cumae on the Bay of Naples, perhaps originally its port, first famous for its warm springs containing a variety of minerals and then, from before the time of Cicero, a fashionable Roman resort. Lucullus, Pompey, and Caesar all had villas here, as did the later Roman emperors, and it soon became notorious for its dissipations.

Balbus, common *cognomen* (see NAMES 2) in several Roman *gentes*. It originally denoted one who had an impediment in his speech.

Lucius Cornelius Balbus, a native of Gades (Cadiz), who had Roman citizenship conferred upon him in 72 BC through Pompey's influence, for his services to Rome in the war against Sertorius in Spain, and took a Roman name. He moved to Rome where, with Pompey's favour, he soon became a man of considerable importance. Prudently he cultivated Caesar's favour also, and partly brought about the coalition between Caesar, Pompey, and Crassus in 60 BC. His influence made him many enemies who engineered his prosecution in 56 for illegally assuming Roman citizenship, but he was successfully defended by Cicero in an extant speech. In the civil war he was outwardly neutral while privately favouring Caesar, and subsequently Octavian. In 40 he became Rome's first foreign-born consul. His published diary has not come down to us, but a few of his letters to Cicero survive. (His namesake and nephew is also mentioned in Cicero's correspondence.)

Bandu'sia, Italian fountain made famous by Horace in *Odes* III. 13; it was probably located near Horace's Sabine farm, although there is also evidence suggesting that it was a spring near his birthplace Venusia.

barbarian, onomatopoeic word originally used adjectivally by Homer to describe the speech of the Carians of southwest Asia Minor, though he nowhere speaks of barbarians. The name came later to be applied to all non-Greek-speaking peoples, and was subsequently applied to the Persians in particular when their rise to power threatened Greek freedom in the early fifth century BC. The word thus came to have a cultural rather than a merely linguistic significance, and described people outside the orbit of the Greek city-states, whether or not they spoke Greek; barbarians were therefore thought to be uncivilized, cowardly, cruel, treacherous, and lacking in self-control. However, intellectuals from Democritus and Euripides onwards occasionally emphasized instead the natural unity of all mankind, and *Eratosthenes (2) in his *Geographica*, makes a plea that people should be divided not into Greeks and barbarians but into good and bad: 'for many Greeks are bad, and many barbarians civilized, notably the Indians and Arians, and again the Romans and Carthaginians, who enjoy such admirable forms of government.'

Alexander the Great may have tried to give these ideas some political reality by founding cities where Greeks and bar-

barians could coexist on a basis of complete equality, but the old division prevailed. The Romans adopted the word 'barbarian' and its general significance, but expanded its reference to include anyone not Greek or Roman. The Roman comic poet, Plautus, whose plays were adaptations from the Greek, uses the word from the Greek point of view for comic effect to describe a Roman or Italian.

Ba'ssarids (Bassarides), in Greek, Thracian *Bacchants; also the title of a lost play by Aeschylus. The name appears to mean 'those who wear fox-skins'.

baths. In Greece, bathing was not the social institution it became in Roman times. Public baths existed, but frequent use of warm water was sometimes regarded as excessively luxurious, especially by the Spartans, except to relax the muscles after exercise. A kind of soap was used as well as the strigil (a curved instrument made of metal or bone) to remove oil and dirt from the skin. After bathing both men and women anointed themselves with oil.

The Roman baths are one of the most characteristic of their institutions, found universally in the Roman world and enjoyed by all classes of society. During their earlier history the Romans bathed only for the sake of cleanliness. The earliest known public baths are found at Pompeii and date from the early first century BC. The process of bathing changed radically with the invention of the system for carrying hot air from a furnace through passages under floors (hypocausts), and through ducts embedded in room walls. With this providing warm water and hot air, by the middle of the first century BC the use of public and private baths had become general, and though public baths were intended at first for the poor they were soon made use of by all classes. Baths were communal, each being roughly the size of a small, shallow swimming-pool. The price of a bath was a *quadrans*, the smallest piece of coined money, virtually worthless. The essential rooms for public baths were the changing-room (*apodyterium*), the cold-bath room (*frigidarium*), and a warm-bath room (*caldarium*). Larger establishments might include a warm room (*tepidarium*), a hot vapour bath (*laconicum*), a sweating-room (*sudatorium*), suites of recreational rooms, exercise grounds (it was usual to take exercise before bathing), and gardens. These buildings were the natural medium for the development of concrete vaulted architecture, and the surviving baths strongly influenced the style of Renaissance architecture. Though mixed bathing was not unknown, women more usually had separate (and inferior) baths adjoining those of the men.

Bathy'llus, see PANTOMIME.

Batrachomyoma'chia ('battle of the frogs and mice'), a short Greek mock-epic poem in the style of Homeric epic, sometimes attributed to Homer in antiquity and difficult to date but perhaps of the fifth century BC. The story derives from a fable of Aesop, a mouse Psīcharpax ('crumb-stealer') is invited by a frog Physignathos ('puff-cheek') son of Peleus to ride on his back to visit his watery kingdom. Unfortunately, at the sight of a water-snake the frog dives and the mouse is drowned. But the incident has been seen by another mouse, and a one-day Homeric war ensues between the mice and the frogs, in which the mice seem to be winning. At the request of Athena, Zeus intervenes, and having failed with thunderbolts sends crabs to quell the strife.

Battus, the leader of a body of Dorian Greeks who left the island of Thera in about 630 BC at the bidding of the Delphic Oracle, to colonize *Cyrene in Libya (North Africa). Battus, like other founders, achieved semi-mythical status. He was said to be a descendant of the ancient race of heroes known as the *Minyae and of the *Argonaut Euphemus. His strange name has been variously interpreted, as the Libyan word for king or as meaning 'stammerer' from his supposed speech impediment. His descendants ruled Cyrene for more than two hundred years. The father of the poet Callimachus was a Cyrenaean of royal descent called Battus; hence the poet is often called 'Battiades' ('son of Battus').

Baucis, see PHILEMON.

Bē'driacum, midway between Cremona and Verona in Cisalpine Gaul, the site of two decisive battles in AD 69 when the forces of the Roman emperor Otho were defeated by the supporters of Vitellius, who succeeded to the empire, and whose own forces were defeated some months later by Vespasian's.

Belgae, population group occupying part of Gaul in Roman times. Their area was bounded in the south by the rivers Seine and Marne, in the west by the sea, and in the east and north by the Rhine. They claimed to be of German descent. Some tribes passed into Britain from about 100 BC onwards and settled in the south and south-west. The Belgae of Gaul were subdued by Julius Caesar in 57 BC but continued to give trouble for the subsequent thirty years.

Belisā'rius, outstanding general of the Roman emperor Justinian (reigned AD 527–65). His greatest victories were the recovery of Africa from the Vandals in 533, and in 540 of Italy from the Ostrogoths, whose king and nobles (as well as much treasure) he took back with him when he was recalled through court intrigues to Constantinople, the capital of the Roman empire at that time. He returned to Italy in 546 but was again recalled; the Ostrogoths were not finally crushed until 553, and then by another general, Narses. Belisarius' last victory was against the Bulgarians in 559. In 563 he was accused of a conspiracy against Justinian, and died in 565. There was a tradition that his eyes were put out and that he ended his life as a beggar in the streets of Constantinople. His extraordinary career, his unusual loyalty to the person of the emperor, and his devotion to his influential wife Antonina, a former actress, are all graphically recorded in exhaustive detail by the historian *Procopius.

Belle'rophon (or Bellerophontēs), in Greek myth, son of Glaucus (the son of Sisyphus) and Eurymedē; in some accounts his father was said to be the god Poseidon. His grandson was the Glaucus in the *Iliad*. He was an ancient Corinthian hero, and his adventures sound similar to those of Heracles and Theseus. He spent some time at the palace of Proetus, king of Argos, whose wife Anteia (sometimes called Stheneboea) fell in love with him. When he rejected her Anteia accused him to her husband of trying to seduce her. Proetus, unwilling to violate the laws of hospitality by killing Bellerophon in his house, sent him to Iobates, Proetus' father-in-law and king of Lycia, with a sealed letter requesting the king to execute Bellerophon. The king accordingly set him a number of tasks likely to prove fatal, killing the *Chimaera, defeating the Solymi and the *Amazons, but Bellerophon with the aid of the winged horse *Pegasus was always victorious. He became reconciled to the king and married his daughter. Afterwards he incurred the wrath of the gods by trying to ride Pegasus to heaven, but the horse threw him. He ended his life a lonely outcast.

Bellō'na (in the old form of the name, Duellona), the Roman goddess of war, sometimes thought of as the wife or sister of Mars. She had no *flamen and no festival, and virtually no mythology. Her first known temple was that vowed by Appius Claudius Caecus while fighting the Etruscans in 296 BC and built in the Campus Martius near the Circus Flaminius. Since the temple lay outside the *pomerium* or city boundary of Rome, it was used by the senate to give audience to foreign ambassadors and returning generals (see TRIUMPH) whom it was not considered prudent to admit into the city. Here also stood the pillar symbolizing the enemy's frontier over which the *fetialis* threw a spear when a declaration of war was made. The Greek equivalent of Bellona was recognized to be *Enyo.

Bellum Africum ('the African war'), short record of Julius *Caesar's four months' war in Africa (47–46 BC) against the supporters of Pompey. The author is not known for sure, though some have thought it was *Hirtius; the contents suggest that he was a soldier who took part in the campaign but was not in Caesar's confidence.

Bellum Alexandrī'num ('the Alexandrian war'), a continuation of Julius

*Caesar's history of the civil war (see COMMENTARIES 2), probably written by *Hirtius. It describes the war of 48–47 BC in Egypt, where Caesar, following his pursuit of Pompey, remained to settle the Egyptian succession by restoring *Cleopatra as ruler. It ends with Caesar's victory at Zela in August 47 (see CAESAR 3).

Bellum cīvī'le ('the civil war'). 1. History in three books by Julius *Caesar of the first two years of the civil war between him and Pompey begun in 49 BC; see COMMENTARIES 2.
2. Title of an epic poem by the Latin poet *Lucan on the civil war between Julius Caesar and Pompey, often miscalled *Pharsalia*.

Bellum Gallicum, see COMMENTARIES 1.

Bellum Hispanie'nse ('the Spanish war'), account of Julius *Caesar's final campaign of the civil war fought in Spain in 45 BC against Pompey's sons and Labienus, ending in Caesar's victory at Munda. The author is unknown but was probably a soldier in Caesar's army. The text, written in uneducated Latin, has not been accurately preserved.

Bellum Jugurthī'num, see SALLUST.

Bellum Pū'nicum, see NAEVIUS.

Belus, in Greek myth, king of Egypt, son of Poseidon and of Libya or Eurynomē, twin-brother of *Agenor, father of Aegyptus and *Danaus. Through his sons he became the ancestor of several royal houses in Greece and Africa. Belus was also the name of Dido's father.

Bendis, in Greek myth, a goddess originally worshipped in Thrace and identified with Artemis. Her cult was accepted officially at *Piraeus in 430–429 BC for the benefit of resident Thracians. Her festival, which included a torch-race on horseback, is the occasion of Plato's dialogue the *Republic*.

Beneve'ntum (Benevento), one of the most important cities of Samnium in southern Italy, made a Roman colony with Latin rights in 268 BC. It was of strategic importance to the Romans in the Second *Punic War because of its proximity to Campania. A new colony was established there by Augustus.

Berenī'cē. 1. Born *c.*340 BC, half-sister and third wife of *Ptolemy I Soter, king of Egypt (hence known as Berenice I). Their children were Ptolemy II Philadelphus and Arsinoē II, who married her brother as his second wife (his first wife being Arsinoe I).

2. Daughter of Ptolemy II and Arsinoe I and sister of Ptolemy III, born *c.*280 BC and married to Antiochus II, king of Syria. After his death she and her son were murdered by Antiochus' first wife.

3. Daughter of the king of Cyrene, born *c.*273 BC and married to Ptolemy III Euergetes in 247. In 246 Ptolemy set out for Syria to support, too late, the claims of his sister's son to the throne of Syria (see (2) above). On his departure, his wife Berenice dedicated to the gods a lock of her hair as an offering for his safe return. This lock mysteriously disappeared. Conon, the court astronomer, claimed flatteringly to have discovered it in a hitherto unnamed constellation, seven faint stars near the tail of Leo, thereafter known as *Coma Berenices* (*Berenīkēs plokamos*), 'the lock of Berenice'. This event was celebrated in an ingenious and entertaining poem by *Callimachus, in which the lock of hair addresses the reader. *Catullus' poem 66 is virtually a translation of it into Latin, and Alexander Pope based upon it his *Rape of the Lock* (1712).

4. Born AD 28, daughter of *Herod of Acts 12 (who is usually known as Agrippa I) and great-granddaughter of *Herod the Great, king of Judaea. After the death of her second husband she lived with her brother Agrippa II, and to allay suspicion of incest married the king of Cilicia (AD 54). She soon left him, however, and returned to her brother, with whom she was living when the apostle Paul spoke his defence before them both (Acts 25, where she is called Bernice). She and her brother tried in vain to dissuade the Jews from rebelling against Rome in AD 66, and when war broke out they both sided with the Romans. When Titus, the son of the Roman emperor Vespasian, was fighting in Judaea in 67–70, he fell in love with her, and after she visited Rome with Agrippa in *c.*75 they lived openly together for three or four years. This liaison was unpopular and Titus was compelled to send her away when he succeeded to the throne in 79. *Juvenal mentions her contemptuously in his Satire 6. She is the Berenice who was the heroine of tragedies by Corneille (1606–84) and Racine (1639–99).

Bērō'ssus, priest at Babylon in the third century BC who wrote a history of Babylon in three books in Greek, of which only quotations survive. Also ascribed to him were works on astronomy and *astrology, which are known only from references in later writers.

Bī'as, brother of the Greek seer *Melampus.

Bibra'cte (Mont-Beuvray), in central Gaul, the chief town and hill-fort of the Aedui.

Bi'bulus, Marcus Calpu'rnius, Julius *Caesar's colleague in the aedileship and praetorship and finally in the consulship of 59 BC. After being ineffectual in trying to block Caesar's agrarian laws he shut himself up in his house for the rest of the year, ostensibly to watch for omens and so make Caesar's legislation technically invalid. This gave rise to the joke that it was the consulship not of Caesar and Bibulus but of 'Julius and Caesar'. Upon his proposal Pompey was elected sole consul in 52 BC. He was proconsul of Spain in 51 and commander of Pompey's fleet against Caesar in 49. He died in 48. His wife was Porcia, daughter of Marcus Porcius Cato of Utica, who subsequently married Marcus Brutus, one of Caesar's murderers.

biography

1. *Greek.* Greek biography proper was a late development, though rudimentary forms of it can be seen in the dirge and the funeral oration and in the character sketches of the historians, e.g. of Pausanias and Themistocles in Thucydides. In the fourth century BC appear the *Cyropaedia*, *Memorabilia*, and *Agesilaus* (see under separate titles) of Xenophon, as well as the *Evagoras* of

*Isocrates, which all approach true biography. It was Aristotle's pupils in the fourth and third centuries BC who developed an interest in biography and gave a more systematic form to its composition. The tradition persisted among the Alexandrian scholars who valued biographical information about classical authors as a means of explaining their writings, and among those historians who aimed to entertain their readers by giving prominence to outstanding personalities. (Polybius, the only Hellenistic historian we still possess, is not representative of this school.) None of this work survives except in fragments. Over two hundred years later *Plutarch (second century AD) owed the form of his *Lives* largely to his Hellenistic predecessors, but he clearly distinguished between biography and history, and the scope of his work was original. His biographies were markedly moral in tone, since his aim was to exemplify the virtue displayed by the careers of great men; hence his concentration upon the characters of his heroes. In the early third century AD *Diogenes Laertius wrote a compendium of the lives and doctrines of the Greek philosophers, but it is merely a synthesis of earlier compositions.

2. *Roman*. Roman biography developed from a native tradition of funeral orations and sepulchral inscriptions which listed the achievements of the dead man in considerable detail. Many generals and politicians wrote accounts of their careers in order to justify their actions; Sulla, for example, wrote his memoirs in twenty-two books. Under the empire memoirs were written by the emperor or members of his family, by Augustus and Tiberius, for example. All these works are lost. The most important surviving biographies are those of famous men by Cornelius *Nepos (first century BC), of Agricola by his son-in-law *Tacitus (end of the first century AD), of the Twelve Caesars by *Suetonius (Tacitus' younger contemporary), and of the later emperors by the writers of the *Historia Augusta.

The only autobiography that reveals the writer's own inner life and thoughts is the *Confessions* of St *Augustine (written *c.* AD 397–400), though the *Meditations* of Marcus *Aurelius (AD 121–80) may be compared with it.

Bion. 1. **Bion the Borysthenite** (*c.*325–*c.*246 BC), Greek popular philosopher, born in the Greek colony of Olbia in Scythia, near the estuary of the river Borysthenes (Dnieper). His family was enslaved to a rhetorician but Bion received a good education and was eventually freed. He studied in the various philosophical schools in Athens but became an adherent of no one school. He seemed closest to the *Cynics whose caustic wit and anti-establishment attitudes he shared. Most of his life he spent wandering from city to city, lecturing and teaching for money. He popularized the Greek *diatribē* ('spoken address') as a written sermon, so that it could reach a wider audience; and the connotation of abusiveness which the word has acquired in modern times derives from Bion's humorous but sharp attacks on human faults and weaknesses. His influence on the Latin satires of Lucilius and Horace was notable. Fairly extensive fragments of his writing survive.

2. Of Smyrna, the last Greek pastoral poet known to us by name; he lived at the end of the second century BC, and is generally linked with the pastoral poet *Moschus. Virtually nothing is known of his life; according to the anonymous *Lament for Bion* (attributed to Moschus), he lived in Sicily and died by poisoning. He wrote in hexameters in the (literary) Doric *dialect, and seventeen fragments of his poems (some may even be complete) survive. Since the Renaissance he has been credited with the *Lament for Adonis*, perhaps intended for recitation at a festival. The pastoral element in his work is slight, most of the poems being playfully erotic.

Birds (*Ornithes*, Lat. *Aves*), Greek comedy by *Aristophanes which won second prize at the City Dionysia in 414 BC. In 415 the Athenian fleet had set out on the *Sicilian Expedition and its success was still in the balance. The *Birds* is an escapist fantasy in which two Athenians, Peisetairos ('the persuader') and Euelpides ('the optimist'), dissatisfied with life in Athens and its endless law-suits, go to look for the mythical Tereus (see PHILOMELA) who has been turned into a bird and might know of a more suitable place to live. Tereus suggests various countries, but there are objections to them all. Peisetairos now has a brilliant idea: let the birds all unite and build a great walled city in the air, and they will defy both men and gods; they will intercept the smoke from the sacrifices on which the gods are nourished. The chorus of birds, at first hostile, is won over, and the birds quickly set about building the city, to be called Nephelokokkygia ('cloudcuckooland', from *nephelē*, 'cloud', and *kokkyx*, 'cuckoo'), under the direction of Peisetairos and Euelpides, who grow wings to suit their new condition. Then various unwelcome visitors arrive: a priest, a needy poet with a hymn in honour of the new city, an oracle-monger, *Meton the famous astronomer (to lay out the streets), a superintendent, and a statute-seller. They are all appropriately dealt with. The new city is now finished, when a guard comes in with the news that a god has escaped the birds' blockade. The god, who turns out to be Iris, sent to enquire why sacrifices have stopped on earth, is seized and told that birds are now the gods, and finally goes off in tears to complain to her father. Meanwhile people have become bird-mad and want wings. Further visitors arrive: a father-beater, because young cocks fight their fathers (he is reminded that young storks must feed their fathers); Cinesias the lyric poet, because he wants to soar on airy pinions; an informer, who would find wings useful for serving writs; and the god Prometheus, who hides from Zeus under a parasol while he tells of the food shortage among the gods and advises Peisetairos to make hard terms with them and insist on having Basileia ('sovereignty'), daughter of Zeus, to wife. Then come ambassadors from the gods, Poseidon, Heracles, and a god from the barbarous Triballians (democracy being in full swing among the Olympian gods also). Thanks to the greediness of Heracles, gods and birds are reconciled, Peisetairos gets the sceptre of Zeus as well as Basileia; he is hailed as the highest of the gods, and preparations are made for his wedding.

Bitŏn, see CLEOBIS.

Boadicē'a, the usual, but textually incorrect, English form of *Boudicca.

Bocchus, see JUGURTHA.

Boeŏ'tia, country of central Greece, bordering Attica on the north-west. Its two main cities were Orchomenus and Thebes, and it possessed the two famous mountains of *Cithaeron and *Helicon. In classical times much of the northern plain where Orchomenus stood was covered by the shallow Lake Copāis (now drained). The land was occupied from Neolithic times onward and was clearly important in the Bronze Age. Mycenaean remains at Orchomenus and myths about the wealth of the Minyae who migrated there from Thessaly suggest that this city was older than Thebes, but the rise of the latter and the flooding of Lake Copais contributed to its decline.

Most Boeotian myth centres on the city of Thebes (see CADMUS, HERACLES, OEDIPUS), whose power at any one time determined the importance of Boeotia's role in the history of the period. Thebes was never strong enough, however, to enforce its authority over all the cities of Boeotia and combine them into one state. The fourth century saw the extension of Theban supremacy over the rest of Boeotia, particularly Sparta at Leuctra in 371 and again at Mantinea in 362. Like the rest of Greece, however, Boeotia could not resist the rise of Macedon under Philip II, and after the defeat of Theban and Athenian forces at Chaeronea in 338 and the destruction of Thebes in 335 by Philip's son (Alexander the Great) Boeotia rapidly declined. In Roman times nothing remained of most Boeotian cities except their ruins and their names.

To the Athenians particularly the Boeotians seemed dull and thick-witted, a condition which Cicero and Horace ascribed to the dampness of the atmosphere. It seems true that Boeotia was backward artistically, but its contribution to music and literature was considerable: Hesiod, Corinna, Pindar, and Plutarch were all Boeotians. The *dialect in the

Lesbos and Thessaly, but had some features in common with west Greek and a vowel-system peculiar to itself.

Bŏē'thius (Anicius Manlius Sevērīnus Boethius) (*c.* AD 476–524), Latin philosopher and (Christian) theological writer, belonging to a family which had held many high offices of state in the fourth and fifth centuries. Boethius was himself consul in 510 and *magister officiorum* (head of the civil service) to Theodoric, the Ostrogothic 'King' of Italy (see GOTHS). However, in 523 Boethius was suspected of treachery, was imprisoned, and put to death in 524. He was buried at Pavia and was regarded as a Catholic martyr (because Theodoric was an Arian, i.e. a heretic) and canonized as 'St Severinus'. His importance derives from his being the last Latin-speaking scholar of the ancient world to have a genuine mastery of Greek. After him no one in the West had firsthand acquaintance with Greek philosophy until the rediscovery of Aristotle in the twelfth century (see TEXTS, TRANSMISSION OF ANCIENT 7).

In his early life Boethius' declared aim was to translate and write commentaries upon all the writings of Aristotle and Plato in order to construct a harmony out of the two philosophies. This huge task was never completed, but his translations of and commentaries on Aristotle's logical works and *Porphyry's Introduction (Isagogē) to Aristotle as well as some logical works of his own played a highly influential role in medieval education and ensured that knowledge of Aristotle was never totally extinguished in the western world. His handbooks of arithmetic, music, geometry, and astronomy (the *quadrivium*) were also much used in the medieval schools (the two former books survive). There also survive several Christian treatises, on the doctrine of the Trinity and on the Incarnation. His literary fame depends on the enormously influential book he wrote in prison, the *Consolation of Philosophy*, a dialogue between himself and a personified Lady Philosophy. It consists of five books in prose interspersed with thirty-nine short poems in thirteen different (and metrically accurate) metres in the style of Menippean satire (see MENIPPUS). Philo-sophy, who ousts the Muses, comes to console the prisoner; she reminds him of the sufferings of other thinkers such as Socrates, and invites him to lay bare his troubles. Boethius describes the ingratitude with which his integrity has been met, and laments the triumph of injustice. Philosophy reminds him of the mutability of fortune and the vanity of those things which the world esteems good. The only real good is God. Boethius asks how, under a beneficent God, evil can exist or pass unpunished (book 4), and is answered by a justification of divine government followed by a discussion on free will. It is a moving work, written from the heart, and it provided comfort to innumerable readers of the Middle Ages, as is shown by the hundreds of manuscripts of it which exist today, and the fact that it was translated into more European languages than any other book except the Bible. Its translators include Alfred the Great, Chaucer, and Queen Elizabeth I. Its tone, though theistic, is largely pagan and classical and it ignores the specifically Christian consolations, owing more perhaps to Stoicism and Platonism. Compare CASSIODORUS.

Bona De'a, Roman fertility goddess worshipped exclusively by women, sometimes identified with Fauna. Rites in her honour were celebrated annually at the house of the chief magistrate, under the leadership of his wife assisted by the *Vestal Virgins, and these were attended only by women. It was these rites that *Clodius violated in 62 BC by entering in female disguise.

books and writing

1. Writing had developed in the Near East and Egypt long before the skill reached Greece. In late Bronze Age Greece a script known as *Linear B was used on clay tablets but as far as we can tell only for making official inventories and not for literary purposes, and it did not survive the collapse of this civilization in about 1150 BC. Homer makes an obscure reference to writing (*Iliad* 6. 166ff.) but seems to have thought of the Homeric world as illiterate and bookless. The classical Greeks believed, certainly correctly, that their system of writing

derived from Phoenicia (see CADMUS). Archaeological and literary evidence suggests that writing became widespread in Greece between 750 and 650 BC. See also ALPHABET.

2. Throughout the ancient world the commonest writing material was papyrus. The oldest papyrus roll known to us is Egyptian and is dated to about 3000 BC. We have no firm evidence on when papyrus came into general use in Greece, but it is hard to think that it could be later than the time of the poet Archilochus (c.680–640 BC) when it seems that poetry in general came to be written down. The chief rival to papyrus as writing material was animal skins; Herodotus says that the Ionians used the skins of sheep and goats when papyrus was unavailable. Papyrus was perhaps originally imported into Greece from the Phoenician town of Byblos from which the Greeks took their name for papyrus and thence for book (*biblos*—hence 'bible'). It was made from the pith of a water plant which in antiquity grew mainly in the Nile. Sheets, with a maximum width of about 40 cm. (16 in.) and a normal height of about 23 cm. (9 in.), were pasted together side by side so as to form a continuous roll, the joins being virtually invisible in rolls of good quality. The pasted sheets were called in Greek *kollēmata*. In later times the Greek term for the 'first sheet' of a legal document on which was written the authentication for what followed was *prōtokollon*, hence English 'protocol'. The Library at Alexandria (see ALEXANDRIAN LIBRARY) was probably responsible for introducing standardization in book production. Papyrus was bought in rolls, not sheets, usually about 10 m. (33 ft.) long. With writing of average size such a roll could contain a book of Thucydides, or two of the shorter books of Homer. The work was written in vertical columns of 5–10 cm. (2–4 in.) wide throughout the length of the roll, with a margin between the columns and a broader margin at top and bottom. Scribes seem not to have been concerned to keep a regular number of lines to a column or of letters to a line. The minimum of help is given to the reader. A short stroke under the line (*paragraphos*) often indicated where there was a pause in the sense or a change

of speaker in dramatic texts (but the name of the speaker was hardly ever given). *Accents appear, if at all, only in poetic texts; *punctuation where it exists takes the form of a single point level with the top of the letter; enlarged initial letters are not used. Scribes wrote in black ink made from a dense carbon black. (The Athenian orator Demosthenes mocks Aeschines for having to get up early to 'grind the ink' for his father's school.) A hard reed pen was used for writing. Titles were written at the end of a roll (the part least liable to damage); a roll was usually identified by a label (Gk. *sillybos*, Lat. *titulus*) which hung from it as it lay on a shelf or in a pigeon-hole or box. A roller (Gk. *omphalos*, Lat. *umbilīcus*) might be attached to the end of the papyrus, ornamented with projecting knobs. The rolls comprising a long work or the complete works of an author might be kept together in a cupboard (Lat. *armārium*) or bucket (Lat. *capsa*). A reader would undo the roll with his right hand, and roll it up, as he proceeded, with his left.

The alternative material to papyrus was vellum (Lat. *vellus*, 'skin', 'hide') made from the skins of cattle, sheep, and goats. This material was later known as parchment, a name derived from the city of *Pergamum which was famous for its manufacture. (In modern usage, parchment is made from the skin of sheep and goats, vellum from that of calves, lambs, and kids.)

3. Books to the classical Greeks were essentially a substitute for recitation. It is not till the fifth century BC at Athens that we find the beginnings of a book trade, fostered by the large number of prose books written by the *sophists for educational purposes. Plato has Socrates say that a book by the philosopher Anaxagoras could be bought in the *orchestra* (in the agora at Athens) for a drachma or less. In the fourth century BC books became relatively common and the practice of reading seems to have become firmly established; *Isocrates certainly wrote for private reading (though in antiquity reading always meant reading aloud). Aristotle and his school formed a large collection of books. In the third and subsequent centuries the output of books

greatly increased when educated slaves were employed as copyists and the production of papyrus and later of parchment was organized by the Hellenistic kings. (The story was told that in the second century BC a king of Egypt, jealous of the library at Pergamum, placed an embargo on the supply of papyrus to that city, where parchment was promptly invented.)

4. The Latin word for book, *liber*, 'bark', originated at an early time when books in Rome were written on bark, but the introduction of Greek literature into Rome in the third and second centuries BC propagated the papyrus roll. Very few papyrus fragments of Latin books have survived compared with Greek because the climatic conditions which allow survival are found in Egypt, a Greek-speaking area. On the other hand, Latin literature is much richer than Greek in information about books and the book trade. From the first century BC we hear of booksellers with their staffs of copyists. Cicero had his writings published by *Atticus, and Horace mentions the Sosii as booksellers. The demand for books increased and it became the fashion for rich Romans to have a library. The price of books seems to have been moderate. There was no law of copyright and authors did not profit directly from the sale of their books.

5. A papyrus roll (Lat. *volumen*, English 'volume') was not very convenient to use. It had to be manipulated by both hands and rewound after use. Athenian vase-paintings show readers getting into difficulties with twisted rolls, and they were easily torn. From Homer onwards sets of wooden tablets hinged on a ring or leather thong had been used for notes or letters. The tablets were either whitened and written on in ink or, more usually, coated with wax and the writing scratched on with a stylus (the wax could be smoothed again with the blunt end); thus the Latin verb 'to write', *exarare*, meant originally 'to plough up', because the stylus furrows the wax like a ploughshare. From these tablets there slowly developed from the first century AD the book in modern form, known as a codex, made from folded sheets of papyrus or parchment, put together quire by quire

(eight leaves, sixteen pages), stitched at the spine and bound with wooden boards. The codex had several advantages over the papyrus roll: it was very easy to consult, since the pages could be turned forwards or backwards at will; both sides of the pages could be written on; it could hold four or five times as much text as a roll; and it was longer-lasting. By the fourth century it had superseded the papyrus roll, and parchment was preferred to papyrus. From this and the following century come the earliest surviving manuscripts of classical authors. The roll form was retained for public documents through the Middle Ages to modern times. Paper was introduced from China by the Arabs in the ninth century, but its use did not become common until the twelfth century.

6. *Writing*. Greek books were written with remarkably little change from the time of the early papyri down to the manuscripts of the mid-ninth century AD in a majuscule ('large letters') script known as *uncial. The letters, resembling capitals, were large, rounded, and individually formed. A well-written manuscript in this hand possessed a dignified beauty, but the script was slow to write and took up a lot of room. In the mid-ninth century a new bookhand, minuscule ('small letters'), was introduced which could be written more quickly and economically; see TEXTS, TRANSMISSION OF ANCIENT 3.

The writing of Latin manuscripts followed a similar pattern. During the classical period Latin books were written in majuscule, either in square capitals (for luxury books) or (more usually) in rustic capitals; the latter was a more fluid or careless-looking variety of the former, and it continued in use until the early sixth century AD. Meanwhile, in the fourth century, the uncial form of majuscule emerged as a bookhand, along with a less formal version known as half-uncial, which included some letter forms employed in the everyday business hand. Uncial and half-uncial writing continued until well into the ninth century AD and beyond. Meanwhile in the late seventh and eighth centuries experiments had been taking place in many parts of Europe to find a fast, neat, economical script. In continental Europe a minuscule script developed out of the old Roman *cursive handwriting used for business and official correspondence, whereas in Ireland such a script developed rather out of half-uncial. However, it was in France that a particularly fine and lucid minuscule hand evolved in the eighth century which became the bookhand of Europe. The letters were regular, rounded, and separate. This hand slowly came to predominate, reaching England in the tenth century, and was in use everywhere by the end of the twelfth. See also EPIGRAPHY, LIBRARIES, and TEXTS, TRANSMISSION OF ANCIENT 5.

Bo'reas, in Greek, the north wind (Lat. *aquilo*); in Greek myth, son of the Titan Astraios ('starry one') and Eōs ('dawn'). His native land was said to be Thrace. He carried off as wife the nymph Oreithyia, daughter of Erechtheus, an early king of Athens, and was thus thought by the Athenians to be specially connected with them. They instituted a state cult for him after he destroyed the Persian fleet at Cape Sepias in 480 BC (see WINDS). He was the father of Zētēs and Calăis, mentioned among the *Argonauts.

Bory'sthenēs, river of Scythia (south Russia), the modern Dnieper.

Bo'sporus ('ox-ford'), sometimes 'Bosphorus'. **1.** The Thracian Bosporus, the strait connecting the Sea of Marmora (Propontis) with the Black Sea, and separating Europe from Asia. According to Greek myth it was here that the heifer *Io crossed from one continent to the other (perhaps from Asia to Europe). The strong current and the winding channel made it dangerous to shipping.

2. The Cimmerian Bosporus, the straits connecting the Black Sea with the Sea of Asov. It also is said to derive its name from a crossing made by Io.

Bou'dicca (incorrectly Boadicea), the wife of Prasutagus, king of the Iceni, a tribe living in East Anglia. When he died without a male heir, the Romans annexed and began to despoil his kingdom; Boudicca was flogged and her two daughters raped. While the Roman governor Suetonius Paulinus was campaigning in Anglesey Boudicca led a revolt

(AD 61) during which the British sacked Camulodunum (Colchester), Londinium (London), and Verulamium (St Albans): according to *Tacitus (*Annals* 14), about 70,000 Romans and pro-Roman Britons were killed. At his return the governor routed Boudicca's forces and she is said to have taken poison.

boulē. In those Greek states where the government was carried out by an assembly of citizens and a council, the general Greek name for the latter was *boule*. This was a specially appointed body of citizens, which implemented the decisions of the sovereign assembly and administered the day-to-day running of the state. In classical Athens the boule consisted of five hundred (male) citizens over 30 years old, appointed annually by lot by the *demes (acting as voting districts) of Athens and Attica, from those who were willing to stand and had survived a preliminary scrutiny. No one could serve on the boule more than twice in a lifetime. Hence a large proportion of the male population served at some time in their lives, though there is some evidence that on occasions the well-to-do were over-represented (it must therefore have been possible to interfere with the drawing of lots). *Solon at the beginning of the sixth century BC was credited with the creation of the original boule at Athens, but the origin of the boule as it functioned in classical times lies in the reforms of *Cleisthenes at the end of the sixth century.

bouleutē'rion, at Athens, 'council-chamber'; see METROON.

boustrophē'don (lit. 'as the ox turns'), in Greek *epigraphy, a term used to describe the script on early Greek inscriptions in which the lines of writing run alternately from right to left and from left to right, as the ox pulls the plough in successive furrows. The letters also are turned round to face the appropriate direction. See also ALPHABET.

Bra'sidas (d. 422 BC), the most distinguished Spartan general in the early years of the *Peloponnesian War. In 424 he was sent north to damage Athenian interests in Thrace; there he gained possession of several important cities in alliance with Athens, including Amphipolis and Torone. Brasidas continued operations in Thrace until 422, when he had to face without reinforcements a fresh Athenian army under Cleon sent to recoup the losses. The Athenians took back Torone but failed to recover Amphipolis, and in the battle both Cleon and Brasidas were killed. Brasidas was accorded the singular honour of burial within the walls of Amphipolis, and his tomb received yearly sacrifices as if he were a hero. Thucydides records three speeches in his name and clearly admired his resourcefulness. He permanently damaged the Athenian cause in a vital part of their empire.

Brauron (modern Vraona), in east Attica, one of the twelve ancient Attic townships traditionally united by Theseus into a single Athenian state. It was well known from ancient times for the worship of Artemis, who had an important temple there and in whose honour a festival, Brauronia, was held annually. This was celebrated with particular splendour every fourth year. The cult was in some way associated with *Iphigeneia; local legend said that her sacrifice took place there rather than at Aulis, but that a bear was substituted for her. It was chiefly for women; its notable feature was that young girls between the ages of 5 and 10 wearing saffron dresses 'acted the she-bear', supposedly in atonement for the killing of a bear belonging to Artemis. Originally no girl might be married until she had performed this ritual bear-dance; by classical times the ritual was part of the Athenian state religion and was performed only by the daughters of noble families.

Brennus. 1. Leader of the Gauls (mostly Senones, a Celtic people) who invaded Italy in 390 BC (or 387), defeated the Romans at the river Allia, 19 km. (12 miles) from Rome, and then captured Rome apart from the Capitol. Legend relates that the Gauls massacred the priests and old patricians as they sat silently in their chairs of state in the porticoes of their houses. For the part supposedly played by the Capitoline geese in saving the Capitol, see MANLIUS. Legend also relates that, after six months' siege,

when the gold which the Gauls accepted as the ransom of Rome was being weighed and a Roman tribune complained of false weights, Brennus threw his sword into the scale with the words, 'vae victis', 'woe to the conquered'. Roman pride handed down the story that Brennus and his army were annihilated before they could leave Italy (see CAMILLUS). It has been suggested that the name Brennus was attributed to him in later times from the Gallic chieftain who invaded Greece in 280–279 BC (see below).

2. The leader of a Celtic people from Gaul who in 280–279 BC overran Macedonia and thence Greece. He was checked by a force of Athenians and others at Thermopylae, but finally turned their position as the Persians had done in 480 BC. He was defeated and wounded at Delphi and committed suicide in 278. The Gauls retreated with great loss.

Bria'reos (Lat. Briareus), one of the three hundred-armed giants (see HECATONCHEIRES), the sons of Uranus (Heaven) and Gaia (Earth), to be distinguished (as e.g. Virgil and Callimachus did not) from the other *Giants who were also the offspring of these parents. Briareos was also called Aegaeon. He and his two brothers fought with Zeus against the *Titans and were rewarded by being set to guard the Titans imprisoned in Tartarus. When the other Olympian gods were about to put Zeus in chains, Briareos, summoned by Thetis, saved him.

Briga'ntes, numerically the largest tribe in Britain, whose territory in the north of England stretched from coast to coast and from Hadrian's Wall (and, in the west, beyond it) to as far south as a curved line between the Mersey and the Humber, taking in the Peak District but excluding east Yorkshire. The territory was annexed by Rome in the seventies AD.

Brise'is, in the *Iliad*, Achilles' captive slave-concubine taken from him by Agamemnon, when the latter at the wish of Apollo had to return his own concubine Chryseis to her father. Hence the anger of Achilles, which is the theme of the *Iliad*.

Britain

Britain probably became known to the Mediterranean world in the fifth century BC through the Phoenicians of Carthage, the great traders and voyagers of the ancient world, because south-west Britain was one of the few sources of tin, a necessary component of bronze very scantily diffused in the Mediterranean area. Greeks of the fifth century heard only vague stories about the 'Tin Islands' (*Cassiterides), but in the late fourth century a Greek navigator from Massilia (Marseilles), *Pytheas, visited Cornwall and the tin-depot at St Michael's Mount on his circumnavigation of Britain. By the second century BC regular trade routes between Britain and the Mediterranean were established.

Julius *Caesar invaded Britain in expeditions in 55 and 54 BC, perhaps feeling that his conquest of Gaul was hardly secure without at least a show of Roman strength in Britain (Britons fought in the Gallic armies and rebellious Gauls sought refuge in Britain); total conquest may not have been his intention. The first invasion was in the nature of a reconnaissance, but the second was a more serious affair, involving a fleet of over 800 vessels and probably more than 20,000 men, including 2,000 cavalry. Caesar crossed the river Thames (Tamesis or Tamesa) to attack the British commander Cassivellaunus, king of the Catuvellauni, the most powerful of the southern tribes. Cassivellaunus was forced to give hostages and pay tribute, then Caesar withdrew to Gaul, where he feared an uprising.

Britain was now a recognized part of the Roman world, though Rome was not to invade again for another century. In the thirties and twenties BC the Latin poets Virgil and Horace sometimes speak as if the emperor Augustus was on the verge of annexing Britain, but nothing came of it and it was the emperor Claudius who made the conquest, sending a force of perhaps 40,000 men in AD 43; he arrived in person for the capture of Camulodunum—Colchester—although whether he played an active part in the fighting is disputed. Claudius pursued the policy of having client kingdoms around the province: such were the Iceni of Norfolk and the Brigantes in the north, though the latter felt themselves to be largely independent. An important client king was *Cogidubnus, whose land centred on the Chichester area of west Sussex (the palace excavated at Fishbourne is almost certainly his). Aulus Plautius, who had led the invasion, was made governor of the province with orders to secure the rest of the country and by 47, when his term as governor ended, the whole area south of the Humber and east of the Severn was under Roman control. Ostorius Scapula, governor from 47 to 52, made advances into Wales, and in 51 defeated *Caratacus, who had become the leader of British opposition to Rome. Gaius Suetonius Paulinus, governor from 58 to 61, quashed the much more serious revolt of *Boudicca, ushering in a long period of stability in the south. In the 70s the whole of Wales was subdued, and *Agricola (governor 77/8–84) advanced into Scotland, reaching the line of the Forth and the Clyde in 81. In 83 he moved further north and in 84 inflicted a famous defeat on the Caledonians at Mons Graupius. He sent a fleet around the north of Britain, and thus confirmed that it was an island. By the end of the century, or soon after, however, Scotland beyond the line of the Forth and the Clyde was abandoned, and the opportunity never came again to embrace the whole island in one province.

Under the emperor Trajan (98–117) there seems to have been a withdrawal from the south of Scotland and a new boundary created along the line between the Solway and the Tyne, confirmed by the subsequent emperor Hadrian (117–138) with the most elaborate frontier in the Roman world—'Hadrian's Wall'—which was begun after the emperor's visit in 122, and ran from Wallsend-on-Tyne in the east to Bowness-on-Solway in the west, 118 km. (74 miles) in all. It acted as a base for patrols, cut off raiders from the north, and produced settled conditions in the south in which the economy and the arts of peace could flourish.

Soon after Antoninus Pius became

emperor in 138 he initiated a sudden change of policy. The governor of Britain, Q. Lollius Urbicus, advanced once more into southern Scotland, reconquered the lowlands, and built a new frontier wall of turf—the Antonine Wall—across the line of the Forth and the Clyde, 60 km. (37 miles) long, less elaborate than Hadrian's Wall but of the same basic plan, with forts interspersed with smaller stations. The history of this period is confused, but the Antonine Wall seems to have been abandoned in c.163. Not long after 180 what is described as the greatest war of the emperor Commodus' reign occurred in Britain. Tribes from the north swept over Hadrian's Wall, ravaged widely, and destroyed a Roman force. A punitive campaign was successfully waged in 184, followed by withdrawal to the Wall. Roman influence was accepted in the lowlands but the tribes remained autonomous.

After the assassination of the emperor Commodus in 192, Clodius Albinus, governor of Britain, became a rival to the new emperor, Septimius Severus, and eventually claimed the throne. In 196 he crossed with an army to Gaul, where he was defeated by Severus in 197 and committed suicide. His withdrawal of troops from Britain gave the opportunity to those who hated Rome, especially those beyond the Wall, to vandalize and loot. In 208 Severus himself arrived in Britain and directed a punitive expedition into Scotland; he was planning a further campaign when he died in 211. At some time in the early third century Britain was divided into two provinces, the northern having its centre at York and the southern at London. For the rest of the century it remained relatively undisturbed and moderately prosperous, untypically so if it is compared with the convulsions elsewhere in the empire in this period.

In 286 or 287 Carausius, commander of the British fleet, declared himself emperor of Britain, making the island independent of the central government in Rome. Carausius was left in peace and his government was efficient and successful, but in 294 he was assassinated by one of his chief associates, Allectus, who him-

self seized the provinces of Britain. In 296 Constantius launched an invasion against Allectus, and the latter was killed in battle. Constantius thereby regained the provinces, which needed considerable reconstruction. In 306, when Constantius had become senior Augustus (emperor), he was joined by his son *Constantine for another invasion of Scotland, and won a great victory. Shortly after, he died at York and his son succeeded as Caesar. Constantine had soon to leave for Gaul, but during the first half of the fourth century Britain enjoyed peace and prosperity.

In 337 Constantine died and out of the ensuing chaos his son Constantine II emerged as senior Augustus with command over Britain, Gaul, and Spain. He invaded Italy, the domain of his brother Constans, in 340, and was killed in battle. Some unknown crisis brought Constans unexpectedly to Britain in 343, perhaps attacks by Picts and Scots beyond the Wall and by Saxon and Frankish marauders in the south. By 368 the threat to British security was alarming, and in that year a concerted attack was made by the tribes in the north, the west coast, and the south-east; the country was overrun and London threatened. It was two years before a military commander Theodosius (the Elder), a Spaniard, sent by the emperor Valentinian, could restore order. He drove out the invaders and again repaired the Wall. Once more Britain had a firm government and secure defences, but the growing power of barbarians outside the empire threatened all Europe and from 383 there were repeated withdrawals of troops from Britain to defend Italy. Soon after 400 effective occupation of Hadrian's Wall had ceased, but there was no sudden conclusion to Roman rule in Britain—rather it was a gradual process spread over several decades. By c.450 the barbarians were in Britain to stay.

Brita'nnicus (Tiberius Claudius Britannicus) (AD 41–55), son of the Roman emperor *Claudius and his wife *Messal-(l)ina. He was displaced as heir by the young *Nero, after whose accession he soon died, perhaps by poison.

Britoma'rtis, Cretan goddess of hunters

and fishermen, frequently identified with the Greek goddess *Artemis after the introduction of the latter into Crete. Her name is said to mean 'sweet maiden'. *Minos king of Crete pursued her for nine months, and finally to avoid him she leaped over a cliff into the sea but was caught and saved by fishermen's nets— hence she is also called Dictynna (from the Greek word meaning 'net'). She escaped to Aegina, where she was worshipped under the name of Aphaia, in a temple whose ruins still survive.

Bro'mius, name of the Greek god *Dionysus meaning 'noisy', 'boisterous', from the Greek verb meaning 'to roar'.

Brontēs, see CYCLOPES.

Bronze Age, in mainland Greece, the period from c.2800 to c.1050 BC; in Crete and the Aegean islands it began a little earlier, c.3000 BC. It was followed by the Iron Age, c.1050–850 BC (which mostly coincides with the Greek *Dark Age). The various periods into which the Greek Bronze Age is subdivided for more precise reference are called Helladic I, II, etc. (see MYCENAE). Similar subdivisions of the Cretan Bronze Age are known as *Minoan I, II, etc. In Italy the Bronze Age was the period from c.1800 to c.1000 BC.

Brundi'sium (modern Brindisi), the best harbour on the east coast of Italy, situated on the heel, and the nearest Italian town to the eastern Adriatic coast. It was made a Latin colony in 246 BC. Connected to Rome by the Via Appia, it was the regular port of embarkation for Greece and Epirus. It was from Brundisium that Cicero and Ovid set out on their respective exiles, and it is a journey to Brundisium in company with, among others, Virgil, that Horace describes in *Satires* 1. 5. Here Virgil subsequently died, in 19 BC, on his way home from Greece. Lucan in the *Pharsalia* relates Pompey's departure from the same port, and Tacitus (*Annals* 3. 1) the arrival there of Agrippina bringing home the ashes of Germanicus. The Treaty of Brundisium was made in 40 BC between Mark Antony and Octavian, at the insistence of soldiers in both armies when war between the two seemed imminent.

Brutus, name of a Roman plebeian family of the *gens Junia*, the Junian clan, which traced its descent from L. Junius Brutus (see 1 below) and included the Brutus (see 2 below) who murdered Julius Caesar.

1. **Lucius Junius Brutus,** the traditional founder of the Roman republic and probably a historical figure, although accounts of him in ancient sources contain legendary elements. He pretended to be an idiot (*brutus*) in order to escape the fate of his brother who had been murdered by their uncle, Tarquinius Superbus, the (last) Roman king. When *Lucretia was raped by Tarquinius' son, Brutus led an insurrection that ousted the Tarquin family, and was elected the first consul (traditionally in 509 BC) with L. Tarquinius Collatinus (Lucretia's husband). He was famous for his strict justice and put to death his own two sons who were attempting to restore the Tarquins. He was killed fighting an Etruscan army which was engaged in the same attempt.

2. **Marcus Junius Brutus,** c.85–42 BC, the prime assassin of Julius *Caesar. In 49 BC he joined in the civil war on Pompey's side against Julius Caesar, but after the former's defeat at Pharsalus he sought Caesar's pardon, which was granted. In c.45 he married Porcia, the daughter of M. Porcius *Cato whom he greatly admired and by whose republican sympathies he was influenced. In 44 Caesar appointed him as praetor, and he appeared to bear Caesar's dictatorship with equanimity, but *Cassius, a fellow-praetor, prevailed upon him to lead a conspiracy to murder Caesar, playing upon his patriotic desire to follow his famous ancestor and restore the republic. It is related by Suetonius that Caesar gave up the struggle against his murderers when he saw Brutus among them, exclaiming in Greek, *kai su, teknon* ('even you, my child!'). (The Latin version, 'Et tu, Brute!' ('even you, Brutus!') was made famous by Shakespeare.) Soon after the assassination Brutus was forced to leave Italy through public hostility and went to Greece, and with Cassius he prepared to resist the army of the *triumvirs Antony, Lepidus, and Octavian. In the autumn

of 42 Antony and Octavian defeated Brutus and Cassius at *Philippi in eastern Macedonia, and Brutus committed suicide.

In his youth Brutus acquired a love of learning which never left him. He was one of Cicero's favourite literary adversaries, and Cicero seems to have felt affection for him, while failing to win him over to his own way of thinking in oratory, philosophy, or politics. In his treatise *Brutus* (see below) Cicero made him one of the speakers, and he dedicated to Brutus his *Orator*, *De finibus*, and *Tusculan disputations*. In Cicero's correspondence some letters of Brutus survive from which we learn of his financial dealings with the people of Salamis (in Cyprus); these throw a different light on his character: he lent money to the town at 48 per cent interest, and was prepared to go to any length to recover the debt.

3. Decimus Junius Brutus, one of the assassins of Julius Caesar (not to be confused with Marcus Junius, 2 above, to whom he was only distantly related). As a young man he served under Caesar in Gaul and fought for him in the civil war against Pompey. Caesar trusted Brutus so completely that he promised him the governorship of Cisalpine Gaul and allowed him to be his escort to the senate house on the day of his assassination. After Caesar's murder Brutus retired to Cisalpine Gaul and refused to surrender it to Mark Antony. The latter proceeded to besiege him and his republican forces in Mutina (43 BC), but with the aid of a senatorial army Brutus succeeded in repulsing him. Later, however, finding himself under attack by both Octavian and Antony, he tried to cross over to M. Brutus (2 above) in Macedonia, but was betrayed and killed.

Brutus (or *De claris oratoribus*), treatise by *Cicero ((1) 5) on eminent Roman orators. Written in 46 BC with the purpose of defending Cicero's own oratorical practice, it gives interesting details of his early life and training as an orator and his gradual rise to the highest position. It purports to record a recent conversation between Cicero, M. Junius Brutus (see previous entry), and *Atticus, in which

Cicero ends an introductory section on Greek orators by referring to the Attic, Asianic, and Rhodian schools of *oratory, commending some of the qualities of the Asianists as well as of the Atticists. He reviews the long series of Roman orators from Brutus the Liberator (supposedly consul in 509 BC), but more particularly from Cethēgus, consul in 204 BC, 'the marrow of persuasion' according to Ennius, to his own times, giving a brief description of each.

Būce'phalas ('ox-head'), the black horse of Alexander the Great, his favourite for twenty years, which died probably of wounds at the battle fought against the Indian Porus at the river Hydaspes (Jhelum) in 326 BC. In his memory Alexander founded the town of Bucephala (probably Jhelum on the west bank of the river in west Pakistan) near the site of Bucephalas' last river crossing. The popular story was that the horse had proved unmanageable until the 12-year-old Alexander, observing that it shied at its own shadow, turned its head to the sun, soothed, and then mounted it.

bucolic poetry, pastoral poetry. The name 'bucolic' is derived from the Greek word for herdsmen, *boukoloi*, and was first used to describe the poems (known as *idylls) of the Greek poet *Theocritus, who invented the genre of pastoral poetry. These were imitated by the Greek poets *Bion and *Moschus, and later and most notably by the Roman poet Virgil (in the *Eclogues); it was Virgil who gave the genre its location (Arcadia in Greece), its typical form, and many of the motifs subsequently used by later European pastoral poets. In the typical pastoral poem the herdsmen-poets sing of themselves, their loves, and their music in a stylized Greek landscape with Pan and the nymphs. At its best the artful simplicity of pastoral poetry conceals a subtlety of composition that most appeals to a sophisticated taste able to appreciate its studied remoteness from the realities of a shepherd's life. Many of its features are found in Milton's poem *Lycidas* (1637). Because of its limited subject-matter and easily recognized conventions pastoral poetry came to be used as a vehicle for *allegory or veiled social comment as early as Virgil. See also GENRE and ELEGY.

Burrus, see SENECA (2) I.

Būsī'ris (Bousīris), in Greek myth, a king of Egypt, son of Poseidon, who, in order to end a drought, on the advice of a seer, sacrificed to Zeus all strangers who arrived in his kingdom. The seer himself, being a visitor from Cyprus, was the first victim. Soon afterwards *Heracles arrived and killed Busiris and his son and all his attendants.

Byzantine age, term describing Greek history and culture of the period from (at its widest) AD 330 until 1453, derived from the name of the capital of the eastern Roman empire, the Greek city *Byzantium. The period begins when the emperor *Constantine the Great transferred his residence from Rome to Byzantium and renamed the city Constantinople. In AD 395, at the death of the emperor Theodosius the Great, the empire was divided between his two sons, Arcadius ruling from Byzantium/Constantinople in the East and Honorius from Rome in the West. Thereafter there was complete separation of administration and even of succession. When the western empire collapsed in the fifth century (see FALL OF ROME) relations between east and west declined. The last eastern emperor to use Latin as the official language of imperial government at Byzantium was Justinian, with whose reign (527–65) the Byzantine age (or Byzantine empire) is sometimes said to begin. Greek literature, no longer pagan, was now centred on Byzantium, and had lost its classical stamp under Roman, Eastern, and Christian influences. The Greek pronunciation had changed, syllables in Byzantine Greek having different quantities from classical Greek (see METRE, GREEK I), with the result that after the second century AD it was no longer possible, except for a few deliberately archaizing poets, to write verse in the old classical metres. New literary genres appeared, such as Christian hymns and saints' lives. The kind of Greek used by authors varied widely, from the most ornate imitations

of classical literary Greek to the very different near-vernacular. It was primarily an age of prose, of theology and history particularly; notable historians include *Procopius, Anna Comnena (1083–after 1148), and Michael Psellus (c.1019–c.1078) (the last two outside the scope of this work). Many writers were occupied with lexicons, abridgements of classical works, and commentaries on them, and played an important part in the preservation and transmission of the ancient authors. The period ended in 1453 with the fall of what was still officially the eastern Roman empire and the capture of Byzantium/Constantinople by the Ottoman Turks. See also SOPHISTIC, SECOND and TEXTS, TRANSMISSION OF ANCIENT 2 and 3.

Byzantium, Greek city by the Propontis (the Sea of Marmora), at the southern end of the Bosporus on the European side, later renamed Constantinople (see below) and now Istanbul. It was magnificently situated, commanding the two opposite shores of Europe and Asia with the advantages of security and great facility for trade. It was originally founded by Megarians in the seventh century BC, opposite Chalcedon (the 'city of the blind', so called by the Delphic oracle because its earlier Megarian founders had failed to choose the superior site of Byzantium). Ruled by Persia from 512 to 478 BC, then alternately under Athenian and Spartan dominion in the fifth and fourth centuries, Byzantium was a formal ally of Athens from c.378 to 357 BC, and then again when successfully resisting Philip of Macedon in the famous siege of 340–339. The help supposedly given by the goddess Hecatē on this occasion was commemorated on Byzantine coins by her symbol of crescent and star (adopted by the Turks as their device after they captured the city in AD 1453). The city suffered severely from the Celtic (Gallic) invasions of the third century BC (see GALATIANS) and subsequently passed into the Roman empire, while remaining Greek in culture. It was chosen by the emperor *Constantine for his new capital (AD 330), to be known thereafter in the West as Constantinople. When the Roman empire in the West finally collapsed in the fifth century under barbarian invasions (see FALL OF ROME) the eastern empire and its capital, firmly in the Greek world, flourished. The city's position as the capital of the eastern empire was interrupted in 1204 when it was captured by the French and Venetians (collectively known as Latins) during the Fourth Crusade, and became the seat of the Latin empire until restored to Greek possession in 1261. The last emperor, Constantine XIII, was killed when the city and empire fell to the Turks in 1453. See also BYZANTINE AGE.

C

Cabei'ri (Kabeiroi), in Greek religion, gods apparently non-Greek in origin (their name has been thought to have Semitic connections) who, together with a mother goddess, were the object of a *mystery cult since early times. Their genealogy was variously given; sometimes they were described as the sons of *Hephaestus. Aeschylus gave the name *Kabeiroi* to one of his plays, now lost, in which they appeared as the chorus, receiving the Argonauts on Lemnos, and describing themselves as great wine-drinkers. Their mysteries were celebrated from early times on the north Aegean islands of Lemnos and Samothrace in particular, and from before the sixth century at Thebes. By the fifth century they were known in Athens; the historian Herodotus was an initiate. After the time of Alexander the Great (late fourth century BC) their cult spread rapidly over the Greek world, but little is known about it.

Cācus, in Roman myth, a fire-breathing monster, son of Vulcan, who was supposed to have lived on a hill at Rome (Aventine according to Virgil) and who terrorized the country. As *Hercules was driving home to Greece the cattle he had stolen from the monster Geryon, he rested at the site of the future Rome, where he was entertained by *Evander. Cacus stole some of the cattle and dragged them into his cave tail first so that it was impossible to follow their traces. When the remaining cattle passed the cave those within began to bellow and were thus discovered; Hercules then killed Cacus. Virgil may have invented this story. Cacus seems to have originated in Etruscan myth, where he was a seer on the Palatine.

Cadmē'a (Kadmeia), the citadel of Thebes, named after the city's founder *Cadmus.

Cadmus. 1. In Greek myth Cadmus was the legendary founder of the city of Thebes (in Boeotia), son of Agenor king of Tyre (in Phoenicia), who was sent to look for his sister Europa after she had been carried off by Zeus in the shape of a bull. By the advice of the Delphic Oracle he abandoned the search; he was told that he would meet a cow which he should follow until it lay down; there he should found a city. The cow led him to the site of Thebes; when he sent his companions to fetch water for sacrifice from a nearby spring they were all killed by the dragon guarding it. Cadmus slew the dragon and at the instruction of the goddess Athena sowed half the dragon's teeth (Athena kept the other half for Aeētēs, king of Colchis, to give to Jason). A crop of armed men sprang up whom he set fighting by throwing a stone among them, and they fought each other until only five survived. These five, the Spartoi ('sown men'), helped to build the *Cadmea and in historical times were held to be the ancestors of the Theban nobility. Zeus gave Cadmus as bride Harmonia, the daughter of Ares and Aphrodite, and all the gods attended the wedding. Cadmus gave his bride as a present a necklace made by Hephaestus which subsequently was to play a fatal part in the Theban story (see AMPHIARAUS and ALCMAEON). Their daughters, all of whom met disaster, were Ino, Semelē (mother of *Dionysus), Autonoē, and Agavē (mother of Pentheus). Cadmus eventually abdicated in favour of Pentheus, but returned after the latter's death (see BACCHAE). He and his wife finally withdrew to Illyria, where they were changed into snakes and carried off by Zeus to Elysium. Cadmus was said to have civilized the Boeotians and taught them the art of writing with Phoenician letters (from which in fact the Greek *alphabet is derived). A large number of objects from the Near East has been found in the Kadmeion or royal palace of Thebes, suggesting possible Phoenician influence. Because in Theban mythical history victory so often entailed disaster for the victors, a 'Cadmean victory' was proverbial in Greek (compare 'Pyrrhic victory'; see PYRRHUS).

2. Of Miletus, see LOGOGRAPHERS.

Caeci'lius Stā'tius, Gaul from northern Italy, probably Mediolanum (Milan), taken prisoner of war in 223 or 222 BC, brought to Rome as a slave and manumitted, and subsequently the chief Roman comic dramatist of his day. He was the friend of the poet Ennius and came in point of time between the dramatists Plautus and Terence. He was still alive in 166 to pass judgement on the latter's *Andria*. No complete play of his survives, but some forty-two titles are known, of which sixteen derive from Menander, the Greek writer of New Comedy. Some fragments survive in quotations. See COMEDY, ROMAN.

Cae'lius Rufus, Marcus (82–48 BC), young Roman with political ambitions, friend and pupil of Cicero from 66 to 63, when he broke away and associated with Catiline for a while. After a successful prosecution in 59 of Antonius, Cicero's colleague in the consulship in 63, Caelius became popular in fashionable circles and rented a house in the desirable Palatine quarter near *Clodia, perhaps supplanting the poet Catullus in her affections, if he is the Rufus whom Catullus mentions. Their affair was over by 56, the year in which he was prosecuted by L. Sempronius Atratinus after he had himself successfully prosecuted the latter's father earlier in the year. It would appear that Clodia was the driving force behind the case. Cicero defended him in a notable speech which still survives (see CICERO (1) 4), and Caelius was acquitted. Clodia thereafter disappears from view, a coincidence which may indicate the social importance of Caelius' victory. He was tribune in 52, a supporter of Milo and enemy of Pompey. In 51 Cicero went to Cilicia as governor, and during his year's absence Caelius kept him informed of home affairs in seventeen witty and politically acute letters which survive in Cicero's correspondence. In 49, as civil war became imminent, he declared for Caesar, but soon grew discontented; he joined Milo in raising a rebellion in south Italy, but it was easily suppressed by Caesar, and Caelius and Milo were both killed.

Caesar, the name of a Roman patrician family of the *gens *Julia*, one of the most ancient clans in Rome, which traced its origin back to Iulus, son of Aeneas. The name 'Caesar' (see 6 below) survived into modern times in the Russian 'Tzar' and German 'Kaiser'. Julius Caesar's adopted son *Octavian (later the emperor Augustus), added it to his own name, as did his adopted son, the emperor Tiberius, and his successors. Although the Caesarian branch of the Julian clan became extinct with the death of Nero, succeeding emperors tended to assume the name as a title, until '*Augustus' became the title of the reigning emperor, 'Caesar' that of the emperor's designated heir or second-in-command.

Gaius Julius Caesar, Roman general, statesman, and dictator, b. 12 or 13 July 100 BC, assassinated 15 March (the Ides) 44 BC.

1. *100–62 BC.* He came of a patrician family, but from the beginning was associated in politics with the popular party (see POPULARES). In 81 he served his first military campaign in Asia, but he came to public attention by two (unsuccessful) prosecutions in Rome. He then retired to Rhodes to study under a Greek rhetorician (M. Antonius Gnipho, who also taught Cicero), but on the way was captured for ransom by pirates whom, soon after his release, he caught and crucified, as he had told them he would during his captivity. He returned to Rome in 73 and became a senator before 70, supporting *Pompey when the latter as consul repealed some of Sulla's revisions of the constitution. In 68 he went as quaestor to Hispania Ulterior (Further Spain). His wife Cornelia died, and on his return in 67 he married one of the Pompeian family, no doubt in order to cement an alliance. In 65 he was elected to the aedileship, an office whose holder was expected to spend lavishly on buildings and public entertainments. Caesar spent with unparalleled generosity. In 63 he was elected *pontifex maximus*, to the shame of his aristocratic rivals, and to the praetorship for 62. The end of his

praetorship was marked by the scandal arising from *Clodius' profanation of the Bona Dea mysteries in Caesar's house by appearing disguised as a woman. As a consequence Caesar divorced his wife Pompeia because, according to Plutarch, 'his wife must be above suspicion'.

2. *61–50 BC*. Caesar's successful governorship of Further Spain in 61 established his reputation as a general. On his return he made an informal alliance with Pompey and *Crassus (often called by modern scholars 'the first triumvirate'), and was elected consul for 59 together with *Bibulus whose vetoes he notoriously disregarded. His legislation satisfied the personal ambitions of Pompey and Crassus, and as proconsul in 58 he took for himself the governorship of Illyricum (Dalmatia), Cisalpine Gaul (northern Italy), and Transalpine Gaul (southern France).

The next nine years were occupied in the conquest of the rest of *Gaul (the Gallic War), brilliantly described in his *Commentaries*. In the early years there is no evidence of discord with Pompey, who in 59 married Julia, the daughter of Caesar by his first wife Cornelia. Caesar himself married as his third wife *Calpurnia, the daughter of L. Calpurnius Piso who was consul in 59. By 56 Caesar regarded the conquest of Gaul as complete, and spent 55 and 54 in sending expeditions to *Germany and *Britain. The compact with Pompey and Crassus had been renewed at Luca (Lucca) in 56; these two became consuls for 55 and renewed Caesar's command for a further five years. However, in 53 Crassus was killed fighting the Parthians, and Pompey and Caesar were left alone at the head of the state. Pompey's wife Julia, who had formed a bond between them, had died in childbirth the previous year. Sporadic revolts in Gaul in 53 culminated in a general rising in 52 under Vercingetorix, which Caesar put down after the most difficult fighting of his career. The pacification of Gaul was completed by 50. Meanwhile civil disturbances at Rome led to the appointment of Pompey as sole consul for 52, and his measures included a law that allowed Caesar to stand for the consulship in his absence. Caesar's governorship expired

in 49 and he therefore needed the consulship for 48 if he was not to become a private citizen, liable to prosecution by his political enemies in Rome. The senate wished to recall him before there could be any risk of his becoming consul while still at the head of his army, and the consul C. Marcellus proposed that he should lay down his command by 13 November. Pompey hesitated whether to give his support, but finally threw in his lot with Caesar's enemies.

3. *49–44 BC*. On 7 January 49 the senate ordered Caesar, now at the river *Rubicon, the boundary between Cisalpine Gaul and Italy, to disband his army. On 10 January Caesar nevertheless crossed the Rubicon with his army, and the civil war was launched. Pompey was entrusted by the senate with the whole management of the war on behalf of the republic, but he was outmanœuvred and fled to Greece, and within three months Caesar was master of Italy with a large measure of popular support. He was prudently merciful to the defeated, in strong contrast with earlier Roman leaders and their proscriptions. Rather than pursue Pompey to Greece he went to Spain, where in a brief and brilliant campaign he forced the surrender of the Pompeian army at Ilerda (Lerida). In 48 he followed Pompey to Epirus in Greece and suffered a reverse at Dyrrhachium from the latter's powerful army; however, he defeated Pompey at *Pharsalus and pursued him to Egypt, but on his arrival found him already murdered. After Ilerda, Caesar had been appointed dictator in order to hold the consular elections (in which he was elected consul) and pass some necessary legislation, but, that done, he had laid down the dictatorship. When news of his victory at Pharsalus reached Rome he was again nominated dictator, this time for a year. Throughout the winter of 48 he was occupied with a difficult war (the Alexandrian War; see BELLUM ALEXANDRINUM) to establish *Cleopatra VII, now his mistress, on the throne of Egypt; and he thereby gave the Pompeian forces time to regroup. Soon afterwards Cleopatra had a son (*Caesarion), claiming him to be by Caesar. Before returning to Rome, Caesar marched through Syria and Pon-

tus to defeat Pharnaces, king of Pontus and son of the famous Mithridates. This he did in 47 at Zela, a victory which he announced with his famous boast, *veni, vidi, vici*, 'I came, I saw, I conquered'. In Rome he was elected to his third dictatorship, but before the year ended he set out for Africa where he defeated the Pompeians (i.e. republicans) at Thapsus in 46 (the consequent suicide of *Cato at Utica became an inspiration for later republicans). On his return to Rome he was given the dictatorship for another ten years and in four magnificent triumphs celebrated his victories over foreign enemies (not those over other Romans).

He now turned to legislation, using his amazing ability and energy to bring about many much-needed reforms, none of such long-lasting benefit as the reform of the *calendar. This (Julian) calendar remained in operation until it was further reformed in the sixteenth century. In the midst of these activities Caesar was called to Spain where a republican revolt had broken out, led by Pompey's two sons and Caesar's own former officer Labienus. They were finally defeated in the hard-fought battle of Munda (45). Among the army and the people Caesar's popularity was enormous, and the senate granted him virtually monarchical power as well as extraordinary emblems of monarchy; but, although he attempted to conciliate powerful senators by merciful treatment of his enemies, his evident intention of putting an end to republican government for ever and keeping the supreme power within his own family led to a conspiracy against his life, led by *Cassius and *Brutus, and he was stabbed to death in the senate house in 44 BC. (Dante in the *Inferno* put these two with Judas Iscariot in the lowest circle of Hell.)

4. Caesar's *Commentaries* (i.e. 'notes') on the Gallic war, and the (unfinished) three books on the civil war are his only writings that survive entire. The title of the former was chosen deliberately to suggest that it was not history that was being written but rather a bald record of events written in the third person, and therefore an objectively truthful account. Caesar wished, in fact, to create the impression that he was a simple soldier fighting necessary wars for the good of Rome, so as to refute the charges of his political enemies that he was fighting for personal aggrandizement. Nevertheless, despite its political purpose, the *Gallic War* is unique as a contemporary account of a foreign war written by a Roman general, in lucid, unrhetorical Latin. Each book seems to have been composed at the end of the year with which it deals and perhaps sent individually to Rome. The work was published as a whole probably in 51 BC. The *Civil War* is rather more obviously a political pamphlet, with the theme that his enemies had forced war upon him, but the narrative is occasionally relieved by a human touch or a flash of sardonic humour. The *Bellum Africum*, *Bellum Alexandrinum*, and *Bellum Hispaniense* were written by members of Caesar's staff.

5. Caesar also wrote a number of other books which have not survived: a collection of jokes and sayings, later suppressed by Augustus as too frivolous; a grammatical work on declensions and conjugations, composed while he was crossing the Alps and dedicated to Cicero; an irritated reply, *Anticato*, to Cicero's panegyric of Cato (see 3 above), and a number of poems, of which a verse epigram to Terence survives. He was an outstanding orator, described by Cicero as the most eloquent of Romans. We have Lives of Caesar by Plutarch and Suetonius. Several portrait busts considered authentic show a clean-shaven, austere face, with hair combed forward in later life to conceal baldness, as Suetonius described him. He was tall, pale, with keen black eyes, and took pains over his appearance. It was related that he was born by being cut from his mother's womb, the so-called Caesarian section, but this story is also told of the first member of the Julian *gens* to take the name Caesar, in order to explain the name by deriving it from *caesus*, 'cut'.

For 'Caesar' as a title under the Roman empire SEE AUGUSTUS.

Caesa'rion, the nickname given by the Alexandrians, and generally accepted, to Ptolemy XV (Ptolemaeus Caesar), the son of Cleopatra VII, born in 47 BC and said by her to have been fathered by

Julius Caesar. Octavian, Caesar's adopted son and heir, had him executed in 30 BC, perhaps seeing him as a rival.

caesü'ra ('cut'), place in a metrical line where a break between words regularly occurs, dividing the line into two unequal parts; see METRE, GREEK 2.

Calabria, in ancient times the heel of Italy, not, as now, the toe. It was very fertile despite its dryness and its great heat in summer. It was famous for olives, fruit, wine, and horses. Brundisium was its chief city.

Ca'laïs and Zētēs, in Greek myth, sons of Boreas, the north wind. They were of human shape but had wings on their shoulders. They took part in the expedition of the *Argonauts to recover the Golden Fleece, in the course of which they saved *Phineus from the Harpies. On their way home they were killed in revenge by Heracles on the island of Tenos, because on the voyage to Colchis they had persuaded the other Argonauts to leave him behind on the coast of Bithynia (on the Propontis) when he was frantically searching for the lost *Hylas. Heracles erected two pillars over their grave, one of which moved whenever the north wind blew.

Calchas, the seer of the Greek army in the Trojan War. At the opening of Homer's *Iliad* he reveals the reason for the plague in the Greek camp. After Homer he is introduced into several narratives relating to the capture of Troy, such as Agamemnon's sacrifice of his daughter Iphigeneia and the construction of the Trojan Horse. See also MOPSUS.

Caledō'nia, the name used by Tacitus and other Romans to describe Britain north of the Firth of Forth.

calendars
Virtually all peoples have used the lunar month as a measure of time, although, since this period comprises 29½ days, the months inaugurated by each new moon cannot contain a constant number of whole days. The succession of seasons is determined by the yearly cycle of the earth around the sun in roughly 365¼ days, that is, the solar year, which is about eleven days longer than twelve

lunar months. Hence, when the solar year is divided into twelve months, the beginning of each month cannot in general correspond exactly with the appearance of the new moon.

The Greek calendar
All Greek states had a civil year of twelve months with 29 and 30 days alternately, each month beginning with the new moon. Since the year thus contained only 354 days, adjustment to fit the solar year had to be made, and the magistrates did this by adding ('intercalating') extra months or fractions of months as need arose.

The civil year at Athens began in July and was named after the chief archon. The days within the Greek month or the prytany were sometimes divided into three periods of (mostly) ten days (decades) and the days within each decade denoted by number, but there were many variations.

The Roman calendar
The original Roman calendar ran from March to December ('month ten', *decem*), with an uncounted gap in the winter when no agricultural work was possible. By Caesar's day the Roman year consisted of 355 days divided into twelve months, which corresponded with neither the sun nor the moon, and by 46 BC the civic and solar years were discrepant by about three months. Caesar gave the year 46 BC 445 days to remove the discrepancy, and from 1 January 45 made the year consist of 365 days, with the individual months having essentially the same length as in the modern calendar; he also introduced the leap year. In this Julian calendar the year is about eleven minutes longer than the solar year, and by the late sixteenth century the accumulated difference amounted to ten days; accordingly Pope Gregory XIII omitted ten days from 1582 and suggested that three intercalary days be omitted every four hundred years. The modern calendar is essentially the Julian, which is still used for dates before 1582.

The Romans dated their year by the names of the consuls. The method of dating by magistrates is only effective if the series of names continues uninterrupted. Dating by eras, where the years are numbered consecutively from an agreed starting-point, e.g. the foundation of Rome, has obvious advantages. In the fifth century BC some Greeks had used to establish an era the Olympian games, whose first recorded victor won in 776 BC and which recurred every four years. The numbering of Olympiads (the four-year periods between games) and the counting of years within an Olympiad probably goes back to the third century BC, and this system lasted until the Byzantine age. The Romans did not widely use the era *ab urbe condita* ('from the foundation of Rome', abbreviated to AUC), perhaps because the date we now accept as traditional, 753 BC, was disputed.

The method of dating by the years of the Christian era was introduced in the mid-sixth century by Dionysius Exiguus, a Scythian monk who lived at Rome.

Cali'gula ('little boot'), the popular name of the Roman emperor *Gaius Caesar, derived from the heavy hobnailed boot (caliga) worn by Roman soldiers.

Ca'llias, rich and distinguished fifth-century Athenian politician who was said to have negotiated the 'Peace of Callias' *c*.450 BC which finally ended the wars between Athens and Persia. Thucydides' failure to mention this treaty in his history has led some scholars to deny its existence, but hostilities between Athens and Persia ceased at this period until 413 BC. Callias was remembered for having married *Cimon's sister (or half-sister) Elpinicē for love and without a dowry.

Calli'cratēs, Greek architect of the fifth century BC, associated with Ictinus and Pheidias in the building of the *Parthenon.

Calli'machus, Greek poet and scholar of the Hellenistic age, who was born *c*.310–305 BC in Cyrene (North Africa) and died *c*.240. He is occasionally referred to as Battiades (i.e. 'son of *Battus'). During the reign of Ptolemy II Philadelphus, king of Egypt 285–246 BC, he arrived at Alexandria and was commissioned by the king to prepare the great catalogue (*pinakēs*) of all the books in the *Alexandrian Library. This enormous undertaking (the catalogue ran to

120 volumes) not only benefited the library but also influenced the poet's style: like other Hellenistic poets who combined poetry with scholarship he found in his researches material to be polished and incorporated in his verse. During this time Callimachus produced several prose works of scholarship which have not survived. Of his many poetical works the only ones to survive intact are the six Hymns and perhaps sixty-one short epigrams. The Hymns were modelled on the (so-called) *Homeric Hymns but were not, like the latter, intended for recitation at festivals. Rather they were complex literary compositions, designed to be recited to, or read by, a cultivated audience appreciative of an intriguing narrative and a learned and sometimes ironic imitation of an earlier form. Hymn 1 is to Zeus, 2 to Apollo, 3 to Artemis, and 4 to Delos; Hymn 5, 'The Baths of Pallas', is written in elegiac couplets, unlike the others which are in hexameters; Hymn 6, to Demeter, tells the gruesome story of the insatiable hunger of Erysichthon. In the *epigrams Callimachus plays subtly with the conventions of this (relatively new) literary form. The epigrams which appeal most to us seem to reflect the poet's own experiences and emotions.

The rest of Callimachus' surviving poetry exists only in fragments, most of it on papyri discovered in the twentieth century; it includes the *Aitia*, the *Hecălē*, the *Iambi*, a lyric poem called *Apotheosis of Queen Arsinoe*, and an elegiac poem, *Victory of Sosibius*. The *Aitia* ('causes') was an elegiac poem in four books, comprising about 7,000 lines. The first two books have an elaborate framework: the poet is transported in a dream to Mount Helicon where (like the poet Hesiod) he is instructed by the Muses, in his case in the origins of all kinds of mythical lore connected with Greek history, customs, and religious rites. None of the stories except for one is known from earlier literature, and the sources appear to have been local histories. The style is learned and allusive but it is enlivened by dry humour and is not without true poetic touches. The third and fourth books, which were probably composed much later, do not have this framework, and are a collection of separate 'causes'. The first and last poems are in praise of the queen Berenice, the last being the famous *Plokamos* (Lat. *Coma*) or *Lock of *Berenice*. The *Aitia* was also imitated by Ovid in his *Fasti*. By way of introduction to the whole work Callimachus composed the *Answer to the *Telchines*, apparently his critics, who belittle his achievement because he has not written one long continuous poem on an epic theme. His reply is that the small-scale poem is more attractive; moreover Apollo himself has commanded the poet to 'cultivate a slender Muse' and 'tread an unworn path'. As he reputedly said elsewhere, 'a big book is a big evil'; poetry should aim at small-scale perfection. A late tradition relates that chief among his opponents was the epic poet *Apollonius Rhodius, who was thought to be the object of Callimachus' (lost) verse invective, *Ibis*, later translated and adapted to his own purposes by Ovid. (See also ANTIMACHUS.)

Hecale is an example of the kind of epic Callimachus approved, an *epyllion perhaps about a thousand lines long (now known only in fragments) in which the poet tells how Theseus was on his way from Athens to Marathon to fight the Marathonian bull when a storm arose and the hero took shelter in the hut of an old woman, Hecale, who prepares a simple meal for him (the source perhaps of a similar meal in the hut of Philemon and Baucis in Ovid's *Metamorphoses*). When Theseus returns from killing the bull he finds that Hecale has died and men are digging her grave.

The fragmentary *Iambi* consist of thirteen short poems, in iambic and choliambic metres, which look back to the sixth-century vituperative poet *Hipponax; they are satirical in tone and often criticize contemporary literary attitudes.

Callimachus was a writer of astonishing output (reputedly 800 volumes) and remarkable originality and versatility, who aimed to be both a poet and a man of taste and erudition. His contribution to the development of a new literary taste in a new cosmopolitan society was very considerable (see HELLENISTIC AGE). His blend of sensitivity and detachment, elegance, wit, and learning, had a profound influence on later Roman poets, especially Catullus, Ovid, and Propertius (the last thought of himself as the Roman Callimachus), and through them on the whole European literary tradition.

Calli'nus (first half of the seventh century BC), the first Greek poet known to have written in elegiac couplets (see METRE, GREEK 4). He lived in the Greek city of Ephesus in Ionia on the coast of Asia Minor, and the few fragments of his poetry which survive refer to the barbarian invasions of '*Cimmerians and Trerians' from south Russia. In the only fragment of any length he exhorts his fellow-countrymen to take up arms and defend their country.

Calli'ope ('fair-voice'), in Greek (and Roman) myth one of the *Muses. When, in later Greek literature and art, each Muse is made the patron of a particular branch, Calliope is represented as the Muse of epic poetry, with writing tablet and stylus. Orpheus was sometimes said to be her son.

Calli'rhoë ('fair-flowing'). 1. Daughter of Oceanus and mother of Geryon.

2. The famous spring at Athens.

Calli'sthenēs, Greek historian, born *c.*370 BC, a relation of Aristotle under whom he studied at Stageira. All his works, including his history of Alexander the Great, are lost. He collaborated with Aristotle in the preparation of a complete list of the victors at the Pythian games from the earliest time. He accompanied Alexander on his expedition east as the historian of the campaigns; his biography of the king, which was widely read, extolled him as the champion of panhellenism, claiming him to be the son of Zeus. However, he quarrelled with Alexander, was suspected of being involved in Hermolaus' conspiracy against him, and was put to death in 327. This murder earned for Alexander the strong hostility of the school of Aristotle. Because of his adulatory and rhetorical style of history, Callisthenes' name became attached to an early version of the popular *Alexander Romance* (see ALEXANDER).

Calli'sto, in Greek myth, nymph attendant upon the goddess Artemis; she was loved by Zeus and became mother of

Arcas, the mythical ancestor of the Arcadians. She was changed into a bear, either by Zeus, to save her from the anger of his consort Hera, or by Hera or Artemis out of vengeance. In this form she wandered about until her son, now grown up, met her when out hunting and would have killed her with his spear. But Zeus turned both into constellations, the Great Bear and the Little Bear (Arctophylax, also known as *Boötēs).

Calli'stratus (d. *c*.355 BC), Athenian orator and statesman. He was elected *strategos in 378 and influenced Athenian policy from 371 to 361. He realized that Thebes was becoming more of a threat to Athens than was Sparta, but he and others nevertheless allowed the Thebans to gain possession of Oropus in 366. He was subsequently prosecuted, but successfully defended himself in a speech which is said to have inspired *Demosthenes to study oratory. In 361 he was again prosecuted and went into exile before the death sentence was pronounced. He eventually returned to Athens, miscalculating the popular mood, and was then put to death.

Calpu'rnia. 1. The daughter of *Piso Caesonius (the object of Cicero's speech *In Pisonem*), and the third wife of Julius Caesar, whom she married in 59 BC. Calpurnia's affection for Caesar survived his proposal, made in 54 after the death of his daughter Julia, Pompey's wife, that he should divorce her and marry Pompey's daughter to keep up the family connection, and she tried to keep him from the senate on the day of his murder. **2.** Third wife of *Pliny the Younger, whom she accompanied to Bithynia.

Calpu'rnius Si'culus, Titus, the otherwise unknown Latin author of seven pastoral poems (an additional four appended and attributed to him in the manuscripts are by Nemesianus), usually thought to be writing between AD 50 and 60. Three of these poems, Eclogues 1, 4, and 7, are courtly poems aimed to flatter the emperor (Claudius or Nero), while the remainder are more strictly pastoral. They are full of reminiscences of Augustan poetry and especially of Virgil's *Eclogues*.

Calvus, Gaius Lici'nius, 82–*c*.47 BC, son of the Roman annalist Licinius Macer (see ANNALS), a celebrated love poet in his day and a successful lawyer, who employed the austere Attic style of *oratory; his speeches against Vatinius were still used as models of oratory a century later. He was also a friend of Catullus, the *salaputium disertum* ('eloquent dwarf') of the latter's poem 53 (and the recipient of poems 14, 50, and 96). The very scanty fragments of his verse that survive—from epithalamia, a narrative poem, and satiric epigrams (attacking Pompey and Caesar)—at least show that his range was similar to that of Catullus.

Ca'lydon, Greek town in Aetolia, in Greek myth ruled over by Meleager, and famous for being once ravaged by a boar sent by Artemis. For the Calydonian boar-hunt see MELEAGER.

Caly'pso, in Greek myth, a goddess or nymph, the daughter of Atlas, who lived on the island of Ogygia where *Odysseus was washed up after being shipwrecked. She kept him there for seven years and promised to make him immortal if he would be her husband, but Zeus sent Hermes to order her to release him, and she gave him materials to make his own boat. Some stories make her the mother by Odysseus of Auson, the eponymous ancestor of the Ausonians of Italy.

Cambÿ'sēs, king of Persia 530–522 BC, son of Cyrus the Great. His main achievement was the conquest of Egypt in 525 BC, which established Persian rule there for two centuries. Greek writers, perhaps following a hostile Egyptian tradition, represent him as impious and tyrannical.

Camē'nae, Italian goddesses perhaps originally associated with water, and identified with the Greek Muses since *Livius Andronicus invoked the Camenae at the beginning of his Latin translation of Homer's *Odyssey*. They had a grove and a spring outside the Porta Capena at Rome from which the Vestals drew water daily for their rites.

Cami'lla, known only from Virgil's *Aeneid* and perhaps a Virgilian invention, a maiden-warrior of the Volsci, and ally of Turnus. When she was a baby her father Metabus, king of the Volscians, was driven out for his cruelty, and arrived with his baby daughter at the flooded river Amasenus. He tied her to a spear, dedicated her to the goddess Diana (Lat. *camilla*, 'religious attendant'), and threw her across the river to safety. He then swam across himself. In the *Aeneid* she is killed by the Etruscan Arruns.

Cami'llus, Marcus Fū'rius (d. *c.*365 BC), Roman statesman and general. His exploits were greatly embellished in later times and according to Livy he was 'the saviour of his country and second founder of Rome' after its occupation by the Gauls *c.*390 BC. His most famous victory was the capture of the Etruscan town of Veii in 396 BC, after which he dedicated a golden basin to Apollo at Delphi in fulfilment of a vow. Soon afterwards Camillus captured another Etruscan town, Falerii. To this campaign belongs the famous story of the local schoolmaster who brought his pupils to Camillus' camp with the suggestion that they should be used as hostages to secure the town. Camillus, refusing to profit by treachery, returned the children safely, and sent the schoolmaster back in chains. The citizens were so struck by this example of Roman justice that they surrendered.

According to tradition Camillus was accused of appropriating booty and went into exile, but was recalled as dictator when the Gauls captured Rome *c.*390 (see BRENNUS). He is supposed to have annihilated the Gauls and later conquered the Volsci and the Aequi. He was a moderating influence during the civil strife between patricians and plebeians that ended in 367, and marked the return to peace by founding a temple to Concord built at the foot of the Capitoline hill. He was five times dictator, and a reform of Roman military organization is attributed to him.

Campā'nia, territory in Italy south of Latium, lying between the Apennines and the Tyrrhenian Sea, and extending south to the Surrentine promontory (Sorrento). A volcanic plain, it is exceptionally fertile, and many wealthy Romans had villas there. It included the port of Puteoli and the towns of Cumae, Capua, Baiae, Neapolis (Naples), Pompeii, and

Herculaneum. The Sabelli conquered Campania in the fifth century BC and brought with them their language, *Oscan, which was still spoken at Pompeii in the first century AD. The Campanians surrendered their territory to Roman authority in 343 BC. The emperor Augustus joined Campania to Latium, which thereby acquired the former name, the Campagna of today.

Campus Martius ('field of Mars'), at Rome, the park and recreation ground of the Romans. Situated outside and to the north-west of the city boundary, in early times it was the exercise ground of Roman armies and the meeting-place of the *comitia centuriata*. It took its name from an altar to Mars erected there. Public buildings were gradually erected on it, and in 221 BC the censor C. Flaminius constructed there the circus that bore his name. Later, in 52 BC, Pompey built close to this the first permanent theatre in Rome. In the late republic and during the empire imposing buildings and colonnades were erected there.

Canacē, in Greek myth, daughter of Aeolus and Enaretē. She fell incestuously in love with her brother Macareus, and for this reason was put to death by her father, or, according to some accounts, committed suicide.

Candau'lēs, king of Lydia, killed by *Gyges *c.*685 BC.

canē'phori, 'basket-bearers', in Greece, maidens who bore baskets on their heads in religious processions; in particular, those from noble families who did so in the procession to the temple of Athena Polias at the *Panathenaea at Athens, and who were required to be chaste. To be rejected as unsuitable, as *Harmodius' sister was by Hipparchus, was a grave insult. The baskets contained all that was needed in the sacrificial ceremony.

Canī'nius Re'bilus, Roman senator who achieved fame when Julius Caesar appointed him consul at noon on the last day of the year 45 BC for the remainder of the day (the consul of that year having died on his last day of office). This was the consulship in which, according to

Cicero's joke, no one breakfasted and the consul never slept.

Cannae, village in Apulia in Italy, the scene of a great defeat inflicted on the Romans by Hannibal in 216 BC. The consul Aemilius Paulus and (it was said) 50,000 Romans and their allies were killed in the battle. See PUNIC WARS.

canons, selective lists of Greek authors, dating from ancient times. By the mid-fourth century BC it was recognized at Athens that there were only three outstanding tragic dramatists, Aeschylus, Sophocles, and Euripides, who comprised the tragic canon, but the first authoritative lists, at least of the poets, seem to have been drawn up by the Hellenistic scholars, *Aristophanes of Byzantium and *Aristarchus, in the third and second centuries BC. These lists can only be reconstructed from later references and there is no unanimous agreement on their contents, but it seems clear that they named as the best *iambographers Archilochus, Hipponax, and Semonides; as the best epic poets Homer and Hesiod; as the best writers of Old Comedy Eupolis, Cratinus, and Aristophanes; and of lyric poetry Pindar, Bacchylides, Sappho, Anacreon, Stesichorus, Simonides, Ibycus, Alcman, and Alcaeus. Lists of orators, historians, and philosophers were subsequently compiled, although only that of the Attic orators rivalled in fame the lists of the poets. The ten best Attic orators were deemed to be Antiphon, Lysias, Andocides, Isocrates, Isaeus, Demosthenes, Aeschines, Lycurgus, Hypereides, and Deinarchus. The authors themselves were called in Greek, *hoi enkrithentes*, 'those selected', and in Latin, *classici*, i.e. 'of the first class' (see also CLASSIC), but there was no term for 'selective list' until the German-Dutch scholar David Ruhnken in 1768 originated the use of 'canon' in the sense (Gk. *kanonĕs*—originally 'rods', then carpenters' 'rules', hence metaphorically 'standards of excellence').

ca'ntica, in Roman comedy and particularly in Plautus, the parts that were sung or recited to a musical accompaniment. They were an invention of Roman

dramatists. See COMEDY, ROMAN 2 (at the end).

cantō'res Euphoriō'nis, see EUPHORION 2.

Căpănē'us, in Greek myth, one of the *Seven against Thebes. He climbed the walls of Thebes boasting that not even Zeus would stop him, and was destroyed by Zeus' thunderbolt. His wife Evadne committed suicide by throwing herself on to his funeral pyre.

Cape'lla, Martiā'nus, see MARTIANUS CAPELLA.

Capitō'lium or **mons Capitōlī'nus,** the Capitoline hill, one of the hills of Rome; it had two peaks, the south-west summit known as the Capitol and the northern one known as the *arx* ('citadel'). However, these two last terms are used indiscriminately by ancient as well as modern writers to signify the whole hill as well as one or other of the summits. From earliest times the hill was used not so much for habitation as for a citadel and a religious centre. The Capitol was the site of the temple to Iuppiter Optimus Maximus, 'Jupiter best and greatest', and his companions, the goddesses Juno and Minerva; it was therefore the most sacred part of Rome. According to tradition it was begun by the king Tarquin and dedicated in the first year of the republic, 509 BC. Here sacrifice was offered by magistrates on taking office, and by victorious generals in a *triumph. It was burnt in 83 BC but subsequently rebuilt. On the Capitol also stood the ancient temple of *Jupiter Feretrius, associated with an oak-tree, and reputedly founded by Romulus. The *Tarpeian Rock lay close to the Capitol. For the legend of the saving of the Capitol from the Gauls by the sacred geese see MANLIUS CAPITOLINUS.

Captī'vī ('prisoners of war'), Roman comedy by *Plautus, the Greek original of which has not survived. There are no women in the play, and the characters are more high-minded than is usual in Plautus.

One of the two sons of Hegio has been taken prisoner by the Eleans; the other was kidnapped when a child by a slave and has not been heard of since. Some

Eleans have now been taken prisoner in a war and Hegio has bought two of them, Philocrates and his slave Tyndarus, in the hope of effecting an exchange for his captured son. The slave is to be sent to Elis to negotiate, but he secretly changes identity with his master in order to release him. The trick is revealed unintentionally by an Elean fellow-prisoner and Hegio, thinking that he will not now recover his son, sends Tyndarus loaded with fetters to work in the quarries. Presently Philocrates returns bringing with him Hegio's captive son and the slave who stole his second son. The slave reveals that the boy had been sold to the father of Philocrates and is in fact Tyndarus. The dramatic ironies and the dignified behaviour of the two prisoners make this one of Plautus' most interesting plays.

Ca'pua, in western Italy, the chief city of *Campania, to which it gave its name, and famous for its luxury. In 216 BC after the Roman defeat at Cannae in the *Punic Wars it went over to the Carthaginian side, but was recaptured by Rome in 211 and severely punished: its leading citizens were beheaded, the others exiled, and its territory became the property of the Roman state.

Caraca'lla, nickname of Aurelius Antoninus, Roman emperor AD 211–17; it was derived from the long, hooded Celtic cloak which he introduced. The son of Lucius Septimius Severus and *Julia Domna, he was mentally unstable, and murdered his younger brother Geta. His most significant act was to grant citizenship to all free inhabitants of the Roman empire in 212.

Carā'tacus (the spelling Caractacus is incorrect), in Welsh, 'Caradoc', British king AD 42–51, the son of Cunobelinus (Shakespeare's Cymbeline). After the death of his father and brother and the capture by the Romans of his capital Camulodunum (Colchester) in AD 43, Caratacus escaped to Wales and organized resistance to Rome. After being again defeated in 51 he fled to Cartimandua, queen of the Brigantes in Yorkshire, but she handed him over to

the Romans. Thereafter he lived in honourable captivity in Rome.

Carau'sius (Marcus Aurēlius Mausaeus Carausius), general from the Low Countries who in AD 286 or 287 seized the provinces of *Britain.

Ca'ria, region in south-west Asia Minor south of the river Maeander, inhabited largely by a people who claimed to be indigenous, but including the Dorian Greek cities of Cnidus and Halicarnassus. Under the rule of *Mausolus in the fourth century BC the country became thoroughly Hellenized. Carian *hoplite soldiers of the seventh century BC are said to have been the first to fight as mercenaries.

Cari'stia, Roman family feast. See PARENTALIA.

Carmen Saeculā're, choral hymn in the sapphic metre written by *Horace in 17 BC at the command of the emperor Augustus, to be performed at the *ludi saeculares ('secular games') by a choir of twenty-seven boys and twenty-seven girls. A marble inscription recording the ceremony and the part played by Horace still survives. The ode is in the form of a prayer addressed to Apollo and Diana, and the achievements of Augustus are commemorated.

Carme'ntis or **Carme'nta,** in Roman myth, a prophetic goddess, mother of *Evander the first settler at Rome. She may have been a water-goddess, and she was certainly a goddess of protection in childbirth, worshipped by matrons. A minor *flamen was assigned to her, and her festival, the Carmentalia, was on 11 and 15 January. It was said to have been inaugurated by the senate in the third century BC to mark the successful protest of Roman women who refused to have children until the senate restored their right, recently taken away from them, to ride in carriages (see CAMILLUS). One of the gates of Rome near the foot of the Capitoline hill was named after her, the Porta Carmentalis.

Carnē'a (Karneia), festival held at Sparta and in other Doric states at harvest time, from which the Doric name of the month Karneios (August–Septem-

ber) is derived. It was held in honour of
Apollo, who had probably ousted some
earlier god Karnos or Karneios. It in part
symbolized the military life of Sparta, but
it also had a rural character, and included
a race between boys carrying bunches of
grapes. A musical contest was added,
which attracted poets and musicians from
all parts of Greece.

Carne'adēs, c.213–129 BC, of Cyrene
(North Africa), an important Greek
philosopher, a *Sceptic whose headship
of the *Academy at Athens marks a new
turn in the development of Scepticism
(which had been originated by *Pyrrho in
the fourth century BC and taken up by
Arcesilaus in the third). He was already
head of the Academy in 155 BC, when he
was sent as one of three philosophers on
an embassy to Rome; there he won fame
for giving, on two consecutive days, first a
lecture in praise of justice and then
another in which it was proved not to be a
virtue but a civil compact to maintain
society. He followed the fashion of his
Sceptic predecessors and published
nothing, but his arguments were recorded
by his pupils, notably by Clitomachus,
through whom they have survived in the
philosophical writings of *Cicero ((1) 5).
His influence was considerable. He
argued at length against the Stoic belief
that knowledge about the world was
attainable if it was based upon sense
impressions which recorded the facts (or
objects) correctly, and that the percipient
could be sure that the sense impressions
were correct through their complete conformity with the facts perceived. Carneades did not believe that the percipient
could be sure; sense impressions have no
particular characteristics by which one
may distinguish those that are correct
from those that are not. Therefore he
thought, like Arcesilaus, that knowledge
was unattainable, but he allowed that
some sense impressions are 'persuasive',
i.e. seem probable, while others are not.
For the purposes of life we have to
assume the truth, or the falsity, of many
sense impressions, but we should not
assert it, because the truth about facts or
objects may actually be quite different
from our perception of them.

Carneades attacked many Stoic and
Epicurean dogmas, exposing their
improbabilities and the often shaky arguments on which they were based. The
Stoics modified some of their theories in
the light of his criticism. After Carneades
the tradition of (moderate) Scepticism in
the Academy was continued by Philo of
Larisa (head of the Academy 109 BC).
Cicero declared himself an adherent of
the 'New' Academy of Arcesilaus, Carneades, and Philo.

Carrhae, city in northern Mesopotamia,
scene of the defeat of the Roman general
M. Licinius *Crassus by the Parthians in
53 BC.

Carthage, city occupying a strong strategic position on the Tunisian coast of
North Africa, founded by colonists from
Phoenician Tyre, traditionally in 814 BC
though the earliest archaeological
evidence dates from a century later. For
its foundation legend see DIDO. It gradually outstripped other Phoenician cities in
North Africa (Utica was the chief rival)
and became the centre of a powerful
empire whose wealth was based on agriculture and commerce; it carried on trade
all along the coasts of the Mediterranean
and maintained control of sea-routes to
the west, especially the important tin-
routes. Carthage eventually ruled all the
islands of the Western Mediterranean,
but it never achieved complete control
over *Sicily. Greeks and Carthaginians
fought over the island for three centuries,
and Carthaginian interests also came into
conflict with those of Rome, leading to
the *Punic Wars, which began in 264 BC.
When they ended in 146 BC Carthage was
utterly destroyed. Rome decreed that no
house should be built nor crop planted,
but the city was refounded by Julius
Caesar in 44 BC and became the capital of
the enlarged province of *Africa. By the
second century AD Carthage had become
the largest city in the west after Rome.
Under the empire Carthage became first
a famous educational centre, especially
for law and rhetoric, and then a focus for
Christianity in the west, especially in the
time of Tertullian and Cyprian (second
and third centuries AD). Carthage fell to
the Vandals in 439 and became the
capital of their king Gaiseric, but after
the victory of Belisarius in 533 it

remained loyal to the Roman empire in the east until the Arab conquest at the end of the seventh century.

Cartima'ndua, British queen of the *Brigantes who made a treaty with the Roman emperor Claudius. In AD 51 she handed over the fugitive *Caratacus to Rome. She divorced her husband Venutius and married one of his officers, but in 68 Venutius defeated Cartimandua and regained the kingdom. In order to rescue the queen the Romans advanced further north into Britain.

Caryǎ'tids (Karyātiděs), the Greek name for columns carved in the form of women in long drapery. The most famous are the six which supported the roof of the small porch on the west end of the *Erechtheum, one of which is now in the British Museum. The derivation of the name is unknown; one suggestion is that it means 'maidens of Caryae', a place in Laconia, and it is perhaps connected with the girl dancers who performed there in honour of Artemis.

Casca. Two brothers so named joined the conspiracy against Julius Caesar in 44 BC. One of them, Publius Longus, was the first to strike Caesar at his assassination. Both killed themselves after the defeat of the republicans at Philippi in 42 BC.

Ca'sina, Roman comedy by *Plautus, adapted from a play by the Greek writer of New Comedy, Diphilus (see COMEDY, GREEK 6).

An elderly Athenian and his son have both fallen in love with Casina, a slave-girl who has been rescued from exposure as a baby and brought up in their household. The father wants to have her married to his bailiff, the son to his own attendant Chalinus, each for his own purpose, while the father's wife, aware of her husband's scheme, plots on her son's behalf. Lots are drawn to settle the matter and the father wins, but at the wedding the bailiff is fobbed off with Chalinus dressed as a bride, who beats both bailiff and father. Casina is found to be a free-born Athenian and marries the son.

Cassa'nder (Kassandros), c.358–297 BC, Macedonian, son of the general Antipater who helped Alexander the Great to succeed to the throne of Macedon after the death of his father Philip II. Cassander was sent to Alexander at Babylon in the last months of the latter's life; he seems to have personally disliked Alexander. After the latter's death he was involved in the power-struggles among the generals and eventually procured the deaths of Alexander's mother, wife, and son. He managed to establish himself as his father's successor and ruled over Macedon and most of Greece, but spent the rest of his life trying to keep his territory. He founded the city of Thessalonika (Salonika) and rebuilt Thebes.

Cassa'ndra (also called Alexandra), in Greek myth, the prophetic daughter of *Priam, king of Troy, and Hecuba his wife. For Homer, who knows nothing of her prophetic gifts, she is the most beautiful of Priam's daughters. It was according to a later tradition that she was loved by Apollo and given the gift of prophecy, but when she refused his love he condemned her to the fate of always prophesying truthfully but never being believed. She appears in Greek tragedy in this role, vainly foretelling the fall of Troy. When Troy was captured, Ajax the Locrian, son of Oileus, found her in the temple of Athena clinging to the sacred statue of the goddess (the *Palladium), dragged her away, and raped her. To expiate this sacrilege the Locrians were obliged to send two maidens to Troy every year for a thousand years to serve as slaves in Athena's temple; if they were caught by the inhabitants before reaching the temple they were executed. This obligation continued into the second century BC. After the sack of Troy Cassandra was awarded to the Greek commander *Agamemnon as his concubine, but on their return to Mycenae she was murdered by his wife Clytemnestra.

Cassiodō'rus (Flāvius Magnus Aurēlius Cassiodōrus), c. AD 490–583, Christian Roman statesman and writer. Born in south Italy the son of a praetorian prefect of Theodoric, king of the *Goths, he too served Theodoric, was consul in 514, and pursued a public career until the 540s. He then retired to his estates to devote himself to scholarship and the Christian life, as a monk in the monastery he founded at

Vivarium in Bruttium (Calabria). He published twelve books of his *Variae epistulae* ('various letters'), the most important letters and edicts he had written for the Gothic kings to the notable personages of the day, and a valuable source to us for sixth-century history. Among his other writings were a *History of the Goths*, of which a summary survives, a brief history of the world down to AD 519, very popular in medieval times, and some grammatical works. The chief literary work of his later life was the *Institutiones* ('institutions'), a guide to the religious and secular education of his monks, the secular part being based on the *seven liberal arts. It also gives instruction about the copying of manuscripts, in which Vivarium was very active, but not, as far as can be seen, in the area of classical Latin texts. Nevertheless Cassiodorus played a part in the transmission of a literate culture to the western medieval world. Compare BOETHIUS.

Cassiope'ia or **Cassiepeia**, in Greek myth, wife of Cepheus king of the Ethiopians; she boasted that her daughter *Andromeda (or possibly she herself) was more beautiful than the Nereids; in consequence Poseidon sent a sea-serpent to ravage the land, to which Andromeda was to be sacrificed until *Perseus saved her life. After their deaths Cassiopeia and her family became constellations.

Cassite'rides ('tin islands'), name given by the Greeks to all the unknown lands in the north-west of Europe producing tin, but probably with special reference to the west of England and the Scillies.

Ca'ssius, Gaius Longī'nus, one of the murderers of Julius Caesar in 44 BC; he was *quaestor to M. *Crassus at the battle of Carrhae in 53 BC where he succeeded in extricating a division of the Roman army from the disaster. He supported Pompey in the civil war and was given a naval command, but on hearing of Pompey's defeat at Pharsalus in 48 BC, abandoned the war and later obtained Caesar's pardon. He was *praetor peregrinus* in 44 when he played a leading part in the conspiracy against Caesar. After the assassination he had to withdraw from Rome and in the senate's dis-

tribution of provinces was allocated Syria, where he defeated Caesar's supporter Dolabella. After Caesar's murderers were outlawed in the autumn of 43, he joined Brutus in Thrace to meet the triumvirs. In the first battle of Philippi in 42 his camp was captured and he ordered his slave to kill him.

Ca'ssius Dīo, Coccēiā'nus, also known as Dio Cassius, *c.* AD 150–235, Roman historian from Nicaea in Bithynia. He was twice consul at Rome and governor of Africa and Dalmatia. He wrote a small book on dreams and portents, and a history of the civil wars of 193–7 (both lost), but his major work was the history of Rome (written in Greek) in eighty books, from the landing of Aeneas in Italy down to AD 229. Books 36–54, covering the years 68–10 BC, survive complete, books 55–60 (9 BC–AD 46) in an abbreviated form, and books 79–80 (AD 217–20) in part. The rest of the history has to be pieced together from the summary descriptions of Byzantine historians of the eleventh and twelfth centuries. He is an important witness for contemporary events and a valuable commentator on the political aspects of history through his own experience, but he is unreliable about republican institutions and the style is coloured by his rhetorical training.

Cassivellau'nus, king of the British tribe of Catuvellauni, the most powerful of the southern tribes, and commander of the British forces that resisted Julius Caesar's second invasion of Britain in 54 BC. When Caesar discovered and captured his stronghold, perhaps at Wheathampstead in Hertfordshire, Cassivellaunus was forced to make terms.

Castā'lia, in Greek myth, the nymph who, when pursued by Apollo, threw herself into the spring on Mount Parnassus near Delphi. The spring was held sacred to Apollo and the Muses. All who wished to consult the Delphic Oracle were required to purify themselves in its waters. It may still be seen a little to the north-east of *Delphi. To the Romans, 'drinking the waters of Castalia' signified poetic inspiration, since Apollo was the god of poetry.

Castor and Pollux (Gk. Polydeukēs), twin sons of Leda, brothers to Helen of Troy. For their story see DIOSCURI.

catalectic, catalexis, see METRE, GREEK 6.

Catale'pton, see APPENDIX VIRGILIANA.

Catalogue of Women (Gk. Ē(h)ōīai, Lat. Ē(h)ōeae), Greek hexameter poem ascribed to *Hesiod in antiquity but probably not earlier than the sixth century BC. It was a continuation of his *Theogony* in five books, containing accounts of the women who had been loved by the gods and become the mothers of heroes. Some parts of the work survive in quotation and in papyrus fragments. The title was derived from the Greek words introducing each new group of heroines, ē hoiai ('or such as . . .').

Categories (*Katēgoriai*, Lat. *Categoriae*, 'predicates'), one of the six logical works which comprise Aristotle's *Organon* (see ARISTOTLE 4 (i)), a treatise on the ten different types of predicate, or classes, into which the attributes of things (e.g. their substance or their size) may be divided.

catharsis, see POETICS.

Ca'tiline (Lucius Sergius Catilīna) d. 62 BC, a Roman patrician of disreputable character from a relatively obscure family, legate of Sulla, who rose to political prominence in the 60s of the first century BC. He was praetor in 68, governor of Africa for the following two years, and on his return was prosecuted for extortion and so prevented from standing for the consulship until he was finally acquitted. He was defeated for the consulship of 63 by Cicero, who captured the vote of the *optimates*; they might otherwise have supported Catiline but were alarmed by what his intentions might be. He was exploiting the widespread unrest in Italy at that time among many classes of society and proposing the cancelling of debts, and was said to have had the support of Julius Caesar. Defeated for the consulship of 62 also, he laid plans for revolution, against which Cicero could not take action until he had manœuvred Catiline into leaving Rome,

and had obtained written evidence to convince the senate of Catiline's intentions. The *senatus consultum ultimum* was passed late in 63 and the leaders of the conspiracy still in Rome were arrested and executed. Catiline was now in open rebellion against the state; the consul Antonius marched out with an army, and defeated and killed him early in 62. Catiline's severest critics, Cicero and Sallust, credit him with bravery and qualities of leadership, but his actions were prompted by a desperate ambition. See also CICERO (I) 2.

Cāto, Marcus Po'rcius. I. 'The Elder' or 'the Censor', 234–149 BC, Roman statesman and moralist. He was born of peasant stock at Tusculum, fought in the Second *Punic War as military tribune, and embarked on a political career under the patronage of L. Valerius Flaccus who was impressed by Cato's stern morality. He was quaestor in Sicily, and returning to Rome via Sardinia he is said to have found the poet Ennius there and brought him to Rome. He was praetor in 198 and consul with Flaccus in 195, when he unsuccessfully opposed the repeal of the Oppian law limiting women's finery. He was governor in Spain where he won a *triumph for his military operations. During the 180s Cato was prominent in attacking the *Scipios, and hostile to their attempts to introduce Greek culture to Rome (although this did not prevent him from learning Greek himself in his later years). He was elected to the censorship in 184, an office he held with a severity which became proverbial. He applied himself to reforming the lax morals of the Roman nobility and checking the extravagance of the wealthy. His ideal was a return to the primitive simplicity of a mainly agricultural state. Late in life he went as a commissioner to Carthage and was so impressed by the danger to Rome from her reviving prosperity that, henceforth, when asked for his opinion in the senate, whatever the subject under debate, he always declared 'Carthage must be destroyed' (*Carthago delenda est*). He had the satisfaction of seeing the Third Punic War under way before his death.

Cato wrote treatises for his son on

varied topics. *Origines* ('beginnings') in seven books dealt with the foundation legends of Rome and the Italian cities (whence the title), and the history of recent wars. This discursive work (now lost) was the first of its kind in the Latin language (earlier Roman annalists wrote in Greek; see HISTORIOGRAPHY, ROMAN), and as well as stimulating the study of history it laid the foundation of Latin prose style. He wrote with greater sophistication than is suggested by his precept, *rem tene: verba sequentur* ('stick to the meaning: the words will follow'). His *De agri cultura* ('on agriculture'), sometimes known as *De re rustica*, which in large part survives, deals with the cultivation of vines, olives, and fruit, and cattle-grazing for profit, the precepts and recipes based on his experience, with prayers and spells included as well. His advice to sell off a slave when he is too old to be profitable is notorious. Cato was also a successful orator; one hundred and fifty of his speeches were known to Cicero. The surviving fragments show shrewdness and wit, honesty and simplicity. He kept his vigour into old age, and Cicero makes him the principal interlocutor in his dialogue *De senectute*. For an anecdote concerning his views on divination see *De divinatione*.

Dicta Catōnis, 'the sayings of (Marcus) Cato', a collection of Latin moral maxims in prose and (mostly) verse, was an immensely popular school-book in the Middle Ages, translated into several European languages. From the sixteenth to the nineteenth century, editions of the work have called the author, erroneously, 'Dionysius Cato'.

2. 'Of Utica' (Lat. Uticensis), 95–46 BC, great-grandson of Cato (1), a man of unbending Stoic principles and absolute integrity, who was impelled by his devotion to the Roman tradition and his desire to emulate the virtue of his great-grandfather to support senatorial government and the republican cause. He was influential in persuading the senate to execute Catiline's fellow-conspirators in 63 BC (see CICERO (1) 2), accusing Julius Caesar of being an accomplice, and was the chief antagonist of the so-called 'first triumvirate' of Caesar, Pompey, and Crassus. He was so much of an annoyance to them that they arranged for Clodius to propose a law which sent him away to annex Cyprus. After his return Cato continued to oppose the triumvirs, and when Pompey became sole consul in 52 Cato felt that Pompey had abandoned republican principles. He withdrew from public life and, after the civil war began in 49, despaired of Rome. Nevertheless he held Sicily for the senate. When Caesar's supporter Curio landed, he withdrew to join Pompey, but was not present at the battle of Pharsalus. He proceeded to Africa, where his march around the Great Syrtis (gulf of Sirte) became famous as a feat of endurance. There he heard of Pompey's death and, subsequently, of Caesar's victory over the senatorial party at Thapsus. All Africa, except Utica, surrendered to Caesar, and Cato, after seeing to the safety of his friends, committed suicide, having spent the previous night reading Plato's *Phaedo*. One letter of his survives in Cicero's correspondence, civilly refusing to use his influence in procuring Cicero a triumph. His death conferred its own nobility on the losing republican side, to inspire Romans with a republican ideal long after republicanism was dead. Virgil in the *Aeneid* (book 8) makes him a judge in Elysium.

Catu'llus, Gaius Vale'rius, *c.*84–*c.*54 BC, Roman poet, born in Verona, son of a wealthy man whose acquaintances included Julius Caesar. As a young man he went to Rome and joined the fashionable literary circle (see NEOTERICS), addressing poems to Cicero, Cornelius Nepos, and Hortensius among others, and freely insulting Caesar and Mamurra. Very little is known of his life except what can be gleaned from his poems: that he spent a year (57 to 56) with his friend *Cinna in Bithynia on the staff of the governor, Gaius *Memmius; that he saw his brother's grave in the Troad; that he returned from abroad to a villa at Sirmio on Lake Garda. At Rome he fell in love with a married woman of some social standing whom he calls Lesbia, but whose real name was probably *Clodia. Some poems suggest that she deserted Catullus for Cicero's young protégé *Caelius. Catullus addressed twenty-five poems to Lesbia which chronicle his love affair from an idyllic beginning to final disillusionment.

His poems fall into three groups. 1–60 are short pieces, in hendecasyllables or other lyric metres (iambics, scazons, and in one case glyconics) or in elegiacs (see METRE). They are varied in subject and manner, embracing incidents of daily life, expressions of friendship, satires, political lampoons, love poems, even a hymn to Diana; poem 51 is a translation of an extant poem by the Greek poet Sappho. This collection was for the most part made by the author and shows traces of a careful arrangement. The second group, 61–64, are longer poems: 61 is an epithalamium for a friend, 62 another wedding song, 63 an extraordinary metrical feat, a poem in galliambics (see METRE, LATIN 3 (iii) d) on the legend of Attis, a young man who, in religious frenzy for the goddess Cybelē, emasculates himself and lives to regret it; 64 is an *epyllion on the marriage of Peleus and Thetis, consisting mostly of a digression on the story of Ariadne. The first four poems of the third group, 65–68, are longer elegiac poems, 66 being a translation of *Callimachus' poem, *The Lock of *Berenice*; 69–116 form a sequence of epigrams in elegiacs on a wide range of subjects. The second and third groups of poems were perhaps collected and arranged by an editor. The first and third groups both contain love poems, expressing happiness and disillusionment, and witty and malicious occasional poems, but the poems of the third group are not perhaps so adventurous or experimental; they express the poet's feelings in more traditional Roman terms. Groups one and two were more obviously written under the influence of Hellenistic Greek poetry in racy, often erudite language (the blend of the fashionable colloquial and the obscure is peculiarly Catullus' own), sometimes ingeniously fitted to metres hitherto purely Greek. Catullus was the leading figure among the new poets of the day who were looking for inspiration not to past Romans but to the Greeks, both to the learned, polished poets of the Hellenistic age and to the more direct lyric poets of earlier centuries, such as Sappho. Part of his appeal lies in his versatility, but it is as a love poet that he is chiefly remem-

bered. He was the first ancient poet to describe the progress of one deeply felt love affair, and in this he exerted a wide influence on his successors, on Tibullus, Propertius, and Ovid and others whose works are lost. We are fortunate to have his poems, for they nearly perished. The three manuscripts in which they are preserved are descended from the only text of the poems known to have survived into the fourteenth century. See TEXTS, TRANSMISSION OF ANCIENT 6.

Ca'tulus, Quintus Lutā'tius, Roman consul in 102 BC with *Marius and joint victor over the Cimbri in 101 BC, also with Marius. Catulus, resentful of his colleague's greater reputation, became one of his chief opponents. When Marius and Cinna captured Rome in 87 BC they not surprisingly proscribed him (see PROSCRIPTION), and he committed suicide. He was a cultured man, a competent orator— Cicero introduced him into his *De oratore*—and a writer of epigrams, two of which survive. His son of the same name is an interlocutor in Cicero's *Academica*.

Catuvellau'ni, the most powerful tribe in south-east Britain at the time of Julius Caesar's invasions, ruled by *Cassivellaunus.

Caudine Forks (Furculae Caudīnae), the defile of Caudium in Samnium where the Roman army in 321 BC was obliged to surrender to the Samnites—a notorious disaster for Rome. The site has never been certainly identified.

Cavalry Commander, The (*Hipparchikos*), a treatise by the Athenian *Xenophon on the duties of a cavalry commander, perhaps written c.357 BC.

Cēbēs, of Thebes, a Pythagorean philosopher and associate of Socrates who plays an important part in the discussions in Plato's *Phaedo*. In the *Crito* he is one of those who are prepared to help Socrates escape from prison. An allegorical composition on the life of man, known as the *Pinax* ('picture') of Cebes, has been wrongly ascribed to him.

Cecrops, the mythical first king of Athens, sprung from the earth (i.e. aboriginal) and represented as serpent-shaped below the waist. The state of Attica was sometimes called Cecropia after him. By Aglaurus he had three daughters (for their story see ERICHTHONIUS). The contest between Athena and *Poseidon for possession of Attica took place in his reign, and in some accounts he was the judge, awarding the land to Athena.

Ce'lĕus, see DEMETER.

Celsus. 1. Aulus or **Aurelius Cornelius Celsus,** Roman encyclopaedist of whom very little is known. He lived in the reign of the emperor Tiberius (AD 14–37). Of his encyclopaedia, *Artes* ('arts'), eight books, on medicine, survive. After giving a brief history of medicine, which is important for reconstructing Hellenistic doctrines, he surveys the whole field of medical science as it was known at Rome in his day, but without adhering to any one school. Consideration of diet and of the general principles of treatment are followed by a survey of diseases, classified as internal or external, and their treatment, and a discussion of pharmaceutical preparations; the final two books deal with diseases that are to be remedied by surgery, perhaps the most interesting and advanced part of the work. Much of the practice described was not superseded until the nineteenth century. Celsus' book was largely unknown until it was rediscovered and printed in the fifteenth century, from which time it became immensely popular, in part because of the simple and elegant style of the Latin in which it was written.

2. Greek-speaking Platonist philosopher of the second century AD who wrote the first comprehensive attack on Christianity; large parts of it survive in *Origen's reply, *Contra Celsum* ('against Celsus').

Celts, term used by ancient and modern writers to describe a population group occupying in prehistoric and historic times lands mainly north of the Mediterranean, from the Spanish peninsula and the British Isles in the west to Galatia in central Asia Minor (see GALATIANS). Their unity can be recognized from the fact that they had a common speech, evinced in place-names, and from a common artistic style. It is generally thought

that the Celts spread from the region of the Upper Danube during the Bronze Age. Celtic tribes invading from across the Rhine and settling in Gaul came to be known themselves as Gauls. Hence the invaders of Italy who sacked Rome in c.370 BC and who entered the Balkans and raided Delphi in 279 BC and crossed the Hellespont in 278 are referred to either as Celts or as Gauls. The latter gave their name to the territory of Galatia, where Celtic was still spoken in the fifth century AD. The Celts in Europe were overrun by invading Germans crossing the Rhine from the third century BC onwards and by the migrations of the Cimbri and Teutones soon after 120 BC, and so they withdrew from Bohemia and south Germany. They were also conquered by Rome in the Gallic wars and some, e.g. the Belgae, became assimilated to their invaders.

censors, magistrates at Rome, two in number, who were elected every five years but held office for eighteen months only, in order to take the census, i.e. make up the official list of citizens and carry out the solemn purification, *lustrum,* which concluded it and which gave its name to the interval of five years between each purification. The registration of citizens took place in a special building on the Campus Martius. The censors' power and prestige derived from their duty of revising the roll of senators, removing those who had acted against law and morality and replacing them by others. Throughout the middle and late republic the censorship stood at the head of the *cursus honorum,* but its authority was reduced by the legislation of *Sulla.

centaurs, in Greek myth, a race of creatures with the body and legs of a horse but the chest, head, and arms of a man, said to be the offspring of *Ixion and Nephelē ('cloud'). They lived on Mount Pelion in Thessaly, and symbolized for the Greeks the appetites of animal nature and perhaps barbarism. When their neighbours the Lapiths were holding a feast for the wedding of their king Pirithous with Hippodamia, and invited the centaurs, the latter tried to carry off Hippodamia and other women. The centaurs were routed and driven from Thessaly to the Peloponnese. Individual centaurs have myths of their own; see NESSUS, PHOLUS, and CHIRON.

centu'mviri, 'the hundred men', at Rome, a special civil court numbering in fact 105 men during the republic, three from each of the thirty-five tribes, and increased under the empire to 180; these sat as jury for certain trials, mostly relating, it seems, to property and inheritance.

Ce'phalas, see ANTHOLOGY I.

Ce'phalus. 1. In Greek myth, the husband of Procris, daughter of Erechtheus. Eos ('dawn') fell in love with him, causing dissension between husband and wife. Artemis (or Minos) gave Procris a hound which always caught its quarry and a spear which never missed its mark; these Procris gave to Cephalus and a reconciliation followed. But Eos made Procris jealous of the time Cephalus spent hunting. Procris hid in a bush to watch him and he, thinking that he heard an animal stir in the bush, hurled his spear and killed her. These two are 'Shafalus' and 'Procrus' mentioned in the Pyramus and Thisbe playlet of Shakespeare's *A Midsummer Night's Dream*.
2. The old man in Book I of Plato's *Republic*, the father of the Attic orator *Lysias.

Cēphī'sus or **Cephissus. 1.** The main river of the plain of Athens, rising in Mount Parnes, flowing past Athens about 3 km. (2 miles) to the west and into the bay of Phalerum. Its clay bed provided the material for Athenian pottery.
2. The main river of Phocis and Boeotia, emptying into the lake Copaïs.

Ceramī'cus (Kerameikos), the potters' quarter at Athens, an area north-west of the Acropolis. When the Themistoclean city wall was built this quarter was divided into the Inner and Outer Ceramicus. The part outside the walls was used as a burial ground; the agora was included in the inner part.

Ce'rberus, in Greek myth, monstrous dog guarding the entrance to the Underworld, the offspring of *Typhon and *Echidna. He had three (or fifty) heads and a mane or tail of snakes. As one of the labours imposed on him by Eurystheus, Heracles dragged Cerberus out of the Underworld, showed him to Eurystheus, and then returned him. Aeneas on his descent was told to drug him with a specially prepared cake: hence the expression 'a sop to Cerberus'.

Ce'rcidas, *c.*290–*c.*220 BC, Greek poet and statesman from Megalopolis in Arcadia of whose poems only seven fragments survive.

Cercō'pes, in Greek myth, a pair of monkey-like dwarfs whose mother Theia told them to beware of a certain Melampyges ('black-buttocks'). *Heracles caught them trying to steal his armour and slung them upside down from a pole borne across his shoulders. They found themselves staring straight at his buttocks, covered with black hair, and thus understood the warning. Their jokes at his hairiness so amused Heracles that he let them go.

Cērēs, an Italian divinity representing the generative power of nature, in later times identified with the Greek *Demeter. In cult she was associated with *Tellus, the earth-goddess. Her worship at Rome was very ancient, as is clear from the existence of a *flamen cerialis* and the occurrence of the festival of the Cerialia (held on 19 April) in the calendars, but very little is known of it. Her most famous cult was that on the Aventine hill at Rome. In 496 BC under the stress of famine the Sibylline books were consulted and recommended the introduction of the worship of the Greek gods Demeter, Korē, and Iacchus, to be identified with the Roman Ceres, Liber, and Libera. The temple was completed in 493 and became a centre of plebeian activities. Games were instituted which became a prominent feature of the Cerialia. Little is known about the ritual of the festival, except the peculiar custom of tying lighted brands to the tails of a number of foxes which were then let loose in the Circus Maximus. As a deity of the earth Ceres also received sacrifice after a funeral, as a means of purifying the house of the deceased.

Cē'yx, in Greek myth, husband of *Alcyonē.

Chae'reas and Calli'rrhŏē, title of a Greek *novel by Chariton.

Chaeronē'a (Khairōneia), in Boeotia, the scene of the defeat of the Thebans and Athenians by *Philip II of Macedon in 338 BC, commemorated by the erection of a large stone lion; by whom or when is not known. The lion was smashed in the Greek War of Independence (1821-2) and restored in the late nineteenth century. Under it were found the bones of some two hundred and fifty-four men, perhaps of the *Sacred Band. Chaeronea was also the scene of the defeat of Mithridates by Sulla in 86 BC, and the birthplace of Plutarch.

Chalcē'don, Megarian colony on the Asiatic side of the Bosporus opposite Byzantium, called by the Delphic Oracle 'the city of the blind' because its colonizers missed the then unoccupied and superior site of Byzantium across the channel.

Chalci'dicē, promontory in Macedonia between the Thermaic and Strymonic Gulfs terminating in three smaller peninsulas. It was first colonized by Chalcis in the eighth century BC.

Chalci'dic League. A confederacy formed by the cities of *Chalcidicē, after revolting from the *Delian League and Athenian imperialism in 432 BC. The capital was at *Olynthus. In the 380s the League expanded to embrace part of Macedonia including the capital Pella, and its ambitions grew to include its less willing neighbours, by force if necessary. Sparta, asked to intervene by some of the threatened cities, forced the League to capitulate in 379 and become subordinate allies. The Chalcidians soon joined a league with Athens, but were conquered by Philip II of Macedon in 348 BC.

Chalcis, chief city in Euboea, on its west coast, and separated from the mainland of Greece only by the narrow strait of the Euripus. It was an important link with trading routes from Greece to the east in the eighth century BC. Chalcis planted colonies in Italy, Sicily, and the north Aegean and became a great manufacturing and trading city, but was subject to Athens during the greater part of the fifth and fourth centuries BC.

Chāos ('gaping void'), in Greek mythical cosmogony the first created being. It was scarcely personified at all but was that out of which came the primeval deities Gaia (Earth), Tartarus, Erebus (Darkness), and Nyx (Night).

Charactē'rĕs, see THEOPHRASTUS.

Chara'xus, brother of *Sappho.

Chārēs, c.400–c.325 BC, famous Athenian general and commander of naval operations, notably against Philip II of Macedon. His troops were mercenaries whose pay he had to find himself. He fought at *Chaeronea and continued to hold commands until his death.

Chariclē'a and Theā'genēs, alternative title of the novel *Aethiopica* by Heliodorus. See NOVEL 1.

Cha'rites (sing. Charis), see GRACES.

Cha'riton, author of a Greek novel, *Chaereas and Callirrhoe*; see NOVEL 1.

Cha'rmidēs, title of a dialogue by *Plato in which Charmides plays a large part. He was from an aristocratic Athenian family, cousin of Critias, uncle of Plato, and friend of Socrates. He took part in the oligarchic revolution of 404 BC and died with Critias fighting against Thrasybulus in 403.

Chāron. 1. In Greek myth, the ferryman who conveyed the dead in his boat across the river Styx to their final abode in the Underworld, provided they had received the proper rites of burial and paid the fare (an obol, placed in the mouth of the corpse). He is unknown to Homer, but is mentioned by Aeschylus, and plays memorable parts in the *Frogs* of Aristophanes and book 6 of Virgil's *Aeneid*.

2. Of Lampsacus, see LOGOGRAPHERS (1).

Chary'bdis, in Greek legend, a whirlpool in a narrow channel of water, traditionally sited in the Straits of Messina. Homer (*Odyssey* 12) pictured it as a female monster, daughter of Poseidon and Gaia, who sucked in seawater and spewed it out three times a day. The equally dangerous *Scylla was on the opposite shore, so that Odysseus had to decide which to avoid as he sailed between them. The two have become proverbial to describe equally unpleasant alternatives.

Cheiron, see CHIRON.

Che'rsonese (chersonēsos, 'peninsula'). 1. Thracian Chersonese (Gallipoli), projecting into the north-east of the Aegean Sea, separated from Asia Minor by the Hellespont. It was important as a wheat-growing district and more especially because it lay on a main route between Europe and Asia and so controlled the corn-supply from the Crimea. It was acquired by the elder *Miltiades c.560 BC and remained a family possession until the younger Miltiades abandoned it to the Persians in 493 BC. After the Persian Wars the Athenians planted *cleruchies there. It was threatened by *Philip II of Macedon, and this threat was one of the chief grounds of hostility between Athens and Macedon. It was finally ceded to Philip in 338 BC.
2. Tauric Chersonese, in the Black Sea, the modern Crimea.

Chersonese, On the, political speech by Demosthenes. See DEMOSTHENES (2) 4.

chia'smus (from the form of the Greek letter chi, X), figure of speech in which the terms in the second of two parallel phrases are in reverse order to the corresponding terms in the first; e.g. odit *populus Romanus* privatam *luxuriam*, publican *magnificentiam* diligit (Cicero, *Pro Murena* 32): 'The Roman people *hate private* luxury but *public* display they *love*.'

Chilon, *ephor at Sparta in 536 BC, famous for his wisdom. His exact contribution to the political life of sixth-century Sparta is uncertain but he may have helped to extend Spartan influence through the *Peloponnesian League. He was included among the *Seven Sages of Greece.

Chi'maera, in Greek myth, a fire-breathing monster with the head of a lion, body of a she-goat, and tail of a snake, the offspring of *Typhon and *Echidna. It was killed by *Bellerophon, mounted on the winged horse Pegasus.

Chios, large island in the Aegean Sea off the coast of Asia Minor, settled by Greeks from Ionia. It became part of the Persian empire under Cyrus in the sixth century BC and its citizens fought bravely in the unsuccessful Ionian revolt against Persia in the 490s. As a member of the *Delian League it remained loyal to Athens until 413 BC. At its defection, Athens laid waste the island but failed to take the city. It was allied to Athens again in the first half of the fourth century BC, but again revolted and regained its independence in 354. The island was famed in antiquity for its wine and figs, and had a distinguished literary tradition, claiming to be the birthplace of Homer; see HOMERIDAE.

Chiron (Kheirōn), in Greek myth, a *centaur, but, unlike the others, the son of Philyra and Cronus; he owed his shape, half man and half horse, to the fact that Cronus assumed the shape of a horse when he approached Philyra so as to escape the jealous notice of his wife Rhea. In consequence Chiron's nature was different from that of the other centaurs; he was wise and kind, and instructed by Apollo and Artemis he was skilled in medicine, music, hunting, and the art of prophecy. He became the tutor of some of the most famous of the Greek heroes, Asclepius, Jason, and Achilles. He was the grandfather (through his daughter Endeis) of Peleus, saving him by restoring his sword when he was abandoned weaponless by Acastus on Mount Pelion, the Thessalian home of the centaurs. Chiron also helped him to win his bride Thetis. Like the other centaurs he was driven out of Thessaly into the Peloponnese by the Lapiths. When Heracles came in pursuit of the Erymanthian boar and was involved in a fight with the centaurs, one of his poisoned arrows scratched Chiron. Although immortal, Chiron suffered great pain and, wishing to live no longer, transferred his immortality to the Titan Prometheus. Zeus set him in the sky as the constellation Centaurus.

Chloris, see FLORA.

Chŏē'phoroe or **Chŏē'phori** (Khŏēphoroi), 'Libation Bearers', the second tragedy in the *Oresteia* trilogy by Aeschylus.

chŏes, see ANTHESTERIA.

chōlia'mbic (or scazon), in metre, the so-called 'limping iambic' line in which the penultimate syllable, short in an iambic line, is long (see METRE, GREEK 5 (iii)).

choral lyric, see LYRIC POETRY 1.

chorē'gia, at Athens, a form of *liturgy or public service in which individual wealthy citizens were expected to bear the expense of providing a chorus for one or other of the various lyric and dramatic contests (at the *Panathenaea, *Thargelia, *Dionysia, and *Lenaea), and hence were known as *choregoi*. The expense was considerable.

chŏ'riamb, in *metre, the metron $- \cup \cup -$.

chorodida'skalos, in Athens, the trainer of a chorus performing in one of the various lyric and dramatic contests, usually the poet himself. See CHOREGIA.

chōrus (*chŏros*, 'dance'). In Greece the dance was an important part of public religious ceremonies, performed by a troupe to whom the name 'chorus' was also given. By archaic times the chorus sang as well as danced in performances of choral *lyric poetry, usually under a leader. As well as this the chorus had a role in tragedy and comedy. It is generally believed that Attic tragedy had its origin in the kind of choral lyric known as the dithyramb, sung and danced in honour of the god Dionysus (see TRAGEDY 1), and that comedy likewise developed out of the cheerfully insulting songs sung by bands of revellers as they accompanied the *phallus in Dionysiac processions (see COMEDY, GREEK 2). If this is the case, the fact that the chorus continued to play an important role in all fifth-century drama is entirely natural. The chorus sings the lyric passages (which are themselves referred to as 'the choruses') to flute accompaniment. Like the actors the chorus was masked (as in Dionysiac ritual). In tragedy it always performed in character as a group of people involved in the action; the chorus-leader, known as the *coryphaeus* or *hēgemon*, is sometimes made to converse briefly with the characters. Sophocles was said to have raised the number of the tragic chorus from twelve to fifteen, as it remained thereafter. It entered the *orchestra* (see DIONYSUS, THEATRE OF) on the audience's right in quadrangular form, three or five abreast. The chorus-leader stood in the middle of the row nearest to the audience; sometimes this role was taken by the *choregos* (see CHOREGIA). The chorus in Old Comedy comprised twenty-four members and was of central importance, the characters represented often giving the play its name, e.g. *Frogs* and *Wasps*, and their entry being a high point in the play. They threw off their assumed character in part at least of the *parabasis* (see COMEDY, GREEK 3 (iv)) and addressed the audience on behalf of the poet. After the fifth century the role of the chorus in tragedy and especially in comedy became much reduced: in Middle and New Comedy its role became entirely non-dramatic, and a song from a chorus (not included in the text of the play) became merely a device for dividing one act from the next. The Roman adaptations of Greek tragedy and the comedies of Plautus and Terence did not include a chorus.

Chremōnidē'an War. The Athenian nationalist statesman Chremonidēs carried a decree, probably in 266 BC, by which Athens joined the Peloponnesian anti-Macedonian coalition and led a revolt against Macedon and its ruler Antigonus Gonatas. Athens was besieged and surrendered in 262 BC.

Chrēstoma'thia, see PROCLUS.

Chronica, see NEPOS and EUSEBIUS.

chroniclers. For Greek, see LOGOGRAPHERS; for Roman see ANNALS.

Chrȳsē'is, in Homer's *Iliad*, the daughter of Chrȳsēs, priest of Apollo on the island of Chrȳsē near Troy. When the Greeks sacked the island they gave her to Agamemnon as his gift of honour. He took her as his concubine, declaring that he preferred her to his wife Clytemnestra, and refused the rich ransom offered by Chryses. Chryses prayed to Apollo, and after the Greeks suffered in consequence nine days of pestilence Agamemnon agreed to return Chryseis on condition that he should receive in compensation the girl Briseis who had been given as a prize of war to Achilles. Hence arose the anger of Achilles, one of the main themes of the *Iliad*.

chryselepha'ntine ('of gold and ivory'), term used to describe certain Greek statues made of wood overlaid with gold and ivory, such as *Pheidias' statue of Athena in the Parthenon.

Chrȳsi'ppus, *c.*280–207 BC, Greek *Stoic philosopher. He became head of the Stoa in succession to *Cleanthes by whom he was converted to Stoicism after being educated at the Academy under the *Sceptic Arcesilaus. His voluminous writings (now lost) gave Stoicism coherence and logic, and became recognized as Stoic orthodoxy.

Chrȳsö'themis, see ELECTRA (1).

Ci'cero. 1. Marcus Tu'llius Cicero, 106–43 BC, Roman orator and statesman.

1. *Early life, 106–64 BC.* Cicero was born on 3 January 106 at Arpinum (Arpino) some 110 km. (70 miles) south-east of Rome, the elder of two sons of a wealthy *eques,* the family being distantly related to the general Gaius *Marius. His early promise suggested a career as advocate and politician, and he was sent to Rome to study law under the two great lawyer-politicians of the day, the *Scaevolas (3 and 4), as well as philosophy under Philo, the former head of the Academy at Athens, and Diodotus the Stoic. At the age of 17 Cicero saw military service in the *Social War, serving under Pompeius Strabo, the father of *Pompey the Great, whose acquaintance Cicero probably made at this time. Throughout his life Cicero was to remain a supporter of Pompey, seeing him as the one man who could save Rome from external enemies and internal lawlessness while preserving the republican constitution. Also serving under Strabo was the young *Catiline (see 2 below). During the turbulent eighties Cicero completed his forensic education. His earliest surviving speech is

Pro Quinctio of 81, a complicated partnership case; the result is unknown, but we know that the opposing advocate was Hortensius, the greatest orator of the day. Cicero's reputation was established in the following year (80) by his successful defence of Roscius of Ameria (*Pro Roscio Amerino*) on a charge of parricide. Both speeches had a political aspect; in the latter Cicero courageously attacked Sulla's powerful freedman Chrysogonus. At this point (79) Cicero left Rome to spend two years abroad to improve his health and pursue his studies under the Greek masters of rhetoric and philosophy. At Athens he studied with another young Roman, Titus Pomponius *Atticus, who was to become his lifelong friend and, since Atticus spent most of his life away from Rome, his most valued correspondent (see 7 below). In Rhodes Cicero visited *Posidonius, the great scholar and Stoic philosopher.

At about this time, either before he left for Greece or soon after his return in 77, he married his wife Terentia. Perhaps to this period after his return belongs his defence of his friend the comic actor Roscius (*Pro Roscio comoedo*). In 76 he was elected quaestor at the minimum age (of 30), as with every subsequent office he held, and so qualified for membership of the senate, remaining a member until his death. He served his quaestorship (75) at Lilybaeum (Marsala) in west Sicily; after his return to Rome in 74 he never willingly left Italy again (but see 4), refusing provincial governorships both after his praetorship and after his consulship. In the next few years he was occupied with legal work in the courts, particularly on behalf of the *equites,* through which he gained wealth and eventually political support. His reputation was unshakeably established in 70 with his brilliant prosecution of C. *Verres, the corrupt governor of Sicily from 73 to 71, at the request of the Sicilians. Verres was defended by the famous Hortensius, but the latter was never called upon to speak: after Cicero's first speech for the prosecution (*actio prima*) Verres threw up the case and retired into exile in Massilia (Marseilles). Cicero's immense labours in gathering evidence for this case were not to be wasted; he published as well as his first speech the five long sections that were to comprise the *actio secunda* ('second stage' of the trial), and they made his reputation as Rome's leading advocate and fearless opponent of corruption.

In 69 Cicero became aedile, and in 66 praetor at the minimum age of 40. In this year he delivered in public assembly his first purely political speech, **Pro lege Manilia*, in which he supported, against strong **optimate* opposition, the proposal of the tribune Manilius that Pompey should be appointed to the command of the war in the East against Mithridates. In this Cicero was to some extent motivated by self-interest: it would be invaluable to his political ambitions to have the backing of the powerful Pompey. His other important speech of this year was *Pro Cluentio*, a forensic masterpiece in which he successfully defended the rich *eques* Cluentius on a charge of poisoning his stepfather.

During the years from 66 to 63 Cicero gradually moved away from his earlier reformist position and moved closer to the position of the conservative *optimates*, while men like Publius Crassus, Julius **Caesar*, Gaius Antonius, and Catiline (the last two Cicero's rivals for the consulship in 63) propagated schemes for radical social reform.

2. *63–62 BC: Cicero's consulship*. In the elections of 64 Cicero, a **novus homo*, a 'new man' with no advantages of birth, stood for the consulship of 63 and came top of the poll, *consul prior*, at the earliest permissible age, 42, *suo anno*, 'in his own year'. His candidature was successful partly because the *optimates* were alarmed by the revolutionary inclinations of Catiline, who might otherwise have been their candidate. His colleague in the consulship was Gaius Antonius, an ally of Catiline. As consul in 63 Cicero delivered the speeches *De lege agraria* (or *Contra Rullum*), arguing successfully that the legislation proposed by the tribune P. Servilius Rullus to bring about the distribution of land was fraudulent. The speech *Pro Rabirio* of the same year was in defence of an elderly *eques* charged by the popular party (at the instigation of Caesar; see also LABIENUS) with having killed, thirty-seven years before, the

tribune Saturninus after the **senatus consultum ultimum* had been passed by the senate. The prosecution was in fact questioning the validity of such a resolution and drawing popular attention to the possibility of its abuse. The trial was abandoned, but Cicero was clearly seen to be a moderate conservative, in opposition to Caesar and the popular party who had brought about the prosecution. At the elections held in 63 for the consulship in 62, Catiline was again a candidate, and the natural leader of those desperate for much-needed economic reform. Again he was defeated. He seems to have hoped for some sort of aid from Cicero's colleague Antonius, but Cicero won over the latter by offering him the governorship of the more profitable province of Macedonia instead of Cisalpine Gaul. Catiline saw that his only chance of success lay in the violent seizure of power. Cicero discovered his plans and, having convinced the senate of the imminence of an uprising followed by a massacre at Rome, persuaded them to pass the *senatus consultum ultimum*. He still had no firm evidence against Catiline, however, and when he addressed the senate on 8 November 63 in the most famous of all his speeches, his first *In Catilinam*, Catiline was present. Immediately afterwards Catiline left Rome. His departure was followed by Cicero's exposition of events to the people on 9 November (his second speech *In Catilinam*), and the arrest of five prominent citizens, who were leading conspirators in treasonable correspondence with envoys of the Allobroges (a Gallic tribe), on 2–3 December. In a third speech Cicero explained the new developments to the people. The fourth was delivered in the senate (5 December) on the question of the punishment of the prisoners, a speech of studied impartiality. The consul designate Silanus proposed the death penalty; Caesar proposed life imprisonment, a novel penalty in Roman law. Marcus **Cato* spoke powerfully in favour of the death penalty and carried the senate with him. Cicero had the sentence carried out at once. He never doubted that he had saved the state from grave danger, and he wrote of his action in prose and verse, both in Latin and in

Greek (see 8 below). During this crisis Cicero found himself called upon to defend (and did so successfully) the second consul designate, L. Murena, on an ill-timed charge, brought by Marcus Cato, of bribery in the elections (see PRO MURENA).

3. *From 62 to Cicero's banishment in 58.* Cicero never forgot, nor allowed anyone else to forget, the glory of 63, and Marcus Cato saluted him as 'father of his country' (*pater patriae*). But the legality of the execution of the arrested conspirators (who had been denied a trial) was soon questioned by the popular party. Cicero thought that he could bring about a union of all sound and respectable men of property from both the senatorial and equestrian classes, his *concordia ordinum*, 'harmony between the *orders', but by the end of 61 it became clear that this was a delusion. In 62 he had delivered two speeches, *Pro Sulla and *Pro Archia. At the end of that year Publius *Clodius, who later emerged as a powerful popular leader, was detected while in disguise as a woman at the (female) mysteries of the Bona Dea, and prosecuted. Although he obtained an acquittal by bribery, his attempt to set up an alibi was defeated by the evidence of Cicero, who thereby incurred Clodius' hatred. Also at the end of the year Pompey returned from the East to Italy. The jealousy and hostility of the senate frustrated his political ambitions, but when Caesar returned from his governorship of Spain in 60 and was about to enter on his consulship in 59, he and Pompey formed a political alliance with Crassus, called in modern times 'the first triumvirate'. It appears that Caesar made advances to Cicero with a view to including him in the alliance, but Cicero could not reconcile himself to Caesar's unconstitutional attitude and bravely but unwisely adopted a course of opposition. Cicero's only surviving speech of this year (59) was *Pro Flacco*, a defence on a charge of extortion in his province of one of the praetors of 63 who had effected the arrest of the Catilinarians. In it he took the opportunity to appeal to popular sentiment in his own favour. When Caesar renewed his overtures and Cicero again refused, Caesar seems to have allowed

Clodius to get his revenge. As tribune for 58 Clodius brought in a bill aimed at Cicero, proposing to outlaw anyone who had put Roman citizens to death without trial. Cicero found himself without any obvious support; he therefore yielded to Clodius' threats and left Rome for exile in March 58.

Clodius now carried a decree exiling Cicero by name and confiscating his property. Cicero's magnificent house on the Palatine was destroyed (and part consecrated to *Libertas*, 'liberty', an ironic touch by Clodius), and his villa at Tusculum badly damaged. He spent his exile in Macedonia, at Thessalonika in 58 with the quaestor Gnaeus Plancius, moving at the end of the year to Dyrrhachium. He was utterly crushed by his misfortune and consumed by self-pity. But Pompey lost little time in starting to bring about Cicero's recall, with the support of the tribune *Milo, who employed violence as freely as Clodius.

4. *57–45*. Cicero was recalled by a law of the people on 4 August 57 and reached Rome a month later, to an enthusiastic welcome. In the two speeches *Post reditum* (whose authenticity has been questioned) he thanked the senate and people for his recall. His speeches during the ensuing period arise out of his struggles to secure public compensation for the damage to his property (*De domo sua* and *De haruspicum responso*) and out of his support for those responsible for his recall. Thus in 56 he defended P. Sestius (*Pro Sestio*), a tribune who had exerted himself on his behalf, against a charge of rioting brought by Clodius. This speech, largely occupied with Cicero's own services and an attempt to rally aristocratic feeling against the triumvirs, contains some of the orator's finest passages. The speech *In Vatinium* was an attack on Vatinius, one of the witnesses, a supporter of Caesar's who had tried to get Sestius convicted. The speech *Pro Caelio* succeeded in obtaining the acquittal of a fashionable young friend, M. *Caelius Rufus, on charges that included conspiracy to murder an Egyptian envoy and the attempted poisoning of Caelius' former mistress Clodia, the sister of Clodius (and almost certainly the 'Lesbia' of *Catullus). The attack on

Clodia herself is Cicero's most brilliant *tour de force*.

Cicero hoped that the political manœuvrings of 57 and 56, which took place against a background of increasing civil violence, would end in the break-up of the triumvirate, but in April 56 Caesar, Pompey, and Crassus renewed their political union and Cicero was forced to accept the situation and make his peace with Caesar, who always behaved with generosity towards him. Cicero's capitulation was evident in the speeches of 56, *De provinciis consularibus* ('on provinces governed by consuls') in favour of the prolongation of Caesar's command in Gaul, and *Pro Balbo*, a defence of the citizenship procured by Pompey for a rich Spaniard, Balbus, who was also a friend of Caesar's. In letters to his close friends Cicero reveals the blow that his pride has suffered. He had some satisfaction in speaking against his old enemy L. Calpurnius *Piso (In Pisonem) when the latter had been recalled from the governorship of Macedonia largely as a result of Cicero's attacks on him in *De provinciis consularibus* (see above). In 54 he defended his friend Plancius, who had received him during his exile in Macedonia (see 3 above), on a charge of electoral corruption (*Pro Plancio*), and Rabirius, a partisan of Caesar, on a charge of extortion (*Pro Rabirio Postumo*) as well as M. Aemilius Scaurus, ex-governor of Sardinia, on a similar charge (of this speech we have only fragments). The worst humiliations came in 54 when, at the behest of the triumvirs, he was forced to defend his enemies, Vatinius for bribery (successfully), and (unsuccessfully) on a charge of extortion the hated Gabinius, who as consul in 58 had made no attempt to prevent Cicero's exile. He was mortified by his failure in 52 to defend Milo successfully when the latter was charged and condemned for the murder of Clodius, and had to content himself with sending to the exiled Milo the speech *Pro Milone*, perhaps the finest of all his speeches. It is an elaboration of the one he tried to deliver when he lost his nerve, presented as he was with a court room packed with Clodian supporters and the hostile soldiers of Pompey. Milo is said to have congratulated himself

that it was not delivered, otherwise he would have been acquitted and never have known the excellent seafood for which Massilia (Marseilles) was already famous. In 53 Cicero was somewhat comforted by being elected augur.

During the 50s, as he withdrew from the collapsing world of republican politics, he found consolation in writing on philosophy and rhetoric, and arguing against his literary antagonists, who were principally Julius Caesar, *Calvus, Marcus *Brutus, and Asinius *Pollio. By the end of 55 he had finished *De oratore*, a treatise in three books on rhetoric, designed to replace his early work on the same subject, *De inventione* ('on invention'), written before he was 25; it was followed, perhaps in the late 50s, by a briefer essay on rhetoric, *Partitiones oratoriae* ('divisions of oratory'), in which Cicero answers his young son's questions on the orator's craft. From this period also comes the *De republica (of which we have only parts, including the *Somnium Scipionis), and *De legibus ('on laws'), which seems to have been begun in 52, though it was not completed until 45 and was probably published after Cicero's death. There was to be a further outpouring of philosophical works between 46 and 44. Meanwhile Cicero was reluctantly obliged to govern the province of Cilicia from summer 51 to summer 50 under the new regulations of Pompey's law for the government of the provinces. He disliked leaving Rome but he carried out his duties honestly and efficiently, winning a victory over the brigands and returning to Rome with the *fasces of his lictors wreathed in fading laurels. He found Rome on the brink of civil war, and when war did break out he left the city, with many of the senatorial party. Pompey had accepted the command of the republic's forces in Italy, but after he withdrew with them to Epirus in Greece Cicero was in the deepest trouble and perplexity. He decided to remain in Italy, and followed Pompey only at a later stage. After the defeat of the Pompeians at Pharsalus in the summer of 48 (at which battle he was not present because of illness), he returned to Italy. A period of anxious suspense was ended in 47 when Caesar came to Italy and the two were completely reconciled. At last Cicero could return to Rome.

At first he remained detached from public life, attending meetings in the senate but not speaking, regarded with suspicion by both sides. But he began to entertain the faint hope that when the civil war was finally over Caesar might perhaps set about restoring constitutional government. In 46 he delivered his first important speech for five years, *Pro Marcello*, a speech of thanks to Caesar for pardoning M. Marcellus who as consul in 51 had launched the attack on him which ultimately precipitated the civil war (see CAESAR 2); it contains a famous sentence, *satis diu vel naturae vixi vel gloriae* ('I have lived long enough for the demands of nature or fame'). In 45 he spoke *Pro Ligario*, a defence of Q. Ligarius, tried as an enemy of Caesar, a speech whose eloquence is said to have moved Caesar to acquit the accused; and in the same year he delivered the speech *Pro rege Deiotaro*, defending the tetrarch of Galatia on a charge of attempting to murder Caesar. Shortly after Cato's death at Utica (Utique) in 46, Cicero, at Brutus' suggestion, wrote a panegyric on him, now lost. It displeased Caesar, who replied to it in a work, also lost, called *Anticato*.

In 46 Cicero divorced his wife of some thirty years, Terentia, and shortly after married Publilia, who had been his ward. In 45 his beloved daughter *Tullia died, and Cicero was overwhelmed with grief. A famous letter of consolation (*Epistulae ad familiares* IV. 5) was written to him by the jurist *Sulpicius. Publilia offended Cicero by her lack of sympathy, and this second marriage also ended in divorce. These personal blows were made harder to bear by Cicero's growing realization that Caesar was never going to attempt to restore the republican constitution, and he took what consolation he could in literary composition.

5. *Philosophical and literary writings*. Between 46 and 44 Cicero wrote *Brutus*, a history of Roman oratory, *Orator*, a picture of the accomplished speaker, and other works on rhetoric: the *Topica* ('matters relating to commonplaces'), dealing with kinds of arguments, supposedly derived from Aristotle's work of

the same name; *De optimo genere oratorum* ('on the best kind of orators', perhaps written in 52), of which only a part survives; a preface to his (lost) translations of the two Greek orations *De corona* of Demosthenes and *Against Ctesiphon* of Aeschines (this work may not be by Cicero). In 45 he wrote the *Consolatio* ('consolation') on the deaths of great men, a work (of which fragments survive) occasioned by the death of Tullia; *Hortensius* (now lost), a plea for the study of philosophy which greatly moved St Augustine; *Academica*, on the views of the Athenian 'New' Academy, and in particular of *Carneades; and *De finibus bonorum et malorum*, on the different conceptions held by philosophers of the 'chief good'. After these works he wrote during 45 and 44 *Tusculanae disputationes* ('*Tusculan Disputations') on the conditions of happiness, the most intensely felt and expressed of all his philosophical works; *De natura deorum*, the views of different philosophical schools on the nature of the gods; *De fato* ('on fate', of which only fragments survive), a discussion of free will; the two charming essays *De senectute and *De amicitia; *De divinatione*, the examination of Stoic belief concerning fate and the possibility of prediction, published soon after Caesar's murder; and his last work on moral philosophy, *De officiis*, finished in November 44 and written for the edification of his son. It was altogether a wonderful output for two or three years.

As a philosopher Cicero claimed to be a follower of the 'New' Academy of Carneades which held that certain knowledge was impossible, and that practical conviction based on probability was the most that could be attained. But while his general attitude was that of the New Academy, he was an eclectic, that is to say he did not adhere to any one school, but picked from among the doctrines of the various Greek schools those which commended themselves to his reason; and in questions of morality he was inclined (e.g. in *De finibus*, the *Tusculan Disputations*, and *De officiis*) to accept the positive Stoic teaching. He believed in the existence of a divine being, and maintained that it is prudent to keep up traditional rites and ceremonies. Finally, in *De fato* he shows his belief in the freedom of the will against Stoic fatalism. He did not claim that his philosophical works were original but he popularized Greek thought and created a Latin philosophical vocabulary. The works *De senectute*, *De amicitia*, *De officiis*, the *Tusculan Disputations*, and the *Somnium Scipionis* (detached from the *De republica* which was ultimately lost) had considerable influence on the Fathers of the early Church. In the Middle Ages, when Cicero's political and oratorical works had yet to be rediscovered (see TEXTS, TRANSMISSION OF ANCIENT 8), these books were studied extensively, and handed on to the European world a knowledge of Greek philosophy which was not otherwise attainable.

6. *The Philippics and Cicero's death, 44–43.* When a heterogeneous collection of men, united only in their desire to put an end to despotic rule, murdered Caesar in 44, Cicero was not invited to join them, although he greeted the news with delight. For several months he remained aloof from politics, but he still ardently desired to see the restoration of the republic. When, after several months of confusion and perplexity, the political alignments were becoming clear, and Mark *Antony had left Rome for Cisalpine Gaul to lay siege to the republicans under Decimus *Brutus at Mutina, Cicero put himself at the head of what was left of the senatorial party. He gave full expression to his hatred of the Caesarian tyranny in fourteen orations against Antony which he entitled *Philippics*, after the patriotic speeches delivered by the Athenian orator Demosthenes against Philip II of Macedon. The *First Philippic* was in fact delivered to the senate on 2 September, before Antony left for Cisalpine Gaul; the *Fourteen Philippics*—the last of all Cicero's surviving speeches—was delivered on 21 April 43. It celebrated the defeat of Antony at Mutina, but the rejoicing was premature. Cicero mistakenly believed that *Octavian intended to destroy Antony, but instead Octavian marched on Rome with his legions to demand the consulship, and obtained it on 19 August 43. He then proceeded to make his peace with

Antony, rescinding sentences outlawing the latter and Lepidus, and at the end of October all three met to agree on a threefold division of power, the (second) triumvirate. They were to prosecute the war jointly against Brutus and Cassius in the East, money and land were to be obtained to satisfy their troops, and old scores settled by widespread *proscriptions. On the first list sent to Rome Antony wrote Cicero's name. On 7 December 43 his soldiers caught Cicero in a not very resolute attempt to escape by sea, and he bravely submitted to execution. His head and hands were displayed on the *Rostra in Rome.

7. *Letters.* Perhaps, ironically, to his detriment, Cicero is known to us more intimately than anyone else in the ancient world through his voluminous correspondence covering the period 68 to 43. Over 800 of his letters survive in which, with complete candour and mostly with little thought of publication, he recorded his moods and actions. The first we hear of publication is in July 44 when he writes about making a small collection of his letters to *Tiro and Atticus (see also 1 above). Because he was closely involved in the politics of a momentous period in history, and wrote to correspondents of the most diverse political views as well as to members of his household, the letters are an invaluable historical source. They have come down to us in four collections, which include some letters from his correspondents, and comprise: those written to Atticus (*Epistulae ad Atticum*) between 68 and 43; those written to more than ninety other friends and relations (*Epistulae ad familiares*) published by Tiro; those to his brother Quintus (*Epistulae ad Quintum fratrem*; see (2) below) written when the brothers were separated, chiefly between 59 and 54; and twenty-five letters written to Marcus Brutus (*Epistulae ad Brutum*) all written in 43. There are no letters for the years of Cicero's consulship (63) or the preceding year.

8. *Poems.* Cicero's very early poetry has perished but there survive a large part of the *Aratea* (469 consecutive hexameter lines and some fragments) and his translation of the *Phaenomena* of *Aratus, a Greek didactic poem; his

philosophical works also contain snippets from Homer and the Greek tragedians in his own Latin version, and a few lines survive of an epic *Marius*. His famous poems were the autobiographical ones of self-glorification, the three books *De consulatu suo* ('on my consulship') written in 60, and, some five years later, three further books *De temporibus suis* ('on my times'). Little has survived of them except a passage of seventy-two lines on his consulship and the two notorious lines which aroused the derision of his contemporaries for their jingling sound and boastful expression, *cedant arma togae, concedat laurea laudi* (or *linguae*) ('Let arms submit to civil power, let military laurels yield to praise' or 'speech'), and *o fortunatam natam me consule Romam* ('O happy Rome, born in my consulship'). Despite his poetic failings he furthered the development of the Latin hexameter and had some influence on *Lucretius and perhaps Catullus.

9. *Cicero's influence on literature and thought.* Cicero was a man of great versatility of intellect. Lasting political success eluded him because of his support for what turned out to be a lost cause. His consulship in 63 was famous; he was a political force of whom serious account had subsequently to be taken by whoever aimed at controlling the political scene; his devotion to his country was selfless and never in doubt. But his immense success as consul left him with an exaggerated idea of what it was possible for him to achieve politically, and his enthusiasm for the restoration of the old form of the republic was sadly unrealistic; he was not able—nor was anyone—to deal with the serious economic and social issues which lay behind the politics of the day, and it is often said that he lacked judgement and constancy of purpose. His lasting greatness lies in his exceptional mastery of the Latin language. He was the greatest orator that Rome produced. In his prose treatises as well as in his oratory, he wrote in lucid and unaffected Latin and in a complex periodic style that was logical and coherent, rhythmical and sonorous. His prose became a model for later writers in Latin and helped to mould the style of many authors writing in the languages of modern Europe.

In his forensic speeches, mostly written for the defence, he was adept at selecting those aspects of a case on which he might speak to his client's advantage, at relating an engrossing narrative that furthered his cause, at rising to heights of emotion where appropriate, and at employing his considerable powers of wit, irony, and ridicule. He was unusual in being able to expound the theory of his art in a series of valuable treatises on rhetoric. He exemplified his own precept that an orator needed to have a wide knowledge by constant reading and study, especially of the Greek philosophers. Hitherto the Latin language was not adapted to expressing general philosophic ideas and lacked a suitable vocabulary. Cicero succeeded in expounding the Greek philosophical systems partly by introducing into Latin a range of new words to express the ideas. These ideas were not arid theories but, adapted to the Roman environment and Roman attitudes, underpinned Cicero's life as a practical man of action. Though ultimately suspending belief in the existence of gods he was, nevertheless, convinced of the essential rightness of the Stoic doctrine that all humans possessed a spark of the divine, which bound man to man and demanded that we treat each other with a common respect.

Cicero's reputation was somewhat eclipsed in the two centuries after his death; his views on rhetorical education had little influence, and Latin prose style tended to avoid Ciceronian fullness and balance in favour of what was striking and epigrammatic. His letters were probably published in the course of the first century AD but aroused no particular interest, nor was his philosophy much read. Some Christians saw him as a symbol of the pagan culture which should be rejected, but his good sense and his style ensured that he was studied by Christian apologists needing an acceptable language to express their beliefs to a pagan audience, and sometimes needing the arguments too. Those books that seemed to prefigure or echo Christian wisdom were especially favoured in Christian reading and education: *Somnium Scipionis*, *De officiis*, *De amicitia*, *De senectute*. From the early Middle Ages until the nineteenth century

Cicero's influence on literature and ideas was profound. Renaissance scholars admired and imitated his language and style, but, more importantly, saw him as the ideal of civilized man, brilliant, humane, practical in the discharge of civic duties, and enjoying a refined leisure. Interest in his Latin style became less intense towards the end of the sixteenth century when taste turned to Seneca and Tacitus, and in any case the various vernaculars established themselves as respectable vehicles of composition, themselves much influenced by Ciceronian style. In England in the seventeenth century the language of John Milton and of the Authorized Version of the Bible show their indebtedness. The eighteenth century with its cool rationalism felt a special affinity to Cicero, and in France (and America) his freedom from dogma and his open-minded speculations struck a chord among aspiring revolutionaries. In the nineteenth century his reputation as a statesman collapsed; his philosophical writings too ceased to exert their previous influence and seemed unoriginal and excessively moralistic, and interest turned towards their Greek sources. Nevertheless, Ciceronian 'humanity' is still the ideal that lies at the base of much of modern civilization.

2. Quintus Tu'llius Cicero, 102–43 BC, younger brother of the orator ((1) above), an able soldier and administrator. He was praetor in 62, and governor of Asia 61–59, where he received from his brother two long letters of advice (*Epistulae ad Quintum fratrem* I. 1 and 2). He served as legate with Caesar in Gaul during 54–51, taking part in the invasion of Britain, and then joined his brother in Cilicia. He followed Pompey in the civil war, was pardoned after Pharsalus, and took no further part in public life. He and his son died in the proscriptions of 43. He had wide literary interests but his works do not survive, except for four letters to his brother. He married Pomponia, sister of his brother's friend Atticus.

3. Marcus Tu'llius Cicero, born 65 BC, only son of the orator ((1) above) and his wife Terentia. He was taken out to Cilicia with his father in 51. He fought with a squadron of cavalry in Pompey's army in 49/8, was pardoned after the battle of Pharsalus, joined Sextus Pompeius after Philippi, but took advantage of the amnesty after 39 to return to Rome. He was consul with Octavian for a brief period in 30; subsequently he governed Syria and after that we hear no more of him. An apologetic letter survives (*Ad familiares* XVI. 21) written by him to *Tiro in response to letters from his father and Atticus which expressed displeasure at his idle life while a student in Athens. In it he gives a careful account of his reformed mode of life.

Ciceronian age, of Roman literature, a term sometimes used to signify the period in Latin literature that roughly coincided with the manhood of Cicero and the last years of the republic, about 70 to 30 BC. The writers of the period apart from Cicero include Lucretius, Catullus, Sallust, and Varro. Virgil is generally associated with the Augustan age although he had written the *Eclogues* and *Georgics* by 30 BC.

Cili'cia, country on the eastern half of the south coast of Asia Minor. In Homer's *Iliad* the Cilices, after whom the country is named, inhabited the southern Troad, but after the Trojan War some Greeks, under the leadership of *Mopsus the seer, applied the name to this new region in which they settled. The western area was rough and mountainous, but the east consisted of a large and very fertile plain. In the second century BC it became a pirate stronghold and the Romans constituted it as a province in 102 BC to deal with the menace. The pirates were not suppressed until Pompey's campaign of 67 BC. Cicero was governor of Cilicia in 51–50 (see CICERO (1) 4). Its most important city, autonomous until annexed by Pompey in 66 BC, was Tarsus, the seat of a famous school of philosophy and birthplace of the apostle Paul.

Cimme'rians (Kimmerioi), a people who belong partly to legend and partly to history. In Homer's *Odyssey* (book 11) they are a fabulous people living on the edge of the world by the shore of *Oceanus, shrouded in mist and in perpetual darkness. Here Odysseus gained access to the spirits of the dead. In Herodotus they are a historical people driven from their home (the biblical Gomer) north of the Black Sea in the eighth and seventh centuries BC by nomadic Scythian tribes. In the early seventh century they overturned Midas' kingdom of Phrygia (at which Midas took poison), attacked Lydia, killing the king Gyges, and in c.644 BC, during the reign of his son Ardys, took the capital Sardis, except for the citadel. The Greek poets Callinus and Archilochus bear witness to the terror they inspired in Ionia. Then plague struck them and they retreated east. Some who remained were finally expelled about 600 BC by Alyattes, king of Lydia.

Cīmon (c.510–c.450 BC), Athenian statesman and soldier. He was the son of *Miltiades and the Thracian Hegesipylē, and it seems to have been thought that he owed some of his features—his great height, shaggy hair, and slowness of wit—to his Thracian ancestry. Cimon entered politics shortly after 480. He was *strategos* in 478, thereafter held that office frequently, and from 476 to 463 was commander in nearly all the operations of the *Delian League. In 475 he conquered the island of Scyros, drove out the pirates, and brought back in triumph to Athens what were supposed to be the bones of the Athenian hero Theseus who was said to be buried there. Cimon's greatest military achievement was the defeat of the Persian fleet at the mouth of the Eurymedon, perhaps in 466. Subsequently he reduced Thasos in 463 after a two-year siege when that island revolted from the Delian League. Cimon's benevolence towards Sparta was unpopular, however, leading to his exile in 461. Tradition states that he was recalled before the full ten years of exile had elapsed in order to conduct the delicate Athenian peace negotiations in the war with Sparta and the Peloponnesians. In c.451 Athens and Sparta concluded a five years' truce. Cimon led a last campaign against Persia to recapture Cyprus and died there c.450.

Cincinnā'tus, Lucius Quinctius, a legendary Roman hero who, according to tradition, was called from the plough to be dictator in 458 BC, when the Roman army under the consul Mincius was blockaded by the Italian tribe of the Aequi on Mount Algidus. He defeated the enemy, resigned his dictatorship after sixteen days, and returned to his farm. He is often cited as an exemplar of old-fashioned Roman simplicity and frugality.

Cinē'sias, Athenian *lyric (especially dithyrambic) poet who lived in the second half of the fifth century BC. Of his work nothing of interest survives. He was much mocked by his contemporaries, especially Aristophanes, for his free style of music.

Cinna. 1. **Lucius Cornelius Cinna,** brother of Julius Caesar's wife Cornelia, praetor in 44 BC. He had republican sympathies and expressed approval of Caesar's murder. He may have died in the later proscriptions. See also (2) below.

2. **Gaius Helvius Cinna,** Roman poet and friend of *Catullus, whom he accompanied to Bithynia in 57 BC; his *epyllion *Zmyrna* was greatly admired by his contemporaries for its vast erudition in the Alexandrian manner. He also wrote erotic poetry in various metres, of which only very small fragments survive. The ancient sources identify him with the tribune of 44 BC who, after the murder of Caesar, was lynched by the angry mob in mistake for Cornelius Cinna (see above) who had spoken publicly against the dictator on the previous day (or 'for his bad verses' according to Shakespeare).

Ci'nyras, mythical king of Cyprus and founder of the cult of Aphroditē in that island. He was the father of *Adonis through an unwitting union with his daughter Zmyrna (or Myrrha). He was regarded as a seer and musician, and sometimes said for that reason to be the son of Apollo. (See also PYGMALION.)

Circē, in Homer's *Odyssey* (book 10), a goddess living on the fabulous island of Aeaea (later identified by the Romans with the promontory of Circeii in Latium), powerful in magic, who turned Odysseus' men into swine. Odysseus resisted her magic by means of the mythical herb moly. Circe was the daughter of *Helios and Persē, and the sister of Aeëtēs; by Odysseus she was the mother

of two or three sons, one of whom was
*Telegonos. Milton in *Comus* makes the
magician Comus the son of Circe and
Bacchus.

circe'nsēs, at Rome, contests and other
displays in the circus, including chariot-
races. *Panem et circenses* ('bread and
circuses') were, according to the poet
Juvenal (10. 81), the only things that the
degenerate Roman people cared about.

Ciris, see *APPENDIX VIRGILIANA*.

Cirrha, see CRISA.

Cisal'pine Gaul, see GAUL.

Cistellā'ria ('casket'), Roman comedy
by *Plautus, adapted from a comedy by
the Greek comic poet *Menander,
Synaristōsai ('breakfasters'). The plot
turns on the discovery by means of a
casket of the true parentage of a found-
ling girl, Selēnium, who has passed into
the care of a courtesan and has become
the mistress of a young man
Alcesimarchus. She is found to be the
daughter of a citizen, Dēmipho, and is
thereupon married to her lover.

Cithae'ron, the westerly part of the
mountain range which separates the
north of Attica from Boeotia. The summit was sacred to Zeus, but the mountain
was also sacred to Dionysus, and on one
of the crests was a famous cave of the
*nymphs. It was the scene of several
myths and legends including the
metamorphosis of *Actaeon, the death of
Pentheus (see BACCHAE), and the
exposure of *Oedipus.

cǐ'thara, see MUSIC.

civil war, at Rome. This term denotes
any one of three periods of civil war at
Rome, first between Marius and Sulla
from 88 to 82 BC, secondly between
Pompey and Julius Caesar from 49 to 45
BC, and thirdly between Antony and
Octavian from 44 to 30 BC.

Civil War, commentaries by Julius
Caesar; see *COMMENTARIES* 2.

clan, see GENOS and GENS.

classic (classics, classical). The English
terms are derived from the Latin adjective *classicus* meaning 'of the highest
class' (of the five classes of Roman

citizens divided by Servius Tullius on a
property basis). Aulus Gellius in the
second century AD seems to have been
the first to use the adjective figuratively
to describe a writer, but Cicero had
already taken the noun *classis* ('class')
from its political and military sphere and
used it to describe a 'class' of philosophers (see also CANONS). Renaissance
scholars writing in Latin adopted the
adjective to describe Greek and Latin
authors in general, and from this the
modern usage is derived. The terms are
sometimes used with a narrower,
temporal meaning to describe what is
thought to be the best period, in a
cultural sense, of the Greek and Roman
civilizations. Thus, the classical period of
ancient Greece was most of the fifth and
fourth centuries BC, roughly from the
defeat of the Persians in 480 to the death
of Alexander the Great in 323 BC, and
that of Rome the first century BC and the
following century up to the death of
Augustus in AD 14, sometimes referred to
as the Golden Age.

Claudian (Claudius Claudiānus) (d.
c. AD 404), the last great Latin poet in the
classical tradition. He was born at Alexandria in the late fourth century AD and
came to Italy before 395. Although a
native Greek speaker, he turned to composing in Latin and became immediately
successful as a court poet under
Honorius, the young emperor in the
West, writing in hexameters a number of
eulogies of him and his ministers and, in
particular, a three-book panegyric of the
general and regent *Stilicho. (The date of
his death is inferred from his silence
about Stilicho's achievements after 404.)
He also wrote poems savagely abusing
Honorius' political enemies, mostly in
the eastern empire (ruled by Honorius'
young brother Arcadius), attacking in
particular Rufinus, the guardian of
Arcadius, and the eunuch Eutropius,
Rufinus' successor. He wrote an (incomplete) *epyllion of 526 lines on the defeat
of Gildo who led an uprising in Africa,
and another on Stilicho's defeat of the
Visigothic king Alaric at Pollentia (Pol-
lenza). In these poems Claudian shows
sincere enthusiasm for the Roman
empire, great technical and rhetorical

skill, and a vigour at times reaching high eloquence, although both his panegyric and his invective are extravagant. He makes abundant use of allegory and mythological episode and allusion. In addition to the political poems he wrote an epithalamium and four shorter poems for Honorius' marriage to Stilicho's daughter Maria. His finest work, as it seems today, is *The Rape of Proserpine*, divided into four books, of which 1,100 lines survive; he tells with great charm the familiar story of Proserpine's abduction by Pluto in the field of Enna. He also wrote a number of short pieces, idylls and epigrams, mostly in elegiacs (see METRE, GREEK 4), on a great variety of subjects— the Nile, the phoenix, a porcupine, a lobster, a statue, a landscape, etc. The best-known is the idyll on the 'Old man of Verona', imitated from Virgil's description of the old gardener of Tarentum (*Georgics* 4. 125). Although Honorius' court was Christian, Claudian's poetry shows a predilection for the old pagan religion and it is probable that he remained unconverted. He was honoured for his work by a bronze statue erected in the Forum of Trajan, the inscription from which has survived and is in Naples.

Claudius. 1. Appius Claudius, Roman patrician leader of the decemvirs (**decemviri*, commission of ten men) appointed in 451 BC to draw up a written code of laws, the *Twelve Tables, in response to the agitation of the *plebs*. The traditions concerning these events are inextricably confused. The decemvirs, when reappointed for a second year, appear to have become oppressive, and Appius' conduct towards *Virginia provoked their overthrow in 449. Appius was arrested but committed suicide before he was brought to trial (Livy 3. 33). To later Romans he came to symbolize aristocratic arrogance.

2. Appius Claudius Caecus ('blind'), the famous Roman censor (in 312 BC), reputedly a proud and obstinate man with original and broad views. He used his censorship to extend membership of the senate to rich citizens of the lower classes, and even to the sons of freedmen. Their support as well as heavier taxation enabled him to build Rome's first

aqueduct, Aqua Appia, and the Via *Appia. In his old age, when blind, he successfully attacked the proposals of *Pyrrhus for peace (279/8 BC), in a famous speech still circulated in Cicero's day. He is the first Roman prose-writer whose name is known to us. Cicero says that he was a notable orator, and that some of his funeral orations were still read. He composed aphorisms in Saturnian verse (see METRE, LATIN 1) of which a few have survived; they include 'a man is the creator of his own fortune', *faber est suae quisque fortunae*.

3. Tiberius Claudius Nero Germa'nicus (10 BC–AD 54), son of the elder *Drusus and Antonia, daughter of Mark Antony, the Roman emperor Claudius from 41 until his death. Hampered by some physical disability and the general belief that he was mentally deficient, he led a retired life and devoted himself to scholarship, producing a history of the reign of Octavian and another from the death of Julius Caesar, as well as histories of Etruria and Carthage, and an autobiography. None of these works has survived. When the emperor *Gaius (Caligula) was murdered, Claudius was the only surviving adult male of the Julio-Claudian line, and was proclaimed emperor by the praetorian guard almost, it seemed, by accident, after being discovered in hiding, and against the wishes of the senate who wanted to restore the republic. Claudius took part in the invasion of Britain in AD 43 and was present at the capture of Camulodunum (Colchester). In 48 he divorced his wife *Messallina, by whom he had a daughter Octavia and a son Britannicus, for her infidelity, and married his niece *Agrippina, whose son *Nero he adopted. It was generally believed that his death four years later was caused by a dish of mushrooms poisoned by Agrippina. His subsequent deification was the subject of a satire by *Seneca (2), entitled *Apocolocyntōsis*.

clau'sula ('sentence-ending'). In Greek and Latin rhetoric, the closing words of a sentence (or of a clause ending in a strong stop) are rhythmically very important and often follow a regular metrical sequence based on syllable length.

Clea'nthēs (*c*.331–*c*.232 BC), of Assos in

the Troad, successor of Zeno, the founder of *Stoicism, as head of that school of philosophy from *c.*261 to his death. He was said to have defined Zeno's instruction to 'live consistently' as meaning 'to live consistently with nature'. In his ethical teaching he stressed disinterestedness, saying that to do good to others with a view to one's own benefit was no different from feeding cattle in order to eat them. His Stoicism was pervaded by a religious fervour expressed in the thirty-eight surviving hexameter lines of a hymn to Zeus, in which Zeus is envisaged as the spirit that permeates and rules the universe, and human beings as the only living things that have a semblance to him. Parts of the poem express the Stoic view that all events are the will of a perfect God, and that men's acceptance of this fact will bring them peace of mind. Other small fragments of Cleanthes' works survive.

Clei'sthenes. 1. Tyrant of Sicyon *c.*600–570 BC. His policy was consistently anti-Dorian and anti-Argive (Sicyon had originally been occupied by Dorians from Argos but retained a large pre-Dorian element in its population) and led to war with Argos. Earlier, Cleisthenes had taken a leading part in the *Sacred War of *c.*590 in support of Delphi against Crisa. His daughter Agaristē married the *Alcmaeonid Megacles and was mother of the Athenian Cleisthenes: see (2) below. For her marriage see HIPPO-CLEIDES.

2. (d. after 507 BC), the founder of Athenian democracy, grandson of Cleisthenes, tyrant of Sicyon (see 1 above). He was *archon under the tyrant *Hippias in (perhaps) 525. When Hippias was expelled by the Spartan king *Cleomenes I in 510 and those exiled had returned, there was a movement in favour of oligarchy by the aristocracy in Athens, led by Isagoras and supported by Cleomenes. At this point Cleisthenes put himself forward as the champion of democracy and overthrew the aristocrats. He then proceeded to pass far-reaching political reforms of a democratic nature. He broke up what remained of the old political organization based on family groups, and substituted a new system based on topography. He divided the territory of Attica, including the city of Athens, into *demes (*dēmoi*), local communities or parishes, possibly on the basis of existing demes. Cleisthenes then grouped all the demes into ten new tribes so as to ensure that no tribe had a continuous territory or represented a local interest; on the contrary, each contained groups of demes (*trittyes*) from the city region, from the coast, and from the interior. By these means groups of people in various parts of Attica were brought together and required to act in common, and the old parties acting out of purely local interest were abolished. The organization of the army depended on the tribes, each of which contributed a regiment of hoplites and a squadron of cavalry. Cleisthenes subordinated the *boule* and the *Areopagus to the supreme authority of the *ecclesia*, 'assembly' of all the citizens, which met regularly and might deal with any important state matter. In one respect Cleisthenes was conservative: he seems to have retained *Solon's restrictions on eligibility for the higher offices of state. The archons could be chosen only from the two wealthiest classes of the population, and the *Eupatridae retained the monopoly of priestly offices. At his death Cleisthenes received a public burial in the *Ceramicus.

Cleitus, brother of the foster-mother of Alexander the Great and one of his cavalry commanders. He saved Alexander's life at the battle of the Granicus (334 BC), but was subsequently murdered by him in a drunken brawl in 327.

Cle'obis and Bitōn, sons of the Argive priestess of Hera, who were described by Solon to Croesus, according to a story in Herodotus (1. 31), as having been among the happiest of men. When on one occasion the oxen for the priestess's chariot were not brought in time, her sons drew it for some distance to the temple. She prayed to Hera to grant them the greatest blessing possible for mortals, and the goddess caused them to fall asleep in the temple and die in their sleep. Their statues, erected by the Argives at Delphi in the early sixth century BC, are now in the museum there.

Cleo'menēs. 1. **Cleomenes I,** from c.520–c.490 BC king of Sparta of the *Agiad line. He expelled the tyrant *Hippias from Athens in 510. In 508 he supported the aristocratic faction in the city, led by Isagoras, against *Cleisthenes, and by invoking the hereditary curse of the *Alcmaeonidae, to which family Cleisthenes belonged, compelled him and his supporters to retire. When Cleomenes arrived in Athens and attempted to set up Isagoras and his friends in a narrow oligarchy, there was a popular uprising; after being besieged in the Acropolis both were obliged to withdraw, and Cleisthenes was able to return. Later Cleomenes failed in attempts to restore first Isagoras and then the tyrant Hippias, obstructed in both cases by his fellow king Demaratus. The latter also prevented him from punishing Aegina in 491, when that island was suspected of favouring Persia before the outbreak of the Persian War.

2. **Cleomenes III,** b. c.260 BC, king of Sparta from 235 to 219. Following the social ideals of his predecessor Agis IV, whose widow he married, he attempted to restore Spartan power by a series of idealistic reforms designed to rehabilitate the constitution of *Lycurgus. This was in 226–225, when Cleomenes had already built up a strong position in the state by his successful wars against the *Achaean League. The reforms were in part carried out, but in 222 Cleomenes was defeated at Sellasia by the Achaeans under Aratus of Sicyon and fled to his patron Ptolemy III Euergetes in Egypt; there he committed suicide in 219. He was a nationalist and an idealist whose ideals lived on after him, but in practical terms he made no lasting gains.

Clēon (d. 422 BC), Athenian politician prominent during the first part of the *Peloponnesian War, the son of a rich tanner. His first known political acts were attacks on *Pericles in 431 and 430. After Pericles' death in 429 he succeeded him as the most influential politician of his day. In 427 he proposed the decree (carried but rescinded the following day) to execute all the men of Mitylene after the suppression of its revolt. He favoured the ruthless pursuit of victory in the war, by

any means so long as it brought power, glory, and wealth to the Athenian people. After the Athenian victory at Pylos in 425 he thwarted the Spartan peace proposals. He attacked for incompetence the generals who were unsuccessfully besieging the Spartans on the island of Sphacteria, and when Nicias proposed to hand over the command to him he was forced to accept. With the help of the general Demosthenes, Cleon was able to make good his promise to take Sphacteria and bring home the prisoners within twenty days. He gained popularity with the people at this time by raising the pay for jury service from two to three obols, and would certainly have supported, if he did not originate, the measure greatly increasing the tribute paid by the allies (see DELIAN LEAGUE). In 423 he secured a decree for the destruction of Scione and the execution of its citizens (carried out in 421). After Athenian setbacks in Thrace he was elected *strategos* and commanded the expedition to that area, but after some successes he was defeated and killed at Amphipolis by the Spartan general Brasidas, who was himself mortally wounded (422). His death and that of Brasidas removed the principal obstacles to the Peace of Nicias, which was concluded in 421.

A vivid but hostile picture of Cleon as a coarse and unscrupulous *demagogue is presented by Thucydides and by Aristophanes, and we have no independent witnesses who might give a less prejudiced view. His influence lay in his forceful and bullying style of oratory, anti-intellectual and anti-aristocratic in tone, and his appeal to the emotions and prejudices of the people. He seems to have aimed at short-term goals, but Athens' poor stood to benefit by his policies, at the expense of her allies.

Cleopa'tra VII (69–30 BC), daughter of Ptolemy XII Auletēs, king of Egypt (d. 51 BC), appointed by him as his successor with her younger brother, Ptolemy XIII, to whom she was nominally married. (By Ptolemaic custom she could not rule alone.) She was expelled in 48 by her brother's party but reinstated by Julius *Caesar (see 3), who was in Egypt in pursuit of Pompey. When in the consequent war, the Bellum Alexandrinum, Ptolemy XIII lost his life Cleopatra married another younger brother, Ptolemy XIV, but was effectively sole ruler. By now she was Caesar's mistress. In 47 she gave birth to a son, *Caesarion, declaring that Caesar was the father. In 46 she followed Caesar to Rome, returning to Egypt after his murder. When Ptolemy XIV died soon after, perhaps poisoned by her, she made her son co-ruler. In the Roman civil war following Caesar's murder she naturally sided with the triumvirate against the murderers. In 41 she met Mark *Antony at Tarsus in Cilicia; he spent the winter of 41–40 in Alexandria, and she bore him twins, a son and a daughter. After 37 she and Antony were in permanent association, and by 32, when Rome declared war on Cleopatra (alone), the association was seen as a threat to the Roman empire and to Octavian. After their defeat in the sea-battle at *Actium (31), Cleopatra and Antony sought peace terms from Octavian, but without success. Alexandria was surrendered in 30 and Antony committed suicide. Cleopatra was ordered to leave for Rome, and apparently committed suicide to avoid the shame of participating in Octavian's triumph. The story that she died by the bite of an asp (said to be painless) was accepted enthusiastically by the Romans as appropriate for a barbarian queen, and reported with some reservations by the historians.

Cleopatra was Greek by descent (the name is found in Homer), from Alexander's general Ptolemy Soter, and with her ended the Macedonian dynasty of the *Ptolemies in Egypt. We do not know her true character behind the romantic tales, but she clearly had personal courage and magnetism, and she wielded sufficient power to be feared by the Romans.

Cle'ophon, Athenian politician prominent in the latter part of the Peloponnesian War, and a leader of the people (*demagogue) after the restoration of democratic rule in 410 BC. He introduced a dole of two obols a day for poor citizens. His manner was as aggressive as *Cleon's, and he prevented the

Athenians from accepting Sparta's peace offers in 410 and 405. He was prosecuted and condemned to death by the *oligarchs in 404.

clēruch (*klērouchos*), Athenian citizen who held an allotment (*klēros*) of land in a foreign country.

client, at Rome, in early republican times, a free man who entrusted himself to a powerful *patron to whom he rendered services and from whom he received protection; a freedman became automatically the client of his former owner. The *Twelve Tables recognized the tie of clientship as legally binding. Under the empire the client became almost indistinguishable from the *parasite, the subservient hanger-on, familiar from the satires of Juvenal and Martial. Certain conquered foreign states are sometimes spoken of as 'clients' of Rome, and some individuals and families in Rome built up a large following of foreign 'clients'.

Clīo (Kleiō), see MUSES.

Cloā'ca Ma'xima, the great sewer of Rome, originally an open watercourse, later vaulted and paved. Its construction was attributed to the Tarquins, and more particularly to Tarquinius Superbus in the late sixth century BC. It was first enclosed in the third century BC, and much of the existing sewer is the work of M. Vipsanius *Agrippa in c.33 BC. It still forms part of the drainage system of the modern city. (See CRATES 4.)

Cloa'nthus, in Virgil's *Aeneid*, a companion of Aeneas. He figures in the boat-race (book 5).

clocks (*horologia*; sing. Gk. *hōrologion*, Lat. *hōrologium*). In ordinary life the Greeks and Romans referred to the time of day in descriptive terms, 'first light', 'midday', etc. The hour, when used, was not a twenty-fourth part of the astronomical day but one-twelfth of the time from sunrise to sunset (or sunset to sunrise), and its length therefore varied with latitude and season. The clocks which were used to measure these hours in the ancient world were all variants of two basic kinds, the shadow-clock or sundial and the water-clock (clepsydra).

This was a vessel with a small opening at the bottom through which water was allowed to trickle. It appears to have been in common use at Athens from the fifth century BC. The earliest preserved examples have been found in Egypt. The shadow-clock had disadvantages other than its dependence on sunshine: it required different scales according to latitude, and for dividing the period of daylight into equal parts it required, like the water-clock, seasonal correction. The first clocks brought to Rome in the third century BC were shadow-clocks in the form of sundials, *sōlāria*, erected in public view. The most famous was one captured in Sicily in 263 BC and set up on a column behind the Rostra, but it was unfortunately not adapted to the latitude of Rome. In 159 BC, P. Scipio Nasica erected a public clepsydra which told the hours of day and of night. A magnificent shadow-clock was erected by Augustus in the Campus Martius, its *gnomon* an Egyptian obelisk. Clocks were also kept by private individuals (see HEROPHILUS); Cicero sent one to Tiro. The Alexandrian inventor Ctesibius was said to have designed a water-clock in which dripping water turned wheels which gradually elevated a small statue whose pointing stick indicated the passing hours. Clepsydrae were used by the Romans in their military camps to measure the four watches into which the night was divided.

Clō'dia, in Rome, b. *c.*95 BC, second of the three sisters of P. *Clodius and wife of Q. Metellus Celer (consul in 60), notorious for her profligacy. Among her lovers was the poet *Catullus, who celebrated her as 'Lesbia' (the identification is virtually certain). Cicero paints a vivid picture of her in his letters and especially in his speech of 56, *Pro Caelio* (see CICERO (1) 4). She may have been still alive in 45 BC.

Clō'dius. 1. Publius Clodius Pulcher, b. *c.*92 BC, Roman patrician of the famous Claudian *gens*, who, like his sister Clodia (see above) and some other members of the *gens*, used the plebeian form of the name. He was notorious for his violence and profligacy, and as the enemy of Cicero. For his profanation of the mysteries of the Bona Dea in 62 BC, his

hatred of Cicero, resulting in the latter's exile in 58, his feud with Milo, and his violent death in 52 see CICERO (1) 3 and 4.

2. Decimus Clodius Albīnus, governor of Britain at the end of the second century AD.

Cloe'lia, according to Roman legend, one of the Roman hostages given to the Etruscan king Lars *Porsen(n)a in the course of his war with the newly founded Roman republic (510 BC). She escaped by swimming across the Tiber to Rome, but had to be handed back to Porsenna; he freed her, however, together with some of her companions, in admiration of her bravery, thus initiating a reconciliation between the two sides. The Romans erected an equestrian statue to her on the Via Sacra.

Clōtho, 'spinner', one of the three Greek *Fates.

Cloudcuckooland, see BIRDS.

Clouds (*Nephelai*, Lat. *Nūbēs*), Greek comedy by *Aristophanes, ridiculing Socrates as a typical *sophist and corrupt propagator of ridiculous new ideas among the young. The play was originally produced at the City *Dionysia of 423 BC but won only third (and last) prize, and Aristophanes, who seems to have thought it his best play to date, set about rewriting it. We have only the (incompletely) revised version dating from the period 418–416, which was never performed.

Strepsīadēs ('twister'), an elderly dishonest farmer, has been financially ruined by his fashionable wife and horse-loving son Pheidippidēs. He has heard of Socrates, a man who can make the worse cause appear the better, and hopes that he will teach his son how to defraud his creditors. As his son refuses to enter Socrates' school (the *phrontistērion*, 'think-shop'), Strepsiades decides to go himself. He is told he must resign himself to hard work and simple living, and is introduced to the Clouds who (and not Zeus, as generally believed) are the deities who produce thunder and rain. But Strepsiades is too stupid and too much concerned with his debts to learn very much, and Pheidippides has to take his place as pupil. Socrates hands

Pheidippides over to be instructed by Right and Wrong in person. A contest between these two (one of the substituted scenes) follows, in which Wrong is victorious. Strepsiades, by the aid of what little he has learnt, is able to confute his creditors. But the tables are turned on him when, as a result of the same learning, Pheidippides starts to beat his father (and threatens to beat his mother too), and proves that he is justified in doing so. Strepsiades, disgusted with the new education and repenting of his dishonesty, sets fire to Socrates' school and drives the inmates away.

Clytemne'stra (Klўtaim(n)ēstrā), in Greek myth, daughter of Tyndareus king of Sparta, and Leda; sister of Helen (of Troy), Castor, and Polydeuces (Lat. Pollux). She married Agamemnon king of Mycenae and became the mother of Iphigeneia (or Iphianassa), Chrysothemis, Electra (or Laodicē), and Orestes. During Agamemnon's absence in the Trojan War she took Aegisthus as lover, and upon Agamemnon's return with Cassandra, his Trojan concubine, she killed them both, Agamemnon in the bath. When Orestes reached manhood he killed his mother and Aegisthus. The chief interest of her story for the authors who related it is the variety of motives it admits for the murder of Agamemnon, and the different characterizations it therefore makes possible.

Cnidus, Greek city on the coast of Caria in south-western Asia Minor, a Lacedaemonian colony, and one of the six Dorian colonies in Asia Minor known collectively as the Dorian Hexapolis, namely Cnidus, Cos, Halicarnassus (before its expulsion), and the three cities of Rhodes: Lindus, Ialysus, and Camirus. Owing to its favourable situation it acquired great wealth from trade. Famous citizens include *Ctēsias and *Eudoxus. Aphroditē was worshipped there, and the Cnidians, who seem to have been fond of art, possessed the statue by *Praxiteles of the goddess naked; they refused the king of Bithynia's offer to pay their public debt in exchange for it. (See also DELPHI.) In the fifth century BC Cnidus developed a flourishing medical school; with Cos it

became the main centre for teaching medicine, with its own particular doctrines and practices.

Cnossus (Knōsos or Knōssos), the most famous city of *Crete in ancient times, situated near the middle of the north coast of the island about 6 km. (4 miles) inland. Its foundation was attributed to the legendary king *Minos who also built there the *labyrinth to contain the Minotaur.

Cock, The, see LUCIAN.

Coclēs, Publius Horā'tius, the legendary Roman hero Horatius, the subject of the best known of the *Lays of Ancient Rome* (1842) by Thomas Macaulay. With two companions, Sp. Larcius and T. Herminius, Horatius held at bay the whole Etruscan army under Lars *Porsen(n)a while the wooden Sublician bridge over the Tiber into Rome was being cut down behind them. At the moment of its collapse he sent back his two companions and held the position single-handed, finally jumping into the river and swimming back to the city.

Cocy'tus, in Greek myth, one of the rivers of *Hades. It was also the name of a tributary of the Acheron in Epirus.

cōdex, see BOOKS AND WRITING and JUSTINIAN.

Codrus, in Athenian legend, son of Melanthus, descendant of *Neleus, and a member of the Messenian royal family. When the Dorians captured Messenia, Codrus came to Athens; there he became king at the time when the Dorians conquered the Peloponnese. When they invaded Attica (roughly in the eleventh century BC; see DORIAN INVASION) they were told by an oracle that they would be victorious if they spared the king. Codrus, hearing this, entered the Dorian camp in disguise, provoked a quarrel, and was killed; the Dorians then withdrew. One tradition said that because no one was thought worthy to succeed such a king, the kingly office was thereafter abolished, and *archons appointed instead. The first archonship was held by Codrus' son Medon, from whom *Solon and *Peisistratus claimed descent.

Another tradition made a later descendant the first archon.

cognō'men, SEE NAMES 2.

cohort, in the Roman army, the tenth part of a legion, nominally 600 men.

Cōlax ('flatterer'), Greek comedy by *Menander, made use of by Terence for his own *Eunuchus*. Some fragments of *Colax* have been recovered from papyri but it is difficult to reconstruct the plot. It concerned an arrogant Greek professional soldier.

Colchis, country at the eastern end of the Black Sea, bounded on the north by the Caucasus, famous in Greek legend as the destination of the *Argonauts and the home of *Medea. It was also known as Aea. Its river, Phasis, was sometimes regarded as forming the boundary between Europe and Asia, its navigable waters taking sailors from the Black Sea as far east as they could go.

Colline Gate, at Rome, on the northeast side of the city, the scene of a battle in 82 BC in which *Sulla, after his return from the first Mithridatic War in the East, finally overcame the Marian forces and made himself master of Italy.

cōlon, SEE METRE, GREEK 8 (i).

Colō'nus, deme or district of Attica, about 1.5 km. (1 mile) north-west of the *Dipylon at Athens, the legendary scene of the death of *Oedipus, and the birthplace of Sophocles.

Colosse'um, the great amphitheatre of Rome, begun by the emperor Vespasian and dedicated by his son Titus in AD 80. It stands on a site previously occupied by part of the *Golden House of Nero and the name derives from a large statue (see COLOSSUS) of Nero that stood nearby. The Colosseum was capable of holding at least 50,000 people. It was used for gladiatorial and wild-beast shows and the arena could be flooded for mimic sea-fights (see NAUMACHIAE), but the tradition that it was the scene of many Christian martyrdoms has been questioned.

Colo'ssus of Rhodes (Gk. *kolossos*, 'a more than lifesize statue'), a bronze statue of the Greek sun-god Helios, one of the *Seven Wonders of the ancient world. Erected to commemorate the successful defence of the city against a siege in 305–304 BC, it stood at the entrance of the harbour (the tradition that it stood astride the entrance is discredited), and was 70 cubits high (30–5 m., 100–15 ft.). It was completed *c.*280 BC and overthrown by an earthquake *c.*224 BC.

Colume'lla, Lucius Junius Moderā'-tus, Spaniard from Gades (Cadiz) in Spain who served as a tribune of the Roman army in Syria. In about AD 60–5 he composed a treatise on farming, *De re rustica*, in twelve books. It deals with the various aspects of a farmer's life and work, the choice of a farm, its cultivation, livestock, fishponds, bees, and gardens, while the last two books expound the duties of the bailiff and his wife. All the books are written in prose except for book 10, which in rather uninspired hexameters deals with gardens, a topic which Virgil, in the last book of the *Georgics*, had said he was leaving to others. Columella writes as a practical farmer who is distressed by the decline of Italian agriculture, remedy for which he sees in knowledge, hard work, and interest on the part of the landowner. He is a warm admirer of the *Georgics*. His prose is simple and dignified, without affectation. He also wrote a shorter manual on agriculture, of which one book on trees, *De arboribus*, is extant.

comedy. 1. Greek. The only Greek comedy we possess is Athenian. For that reason it is also known as Attic comedy (from the state of Attica, of which Athens was the chief city).

1. *Background.* Comedies at Athens, like tragedies, were produced under the auspices of the state and were a matter for competition (compare TRAGEDY 1). They were first produced at the annual festival of the City *Dionysia in 486 BC and at the *Lenaea (another Dionysiac festival) *c.*440 BC. Before and after the Peloponnesian War (431–404 BC), five comedies were performed annually at each festival; during the war the number is said to have been reduced to three for reasons of economy. Comic dramatists (often called comic poets because the

plays were written in verse) who wished to have their plays performed 'applied for a *chorus' to the magistrate in charge of the festival, who chose the successful applicants. The duty of providing a chorus fell upon rich citizens (see CHORE-GIA). The dramatists, who received payment, usually presented only one play each, and were in competition for first prize, which may have been no more than a garland of ivy. At the Lenaea a prize seems also to have been given for the best comic actor, but not at the City Dionysia until the late fourth century. Ten judges were appointed by lot from among the citizens, according to an elaborate method designed to avoid corruption. It seems to be the case that no Greek wrote both tragedies and comedies; when, at the end of Plato's *Symposium*, Socrates forces Agathon, who wrote tragedies, and *Aristophanes, who wrote comedies, to admit that the same man could write both, the admission was intended to be paradoxical (but see ION OF CHIOS).

2. *The origin of Greek comedy*. The earliest comedy we possess, the *Acharnians* of Aristophanes, was produced in 425 BC; we do not know how it differed from the earliest comedies performed in Athens, nor how comedy started in the first place.

3. *Old Comedy (Aristophanic Comedy)*. The term 'Old Comedy' denotes the comedies produced in Athens in the fifth century BC. Of all these works the only complete plays surviving are eleven by Aristophanes, and of these the last two (*Ecclesiazusae* and *Plutus*) were written in the fourth century BC and are different in character from the rest, notably in the much reduced role of the chorus. Our knowledge of Old Comedy therefore depends upon Aristophanes' other nine plays, all produced in the last quarter of the fifth century. However, there are sufficient resemblances between these plays, late in the tradition though they are, and the fragments of the other playwrights (see 4 below), to allow cautious generalizations about the nature of Old Comedy.

An Aristophanic comedy is elaborate in structure and may be divided into the following parts (found with some variations in the first nine plays).

(i) *prologos*, 'prologue', an expository opening scene before the entrance of the chorus.

(ii) *parodos*, 'the entry of the chorus', a scene in which the chorus enters and is characterized and introduced to the audience; it is usual for it then to oppose either the hero or the hero's enemies with great vigour. The *parodos* ends with a short scene that effects a transition to the next section.

(iii) *agon*, 'debate', between two adversaries with arguments for and against the crucial issue of the play.

(iv) *parabasis*, 'coming forward'. After the *agon* all the characters leave the stage, the chorus 'comes forward' and the chorus-leader addresses the audience directly in anapaestic tetrameters, the subject-matter having little to do with the plot. The anapaests end in a long sentence to be spoken in one breath (*pnīgos*, 'the choke').

(v) Following the *parabasis* comes a number of episodes (*epeisodia*), separated by brief choral songs, sometimes carrying on the main plot, but usually only illustrating the conclusion arrived at in the *agon*.

(vi) *exodos*, final scene, in which the predominant note is rejoicing, generally leading up to a feast or wedding. The play may conclude with a *cordax* or riotous dance.

A comedy required for its performance three or four actors, occasionally with the support of supernumeraries, and a chorus of twenty-four members (all men). The chorus was of primary importance. Many plays took their titles from the chorus (e.g. *Acharnians*, *Wasps*, *Birds*), whose costume and dances provided spectacle. The actors' costumes were an exaggeration of reality, with grotesque masks (which included hair) and body padding and, probably, a large phallus for male characters. The costume was consonant with the robust nature of Old Comedy, in which the jokes were much concerned with sex and excretion and expressed in uninhibited language. The comedy took as its starting point a fantastic scheme on the part of the hero, the achievement of which, wholly impossible in real life, constituted the plot. A few prominent citizens were mercilessly ridiculed; in some comedies they figure in major roles, either in their own names, e.g. Socrates in *Clouds*, Euripides in *Thesmophoriazusae*, or in thin disguise, e.g. Cleon as the Paphlagonian in *Knights*. Topical comment on personalities, events, and institutions of the day (e.g. the lawcourts in *Wasps*) was pervasive. The more extreme aspects of contemporary democratic politics, the more ridiculous developments in education, music, and literature, even the indignities of war, were seized upon and exaggerated for comic effect. The gods, or certain gods, were similarly treated with irreverence, but never in such a way as to deny their reality. It is difficult to see how far serious social comment lay behind the jokes. Altogether, Old Comedy was a humane blend of religious ceremony, satire and criticism (political, social, and literary), wit and buffoonery.

4. *Authors of Old Comedy*. Of the authors of Old Comedy other than Aristophanes we know little. The two greatest after Aristophanes, as the Greeks thought, were Cratinus and Eupolis. Only fragments survive.

5. *Middle Comedy*. This term is used to describe Athenian comedy of the period *c*.400–*c*.323 BC (between Old and New Comedy), almost all of which is lost. It was a period of experimentation and no single type of play can be said to represent it exclusively. The defeat of Athens at the end of the Peloponnesian War (404 BC) was reflected in comedy by the evolution of a type that was cosmopolitan and less Athenian in character. Aristophanes' *Ecclesiazusae* (probably 391) and *Plutus* (388) are thought of as typical early examples. The *parabasis* disappeared, the role of the chorus declined sharply, the padded costume and the phallus were given up. Plots based on mythology continued to be popular in the first half of the period, but political themes and comment gradually disappeared, to be replaced by satire of familiar types in society, the professional soldier and the courtesan, for example. Emphasis came to be put on the realities of ordinary life. We know the names of about fifty dramatists of this period, of whom the most famous (after Aristophanes) were Antiphanēs, Eubulus, and *Alexis; but Aristophanes

apart, no complete play survives, although we have a large number of fragments.

6. *New Comedy*. New Comedy is the name given to Athenian comedy of the period *c*.323–*c*.263 BC, that is, from the death of Alexander the Great to the death of Philemon, the last great dramatist of New Comedy. (The latter's death is memorably described in the *Florida* of Apuleius.) The plays of New Comedy adhere to a recognizable pattern which is a final development from Old Comedy. They were divided into five acts, separated by irrelevant choral interludes performed by a chorus which took no other part in the play and whose songs have not survived. Padded costume had been abandoned but masks were retained; in other respects the actors wore ordinary Athenian dress. The dramatists set their plays in Athens and were themselves based in Athens, but many of them were drawn there from other cities. They made few references to prominent Athenian citizens or politicians, and in general political comment was rare. Their plots were concerned with some stereotyped but relatively realistic episodes in the private life of the well-to-do family, cosmopolitan rather than narrowly Athenian. Their success lay in the delineation of character, especially as expressed by mood and feeling. These characteristics gave New Comedy a wide and long-lasting appeal, and the plays enjoyed great popularity for many centuries in the Graeco-Roman world. It is ironic therefore that the Attic Greek in which they were written, foreshadowing the international *koinē* (see DIALECTS (1) 3), was considered in the Byzantine age to be inferior to Attic speech of the fifth century BC, and thus unsuitable for the Byzantine schoolroom. As a result manuscripts of the plays were not circulated or copied and none has survived to the present day. However, a number of papyrus finds (see PAPYROLOGY) has restored to us large parts of several plays of *Menander, and we have fragments of some other dramatists. Apart from Menander, the most famous was Philemon (*c*.361–263 BC). He was probably born in Syracuse, but became an Athenian citizen. Sixty titles are known

and over two hundred fragments. His technique can be gathered from Plautus' adaptation of his plays. Dīphilus from the Milesian colony of Sinopē on the Black Sea was another dramatist of the second half of the fourth century BC. Again, about sixty titles are known, and a few of his plays were adapted by Plautus.

2. Roman

1. *Background*. Drama at Rome had its origin in the third century BC, but two centuries later there was disagreement as to how, when exactly, and where it arose. Livy's version of its origin (see below) is only one of several. He states (7. 2) that it began with the dances, accompanied by the flute, of players brought from Etruria in 363 BC to propitiate the gods because of an outbreak of plague. Young men of Rome imitated these dances, adding a dialogue in verse, roughly improvised and, according to Livy, similar to the *Fescennine verses (whatever these may have been) which Horace saw as the origin of comedy. These entertainments were thought of as giving place to a somewhat more developed but still plotless dramatic performance, the *satura* or medley (see SATIRE), with appropriate musical accompaniment. *Livius Andronicus (c.284–204 BC), a Greek from Tarentum, was the first, according to Livy, to abandon the *satura* and compose a play with a plot. With him a more serious and artistic form of drama became established. Probably several elements went to the development of Roman comedy: Etruscan mimetic dances (*persona*, 'mask', and *scaena*, 'stage', are Etruscan forms of the Greek words *prosōpon* and *skēnē*) and perhaps Fescennine dialogue; *satura*; and *Atellan farce, familiar in Rome by the end of the third century BC, but perhaps imported much earlier. The *mime too was known in Rome well before the end of the third century. With audiences prepared by these primitive dramatic forms, Greek (New) Comedy was first introduced by Livius Andronicus in translation in 240 BC and gained a temporary hold. Greek comedy found its first important native Italian exponent in *Naevius, more than thirty of whose comedies have titles known to us, mostly, it would seem, translations of Greek New

Comedy, but possibly including original comedies set in Italy. He was followed by *Plautus, *Caecilius Statius, and *Terence, all imitators and adaptors of New Comedy; their plays were known in consequence as *fabulae *palliatae*, 'plays in Greek cloaks'. But some attempts were made, by the middle of the second century BC, to write comedies in which characters and scenes were Italian although the structure was Greek. These were called *fabulae *togatae*, 'plays in togas'. Unfortunately none of these plays survives, except for a few brief quotations. Lucius Afranius (b. *c.*150 BC) was the most famous of their authors. Roman comedy practically ceased to be written in the first century BC, supplanted by the more popular mime, which had no claim to literary merit. The last recorded revival at Rome of a comedy by Plautus, *Pseudolus*, was staged in Cicero's day.

2. *Performance of Roman comedy*. There had always been an audience at Rome for dramatic performances of one sort or another. From the third century BC days were set aside for stage performances at the public games (see LUDI), and besides regular festivals there were occasional performances at such events as the funeral games of distinguished men. Audiences were drawn from all social classes, but, in general, Roman audiences were less knowledgeable and appreciative than their counterparts in Athens, and had less respect for actors and for the occasion. Horace alleged that an audience will demand a bear or boxers in the middle of a play. Plautus in the prologue to *Poenulus* enumerates an amazing list of activities he would prefer the audience to desist from, of which letting the baby cry is the least. Roman actors, always men except in mimes, were generally slaves (see THEATRE), and if free men, were thought too disreputable to vote or to serve in the army (but see ROSCIUS). There was no strict limitation upon the number of actors, as there was in Greece, and many plays require at least five speaking actors. Oddly enough, it is not known for sure if masks were worn in Roman adaptations of Greek drama, but they were worn in the native Atellan drama. Though the texts of the plays of Plautus have been divided into

five acts since the Renaissance, and those of Terence since ancient times, they were written to run continuously, and they did not employ a chorus, although they included parts that were declaimed or sung. The scenes of spoken dialogue were written in iambic senarii and are called *dīverbia*. All other parts are called *cantica*, and include (*a*) trochaic and iambic septenarii, forming melodramatic recitals, declaimed by the actor to a musical accompaniment, and (*b*) the lyric parts sung by the actor (or a concealed substitute) with a flute accompaniment. For the metre of Roman comedy see METRE, LATIN 2. (See also PANTOMIME and SOCCUS.)

comi'tia (plural noun), name given to a (political) assembly of the Roman people to vote on business presented to them by magistrates. The resolutions of the comitia had to be ratified by the senate. The meetings had to be held on the proper day, after the auspices had been taken, on an inaugurated site (see COMITIUM). (When the people were summoned as a whole and not by particular groups, the assembly was called a *contio*; when only a part of the people was summoned, the assembly was properly called a *concilium*). The *comitia* continued to exist at least formally until the third century AD. See REPUBLIC, ROMAN.

Comi'tium, the chief place of political assembly in republican Rome, a paved area about 75 sq. m. (90 sq. yds.) on the north-west side of the Roman Forum. It was a *templum*, or inaugurated area, and here in early republican times took place most of the assemblies of the Roman people for purposes other than elections (see CAMPUS MARTIUS). On the north side of it stood the *Curia, and on the south the *Rostra.

Commentaries, on the Gallic War and on the Civil War (*Commentarii de bello Gallico* and *Commentarii de bello cīvīli*), memoirs by Julius *Caesar concerned with, respectively, his campaigns in *Gaul from 58 to 52 BC and the civil war against *Pompey which culminated in the battle of Pharsalus (48 BC).

1. *The Gallic War*
Book 1. After a brief geographical de-

scription of Gaul, Caesar starts with an account of the migration of the *Helvetii into Gaul, of how the Romans pursued them and drove them back, and finally resettled them in their old homes. He then relates the increasing invasion of Gaul by Germans, his decision to put an end to it, the fruitless negotiations with their king Ariovistus, and the great battle north-east of Vesontio (Besançon) in which the Germans were routed (58).

Book 2. The Belgic tribes (see BELGAE), threatened by the Roman advance and stirred up by discontented Gauls, combine for war against Rome. The prompt movement of Caesar against them upsets their plans; a series of fights ends in a critical battle against the Nervii (a Belgic tribe) on the river Sabis (Sambre) and they are virtually exterminated. An expeditionary force under P. Crassus meanwhile subdues the tribes on the Atlantic seaboard, and the whole of Gaul is temporarily reduced to quiet (57).

Book 3. Some predatory African tribes are subdued by Servius Galba. Certain Armorican tribes (in Brittany) led by the Veneti (from south Brittany) revolt, and although the Romans have little experience of their kind of naval warfare the rebels are defeated by the makeshift Roman fleet and its unexpected tactics. Their allies are dealt with in smaller campaigns.

Book 4. The German tribes of the Usipetēs and Tencteri invade Gaul and are crushed by Caesar near the river Mosa (Meuse). Caesar follows up this success by crossing the river Rhenus (Rhine) to demonstrate Roman power. He makes his first expedition to Britain, which had supported Gaul against the Romans. A small force lands in Kent in face of fierce opposition. Caesar's fleet at anchor is badly damaged by storm, and the British manner of chariot-fighting throws his troops into confusion. He withdraws his force from Britain in September (55).

Book 5. The second invasion of Britain with a larger force. After its landing, a storm again destroys many of the transports. Caesar reaches and fords the Thames, captures the stronghold of the chief Cassivelaunus, and obtains his surrender. Caesar takes hostages, fixes the tribute payable by Britain, and withdraws to the Continent (at this point the book includes a geographical description of Britain). During the winter the Gauls revolt, taking advantage of the dispersal of the legions in widely separated winter quarters. The Eburones under Ambiorix annihilate the Roman garrison at Aduatuca and then, gathering their allies, lay siege to the camp of Q. *Cicero in the territory of the Nervii. Cicero is rescued from a dangerous situation only by the rapid advance of Caesar with two legions from Samarobriva (Amiens). Further signs of revolt appear during the winter. Idutiomārus, leader of the rebellious Treveri, is killed in a surprise attack by the Romans (54).

Book 6. Various punitive expeditions are made by the Romans in the north-east of Gaul, the chief of them directed against Ambiorix (the leader of the Eburones in the capture of Aduatuca; see book 5). His kingdom is ravaged but he himself escapes. A company of German horsemen cross the Rhine to plunder what they can in the territory of Ambiorix, but at the suggestion of one of their Gallic prisoners they attack instead Aduatuca, where the baggage of the Roman army is stored. They nearly capture this fort by their surprise attack, but the Romans drive them off (53). The book contains an account of the customs of the Gauls and Druids, and of the Germans.

Book 7. The disturbed state of Italy (*Clodius having been murdered early in 52 BC; see CICERO (1) 3 and 4) encourages the Gauls to a general revolt, begun by the Carnūtēs, who massacre the Roman residents in Cēnabum (Orleans). A coalition of the principal tribes is formed under Vercingetorix, leader of the Arverni (who gave their name to Auvergne), and threatens the frontier of the Roman province of Transalpine Gaul. Caesar hastens back from Italy, makes the province secure, and crosses the Cevennes in midwinter, drawing Vercingetorix south to defend Auvergne. Leaving behind D. *Brutus to divert Vercingetorix' attention Caesar himself rapidly travels to the country of the Lingones (Langres) and gathers his troops together. He recaptures Cenabum and besieges Avaricum (Bourges),

capital of the Bitūriges. In spite of the attempts of Vercingetorix to relieve the town, and hardships suffered from the cold and from scarcity of supplies, the Romans occupy it and in revenge for past sufferings butcher all the inhabitants. Caesar moves to attack Gergōvia, capital of the Arverni. During the siege of this very difficult position, the rashness of some of the Roman troops in the course of a carefully planned attack, leading to an over-hasty assault on the town gates, results in heavy loss. This and news that the Aedui, hitherto faithful allies of Rome, were planning to revolt, leads Caesar to withdraw from Gergovia and make for the territory of the Aedui. Without hindrance from Vercingetorix he rejoins *Labienus in the north. Labienus has been sent out against the Senonēs (who gave their name to Sens) and the Parisii, but an uprising of the Bellovaci, as a consequence of their hearing that Caesar has retreated from Gergovia, has put him in danger. He extricates his troops by a skilful manœuvre and joins Caesar at Sens. The united army moves against Vercingetorix, who is again threatening the province of Transalpine Gaul, follows him to his stronghold Alēsia (Mont Auxois), lays siege to it, and in spite of the efforts of a great army of Gauls to relieve it, captures the stronghold as well as Vercingetorix after fierce fighting (52).

Book 8, a continuation of the others, was written by A. *Hirtius. Books 1–7 were published in 51 BC.

2. *The Civil War*

Book 1 narrates the opening of the war, after the senate had voted that Caesar should lay down his military command and he, in defiance, had crossed the *Rubicon with his army. Caesar rapidly overruns Italy, and Pompey, under pressure, retires first to the south Italian port of Brundisium (Brindisi) and then across to Epirus in north-west Greece, before Caesar can close the harbour. Caesar therefore turns west to Massilia (Marseilles), starting to lay siege to it, and then to Spain, where his strategy in the neighbourhood of Ilerda (Lerida) secures the surrender of Pompey's lieutenants Afrānius and Petrēius.

Book 2 relates the continuation of the

siege of Massilia and its surrender, the conquest of western Spain, and the disastrous North African campaign of Caesar's lieutenant, C. Curio, whose rashness brings about the annihilation of his force by king Juba. All the events of the first two books take place in 49 BC.

Book 3 relates the operations of Caesar in 48 against Pompey in Epirus, the unsuccessful attempt to blockade Pompey at Dyrrhachium, Caesar's withdrawal to Thessaly where he is reinforced by fresh troops, the battle of Pharsālus where Caesar's veterans defeat Pompey's numerically superior forces, and Pompey's flight to Egypt, where he is murdered through the agency of the Egyptian king's advisers. The work ends with an account of the political situation in Egypt, Caesar's activities there, and the grave danger to which he and his forces are exposed.

commercium and conubium, rights of, see LATIN RIGHTS.

Co'mmodus, Lucius Ae'lius Aurē'lius (AD 161–92), Roman emperor from 180 to his death, elder son of Marcus *Aurelius. Late in his reign he became insane, renamed Rome Colonia Commodiana ('colony of Commodus'), and believed himself to be the reincarnation of Hercules. When he determined to appear in public as consul and gladiator, his ministers had him strangled by an athlete called Narcissus.

commū'nes loci, 'commonplaces'; in *rhetoric, 'arguments that can be transferred to many places', which were published in handbooks of rhetoric and practised in schools. They seem to have originated with the Greek *sophists Gorgias and Protagoras.

Compitā'lia, at Rome, the festival of the *lares of the crossroads (compita). The festival was a movable one, held on a day announced by the city praetor early in January (see FERIAE) to mark the end of the agricultural year. It was said to have been instituted by the king Servius Tullius, the son of a slave-woman by the lar familiaris. Slaves had a share in the festival and were allowed a great deal of licence. It fell into disuse during the civil wars but was restored by Augustus.

cōmus, see COMEDY, GREEK 2.

conceptī'vae, fē'riae, see FERIAE.

conci'lium plē'bis (also known as the comitia tributa), at Rome, the meeting of the *plebeians by *tribes, under the presidency of their *tribunes, instituted around the mid-fifth century BC. Patricians were excluded from the meetings. Its resolutions, plēbi scita, were recognized as binding on patricians and plebeians alike after 287 BC. It elected the tribunes and (plebeian) *aediles.

Concord, Temple of. According to tradition the first Temple of Concord at Rome was dedicated by M. Furius Camillus in 367 BC to celebrate the end of civil strife over the Licinian rogations (see LICINIAN–SEXTIAN LAWS). It was restored by L. Opimius in 121 BC after the death of C. Gracchus and again by the emperor Tiberius in AD 10 from the spoils of his German campaigns. It stood in an elevated position at the west end of the Forum. The senate often met there and it was the setting for some of Cicero's great political speeches. It was there too that Sejanus was condemned to death.

conco'rdia o'rdinum, see CICERO (1) 3.

confarreā'tio, at Rome, the oldest and most solemn form of *marriage, in classical times only necessary for and perhaps confined to certain priesthoods. Bride and bridegroom sat with veiled heads on joined seats covered with the skin of a sacrificed sheep. A cake made of far (coarse wheat) was of some significance in the ceremony; it may have been offered to Jupiter Farreus, in whose honour this marriage ritual was performed. The *flamen dialis and *pontifex maximus were present. The marriage was indissoluble except by an elaborate ceremony.

Cōnon. 1. One of the Athenian commanders at the battle of Aegospotami between Athens and Sparta at the end of the *Peloponnesian War (405 BC). He escaped from the Athenian disaster with eight ships, and made his way to *Evagoras in Cyprus where he helped revive Persian sea-power. He was subsequently appointed with Pharnabāzus to command the Persian fleet against Sparta, and in

394 defeated the Spartans at Cnidus, destroying their naval power and avenging Aegospotami. He returned to Athens and with the help of the Persian fleet completed the rebuilding of the *Long Walls.

2. Of Samos (third century BC), mathematician and astronomer, who settled in Alexandria. He is best known for his discovery (*c*.245) of the new constellation, the Lock of *Berenice (see also CALLIMACHUS), and he worked on solar eclipses; nothing of his writings survives. He was a close friend of Archimedes, who writes of him with admiration.

Consōlā'tio ad Lī'viam ('consolation to Livia'), a Latin elegiac poem, incorrectly attributed to Ovid, ostensibly written on the death of the empress Livia's son Drusus (see GERMANICUS) while campaigning in Germany in 9 BC.

Consōlā'tio ad Ma'rciam, ad He'lviam, ad Poly'bium, see SENECA (2).

Constantine I, the Great (Flāvius Valerius Constantīnus Augustus), *c*. AD 285–337, emperor of Rome, son of Constantius, the *Augustus in the West. He was with his father in Britain at the latter's death (AD 306) at York, and was there proclaimed Augustus by the army; Galerius, the Augustus in the East, granted him only the rank of Caesar, and Severus became Augustus in the West. A complicated power struggle between rival claimants occupied the following years, brought to a head by the death of Galerius in 311. Early in 312 Constantine invaded Italy and marched on Rome. In a battle near the Milvian bridge across the Tiber he defeated Maxentius who had declared himself Augustus in the West; Maxentius was drowned in the Tiber while attempting to escape. Welcomed as deliverer by the senate, Constantine thus became the senior Augustus. *Eusebius says that years later Constantine told him that in the course of his march on Rome he had seen a vision of the cross of Christ against the sun, and beneath it the words 'In this conquer'. Before the walls of Rome Constantine saw a further vision telling him to have the soldiers mark their shields with the Christian monogram, the Greek letters chi and rho (the first two letters of the Greek word *Christos*, Christ) intersecting. Constantine regarded his victory as showing the favour of the Christian God. In 313 Constantine and Licinius, an imperial claimant, met at Milan and agreed to grant Christians complete religious freedom. It is sometimes thought that a formal proclamation of this policy was made, and it is referred to as the Edict of Milan. Later that year Licinius became Augustus in the East. In 316 (probably) and again in 323 war broke out between Constantine and Licinius, and the latter began to persecute the eastern Christians. In 324 Constantine, after several battles, forced the surrender of Licinius, whom he soon executed for fresh intrigues. Constantine was now sole Augustus and emperor. One of his early decisions was to establish a new imperial residence at *Byzantium for strategic reasons, the site proving commercially advantageous also. In 330 the new residence was formally dedicated and the city renamed Constantinople. It was predominantly a Christian city, and Constantine desired a unified Christian Church as an essential for a united empire. His success in this aim, however, was neither complete nor lasting. Constantine died in 337, having been baptized a Christian on his deathbed (such a postponement was not unusual at the time). In the Eastern Church he is venerated as a saint. Having put to death in 326 his eldest son Crispus (whose tutor was *Lactantius), he was succeeded by his three remaining sons who each took the title Augustus and divided the empire between themselves.

Constantinople, see BYZANTIUM, BYZANTINE AGE, CONSTANTINE I, and JUSTINIAN.

Constantius, see CONSTANTINE I.

Constitution of the Athenians (*Athēnaiōn politeia*). **1.** Political treatise by Aristotle; see ARISTOTLE 3 (ii).

2. Short pamphlet attributed in antiquity to Xenophon but probably written in the 420s BC, and so too early to be by him. Its author is an Athenian of oligarchic sympathies who is critical of the policy and system of contemporary Athenian democracy, and hence is often called the Old Oligarch. Despite its evident bias, the pamphlet concedes that as far as democracies go the Athenian version is efficient, and it is useful for its attempt to explain how democracy at Athens worked.

Constitution of the Lacedaemonians (*Lakedaimoniōn politeia*), minor work of *Xenophon, written *c.*388 BC, a largely admiring account of the Spartan way of life. Xenophon attributes the power of Sparta to the traditional institutions of *Lycurgus which he describes: the marriage system, the physical training of both sexes, the unusual manner of educating the young, the system of eating in public messes, the discouragement of private property, the preference for an honourable death to a disgraceful life, the army system, and the position and function of the kings. In ch. 14, perhaps written later, he laments the decline of the old ways in the Sparta of his day. Of the actual Lacedaemonian constitution, in spite of the title, he tells us very little.

Consuā'lia, see CONSUS.

consuls (Lat. *consules*), at Rome under the republic, the supreme civil and military magistrates (originally called *praetors, *praetores*, perhaps, until the reforms of the *decemvirs in 451 BC), two in number with equal powers (see COLLEGIUM I). Consuls were elected annually by the people, but as the candidates were required to be senators their choice was restricted (see SENATE). After about the middle of the fourth century BC one consul was always *plebeian. The consuls' power was in course of time reduced by the creation of new magistracies, notably the censorship (see CENSORS). The chief functions retained by the consuls were those of military command. Later they received as 'proconsuls' an extension of their authority after the termination of their year of office, to enable them to carry on a military command or govern a province (see PROCONSUL). In the Roman calendar the years were dated by naming the consuls. Under the emperors the consulship increasingly became a mainly honorary office; consuls were generally appointed for no more than two to four

months, only those who entered office on I January giving their name to the year. The consuls retained some judicial functions and introduced legal cases before the senate. See CURSUS HONORUM and IMPERIUM.

A *consul suffectus* was appointed to succeed a consul unable to complete his term of office, or, under the emperors, appointed after the term of *eponymous consul (see above) had expired.

Consus ('storer'), in Roman religion, an ancient god of the granary whose festivals, Consuālia, in August and December, suggest that he was connected with the harvest and the autumn sowing. He had an underground barn and altar in the Circus Maximus which was uncovered only during his festival. The Romans later thought he had something to do with *consilium*, 'counsel', and because they also associated him with horses they sometimes identified him with the Greek god *Poseidon.

co'ntio, public gathering at Rome; see COMITIA.

Contra Rullum ('against Rullus'), or *De lege agraria* ('on the agrarian law'), three speeches delivered by Cicero in 63 BC; see CICERO (I) 2.

contrŏve'rsiae, Latin rhetorical exercises in the oratory of the law-courts; see SENECA (I) and NOVEL.

Cōpa, short Latin elegiac poem doubtfully attributed to Virgil; see APPENDIX VIRGILIANA.

Cōpā'is, lake in *Boeotia.

Corax, of Syracuse (first half of the fifth century BC), said to have been the first Greek teacher of *rhetoric.

Corcy'ra (Kerkyra, modern Corfu), an island in the Ionian Sea in north-west Greece, off the coast of Epirus, identified by the ancients with Scheria, the land of the Phaeacians in Homer's *Odyssey* (book 5). It was colonized first perhaps by Eretrians, and then in 733 BC by Corinthians. In consequence of a quarrel with its mother city in 435 BC it made an alliance with Athens in 433. Serious political strife between oligarchs and democrats in 427 resulted in wholesale massacre, memorably described by Thucydides (3. 69 and 4. 46–8). Corcyra remained an Athenian ally until 410, and rejoined the Athenian League in the fourth century BC.

cordax, comic dance performed in Old Comedy (see COMEDY, GREEK 3), associated with lewdness and drunkenness. Aristophanes claimed to exclude it from his plays (but see WASPS).

Corē ('the maiden'), in Greek myth, *Persephonē.

Cori'nna. 1. Greek lyric poetess from Tanagra in Boeotia, thought in ancient times to be an older contemporary of her fellow-countryman the poet Pindar, and thus of the second half of the sixth century BC. But her spelling of the Boeotian dialect and the lack of early references to her have led to the suggestion that she lived *c.*200 BC. The question is still unresolved. The fragments of her poetry which survive in quotation have been augmented by the substantial remains of two poems found in a papyrus. One concerns a singing contest between the mountains Cithaeron and Helicon, each traditionally associated with the Muses and so with poetry; the other is a catalogue poem in the manner of Hesiod concerning the genealogies of Boeotian heroes and heroines. The poems are written in regular stanzas using simple lyric metres. According to an ancient anecdote Corinna criticized the absence of myth from one of Pindar's poems; when he thereupon went to the other extreme she remarked that one should 'sow by handfuls, not with the whole sack', an expression which became proverbial.

2. In Ovid, see AMORES.

Corinth (Korinthos), mentioned in Homer's *Iliad*, where it is also referred to by the name Ephyrē, one of the most important cities of ancient Greece, strategically situated on the Isthmus joining north Greece to the Peloponnese, between two important seas (the Ionian and Aegean), and therefore destined to be a great maritime power. Also, it was situated at the focal point of north–south and, more importantly, east–west trade routes. It was easier to drag small ships across the Isthmus (see next entry) or unload from ships on one side and reload

on to different ships on the other, than to undertake a long and stormy voyage around the Peloponnese.

Corinth is connected with the early history of Greek literature through *Arion and *Eumelus. In myth it is associated with *Sisyphus and his descendants; *Medea and Jason fled there after the former contrived the murder of Jason's uncle Pelias. It was occupied by the *Dorians *c.*900 BC. The tradition was that from 747 until 657 BC the city was ruled by the Dorian oligarchy of the *Bacchiadae, under whom Corinth founded *Corcyra and Syracuse in 733, and remains found on the site attest the city's widespread foreign contacts. In 657 the Bacchiads were overthrown by the tyrant *Cypselus and under him and his son *Periander (*c.*625–585 BC) Corinthian power and prosperity reached their zenith. Three years after Periander died, to be succeeded by his nephew Psammetichus, the tyranny fell and was replaced by an oligarchy which maintained friendship with Sparta and Athens. With the growth of Athenian imperialism in the second half of the fifth century relations with Athens deteriorated, and disputes between Athens and Corinth over Corcyra and *Potidaea (another Corinthian colony) led to the outbreak of the Peloponnesian War in 431. Corinthians were one of the most active and persistent opponents of Athens throughout the war, but Corinth later joined Athens, Argos, and Boeotia to make war against the tyrannical rule of Sparta (the Corinthian War, 395–386 BC). The war ended with the Peace of Antalcidas (a Spartan general), engineered with the aid of Persia. In the war against Philip II of Macedon, Corinth joined Athens in the cause of Hellenic freedom. After the defeat of the Athenians and Thebans at Chaeronea (338), it was at Corinth that Philip summoned a congress of Greek states to form a confederacy under Macedonian supremacy. Later, Corinth became one of the principal strongholds of the *Achaean League. It afterwards passed into Macedonian control until Flaminius' victory over Macedon in 198–196, when it was declared free like all other Greek cities and became the chief city of the Achaean League. In the course of Rome's operations against the League it was completely sacked by Mummius in 146 BC in revenge for the insults suffered by the Roman ambassadors, and its population slaughtered or enslaved. It was the extinction, as Cicero said, of 'the light of all Greece'. The Greek Anthology contains a moving lament by a contemporary poet (9. 151). After a century's desolation it was refounded by Julius Caesar as a colony (46 BC). When the apostle Paul visited it about a hundred years later it was the capital of the Roman province of Achaea, and a prosperous and populous city. It became notorious for luxury and excessive refinement; the adjective 'Corinthian' was in former times used in English with this connotation.

Corinth, Isthmus of. The Isthmus, 6 km. (4 miles) wide at its narrowest, is the neck of land east of the city of Corinth across which merchandise was transported from one sea to the other and ships were dragged along a portage-road (*diolkos*), still visible in part, perhaps built by *Periander. It was also the site of the Isthmian games. Octavian's fleet was dragged across when Octavian pursued Antony and Cleopatra after defeating them at Actium in 31 BC. The emperor Nero undertook the work of cutting a canal through the Isthmus (as others, from Periander onwards, had contemplated before him), and actually started it with his own hands and a golden pickaxe; but it was discontinued after a considerable amount of excavation had been done.

Corinthian War, 395–386 BC, Corinth, Athens, Argos, and Boeotia against Sparta. See CORINTH.

Coriolā'nus, Gnaeus Ma'rcius, one of the great legendary heroes of Rome, a general who according to tradition won his name (*cognomen*) from the capture of the Volscian town of Corioli in 493 BC. His arrogance towards the people during a corn shortage led to his prosecution by the tribunes on the charge of aspiring to become tyrant, and subsequent exile. He withdrew to his old enemies the Volscians, led them against Rome, and approached within five miles of the city.

Moved by the pleas of his mother Veturia and his wife Volumnia (the names vary in the sources), he withdrew his army and returned to the Volscian city of Antium (Anzio), where he was put to death by the Volscians. His story is told by Livy (2. 33). Shakespeare's play *Coriolanus* depends upon the Life written by Plutarch, whose source was Dionysius of Halicarnassus.

Cornē'lia (second century BC), mother of the *Gracchi, famous in her day and after as the ideal Roman matron, distinguished for her virtue and accomplishments. She was the second daughter of *Scipio Africanus, and married Ti. Sempronius Gracchus (d. 153). Among her twelve children were the two famous tribunes Tiberius and Gaius Gracchus, and a daughter Sempronia who married Scipio Aemilianus. After her husband's death she devoted herself to the management of her estate and the education of her children. She remained an important influence on her sons. Tiberius was said to have been urged on to propose his laws by his mother's reproach that she was known as the mother-in-law of Scipio, not the mother of the Gracchi. Plutarch tells the well-known story that when a visitor asked to see her jewels she produced her sons, saying 'These are my jewels'. The authenticity of two fragments of letters from her to Gaius which have survived in quotation has been disputed.

Cornē'lius Gallus, see GALLUS.

Cornē'lius Sevē'rus, Roman epic poet of the late first century BC; see EPIC 2.

Corno'vii, British tribe which occupied what is now Staffordshire, Cheshire, and Shropshire, centred on Viriconium (Wroxeter).

Cornū'tus, Lucius Annae'us, philosopher at Rome in the first century AD. See LUCAN and PERSIUS.

Corōnē'a (Korōneia), in Boeotia, the scene of two battles. 1. In 447 BC, the Athenians, under Tolmidēs, were defeated by the Boeotians and had to surrender the sovereignty they had exercised over Boeotia for the previous ten years. 2. In 394 BC the Spartans under

*Agesilaus defeated the Boeotians and their allies, including Athens.

Corō'nis, in Greek myth, mother of *Asclepius.

Corpus Iūris Cīvīlis ('the complete civil law'), a volume of Roman law compiled by *Justinian containing all imperial legislation still in force in his day.

correption, in metre, the shortening of a long vowel or diphthong at the end of a word when the following word begins with a vowel. It occurs frequently in Homer, much less frequently in other poets.

Coryba'ntēs, male priests associated with various gods who had orgiastic cults (see ORGIA), and in particular the companions of the Asiatic goddess *Cybelē, whom they followed with wild dances and music. They were often confused with the *Curetes.

Cory'cian cave. 1. In Greece, a celebrated cave on Mount Parnassus above Delphi, sacred to *Pan and the nymphs. The Delphians used it as a refuge in 480 BC during the Persian invasion; it was the scene of one of the miraculous happenings that brought about the Persians' precipitate retreat from Delphi (Herodotus 8. 36).
2. A cave at Corycus in Cilicia (on the southern coast of Asia Minor), the reputed dwelling of the giant *Typhoeus (Typhon), and famous for its saffron-producing crocuses. Corycus was the home of Virgil's *Corycius senex*, 'old man of Corycus', the gardener of *Georgics* 4. 125.

coryphae'us, chorus-leader; see CHORUS.

Cos, one of the Sporades islands off the south-west tip of Asia Minor, opposite Halicarnassus, colonized by *Dorians. It won fame in the Hellenistic age, in the fourth and third centuries BC, as a literary centre under the patronage of the Egyptian kings the Ptolemies, and was the home of the Greek poets Philetas and Theocritus. It was the birthplace of *Hippocrates (fifth century BC), the father of Greek medicine and a member of a famous medical family in that island, reputedly descended from *Asclepius.

cothu'rnus (*kothornos*), 'buskin' or calf-length laced boot of soft leather with a thin sole and turned-up toes worn by actors playing heroic roles in Greek tragedy, and hence the symbol of high tragedy. The famous tragic buskin with a sole several inches high was an invention of the late Hellenistic Age. Since the boot could be worn on either foot, the word was used as a nickname for a politician prepared to support either side, a 'trimmer' (see THERAMENES). See also CREPIDATA and SOCCUS.

Cottus, see HECATONCHEIRES.

Crannon, town in Thessaly, the home of the powerful family of the Scopadae (see SIMONIDES). The battle of Crannon (322 BC) was a Macedonian victory over the Athenians in the *Lamian War.

Crantor, of Soli in Cilicia (on the southern coast of Asia Minor), *c.*335–275 BC, a Greek philosopher belonging to the *Academy at Athens, who wrote a commentary on Plato's dialogue *Timaeus*. His work 'On grief' was much admired by later writers including Cicero, who used it as a model for his own 'Consolation' written to comfort himself on the death of his daughter Tullia (see CICERO (1) 4).

crāsis, in Greek grammar, the running-together of a vowel or diphthong at the end of a word with a vowel or diphthong at the beginning of the next, the two words being thus joined together. Compare SYNIZESIS, where the spelling of the two words remains unaffected.

Crassus. 1. Lucius Lici'nius Crassus (140–91 BC), the outstanding Roman orator of his day, exemplar for Cicero, who makes him the chief speaker in his *De oratore. He was a strong supporter of the aristocracy. His speeches have not survived, but a saying has: see AHENOBARBUS.
2. **Marcus Lici'nius Crassus** (115–53 BC), the triumvir, one of *Sulla's lieutenants, who had made a fortune in the *proscriptions. In 71 he put down the slave revolt led by *Spartacus, who had defeated the consuls in the previous year. He was consul in 70 with *Pompey whom he now felt to be his rival. They greatly modified Sulla's constitution and diminished the power of the senate. In

the following years Crassus increased his fortune, and by helping suitably eminent or promising men in need (such as Julius *Caesar) he gained much influence. When Caesar returned from Spain, he, Pompey, and Crassus made an informal coalition, known in modern times as 'the first triumvirate', with the purpose of enabling each man to achieve his particular aim. Crassus helped Caesar to become consul in 59. In 55 Caesar procured the consulship for both Pompey and Crassus, and arranged for Crassus to proceed afterwards to the province of Syria, which the latter reckoned to be the place to acquire wealth and military glory by a victory over the Parthians. In the event the Romans suffered an appalling defeat at Carrhae in 53 and Crassus was subsequently murdered by the Parthians. The Parthian king was celebrating the marriage of his son and entertaining the wedding party with a performance of Euripides' *Bacchae*, when a messenger arrived with the head and hand of Crassus. To the delight of the spectators the actors applied to Crassus' head the lines in the play referring to that of Pentheus.

Cratī'nus, writer of Greek Old Comedy; see COMEDY, GREEK 4.

Cra'tylus, dialogue by *Plato on the origin of language, written c.384 BC. Cratylus was a philosopher of the school of *Heracleitus and a friend, or teacher, of Plato. According to the views expressed in the dialogue by Cratylus and Socrates, all words in all languages are by nature appropriate to the things they describe, being imitations of them, but in language there are also elements of chance, of design, and of convention. Cratylus is represented as accepting Socrates' fanciful etymologies.

Crĕ'mera, see FABIA GENS.

Cremū'tius Cordus, Aulus, Roman historian who wrote in the first century AD a history of the civil wars. He committed suicide when prosecuted by the emperor Tiberius because, it was said, he called *Cassius (one of Caesar's murderers) 'the last Roman'. His work has not survived.

Crēon ('prince'), name given to several

figures in Greek myth; compare CREUSA, 'princess'.

1. King of Corinth, with whom Jason and Medea took refuge (see ARGONAUTS). Jason abandoned Medea in favour of marriage with the king's daughter, and in revenge Medea contrived the death of father and daughter.

2. Brother of Jocasta, the wife of *Oedipus, king of Thebes. He ruled Thebes on three occasions: after Laius' death, after Oedipus' downfall, and again after the death of Oedipus' son Eteocles (see ANTIGONE). He gave his daughter Megara in marriage to Heracles (see HERACLES, MADNESS OF).

crepidā'ta, fa'bula, term applied to a Roman tragedy on a Greek theme, such as the tragedies of Accius and Pacuvius; from *crepida*, the Latin word for the high boot, *cothurnus*, worn by Greek tragic actors.

Crete (Krētē, Lat. Crēta), Mediterranean island to the south-east of Greece and the south-west of Asia Minor. Its position makes it a natural stepping-stone from Europe to Egypt, Cyprus, and Asia. Holding therefore an intermediate position in early times, between the ancient civilizations of the Near and Middle East and barbarian Europe, it was well suited to become the site of the earliest European high civilization.

The British archaeologist Sir Arthur Evans, who began excavations on the island in 1899, named this Bronze Age culture Minoan civilization after Minos, the legendary early king of Crete. Evans divided the civilization into three main phases that covered the period c.3000–c.1000 BC, Early, Middle, and Late Minoan (EM, MM, LM), and each phase into three sub-periods, I, II, and III. Further subdivisions have since been made, e.g. LMIIIA, LMIIIA1. Sixteen or more successive periods can be recognized by changes in the shape and decoration of Minoan pottery. The chief sites are at *Cnossus, Phaestus, Mallia, and Khania (in classical times known as Cydonia); other smaller sites have also been excavated.

The Early Minoan period (c.3000–2200 BC), which succeeded a long Neolithic Age, was marked by a striking new style of pottery, indicating the arrival of a new (and non-Greek) people from western Asia, from Anatolia perhaps, or a Semitic people from Syria or Palestine. The end of this period marked the start of the great period of Minoan civilization, c.2200–1450 BC (MMI–LMI). The island seems to have been peaceful (there were few defences) and prosperous; writing existed in the form of pictograms on stone seals, out of which developed a simplified script (see LINEAR A) found on clay tablets and in inscriptions and graffiti. This script has not yet been deciphered. In MMII, perhaps at the end of the eighteenth century BC, the great palaces at Cnossus and Phaestus were destroyed, probably by earthquake rather than war. Afterwards they were entirely rebuilt, and the period following the rebuilding is sometimes referred to as the 'second palace period'. However, Cnossus and other Cretan sites suffered further destruction c.1500 BC, in consequence, it has been thought, of the great volcanic explosion of *Thera, which caused widespread damage and may have been followed in some places by foreign conquest. After these disasters only Cnossus seems to have recovered her former prosperity in the succeeding period, LMII (c.1450–1400 BC). During this time a new influence becomes apparent, both in pottery styles and in writing. Clay tablets appear late in the period (the dating is uncertain) written in a different script, *Linear B, which is also known from several sites on the mainland of Greece. This has been deciphered as an early form of Greek, different from the language of the earlier scripts and probably indicating that the island rulers were by this time Mycenaean Greeks from the mainland whose power was expanding as that of Crete declined (see MYCENAE).

A final catastrophe, accompanied by fire and looting, overwhelmed Cnossus in the 'last palace' period, c.1375 BC (LMIIIA); there is no clear evidence to show the origin of the catastrophe, whether it was natural or caused by revolution or foreign invasion. By the end of the Bronze Age (towards 1000 BC), Minoan culture was in sharp decline. Cnossus, however, remained an import-

ant city into the Early Iron Age, c.1000 BC, and Crete's strategic position ensured its continuing fame. Homer talks of 'Crete of the hundred cities' (more than half of which are known). In historical times Crete was predominantly *Dorian; it was governed by an aristocracy and its important cities were Cnossus (still), Gortyn, and Lyttos, and later Cydonia (Khania). It had a reputation for producing good slingers and archers, and also lawgivers (see GORTYN). During the fifth and fourth centuries BC the island lay outside the mainstream of Greek history. By the late third century BC, the notoriety of Crete as a refuge for pirates rivalled that of Cilicia. The pirates supported *Mithridates VI, king of Pontus, against Rome, but those in Crete were crushed in 68–67 BC by the Roman general Q. Metellus who captured many cities and destroyed Cnossus. Thereafter Crete became a Roman province.

Cretheus, son of *Aeolus (2) and Enaretē, father of Aeson (see ARGONAUTS).

cretic, in metre the sequence – ◡ –; see METRE, GREEK 1.

Crĕu'sa, 'princess' (the feminine equivalent of 'Creon'), in myth the name of several heroines of whom the best-known are the following.

1. Daughter of Erechtheus, king of Athens, and mother, by Apollo, of *Ion.

2. Daughter of the Trojan king *Priam and his wife Hecuba, wife of Aeneas and mother of Ascanius; she died in the flight from Troy after its capture by the Greeks. In Virgil's Aeneid her ghost warns Aeneas of the adventures that lie before him.

Crīmī'sus, river in the west of Sicily, near which Timoleon of Corinth defeated the Carthaginians in 339 BC.

Crina'goras, born c.70 BC, a Greek elegiac poet of Mitylene who went to Rome; some of his verse is preserved in the Palatine Anthology (see ANTHOLOGY 1).

Crīsa (or **Crissa** or **Cirrha**—whatever the original differences, the names were used interchangeably in classical times), in Phocis, one of the most ancient of Greek cities; the territory of Crisa included a fertile plain. The name is often used to denote Delphi, which was situated a few kilometres to the north-west. See SACRED WARS.

Cri'tias (c.460–403 BC), at Athens, an extreme oligarch, from an aristocratic family, a cousin of Plato's mother. After playing a part in the oligarchic revolution of the Four Hundred in 411, he went into exile c.406, but returned when Sparta defeated Athens at the end of the Peloponnesian War (404). Being strongly pro-Spartan he became one of the *Thirty Tyrants; he may have helped to bring about the death of his more moderate colleague Theramenes. He was killed fighting at Munychia in the civil war that ended the tyranny of the Thirty. In his lifetime he associated with the sophists and with Socrates. He wrote elegiac poems and tragedies, some fragments of which survive. Plato, who disapproved of the excesses of the Thirty, nevertheless made him figure in his dialogues *Protagoras*, *Timaeus*, and *Critias* (see PLATO 2).

Cri'tias, dialogue by Plato; see PLATO 2.

Crīto (*Kritōn*), dialogue by *Plato.

Socrates is in prison, awaiting the time when he must submit to the death penalty by drinking hemlock. His friend Crito comes to him and proposes a means of escape, urging his duty to his children. Socrates replies that the only question is whether an attempt at escape would be a just act; evil must not be done in return for evil suffered. Suppose the laws of Athens should remonstrate with him and ask why he, who was born and has lived under them, should now try to overturn them? Moreover, how will he gain by a life of exile? The requirement of the laws is that he should first act justly, and only afterwards think of life and children: that is what the laws say to him. Crito admits that he has no reply.

Critolā'us, head of the *Peripatetic (Aristotelian) school of philosophy at Athens in the second century BC. Only a few fragments of his writings have survived. Like Plato he was severely critical of rhetoric, but he recognized the outstanding qualities of the orator Demosthenes. See PHILOSOPHY 2.

Crœ̄'sus, the last king of *Lydia, c.560–546 BC, son of Alyattes and proverbial for his great wealth. He subdued the Greek cities on the coast of Asia Minor, but in general he showed favour to the Greeks, making rich offerings to Greek shrines, especially Delphi. The rise of Persia as a rival power led him to seek a decisive battle, and emboldened by an oracle from Delphi which in the event proved ambiguous ('If you cross the Halys you will destroy a great realm') he crossed the river Halys, the boundary of his empire, in an expedition against the Persian king Cyrus. Croesus was utterly defeated and his capital Sardis taken. Legends telling of his fate seem to have sprung up soon after: that he set himself on his own funeral pyre, but was saved by Apollo out of gratitude for the gifts to Delphi, or that he was spared after being put on a pyre by Cyrus, who, hearing Croesus recall the warning of Solon about the uncertainty of life, reflected on his own mortality, and repented of his murderous intention (see also CLEOBIS AND BITON).

Crŏnus, in Greek myth, the youngest and most important of the *Titans, the older gods who preceded the Olympian *gods. The Titans were the children of *Uranus and *Gaia, Heaven and Earth. On the advice of his mother Gaia, Cronus castrated his father Uranus, releasing the other Titans from inside Gaia where Uranus had forced them to remain confined. Cronus then took as wife his sister Rhea, and they became the parents of many of the important Greek gods. Because Cronus knew he was fated to be supplanted by one of them, he swallowed them all at birth, but when *Zeus was born Rhea handed Cronus a stone instead and hid the baby in Crete (see CURETES). When Zeus grew up he made Cronus disgorge the stone and all the rest of his children (a stone set up at *Delphi is by tradition the one disgorged). Cronus and the other Titans (with the aid of the *Giants and *Typhoeus) waged war against Zeus and the new gods (who were helped by the *Cyclopes and the *Hekatoncheires), but the Titans were eventually overwhelmed and consigned to *Tartarus. The extraordinary narrative of this succession myth is paralleled by myths current among eastern peoples, notably the Phoenicians and the Hittites, in the second millennium BC, and it is likely that it reached Greece from these sources. The act of castration represents the separation of heaven and earth, a common motif in mythology from many parts of the world. A different group of stories represents the period when Cronus ruled, after he had overthrown Uranus, as a Golden Age on earth. Cronus is mainly a figure of myth (rather than of religion) and rarely the object of a cult. The Romans identified him with *Saturn.

Crŏton (Krŏtōn, Lat. Crŏtōna or Cortōna; modern Crotone), Greek colony on the west coast of the Gulf of Tarentum in south Italy, somewhat south of its rival *Sybaris, settled by *Achaeans from the Peloponnese in 709 BC. It became a large and flourishing city, founding its own colonies, and famous for its doctors and athletes. It won a notable victory against Sybaris at the river Crathis in 510 BC (its army led by its most famous athlete, *Milo), reaching the height of its power as a consequence. *Pythagoras settled there c.530 BC and founded his school. The Pythagoreans came to dominate the politics of the city, but were overthrown by a democratic revolution c.450 BC. Croton was conquered by Dionysius I of Syracuse and suffered severely in the Roman wars against Pyrrhus and Hannibal. It is ironic that the Greek pastoral poet *Theocritus chose it in Idyll 4 as the scene of tranquil country life at a time when it was being ravaged by war (first half of the third century BC). In 194 BC it was recolonized by the Romans, but without lasting success.

Crown, On the (*Peri tou stephanou*, Lat. *De corona*), speech by Demosthenes in reply to Aeschines' general indictment of his policy. See DEMOSTHENES (2) 1 and 4.

Ctē'sias, of *Cnidus in Asia Minor, a Greek physician of the early fourth century BC, who lived for a number of years at the Persian court. He wrote a history of Persia in twenty-three books (*Persika*), as well as the first book to be devoted entirely to India (*Indika*). We possess a few fragments of these and synopses made by *Photius (*Bibliotheca* 72).

Ctē'siphon, see AESCHINES.

Cu'lex ('gnat'), Latin poem in hexameters doubtfully attributed to Virgil (see APPENDIX VIRGILIANA).

cult, the worship of a god or hero with rites and ceremonies. Believing in, respecting, or recognizing the gods was to both Greeks and Romans primarily a matter of observing their cult by performing acts of worship. Worship consisted of correct action rather than intense personal conviction or spirituality. The most important aspect of cult was making an offering to the god by *sacrifice, *libation, or dedication (i.e. gift of an object). The offering was accompanied by prayer, on the principle of *do ut des*, 'I give (to you) so that you will give (to me)'.

Cūmae (Kȳmē), the earliest and for some time the most distant Greek settlement in Italy, on the coast a little north of the Bay of Naples. It was founded by Euboeans from the cities of Chalcis and Eretria soon after 750 BC, but it took its name from the city of Cyme in Aeolis in Asia Minor, the home town, it was said, of one of the founders. Having excellent harbours nearby and surrounded by very fertile country it rapidly acquired wealth, the period of its greatest prosperity being 700–500 BC. In the late sixth century, when the Etruscans threatened the city, the leader of the people, Aristodemus, successfully drove them off and afterwards made himself tyrant (c.505 BC). He died c.492. In 474, with the aid of Hieron, tyrant of Syracuse, Cumae crushed the combined fleets of Etruria and Carthage in a famous victory, but c.421 was conquered by the (Italian) Samnites and thereafter ceased to be a Greek city. It came under the control of Rome in 338, and steady decline set in. The cave of the Cumaean *Sibyl was here, and may still be seen, and nearby is Lake *Avernus.

Cunobelī'nus, 'Cymbeline', British king in the first half of the first century AD. He figures in medieval legends; Holinshed's *Chronicles* (1577) were the source for Shakespeare's *Cymbeline*.

Cupid (Lat. *cupīdo*, 'desire'), the

Roman boy-god of love, son of Venus and Vulcan, an adaptation of *Eros, the childlike god of Hellenistic Greece with wings and a quiverful of arrows, and a figure of literature rather than of cult. He is familiar in the Latin poets, and especially in the first book of Virgil's *Aeneid* where Venus sends him to take the place of Ascanius, and to excite the love of Dido for Aeneas. Later he appears in the fairy story of Cupid and *Psychē, set in the narrative of the *Golden Ass*, a Latin novel of the second century AD by *Apuleius. Cupids appear on ancient coffins as a symbol of the life after death promised to initiates of the mystery religions, and hence into churches as winged cherubs.

Cupid and Psyche, see PSYCHE.

Curcu'lio ('weevil'), Roman comedy by *Plautus.

Phaedromus is in love with Planesium, a slave-girl, but lacks the funds to buy her from the pimp Cappadox. Curculio, a *parasite of Phaedromus, steals a sealring from the boastful soldier Therapontigonus, who has deposited with a banker a sum of money in order to buy Planesium for himself. By means of a letter sealed with this ring Curculio secures the girl for his master. Therapontigonus is furious at the fraud, but the ring reveals the fact that Planesium is his freeborn sister, and so he gets his money back and Phaedromus marries the girl.

Cūrē'tēs, attendants of the goddess *Rhea. They were thought to be originally semi-divine people inhabiting Crete in mythical times, to whom the infant *Zeus was entrusted by his mother Rhea for protection against his father *Cronus; to conceal the child they danced around him, drowning his cries with the clashing of their weapons (see also AMALTHEA). They are often confused with the *Corybantes, who were properly the attendants of the Asiatic goddess Cybelē, because she was often assimilated to Rhea and to other mother-goddesses.

Cū'ria, originally, one of the groups into which the Roman people was divided in earliest times, thirty in number, ten to each *tribe. They were the basis of the political and military organization of the state, such as it was. Each *curia* had its own meeting-place, whence the word came to mean 'a place of assembly', and in particular denoted the senate-house of Rome, situated on the north side of the *Comitium in the Roman Forum. This was known as the Curia Hostīlia because its erection was ascribed to Tullus Hostilius, king of Rome in the midseventh century BC. It was burnt down by the mob in 52 BC when Clodius' body was placed on a pyre made up of its furnishings, and a new one was begun near the site of the old by Julius Caesar in 44 BC.

Curiā'tii, see HORATII.

Cu'rius Dentā'tus, Mā'nius (d. 270 BC), Roman general, regarded as epitomizing the Roman values of simplicity and severity. As consul in 290 and in 275 BC he defeated first the Samnites, bringing the Samnite War to an end, and secondly *Pyrrhus at Beneventum (Benevento). His triumphal procession was adorned by four elephants, the first ever seen at Rome. He was consul for a third time in 274, and defeated Pyrrhus' Italian allies who were still in arms. When the Samnites had tried to bribe him with costly presents, he replied that he preferred ruling over those who possessed gold to possessing it himself.

cursive (script), name given to fluent, everyday handwriting and in particular to that used in the early centuries of the present era not only privately but by Greek and Roman scribes for official letters and documents. It was an influence in the development of the later book-hand known as minuscule (see BOOKS AND WRITING 6). Some letter forms are unexpected; e.g. in Roman cursive E was written ||, N |||, and M ||||.

cursus honō'rum ('the sequence of magistracies', i.e. political offices), at Rome, a term signifying the various political offices in the order in which they were to be held, and the periods of time which were required to elapse between the tenure of successive offices. It was determined by custom at an early date and first fixed by law in 180 BC, with later amendments, notably by Sulla after 82 BC. The required pattern was service in the army followed by the offices of quaestor, praetor, consul, and censor. If the aedileship was held (which was not obligatory) it came after the quaestorship. The minimum age at which a consulship might be held did not vary much, being in general 42. To gain a magistracy 'in one's own year' (*suo anno*) meant at the earliest possible age (see CICERO (1) 2).

Curtius, hero of a Roman legend invented to explain a depression or pit known as Lacus Curtius, 'Curtius' pond', in the Roman Forum, which had dried up and was paved over in Sullan times (beginning of the first century BC). There were three versions of the legend: (i) a Sabine, Mettius Curtius, pursued by Romulus and the Romans, leaped with his horse into the swamp which covered the later site of the Forum; (ii) the consul Curtius in 445 BC had the area enclosed as sacred because it had been struck by lightning; (iii) (most famously) after a cleft had opened in the Forum (supposedly in 362 BC) and an oracle had said that the chief strength of Rome must be thrown into it before it would close, a soldier Marcus Curtius, understanding the oracle's meaning, rode fully armed into the cleft.

Cu'rtius Rufus, Quintus, Roman historian of the first century AD who wrote a history of Alexander the Great in ten books, of which the first two are lost. The extant books start in 333 BC with Alexander's march through Phrygia and the cutting of the Gordian knot. The narrative is dramatic and romantic, with vivid detail, but with little critical sense or grasp of Alexander's place in history.

curule magistracies, in Rome, important magistracies which entitled the holders to use the *sella curūlis*, or 'chair of state', as a symbol of their authority. The 'chair' was in fact more like a folding stool, inlaid with ivory; it originated in Etruria, where it had been used in the royal chariot from which justice was administered. The entitled magistrates were censors, consuls, praetors, and the two 'curule' aediles. It was also the prerogative of a dictator and those immediately under him, and the *flamen dialis*.

Cy'belē (Kybelē or Kybēbē), the great mother-goddess of Phrygia associated in myth and cult with a young male consort *Attis. Her fame spread all over the ancient world. The centre of her cult was on Mount Dindymus, at Pessīnus, where she was called Agdistis, and where her image, of stone, was believed to have fallen from heaven. She was primarily a goddess of fertility, but also a goddess of wild nature, symbolized by her attendant lions. She was said to cure (and send) disease, and protect her people in time of war. By the fifth century she was known in Greece and was soon identified with the local 'mother of the gods' and Demeter. In 204 BC in the stress of the Second Punic War, and in accordance with a prophecy in the Sibylline books and advice from Delphi, the Romans sent a distinguished embassy to Pessinus on the delicate diplomatic mission of taking back to Rome the sacred stone. On its voyage it had an escort of five quinqueremes. The temple built for the goddess's reception stood on the Palatine, but the cult was kept under surveillance until the end of the republic, and participation in priesthoods and rituals was forbidden to Roman citizens (except that they might join in her festival, the *Megalesia); she was kept to her temple and served only by oriental priests (see GALLI) although processions of the priests were allowed (as described by Lucretius, 2. 600). These restrictions were lifted by the emperor Claudius; worship of Cybele and Attis became part of the state religion, and one of the important *mystery religions of the Roman empire.

Cy'clades, group of islands in the southern part of the Aegean Sea, so called because they form roughly a circle (*kuklos*). They include Delos, Ceos, Naxos, Paros, Andros, and Tenos. During the early and middle Bronze Age (which in Greece was c.3000–c.1000 BC) they enjoyed an independent culture (sometimes called 'Cycladic'). Towards the end of the Bronze Age several of the islands were settled from Minoan Crete and later came under the influence of Mycenean Greece. In about 1000 BC they were occupied by Ionic-speaking Greeks. After the Persian Wars they joined Athens' Delian League.

cyclic poems, see EPIC CYCLE.

Cyclō'pēs (sing. Cyclops), in Greek myth, one-eyed giants, according to Homer, dwelling on a distant island. *Odysseus visited the cave of one of them, *Polyphemus. In Hesiod they were the sons of *Uranus (Heaven) and Gaia (Earth), three in number, called Brontēs, Steropēs, and Argēs ('thunderer', 'lightener', 'bright'), who made the thunderbolts of Zeus and aided him in his war against the Titans. They often appear as Hephaestus' workmen, and were credited with the construction of ancient walls, such as those of Tiryns and Mycenae. In these cases they have little in common with the Cyclopes of the *Odyssey*. See also ASCLEPIUS, and CYCLOPS below.

Cȳclops, *satyric drama by *Euripides, produced perhaps in 412 BC.

The Greek god *Dionysus having been captured by pirates, Silenus has set out in pursuit, accompanied by his satyrs, and has fallen into the power of the Cyclops *Polyphemus. Odysseus and his crew arrive and bargain with Silenus for food in exchange for wine. Polyphemus returns and makes prisoners of Odysseus and his men. The blinding of the Cyclops and the escape of Odysseus are told much as in the *Odyssey*. The whole subject is dealt with humorously.

Cycnus, see SHIELD OF HERACLES. There are several figures of this name in Greek myth. The best known are the following.

1. Son of Arēs, who robbed and killed travellers taking offerings to Delphi, and tried to build a temple to Apollo out of their skulls. He was killed by Heracles when the latter was on his way to fetch the apples of the Hesperides (see HERACLES, LABOURS OF 11).

2. Son of Poseidon, ally of the Trojans in the Trojan War, invulnerable to human weapons but strangled by the Greek hero Achilles when he tried to prevent the Greeks landing at Troy. The story is not found in Homer.

Cȳlon, Athenian noble who married the daughter of Theagenes, tyrant of Megara, and with his help seized the Acropolis at Athens with a view to setting himself up as a tyrant (c.632 BC). The Athenians under the archon Megacles laid siege to the Acropolis, and after Cylon and his brother managed to escape to Megara, killed their associates who had taken refuge at the altar of Athena. Those responsible for this sacrilege, especially Megacles and his family, the *Alcmaeonidae, were said to have incurred *pollution, and this was frequently invoked against them in later political disputes at Athens.

Cȳmē, see CUMAE. See also HESIOD.

Cynēge'tica, see OPPIAN and GRATTIUS.

Cynēge'ticus ('hunting'), a treatise by *Xenophon.

After an exordium, exceptional in Xenophon's works, tracing the invention of hunting game with hounds to Apollo and Artemis, who handed it on to Chiron, and he to a number of heroes, the author urges all young men to take up hunting, especially of hare and deer on foot, with hounds. He begins by describing the necessary equipment, the nets, the hounds, and their points, but wanders on to the question of scent and the habits of the hare. He then returns to the trappings of the hounds, the proper way to fix the nets, and the actual hunt; here Xenophon shows his enthusiasm. A passage follows on the breeding, training, and naming of hounds (forty-seven names to choose from, all disyllabic for easy calling). The author next describes the hunting of deer (for which hounds and snares were used) and of wild boar (with hounds, nets, javelins, and spears), and gives a short chapter to the hunting of big game in foreign countries. He then enumerates the benefits of hunting, in respect of health, military service, and moral education. The treatise concludes with an attack on sophists as useless and untrustworthy.

*Arrian also wrote a book on hunting, which still survives, in the style of Xenophon and as a supplement to his treatise.

Cynic philosophers, those following the principles of Antisthenes and Diogenes of Sinopē.

Anti'sthenēs (c.445–c.360 BC), at Athens, a pupil and friend of Socrates, but differing in his views from the latter's most famous follower, Plato; he was considered the founder of the sect, and influenced its best-known exponent Diogenes of Sinope, from whose nickname, *kyōn*, 'the dog', the sect derived its name (see below, and CYNOSARGES). Antisthenes believed that happiness is based on virtue, that virtue consists in action, and that it is a practical quality which can be taught; thus to him the life of the mythical hero Heracles epitomized the ideal. Since happiness results only from virtuous action, most pleasures do not contribute to it. The knowledge of virtue, once acquired, cannot be lost; the wise man cannot act unwisely. Antisthenes' voluminous writings, except for some fragments, have been lost, but it is known that he was interested in literature, linguistic theory, and dialectic.

Dio'genēs (*c.*400–325 BC), after his arrival in Athens, seems to have been attracted by the austere character and way of life of Antisthenes, which perhaps influenced him in his fanatical espousal of the 'natural' life, the subject of many anecdotes. While in Athens he was supposed to have lived in a tub (of earthenware) belonging to the Metrōon (temple of the Mother of the gods). It is said that his later life was spent in Corinth, as a result of the voyage in which he was captured by pirates and sold as a slave to a Corinthian. Here he is reputed to have met Alexander the Great. If he in fact wrote any of the works attributed to him, nothing has survived. He rejected all conventional views of what constituted a person's happiness; for him it consisted of satisfying one's barest natural needs for things outside oneself, for food and shelter for example, in the cheapest and easiest way, and for the rest living on one's own natural endowments, renouncing all possessions and relationships. This self-sufficiency could be achieved by physical and mental self-discipline, and by losing the conventional sense of shame. It was supposed to be on account of this last characteristic that Diogenes was nicknamed 'dog'. He illustrated his principles in his way of life and in caustic utterances. His philosophy and way of life were spread by his disciple Crates.

Cratēs (*c.*365–285 BC), who came to Athens from Thebes and was won over by the example of Diogenes, became famous for the wholehearted way in which he embraced Cynic doctrine. Having renounced his large fortune, and restricting himself to absolute necessities, he achieved a high degree of self-sufficiency. Hipparchia, the daughter of a rich family, threatened suicide in order to persuade her parents to let her share his life. (See also ZENO.)

The Cynics developed no elaborate philosophical system and were never organized into a school, so in practice they embraced a range of beliefs while maintaining as their central tenet that self-sufficiency could bring contentment in all the vicissitudes of life. Crates originated the type of Cynic philosopher who wandered the Greek world with stick and knapsack, the frequent object of mockery. Cynic beggars of this kind suddenly proliferated in the first and second centuries AD, and still existed in the sixth; the contrast between them and true Cynic philosophers became a literary commonplace. See also STOICS.

Cynosa'rges, a gymnasium outside the city of Athens sacred to Heracles, for the use of those who were not of pure Athenian blood. Antisthenes is said to have started teaching there, and on this has been based an alternative explanation for the name 'Cynic' (see CYNIC PHILOSOPHERS).

Cynosce'phalae, in Thessaly, scene of the defeat in 197 BC of Philip V of Macedon by the Roman Q. Flamininus. For an earlier battle there see ALEXANDER OF PHERAE.

Cynthia, Cynthius, epithets given to the Greek deities Artemis (equivalent to the Roman Diana) and Apollo, derived from Mount Cynthus in their native island of Delos. 'Cynthia' was the name given by the Roman poet *Propertius to his mistress (compare Lesbia, the object of Catullus' love poems, named from the island of Lesbos, and *Delia).

Cy'pria (perhaps 'the epic composed in Cyprus'), a lost poem of the Greek *Epic Cycle. It recounted, in eleven books, the events that led up to the point in the Trojan War at which Homer's *Iliad* begins, including the wedding of Peleus and Thetis, the judgement of Paris, the abduction of Helen, the assembly of the Greek fleet, the rescue of Iphigeneia by Artemis at the moment of sacrifice, and the first engagements at Troy. The epic is sometimes ascribed to Stasinus of Cyprus, hence the title (otherwise unexplained).

Cẏprus, island in the north-east Mediterranean. In the early Bronze Age it was populated from Anatolia, but by the end of the thirteenth century BC the native culture seems to have been submerged, perhaps by Mycenaean Greeks fleeing from destruction on the mainland. Modern Enkomi appears to have been the site of the chief Mycenaean city. During this Mycenaean period the Cypriots used a syllabic script derived from Cretan *Linear A, and now known as Cypro-Minoan, which was the ancestor of a syllabic script used from the seventh to the third centuries BC to write Cypriot Greek (see DIALECTS). Settlers later came in large numbers from Phoenicia, and their influence grew until in the fourth century BC much of central Cyprus was in their control. In 525 BC Cyprus fell to the Persians, but it enjoyed a brief period of independence after the efforts of the philhellene *Evagoras in 411. In the late fourth century BC the island came under the control of the Ptolemies of Egypt for nearly two and a half centuries. It was annexed by Rome in 58 BC and attached to the province of Cilicia. The sanctuaries of *Aphroditē on the island, at Păphos and Amathus, were especially renowned, so that the goddess was often called simply 'the Cyprian' (Gk. Kypris, Lat. Cypria). According to one myth, it was at Paphos that she was born from the sea-foam.

Cy'pselus, tyrant of *Corinth, who overthrew the oligarchy of the *Bacchiadae and founded a dynasty of tyrants, ruling himself from c.657 to c.625, when he was succeeded by his son *Periander. Under him Corinth grew in power and prosperity. His name was explained by a story, that his father Eĕtion was of humble birth but had managed to marry a Bacchiad wife, Labda, because she was lame. As the result of an oracle prophesying their overthrow the Bacchiads tried to kill the son of the marriage, but his mother had hidden him in a chest, *kypselē*, and he survived. A magnificent chest of cedar wood carved and decorated with figures in ivory and gold, purporting to be that of Cypselus, was dedicated by the Corinthians at Olympia and was seen there many centuries later by Pausanias. His description suggests that it was not made until the sixth century BC.

Cẏrena'ic school of philosophy, founded at Cyrene by *Aristippus.

Cyrē'nē, Greek colony in Libya (North Africa), on a high plateau a few kilometres inland, roughly midway between the Egyptian delta and Tunisia. Being cut off from other civilized regions of Africa by deserts and great distances, it looked naturally towards Greece. It was originally colonized from Thera in 630 BC, but received more settlers from Greece on several occasions. The colony attained great prosperity, its territory (Cyrenāica) being rich in corn, wool, oil, and the mysterious plant silphium, trade in which was a monopoly of the rulers. Unknown today, it was greatly valued in classical times as a universal medicine and was exported on a large scale. Cyrene was unique in that its founder *Battus established a long-lasting royal dynasty, unbroken until it was overthrown some time after 460 BC; the rulers were named Battus and Arcesilaus alternately. It was made a Roman province in 74 BC. Cyrene was the birthplace of Aristippus, Carneades, Synesius, and Callimachus, who was occasionally called 'Battiadēs', (son of Battus) in allusion to his royal descent.

Cẏropaedī'a (*Kyrou paideia*, 'education of Cyrus'), narrative by *Xenophon, in eight books, of the career of *Cyrus the Great, king of Persia, in which characters and historical facts are modified to suit the author's didactic purpose. Writing roughly at the same time as Plato, who in the *Republic* argues for *his* conception of the education of an ideal ruler, Xenophon sets out his own in the *Cyropaedia*, a work which strongly resembles a historical novel with a moral purpose. Cyrus himself is an idealized character, the perfect statesman, ruler, and general, drawn partly from the character of the younger Cyrus who was known to Xenophon and appears in his *Anabasis*. The constitution of Persia, and the method of education described, similarly represent Xenophon's ideals (based in part on the institutions of Sparta). The military precepts and the tactics described are Xenophon's own. There are numerous minor characters, kings, soldiers, and councillors, and among them the Indian tutor of the Armenian king's eldest son, Tigranes, unjustly put to death—a portrait intended to suggest Socrates. The tedium of the work (for most modern readers) is somewhat relieved by the romantic episode of the farewell of Abradatas (who is about to die in battle) to his wife Panthea. After the narrative of Cyrus' military campaigns is concluded with the capture of Sardis and Babylon, the work ends with a description of the organization of the Persian empire and the death of Cyrus. But by the time Xenophon came to write the end of the book it had become apparent that the Persian system was neither efficient nor progressive; the final chapter, describing the confusion resulting from Cyrus' death, was perhaps intended as a counterweight to the earlier admiration.

Cȳrus. 1. Cyrus the Great (559–529 BC), the founder of the Persian empire. He was the son of Cambyses, of the Persian family of the Achaemenids, and the vassal of Astyages, king of Media. He ousted Astyages from his throne and by 547 had extended Persian rule as far east as the river Halys. He then overthrew and captured *Croesus, king of Lydia, and gained control over Asia Minor, Babylonia (thereby liberating the Jews from captivity), Assyria, Syria, and Palestine. He administered a vast empire with wisdom and tolerance; to Xenophon he was an example of the ideal ruler (see CYROPAEDIA). His grave is at the Persian city of Pasargadae, near the place where he defeated Astyages. He was succeeded by his son Cambyses.

2. Cyrus the Younger, descendant of Darius I, the second son of Darius II, king of Persia 424–405 BC. His friendly relations with the Spartan general Lysander were fatal for Athens at the end of the Peloponnesian War. After the death of his father he gathered together a mercenary army, which included Xenophon, ostensibly for an expedition against Pisidia, but in reality to oust his elder brother Artaxerxes from the throne. A pitched battle was fought at Cunaxa in 401; Cyrus' army was defeated and he himself killed. The westward march of the Greek mercenaries to the coast is the subject of Xenophon's *Anabasis*.

Cythē'ra, island off the south coast of Laconia in the Peloponnese. Some Greek myths relate that Aphrodite landed there after being born from the sea-foam, hence she is sometimes called 'Cytherean' (but see also CYPRUS).

Cythē'ris, see GALLUS.

D

dactyl (*daktylos*, 'finger'), in metre, the sequence – ◡ ◡. See METRE, GREEK 1.

Dactyls, Idaean, in Greek myth, magical smiths, the subject of obscure and conflicting stories. They were located on either the Cretan or the Phrygian Mount Ida. Hence they are sometimes associated with Rhea, as the beings in Crete to whom the infant Zeus was entrusted (thus being identified with the *Curetes), or with *Cybelē (being then confused with the Corybantes).

da'ctylo-e'pitrīte, see METRE, GREEK 3.

Dae'dalus ('cunning worker'), legendary Athenian craftsman and inventor, thought of as living in the age of *Minos, in whom the Greeks personified the development of sculpture and architecture through mechanical inventions; his impossibly ingenious devices provided the plot of many exciting stories. It was said that his statues could move themselves. Being afraid that his nephew and pupil Talōs would outdo him (for the latter invented the saw and the potter's wheel), Daedalus threw him down from the Acropolis (*Pausanias (2) saw his reputed grave at Athens in the second century AD) or into the sea (when Athena changed him into a partridge, *perdix*, by which name Talōs was also known). Daedalus was condemned for his crime by the Areopagus and fled to Crete, where he constructed the *labyrinth for king Minos. Afterwards, Minos would not let him go; Daedalus then made wings for himself and his son Icarus out of wax and feathers, and they flew away. But Icarus flew too near the sun; the wax of his wings melted and he fell into the sea and was drowned. Daedalus landed on the island in the Sporades now called Ikaria and buried his son's body. He then escaped to king Cocalus in Sicily, whither Minos pursued him; enticed into Cocalus' palace Minos was scalded to death in a bath of Daedalus' invention. Virgil at the beginning of book 6 of the *Aeneid* describes Daedalus arriving at Cumae in his flight from Minos and dedicating a temple there. Pausanias saw several statues said to have been sculpted by Daedalus, and accepted that he really existed.

daimon (pl. *daimonĕs*), in Greek, 'divine spirit', commonly interpreted etymologically as 'he who allots'. The word is used loosely in Greek poetry to mean 'god' or 'the gods'; but in general *daimones* did not have this equivalence; there were no images of them and they received no cult, except that the first *libation at a wine-drinking was made in honour of the Good Daimon. In general *daimon* describes an aspect of divine power which cannot be identified with a particular god, and is only rarely used to designate one of the Olympian gods. It is this power which gives a man good or bad fortune at any time, so that he may feel that he has the *daimon* on his side, or else that he is struggling against it; thus *daimon* approximates in meaning to irresistible fate. (Heracleitus declared in a famous utterance that an individual's character is his *daimon*, thereby asserting that a person's destiny is under his own control.) Hesiod says that after death the men of the *Golden Age were transformed by Zeus into *daimones*, able to confer prosperity on mankind. Perhaps this was the basis for honouring great and powerful men when they had died, as for example in the case of the Persian king Darius, who was conjured up as a *daimon* in the *Persae* of Aeschylus; Plato thought those who died fighting for their country should be honoured as *daimones*. The notion of *daimones* as intermediate beings between gods and men may long have existed in popular superstition, but is introduced into literature by Plato. His followers extended the idea to include *daimones* as evil spirits, 'demons'. For Socrates' 'divine sign' (*daimonion*) see SOCRATES. See also EMPEDOCLES.

Dama'stēs, another name for the

legendary Greek brigand *Procrustēs.

damna'tio memo'riae ('obliteration of the record'), at Rome, punishment for a crime against the state, whereby use of the *praenomen* (see NAMES) of the condemned man was forbidden in his family, every image of him destroyed, and all public mention of him erased.

Da'moclēs, a courtier of Dionysius I, tyrant of *Syracuse in the fourth century BC. When he praised to excess the happiness of a tyrant, Dionysius invited him to experience it for himself. He placed Damocles at a banquet where presently the latter observed a naked sword hanging over his head by a single hair, symbolizing the precarious nature of such happiness.

Damon, Pythagorean philosopher from Syracuse, proverbial for his friendship with Pythias (whose name in fact seems to have been Phintias). The latter, condemned to death, left Syracuse in order to arrange his affairs, leaving Damon to stand surety for him, and returned in time to redeem his friend. The tyrant was so impressed by their friendship that he pardoned the criminal.

Dana'ans (Dănăoi), general name for the Greek nation in Homer and later poets; more particularly, a Peloponnesian Greek people inhabiting the region of Argos in early times; thus the name Danaans sometimes signifies Argives. For their supposed origin see DANAUS.

Dă'năē, in Greek myth, daughter of Acrisius king of Argos (brother of Proetus). An oracle foretold that Acrisius would be killed by his daughter's son, and he therefore confined Danae in a bronze tower, so that no man might approach her. But Zeus descended on her in a shower of gold, and she bore a son Perseus. Acrisius placed Danae and the child in a chest and cast them adrift in the sea (for a Greek lyric poem on the subject see SIMONIDES), but they landed on the island of Serīphos, where they were sheltered by Dictys, brother of Polydectēs, the king of the island. See also PERSEUS.

Da'naids (Danăidĕs), in Greek myth, daughters of *Danaus.

Dă'năus, in Greek myth, son of *Belus, king of Egypt, descendant of *Io, and brother of Aegyptus. The brothers' names show that they were regarded by the Greeks as the ancestors of the *Danaans and the Egyptians. Aegyptus had fifty sons, Danaus fifty daughters (the Danaids). Belus gave Aegyptus the kingdom of Arabia and Danaus Libya, but the latter, feeling threatened by his brother's conquest of Egypt, sailed away with his daughters to Argos, the city from which Io had come, and became king, the inhabitants being called in consequence Danaoi. The sons of Aegyptus pursued their cousins to Argos in order to marry them, though they were unwilling. Danaus was forced to consent, but ordered his daughters to stab them with daggers which he provided, on their wedding night. This they all did except Hypermnestra, who spared her husband *Lynceūs. She was imprisoned and put on trial by her father, but the Argive court, perhaps through the intervention of the goddess of love, Aphroditē, acquitted her. Pindar tells how Danaus, in order to select other husbands for his daughters, set these at the end of a race course and let their suitors run for them. After their deaths the other Danaids were punished for their crime in the Underworld by having to try to fill leaky jars with water.

Daphnē ('laurel'), in Greek myth, a nymph, daughter of a river-god (generally Ladon in Arcadia but also represented as Pēnēus in Thessaly). She was a huntress and wanted no lovers, but was pursued by Leucippus who joined her hunting companions disguised as a girl. When Daphne and her companions bathed after the hunt Leucippus was found out and killed. She also rejected the love of the god Apollo and fled from him, praying to the river-god Peneus for deliverance; she was thereupon changed into a laurel tree.

Daphnis, legendary Sicilian herdsman, a recurring figure of bucolic (i.e. pastoral) mythology, said to be the originator of bucolic song. His father was sometimes said to be the Greek god Hermes, his mother a nymph who exposed him under a laurel bush (*daphne*), from which his name is derived. He himself was mortal. He was loved by a nymph to whom he vowed eternal fidelity, but he was made drunk and seduced by a princess. Thereupon the nymph blinded him, and he spent the rest of his life composing mournful songs on his unhappy fate, the supposed origin of bucolic poetry. There are variations on this story, notably in *Theocritus where Daphnis appears to die of love. Daphnis epitomizes the musician-shepherd, the ideal inhabitant of the idyllic pastoral world, his life and death powerfully signifying that even in such a world there is no escape from the pangs of unhappy love and death.

Daphnis and Chloe, Greek *novel by Longus.

Da'rdanus, in Greek myth, son of Zeus and Electra, the daughter of the Titan *Atlas. He was the ancestor of the kings of Troy, and was said to have lived in Samothrace (in the north Aegean), from where he went to Phrygia. The local king Teucer welcomed him and gave him his daughter as wife and part of his territory. Dardanus built a city on the slope of Mount Ida (south-east of the future site of Troy) and called it Dardania. Hence the Trojans are sometimes called 'Dardanians'. In the Trojan war, the enmity of Zeus' wife Hera towards the Trojans in part originated from her jealously of Electra for having won the love of Zeus.

Darēs, in Virgil's *Aeneid*, a companion of Aeneas; he figures in the boxing match (book 5).

Darēs Phry'gius, in Homer's *Iliad*, the priest of Hephaestus at Troy. He was thought by later Greeks to have existed in fact and to be the author of a pre-Homeric poem on the destruction of Troy, a supposed translation of which into Latin prose survives, written no earlier than the fifth century AD. This work was subsequently ascribed to Cornelius *Nepos because it was prefaced by a forged letter purportedly written by Nepos to Sallust, explaining how he had discovered the original in Athens. During the fifteenth and sixteenth centuries the poem enjoyed great popularity because of its subject-matter (the *Iliad* does not give an account of the fall of Troy), as did the similar work of *Dictys of Crete.

Darī'us (Dāreios). **1. Darius I the Great,** king of Persia from 521 to 486 BC, a member of the *Achaemedid family. A brilliant administrator, he restored order after anarchy and reorganized the empire, creating twenty provinces called satrapies. In 499 the Greek cities of Ionia, which were his vassals, revolted, but by 494 the revolt was suppressed. The cities of mainland Greece had been implicated and in 491 Darius sent envoys to Greece demanding submission. When this was not forthcoming he sent an army, which was defeated at Marathon in 490 (see PERSIAN WARS). Darius died four years later and was succeeded by his son *Xerxes, who continued the war against Greece.

2. Darius III Codomā'nus (*c.*380–330 BC), the king of Persia overthrown by *Alexander the Great.

Dark Age(s). This term is applied to various turbulent periods of history when civilization was endangered and few records handed down. In the ancient world it refers to the following two periods.

1. In Greece, the period from, very roughly, the twelfth to the ninth century BC. It begins with the invasions that resulted in the final destruction of *Mycenae and ends with the emergence of Athens as a cultural force in Greece.

2. In the later Roman empire, the period of the barbarian invasions and their aftermath, very roughly from the sixth to the ninth century AD.

Davus, name of the cunning slave in Terence's *Andria*, and also of the slave who lectures Horace in *Satires* II. 7.

De'a Dīa, a Roman corn-goddess; her cult was promoted by the *arval priests.

De agri cultū'ra or ***De re rustica*** ('on agriculture'), treatise by M. Porcius *Cato the Censor, the oldest piece of Latin prose of some length to survive. It is a concise, practical handbook, dealing with the cultivation for profit, in Latium and Campania, of vines, olives, and fruit, and with cattle-breeding. Cato discusses the purchase of a farm; the duties of owner, overseer, housekeeper, and slaves; the tilling of the soil; the care of livestock; and a few minor matters, such as a prescription for treating a sick ox, recipes for curing hams and making cheese-cakes, and religious and superstitious formulas. It is written in a curt, abrupt style, without much organization of material, but it was widely read and quoted from in ancient times.

De amīci'tia ('on friendship'), also known as *Laelius*, dialogue by *Cicero ((1) 5) composed in 44 BC and addressed to *Atticus. The dialogue is supposed to take place in 129 BC shortly after the death of *Scipio Aemilianus. The interlocutors are *Laelius, the intimate friend of Scipio, and his two sons-in-law, C. Fannius and the augur Quintus Mucius *Scaevola. Cicero in his youth had received instruction in the law from Scaevola and had heard him, he tells us, repeat the conversation. Laelius in his discourse discusses the nature of friendship and the principles by which it should be governed. The conclusion is that friendship is founded on, and preserved by, virtue; for it owes to virtue the harmony, permanence, and loyalty that are its essential features. This is one of the most admired of Cicero's dialogues for its dignity and calm and for the melodious quality of its prose. It was one of the two books in which Dante found consolation for the death of Beatrice.

De architectū'ra ('on architecture'), *Vitruvius' treatise on building, written towards the end of the first century BC.

De be'llo cīvī'li and *De be'llo Ga'llico*, see *COMMENTARIES.*

De benefi'ciis ('on benefits'), treatise in seven books by *Seneca (2).

De brevitā'te vī'tae ('on the shortness of life'), dialogue by *Seneca (2), considered one of his best essays.

De causis planta'rum ('inquiry into plants'), treatise by *Theophrastus written towards the end of the fourth century BC.

Decelē'a (Dekeleia), an Attic deme north-east of Athens near the pass east across Mount Parnes. It was about 22 km. (14 miles) from Athens and visible from there; ships entering Piraeus were in its view. Its occupation by the Spartans in 413 BC, during the Peloponnesian War, at the suggestion of the Athenian Alcibiades, put a stranglehold on Athens for the rest of the war. The term 'Decelean War' is sometimes used to describe the last period of the Peloponnesian War, from 413 to 404.

decemviri, decemvirs, 'ten men'. In Rome the name was given to several boards of ten men set up for particular purposes. The most famous were the *decemviri legibus scribundis* (an early form of the classical Latin *scribendis*), 'decemvirs for writing down the laws', appointed in 451 BC with Appius *Claudius as their leader. Before that time the laws at Rome remained unpublished and inaccessible to the people, and it was thus easier for the ruling patricians to manipulate justice to their own advantage. *Decemviri stlitibus* (an early Latin form of *litibus*) *iudicandis* were 'decemvirs for judging cases'; they acted as a jury to decide whether an individual was a slave or free.

Dĕ'cius Mus, Publius, one of the Roman consuls in 340 BC during the war with the Latins. According to legend he gained the victory for Rome by 'devoting' himself and the enemy to the gods below (see DEVOTIO), and then charging into the enemy ranks to his death. His son of the same name played a similar part in 295 BC at the battle of Sentīnum (Sentino) against the Samnites. The latter instance of *devotio* is more likely to be historical (see FABIUS MAXIMUS RULLIANUS).

dēclāmātiō'nēs (Gk. *meletai* or *scholastikai*, 'declamations'), in Roman oratory (but originating in Greek practice of the third and second centuries BC), the technical term for the exercises performed by young would-be orators in the rhetorical schools. These pupils were required to speak on invented themes (*thesēs*), some highly implausible. For judicial declamations, *controversiae*, and deliberative declamations, *suasoriae*, see SENECA (1) and QUINTILIAN.

De clāris orātō'ribus ('on famous orators'), an alternative title to Cicero's treatise *Brutus*, written about 45 BC.

De clēme'ntia ('on clemency') (AD 55–6), treatise by *Seneca (2) in three books, of which the first and part of the second survive, on the need for clemency in a ruler. It was written in the second year of the emperor Nero's reign. Its theme was suggested by his exclamation when unwillingly signing a death warrant, 'Would that I had never learnt to write!' The praise of Nero that it contains must be judged in relation to the comparative mildness of his rule in the first years.

De compendiō'sa doctrī'na ('epitome of learning'), Latin encyclopadia of the fourth century AD by *Nonius Marcellus.

De consōlatiō'ne ad Ma'rciam, ad Poly'bium, ad He'lviam, three 'consolations' written by *Seneca (2) between AD 40 and 43.

De consta'ntia sapie'ntis ('on the constancy of the wise man'), written by *Seneca (2) after AD 47.

De corō'na (*Peri tou stephanou*, 'on the crown'), title of a speech by Demosthenes (see DEMOSTHENES (2) 1 and 4).

De dīvinātiō'ne ('concerning divination'), dialogue by Cicero composed as supplement to his *De natura deorum* ('on the nature of the gods'; see CICERO (1) 5) and published in 44 BC soon after Caesar's murder. It examines *Stoic beliefs about fate and the possibility of prediction. Cicero here shows little sympathy with Stoic views, but affirms his belief in a divine being. The dialogue takes place at Cicero's villa at Tusculum, and the interlocutors are his brother Quintus and himself (Marcus). Quintus expounds, with a wealth of illustration and quotations from the Stoics (and also from Cicero's own writings) his reasons for believing in certain forms of *divination. Marcus explodes the belief in divination in general by this dilemma: future events are either at the mercy of chance or are foreordained by fate. If the former, no one, not even a god, can have foreknowledge of them; if the latter, there is no use in divination (i.e. investigation into the future in order to avoid unpleasant events) because what is foreordained cannot be avoided. Marcus thinks that divination on state matters by official augurs should be maintained for reasons of prudence but ridicules its absurdities, quoting in passing the saying of Cato (the Censor) that he wondered how a soothsayer (*haruspex*; see HARUSPICES) could meet another soothsayer without laughing. Marcus recognizes an art of *augury, but denies a science of divination. He similarly demolishes other methods of prediction based on dreams, omens, astrology, and 'inspired' prophecy. The work contains the much-quoted observation, 'there is nothing so ridiculous that some philosopher won't say it' (*nihil tam absurde dici potest quod non dicatur ab aliquo philosophorum*).

De do'mo sua ('concerning his house'), speech delivered by *Cicero ((1) 4) to the College of Pontiffs (see PONTIFICES).

When Cicero was exiled in 58 BC, *Clodius had his house on the Palatine destroyed, consecrated the site, and erected on it a monument to Liberty. Cicero asks the College of Pontiffs to annul the consecration on the grounds that Clodius' tribunate was irregular, that his law banishing Cicero was unconstitutional, and that the dedication was unjust. The College decided in Cicero's favour.

De falsa lēgātiō'ne (*Peri tou pseudous symbaseōs*, 'on the false embassy'), speech by Demosthenes; see DEMOSTHENES (2) 4.

De fāto ('on fate'), see CICERO (1) 5.

De fī'nibus bono'rum et malo'rum ('on the different conceptions of the chief good and evil'), treatise by Cicero in five books, addressed to M. *Brutus, in which he sets out and criticizes the ethical systems of the Epicurean and Stoic schools, before giving the views of the 'Old' *Academy. It was written in 45 BC (see CICERO (1) 5).

De gente po'puli rōmā'ni ('on the Roman nation'), a lost treatise by *Varro on the prehistory and early chronology of Rome.

De gramma'ticis ('on the grammarians'), book of short biographical sketches by *Suetonius on about twenty-one Roman grammarians, of which some part survives.

De haru'spicum respo'nso ('concerning the response of the soothsayers'), see CICERO (1) 4.

De histo'ria conscrībe'nda (*pōs dei historian syngraphein*, 'the way to write history'), by *Lucian, perhaps the best of his critical works.

Dēianei'ra, in Greek myth, the wife of *Heracles.

de'i conse'ntēs, see DI CONSENTES.

Dēidamī'a (Dēidameia), in Greek myth, the mother of Neoptolemus by *Achilles.

De impe'rio Cn. Pompeii ('concerning Pompey's command'), alternative title for Cicero's speech *Pro lege Manilia* in support of the proposal in 66 BC to extend Pompey's command in Asia.

Deina'rchus, (*c*.360–*c*.290 BC), a distinguished Greek orator, Corinthian by birth, who lived in Athens. Not being an Athenian citizen he was debarred from addressing the assembly, but he composed a large number of speeches for others, including a speech *Against Demosthenes* connected, like his other two surviving speeches (*Against Aristogeiton* and *Against Philocles*), with the Harpalus affair (see DEMOSTHENES (2) 1). Three other speeches surviving in the manuscripts of Demosthenes have sometimes been attributed to Deinarchus: *Against Boeotus II*, *Against Theocrines*, and *Against Mantitheus*.

De interpretātiō'ne (*Peri hermeneias*, 'on interpretation'), title of a short treatise on logic by *Aristotle (4 (i)).

De inventiō'ne ('on invention'), an early work (*c*.84 BC) on oratory by *Cicero ((1) 4). It explains how the subject-matter should be chosen and arranged, how the speech should be divided into sections, and what kind of treatment is appropriate to each section.

Dēi'phobē, name of the Cumaean *Sibyl in Virgil's *Aeneid*.

Dēi'phobus, in Greek myth, son of *Priam, king of Troy, and of Hecuba. He

took a prominent part in the fighting at Troy. After the death of Paris he married Helen and was subsequently killed at the fall of Troy. His body disappeared, but Aeneas erected a cenotaph to him on Cape Rhoeteum; on his visit to the Underworld Aeneas heard the story of his death from Deiphobus himself (see AENEID 6).

Deipnosophi'stai, title of a literary work by *Athenaeus.

De īra ('on anger'), treatise in dialogue form by *Seneca (2), addressed to his brother Novātus.

De īra Dei ('on the wrath of God'), a Christian work by *Lactantius.

De lau'de Pīsō'nis ('in praise of Piso'), Latin verse panegyric in 261 hexameters by an unknown author sometimes thought to be *Calpurnius Siculus. The Piso of the poem may be Gaius Calpurnius Piso who was executed for plotting against Nero in AD 65.

De lēge agrā'ria ('on the agrarian law'), or *Contra Rullum* ('against Rullus'), see CICERO (1) 2.

De lē'gibus ('on laws'), dialogue by *Cicero ((1) 4), a sequel to *De republica*, probably begun about 52 BC. The date of its completion (if it ever was completed) is unknown; Cicero seems not to have published it. Most of the first three books survive.

The interlocutors are Cicero, his brother Quintus, and Atticus; the scene is Cicero's estate at Arpīnum.

Dē'lia, name of the woman celebrated in his poems by the Roman poet *Tibullus. (Compare CYNTHIA.)

Dē'lian League, the modern name given to the alliance of Greek states against the Persians created in 478 BC after the expulsion of the Persian invaders from Greece. The alliance comprised mainly Athens, the Ionian Greek cities on the coast of Asia Minor, the Hellespont, the Propontis, and most of the islands in the Aegean. At the allies' request Athens took over the leadership (see PAUSANIAS (1)). The island of *Delos, sacred to Ionians everywhere, was the venue for meetings of the League and provided the treasury for League funds. Some states with strong navies, e.g. Chios, Samos, and Lesbos, contributed ships; the remainder paid tribute (money). At first the League undertook military operations against the Persians, thereby extending Greek control along the whole coast of Asia Minor, but its character changed to become an alliance of cities controlled by Athens, i.e. her empire. With the defeat of Athens in the Peloponnesian War (404) the League came to an end.

De lingua latī'na ('on the Latin language'), treatise by *Varro in twenty-five books of which books 5–10 survive (with gaps).

Dēlos, small island (less than 5 sq. km. (2 sq. miles) in area) in the Aegean sea, in the midst of the Cyclades, according to Greek myth the birthplace of Artemis and Apollo. The Homeric Hymn to Apollo attests that already in the eighth century BC Delos was the scene of a festival to the god, with song, dance, and games, attracting Ionians (including Athenians) from the islands and coasts of the Aegean. In later times it was said that the Athenians instituted the festival to commemorate the safe return of Theseus and his companions from Crete. Every year, reputedly since the days of Theseus, the Athenians sent a sacred embassy to Delos. During the absence of the state ship on this mission Athens was kept in a state of ceremonial purity, when no criminal might be executed. (It was this which delayed the execution of Socrates.) Delos was also chosen as the centre of the *Delian League.

From early times the island had commercial importance owing to the business transacted there during the festival of Apollo and in the third century BC it became a great corn-market. Its prosperity increased again after 166 BC when Rome, putting Delos under Athenian control, made it a free port (i.e. abolished all duties on the movement of goods) in order to damage the trade of Rhodes, a free city and an object of Roman jealousy. The island was sacked in 88 BC by soldiers of Mithridates of Pontus, a great enemy of Rome, and 20,000 inhabitants were killed. It was devastated again by pirates in 69 BC.

Before the end of the first century BC trade routes had changed; Delos was replaced by Puteoli as the chief focus of Italian trade with the East, and as a cult-centre too it entered a sharp decline.

Delphi (Delphoi), city in the Greek state of Phocis and the site of the famous oracle of Apollo. It was situated on the southern slopes of Mount *Parnassus, enclosed in a narrow valley but occupying the central area of a great natural theatre. There was a small settlement here in Mycenaean times (c. 1400 BC) but it seems to have been destroyed in the *Dark Age and a fresh start made in the eighth century BC. The famous crossroads where Oedipus was said to have murdered his father Laius is found on the road from Thebes to Delphi, which was precipitous and difficult in places.

Above the town was the sanctuary and oracle of Apollo. Inside the wall surrounding the sanctuary and oracle stood the many statues dedicated by successful athletes in the Pythian games held at Delphi, and also the treasuries built by various Greek cities to hold their most valuable offerings to Apollo. Only the Athenian treasury, dating perhaps from the 490s, still stands (rebuilt using the original stones), but remains of other buildings and monuments have been excavated. In front of the temple, in the open air, stood the great altar of Apollo. The original temple dated from about 600 BC but was destroyed by fire in 548. A new temple was built by the Athenian family of the *Alcmaeonidae, then living in exile at Delphi; this was destroyed by earthquake in 373 and a third temple replaced it. On the front of the temple were engraved the maxims ascribed to the *seven sages, *gnōthi sauton*, 'know yourself' (i.e. know your human weakness in contrast with the power of the gods), and *mēden agan*, 'nothing in excess'; also set up was the Greek letter E, the exact significance of which remains obscure (see PLUTARCH 3).

Inside the temple was the hearth beside which the priest of Apollo was said to have killed *Neoptolemus, and beside it the iron chair of Pindar, from which he reputedly sang his hymns to Apollo. On the hearth burned a perpetual fire. Further inside was the *omphalos*, the navel-stone, supposed to mark the mid-point of the earth, determined by Zeus as the place at which two eagles met, after flying one from the eastern and one from the western boundary of the world. In Aeschylus' tragedy *Eumenides* the Pythia (prophetess of Apollo), passing through the temple to the inmost sanctuary (*adyton*), catches sight of Orestes sitting upon the *omphalos*. In the *adyton* the Pythia gave oracular responses to those who came to consult her.

North of the temple, still in the sacred enclosure, was the tomb of Neoptolemus, and beyond it the stone which, according to Greek belief, *Cronus swallowed in place of his son Zeus. Here also was the spring (where Apollo slew the serpent Python; see DELPHIC ORACLE), which watered the sacred grove of myrtles and laurels and perhaps provided water for the *adyton*. To the west of this area lay a small theatre where the musical contests in the Pythian games were held, and a little further north the Leschē or public room (dedicated by the Cnidians), famous for its two large paintings by *Polygnōtus, *The Fall of Troy* and *The Descent of Odysseus into Hades*, both crammed with incident. About 10 km. (6 miles) north-east of Delphi was the famous *Corycian cave.

In AD 391 the sanctuary of Apollo was closed for ever along with all other pagan temples by the Roman emperor Theodosius, in the name of Christianity.

Delphic Oracle, at *Delphi, the most important *oracle in Greece, belonging to the god *Apollo. In his temple the priestess of Apollo, known as the Pythia, speaking under the inspiration supposedly of the god, answered questions put to her by worshippers. The Pythia was over the age of 50 when she was appointed, and thereafter lived a secluded and dedicated life; how she was selected is never explained, but the Delphian authorities may have chosen her from among a band of holy women whose task it was to tend the hearth in the temple (see DELPHI). When prophesying the Pythia sat on a tall tripod similar in style to the cooking utensil (i.e. three metal legs supporting a bowl), said in late

antiquity to be placed over a chasm from which fumes were exhaled (but for which there seems to be no archaeological or classical evidence). Plutarch records that in early times the Pythia gave oracles on only one day a year, in early spring; at a later date, perhaps in the sixth century BC, on one day a month, with the exception of the three winter months which the god spent with the *Hyperboreans. The day had to be declared auspicious by the priests, after they had tested the omens. Each enquirer, or indeed anyone who was in Delphi for a religious purpose, was required first to purify himself. It seems that the enquirer addressed his question to the Pythia directly and was answered directly, occasionally in verse, more often in prose. A priest or *prophētēs* ('mouthpiece') may have been in charge of the proceedings, and may even have 'interpreted' the Pythia's response, or put it into hexameter form. An enquirer might have let the priest know his question in advance, especially if bribery of the priests or Pythia was involved. With the reply, the consultation ended.

The impressiveness of the wild scenery at Delphi as well as of the ritual no doubt contributed to the importance of Apollo's oracle. In religion its authority was for many centuries supreme, especially in the matter of cult laws and institutions. Every four years, at the Pythian games, Delphi was the centre for a panhellenic concourse. In Hellenistic times its decline began. Some of the functions of Delphi were taken over by defunct oracles in Asia and Europe which were revived after Alexander the Great had destroyed Persian domination. Sharp decline did not set in until the first centuries BC and AD as a consequence of increasing secularism and perhaps because of the rising interest in astrology. The oracle enjoyed a brief revival under the emperor Hadrian, but by the time of the fervently pagan Julian (emperor AD 360–3), it was beyond resuscitation as its last message to the emperor, reported by a later historian, makes clear: 'Tell the emperor that the finely wrought hall is fallen to the ground; no longer has Phoebus his shelter, nor his prophetic laurel, nor his babbling spring; the water of speech is dried up.'

Dē'madēs (*c.*380–319 BC), Athenian politician and orator who realized that in order to survive Athens must come to terms with Philip II of Macedon. After the Athenian defeat at Chaeronea in 338 BC he secured an honourable settlement for Athens. When in 322 BC Antipater, the governor of Macedonia, had put down a revolt against Macedonian rule in which Athens took part, Demades procured the deaths of the politicians opposed to peace with Macedon, Hypereides and (indirectly) Demosthenes. In 319, caught in the political intrigues after the death of Antipater, he was himself executed by *Cassander. Only a few phrases from his speeches survive. See DEMOSTHENES (2) 1.

de'magogue (*dēmagōgos*, 'leader of the people'). This term to describe a leader of the people arose in Athens in the late fifth century BC and it usually had the pejorative sense of an unprincipled mob orator. The most notable demagogues were *Cleon, *Hyperbolus, *Cleophon, and Androcles.

De mercē'de condu'ctis (*Peri tōn epi misthōi synontōn*, 'on salaried posts'), satirical dialogue by *Lucian.

demes (*dēmoi*), local communities or parishes in Attica, eventually numbering about 170. In the reforms of *Cleisthenes (2), they replaced kinship groups as the basis of the democratic constitution in Athens. Cleisthenes arranged the demes into ten tribes (*phylai*) and each tribe into three *trittyes* (see TRITTYS); in each tribe one *trittys* comprised demes from the city region, another demes from the interior, and the third demes from the coast. In this way each tribe was made representative of the whole. Each deme had its own finances and its demarch (deme leader), elected by its assembly (*agora*) which dealt with local affairs. After Cleisthenes, membership of a deme was hereditary and did not change with change of residence. On reaching the age of 18 every male Athenian citizen was registered in his family deme.

Demē'ter, in Greek myth, daughter of Cronus and Rhea, sister of Zeus, a corn-goddess, patroness of agriculture in general and goddess of the Eleusinian

*mysteries. By Zeus she was the mother of *Persephonē (Lat. Proserpina), and by *Iasion the mother of *Plutus. The Romans identified her with the Italian goddess of the corn, *Cerēs. She was also identified sometimes with the Egyptian Isis and the Phrygian *Cybelē. Most of the myths concerning her relate to the rape of Persephone by Hades, god of the Underworld. Demeter sought her daughter all over the world, fasting, with hair untied, and carrying torches, and the earth became barren as a result of her neglect. To appease her, Persephone was released for part of the year. This myth has always been interpreted as an allegory of nature: Persephone must descend like seed into the earth so that the new corn may germinate. In her wanderings Demeter came to Eleusis where, in the guise of an old woman, she was hospitably received by the king, Celeus, and his wife Metaneira, and tended their new-born son Dēmoph(o)ōn (or *Triptolemus). She was discovered holding the child in the fire, to make it immortal by purging away its mortality. She explained her action by revealing her divinity, and ordered that rites, known thereafter as the Eleusinian mysteries, should be instituted at Eleusis in her honour. It was at Eleusis that Persephone was restored to her. She also sent Triptolemus about the world teaching the art of agriculture. See also ERYSICHTHON.

Dēmē'trius. 1. Demetrius of Phalērum (*c.*350–*c.*283 BC), Athenian statesman and philosopher. He was pro-Macedonian and favoured *Cassander's cause. When most of the Greek states including Athens surrendered to Cassander in 318, the latter made Demetrius governor of Athens, where he ruled in an enlightened manner for ten years. He went into exile when the Macedonian Demetrius Poliorcetes took Athens in 307, and later joined the Egyptian court of Ptolemy I Soter at Alexandria. He had studied at the Peripatetic school of philosophy in Athens as the pupil of *Theophrastus, and it is probable that he advised Soter about the foundation of the *Alexandrian Library and possibly about the *Museum too. He is thus partly responsible for their being organized in the Peripatetic fashion and spirit, which accounts for the nature and trend of much of the intellectual life of Alexandria. After Ptolemy II Philadelphus became sole ruler in 283 BC Demetrius was exiled to Upper Egypt where he died. He was an outstanding orator and the author of many scholarly works of which only fragments survive.

2. Demetrius Poliorcē'tēs, Macedonian general, famous for his unsuccessful siege of *Rhodes in 305–304 BC, commemorated by the *Colossus of Rhodes.

3. Greek author of a treatise 'On Style' (*Peri hermeneiās*), traditionally said to be Demetrius of Phalerum (see above), but the style and contents suggest a date at least a century later, and the work perhaps belongs to the first century BC. The author analyses style (*charactēr*) under four headings (rather than the more usual three; compare ORATOR): plain (*ischnos*), grand (*megaloprepēs*), elegant (*glaphyros*), and forceful (*deinos*); the last category is a novelty in this kind of criticism. He also gives an account of style in letter-writing, a literary genre usually ignored by other ancient critics.

Demiu'rge (*dēmiourgos*), in Greek, originally 'skilled workman', later 'creator', 'producer', and so, in Plato (see TIMAEUS), the creator of the visible world, and in Greek Christian writers God the Creator of all things. The Gnostics (see GNOSTICISM) used the term to denote the inferior deity who created the material universe, as distinct from the supreme God. The name *Demogorgon, taken in later times to mean the primeval god of ancient mythology, is probably a corruption of this word.

democracy (*dēmokratia*, 'rule of the people', i.e. of the *demos*). Democracy in the sense of government by the majority vote of all male citizens is first known in ancient Greece, and this ideal was most nearly achieved at Athens in the fifth century BC, established in essentials by *Cleisthenes (2).

Demo'critus, Greek philosopher, with Leucippus founder of the Greek atomic theory. He was born in Abdera (in Thrace) in 460 BC and reputedly lived to a very great age, dying *c*.357. In his early

years he is said to have travelled very widely in Asia. Plato never mentions him by name, but Aristotle refers to him frequently and in several connections, always with respect. He wrote copiously on a wide variety of subjects including natural sciences, mathematics, mechanics, grammar, music, and philosophy, but comparatively little has survived, and all of that in quotation. These few fragments deal mostly with ethics. Since the works of Leucippus, who was said to have been his teacher, have also perished, it is impossible to separate the contribution of each to the atomic theory. The atomists' arguments aimed to explain the perceptible world as it appears to the senses, containing multiplicity and diversity as well as motion and change.

Earlier philosophers, known as the Eleatics (see PHILOSOPHY I), had argued that 'what exists' (i.e. the cosmos and all that it contains) is single, indivisible, and unchanging, despite appearances to the contrary: the opposite to 'what exists', namely 'what is non-existent', their argument ran, is not there to be thought about and therefore cannot exist. The atomists' answer was that 'nothingness' exists and is as real as 'a thing', and might separate parts of 'what exists' from other parts. 'What exists' is indeed single, indivisible, and unchanging, but it is in the form of particles, indivisible small solids (*atoma*, 'things which cannot be divided'), differentiated from each other only in shape and size, randomly moving for ever in limitless 'nothingness', i.e. the void. All worlds—ours is not unique—first came into being through randomly colliding atoms causing a rotary movement in which atoms became attached to each other; different arrangements of atoms form different compounds, hence the variety of the world as we perceive it. Our world like every other came into being by accident and developed by necessity; its intelligibility does not depend upon its having been created by some sort of divine intelligence. The gods, if they exist, though superior to the human race are still creatures which have come into being and will eventually perish. People's consciousness and perception are entirely physical, to be accounted for by the arrangements of atoms which are by themselves not capable of consciousness. Consciousness resides in the soul (which is also the cause of life) because the soul is made of particularly fine atoms, though it is as perishable as the body. Perception comes about through the impact made on the soul (mediated through the sense-organs) by fine films emanating from the objects perceived. In his treatise *On Cheerfulness* (*Peri euthymiēs*) Democritus states that to achieve cheerfulness the atoms forming the soul must be protected from violent disturbance, thus expressing for the first time the idea (later developed by *Epicurus) that men should aim at the happiness which derives from peace of mind, itself based on knowledge of the physical basis of life. Most later Greek philosophers did not take up the atomic theory of matter; Democritus' most influential followers were Epicurus and (the Roman) *Lucretius. A tradition in the Latin writers represented Democritus as 'the laughing philosopher' unable to restrain his mirth at the spectacle of human life (in contrast with the melancholy Heracleitus).

Dēmo'docus. 1. In Homer's *Odyssey*, a bard at the Phaeacian court of king Alcinous, who sings of the love of Arēs and Aphroditē.

2. In Virgil's *Aeneid* (10. 413) a companion of Aeneas.

Dēmogo'rgon. This ominous name (compare GORGON), used by writers from the fifteenth century to denote the primeval god of ancient mythology, seems to have originated with a medieval scribe's miswriting of the name *Demiurge. The Italian poet Boccaccio (1313–75) copied this ghostword from the scholia to *Statius' *Thebaid* 4. 516 (see SCHOLIUM), and thence it entered literature.

Dēmō'nax, of Cyprus (second century AD), a Cynic philosopher known only by the biography of him ascribed to *Lucian.

De mo'rtibus persecūto'rum ('on the deaths of the persecutors'), essay by the Christian *Lactantius on the downfalls of the Roman emperors who persecuted the Christians. It was written c.318.

dēmos, in Greece, 'the people'; the term sometimes denoted the whole citizen body (and its assembly), sometimes only the lower classes in contrast with the upper.

Dēmo'sthenēs. 1. (d. 413 BC), prominent Athenian general during the Peloponnesian War. After earlier successes in the war his occupation of Pylos in 425 BC led to the capture of a body of Spartan hoplites on the neighbouring island of Sphacteria (see CLEON). In 413 after less successful campaigning he was sent with reinforcements for Nicias in Syracuse, but failed to persuade that general to withdraw from the city until the Athenians lost control of the sea and had to attempt an escape by land. In that retreat he commanded the rearguard but was forced to surrender to the Syracusans and Spartans and was subsequently executed.

2. (384–322 BC), the greatest of the Athenian orators.

1. *Life.* Demosthenes was born at Athens, in the deme of Paiānia, the sickly son of a wealthy father of the same name, who manufactured couches as well as swords and cutlery (hence the orator's nickname *machairopoios*, 'the cutler'). When Demosthenes was 7 his father died, and he was left to the care of three guardians appointed in the will; these so mismanaged the property that Demosthenes at 18 found himself almost without funds. He had already been inspired to become an orator by witnessing as a child the trial of the statesman Callistratus. He now prepared to sue his guardians, and for three years tried unsuccessfully to obtain restitution, during this time studying rhetoric and legal procedure, perhaps under *Isaeus. In 363 he brought an action against his guardians and won it, but probably recovered little (see 2 below). In the political sphere, his early attempts to address the assembly at Athens were said not to have been a success (he could not pronounce his r's and was given the nickname *batalos*, 'the stammerer'); he thereupon made strenuous efforts to improve his delivery (practising with pebbles in his mouth, for example), and studied literature and the

orators. He also became a speech-writer (*logographos*) for those who had to plead private suits in the law-courts, and he taught pupils. His growing reputation brought him employment as a speech-writer for public trials also, and he wrote speeches for the prosecution of Androtion in 355, Leptines in 354, and Androtion's associate Timocrates in 353. Demosthenes himself delivered the speech against Leptines, and it is possible that he was personally opposed to the policy Leptines advocated (see 2 below). This would be consistent with his attitude in the speech *On the Taxation Groups* (*Symmoriai*) in 354 (see 3 below).

Demosthenes became prominent as a politician by constantly urging resistance to the encroachments of *Philip II of Macedon. His first oration against Philip, the so-called *First Philippic*, advocating a vigorous policy of resistance was delivered in 352. In 349 Philip attacked Olynthus, a city that had made overtures of friendship to Athens. Demosthenes delivered three orations urging help (the *Olynthiacs*), but a faction inside Olynthus betrayed the city to Philip in the following year and it was destroyed. The Peace of Philocrates followed, in which Demosthenes was one of the negotiators. Despite this, as soon as the Peace was agreed Demosthenes became convinced that Philip was breaking it; he set about undoing it, but advised caution in his speech *On the Peace*. In 344 he persuaded the assembly to refuse Philip's offer to renew the Peace (the *Second Philippic*). In 342 Philip intervened more directly in the affairs of Greece and Demosthenes tried to organize a Greek alliance against him; in 341 in his speech *On the Chersonese* (followed by the *Third Philippic*) he defended the aggression in Thrace of the Athenian general Diopeithes, by arguing that Philip's actions were already tantamount to war. The *Fourth Philippic*, if genuine, would have been delivered soon afterwards.

When Philip's activities in Thrace reached *Byzantium, Athens, anxious for the security of her corn-route, sent aid to the Byzantines, and open war with Philip was begun; Demosthenes was the most influential voice in Athens at this time. In 339 Philip moved south and was at Elatea

in Phocis before the end of the year. Demosthenes procured an alliance with the Thebans, and both sides met at Chaeronea in autumn 338, Philip winning a decisive victory. Demosthenes, who was present at the battle, delivered the funeral oration over the dead, a speech which has not survived. There was no need for Philip to impose a direct political settlement on Greece: in most cities pro-Macedonian politicians and policies naturally came to the fore. Despite the defeat at Chaeronea, a battle which Demosthenes had actively sought, his friend Ctesiphon proposed soon afterwards that he should be honoured with a gold crown at the Great *Dionysia for his service to the city. *Aeschines charged Ctesiphon with the alleged illegality of the proposal, but the case did not come to trial until 330. In his speech (*Against Ctesiphon*) Aeschines reviewed Demosthenes' career and blamed on him all the recent misfortunes of Athens, but the latter's reply (*On the Crown*) was a masterpiece and secured an overwhelming vote in his favour; fewer than one fifth of the jury voted for Aeschines (who then retired to Rhodes, where he died). Meanwhile, Alexander the Great had succeeded to the throne of Macedon after Philip's assassination in 336, and had quickly indicated that he did not intend to let Greece slip from Macedonian control.

Demosthenes remained to the fore in public affairs, but the later part of his career was clouded by the affair of Harpalus, the fugitive treasurer of Alexander the Great, who decamped to the coast of Attica in 325 with a vast sum of money. Demosthenes seems to have proposed first that Harpalus should be kept prisoner and his money stored on the Acropolis, and later, after Harpalus had escaped, that the *Areopagus should investigate the disappearance of some of it. Demosthenes' actions and motives are by no means clear, but he was accused and found guilty of appropriating a large sum from it for himself and was fined fifty talents (see DEINARCHUS and HYPEREIDES). He retired into exile, but after the death of Alexander in 323 he was active once again in stimulating concerted Greek resistance to Macedon, and returned to Athens in triumph. When the defeat at

*Crannon in 322 led to the breakup of the Greek alliance, each state made its own separate peace with Antipater, Alexander's successor. The terms for Athens were that the chief agitators against Macedon should be surrendered; Athens refused, but when the Macedonians marched upon the city Demosthenes and his supporters fled. *Demades' proposal that they should be sentenced to death was carried. Rather than be taken alive from the temple on Calaureia (an island off the east coast of Argolis) where he had sought refuge, Demosthenes took poison. The Greek traveller Pausanias who visited Athens in the second century AD summed up his life: 'Demosthenes loved the Athenians too much, and this is what came of it. It seems to me a true saying that a man who devotes himself unsparingly to his country's affairs and trusts his people never comes to a good end.'

Sixty-one speeches have come down to us under the name of Demosthenes, but the authenticity of some of them, particularly among the speeches relating to civil cases, has been doubted. Among the speeches generally accepted as genuine the following are the most important.

2. *Speeches in the law-courts.* Demosthenes' first private speeches in the law-courts were the three delivered against his fraudulent guardian Aphobus in 363; his last was against Dionysodorus in 322. He won his suit against Aphobus but could recover no more than a fraction of his property. This was followed by further fruitless proceedings, against Onetor, brother-in-law of Aphobus, in which Demosthenes delivered two speeches. The private speeches cover many subjects, including bottomry loans, mining rights, forgery, and trespass. Speeches on behalf of Phormio (350) and against Stephanus (349) concern the wealthy banker *Pasion, whose chief clerk Phormio was. A speech *Against Boeotus* (348) attempts to prevent an illegitimate son from claiming the name of his legitimate half-brother (with implications for his legitimacy). In a speech *Against Meidias* (347), which was never delivered, Demosthenes prosecutes an old personal and political enemy who had slapped the orator's face at a public festival. After long delay the suit was settled out of court, Demosthenes receiving a considerable sum in damages. *Against Conon* (341) is a brilliant and entertaining speech for the prosecution of Conon and his rowdy sons, for assault upon a virtuous young man. The speech *Against Callicles*, of uncertain date, alleges with touches of humour that the defendant has caused the plaintiff's land to be flooded by blocking a watercourse.

Against Androtion is Demosthenes' earliest speech in a public prosecution, in 355. Androtion had proposed that crowns be awarded to the outgoing members of the council (*boulē*); Demosthenes supports a certain Diodorus in raising objections, on the grounds that the navy has not been increased during the year. In *Against Timocrates* (353) Demosthenes again supports Diodorus, in an embezzlement case. *Against Aristocrates* (352) is an attack on the politician Charidemus for his dealings in Thrace. None of these was actually delivered by Demosthenes, but he himself spoke *Against Leptines* (in 354; see 1 above). Leptines had proposed, in view of the financial difficulties of the state, to abolish all hereditary exemptions from taxation granted as a reward to benefactors of the state. Demosthenes argues that the proposal is contrary to good policy and that the saving will be negligible.

3. *Early speeches on public policy.*

On the Taxation Groups (or symmories, Gk. *symmoriai*) (354). The duty of equipping triremes (i.e. warships) had in 357 been laid on the twelve hundred richest citizens, divided into twenty groups, the members of which each paid the same share of the cost, however much property each had. The system worked unfairly, and in this speech Demosthenes proposes its reform. At the same time he opposes war with Persia.

For the Megalopolitans (353). Demosthenes advocates alliance with Megalopolis, the capital, recently founded with Theban help, of a newly confederated Arcadia. While Thebes was occupied with the *Sacred War against Phocis, Sparta was trying to regain her former control over Arcadia. Some of the Athenian assembly, out of hostility to Thebes, did not wish to take any action unfavourable to Sparta. Demosthenes, on the contrary, urges the maintenance of a balance of power between Sparta and Thebes: if Sparta reduces Arcadia she will become too strong. (Subsequent events seem to show that Demosthenes greatly exaggerated Sparta's aggressive power at that time.)

On the Liberty of the Rhodians (351). Rhodes had revolted from the Athenian League; oligarchs were in control and the leading democrats in exile. Demosthenes urges the Athenians to restore the democrats and follow their traditional role of liberators.

4. *The* Philippics *and other speeches on* Macedon.

First Philippic (351). Philip's aggressive policy in Thrace threatened not only Athens' corn-route and the cleruchy in the Chersonese, but also Olynthus, which had concluded a peace with Athens in 352. Demosthenes urges the Athenians to rouse themselves, and details the measures they ought to take: the immediate dispatch of a small expedition and the preparation of a larger permanent force to meet Philip's rapid movements in whatever direction. The citizens themselves must form part of the force; they must not rely entirely on mercenaries.

Olynthiacs (349). Philip had resumed his threat to Olynthus and had captured some other Chalcidian towns, although not Olynthus itself. The Olynthians appealed to Athens in 349. In the three *Olynthiacs*, speeches delivered in quick succession, Demosthenes urges the fullest support, including the suggestion that the *theoric fund (used to pay for festivals) should be diverted to military purposes. He contrasts the public-spiritedness of the citizens in former days with present-day indolence fostered by public doles distributed without regard to public service.

On the Peace (346). In mid-348 before the fall of Olynthus Demosthenes had successfully defended Philocrates against the charge that the latter's proposal to open negotiations with Philip was illegal. His friendship with philocrates continued and he took part in the embassies that resulted in the Peace of Philocrates (346). However, soon after that Philip had extended his conquests in Thrace, advanced into Greece, subdued the Phocians, and secured a place on the Amphictyonic Council. Demosthenes, who subsequently did all he could to repudiate the Peace, considered that for the time being resistance was impossible and in this speech advises a pacific policy.

Second Philippic (344). After an interval Philip had resumed his interference in Greece, strengthening his position in Thessaly, and in the Peloponnese supporting the Argives and Messenians against Sparta. Demosthenes went on an embassy to those cities to warn them of the dangers of consorting with Philip, who promptly protested. This speech is his reply to Philip's protests. He exposes Philip's designs for empire and proposes a reply to him (the text of which has not survived).

On the False Embassy (343). There had been serious disagreements between Demosthenes and his fellow ambassadors at the time when the Peace of Philocrates was made. The terms agreed upon were that Athens and Macedon should each retain the territories they possessed to date. As Philip was constantly engaged on fresh conquests it was urgent, when once Athens had accepted the terms, that the second embassy sent to receive Philip's oath of ratification should act with all speed. In spite of Demosthenes' protests the embassy delayed and Philip delayed further, so that by the time the Peace was ratified Philip had subdued Thrace. Moreover, on the embassy's return to Athens Aeschines gave so favourable an account of Philip's intentions with regard to Athenian interests that the assembly voted to extend the treaty to Philip's descendants, allowed him to occupy Thermopylae, and left Phocis, whose appeal for help Athens had earlier answered (see SACRED WAR), to surrender to him. In 343, when feeling at Athens had been roused by Philip's continuing aggressions, Demosthenes prosecuted Aeschines for the delays which had resulted in Philip's intervention in Phocis, and for giving false reports, suggesting that bribery was the cause of his pro-Macedonian stance. Aeschines' reply (which we possess; see AESCHINES) secured a decision in his favour by a narrow majority.

On the Chersonese (341). Demosthenes in this speech (and in the *Third Philippic*; see below) is seeking to end the Peace by persuading the Athenians that Philip has already broken it. Philip was in Thrace, in dangerous proximity to the Chersonese and projecting an attack on Byzantium. After the Peace of Philocrates Athens had sent settlers to the Chersonese under Diopeithes. The town of Cardia refused them admission, and Philip sent an expedition for the town's protection. Diopeithes, ill-provided with funds by Athens, made piratical raids in various directions, among others into Philip's Thracian territory, and Philip sent a protest to Athens. In his speech Demosthenes urges that Diopeithes should be vigorously supported. The speech is distinguished by the passion with which Demosthenes expresses his feelings about Philip's fundamental and implacable ambition.

Third Philippic (also 341, a few months after the previous speech). The threat to the Chersonese and Byzantium was closer and Philip was also interfering in Euboea. Demosthenes wants to unite the Greek cities against Philip and, trying to rouse the Athenians to the imminence of their danger, proposes the immediate dispatch of forces. This is one of the finest of Demosthenes' speeches, marked by gravity and deep anxiety; in one notable passage he contrasts the ancient spirit of Athens with her present degeneracy. (The *Fourth Philippic*, if genuine, would have been delivered soon after the *Third*.)

On the Crown (330). This is Demosthenes' greatest oration, rebutting the attack of his rival Aeschines (for the background see 1 above). Demosthenes defends in detail his policy from the Peace of Philocrates in 346 to the defeat at Chaeronea in 338, maintaining that his advice has always been in accordance with the honourable traditions of Athens which has never 'preferred an inglorious security to the hazardous vindication of a noble cause'. He includes a virulent attack on Aeschines, ridiculing, perhaps without strict regard to truth, his humble origins, and endeavouring to prove from the facts of his career that he was a traitor, bribed by Philip's money. Two passages are especially famous: the description of the confusion at Athens when the messenger came with the news that Philip was at Elatea (in Phocis) and so on Athens' doorstep (ch. 169); and the invocation of the Athenians who had fought the Persians at Marathon, Salamis, and Plataea a century and a half earlier (ch. 206).

5. Demosthenes' claim to greatness rests on his character as well as his oratory, his sincere and far-sighted patriotism trenchantly expressed in simple language. His speeches are marked by a passionate earnestness expressed in a great variety of tones: anger, irony, sarcasm, invective; pathos and humour rarely appear. A striking feature of his eloquence is that it is at once elevated and practical: there is no fine speaking for its own sake; all is directed to the persuasion of his hearers' minds, but in a form calculated to appeal to a popular audience. He is sometimes criticized for the artificial expression and the sophistic character of some of his arguments. But the development of his arguments and the arrangement of his topics, although often intricate, are lucid and compelling. He writes in pure Attic Greek, with bold metaphors rarely but aptly placed, and likes vivid examples: the Athenians in their warfare with Philip are like barbarians boxing, 'Hit one of them, and he rubs the place; hit him on the other side, and there go his hands; but as for guarding, or looking his opponent in the face, he neither can nor will do it' (*Philippic* 1. 40). The speeches were most carefully prepared but the style aims to conceal this fact, long, periodic sentences often being followed by short, pithy statements, which gives an impression of spontaneity. In all his speeches Demosthenes deliberately avoided hiatus (the placing of a word ending in a vowel before a word beginning with a vowel) except in unavoidable cases, such as those involving the use of 'or' ($\bar{e}$) or 'and' (*kai*); in his early speeches he was strict in the observance of this rule. As a further aid to euphony he avoided as far as possible a run of more than two short syllables. (For length of syllables see PROSODY.)

The oratorical method of Demosthenes

was much studied by subsequent orators, and by none more than *Cicero (1) 6. 'Philippics' was used by him as the title of his own speeches against Mark Antony, and hence adopted as a general title for speeches of political invective. *Quintilian thought that Demosthenes' speeches should not only be examined but learnt by heart by students of rhetoric; *Longinus admired his intensity and sublimity.

demotic, see ROSETTA STONE.

De nātū'ra deo'rum ('on the nature of the gods'), philosophical dialogue in three books by Cicero, written in 45 BC after the death of his daughter, in which he sets out the theological tenets of the three principal Greek schools of philosophy in his day, the Epicurean, Stoic, and Academic. The work is addressed to M. Brutus. (See CICERO (1) 5.)

Dentā'tus, Mā'nius Cu'rius, see CURIUS DENTATUS.

De offi'ciis ('on [moral] duties'), by Cicero, his last work on moral philosophy, finished in November 44 BC (see CICERO (1) 5), in the form of a letter to his son Marcus then studying philosophy at Athens. It consists of three books of moral advice, based on Stoic precepts and, in the first two books, on the teaching of *Panaetius; the third is based on that of *Posidonius and others.

The first book deals with the four cardinal virtues, wisdom, justice, fortitude, and temperance, develops the various duties that devolve from these, and passes on to their application to individual people who vary in age, position, abilities, etc. The second and third books discuss the application of the above principles to the pursuit of success in life: the reconciliation of expediency with virtue. The two are shown to be in reality identical, even in cases of apparent conflict; for material gain cannot compensate for the loss of the sense of honour and justice. Cicero's doctrine is illustrated throughout with examples from Greek and Roman history. Noteworthy are the highly practical character of his precepts, his condemnation of abstention from public activities (in opposition to the Stoics), and his insistence on the social

character of a man and the duty of men to their fellow human beings, something beyond patriotism. This work received high praise in later ages and was a pervasive influence in its exposition of the virtuous political life.

De opifi'cio Dei ('on the handiwork of God'), Christian work by *Lactantius.

De o'ptimo ge'nere ōrātō'rum ('on the best kind of orators'), by Cicero, an introduction to translations of the Greek orations *De corona* of Demosthenes and *Against Ctesiphon* of Aeschines (see CICERO (1) 5), which is only partially preserved. Cicero argues that Demosthenes, who wrote in Attic Greek, had such a command of every oratorical style that it is inappropriate to use the term Atticism to describe a plain style of *oratory (see 1).

De ōrātō're ('on the orator'), work in three books by *Cicero ((1) 4), the most finished of his treatises on oratory, completed in 55 BC after his exile and addressed to his brother Quintus. The dialogues which it comprises are supposed to take place in 91 BC and the chief interlocutors are the eminent lawyers L. Licinius *Crassus and M. *Antonius; Q. Mucius *Scaevola, another great lawyer, is also present; and after the first dialogue Q. *Catulus, consul with the general Marius, and C. Julius Caesar Strabo the orator. The scene of the dialogues is the villa of Crassus at Tusculum. Cicero's aim is to describe the general principles underlying the practice of oratory.

Deo'rum conci'lium, satirical dialogue by *Lucian.

Deo'rum dia'logi, short dialogues by *Lucian, making fun of Greek myths.

De ō'tio ('on leisure'), dialogue by *Seneca (2), advocating that leisure should be spent in contemplation.

De philoso'phia ('on philosophy'), lost treatise by *Varro, apparently an outline of the doctrines of the different philosophical schools.

De prōvide'ntia ('on providence'), dialogue by *Seneca (2), addressed to his friend Lucilius (the Younger), in which he discusses the question why good men meet with misfortune when there exists a providence. The answer is that misfortune serves a useful purpose: it is a school of virtue. Stoicism provides the remedy of suicide when misfortune becomes intolerable.

De prōvi'nciis consulā'ribus ('on provinces governed by consuls'), speech by Cicero in 56 BC (see CICERO (1) 4), advocating the prolongation of Caesar's command in Gaul.

De re eque'stri (*Peri hippikēs*, '*horsemanship'), treatise by *Xenophon.

De repu'blica ('on the state'), dialogue in six books on political science by *Cicero ((1) 4), begun in 54 BC and published by early 51 BC. We possess the greater part of the first three books and fragments of the others, including the *Somnium Scipionis*, 'dream of Scipio', which formed the conclusion of the work and is preserved mainly in a commentary by Macrobius. The dialogue is modelled to some extent on Plato's *Republic*. It is supposed to take place in the course of three days in 129 BC, in the garden of *Scipio Aemilianus, and the principal interlocutors are Scipio and *Laelius.

De repu'blica Athenie'nsium ('on the Athenian constitution'), short political pamphlet attributed to *Xenophon; see CONSTITUTION OF THE ATHENIANS (2).

De re ru'stica ('on farming'). 1. Of M. Porcius *Cato; see DE AGRI CULTURA.

2. Treatise on farming written in dialogue form by M. Terentius *Varro when his eightieth year admonished him 'that he must be packing his baggage to depart this life'. The treatise is in three books and takes the form of conversations, to some extent in a dramatic setting: the first conversation is interrupted by news of a murder, and the third by incidents in an election. Book 1 deals with the farm itself, its buildings and equipment, and the agricultural year in general; book 2 with cattle- and sheep-breeding; book 3 with the smaller livestock on a farm, aviaries, poultry, bees, game preserves, and fishponds. The work is written in a more literary form than that of Cato, and is animated by touches of wit and a feeling for the country life.

3. Treatise by *Columella.

De rerum nātū'ra, philosophical poem by *Lucretius.

De rhēto'ribus ('on the orators'), brief biographical sketches of sixteen Roman orators by *Suetonius, of which some part survives.

Derveni papyrus, the only ancient book to have been found in Greece (see PAPYROLOGY), consisting of the upper half of a papyrus roll of the late fourth century BC, found at Derveni, c.9 km north of Thessaloniki, and now in the Museum at Thessaloniki. It had been carbonized (and so preserved) from being placed on a funeral pyre. It contains a commentary on an Orphic religious poem.

De senectū'te ('on old age'), dialogue by *Cicero ((1) 5), whose title for it was *Cato Maior de senectute*, probably written just before Julius Caesar's murder in 44 BC. The work is dedicated to *Atticus. The conversation is supposed to take place in 150 BC, when M. Porcius *Cato (the Censor) was in his eighty-fourth year. At the request of his young friends *Scipio Aemilianus and *Laelius, Cato expounds how the burden of old age may best be borne; he describes its compensations and consolations, drawing illustrations from his own experience, from reminiscences of old men he has known, and from his reading (notably of Plato and Xenophon). He concludes with a reasoned statement of his belief in the immortality of the soul. The early part of the dialogue is imitated from the conversation of Socrates and Cephalus in book 1 of Plato's *Republic*.

De situ orbis ('the geography of the world'), treatise by Pomponius *Mela.

De sophi'sticis ele'nchis ('refutations in the manner of the sophists'), treatise on logic by Aristotle; see ARISTOTLE 4 (i).

De tranquillitā'te a'nimi ('on tranquillity of the soul'), dialogue by *Seneca (2); see 2.

Deuca'lion, in Greek myth, the son of *Prometheus. When Zeus was so angry at the crimes of men that he decided to destroy them by a flood, Deucalion, warned by Prometheus, built a boat for himself and his wife Pyrrha; they floated in it until the water subsided and they grounded on Mount Parnassus. Advised by an oracle to throw their mother's bones over their shoulder, they realized that this meant the stones of the earth and did so, those thrown by Deucalion becoming men and those thrown by Pyrrha women. The new race was called the Leleges. Subsequently Deucalion and Pyrrha became the parents of *Hellen, the eponymous founder of the Greeks.

de'us ex ma'china, SEE THEATRE 1.

De verbo'rum significā'tu ('on the meaning of words'), an encyclopaedic work by *Verrius Flaccus.

De viris illu'stribus ('on famous men'), collection of biographical sketches of Roman literary figures by *Suetonius, of which only fragments survive.

De vīta beā'ta ('on the happy life'), dialogue by *Seneca (2).

De vīta Cae'sarum ('the lives of the Caesars'), biographies of the Twelve Caesars from Julius to Domitian (d. AD 96) by *Suetonius.

De vīta po'puli rōmā'ni ('the manner of life of the Roman people'), history of Roman culture and society by *Varro.

dēvō'tio. If a battle was going against a Roman general it was possible for him to dedicate himself and the enemy army to 'Tellus and the Manes', i.e. the gods of the Underworld, by a fairly elaborate ritual. He then sought to be killed among the enemy, on the understanding that if the gods accepted his 'dedication' of himself they must also accept the enemy army. See DECIUS MUS.

dia'dochoi ('successors'), the name given to the Greek rulers who succeeded to various parts of the empire of *Alexander the Great after his death in 323 BC. See ATTALIDS, PTOLEMIES, and SELEUCIDS.

diae'resis, see METRE, GREEK 2.

Dia'goras, famous boxer of Rhodes, from a family of athletes. One of Pindar's Olympian Odes (no. 7) is devoted to him.

dia'krioi, in Athens of the sixth century BC the 'men of the hills' organized by *Peisistratus as a revolutionary faction.

dialectic (*dialektikē*), term of Greek philosophy, derived from the verb meaning 'to converse', 'to discuss'; in Plato and others, a method of philosophical inquiry conducted by question and answer. The inventor of dialectic was said to have been the philosopher *Zeno the Eleatic, whose characteristic method was to take an opponent's hypothesis and deduce from it two contradictory conclusions, thereby rendering it absurd. The dialectical method of Socrates (see ELENCHUS), as it appears from the dialogues of Plato, had as its aim the testing of the truth of a proposition by question and answer, in a manner roughly resembling ordinary conversation. It was destructive rather than constructive, in that it demonstrated flaws in a suggested proposition but arrived at no better substitute. Plato's own dialectic is a development from that of Socrates. At its simplest it starts from an assumption taken to be true for the purposes of argument (as did Zeno's), and proceeds through question and answer (as did Socrates') in a methodically rigorous way until a conclusion is reached. It seemed to Plato that his method made it possible to acquire knowledge, and provide explanations for what is known, positively and systematically. For Plato dialectic was the only way to reach the true end of philosophy, knowledge of the Good, and sometimes therefore signified philosophy itself rather than simply a philosophical method. In the logical works of Aristotle, the term dialectic describes reasoning from a hypothesis; as a philosophical method Aristotle thought it inferior to deduction, which starts from premisses known to be true. In modern usage, which is sometimes at a considerable remove from the ancient meaning, the term often describes the general arguments or ideas of a work or an author.

dialects. 1. Greek. (For the origins of the Greek language see GREECE.)

1. The evidence of inscriptions (see EPIGRAPHY) and of literary texts shows that in classical times the Greek language existed in a number of dialects. The differences between them, small enough to allow each Greek city to understand the others, reflect the movement of Greek peoples in early times into and within

Greece, and into the Aegean islands and the west coast of Asia Minor. The later predominance of the Attic dialect reflects the ascendancy of Athenian literature and culture generally (see 3 below).

The dialects of Greece in classical times fall into two broad divisions, West Greek and East Greek. These divisions subdivide further: West Greek comprises North-West Greek, spoken in Phocis, Locris, Elis, and Aetolia, and Doric, spoken throughout the Peloponnese and in the places colonized by Doric speakers, namely the southern group of Aegean islands, Crete, Rhodes, the south-west coast of Asia Minor, and many colonies in Sicily and Magna Graecia (south Italy). East Greek subdivides into Ionic, Aeolic, and Arcado-Cyprian. Ionic was spoken in Ionia (on the coast of Asia Minor), Euboea, and the islands in the Aegean colonized by Ionic speakers; its offshoot Attic was spoken in Attica and so by the Athenians. Aeolic was spoken in the island of Lesbos and in the neighbouring part of Asia Minor, and, with an admixture of West Greek, in Thessaly and Boeotia. The name Arcado-Cyprian (invented in modern times) expresses the close relationship between the dialect of Arcadia, in the centre of the Peloponnese, and that of Cyprus, far away in the eastern Mediterranean; for this dialect there are no literary texts. It has been suggested that the Arcadian and Cyprian dialects preserve some of the forms present in the *Mycenaean Greek of earlier times because these parts were difficult of access and relatively isolated. The Dorians were a people of Greek stock who were thought to have arrived from the north-west c.1100 BC (see DORIAN INVASION), and who spoke a dialect not substantially different from that spoken in Greece before they arrived (see LINEAR B).

2. The dialect used by a Greek author is not necessarily that of his native speech nor that of the city in which he wrote. It is characteristic of the conservatism of Greek literature in its formal aspects that the dialect in which a literary genre originated remained the dialect of that genre in later times. Thus, because choral lyric poetry originated in a Doric-speaking region, all such poetry is written in a

(literary) form of Doric, even when it is composed by a Boeotian (Pindar) or by an Ionic speaker (Bacchylides) or is found in Attic tragedy. All the dialects that appear in literature are modified so as to present their most conspicuous characteristics while avoiding the parochial or undignified; in the choral lyric of tragedy, for example, the Doric element became a conventional means of enriching and ennobling the diction.

The dialect of Homer's epic is an artificial amalgam of Ionic and Aeolic elements never spoken in conjunction at any one time in any one place. It was the product of a long tradition of epic poetry, the composition of which seems to have passed from an Aeolic- to an Ionic-speaking area. Hesiod, a Boeotian, wrote his poems in hexameters, the metre of Homeric epic, and so his dialect is virtually identical with Homer's, as was that of all later epic, e.g. the *Argonautica* of Apollonius Rhodius. Elegy (whose metre is hexameter followed by pentameter) was the invention of the Ionians, but since the hexameter was also the metre of Homeric epic, the dialect of elegy too is quite strongly epic, but with a larger admixture of Ionic forms. Tragedy and comedy at Athens were written in Attic, the local dialect and a branch of Ionic, except for the choral lyric parts, which were written in a form of Doric (see above). The lyric poetry of Sappho and Alcaeus was written in the native dialect of Lesbos, a branch of Aeolic. Anacreon wrote in his native Ionic, and Corinna in her local Boeotian. Iambic and trochaic poems were written in Ionic, although the Athenian Solon when writing in these metres used many forms taken from his native Attic. Pastoral poetry, a genre created by Theocritus, is mostly written in an artificial Doric made up of a variety of forms, some in general use, some purely local, others made up by false analogies; it also has a sprinkling of Aeolic and epic features. The modern sense of Doric meaning 'rustic' derives from the use of this dialect in pastoral poetry. Because prose literature first arose in Ionia, Ionic became the dialect of historical and scientific works. Even the Athenian historian Thucydides, writing mainly in Attic, avoided using peculiarly

Attic forms so as not to depart too obviously from the appropriate dialect.

3. The *koinē* ('common tongue'). The political unification of Greece which began under Philip II of Macedon (reigned 359–336 BC), and the absorption of large tracts of the East into a Greek empire, brought about the decline of the separate dialects and the rise of this new, uniform Greek. The Athenian *Xenophon, who spent most of his life abroad, may be considered the first writer of the new *koine*. The basis of it was Attic, officially adopted by Philip II in preference to the semi-barbarous Macedonian dialect, and it spread, with the conquests of his son Alexander the Great, throughout the Greek empire. (The poets of the Hellenistic age could reproduce the old dialects only by studied effort.) The *koine* was the language in which the *Septuagint and the Greek New Testament were written. In the first century AD there was an attempt to write Greek prose literature in the classical Attic dialect; of this revival Lucian is the best example. See SOPHISTIC, SECOND.

2. **Italic.** The Italic languages (a branch of Indo-European) consist of Latin, Oscan, and Umbrian, as well as the dialects of various mountain tribes of central Italy. When the Latin language was still confined to Rome and Latium, Oscan was the chief language of central Italy. See LATIN LANGUAGE.

dialogue, literary genre, Greek in origin, in which characters, usually real but sometimes imaginary, conduct a conversation, pursuing a single theme but admitting some of the digression and inconsequence found in normal conversation. The *mimes of Sophron of Syracuse (fifth century BC) are an example, said to have been admired by Plato, whose Socratic dialogues may have taken their form from the mimes while their content was based on the actual conversations of Socrates. Xenophon and Aristotle wrote similarly, the latter's dialogues surviving only in fragments. This literary form reappeared in the second century AD in the dialogues of *Plutarch and *Lucian. These were modelled on Plato's but in the case of Lucian served satirical rather than philosophical ends and were a witty

and biting form of entertainment. In the *Deipnosophistai* *Athenaeus relates in fifteen books the conversations of learned men meeting over dinner and discussing food in all its aspects.

In Roman literature the chief examples of the dialogue are to be found in Cicero's political, rhetorical, and philosophical treatises and in the *Dialogus de oratoribus* of Tacitus. In these it is the usual pattern for the leading role to be taken by one interlocutor (sometimes the author himself), who expounds his view at length, the other characters' parts being conspicuously less important. In *Seneca's dialogues the dramatic element is reduced to a minimum. The *Noctes Atticae* ('Attic nights') of Aulus *Gellius is an idiosyncratic compilation of learning, some of it purporting to record past conversations.

Dialogues of the Dead, of the Gods, of the Sea-Gods, see LUCIAN.

Dia'logus de ōrātō'ribus ('dialogue on orators'), dialogue attributed to *Tacitus and now generally accepted as by him, in spite of differences in style from his later work, which may be the result of its belonging to a different literary genre. It is no longer thought to be an early work; since it is dedicated to Lucius Fabius Justus, consul in AD 102, it was probably published in that year or soon after. The claims of oratory against other branches of literature are discussed, and the reasons why oratory has declined since Cicero's day. The scene is set in the house of Curiātius Māternus, a poet. The other interlocutors are two distinguished orators, Marcus Aper, an advocate, and Julius Secundus, both of Gallic birth and both teachers of Tacitus; and Vipstanus Messalla, a man of distinguished birth. The date is supposed to be *c.* AD 75. The first twenty-seven chapters are introductory. Aper, a practical, utilitarian lawyer, maintains the superiority of oratory over poetry, for the rewards it brings. Maternus, a meditative idealist, disdains wealth and power and prefers a quiet life and the companionship of the Muses. Aper admits no decline in oratory. Messalla, a champion of former times, criticizes the modern speakers. At the request of Maternus he passes to the causes of the alleged decline (ch. 28), which for the purposes of the discussion is to be assumed. These causes Messalla finds in the lax education of the young, contrasted with the careful methods of former days; and in the defective training given to orators in the schools of rhetoric. After this there is a gap of several pages in the manuscript. When the text resumes someone else (probably Maternus) is speaking. He argues that the decline in oratory is due to the changed conditions of public life. Oratory flourished under the republic in times of disorder and revolution, when orators were inspired by political enthusiasm. The calmness of political life under the emperors has removed these incentives, but has brought compensations.

Oratory was seen by Tacitus to be in an inevitable decline, linked as it was to political institutions themselves in decline. It is interesting to compare this work with the near-contemporary *Education of an Orator* (published in the 90s) by *Quintilian, whose concern is rather with the technical and literary aspects of oratory.

Dia'na, Italian goddess of woodland and wild nature, protector of women, identified with the Greek *Artemis; her cult was widespread in Italy. From very early times she had a temple at Rome on the Aventine, traditionally founded by the king Servius Tullius (578–535 BC). Catullus' poem 34, *Hymn to Diana*, describes her role. Her most famous cult was at Arīcia, on the shore of Lake Nemi in the Alban hills. Her shrine there stood in a grove where she was worshipped in association with *Egeria and with a male god of the forest named Virbius, later identified with the Greek Hippolytus. The priesthood of this shrine was given to a runaway slave, called *rex* ('king'), after he had broken off a branch from a certain tree in the grove (see GOLDEN BOUGH) and killed his predecessor. Diana may have been thought of as a moon-goddess. From being worshipped (like *Hecatē) at crossroads she derives her title 'Trivia' (*trivium*, 'place where three roads meet').

diatribe (*diatribē*, 'spoken address', 'lecture'), in Greek, the name given to a short, ethical discourse, particularly of the kind composed by Cynic and Stoic philosophers (see EPICTETUS). These popular moral lectures were often polemical in tone, and 'diatribe' soon acquired the modern sense of 'invective'. Many Roman writers produced diatribes, as did Christian polemicists.

Dicaea'rchus (third to second century BC), of Messana in Sicily, Greek scientist and pupil of Aristotle, whose works are lost. He wrote biographies of earlier Greek writers as well as philosophical, political, and geographical works. His most interesting was a treatise on life in Greece (*Bios Hellados*), which was the first universal history of culture from the (imagined) *Golden Age to Dicaearchus' own day, and included a description of the known world. He was an important influence upon Eratosthenes, Cicero, Josephus, and Plutarch. Cicero admired him greatly, and took him as exemplar of the 'practical life' (see DE OFFICIIS).

dicasts (*dikastai*), in Athenian law-courts, the members of the jury.

di conse'ntes (perhaps 'the gods that are'), in Roman religion, the twelve great gods, six male and six female; according to two hexameter lines of the poet Ennius,

> Juno, Vesta, Minerva, Ceres, Diana,
> Venus, Mars,
> Mercurius, Jovi', Neptunus,
> Volcanus, Apollo.

Dicta Catōnis, see CATO (1), end of entry.

dictator. At Rome, the dictatorship was an *ad hoc* magistracy, admitted to the Roman constitution soon after the expulsion of the kings in 509 BC to allow supreme authority to be entrusted temporarily to one individual in times of grave crisis (compare COLLEGIUM 1). The dictator was appointed by the nomination of a consul on the senate's proposal. He had supreme military and judicial authority, which was not subject to appeal, and he could not be called to account for his actions. The dictator, who was also known as *magister populi*, 'master of the infantry', immediately appointed as his assistant a *magister equitum*, 'master of the horse'. The other magistrates remained in office but were subordinate to the dictator, who held office for six months at most. This time limit meant that the office was of little use outside Italy, and it declined in importance in the third century BC. However, in 82 BC Sulla was appointed dictator 'to restore the republic', i.e. for an indefinite period. Similarly, Julius Caesar was appointed dictator first in 49 BC for the specific purpose of holding the elections for 48; secondly in 48, perhaps for a year; thirdly in 46 for ten years; and finally in 44, for life. These dictatorships obviously were different in intention from the earlier office. After Caesar's murder the dictatorship was formally abolished, and Augustus refused to revive it.

Dictē, mountain in the east of Crete, an important centre since Minoan times of Zeus' cult; the site of his archaic temple has been found at Palaikastro. There is no good evidence for the existence of the 'Dictaean cave' in which Zeus was said by some writers to have been born or brought up. This seems to be the result of a confusion with the cave, also associated with Zeus, on Mount Ida. Zeus presumably took the place of an earlier Minoan deity. See also DICTYNNA below.

Dicty'nna, '(the goddess) of Mount *Dicte', a (Minoan) Cretan goddess, whose proper name was *Britomartis; she was later identified with Artemis. The derivation of her name is from the mountain rather than from the Greek *diktys*, 'net', as was sometimes supposed. This gave rise to the story that she fled from King Minos, who was in love with her, but became entangled in fishermen's nets.

Dictys Crēte'nsis, Dictys of Crete, said to have accompanied *Idomeneus (leader of the Cretans) to the Trojan War and to have written a diary of the events. This work, inscribed in Phoenician characters (the earliest alphabet used by the Greeks; see CADMUS), was supposed to have been discovered during the reign of the emperor Nero (AD 54–68), and subsequently transliterated into Greek letters and deposited in a library. (A fragment of the Greek version has been found on papyrus.) It was rediscovered by a certain Lucius Septimius in (perhaps) the fourth century AD and

translated into Latin, under the title *Ephemeris belli Troiani*, 'diary of the Trojan War'. This work of fantasy, together with that attributed to *Darēs, provided the principal material for medieval writers on the story of Troy.

didactic poetry, poetry designed to give instruction. Before writing came into general use, instruction was conveniently expressed in verse, as being more easily remembered than prose. The Greeks did not recognize didactic poetry as a separate literary genre; since, like epic, it was written in hexameters (see METRE, GREEK 3) they regarded it as a form of epic poetry. For early examples of didactic poetry see HESIOD, EMPEDOCLES, and PARMENIDES. In Greece this kind of composition died out in the fifth century BC with the rise of prose literature, but was revived in the Hellenistic age: see ARATUS and NICANDER. For later works see DIONYSIUS PERIEGETES and OPPIAN.

Didactic poetry found favour in Rome quite early: *Ennius translated from Greek a poem on nature falsely attributed to the Sicilian Epicharmus. In the first century BC there are Lucretius' *De rerum natura* and Virgil's *Georgics*; in the following century Ovid's *Fasti*, the *Astronomica* of Manilius, and the *Aetna* of an unknown author. See also COLUMELLA (book 10).

didasca'lia, at Athens, the 'teaching' of a *dithyramb, comedy, or tragedy to the chorus and actors who were to perform it, by the dramatist (or his representative). The word came to be used to describe the official record of a dramatic performance, giving the name of the festival at which the work was produced and that of the *eponymous archon; in the case of drama, the names of the dramatists in order of success (Greek drama was always a matter for competition; see TRAGEDY 2), and of the plays which each dramatist entered; the names of the protagonists, the best actor, and the *choregos* of the winning play; in the case of the dithyrambic competitions, the name of the victorious tribe (each of the ten tribes provided a chorus) and the best flute-player. This information has in some cases survived on inscriptions. Aristotle in the fourth century BC compiled a book of *didascaliae* which has not survived but which was used by Hellenistic scholars, some of whose records found their way into the manuscripts of extant plays, providing valuable information concerning dates and names.

Dido, legendary daughter of a king of Tyre called Belus by Virgil. She is said to have had the name Elissa at Tyre, but subsequently, at Carthage, Dido. She was married to her uncle Sychaeus, who was murdered for his great wealth by her brother Pygmalion when the latter was king of Tyre. Dido fled with some followers to Libya and founded the city of Carthage: Iarbas, a local king, had given her as much land as might be covered by an ox-hide; this she had cut into strips and stretched. To escape marriage with Iarbas she built a pyre as though for an offering and threw herself on to the flames. For Virgil's adaptation of her story see AENEID.

Di'dymus (*c*.65 BC—*c*. AD 10), of Alexandria in Egypt, a notable Greek scholar, nicknamed *Chalkenteros* ('brazen-guts') on account of his enormous industry (he was said to have written four thousand books). None of his works has survived entire, though some fragments have turned up on papyrus, yet the results of his labours can be seen in the learned notes (*scholia) on ancient texts that are found in some manuscripts, in the lexica and etymologies compiled by scholars in later centuries, and in the collections of out-of-the-way learning represented by works such as the *Deipnosophistai* of *Athenaeus. As a compiler and abstracter of earlier researches Didymus has been invaluable in preserving some of the Hellenistic scholarship of the previous two and a half centuries which would otherwise have been completely lost. Perhaps his most important commentaries were on Homer and on Attic comedy, the contemporary background of which needed systematic elucidation, but he also wrote on Pindar, Bacchylides, the tragedians Sophocles and Euripides (there is no certain evidence that he wrote on Aeschylus), and the orators, especially Demosthenes. His many important monographs included one on the classification of Greek lyric poetry and another on proverbs.

di'es fasti, nefa'sti, at Rome, lawful and unlawful days for conducting public business. In the Roman calendar, a day marked F for *fastus* was a day 'of speaking', when it was permitted to transact legal business by speaking the formal words necessary; conversely, the sign N indicated a *dies nefastus*, 'day of not speaking', when for religious reasons the courts were not open. See FASTI.

Die'spiter, archaic Latin nominative form of *Jupiter, generally replaced by the vocative Iuppiter.

diga'mma, or vau, name given to a Greek consonant equivalent to the English w, in written form resembling F (hence its name 'double-gamma'), a sound originally in use in all the Greek dialects but which gradually disappeared from most of them. It started to disappear from Attic-Ionic before 1000 BC, from the other dialects later. The earliest Greek literature we possess, the *Iliad* and *Odyssey* of Homer, was composed in perhaps the eighth century BC but our text of these poems is based on that established by the Alexandrian scholars in the third century BC. It thus has no written indication of the digamma, but metrical effects indicate that the sound must originally have been present in many words; the most obvious example is *hiatus (where a word ending with a vowel precedes one beginning with a vowel): hiatus is normally very rare in Greek poetry, but appears with unusual frequency in Homer. It was observed (by the English scholar Richard Bentley, 1662-1742) that if in these cases the lost initial digamma was restored to the second word, hiatus was removed. The digamma must still have been used in the spoken language when these words were incorporated into Homer's epic poetry, but as it dropped out of the spoken language it disappeared from epic also, with consequences for the metre. Although the sound was lost in Greek, it was preserved in languages cognate to Greek, e.g. English *wine*, Latin *vinum*: Greek (w)*oinos*. See also ALPHABET.

dige'sta ('system'), in Roman jurisprudence, a body of law arranged systematically; the name was applied especially by the Roman emperor *Justinian to the main part of his codification.

di i'nferi, 'gods of the Underworld' in Roman religion.

Dikē ('justice'), in Greek myth, the personification of justice. See ASTRAEA.

di mānēs, pare'ntēs, see MANES, PARENTALIA.

dī'meter, metrical line containing two metra or metrical sequences; see METRE, GREEK I.

Dī'narchus, see DEINARCHUS.

Dindymē'nē, name of the goddess *Cybelē from Mount Dindymon in Phrygia, where stood one of her early shrines.

Dio, see DION.

Diocle'tian (Gaius Aurēlius Valērius Dioclētianus, originally named Dioclēs), Roman emperor AD 284–305. He was a Dalmatian of humble birth, elevated by the army. His genius was for administration, and many of his measures lasted for centuries. He made the empire into a tetrarchy (i.e. he divided the rule into four), in order to make government more effective and to bring about an ordered succession to the throne (see AUGUSTUS, THE). Many provinces were divided so as to become smaller administrative units, the frontiers were strengthened by fortifications and the size of the army was greatly increased. Diocletian's anxieties for the unity of the empire made him favour the old Roman ways, and it was probably this which led to his notorious persecution of the Christians, begun in 303 and felt particularly in Palestine and Egypt. As a consequence the Coptic and Ethiopian Churches reckon the years of the Christian era from the accession of Diocletian in 284 ('era of the martyrs'). See also EUSEBIUS.

Diodō'rus Si'culus, Sicilian Greek historian who wrote between c.60 and 30 BC a world history (*Bibliothēkē historikē*), centred on Rome, in forty books. Books 1–3 comprise the ancient legends of Asia and North Africa, books 4–6 those of Greece and Europe. All these books are fully preserved except for 6, which is frag-

mentary. Books 7–17 cover the period from the Trojan War to Alexander the Great; 7–10 survive in fragments, 11–17 are fully preserved. Books 18–40 cover the period from the Diadochoi (successors of Alexander) to Julius Caesar (54 BC); 18–20 are fully preserved, 21–40 survive in fragments. A complete copy is said to have perished in the sack of Constantinople by the Turks in 1453. The work is an uncritical compilation, and confused when Diodorus changes sources, but valuable for preserving the evidence of these sources: for example, his evidence is very important when, for the events in Greece around 400 BC he draws on the history of which *Hellenica Oxyrhynchia* is a part (see OXYRHYNCUS HISTORIAN). In the early books he is a useful source of mythological information. Concerning the gods his view is somewhat euhemerist (see EUHEMERUS).

Dio'genes. 1. Of Sinōpē, see CYNIC PHILOSOPHERS.

2. Of Oenoanda, see EPICURUS.

3. **Diogenes Lāe'rtius** (i.e. of Laertē in Cilicia), the Greek author of *Lives and Opinions of Eminent Philosophers* (generally known as *Lives of the Philosophers*). He probably lived in the first half of the third century AD but about his life nothing is known. His work, in ten books, purports to give an account of the principal Greek thinkers (including in the term such men as Solon, the Athenian poet and reforming politician, and Periander, tyrant of Corinth), eighty-two in number, from Thales (c.600 BC) to Epicurus (fourth century BC). Diogenes was industrious, but he compiled his book from the works of earlier biographers and epitomizers of philosophical doctrines, so that he is often at several removes from the works of the philosophers themselves. Fortunately, he usually names his sources, and thus it is to some extent possible to tell when his evidence may be relied upon. He is most valuable in his preservation of the maxims and three epistles of *Epicurus, and he preserves the epigram of *Callimachus upon the death of his friend Heracleitus. Diogenes also wrote (rather bad) poetry, some of which he quotes in the *Lives*.

Diomē'dēs (in English often Dio'mede).

1. In Greek myth, a Thracian, son of Arēs and a nymph Cyrenē, king of the Bistones, whose man-eating horses Heracles captured as one of his Labours.

2. In Greek myth, son of *Tȳdeus and of Dēïpylē, daughter of Adrastus. He took part in the expedition of the *Epigonoi against Thebes, and was leader of the men of Argos and Tiryns in the Trojan War. With the help of Athena he wounded Aphroditē and even the war-god Arēs, and killed a number of Trojan warriors, but behaved chivalrously to his guest-friend *Glaucus of Lycia although he was on the enemy side. He and Odysseus raided the Trojan camp and killed Rhesus. He plays an important part in the poems of the *Epic Cycle which describe what happened to the Greek heroes after the fall of Troy. With Odysseus he brought *Philoctetes from Lemnos and stole the *Palladium from Troy. When on his return home from Troy he found that his wife Aigialeia had been unfaithful to him, he left again and wandered to Italy where he founded various towns in Apulia; on his death he was buried on one of the 'Islands of Diomedes' (*Diomedeae insulae*; modern Tremiti Is.) near the Apulian coast. In *Aeneid* 11 he is represented as refusing to join in the resistance to Aeneas.

Dīo(n). 1. Ruler of *Syracuse (see SYRACUSE and PLATO 1).

2. **Dio(n) Chry'sostom** (*Chrysostomos*, 'golden mouthed'), properly Dio(n) Cocceiānus (c. AD 40–after 111), also known as Dio Prūsius, 'of Prusa' in Bithynia, Greek orator and popular philosopher. A member of a wealthy family from Prusa, he came to Rome and fell under the influence of the Stoic philosopher Musonius. Banished from Rome and Bithynia because of opposition to the emperor Domitian, he travelled widely through Greece and Asia Minor preaching Stoic-Cynic philosophy. He was highly thought of by the enlightened emperors Nerva (who succeeded Domitian in AD 96) and his successor (in 98) Trajan. Some of his eighty or so surviving speeches are genuinely political, dealing with real situations in Bithynia, but the rest are 'display pieces' on a variety of popular themes, delivered

to inform, improve, and entertain a variety of audiences while he was on his travels. He aims at the style and language of Attic Greek, in the easy manner of Plato and Xenophon, and his philosophy reflects conservative values of virtue and charity towards others. His speeches give a vivid picture of his life and times.

3. **Dio(n) Ca'ssius,** see CASSIUS.

Diō'nē, consort of Zeus at Dodona, the only seat of her cult, and by him the mother of *Aphroditē. The name is the feminine of Zeus.

Diony'sia, name given in Greece to festivals of the god Dionysus, which included dramatic performances (see also LENAEA). Attica celebrated two festivals annually under this name, the Rural (or Rustic) Dionysia in the month Poseideon (December), whose procession is memorably imitated by Aristophanes in the *Acharnians*, and the Great (or City) Dionysia at Athens itself in the month Elaphebolion (March), the sobriquet 'Great' being given because of its importance. This latter festival was instituted, or at any rate considerably augmented, in 534 BC by the tyrant Peisistratus, who brought the cult to Athens from Eleutherae (on the border between Attica and Boeotia, north of Eleusis). The god's image was placed in the old temple of Dionysus within the precinct of the theatre (see DIONYSUS, THEATRE OF). A day or two before the festival began the image was taken from its temple to another outside Athens near the *Academy, so that by escorting it in a torchlight procession back to the theatre the Athenians might re-enact its original arrival in the city from Eleutherae; it was thus present throughout the dramatic performances staged in the god's honour. The Great Dionysia proper began on the tenth day of Elaphebolion with a spectacular religious procession (in which one conspicuous element was the carrying of phalluses in honour of the god) leading up to the sacrifices and libations poured by the 10 *strategoi* in the precinct of Dionysus' temple. The procession included the *choregoi* of the various dramatic performances, dressed in their robes. Except for the period of the Peloponnesian War the festival seems to have lasted for five days, when five comedies were performed, one on each afternoon, preceded on two days by dithyrambic competitions and on three days by tragedies and satyr plays, the activities beginning at daybreak. During the war, to save expense and time, the festival was curtailed by one day and the number of comedies performed reduced to three.

At the time of the Great Dionysia, when the winter was over, the seas were navigable and there might be many visitors in Athens (as there were not at the earlier Lenaea in winter). The festival thus became for Athenians a patriotic display of the cultural and political superiority of their city.

Diony'sius. 1. Dionysius I and **II,** tyrants of Syracuse; see SYRACUSE.

2. Dionysius the Thracian (Dionysios Thrax) (*c.*170–*c.*90 BC), of Alexandria, a pupil of *Aristarchus and later a teacher of grammar and literature at Rhodes. His only surviving work is a Greek grammar (*Technē grammatikē*), which remained a standard work for many centuries. Latin grammar fell under its influence, and through Latin most of the modern grammars of Europe are indebted to it. Its influence spread through Syriac and Armenian adaptations, and a large body of comment grew up around it. The Greek verb *typtō* ('I beat') was used to exemplify voices, numbers, and persons, but the full paradigm with all possible moods and tenses was introduced later.

3. Dionysius of Halicarnassus, Greek *rhetor and historian who lived at Rome for many years from 30 BC. As a literary critic of good judgement he wrote (in Greek) a number of treatises: criticism of the Greek orators Lysias, Isocrates, Isaeus, and Demosthenes, showing in the introduction his preference for the Attic style of rhetoric over that of the Asianic school (see ORATORY 1); some minor works on Deinarchus, Demosthenes, and Thucydides, and a letter on Plato, of whose 'dithyrambic' style Dionysius was very critical; and, the most interesting of his works, a treatise *On the Arrangement of Words* (*Peri syntheseōs onomatōn*), the only surviving ancient work on word-order and euphony. To this we owe the best preserved text of Sappho's *Ode to Aphrodite* and the fragment from the *Danae* poem of Simonides. As a historian Dionysius had a great enthusiasm for Rome, expressed in the twenty books of his *Roman Antiquities* (*Rōmaïkē archaiologia*), of which books 1–9 and large parts of 10 and 11 survive. It went from mythical times down to the outbreak of the First Punic War (264 BC), the point at which the history of Polybius begins, but the surviving part breaks off in 441 BC. It is a painstakingly detailed composition made from the Roman annalists, and a valuable supplement to Livy. It contains the observation, much repeated since the writer's day, that the style is the man (1. 3).

4. Dionysius the Areo'pagite, see NEOPLATONISM.

5. Dionysius Periēgē'tēs ('the guide') (probably second century AD), the Greek author of a *Description of the World*, a didactic poem in 1,185 hexameters, repeating the views of the Hellenistic scholar *Eratosthenes, who was by then somewhat out of date. It enjoyed great popularity in later times. *Eustathius in the twelfth century wrote a valuable commentary on it.

Diony'sus, in Greek myth, the god of wine and of ecstasy, son of Zeus and Semelē, the daughter of *Cadmus, king of Thebes. When Semele was made pregnant by Zeus, his jealous wife Hera, in human disguise, persuaded her to pray to Zeus to visit her in all the splendour of a god. This he did and she was consumed by his lightning; but he rescued her unborn child from the ashes and placed him in his thigh, from which in due time he was born. The child was entrusted to Ino, sister of Semele and wife of *Athamas, but Hera, still jealous, punished them by driving them mad, so that Athamas killed his son Learchos and Ino leaped into the sea with her other son Melicertes. Ino was transformed into a sea-goddess Leucothea, and Melicertes became the sea-god Palaemon. Dionysus was now handed over to the nymphs of Mount Nysa (variously located), whence he derived his name, where he was worshipped, and where he introduced the cultivation of the vine. He was persecuted by those who refused to recognize his divinity, but overcame them and extended his conquests far into Asia and into India. The most famous of these persecutions was that of Pentheus, king of Thebes, which forms the subject of the *Bacchae* of Euripides. The daughters of Proetus, (see BELLEROPHON), king of Argos, also opposed him and were driven mad; their madness was cured by the intervention of the seer *Melampus. For another similar legend see MINYAS. Dionysus is represented as accompanied on his conquests by a host of votaries, male and female, *Satyrs, *Sileni, *Maenads, *Bassarids, dancing about him, intoxicated or possessed. They were known as *Bacchi* (fem. *Bacchae*), sharing with the god his other name, Bacchus. The seventh *Homeric Hymn relates how pirates found and kidnapped him, tying him up on shipboard; but the bonds fell off him, a vine grew about the mast, and the captive turned into a lion. The pirates in terror jumped into the sea, whereupon they were transformed into dolphins. For other myths about Dionysus see ARIADNE and ICARIUS.

Dionysus scarcely appears at all in Homer, and this fact, combined with the stories of his coming to Greece from Thrace and having to overcome resistance before being accepted, has suggested to some that he was a new god, accepted late into the Greek pantheon of Olympians (see GODS I). However, his name has been found in Greece in the late Bronze Age on *Linear B tablets, perhaps even in connection with wine, and archaeological evidence seems to suggest that he was worshipped in the island of Ceos from the fifteenth century BC onwards; moreover, the Dionysiac festival of wine, the *Anthesteria, predates the Ionian migrations (in about the tenth century BC). This evidence seems to indicate that his name and cult may be Mycenaean in origin. He is a god of an essentially different type from the Olympian deities, a giver of joy and a soother of cares (the latter described by his epithet Lyaios), experienced by the worshipper through intoxication; he is also experienced through ecstasy, felt as intensified mental power and the surrender of everyday identity. But he had another aspect, seen when his ecstatic

worshippers seized a wild animal and tore it apart in order to eat it raw (the act known as a *sparagmos*) believing that they were then incorporating in themselves the god and his power. This side of Dionysiac possession and the dire results it could lead to are often shown in myths. Characteristic of the cult of Dionysus is the mask, symbol of the surrender of identity, and a means of transforming identity. At its simplest his image consisted of a mask on a column draped with a piece of cloth. Important in connection with his worship were the *dithyramb (a variety of Greek choral lyric poetry), tragedy, and comedy, all of which were performed at his festivals (see DIONYSIA and LENAEA). Dionysus is frequently represented as a rather effeminate youth, with luxuriant hair, reclining with grapes or a wine-cup in his hand, or holding the *thyrsos*, a rod with a bunch of ivy leaves fastened to the top. The Greeks identified him with the Egyptian god Osiris, and the Romans with their wine-god Liber, also called Bacchus. See also DIONYSUS ZAGREUS, IACCHOS, and BACCHANALIA.

Dionysus, Theatre of, at Athens. The theatre at Athens was situated in the open air in a hollow on the southern slope of the Acropolis; it was within the precinct of the old temple of the god Dionysus, who thus gave the theatre its name and whose image watched over the dramatic performances of the Great *Dionysia and of the *Lenaea. An altar of the god (*thymelē*) stood in the centre of the dancing-floor (*orchestra*). The oldest remains of buildings on the site go back perhaps to the sixth century BC (see THEATRE I).

Dionȳ'sus Za'greus. The myth of Dionysus Zagreus played an important role in the beliefs of the Greeks who practised the mysteries of *Orpheus. Zagreus was the son of Persephonē and Zeus, who came to her in the form of a snake. He gave the rule of the world to the child, sat him on a throne and had the *Corybantes guard him. At the instigation of the jealous Hera (wife of Zeus) the *Titans distracted the child's attention with toys, then seized him, tore him to pieces, and devoured him, all but the heart; this

Athena saved and took to Zeus. From the heart Zeus remade his son and implanted him in Semelē (see DIONYSUS), from whom was later born a new Dionysus Zagreus. He punished the Titans by striking them with his lightning, and from the rising soot sprang the human race, rebels against the gods but having in them some portion of the divine. This story is known only from writers of the Hellenistic age, but it seems to have been current earlier. The association of Dionysus with the Underworld (through his mother Persephone, wife of Hades and queen of the Underworld) is significant in the *mystery religions which were primarily concerned with judgement after death, freedom from punishment, rebirth, and eventual blessedness.

Diosco'rides, see DIOSCURIDES.

Dio'scŭri (*Dios kouroi*, 'sons of Zeus'), in Greek myth, Castor and Polydeuces (Lat. Pollux). They were native to Sparta, where they were worshipped. In Homer and in Hesiod they are the twin sons Tyndareus and *Leda, and the brothers of Helen (of Troy). Later, Polydeuces is represented as the son of Zeus, and immortal. When Castor, the mortal son of Tyndareus, is fatally wounded (see below), Polydeuces chooses to share his immortality with his brother, so that they both spend half their time in the Underworld and the other half with the gods on Mount Olympus. Other accounts make them both sons of Zeus, born like Helen from an egg. They occur in three mythical stories. When *Theseus carried off Helen as a child they made an expedition to Attica, recovered her, and took Theseus' mother Aethra as well to be Helen's slave. Helen's place of concealment had been revealed by the hero Akademos (see ACADEMY), whose land was always spared in consequence by invading Lacedaemonians. In another story they took part in the voyage of the *Argonauts, Polydeuces distinguishing himself in the fight against *Amycus. Finally they carried off the two daughters of a certain Leucippus, Hilaēira and Phoebē, who were betrothed to their cousins Idas and Lynceus. In the ensuing fight (or, in some versions, in a cattle raid) Castor and both opponents were killed. It was on this occasion that Polydeuces gave Castor a share of his immortality (see above). The Dioscuri are often identified with the constellation Gemini (the Twins). They were commonly regarded as protectors of sailors, to whom they appeared during storms as the lights of St Elmo's fire. They were also notable boxers and horsemen, frequently called 'riders of white horses', and therefore the patrons of athletes and athletic contests.

In Roman religion the worship of Castor and Pollux was introduced in early times, Castor always being the more popular. Their temple at Rome (nearly always known as the temple of Castor) was vowed by the dictator Aulus Postumius during the battle of the Romans against the Latins at Lake Regillus (496 BC). The story was that they then fought at the head of the Roman army and after the battle brought the news of the victory to Rome; they were seen watering their horses at the Lacus Iuturnae ('pool of Juturna', a fountain in the Forum) and their temple was erected on that spot, beside that of Vesta. According to another story (related in Cicero, *De natura deorum*), Publius Vatinius (grandfather of the famous tribune) informed the senate that he had met two youths on white horses who told him of the capture of Perseus of Macedon on that day (168 BC); he was thrown into prison until his statement was confirmed by dispatches. The Roman *equites* regarded the brothers as their particular patrons. The common oaths *mecastor* and *edepol*, based on their names, are evidence of their popularity.

Dioscŭ'rĭdēs (Dioskourĭdēs) (first century AD), Greek physician who served with the Roman army. He was the author of a *Mātĕria mĕdica* (*Peri hȳlēs iatrikēs*, 'pharmacopoeia') in five books in which he described the medicinal properties of some six hundred plants and nearly a thousand drugs, some produced from minerals. Dioscurides is a careful observer and unsuperstitious, but the herb lore he preserves is irrational and very few herbs seem to have the properties he ascribes to them; nevertheless his work, with the numerous commentaries on it, was the standard text-book of pharmacy for many centuries.

Dī'philus, see COMEDY, GREEK 6.

Di'pylon ('double gate'), the principal gate of Athens, on the north-west of the city in the Ceramicus (potters' quarter). Through it passed a road leading from the agora to the Academy; bordering it outside the walls were the tombs of those who died in war. Here *Pericles delivered the Funeral Oration.

Dīrae or **Furiae,** the Roman counterparts of the Greek Erinyes or Eumenides; see FURIES.

Dīrae ('Furies'), Latin poem in hexameters attributed to Virgil; see APPENDIX VIRGILIANA.

Dircē, in Greek myth, wife of Lycus, regent of Thebes. She was killed by the sons of *Antiopē in revenge for her treatment of their mother; they tied her to the horns of a bull and she was dragged to death. After her death she was changed into the stream that bore her name, symbolic of Thebes in Greek literature: for example, the 'swan of Dirce' signifies the poet Pindar.

dirge (Gk. *thrēnos*), in Greek literature, lyric poem of lament sung over the dead. The dirges of Simonides and Pindar were famous, but only a few fragments survive. Compare NAENIAE at Rome.

Dis, in Roman religion, the ruler of the Underworld, the equivalent of the Greek god Pluto (another name for *Hades), of whose name Dis (i.e. Dīvēs, 'rich') is perhaps the Latin translation. During the Punic Wars foreign religious rites were from time to time introduced at Rome by order of the senate to hearten the people. In 249 and 207 BC the senate appointed special festivals of appeasement to the Roman equivalents of the Greek Underworld deities Pluto and Persephone, namely Dis and Proserpina. In classical Roman literature Dis has become merely a symbol of death.

Disciplī'nae, lost treatise on the liberal arts by *Varro.

Discord, Apple of, see ERIS.

Dis exapatō'n ('twice a swindler'), Greek comedy by *Menander, very prob-

ably the original of Plautus' *Bacchides*. A papyrus fragment from the play is clearly the source of lines 494–562 of *Bacchides*, and is the first passage in Menander of any length which has been found to correspond to a later Roman adaptation.

di'thyramb (*dithyrambos*), in Greek, form of choral *lyric sung to the god Dionysus; the word is of unknown origin, almost certainly not Greek. Its development into a literary genre was the work of the poet *Arion in Corinth in the last quarter of the seventh century BC. From Corinth it was brought to Athens by *Lasus of Hermione, and in 509 BC it became a subject for competition at the festivals of Dionysus (see DIONYSIA). Simonides, Pindar, and Bacchylides all wrote dithyrambs; of the first two only fragments exist, but several of Bacchylides' survive almost entire. The dithyrambic chorus did not wear masks; they danced and sang in a circle in the *orchestra* (see DIONYSUS, THEATRE OF). Narrative plays a large part in these poems, but its subject-matter is not particularly connected with Dionysus. At the Great Dionysia at Athens each tribe entered two choruses for the dithyrambic competitions, one of boys and one of men, each under the charge of a *choregos* (see CHOREGIA) chosen from the tribe. Lots were drawn to determine the order for selecting poets and flute-players; the *choregos* also needed the services of a good chorus-trainer. The inscriptions preserving the lists of victors in the dithyrambic contests at Athens (see DIDASCALIA) preserve the names of the victorious tribes and their *choregoi* but not the names of the poets, no matter how famous. The successful *choregos* received, as the representative of his tribe, a *tripod, which he erected at his own expense upon a monument, with an inscription. After Bacchylides the musical component of the dithyramb seems to have increased in importance at the expense of the words, but since no music has survived it is hard to discern what happened. Up to this time the dithyramb had been composed in regular form in *strophes and antistrophes, but now this correspondence was abandoned in favour

of a freer style of composition, with solo
songs, and the language became far-
fetched and artificial. The names chiefly
associated with these changes are
Melanippides of Melos (flourished c.480
BC) who introduced lyric solos, Philo-
xenus of Cythera (c.436–380) who introduced in his *Cyclops* a solo sung to
the lyre, *Cinesias of Athens, and
*Timotheus of Miletus. After the fourth
century BC it seems that the dithyramb
was no longer an important form of literary composition, although the competitions survived into the time of the Roman
emperors.

Dīus Fī'dius, in Roman religion, a god
sworn by in oaths, perhaps a title of
Jupiter.

dīver'bium, name given to dialogue in a
Roman comedy, as distinct from *cantica*,
the parts declaimed by the actors to a
musical accompaniment.

divination. The prediction of the future
by supernatural means, called by the
Greeks *mantikē*, was practised by the
Greeks and Romans in many ways. The
most important source of our knowledge
is Cicero's *De divinatione*. Divination
may be divided into two kinds, natural
and artificial. The most obvious form of
natural divination is based on dreams,
which the dreamer might interpret for
himself or take to professional interpreters (for an ancient 'dream-book' see
ARTEMIDORUS). As the result of a dream
the father of the young *Galen directed
his son to the study of medicine. The
emperor Marcus *Aurelius was thankful
to have received advice from a similar
source on how to cure his ailments. In the
practice of incubation, a sick person
would sleep in the temple of a healing
god, most usually *Asclepius, so as to
receive from the god a dream which
would suggest a cure. Another form of
natural divination is prophecy from the
speech of someone acting as the mouthpiece (*prophētēs*) of a divine power which
possesses him. This kind of divination
became institutionalized, with a succession of prophets, at the great oracular sites
of Delphi, Dodona, Oropus, Ammon,
and the various Sibylline sites.
Artificial divination is based on

external observations of animals, plants,
or objects; the best known form is
*augury, observation of the behaviour of
birds, which at Rome was entrusted to a
college of augurs. Widely used also was
observation of the entrails of sacrificial
animals (see HARUSPICES). Predictions
were sometimes based on certain
involuntary human actions, a twitch
or a sneeze for example. Exceptional
plant growth might also be meaningful.
Divination by throwing dice or drawing
lots was common, and localized at
certain sites. In later times, random
consultation of the works of famous
poets was favoured, perhaps because
they were considered divinely inspired:
hence the *sortes Homericae* and *Virgilianae*
('Homeric, Virgilian consultations');
see VIRGIL. Unusual meteorological phenomena were considered significant at
all times, and at Rome were recorded
in the *annales maximi* (priestly records;
see ANNALS). *Astrology became very
popular after increased contact with
the East following the conquests of Alexander the Great (second half of the
fourth century BC). Necromancy, calling
up the spirits of the dead, was practised
at all periods but never acquired
respectability.

Most people accepted the forms of
divination that had become established
by their own day but looked with suspicion upon any new forms. The attitudes
of philosophers to divination seem to
have varied with the individual, though
Epicureans rejected it, as did some
Sceptics. Prophecy by inspired utterance
was more acceptable. Stoics, by the
nature of their beliefs, defended most
types. Early Christian writers saw pagan
divination as the work of evil demons; the
edict of the emperor Theodosius in AD
391, banning all forms of pagan cult, put
a formal end to the practice.

division of the Roman empire, into
eastern and western halves in AD 395, see
BYZANTINE AGE.

Dīvitiā'cus (first century BC), pro-
Roman chief of the Gallic tribe of the
Aedui, who appealed for Roman help
against the invading Germans led by
*Ariovistus. He assisted Caesar in his

operations in Gaul (see COMMENTARIES I
(books I and 2)).

do'chmius or **do'chmiac**, see METRE,
GREEK I.

Dōdō'na, see ORACLES, GREEK.

Dolabe'lla, Publius Cornēlius (c.80–
43 BC), husband of Cicero's daughter
*Tullia, a dissolute and debt-ridden
aristocrat, a legate of Julius Caesar in the
civil war, nominated by Caesar before his
death to stand in for him as consul during
his absence in Parthia. After Caesar's
murder Dolabella briefly turned republican for his own advantage, but reverted.
He was finally defeated by the republican
Cassius in Syria and committed suicide.

Dōlon, in Homer's *Iliad* and the *Rhesus*
of Euripides, a Trojan spy killed by
Odysseus and Diomedes.

Domi'tian (Titus Flāvius Domitiānus)
(AD 51–96), Roman emperor from 81 to
his death, younger son of the emperor
Vespasian, and the last of the Flavian
emperors.

Domus Au'rea, of Nero, see GOLDEN
HOUSE.

Domus Pu'blica, official residence at
Rome of the *pontifex maximus*.

Donā'tus. 1. Ae'lius Donatus (fourth
century AD), Latin grammarian, teacher
of *Jerome. He wrote two books of Latin
grammar which remained in use
throughout the Middle Ages, to the
extent that 'donat' or 'donet' was used
generally to mean 'text-book'. He also
wrote a commentary on Terence which
survives, combined with the notes of
other commentators, in the *scholia on
that author; and most valuably a commentary on Virgil. Of this only the preface and the Life, with an introduction to
the *Eclogues*, survive entire, but it was
extensively used by *Servius in his
commentary.

2. Tiberius Claudius Donatus (late
fourth century AD), the author of a
rhetorical and stylistic commentary in
twelve books on Virgil's *Aeneid*, which
has no connection with the commentary
of Donatus (1).

Do'rians, Dorian Invasion. According
to Greek myth, it had been the will of

Zeus that *Heraclēs should rule over the
country of *Perseus at Mycenae and
Tiryns. After Heracles' death, however,
these cities came into the hands of the
descendants of *Pelops, and at the time
of the Trojan War Agamemnon ruled at
Mycenae. The Greeks believed as historical fact the legend that two generations
after the Trojan War, c.1100 BC, there
was an invasion into Greece from the
north by a new, Greek-speaking people
known as Dorians (for the name see
DORUS). They accompanied the sons of
the hero Heracles (see AEGIMIUS), who
were returning to the Peloponnese to
claim their father's inheritance, first the
city of Tiryns and then, by conquest, the
whole Peloponnese. By this legend many
historical facts were explained and the
Dorian invasion may also account for a
historical fact of which the Greeks themselves were scarcely aware, that the cities
and civilization of Mycenaean Greece
were destroyed in successive attacks in
the twelfth century BC, to be succeeded
by migrations overseas to the coast of
Asia Minor from c.1050 to 950, and by
poverty and deprivation in Greece itself.
There is no archaeological evidence for
the identity of the people who destroyed
the Mycenaean culture, and no positive
signs of an influx of new people. This
makes sense if the invaders were of
related Greek stock from the fringes of
the Mycenaean world. It has also been
argued that there was in fact no Dorian
invasion, that different groups of Greeks
had been present in Greece since the
beginning of Mycenaean culture, and that
the destructions were caused by
spasmodic raids or local uprisings of a
suppressed population. However, a
strong sense of discontinuity following
the destructions as well as the legends
themselves tell in favour of the essential
historicity of the Dorian invasion.

Doric. 1. See DIALECTS, GREEK I and 2.
2. See ARCHITECTURE.

Dō'richa, the Egyptian courtesan loved
by *Sappho's brother.

Dōrus, in Greek myth, son of *Hellen,
the eponymous ancestor of the Hellenes
(Greeks), himself the son of *Deucalion.
Hellen became, by the nymph Orseïs, the

father of the mythical ancestors of the three great branches of the Greek race, Aeolus (of the Aeolians), Xuthus (of the Achaeans and Ionians), and Dorus (of the Dorians). See also AEGIMIUS.

drachma, in Greece, a coin worth six obols (see MONEY 1). The word dates back to the days when Greece had a primitive iron currency; it means 'a handful', i.e. of obols (*oboloi*, 'spits').

Drāco (Drăkōn), an Athenian legislator, who received special authority to organize and codify the laws in 621 BC, the first time the Athenian laws were put down in writing. Details of his legislation are not now known, but the laws were notoriously harsh (hence the adjective 'Draconian') with nearly all offences (including idleness) punishable by death. When asked why he decreed death as the penalty for most offences he said that small offences deserved death and he knew of no severer punishment for great ones. All his laws were repealed by *Solon except those dealing with homicide (which entrusted trials for murder to the *Areopagus), but although no one at Athens in the fifth and fourth centuries BC doubted that the homicide laws then in force were those of Draco, it cannot be assumed that in fact they had remained unchanged since his day. The constitution attributed to Draco by Aristotle (*Constitution of the Athenians*, ch. 4) is now rejected as a later compilation.

drama, see CHOREGIA; CHORUS; DIDASCALIA; DIONYSIA; DIONYSUS, THEATRE OF; DRAMATIC COMPETITIONS; THEATRE; TRAGEDY; COMEDY; MIME; and PANTOMIME.

dramatic competitions. At Athens, from the late sixth century BC onwards, tragedies and comedies were performed at festivals, under state supervision, by dramatists in competition with each other to win the prize for the best play. See TRAGEDY 2 and COMEDY, GREEK 1.

Drancēs, in Virgil's *Aeneid* (11. 336), the Italian chief who taunts the Rutulian king Turnus. Virgil is said to have modelled him on Cicero.

dreams, see DIVINATION.

Dreams (Gk. Oneiroi, Lat. Somnia). Dreams are frequently personified in

Greek and Latin literature; according to Hesiod, they are the daughters of Night. In Homer's *Odyssey* (24. 12) they live beyond *Oceanus, near the gates of the sun. Later poets wrote of a god of dreams, Morpheus (hence 'morphia' etc.), who made human shapes (*morphai*) appear to dreamers. Virgil says (in *Aeneid* 6. 893) that the spirits of the dead send dreams to men from the Underworld, those which are true through a gate of horn, false dreams through a gate of ivory. He thus adapts what Homer says, very similarly, in *Odyssey* 19. 562.

Drūsus. For the various members of the Roman Julio-Claudian family who bore this name see below and see also GERMANICUS.

1. **Marcus Li'vius Drusus,** tribune of the plebs in 122 BC, a supporter of the aristocracy against C. *Gracchus.

2. **Marcus Livius Drusus,** son of (1), grandfather of *Livia, the wife of the emperor Augustus, tribune of the plebs in 91 BC, who proposed, besides various democratic measures, to give the franchise to the Italian allies. His various enemies combined against him, and he was assassinated. His proposals and the consequent upheavals brought about the *Social War.

3. **Nero Claudius Drusus** (38–9 BC), second son of Ti. Claudius Nero and *Livia. Since Livia was later the wife of Augustus he became the latter's stepson. His older brother was Tiberius (Augustus' successor as Roman emperor). He was commonly known as Drusus the Elder to distinguish him from Tiberius' son Drusus the Younger (see below). He married Antonia Minor (daughter of Mark Anthony and Octavia), and was the father of Nero Claudius Germanicus and of the emperor Claudius. He was brilliantly successful in a series of campaigns against Germany during the years 12–9 BC, but died in the latter year from injuries received in a fall from his horse. After his death he was given the cognomen Germanicus; it is rarely used to describe him, but the name passed to his descendants.

4. **Drusus Julius Caesar** (c.13 BC–AD 23), Drusus the Younger, son of Tiberius (later emperor) and his first wife Vipsania

Agrippina, daughter of *Agrippa. His original name, before the adoption of his father by Augustus, is not known. After the death of Germanicus, in AD 19, he became his father's principal collaborator and appears to have been designated to succeed him, but he died in 23, poisoned, it was later suspected, by his wife, who had been seduced by *Sejanus (Tiberius' ambitious minister).

dryads, *nymphs of trees.

Dy'scolus ('bad-tempered man'), Greek comedy by *Menander, produced at the *Lenaea of 317 BC and awarded first prize.

During a hunting-party a rich young man Sōstratus catches sight of a country girl praying to Pan and the nymphs at a shrine, and immediately falls in love and decides to marry her (this happens by the will of Pan, as the god himself reveals in a prologue). Unfortunately the girl's father Cnēmōn is a misanthrope (the *dyscolus* of the title) who lives a deliberately solitary life with only his daughter and a servant for company. His unpleasant nature has driven his wife to leave the house, and she has gone to live on the next farm with her son by a previous marriage, Gorgias. Sostratus now asks him for his help. Gorgias tells him that the only kind of son-in-law Cnemon will contemplate is one like himself. Sostratus tries to impress Cnemon with his hard work on the farm but Cnemon does not see him. Sostratus' mother has a bad dream and proposes a sacrifice at the shrine of the nymphs and Pan. At this juncture Cnemon falls down a well, is rescued by Gorgias, with the help of Sostratus, and emerges cured to some extent of his liking for a solitary life. He takes back his wife and entrusts his property and daughter to Gorgias, who bestows the daughter on Sostratus. The latter then persuades his father to give his sister to Gorgias as wife, and the play ends with the teasing of Cnemon to make him join the feast.

E

ecclē'sia, assembly and sovereign body at Athens, comprising all the adult male citizens over the age of 18, all equally entitled to address the assembly and to vote. It normally met forty times a year on the *Pnyx, with extra sessions as required, and was presided over by the chairman of the *boulē (executive council) who had been chosen by lot for the day. Voting was by simple majority and generally by show of hands. The assembly elected the *strategoi (military commanders) and served as a law court in the matter of grave crimes threatening the safety of the state, but its chief work was the passing of decrees (*psephismata*) dealing in detail with every sphere of government, including foreign affairs, finance, naval and military operations, and the corn supply. The agenda for meetings were prepared by the boule and any citizen might submit a matter for inclusion. No motion might be debated unless it appeared on the agenda and had been duly advertised: snap decisions were thus avoided. The only restraint on the powers of the assembly was that of the laws. If a motion proposed was illegal or even inexpedient, the proposer was liable to prosecution. The normal peacetime attendance was well over 5,000, a good proportion of the male citizen-body. From perhaps 403 BC, to ensure that every citizen could exercise his political rights, payment of one obol to those attending was introduced, the rate becoming more liberal in the course of time. During the fifth and most of the fourth centuries the assembly functioned in a fully democratic way (given that women, slaves, and *metics were excluded). The boule exercised no control, and the initiation of policy lay entirely in the hands of the citizens. Continuous policy was achieved only when one man, or a group of men, holding the confidence of the people over a period of time, was repeatedly elected to the office of *strategos. These semi-professional politicians were sometimes aristocrats, sometimes men of no family who were skilled orators, occasionally accepting fees from others in return for promoting certain measures in the assembly. They were the men who by and large proposed motions, and they wielded considerable influence in the assembly. See also DEMOCRACY, DEMAGOGUE, SOLON, CLEIS-THENES, PERICLES, CLEON, DEMOSTHENES, and EUBULUS.

Ecclēsiazū'sae (*Ekklēsiazousai*, 'women at the assembly'), Greek comedy by *Aristophanes produced probably in 392 BC (the *didascalia has not been preserved). The theme of the play, women taking over the running of the city (from which they were in reality excluded; see DEMOCRACY) and introducing community of property, has something in common with *Lysistrata; both plays depict the women of Athens seizing the political and social initiative under the guidance of a powerful female character, here Praxagora. A remarkable feature of the play, foreshadowing the way drama was to develop in the fourth century, is the greatly reduced role of the chorus, who do not sing a song until the end (see COMEDY, GREEK 5). It is likely that the comic poet was no longer writing his own lyric passages, and these were not now integral to the drama but served simply as entertainment at breaks in the action. There is no *parabasis*, no boisterous attack on politicians, and there is a new style of quiet witty dialogue of the kind found later in New Comedy. The similarity between Praxagora's reforms and Plato's intention for the ruling class in his ideal republic (see REPUBLIC), that they should not possess any private property, has suggested the possibility that Aristophanes is satirizing Plato, but this is unlikely on chronological grounds and in view of the lack of evidence in the text.

As a result of a conspiracy of women

led by Praxagora, she and her fellow conspirators, disguised as men, pack the assembly, and carry by a large majority a motion transferring control of the affairs of state from men to women. Praxagora, having been appointed head of the new government, returns to her husband, who has been put to great inconvenience by her having borrowed his clothes. She explains the new social system that is to be introduced: community of property, community of women and children; a fair share in sexual relations for the old and ugly, men and women alike, to be secured by legislation. Then she goes off to the agora to arrange for the reception of all private property and administer the drawing of lots for dinner. A law-abiding citizen hastens to hand in his property; a sceptic waits to see what will come of the new system. The sexual consequences become immediately apparent. A young man arrives to find his girl, but three old women assert their prior rights to him, and one succeeds in carrying him off. The play ends with the chorus hurrying away to a communal dinner (where one of the dishes has a name seven lines long).

Echi'dna, 'snake', in Greek myth, a monster, half woman and half serpent. Her genealogy as found in Hesiod's *Theogony* admits of various interpretations. She was most probably the daughter of Phorcys and Ceto (compare GORGONS) and lived in the Underworld. She bore, by Typhon, Orth(r)us (Geryon's hound), Cerberus, and the Hydra; some would add the Chimaera, and, by Orth(r)us, the *Sphinx and the Nemean lion (see HERACLES, LABOURS OF 1).

Echo. 1. Nymph unsuccessfully wooed by the god Pan; in revenge he sent madness upon the local shepherds so that they tore her to pieces and only her voice survived.

2. Nymph who was punished by the goddess Hera for engaging her in talk when the goddess wanted to spy on the amours of Zeus, her husband, with other nymphs. She was deprived of speech except for repeating the last words of her interlocutor. Having fallen in love with *Narcissus and been rejected by him, she wasted away to a voice.

eclogue (Gk. *eklogē*), an occasional poem or passage 'selected' from a larger collection or work; in the plural the word was used to describe any short poems and in that sense was applied to Virgil's pastoral poems (see ECLOGUES below) although having itself no pastoral connotation. Since this title was also given to the later pastoral poems of *Calpurnius and *Nemesianus, it was appropriated by the poets of Charlemagne's court to describe their own pastoral poems written in imitation of Roman models and thence applied to the Latin pastoral poems of the Middle Ages and the Renaissance. Once the identification of eclogue and pastoral had been made, scholars attempted to find an etymological connection. From the ninth century throughout the Middle Ages 'eclogue' was understood by false etymology to mean 'goatish speech', and in the late sixteenth century when the English poet Edmund Spenser was writing his own pastorals, to mean 'goatherds' tales' (*aigōn logoi*); but by the middle of that century the scholar J. C. Scaliger in France had already given the correct derivation.

Eclogues (Lat. *Eclogae* or *Būcolica*) of *Virgil, ten unconnected pastoral poems written in imitation of Theocritus, Idylls 1–11, those Idylls which are mainly *bucolic (i.e. pastoral), at the suggestion of *Pollio, Virgil's literary patron at the time. (For the meaning of 'eclogue' see above.) *Eclogues* seems not to have been the title used by Virgil, who apparently called the book (and the poems) *Bucolica*. The ancient authorities state that Virgil began the *Eclogues* when he was 28, i.e. in 42 BC, and that he spent three years in their composition. The second and third Eclogues are generally considered the earliest, written 42–41. However, not all were written between 42 and 39. Eclogue 10 is later, and Eclogue 8 may well be dedicated not to Pollio but to *Octavian and refer to his campaigns of 35 BC. Universal agreement on dates cannot be reached, but Virgil was certainly engaged in the composition of the *Eclogues* from 43 to at least 37, and they probably circulated among the poet's friends before publication. They won immediate popular success; they were recited in the theatre, where their author was publicly acclaimed. Their present arrangement is not chronological but governed by artistic considerations of symmetry and contrast. The odd-numbered poems are dialogues, the even-numbered are narratives for only one speaker. (The following Eclogues are discussed in roughly chronological order.)

In Eclogue 2 the shepherd Corydon laments that his love for the boy Alexis is unrequited. This theme, of 'the passionate shepherd to his love', and much of the detail, are taken from *Theocritus (Idylls 3 and 11). Eclogue 3 is also indebted to Theocritus for its form and characters—an exchange of banter between two rival shepherds, Damoetas and Menalcas, leading to a singing match (see AMOEBOEAN VERSE)—and some of the content: the two pairs of cups, for example, offered as the stake in the contest, recall the description of the cup of Idyll 1. In Eclogue 5, also rich in echoes from Theocritus, two shepherds celebrate in song the death and deification of *Daphnis. The shepherd Menalcas reveals himself as the composer of Eclogues 3 and 4 and the way is thus open to see Daphnis too as an allegorical figure, concealing an identity relevant to Virgil's own times. Since after the assassination of Julius Caesar in 44 BC it had been decreed that divine honours should be paid to him as if he were a god, some scholars, from antiquity onwards, have thought that Daphnis represents Caesar, if not in particular at least in general terms. Eclogue 7, of uncertain date, describes a singing match between Corydon and Thyrsis, two Arcadian herdsmen (the first reference to Arcadia in connection with pastoral poetry); by staging this on the banks of his native river Mincius, Virgil demonstrates the detachment of his pastoral world from any specific landscape. The poem is notable for the grace and beauty of the pastoral songs. Eclogues 1 and 9 are concerned with shepherds whose farms have been confiscated for the settlement of soldiers after the battle of Philippi in 42, when Virgil perhaps lost his own farm. Both poems may have been coloured by the poet's own experiences but they are not autobiographical: his concern is a general

one for the sufferings inflicted by war. Eclogue 1 contrasts the good fortune of Tityrus, who made his first journey to Rome under the threat of eviction and was rewarded by being allowed to keep his farm through the intervention of 'a young man', with the enforced exile of Meliboeus who had not left his home. Eclogue 9 depicts a similar situation. Two countrymen fall into conversation on the way to town; Moeris has just been evicted, and Lycidas recalls how Menalcas, a poet, tried to save the district by his poetry but failed.

In Eclogue 4, which owes nothing to any Greek predecessor, the poet looks forward to the birth of a child who will inaugurate a new era. This poem has been more discussed than any other short poem in Latin; throughout the Middle Ages it was accepted as a Messianic prophecy of the birth of the Christ-child given under divine inspiration. St Jerome was exceptional in expressing disbelief. Several contemporary children have also been suggested as the subject: a child of Pollio, an expected child of Mark Antony and Octavia, a child of Octavian and Scribonia, even Octavian himself. The poem can be dated to 40 BC, near the time of the Treaty of *Brundisium. It may well be that the child is for Virgil simply a symbol of the forces which he hoped would bring about the dawn of a new age. Eclogue 8 is dedicated to an unnamed person, usually thought to be Pollio, the campaigns referred to taken to be those of 39; *Servius, however, says that the dedicatee is Octavian, and it has been suggested that the campaigns are his of 35. The Eclogue is modelled mainly on Idylls 1 and 2 of Theocritus, and consists of a singing match between Damon and Alphesiboeus: the first sings a lament for his faithless mistress, the second relates the incantations and magic by which a girl hopes to win back her lover. Eclogue 6 remains obscure to us because we know little of its literary background; it does not have much to do with pastoral and bears little resemblance to Theocritus. It consists of a song sung by *Silenus in which he recounts the creation of the world in the style of *Lucretius as a prelude to some allusively narrated myths. The narrative is interrupted by a description of Virgil's friend and fellow-poet *Gallus accepting his vocation as a poet, in language reminiscent of *Callimachus in the *Aitia*. Eclogue 10, possibly the last to be written, in 37 (but see Eclogue 8 above), has Gallus as the subject, represented as dying of hopeless love for his absent mistress Lycoris. This is the boldest juxtaposition of the Arcadian and the real world that Virgil aspires to, and one that was to have great influence on the style and content of later pastoral poetry (see below).

Virgil extended the character of pastoral in new directions. The *Eclogues* became the models of pastoral poetry and the inspirers of pastoral romance and drama in later ages (for the Idylls of Theocritus were little read until the Renaissance). Unlike Theocritus in general (whose Idyll 7 is the exception) he allowed elements of contemporary reality to intrude into his Arcadian world, using myth and symbolic imagery to allude to recent history. This was an innovation decisive for the later development of pastoral, providing a precedent for the introduction of elaborate *allegory into the genre. Virgil was also the first to use pastoral as a vehicle for moral criticism of the society of his own day. From Petrarch and Boccaccio onwards pastoral became a recognized form for expressing political and ecclesiastical controversy and eulogy.

Virgil created a simple world which is an image of life but distinct from it, and his *Eclogues* derive their haunting quality from the implied relationships between the two. But not many later pastoral poets were content merely to imitate Virgil. *Calpurnius (first century AD) and *Nemesianus (third century) enlarged the scope of this literary mode by using it more enthusiastically than had Virgil as a vehicle for panegyric, and in this they were followed by the eighth- and ninth-century poets of Charlemagne's court. Virgil's *Eclogues* were interpreted as allegory by generations of commentators, and as a result allegory was thought to be an essential feature of the mode. Latin pastoral written in the Middle Ages thus came to have very little to do with shepherds unless they were specifically allegorical (in contrast with an entirely

independent vernacular pastoral where the shepherd was the key figure). Petrarch, for example, used the eclogue form to inveigh against the bad government of specific popes and rulers. The richness of English Renaissance pastoral, exemplified by the poets Sir Philip Sidney, Edmund Spenser, Michael Drayton, and Shakespeare, springs from the successful blending of the Virgilian and the vernacular traditions, as well as the poets' own belief in the mode as one that could be taken seriously. But by the eighteenth century pastoral had lost its vitality and degenerated into the witty parodies of John Gay or the saccharine effusions of Alexander Pope's imitators.

e'cphräsis, type of rhetorical exercise taking the form of a description of a work of art. The earliest extant collection of ecphrases is the *Eikones* ('Images') of *Philostratus, probably dating to the third century AD.

Ege'ria, in Roman religion, Italian water-nymph, to whom pregnant women sacrificed to secure easy delivery. She was worshipped in association with the goddess *Diana at Aricia in Latium, and with the *Camenae at a grove outside the gate known as the Porta Capena at Rome, where from a spring the *Vestal Virgins drew water daily. She was said to be the consort and adviser of *Numa Pompilius, legendary second king of Rome (715–673 BC), whom she used to meet by night at the Porta Capena and instruct in statesmanship and religion. At his death she was said to have moved to Africa.

Egypt (Gk. Aigyptos, Lat. Aegyptus). Archaeological evidence testifies to the existence of trading relations between Egypt and the Greek world in Mycenaean times (second half of the second millennium BC). Literary evidence becomes available in the eighth and seventh centuries and Homer tells the story of Menelaus' visit to Egypt (*Odyssey* 4. 351). With the establishment of Greek settlements on the North African coast in the seventh century, it was not long before the Greeks secured a foothold in Egypt. They were profoundly impressed by the great antiquity of the country, as well as by its religion, monuments, and customs. They thought that Egypt above all other lands was the repository of ancient wisdom and many Greeks proverbial for their wisdom were supposed to have visited the country in the seventh and sixth centuries (some are known to have done so). Solon is said to have visited the pharaoh Amasis, Thales to have invented geometry after studying 'land-measurements' in Egypt. Herodotus travelled widely in Egypt in the mid 5th century and devoted the second book of his history to giving an account of the country. In 462 a large Athenian fleet assisted in an unsuccessful Egyptian revolt against Persian rule (*Cambyses had conquered the country in 525), and when the hated Persian monarchy was finally overthrown in 332 BC by Alexander the Great (a Macedonian Greek), the change was not wholly resented. The Macedonian kings who thereafter ruled Egypt were known as the *Ptolemies (and Egypt under their rule as Ptolemaic Egypt). In their time the city of *Alexandria which Alexander founded became a centre of Greek culture. The Greeks were at first the dominant race there, and the native Egyptians were not regarded as full citizens. Later the Greek element became Egyptianized; the official language was Greek, but Egyptian persisted, to emerge in the Christian period as Coptic. (See also ROSETTA STONE.) The Greek gods were known only as names for local deities (see HARPOCRATES).

Greek rule was in turn brought to an end by the Roman Annexation of Egypt in 30 BC (after the battle of *Actium) when the country became a province of peculiar status, being governed by the emperor through an equestrian prefect rather than, as in all other important provinces, a senatorial legate. This special status indicates the value Augustus put upon the province and his appreciation of the temptation it presented to a governor ambitious for wealth and independence. No senator was allowed to set foot in Egypt without the emperor's permission. The first prefect was the soldier-poet *Gallus. Egypt with the rest of North Africa was the granary of Rome, eclipsing Sicily in that respect. It had a monopoly in the production of

papyri (see BOOKS AND WRITING 1), and was the starting-point for the Indian trade. A general survey of the Nile valley was made and to this we owe the accurate description of it that appears in book 17 of Strabo's *Geography* (first century AD). The only serious revolt against Roman rule lasted from AD 162 to 166 before being finally put down. In the reign of Caracalla (early third century) Egyptians entered the Roman senate for the first time, and the worship of the Egyptian goddess *Isis was publicly sanctioned at Rome. Nevertheless, the province was never Romanized, and Greek and native Egyptian elements were united in opposition to Roman government. The Roman era came to an end with the Arab conquest of Egypt in 640.

Ēhoe'ae or **Ēhoiai,** see CATALOGUE OF WOMEN.

Eido'thea (or Īdothea), in Greek myth, nymph, daughter of *Proteus, a sea-god. In Homer's *Odyssey* Menelaus tells Telemachus that, on the way home from Troy, when his ship was becalmed off the coast of Egypt and he nearly starved, Eidothea showed him how he might secure her father, despite his attempts to escape by assuming different forms, and force him to reveal the cause of the misfortune.

Eileithyī'a(e), the Greek goddess of childbirth, sometimes referred to in the plural (compare PAN and SILENUS); she was a lesser deity, not one of the twelve Olympian gods (see GODS 1). Her name may mean the 'coming', i.e. of the child. Hesiod makes her the daughter of Zeus and Hera, who was herself a goddess of birth and therefore is sometimes given this title. Perhaps a Minoan mother-goddess in origin, her cavern-sanctuary in Crete at Amnisos, mentioned by Homer and appearing on the *Linear B tablets from Cnossus, has been excavated and shows continuous cult from neolithic to classical times. She has no myth of her own but appears in various stories of birth, often in association with Artemis and Hera. The Romans identified her with Lucina (see JUNO).

Eisagō'gē, see PORPHYRY.

e'kphrasis, see ECPHRASIS.

Elaga'balus (incorrectly, Heliogabalus), Roman emperor AD 218–22. His resemblance to the emperor *Caracalla (to whom he was related) caused him to be proclaimed the latter's successor when he was only fifteen, in the belief that he was Caracalla's bastard son. He was a Syrian from Emesa, and he took the name of the Syro-Phoenician sun-god, worshipped in the form of a black conical stone, whose priest he was and to whom he was fanatically devoted. The stone was brought to Rome and passing through streets strewn with gold-dust was installed in a magnificent temple on the Palatine. Elagabalus' ludicrous and obscene excesses outraged the army, and he was murdered by the *praetorian guard. He was said to have been the first man at Rome to wear garments of pure silk.

Elatē'a (Elateia), in Greece, a city of Phocis, three days' march from Athens, of great strategic importance in that it commanded the passes into southern Greece from the north. Philip II of Macedon occupied it in 339 BC, thereby threatening Boeotia and Athens. In the ensuing panic at Athens, described in his *De corona*, Demosthenes proposed and brought about an alliance between Athens and her old enemy Thebes; the two fought together and were defeated by Philip at the battle of Chaeronea in the following year.

E'lea (Lat. Velia), Greek colony on the west coast of south Italy founded by Phocaea (in Ionia) *c*.540 BC, when the whole population left the city at the threat of Persian conquest (the story is told by Herodotus, 1. 164). It is chiefly famed for its school of philosophers (see below).

Eleatic School, Greek philosophical school of thought originated by *Parmenides of Elea at the end of the sixth century BC. Parmenides believed that 'what exists', the essential matter of the universe, is single, indivisible, and unchanging, and this monistic theory was subsequently defended by *Zeno and by Melissus, who lived in the mid-fifth century BC and was the last important member of the school.

Ele'ctra. 1. In Greek myth, daughter of *Agamemnon and Clytemnestra. She does not appear in epic, but in the tragedies of Aeschylus (especially *Choephoroe*; see ORESTEIA), Sophocles, and Euripides she becomes a heroic figure in the story of the House of Atreus (see PELOPS), represented as implacably hostile to Clytemnestra and her lover Aegisthus, faithful to her father's memory and devoted to her brother Orestes, whom she supports in the vengeance he takes on Clytemnestra and Aegisthus. She eventually marries Orestes' faithful friend Pylades. Her supposed tomb was shown in later times at Mycenae.

2. In Greek myth, daughter of the Titan *Atlas, mother by Zeus of Dardanus (see TROY).

Electra. 1. Greek tragedy by *Sophocles, of uncertain date but very probably produced between 418 and 410 BC. It is disputed whether it preceded or followed Euripides' *Electra* (see below) of perhaps 417. For the myth on which it is based see PELOPS.

Orestes arrives at Mycenae, accompanied by Pylades and an old man, Orestes' childhood attendant (*paidagogos*), to avenge the murder of his father Agamemnon, in obedience to the *Delphic Oracle. The old man is sent on to tell Orestes' mother Clytemnestra that Orestes has been killed in a chariot race, and the others prepare to follow in disguise, taking with them an urn supposed to contain his ashes. Meanwhile Clytemnestra, having had a dream of ill omen, has sent her daughter Chrysothemis to pour libations on the tomb of Agamemnon, the husband she has killed. Her other daughter Electra, who is living a wretched life, bullied by Clytemnestra and Aegisthus on account of her constant mourning for her murdered father, meets Chrysothemis and persuades her to substitute for the polluted offerings of Agamemnon's widow and murderer other more personal offerings from his daughters. Clytemnestra appears and abuses Electra, who retorts in kind, but they are interrupted by the arrival of the old man, and learn, the former with scarcely concealed joy, of the death of Orestes. Electra, on the other hand, is reduced to despair. The announcement of Chrysothemis that she has found a lock of hair on Agamemnon's tomb which is clearly Orestes' seems only to mock her sorrow. She determines, now that the expected help of Orestes is lost, to kill Clytemnestra and Aegisthus herself. The more prudent Chrysothemis refuses to share in the murder. Orestes and Pylades now approach, and Orestes tells Electra by degrees who he is. He and Pylades enter the palace, and the cries of Clytemnestra are heard as they kill her. Aegisthus then approaches. He is lured into the palace to see what he supposes to be the corpse of Orestes, but finds to be that of Clytemnestra. He is driven at the point of a sword to the room where Agamemnon met his death and there killed. The chorus of Mycenaean women rejoice at the final passing of the curse which has rested on the house of Atreus.

The greater complexity of plot and situation open to the Greek tragedians after the introduction, by Sophocles, of the third actor (see TRAGEDY 2) is very apparent in *Electra*. One might note the three-cornered scene where the messenger's false narrative about the death of Orestes has very different effects upon Clytemnestra and Electra, and the action preceding the recognition-scene where Sophocles is able to portray Electra faced by a rapid progression of people and events. It has seemed to many readers that Sophocles has chosen to ignore the moral issue, which is so important to Aeschylus and Euripides, as to how far the matricide is justified.

2. Greek tragedy by Euripides, often dated to 413 BC because of a supposed reference to the Sicilian Expedition, but perhaps a few years earlier (compare the date of Sophocles' *Electra*, above).

The theme of the play is the same as that of (1) above, but there are differences of detail. Aegisthus has married Electra to a poor farmer so that no son of hers may aspire to lay claim to the kingdom of Mycenae. This farmer, though poor, is of noble descent and high character, and refuses to consummate the marriage, considering that her marriage to him is beneath her dignity. Electra takes her share with Orestes in the murder of their mother, an act of justice but morally horrifying. The play is an interesting character study of the exiled Orestes and the haunted Electra. By making the latter the wife of a poor farmer, and by dwelling upon her physical privations and mental suffering, Euripides has brought the myth down from the heroic plane and placed the matricide in a setting of everyday life, where the characters bear the marks of human experience.

Plutarch relates that after the Spartan capture of Athens in 404 BC, the Spartan admiral Lysander was moved to spare the city by hearing a Phocian singing the opening chorus of *Electra*.

Ele'ctryon, in Greek myth, son of Andromeda and *Perseus, whom he succeeded as king of Mycenae. He became the father of Alcmena (later the mother of Heracles), and six sons. He was accidentally killed by his nephew Amphitryon to whom he had betrothed his daughter. By a Phrygian woman Midea he was the father of a seventh son Licymnius.

elegī'ac, see METRE, GREEK 4.

elegy, in Greek and Latin literature, any poem written in elegiacs (also called elegiac couplets), that is, in alternate lines of hexameter and pentameter (see METRE, GREEK 4). The ultimate derivation of the name is uncertain, but it was perhaps connected with a word for 'flute', an instrument which seems originally to have accompanied its recitation (compare LYRIC). In antiquity the elegiac metre was considered to be primarily the metre of lament, but it was used for a variety of poems, and the earliest lines we possess, written in Greece at the end of the eighth century BC, bear no resemblance to lament. Elegiac poetry was the medium for expressing personal sentiments (as distinct from narrative): for description, for exhortation to war or to virtue, for reflection on a variety of subjects, serious and frivolous, for epitaphs and laments, and for love-poems. The use of elegiacs for inscriptions to commemorate the dead seems to have become popular in the middle of the sixth century BC and persisted throughout antiquity; those attributed to Simonides are the most famous (see EPIGRAM). Among the principal early elegiac poets of Greece were Tyrtaeus, Mimnermus, Solon, Phocylides, Callinus, and Theognis. Love poems in elegiacs are said to have been first written by Mimnermus; they may have been a development from the cheerful sympotic elegies such as were written by Archilochus. The Hellenistic poets in particular used this form for love poetry, and also introduced a number of metrical refinements.

The history of Latin elegy begins in the first century BC when it was developed at Rome under Greek influence chiefly as a medium for love poetry. The Romans gave elegy a new direction by using it for a cycle of short poems centred on the poet's relationship with a single mistress. Almost every individual feature of Latin love-elegy is derived from Greek models, but the whole effect is of something completely original. The principal Roman poets were Cornelius Gallus, whose work has not survived, Catullus, Tibullus, Propertius, and Ovid. Ovid also refined the already strict metrical rules for Latin elegiac still further, and extended the range of subjects to be treated in this metre. After Ovid, the metre was used chiefly for short occasional poems and for epigrams. Martial is the most famous practitioner of the epigram and he sometimes rivals Ovid in metrical virtuosity.

Only in comparatively modern times, since the sixteenth century, has the term elegy come to denote specifically a poem of lament for an individual or a poem of serious, meditative tone. Several famous elegies in English literature are written using the conventions of pastoral (see BUCOLIC), one of the earliest being Edmund Spenser's *Astrophel*, on the death of Sir Philip Sidney (1586). The origin of the pastoral lament or elegy is to be found in *Theocritus'* first Idyll; this poem, however, being written in hexameters and not in elegiacs, is not, in classical terms, an elegy.

ele'nchus, 'cross-examining', a term used to describe *Socrates'* method of philosophical inquiry. In his search for knowledge it was his practice to ask for definitions ('what is courage? goodness?' etc.) on the grounds that if one could define or give an account of e.g. goodness one would have clearer ideas about the

good life and a basis for further investigation. The answerer's definition was then submitted to rigorous testing by means of question and answer (*elenchus*). This, however, turned out to be a negative process: the answerer's definition was found to be inconsistent with his other assumptions, and was thus revealed as defective or inadequate, while no satisfactory alternative could be arrived at to take its place. The answerer was left in a state of helplessness, *aporia*, but his gain was that he now knew the extent of his ignorance. The method was further developed by Plato, who uses the term *dialectic to describe it.

Eleusi'nian mysteries, SEE MYSTERIES.

Eleusi'nion, at Athens, a temple below the Acropolis, east of the Panathenaic Way, dedicated to the goddesses Demeter and Persephonē, dating from the time when Eleusis was finally amalgamated with Athens, perhaps at the end of the seventh century BC. Here were kept the sacred objects of the Eleusinian *mysteries.

Eleu'sis, the most important town of Attica after Athens and Piraeus, situated about 20 km. (12 miles) north-west of Athens near the sea. It remained independent of Athens till perhaps as late as the seventh century BC. The myth of *Erechtheus may reflect the Athenian conquest. According to ancient tradition it was at Eleusis that Persephone, who had been snatched away by Hades, god of the Underworld, was restored to her mother *Demeter. Eleusis owed its fame to the *mysteries traditionally instituted by Demeter herself and celebrated primarily in her honour. These attracted visitors from all over Greece and were much venerated. There is evidence that a cult was practised on that site in Mycenaean times; the magnificent *telestērion* ('hall of initiation') dates from the time of Peisistratus in the sixth century BC. There was much building in Roman times, including the great Propylaea ('gateway') finished by Marcus Aurelius (emperor AD 161–80). The sanctuary ceased to function after being sacked by Alaric and the Visigoths in AD 395. See also ELEUSINION.

Eleuthe'ria, a festival instituted at Plataea after the victory over the Persians in 479 BC during the Persian Wars, and celebrated every five years.

Eleven, the (*hoi hendeka*), at Athens, magistrates responsible for the care and management of the public prison, and for seeing that sentences, including the judicial torture of slaves, were carried out.

Elgin Marbles, see PARTHENON.

ēliai'a, see HELIAIA.

Ēlis, Greek state in the north-west Peloponnese, comprising a rich plain in which Olympia is situated; it was famed for horse-breeding. From 471 BC the Eleans presided formally over the Olympian festival and games, a right disputed from time to time in previous centuries with their small neighbour *Pisa (see also OLYMPIA). There is evidence for occupation at Elis since Mycenaean times. Elis was an early and loyal ally of Sparta until 420 BC when, upon Sparta's challenging the independence of her small neighbour Leprium, she changed allegiance to Athens. For this Sparta severely punished her in 399. Sparta gave the Athenian historian *Xenophon an estate near Olympia to live in during his exile, but Elis in defiance of Sparta obliged him to leave in 371.

elision, in Greek and Latin speech and writing, the 'thrusting out', i.e. dropping, of a vowel at the end of one word before a vowel at the beginning of the next; in Greek this feature was confined mainly to the short final vowels a, e, o, and sometimes i; in Latin it extended to the dropping of long final vowels also, and of syllables ending in m; early Latin writers sometimes elided final s. In Latin poetry the elided vowels are printed but dropped in scansion (compare CRASIS).

Eli'ssa, name by which *Dido, queen of Carthage, was said to have been known at Tyre, where her father was king.

Elpē'nōr, in Homer's *Odyssey*, companion of Odysseus who fell from the roof of Circē's dwelling and was killed and left unburied. His is the first shade Odysseus meets in the Underworld; Odysseus grants his request to be buried and to have his oar planted on his grave.

Elpini'cē, daughter of the younger *Miltiadēs and wife of *Callias.

Ely'sium, also known as the Isles of the Blest (*makarōn nēsoi*), thought of by Homer and Hesiod as a place in the far West beyond the stream of *Ocean where certain favoured heroes are sent by the gods instead of dying, to enjoy a full and pleasant after-life. It has been suspected that this Elysium, at variance with the idea that all the dead dwell together in the Underworld (or *Hades), is a survival from Minoan religion. It seems probable that the attainment of Elysium was promised to the initiates of the *mysteries of Eleusis. In later myth Elysium was represented as part of the Underworld ruled over by *Rhadamanthys (and Cronus). That is where Virgil locates it in *Aeneid* 6; for him as for Plato it is the place where the good soul temporarily rests before being reborn.

Ema'thion, see EOS.

E'mathus, in Greek myth, son of Macedon and brother of Pierus, from whom Emathia (the Homeric name for Macedonia) was believed to have derived its name. The daughters of Pierus, the Pierides, are sometimes called Emathides. 'The Emathian' is Alexander the Great.

Embassy, On the False (*De falsa lēgātiōne*), political speech by Demosthenes. See DEMOSTHENES (2) 4.

embo'lima, see TRAGEDY 3 (iv).

emmelei'a, see TRAGEDY 2.

Empe'doclēs (*c*.495–*c*.435 BC), Greek Presocratic philosopher of versatile genius, with the reputation of being a statesman, healer, philosopher, mystic, and wonder-worker. He was born of aristocratic family at Acragas in Sicily and after the fall of the tyranny *c*.468 BC was offered but declined the kingship, being an ardent democrat. Political upheavals led to his exile, and he travelled to south Italy and Greece. He was an accomplished orator, credited by Aristotle with the invention of rhetoric; *Gorgias is said to have been his pupil. He also won fame as a scientist and healer; Galen called him the founder of the Sicilian school of medicine. However,

it is as a thinker of far-reaching importance that he is chiefly known, and like
*Parmenides, by whom he was strongly
influenced, he expressed his thought in
hexameter verse, much read until late
antiquity. Only some 450 lines survive, in
quotation in other authors, but this is
enough to give a fairly clear idea of
Empedocles' meaning. According to
*Diogenes Laertius he composed two
poems, *On Nature*, addressed to a friend,
and *Purifications* (*Katharmoi*), addressed
to the people of Acragas. In these
Empedocles attempts to explain the
world on scientific and rational grounds.

He accepts the thesis of the *Eleatic
School that 'what exists' cannot come
into being nor pass away, but he denies
that it is a unity and unchanging. There
are four eternally persisting elements
from which all other things are formed,
earth, air, fire, and water, and the
rearrangement of these elements gives
rise to change; Empedocles uses as
analogy the painter's depiction of a great
variety of objects by mixing a limited
number of pigments. He introduces two
further principles, Love and Strife, also
eternal, but having no perceptible qualities of their own and apprehended only
by their effect on the other four. The
universe is under their alternate domination: Love maintains a properly balanced
mixture in things, but Strife dissolves this
mixture into constituents that war against
each other; the universe is recurringly
brought together and then fragmented
in a cosmic cycle. Strife, Empedocles
believed, was increasing at the time in
which he lived. Part of his work is
devoted to cosmogony, the gradual
development of the present world, the
evolution of animals, and many topics in
biology. He relies on metaphor and
analogy for giving clarity to his explanations. In the fragments which have been
attributed to *Purifications* Empedocles
gives an account of the primal sin and
collective fall of mankind (though not
apparently precluding the particular fall
of the individual soul) from a state of
innocence when Love ruled the universe.
The sin appears to be that of bloodshed
and meat-eating. The fallen soul, an
exiled god, *daimōn*, is punished by successive incarnations in animal (and even

vegetable) forms; it feels a homeless exile
until it regains its original purity and rises
up the scale of lives to the highest rung,
'prophets, bards, doctors, and princes'—
Empedocles himself has been thought to
be all these—and thence escapes back to
its original incorporeal state of divinity.
In some surviving lines Empedocles
declares that he has attained this state
and is no longer a mortal but an immortal
god. Much of this is clearly close to
Pythagorean teaching (see PYTHAGORAS)
and the Orphic poems (see ORPHEUS).

The Roman poet *Lucretius was
inspired by Empedocles to compose his
own scientific poem, *De rerum natura*, in
which he praises his predecessor for 'the
songs of his godlike heart'. Empedocles'
death is variously recounted, most
notably in the story that he committed
suicide by throwing himself into the
crater of Mount Etna.

emperors, empire, Roman, see ROMAN
EMPIRE, PRINCIPATE, BYZANTINE AGE, and
FALL OF ROME.

empire, Athenian, see DELIAN LEAGUE.

enco'mium (*enkōmion*), Greek choral
hymn (see LYRIC POETRY 1) in celebration
not of a god but of a man. By derivation
the word means a song 'at the *kōmos*', in
this context the revel at the end of a
banquet, and so suggests a eulogy of the
host and guests. The word came to cover
eulogies in general; the first poems of a
generally eulogistic nature so described
were those of Simonides. The *epinikion*
or epinician ode, a triumphal ode for victory in the Games, and the *thrēnos*, a
funeral dirge, are developments of the
encomium.

Endy'mion, in Greek myth, a beautiful
young man, famed for his eternal sleep
on Mount Latmus in Caria. He was the
son of Calycē, daughter of Aeolus, and
Āethlius or Zeus, and was king of Elis.
He was especially loved by *Selenē
(Moon); according to one tradition he
came from Elis to Mount Latmus and
while he was sleeping in a cave Selene
came down to him. His eternal sleep is
variously explained, one version being
that Selene sent it upon him, wishing to
embrace him unobserved. One of his chil-

dren (not by Selene) was Aetōlus, the eponymous hero of Aetolia.

E'nneads, see PLOTINUS.

enneakrou'nos ('nine springs'), fountain-house at Athens built by the tyrant *Peisistratus.

E'nnius, Quintus (239–169 BC), one of the greatest and most versatile of the early Roman poets, born at Rudiae in Calabria; since that was an area of Italy partly *Oscan and partly Greek, Ennius spoke Oscan and Greek, as well as Latin. He seems to have been in Sardinia (perhaps as a soldier) when he met Cato the Elder, quaestor there in 204, who took him to Rome. There he won a reputation in the 190s for writing tragedy. In 189 he accompanied M. Fulvius Nobilior on his Aetolian campaign (probably in order to celebrate his patron's achievements) and on his return had Roman citizenship conferred on him. He lived in modest style on the Aventine, teaching and writing. Anecdotes told by Cicero connect him with *Scipio Africanus, *Scipio Nasica, and Ser. Sulpicius Galba. It was at this time that he began the *Annales* ('annals'), which, with his tragedies, constituted his principal work. Ennius also wrote comedies, of which only four separate lines survive; *fabulae *praetextae*; *saturae* (see SATIRE), four books of mixed verse of which seventy lines are extant; *Epicharmus*, a poem on the nature of the universe; the *Hēdyphagētica* ('of sweet eating'), a mock-heroic poem on gastronomy; and a poem in special celebration of Scipio Africanus. The *Euhēmerus* was a prose work which adopted the rationalist theory of *Euhemerus on the origin of the gods. Of his tragedies some twenty titles are known, of which perhaps twelve are derived from Euripides, perhaps three from Aeschylus, and one from an obscure contemporary of Euripides. The fragments remaining allow interesting comparison with the Greek originals, particularly in the case of *Medea*. The natural ease of the Greek has been replaced by a rather grand and high-flown style, but Cicero's admiration for it is understandable.

The *Annales*, an epic poem chronicling Roman history in eighteen books, occupied Ennius up to the time of his death. Fewer than 600 lines survive, which do no more than indicate the general scope of the work. The poem inaugurated a new era in Roman literature, being composed not in the saturnian metre used by Naevius and Livius Andronicus (see METRE, LATIN 1) but in the hexameter of Greek epic (see METRE, GREEK 3). To emphasize the connection with Greek poetry Ennius began his work by recounting a dream in which he had been told by Homer that he was the latter's reincarnation. The *Annales* presented the history of Rome from the time of Aeneas to the wars of the poet's own day, including a series of descriptions of great Romans. The First Punic War was omitted, having been dealt with by Naevius. The events of living memory seem to have occupied the second half of the work. It was from reading Ennius that Roman schoolboys learned about the heroes of old and the Roman virtues. The famous line on Fabius Maximus Cunctator: *unus homo nobis cunctando restituit rem*, 'one man by delaying restored the state for us', was much quoted. Clumsy though the hexameters are, the style is grave and sonorous and suited to the poet's grand conception of his subject. Ennius was regarded by the Romans as the father of their literature; Lucretius and Virgil were considerably influenced by him, Cicero admired and quoted him. He reputedly composed his own epitaph:

nemo me lacrumis decoret neu funera
* fletu faxit. Cur? volito vivo' per ora*
* virum.*

('Let no one honour me with tears or attend my funeral with weeping. Why? I fly, still living, through the mouths of men.')

The poet Pacuvius was his nephew and heir.

Enȳ'o. 1. One of the *Graiae. **2.** Greek goddess of war, secondary in importance to *Arēs. The Roman *Bellona was identified with her.

Ēoē'ae or **Ēōīai**, see CATALOGUE OF WOMEN.

Ê'ōs, in Greek myth, the dawn-goddess (Lat. Aurora), who figures in story rather than in cult, daughter of *Hyperion and Theia (Ovid calls her a daughter of Pallas the Titan or Giant), and sister of Helios (Sun) and Selenē (Moon). She carried off several youths celebrated for their beauty: *Tithonus, by whom she became the mother of Emathion and Memnon; *Orion, whom Artemis killed; Cleitus, son of Mantius; and *Cephalus the husband of Procris.

Epamino'ndas (Epameinōndās) (d. 362 BC), Theban general and statesman who with his friend *Pelopidas raised Thebes to be for a time the most powerful city in Greece. When Sparta invaded Boeotia in 371, the Thebans, under Epaminondas' brilliant command, won a decisive victory at Leuctra, bringing Sparta's supremacy in Greece to an end and making Epaminondas famous. He invaded the Peloponnese in 370/69 to help the Arcadians throw off Spartan control (see MEGALOPOLIS), and he established the independence of *Messenia. He invaded again in 369 and in 366, with less effect. In 364 he even challenged Athens' naval supremacy at sea. In 362 he invaded the Peloponnese once more in order to reassert Theban influence there. This time the Thebans and their allies had to face an alliance of Athenians and Spartans. The armies fought at *Mantinea and the Thebans were in fact victorious, but the victory turned into defeat when it was known that Epaminondas had been killed. His creation of independent Arcadia and Messenia survived him, but he left behind no constructive policy for Thebes or Boeotia which others could continue, and he had no successors. He was one of the greatest generals of antiquity and his tactical innovations were studied by Philip II of Macedon and his son Alexander the Great. See also SACRED BAND.

Epaphrodī'tus, freedman and secretary to the emperor Nero whom he accompanied in his final flight and helped to commit suicide. He was subsequently secretary to the emperor Domitian, by whom he was killed in AD 95. The philosopher *Epictetus was his slave.

Epei'os, maker of the *Trojan Horse.

epeiso'dion, see EPISODE.

ephē'boi ('youths'), in Greek, term normally used of boys of any age between 15 and 20, but in Athens in the fourth century BC used specifically to denote members of the *ephebīa ('ephebic college'). Founded c.335 following the defeat of Athens by Macedon at Chaeronea in 338, this institution gave the young men of 18 to 20 a compulsory and efficient military training, and spread rapidly throughout the Greek world. In their characteristic dress of dark mantle and broad-brimmed hat they were during their existence a graceful feature of the Athenian scene. With the end of compulsory military service in about 300 BC and the abolition of the allowance, the *ephebia* became a largely educational institution for a wealthy élite and by the end of the second century BC it had been remodelled into a school especially of literature and philosophy.

ephēme'ridēs, 'diaries', a term especially applied to the diaries of *Alexander the Great, supposedly kept by his secretary Eumenes and thought to have been consulted by contemporary historians.

Ephesi'aca (or *Habrocomes and Antheia*), *novel by Xenophon of Ephesus.

E'phesus, one of the principal Ionian Greek cities on the west coast of Asia Minor, at the mouth of the Caÿster. It was founded by Ionian Greek settlers under Androclus, son of the Athenian king Codrus. They were reputed to have found the worship of Artemis (presumably the Asiatic Mother-goddess; see CYBELE) already established there. Ephesus survived the Cimmerian invasions (seventh century BC) but was captured in the mid-sixth century by Croesus, king of Lydia, who contributed to the rebuilding of the great temple of Artemis, the fourth to be built on the site. Fragments of some of the columns dedicated by Croesus are now in the British Museum. In the later sixth century Ephesus, like the rest of the Ionian seaboard cities, passed under the domination of the Persians. In the fifth century, after the defeat of the Persians (see PERSIAN WARS) it became a member of the *Delian League, but revolted from Athens c.412 BC and sided with Sparta.

In 334 the city passed into the control of Alexander, and in 133 BC, with the kingdom of Attalus III (see ATTALIDS), to the Romans. In Roman times Ephesus became the chief city (although Pergamum was the capital) of the province of Asia, and the seat of the governor. Strabo in the early first century AD describes it as 'the greatest place of trade of all the cities of Asia west of the Taurus' (a mountain range in Cilicia). Acts 19 gives a lively picture of the city in the mid-first century AD. Its famous citizens included the philosopher Heracleitus, the poet Hipponax, and the painter Parrhasius (Apelles too was connected with Ephesus). In AD 391 the emperor Theodosius suppressed all pagan worship, and the temple of Diana (the Roman goddess corresponding to Artemis) was closed.

Ep(h)ia'ltēs. 1. In Greek myth, brother of *Otus; they were the giant sons of Aloeus. It was also the name of the demon of nightmare.

2. Of Trachis, the Greek traitor said to have shown Xerxes the path by which the Persians outflanked Leonidas at Thermopylae (see PERSIAN WARS).

3. An Athenian statesman who became the leading politician on the democratic side after about 465 BC and the opponent of the aristocratic *Cimon. He took advantage of Cimon's absence in Sparta, or eclipse in popularity following his ignominious return, to put into effect a number of radical reforms—depriving the *Areopagus of its main powers—necessary for the institution of democracy. In this he was supported by the young Pericles. The *Eumenides* of Aeschylus, performed in 458, testifies to some extent to the thoughts and feelings aroused by the new measures. Ephialtes was murdered in 461.

ĕphors, at *Sparta a body of magistrates, by the late fifth century BC five in number, elected annually by the citizens and exercising general control over the kings' conduct; two ephors always accompanied a king on campaign.

E'phorus, of Cyme, one of the most influential Greek historians of the fourth century BC, the author of a history of the cities of Greece and Asia Minor in thirty books, no longer extant; it began with the 'return of the *Heracleidae' (i.e. the *Dorian Invasion c.1100 BC) and continued to the siege of Perinthus by Philip II of Macedon in 341 BC, including myths and legends, geography and ethnography, political and military history. Ephorus consulted numerous authorities now lost to us, and his work was known to Polybius and extensively used by Strabo and Diodorus, books 11–16 of whose history are almost entirely dependent on him as well as being the main source of our knowledge of him. See also OXYRHYNCHUS HISTORIAN.

Ephy'ra, the name of several cities in Greece in early times, including Corinth and Crannon.

epic (from Gk. *epē*, 'hexameters'; see METRE, GREEK 3). In literature, an epic is a narrative poem on the grand scale and in majestic style concerning the exploits and adventures of a superhuman hero (or heroes) engaged in a quest or some serious endeavour. The hero is distinguished above all men by his strength and courage, and is restrained only by a sense of honour. The subject-matter of epic includes *myth, legend, history, and folk tale. It is usually set in a heroic age of the past and embodies its country's early history and expresses its values. Battles and perilous journeys play a large part, as do gods, the supernatural, and magic; scenes are often set in the Underworld or in heaven. Certain formal features are conspicuous: the narrator vouches for the truth of his story; there are invocations, elaborate greetings, long speeches, detailed similes, digressions, and the frequent repetition of 'typical' elements, for example the stock adjective or *formula, the stock scene such as the hero arming for battle. Epic expresses a delight in the physical world, shown by painstaking descriptions of such things as arms, clothing, or ships.

1. *Greek epic and the Epic Cycle*. Epic poetry in the shape of the *Iliad* and *Odyssey* of Homer is the earliest surviving form of Greek literature; the origins of these poems are lost, but they probably go back to Mycenaean times. From the

incident of Odysseus asking the bard Demodocus (*Odyssey* 8) to sing of the ruse of the Trojan Horse it is clear that there was a corpus of sagas on which a bard could draw. What the bard recited (or rather chanted, to the lyre) would be a story taken from an existing body of myth but with no fixed text (and before literacy with no written text at all); rather it was an improvisation made up for each occasion with the help of stylized elements of phrasing or formulae, previously memorized, developed by a long succession of bards. The relationship between the early type of oral epic narrative and the Homeric poems as they now exist is still far from clear, but it is commonly thought that with the advent of alphabetic writing into the Greek world in the second half of the eighth century BC the Homeric poems were committed to writing in something like their present form, perhaps by a bard called Homer. It is at least clear that they embody traditional material of a much earlier date.

The *Epic Cycle* is the name given to a collection of epics (excluding the *Iliad* and *Odyssey*), of which only some 120 lines now survive, written by various poets in the seventh and sixth centuries BC, which could be arranged so as to make a chronological narrative extending from the beginning of the world to the end of the heroic age. Some of these poems were occasionally ascribed to Homer. They seem to have been well known in the fifth and fourth centuries BC but little read later; a writer of the sixth century AD declares that they are no longer to be found, and our knowledge of their contents derives in part from summaries made in antiquity by *Proclus. There was a Trojan cycle completing the story of the Trojan War. The epics comprising it are the *Cypria* (covering the preliminaries of the Trojan War), *Aethiopis*, Little *Iliad*, *Iliupersis*, *Nostoi* ('home-comings' of the heroes), and the *Telegonia* (concerning Telegonus). There was also a Theban cycle, the narrative of the legends of *Thebes, which included the *Thebaïs*. These formed the storehouse from which Greek dramatic and lyric poets drew many of their subjects.

The last great epic poet of archaic Greece seems to have been Panyassis, a kinsman of Herodotus, who flourished in the early fifth century BC and wrote an epic on Heracles. By the end of the fifth century Greek epic writing had lost its spontaneity and was becoming allusive and even pedantic, as is clear from the sparse fragments of Antimachus of Colophon and Choerilus of Samos (the latter noteworthy in having composed an epic, the *Persica*, on a historical subject, the Persian Wars). Some later epic still survives. In the third century BC the Hellenistic poet *Apollonius Rhodius wrote the *Argonautica* in four books; in the fourth century AD *Quintus of Smyrna wrote the *Posthomerica* in fourteen books, to fill the gap between the events of the *Iliad* and of the *Odyssey*, and in the fifth century AD *Nonnus wrote the *Dionysiaca* in forty-eight books.

2. *Roman epic*. Epic was introduced at Rome in the third century BC in a Latin version of Homer's *Odyssey* rendered into saturnian metre (SEE METRE, LATIN I) by *Livius Andronicus. It seems from the remaining fragments to have been an adaptation rather than a translation of Homer, but it became a famous and influential work. *Naevius in the late second century BC undertook an entirely original piece of work by composing an epic in saturnian metre on the Punic Wars. The *Annales* of *Ennius, an epic in eighteen books on the history of Rome, was a work in which the dactylic hexameter was applied to Latin epic for the first time. The greatest Roman epic was the *Aeneid* of Virgil, who was influenced in its composition not only by the Homeric Greek epics but also by Ennius and other Latin hexameter poets. In the Silver Age Latin epic became rhetorical in character and seems written with the intention that it should be declaimed. The best epic of that age was Lucan's *Pharsalia*. Other epic poets of the empire whose works survive in part were *Silius Italicus, *Valerius Flaccus, *Statius, and *Claudian. Among those whose works are lost were Cornelius Severus (praised by Ovid and Quintilian) who wrote historical poems, and Albinovanus Pedo, author of a *Theseid* and a poem on the campaigns of Germanicus.

epice'dion, see DIRGE.

Epicha'rmus, Greek writer of comedy from Sicily, who was active perhaps in the late sixth and certainly in the early fifth centuries BC. He was at the court of Hieron of Syracuse in the 470s. No play survives, but many titles are known, and quotations and papyrus fragments give some idea of the contents. He seems to have enjoyed writing mythological burlesque, with Odysseus and Heracles the favourite heroes. It would appear that he also introduced various types of character, e.g. the *parasite, the sight-seer, the philosopher, and an ancient writer asserts that he was the first to bring a drunkard on to the stage. Some of these characters were to appear later in literary *mime as well as in Attic comedy. The plural titles of some plays suggest that he employed a chorus, but there is no firm evidence in the fragments that he did so, nor do we know how many actors he employed, nor how long the plays were. His language is Sicilian Doric, used as wittily as the Attic of Old Comedy (see COMEDY, GREEK 3). Many of the comic aspects of language familiar from Aristophanes are present: parody, word-play, the coining of long words, and the rattling-off of lists of things good to eat. There is no evidence that he used a variety of metres and there are no lyrics among the extant fragments. In antiquity Epicharmus was regarded as the author also of a number of philosophical and quasi-scientific works, but these are no longer thought to be genuinely by him.

Epicte'tus (*c.* AD 50–*c.*120) of Hiera-polis, in Phrygia, *Stoic philosopher, born a slave, owned and later freed by Epaphroditus, freedman and secretary of the emperor Nero. He attended the lectures of *Musonius Rufus at Rome and then gave lectures there himself; after Domitian banished the philosophers in *c.*89 he migrated to Epirus in Greece where he spent the rest of his life. His lectures there were attended by the historian *Arrian, who took careful notes of what he said and published them; four books of *Diatribai* ('lectures') survive (see DIATRIBE). Later Arrian published a summary of Epictetus' philosophy, the *Encheiridion* ('manual').

These works strongly influenced the emperor Marcus *Aurelius. The *Manual* is a rather formal statement of Epictetus' views but the *Diatribai*, which are his comments on various Stoic writings, have a vivid informality, enlivened by anecdotes and imaginary conversations, and Arrian reproduces the *koinē* Greek in which Epictetus spoke (see DIALECTS). He taught that the universe is governed for the best by an all-wise Providence, and that all men are brothers. Unlike many Stoics he taught for the many and the humble, rather than for those few to whom Stoicism had an intellectual appeal, thereby continuing a tradition of popular preaching which began with the *Cynics in the third century BC. Only those who knew their own weakness and misery, he said, could benefit from philosophers. Like the other early Stoics he wanted to make men independent of their circumstances and of the vicissitudes of life. Having experienced slavery himself, he lays emphasis on that part of a man over which no one else has control, his mind. He is said (by Aulus *Gellius, 17. 19) to have preached that people should take to heart two words, *anechou* and *apechou*, 'endure' and 'abstain'. He shows a robust faith in the power of the human will to surmount trials, and is more positive than Marcus Aurelius, with whom it is natural to compare him. The nineteenth-century British general Gordon (of Khartoum) used to present his friends with the works of both.

Epicū'rus (Epikouros) (341–271 BC), Greek philosopher of the Hellenistic age and founder of the Epicurean school of philosophy. He was born in Samos, the son of a schoolteacher who had Athenian citizenship. In his youth he studied and was impressed by the atomist philosophy of *Democritus, and established his own philosophical circles at Mytilene and Lampsacus. He settled in Athens in 307 and bought a house with a garden (*kēpoi*), which gave its name, the Garden, to the school of philosophy which he set up in it. At his death he bequeathed this property to his successor Hermarchus. Epicurus resembled Socrates in the affection and respect he inspired among his friends, who sought out his company. His school, perhaps better called a community, consisted of a group of like-minded people, including women and slaves, who lived with him in austere seclusion. It attracted ridicule and accusations of profligacy because of its communal life and Epicurus' philosophical hedonism (see below), the serious aspects of which were ignored. Although Epicurus wrote prolifically most of his work is lost. *Diogenes Laertius preserves three important letters summarizing his teaching, together with a collection of forty aphorisms, *Kyriai doxai* ('principal doctrines'); some eighty further aphorisms survive in a manuscript. Of the thirty-seven books of his great work *On Nature*, fairly substantial fragments have been recovered from carbonized papyrus rolls found in a villa excavated at *Herculaneum, the study of which is yielding results. For our knowledge of Epicurus' thought we also depend largely on the poem of *Lucretius, *De rerum natura*, which expounds his physical theory and to some extent his moral theory too.

Epicurus' aim was the wise conduct of life, to be attained by reliance on the evidence of the senses, and the elimination of superstition and of the belief in supernatural intervention. He accepted from Democritus that the world consisted of (unchanging and indestructible) atoms and void, change being brought about by the rearrangement of atoms. He gives a strictly mechanistic account of all phenomena: the universe came into being through a chance combination of atoms, and will eventually perish through their dispersal. Gods exist, but have no part in the ordinary processes of nature and take no thought for humankind. The latter is merely an ephemeral compound of atoms, and the human soul, also compounded of atoms, perishes with the body. Epicurus makes atomism serve a moral purpose. Happiness consists in attaining tranquillity of mind, an attainment achieved by a proper understanding of nature. Epicurus' moral theory is summed up in a sentence from one of his letters: 'We say that pleasure is the beginning and end of living happily.' Thus for Epicurus pleasure is identical with the good. It is in the nature of people

to seek pleasure; pain, which is a disturbance of the natural state, is caused by unsatisfied desire, and pleasure is experienced when the natural state is restored. Therefore one must satisfy desire, and this is pleasure. But some pleasures bring pain in their wake. Therefore one must satisfy desires which are natural and necessary, but accept as the limit of pleasure the onset of pain. Hence pleasure may lie in limiting desire. (Epicurus is perhaps uniting under the term 'pleasure' both positive enjoyment and the absence of pain.) Mental pleasure is far greater than physical pleasure (as mental suffering is worse than physical suffering), and is found in *ataraxia*, 'freedom from disturbance'. This can be achieved in three ways: by learning the nature of the universe and of death, which removes fear of the supernatural (the worst mental pain), by withdrawing from the turmoils of public life, and by avoiding emotional commitments.

The meaning given in modern times to the word 'epicure' (a gourmet or person devoted to sensual pleasures) represents widespread hostility to and misunderstanding of Epicurean philosophy (not helped by Horace's ironic description of himself, *Epistles* 1. 4. 16, as 'a hog from the sty of Epicurus'). Particular antagonism was felt by the *Stoics; nevertheless Epicureanism spread, first to Antioch and Alexandria, then into Italy, and for a brief time during the late republic it won the adherence of men like Calpurnius Piso, Cassius, and Cicero's friend Atticus. Naturally the early Christians regarded Epicureanism with abhorrence because it stated that there was no providential God and no survival after death, that the universe had been created by accident, and that the aim of life was pleasure. A remarkable testimony to the continuing vitality of the philosophy was a very large public inscription (of which fragments survive) erected in AD 200 at Oenoanda in the interior of modern Turkey by a certain Diogenes, giving passages of Epicurean doctrine together with a concise summary of Epicurus' teaching.

Epidau'rus, small Greek state on the Argolis peninsula in the north-eastern

Peloponnese, chiefly famed for its sanctuary of *Asclepius. This contained several public buildings, mainly built in the 4th century BC, of which substantial remains survive. Many inscriptions from the sanctuary also survive, attesting cures effected by *incubation (sleeping in a dormitory attached to the temple) and by following the prescriptions of the priests.

epidei'ctic oratory, the oratory 'of display', that is, speeches for delivery at festivals (panegyrics), and funeral orations; epideictic is distinguished from forensic oratory (of the law-courts) and deliberative (symbouleutic) or political oratory.

Epi'dicus, Roman comedy by *Plautus. The complicated plot turns on the deceits of the slave Epidicus. He tricks his old master out of money, first to pay for a harp-girl to whom the old man's son has taken a fancy; then to pay for a captive whom the son, who has gone off to the wars and transferred his affections, has bought with borrowed money. The fraud is discovered, but as the captive turns out to be the old man's lost daughter, Epidicus is forgiven and freed.

Epi'gonoi ('successors'), in Greek myth, the sons of the *Seven against Thebes who, under the leadership of *Adrastus, the only survivor of the original Seven, took and destroyed Thebes, an event supposed to have occurred shortly before the Trojan War. Their names (with some variations in the sources) were usually given as Alcmaeon and Amphilochus, sons of Amphiaraus; Aegialeus, son of Adrastus and the only one of the Epigonoi to be killed in the expedition; Diomedes, son of Tydeus; Polydorus, of Hippomedon; Promachus, of Parthenopaeus; Sthenelus, of Capaneus; and Thersander, of Polyneices. The term epigonoi was also applied to the officers of Alexander the Great who 'succeeded' to his empire (see DIADOCHOI).

epigram (*epigramma*, 'inscription'), a verse inscription. In Greece, epigrams were written at first in hexameters, later in elegiacs (see METRE, GREEK 3 and 4). The early epigrams (of the seventh century BC) were placed on gravestones or votive tablets, composed so as to suggest that the dead man or the dedicator was directly addressing the reader, giving him the bare facts in a severely laconic style which became the artistic hallmark of the epigram. The first famous epigrammatist was *Simonides of Ceos, to whom many anonymous epigrams have been falsely attributed. The few which we know to be genuinely his combine intensity of feeling with great simplicity of expression. Quite a few Greek epigrams purport to survive from the classical period attached to famous names, among them Euripides, Plato, and Aristotle, but they are almost certainly spurious. It was not until the fourth century BC that epigrams were written simply as literature (though real inscriptions in verse were still being composed) and the term was extended to mean a brief poem suggested by a single event, serious or trivial. Thus *Callimachus' epigram on the death of his friend Heracleitus, well known in English poetry through the nineteenth-century translation of William Cory, 'They told me, Heraclitus . . .', is a direct address by the poet to the dead man, in which he voices his personal sorrow in a manner very different from the impersonal style of the classic inscriptional epigram. *Asclepiades was one of the earliest and most influential of the Hellenistic epigrammatists. The subjects they treated were very varied, but the themes of love and wine predominated. Whatever the subject-matter, brevity and elegance of expression were essential. In the first century BC *Meleager compiled the first large anthology of epigrams written during the previous five centuries, the *Garland*, which was supplemented by later anthologists (see also ANTHOLOGY 1). Marcus Argentarius in the first century AD introduced that final refinement of the epigram which is now considered its characteristic feature, an unexpected twist—a pun or a paradox—in the last few words. Epigrams continued to be written in Greek throughout the Byzantine period, sometimes upon Christian themes but often in a markedly pagan spirit; the poets best remembered are *Palladas, *Paul the Silentiary, and *Agathias.

The Romans had their own tradition of

funerary epigrams, but their first literary epigrams, written in the late second century BC in elegiacs, were Greek in inspiration and were all on the theme of love. *Catullus wrote epigrams of both love and hate, and after him epigrams were said to have been written by most of the prominent men of the late republic and early empire, but very few have survived. The literary form of the Latin epigram culminated in the work of *Martial, who cultivated especially the witty, paradoxical ending that is imitated by all modern writers of epigrams.

epigraphy, study of inscriptions in respect of both their form and their content, an inscription being taken to mean any writing cut, scratched, or impressed on any durable material such as stone or metal, either in official form or casually by an individual (in the latter case known as a graffito). Coins are excluded, their inscriptions being within the province of the numismatist, and it is usual to exclude painted inscriptions and texts written in ink, on whatever material.

1. *Greek*. The earliest surviving Greek inscriptions are dated to the middle of the eighth century BC and consist merely of names or brief personal comments scratched on pots. By the early seventh century inscriptions are of a more formal nature—dedications to gods or names of the dead on gravestones. Like the Phoenicians the Greeks originally wrote from right to left (retrograde); if a second line of writing was required to complete the inscription, it was often written underneath the first line but proceeding in the opposite direction, creating a hairpin-like pattern. This pattern of writing was known as *boustrophēdon, 'as the ox turns', and was helpful for the inexperienced reader whose eye could then continue to read without interruption at the end of a line. It sometimes seems from the inscriptions of the seventh and sixth centuries that the lines of writing need not even be horizontal: the words could apparently be as easily read when written vertically. It was not until the Greeks set up formal inscriptions, as opposed to using words merely to identify, say, figures on a vase, that they adopted a consistent left-to-right direction. In

the sixth century the Greeks, and notably the Athenians, adopted a style of inscription which suited their feeling for symmetry and uniformity, in which the letters were exactly aligned both horizontally and vertically (the *stoichēdon*, 'in a line', style). This persisted until the end of the fourth century BC, but had disappeared almost entirely by the end of the third.

Greek inscriptions survive in their tens of thousands, including hundreds of poems of various kinds which would otherwise be unknown to us. They immeasurably enrich our knowledge of Greek history, thought, and speech by being first-hand, contemporary records, in the authentic language of the time, of every aspect of Greek life. Among the more important Greek historical inscriptions are the Athenian *tribute lists, the law-code of *Gortyn in Crete, and the chronological table known as the Parian Marble (see MARMOR PARIUM).

2. *Latin*. Latin inscriptions earlier than the third century BC are rare, and unfortunately so, since those we have provide valuable evidence of linguistic usage at a period earlier than that of most surviving Latin literature. Most Latin inscriptions date from the early empire, but they continue beyond the collapse of Rome in the fifth century AD. Inscriptions from the provinces of the empire are of particular historical value. The Latin script was originally very like that of the early Greek alphabet used by the Greek settlers at Cumae (on the coast near Naples, founded *c*.750 BC), from which the Latin alphabet was ultimately derived. By the first century AD the cutters had developed the beautiful Roman capital lettering, seen at its best on the base of Trajan's Column. Latin inscriptions, like Greek, are an invaluable source of information on politics and law, social, religious, and military administration, and other aspects of Roman life which without them would remain obscure to us. Christian inscriptions throw light on the development of Christian society and religious thought. Important Latin historical inscriptions include the so-called *Monumentum Ancyranum*, the emperor Augustus' official autobiography, written in both Latin and Greek.

Epime'nidēs, semi-legendary Cretan poet, prophet, and wonder-worker, variously dated to between 600 and 500 BC, and credited with remarkable longevity, with wandering out of the body and with a miraculous sleep of 57 years (compare ARISTEAS). He is supposed to have visited Athens in about 600 BC to purify the city after the murder of Cylon's associates (see ALCMAEONIDAE). Tradition ascribed to him a theogony and other poems of a mystical nature. The quotation in St Paul's Epistle to Titus 1: 12, 'Cretans are always liars', is said to be from his work.

Epimē'theus ('afterthought'), in Greek myth, brother of *Prometheus.

epinī'kion (Lat. *epinīcium*), epinician ode, a form of Greek choral *lyric composed in the grand manner in honour of a victory in one of the great Games in Greece, and publicly performed usually upon the victor's return to his city. The principal epinician poets whose odes are still largely extant are *Pindar and *Bacchylides. Of *Simonides' epinicians only a few lines survive. Virtually all the odes adhere to a standard pattern: they are usually written in *triads, they eulogize the victor and his family and city, they narrate a myth, and they relate the victory to life in general, often by means of moral reflections and exhortations which may seem sombre in the context of victory and celebration.

epirrhē'ma ('what is said afterwards'), in Greek Old Comedy, passage spoken by the *coryphaeus* (chorus-leader) after the chorus has sung a short lyric at the end of the *parabasis*. See COMEDY, GREEK 3 (iv). It often satirizes various Athenians or admonishes the audience. The metre is trochaic.

episode (*epeisodion*), in Greek tragedy, the dialogue between two choral odes, corresponding to the modern 'act' (see TRAGEDY 3). In Old Comedy, episodes are the brief scenes following the *parabasis*, separated by choral songs and illustrating the consequences of the hero's achievement of his aim (see COMEDY, GREEK 3 (v)).

Epistles (*Epistulae*, 'letters'), of *Horace, two books of Latin hexameter poems of a reflective nature and written ostensibly as letters to friends, a literary genre which had no obvious antecedent in Greek. The first book was probably published in 20 or 19 BC; in the opening poem Horace professes to have abandoned lyric poetry (*Odes* I–III were published probably in 23 BC) and to have turned to philosophy. This 'philosophy' is not that of the professionals, which he treats with irony and humour (for his own description of his Epicureanism see EPICURUS), but is rather a matter of the morals of everyday living—the contentment to be found in a simple life, the dangers of avarice, and above all the advantage of moderation in all things, themes which the form of the *Epistles* enables him to treat conversationally from a personal view-point, with wit and good sense. It is a matter of debate whether the *Epistles* are entirely fictitious, merely providing a convenient framework for composition, or are real letters sent on particular occasions to particular persons.

Book I contains twenty epistles, and is memorable for its many telling passages and felicitous phrases: the comparison of the man who puts off the hour of right living with the countryman who waits for the river to flow by: *dimidium facti qui coepit habet: sapere aude* ('he who has begun his task has half done it; have the courage to be wise', 2. 40); the folly of men who look for peace of mind in a new place: *caelum non animum mutant* ('they change the sky but not their state of mind', 11. 27); *ira furor brevis est* ('anger is a short madness', 2. 62); *naturam expellas furca, tamen usque recurret* ('you may drive nature out with a pitchfork but she will return every time', 10. 24); the 'by-ways of a quiet life', *fallentis semita vitae* (18. 103). Epistle 4 is interesting as addressed to the poet Tibullus; Epistle 6 is a series of reflections on peace of mind, *nil admirari*, 'to wonder at nothing' (the *ataraxia* of Epicurus); Epistle 9 is a letter introducing a friend to the future emperor Tiberius; Epistle 16 contains a description of the poet's farm. Book II contains only two epistles (but see below), the first to the emperor Augustus, written perhaps in 15 BC, and the second to Julius Florus, a young companion of Tiberius with literary aspirations, written in 19 or 18 BC. Both concern literature; in the first Horace surveys the development of Latin poetry and defends the refinement of contemporary poetry under the influence of Greek literature; in the second Horace gives his reasons for abandoning lyric poetry in favour of philosophy. There are other interesting autobiographical passages and some literary doctrine; unsparing self-criticism in an author is especially recommended. For a third epistle see ARS POETICA, a name it has been known by since Quintilian.

Epistle to the Pisos (*Epi'stula ad Pisōnēs*), see ARS POETICA.

Epi'stulae ex Ponto ('letters from the Black Sea'), four books of elegiac poems written by *Ovid in the latter years of his exile at Tomis. Books 1–3 were published in AD 13; book 4 probably appeared posthumously. Like the poems of books 3–5 of the *Tristia*, these describe the rigours of his exile and plead for leniency; they differ only by being addressed to individuals by name. Ovid's hopes rested largely on the genial character of Germanicus, nephew and adopted son of the emperor Tiberius, who is addressed or mentioned in several places.

epitaphs, see EPIGRAM.

epithala'mium (Gk. *epithalamion*), 'at the bedroom', in Greek and Latin poetry, a marriage-song, sung by young men and girls outside the bedroom on the wedding-night (compare HYMENAEUS). Sappho is the first poet known to have used it as a literary form; only a few lines survive of her epithalamia (which probably made up book 9 of her poems); Theocritus' Idyll 18 is also an epithalamium. The most famous Latin examples of this genre are Catullus' poems 61 and 62, which show the influence of Sappho.

epithets, divine. Particular epithets or adjectives are often applied to Greek and Roman gods, especially in *epic literature. Many of these are purely ornamental or poetic, often joining with the proper name to form a convenient metrical unit, but others are known to have been used in cult. It can be difficult to decide to which category a particular epithet belongs. Some obviously indicate the place where the deity is worshipped; others more interestingly, sometimes more importantly from a historical point of view, indicate an association with another deity. The largest class of epithets refers to the functions of the deity. Thus Zeus has many titles referring to his function as a weather god; he is the cloud-gatherer, loud-thunderer, rain-sender, the god 'who descends' (in lightning and the thunderbolt). Sometimes the epithet refers not to the characteristics of the god but to those of the worshipper. In one place Hera was addressed as 'girl', 'wife', and 'widow' because she was worshipped by women of all ages and conditions (Pausanias VIII. 22. 2). More rarely deities are described by an epithet referring to their moral or civic qualities (e.g. Apollo Archēgetēs, Apollo in his role as the god who approved schemes of colonization).

For Homeric epithets see HOMER 3 and ORAL POETRY.

Epitrepo'ntes ('arbitrants'), Greek comedy by *Menander, of which half is preserved intact on several papyri and a further sixth in fragments.

During the absence of her husband Charisios, Pamphilē has borne a child five months after her marriage, and has exposed it with the help of her old nurse Sophronē. Charisios, told of this by his slave Onesimos, leaves home to stay with a friend Chairestratos and invites the harp-girl Habrotonon to join him, to the great indignation of Pamphile's unpleasant father Smikrines. A shepherd Daos finds the child and gives it to a charcoal burner Syriskos whose wife has lost her own baby, but Daos and Syriskos dispute possession of some trinkets found with the child and agree to submit to the arbitration of a passer-by. This chances to be Smikrines, who judges that the trinkets, being evidence of parentage, should accompany the child. Onesimos recognizes one as being his master's ring, and thus Charisios, already repenting of his priggish self-righteousness, is eventually revealed as having himself seduced Pamphile at a festival before their marriage and being the father of her exposed child. With the kindly help of Habrotonon all are reconciled and the play ends with the discomfiture of the objectionable Smikrines who, unaware of the turn of events, arrives determined to remove his daughter.

Terence's *Hecyra* resembles the *Epitrepontes* in plot.

e'pitrīte (*epitrītos*), see METRE, GREEK 8 (iii).

epode ('sung after'). For the *Epodes* of Horace see ODES AND EPODES; see also TRIAD.

E'pŏna, 'great mare', Latin name of a Celtic goddess associated with horses and mules and known from a large number of western European dedications.

eponymous ('that gives his name'), term used both of those who gave their names to places, as the goddess Athena to Athens, and of the chief magistrate of a city (in Athens the principal archon, in Rome the two consuls) who gave his name to the year in which he held office, thereby identifying it (see CALENDARS). When *Cleisthenes (2) divided the Athenians into ten tribes, the Delphic Oracle chose ten Attic heroes to be their eponyms (*epōnymoi*).

epy'llion (Greek diminutive of *epos*, 'epic'), in Greek and Latin literature, a very brief epic, i.e. a narrative poem a few hundred lines long, in hexameters, usually on the subject of the life and especially the loves of a mythical hero or heroine, and popular from the Hellenistic age (Theocritus' Idyll 24 on the infant Heracles is an example) to Ovid. The use of the word as a descriptive term appears to be modern.

equestrian order (Lat. *equēs*, 'knight', pl. *equitēs*), an important social class of Roman citizens, originally enrolled, according to tradition, by the kings of Rome to form the cavalry section of the army. They had to be wealthy as well as physically and morally worthy, and the term 'equestrian order' thus came to denote a wealthy social class. In the second century BC the original *raison d'être* of the equites gradually disappeared when the cavalry contingents, if needed at all, were raised outside Italy.

From this time on the military function of the equites changed to service as staff officers. By the end of the republic the term equites denoted all well-to-do citizens who did not belong to the senatorial class and they were capable of exerting considerable political force. Under the empire the order lost its political significance, but individual equites continued to be of importance in the civilian and military administration. In the 4th century AD the wide diffusion of honours among officials blurred the distinctions of class, and the equestrian order ceased to be a recognizable element in the state.

Erasi'stratus, of Ceos (third century BC), famous physician who may have practised at Alexandria, the leading medical centre of the time, or more probably at Antioch. He was the first to expound a complete physiological scheme of the body, which he saw as a mechanism. Unlike *Herophilus whose anatomical and physiological investigations he continued, Erasistratus abandoned the doctrine of humours as an explanation of the origin of disease and instead ascribed the latter to the repletion of the body through undigested nutrition. Since it was his view that the heart is the centre and source of both the arterial and the venous systems and that there are very fine interconnections between arteries and veins, he was not far from the conception of the circulation of blood, which was not accurately described until 1628 (by the English physician William Harvey). His writings were still being read in the fourth century AD, but survive today only in quotation.

E'rato, see MUSES.

Erato'sthenes. 1. At Athens, one of the *Thirty Tyrants, prosecuted by *Lysias.

2. Of Cyrene (b. *c.*285–80, d. *c.*194 BC), head of the Library at Alexandria, the most versatile scholar of his time, styled *pentathlos*, 'all-rounder' (properly, in athletics), and *beta* because he was next best to the (*alpha*) specialist in every subject (for the terms see ALPHABET). From *philologia*, 'love of learning', he coined to describe himself the word *philologos*, 'scholar'; it is apt for one who was philosopher, mathematician, astronomer, chronographer, geographer, grammarian, and poet. Nothing of his work survives except for scattered quotations. Of his literary works the most interesting was his book *On Ancient Comedy*, but his most important works were the *Chronographia* (for which he was indebted to *Timaeus), the *Geographica*, and *On the Measurement of the Earth*. The *Chronographia* presented in the form of tables a reasonably clear and accurate chronological system of Greek history, free from myth, beginning with the fall of Troy (which he dated to 1184 BC) and ending with the death of Alexander the Great (323 BC). The three books of the *Geographica* were the first complete description of the inhabited world, and the work was completed by a world-map of tolerable accuracy. (See also BARBARIANS.) In *On the Measurement of the Earth* he used an ingenious method to make a remarkably accurate calculation of the earth's circumference. His calculations were based on observations of the angles of the sun's rays at Alexandria and Syenē (Aswan), which were (almost) on the same longitude and a known distance (about 800 km.) apart. He concluded that the distance from Syene to Alexandria must be 1/50th part of the earth's circumference, and on some estimates of the unit of distance (the 'stade') used by Eratosthenes, his result is within 1 per cent of the modern figure (40,075 km.).

E'rebus (Darkness), in Greek mythical cosmogony, one of the primeval deities sprung from *Chaos (Void); the others are Gaia (Earth), Tartarus, Eros (Love), and Nyx (Night). Nyx and Erebus became the parents of Aether and Day, and of the *Hesperides.

Erechthē'um (Erechtheion), at Athens, the temple that housed the most famous cult of Athena, under the title of Athena Polias, 'goddess of the city', erected on the *Acropolis north of the Parthenon; it was probably begun after 421 BC and after a short interruption completed in 406. Its name reflects the fact that Erechtheus (see below) was also worshipped there, and this joint cult was known to Homer. The design is very complicated, primarily because it had to incorporate certain

spots sacred to the Athenians: the tombs of the mythical kings *Cecrops and Erechtheus; the sacred olive tree which Athena called forth from the earth in her contest with Poseidon for possession of Attica (see POSEIDON), burnt with the previous temple but miraculously surviving; and the well of salt water which Poseidon produced at the stroke of his trident on a rock. It is likely that the cella or chamber contained the Palladium, the most ancient statue of the goddess in Athens, made of olive wood and said to have fallen down from heaven (and referred to in Aeschylus' *Eumenides* when Athena tells Orestes to grasp it in supplication). This was the statue to which the Athenians originally dedicated the *Panathenaic robe (before the erection of the Parthenon); in front of it a golden lamp designed by the sculptor Callimachus burned perpetually. The temple also contained an altar to Poseidon and Erechtheus (the reason for the combination of these two names is obscure), and other altars to Erechtheus' son Butēs and to Hephaestus.

Ere'chtheus, mythical king of Athens, sometimes confused with the hero Erichthonius, and like him said to have sprung from the earth and to have been nurtured by Athena. According to Homer, Athena installed him in her temple, the Erechtheum, at Athens and made him her companion. The chief myth concerning him relates that when the Eleusinians and Eumolpus the Thracian, son of Poseidon, invaded Attica, Erechtheus, having enquired of the Delphic Oracle and been told that victory would be his only if he sacrificed one of his daughters, performed the sacrifice and duly defeated the Eleusinians, killing Eumolpus. Poseidon in anger caused the death of Erechtheus and all his house. The story was the subject of a popular tragedy by Euripides, now lost.

Erichtho'nius, Attic hero and mythical king of Athens, usually said to be the son of *Hephaestus, whose semen fell upon the earth as he struggled to ravish Athena. Gaia (Earth) gave birth to the child and Athena took him and hid him in a chest which she gave to the daughters of *Cecrops, king of Athens, to guard, instructing them not to open it. They disobeyed, and terrified by what they saw (either the child in serpent form or attended by serpents), leaped from the Acropolis to their deaths. Erichthonius became king of Athens and received from Athena two drops of the *Gorgon's blood, one of which poisoned and the other healed. He was later worshipped at Athens in the form of a serpent. In some stories his son and successor is *Pandion.

Eri'danus. 1. Legendary amber-bearing river, vaguely located by the Greeks in the far north-west, into which *Phaethon supposedly fell, the amber being the tears wept by his sisters who were transformed into poplar trees. Herodotus reported that he had heard of it as the source of amber but did not believe it existed. Later Greeks identified it with the river Po (Lat. Padus) in north Italy, and the Roman poets and occasionally prose writers adopted the name.
2. Name of a small tributary of the river Ilissus at Athens.

Eri'gone. 1. In Greek myth, daughter of *Icarius of Attica who was killed by his drunken fellow-countrymen after introducing them to wine. When Erigone, aided by their dog Maera, found his body she hanged herself for grief. She was loved by *Dionysus.
2. In Greek myth, daughter of Aegisthus and Clytemnestra.

Eri'nna, Greek poetess of the island of Telos near Rhodes, probably of the fourth century BC, who died at the age of 19. She was famous for a poem of 300 hexameter lines, *The Distaff* (*Élakatē*), which has not survived except for a few quotations and papyrus fragments; it was written in memory of her friend Baucis from whom she had been separated by the latter's marriage and death.

Eri'nyes, SEE FURIES

Eriphy'le, in Greek myth, sister of Adrastus and wife of *Amphiaraus.

Eris, in Greek myth, the personification of strife (see PARIS, JUDGEMENT OF).

Eros, in Greek myth, the god of love, the Roman Cupid. He does not appear in Homer, but Hesiod includes him as one of the first created gods (see EREBUS),

signifying the power of love over gods and men. Eros in this cosmogonic sense sometimes figures in the thought of the early Greek philosophers. In the lyric poets however he is the personification of physical desire, cruel and unpredictable, but embodying those qualities that inspire love, and hence young and beautiful. This Eros is the companion, often the son, of Aphrodite. His bow and arrows, first mentioned by Euripides, and later his torch, figure prominently in his role of mischievous boy assigned to him by the Hellenistic poets and artists. Quite often he is expanded into a plurality of Erotes. Eros was not, however, simply a literary conceit; he was also an object of worship in several ancient cults. See also IRIS.

Eryma'nthus, range of mountains in Arcadia, famous as the haunt of the fierce boar destroyed by Heracles (see HERACLES, LABOURS OF 3).

Erysi'chthon, in Greek myth, man who cut down a grove sacred to Demeter, by whom he was punished with insatiable hunger which ruined all his household. See CALLIMACHUS (Hymn 6).

Eryx, mountain above Drepana in west Sicily, the site of a famous temple of Aphrodite built according to some by Eryx, a son of Aphrodite, but according to Virgil by Aeneas. From Sicily the worship of Aphrodite (Venus) Erycina was introduced at Rome.

E'squiline (Lat. Esquiliae or later Mons Esquilinus), one of the *seven hills of Rome, on the eastern side of the city; it gave its name to one of the four regions (with the Suburbana, Collina, and Palatina) into which the republican city was divided.

E'teocles, in Greek myth, the elder son of *Oedipus and Jocasta, brother of Polyneices, Antigone, and Ismene.

Etesian winds, winds blowing steadily and often strongly from the north over the Aegean Sea from mid-June for up to three months, making northward navigation difficult.

Ether, SEE AETHER.

Ethiopia, the land of the 'burnt-faced men' (Aithiŏpĕs) according to the Greeks, situated with vague delimitations in north Africa, between the equator, the Red Sea, and the Atlantic, but especially describing the lands south of Egypt. Aeschylus had the Ethiopians extend to India, and Herodotus distinguishes between straight-haired (Asian) and curly-haired (Libyan) Ethiopians. Neither Greeks nor Romans penetrated further south than Meroë, and consequently their accounts of the various Ethiopian tribes are scanty and confused.

Etna, see AETNA.

Etrū'ria, in Italy, the country of the Etruscans (see below).

Etruscans, called Tyrrhenians by the Greeks, Tusci or Etrusci by Latin speakers, a pre-Roman people of central *Italy and in early times Rome's principal rivals for the control of that area. Etruscan culture came into being *c.*700 BC, apparently as a development from that of the early Iron Age Villanovans, which flowered briefly in that region. Politically the Etruscans made up a loose confederation of independent cities, and at the height of their power, from *c.*620 to *c.*500 BC, they controlled an empire reaching from the Po in the north to Campania in the south, including early Rome. The Roman king Tarquinius Priscus was said, probably rightly, to have been of Etruscan origin. After the expulsion of the Tarquins from Rome at the end of the sixth century, the Etruscans gradually lost their southern territory, suffering a famous defeat at Aricia *c.*504, and had perhaps already surrendered their northern lands to invading Celts. Their naval supremacy was destroyed in a sea-battle off Cumae in 474 when they were defeated by a fleet of Cumaeans and Syracusans under Hieron, tyrant of Syracuse. By the end of the third century BC Rome held the whole of Etruria.

The origin of the Etruscans was already a subject for antiquarian speculation in the middle of the first century AD when the emperor Claudius wrote their history (which has not survived). The Greek historian Herodotus thought they came from Lydia in Asia Minor (and the language might well be Anatolian; see below); but others (including Dionysius

of Halicarnassus) have thought them indigenous to Italy. There exist thousands of inscriptions written in a Greek alphabet, mostly epitaphs, dating from the seventh century to the time of the emperor Augustus, but their language seems not to be Indo-European, nor directly related to any other, and it remains largely undeciphered, although the phonetics and morphology are understood.

Eubū'lus (Euboulos) (*c.*405–*c.*335 BC), an important Athenian statesman who greatly influenced Athenian financial policy to the city's advantage, and was an advocate of peace with *Philip II of Macedon in opposition to *Demosthenes and the war-party. See also ISOCRATES 5.

Euclid (Eukleidēs), Greek mathematician, who lived in Alexandria *c.*300 BC, but of whose birthplace and life nothing reliable is known. His fame rests on his great textbook, *Stoicheia* ('elements'): books 1–4 and 6 on plane geometry, 5 on proportion, 7–9 on arithmetic and the theory of rational numbers, 10 on irrationals, 11–13 on solid geometry; books 14 and 15 are not by Euclid. This work caused the name 'Euclid' to become almost synonymous with 'geometry'. One of the few anecdotes told about him says that when Ptolemy I of Alexandria asked him if there was a shorter way to understand geometry than that of the *Elements*, he replied that there was no 'royal road' to geometry. His work drew extensively on the discoveries of his predecessors, but its great value lies in its rigorous exposition of the geometrical knowledge acquired by the Greeks from the time of Pythagoras, arranged systematically and in logical sequence. As soon as it was published Euclid's textbook became the subject for study and comment, and the edition (or reworking) of *Theon (fourth century AD) was widely used; most valuable is the commentary of *Proclus (fifth century AD) on book 1.

In western Europe Euclid's work suffered the common fate of Greek science and mathematics, being known only to the Arabs until in the first half of the twelfth century an Englishman, Adelard of Bath, translated the Arabic version of the *Elements* into Latin. (See TEXTS,

TRANSMISSION OF ANCIENT 7). The original Greek was not generally known until a text was printed at Basle in 1533. The vernacular translations date from the middle of the sixteenth century; although in Europe geometrical textbooks gradually incorporated modern advances in the subject, in Britain the *Elements* held their ground more or less unadulterated until the end of the nineteenth century. Euclid seems to have been the source of the words put at the end of mathematical proofs, in Greek, *hŏper edei deixai*, 'which was to be proved', but usually known in the Latin version, *q(uod) e(rat) d(emonstrandum)*. He wrote a number of other mathematical works, some of which survive in Greek and others in the Arabic translations only. He also wrote a treatise on music, still extant.

Euclī'dēs (Eukleidēs), of Megara (*c*.450–380 BC), associate of Socrates and present at his death; founder of the Megarian school of philosophy and, apparently in the tradition of the *Eleatic school, identifying the single principle of the latter with moral good.

Eu'clio, the old miser in the *Aulularia*, a Roman comedy by Plautus.

Eudē'mus (second half of the fourth century BC), friend and pupil of *Aristotle; his writings have not survived. He used to be regarded as the author of the *Eudemian Ethics*, preserved among the works of Aristotle, but this work is now usually attributed to Aristotle himself (see 4 (iv)).

Eudo'xus, of Cnidus (*c*.400–*c*.350 BC), outstanding mathematician and astronomer in the half-century before Euclid, a younger contemporary of Plato and an associate of his in the Academy. His writings are lost but their contents are fairly well known from later writers. He is largely responsible for the discovery of the theory of proportion between incommensurables (covered by Euclid in *Elements*, book 5) and, in showing that a proportion could be established between any magnitudes, for removing the check given to geometry when irrational numbers were discovered. In solid geometry he showed that the volume of a pyramid was one third of that of a prism of equal height on the same base, and correspondingly that the volume of a cone was one third that of its containing cylinder. In astronomy his work marks the beginning of a new epoch, for he was the first to give a mathematical account of the movements of the heavenly bodies that tried to explain the fact that the planets occasionally appear to interrupt their movement eastward (relative to the fixed stars) along the zodiac, and for a time to move backwards from east to west (retrogression). Eudoxus suggested that the paths of the sun and moon and planets were produced by the circular movements of concentric spheres, rotating at different speeds and about different axes with the earth at rest at their common centre. The system showed great mathematical skill and managed to account fairly successfully for a wide variety of phenomena. It was modified by Callippus to remove the most obvious inconsistencies with observable fact, and in this form it was accepted by *Aristotle. Eudoxus' astronomical calendar of the risings and settings of the constellations formed the basis of *Aratus' astronomical poem the *Phaenomena*.

Euhē'merus (Euēmeros), of Messene, author *c*.300 BC of a fantasy travel novel in Greek, *Sacred Scripture* (*Hiera anagraphē*), now surviving only in fragments, but influential in its day. In it he describes an imaginary voyage to an island Panchaia in the Indian Ocean where he found documentary evidence that the gods of mythology were originally great kings, deified by their grateful people, a theory known to the modern world as 'euhemerism'. The idea was very relevant to the contemporary Hellenistic world where rulers might demand worship from their subjects, and where a rationalizing atheism was part of the new view of life. *Ennius wrote in Latin a prose work based on the *Sacred Scripture*, impugning the majesty of Jupiter Optimus Maximus. That likewise has not survived but it is quoted extensively by the Christian apologist *Lactantius, who used it as evidence of the fraudulent nature of the Greek gods.

Eumae'us, in Homer's *Odyssey*, the faithful swineherd of Odysseus; he entertained Odysseus in his hut when the latter returned to Ithaca and afterwards helped him to destroy the suitors. His story is told in *Odyssey* 15.

Eumē'lus, of the Bacchiadae of Corinth, Greek epic poet of the second half of the eighth century BC, author of an epic on the mythical and heroic history of Corinth (and perhaps other epic poems). He also wrote a famous *prosodion* (procession-song; see LYRIC POETRY 1) for the Messenians to sing at the festival of Apollo at Delos. The small fragment which survives in quotation is interesting as a very early specimen of lyric.

Eume'nidēs, 'the kindly ones', euphemistic name for the *Furies and the title of a Greek tragedy by Aeschylus (see ORESTEIA).

Eumo'lpus, in Greek myth, a Thracian, the son of Poseidon, who while in exile from Thrace as punishment for rape visited Eleusis where he founded, or became connected with, the Eleusinian *mysteries. He succeeded to the throne of Thrace, but was sent for by the Eleusinians to help them against *Erechtheus, king of Athens, in which campaign he was killed. He was the eponymous ancestor of the family of the Eumolpidae, who officiated at the mysteries.

Eunū'chus ('eunuch'), Roman comedy by *Terence adapted from a Greek comedy of the same name by *Menander, with the characters of the *parasite and the soldier added from Menander's *Colax*. It was performed in 161 BC with great success, well-earned by its varied action and lively dialogue.

Phaedria, a young Athenian, is in love with the courtesan Thāis, who is also loved by the boastful soldier Thraso (always attended by the parasite Gnatho). Thraso wants to give her as a bribe a young slave-girl bought in Rhodes whom Thais, knowing her to be of Athenian birth and stolen in childhood, wishes to own so as to restore her to her family. She therefore persuades Phaedria to let her pretend to give in to Thraso. Phaedria, meanwhile, has himself bought a present for Thais of a eunuch, but his brother Chaerea, having seen and fallen in love with the Rhodian slave-girl on her

way to Thais' house, exchanges clothes with the eunuch and assumes his character in order to gain access to her. In this he succeeds, and when Thais reveals the girl's Athenian birth they are betrothed. Thraso, repulsed by Thais as soon as she has gained possession of the slave-girl, tries unsuccessfully to carry her off, but a compromise is reached by which both he and Phaedria share her favours.

The prologue contains a line which subsequently became well known, *nullumst iam dictum quod non dictum sit prius*, 'nothing is said which has not been said before'. The play was imitated by Nicholas Udall (headmaster successively of Eton and Westminster) in the later scenes of *Ralph Roister Doister* (c.1554), the earliest known English comedy.

Eupa'tridae ('well-born'), the aristocracy at Athens, i.e. those born into one of the sixty or so named *genē* (see GENOS) or families which each claimed descent from a heroic ancestor who was himself the son of a god. They were generally rich landowners who could muster political support from their own territory. Until the end of the sixth century BC they monopolized the offices of government, and even when the city became more democratic they were still influential.

Eupho'rion. 1. Son of the Attic tragedian Aeschylus, who is said to have won victories in the drama festivals with tragedies written by his father but not produced in his lifetime. In 431 BC he defeated both Sophocles and Euripides (one of whose plays was *Medea*), but with what plays is not known.

2. Of Chalcis in Euboea, a Hellenistic Greek poet of the third century BC who lived most of his life in Antioch in Syria where he was librarian. The scantiness of his surviving work makes it difficult to assess, but he seems mostly to have written epic-style poetry on mythological subjects. He exercised a considerable influence on later poets; at Rome his *epyllia were greatly admired by Catullus and his contemporaries (hence Cicero's description of these poets as *cantores Euphorionis*, 'those who sing the praises of Euphorion') but he did not write love elegies in the Roman manner, as used to be thought. Probably the *Ciris* reproduces his manner most closely (see APPENDIX VIRGILIANA).

Eu'polis, one of the trio of famous Athenian writers of Old Comedy, the others being Cratinus and Aristophanes (see COMEDY, GREEK 4). He was contemporary with the latter, producing his first play in 429 BC and dying at some time after 415. None of his plays survives in manuscript, but we have nineteen titles and numerous quotations as well as some papyrus fragments. His comedies are similar in subject-matter and style to those of Aristophanes. In *Marikās* (a non-Greek word meaning 'catamite') he attacked Hyperbolus much as Aristophanes did Cleon in *Knights*; in *Demoi* ('demes') great Athenians of the past were brought up from the Underworld to give the city good advice, and in *Taxiarchoi* ('corps-commanders') he represented the god Dionysus undergoing hard military training, recalling themes in Aristophanes' *Frogs* and showing that he and Aristophanes, as well as being rivals, were imitators of each other's work.

Euri'pidēs (*c.*485–406 BC), the youngest of the three great Athenian tragedians. We have little reliable information about his life, most of the anecdotes told about him being ultimately derived from the hostile jokes of the comic poets, such as the references to his mother selling herbs in the market. The story that he wrote his plays in a cave on Salamis confirms other reports of his solitary disposition, and he was not prominent in politics. He was associated in people's minds with the *sophists, whose influence is discernible in his work, and said to be acquainted with Anaxagoras, Socrates, and Protagoras; it was supposed to have been at his house that Protagoras gave the first public reading of his sceptical work *On the Gods*. Euripides won the dramatic competitions with the trilogy containing *Hippolytus* in 428, and posthumously with the trilogy containing *Bacchae* and *Iphigeneia at Aulis*, produced probably in 405, and on only two other occasions. In about 408, embittered, it was said, by his unpopularity, he withdrew from Athens to the court of Archelaus, king of Macedon. There he died, allegedly torn to pieces by Archelaus' dogs, not long before the Dionysia of 406, at the *proagon* of which Sophocles commemorated his death by presenting his own tragic chorus ungarlanded.

We possess nineteen of the ninety-two plays Euripides is said to have written, and know the titles of about eighty. The plays we possess are of two classes:

(i) a selection of ten plays perhaps made *c.* AD 200 and transmitted with *scholia, consisting of *Alcestis* (438, second prize), *Medea* (431, third prize), *Hippolytus* (428, first prize), *Andromache* (date not known; *c.*426), *Hecuba* (date not known; *c.*424), *Trojan Women* (415, second prize), *Phoenician Women* (see PHOENISSAE; between 412 and 408), *Orestes* (408), *Bacchae* (405; the scholia are lost), and *Rhesus* (perhaps not genuine);

(ii) part of an alphabetic arrangement of his work comprising plays whose (Greek) titles begin with the Greek letters E to K, namely, *Helen* (412), *Electra* (date not known; *c.*417), *Children of *Heracles* (*Heracleidae*) (date not known; *c.*430), *Madness of *Heracles* (date not known; *c.*417), *Suppliant Women* (see SUPPLIANTS 2; date not known; *c.*422), *Iphigeneia at Aulis* (405; produced with *Bacchae*), *Iphigeneia in Tauris* (date not known; *c.*414), *Ion* (date not known; *c.*410), and *Cyclops* (a satyric drama, probably late). In this second group we therefore have some plays of Euripides that may be considered a representative selection of his work rather than plays selected for a purpose, such as a school curriculum. Very fragmentary remains of several lost plays have turned up on papyri in the twentieth century.

Euripides' tragedies derive their characteristic tone from the author's departure from the orthodoxies of Aeschylus and Sophocles, his giving prominence to unconventional and untraditional views and to socially insignificant people like women and slaves, as well as his reappraisal of old stories in the light of late-fifth-century scepticism. His mythical heroes and heroines, clothed in garments appropriate to their sufferings—the Athenians never forgot that in the *Telephus* he depicted the hero dressed in rags—describe their misfortunes in contemporary language and human terms, while a slave may reveal an inherent nobility of mind at odds with his status. Aristotle, in the *Poetics*, quoted in this connection Sophocles' saying that he, Sophocles, represented people as they should be, Euripides as they are. Euripides was often censured in antiquity for making his characters, and especially his women, unnecessarily bad. He was clearly attracted by stories of violent and bizarre passion—Phaedra falling incestuously in love with her stepson Hippolytus, Medea taking vengeance on her husband by murdering their children, Heracles' madness; but what interested him also was the conflict that arose in the minds of such people. Nineteenth-century critics liked to call him a rationalist because of his sceptical attitudes to traditional religion and morality, but in more recent times he has been called, no less justly, an irrationalist, because he depicts people struggling with powerful irrational forces within themselves. In construction the plays sometimes seem awkward. Characters speak what is rhetorically appropriate, especially in the set debates of which Euripides was so fond, or raise questions relevant to the thought and events of the late fifth century (and in particular to the Peloponnesian War), but the speeches often seem incongruous in the context and the characters themselves less credible therefore. Eleven plays are brought to a conclusion by 'a god in a machine' (*deus ex machina*; see THEATRE 1). Aristophanes parodied Euripides brilliantly in *Frogs*, and to a lesser extent in *Acharnians* and *Thesmophoriazusae*. Aristotle called him 'the most tragic of the poets' (i.e. best at arousing pity and fear; see *POETICS*), a description particularly apt to his depiction of the horrors of war. It was said that some Athenian prisoners after the *Sicilian Expedition won their liberty by reciting passages from his plays. (See also *ELECTRA* 2.)

Eurī'pus, in Greek, word meaning any strait where the flow of the tide is violent, the name in particular of the strait separating Euboea from Boeotia.

Eurō'pa ('broad-browed'), in Greek myth, daughter of Agenor, king of Tyre. Zeus loved her and so took the form of, or sent, a beautiful bull which swam to the sea-shore where she was playing and seemed so mild that she climbed upon its back. Thereupon it swam away with her to Crete, where to Zeus she bore *Minos, *Rhadamanthys, and, in post-Homeric accounts, *Sarpedon. The bull became the constellation Taurus. Europa was identified with a Cretan goddess and worshipped on the island.

Europe. The continent of Europe was said to have been named from the mythical *Europa, although Herodotus (4. 45) found this implausible since she was from Phoenicia and never entered mainland Europe. The name as used by the ancients does not correspond with the modern continent. Not mentioned by Homer, it is first found in the *Homeric Hymn to Apollo (seventh century BC) where it is an unspecified area (around Greece) distinct from the Peloponnese and the Greek islands. Herodotus and his contemporaries in the mid-fifth century BC considered the whole of the known earth as one continent divided into three main parts, Asia, Libya, and Europe. The last was naturally bounded by the Mediterranean and the Atlantic; its western boundary was signified by the Pillars of Hercules (the Straits of Gibraltar) beyond which the Greeks rarely penetrated, while in the east Europe was divided from Asia first by the river Phasis (modern Rioni) which flows to the eastern shore of the Black Sea, and later by the Tanais (modern Don). The northern boundary was the mountain-chain which runs north of Thrace, Italy, and Spain. The Greeks hardly explored beyond south Russia; central and northern Russia and Scandinavia were unknown and fabulous regions. The land exploration of Europe was chiefly accomplished in the first centuries BC and AD by the Roman army surveyors under Julius Caesar and the generals of the emperor Augustus.

Eurō'tās, the chief river of Laconia.

Eurus (Gk. *euros*), in Latin literature, the east or south-east *wind.

Eury'alē, one of the three *Gorgons.

Eury'alus, in Virgil's *Aeneid*, the friend of *Nisus.

Euryclei'a, in Homer's *Odyssey*, the old nurse of Odysseus.

Eury'dicē, the name of several women in Greek myth, including the wife of Creon, king of Thebes (see *ANTIGONE* of Sophocles). The best-known was a nymph and the wife of *Orpheus. While pursued by Aristaeus she was bitten by a snake and died. Orpheus followed her to the Underworld where the charms of his lyre suspended the tortures of the damned and persuaded Hades to allow him to bring her back, provided that he did not look round at her before he reached the upper world. He broke this condition and thus lost her forever. Through Virgil (*Georgics* 4. 453) and Ovid (*Metamorphoses* 10. 1) the story became well known to the Middle Ages. The story was sometimes given a happy ending as in Gluck's opera, where Eurydice was restored by the gods' forgiveness. The theme easily lent itself to a variety of symbolic interpretation, in ancient as well as modern times.

Eury'medon, one of the principal rivers of Pamphȳlia (in the south of modern Turkey), at the mouth of which the Athenian general Cimon destroyed a Persian fleet and then won a victory on land in or about 467 BC. The ruins at Aspendus (modern Belkis), some 12 km. (7 miles) upstream, include a well-preserved Roman theatre and aqueduct.

Eurypo'ntid, the name of the junior branch of the royal house at Sparta, descendants of Eurypon, grandson of Procles (see HERACLEIDAE). (The senior branch was the *Agiad.)

Eury'stheus, in Greek myth, king of Tiryns in Argos, son of Sthenelus and Menippē, a descendant of *Perseus. When Zeus swore on oath that the first descendant of Perseus to be born on a certain day would rule the surrounding peoples, intending that it should be his son Heracles, Hera in jealousy contrived that Eurystheus was born first. In the usual version of the myth, after Heracles in madness had killed his wife and children, the oracle at Delphi ordered him to live at Tiryns and serve Eurystheus for

twelve years in expiation. Eurystheus imposed upon him many dangerous tasks, known later as the Twelve Labours (see HERACLES, LABOURS OF).

Eury'tion. 1. In Greek myth, the herdsman of Geryon (see HERACLES, LABOURS OF 10).

2. In Greek myth, the *centaur whose misbehaviour at the wedding-feast of Pirithous, king of the Lapiths, began the quarrel between centaurs and Lapiths.

Eu'rytus, in Greek myth, king of Oechalia and father of Iolē; see HERACLES.

Eusē'bius (*c.* AD 260–*c.*340), Greek Christian writer, bishop of Caesarea in Palestine. His most important work, for which there was no precedent, is the *Ecclesiastical History*, which has earned him the title of father of Church history. It is divided into ten books, and is the main source for the history of the early Church in the East from its foundation to 324 (in the final version). It survives in the original Greek and also in Latin, Syriac, and Armenian versions. Among his other works is 'The Martyrs of Palestine', an eyewitness account of the persecutions (from 303 to 310) of the emperor *Diocletian. The *Praeparatio evangelica* ('preparation for the gospel'), in which he shows that the Greek tradition is inferior to the Hebrew and that the best of Greek philosophy merely coincided with or was derived from biblical teaching, is incidentally valuable in that it includes many quotations from classical authors now lost. Of importance for the study of ancient history are the two books of the *Chronikon* ('chronicle'), of which the first is an outline history of several ancient nations, and the second consists of synchronical tables with catalogues of rulers and striking occurrences from the birth of Abraham (reckoned as 2016 BC) to AD 328. It is a valuable adjunct to, and sometimes the only source for, our knowledge of dates and events in Greek and Roman history. The original Greek text survives only in a few fragments, but we have a Latin adaptation by Jerome and an Armenian translation.

Eustā'thius (latter half of the twelfth

century AD), a native of Constantinople, archbishop of Thessalonika, the most learned man of his age, whose commentaries on ancient Greek writers embody much valuable scholarship which has not survived elsewhere. His classical commentaries consist of an *Introduction* to Pindar, a *Paraphrase* of Dionysius Periegetes, and *Commentaries* on Homer's *Iliad* and *Odyssey*; these last are of great length and deal with the history, geography, language, and mythology of the two works, incorporating much ancient learning not found elsewhere. Eustathius is regarded as a saint by the Orthodox Church.

Eute'rpē, one of the *Muses, in late authors specified as the muse of flute-playing.

Euthyde'mus, title of one of the earlier Greek dialogues of *Plato, taken from the name of the sophist of Chios.

Socrates narrates to his friend Crito, who is pondering how best to educate his son, a recent debate in the wrestling school, in which Cleinias, an aristocratic Athenian youth in danger of being corrupted unless properly educated, is presented with two opposing principles of education, the sophistic (see SOPHISTS), represented by Euthydemus and Dionysodorus, and the Socratic. The sophist would teach 'virtue', *aretē*, understood as meaning success in public life; Socrates expresses doubt as to whether *arete* can be taught at all. Crito, reinforced by an anonymous bystander who concluded that philosophy was worth nothing, doubts whether he should entrust his son to any of them.

Eu'thyphrō (*Euthyphrōn*), title of an early Greek dialogue by *Plato.

Socrates, awaiting his trial for impiety, meets outside the court house Euthyphro the seer, who some years earlier had prosecuted his own father for unintentional homicide in order to clear himself of the pollution attendant on being connected with a murder. Socrates, appropriately, asks him for a definition of piety, but can only elicit the answer that piety is what is pleasing to the gods, and this turns out to be a matter of asking the gods for things and giving things to them. The dialogue is a gentle satire on an unworthy conception of religion.

Eutro'pius, Roman historian who published during the reign of the emperor Valens (AD 364–378) a survey of Roman history (*Breviarium ab urbe condita*) in ten books, from the time of Romulus to the death of the emperor Jovian in 364, ending with events of which the historian had personal knowledge. The early books are based on the epitome of Livy. The work is concise, well-balanced, and impartial.

Euxine, the 'hospitable' sea (Gk. *euxeinos*; originally *axenos*, 'inhospitable'), the euphemistic Greek name for the stormy Black Sea. It was opened up in the seventh century by explorers from Miletus and other Ionian Greek cities, an event perhaps reflected in the legends of the voyage of the Argonauts to Colchis, at the eastern end. By 600 BC its shores were dotted with Greek colonies, founded largely for the sake of trade. The earliest surviving description of it is given in the history of Herodotus, book 4.

Eva'dnē (Euadnē). **1.** In Greek myth, daughter of *Poseidon, by Apollo mother of Iamus, ancestor of the prophetic clan of the Iamidae who performed priestly functions at Olympia.

2. In Greek myth, wife of Capaneus, one of the *Seven against Thebes, who threw herself on his funeral pyre.

Eva'goras (*Euagoras*) (*c*.435–374 BC), king of Salamis in Cyprus, reputedly descended from *Teucer (2). He was friendly towards Athens and received many Athenian exiles at the end of the Peloponnesian War. His Hellenism brought him into conflict with Persia, by whom he was finally defeated. He died by assassination in a palace intrigue.

Eva'nder (Gk. Euandros, 'good man'), in Greece a minor deity associated with Pan and worshipped in Arcadia, especially at Pallantion. In Roman legend he was regarded as the first to make a settlement on the site of the future city of Rome. He was the son of Hermēs (or of a human father) and a nymph, identified with the Roman goddess Carmentis, and he led a small colony from Arcadia to the future site of the city on a hill called, after his native city, Pallanteum. This became known as the Palatine, and there he instituted the festival of the *Lupercalia, connected with the worship of Faunus, in reminiscence of the Arcadian festival of the Lycaea, which was connected with Pan. Hercules visited him on one occasion and killed the monster *Cacus. In commemoration Evander established the cult of Hercules at the Ara Maxima. Virgil in the *Aeneid* represents Evander as still alive when Aeneas arrives in Italy and as forming an alliance with him against the Latins. His son Pallas was killed fighting Turnus; it was to avenge him that Aeneas refused to spare Turnus. The story of Evander illustrates how the Romans created a connection in legend between Greece and Rome which included place-names and cults.

Exe'mpla ('examples'), a lost work of Cornelius *Nepos consisting of a collection of anecdotes from Roman history.

exile, a form of penalty for criminal offences used in Athens and Rome. In Athens it was imposed for unintentional homicide and sometimes for treason, but not for other offences, though it was permissible to go into voluntary exile in order to escape the death penalty. (*Ostracism, which meant banishment for ten years, was a political expedient and not a penalty for an offence.) Exile could be augmented by other penalties— the loss of property and of the right to be buried in Attic soil, the destruction of one's house, for example—but most of those who had committed unintentional homicide could keep their property and live abroad in freedom provided they avoided the great religious festivals and games, so as not to be a *pollution. If a man suffering penal exile was found in Attica, he ran the risk of imprisonment and perhaps execution. Exile lasted for life unless the sufferer obtained pardon.

In Rome, as in Athens, a defendant on trial for a capital crime might choose to go into exile (*exsilium*) before judgement was pronounced. However, in the last century of the republic exile became a substitute for the death penalty when magistrates were obliged to allow a condemned person time to escape before executing sentence, after which he was deprived of all legal protection and threatened with death ('denied fire and water') if he returned. There were varying degrees of voluntary and prescribed banishment, from the mild *relegatio* up to the severe *deportatio* (introduced by the emperor Tiberius), a perpetual banishment to a certain place, confiscation of property, and loss of citizenship. The term 'exile' came to be applied to them all.

e'xodos, in Greek drama, the final scene; in *tragedy, it is the action following the final *stasimon* (choral ode); in comedy it is the final rejoicing following the last *episode.

exo'rdium, in *rhetoric, the introduction (or proem) of a speech.

ex Ponto, Epi'stulae, see EPISTULAE EX PONTO.

F

Fa'bia, gens, one of the most ancient patrician clans at Rome which traced its origins to *Hercules and *Evander. Its greatest fame derives from an exploit in 479 when the *gens* offered to pursue the war against the Etruscan town of Veii entirely on its own; 306 men withdrew from Rome and built a fortress on the Cremera (Fosso Valchetta), a small stream which falls into the Tiber a few miles above Rome. They were caught in an ambush and all perished with the exception of one youth, from whom all later members of the *gens* were descended. The later battle at the *Allia was generally believed to have occurred on the same day of the year (18 July).

Fa'bius Ma'ximus Rullia'nus (or Rullus), Quintus, a famous Roman general of the Samnite wars, five or six times consul, dictator in 315 BC and perhaps again in 313, censor in 304. He celebrated *triumphs over Samnites, Etruscans, and Gauls. Livy's account of his numerous exploits in books 8–11, based on Fabius Pictor and the later annalists, is untrustworthy and introduces incidents from the life of his great-grandson, Fabius Cunctator (see below). When consul for the fifth time in 295 he and his colleague P. *Decius Mus defeated an alliance of Samnites, Gauls, and others at Sentinum (Sassoferrato) in the decisive battle for the supremacy of Italy.

Fa'bius Ma'ximus Verruco'sus, Cuncta'tor, Quintus (*c.*275–203 BC), the famous Roman general and consul of the Second Punic War, dictator in 221 and again in 217 after Hannibal destroyed the consul Flaminius and the Roman army at the battle of Lake Trasimene. During the six months of his second period of office he fought a defensive war against Hannibal (see PUNIC WARS), and was called in consequence Cunctator, 'delayer', by doggedly following Hannibal's movements while avoiding a direct encounter. After Rome ventured on a pitched battle at Cannae in 216 and was disastrously defeated, Fabius' evasive strategy had to be resumed. The name derisively given to him took on an honourable connotation, and was incorporated in a famous line by the poet Ennius: *unus homo nobis cunctando restituit rem* ('one man by his delaying restored the situation for us'). Fabius was consul (and leader of the senate) for the fifth time in 209 when he recovered Tarentum (Taranto) from the Carthaginians. He strenuously opposed the plans of Scipio (Africanus), who had driven the Carthaginians out of Spain by 205, to take the war into the enemy's country by invading Africa; he died in 203, at about the time of Hannibal's departure from Italy, before the favourable conclusion of the war. Fabius was rightly called the Shield of Rome and was admired by later generations for his (perhaps unimaginative) courage and his old-fashioned patrician virtues. In British politics 'Fabianism' describes a socialist policy of cautious advance, as opposed to immediate revolution.

Fa'bius Pictor ('painter'), **Quintus,** the earliest Roman historian, whose work survives only in quotations in later writers. (The family name derives from his grandfather who painted a temple *c.*302 BC.) He was a senator, fought in the Second Punic War (218–201 BC), and was sent to consult the Delphic Oracle after the Roman defeat at Cannae in 216. His history of Rome, which began with its foundation (dated by him to 748 BC) and continued to his own day, was written in Greek partly because Latin prose was not yet a literary medium but also with the purpose of justifying Roman policy to the Greeks. His work probably used pontifical records (see FASTI) and lists of magistrates. He was reliable, and used by Livy and Polybius.

fable, in literature, an anecdote with a moral in which the characters are animals behaving as humans. The fable was a popular literary genre in Greece, as in other countries, at all times. Quintilian observes that it appeals particularly to the simple and uneducated. It is not found in Homer, but occurs in Hesiod (see WORKS AND DAYS) and *Archilochus. By the end of the fifth century BC Greek fables were generally attributed to *Aesop; they were probably written in prose. A collection of 'Tales of Aesop' was made by *Demetrius of Phalerum. The earliest surviving collection of fables is that of *Babrius, probably of the second century AD, written in choliambic verse (see METRE, GREEK 5 (iii)). It enjoyed wide popularity.

Latin authors frequently refer to fables which we know from Aesop. The earliest Latin collection was that of *Phaedrus, of the first century AD, written in iambic verse (see METRE, GREEK 5).

Fabri'cius Luscī'nus ('blind in one eye'), **Gaius**, a hero of the Romans' war with *Pyrrhus (280–272 BC), a *novus homo* who was twice consul and was admired in later times for his old-style virtues of austerity, high principle, and incorruptibility. He refused bribes from Pyrrhus when he was sent to him by the Romans in 280 to negotiate an exchange of prisoners; and in the campaign of 278 when he was consul and in command of the Roman forces, he sent back to Pyrrhus the latter's treacherous doctor who had offered to poison him. This generous act paved the way for Pyrrhus' withdrawal from Italy. Fabricius was a notably strict censor in 275. At his death he left no money to provide his daughters' dowry, which was given by the senate.

fā'bula, besides meaning 'story', the general Latin word for 'play', frequently combined with an adjective defining the subject. The commonest types were the *fabula* *Atellāna*, farce, *f.* *crĕpidāta*, Roman tragedy on a Greek theme, *f.* *palliāta*, adaptation of a Greek comedy, *f.* *praetexta*, a serious play on a Roman historical subject, and *f.* *tŏgāta*, a Roman comedy with a native theme concerning low life in Rome.

Fali'sci, an Italian Iron Age people

closely related to the Latins, who lived on the right bank of the Tiber north of Latium.

Fall of Rome. Between AD 395 (when the Visigothic leader *Alaric began to ravage inside the Roman imperial frontiers in Thrace and Macedonia) and 495 (when Theodoric the Great, king of the Ostrogoths, was proclaimed king of Italy), the Roman empire in the West was no longer capable of resisting barbarian incursions. Italy and the western provinces were gradually occupied by Germanic peoples mostly migrating under pressure from the advancing Huns. In 401 and again in 403 Alaric invaded Italy but was forced to withdraw by *Stilicho. After the latter's death in 408 there was no general able to defeat the Visigoths, and on 24 August 410 they entered Rome and sacked it, the first time the city had fallen to a foreign enemy since its capture by the Gauls in 390 BC. In 452 the Huns devastated parts of Italy, but their king Attila (known as the 'Scourge of God') was persuaded by Pope Leo I, the Great, to withdraw without entering Rome. Three years later the city fell to Gaiseric, king of the Vandals, who stayed for a fortnight in the city to plunder its treasures. The last Roman emperor in the West was the young Romulus Augustulus who reigned briefly 475–6. He was deposed and banished by Odo(v)acer, German commander of the imperial guard, who was proclaimed king of Italy by the army and accepted the emperor in the East as his overlord. With him the Roman empire in the West came to an end. (For the division of the empire into two halves see BYZANTINE AGE.)

fascēs, 'bundle of rods', bound together by red thongs and carried on their shoulders by *lictors before important Roman magistrates as a symbol of their power. The practice seems to have been of Etruscan origin. Under the kings each bundle enclosed an axe, symbolizing the king's right to scourge and execute, but from the early republic onwards only dictators were allowed axes in Rome; other magistrates retained the axe when outside Rome and at the head of an army. In the case of a general who had won a victory and been saluted as Imperator by his soldiers, his *fasces* were always crowned with laurel. From the Italian equivalent *fascio* the Italian Fascist party took its name, with the *fasces* as its symbol.

fasti, the name given to the old Roman *calendar which originally indicated *dies fasti* and *nefasti*, the days on which it was or was not permissible to transact legal and public business. Later were included lists of consuls (*fasti consularēs*), priests (*fasti sacerdotalēs*), and records of triumphs. They were published in 304 BC by Gnaeus *Flavius. Some fragments survive in inscriptions. (Compare ANNALS.)

Fasti, *Ovid's poetical calendar of the Roman year, with its various observances and festivals, written in elegiacs. It was incomplete at the time of his exile in AD 8, and we have only the first six books (January to June), partially revised at Tomis. Ovid's models were Hellenistic poems, for astronomy the *Phaenomena* of *Aratus, and for his explanations of the origins of Roman history and religion the *Aitia* of *Callimachus, though he may have also been influenced by *Propertius' last book of elegies which contains a large number of Roman legends.

Ovid's design, as stated in the preface to the poem, is to study the calendar in the light of old annals, and to show what events are commemorated on each day and the origins of the various rites. It accordingly records day by day the rising and setting of the constellations (not without mistakes), and explains the origins of the fixed festivals and the rites noted in the calendar, such as the *Lupercalia on 15 February. It also relates the legends connected with particular dates, such as that of the founding of Rome on 21 April, and that of the expulsion of the Tarquins on 24 February. The scheme provides opportunity for telling afresh some of the old Greek myths, such as the tale of Proserpine; and for excursion on a multitude of customs and beliefs, such as those connected with New Year's Day, the unluckiness of marriages in May, and the casting of straw men into the Tiber (see ARGEI).

Fates (Gk. Moirai; Lat. Fāta or Parcae). The Greek Fates, to which the Latin Parcae (so called from *parĕrĕ*, to bring forth) were in all respects assimilated, were represented from Homer onwards as old women spinning, three in number according to Hesiod, the children of Nyx (Night) or, somewhat allegorically, of Zeus and Themis (Righteousness). The three were called Klōtho ('spinner'), who held the distaff, Lachĕsis ('apportioner'), who drew off the thread, and Atrŏpŏs ('inflexible'), who cut it short, Milton's 'blind Fury with th'abhorred shears'. The Parcae were named Nōna, Decuma, and Morta, meaning respectively, a nine-months' birth (premature, by Roman inclusive reckoning), a ten-months' (full-term) birth, and a still-birth. They could have been in origin birth-goddesses who became abstract powers of destiny only later. Their spinning may be thought of as completed at the moment of birth or continuing throughout life until all the thread is drawn off the distaff. They may also weave; the images in the poets are various. They are present at all great beginnings, as at the marriage of *Peleus and Thetis, where they also sang. The Moirai could be worshipped as birth-goddesses—Athenian brides offered them locks of hair, and women swore by them.

Faunus, in Roman myth, son of Pīcus, grandson of Saturn, and father of Latīnus, king of the Latini when Aeneas arrived in Italy. He was an Italian pastoral god, connected with the *Lupercalia, a hunter and promoter of agriculture, whose festival on 5 December was celebrated by cheerful celebrations in the countryside. He was also an oracular god (hence his title Fātŭus, 'the speaker') who revealed the future by dreams or supernatural voices in sacred groves, of which there was one near Tibur and another on the Aventine. The spectral appearances and terrifying sounds he was believed to make in wooded places caused him to be visualized as a monster with the legs and horns of a goat. Hence he was identified with the Arcadian god Pan and, as in the case of the latter, the idea grew up of a plurality of Fauni (fauns), who were identified with the Greek satyrs but usually thought of as more gentle.

Faustī'na, A'nnia Gale'ria. 1. The

Elder, aunt of the Roman emperor Marcus *Aurelius and wife of Antoninus Pius, emperor AD 137–61. She died in 140; Antoninus named after her a charity for the maintenance of poor children.

2. The Younger, daughter of (1) above, who married her cousin M. Aurelius, emperor AD 161–80, in 145, and bore him at least 12 children. She accompanied her husband during his northern campaign in 170–4 and to the East, where she died in 175. She too, like her mother, was said by ancient writers to be faithless and disloyal, but it seems from his *Meditations* that she was loved by her husband, who also founded a charity in her memory.

Fau'stŭlus, in Roman legend, the herdsman who found Romulus and Remus in the she-wolf's den, and whose wife Acca Larentia brought them up.

Favō'nius, in Latin, the west wind, also known as Zephyrus, and associated with spring-time. See WINDS.

Favorī'nus, orator and teacher of Greek rhetoric in the second century AD (see SOPHISTIC, SECOND); born at Arelatē (Arles) in Gaul he learned Greek at Massilia (Marseilles), and always seems to have written and spoken it in preference to Latin. Two of the speeches handed down in the works of Dion of Prusa (37 and 64) are probably by him, and a fragment of his treatise *On Exile* survives. His powers of oratory and his philosophical knowledge brought him high distinction in Greece and Rome, and for a time he enjoyed the favour of the Roman emperor Hadrian. He was banished to Chios c.130, but Hadrian's successor Antoninus Pius allowed him to return to Rome where he remained until his death in about the middle of the century. He used to boast of three things: that being a (natural) eunuch he had been charged with adultery, that being a native of Gaul he wrote and spoke Greek, and that he continued to live despite having offended the emperor.

Fēli'citās, the Roman goddess of good luck, unknown until the mid-second century BC, when L. Licinius *Lucullus dedicated a temple to her; another was planned by Julius Caesar and was erected

after his death. She was important in official cult under the emperors.

Fērā'lia ('commemoration of the dead'), in the Roman calendar, the festival of the dead held on 21 February, the last day of the *Parentalia, when food was carried to tombs for the use of the dead.

fē'riae, Latin term for a festival or holiday which involved visiting temples and making sacrifice to the gods. Holidays were either public, observed by the state, or private, observed by a family to celebrate e.g. a birthday. Abstention from work, including legal and political business, was obligatory during public holidays (which were thus *dies nefasti*), so that the sacred time should not be polluted. There exist interesting decisions made by the pontiffs as to what kind of work might be permissible; the pontiff Scaevola permitted any work in which delay might cause injury or suffering, such as rescuing an ox which had fallen into a pit (compare Luke 14: 5). See FERIAE LATINAE below; and also COMPITALIA, FERALIA, FORDICIDIA, FORNACALIA, LEMURES, LIBER, LUPERCALIA, LUDI, MEGALESIA, PAGANALIA, PALES, QUINQUATRIS, SATURNALIA, and VESTA.

fē'riae Lati'nae ('Latin festival'), a joint religious celebration of the Romans and the Latins in honour of Jupiter Latiāris, in his role as god of the *Latin League, held on the Alban Mount annually, usually at the end of April. It dated back to the period when *Alba Longa and not Rome was the chief city of Latium. The flesh of the sacrificial victim (a white heifer) was eaten in a communal meal by representatives from all the cities of the League. It was an important occasion, attended by all the magistrates; the festival was still celebrated in the third century AD.

Fērō'nia, an Italian goddess of widespread cult; of her functions and the etymology of her name nothing is known.

Fesce'nnine verses (*versus fescennīni*), in Latin, one of the earliest kinds of Italian poetry, ribald songs or dialogues in extempore verse, produced for amusement at festivals and also sung at weddings; they were of the same nature as the abusive songs sung by soldiers at triumphs and the term was used of scurrilous verse in general. Livy and Horace thought the original Fescennine verses were a crude form of metrical repartee exchanged extempore between rustics, and the origin of Italian drama, perhaps in imitation of the Aristotelian theory of the origin of drama in Greece (see COMEDY, GREEK 2; TRAGEDY 1). The ancients derived the name either from Fescennium, a town in Etruria (which has no obvious connection), or from *fascinum* ('enchantment', the 'evil eye'), which the songs, like the phallic emblem worn by children (also called *fascinum*), were supposed to ward off.

festivals, in the ancient world, a day or days set aside by a city, state, or country for the worship of gods. Although festivals were always in some aspect religious and never purely secular, no rigid distinction was made between religious and secular activities, and they were frequently occasions of general merrymaking. Feasting, athletics, play-acting, and bawdiness were all considered appropriate constituents of certain festivals.

For individual festivals, see the following. For the major Greek athletic festivals: OLYMPIA (and OLYMPIAD), ISTHMIAN GAMES, NEMEAN GAMES, PYTHIAN GAMES. For Athenian festivals: PANATHENAEA, DIONYSIA, LENAEA, ANTHESTERIA, OSCHOPHORIA, THESMOPHORIA, SCIROPHORIA, THARGELIA, PYANEPSIA. For Apaturia see PHRATRIAI. For Spartan festivals: GYMNOPAEDIAE and CARNEA. For Argos: HERAEA. See also ELEUTHERIA, LYCAEUS, and MYSTERIES.

For Roman festivals see FERIAE.

Festus, Sextus Pompē'ius, see VERRIUS FLACCUS.

fētiā'lēs, *college of Roman priests, selected for life from among the nobles, who represented the people in their dealings with other nations; the origin of their name is uncertain, but it may be connected with words meaning 'ordinance'. They were concerned particularly in the rituals of making a treaty and declaring war. In the former case a fetial would pronounce a curse on Rome in the event

that she should break the treaty first, and confirm it by killing a pig with a flint; in the latter case the fetial cast a specially hardened spear across the border into the offending country, if it was a neighbour, or into a special piece of land near the temple of Bellona that by a legal fiction was constituted as enemy territory. The office seems to have lapsed in the last century of the republic but to have been revived under Augustus.

fiscus ('basket', 'money-bag'), the term which came to denote the funds of the Roman emperor, as opposed to the public *aerarium*; it was instituted as a separate treasury in the first century AD (at what point exactly is not known), and possessed certain rights in law.

Five Thousand (at Athens), see FOUR HUNDRED.

Flaccus, Ve'rrius, see VERRIUS.

flamen (apparently meaning 'priest' or 'sacrificer'), at Rome, a priest appointed to the service of one particular god from among the most ancient Roman deities, further distinguished by an epithet derived from the god's name. Fifteen in number, the flamens were part of the college of pontiffs (see COLLEGIUM) under the authority of the *pontifex maximus*. The most ancient and dignified (*maiorēs*) were the *flamen dialis* of Jupiter, *martialis* of Mars, and *quirinalis* of Quirinus, all chosen from among the patricians, the rest (*minorēs*) being plebeian. They were nominated by the people and elected for life. After the deification of the emperors, starting with Julius Caesar in 42 BC, flamens were appointed in Rome and in the provinces to superintend their worship also.

Flāminī'nus, Titus Qui'nctius (d. 174 BC), Roman statesman and general, consul 198 BC. In 197 he was sent to Macedonia where Rome was engaged in the Second Macedonian War against Philip V of Macedon. Flamininus won a pitched battle against him at Cynoscephalae in Thessaly, and by this victory the Romans found themselves responsible for the settlement of a newly-liberated Greece. When Flamininus announced the liberation of Greece to the crowds gathered at Corinth for the

Isthmian games of 196, he was hailed as a saviour. In 194 he left Greece, where, however, peace was short-lived (see MACEDONIA). In his philhellenism Flamininus was comparable with *Scipio Africanus.

Flavian emperors, the emperors of Rome from AD 71 to 96 who belonged to the *gens Flāvia*; they were *Vespasian (71–9), his elder son *Titus (79–81), and his younger son *Domitian (81–96).

Flā'vius, Gnaeus, secretary to *Appius Claudius Caecus (censor 312 BC), aedile in 304 BC, famous in the annals of Roman law for having been the first to publish and therefore make known to the people the rules of the calendar (see FASTI) which determined what legal acts might be done on which days, and probably also the *formulae* or form of words which in law had to be used to state a claim or make a defence. This knowledge had formerly been the monopoly of the pontiffs, who were patrician, and the patricians were indignant to see it broken.

Flōra, an Italian goddess of flowers and spring whose antiquity is proved by the assignment to her of a *flamen floralis*, but who was not given a temple until 238 BC. At this temple, near the Circus Maximus, cheerful and ribald celebrations in her honour were held every April, reaching their climax on the first of May. Ovid tells the story of Chlōris who, when pursued by Zephyrus, changed into Flora and breathed out flowers which spread over the countryside; this myth is depicted in Botticelli's *Primavera*.

Flōrus, author of the Latin history known as the 'Epitome of all the Wars during Seven Hundred Years', an abridgement of Roman history up to the age of Augustus with special reference to the wars, and designed as a panegyric of the Roman people. Some manuscripts describe it as an epitome of Livy, but it is sometimes at variance with that historian while it draws on the work of Sallust and Caesar and perhaps Virgil and Lucan. The style is markedly rhetorical, and the author is sometimes brief to the point of obscurity. Florus' identity and other names are not known for certain, though he is commonly called Lucius Annaeus.

He lived in the second century AD and is variously identified with the Florus who was poet-friend of the emperor Hadrian and with the author of a dialogue, imperfectly preserved, entitled 'Is Virgil an orator or a poet?'

Fordicī'dia, at Rome, a religious festival held on 15 April, at which a pregnant cow (*forda*) was sacrificed in each of the thirty wards (*curiae*) of the city. The intention was to promote the fertility of the cattle and fields. The unborn calves were removed from the womb and burnt, and the ashes subsequently used in a purificatory rite at the festival of the Parilia (see PALES).

Fo'rmiae (Formia), an ancient Volscian town on the Appian Way, identified by the Roman poets with Lamus, the city of the Laestrygonians in Homer's *Odyssey*. In the classical period it became a fashionable pleasure resort where many Romans had villas, including Cicero, who was killed nearby.

Forms, Platonic, see PLATO 4.

formulae, Homeric and formulaic verse. Homeric epic is in its origin *oral composition, and every performance was an improvisation. In order to facilitate improvisation within the strict constraints imposed by the metre, the bard memorized what have been called in modern times 'formulae', groups of words of various metrical patterns which express a commonly repeated idea or action and can fit into many contexts. Formulae may vary in length from a noun plus adjective—'swift-footed Achilles', 'wily Odysseus'—to several lines, such as those describing a hero arming for battle. The use of formulae accounts for the repetitive nature of Homeric verse.

Fornācā'lia, at Rome, religious festival celebrated by the wards or *curiae*, held in early February on a day to be decided by the leaders of the *curiae*. Its purpose was in some way to prosper the ovens, *fornacēs*, which parched the grain.

Fortū'na or **Fors Fortuna,** Italian goddess, perhaps originally the 'bringer' of fertility (Lat. *ferre*, 'to bring'), but identified with the Greek *Tȳchē and so the goddess of chance or luck. She had an ancient temple in the Forum Boarium at Rome. Her cult was said to have been introduced into Rome by *Servius Tullius; she was not, therefore, one of the most ancient deities, a fact confirmed by her not having a *flamen. She was worshipped at Antium and at Praenestē, where she had an oracular shrine. At Rome her festival on 24 June was a popular holiday, and large crowds including slaves flocked to her shrine, near the river Tiber about 2 km. (1 mile) downstream from the city, to witness the sacrifices. The Romans addressed her by a variety of epithets expressing either particular kinds of good luck or the kinds of people to whom she granted it.

Forty, the, at Athens, the magistrates (four picked by lot from each of the ten tribes) responsible for deciding private law-suits if the amount of money involved did not exceed ten drachmas.

forum ('market-place'), a levelled rectangle of ground in the centre of every large Roman town and a constant feature of Roman town-plans even in the provinces. Although there was a tendency over the years for trade to be transferred to shops in other quarters, the forum remained the focus of the town's political, social, and commercial life, and was surrounded by the chief civic buildings. It sometimes gave a town its name, e.g. Forum Julii (Fréjus). The various fora in Rome itself are as follows.

Forum Augu'stum, a forum that was also the very large precinct (110 m. by 83 m., 360 ft. by 270 ft.) of the temple of Mars Ultor ('avenger'). The temple was dedicated in 2 BC by the emperor Augustus, having been vowed by him during the battle of Philippi in 42 BC. The forum was built to provide additional room for the law-courts and to meet other needs of the increasing population. Augustus placed in it bronze statues of all successful Roman generals, many of whose inscriptions have been found. It was from here that provincial governors ceremonially set off, and here they were received upon their return.

Forum Boā'rium, the 'cattle-market'

and also an important centre for traffic, situated between the Palatine hill and the river Tiber.

Forum Ju'lium or *Cae'saris*, dedicated by Julius Caesar in 46 BC as a centre for business. In it he erected a temple to Venus Genetrix, mythical ancestress of the *Julian gens*, which he had vowed at the battle of Pharsalus in 48, and in front of it placed an equestrian statue of himself.

Forum Rōmā'num, the ancient marketplace and later the political, commercial, and religious centre of Rome, occupying what was originally a marshy valley which served as one of the defences of the first city on the Palatine hill and separated it from the Capitoline and Quirinal hills (SEE SEVEN HILLS OF ROME). It is this which is normally referred to as 'the forum' at Rome. For early features of it see JUTURNA, REGIA, and VESTA. Its earliest monuments were the first temples to Saturn (497 BC), Castor (484), and Concordia (336). The speaker's platform (*rostra*) was in existence by 338 BC. The first overall plan of the forum is in large part due to Sulla who at the beginning of the first century BC paved much of the area, built a new basilica, and restored the Rostra. Julius Caesar's further designs for it were largely carried out by the emperor Augustus, who transformed it, and most of the surrounding buildings have come down to us much as he left them—the rebuilt temples of Saturn, Castor, and Concordia, the temple of Julius Caesar, two basilicas, and the restored Rostra.

Forum Trāiā'ni (sometimes called the Forum Ulpium), built by the emperor Trajan in AD 113 between the Capitoline and Quirinal hills, the last and most magnificent of the Roman fora erected by the emperors. It contained the Basilica Ulpia (a lawcourt), the Bibliotheca Ulpia (a library comprising two halls, one for Greek and the other for Latin books), and Trajan's Column. After Trajan's death Hadrian erected in the forum a temple dedicated to him. Trajan's Column, 38 m. (125 ft.) high and hollow, with a spiral staircase leading to the top, still stands in a good state of preservation. It is decorated with a spiral frieze illustrating the events of the Dacian Wars and once contained Trajan's ashes in a golden urn.

Four Hundred, the, a revolutionary oligarchic council (see OLIGARCHY) that seized power from the democratic council of five hundred (the boulē) and ruled Athens for three months in 411 BC before being deposed. It came into being because some Athenians believed that if democratic rule at Athens were replaced by an oligarchy the king of Persia would support Athens in the *Peloponnesian War. The Four Hundred were deposed in September 411 and replaced by an assembly of 5,000 citizens (the Five Thousand), but in 410 the democracy was restored, with its old council of five hundred.

Franks (Franci, 'free men'), a coalition of small German tribes on the Lower Rhine who took this name in the third century AD. In the fourth century they were permitted by Rome to occupy a large area in the region of modern Belgium. They expanded further into Gaul in the fifth century, and in 486, led by their king Clovis, of the Merovingian family, they defeated Syagrius, the last Roman ruler in Gaul. Clovis, who became a convert to Christianity, and his descendants succeeded in uniting under their rule the whole area of modern France (Francia).

fratres arva'les, SEE ARVAL PRIESTS.

freedmen (Lat. liberti, libertini), slaves who had been freed ('manumitted') by their masters, and a class of people who figured much more prominently in Roman society than in Greek. Freedmen in Rome have been regarded as almost comprising a middle class in the society of the late republic and early empire, and they included many people of intelligence, energy, and ambition. In Athens manumission required no formal procedure; a manumitted slave was registered as a metic (resident alien) with his former owner as sponsor. This meant that he was not a citizen and could not normally become one.

It was an extraordinary feature of Roman law that a slave manumitted in proper legal form by a Roman citizen owner became himself a Roman citizen, though ineligible for high rank because he was not himself free-born (which his children would be). A freedman whose former owner or his children still lived owed obligations to the family which were enforceable at law (see CLIENT). Romans liked to think of the relationship between freedmen and patron as filial, and certainly bonds of affection existed, as for example between Cicero and his family and their freedman *Tiro.

By the end of the republic freedmen constituted a large proportion of the Roman citizen body; the distinction between citizens of servile birth and those of free birth became blurred, and was replaced by the distinction between the rich and the poor. *Petronius' imaginary freedman Trimalchio is an extravagant satire on the characteristics of the class. Many of the higher posts in the bureaucracy during the first century AD were held by freedmen, who were ineligible for the *curule magistracies. These men often came to exercise great power, and incurred widespread hatred.

Frogs (Batrachoi, Lat. Rānae), Greek comedy by *Aristophanes which won the first prize at the *Lenaea in Athens in 405 BC and earned its author a crown of sacred olive, as well as the right to produce it a second time. It gives expression to the city's literary attitudes and political plight at that time. The great tragic poets, Aeschylus, Sophocles, and Euripides, are all dead, the last two only recently; Athens, despite her victory in the sea-battle at Arginusae the previous year, is exhausted; she badly needs sound advice such as might be given by the best poets. The play opens with the patron god of tragedy Dionysus, characterized as possessing the human failings of the Athenian people—he is weak, conceited, credulous, and has a passion for Euripides—setting off for Hades disguised as Heracles in order to bring back Euripides. The journey in Charon's boat across the lake is accompanied by the croaking of a (secondary) chorus of frogs, who give their name to the play; the main chorus comprises initiates in the Eleusinian mysteries (see MYSTERIES). After arriving in Hades Dionysus has various adventures in consequence of being mistaken for Heracles, but is finally identified and asked to judge a dispute between Aeschylus and Euripides for possession of the throne of tragedy, Sophocles having relinquished his claim in favour of Aeschylus. Aeschylus represents his plays as superior in grandeur and moral purpose, Euripides his as more realistic and human, but each produces telling criticism of the other. Both agree that the duty of the poet is to make men better; Aeschylus says his heroes were models to be imitated, Euripides that he made the audience think; but Aeschylus objects that Euripides' depraved characters are the cause of the decline in morals. The poets then attack the construction of each other's plays, their language, metre, and music. The final test whereby each poet speaks a line into a pair of scales to determine whose poetry is the weightier is easily won by Aeschylus. Dionysus, still undecided as to which poet he prefers, asks each for advice on how to save the city. Euripides makes a characteristically enigmatic reply, and Dionysus chooses Aeschylus as representative of the old Athenian spirit.

Fronti'nus, Sextus Julius (*c.* AD 30–*c.*104), consul in 73 or 74, after which he was sent as governor to Britain, where he subdued the Silures in south-east Wales. Of his writings there survive the *Stratēgēmata* in four books, a manual of Greek and Roman strategy for the use of officers; fragments of a work on land-surveying; and his most famous work, *De aquis urbis Romae* ('on the waters of Rome'), in two books written after he was appointed curator of the Roman water-supply (*curator aquarum*) in 97. He describes for the benefit of his successors the *aqueducts and their history, the regulations governing them, and technical details concerning the quality and distribution of supply. Frontinus' writings have a straightforward style in keeping with their subject-matter.

Fronto, Marcus Cornelius (*c.* AD 100–*c.*176), the leading Roman orator of his day. He was born in North Africa, but lived most of his life in Rome. His political importance was negligible although he was consul in 143 (with *Herodes Atticus the Greek sophist). He was influential as a literary figure, however, and was tutor to the future emperors Marcus *Aurelius and Lucius Verus. Very little of his work was known until a collection of his letters (partly in Greek) was discovered in the early nineteenth century at Rome and Milan. Disappointing as historical sources, despite being written to and including letters from the leading figures of the day, they are more revealing on personal and literary matters. A cordial friendship between Fronto and M. Aurelius is apparent, although the latter ultimately rejected rhetoric as being unworthy of serious pursuit. Fronto's interest in rhetoric is largely confined to matters of language and style, and he was attracted by archaic and recondite Latin words. His most admired models of life and speech were the old Romans down to Cicero and Sallust; he disliked Seneca. The few rhetorical exercises of his which survive are in a vigorous and straightforward Latin.

Fu'lvia, first wife (by 45 BC) of Mark *Antony (she had previously been the wife successively of P. Clodius and C. Scribonius Curio), who played an important part in the political struggles after the death of Caesar in 44 BC. She is said to have taken an active part in the proscriptions and gazed with delight at the corpse of Cicero, who had attacked her in his speeches. In 41 BC, while Antony was entertaining himself with Cleopatra, she engaged in civil war (SEE PERUSINE WAR) with Octavian. When Octavian was victorious she was allowed to escape to Greece, where she met Antony in Athens. He is said to have been so angry at Fulvia's action in promoting discord between himself and Octavian that she lost all interest in life and died in 40. Her death was opportune for a reconciliation between Octavian and Antony, who then married Octavian's sister.

funeral games. In Greek epic poetry, the deaths of heroes were marked with athletic competitions, as were those of great men in early historical times. At such an occasion the poet Hesiod won a tripod in a competition for a funeral song.

Funeral Oration, SEE PERICLES.

Fu'riae or **Dīrae,** Roman equivalent of

the Greek Erinyes or Eumenides (see FURIES). There is no proof that they were ever the object of cult in Italy.

Furies (Gk. Erīnўěs), also known by the propitiatory names of Euměnĭděs, 'kindly ones', and Semnai, 'the holy ones', in Greek myth, spirits of punishment avenging without pity wrongs done to kindred and especially murder within the family. According to Hesiod they were the daughters of Gaia (Earth), conceived from the drops of blood spilt when Cronus castrated his father *Uranus (Heaven), i.e. they were born of a crime committed by a son against a father. Authorities differ as to their parentage, but they are always represented as more ancient than the Olympian gods and not under the rule of Zeus, although they honour him. They also punished perjurers and those who had violated the laws of hospitality and supplication, and came to assume the character of goddesses who punish crimes after death and seldom appear on earth. They were represented as carrying torches and scourges, and wreathed with snakes. Later writers make them three in number with the names Tīsiphŏnē, Megaera, and Allecto. Their cult was rare, but they had a sanctuary at the foot of the Acropolis.

Fūrī'na, see FURRINA.

Fu'rius Cami'llus, Marcus, see CAMILLUS.

Furrī'na or **Fūrīna,** ancient Italian goddess whose nature and function had, by Cicero's day, become a matter of conjecture. Nevertheless she possessed a grove on the slopes of the Janiculum near the Pons Sublicius, a *flamen, and an annual festival (Furrinalia, 25 July), although in classical times this was celebrated only by the priests connected with the cult. It was in the grove of Furrina that C. *Gracchus had his slave kill him in 121 BC.

G

Gadēs (Cadiz, Gk. Gadeira), colony founded by the Phoenicians from Tyre, traditionally in 1100 BC, on a small island off the Spanish mainland north-west of the Pillars of Hercules (Gibraltar), and for a long time the westernmost point of the world known to the Greeks and Romans. It was sometimes identified with and sometimes said to be near the mythical island of Erytheia, where *Geryon grazed the cattle which were later carried off by Heracles (see HERACLES, LABOURS OF 10). Occasionally it was confused with the region of southern Spain known as Tartessus. For a long time it was dependent on Carthage, and from 237 BC was *Hamilcar Barca's base in his Spanish campaigns. In 206 BC during the Second Punic War it surrendered to Rome on favourable terms, and was later made a Roman *municipium* by Julius Caesar. For a long time it was the most important commercial shipping port in the West, and enjoyed considerable wealth.

Gaia, in Greek myth, the Earth, personified as a goddess, the daughter of Chaos, the mother and wife of *Uranus, Heaven; their offspring included the Titans and the Cyclopēs. On the advice of Gaia, Cronus, the youngest of the Titans, castrated his father; fertilized by the blood, Gaia became the mother of the Giants and the Furies. Later she bore Typhon to her son *Tartarus. Her cult can be traced in many places in Greece, but for the most part it was superseded in classical times by that of later gods; at Delphi she seems to have been thought of as the original holder of the oracular shrine, before Apollo seized it by killing the serpent Python. Her characteristic function was to be a witness to oaths, as one who knows all that is done on earth.

Gaiseric, see VANDALS.

Gaius (second century AD), one of the most distinguished Roman jurists, who lived in Rome and wrote extensively but whose full name and origins are unknown; he was never quoted by contemporary or near-contemporary jurists. It is likely therefore that he was a teacher rather than a practical jurist, and did not in his lifetime have *ius respondendi*, 'the right to give a legal opinion', i.e. his opinions could not be cited as authority for subsequent legal decisions. This prerogative was granted posthumously in AD 426 when his writings were given equal authority with those of *Papinian, *Paulus, and *Ulpian. His best-known, though perhaps not wholly original, work is the *Institutionēs* ('institutes'), which was taken by *Justinian, the Roman emperor at Constantinople, as the basis of his own *Institutiones* in AD 533 and thereby exerted immense influence on later legal thought. This work was known only in an abbreviated version until its discovery on a palimpsest at Verona in 1816, the Letters of St Jerome having been written over it. It is the only classical legal work to have come down to us in substantially its original form.

Gaius Caesar, properly Gaius Julius Caesar Germanicus, popularly known as Caligula (AD 12–41), Roman emperor, the son of *Germanicus and Agrippina. In AD 14–16 he was on the Rhine with his parents, where he was nicknamed Caligula ('little boot') because of the military boots he wore. After the death of his brother Drusus in 33 he became next in succession to the principate, being the only surviving son of Germanicus. Soon after his accession in 37 at the death of Tiberius, he fell seriously ill; *Philo the Jew, who went on an embassy to Rome in 40, suggests that the illness affected his mind. Certainly his behaviour afterwards became increasingly despotic and mad, marked by wild extravagance, arbitrary executions, and aspirations towards deification. He was murdered in 41.

Galatē'a (Galateia, 'milk-white'), Greek sea-nymph, daughter of *Nereus and Doris. The story of her wooing by the ugly *Cyclops Polyphemus was frequently told, by the bucolic poets (Theocritus, Idyll 11; Virgil, Eclogue 9; Ovid, *Metamorphoses* 13); and by the early eighteenth-century English poet John Gay in his libretto to Handel's *Acis and Galatea*. Ovid tells how she loved a young shepherd Acis but was discovered by Polyphemus who hurled a rock at him. As it fell Galatea turned Acis into a river which henceforth bore his name. A later story made her bear a son to Polyphemus who became the eponymous ancestor of the Gauls ('Galatians'; see below).

Gala'tians (Galătae), a Gallic people (i.e. *Celts) who crossed the Hellespont from Europe into Asia Minor in the third century BC and settled in Phrygia, in the area surrounding modern Ankara in central Turkey. In a Greek-speaking part of the world they maintained their tribal system and language for several centuries. A warlike people, they terrorized western Asia for more than a century. Attalus I of Pergamum inflicted a notable defeat on them some time before 230 BC and they were finally subdued in 188 BC by the Roman proconsul Manlius Vulso. The emperor Augustus created the province of Galatia in 25 BC by adding adjacent territories to Galatia proper. The apostle Paul passed through the latter region on his second missionary journey, but it is uncertain whether his Epistle was written to the inhabitants of Galatia proper or to churches in the whole province.

Galba, Se'rvius Sulpi'cius (*c*.3 BC–AD 69), Roman emperor for about six months in 68–9 in succession to Nero. He came from a patrician family and had enjoyed the favour of previous emperors. After a distinguished military career he was from AD 60 governor of eastern Spain, until Vindex, governor of western Gaul, rebelled against the emperor Nero in 68 and invited Galba to replace him. Vindex was soon defeated, but then the praetorian guard, after bribery, deserted Nero and declared for Galba. Encouraged, he took the title of Caesar and slowly marched to Rome with Otho, governor of Lusitania, who hoped to be named as Galba's heir. Disappointed in this hope, Otho took advantage of the unpopularity Galba had incurred by his severity and meanness, to conspire with the praetorian guard, and they murdered Galba in AD 69 and proclaimed Otho emperor. Tacitus describes Galba's career and character in book 1 of his *Histories*.

Galen (Gălēnos), of Pergamum (AD 129–99), Greek physician, whose outstanding influence on medicine in ancient and modern times has not been equalled. As a young man he studied and travelled widely, but he spent most of his life at Rome as physician to the emperor Marcus Aurelius, his son Commodus, and Septimius Severus. He was the most learned scientist of his day, satisfying the popular taste of the time with anatomical displays, lectures, and handbooks on medical topics. He was a voluminous writer; almost all his extant works are medical and cover every branch of health and disease, especially physiology and anatomy, but he believed that there was a close connection between medicine and philosophy and wrote a number of commentaries on works of Plato, Aristotle, and Theophrastus as well as on general philosophical and philological topics. He wrote in elegant if somewhat prolix Greek, and was in many ways typical of the cultural life of his time (see SOPHISTIC, SECOND and ATHENAEUS). In his day the medical profession was divided into several mutually antagonistic sects, but Galen was eclectic; he professed allegiance to none and preferred to take from each what seemed to him to be true. After his death his influence caused the various sects to die out. He was a profound admirer of *Hippocrates whose doctrines he professed to be merely reinforcing and augmenting. Much of his physiology was traditional, but his discourses on anatomy and physiological processes reveal his close observation which brought to light many new facts. He followed *Herophilus in maintaining that the arteries contained blood, not air. It appears that he seldom, perhaps never, dissected human bodies, for which opportunities were rare, but used animals of various kinds, preferably apes.

Galen's writings formed the basis of all later medical works. After the ninth century, and the translation of his works into Arabic, he became the standard of medical perfection. His fame in Europe in the Middle Ages probably derived from the influence of the Arabic medical writers, and his opinions and his name were universally invoked even when his writings were little read.

Gale'rius, see CONSTANTINE I.

Galli (Galloi), the eunuch priests of *Cybelē, supposedly named from the river Gallus in Galatia, which flowed near the original temple of Cybele and whose waters were said to madden anyone who drank from them. The priests were thought to castrate themselves in imitation of the act of *Attis, Cybele's cult-partner.

galliambic, see METRE, LATIN 3 (iii).

Gallic, see GAUL, GALATIANS, and CELTS.

Gallic War, the campaigns in which Julius Caesar completed the conquest of Gaul between 58 and 51 BC, and the name by which his commentary on the conquest (in seven books) is commonly known. The narrative is one of the best examples we have of unadorned Latin prose (see *COMMENTARIES* I).

Gallus, Gaius Cornelius (*c.*69–26 BC), soldier and poet, friend of the emperor Augustus and of Virgil. Born at Forum Julii (Fréjus), possibly of a Gallic family, he went to Rome at an early age and rose to equestrian rank. He fought in the civil war on Octavian's side and was one of the commissioners appointed by him in 41 to confiscate land in north Italy and distribute it among his veterans (see VIRGIL). Octavian made him the first prefect of Egypt in 30 BC but after four years he was recalled in disgrace for an offence which remains obscure; Octavian (now called Augustus) formally renounced his friendship, and Gallus committed suicide. Virgil is said to have rewritten the latter half of the fourth Georgic which had formerly contained a eulogy of Gallus.

His poetry, of which only one pentameter line and perhaps tiny papyrus fragments survive, included four books of love-elegies centred upon the poet's mistress, the famous actress Cytheris (also loved by Mark Antony), under the pseudonym of Lycōris. This was a genre which he appears to have originated (see ELEGY). His poetry was influenced by the Hellenistic Greek poets Callimachus and Euphorion, and the Roman *neoterics. Virgil in his tenth Eclogue worked some of Gallus' own lines into his poem.

games, public, see FESTIVALS.

Ga'nymēde (Ganymēdēs), in Greek myth, son of Tros (or Laomedon), king of *Troy, carried off by the gods or the eagle of Zeus or Zeus himself because of his beauty, to be the cup-bearer of Zeus, who gave in exchange to his father a pair of divine horses. In later times he was thought to be immortalized as the zodiacal sign Aquarius. From the Latin version of his name (Catamītus) is derived the word 'catamite'. For the Middle Ages he typified homosexual love, but during the Renaissance his ascent to Zeus symbolized for some the soul's ascent to the absolute.

Garden, the, see EPICURUS.

Gates of Dreams, see DREAMS.

Gaugamē'la, small village east of the river Tigris in Assyria, the scene of the final victory of Alexander the Great over Darius III, king of Persia, in 331 BC.

Gaul (Gallia)
1. *Cisalpine Gaul.* This is the name which the Romans before 42 BC gave to the region of north Italy that lies between the Apennines and the Alps, denoting 'Gaul this side (i.e. south) of the Alps' (as opposed to Transalpine Gaul, or 'Gaul beyond (i.e. north of) the Alps'). The Romans gave the name Galli to the Celtic invaders (see CELTS) who, originating perhaps in the Upper Danube, moved westwards across Europe in the eighth and seventh centuries BC and passed into north Italy *c.*400 BC. Their marauding bands terrorized the country and in 390 BC even captured Rome (see ALLIA). They were a constant menace to Italian security until in the latter part of the third century BC, after a particularly dangerous incursion of a coalition of four Gallic tribes, Rome decided to put an end to the danger by annexing Cisalpine Gaul. This was largely effected by the campaigns of 224–2 but the area was mostly lost again

through Hannibal's invasion of 218. It
was regained in the 190s and by 150 few
Gauls remained in the Cisalpine plain.
The name Gallia Togata was often
applied to this area after it was settled by
the Romans, indicating the numerical
superiority of the togati ('those who wear
the toga', i.e. Romans) over the Gallic
population. Those inhabitants north of
the river Padus (Po) were sometimes
called Transpadani. Cisalpine Gaul was
constituted a Roman province by Sulla in
his settlements of 82 BC, with the river
*Rubicon as its southern boundary. In 42
BC the province was incorporated into
Italy. Under the emperor Augustus the
tribes of the Alpine foothills were conquered, and the Alps thus became the
frontier of Italy.

2. *Transalpine Gaul.* This is the area
that is commonly denoted by the single
word 'Gaul', i.e. modern France. It was
occupied by a population predominantly
Celtic advancing from the Upper Danube
(see 1 above), superimposed upon a race
of earlier inhabitants generally known as
Ligurians. Gaul first came into contact
with the Mediterranean civilization
through the foundation in about 600 BC of
the Greek colony of Massilia (Marseilles). Rome's first interest in Transalpine Gaul arose from the need to secure
communications with her trading ally
Saguntum (Sagunto) in Spain. Communication was usually safeguarded by Massilia but when, in the second century BC,
that city was threatened first by Ligurian
invaders and then by the Celtic tribes of
the Allobrogēs and the Arverni, the
Romans themselves fought and finally
defeated them. These campaigns gave
Rome possession of the Gallic territory
between the Alps and the Rhone as far
north as Geneva; in 121 it was formed
into a province, at first called simply Pro-
vincia (modern Provence). Its territory
was subsequently extended westwards
when in 118 the Roman colony of Narbo
(Narbonne) was established, and the
province was then called Gallia Narbonensis; the Romans thereby commanded the road into Spain through
the eastern Pyrenees. Narbo became a
commercial rival to Greek Massilia,
which remained nominally independent.
The next threat came from incursions

of Northmen, the Cimbri and Teutones,
who caused terrible devastation in Gaul
at the end of the second century BC.
These were finally crushed by Marius in
101, after which there was no great movement of peoples until 58. In this year
Julius Caesar, after the expiry of his consulship in 59, obtained Cisalpine and Narbonese Gaul for his province at a time
when Transalpine Gaul had already suffered an invasion of Germanic peoples
under Ariovistus, and an invasion from
the Helvetii was threatening. For the
events of the next few years see COMMEN-
TARIES 1. By 51 Caesar had finally subjugated the whole of Transalpine Gaul, a
country twice as large as Italy, and given
it the structure of a province. He divided
the country into three parts (excluding
Narbonese Gaul, a fourth), namely
Aquitania, Celtica, and Belgica. The
final settlement of Gaul was the work of
Augustus: between 27 and 13 BC Narbonese Gaul became a senatorial province; the other three parts, often known
collectively as Gallia Comata ('long-
haired'), became one imperial province
which was eventually redivided into
three, the divisions deliberately cutting
across ethnic boundaries. Celtica disappeared and the division known as Lug-
dunensis came into being, named after
the new settlement at Lugdunum
(Lyons).

Romanization was very rapid, and in
the late empire Gaul produced several
interesting Latin writers, including
*Ausonius, Paulinus of Nola, and *Sido-
nius. The Roman empire in Gaul came
to an end in the fifth century AD with the
withdrawal of the garrisons and the
gradual development into separate kingdoms of those settlements made by the
barbarian invaders of the fourth and fifth
centuries. See FALL OF ROME and FRANKS.

Gē, alternative form of *Gaia.

geese, sacred, see MANLIUS CAPITOLINUS.

Gēla, Greek city on the south coast of
Sicily founded in 688 BC by Cretans and
Rhodians, itself colonizing *Acragas a
century later. Under the tyrants Cleander
and Hippocrates it became the most
powerful city in the island, but in 485 its

tyrant *Gelon transferred himself and a large proportion of the population to Syracuse, leaving his brother Hieron in control at Gela. It was repopulated in 466 and prospered; Aeschylus died there in 456. After being sacked by the Carthaginians in 406, together with Acragas and Camarina, it was abandoned by the tyrant of Syracuse, Dionysius I, and in 280 BC the remaining inhabitants departed to a new foundation. One remarkable surviving monument is the fortifications built by *Timoleon, the great Corinthian general of the fourth century BC and liberator of Sicily.

Ge'llius, Aulus (*c.* AD 130–perhaps 180), the (Latin) author of *Noctes Atticae* ('Attic nights'), in twenty books, of which all survive except the beginning of the preface and book 8 (for which we have chapter headings). His birthplace is unknown, but he studied literature at Rome before proceeding to Athens where he visited *Herodēs Atticus. His book is a random collection of short essays, based on the Greek and Latin books he had read and the conversations and lectures he had heard, and deals with a great variety of topics: philosophy, history, law, grammar, literary and textual criticism, antiquarian knowledge, and many other subjects. He began collecting his material during the winter nights in Attica and arranged it in later life for the amusement and instruction of his children. It contains thousands of curious and interesting passages from works no longer extant, and is a mine of information on Greek and Latin authors; we are particularly indebted to him for the preservation of many passages from early Latin literature, and, among many good stories, for that of Androclus and the lion (5. 14).

Gelon (*c.*540–478 BC), tyrant of *Gela (*c.*491–485) and subsequently of Syracuse (485–478), in (Greek) Sicily. During his tyranny Syracuse became the leading Hellenic power of the time; the mainland Greeks sought his aid against Persia (in the Persian Wars), but withdrew on his making it a condition that he should have supreme command. In alliance with *Theron, tyrant of Acragas, he defeated at Himera in 480 a great Carthaginian expedition, traditionally on the same day as the Greeks defeated the Persians at Salamis.

gē'nius, literally 'the begetter', in Roman belief a man's guardian spirit, which enabled him to beget children; the marriage-bed, *lectus genialis*, was its sphere. A household worshipped the *genius* of the house on the birthday of the *paterfamilias*, head of the family, in whom it was thought to reside. Its symbol was the house-snake; by many it was identified with the *lar*. The idea was extended so that places and even corporations might be said to have their own genius. We hear of a *genius populi Romani*, 'genius of the Roman people', and a *genius urbis Romae*, 'genius of the city of Rome', and the practice of slaves venerating the genius of their master led in imperial times to the cult of the emperor's genius. Although in the post-classical period the word sometimes refers to 'talent' or 'inspiration' in literature, it seems not to have had the senses it usually has in modern English, intellectual power of a very high order, or the person possessing it, or the prevalent spirit of a nation, age, language, etc. The corresponding spirit in women was known as *Iuno* (Juno).

gĕnos (pl. *genē*), in the Greek social system, a 'clan' or group of families claiming descent in the male line from one ancestor; it was narrower than a *phratry. Naturally most is heard about noble families whose ultimate ancestor was reputedly a hero or god; their family name was usually in patronymic form (see NAMES), meaning 'the descendants of . . .'. Not all citizens were members of a *genos*; the Athenian *gene* were probably entirely aristocratic. Powerful *gene* at Athens were the Philaidae (the clan of Miltiades and Cimon) and the *Alcmaeonidae. The *genos* could come together as a body for the specific function of worshipping the ancestor; it generally met at least once a year to elect officials, pass decrees, and enrol new members, who had to be the lawful (including adopted) sons of existing members. At Athens the *gene* were often referred to as the *Eupatridae.

genre, in literature, a class or type of literary work, such as epic, lyric, tragedy, or comedy. In classical literature the genres were carefully distinguished from each other not only by subject-matter but also by formal aspects such as dialect (in Greek), vocabulary, and metre, and the conventions of each genre were strictly adhered to. Ignorance of these has sometimes resulted in misplaced criticism, as when Samuel Johnson found 'inherently improbable' the poet Milton's pastoral elegy *Lycidas*.

gens (pl. *gentēs*), in the Roman social system, a 'clan' or group of families bearing a common name or *nomen* (see NAMES) and descended in the male line from one ancestor whom, in distinction from the Greeks, they neither recorded nor worshipped (compare *genos*). Originally the *gentes* were aristocratic, *patrician families, but in early times the wealthiest *plebeian families organized themselves also into *gentes* and some probably gained admission to the patrician *gentes*. This supposition, if correct, would explain the existence of both patrician and plebeian families within the same *gens*. A *gens* had certain common property (including a burial ground), held meetings of its members, and performed religious rites in common.

Geogra'phica, see STRABO.

geography, (*geōgraphia,* 'description of the earth'). For Homer and Hesiod the earth was a plane land mass of circular contour around the Mediterranean basin, surrounded by the stream of Ocean, and the first world maps drawn by Anaximander and Hecataeus in the sixth century BC largely supported this view. The Greeks and Romans knew of three continents, *Europe, *Asia, and *Africa (Libya), but of none of them fully. It was generally believed that the distance from east to west was twice that from north to south. During the fifth century works of descriptive geography began to be written. Herodotus' *Histories* contain much geographical and ethnological material. *Ctesias wrote a geographical treatise and the first separate work on India. Two fourth-century historians, *Ephorus and *Timaeus, devoted several books to de-scriptive geography. The conquests of Alexander the Great and the opening up of western Europe by the Romans in the second and first centuries BC resulted in many treatises being written. The most notable work of descriptive geography to survive is that of the Greek *Strabo (first century BC to first century AD) who combined physical, historical, political, and mathematical geography. This last had been made possible by Aristotle's proof (*c*.350 BC) of the earth's sphericity and his introduction of the general principle of dividing the globe into zones. *Eratosthenes (*c*.275–194 BC) established mathematical geography as a science and *Ptolemy applied its principles in the first half of the second century AD. Unfortunately the scientific geographers did not oust the traditional and erroneous beliefs of older writers, which were perpetuated in the compilations of late antiquity. (See also POMPONIUS MELA.)

Geometric age, name given to one of the five periods of the Greek era (based on the differences in pottery styles), denoting very roughly the period 875–750 BC. (Compare PROTO-GEOMETRIC, ORIENTALIZING, ARCHAIC, and CLASSIC. See also IRON AGE.)

Georgics (*gĕōrgica,* 'husbandry'), *Virgil's didactic poem (in four books and over 2,000 hexameter lines) written in imitation of the *Works and Days* of the early Greek poet Hesiod. Virgil spent seven years (36–29 BC) on its composition and dedicated it to his patron Maecenas. His debt to the *Works and Days* is relatively small. The *Georgics* are much more sophisticated in thought and in technique, and owe something to the polished versification of the later Greek didactic poets such as *Aratus of Soli and *Nicander. The poet derived some factual information from *Varro's prose handbook *De re rustica* ('on farming') published in 37 BC (and he was perhaps also influenced by its moral and patriotic tone). However, Virgil resembles Hesiod in that his intention is not to compose a handbook of instruction for those who wish to be farmers; rather he is presenting a picture of the (Italian) farmer's life as the ideal: it is frugal and austere, prone to setbacks and not free from suffering, but, lived in harmony with nature and with the divine scheme of things, it is morally satisfying and it brings the reward of peace and contentment (2. 458 ff.); it is also the basis of Italy's greatness. For Virgil, as for Hesiod, hard work, *labor improbus*, is essential; he sees the individual as an oarsman rowing upstream whom the current will carry backwards if he slackens his effort (1. 199). Virgil's greatest debt is perhaps to *Lucretius, to whom he alludes obliquely in 2. 490. He recalls that poet not only in phrasing and in style but also in the passion with which he expounds his subject. Nevertheless the *Georgics* are a rebuttal of Lucretius' Epicureanism which asserted that the gods did not intervene in the world; Virgil reasserts divine providence, and dwells affectionately on the gods of the countryside. It was Virgil's deep sympathy for all living things and his sense of the need for men to co-operate with nature that led his English translator John Dryden (1631–1700) to call the *Georgics* 'the best poem of the best poet', a judgement also supported by Virgil's mature mastery of expression. The poem must therefore be seen as far more than a practical guide to farming, which its omissions and inaccuracies could not allow it to be, and to which the philosophical 'digressions' are irrelevant. Ancient critics soon observed that Virgil's aim was to give pleasure rather than instruction.

Book 1 deals with the raising of crops and the signs of the weather, ending emotionally with a description of the horrors suffered by Italy as a consequence of the murder of Julius Caesar; book 2 covers the growing of trees, chiefly the olive and the vine, and also contains magnificent praise of Italy (136 ff.); book 3 deals with the rearing of cattle (concluding with the notable description of the cattle-plague in the Alps); in book 4 Virgil describes beekeeping, treating the bees with affectionate irony as exemplars of the ideal citizen body, 'little Romans' (*parvi Quirites*). The work ends with the episode of *Aristaeus together with the story of Orpheus and Eurydicē. The reason for this latter inclusion is hard to discern; the ancient commentator Servius implausibly suggests that it was written to replace an earlier panegyric of the Roman poet *Gallus which had to be excised after the latter's disgrace. Whatever the reason, it contains some of Virgil's most haunting poetry, and the effect of the highly individualized, hapless love of the poet Orpheus for his beautiful wife Eurydice, following after the description of the busy, orderly, useful, and sexless lives of the bees, is deeply moving.

Geō'rgos ('farmer'), Greek comedy by *Menander, a fragment of which has been recovered from a papyrus. The plot revolves around two neighbours, one a poor widow, Myrrhinē, with a son and a daughter, the other a rich man with a son, by a previous marriage, and a daughter. The rich man's son wishes to marry Myrrhine's daughter, who is already pregnant by him, but his father is arranging to marry him to his half-sister. The farmer of the title, Kleainētos, apparently also wishes to marry the widow's daughter. Presumably in the end it is the rich neighbour's son who succeeds in doing so.

Germā'nia ('Germany'), the name commonly given to a monograph by *Tacitus on the origin, geography, institutions, and tribes of the Germans, published in AD 98. It describes the various tribes north of the Rhine and the Danube, their appearance, political and social customs, and dress; the organization of their army; their religion and land tenure; their sloth alternating with warlike activity; their intemperance and gambling; the exemplary morality of their family life (sarcastically contrasted with the laxity prevailing at Rome). Tacitus then passes on to the geography of the area and the particular characteristics of the several Germanic tribes (including the Swedes and ending with the Finns). As an ethnological work it is somewhat incoherent and some of the material was out of date when Tacitus wrote it, but there seem to be other motives underlying its composition—a desire to point out the corruption of Rome by contrast with the purer morals of the barbarian, and to emphasize the threat Germany posed to Rome's security: 'Germany has afforded more triumphs than victories to Rome'.

Germa'nicus, *cognomen* (see NAMES)

borne by various members of the Julio-Claudian family in Rome. It was originally bestowed by the senate as a title of honour upon Nero Claudius *Drusus (39–8 BC) and his descendants for his victories over the Germans. He was the son of Tiberius Claudius Nero and Livia, and brother of the future emperor Tiberius; he is usually known as Drusus the Elder. The name Germanicus by itself commonly designates Nero Claudius Germanicus (15 BC–AD 19), the elder son of the above Drusus and Antonia Minor (daughter of Mark Antony and Octavia), who was adopted by his uncle Tiberius in AD 4 when the latter was himself adopted by Augustus. Germanicus thus became a member of the Julian *gens*, in line to succeed to the imperial throne, and took the name Germanicus Julius Caesar. Emulating his natural father he too waged successful wars against the Germans (AD 14–16) and won his troops' affection, on which he was able to rely when he quelled the mutiny of the Rhine army in 14. In 17 he was given command over all the eastern provinces, but Tiberius (who perhaps feared his popularity) appointed Cn. Piso as governor of Syria with the open intention of having him as a restraining influence on Germanicus. The two quarrelled and Germanicus ordered Piso to leave his province. Soon after, Germanicus died in mysterious circumstances and his friends accused Piso and his wife Plancina of having poisoned him with the connivance of Tiberius. The death of so admired and popular a leader—he was commonly compared with Alexander the Great—caused widespread grief and resentment in Rome (see Tacitus' vivid description in *Annals* 2. 82). By his wife Agrippina (the Elder) he had nine children who included the future emperor *Gaius (Caligula) and Agrippina (the Younger), the mother of the emperor Nero. He had literary tastes; he is said to have written comedies in Greek, but all are lost; fragments of his Latin translation of the *Phaenomena* of *Aratus still survive, with a few epigrams.

Germany, for the Romans an undefined area east of the Rhine (Rhenus) and north of the Danube (Danubius or Ister).

In the north it comprised what are now Denmark, Sweden, and Norway. The German tribes originated in south Scandinavia and Jutland, and from about 1000 BC they expanded southwards and westwards. According to Tacitus one of the tribes was called Germani, and this name was first used by the Gauls to designate the whole race. It was not until shortly after 120 BC that they entered Roman history, when the tribes of the Cimbri and the Teutones, invading southeast Gaul and, later, northern Italy, inspired great terror at Rome; they were finally destroyed by Roman armies under Marius. Early in the first century BC another German tribe, the Suebi, moved south-west to the area of the rivers Main (Moenus) and Rhine. Their inroads into Gaul in 58 BC led Julius Caesar to drive them back across the Rhine (as related in the first book of Caesar's *Gallic War*), which river became a frontier of the Roman empire. Later, under Augustus, Roman invasions of German territory were systematically undertaken, but the Roman ascendancy in this region was brought to an end in AD 9 when the Roman forces under P. Quinctilius Varus were destroyed by the German chief Arminius. After this disaster Augustus abandoned all attempts to establish a frontier beyond the Rhine, although in the east he established the river Danube as a frontier against tribes from the north. Around AD 90 Domitian formally established the two provinces of Germania Superior (Upper Germany) in the south and Germania Inferior (Lower Germany) in the north. During the reign of Marcus Aurelius (AD 161–80) there occurred a dangerous invasion across the Danube by the Marcomanni, a German tribe who advanced even into Italy and besieged Aquileia (near the coast at the head of the Adriatic Sea). The resulting war continued to the end of the emperor's life, and his successor Commodus had to make a compromise peace with the Germans. During the next three centuries the German tribes, especially the Alemanni and *Franks, harassed Gaul by frequent invasions and finally crossed in great numbers over the Rhine, the Danube, and the Alps, conquering Gaul, Italy, and Spain and even penetrating into Africa. Other tribes such as the Angli and the Saxons had by that time crossed over into Britain. Nearly the whole of western Europe was thus overrun by German tribes. (See also FALL OF ROME.)

gerou'sia, at *Sparta, the council of elders composed of the two kings and twenty-eight other members over 60 years of age, elected for life from certain aristocratic families by measuring the acclamation of the citizens (a method which Aristotle thought childish). As a deliberative body they prepared business for the assembly (see APELLA); as a judicial body they heard cases involving death, exile, or disenfranchisement and could even put the kings on trial.

Ge'ryon (Gēryōn, Gēryonēs, or Gēryoneus), in Greek myth, son of *Chrysaor and Calirrhoē, a three-headed or three-bodied giant living in the far West on an island, Erytheia, in the stream of *Ocean beyond the Pillars of Hercules; there he pastured a herd of magnificent cattle, aided by his herdsman Eurytion and his dog Orthrus. It was one of the labours of Heracles to steal the cattle and drive them back to Greece (see HERACLES, LABOURS OF 10).

Giants (Gigantēs), in Greek myth, monstrous beings of vast size, according to Hesiod sons of Gaia (Earth), conceived from the blood of *Uranus that fell upon the earth when he was castrated. In post-Homeric legend they rebelled against Zeus and the Olympian gods, who, learning that they would not win unless they were assisted by a mortal, called in Heracles. The Giants were defeated at Phlegra (Pallēnē, the westernmost prong of Chalcidice), and were believed to be buried under volcanoes in various parts of Greece and Italy. The Battle of Gods and Giants was a very popular myth in Greece, especially among sculptors, and was sometimes thought of as symbolizing the fight of civilization against barbarism. The events of the three attacks on the Olympian gods made respectively by the *Titans, the Giants, and *Otus and Ephialtes were often confused by the poets. See also HECATONCHEIRES.

gladiators, men who fought with one another in Roman amphitheatres for the amusement of the spectators. Gladiatorial combats were said to have originated in Etruria. They were introduced at Rome in 264 BC, and were at first confined to public funerals, until the games held by Julius Caesar in 46 BC which were only partly commemorative (of his daughter Julia). Under the empire the passion for this amusement reached its height and contributed to the decline of drama at Rome; five thousand pairs fought in the games given by Trajan in AD 107 to celebrate the conclusion of the Dacian War. Gladiators were selected from prisoners of war, condemned criminals, slaves bought for the purpose, or volunteers who took part for a fee. In late republican times large numbers were trained in gladiatorial schools and retained by private individuals, becoming a danger to law and order (see MILO). It was from a school in Capua that *Spartacus escaped to lead a slave revolt in 73 BC. There were several types of gladiator: the *murmillo*, who fought with helmet, oblong shield, and sword, and had a fish for crest on his helmet; he usually fought a *retiarius*, who was lightly clad and armed only with a net and trident; there were also the Samnite, armed with oblong shield, visored helmet, and sword, and the Thracian, with round shield and curved scimitar. The poet Statius mentions women and dwarfs among the combatants. A repeatedly successful gladiator might receive by favour of the people a wooden sword (*rudis*), a token of his discharge from service. A wounded gladiator raised his forefinger to ask for the mercy of the spectators. They signified their decision either by pressing the thumb against the forefinger (*premere pollicem*) as a sign of good omen (apparently), thereby sparing his life, or by turning the thumb upwards or towards the breast (*vertere pollicem*) to signify the death-stroke. See also VENATIONES.

Glau'cia, Gaius Servi'lius, Roman politician. As tribune (101 BC) and praetor (100) he co-operated with Marius and *Saturninus, and passed a law restoring the *repetundae* court to the equites. He hoped to be consul for 99 BC but his candidature was disallowed. He fled with Saturninus, but the senate had them arrested and they died in prison.

Glaucus. In Greek myth, the name of several characters, including the following.

1. A fisherman from Anthedon in Boeotia who saw a fish which he had caught come to life when he laid it on a certain herb. He ate the herb, sprang into the sea, and became immortal, turning into an oracular god of the sea. He figured in some versions of the story of the *Argonauts.

2. Son of Sisyphus and Meropē and (usually reputed to be) father of *Bellerophon. He inherited his father's kingdom of Corinth but kept a team of mares at Potniae in Boeotia. These he did not allow to breed, but the goddess Aphroditē, angered, drove them mad (or they went mad because Glaucus fed them on human flesh, or for some other reason); they killed Glaucus when he lost the chariot race at the funeral games of Pelias, and ate him. His ghost, known as Taraxippus, was supposed to haunt the stadium and frighten the horses at the Isthmian games (held near Corinth). Aeschylus' tragedy *Glaucus Potnieus* ('Glaucus of Potniae') was one of the trilogy that included the *Persae*, produced in 472 BC. Only fragments survive.

3. In Homer's *Iliad*, a grandson of Bellerophon and leader (after *Sarpedon) of the Lycian allies of the Trojans. During the battle he confronted the Greek Diomedes, but when they found that their grandfathers were bound by ties of hospitality they exchanged armour, Glaucus giving Diomedes his equipment, made of gold and worth a hundred oxen, and receiving the other's of bronze, worth nine. He was killed by Ajax, son of Telamon.

glyco'nic, see METRE, GREEK 8 (i).

Gnātho, the parasite in the *Eunuchus* of Terence.

gnō'mē, gnōmic verse. *Gnōmē*, in Greek, literally 'expression of opinion', is used to describe the pithy expression of an acknowledged truth. The most famous *gnomai* are those inscribed on the temple at Delphi, *gnōthi sauton* ('know thy-

self') and *mēden agan* ('nothing in excess'). They are frequent in the poetry of Hesiod and Euripides. Gnomic poetry, usually written in elegiacs and embodying popular wisdom, can be traced back to *Phocylidēs and *Theognis in the mid-sixth century BC.

gno'sticism, the name (derived from the Greek *gnōsis*, 'knowledge') given to a complex religious movement based on a myth of redemption. It was perhaps pre-Christian in origin, but it became prominent in the second century AD and had Christian as well as pagan forms. Gnosticism distinguished between a remote and unknowable divinity and a *Demiurge descended in some way from the former, who was the (imperfect) creator and ruler of the world, his imperfect creation. Some individuals, however, possessed a spark of the divine spiritual substance and these might hope, by correct observances in this world, to return to the divinity after death. A redeemer was sent, perhaps Christ (or there might be another redeemer still to come), from the divinity, who brought *gnosis* and temporarily inhabited the body of a human being. Gnosticism in various forms persisted for many centuries.

gods

1. *Greek*. The Greeks thought of their most important gods as living on Mount *Olympus and numbering twelve. The number was fixed, although some slight variation of names was possible. The Olympian gods who appear as the central group on the east frieze of the Parthenon are Zeus, Hera, Poseidon, Athena, Apollo, Artemis, Aphroditē, Hermes, Demeter, Dionysus, Hephaestus, and Arēs. It is likely that Hestia was originally one of the canonical twelve and was replaced by Dionysus. Lesser gods who were sometimes important in cult include Asclepius, Cabeiri, Charitēs, Cybelē, Eileithyia, Enyalios, Eros, Hadēs, Hecatē, Helios, Leto, Leucothea, Muses, Pan, Thetis, Titans, and various sea-gods (Glaucus, Nereus, Pontus, and Proteus). For each of these, see under the name.

2. *Roman*. See DIANA, FLORA, JANUS, JUNO, JUPITER, LARES, MAIA, MARS, MERCURY, MINERVA, PENATES, QUIRINUS, TERMINUS, VENUS, VESTA, and VULCAN.

Golden Age. The Greek poet Hesiod was the first to describe earlier races or generations of men who lived in happier times than we, and the earliest, whose life was most idyllic, was the Golden race, who lived at a time when the ruling god was not yet Zeus but his father *Cronus (Saturn at Rome). This race was succeeded by progressively inferior races, those of silver, bronze, and iron, the last being our own; the deterioration was interrupted by the race of *heroes (those who fought in the Theban and Trojan wars) who immediately preceded us. The Roman poets Horace, Virgil, and Ovid all borrowed the idea, but the Romans, in translating the Greek word *genos*, 'generation' or 'race', by the Latin *saeculum*, incidentally introduced the additional meaning of the latter, namely 'age' or 'long period of time'. Hence there came about the idea of a Golden Age.

The term 'Golden Age' has also been used by literary critics to describe the *Ciceronian and *Augustan ages of Latin literature.

Golden Ass, see APULEIUS.

Golden Bough. In Virgil's *Aeneid*, book 6, Aeneas is told by the Cumaean Sibyl that he must find and pluck a 'golden bough' for Proserpine before he can enter the Underworld. This idea seems to be an invention of Virgil's own; Servius, the fourth-century commentator on Virgil, associated it with the cult of the goddess *Diana at Aricia, where there was a sacred tree from which a branch had first to be broken off by the runaway slave who wished to kill the priest and take his place. This legend of ritual killing can be paralleled in other societies, and from this starting-point Sir James Frazer developed his great work on the evolution of religious beliefs and institutions, the *Golden Bough* (1890–1915).

Golden Fleece, the fleece of the ram that had carried away Phrixus and *Hellē, sought by Jason and the *Argonauts.

Golden House (Domus Aurea), the vast palace built by the emperor Nero in Rome after the great fire of AD 64, covering, it is calculated, about 50 hectares (125 acres) between the Palatine and Esquiline hills; the centre-piece was an ornamental lake in the valley later occupied by the Colosseum.

Golden Milestone, see MILIARIUM AUREUM.

Gordian knot. Alexander the Great, on his arrival at Gordium in Phrygia, found in the acropolis there an ox-cart of which the pole was fastened to the yoke by a knot of cornel-bark. According to legend, in ancient times a Phrygian peasant called Gordius, his wife, and son *Midas chanced to arrive in this cart at an assembly of the Phrygians, who had just been told by an oracle that a cart would bring them a king to put an end to the civil disturbances. The Phrygians at once made Gordius king, and he dedicated to Zeus in the acropolis at the town subsequently named Gordium his cart and the yoke to which the oxen had been fastened. A further oracle declared that whoever could untie the knot, which had defeated all attempts to undo it, should reign over Asia. Alexander cut the knot with his sword and applied the oracle to himself. 'To cut the Gordian knot' thus signifies drastic action to solve a difficulty.

Go'rgias, of Leontini in Sicily (*c*.483–*c*.385 BC), one of the most influential of the Greek *sophists whose particular expertise was the teaching of rhetoric, based less upon systematic treatment of the subject-matter than upon mannered, poetic, and effective expression. He made his pupils learn typical passages by heart. He appears in one or two of Plato's dialogues (see below), where he is treated with a certain amount of respect (although Agathon's speech in the *Symposium* is a telling parody of his style). His speeches delivered in Athens in 427 when he headed an embassy from his home-town stunned the Athenians with the brilliance and novelty of their style (see RHETORIC). His extant *Encomium of Helen* and *Defence of Palamedes* illustrate both his confidence that the well-taught orator could with ingenuity find arguments to support any case and also his remarkable prose style, with its short symmetrical clauses, rhythmically balanced antitheses, verbal echoes, and play on words. Part of a funeral oration also survives, and a fragment on the paradoxical theme that 'nothing exists'. Gorgias later travelled about Greece giving lectures, dying at a great age at Larisa in Thessaly. His influence has been detected in Antiphon, Thucydides, and especially in the speeches of *Isocrates.

Go'rgias, dialogue by *Plato named after the famous sophist (see above). Socrates opens the dialogue by asking Gorgias to define rhetoric. The latter replies that it is the most important of human concerns because successful statesmanship depends not upon knowing what should be done and advising accordingly, but upon having the knack of persuasive speech. A successful orator can therefore act as he pleases, justly or unjustly. When Gorgias retires his pupil Polus takes up the argument; Socrates makes him agree, against his will, that it is better to suffer injustice than to do it, and that when one has done evil it is better to be punished than to go unpunished. When Polus retires his place is taken by a certain Callicles (otherwise unknown to us), who in a manner foreshadowing Nietzsche argues that virtue and happiness are to be found in the exercise of lawless self-will, for those who are capable of it. The issue of the dialogue is suddenly seen to be the choice a man has to make between a life of action of the kind Callicles stands for and a life of philosophy represented by Socrates. Socrates reinforces his own choice of philosophy with a passionate denunciation of the 'great' Athenian statesmen of the past, Pericles, Cimon, and Miltiades, and emerges himself as the only true statesman because he alone improves his fellow citizens. At the climax of the dialogue there is a myth, the earliest in Plato, of the judgement of the soul after death, perhaps as an additional incentive to avoid injustice.

Gorgons (Gorgonēs), in Greek myth, female monsters. Homer seems to know only one Gorgon: in the *Iliad* her head adorns the *aegis of the goddess Athena and inspires terror. According to Hesiod there were three Gorgons, Sthenno ('mighty'), Euryalē ('wide-wanderer'), and Medusa ('queen'), living in the far West, by the stream of Ocean, daughters of the sea deities Phorcys and his sister Ceto, and sisters of the Graiae. They are often given monstrous features such as serpents in their hair and glaring eyes. Medusa, who alone was mortal, and whose head was so fearful that anyone who looked at it was turned to stone, was loved by Poseidon and pregnant by him when *Perseus killed her. At the moment of her death she gave birth to Pegasus and Chrysaor ('golden-sword'). The head of Medusa was said to be buried under a mound in the agora of Argos, where it was probably thought to have apotropaic power, and the representation of the head or Gorgoneion was often carved as a protective figure on armour and walls. In the art of the fifth century BC the head is humanized, and later is often shown as beautiful in death.

Gortyn, an ancient and important city of Crete. Much has been excavated and among the many inscriptions found is the famous 'code of Gortyn', dating from *c.*450 BC, which enumerates many of the city's laws and is the most important source of prehellenistic Greek law.

Goths, a Germanic people originating in the Baltic area who moved southwards and settled to the north of the Black Sea, whence in the third century AD they attacked the territory of the Roman empire. Around 370 the Ostrogoths (East Goths) of the Ukraine were overwhelmed by the *Huns, as later were the *Visigoths (West Goths) on the river Tyras (Dniester). The latter subsequently moved into Italy; the former migrated in the fifth century, and eventually, in 489, under their leader Theodoric the Great, reached Italy also, having been ordered by the emperor in the East to 'secure' it from the first barbarian king, *Odo(v)acer. Peace was made between the two in 493; Theodoric was proclaimed king of Italy and took *Ravenna as his capital. He appears in the medieval German poem the *Nibelungenlied* as 'Dietrich von Bern' (i.e. Theodoric of Verona). The Gothic language is the most primitive German language known to us. See also ANTHIMUS and FALL OF ROME.

Gracchi, the, Roman statesmen and social reformers, the two brothers Tiberius Sempronius Gracchus (*c.*164–133 BC) and Gaius Sempronius Gracchus (*c.*153–121 BC). They were among the twelve children of Tiberius Sempronius Gracchus, the censor, a man of high character and liberal thought, famous for his austerity. He married *Cornelia, the daughter of Scipio Africanus, and died in 154 BC.

1. Tiberius Sempronius Gracchus, like his father, served with distinction in Spain, winning popular acclaim by negotiating a treaty that saved many Roman lives. In 133 he was elected tribune, and—alarmed by the concentration of land and wealth in the hands of a few—proposed a law aimed at alleviating poverty by redistributing public land. The law was passed, but in haste and by unconventional means that included deposing a hostile tribune, M. Octavius. When Tiberius further proposed that the property of Attalus III of Pergamum, bequeathed to Rome, should be used to finance the new allotment-holders, and when he unconstitutionally sought re-election, the senate was persuaded that he was aiming at a tyranny. His cousin Scipio Nasica led a mob of senators and their clients against Tiberius, killing him and many of his supporters on the Capitol. Tiberius' tribunate marks the advent of violence upon the Roman political scene, and the beginning of the disintegration of the senate's power under the attacks of its own members who supported the people.

2. Gaius Sempronius Gracchus, the younger brother of Tiberius, was with Scipio Aemilianus in Spain in 133 when news of Tiberius' murder arrived. He returned to Rome, where he was already a member of the agrarian commission, but he seems not to have been very active in public life until he gained the quaestorship in 126 and was sent to Sardinia. After two years there he returned to Rome and was elected tribune for 123 and again for 122. The first laws he proposed were aimed at taking vengeance on his brother's enemies; he then passed a series of laws aimed at alleviating poverty as well as winning the support of the people. Other laws were aimed at limit-ing the power of senators. He proposed to establish a number of colonies, mainly in Italy, but including one on the site of Carthage, and early in 122 set out for Africa to supervise the settlement of this. During his absence the tribune Livius Drusus (who enjoyed senatorial support) managed to turn the people against him. Gaius failed to obtain re-election for 121, and violence broke out between the Gracchans and their enemies. The senate declared a public emergency (the first recorded use of the *senatus consultum ultimum*), and Gaius, finding himself cut off, ordered a slave to kill him (see FURRINA).

Gaius was the more able of the Gracchi; an astute politician and impassioned orator (some fragments of his speeches survive), he used his skills to promote the radical reforms he saw were necessary, but which his enemies' success nullified. The results were disastrous for Rome, leading to the civil wars of the next century.

Graces, the (Gk. Charĭtĕs, Lat. Gratiae), in myth, minor goddesses, usually said to be daughters of Zeus and to be three in number, called by the Greek poet Hesiod Euphrosynē, Aglaia (sometimes said to be Hephaestus' wife), and Thalia. They are the personification of the grace and beauty that enhance the enjoyment of life. Thus they accompany the Muses, and the most perfect works of art are called the work of the Graces; they give wisdom its charm, they moderate the exciting influence of wine, and they accompany Aphroditē and Eros. For later Romans they were also the symbols of gratitude. They had cults of their own in various parts of Greece (notably an ancient one at Orchomenus in Boeotia), and are often made attendants on other gods. In early times the Graces were portrayed clothed, but later they were always shown naked.

Gradi'vus, a name often applied to *Mars, probably signifying 'he who marches forth'.

Graiae, in Greek myth, Pemphrēdo, Enўo, and Deino, daughters of Phorcys and Ceto and sisters of the *Gorgons, the personification of old age, grey-haired from birth, with one eye and one tooth between them. *Perseus stole their eye and so made them tell him where to find the Gorgons.

Gra'ttius (less correct Grātius), Augustan poet mentioned by Ovid, the author of a Latin poem on hunting (*Cynē-getica*) of which 536 hexameters survive.

Greece. In the ancient world Greece comprised an area of the Balkan peninsula comparable with that of modern Greece. It may be divided into three parts: (i) the peninsula south of the Isthmus of Corinth, known as the Peloponnese; (ii) the land north of the Isthmus roughly as far as the Ambracian Gulf in the west and the river Peneius in the east, which includes Thessaly and is in many contexts known as Greece proper (or mainland Greece); and (iii) the northern regions comprising Epirus, Macedonia, and Thrace, whose inhabitants were regarded as scarcely Greek by the states in the southern regions. For the main ethnic divisions of the Greek people in historical times, see HELLEN. To a large extent the north of Greece was cut off from the rest by the mountain ranges in that area, and Greece itself from the rest of Europe by the high mountain chain that runs from Thrace to Italy. Greece is a land dominated by mountains, which have been held to be the reason for the political development of the country into a scatter of independent states each centred on a pocket of arable land.

Despite the fact that Greece was made up of a large number of independent communities, the Greeks formed a single people, with one and the same civilization (see HELLAS); they spoke the same language and were distinguished thereby from the '*barbarians'; there was a broad similarity in their political institutions (government in city-states, normally under oligarchic or democratic constitutions); they had a common religion and respected the same oracular shrines; they had a common heritage of literature from Homer onwards and their art, despite certain diversities, had unity; many of the Greek colonies were founded in common by emigrants from more than one state. The social unity of Greece manifested itself in the common festivals and games; and some degree of political unity was shown in the combined resistance to Persia. But the various attempts, such as that of Pericles, to consolidate this unity always collapsed before the jealously independent spirit of the different states.

The Greeks called their country Hellas and themselves Hellenes (originally the name of a tribe in south Thessaly). Graii, the local name of a tribe in west Greece, became the Latin name for the Greeks in general; *Graeci* and *Graecia* ('Greeks' and 'Greece') are derivatives from Graii. It has been suggested that the Graii took part in the colonization of Cumae, the oldest Greek colony in Italy, and from them the name was applied more widely. When the Romans created the province of Greece in 27 BC they called it Achaea.

The phrase 'Greek world' describes that part of the world at the time in question in which Greek was, or had become, the principal language, or was the language of the rulers and the administration. Apart from Greece and the Peloponnese, together with Epirus, Macedonia, and Thrace, it might include Magna Graecia and Sicily (during the Greek classical period; both were slowly Romanized), Egypt and Cyrenaica (see CYRENE), Asia Minor, and to a varying extent lands to the east and south: Syria, north Arabia, and even Mesopotamia (Iraq) and beyond. Rome began to take over the Greek world in the second century BC and had done so before the end of the first century BC.

griffin or **gryphon** (Gk. *gryps*), fabulous animal with the body of a lion and the head and wings of an eagle, supposed to dwell in the far north between the Hyperboreans and the one-eyed Arimaspians, guarding the gold of the north. The conception would seem to be eastern in origin.

groma'tici, Roman land-surveyors (Lat. *groma*, a measuring rod). During the empire several Latin authors wrote on surveying, including *Frontinus and *Hyginus; the former's treatise is known to us only in extracts.

Gyas, in Virgil's *Aeneid*, a companion of Aeneas; he figures in the boat-race (book

5). Also, the name of a Latin slain by Aeneas (*Aeneid* 10. 318).

Gy'es, see HECATONCHEIRES.

Gygēs, king of Lydia (*c*.685–*c*.657 BC); he founded the dynasty of the Mermnadae by killing the king Candaules (called Myrsilus by the Greeks). According to Herodotus he was the favourite officer of Candaules who, being proud of his wife's beauty, insisted that Gyges should see the queen naked while remaining himself hidden. The queen, however, sensed his presence, and later summoned Gyges to offer him the choice of dying himself or murdering the king and taking the kingdom, with her as his queen. He chose the latter course. Plato in *Republic*, book 2, tells the story that Gyges won the queen and the kingdom by means of a magic ring of invisibility, to illustrate the view that men are not virtuous when they need not fear the consequences of their actions. 'Gyges' ring' subsequently became proverbial, as did 'the riches of Gyges'. He reputedly sent rich gifts to Delphi in gratitude for an oracle which established his right to the throne. He was the first Lydian king to try to extend his rule over the Greek cities of the Ionian coast.

Gyli'ppus, Spartan general sent in 414 BC to help the Syracusans against the Athenians during the Peloponnesian War. Under his leadership the Athenian fleet and army were utterly destroyed. He was convicted at Sparta in 405 of embezzling public funds and went into exile.

gymnasia'rchia, see GYMNASIUM and LITURGY.

gymna'sium (Gk. *gymnos*, 'naked'), in Greece, a (gymnastic) school, its name derived from the practice among Greek boys and men of exercising naked. Education to the Greeks meant a training both intellectual and physical (in preparation for war), and the gymnasia catered for both. While intellectual training ceased after youth, gymnastics were practised at all ages. In Sparta there were no gymnasia since all male citizens from the age of 7 were engaged exclusively in military training. At Athens, on the other hand, three gymnasia, the *Lyceum, the *Academy, and the *Cynosargēs, became famous schools of philosophy. By the Hellenistic age the gymnasium had become an essential element of Greek life, and a hallmark of Hellenism.

Gymnopae'diae, an annual festival 'of the naked youths' at Sparta. It was held in July, lasted for several days, and included displays of gymnastics and dancing by boys and men; hymns were sung in honour of the gods and Spartan heroes.

H

Habro'comēs and Anthei'a (or *Ephesiaca*), *novel by Xenophon of Ephesus.

Hādēs (Haidēs, Ăidēs, or Ăidōneus), also known as Plūto (the Latin form of the Greek Ploutōn, 'the wealth-giver'), or Dis (the contracted form of Latin *dives*, 'rich'); in Greek myth, one of the three sons of Cronus and Rhea, and brother of Zeus and Poseidon. When the three cast lots for their domains (see ZEUS), Hades obtained the Underworld. He and his wife *Persephonē are the rulers of the dead. Although he is therefore a grim and dreaded god, he is not an enemy to mankind, nor to his brothers. Plato observes that out of fear people prefer to call him by the euphemistic name of Plouton because all metals are found under the earth. The etymology of Hades is uncertain; it may mean 'the unseen one'. The name in Greek nearly always designates the god, not his kingdom, to which it was later extended by natural usage: the dead were said to go 'to (the house of) Hades'. His kingdom was thought of as underground, despite the tendency of Greeks to locate the abode of the dead in the West. The two ideas were reconciled by supposing the entrance to be at some locality in the West. In Homer's *Iliad* it is in the far West beyond the stream of *Ocean (which was believed to encircle the earth). Later it was thought to be approached by various natural chasms. Details in the description of the realm of Hades also vary. It contains the dreary Plain of Asphodel, where the ghosts of the dead lead a vague, unsubstantial life. A few fortunate ones escape this fate and are taken to *Elysium, while those who have been enemies of the gods are removed to *Tartarus for punishment. Generally the realm of the dead is separated from that of the living by one of the rivers of Hades, *Styx or *Acheron. Across this the dead, provided they have been duly buried, are ferried by *Charon. At the entrance of the Underworld stands the watch-dog *Cerberus who prevents any of the dead from going out again. Within sit the judges of the dead, *Minos, *Rhadamanthys, and *Aeacus, who assign to each ghost its appropriate abode. Besides Styx and Acheron, three other rivers intersect the Underworld, Phlegethon or Pyriphlegethon ('the fiery one'), *Cocytus, and (in Latin poetry) *Lēthē. Black sheep were sacrificed to Hades but he had very little cult, and few statues of him exist. He figures little in myth except for the story of Persephone. See also AFTERLIFE.

Hadrian (Publius Aelius Hādriānus), Roman emperor AD 117–38. He was born in 76 in Spain, and when left fatherless entered the household of Trajan, to whom he was distantly connected. He won favour and held significantly high offices, but his adoption by the childless emperor Trajan on the latter's deathbed surprised and displeased some; nevertheless the senate sanctioned his succession. He passed the years 120–31 in touring the provinces, visiting *Britain in 121 or 122 and spending at least two years in Athens, a city he greatly loved. While he was in Egypt in 130 his favourite companion *Antinŏus, then aged about 20, was drowned. These travels reinforced his intention to aim at peace and sound defences in his foreign policy—hence the Wall across Britain; he renounced those eastern conquests of Trajan which could not be secured. A revolt in Judaea, 132–5, was the only serious war of his reign.

Hadrian was the most intellectual and cultivated of all the emperors, and a generous patron. Most places he visited benefited from his liberality. In Rome he founded the Athenaeum, an institute for lectures and recitations, built the *Pantheon, the temple of Venus and Rome, and his mausoleum (modern Castel S. Angelo) together with the bridge, Pons Aelius, by which it was approached. He also built an extensive villa at Tibur

(Tivoli), which has been a rich source of art treasures. His attitude towards Christianity was tolerant as far as was consistent with good order. Hadrian died reputedly with a poem addressed to his soul on his lips, '*animula, vagula, blandula*' ('little soul, wandering, pleasant . . .'). His other works, which include speeches, letters, and an autobiography, are lost.

Hadrian's Wall, see BRITAIN.

Haedui, see AEDUI.

Haemon, son of Creon; see OEDIPUS.

Halicarna'ssus, city in *Caria on the south-west coast of Asia Minor near the island of Cos, the birthplace of Herodotus and Dionysius. In classical times its culture was Ionian. The strength and beauty of its position led *Mausolus, king of Caria in the fourth century BC, to make it his capital.

Halieu'tica. 1. Latin poem wrongly attributed to *Ovid, of which a fragment survives.
2. Greek didactic poem in five books of hexameters by *Oppian.

hamadry'ads, *nymphs of trees, whose lives were co-terminous with their trees.

Hami'lcar. 1. Carthaginian general at the battle of Himera (480 BC) in which he was defeated and killed by *Gelon, tyrant of Syracuse. He was the first to organize the Carthaginian army.
2. **Hamilcar Barca** (d. 229 BC), general appointed at a young age to command the Carthaginian forces in Sicily during the First *Punic War against Rome in 247 BC. He seized Herctē on the north coast of Sicily in the midst of enemy territory and held it for three years while raiding the Italian coast as far as Cumae. In 244 he abruptly left and took the town at the foot of Mount Eryx, where he defied the Romans for another two years. After the Carthaginian naval defeat at Aegates Insulae in 241 he negotiated the terms of peace and resigned his command. In 237 he went to Spain, perhaps intending to form there a new empire for Carthage, to compensate for the loss of Sicily and Sardinia, and to provide wealth and manpower for a new onslaught against the hated Romans. He was drowned during the siege of a Spanish town, leaving three sons, *Hannibal, *Hasdrubal, and Mago, all of whom distinguished themselves in the Second Punic War.

Ha'nnibal (247–183/2 BC), eldest son of *Hamilcar Barca and the great leader of the Carthaginians against Rome in the Second *Punic War. Hamilcar took him to Spain in 237, after making him swear eternal hatred to Rome, a story told by Hannibal himself. When *Hasdrubal (1) was assassinated in 221, the army elected Hannibal commander-in-chief. For two years he extended Carthaginian power in Spain and then in 219 besieged Saguntum, a city in alliance with Rome, thus, as he expected, precipitating war with Rome. In 218 he reached Italy after an arduous winter journey over the Alps, during which many of the war elephants he brought with him perished (according to *Appian he started with thirty-seven). After fifteen years of continuous warfare in Italy he was ordered in 203 to withdraw his undefeated army and return to Africa in order to defend Carthage from the invading Romans. Finally defeated by *Scipio Africanus at Zama in 202, he escaped to Carthage and urged an immediate peace. When his enemies informed Rome that he was conspiring with Antiochus of Syria, Hannibal left to join Antiochus, who was on the verge of war with Rome. Hannibal was defeated in a naval engagement at Sidē, and subsequently fled to Crete and thence to king Prūsias of Bithynia. The Romans were uneasy as long as he remained alive, and eventually demanded his surrender. Hannibal, seeing all ways shut to him, took poison in 183 or 182. Acknowledged to be one of the world's greatest soldiers, Hannibal inspired the utmost loyalty in his troops (even in defeat and hardship) and dread among his enemies. He lived on in the imagination as the archetypal enemy of Rome, and Roman mothers frightened their children with the nursery threat: *Hannibal ad portas* ('Hannibal is at the gates').

Harmo'dius and Aristogei'ton, two (male) lovers who killed Hipparchus, the younger brother of the Athenian tyrant Hippias, at the festival of the Panathenaea in 514 BC. The story was that Hipparchus had arranged a public insult to Harmodius' sister after he had made advances to Harmodius and been rejected. The two then made an attempt to overthrow the tyranny but failed and were killed. The tyranny lasted until 510 BC, but they were later honoured by the Athenian people as if they had succeeded. A statue to them was erected in the agora with an epigram by Simonides inscribed on the base, fragments of which have been found. See ALCMAEONIDAE and PEISISTRATUS.

Harmo'nia, necklace of. Made by the god Hephaestus, it was given as a wedding present to Harmonia, daughter of Arēs and Aphroditē, by her husband Cadmus. It did harm to all who subsequently possessed it. (See CADMUS, AMPHIARAUS, and ALCMAEON).

harmony or **music of the spheres,** a Pythagorean concept (see PYTHAGORAS), harmony having cosmic significance for the Pythagoreans. It seemed to them, as to others, that the heavenly bodies (the spheres) must, like other large bodies moving at speed, produce a sound as they whirl through space, and that since the bodies move at different speeds they must each produce different (but harmonious) notes. Plato's version of this idea, expounded in the Myth of Er (*Republic*, book 10), is that on each of the eight concentric circles in which the bodies rotate stands a *Siren uttering a note of constant pitch, the eight notes together making up a scale. Because the sound is with us constantly from birth and there is no contrasting silence we are unaware of it.

ha'rmosts (*harmostai*, 'regulators'), name given to Spartan military governors abroad, especially to those sent to the cities occupied by Sparta after the latter defeated Athens at the end of the Peloponnesian War in 404 BC.

Ha'rpalus, unreliable treasurer of Alexander the Great; see DEMOSTHENES (2) 1 and DEINARCHUS.

Harpies (harpŭīai, 'snatchers'), in Greek myth, the daughters of Thaumas (son of Pontus, Sea) and Electra (daughter of *Oceanus). They appear to have been regarded by Homer and

Hesiod as personifications of violent winds which carried off the daughters of Pandareus, Cleothera and Meropē, to be slaves to the Furies. Among their names were Aĕllo ('storm-wind'), Ōcypetē ('swift-flying'), Podargē ('fleet-of-foot'), and Celaino ('dark'). They are represented as birds with the faces of women. In the story of *Phineus the Harpies carry off or defile all his food. Virgil makes Aeneas encounter them at the islands of the Strophades (*Aeneid* 3. 225).

Harpo'cratēs, Greek name for the Egyptian god *Horus.

haru'spicēs (sing. *haruspex*), name given in Rome to Etruscan diviners, believed to be interpreters of the will of the gods, as conveyed through the state of the entrails (*exta*) of sacrificial animals, or through *monstra*, 'prodigies' (unusual births or growths), or *fulgura*, 'lightning', the two last categories being considered as sent from the gods as warnings. See DIVINATION.

Ha'sdrubal. 1. Carthaginian general and son-in-law of *Hamilcar Barca, upon whose death in 229 BC he became the commander in Spain. He extended the Carthaginian empire in Spain to the boundary of the river Ebro, but in 221 was murdered by a Celtic slave, and was succeeded in the command by Hannibal.

2. Son of Hamilcar Barca and brother of Hannibal, left in command of the Carthaginians in Spain when Hannibal invaded Italy in 218 BC (Second Punic War). From 218 to 208 he fought in Spain against the Roman generals Publius Cornelius *Scipio and his son Scipio Africanus. Having evaded the Roman army he then marched to Italy to the relief of Hannibal (207), but he was intercepted in the valley of the river Metaurus, defeated, and killed, in a significant victory for the Romans.

Heau'ton timōrū'menos ('self-tormentor'), Roman comedy (with Greek title) by *Terence, adapted from a Greek comedy of the same name by *Menander, and produced at Rome in 163 BC.

The self-tormentor is an Athenian father, Menedēmus, who imposes hardships on himself in penitence for the harshness which has driven his son Clīnia

out of the country on account of his love
for Antiphila, supposed to be the
daughter of a Corinthian woman of small
means. His neighbour Chremēs, per-
plexed by his behaviour, intervenes:
homo sum; *humani nil a me alienum puto*
('I am a man; I reckon nothing human to
be foreign to me'), he says in explanation, and somewhat officiously lectures
Menedemus on a parent's duty of
indulgence. Clinia returns to Athens,
making his home with his friend Clītipho,
son of Chremes, who, unknown to his
father, is spending his money on the prostitute Bacchis. It is arranged that Bacchis
shall come to the house of Chremes, in
the character of Clinia's friend, bringing
with her Antiphila as a companion. By a
trick of the slave Sўrus, Chremes is
cheated out of some money for the benefit of his son's extravagant mistress, and
when Chremes discovers this and what
has been going on in his house, he angrily
disinherits the boy, repudiating his own
doctrine of parental duty. His wife inter-
cedes for their son, and Clitipho is let off
on condition of a suitable marriage (not,
however, with 'the red-headed, cat-eyed
girl' first proposed to him). Meanwhile
Clinia has been restored to his repentant
father, and Antiphila has been discovered to be the daughter of Chremes,
who gives her in marriage to Clinia.

Hebdo'madēs ('sevens'), lost work by
Marcus Terentius *Varro, an illustrated
biographical dictionary of famous
Romans and Greeks, containing seven
hundred portraits.

Hēbē, in Greek myth, daughter of Zeus
and Hera, the cup-bearer of the gods and
wife to *Heracles after his death and
translation to Olympus. She is the personification of the Greek word for youth.
The Roman goddess Juventas was identified with her.

He'calē, *epyllion by the Hellenistic
Greek poet *Callimachus, describing
how Theseus was once hospitably
entertained by a poor old woman of this
name while on his way to kill the bull of
Marathon. The poem was intended to
explain the name and cult of the Attic
deme of Hecale.

Hecatae'us (d. *c*.476 BC), of Miletus (an

Ionian Greek city in Asia Minor), one of
the earliest composers of Greek prose
history and geography (see LOGOGRA-
PHERS). The results of his extensive
travels in the Persian empire, Egypt,
Greece, and around the coasts of the
Mediterranean and Black Sea were
embodied in a map of the world, showing
a flat, circular earth with a hole in the
middle, representing the Mediterranean,
and the stream of *Ocean running like a
river around the outside. (This was said
to be the second map made in Greece:
see ANAXIMANDER.) Makers of this style
of map were much derided by Herodotus
for their ignorance. Hecataeus wrote in
(Ionic) Greek a *Periēgēsis* (or *Periodos
gēs*, 'guide') to illustrate his map, many
fragments of which survive in quotations,
mostly too short to be illuminating.
Herodotus seems to have made extensive
use of this work without acknowledgement. Hecataeus also wrote a work entitled the *Histories* or *Genealogies*, the few
surviving fragments of which show that
he was tracing back to mythical times the
families (including, apparently, his own)
of those who claimed a god or hero as
their ultimate ancestor. The first sentence
is famous for embodying a new critical
approach: 'I write these things as they
seem to me; for the stories of the Greeks
are many and ridiculous in my opinion.'

He'catē, an ancient and somewhat
mysterious Greek goddess, unknown to
Homer, but according to Hesiod the
daughter of the *Titans Persēs and
Asteriē (sister of Leto). Hesiod described
her as the source of innumerable blessings for men—wealth, victory, wisdom,
good luck to sailors and hunters, and so
on, and as uniquely honoured among the
Titans for being allowed to keep her
powers under Zeus' rule. She was
frequently confused with Artemis (at
Rome, Diana), whose functions overlap
hers to some extent. But generally in
Greece she was associated with the ghost
world, an attendant upon *Persephonē,
queen of the Underworld, and so in some
sense herself a ruler over the souls of the
dead. At night she sent ghosts and
demons into the world, and wandered
about with the souls of the dead, her
approach signalled by the howling of

dogs. She was associated with sorcery and black magic, and is invoked by Medea in Euripides' play and by Simaetha in the second Idyll of Theocritus. She was worshipped at cross-roads (i.e. wherever one road meets another), where dishes of food were put out for her at the end of every month as a purificatory rite; the usual sacrifice to her was of dogs. In statues she was often represented in triple form (perhaps looking along three roads).

he'catomb, in Greece, originally the sacrifice of a hundred oxen (*hekaton bous*); the term came to be used even in Homer of any great sacrifice of animals. *Hekatombaion* was the name of a month at Athens, 'the time when hecatombs are offered'.

Hecatonchei'res ('hundred-handed'), in Greek myth, three monstrous giants, Briareus, Cottus, and Gyēs, sons of Uranus (Heaven) and Gaia (Earth), who helped Zeus in his war against the Titans.

Hector, in Greek legend, the eldest son of *Priam, king of Troy, and of his wife Hecuba, the husband of Andromachē and father of Astyanax, the leader and the bravest of the Trojans during the siege of Troy (see ILIAD). In the early books of the *Iliad* he takes a prominent part in the fighting and arranges the single combat between Paris and Menelaus. In book 6, having left the fighting to advise the Trojan women to supplicate the gods, he sees Andromache and Astyanax for the last time in a memorable scene of farewell. After his return to battle his challenge to single combat is taken up by Ajax, son of Telamon, who is his superior though the fight is inconclusive; in the battles that follow, while Achilles is absent from the field, Hector plays the leading part in the Trojan successes which culminate in his slaying of Patroclus. When Achilles returns to battle and the Trojans are routed, Hector alone awaits Achilles before the walls of Troy. Achilles pursues him around the city but eventually Hector halts, deceived by the goddess Athena into thinking that his brother Deïphobus has come to his aid. When he realizes the deception he knows that he must die. Achilles kills him

and mutilates the body by dragging it behind his chariot to the Greek ships. In a moving scene Priam calls upon Achilles in order to ransom his son's body, and Hector's funeral ends the *Iliad*.

Hector is the greatest hero on the Trojan side; on his life alone the survival of Troy depends. He is always inferior to the Greek hero Achilles, but noble and chivalrous, regarded by his countrymen as god-like. He dies gloriously defending Troy, and his death not only portends the complete destruction of the city but is in itself an event of extreme pathos as the hero is shorn of his god-like qualities to become merely a mutilated corpse.

He'cuba (Hekabē), in Greek myth, the (chief) wife of Priam, king of Troy, and mother of nineteen of his children including Hector, Helenus, Troilus, Paris, Cassandra, Creusa, and Polyxena. In the *Iliad* she remains in the background fulfilling the role of the bereaved queen destined to survive the sack of Troy and the loss of her husband and nearly all her children. In Greek tragedy this latter part of her life becomes a favourite subject, being rich in dramatic possibilities. In the *Trojan Women* of Euripides she is allotted as spoils of war to Odysseus, and has to endure the sacrifice of her daughter Polyxena on Achilles' tomb and the murder of Hector's only son Astyanax. In the *Hecuba*, also by Euripides, she discovers the murder of her last remaining son Polydorus (see below), and the prophecy is made that she will be metamorphosed into a bitch. Later legend elaborated upon this topic.

He'cuba, Greek tragedy by *Euripides written perhaps in 424 BC.

Troy has fallen to the Greeks, the women of Troy have been apportioned to the victors, but the return home of the Greek fleet is delayed by contrary winds. The ghost of the Greek hero Achilles has demanded the sacrifice to him of Polyxena, daughter of Hecuba and Priam, king of Troy. The Greek hero Odysseus comes to lead her away. He is unmoved by Hecuba's despair and by her reminder that he once owed his life to her. But Polyxena, a striking figure, prefers death to slavery, and willingly goes to her sacrifice. As Hecuba prepares for the burial, she suffers a further sorrow. Her youngest son Polydōrus had been sent for safety to Polymēstor, king of the Thracian Chersonese (where the Greek fleet is now detained), with part of the treasure of Priam. When Troy fell, Polymestor had murdered the boy in order to secure the treasure for himself, and had thrown his body into the sea. It has now been washed up and is brought to Hecuba. She appeals to the Greek leader Agamemnon for vengeance; but he, though sympathetic, is timid. Hecuba thereupon takes vengeance into her own hands. She lures Polymestor and his sons to her tent, where her women put out his eyes and kill the sons. Agamemnon orders the blinded king to be left on a deserted island; he then prophesies that Hecuba will turn into a bitch, and that the site of her tomb will be commemorated by the name Cynossēma ('dog's tomb') on the east coast of the Thracian Chersonese).

He'cyra ('mother-in-law'), Roman comedy by *Terence adapted from the Greek original by Apollodorus of Carystus, a writer of New Comedy (see COMEDY, GREEK 6). The plot also resembles that of Menander's *Epitrepontes*. The *Hecyra* lost its audience at its first two productions, first in 165 BC to the rival attractions of rope-dancers and a boxing match, and secondly in 160 to a gladiatorial combat, and was successfully performed only at its third attempt in the same year. It has never been a popular play.

Pamphilus has been reluctantly persuaded by his father to give up the prostitute Bacchis and to marry. Soon after the marriage he is sent away by his father on business. During his absence his wife leaves her mother-in-law's house on a pretext and returns to her own mother's house. There she gives birth to a baby conceived before her marriage, having been seduced by an unknown man under cover of darkness. This man had taken from her a ring, subsequently discovered in the possession of Bacchis. With the latter's help it is discovered that the wife's seducer was Pamphilus himself, who is after all the father of his wife's child. Pamphilus, who had reluctantly felt that he must separate from his wife, therefore

returns to her. The title of the play is derived from the carefully drawn characters of the two mothers-in-law.

Helen. In Greek myth, Leda, the wife of Tyndareus king of Sparta, bore four children, the twins Castor and Polydeuces, Clytemnestra, and Helen, of whom the last at least was fathered by Zeus. According to the usual story, Zeus visited Leda in the form of a swan, Leda laid an egg, and from this Helen was hatched. Helen and her brothers were worshipped as important deities in Sparta, but in the literary tradition, starting with Homer, she is the entirely human wife of King Menelaus of Sparta, the younger brother of Agamemnon, the latter being married to Helen's sister Clytemnestra. Of outstanding beauty, Helen was said to have been carried off in her youth by Theseus to Attica; but during Theseus' absence in the Underworld her brothers rescued her and took her back to Sparta together with Theseus' mother Aethra. She was subsequently wooed by all the leading men in Greece; at the suggestion of Odysseus she was allowed to choose whom she pleased, and the rest swore to abide by her choice and support her husband's rights. She married Menelaus and bore him a daughter Hermione, but while he was absent in Crete Paris arrived in Sparta, and either persuaded Helen to flee with him or carried her off by force to Troy. (The goddess Aphrodite had promised him the most beautiful woman in the world as his wife; see PARIS, JUDGEMENT OF.) On his return Menelaus and his brother Agamemnon raised an expedition against Troy. Another tradition, apparently as old as the poet Stesichorus (sixth century BC), has it that Helen was carried for safe keeping to King Proteus of Egypt, while Zeus and Hera allowed only a phantom resembling her to accompany Paris to Troy, thus providing a pretext for the Trojan War, which Zeus had already decreed should take place so as to reduce the wickedness and the multitude of men. After the war Menelaus found Helen in Egypt and took her home.

In the *Iliad* Helen is a tragic figure, compelled by Aphrodite to be the wife of Paris and aware that her wrong-doing has caused suffering for everyone. She reproaches herself, but is not generally reproached by the Trojans and never, as she says, by Priam or Hector. In a memorable scene on the battlements of Troy the old men, seeing her, observe that such beauty puts her beyond blame. In the *Odyssey* she lives peacefully in Sparta reconciled with her husband, but is an enigmatic figure. Later writers, Greek and Roman, were generally hostile to Helen, and the speeches in her defence composed by *Gorgias and *Isocrates are little more than rhetorical demonstrations of how to defend the patently guilty.

Helen, Greek tragedy (with a happy ending) by *Euripides, produced in 412 BC. The plot is based on the legend (see above) that it was not the real Helen but her phantom which accompanied Paris to Troy.

Helen herself has been magically conveyed by the god Hermes to the court of Proteus, king of Egypt, where she awaits the return of her husband Menelaus from Troy. But Proteus is now dead, and his son Theoclymenus is trying to force her to marry him. She has taken refuge at the tomb of Proteus. The Greek hero Teucer, the brother of Ajax, arrives and tells her of the fall of Troy seven years previously, and of the probable death of Menelaus. While she is lamenting, Menelaus himself appears. He has been shipwrecked on the Egyptian coast, has left the 'Helen' whom he was bringing from Troy in a cave, and has come to the palace for help. A curious scene of reconciliation follows, for Menelaus is puzzled by the two Helens and is convinced of the reality of the 'Egyptian' Helen only when he learns that the other has disappeared into the air after revealing the deception. Helen now devises an escape for both of them from Egypt, a difficult matter, for Theoclymenus not only is determined to marry her, but will kill any Greek whom he finds in the land. With the help of Theonoē, a priestess and the sister of the king, Theoclymenus is fooled with a pretence of a funeral ceremony at sea for a supposedly dead Menelaus, and Menelaus and Helen escape on the ship provided for the

purpose. Castor and Polydeuces, Helen's deified brothers, appear at the end to avert the king's wrath against Theonoe for her complicity. The chorus consists of Helen's attendants, captured Greek maidens.

The poet does not fail to point out the grim humour of the situation: the ten years' siege of Troy has all been for nothing; and the lore of seers is not worth much, for *Calchas and *Helenus gave no indication whatsoever of the deception.

Helen, Encomium on, see GORGIAS and ISOCRATES.

He'lenus, in Homer's *Iliad*, son of Priam, king of Troy, and his wife Hecuba, gifted with prophecy. According to later legend (not in Homer) he was captured by Odysseus and revealed that the Greeks would take Troy only if *Philoctetes was brought there with his bow and arrows. After the fall of Troy, Helenus became the captive of Neoptolemus, and after the latter's death married Andromachē and became king of Chāonia, a part of Epirus. *Aeneas, in the course of his wanderings, visited him there and received advice on the direction he should follow.

He'licon, largest mountain of Boeotia in Greece, celebrated as one of the two favourite haunts of the Muses (the other is Pieria) who had an ancient sanctuary there. On its slope was the village of Ascra, the home of the poet Hesiod, who tells how he met the Muses while tending sheep on the mountainside. The fountains of Aganippē and Hippocrēnē on the mountain, which supplied the streams Olmeios and Permessos, were believed to inspire those who drank from them; see PEGASUS.

Hēliodō'rus, of Emesa in Syria, author of the Greek novel the *Aethiopica* (or *Theagenes and Charicleia*). Nothing certain is known of his life, which is dated variously in the third and fourth centuries AD, but he has been identified with a Christian bishop in Thessaly of that name. See NOVEL 1.

Helioga'balus, see ELAGABALUS.

Hē'lios, in Greek myth, the Sun, personified as a god, son of the *Titans Hyperion and Thea, brother of Selēnē (Moon) and Eōs (Dawn), and the father of Aeētēs, Circē, and *Phaethōn. (Homer occasionally calls him Hyperion, a practice imitated by other poets.) He is generally represented as a charioteer driving daily from east to west across the sky, and floating back to the east during the night in a golden cup on the stream of Ocean, the cup that Heracles once borrowed (see HERACLES, LABOURS OF 10). He had cattle and sheep in the island of Thrinacia (see ODYSSEY (book 12) and SICILY). His cult was not widespread in Greece, although he is often appealed to as a witness because he sees and hears everything. This aspect perhaps contributed to his occasional identification with Apollo, the all-knowing god, after the fifth century BC. In Rhodes, however, he appears to have been the chief national god, who chose the island as his own before it rose above the surface of the sea. The famous *Colossus erected by the harbour entrance was a statue of him.

Hellanī'cus, of Mitylene in Lesbos, a Greek *logographer of the fifth century BC. He was a prolific writer, of whose books some fragments survive. His most important works were a *History of Attica* (see ATTHIS), a list of the priestesses of Hera at Argos, which he used as a chronological basis for his history, and a list of victors at the Carnea.

Hellas, Hellenes, names used by the Greeks in classical times to denote Greece and the Greeks. Homer (who did not have a comprehensive name for the Greeks, calling them Achaeans, Argives, or Danaans) used these names to denote a small region of south Thessaly and its inhabitants; by 'Panhellenes' he seems to mean the northern, as opposed to the southern, Greeks. Hesiod, however, uses Hellas in the general sense of Greece, and from about the seventh century onwards the Greeks called themselves and their country by these names, deriving them from a mythical ancestor *Hellen. In classical times the name Hellas embraced all lands inhabited by Hellenes, including not only the mainland of Greece, the Peloponnese, and the Greek islands, but also the colonies and the

Greek cities on the coast of Asia Minor. From the fourth century AD onwards the Greeks of the eastern Roman empire called themselves *Rhōmaioi* ('Romans'); by that time the name 'Hellenes' denoted pagans. (See also GREECE.)

Hellē, in Greek myth, sister of Phrixus. While she and her brother were flying through the air on the back of the ram with the golden fleece to escape from their father *Athamas and step-mother Ino, Helle fell off into the sea and drowned. In consequence the sea was called the Hellespont, 'sea of Helle'.

Hellēn, in Greek myth, the eponymous ancestor of the Hellenes, usually described as the son of Pyrrha and *Deucalion. He was the father of Dorus, Aeolus, and Xuthus, whose sons were Ion and Achaeus; thus he engendered the ancestors of the main ethnic divisions of the Greeks in historical times, Dorians, Aeolians, Ionians, and Achaeans. (Some regions of Greece, e.g. Phocis, Elis, and Arcadia, lay outside these divisions.)

Hellē'nica. **1.** History of Greece from 411 to 362 BC by *Xenophon, who lived through the events he describes. The work was not conceived as a unity, but was written in instalments which were probably published together but without revision. Xenophon begins his narrative at the point in the Peloponnesian War where Thucydides' history stops, and books 1–2 cover the years 411 to 403, the rule and overthrow of the Thirty at Athens. After leaving a gap for the events of 402 to 400, he covers the years 399 to 379 in books 3–5: the Spartan war against the Persians (399–387); the attempt of various Greek states to check the growing power of Sparta (the Corinthian War, 394–387, ended by the Peace of Antalcidas); the rivalry of Sparta and Thebes. The second half of book 5 and books 6 and 7 take the reader from 379 to 362, and cover the triumph of Thebes at the battle of Leuctra (371) and her supremacy under the general Epaminondas, ending with his death at the battle of Mantinea in 362.

2. History by *Theopompus, of which only fragments survive.

Helle'nica Oxyrhy'nchia, see OXY-RHYNCHUS HISTORIAN.

Hellenism, the national character and culture of the (ancient) Greeks; see HELLAS.

Hellenistic, term used to denote the civilization, language, art, and literature of the Greek world from the late fourth to the late first centuries BC. (For the Greek world see GREECE; for the term 'classical' referring to the fifth and fourth centuries BC in Greece, see CLASSIC.) See also HELLENISTIC AGE, below.

Hellenistic age, the period of Greek culture which may be said to start from the death of Alexander the Great in 323 BC and which ended with Rome's absorption of Greece and the Greek East in the latter part of the first century BC (the conventional terminal date is often put at 31 BC—the Battle of Actium—or 27 BC—when Augustus became the first Roman emperor). Before Alexander, Greek culture had little influence outside *Hellas; after his conquest of the Persian empire, important centres of Greek civilization and economy were to be found in Egypt and Asia, and the dominant culture of the East was Greek. The new city of Alexandria in Egypt was its focus, whence the period is sometimes known as the Alexandrian age, but the cities of Pergamum (north-west Asia Minor), Antioch (in Syria on the river Orontes), and Athens were cultural rivals.

What remains of Hellenistic literature is only a small and unrepresentative fraction of the vast amount produced by the age. Out of hundreds of histories only five books of Polybius survive entire; important histories such as those of Timaeus, Hieronymus of Cardia, and Posidonius survive only in fragments. Such literature as survives is largely in verse. Even so, almost nothing remains of the scores of tragic poets, not even of the so-called *Pleiad. Comedy retained its vigour at Athens in the early years of the Hellenistic age, in the so-called New Comedy of Menander and Philemon (see COMEDY, GREEK 6); although it cannot be said to have survived in manuscript to the present day, our knowledge of it has been considerably enhanced by substantial papyrus discoveries made in the twentieth century (see PAPYROLOGY). Among other poetry which has perished are the works of poets who considerably influenced later Latin literature, like Philetas of Cos and Euphorion; but they seem to have resembled, in small scale and exquisite refinement, the surviving works of their contemporaries Callimachus and Theocritus. By contrast Apollonius of Rhodes wrote an epic about the voyage of the Argonauts (which survives), and there is a tradition that Callimachus quarrelled violently with him over his use of this genre, outdated in its large scale. Didactic poetry was popular on a variety of topics such as geography, astronomy, and fishing; the *Phaenomena* of Aratus is the chief example of the class. A novel Greek literary form, the mime, came to light when eight of these miniature dramas by Herodas turned up on a papyrus discovered at the end of the nineteenth century.

In the second and first centuries BC the rise of Rome, accompanied by constant wars and widespread destruction in the Greek world, brought about the decline of science and literature. But early in the first century BC the poet Meleager published an anthology of epigrams from Archilochus (seventh century BC) to his own day, called 'the Garland' (*Stephanos*), the first large critical anthology of poems of which we have knowledge; each of the fifty or so poets represented was likened to a flower. By now the oratory of the city-state, which largely depended on political stimulus, had died (with the exception of a few political speeches), but rhetoric, outliving it, had become the chief tool of education. It flourished in Greek Asia, where particularly exaggerated importance was attached to form and to a mannered and florid style ('Asianism'; see ORATORY 1) against which later Greeks (and some Romans; see *BRUTUS*) were to react.

With the decline of the city-state and the loosening of the bond which united its citizens, philosophies arose that gave support to people as individuals and aimed to bring them peace of mind. The Hellenistic age saw the rise of two new systems, that of Epicurus and that of Zeno and the

Stoics; the doctrine of the latter exerted an immense influence not only on the Greek world but later on Rome and ultimately on Christianity. The other schools occupied from now onwards a secondary position. After Aristotle's death (322 BC) the Peripatetics under Theophrastus and his successor Strato continued his interest in problems of natural science, but their importance thereafter came to an end. Plato's Academy was likewise eclipsed, until under Arcesilaus and Carneades it resumed some prominence by its adoption of Scepticism.

The Hellenistic age saw a striking advance in scholarship and scientific knowledge, the Library and Museum at *Alexandria being great centres of study and research. The leading names in this area were Zenodotus, Aristophanes of Byzantium, and Aristarchus of Samothrace. Hellenistic achievements in the fields of mathematics, astronomy, biology, and medicine are known to us mainly through the works of later writers. The great names in mathematics and astronomy are Aristarchus of Samos, Archimedes, Hipparchus, Euclid, and the polymaths Eratosthenes and Posidonius. In biology and medicine the two great names were Herophilus and Erasistratus.

He'llespont, the Dardanelles; the strait which connects the Aegean Sea in the north-east to the Propontis (Sea of Marmora), and divides Europe from Asia. For the name see HELLE. In 1810 the English poet Lord Byron swam the Hellespont from Abydus to Sestus, in emulation of the mythical lover *Leander, at roughly the place where the Persian king Xerxes had built his bridge of ships during the Persian Wars.

helots (*heilōtĕs*), word of uncertain derivation applied to the serfs at Sparta.

Helve'tii, Celtic tribe which tried to settle in Gaul in the first century BC by moving from its territory roughly north-east of Lake Geneva through the Roman province of Narbonese Gaul to settle in Gaul proper. They were halted by the Romans and the remnants

driven back to their old territory. See COMMENTARIES I (book I).

Helvi'dius Priscus (first century AD), son-in-law of Paetus *Thrasea, whose political views he shared, a member of the Stoic and republican opposition to the emperor Nero. He was exiled in AD 66, but returned to Rome two years later. He became violently opposed to the emperor Vespasian and after being again exiled was put to death (perhaps in 75). Helvidius' son (of the same name) by his first marriage was a friend of Tacitus and Pliny the Younger.

hendecasy'llable, see METRE, GREEK 5.

Hēphae'stion. 1. Macedonian, son of Amyntor, military commander and closest friend of Alexander the Great. He died suddenly in 324 BC.

2. Of Alexandria, second century AD, a Greek metrist. He was the author of a treatise on Greek metres in forty-eight books, of which only an epitome survives; he analysed metres into feet and cola (see METRE, GREEK 1 and 8 (i)). Much of his value lies incidentally in his quotations from many otherwise lost Greek poems.

Hēphae'stus, Greek god of fire and of crafts, particularly those in which fire is employed. His origin, like his name, may be non-Greek, and perhaps Asian. In Greek myth he was the child of Zeus and Hera, or of Hera alone, and because he was lame from birth Hera threw him out of Olympus. He fell on Lemnos, an important centre of his cult. According to another version, he intervened on his mother's side in a quarrel between Zeus and Hera, whereupon Zeus seized him by the foot and hurled him down to earth. Hephaestus revenged himself on Hera by ensnaring her in an ingeniously constructed throne where she had to remain until Dionysus made him drunk and brought him back to Olympus to release her. This episode became a favourite subject for vase-painters. With a net of his own devising he also trapped his unfaithful wife Aphroditē with the god Arēs. His many famous works of craftsmanship include the armour of Achilles and the necklace of *Harmonia. Hesiod has him create the first woman, Pandora. In

Athens, where he was the father of the first king *Erichthonius and so in a sense the ancestor of the Athenians, he had a special cult and a temple above the *Ceramicus, where the shops of the smiths and braziers (as well as the potters) were to be found.

Hēra, with whom *Juno was identified by the Romans, in Greek myth, the daughter of *Cronus and Rhea, and the sister and wife of Zeus, from which position she derived her authority as queen of the gods. Her children by Zeus were *Hephaestus, *Arēs, *Hēbē, and *Eileithyia. She is essentially the goddess of marriage and of married women; but she is never invoked as a mother and never represented as a mother with a child. Her depiction in myth is often as the jealous wife outraged by her husband's infidelities and pursuing with vindictive hatred his children by other mothers, e.g. Dionysus and Heracles, as well as the other women he loved, e.g. Io. For her part in the Judgement of Paris see PARIS, JUDGEMENT OF. Her principal temples were at a sanctuary between Argos and Mycenae (see HERAEUM), and at Samos, where she was said to have been born. But she was worshipped all over Greece, and many important Greek temples are dedicated to her.

Heraclei'dae, the children or the descendants of *Heracles, who was father by Deianeira of several sons, of whom Hyllus was the eldest, and of one daughter Macaria. For their story see *HERACLES, CHILDREN OF.* The phrase 'Return of the Heracleidae' was often used by the Greeks to refer to the *Dorian Invasion; the Dorians claimed connection with Heracles through their kings who were descended from him, and his son Hyllus became a Dorian by adoption: see AEGIMIUS. Hyllus consulted the Delphic Oracle to ask how he and his brothers should claim their father's kingdom of Tiryns in Argos (or, according to the Dorians, the whole Peloponnese; in this way they legitimized the Dorian Invasion). He was told to await 'the third fruit'. Misunderstanding this to mean the third harvest he duly made his attack on Tiryns three years later but failed and was killed in single combat by Echemus the

Tegean. It was subsequently learnt that 'third fruit' meant 'third generation', and when this was reached Tēmenus and the other Heracleidae conquered the Peloponnese. The territory was divided into three portions: Cresphontēs (see MEROPE) took Messenia, Temenus took Argos, and the sons of Aristodemus, Eurysthenēs and Proclēs, received Lacedaemon, thus founding the dual kingship of Sparta; the line of the elder twin Eurysthenes had seniority and greater honour. The Spartan kings traced their ancestry back in the male line to *Perseus (whose father was Zeus). Perseus' mother, however, was *Danaē, descendant of the Egyptian Danaus. Herodotus (6. 52) speaks as if the Egyptian element was well known.

Heraclei'tus. 1. (c.540–c.480 BC), Greek philosopher who was born and lived his life at Ephesus. He came from a royal family but surrendered his hereditary privileges to his brother. He was notorious for misanthropy, and for arrogance towards the reputations of those who were generally admired for wisdom: Homer, Hesiod, Archilochus, Hecataeus, Xenophanes, Pythagoras. Although he is said to have written a book entitled 'On Nature', many of the eighty or so fragments that survive in quotations rather suggest a collection of aphorisms, striking and paradoxical, but, lacking a context, difficult to interpret. The Greeks themselves complained of the obscurity of his writings. He believed that it is impossible to comprehend fully the reality of things and that appearances are unreliable, but nevertheless that some sort of knowledge is attainable. Wisdom lies in understanding that the world has an underlying coherence and is a unity; this unity depends upon a balance between opposites; change in one direction leads to change in the other. Therefore 'all things are in a state of flux' (*panta rhei*). The essential stuff of the universe is pure fire, of which some is always being kindled and some being extinguished to form sea and earth; the soul too is composed of fire, and after death the souls of the virtuous join the cosmic fire. In Roman times Heracleitus became known as 'the weeping philosopher' (in contrast with 'the laughing philosopher' *Democritus), weeping at the spectacle of human life.

2. Of Halicarnassus, a poet and friend of the Hellenistic poet *Callimachus, who wrote a famous epigram on his death.

He'raclēs (Hēraklēs, Lat. Herculēs), son of Zeus and Alcmena, and most famous of the Greek heroes; his exploits were known and his cult was observed throughout the Greek world. He was descended from *Perseus and through Perseus' mother *Danaē from *Danaus. Famous for his strength, courage, endurance, good nature, and compassion, he was also known for his appetites, gluttony and lust. Being considered the universal helper, he was invoked on every occasion, and commonly called *Alexikakos*, 'averter of evil'. He later became an ideal of human behaviour: as the noble ruler who acts for the good of mankind and is finally elevated to the gods (Alexander the Great stamped the image of Heracles on his coins), and the ordinary mortal who, at the end of a life of toil, may hope to join after death the company of the gods. The Stoics and Cynics saw him as an exemplar of fortitude, to the neglect of his other qualities. At all times he caught the popular fancy, and myths, some of them transferred from less-known heroes, accumulated about him, including those of the Labours (see HERACLES, LABOURS OF, below). For the story of his birth at Thebes see AMPHITRYON.

In his cradle Heracles strangled two snakes which Hera had sent to kill him; for she, always roused to jealousy by Zeus' union with other women, human or divine, pursued him with implacable anger throughout his life. (It is inexplicable why he should have a name that seems to mean 'glory of Hera'.) He was instructed in the various arts by all the greatest experts: by Eurytus, grandson of Apollo, in the use of the bow; by *Autolycus in wrestling; by Polydeuces (see DIOSCURI) in the use of arms; by *Linus in music. When the last tried to correct him, Heracles killed him with his own lute. Amphitryon then sent Heracles to tend his flocks on Mount Cithaeron, and there, when eighteen, he killed a huge

lion. Cithaeron was also the setting of 'The Choice of Heracles': as he was pondering which course of life to follow, two women appeared before him, Pleasure and Virtue, one offering a life of enjoyment, the other a life of toil and glory; he chose the latter. On his return to Thebes, he relieved the city of a tribute it had been forced to pay to Orchomenus, and *Creon, king of Thebes, in gratitude gave him his daughter Megara to marry. Creon's younger daughter married Iphicles (Heracles' twin brother) who already had a son Iolāus. The latter became Heracles' faithful companion and charioteer. After some years Hera sent a fit of madness upon Heracles, so that he killed Megara and his children under the delusion that they were his enemies. After this calamity he went into exile and sought advice from the Delphic Oracle on how he might be purified. He was told to go to Tiryns and serve Eurystheus, king of that city, for twelve years, and win immortality by performing the labours that Eurystheus imposed. There are many different versions of the events of Heracles' life: Euripides' version of Heracles' madness, for example, makes it come upon him after the performance of the Labours; and various reasons are given why Heracles served Eurystheus. Eurystheus is sometimes represented as a coward who would take refuge in a bronze tub when Heracles returned with some monster or other. Subsequently Heracles married Dēianeira, daughter of Oeneus of Calydon, winning her by defeating the river-god Achelōus in wrestling. When he and Deianeira departed, they came to the flooded river Evēnus (in Aetolia). A centaur, Nessus, carried Deianeira across and tried to rape her, whereupon Heracles shot him with a poisoned arrow. As he lay dying the centaur advised Deianeira, apparently with friendly intention, to keep some of his blood, which, smeared on a garment, would win back the love of Heracles if he was ever unfaithful to her; this Deianeira did.

The adventures ascribed to Heracles are too numerous to relate more than a few. He accompanied the *Argonauts (see also HYLAS) on the early part of their voyage. He rescued Alcestis, wife of

*Admetus, from Death. He fell in love with Iolē, daughter of Eurytus, king of Oechalia, but her father and brothers would not give her to him. One of these brothers, Iphitus, who had come to Tiryns in search of some lost cattle of his father's, was thrown by Heracles, in a fit of madness, from the walls of the city. For this murder the Delphic Oracle sent him into slavery for a year, and he was sold to Omphalē, queen of Lydia. There he was set to do a woman's work, in woman's dress, while Omphale took over his lion's skin and club. When his period of servitude was over he led an expedition against *Laomedon, king of Troy. Poseidon at an earlier time had sent a sea-serpent against Troy, and Laomedon had promised Heracles his famous horses if he would kill it, but when the feat was done he refused the reward. Heracles now gathered an army, which included Telamon (father of Ajax) and Peleus (father of Achilles), attacked the city, and captured it. Heracles gave Laomedon's daughter Hēsionē to Telamon, by whom she became the mother of Teucer.

Finally Heracles attacked Oechalia and carried off Iole. Deianeira, to win him back, followed the advice of Nessus and sent Heracles a robe smeared with the centaur's blood. But this blood had been poisoned by the blood of the Hydra, in which Heracles dipped his arrows (see HERACLES, LABOURS OF 2); the robe clung to Heracles' flesh and caused terrible suffering. To escape from it he had himself carried to the summit of Mount Oeta and placed on a pyre. He gave Iole to his son Hyllus (see HERACLEIDAE) and persuaded Poias, father of *Philoctētēs, by the gift of his bow and arrows, to light the pyre. He was then carried up to Olympus, reconciled to Hera, and married to her daughter Hēbē.

Among the numerous opponents of Heracles at one time or another were Cycnus, a son of Arēs, who robbed Apollo of the hecatombs intended to be sacrificed to him at Delphi (the subject of the poem *The *Shield of Heracles* attributed to Hesiod); Busiris, king of Egypt, who in order to avert a drought sacrificed strangers who came to his country and attempted to sacrifice Heracles too while the latter was on his way to the Hesperides (see HERACLES, LABOURS OF 11); and Eryx, the legendary king of the mountain of that name in Sicily, whom Heracles wrestled with and killed while searching for one of Geryon's cattle which had wandered into his territory. See also PROMETHEUS, ANTAEUS, CHIRON, and CERCOPES.

The legends of Heracles connected him with both Thebes and Tiryns. For the claim of his descendants to the latter (extended to the whole Peloponnese) see HERACLEIDAE.

Heracles, Children of (*Hērakleidai*), Greek tragedy by *Euripides, perhaps produced in the early part of the Peloponnesian War (i.e. *c.*430 BC), possibly intended to remind the audience of the gratitude due to Athens for saving the children of Heracles (the founders of the Dorian race) from the persecution of *Eurystheus, king of Argos.

The children of Heracles, who is now dead, with his nephew and former comrade-in-arms Iolāus, now an old man, have taken refuge from the unremitting persecution of Eurystheus at the altar of Zeus at Athens. The herald of Eurystheus demands their surrender, and, on the refusal of Dēmophōn, king of Athens and son of Theseus, declares war. The soothsayers announce that the sacrifice of a nobly-born maiden is necessary to secure the success of the Athenian army, and Macaria, daughter of Heracles, voluntarily offers herself as the victim and is sacrificed. As the army of Eurystheus approaches, Hyllus, eldest son of Heracles, comes to the aid of Athens, and Iolaus, miraculously made young again, joins in the fight and captures Eurystheus. The captive is brought before Alcmēna, mother of Heracles, is reviled by her, and ordered off to his death.

Heracles, Labours of. The number of Labours seems to have been canonized as twelve by the scholars working at Alexandria in the third century BC, but Euripides had already spoken of twelve, and twelve were depicted on the metopes of the temple of Zeus at Olympia (*c.*460 BC). They were imposed on Heracles by

*Eurystheus and according to the most commonly accepted list were as follows.

The Peloponnesian Labours

1. The Nemean Lion, an invulnerable monster, the offspring of *Echidna and *Typhon or Orthrus, sent to Nemea in Argos by Hera, to destroy Heracles. Heracles choked the monster in his arms, and clothed himself with its skin, using the beast's own claws, by which alone the skin was penetrable, to separate it from the body.

2. The Hydra, the offspring of Echidna and Typhon; it was a poisonous water-snake which lived in the marshes of Lerna near Argos. It had numerous heads; when one was cut off another grew in its place. Moreover Hera sent a huge crab to help it, hence the proverb 'Not even Heracles can fight two', spoken by the hero as he summoned his comrade-in-arms Iolaus. The latter, as Heracles cut off the heads, seared the stumps with burning brands. Heracles then dipped his arrows in the Hydra's blood, which made their wounds incurable (fatally for himself, as it proved; see HERACLES). There were various elaborations of the legend, as that the Hydra had one immortal head, which Heracles buried under a rock. The crab, which Heracles killed by crushing it under foot, became the constellation Cancer.

3. The Erymanthian Boar. Heracles' labour in this case was to catch alive the boar that lived on Mount Erymanthus in Arcadia. He drove it into a snowfield, tired it out, and caught it in a net. It was while searching for the boar that he was entertained by Pholus the centaur, to whom he gave wine. The other centaurs, lured to the cave by the smell of wine, got drunk and attacked Heracles; in defending himself he killed many of them with his poisoned arrows.

4. The Cerynitian Hind. In the usual version Heracles captures the hind alive after a year-long chase which takes him to the land of the Hyperboreans. Though female and therefore by nature hornless, this creature was said to have gilded horns and to be sacred to Artemis. According to some it lived in the woods of Oenoë in the Argolid. Its connection with the Achaean town Ceryneia or river Cerynitës is obscure.

5. The Stymphālian Birds, which infested the woods round lake Stymphālus in Arcadia. Various reasons are given about the need for their destruction, e.g. they used their bronze-tipped feathers as arrows and killed and ate men and beasts. Heracles scared them by means of a bronze rattle (made by Hephaestus), then shot some with his arrows and drove the rest away.

6. The Augēan Stables. Augēas, king of Elis, had enormous herds of cattle, like his father Helios, and Heracles was required to clean in one day their stables which had never been cleaned before. This he did by diverting the river Alphēus so that it flowed through the yard.

Labours outside the Peloponnese

7. The Cretan Bull, either the bull with which Pāsiphaē (see MINOS) fell in love, or the one which bore *Europa to Crete. Heracles caught it alive, brought it back to show Eurystheus, and let it go. It wandered throughout Greece and finally settled down near Marathon (see THESEUS).

8. The Horses of Diomēdēs. Diomedes was the son of Arēs and a nymph Cyrēnē, and king of the Bistones in Thrace. His horses were fed on human flesh. Heracles killed Diomedes and fed his body to the horses, whereupon they became tame and Heracles brought them to Argos.

9. The Girdle of the Amazon. The girdle given to Hippolytē, queen of the Amazons, by her father Arēs, was desired by the daughter of Eurystheus, and Heracles was sent to procure it. Hippolyte would have handed it over, but Hera stirred up war; in the ensuing battle Heracles killed Hippolyte and removed the girdle from her dead body. In another version he captured Hippolyte's second-in-command Melanippē who handed over the girdle as the price of freedom.

10. The Cattle of Geryon. In order to obtain the cattle Heracles had to travel to the extreme west where they were pastured on the mythical island of Erytheia ('red island') in *Ocean. Helios (Sun) so much admired Heracles' boldness in drawing his bow on him when annoyed by the heat that he gave him his golden cup in which to sail to Erytheia. At the end of the journey Heracles erected two pillars (Calpē and Abyla),

the Pillars of Hercules, one on each side of the Straits of Gibraltar. Having reached the island Heracles killed the dog Orthrus, the herdsman Eurytion, and lastly Geryon himself, who was a three-headed ogre, and brought away his cattle either in the golden cup, or by a long overland route through Spain, France, Italy, and Sicily, reaching even the Black Sea, and thus having opportunity for many more adventures (see CACUS, and ARA MAXIMA) before he reached home safely.

11. The Golden Apples of the Hesperides ('daughters of Night'). These were the apples given by Gaia to Hera as a wedding present, and kept in a garden at the edge of the world. Heracles, who had to bring back the apples, had much difficulty in finding the way and forced *Nereus to give him directions to the garden. Having killed Ladon, the dragon that guarded it, he carried off the apples. According to another version he induced *Atlas to fetch the apples, holding up the sky in his place while he did this. Some say that Atlas then refused to resume his burden, and had to be tricked into doing so.

12. The Descent to the Underworld for *Cerberus (Heracles' last labour and the only one explicitly mentioned in Homer). Heracles, after preliminary initiation into the Eleusinian mysteries, and with the help of the gods Hermes and Athena, descended to the Underworld near Cape Taenarum in Laconia. While there he freed Theseus, but was unable to free Pirithous. (See also HERACLES, MADNESS OF, below.) This may have been the occasion on which Heracles wounded Hades himself with an arrow, as Homer mentions. Heracles captured and bound the dog Cerberus, brought him to Eurystheus, and then returned him to the Underworld. This myth perhaps suggests that by conquering death Heracles earns his final immortality (see also ALCESTIS). For Heracles at Rome see HERCULES.

Heracles, Madness of (*Hēraklēs mainomenos*, Lat. *Hercules furens*), Greek tragedy by *Euripides, of uncertain date but perhaps produced *c*.417 BC. It was originally called simply *Heracles*.

Heracles, engaged on the last of his twelve labours, has gone down to the Underworld to bring up the dog *Cerberus. During his long absence Lycus, supported by a faction of Thebans, has killed Creon, king of Thebes and father of Heracles' wife Megara, and seized power. He threatens with death Megara and the three young sons of Heracles (fearing their vengeance in the future) and Heracles' reputed father the now aged Amphitryon. They have taken sanctuary at the altar of Zeus, but Lycus threatens to burn them to death there, and they prepare themselves. At this point Heracles returns, rescues his family, and kills Lycus. But his persistent enemy the goddess Hera sends Lyssa ('madness') who reluctantly seizes on Heracles and drives him to kill his own children (under the impression that they are the children of Eurystheus) and his wife. Upon recovering from his madness, Heracles is filled with despair. Thereupon Theseus (whom Heracles brought back from the Underworld in his final Labour) arrives upon the scene, helps to restore his courage, and takes him away to Athens to be purified. For the *Hercules furens* of Seneca see that entry.

He'raclids, see HERACLEIDAE and HERACLES, CHILDREN OF.

Heracli'tus, see HERACLEITUS.

Hērae'a, Greek festival held at Argos every four years in honour of Hera, and celebrated with a procession to the *Heraeum, the priestess riding in a chariot drawn by oxen (see CLEOBIS AND BITON); there was a hecatomb, and athletic contests in the stadium near the temple, for which the prize was a bronze shield.

Hērae'um, 'temple of *Hera', the most famous being that in Argos, 3 km. (2 miles) south-east of Mycenae. An early wooden temple there was destroyed by fire in 423 BC; the new temple, containing the famous gold and ivory statue by *Polycleitus, was built *c*.416 BC.

Herculā'neum, ancient Italian town built on a spur projecting from the lower slopes of the volcano Vesuvius and to the west of it, about 8 km. (5 miles) from Naples. In the first century AD it was a small and wealthy residential town. The eruption of Vesuvius on 24 August AD 79, which also destroyed *Pompeii, overwhelmed it with a mud-flow (rather than volcanic ash). As a result, although the buildings are more collapsed than at Pompeii, the furnishings, being completely sealed in, are better preserved. But the mud set hard so that the town is buried beneath solid rock on which is built the modern town of Resina. Excavation, or rather treasure-hunting, began in the mid-eighteenth century. More systematic excavation has been carried out since 1987. In one of the luxurious villas nearby, excavated in the eighteenth century, and now known as Villa dei Papyri, a fine collection of sculpture was found (now in Naples museum) and a small library of carbonized papyrus rolls containing works on Epicurean philosophy, mainly by Philodemus (fl. 75–35 BC), the influential Epicurean teacher of philosophy, but also by Epicurus himself. See PISO CAESONINUS.

He'rculēs, the Roman adaptation of the Greek hero *Heracles. His was perhaps the earliest foreign cult to be brought to Italy by colonists of Magna Graecia. His altar, the *Ara Maxima, stood in the *Forum Boarium ('cattle market'); here he was worshipped as the god of victory and of commercial enterprise. The *gens *Fabia traced its origin to him. The myth of Hercules and *Cacus, which Virgil makes *Evander narrate (*Aeneid* 8), is probably of Roman origin, perhaps invented to explain the presence of his altar in the Forum Boarium.

Hercules furens, Roman tragedy by *Seneca (2), based on Euripides' play *Heracles* (see HERACLES, MADNESS OF). There are differences of detail: Lycus, instead of threatening to kill Heracles' children, demands his wife in marriage; and Heracles' murder of her and the children forms part of the actual drama.

Hercules Oetae'us ('Hercules on Mount Oeta'), Roman tragedy by *Seneca (2), based on the *Trachiniae* of Sophocles. The play is of great length (part of it is thought to be spurious) and shows variations from the original, presenting Dēianeira not as a gentle and attractive figure but as fiercely jealous,

and adding a scene showing Heracles' death and deification on Mount Oeta in Thessaly.

Here'nnium, Rheto'rica ad, Latin treatise on oratory; see RHETORICA AD HERENNIUM.

Hermae ('herms'), at Athens especially (but also elsewhere in Greece), quadrangular stone pillars bearing an erect phallus and surmounted by a bust of the god *Hermēs (later other gods as well) depicted with old-style pointed beard, set up as boundary-marks at crossroads, by the roadside, near public buildings, and in front of houses; some acted as signposts. They replaced the heaps of stones which were the customary ancient boundary marks. Being phallic they were intended to be apotropaic, i.e. to avert evil influences. At Athens some were set up c.520 BC by Hipparchus, son of the tyrant Peisistratus, with moral maxims engraved on them. They were regarded with reverence; hence the indignation and alarm felt at Athens when in the course of a night shortly before the departure of the *Sicilian Expedition in 415 BC the herms were mutilated.

Hermaphrodī'tus, in Greek myth, son of Hermēs and Aphroditē, who was loved by Salmacis, the nymph of the fountain in which he bathed, near Halicarnassus. She closely embraced him and prayed to the gods to make them one body, which they did. In art Hermaphroditus is accordingly portrayed as a beautiful youth with developed breasts.

Hermēs, in Greek myth, son of Zeus and *Maia. He was born on Mount Cyllēnē in Arcadia. By noon on the day that he was born he had left his cradle and invented the lyre, killing a tortoise and making the instrument from its shell. The same day he drove off fifty cows belonging to Apollo, making them walk backwards so that they should not be traced, and then returned to his cradle. When Apollo, informed by an old man, arrived in a rage, he was mollified by the gift of the lyre and allowed Hermes to keep the cattle he had stolen and gave him in addition various divine powers. This story is told in the fourth *Homeric Hymn. The name Hermes, which appears in the *Linear B tablets, appears to be derived from *herma*, a pile of stones set up to mark a boundary (see HERMAE). He was the god of roads and boundaries, the messenger or herald of the gods, and conductor of the souls of the dead to the Underworld, *psychopompos*; he was also the god of sleep and dreams. Furtiveness and trickery were his attributes as well: he was the god of luck, particularly in the matter of making money, the patron of merchants and thieves; every lucky find was a *hermaion*, gift of Hermes. He was the patron of athletics, and his statue was commonly erected in gymnasia. In many parts of Greece he was the god of herdsmen and of the fertility of herds. Successful communication with enemies and strangers was due to Hermes, hence the Greek word for interpreter, *hermēneus*; and he gives his name to the art of interpretation, 'hermeneutics'. For this reason he was regarded as the patron of oratory with an interest in literature generally. He is represented with wings on his sandals, a winged cap or a broad-brimmed felt hat, and the herald's staff (*kērykeion*, Lat. *cādūcĕus*) on which two serpents are twined in a broken figure-of-eight shape. Hermes was identified by the Romans with their god *Mercury. See also PAN and HERMAPHRODITUS.

Hermēs Trismegi'stus ('thrice-greatest'). This name was given by the *Neoplatonists and the devotees of mysticism and alchemy to the Egyptian god Thoth (who was identified with the Greek god Hermes), the father and protector of all knowledge, who was believed to be the author, under this name, of a collection of Greek and Latin religious and philosophical writings, dating probably from the first to the third centuries AD. The aim of this mystical teaching was the deification of humankind through knowledge of God.

Hermī'onē, in Greek myth, daughter of Menelaus and *Helen (of Troy), wife of *Neoptolemus and later of *Orestēs.

Hermo'genēs, of Tarsus, b. *c.* AD 160, Greek rhetorician, author of several treatises, the most important of which is *Peri ideōn* ('on types of style'). He finds that authors have many different qualities of style, and distinguishes between them with considerable subtlety. Demosthenes is the outstanding exemplar of all qualities. Compare DEMETRIUS (3) and *LONGINUS ON THE SUBLIME*.

herms, see HERMAE.

Hero, heroine of a love story known to us from Ovid but perhaps of Hellenistic origin. For her story see LEANDER.

hero-cult, etc.; see HEROES and CULT.

Herod (Hērōdēs). 1. Herod the Great (*c.*73 BC–4 BC), King of Judaea (a Roman protectorate since 63 BC), his authority being established when Jerusalem was captured by the Romans in 37 BC. He ruled Judaea on the lines of a Hellenistic kingdom, built and adorned cities, and gave peace and prosperity. But he was tyrannical and unscrupulous, and though by his loyalty he retained Augustus' confidence for many years, his high-handed behaviour and his cruelty to his family— he put to death his wife, her two sons, and his own eldest son—lost him Rome's support. Not even his magnificent rebuilding of the Temple won him the affection of the Jews, who hated him for being a foreigner among other things (he was born in Idumaea, south of Judaea, and became a Roman citizen in 47 BC). He is said to have ordered the slaughter of the male children in Bethlehem in order to procure the death of the infant Jesus. His title 'Great' comes from *Josephus.

2. The erroneously called 'Herod' of Acts 12, M. Julius Agrippa (10 BC–AD 44), grandson of Herod the Great, friend of the Roman emperors Caligula and Claudius, who was granted by these emperors territories in Palestine which eventually comprised all the land his grandfather had ruled over. He was a popular ruler; on his death Claudius annexed the whole kingdom. It was before his son, Agrippa II, that the apostle Paul was brought (Acts 25).

Hērō'das or **Herondas** (*c.*300–250 BC), native of Cos or Miletus, a Greek writer of literary *mimes, *mimiambi*, in the Ionic dialect and in scazons (see METRE, GREEK 2). Only a few fragments existed in quotation until the publication in 1891 of a papyrus found in Egypt to which other fragments were later added. There now exist mimes 1–7 complete, and 8 and 9 in a fragmentary state. These are short, dramatic vignettes, probably intended for private reading rather than for solo performance, and present with vividness and humour scenes typical of mime, drawn from city life: the bawd, the pimp, the schoolmaster, the women worshippers, the jealous mistress, the private conversation, the shoemaker, the dream, women entertaining.

Hērō'dēs A'tticus (L. Vibullius Hipparchus Tiberius Claudius Atticus Herodes, AD 101–77), Athenian *sophist and rhetorician, born at Marathon, consul at Rome (with Fronto) in 143. His fame as an orator, teacher, and public benefactor won him the friendship of powerful men: he enjoyed the support of the emperors Hadrian and Antoninus Pius, and was the instructor of the emperor Marcus Aurelius and his co-emperor Lucius Verus. He came of an ancient family which was reputed to trace its descent from the Greek hero *Aeacus. With prodigious generosity he endowed public buildings on a grand scale, including at Athens the stadium (in Pentelic marble), the Odeum, and a temple to Fortune. Aulus *Gellius has left an account of pleasant days spent with him at his villa among the woods of Cephissia (in Attica), which was a literary centre. None of his writings has survived except for one speech doubtfully attributed to him and a Latin translation of another by Aulus Gellius.

Hērō'dian. 1. Aelius Hērōdiānus, son of *Apollonius Dyscolus the Greek grammarian, who lived at Rome under Marcus Aurelius (emperor AD 161–80) and wrote in Greek on a number of grammatical subjects. His principal work was a treatise on Greek accents in twenty-one books, of which only excerpts survive. Two other small works are extant.

2. Of Syria (fl. c. AD 230). He wrote in Greek a history of the Roman emperors in eight books, from the death of Marcus Aurelius in AD 180 to the accession of Gordian III in 238, being a contemporary observer. His authority is generally preferable to that of the *Historia Augusta.

Hero'dotus (c.490–c.425 BC), Greek historian, author of the 'Histories' (historiai, 'inquiries') of the Persian Wars, son of Lyxēs, of a distinguished family in *Halicarnassus in Caria, at that time a city of Ionian Greek culture. He was a kinsman (nephew or cousin) of the epic poet *Panyassis, who was put to death by Lygdamis, tyrant of Halicarnassus, in the political troubles of the 460s. Herodotus withdrew or was exiled to Samos and then travelled widely in Egypt and the Greek world. He visited Athens in the mid-440s, where he is said to have become acquainted with Pericles, before (reputedly) joining the Athenian colony at Thurii (founded 443) near Sybaris in south Italy. He mentions Greek events of 430 but none later, and is presumed to have died before 420.

Herodotus has been called by Cicero and others 'the father of history' because in his account of the Persian Wars he was writing on a scale and with a comprehensiveness that had never been attempted before, and with a grasp of the decisive importance these wars had for the future development of the Mediterranean world. He describes the scope of his work in the opening sentence: it is an investigation, historiē, undertaken so that the great achievements of Greeks and *barbarians (in this case, the people of Asia) may not be forgotten, and in particular, to show how they came to fight one another. He was writing a generation after the wars, and facts were hard to come by. His sources were for the most part not written down; he himself emphasized that his work was based on what he had seen and what he had heard and the conclusions he had drawn. On this basis, he was trying to make a true and systematic record. He sought out those who had the information he needed: aristocrats who preserved their family history (information particularly liable to distortion for political or other reasons), and priests and officials who had access to written records; but in foreign countries where he did not know the language he had to rely on interpreters. His history was shaped in subtle ways by many influences. He may have learned from Homer to divide the world into Greeks and barbarians and to see his purpose as akin to that of epic, namely to preserve the memory of great deeds. He understood the events of history to originate in the characters and actions of individual great men and saw an inexorable moral providence underpinning his whole history: the gods bring it about that overweening pride eventually ends in ruin; the gods intervene in human affairs; their oracles cannot be disregarded. But as well as divinely operated cause and effect Herodotus understood that on a different, non-moral level, scientific cause and effect operated. His search for rational explanations of things and his interest in natural causes reveal his own cast of mind, as well as the influence of earlier Ionian scientists and *logographers, 'those who write accounts of stories', especially *Hecataeus. Herodotus' digressions from the main theme of his history, from mere anecdotes to a whole book on Egypt, for example, may be in the manner of such writers, but the boundless scientific curiosity they display is entirely Herodotus' own. These digressions diversify Herodotus' work so that parts of it are, rather than history, studies in anthropology, ethnography, and archaeology.

The History comprises the struggle between Greece and Asia from the time of Croesus (mid-sixth century BC) to Xerxes' retreat from Greece (478 BC). It has been regarded as unfinished but it is not clear that Herodotus intended to cover events later than the capture of Sestus, which concludes the ninth and last book; the last episode, indicating Persian degeneracy at the end, has a final ring. The division of the work into nine books each named after a Muse is probably the scheme of Alexandrian editors; Herodotus himself divided his work into *logoi*, 'episodes'. So improbable did some of his stories seem to later Greeks that he had the reputation of being a liar: Plutarch accused him also of unfairness and uncharitableness (Plutarch came from Boeotia whose chief town, Thebes, was the bitter enemy of Athens). In modern times Herodotus' attempts to use oral tradition in describing other societies have been better understood and his reputation for veracity restored. His style is simple, clear, and graceful, and his narrative has great charm. He wrote in his native Ionic dialect, using also archaic and poetic forms; the manuscripts, however, include forms that it seems unlikely Herodotus could ever have written, the text having been compiled perhaps by later Greek editors ignorant of the correct usage. The following are the principal subjects of the several books:

Book 1. Blame for the conflict between Greeks and barbarians is attributed to Croesus, whose attack on Cyrus of Persia ruined his own kingdom of Lydia. A digression explains why neither Athens nor Sparta helped Croesus. The conquest of the *Medes by Cyrus is followed by his subjection of the Greeks of Asia Minor, and then an account of the Persian empire under Cyrus, and of Babylon; the book ends with the war of Cyrus against the Massagetae.

Book 2. This book is devoted to a description of Egypt, the pretext for which is furnished by the invasion of that country by Cambysēs, Cyrus' son and heir (the story of Rhampsinītus is in chapter 121).

Book 3. The conquest of Egypt by Cambyses, the story of the Persian usurper, the false Smerdis, and the accession and reforms of Darius (anecdotes of Polycratēs, tyrant of Samos, and his sealring, 40, and of Zōpyrus and the capture of Babylon, 153).

Book 4. The expeditions of Darius in Scythia and Libya (145), with an account of their peoples.

Book 5. The operations of the Persian general Megabazus with a detachment of troops against the Thracians, and an account of the latter; the Ionian Revolt (28) and the burning of the Persian city of Sardis by the Ionians (101).

Book 6. The suppression of the Ionian revolt; the march of the Persian general Mardonius to Macedonia and the wreck of the Persian fleet off Mount Athos (43); the second Persian expedition to Greece under Datis and Artaphernes (94); the Greek victory at Marathon (102); Pheidippidēs' run from Athens to Sparta (105); anecdote of Cleisthenes and Hippocleidēs (126). Events on the Persian side are alternated with events at Sparta and Athens.

Book 7. The death of Darius; preparations by Xerxes, his son and heir, and invasion of Greece; defeat of the Greeks at Thermopylae (201).

Book 8. Victories of the Greeks at Artemisium and Salamis (56); the withdrawal of Xerxes (97).

Book 9. The victory of the Greeks at Plataea and the retreat of the Persians; the victory of the Greeks at Mycalē (98); the capture of Sestus (previously held by the Persians; 114).

heroes (Gk. *hērŏĕs*). In archaic and classical Greece the Greeks thought that in times past there was living in Greece a race of men and women who were bigger, stronger, braver, and more beautiful than the men and women of their own day. These were heroes and heroines, the offspring or descendants of unions between gods and mortals, but still essentially human. The age in which they lived, the Heroic age, was quite short, embracing no more than two or three generations, and not wholly remote; it was the period of the Theban wars (see SEVEN AGAINST THEBES) and the siege of Troy, the latter dated to the early twelfth century BC by the Greeks, who believed both events to be historical. The exploits of the heroes at Thebes and Troy was the stuff of epic poetry, often called in consequence 'heroic' poetry. The fact that Greek myths are dominated by stories about them rather than about gods makes them different from the myths of other cultures and gives them their human scale and interest. The close association of heroes and gods and the latters' interventions in the heroes' lives often give a moral significance to heroic myths and to the characters of the heroes. From the eighth century BC onwards, when the Homeric epics became widely popular (see HOMER), ancient burial sites came to be thought of as the graves of Homer's heroes, and, since they had been superhumanly powerful, sacrifices and rites were performed by the graves in the hope that in return for cult the heroes would actively defend their own locality, rising from the dead when the need arose. Only *Heracles, exceptional in this as in other respects, was both hero and god, his apotheosis following upon his death. Any community would be glad to have its own hero; aristocratic clans often

claimed descent from one. The poet Hesiod, in his myth of the five ages of humankind (see WORKS AND DAYS and GOLDEN AGE), described the heroes as constituting the glorious race that existed before this present sadly degenerate age of iron. In practice, however, not all so-called heroes belonged to the heroic age or were the offspring of gods: ordinary men who were outstanding in some way were sometimes paid heroic honours after death as being the possessors of power that might be channelled to good use: the Spartan general *Brasidas was so honoured after his death in battle in 422 BC.

Heroic age, see HEROES above.

Heroic poetry, see EPIC POETRY.

Hērŏ'idēs (or *Hērōidum epistulae*, 'letters of heroines'), Latin amatory poems in elegiacs by *Ovid, in the form of letters purporting to be addressed by heroines of legend to their lovers or husbands, though they read rather like dramatic monologues. In the first fourteen letters women address men (the authenticity of the fifteenth letter, from Sappho to Phaon, is doubted); letters 16–21 are in pairs, the woman answering the man's letter. It used to be thought that this last group was not by Ovid. The first group was published between the two editions of the *Amores*, i.e. towards the end of the first century BC; the second group perhaps in the earliest years of the first century AD, before Ovid's exile in AD 8. He claimed that they constituted a new literary form, invented by him.

The letters of the heroines are studies of love from the woman's point of view, based perhaps on observation but also on rhetorical training in character-drawing; the sentiments and moral standpoint are those of contemporary Rome. This technique Ovid applies to the characters of Greek epic and drama, and of the Hellenistic poets, as well as of those depicted by the Roman poets, Virgil's Dido and Catullus' Ariadne (poem 64). The heroines are represented in various situations: betrayed or deserted (Dēianeira, Phyllis, Medea, Ariadne, Oenonē, Dido), neglected (Brisēis), bound in a hateful marriage (Hermione), punished for their love (Hypermnestra, Canacē), the victim of unlawful passion (Phaedra), or anxious for their husbands' safety (Penelope, Laodamia). Compare CATA-LOGUE OF WOMEN.

Hērondas, see HERODAS.

Hēro'philē, most ancient of the legendary *Sibyls.

Hēro'philus (first half of the third century BC), from Chalcedon, one of the great founders (with *Erasistratus) of medicine at Alexandria. He made his mark primarily for his study of human anatomy based on human dissection; he is alleged to have practised vivisection on criminals. His writings (which survive only in quotation) included an account of the liver; he correctly opposed the orthodoxy of his day that the veins originated there. His studies of the genital organs, the eye, and the brain were famous; his names for some of the main sections and chambers still survive in their Latin form (the term 'duodenum' is his also, a translation of the Greek *dōdekadaktulos*, 'twelve fingers long'). He established that the brain and not the heart was the centre of the nervous system (as did Hippocrates, *On the Sacred Disease*, ch. 6), maintaining for the first time the distinction between motor and sensory nerves. The vascular system was not understood by the physicians of his day, and no connection was seen between heart beat and pulse beat. Herophilus probably accepted that the arteries contained blood (not air, as was generally thought), and certainly believed that pulse beat was caused by the normal contraction and dilation of the arteries, though he did not understand that the blood circulated through the arteries because of the pumping action of the heart. He invented a portable water-clock (*clepsydra*) to measure pulse beat. He also made increased use of drugs, calling them 'the hands of the gods'. His pathology however showed no advance on that of his predecessors; having no knowledge of bacteria, he believed, as did almost everyone else, that disease was caused by an imbalance of humours. The information about him that survives

attests a man of great intellectual ability, wit, and wisdom.

Hērōs ('hero'), Greek comedy by *Menander.

Hēro'stratus, the man who burned down the temple of *Ephesus in 356 BC 'to make his name immortal', according to *Valerius Maximus.

Hē'siod (Hēsiodos) (lived *c*.700 BC), one of the earliest known Greek poets, and with Homer representative of early Greek *epic poetry. He tells us himself something of his life: his father gave up his livelihood of sea-trading as being unprofitable and moved from Cymē in Aeolis (on the coast of Asia Minor) to Ascra in Boeotia, where Hesiod was born, to become a farmer. As Hesiod was tending the sheep on Mount Helicon he heard the Muses calling him to become a poet and sing of the gods (*Theogony* 22). He once took part in a poetic contest at Chalcis in Euboea and won a tripod. On his father's death the estate was divided between Hesiod and his brother Perses; the latter claimed more than his share and a dispute ensued in which Perses bribed the authorities to favour him. Hesiod is said to have died in Locris, but his tomb was shown at Orchomenus in Boeotia. The story of his meeting and contest with Homer is certainly untrue. Two genuine poems of his survive, the *Theogony* and the *Works and Days*. A third short poem, the *Shield of Heracles*, is not genuine. The *Catalogue of Women*, thought by the ancient Greeks to be by Hesiod, exists only in fragments. Among other works attributed to him, of which only small fragments survive, are the *Precepts of Chiron*, the *Melampodia* (stories of famous seers), and an *Astronomy*. In the *Works and Days* Hesiod sought his subject from outside the field of myth (see DIDACTIC POETRY), and much of the poem seems to derive from his own experience and to reveal his own character. He wrote in the same oral tradition as Homer, using the epic dialect (see DIALECTS), but perhaps at a later stage of its evolution.

Hēsi'onē, in Greek myth, daughter of *Laomedon, wife of *Telamon, and mother of *Teucer.

Hespe'ria, in Latin, 'the western land', from Greek *hespera*, 'west'. From the Greek point of view the term often denotes Italy; from the Roman, Spain.

Hespe'ridĕs, in Greek myth, the daughters of Night (Nyx) and Darkness (*Erebus) who lived in the extreme West on the edge of Ocean, guarding a tree that produced golden apples (see HERACLES, LABOURS OF 11), a present given by Gaia to Hera when the latter married Zeus. The tree was also watched by the dragon Ladon (whom Heracles killed). From the same tree came the apples thrown down before *Atalanta.

He'sperus (Lat. Vesper), the evening star.

He'stia ('hearth'), in Greek myth, the virgin daughter of *Cronus and Rhea, goddess of the hearth and symbol of the home and family. The goddess was never developed, hardly anthropomorphized, and has virtually no mythology; Homer never mentions her. When a new baby was accepted into the family and received its name, someone ran with it round the hearth. A hearth with ever-burning fire was consecrated to her in the chief public building (*prytanēum*) of every capital city (and at Delphi and Olympia); fire from this was taken to every new colony of that city. Sacrifices began with libations to Hestia and she was mentioned first in prayers; the beginning of a meal was marked by small offerings being thrown on to the fire. The Romans worshipped her as *Vesta, and accorded her considerably more importance than the Greeks did Hestia. See GODS 1.

Hēsy'chius (probably fifth century AD), Alexandrian Greek lexicographer, whose lexicon is known from one badly preserved fifteenth-century manuscript, itself a considerable abridgement of the original work. Even so it is a valuable aid for the study of Greek dialects and inscriptions, and it often preserves correct readings which have been replaced in Greek literary texts by easier synonyms.

hetae'rae (*hetairai*, 'female companions'), in Greece, a euphemistic name for prostitutes and courtesans. Many were musicians or dancers, hired to entertain at dinner parties. Some of them

were highly accomplished and became known as the mistresses of distinguished men, as, for example, *Aspasia (mistress of Periclēs), Lais (who loved Diogenēs the Cynic), *Phrynē, and Leontion (who loved Epicurus). *Hetaerae* figured prominently as characters in New Comedy (see COMEDY, GREEK 6), where they inspired infatuation in young men, and are often credited with hearts of gold.

hexa'meter, SEE METRE, GREEK 1.

He'xapla, the six parallel versions of the Old Testament compiled by *Origen.

hiā'tus ('gap'), in Greek and Latin poetry, a break in a line when a vowel at the end of one word is not elided before a vowel at the beginning of the next, as it would be by normal scansion (see ELISION). If the earlier vowel is long it may retain its length or be shortened (for an explanation of 'long' and 'short' in metric see METRE, GREEK 1). Hiatus is common in Greek epic verse (see DIGAMMA), rare in Latin epic.

Hibe'rnia (Gk. Hiernē), the Latin name for Ireland. The Greeks knew of Ireland from *c.*500 BC, and Eratosthenes, writing *c.*235 BC, placed it correctly on his map; Strabo, writing at the end of the first century BC, had heard that its savage inhabitants were cannibals; *Agricola in the first century AD reconnoitred the coast, meditating conquest; Solinus in the third century is the first to observe that there are no snakes in Ireland. Ptolemy a century earlier shows fair knowledge of the whole coast and even mentions seven inland towns; some of his names are still current, e.g. Liboius (Liffey), and Eblana (Dublin).

Hī'eroclēs, probably of Alexandria, *Stoic philosopher of the early second century AD, author of *Elements of Ethics* (*Ēthikē stoicheiōsis*) of which a large part has survived.

Hī'eron I and II (unrelated), rulers of *Syracuse.

Hi'eron, one of the minor works of the Athenian *Xenophon (428–*c.*354 BC), a dialogue between Hieron I, tyrant of Syracuse, and *Simonides, in which the lot of the tyrant and that of the private citizen are compared; Hieron points out the disadvantages of the former, while Simonides shows how a tyrant, by ruling well, may make himself popular and so acquire happiness.

Hiero'nymus. 1. Of Cardia (third century BC), the contemporary and trustworthy historian of the period from the death of Alexander the Great (323 BC) to the death of Pyrrhus, king of Epirus, in 272 BC, or perhaps as far as 263. He served as general and statesman under Eumenēs of Cardia (secretary to Philip II of Macedon and his son Alexander), Antigonus I (one of Alexander's generals), his son Demetrius and his grandson Antigonus Gonatas, and thus had firsthand knowledge of the events he related. His history is lost but is the most important source behind Arrian and Diodorus (books 18–20), and was used by Plutarch for his Lives of Eumenes, Pyrrhus, and Demetrius.

2. See JEROME.

Hi'mera, town on the north coast of Sicily, founded c.648 BC by colonists from Zanclē in the east of the island, itself a Euboean colony founded in the previous century. Its most famous citizen was the poet Stesichorus. It was the scene in 480 BC of a spectacular defeat of the Carthaginians by Gelon, tyrant of Syracuse, and Theron of Acragas.

Hime'rius (AD c.310–c.390), Greek rhetorician from Bithynia, twenty-four of whose ceremonial speeches survive, incidentally valuable for their quotations from Greek lyric poetry otherwise lost. His pupils at Athens included the Christian Fathers St Gregory of Nazianzus and St Basil.

Hippa'rchicus, see CAVALRY COMMANDER.

Hippa'rchia, see CYNIC PHILOSOPHERS: CRATES.

Hippa'rchus. 1. Younger son of Peisistratus, tyrant of Athens, who ruled Athens jointly with his brother Hippias after the death of their father in 527 BC. He was a patron of literature and art. He was murdered by *Harmodius and Aristogeiton in 514 BC. See PEISISTRATUS 3.

2. (c.190–after 126 BC), the greatest of ancient astronomers, a Greek born at Nicaea in Bithynia but living mostly in Rhodes. His only surviving work is his commentary on the *Phaenomena* of *Eudoxus and *Aratus; Hipparchus criticizes the accuracy of Aratus' source, Eudoxus. Most of our knowledge of his other work comes from the *Almagest*, the astronomical textbook of *Ptolemy (second century AD). His principal work was his catalogue of more than 800 fixed stars arranged in categories of magnitude and brightness, their positions fixed by latitude and longitude in relation to the ecliptic (the geocentric path of the sun). He is famous for his discovery of the precession of the equinoxes (i.e. the slight change in timing in each successive year), achieved by comparing his observation of the position of a particular star with the observation made 160 years earlier; his figure differs by only ten seconds from the modern estimate. He calculated more accurately the length of the natural year (from one equinox to the same equinox again), but his retention of the erroneous geocentric theory (as opposed to *Aristarchus' heliocentric theory), made his calculations on the relative size and distance of the sun and moon inaccurate. He is the first person known to have made systematic use of trigonometry, and was probably the inventor of stereographic projection. His researches on the sphere led him to criticize the geographical procedures of *Eratosthenes; he himself applied more rigorous mathematical methods to specify location, and again was apparently the first to use latitude and longitude systematically.

hippeis ('knights', 'the cavalry'), at Athens, one of the names of the top social class; under *Solon, the second of his census-classes, those sufficiently wealthy to keep a horse. For Aristophanes' play see KNIGHTS.

Hi'ppias. 1. Eldest son of Peisistratus, tyrant of Athens, and himself tyrant from 527 to 510 BC. At first a mild ruler, he became harsher as his reign progressed. His brother *Hipparchus was assassinated in 514 BC; during his reign the Spartans invaded and were repulsed, but a second invasion in 510 forced him to withdraw from Athens to the colony of Sigeum and thence to the court of the Persian king Darius. He was with the

Persian forces when they were defeated by the Greeks at Marathon in 490 BC. See PEISISTRATUS 3.

2. Of Elis, a *sophist of the later fifth century BC, a contemporary of Socrates, whose vast range of learning included grammar, poetry, mathematics, and astronomy. He is vividly depicted in two of Plato's dialogues, *Hippias Minor* and *Major* (the latter less certainly by Plato). He is commonly said to have compiled a list of victors at the Olympian games for chronological purposes.

hi'ppikēs, Peri, see HORSEMANSHIP.

hippoca'mpus, in Greek art, a monster on which sea-gods often rode; it had a horse's body and a fish's tail.

Hippoclei'dēs, Athenian who won immortality through an anecdote in Herodotus. He had become the favourite with Cleisthenes, tyrant of Sicyon, to marry the latter's daughter. At the feast at which Cleisthenes' choice was to be made known Hippocleides ordered the flute-player to play a dance and 'probably danced to his own satisfaction', concluding by standing on his head and gesticulating with his legs, but he gravely displeased his intended father-in-law. 'Son of Teisandros, you have danced away your marriage', he was told; his reply, 'Hippocleides doesn't care', became proverbial. (The daughter Agaristē later married Megacles of the family of the Alcmaeonidae: their son was Cleisthenes, the great reformer of the Athenian constitution.)

Hippo'cratēs. 1. The most famous figure in Greek medicine, born in the island of Cos about 460 BC. He lived to at least 370 and he is said to have died at Larisa (in Thessaly). Scarcely anything is known about his life; yet the attitudes apparent in the writings that go under his name as well as the medical practice they describe are attributed to him personally. The former still express the ethical ideal of a doctor, and the latter too has exerted a very strong influence until comparatively recent times. The collection of medical writings known as the Hippocratic Corpus consists of some sixty treatises, all in the Ionic Greek *dialect, most of which were compiled between

c.430 and 330 BC. There is no evidence that Hippocrates wrote any of them personally. The collection as a whole seems to have been made in the third century BC. It may represent the contents of the library of the Hippocratic school of medicine associated with the healing shrine of the god *Asclepius on Cos. The works cover surgery, epidemiology, pharmacology, embryology, and anatomy, including treatises on prognosis and general health care, in some cases propounding widely differing medical doctrines.

Of two fifth-century works, *On Airs, Waters and Places* and *On the Sacred Disease* (epilepsy), the former discusses the effect of climate, water supply, and region on people, and compares the geophysical conditions of life in Europe and Asia; the latter attacks popular superstitions about the disease and demonstrates that, no differently from any other disease, it arises from natural causes. The *Epidemics* contain the interestingly detailed case-book studies of over forty patients with serious illnesses (of which most of the patients died); books 1 and 3 appear to date from the fifth century. The *Aphorisms* or collection of medical sayings contain the famous dictum: 'Life is short, science (*technē*) long, opportunity fleeting, experiment dangerous, judgement difficult.' The Hippocratic Oath seems to have originated in a particular group of medical practitioners, but most of the ideals it expresses are common to all. In the Middle Ages 'Ypocras' became a favourite subject with European storytellers in tales of magic and intrigue, as was 'Bokrát' among Arabic writers, who represented him as studying in a garden near Damascus.

2. Of Chios (*c.*470–400 BC), Greek mathematician whose writings are lost. He was the first to collect together an *Elements of Geometry* (the forerunner of Euclid's *Elements*), which must have contained the propositions known to the Pythagoreans, and presumably contained a certain amount of the geometry of the circle.

Hi'ppocrēne (Hippokrēnē), fountain sacred to the Muses on Mount *Helicon in Boeotia (see PEGASUS), supposedly with the power to inspire with poetry those who drank from it.

Hippodamei'a. 1. In Greek myth, daughter of Oenomaus and wife of *Pelops.

2. In Greek myth, wife of Pīrithŏus, king of the Lapiths (see CENTAURS and THESEUS).

Hippoda'mus, of Miletus (fifth century BC), the most famous Greek town-planner. In the mid-fifth century he planned the town of *Piraeus around the original sea-port, substituting broad straight streets intersecting at right angles in place of crooked, narrow streets. He was also the architect of the Athenian colony of Thurii (near Sybaris) in 443 BC and, according to one tradition, of the city of Rhodes, founded in 408 BC.

hi'ppodrome, in Greece and Rome, track for horse- and chariot-races.

Hippo'lytē (or Hippolyta). 1. In Greek myth, queen of the Amazons, sometimes called Antiopē; see HERACLES, LABOURS OF 9 and THESEUS.

2. In Greek myth, wife of Acastus, sometimes called Astydameia; see PELEUS.

Hippo'lytus, in Greek myth, the son of *Theseus and the Amazon queen Hippolytē; after the latter's death Theseus married *Phaedra, the sister of Ariadne. During his absence Phaedra fell in love with Hippolytus who, being honourable, rejected her advances. Moreover, as a devotee of the goddess Artemis he led a life of perfect chastity. Phaedra subsequently hanged herself, after writing a letter to Theseus denouncing Hippolytus as her seducer. Theseus, not believing his protestations of innocence, banished him, and also used against him one of the three curses which he had been given by the god Poseidon. As Hippolytus drove away from the palace along the shore a monster or bull sent from the sea by Poseidon terrified the horses; Hippolytus was thrown from the chariot and dragged to his death. Theseus learned of his error from Artemis too late. Hippolytus had a cult at Troezen (north-east Peloponnese), the scene of his death, which included laments for him and offerings of hair from girls about to marry. Virgil and other authors relate that Hippolytus was brought back to life by *Asclepius and was conveyed by *Diana (the Roman equivalent of Artemis) to the grove of the nymph Aricia at Nemi in Latium, where under the name of Virbius (*vir bis*, 'a man twice') he lived out his days. His son by Diana, also called Virbius according to Virgil, was among the heroes who resisted the settlement of Aeneas in Latium.

Hippo'lytus, Greek tragedy by *Euripides produced in 429 BC. For the story see above. Euripides makes Phaedra a virtuous woman trying to resist her passion, her feelings betrayed to Hippolytus by her nurse. The false accusation Phaedra makes in the letter to Theseus was motivated, according to Euripides, by shame and anger at Hippolytus' scorn. See also PHAEDRA, the Roman tragedy of Seneca. The subject is treated by the French dramatist Jean Racine in his tragedy *Phèdre* (1677).

Hippō'nax, of Ephesus (mid-sixth century BC), Greek poet of satirical, often scurrilous, verse. He invented his own version of the iambic trimeter, making it end with a spondee, the so-called 'limping iambic' or scazon; see METRE, GREEK 5 (iii). He was banished from Ephesus and moved to Clazomenae, another Ionian city, where according to one of his poems he lived in great poverty. His poems survive only in fragments, but enough remain to show his mordant wit, his realism, and his vigorous use of earthy Greek laced with colloquialisms and words from local dialects. He attacked his enemies with gusto. The best known (apocryphal) story about him relates his quarrel with the sculptor Bupalus and his brother Athēnis, who made a statue caricaturing the features of the poet. He retaliated with such offensive verse that they both hanged themselves. Hipponax is sometimes credited, not impossibly, with the invention of parody.

Hi'rtius, Aulus, one of Julius Caesar's lieutenants in Gaul and consul with Vibius Pansa in 43 BC after Caesar's assassination; in the subsequent fighting Cicero persuaded him to take arms against Mark Antony, who was besieging Mutina. The two consuls, together with Octavian, raised the siege but were both killed (see BRUTUS (3)). Hirtius added the eighth book to Caesar's *Gallic War* (see COMMENTARIES I) and probably wrote the *Bellum Alexandrinum* as well.

Hispa'nia, see SPAIN.

Histiae'us, tyrant of the Ionian Greek city of Miletus who accompanied the Persian king *Darius on his expedition to Scythia, *c.*514 BC. Darius rewarded him with a district in Thrace where he built the strategically important city of Myrcinus, but grew distrustful of Histiaeus, who took to piracy, at one time occupying Byzantium. In 494/3 he was captured by the Persian satrap Artaphernēs and crucified.

Histo'ria Animā'lium ('inquiry into animals'; the usual English title is 'History of Animals'), treatise by *Aristotle; see 4 (iii) (e).

Histo'ria Augu'sta, name given by the Swiss scholar Casaubon in the early seventeenth century to a collection of biographies of Roman emperors, and certain heirs and claimants to the empire, from Hadrian to Numerianus (AD 117–284); there is a gap between 244 and 259. The biographies are attributed to six authors: Aelius Spartianus, Julius Capitolinus, Volcatius Gallicanus, Aelius Lampridius, Trebellius Pollio, and Flavius Vopiscus. Nothing is known of the authors. Of the Lives by the first four, some are addressed to Diocletian, some to Constantine the Great, and it was long assumed that they were written in the reigns of these emperors in the early fourth century. However, study of the style has led some to believe that the collection is the work of only one author, perhaps writing at the very end of the fourth century; the author's purpose in compiling this forgery has been variously described, as intended to entertain readers with sensational stories or even as a veiled pagan attack on Christianity. To others it still seems to be the work of more than one hand. It is clear that the documents cited in the *Historia* are mostly forgeries, and the historical value of the narrative is doubtful.

Histo'riae Phili'ppicae ('Philippic histories'), history of the world by *Trogus.

Historians

1. *Greek.* The following ancient historians wrote in Greek (some on Roman history): Apollodorus, Appian, Arrian, Callisthenes, Cassius Dio, Ctesias, Diodorus, Dionysius of Halicarnassus, Ephorus, Eratosthenes, Eusebius, Herodian, Herodotus, Josephus, Onesicritus, Plutarch, Polybius, Posidonius, Theopompus, Thucydides, Timaeus, Xenophon, and Logographers.

2. *Roman.* The following names include ancient historians who wrote in Latin, and the titles of Latin histories: Ammianus Marcellinus, *Annales*, Caesar, Cremutius Cordus, Curtius, Eutropius, Festus, Florus, Hirtius, *Historia Augusta*, Jerome, Justin, Livy, Nepos, Orosius, Sallust, Sisenna, Suetonius, Tacitus, Trogus, Valerius Maximus, Velleius Paterculus. See also HISTORIOGRAPHY.

Histo'ria plantā'rum ('inquiry into plants'), treatise by *Theophrastus.

Histories, The (*Historiae*), a work by the Roman historian *Tacitus. Originally twelve or fourteen books long, they dealt with the period AD 69–96, from Galba to Domitian, but only the first four books and part of the fifth survive, covering the events of the 'Year of the Four Emperors', 69, and the first nine months or so of 70. They were published, perhaps in instalments, between AD 105 and 108, and were written before the *Annals*. Portions were revised by the Younger Pliny, who sometimes furnished Tacitus with material, e.g. the account of the eruption of Vesuvius in AD 79 which caused the death of Pliny's uncle and namesake.

Book 1 opens with a survey of how, after the prosperous security of the Julio-Claudian dynasty, the empire is shaken by palace conspiracies, sudden murders, the armies moving on Rome from the frontiers, the frontiers themselves overrun by barbarians, the times 'rich in tragedies, terrible with battles, torn by civil strife'; even the Capitol is set on fire by citizens. It describes the brief reign of Galba, his adoption of Piso Licinianus, and the intrigues of Otho with the military which brought about the murder of Galba and Piso and his own accession (69). Tacitus brilliantly portrays the emperor Galba, his mediocrity, 'rather free from vices than endowed with virtues', the stinginess which was his undoing, his high birth and military reputation thanks to which he would have been judged 'equal to the imperial office had he not held it', *capax imperii nisi imperasset*. The narrative passes to the mutinous conduct of the legions in Germany, their adoption of Vitellius as emperor, the movement of his forces under Valens and Caecina, the negotiations between Otho and Vitellius, the shifting allegiances of provinces and legions, and the outbreak of civil war.

Book 2. Tacitus turns to the important role that the commanders Vespasian and Titus were playing in the East, where, except for the resistance of Jerusalem, the war against the Jews had been concluded. Vespasian and Mucianus, governor of Syria, decide to await developments. Tacitus then returns to events in Italy, the fighting around Bedriacum (on the road between Verona and Cremona), and the suicide of Otho, death seeming the only honourable course open to him. The reign of Vitellius is described, the emperor's sloth and gluttony, the disorder in the legions, the wasteful administration, and the threat of the advance of Vespasian's forces under Mucianus.

Book 3 describes the operations of Vespasian's generals against Vitellius, the siege and the terrible sack and burning of Cremona, the fighting in Rome between partisans of the opposing forces, which leads to the burning of the Capitol, the final capture of the city, and the end of Vitellius, discovered wandering forlornly in the deserted palace and put to death (December 69). The author's gift for sombre depiction is seen at its best in this book.

Book 4 and the surviving portion of book 5 are occupied with the reign of Vespasian, the rising of the Batavians under Civilis, and the expedition of Titus

against Jerusalem (the account of the siege is lost).

historiography

1. *Greek*. Greek prose history was first written in the late sixth century BC in Ionia. Coinciding with the development of early science and philosophy in that part of the Greek world, a rational and systematic approach was applied not only to local traditions and the more widespread myths of epic poetry, but also to the information gathered by seafaring people about the coastline and harbours, people, customs, and local history of the Mediterranean. These historians were the so-called *logographers, 'prose writers', of whom the most influential was *Hecataeus of Miletus (*c*.500 BC), but their work survives only in fragments. They wrote both local and general (not necessarily Greek) history. Local histories continued to be written throughout the fifth and fourth centuries; those of Attica for example (see ATTHIS) form much of the basis of Aristotle's *Constitution of Athens*. Lists of annual magistrates and similarly regular recurrences were also compiled with the aim of establishing a chronological framework, e.g. of eponymous archons at Athens, priestesses of Hera at Argos, and victors in the footrace at Olympia.

Greek history proper begins with the full-scale *historiai*, i.e. 'inquiries', of *Herodotus (b. *c*.490 BC); the word soon acquired its more restricted meaning. Herodotus' work established the scale of history, and his all-embracing curiosity, which made him include in his work, as well as history in its restricted sense, archaeology, ethnography, geography, religion, and a fair amount of anecdote, might well have established also its scope. His intellectual successor is in some sense Aristotle, writing treatises over a wide range of historical and scientific subjects. *Thucydides (b. *c*.460 BC) writing a generation later than Herodotus, and choosing to write on contemporary history in which he himself had played some part, was able to apply much more rigorous standards of factual accuracy than had been possible for the latter. He criticizes his immediate predecessors (left unnamed but certainly including

Herodotus) for writing what is merely entertaining to listen to for the moment, rather than what is true and has permanent value. He did not only aim to relate what actually happened; his passion for generalization led him to write on such large matters as the underlying cause of the Peloponnesian War, the behaviour of oligarchs and democrats, and the dynamics of imperialism. His influence narrowed the scope of history, turning it in the direction of politics almost before it had set off along the path Herodotus had indicated. Thucydides' combination of generalization with factual accuracy was difficult to sustain and no later Greek historian made the attempt. The nearest approach to his analytical style is that of *Polybius (b. c.200 BC).

In the fourth century BC a new type of history evolved under the direct influence both in style and moralistic outlook of *Isocrates (b. c.436 BC), but affected too by Plato's preoccupation with moral education. History became the vehicle of moral instruction and political prejudice, and style became more important than content. Isocrates' pupil Ephorus (b. c.405 BC) wrote a universal history, now lost, in which he appears to have regarded it as one of his chief functions to apportion praise or blame. This school of thought had great influence on the Roman historians.

In the Hellenistic age (from c.300 BC), historians generally aimed less at being accurate than at being readable. Careful historians like *Hieronymus of Cardia are the exception; the favoured style was rhetorical and romantic, and because history in this style gave prominence to outstanding individuals, it was the source for later biographers and ultimately Plutarch. Monographs on particular subjects continued to be written, along with histories of cities, memoirs, and other topics similarly limited in scope.

2. *Roman.* The earliest Roman historians, of whom *Fabius Pictor is the most celebrated, working at the beginning of the second century BC, wrote in Greek, both because they wished to glorify Rome's foundation and justify her institutions and policy to the Hellenistic world, and because Latin prose had not yet developed as a literary medium. Thus

they are primarily political writers in intent, within the tradition of Hellenistic Greek historiography; Polybius (b. c.200 BC) worked along the same lines to explore the rise of Rome, and this aim was further pursued but, for the first time in a work of this kind, in Latin, by *Cato (1) in his *Origines*, a history of Rome from its foundation, written between 168 and 149 BC. This great work, which survives only in fragments, inspired further historical study in Rome. The 'old' annalists (see ANNALS), Cassius Hemina and Calpurnius Piso, began the systematic study of Roman institutions which led to the publication after 130 BC of the *annalēs maximi* ('the most important records'). Later writers who depended on this work for their chronological framework also tended to follow its method, describing events as they happened year by year. This basic form was elaborated by historians of the early first century BC, including Valerius Antias and Claudius Quadrigarius, who established in Rome the moralistic tone and especially the rhetorical style of writing history that harked back to Isocrates; this was the style accepted by Livy. On the whole the Romans were more interested in the literary merits of their histories than in giving an accurate report of what actually happened.

The various other kinds of historiography current in Hellenistic times had taken root in Rome by the beginning of the first century BC (see end of 1 above). This was the background against which Sallust and Cicero wrote, and the same tradition was later followed by Tacitus. *Sallust's political thought is intensely moralistic, in the Isocratean manner, but his chief exemplar was Thucydides; his portraits of individuals go back through the biographical tradition to Thucydides, whose severe style he also imitated. He was influenced too by the concise and abrupt style of Cato, and he rejected the amplitude of the oratorical style of his own day. In marked contrast, *Cicero ((1) 5), in his writings on the history of philosophy and oratory, kept to Isocratean standards, and although sincerely aiming at accuracy declared that his merits as a stylist compensated for his lack of philosophical knowledge, and that writing history was the province of orators. *Tacitus (b. *c.* AD 56) in style and content resembled Sallust; and both have been criticized for political bias and inaccuracy. Tacitus, however, united the various traditions of historical writing into work of great power. The biographical tradition was continued with the *Lives* of *Suetonius (b. *c.* AD 69), but degenerated after him into the *Historia Augusta* (fourth century AD). Tacitus' history was continued (from AD 96) and imitated by *Ammianus Marcellinus (b. *c.* AD 330), a Greek writing in Latin for Roman readers. He is considered accurate in general and relatively free of bias, but his work was done in isolation. This was the age of epitomes and outlines of history, and, with the addition of Jewish history to that of Greece and Rome, the start of a tradition of Christian chronicles (see EUSEBIUS).

Homer (Hŏmēros) (probably eighth century BC), Greek epic poet.

1. Homer was regarded in antiquity as the author of two sovereign works, the *Iliad* and the *Odyssey*; other *epic poems were sometimes attributed to him, most popularly *Margites* and *Batrachomyomachia*, but the best authorities rejected these. The Greeks themselves knew no certain facts about his life; various dates were suggested, ranging from the Trojan War (beginning of the twelfth century BC) to five hundred years later. Herodotus dated him to about 850 BC. Modern scholars generally date the poems to the end of the eighth century, long after the events of the Trojan War and its aftermath that they describe. Many cities claimed to be Homer's birthplace, most plausibly Smyrna and Chios, the home of the *Homeridae. The ancient Greeks thought of Homer as a blind minstrel, suffering poverty and hardship in the course of a wandering life before his eventual death and burial on the Aegean island of Ios.

2. The view of some Hellenistic scholars, the 'separatists' (*chōrizontĕs*), that the *Iliad* and the *Odyssey* were not written by the same person, has been adopted by some modern scholars, who argue on the basis of the language, the social customs, and the attitude to the gods, that the *Odyssey* was composed perhaps a generation later than the *Iliad*. Other modern scholars (the 'unitarians'), thinking that the differences between the two poems can be accounted for by their very different subjects, believe, as the ancient Greeks themselves believed, that both poems are the work of one man. Whether two poets or one, it is clear that both poems were composed in an Ionian-speaking part of the Greek world, that the *Odyssey* was intended as a sequel to the *Iliad*, the events of which it presupposes, and that the characters appearing in both have recognizably the same individuality.

3. Not only has it been suggested that there were two poets, it has been doubted whether there was even one. Since the publication of the German scholar F. A. Wolf's *Prolegomena ad Homerum* ('Introduction to Homer') in 1795 Homeric scholarship has been dominated by the problem of defining the authorship, the so-called 'Homeric question'. Wolf and his followers believed that each poem was created out of a compilation of shorter ballad-type poems, 'lays', and brought to its present length by natural accretions and collective effort, or, it might be, by the editorial activity of one man, whose individual contribution it would be impossible to assess. In fact, extensive study of comparable epic material such as that surviving in Yugoslavia into the twentieth century seems to have established that the poems are the culmination of a centuries-old tradition of *oral poetry, and this may account for the disparate elements and for discrepancies which may become apparent to readers able to turn back the pages of a book but which would not be noticed during a recitation. It also accounts for one of the most distinctive features of Homer, the fact that his language is highly '*formulaic', i.e. repetitive; the poet constantly repeats not only epithets and phrases but lines and passages; even scenes are repeated, for example those describing such 'typical' activities as preparing a meal or arming for battle.

4. Some of the traditional elements in the poems may go back, as is often

alleged, to the Mycenaean period of Greek prehistory (say 1400–1200 BC), but these are not very numerous. Perhaps the poems recall a war that was the last concerted effort of Mycenaean Greece against a foreign enemy; archaeology confirms that Troy was in fact destroyed between c.1250 and 1200 BC. Shortly afterwards the Mycenaean civilization itself collapsed, perhaps in the wake of the *Dorian Invasion. The poems vaguely hark back to the glories and the practices of that palace society, but the formative period of Homeric epic and the society it by and large reflects is that of the late Dark Age, the ninth and eighth centuries BC (see HOMERIC AGE).

5. It has been thought likely that the apparent reintroduction of writing into Greece towards the end of the eighth century (see ALPHABET) was the crucial factor in determining the form of the poems, giving an exceptional poet—Homer—the opportunity to meditate and perhaps dictate to a scribe a longer and vastly more complex poem (or poems) than he could otherwise have composed or delivered. The resulting poems were intended for oral delivery (epic was in fact sung or chanted, the poet accompanying himself on the lyre); on the other hand the continuous narrative shows that they were designed to be heard in their entirety, the *Iliad* in particular being difficult to break up into episodes. Their length, however, precludes their being performed at a sitting: uninterrupted recitation of the *Iliad* would take roughly twenty hours, and perhaps would only have been possible at one of the great festivals. It is therefore probable that in general the poems were sung in excerpts by *rhapsodes.

6. The indications, then, are that the poems were each conceived as a unity and composed by an individual poet (or two poets) working in the Ionian tradition of oral composition; it is generally felt that the cohesion and subtle artistry that each poem shows could not have been achieved by mere editorial activity; Aristotle in the *Poetics* singles out Homer's grasp of artistic unity for special praise. Moreover, ancient Greek unanimity about the existence of 'Homer' should not be discounted. A story of doubtful authenticity tells how

the sixth-century Athenian tyrant *Peisistratus, finding the Homeric texts in confusion, was responsible for having them put in order and recited at the Panathenaic festival (see also ONOMACRITUS). The Athenian element in a few episodes, and perhaps even traces of the Attic dialect, indicate that at some stage Athens played a part in the transmission of the text. Indeed, an Athenian version of the text would appear to be the source of all our manuscripts of Homer; it may even be the origin of the division of the poems into 24 books each. At the end of the sixth century BC quotations from and references to Homer begin to appear in fair quantity; from these and subsequent quotations, as well as from papyrus fragments, it is clear that texts at that time contained considerable if superficial variations; for some centuries there was probably an oral transmission maintained by the rhapsodes as well as a written transmission. However, it is upon the editorial labours of the scholars at Alexandria from the third century BC onwards, *Zenodotus, *Aristophanes of Byzantium, and above all *Aristarchus, that the modern text is based.

7. The Homeric poems have been read continuously, first in Greece and then in Europe generally, ever since their creation. Homer was regarded with reverence by most Greeks, the source (with Hesiod) of their knowledge of the gods, the formulator of the heroic code of conduct, a touchstone of wise behaviour. Aristotle in his *Poetics* regarded him as 'in the serious style the poet of poets', 'unequalled in diction and thought', and he was constantly quoted. Passages were frequently imitated or translated by Latin poets (e.g. Lucretius and Virgil); the *Odyssey* was translated into Latin saturnians by *Livius Andronicus. A much-imitated stylistic feature is the Homeric simile which, once the point of comparison is made, develops into an independent vignette; it may be descriptive or it may have an emotional effect or relieve tension, particularly in the *Iliad* where it often introduces into an epic of war a glimpse of ordinary, peaceful life.

8. The first printed edition of Homer appeared at Florence in 1488. Famous English verse-translations of the *Iliad* and

Odyssey were written by George Chapman (1559–1634) (inspiring Keats's sonnet, 'On first looking into Chapman's Homer'), and Alexander Pope (1688–1744). Pope's *Odyssey* contains a line that soon became famous, 'Welcome the coming, speed the parting guest' (15. 74). The late-Victorian prose translations, of the *Iliad* by Lang, Leaf, and Myers (1883), of the *Odyssey* by Butcher and Lang (1879), written in a deliberately archaic and dignified English, keep closely to the original. The translations by E. V. Rieu, racy and colloquial and often rather free, gained an enormous readership—his *Odyssey* (1946) was the first volume published in the Penguin Classics series. A new edition of Rieu's translation appeared in 1991.

For medieval legend connected with the *Iliad* see TROJAN WAR. See also HEROES.

Homeric age. The age which Homer's epic poems, the *Iliad* and the *Odyssey*, dimly reflect is that of Mycenaean Greece in the period before the fall of Troy in the early twelfth century, but the formative period of the epics was the subsequent Dark Age, from about 1000 BC. Many obvious features of Dark Age society have been clearly incorporated into the two poems, but other events of that age which might have been thought to be well known, for example the *Dorian Invasion, have been excluded, it would seem deliberately. In some ways, therefore, the political, social, and economic conditions depicted are an artificial conglomeration. The elements belong to real societies but their combination is in some aspects unreal. Homer's depiction of warfare provides a clear example. The noble still rides to battle in a chariot, which disappeared from warfare at the end of the Mycenaean age, but has forgotten how to use it, preferring to dismount and fight on foot. He fights with a jumble of weapons from different periods which are all made of bronze, although iron is known and used for implements of peace (in historical fact iron seems to have been used for weapons first).

The aristocratic style of life that underlies Homeric society, based on the ethos of the warrior band, never entirely disappeared from Greek society, nor did its morality, with emphasis on competition and on excelling. The influence of the aristocratic clans, with their ramified bases of power, is seen in the success of such families as the Alcmaeonidae at Athens; the comradeship of the Homeric feast survives in the *symposium of classical Athens, and the gifts of guest-friendship in the reciprocal ties of obligation that bound Greeks to each other in later times.

Homeric Hymns (composed during the period from the eighth to the sixth centuries BC), a collection of thirty-three Greek hexameter poems in epic style addressed to gods and minor deities, commonly attributed to Homer in antiquity but denied Homeric authorship by the Alexandrian scholars. It is not known when the collection was put together. The authors were evidently *rhapsodes; the author of the third Hymn describes himself as 'a blind man living in rocky Chios' (thus suggesting Homer). Many of the Hymns are only a few lines long and are preludes to the recitations from epic often given at festivals, invoking the gods whose festivals were being celebrated. Others narrate at length some episode relating to the god. The most notable are: the Hymn to Demeter (hymn 2), which relates the famous myth of the seizing of Persephonē by Hadēs and Demeter's search for her, and ends with the founding of the Eleusinian mysteries; the Hymn to Apollo (3, attributed to Homer by Thucydides and Aristophanes), the first part of which describes the god's birth on Delos and the second the establishment of his oracle at Delphi (the whole may be constituted out of two hymns); the Hymn to Hermes (4), a lively and amusing account of the god's achievements as a baby; the Hymn to Aphroditē (5), which depicts the goddess of love herself yielding to the power of love and marrying Anchisēs; and the Hymn to Dionysus (7), which briefly tells the story of the god's capture by pirates and the subsequent miracles he performed.

Homeridae ('sons of Homer'), name, from the sixth century BC if not earlier, of a clan (*genos*) of *rhapsodes in Chios who claimed descent from Homer and the prerogative of reciting Homer's poems 'by right of succession'. They later developed into a guild by admitting rhapsodes not claiming to be related to Homer.

ho'plites (*hoplītai*), in Greece, the heavy-armed infantry of the city-states, citizens who could not maintain horses but could afford to equip themselves with armour and to provide for their families while they were away on campaign. The style of fighting with hoplites in phalanx formation spread throughout Greece from *c.*700 to *c.*650 BC, giving a sense of cohesion to the middle class with important political consequences: the *hippeis*, 'knights', lost their prestige as battle-winners, and as the new battle-winners hoplites claimed a greater share in the government.

Horace (Quintus Horātius Flaccus) (65–8 BC), Roman poet, all of whose published work survives. A great deal is known about his life from a biography by *Suetonius and the poet's own testimony. He came from Venusia (Venosa, near the river Aufidus in Apulia, south Italy). His father was a collector of payments at auctions, and had acquired a small estate. He gave his son the best education available, first at Rome under *Orbilius, and later at Athens. The civil war following Caesar's murder in 44 BC broke out while Horace was in Greece; in 44–42 he served in Brutus' army (the republican side) as military tribune, and fought on the losing side (and, he says, ran away) at the battle of Philippi in 42 BC. After that he returned to Italy, obtained a pardon from the victors, and purchased a secretaryship in the office of a quaestor. But he had been stripped of his family property, and poverty drove him to write poetry. About 38 BC he was introduced by Virgil and *Varius Rufus to *Maecenas, who after some delay took him under his protection and patronage, and in about 33 BC gave him a villa in the Sabine hills beyond Tivoli which was to be the source of much happiness to him and which he often celebrated in his poetry. Augustus offered him a post as private secretary, but this offer was politely refused.

During the thirties Horace wrote the *Epodes* (see ODES) and *Satires*; the two

books of the latter were perhaps published together in 30 BC, after the defeat of Mark Antony at Actium. The first three books of the *Odes*, composed gradually in the course of some ten years and reflecting the political events of 33–23, were probably published together in 23; the first book of the *Epistles* perhaps in 20. The *Carmen Saeculare* is a long ode written for the Secular Games of 17 BC and commissioned by Augustus, a sign of continuing imperial favour. Book IV of the *Odes* was published in perhaps 13 BC. There remain three literary essays, two of which form Book II of the *Epistles*, while the third is known as the *Epistle to the Pisos* or, more usually, the *Ars poetica* ('art of poetry'). These are generally assigned to the last years of the poet's life, but their exact date is uncertain: Epistle II. 1 may be dated to *c.*16 BC, and II. 2 and the *Ars poetica* are sometimes placed as early as 19 BC. Horace died in 8 BC, a few months after Maecenas, with whom he had maintained a friendship of thirty years. He was never married. Suetonius describes him as short and stout; Horace speaks of himself as (prematurely?) grey.

Horace's position as one of the greatest of Roman poets rests on the perfection of form shown by his poetry and on the depth and detail of his self-portraiture: he shows himself to be one of the most likeable of men, urbane, humorous, tolerant, observant, a lover of the good things of life, a lover of his country. In the *Odes* particularly, his gentle irony and subtle choice of words caused Petronius to refer to his *curiosa felicitas* or 'studied felicity'; Quintilian called him *felicissime audax*, 'most felicitously bold' (in expression). He has been the most quoted of Latin poets, giving lovers of the apt phrase a multitude to choose from. In his lifetime his works were appreciated by his fellow-countrymen, and the *Odes* had become a school text-book before he died. He had few successors to imitate his lyric forms. The *Odes* themselves were not much read in the Middle Ages, but they found particular favour in the Renaissance (as did the *Ars poetica*, accepted as a complete guide to poetry) and again in the eighteenth century, when Horace's philosophy of moderation had particular appeal.

horae, see SEASONS.

Horā'tii and Curiā'tii. According to Roman legend, the struggle between Rome and Alba Longa (in Latium) in the reign of Tullus Hostilius (seventh century BC) was decided by the single combats of three Roman brothers, the Horatii, against three Latin brothers, the Curiatii. Two of the former were killed and three of the latter. As the survivor returned victoriously to Rome he met his sister weeping for the death of one of the Curiatii whom she was to marry. He stabbed her to death, was tried for murder, and eventually acquitted on appeal to the people.

Horā'tius Coclēs, Roman hero of the sixth century from the same family as the Horatii above; see COCLES.

Horse, Trojan, see TROJAN HORSE.

Horsemanship (*Peri hippikēs*, Lat. *De re equestri*), treatise by *Xenophon. The author, himself a keen and experienced horseman, gives advice to his younger friends on the management of horses, under the following heads: buying a colt, the points, beginning with the feet and working upwards; breaking a colt; buying a horse that has already been ridden, age, mouth, behaviour etc., of the animal; stable and yard; duties of a groom; instructions to the rider, mounting, seat, exercises, jumping, dismounting; treatment of a spirited horse; bits; horses for parade; armour for man and horse and arms for the rider. See also Xenophon's treatise the *CAVALRY COMMANDER*.

Horte'nsia, daughter of Quintus *Hortensius Hortalus, famous as having made, in 42 BC, contrary to custom, a speech in the Roman Forum against a proposal of the triumvirs to impose special taxation on the property of wealthy women. Her plea was successful.

Horte'nsius, title of a lost dialogue by *Cicero ((1) 5), composed in 45 BC after the death of the orator after whom it was named (see below). It was an introduction and an exhortation to the study of philosophy, which Cicero defended against Roman prejudices. It was based on the *Protrepticus* of Aristotle (of which only fragments survive). Reading it inspired St *Augustine to seek the 'wisdom' of God (*Confessions* 3. 7).

Horte'nsius Ho'rtalus, Quintus (114–50 BC), generally known as Hortensius, a distinguished Roman orator, consul in 69 BC, eight years older than Cicero and the latter's chief rival in the law-courts. He won fame on his first appearance in 95 BC pleading on behalf of the province of Africa which was accusing a Roman governor of corruption. He was eclipsed by Cicero as the leading orator of the day after Cicero's success in 70 BC at the trial of Verres, whom Hortensius was to defend (see CICERO (1) 1); he had no opportunity to speak since Verres prudently retired after Cicero's opening attack. Hortensius was consul-designate at the time. After Cicero's own consulship of 63 BC he and Hortensius were friends rather than rivals, though Cicero never quite trusted him, and avoided dedicating a work to him until the latter was dead; he praises Hortensius' oratory during the latter's lifetime in *De oratore* (53 BC), and after his death in *Brutus* (about 45 BC). Many stories are told of Hortensius' wealth and of his flamboyance, which extended to his oratorical performances: the pains he took in arranging his toga, and his theatrical deliveries (so that he was called Dionysia after a well-known dancer of the day), were keenly observed by the tragic actors Aesopus and Roscius, as was his florid ('Asianic') style of language (see ORATORY). He also possessed a prodigious memory.

Hōrus, Egyptian god, the child of *Isis, usually called by the Greeks Harpocratēs, corresponding to the Egyptian Harpechrat, i.e. 'Har (or Horus) the child'. After the death of his father Osiris he succeeded in overcoming many obstacles and killing the wicked Set (Typhon to the Greeks). He became popular in Hellenistic times, and is represented as a child holding a finger to his lips, taken to indicate mystery and secrecy; among the Romans he was regarded as the god of silence. Herodotus identified him with Apollo, others with Heracles and Eros.

Hundred-handers, see HECATON-
CHEIRES.

Huns, nomadic people, formidable
horsemen, originating in central Asia, described by the contemporary historian
*Ammianus Marcellinus as savages who
drank the blood of their slaughtered
enemies. Their advance westward in the
fourth century AD to the area north of the
Black Sea caused terror and the widespread migration of *barbarian peoples
across the frontiers of the Roman empire;
see FALL OF ROME, GOTHS, VANDALS. The
Huns subsequently occupied the area of
modern Hungary, Rumania, and south
Russia. Under their leader *Attila they
sacked Italy in 452, but spared Rome.
After Attila's death in 453 his empire was
broken up among his sons and thereafter
ceased to play an important role in
history.

Hyaci'nthus, in Greek myth, a beautiful
youth of Amyclae (an ancient city near
Sparta). He was loved both by the god
Apollo and by Zephyrus (the west wind),
and preferred Apollo. Zephyrus, out of
jealousy, blew a discus thrown by Apollo
so that it struck and killed Hyacinthus.
From his blood sprang a flower bearing
his name, perhaps a kind of iris, with
markings interpreted as reading *aiai*,
'alas, alas'.

Hy'adĕs ('raining ones'), in Greek
myth, five daughters of *Atlas, the
nymphs who supplied moisture to the
earth, and were nurses of Dionysus. They
were placed by Zeus as a group of stars
between the *Pleiades and Orion. The
start of the season of rainy weather was
marked by their setting just before
sunrise at the beginning of November.

Hyda'spēs, river of the Punjab ('land of
five rivers'), now the Jhelum. The classical name is derived from the Sanskrit
Vitasta. It was the scene of the defeat of
Porus by *Alexander the Great and so is
used by the poets to indicate the distant
and romantic East.

Hȳdra, see HERACLES, LABOURS OF 2.

Hygiē'a (Hygieia), the Greek goddess of
health, daughter of *Asclepius.

Hygī'nus, Gaius Julius (*c.*64 BC–AD
17), Spanish freedman of Augustus,
friend of Ovid, one of the greatest
scholars of his day. His writings, now
lost, covered a wide range of subjects,
including a commentary on Virgil, a
treatise on agriculture, historical and
archaeological works, and works on religion. Under his name, though not in fact
by him, two works have survived, a handbook of mythology, *Genealogiae* or
Fabulae, compiled from Greek sources
probably in the second century AD, and a
manual of astronomy, also based on
Greek sources. A work on land-surveying
and the laying-out of camps, probably of
the third century AD, is attributed to a
certain Hyginus *Gromaticus.

Hȳlas, in Greek myth, son of the king of
the Dryopēs. Heraclēs, having killed the
father, carried off the son to accompany
him on the expedition of the *Argonauts.
When the Argo touched at Cios on the
coast of Mysia (Heracles having broken
his oar), Hylas was sent for water. The
water-nymphs, falling in love with him,
drew him into the spring and he was lost.
The Argonauts went on their way, but
Heracles remained to look for him. The
Mysians held a ritual search for him every
year, in obedience to Heracles' orders,
even in Hellenistic times.

Hyllus, eldest son of *Heraclēs by
Dēianeira; see also HERACLEIDAE.

hymenae'us, wedding-song sung by the
bride's attendants as they escorted her
to the groom's house (see also EPI-
THALAMIUM). The name was derived from
the custom at Greek weddings of calling
out, *Hymen o Hymenaie*, supposedly an
invocation to a deity, Hymen, who
presided over weddings.

Hyme'ttus, mountain in Attica overlooking Athens on the coast, famous for
its honey and its marble. The honey is
mentioned by Strabo and Pausanias; the
marble is of a bluish-grey colour. It was
when the glow of sunset appeared on
Hymettus that Socrates drank the
hemlock.

hymns, in Greece, songs sung in honour
of a god or hero. In earlier times the
word had not acquired its later specialized meaning and included hexameter
poetry that was mainly narrative, e.g. the

*Homeric Hymns. Of true cult hymns very little remains; there are a few fragments of those by Alcman, Alcaeus, Pindar, and Bacchylides. The clearest indications of their style are given by some of the choruses in tragedy which are hymnal in form. The cult form consists of an invocation of the god under his several names and titles (clearly the aim was to be comprehensive), and a recital of his deeds, followed by a short prayer. The Latin hymns of Catullus (see poem 34) and Horace were probably modelled on Greek hymns and written to be read rather than performed (but see CARMEN SAECULARE). Horace's hymn to a wine-jar (*Odes* III. 21) is an amusing parody. The greatest Latin hymn, in effect if not in form, is the invocation to Venus at the beginning of the *De rerum natura* of *Lucretius.

Hȳpā'tia (d. AD 415), Alexandrian Greek mathematician and Neoplatonist philosopher, daughter of the mathematician Theon; she was murdered by a Christian mob. See NEOPLATONISM.

Hype'rbolus (d. 411 BC), an Athenian *demagogue during the Peloponnesian War, reputedly a lamp-maker by trade, detested by Thucydides and Aristophanes. After the death of *Cleon in 421 he became a leader of the people. A few years later, perhaps in 417 BC, an *ostracism took place in which he expected to effect the removal of *Nicias or *Alcibiades, but he was outmanœuvred and was himself ostracized. He went to Samos, where he was murdered by revolutionary oligarchs.

Hyperbo'reans ('dwellers beyond the north wind'), a fabulous people believed by the Greeks to live a blessed existence in the distant and inaccessible north, worshippers of Apollo, who traditionally spent the three winter months with them. Those specially favoured by the gods might spend their afterlife with the Hyperboreans.

Hyperei'dēs (389–322 BC), distinguished Athenian orator, a contemporary of Demosthenes. At first he was a professional speech-writer, but becoming involved in politics he made a name as an accuser of prominent men. He supported Demosthenes in the latter's attacks on Philip II of Macedon and proposed a decree to honour him, but in 324 BC at the time of the Harpalus affair (see DEMOSTHENES (2) 1) Hypereides appeared as one of his prosecutors. He was one of the principal promoters of the war of revolt against Macedon (the Lamian War) after the death of Alexander the Great in 323 BC and pronounced the funeral oration (which survives) on the Athenian dead. After the defeat of the Greek alliance, when the Macedonian ruler demanded the surrender by Athens of those hostile to Macedon, he was seized and put to death, along with Demosthenes and others.

Hypereides' works were lost in antiquity and virtually nothing was known of them until in the mid-nineteenth century papyri were discovered containing extensive remains of six speeches, including fragments of *Against Demosthenes*. He was a pupil of *Isocratēs but in general avoids his florid and rather artificial style, resembling *Lysias rather in the grace and simplicity of his language, and using a slightly colloquial vocabulary. One of the best preserved speeches is *Against Athenogenēs* which was found in a papyrus of the second century BC and is therefore one of the most ancient of all classical manuscripts. This speech was praised in the treatise *Longinus on the Sublime. In it Hypereides makes a lively and urbane speech for a client about a contract for the purchase of a perfumery (in order to free a slave, a youth with whom the client was in love). In his speech For Euxenippus (which survives complete) he defends a man accused of reporting a dream falsely after he had slept in the shrine of Amphiaraus in order to ascertain from a god-sent dream the ownership of a piece of land. Among his lost speeches was one in defence of the famous *hetaera Phrynē (he was one of her lovers) when she was accused of profaning the Eleusinian mysteries. At the climax of his speech he had her uncover her breasts, and the jury was so moved by her beauty that she was acquitted. The ancients ranked Hypereides second to Demosthenes. Longinus compared him with the pentathlete who wins the whole competition by being second-best in every particular.

Hȳpe'rion, in Greek myth, one of the *Titans, husband of his sister Thea and father by her of *Helios (Sun), Selēnē (Moon), and Eōs (Dawn). Homer and the poets occasionally give his name to Helios.

Hyperm(n)e'stra, in Greek myth, one of the daughters of *Danaus.

Hypnos, in Greek myth, the god of sleep, the (fatherless) son of *Nyx (Night) and brother of Thanatos (Death) with whom he is usually linked, especially in vase-paintings. He lives in the Underworld, but is kindly to men. Throughout antiquity he is thought of as a winged youth who pours sleep-inducing liquid from a horn, or touches the tired with a branch.

hyporchē'ma (pl. *hyporchēmata*, 'dance-song'), form of Greek choral *lyric in which dance, with mimetic movements, was prominent. The very few surviving fragments of *hyporchemata* by Pindar and Bacchylidēs give little indication of form or content.

hypo'theses, the ancient term used to describe the introductory notes found in the manuscripts of Greek tragedy and comedy. These notes are derived ultimately from Alexandrian scholarship and give basic information about the plays, the outline of the plots, and details of production. See DIDASCALIA.

Hypsi'pylē. According to Greek myth, the women of the island of Lemnos, in consequence of neglecting the rites of Aphroditē, were inflicted by the goddess with a foul smell and so were deserted by their husbands who preferred to have concubines from Thrace. The women jealously killed all the men on the island, except that Hypsipyle spared her father, king Thoas, son of the god Dionysus, and aided his escape. When the *Argonauts came to Lemnos they spent a year there and married the women, fathering the next generation of Lemnians. Hypsipyle bore twin sons to Jason called Euneōs and Thoas. Some time after, she was driven away from Lemnos when it was discovered that she had saved her father; she was captured by pirates and sold to Lycurgus, king of Nemea. When the Seven were marching against Thebes (see SEVEN AGAINST THEBES) and their army halted near Nemea, Hypsipyle, who was nurse of the king's infant son Opheltēs (or Archemorus), laid the child on the ground in order to lead them to a spring. During her absence the child was killed by a serpent. The Seven gave him a splendid funeral and founded the Nemean games in his honour. Hypsipyle was saved from the anger of Lycurgus by the army and finally rescued by her sons who arrived and recognized her. The story is told in the *Thebaid* of Statius.

I

Ia'cchus. At Athens, during the celebration of the Eleusinian *mysteries, the main public event was the procession from Athens to Eleusis along the Sacred Way, in which the crowd shouted *Iakch' o Iakche*, it was presumed in invocation of a deity Iacchus who was being celebrated together with Demeter and Persephonē. He was variously said to be the son of Demeter or of Persephone, or to be Dionysus by another name, because of the similarity between his name and Bacchus (i.e. Dionysus). Herodotus recounts that after the Persians had conquered the Greek mainland shortly before the battle of Salamis a great cloud of dust 'as if caused by thirty thousand men' was seen coming from the direction of Eleusis, and the Iacchus shout was heard proceeding from it. The cloud moved towards Salamis, where the Greek army was stationed; the festival prevented by war was being celebrated supernaturally, with good omen for the Athenians. In Italy Iacchus was occasionally identified with *Liber, as in the temple of Cerēs on the Aventine.

ī'amb (*ĭambos*, Lat. *ĭambus*), **īa'mbic**; see METRE, GREEK 1, 2, 4, and 5.

Ia'mbē, see MYSTERIES.

īa'mbic poetry, that poetry in which the iambic metre prevails (see METRE, GREEK 2). It is the metre in which the dialogue parts of Greek tragedy and comedy are written. Aristotle thought that it was nearest in rhythm to ordinary speech and for that reason was used in satirical and abusive verse. The poet *Archilochus was apparently the first to use the term, and applied it to his own satiric verse written in the iambic metre. *Semonidēs and *Hipponax who also wrote iambic poetry were, like Archilochus, Ionian Greeks. *Solon the Athenian may have imitated them in writing his political poems in iambics, the metre suiting the controversial and prosaic nature of the subject-matter, although the poems were not abusive. The *Iambi* (a book of iambic poems) of *Callimachus are miscellaneous in character, though many are satirical. Iambics were not much used in Latin for personal invective. The iambic trimeter occurs in only three poems of Catullus, though its variant, the scazon (see METRE, LATIN 3 (i)), is used in eight poems. Not all of these poems are abusive. When Catullus refers to his 'iambi' he is probably referring to the satirical nature of his poetry, not to the metre. Horace's claim to have been the first to introduce 'Parian (i.e. Archilochian) iambics' into Latin is probably justified, for his largely iambic *Epodes* contain the elements of Archilochus' poetry—abuse, satire, moralizing, and themes of friendship.

Ia'mblichus. 1. (d. *c.* AD 330), Neoplatonist philosopher with an interest in magic, born in Syria, who studied under *Porphyry in Rome or Sicily. Later he founded his own school in Syria. Among his surviving writings are an 'Exhortation to Philosophy' (*Protreptikos logos*) largely comprising extracts from earlier philosophical works and valuable as a source-book, a work on Pythagoreanism, and a defence of ritualistic magic, *De mysteriis* ('on mysteries'), interesting for the light it throws on fourth-century superstition. A number of his commentaries (now lost) on Plato and Aristotle are much quoted by *Proclus.

2. Author of a Greek novel (of the second century AD), which has not survived.

iambo'graphers, in Greek, writers of *iambic poetry.

Ia'mus, in Greek myth, son of the god Apollo and the mortal Evadne, the mythical ancestor of the prophetic clan of the Iamidae in Greece. Seers from this clan made prophecies from the evidence of the sacrifices on the altar of Zeus at Olympia. The famous seer Teisamenus employed by the Spartans during the Persian Wars was of this clan.

Ia'petus, in Greek myth, one of the *Titans (children of Gaia and Uranus), and father, by Clymenē the daughter of *Oceanus, of Prometheus, Epimetheus, and Atlas. From the Renaissance he was identified with Japhet, son of Noah.

Ia'sion, in Greek myth, brother of Dardanus and lover of *Demeter. He met Demeter at the wedding of Cadmus and Harmonia, and lay with her in a thrice-ploughed field; the offspring of this union was the god *Plutus (Gk. Ploutos, Wealth).

Ībē'ria (or Hibēria), one of the ancient names for *Spain.

Ībis, said to be the title of an abusive poem by *Callimachus, addressed to a certain 'Ibis' who was supposed to have been the poet *Apollonius Rhodius. The poem has not survived. The Latin poet Ovid, while in exile at Tomis, also wrote a poem, in elegiacs, with this name, in the form of a curse directed at an unknown enemy, in which he expresses indebtedness to Callimachus' 'brief poem'. Ovid's poem is full of abstruse mythological learning.

I'bycus, Greek lyric poet of the sixth century BC from Rhegium (in south Italy). It is said that he refused to become tyrant there and withdrew to Samos, where he worked at the court of the tyrant *Polycratēs. The Alexandrian scholars arranged his works in seven books; to judge from the surviving fragments his poems seem to have consisted largely of narrative choral *lyric in the style of *Stesichorus. They also included *encomia of which an interesting specimen, to Polycrates, has turned up on papyrus, and personal love poems. The small fragments of his poems that have survived in quotation show that he had a taste for the colourful and picturesque, and wrote vividly on the power of love.

According to legend Ibycus was attacked and killed by robbers. A flock of cranes was passing overhead and Ibycus exclaimed, 'Those cranes will avenge me'. Soon after, one of the robbers in a crowded theatre, seeing a flock of cranes

hovering overhead, said to his companion, 'There go the avengers of Ibycus'. This was overheard, and the murderers brought to justice.

Īca'rius. 1. In Greek myth, inhabitant of Attica who entertained the god Dionysus and received from him the gift of wine. He gave some to his neighbours, who, feeling the effect and concluding that they were poisoned, killed him (see ERIGONE). He gave his name to an Athenian deme.

2. In Greek myth, of Sparta, father of *Penelope (wife of Odysseus).

Icaromeni'ppus, see LUCIAN.

I'carus, see DAEDALUS.

I'celus, a god of *dreams, who sent to men dreams in the form of monsters.

Īce'nī, a British tribe inhabiting East Anglia; see BOUDICCA and BRITAIN.

Ichneu'tae, see SOPHOCLES.

Icti'nus, Greek architect who worked at Athens in the time of Pericles under the direction of Pheidias. He designed the *Parthenon in collaboration with Callicrates.

ictus, a term in metric, 'beat' or stress. See also ARSIS.

Īda (Idē). **1.** Range of mountains in southern Phrygia, the southern boundary of the Troad. It was there that the Trojan *Paris was said to have been exposed and brought up by shepherds, and to have fallen in love with Oenonē. From its summit Zeus watched the Trojan War.

2. Mountain in the centre of Crete. In a cave on this mountain (or on Mount Dictē) Zeus is said to have been born.

Idae'an Dactyls, see DACTYL, IDAEAN.

Īdas, see LYNCEUS and MARPESSA.

Ideas, Platonic, see PLATO 4.

Ido'meneus, in Greek myth, grandson of *Minos and leader of the Cretans at the siege of Troy. In a storm on his way home he vowed to sacrifice the first living creature that met him, if he returned safe. This proved to be his son. He fulfilled, or tried to fulfil, his vow; in consequence a plague broke out and Idomeneus was driven into exile by the

Cretans (and settled, according to Virgil, on the south coast of Italy).

Ido'thea, see EIDOTHEA.

idyll (apparently from the Greek *eidyllion*, 'little form'), the name given in Roman times to the poems of *Theocritus, which describe some episode or scene from idealized rural life. Hence 'idyllic' is used to describe an idealized state or scene of tranquil happiness, particularly of a pastoral nature.

Ileithyi'a, see EILEITHYIA.

I'lia (or Rhea Silvia), according to Roman legend, the daughter of the Roman king Numitor, a *Vestal Virgin, who became by Mars the mother of Romulus and Remus, and was thrown into the river Tiber by order of her uncle Amulius. The river-god took her as his wife (see Horace, *Odes* I. 2).

I'liad (*Ilias*), Greek epic poem by *Homer in twenty-four books (for this division see HOMER 6). The title is derived from Ilion, another name of *Troy, which was so called from Ilus, its legendary founder.

The subject is the 'wrath of *Achilles', arising from an affront to his honour given by *Agamemnon, leader of the Greek army at the siege of Troy, and the tragic consequences of his wrath. This is an episode in the history of the siege, occupying no more than a short part of its tenth and final year, and yet its action in effect encapsulates the whole war, with the final death of the Trojan hero *Hector symbolizing the fall of Troy that will soon follow. The gods in Olympus are divided in their sympathies and intervene on one side or the other, or even fight among themselves. Their mixture of sublimity and frivolity makes a remarkable contribution to the character of the *Iliad*. The events of the epic are as follows.

Books 1–8: A plague has broken out in the Greek camp, and the seer Calchas declares that it has been brought about by the anger of Apollo on behalf of his priest whose daughter, Chryseis, has been taken prisoner and given to Agamemnon as a gift of honour; if Agamemnon surrenders her the plague will cease. Agamemnon angrily consents but takes in her place Briseis, a slave-concubine belonging to Achilles. The latter, angry at this high-handed act, retires to his tent with his Myrmidons (see AEACUS) and his friend Patroclus and refuses to take further part in the fighting. The Greek army, deprived of his powerful support, suffers serious losses and is driven away from the plain of Troy and back to the camp.

Book 9: Being now hard-pressed, Agamemnon recognizes the wrong that he has done, and sends an embassy to Achilles offering to make handsome amends if he will lay aside his anger. But Achilles has been nursing his grievance and is disillusioned with war and fame; he rejects Agamemnon's offers and announces that he will not fight until Hector fires the Greek ships.

Books 10–17: As a result, he sees the Greeks suffer further losses. His friend Patroclus is stung to shame and regret by their reverses, and obtains Achilles' permission, when the Trojans are actually setting fire to the Greek ships, to join in the fight; moreover Achilles, himself moved by the danger to the Greeks, lends his armour to Patroclus and summons the Myrmidons. The Trojans are driven back, but Patroclus is killed by Hector, and retribution for his anger thus comes to Achilles.

Books 18–22: Achilles, maddened with grief, puts aside his anger with Agamemnon and reveals himself unarmed to the Trojans, who retreat from Patroclus' body. His mother Thetis brings him new armour forged by the god *Hephaestus, and he goes out to avenge the death of his friend. He kills Hector and treats the dead body with gross outrage, tying it by the heels to his chariot and dragging it through the dust.

Books 23–4: The body of Patroclus is then buried and the event marked by funeral games. Priam, the aged king of Troy, comes to Achilles to beg the body of his son Hector and save it from the threatened fate of being thrown to the dogs. Achilles' passion has now spent itself: he feels his common humanity with Priam, pities him, and returns the body. The poem ends with the funeral of Hector.

Side by side with this tragedy we have a picture of life in Troy under the shadow of impending disaster: Priam and *Hecuba bereaved of many of their sons, and finally mourning their dearest, Hector; Hector talking to his wife *Andromachē, his helmet frightening their young son; Helen, conscious of her guilt and the trouble she has brought on Troy, despising Paris, wishing that she had died at birth, and kindly treated by Hector, Priam, and the other Trojans.

A host of other warriors are presented, some of them sharply characterized (see entries for Aeneas, Ajax, Diomedes, Menelaus, Odysseus, Nestor, Sarpedon, Glaucus). Notable passages are the following: the Catalogue of Greek ships, 2. 484–785; the Catalogue of Trojan forces, 2. 786–877; the *Teichoscopia* (the 'viewing from the walls' of the Greek chiefs by Helen and Priam), and the duel of Menelaus and Paris, book 3; the *Epipōlēsis* (Agamemnon's 'review' of his forces), 4. 223–421; the exploits of Diomedes, 4. 422 ff. and book 5; the meeting and recognition of Diomedes and Glaucus, 6. 119–236; Hector's farewell to Andromache, 6. 370–529; the *Doloneia* (the night expedition of Odysseus and Diomedes, the slaying of the spy Dolon and of the Thracian *Rhesus, and the capture of the latter's horses), book 10; the *Diòs apatē* ('deception of Zeus' by Hera), 14. 153–362; the forging of the arms of Achilles, 18. 468–617; the fight of Achilles with the river Scamander, 21. 211–382; the funeral games for Patroclus, 23. 257–897.

For medieval legend connected with the story of Troy see TROJAN WAR.

Iliad, Little (Lat. *Ilias parva*), title of a lost poem of the *Epic Cycle, attributed to Leschēs of Pyrrha or of Mitylene in Lesbos, a sequel to Homer's *Iliad*, in four books. The events it is said to cover are the awarding of the arms of Achilles to *Odysseus; the madness and suicide of *Ajax; the ambushing of *Helenus and his prophecy about the capture of Troy through the agency of *Philoctetes, who kills Paris; the arrival at Troy of *Neoptolemus (Achilles' son); the secret entry of Odysseus into Troy and his stealing of the *Palladium; and the entry of the Wooden Horse. See ILIUPERSIS.

Ilias Latīna ('Latin *Iliad*'), Latin version of Homer's *Iliad* in 1,070 hexameters by an unknown author, perhaps of the first century AD: on internal evidence the author's name may be Baebius Italicus and the date not later than AD 68. The work seems to have been a popular school text.

Ili's(s)us, one of the two streams which water the Athenian plain (the other being the Cephisus). In the neighbourhood of Athens the river-bed is generally dry, but its shady banks and spreading plane trees have been immortalized in Plato's dialogue *Phaedrus*.

I'lium, see TROY.

Iliūpe'rsis (*Iliou persis*, 'sack of Troy'). 1. Title of a lost poem of the *Epic Cycle attributed to Arctīnus of Miletus, a sequel in two books to the Little *Iliad. The events are said to be the following. The Wooden Horse enters Troy; two snakes destroy *Laocŏon and one of his sons; Sinon (see TROJAN HORSE) signals to the departed Greek army to return to Troy, and the Greeks take the city; *Neoptolemus kills Priam, Menelaus finds Helen, and *Ajax son of Oileus tries to carry off Cassandra, pulling over the statue of Athena in the attempt; Odysseus murders *Astyanax, son of Hector, and Neoptolemus takes Hector's wife *Andromachē as prize; the Greeks set fire to the city, sacrifice *Polyxena at the tomb of Achilles, and sail home, with the goddess Athena planning vengeance for Ajax' violation.

2. See STESICHORUS.

Illy'rii, group of tribes, *Indo-European in origin, who occupied a region to the east of the Adriatic Sea bordering on Macedonia and Epirus.

Ilus, see TROY.

Ilȳthī'a, see EILEITHYIA.

Ima'ginēs, dialogue by *Lucian.

Ima'ginum libri XV, see VARRO.

imperā'tor (Gk. *autocratōr*), originally a Roman military title given by acclamation of the soldiers to a general after his victory. He kept the title after his name until he celebrated his *triumph. The first properly attested *imperator* was L. Aemilius *Paullus in 189 BC. The increasing importance of the army in the late republic made the title the symbol of military authority, and Julius Caesar used the title permanently. After 38 BC Octavian (later the emperor Augustus) used the title as a *praenomen* (see NAMES), i.e. Imperator Caesar, not Caesar Imperator. Thus it came to signify the supreme power of the emperor. The use of the title as *praenomen* did not prevent its being applied in the original manner, after the emperor's name, when he had won a victory. The formula *imperator Caesar* was sometimes extended to members of the imperial family who shared the emperor's power (compare AUGUSTUS, THE).

impe'rium, in the Roman constitution, 'power to command', the supreme administrative authority vested in certain individuals, involving command in war and originally the interpretation and execution of the law (including the power to impose the death penalty); later, Roman citizens could not be executed without trial, and had the right of appeal to the people. *Imperium*, originally the authority of the king, was possessed under the republic by consuls, military tribunes with consular power, praetors, dictators, and *magistri equitum* ('masters of the horse'), and by proconsuls and propraetors in their provinces. Sometimes a private citizen was granted *imperium* for a specific purpose.

I'nachus, see IO.

In Catili'nam, see CICERO (I) 2 and CATILINE.

incubation, practice common among Greeks and Romans of sleeping when ill in the temple of a god, most usually of *Asclepius, so as to receive from the god in a dream information about a remedy (or sometimes help in other troubles). Such a cure is described by Aristophanes in his comedy *Plutus*. See also ARISTEIDES (3).

Index rērum a se gestā'rum, epitomized 'summary of the deeds of Augustus by (the emperor) himself', inscribed on bronze in his mausoleum. Copies were placed in various temples of the empire; one of these survives (imperfectly) on the temple of 'Rome and Augustus' at Ancȳra (Ankara), besides

fragments of others; see MONUMENTUM ANCYRANUM.

Indi'getēs, indigitame'nta respectively, a class of Roman gods and a list of religious formulae used in invoking gods, taken from the books of the *pontifices ('priests'). The meaning of the terms is obscure.

i'nferi, di ('gods of the Underworld'), in Roman religion.

Inō, in Greek myth, a daughter of *Cadmus and Harmonia, and wife of *Athamas. See also DIONYSUS for her death and transformation into a sea-goddess. It was she who saved Odysseus when his raft was wrecked, giving him her scarf to keep him afloat (Homer, *Odyssey* 5).

In Pisō'nem, see CICERO (I) 4.

inscriptions, see EPIGRAPHY.

Institūtiō'nēs ('Institutes'), see GAIUS and JUSTINIAN.

Institūtiō'nēs dīvī'nae, see LACTANTIUS.

Institū'tiō ōrātō'ria ('education of an orator'), treatise in twelve books by *Quintilian.

Book I deals with the early education of the future orator; the influence of nurses, parents, slaves; the superiority of school education over education at home; the importance of a thorough study of language as a foundation; and the need for Greek and various other subjects. The subject-matter should not be dictated by commercial consideration.

Book 2, which begins with the boy's entry to the school of rhetoric, is on the general method and aim of training in rhetoric, on the qualifications of a good teacher and the proper treatment of pupils, and on the need in an orator for moral character as well as wide knowledge.

Books 3–7 pass on to technicalities: the three kinds of oratory (judicial, deliberative, laudatory), the parts of a speech (exordium, narrative, etc.), and the arrangement of matters to be dealt with. These are principally related to speeches in the courts, and are illuminating when read in conjunction with the speeches of Cicero.

Books 8–11 deal with style and delivery. Of these book 10 contains the famous discussion of those authors, Greek and Latin, who are to be studied as 'particularly suitable to those proposing to become orators', and Quintilian's judgements on them; it should be remembered that these are made solely from a rhetorical viewpoint. Of the Greeks he places Homer first for his many qualities and in particular his oratorical skills. Pindar is by far the greatest of the lyric poets, especially for his flood of eloquence; Aristophanes, Eupolis, and Cratinus are the greatest of the writers of Old Comedy, Menander of New. Sophocles and Euripides are the most accomplished of the tragedians, for Aeschylus, in spite of his dignity, is often uncouth. In history he sets far above the others Thucydides ('compressed and concise and always pressing on') and Herodotus ('delightful, clear, and discursive'). He discusses Demosthenes and his lesser rivals. He praises Plato's acuteness, and his 'divine and Homeric' gift of eloquence, Xenophon's unaffected style, and Aristotle's knowledge and penetration. Of the Romans he places Virgil first, as most nearly approaching Homer. The style of Lucretius he thinks difficult. Ennius he compares with those ancient sacred groves whose mighty oaks are admired less for their beauty than for their sanctity. Ovid is too much an admirer of his own genius. Satire, for the Roman Quintilian, is 'all our own'; he places Horace as a satirist before Lucilius, and mentions Persius favourably. Horace is also the only lyric poet in Latin worth reading (he mentions Catullus only for the invective of his iambics). He thinks the (now lost) *Thyestes* of Varius the equal of any Greek tragedy, and commends the (also lost) *Medea* of Ovid, but makes no high claim for Roman tragedy. Comedy is Rome's weakest point. In history he regards Sallust as equal to Thucydides, Livy to Herodotus. Cicero is a match for any Greek orator: Quintilian compares his style with that of Demosthenes, and though scrupulously fair to the merits of both cannot conceal the pleasure he feels at Cicero's overall brilliance. Caesar might have been his rival had he devoted

himself to the subject; as it is he equals Cicero in force, acumen, and vigour. Quintilian is critical of Seneca's style and bad influence but admits the value of his subject-matter. Book 11 discusses the manner of delivery.

Book 12 sums up Quintilian's view of the ideal orator, not a speaker merely, but a man of highest character, properly trained in morals as well as in taste; in the words of Cato, *vir bonus dicendi peritus*, 'a good man who knows how to speak'.

interce′ssio, at Rome, the veto which a magistrate might impose upon a motion carried by another magistrate of equal or lower rank. Only the *dictator could not be obstructed by a veto since he had no equal or superior.

interrex, at Rome, originally an individual appointed by the senate at the death of a king to hold temporary power until a new king was appointed. Under the republic, if both consuls should die or resign, *interreges*, who had to be senators and patricians, were appointed until new consuls were elected. The last known example of such an event was in 43 BC when both consuls were killed.

In Vati′nium, see CICERO (1) 4.

Īō, in Greek myth, daughter of Inachus, mythical first king of Argos. When Zeus fell in love with her she suffered disturbing dreams. Inachus, in response to oracles he had consulted, then turned her out of the house. Zeus (or his wife Hera) changed her into a heifer, for purposes of deception; Hera set the herdsman Argus, who had eyes all over his body, to watch over her, and sent a gad-fly to sting her continuously, so that she would not rest long enough for Zeus to make love to her. Zeus sent Hermēs to kill Argus, but Io, now constantly haunted by the herdsman's ghost, was forced by the gad-fly to wander far and wide. Part of the Adriatic Sea was thenceforth called Ionian (Gk. Iŏnios, not derived from Iōnia, for which see ION), and the Bosporus, 'ox-ford', was named after her crossing. When she passed by *Prometheus bound to his rock he prophesied to her what was to come. Eventually she reached Egypt where Zeus changed her back to human form, touched her with his hand, and thus begat his son Epaphus ('he of the touch'). According to one version she was worshipped there as the goddess Isis (Epaphus being identified with the bull-god Apis). Epaphus was the ancestor of Danaus and Aegyptus.

Io'batēs, see BELLEROPHON.

Ioca'stē, see JOCASTA.

Iolā'us, see HERACLES and *HERACLES, CHILDREN OF.*

I'olē, see HERACLES and *TRACHINIAE.*

Īŏn. 1. Eponymous ancestor of the Ionian Greeks (Gk. Iōnes or Iāŏnes). According to Greek myth (as preserved by Euripides; see below), Crĕūsa, daughter of *Erechtheus, king of Athens, was loved by the god Apollo and bore him a son Ion, whom for fear of her father's anger she left in a cave under the Acropolis. Hermes carried the child to Delphi, where he was reared as a servant of the temple. Creusa afterwards married Xuthus (see HELLEN), but as they remained childless they went to Delphi to ask for offspring. At the order of Apollo, Xuthus accepted as his son the first person he met on coming out of the shrine, and this was Ion. Creusa, angered at the adoption of one whom she supposed to be a bastard son of her husband, attempted to kill the boy, but being detected, and in danger of death, took refuge at the altar of Apollo. By the intervention of the priestess, who produced the swaddling clothes in which the infant Ion had been wrapped, Creusa recognized her child, and the goddess Athena revealed what had happened. Ion returned to Athens with Xuthus and Creusa to become, according to Athena's prophecy, the ancestor of the Ionian race.

2. Of Chios (b. *c.*490 BC, d. before 421), Greek poet famed chiefly for his tragedies, which were studied and admired by the Alexandrian scholars and by *Longinus on the Sublime.* None of them has survived. It is possible that he wrote a comedy as well, thus being the exception to the rule that no Greek wrote both (see COMEDY, GREEK 2). Interesting anecdotes link Ion with many of the famous names of the fifth century: he heard Cimon speak in the assembly, met Aeschylus at the Isthmian games and Sophocles when he was *strategos* in 441/40, and was defeated in the tragic contests at the Great Dionysia of 428 when Euripides won with *Hippolytus.* A long quotation by *Athenaeus (*Deipnosophistai* 603), from Ion's prose work *Epidemiai* ('visits'), in which he vividly describes an evening spent with Sophocles, gives cause for regret at the loss of his writings.

Īŏn. 1. Greek tragedy (with a happy ending) by *Euripides, probably written a little after 412 BC. It deals with the story of Ion as in (1) above. The essential features of the plot—a woman seduced, her child exposed, the subsequent recognition, and happy consequences—became typical of New Comedy (see COMEDY, GREEK 6; also MENANDER).

2. Dialogue by *Plato (see 2) named after a *rhapsode of that name.

Iō'nia, Ionians. The country of Ionia comprised a portion of the west coast of Asia Minor, roughly from Smyrna to Miletus (in the south), as well as the adjacent islands, and was inhabited by Ionian Greeks who had migrated there from mainland Greece *c.*1000 BC. Ionians as a Greek people are mentioned once by Homer, the Ionian cities not at all. Ionia was the region in which early Greek literature and *philosophy were principally developed (see also HOMER and HISTORIOGRAPHY 1). For the legendary origin of the name see ION (1). All who traced their origin from the city of Athens and kept the festival of the Apaturia were reckoned as Ionians (see PHRATRIAI). Athens could not claim to be the mother-city of all Ionians, but she may have some claim to have organized the first migrations: the four ancient tribes of Attica, the Geleontes, Aigikoreis, Argadeis, and Hopletes (supposedly named after the sons of Ion) are found among the Ionians also. For their dialect see DIALECTS.

Ionian Revolt (499 BC), see PERSIAN WARS.

Io'nic verse, see METRE, GREEK 3 and 5.

Īphiana'ssa, the name under which *Īphigeneia appears in Homer.

I'phiclēs, half-brother of *Heraclēs.

Ï'phiclus, in Greek myth, son of Phyla-
cus. He imprisoned for a year the seer
*Melampus, who discovered the reason
for Iphiclus' childlessness and cured him.
Iphiclus subsequently became the father
of Podarcēs and *Protesilaus.

Iphigenei'a, in Greek myth, a daughter
of *Agamemnon and Clytemnestra,
whom Agamemnon was forced to sacrifice. The Greek fleet, when about to sail
to Troy, was held by contrary winds
at Aulis (see TROJAN WAR). The seer
Calchas declared that Artemis required
the sacrifice of Agamemnon's daughter
(authorities vary on the reason), and
Agamemnon sent for Iphigeneia on the
pretext that she was to be married to
Achilles. In Aeschylus' *Oresteia the
belief is that she was actually killed; the
version of the *Cypria, followed by
Euripides in *Iphigeneia in Tauris* (see
below), describes how, when she was
about to be sacrificed, Artemis carried
her off to be her priestess in the land of
the Tauri (the Crimea), substituting a
deer for her at the altar. The Tauri had a
savage rite by which all strangers coming
to their land were sacrificed to Artemis,
and Iphigeneia was required to con-
secrate the victims.

Iphigeneia's brother *Orestes, in order
to expiate the blood-guilt incurred by his
murder of Clytemnestra, was ordered by
Apollo to secure the image of Artemis of
the Tauri and bring it to Attica. He had
been separated from Iphigeneia since he
was a child and believed her dead. He
and his friend Pyladēs were captured by
the Tauri and ordered to be sacrificed,
but Iphigeneia discovered her brother's
identity and was persuaded to escape
with him from the country, carrying off
the image of the goddess. The latter was
set up in a temple in Attica—both Halae
and Brauron in historical times claimed
the distinction—where Iphigeneia became the perpetual priestess of Artemis.
Other stories tell that she was married to
Achilles on Leucē or in Elysium.

Iphigenei'a at Aulis (*Īphigeneia hē en
Aulidi*), Greek tragedy by *Euripides,
produced posthumously, perhaps in 405
BC. The text may have been completed by
another hand after Euripides' death. The
play deals with the story of the sacrifice of

*Iphigeneia at Aulis. The poet has
Agamemnon wavering and in despair.
After sending for Iphigeneia, on the urging of his brother Menelaus and on the
pretext of her marriage to Achilles (of
which the latter knows nothing), he
cancels the summons, but the second
messenger is stopped by Menelaus.
Clytemnestra and Iphigeneia arrive.
Menelaus repents of his interference and
offers to give up the expedition, but in
vain; Agamemnon now dreads the anger
of the army if the expedition is called off.
Achilles learns that he has been used in a
deception and boldly tries to save the girl.
But Iphigeneia, after pleading for her
life, changes her mind; resolving to be
sacrificed in order to save the Greek
expedition, she acquiesces.

The tragedy shows important developments: it is concerned almost exclusively
with the interplay of the various characters, and the role of the chorus is
insignificant.

Iphigene'ia in Tauris (the Latin title,
meaning 'Iphigeneia among the
Taurians'; Gk. *Īphigeneia hē en Taurois*),
Greek tragedy by Euripides, produced
probably a little before 412 BC. The play
deals with that part of the legend of
*Iphigeneia which relates to her life in
the land of the Tauri as the priestess of
Artemis. The heroine is represented as a
woman who has long brooded over her
grievances, bitter against the Greeks who
sought to murder her, but longing for
home. The coming of Greeks to the
Tauric Chersonese (Crimea) for the first
time during her priesthood and the discovery that she is required to sacrifice her
own brother arouse her natural affections. A plan of escape is devised. Thoās,
king of the Tauri, is fooled; Iphigeneia,
Orestes, and Pylades escape with the
image of the goddess.

Ï'phitus, SEE HERACLES.

Iris, in Greek myth, the goddess of the
rainbow. She was the daughter of
Thaumās (son of Pontus, Sea) and Electra (daughter of Oceanus), and consequently sister of the *Harpies. Iris is not
only a personification of the rainbow but
also a messenger of the gods, particularly
of Hera. In Virgil the rainbow is the path

along which she travels. According to the early Greek poet Alcaeus she is the mother by Zephyrus of Eros. She had no cult.

Iron Age, the period succeeding the *Bronze Age. In *Greece it lasted from c.1050 to c.850 BC; see also DARK AGE, PROTO-GEOMETRIC, and GEOMETRIC. In *Italy it was the period c.1000–600 BC.

Irus, in Homer's *Odyssey*, book 18, the beggar with whom Odysseus fights.

Isae'us (c.420–after 353 BC), an Athenian orator of whose life little is known. He is represented as either Athenian or Chalcidian by birth, a pupil of *Isocrates and a teacher of *Demosthenes. He was a *logographos* (see LOGOGRAPHERS (2)): all his speeches were composed for others to deliver, and he took no part in political life. Of some fifty speeches with which he was credited, eleven and part of a twelfth have survived. The eleven all deal with cases of inheritance and are important as illustrative of Athenian testamentary law. He was considered 'clever in elaborating pleas for the worse cause' according to Dionysius of Halicarnassus. He is comparable with *Lysias in plainness and simplicity of language but more elaborate in setting out his (sometimes complex) logical proofs, and more vigorous in controversy. In these latter characteristics it may be thought that he influenced Demosthenes.

Isagō´gē, see PORPHYRY.

Isidore of Seville, Saint (c.560–636), theologian and encyclopaedist, archbishop of Seville from 599/600 until his death. An important link between the learning of classical antiquity and the Middle Ages, he tried to keep knowledge of the ancient world alive at an unpropitious time. The most famous of his writings (all in Latin) was an encyclopaedia of arts and science in twenty books, *Etymologiae* ('etymologies') or *Originēs* ('origins'), a work of the same sort as, but superior to, that of *Martianus Capella. It was in widespread use for the following 600 years, and dealt with the seven liberal arts as well as geography, law, medicine, natural history, food and drink, and many lesser topics.

Some of the sections are valuable in preserving the contents of authorities now lost.

Isis, great Egyptian goddess, sister and wife of *Osiris and mother of Hōrus. She represented the female productive force of nature: Herodotus identified her with Demeter, but in the early Hellenistic age she is identified with Aphroditē and also with the Ptolemaic queens. Her symbol was the cow. She was also, with Osiris, thought of as ruler of the Underworld. In Greece, her worship was established in Piraeus by the fourth century BC, by Egyptians living there. Her cult, which in some respects was akin to a mystery religion (see MYSTERIES), spread to Rome in the second century BC.

Islands of the Blest, in Greek myth, islands in the stream of *Ocean in the fabulous far West beyond the Pillars of Hercules (see HERACLES, LABOURS OF 10), where after their death specially favoured mortals, notably the *heroes and the first generation of humankind, the men of the *Golden Age, spent a blissful afterlife, ruled over, it was often said, by *Cronus. Many other fabulous beings were thought to live in the same region: Chrysaor, Callirhoē, the Gorgons, the Hesperidēs, the Hecatoncheires, and the Sirens (see individual entries).

Ismē'nē, see OEDIPUS and ANTIGONE.

Iso'cratēs (436–338 BC), Athenian orator.

1. Hampered by physical weakness, Isocrates played no direct part in the political affairs of his city, but his written speeches no doubt influenced public opinion and provide a valuable commentary on the issues of the day. He was the son of a wealthy Athenian, Theodorus, and fell under the influence of Socrates. (Plato in the *Phaedrus*, writing when Isocrates had become famous, represents Socrates at an earlier period prophesying the young man's future greatness either as an orator or as a philosopher.) He studied under Prodicus, Gorgias, and Teisias (see ORATORY 1 and SOPHISTS) and the moderate oligarch *Theramenēs. His family lost its fortune in the latter part of the Peloponnesian War, and Isocrates appears to have fled from the tyranny of

the Thirty to Chios, where he taught rhetoric, and to have returned to Athens on the restoration of democracy. For a period he wrote speeches for others to use in the courts. (Orations 16–21 belong to this period.) In about 392 he opened a school at Athens and also began to write political discourses. The school was distinguished from those of the sophists by the greater breadth of education it gave and by its emphasis on morals; also by its method, which relied greatly on the efforts and hard work of the pupils themselves. It became famous, and pupils from all parts of the Greek world came to it, including the historians *Ephorus and *Theopompus, Androtion the atthidographer (see ATTHIS), the orators *Hypereidēs and *Isaeus, and the politician *Timotheus (2).

The political writings of Isocrates were chiefly devoted to the cause of Greek unity. When his appeal in the *Panegyricus* met with no success (see 5 below), his panhellenism took another form: he sought a strong man to assume the leadership of a united Greece in an expedition against Persia, his chief hope lying in Philip II of Macedon (see *Philippus*, 5 below). His political speeches (or rather, essays cast in the form of speeches, for they were intended to be read) also include other topics of a more limited scope. Isocrates died at a great age shortly after the Athenian defeat by Philip at Chaeronea in 338 BC, it is said by starving himself to death when his third appeal to Philip failed.

2. Isocrates was the first orator of significance to treat rhetorical prose as a work of art (compare GORGIAS). His rhetoric is of a literary character rather than practical oratory. His sentences are long and flowing, the periods complex and highly wrought so that clarity is sacrificed to form; his avoidance of hiatus and of dissonance is almost total. This is Attic prose at its most elaborate. Owing to the popularity of his school, his influence on literature, Latin as well as Greek, was long-lasting, extending to Cicero. Nine letters (some of which may not be genuine) and twenty-one of his speeches survive.

3. Of the epideictic pieces, the *Busiris* (c.390) and the *Encomium of Helen*

(written in the 380s), are criticisms of the works of other rhetoricians, in which he shows how the themes should have been handled; the **Evagoras* is an *encomium on a king of Salamis (in Cyprus) who had recently died (374); the *Panathēnāicus*, begun when he was ninety-four and completed three years later, perhaps for delivery and publication at the time of the Panathenaic festival of 342, is mainly a laudatory historical review of the deeds and constitution of Athens.

4. Of the two essays on education, *Against the Sophists* (391 or 390) and *On the Antidosis* (353), the first is a protest against what he feels to be the narrow and futile instruction given by the sophists and an exposition of his own principles of teaching. The second is a defence of himself and his educational method, and the chief source of our knowledge of his system of education.

5. The political writings are his most important. The *Panegyricus* ('festival oration'), his version of a conventional subject treated by Gorgias and Lysias (see 1 above), was published in 380 after ten years of composition. It is in structure and expression perhaps his greatest work. Its theme, a plea for the union of the Greek city-states under the joint hegemony of Athens and Sparta, is supported by a historical review. The *Philippus*, written in 346, is generally considered the most important of his works. It is an appeal to Philip II of Macedon as a *Hellene and descendant of Heracles to unite the Greek states under his leadership and undertake an expedition against the Persians. The *Platāicus*, written in 373 after the seizure and destruction of Plataea by the Theban Nīcoclēs, is a plea for Athenian retaliation purporting to be spoken by a Plataean to the Athenian assembly. *On the Peace* (Lat. *De pace*), written shortly before the Social War ended in 355 with Athens' failure to retain her League, is a denunciation of an imperialist policy as a way to bankruptcy; Isocrates urges, in place of the limited peace being made with the allies, a Common Peace, and the foundation of colonies in Thrace as a way out of economic difficulties. It is inspired by strong feeling, and is the most vigorous of Isocrates' speeches, a com-

panion piece to the *Revenues* of Xenophon. Both works illuminate the policies of *Eubulus. The *Archidamus* (366) purports to be spoken by the future Spartan king (Archidamus III) on the Theban proposal that, as a condition of peace, Sparta shall recognize the independence of Messenē. In the *Areopagīticus*, probably written in 355, Isocrates contrasts the degenerate Athenian democracy of his day with the earlier democracy of Solon and Cleisthenes, with particular reference to the function, formerly exercised by the *Areopagus, of censor of public morals. (John Milton's *Areopagitica* of 1644 deals with state censorship of publications.) This uncharacteristic outburst on the ills of Athenian democracy may have been occasioned by the financial and moral impoverishment of Athens after the Social War.

6. The forensic speeches (see 1) are of less importance. They were written for private litigants and include one for the son of (the famous) *Alcibiadēs. An Athenian citizen alleged that the elder Alcibiades had robbed him of a team of horses, and sued his son for their value. The speech is interesting for the defence it contains of the father's character.

Isthmian festival, games, a festival of athletic and musical competitions held every two years in honour of Poseidon at his sanctuary on the Isthmus of Corinth. The prize was a wreath of wild celery. It was at these games in 196 BC that *Flamininus proclaimed the independence of Greece from Philip V of Macedon.

Italy (Italia), a word perhaps meaning 'land of calves' (as if from Vitelia; Lat. *vitulus*, 'calf'); the name appears to have been originally applied to the southern half of the toe of Italy. By 450 BC it meant all of the south-west peninsula (now Calabria), subsequently inhabited by the Bruttii, and by 400 it also included Lucania (the mountainous district of south Italy north of Calabria). By the third century BC it meant the whole Italian peninsula south of Liguria and Cisalpine Gaul. After the death of Julius Caesar in 44 BC Cisalpine Gaul too became part of Italy. At the beginning of historical times, at the end of the sixth century BC, the Italian peninsula as a whole was inhabited by a variety of races: *Celts in the north, *Etruscans south of these, Greeks in the south of the peninsula, and in the centre an agglomeration of kindred tribes, Umbrians, Sabellians, Oscans, and Latins. These peoples differed from each other to a greater or lesser degree in race, language, and culture. The physical characteristics of the country are no less varied, from the Apennines and other mountain ranges, which produced a hardy, frugal mountain people, to the warm southern seaboard, where Greeks led an easy and luxurious life, e.g. at Sybaris and Croton. The achievement of *Rome during the republican period was to conquer and absorb all the inhabitants of the peninsula, receiving from them in return influences which are clearly reflected in Roman literature.

I'thaca (Ithakē), one of the loveliest islands in Greece, but one which played no part in classical Greek history. It is situated off the west coast of Greece, east of the island of Cephallenia. It was the island-kingdom of Odysseus, according to Homer.

Ithō'mē, Mount, isolated and easily fortified mountain in the plain of *Messenia (in the Peloponnese), the rallying point of the Messenians in their struggles for independence against Sparta. In the Third Messenian War, after the great earthquake of 464 BC, the Messenians, having revolted, took refuge there. They were blockaded but did not surrender for a number of years. In 369 BC, when Messenia recovered its independence with the help of the Theban general Epaminondas, a new capital Messenē was founded on the slopes of Mount Ithome.

I'tylus, see AEDON.

Itys, see PHILOLEMA and AEDON.

Iūlus (or Ascanius), the son of Aeneas; see *AENEID*.

Ixī'ōn, in Greek myth, a Thessalian, the ruler of the Lapiths, who married Dia, daughter of Dēioneus (or Ēioneus); their son was Pirithŏus (see CENTAURS). He was traditionally the first Greek to murder a kinsman. When his father-in-law came to fetch the bride-price that had been promised, Ixion contrived that he should fall into a pit of burning coals. For this murder he could obtain purification only from Zeus. When Zeus invited Ixion to Olympus for the rite, Ixion tried to seduce Zeus' wife Hera. Hera complained to Zeus who, to trap Ixion, formed a cloud in the likeness of Hera, and by this cloud, Nephelē, Ixion became the father of the centaurs (or of Centaurus, a monster, who mated with the mares on Mount Pelion to produce the centaurs). As a punishment for his crime Zeus had him bound to a fiery wheel, constantly revolving, in the Underworld.

J

Jāni'culum, the hill on the west bank of the river Tiber opposite Rome (but not one of the seven hills); the name is connected with the early king Janus (see below), who was said to have had a citadel here. From early times it was a defensive outpost of Rome. The grove in which C. *Gracchus died was on the Janiculum.

Jānus, in Roman religion, the god of gates and doorways and subsequently of beginnings in general. The word properly means an archway or gateway, free-standing rather than set in a wall, and used originally for ceremonial purposes. Janus was originally one of the principal Roman gods: the 'god of gods' in the hymn of the *Salii, the first to be named in any list of gods in a prayer, even before Jupiter, and the first to receive a portion of the sacrifice. The first month of the Roman calendar was named after him, and his priest was the *rex sacrorum*. His symbol was a double-faced head, looking in opposite directions. A statue of Janus Bifrons ('with two faces') stood with that of Saturnus in the palace hall of King Latinus (Virgil, *Aeneid* 7. 180). In Rome his temple was a small bronze shrine in the Forum, the Janus Geminus, 'double Janus', consisting of an arched passage with doors at its eastern and western ends. The doors were closed only in time of peace. Livy records that from the time of Numa to his own day the shrine had been closed only twice, after the First Punic War (241 BC) and after the victory of Octavian at Actium (31 BC). The emperor Augustus in the *Monumentum Ancyranum* says that it had been closed on three occasions in his principate. Janus rarely figured in myth. According to one Roman tradition he was an early king of Latium; his son Tiberinus was drowned in the river Tiber, so giving it his name.

Jāson (Iāsōn). 1. In Greek myth, son of Aeson and leader of the *Argonauts.

2. **Jason of Pherae,** tyrant (c.385–370 BC) of the Greek Thessalian town of Pherae who sought control over the whole of Thessaly; he achieved his object in 374, winning over the last important city, Pharsalus, by diplomacy. Ancient sources have suggested that he may have aimed at becoming the dominant power in Greece and even at leading a Greek expedition against Persia. In 370 he alarmed Greece by his plan to display the strength of his army at the next Pythian festival, and to preside at the games, but he was assassinated before he could carry out his plans and his further intentions remain unknown.

Je'rome, Saint (c.347–420), Eusebius Hieronymus (his name in English being a version of the latter), Latin father of the Church. Born at Strido near Aquileia (near the Adriatic coast in north Italy) of a well-to-do Christian family, he was educated at Rome (as a pupil of *Donatus) where he was baptized but continued to enjoy a life of dissipation, and then travelled in Gaul before returning to Aquileia and devoting himself to an ascetic life. In about 374 he went to Antioch, where he started upon theological studies and learned Greek, but remained devoted to classical Latin literature. It was here that he had a nightmare in which he found himself facing the Judgement Seat and, upon being asked his condition and answering that he was a Christian, heard the reply, '*mentiris*; *Ciceronianus es, non Christianus*' ('You lie; you are a Ciceronian, not a Christian'). From 375 to 378 he lived in the desert of Chalcis on the frontier of Syria, where he learned Hebrew with much difficulty. But interference by the other hermits made life there intolerable for him. He returned to Antioch (c.377), where he was ordained priest, but theological disputes there made him decide to go back to Rome. Making his way westwards he stayed at Constantinople (c.379), where he attended the lectures of the great Greek theologian Gregory of Nazianzus. From 382 to 385 he stayed at Rome, acting as secretary to Pope Damasus and preaching asceticism. The Christian women who enthusiastically embraced his teaching included Marcella, Paula, and her daughter Eustochium. His advocacy of asceticism and his suspected aspiration to become Pope aroused hostility, and, accompanied by Paula and Eustochium, he left Rome. He travelled first by way of Antioch to Jerusalem, then to Egypt, and subsequently to Palestine; he settled finally at Bethlehem, where Paula founded a monastery over which he presided, and three convents for women which she herself directed. He spent the rest of his life there in intense scholarly activity and vigorous, often virulent, controversy, and died in 420.

Jerome's scholarship was unsurpassed in the early Church. His Latin is classical in its purity; he had absorbed the works of Cicero (as his nightmare suggested), Virgil, Horace, and others to such an extent that constant echoes of them are to be found in his writings. His most important work was his translation of most of the Bible from the original languages into Latin, the so-called *Vulgate (i.e. the 'common text'). This work had originally been suggested to him by Damasus when he stayed at Rome in the 380s. The purpose of the work was to construct an authoritative text to supersede the Old Latin manuscripts with their serious textual variants which were circulating at the end of the fourth century (Latin texts of the Bible earlier than Jerome's Vulgate are known as the 'Old Latin' versions). He published a revision of the Gospels in 383, using a Greek manuscript as well as Old Latin texts. It is a matter of dispute whether or to what extent he revised the remaining books of the New Testament. Soon after, he produced a revision of the Psalter. After he had settled in Bethlehem he worked on another text of the Psalter, using as a basis *Origen's *Hexapla*. After this he turned to Job and other books of the Old Testament, but he soon became convinced that he needed to work directly from the Hebrew original and to ignore the unsatisfactory Greek translation (the *Septuagint). His Latin translation from the Hebrew occupied

him for about fifteen years. There was at first considerable opposition to Jerome's translations from those who remained faithful to old and familiar versions, but the excellence of his work was gradually realized, and his were the translations chosen when (probably in the sixth century) the various books came to be collected into a single Bible.

His other principal works were the *Chronicle*, a Latin translation from the Greek of *Eusebius, with a supplement covering the period 324–78, one of the most important documents for dating events in the ancient world; *De viris illustribus* ('concerning famous men'), a series of notices of 135 Christian writers, modelled on the work of *Suetonius which has the same title, and closely following Eusebius where the latter had dealt with the same authors; and at least 63 biblical commentaries. There is also a collection of 150 letters (including a number of forgeries), some of which are letters to Jerome and include ten from St *Augustine. These are of great interest and historical importance. Jerome had a passionate nature, and his letters reflect his tender affection for his friends, his hatreds and combative nature in controversy, his attacks on hypocrites and heretics, and his condemnation of himself. In his twenty-second letter he recounts how, when he separated himself from his home and family, he could not separate himself from his library; he would fast, but then afterwards commit the sin of reading the pagan Cicero.

Joca'sta (Iokastē, Epikastē in Homer), the mother and wife of *Oedipus.

Jōsē'phus, Flāvius (AD 37–after 93), Jewish historian. He visited Rome in early adulthood, returning to Jerusalem in 66 on the eve of the Jewish Revolt against Roman domination (Judaea having been a province since AD 6). He tried to persuade the nationalist leaders that war with Rome could lead only to disaster, but without success. When the revolt broke out in the same year, Josephus was given command of Galilee by the Sanhedrin. He survived the siege of Jotapata and was captured; his life was spared when he prophesied to the Roman commander Vespasian that he would become emperor, but he was kept in captivity until his prediction was fulfilled in 69. After the fall of Jerusalem in 70 he did what he could to help his Jewish friends. Subsequently he settled in Rome, where he received Roman citizenship, a house, and a pension. His first work, *Bellum Iudaicum* ('history of the Jewish War against the Romans'), in seven books, was originally written in Aramaic for circulation among the Jews who settled in Mesopotamia after the Diaspora, and later translated into Greek. The rest of his works are in Greek (Jerome called him 'the Greek Livy'). The first part of the *Bellum Iudaicum* deals with the history of the Jews during the two hundred years or so before the revolt; the rest is devoted to the events of the war, many of which he witnessed in person. It ends with the capture of *Masada. His next work was *Antiquitates Iudaicae* ('Jewish archaeology') in twenty books, a history of the Jews from Adam to AD 66, giving a fuller account than the *Bellum Iudaicum* of the events covered by the latter work. Josephus' third work was his *Vita* ('life'), not a full autobiography but a reply to the allegations of his enemy, Justus of Tiberias, that he had instigated and organized the Jewish Revolt in Galilee, a dangerous charge against one who lived in Rome by the favour of the emperor (Domitian at this period). His last work, in two books, was entitled 'Concerning the Antiquity of the Jews' but widely known under the title given it by Jerome, *Contra* (or *In*) *Apionem* ('against Apion', an Alexandrian Greek scholar); this is an eloquent defence of Jews, their religion, law, and customs, against anti-Semitic detractors personified in Apion.

Juba. 1. King of Numidia in North Africa from 60–46 BC, notorious for his cruelty. He sided with Pompey in the civil war and defeated and killed Caesar's ally Gaius Scribonius Curio in 49 BC. He escaped after the republican defeat at Thapsus in 46, but, rejected by all sides, committed suicide.

2. Juba II, son of Juba (1), who while still an infant was led in Julius Caesar's triumph in 46 BC; he was brought up in Italy, and when grown up reinstated in Numidia, receiving in addition the kingdom of Mauretania. He married Cleopatra, the daughter of Mark Antony and the Egyptian queen Cleopatra, and died *c.* AD 23, being succeeded by his son Ptolemy. Juba was a man of great learning who sought to introduce Greek and Roman culture into his kingdom, and made a remarkable collection of artistic treasures. He wrote many books, in Greek (all lost), which are frequently cited by the Elder Pliny: they include a treatise on the medicinal plant euphorbia which he discovered growing on the slopes of Mount Atlas and named after his physician Euphorbus (brother of Antonius Musa, physician to the emperor Augustus).

Judgement of Paris, see PARIS, JUDGEMENT OF.

Jugu'rtha, (d. 109 BC), king of Numidia from 118 BC. In 112, when attacking a rival for his crown, Jugurtha sacked the city of Cirta, and in doing so massacred some Italian businessmen, which led to agitation at Rome to declare war. In spite of Jugurtha's lavish bribery (according to *Sallust), the Romans decided to crush him. After two unsuccessful campaigns (111–110) Metellus, consul of 109, was sent against him. Metellus repeatedly defeated Jugurtha, but found it impossible to subdue him. His legate *Marius, profiting by this, gained the consulship in 107, on the promise of a quick end to the war. Success eluded him too, but the war was ended when Sulla, Marius' quaestor, persuaded Bocchus, king of Mauretania and Jugurtha's father-in-law, with whom Jugurtha had taken refuge, to surrender him to the Romans. Jugurtha was taken to Rome and after Marius' triumph in 104 was put to death. The story of the war, with its many exciting incidents, is vividly told in the *Bellum Iugurthinum* ('Jugurthine war') of Sallust.

Ju'lia. Some of the famous women of the *gens *Julia* (who therefore had this *name) were the following.

1. Wife of Marius and sister of Julius Caesar's father.

2. Sister of Julius Caesar and mother of Atia, who was the mother of the emperor Augustus.

3. Daughter of Julius Caesar and his first wife Cornelia, and wife of Pompey. She died in childbirth in 54 BC.

4. Daughter of Augustus and Scribōnia; she married her cousin, Augustus' nephew, M. Marcellus, in 25 BC, and after his death in 21 married in 21 M. Agrippa, by whom she became the mother of Gaius and Lucius Caesar, Julia, Agrippina, and Agrippa Postumus. Her third marriage, after Agrippa's death, to Tiberius, took place in 11 BC. In 2 BC Augustus finally learned of her adulteries and banished her to a small island; in AD 4 she was allowed to move to Rhegium. Scribonia, who had been divorced from Augustus since 39 BC, voluntarily shared her exile. She died in AD 14.

5. *Livia, the wife first of Ti. Claudius Nero and afterwards of Augustus. Under the latter's will she was adopted into the Julian *gens* and renamed Julia Augusta.

Jū'lia, gens, distinguished patrician *gens* ('clan') at Rome, which claimed descent from Iulus (Ascanius) the son of Aeneas, and through them from the goddess Venus. To this *gens* belonged Julius Caesar and the emperor Augustus (distantly through his mother, properly through being adopted by Caesar and made his heir).

Jū'lia Domna, of Emesa in Syria, the second wife of Septimius Sevērus, Roman emperor AD 193–211, and mother of *Caracalla, reputedly a woman of great intelligence and character who gathered about her a circle of cultivated and learned men, including *Galen and *Philostratus (2). After Severus' death she tried unsuccessfully to reconcile her two sons Caracalla and Geta (Caracalla stabbed Geta to death in her arms). She died or committed suicide at Antioch in 217 on learning of Caracalla's assassination by his successor Macrinus.

Julian (Flavius Claudius Juliānus), Roman emperor AD 360–3, named by Christian writers 'the Apostate' because of his 'renunciation' of belief in Christianity. He was the son of Julius Constantius, half-brother of Constantine the Great. Constantine's son Constantius II put to death all rival members of the imperial family except for his young cousins Julian and his brother. They were brought up in captivity in Cappadocia and given a Christian education, but Julian acquired a passion for the classics and the pagan gods. In 351 he went to complete his education at Ephesus, where he was influenced by the *Neoplatonist philosopher Maximus, and thence to Athens (where a fellow student was the later Greek Father of the Church, Gregory of Nazianzus). After his brother's murder Julian reluctantly gave up his studies when Constantius II, who had no male heirs, summoned him and proclaimed him Caesar, putting him in charge of Gaul and Britain. He was a successful general and very popular with his soldiers, whose hardships he shared. When Constantius demanded some picked troops to be sent to the eastern empire Julian's men mutinied and proclaimed him Augustus (360). Before Julian could reach Constantinople, Constantius died. Julian became sole emperor, openly professed his paganism, proclaimed general religious toleration (but not without some persecution of Christians), and reinstated pagan cults and temples.

Soon after his accession he set out in 361 for Antioch, where he went to make preparations for the invasion of Persia. He met there the pagan orator *Libanius, but found the city hostile, it being both Christian and opposed to his taste for austerity. As a result of his stay there he wrote his *Mīsopōgōn* ('enemy of the beard'), an attack on the high-living, anti-philosophical inhabitants, who shaved, and ridiculed him for allowing his beard to grow. He also wrote a comic satire on the Roman emperors entitled *Caesars* or *The Banquet*, much approved of by the English historian Edward Gibbon. Eighty letters, containing much historical material, eight speeches, and a few poems also survive. The *Commentaries* on his Gallic campaigns are lost, and so too is his important work in seven books 'Against the Christians', refuting the Christian religion. All available copies of this work were destroyed by order of the Christian emperor Theodosius II, and it would have perished entirely but for the many extracts quoted by Cyril of Alexandria in a counter-refutation. Julian embarked on his campaign against Persia early in 363 but was mortally wounded in battle later in the year. The story (in the *Church History* of the fifth-century bishop Theodoret, with later embellishment) that he was murdered by a Christian and died exclaiming, *vicisti, Galilaee!* ('You have conquered, Galilean') is picturesque but unfounded. After his death the pagan revival collapsed. See also DELPHIC ORACLE.

Julius Capitoli'nus, see *HISTORIA AUGUSTA*.

Julius Pollux (second century AD), Greek scholar and rhetorician of Naucratis in Egypt, and teacher of the Roman emperor Commodus. He was a lexicographer and the author of an *Onomasticon*, a list of Attic words and technical terms, a much abridged and interpolated version of which is extant, descended from an epitome possessed by Arethas *c.* AD 900 (see TEXTS, TRANSMISSION OF ANCIENT 3). The arrangement of terms is not alphabetical but according to subject. In its explanation of terms it supplies incidentally a great deal of information on a very wide range of topics in antiquity, perhaps most valuably on music, the ancient theatre, and the Athenian constitution. Its collection of thirty-three terms of abuse for a tax-collector deserves to make it more widely known.

Julius Vale'rius (third to fourth century AD), translator, from the Greek of Pseudo-*Callisthenes, of the romantic history of Alexander the Great, *Res gestae Alexandri Macedonis*, in three books: birth; acts; death. The work is important in connection with the transmission of the Alexander story in the Middle Ages.

Jūno, in Roman religion, the wife of *Jupiter; she was an ancient and important Italian goddess, resembling the Greek *Hera with whom she was identified, closely associated with the life of women, hence sometimes connected with the moon, with fertility, and with the sanctity of marriage. She had many distinctive names indicating her various attributes, e.g. Lucīna, 'she who brings [the child] to light', as the goddess presiding over child-birth, or Opigena, 'who brings help to women in childbirth'. But she also became a goddess of the state; as Juno Regina ('queen') she forms one of the Capitoline triad with Jupiter and Minerva. She had one Roman myth related by Ovid: being annoyed at the birth of *Athena without a mother, she determined to produce a child without a father; at the touch of a herb produced for her by Flora, she became pregnant and bore Mars, the god of war. (In Greek myth Hera, the wife of Zeus, is also the mother of Arēs, the god of war, but Zeus is the father; the child she produces without male assistance is Hephaestus.) The Roman story may have been invented to explain the important festival of the *Matronalia, confined to women, on the first of March, the month dedicated to Mars. 'Moneta' was another of her titles, perhaps meaning 'remembrancer' (i.e. the goddess should remember her previous favours to Rome). The temple of Juno Moneta stood on the northern summit of the Capitoline hill; it had been vowed during a war in 345 BC and dedicated in the following year, and was said to have replaced an older shrine where the sacred geese had been kept (the geese perhaps being originally kept for divination); see MANLIUS CAPITOLINUS. An adjoining building contained the Roman mint: thus from *moneta* is derived the word 'money'. See also LIBRI LINTEI. There was a temple to Juno in the Campus Martius and another on the Aventine. The latter was dedicated in 392 BC by M. Furius Camillus, the conqueror of Veii, who placed in the temple a wooden statue of Juno brought from the captured city. For Juno in the sense of a woman's tutelary spirit see GENIUS.

Jŭ'piter (Lat. Iuppiter), the supreme god of the Romans, originally the Italian sky-god, the name probably derived from an original vocative *dieu-pater* (compare the Greek vocative, *Zeu pater*, 'Father Zeus'), where *dieu* is akin to *dies* ('day') signifying the bright sky (see DIESPITER). He appears to have been originally the power (*numen*) of the sky, responsible for the weather, especially rain and light-

ning. He was worshipped at the rural
*Vinalia (grape-harvest) on 19 August,
when the *flamen dialis* offered a ewe-
lamb to him and cut the first grapes. As
Jupiter Lapis ('stone') he was associated
with the stones used in taking oaths and
presumably thought of as thunderbolts,
by which the perjurer may be struck
down. Hence he seems to be connected
with Fides, the personification of 'good
faith', whose temple was near that of
Jupiter on the Capitol at Rome (see
below).

The Etruscan kings were thought to
have introduced the cult of Iuppiter
Optimus Maximus (i.e. the 'best and
greatest' of all Jupiters) in which the god,
in his temple on the Capitol said to have
been founded by Tarquinus Superbus,
was associated with Juno and Minerva,
the three together known as the
Capitoline triad. This was Jupiter in his
aspect of god of the Roman state. In this
temple the magistrates offered sacrifices
on entering their year of office, and
generals brought their spoils after victorious campaigns. Here every year the
first meeting of the senate was held.

Jupiter Feretrius was also worshipped
on the Capitol, in a temple reputedly
founded by Romulus. The derivation of
the epithet is uncertain; it has been plausibly thought to be connected with Latin
fero, 'I bring', in reference to the institution of dedicating to the god arms taken
in war. The original act of dedication was
supposed to have been made by
Romulus, who hung his *spolia opima* on
a sacred oak-tree on the Capitol. The
temple may have dated from the seventh
or sixth century BC; it had no cult statue
but a sceptre (symbolic of military success) and the *silex*, 'rock' (probably a
meteorite) used in the ritual connected
with the declaration and conclusion of
wars.

Jupiter was also worshipped as Jupiter
Stator, in his aspect of 'stayer of rout',
the protector in battle and giver of victory. Tradition related that Romulus
vowed a temple to him in the midst of a
battle in which the Romans were being
driven back by the Sabines. The temple,
which stood near the highest point of the
Via Sacra, appears not to have been built
until much later, 294 BC, and then in

consequence of a vow made at a critical
moment in a battle against the Samnites,
so the Romulus story appears to be a
later invention. In it was held the meeting
of the senate at which Cicero delivered
his first oration against *Catiline.

For the worship of Jupiter as Jupiter
Latiāris see FERIAE LATINAE.

Justin (Marcus Juniānus Justīnus),
Roman historian of uncertain date
(second or third century AD), who wrote
in Latin an abridgement of the universal
history (*Historiae Philippicae*, now lost)
of *Trogus. It consists of largely
unaltered (or apparently unaltered)
excerpts joined together by colourless
résumés; there are a few striking passages, such as the description of the
multitude of Athenians pouring out to
see *Alcibiadēs on his return from exile
(5. 4), and of *Brennus and his army of
Gauls at Delphi (24). Since Trogus' work
has not survived Justin's book is valuable
for the history of Macedon and the Hellenistic kingdoms. It was widely read in
the Middle Ages.

Justi'nian (Flavius Petrus Sabbatius
Justiniānus) (*c*. AD 482–565), Roman
emperor at Constantinople AD 527–65,
nephew of the emperor Justin, whom he
succeeded. In 522 he married the actress
and courtesan Theodora despite the
scandals of her early life, and remained
devoted to her until her death in 548,
making her an equal and independent
colleague in his imperial office. Justinian
was determined to restore the Roman
empire by recovering the lost provinces
of the West, by codifying and rationalizing the legal system, and by reforming the
administration. All this, he thought,
depended upon God's favour, and this he
resolved to win by suppressing heresy and
paganism. His first aim was achieved
through his great general *Belisarius,
who recovered Africa from the Vandals,
occupied Rome, and overthrew the
Ostrogothic kingdom in Italy (see
GOTHS); finally, part of Spain was freed
from the Visigoths. In his reorganization
of Roman law, Justinian was assisted by
*Tribonian, who set up a commission to
codify the work of previous jurists, an
enormous task, in which the codifiers
employed nearly 2,000 different books.

Throughout his reign Justinian promulgated many new laws himself. The complete collection of his legal work is known by the title *Corpus iuris civilis* ('the complete civil law'). Justinian carried out many reforms of the provincial administration, ridding it of numerous abuses. He kept a careful watch on financial expenditure, but was also a great church-builder, the chief memorial of his reign being the church of Hagia Sophia (532–7) in Constantinople, the supreme masterpiece of Byzantine architecture. In the matter of religion Justinian reinforced the penalties against heretical Christian sects, Jews, and pagans, and strove to achieve orthodoxy throughout the empire. In accordance with this policy and to put an end to *Neoplatonist doctrines, in 529 he closed the schools of Alexandria and Athens.

Jutu'rna, an Italian goddess of fountains. It was at her spring in the Roman Forum that Castor and Pollux were said to have watered their horses after the battle of Lake Regillus (see DIOSCURI). A temple was dedicated to her at Rome in the Campus Martius by C. Lutatius Catulus, vowed in 241 BC during the notable sea-battle off Sicily in the First *Punic War. She is said to have been loved by Jupiter, who rewarded her with immortality and with rule over springs and rivers. Virgil in the *Aeneid* makes her the devoted sister of Turnus, who disguised herself as his charioteer Metiscus, and restored to him his lost sword made by Vulcan. She was compelled by a Fury, sent from Jupiter, to give up her brother to his fate, and returned lamenting to her spring.

Ju'venal (Decimus Junius Juvenālis, flourished early second century AD), the greatest of Roman satirical poets. He was a native of Aquinum (on the Via Latina in Latium) but beyond that fact very little is known of his life. Two inscriptions from that town were found (but are now lost), which may possibly have referred to him, and if so may indicate that he served in the army (as the first step on an official career) and held a local magistracy. The poet *Martial, his elder contemporary, addressed three epigrams to him. The various ancient Lives of Juvenal which survive are of late date, somewhat contradictory, and probably not reliable. They mostly agree in referring to a period of banishment, in consequence of an offence to a favourite (the actor Paris) of the emperor Domitian; it is also stated by one that he practised declamation until middle age (Martial calls him *facundus*, 'eloquent'). Acceptance of what Juvenal says in his *Satires as literally true would require one to believe that he was at one time poor, but later acquired a farm at Tibur (Tivoli), that he could offer hospitality in his house at Rome, and that he had visited Egypt. His sixteen satires, of which the last breaks off short, are arranged in five books (for a résumé of each see SATIRES). Internal evidence suggests they were published between *c*.110 and shortly after 127, in the peaceful reigns of Trajan and Hadrian which followed Domitian's death in 96.

The Satires are notable for their bitter, ironical humour, power of invective, grim epigrams, sympathy with the poor, and a narrow pessimism. Juvenal claims Lucilius and Horace as his masters, but he has none of the latter's mellow humour or gentle irony. The extravagance of his wholesale hatreds and condemnations is effective as rhetoric, but taken as the expression of personal feelings it indicates a man deeply embittered. His gift is for the vivid evocation of scenes of Roman life with a few economical phrases.

Juvenal found many admirers among English satirists, beginning with Chaucer. John Dryden had a high regard for him, translated the Satires, and prefaced them with an essay on the Roman satirists. The satire of Jonathan Swift, with its own *saeva indignatio* ('savage resentment'), is perhaps closest to the spirit of Juvenal.

Juve'ntas, the Roman goddess of youth, identified with the Greek *Hebē.

K

For Greek names with initial K see under C.

kalos ka'gathos (pl. *kaloi kagathoi*), Greek adjective of strong social and moral approval, used to describe men (and actions). It had approximately the meaning and connotations that 'gentlemanly' had in Victorian English; it implied not only that a man so described was of good birth and looks, education, and high position in society, but also that he was active in war and politics, and was expected to be brave, just, and honourable.

knights, at Rome, see EQUESTRIAN ORDER; at Athens, see HIPPEIS.

Knights (*Hippeis*, Lat. *Equites*), Greek comedy by *Aristophanes, produced at the *Lenaea of 424 BC and awarded first prize. It was the first occasion on which Aristophanes produced one of his plays himself. The demagogue *Cleon, the object of attack, was at the height of his fame after his victory at Pylos the previous year. The play is in some sense an allegory; the master of the house is called Dēmos ('the people'), and his slaves Demosthenes and Nicias (the Athenian generals) are terrorized by a new slave, a Paphlagonian (i.e. Cleon; compare *paphlazein*, 'to bluster').

Demosthenes and Nicias are lamenting their ill-treatment at the hands of the Paphlagonian, a spying flatterer of their master, and contemplating desertion as the only remedy. They learn from a collection of oracles that the Paphlagonian is to be ousted from favour by a sausage-seller. One of this trade appears on his way to the market, is told of his destiny to rule over the whole Athenian empire, and has his terror at the prospect of conflict allayed by the assurance that the knights (*hippeis*) will support him against the Paphlagonian. The latter enters threateningly, but the chorus of knights is called and comes charging on to the stage uttering their battle-cry, *paiĕ*, *paie* ('strike! strike!'). The Paphlagonian and the sausage-seller contend with each other for the favour of Demos by flattery, bribes, interpretation of oracles, and mutual abuse. Then they both go off to the *boulē* ('council') to do the same there, the sausage-seller returning to announce his victory. He is immediately followed by the Paphlagonian, and the competition in flattery of Demos continues. The sausage-seller is preferred in this, and in the competition of oracles, and in the final competition to settle who does more for Demos. After this the Paphlagonian discovers that the sausage-seller fits the description of the man fated to overthrow him, and retires in despair; the sausage-seller wins the day, and it is revealed that his name is Agorakritos, 'choice of the assembly', and that he is to be the reformer and saviour of the state. Demos confesses his past gullibility and promises to behave better in future.

koinē, the Greek 'common dialect'; see DIALECTS (1) 3.

kommos, in Attic tragedy, lyric dirge or lament sung by the chorus and one or more of the actors alternately.

Korē ('daughter'), see PERSEPHONE.

krypteia, at Sparta, the equivalent of a secret police force in which selected young Spartan men were authorized by the *ephors to patrol the Laconian countryside and murder any supposedly dangerous *helots. It has been suggested that it was the rationalization of an ancient initiation rite for young men approaching manhood (compare EPHEBOI at Athens). Aristotle ascribed the institution to *Lycurgus.

L

Labe'rius, De'cimus (c.105–43 BC), Roman knight and a distinguished writer of *mimes. According to Macrobius, his outspoken criticism of Julius Caesar brought upon him the humiliation (perhaps in 45 BC) of being required to appear on stage in his own mimes in competition with *Publilius Syrus. Several anecdotes are told of this famous occasion. It is said that at one point all eyes turned towards Caesar when a character said, 'He needs must fear many whom many fear.'

Labie'nus, Titus, Julius Caesar's most senior and trusted officer during a great part of the latter's campaigns in Gaul from 58 to 49 BC. He had been tribune of the people in 63 (the year of Cicero's consulship), and in order to please Caesar had prosecuted Rabirius (see *PRO RABIRIO*), who was defended by *Cicero (see (1) 2). At the outbreak of civil war in 49, he joined Pompey and fought against Caesar until he was defeated and killed at the battle of *Munda in 45.

labyrinth (*labyrinthos*), the complicated building or maze said to have been built by *Daedalus for king *Minos of Crete, where the Minotaur was kept, and from which no one could escape (see THESEUS). The word may be of pre-Greek origin, perhaps derived from *labrys* which, according to Plutarch, is the Lydian word for 'double-headed axe', the royal or religious symbol frequently found represented in the palace remains of Minoan Crete. The original labyrinth was supposed to have been at *Cnossus; the idea was perhaps suggested to later Greeks by the complex ruins of the Bronze Age palace. The complicated figures of the Greek 'crane dance' were supposed to represent the convolutions of the labyrinth.

Lacedae'mon (Lakedaimōn, Lat. Lacōnica, also Lacōnia), the ancient Greek name for Sparta, used by Homer both for the country (in the south-east of the Peloponnese) and its capital. Later Greek writers often called the country Lakōnikē (from *Lakōn*, 'a Spartan', a shortened form of *Lakedaimonios*), although the name Lacedaemon continued to be used. See SPARTA.

Lacedaemo'nians, Constitution of the, a work by Xenophon; see CONSTITUTION OF THE LACEDAEMONIANS.

Lachēs, dialogue by Plato; see PLATO 2.

La'chesis, SEE FATES.

Lacō'nia or **Lacōnica** (Gk. Lakōnikē), the Latin name for Sparta. See LACEDAEMON and SPARTA.

Lacta'ntius, Lucius Caeci'lius (or perhaps Caelius) **Firmiā'nus,** c. AD 245–c.325, Latin author and Christian apologist, a native of North Africa, pupil of the African rhetorician Arnobius. His fame was such that he was summoned by the (pagan) Roman emperor Diocletian (284–305) to teach Latin rhetoric at Nicomedia (a Greek city in Bithynia and Diocletian's eastern capital). It is uncertain when he was converted to Christianity, but at the beginning of the Great Persecution of the Christians (303–313) he seems to have been without employment, probably on that account. In his old age he was summoned to Gaul by the emperor Constantine the Great to become tutor (c.317) to the latter's son Crispus. Only his Christian works survive. Chief among these are De opificio Dei (303–4) ('on God's handiwork'), an attempt to prove the existence of divine providence based on the evidence of design in the human body; De ira Dei ('on the wrath of God'), arguing against some philosophers that anger is a necessary part of the character of God, who must deliver just punishment against evil-doers; and the Institūtiōnes dīvīnae ('divine institutions') in seven books, written between 305 and 313, of which he later produced an epitome. This last is a work of wide scope, a defence of

Christian doctrine as a harmonious and logical system; it is addressed to cultivated pagan readers and appeals not to the scriptures but to the testimony of pagan writers themselves. The first three books are a criticism of polytheism and of Roman philosophers; book 4 turns from criticism to constructive argument, demonstrating that the Christian faith alone provides true unity of philosophy and religion; this is followed by an exposition of the faith, the Christian idea of justice and morality (in book 5), the manner in which homage ought to be paid to God (book 6), and an investigation of the chief good, the purpose of creation, and the immortality of the soul (book 7), concluding with an exhortation to the Christian life. Lactantius has been criticized by Christians for unorthodox beliefs, but he has a grasp of what seem to be the essential principles of the Christian religion. He writes in an oratorical Ciceronian prose (he has been called the Christian Cicero), in a persuasive rather than a polemical tone, seeking to justify faith by reason rather than by authority. An exception to this manner is found in his *De mortibus persecutorum* ('on the deaths of the persecutors'), written in Gaul *c*.318, shortly after the triumph of Christianity (see CONSTANTINE), a blood-curdling description of the successive fates of the emperors who persecuted Christians, particularly in Lactantius' time. Being written by an eyewitness the book has considerable interest; it includes a description of Constantine's vision before the battle of the Milvian Bridge. There also survives a poem generally believed to be by Lactantius, the *Phoenix*; it relates the well-known story of the mythical bird and treats it as a symbol of the resurrection of Christ.

Lādas, runner employed by Alexander the Great, famous for his speed.

Lādōn. 1. River of Arcadia, tributary of the Alpheus.
2. River of Elis, tributary of the Peneus.
3. In Greek myth, the dragon that guarded the golden apples of the *Hesperides.

Lae'lius, Gaius, consul at Rome in 140 BC, and close friend of *Scipio Aemilianus. He was a good soldier and led the decisive assault on Carthage as a legate under Scipio in the Third Punic War (149–146 BC). He was a prominent member of the intellectual, philhellenic circle of Scipio and his friends; Cicero (in *Brutus*) considered him the outstanding orator of his day, and he was given the name Sapiens, 'the wise', for his wide learning and philosophical attainments (or, according to Plutarch, for dropping his proposal for agrarian reform in the face of senatorial opposition). It was said that the comedies of *Terence, who was also a friend of Scipio, owed much to Laelius. Cicero makes him the principal speaker in *De amicitia*, and an interlocutor in *De senectute* and *De republica*. In *De oratore* Cicero tells how Laelius and Scipio liked to go on holiday to the seaside 'where they became incredibly childish and used to collect shells and pebbles on the beach'.

Laelius, see DE AMICITIA.

Lāe'rtes, in Homer's *Odyssey*, the father of Odysseus.

Laestrygo'nians, cannibal giants in Homer's *Odyssey* (book 10).

Lae'vius 'Meli'ssus' (flourished *c*.100 BC; the *cognomen*, sometimes added, depends on identification with a person mentioned by Suetonius), Roman poet of whom little is known except that he wrote *Erōtopaegnia* ('diversions of love'), love poems in a great variety of lyric metres. He was never mentioned in the succeeding two centuries but was discovered by the literary circles of the second century AD who were attracted by his idiosyncracies. He is important as a pioneer of *Alexandrianism at Rome, as an experimenter in metres, and as a predecessor of Catullus in lyric poetry. Only fragments of his work survive.

Lā'ius, in Greek myth, legendary king of Thebes, father of *Oedipus, son of Labdacus, and great-grandson of *Cadmus. See also ANTIOPE.

La'machus, Athenian general of the time of the *Peloponnesian War; he had been *stratēgos c*.435 BC and so was well known by 425 when he was caricatured by Aristophanes in his comedy *Acharnians*. In 415 he was appointed with Alcibiadēs and Nicias to command the *Sicilian Expedition, and he pursued an energetic policy until killed in a skirmish in 414.

La'mian War (323–322 BC), the war that followed the revolt of the Greek states against Macedonian rule after the death of Alexander the Great. Athens joined with the states of northern Greece, and under the Athenian general Leōsthenēs the Greeks were successful for a time and besieged Antipater, regent of Macedonia, in Lamia, a Thessalian town. But after Leosthenes was killed the war ended with a Macedonian victory at the battle of Crannon. The Macedonian fleet played an important part in the war and put an end to the sea-power of Athens. Antipater placed a Macedonian garrison at Piraeus and demanded the surrender of *Demosthenes (see (2) 1).

lampadēdro'mia, see TORCH-RACE.

Lampri'dius, Ae'lius, see *HISTORIA AUGUSTA*.

Lānuvī'nus, Lu'scius, see LUSCIUS.

Lāo'cŏon, Trojan prince, brother of Anchisēs; for his story see TROJAN HORSE. Laocoon is best known through his depiction with his two sons in a statuary group (Vatican Museums) carved by three sculptors from Rhodes—Hagesandros, Athanodoros, and Polydoros—probably in the first century AD. In Rome, it was seen by the Elder *Pliny, who ranked it as the greatest work of art in the world; his description enabled it to be recognized when it was found in the ruins on the Esquiline hill (possibly from Nero's *Golden House) in 1506. The German critic Gotthold Ephraim Lessing made this sculpture the basis of his book *Laokoon* (1766) analysing the different potentialities and limitations of poetry and the visual arts.

Lāodamei'a. 1. In Greek myth, wife of *Protesilaus.

2. In Greek myth, daughter of *Bellerophon and mother of *Sarpedon.

Lāo'medon, in Greek myth, king of *Troy, father of Priam. When the gods Apollo and Poseidon were doomed to serve a mortal for wages (a punishment for revolting against Zeus), Laomedon employed them to build the walls of Troy; when they had finished, however, he refused to pay them. Poseidon then sent a sea-monster against Troy, the danger from which could be averted only if Laomedon sacrificed his daughter Hesionē to the monster. Heracles happened to arrive at Troy and undertook to kill the monster if Laomedon would give him his famous horses (originally a gift from Zeus in exchange for *Ganymede), but Laomedon defrauded him as well. After many years Heracles returned with an army, captured the city, killed Laomedon and all his sons except Priam, and gave Hesione to *Telamon, who had distinguished himself in the attack. There was a story that Laomedon was buried above the Scaean Gate at Troy, and ensured the safety of the city as long as he was undisturbed (the gate was dismantled to admit the Trojan Horse). When the Trojans were called 'sons of Laomedon' it was a hint at possible teachery.

La'pithae, Lapiths, in Greek myth, a Greek tribe inhabiting the north of Thessaly; Pirithous, son of *Ixion, was their king. See CENTAURS.

lārēs, in Roman religion, spirits associated with a particular place. Their origins are disputed, but it seems likely that the *lares* were originally deities of the farmland, invoked (in the words of Tibullus) to 'give good crops and wine', and that the household *lar familiāris* ('of the servants') was introduced into houses at a later time by the farm-slaves. The *lares familiārēs* were sometimes thought of, it has been argued, as the deified spirits of dead ancestors, good and beneficent so long as they were treated with respect. By classical times the *lares familiares* were guardian spirits who had the special care of the house and household. Every household had its *lararium* or shrine, often like a cupboard, containing small images of the *lares*, standing in a corner of the *atrium*. The *lares familiares* had their counterpart in the *lares praestitēs* ('guardians') of the state. These had a temple at the head of the Via Sacra; the figure of a dog stood between their images, symbolic of their faithful guardianship. In later times the *lares* were identified with the *Dioscuri. They have no mythology. See also COMPITALIA, GENIUS, and PENATES.

Lars Po'rsena, see PORSENA.

larvae, see LEMURES.

Lāsus (b. *c*.548 BC), of Hermionē in Argolis, an early Greek *lyric poet, celebrated as the founder of the Athenian school of *dithyrambic poetry (he is said to have instituted dithyrambic contests) and as the teacher of Pindar. He was a contemporary of Simonides, and like him he lived at Athens under the patronage of Hipparchus (brother of Hippias the tyrant). According to Herodotus he revealed *Onomacritus as the forger of oracles supposedly by Musaeus. Virtually nothing of his poetry survives.

latifu'ndia, in Italy, large agricultural estates originating in distributions by lease of *ager publicus* ('state-owned land') in the early second century BC. Each had an extensive farm-house (*villa*) with a large staff of slaves (*familia*) providing plentiful cheap labour with which to exploit the land for profit. In consequence a large number of peasant farmers in Italy (and also in the provinces) were compelled to sell their small-holdings. The small-holder, with his mixed farming and need to make a living, could not compete in the markets, especially since so much land was turned into pasture tended by slave herdsmen. The Elder *Pliny believed the *latifundia* were the ruin of Italy. When slave labour ceased to be cheap, the *familia* was replaced by tenant farmers, *coloni*.

Latin, Latini, Latins. Latini, 'Latins', was the name of a people in Italy who in the early *Iron Age were occupying the southern part of the lower valley of the river Tiber (between, to the south, the Greek culture of Magna Graecia and, to the north, the Etruscan culture of Etruria). They gave their name to this territory, *Latium. See LATIN LEAGUE. For a later use of the name 'Latins' see BYZANTIUM. See also LATIN LANGUAGE.

Latin language
1. Latin was the language of the city of Rome and the territory of *Latium to the south; it spread with the power of Rome until it became the language of most of western Europe. It is known to have been one of several related dialects which formed the Italic group in the Indo-European family of languages, but it is not at all close to Greek, although the latter is also Indo-European. Its nearest Italic relative is *Faliscan, and it is markedly different from the other main branch of Italic, Osco-Umbrian (*Oscan was spoken in the Samnite territories, and *Umbrian in central Italy to the north-east of Rome; both are known only from inscriptions, proper names, and the writings of early grammarians). It is possible that both Latin and Osco-Umbrian developed separately out of one common Italic language, but it is perhaps more likely that Latin resulted from the fusion of one Italic-speaking people with a pre-existing population of Latium. Exactly how and when Italic speakers came into Italy is not clear, nor are the reasons for the development of their different dialects. Other languages spoken in Italy in early historical times were Greek in the south, Celtic in the north, and the (non-Indo-European) language of Etruria, all of which exercised some influence upon Latin. The Latin *alphabet seems not to have been derived directly from the Greek but to be partly of Etruscan origin.

In the course of its long history, Latin has undergone considerable change. Scholars of the late republic and early empire did not find archaic Latin easy to understand or attractive (see LIVIUS ANDRONICUS, SALII, and TWELVE TABLES). Polybius, writing in the second century BC of the 'first Carthaginian treaty' (perhaps 509 BC), says that even the best scholars after much study had difficulty in interpreting some of it.

The following periods can be distinguished: early Latin, up to about 100 BC; classical (or 'Golden Age') Latin, from 100 BC to the death of Livy, occurring soon after the death of the emperor Augustus in AD 14 (the literary activity of Cicero and Caesar gives special importance to the years 81–43 BC; see also CLASSIC); 'Silver Latin', the term which describes the post-classical period up to about AD 150, and marks a falling off from the preceding Golden Age; and late

Latin, from AD 150, which merges into medieval Latin.

2. *Silver Latin*. The period of Silver Latin, broadly from the time of the deaths of Livy and Augustus, say AD 14, to about 150, is a period of what can generally be considered a decline from previous greatness. It is characterized by the development of *rhetoric, which led to a striving for novelty and effect, over and above meaning, and is marked by exaggerated emphases, antitheses, and epigrams. These trends are seen most clearly in the prose of Tacitus and the poetry of Lucan.

3. *Spoken or colloquial Latin*. These terms cover the easy 'everyday speech' (*sermo cotidiānus*) of educated people. The plays of Plautus and Terence provide the best evidence for this style, but also important are the letters of Cicero, especially those to his intimate friend Atticus, with their very free syntax. In similar vein, although poetic, are Horace's Satires and Epistles, and parts of Catullus. Interesting in this respect is the *Satyricon* of *Petronius, which ranges from cultured urbanity to coarse vulgarity.

4. *Vulgar Latin*. Vulgar Latin is the spoken Latin of the uneducated classes in Rome, Italy, and the provinces. It is known from inscriptions and especially graffiti, a few texts such as the *Satyricon* of Petronius (see 3 above), and the early development of the Romance languages. It is marked by slurred or confused pronunciation, resulting in different spellings, a standardization of originally diverse word forms, a break-down of declensions leading to an increased use of prepositions, a much simpler syntax, and a more natural word-order.

Latin League, in Italy, the association of *Latin towns, from the seventh century BC onwards, for, among other things, the joint worship of deities widely recognized among all the Latins. Most important was the celebration of the festival of the Latin Jupiter (Jupiter Latiaris) on the Alban Mount (see FERIAE LATINAE). *Alba Longa traditionally led a Latin League, but the leadership allegedly passed to Rome when she destroyed Alba c.600 BC. After the Latin War of 340–338, in which

the Romans were completely victorious, the Latin League was dissolved and the individual cities had to accept Rome's terms, of incorporation into the Roman state for some (the smaller), and of becoming Roman (subject) allies for the rest.

Latin rights (see also NOMEN LATINUM), rights held by Latin cities that remained unincorporated in the Roman state (such as Tibur and Praenestē) and by Latin colonies. The Latins by their origin (see LATIUM) and special position among Rome's allies (see LATIN LEAGUE) occupied from the Roman point of view an intermediate position between Romans and other Italian allies; they shared many material privileges with Roman citizens including the important rights of *commercium* (the right of transacting business and conducting law-suits at Rome on the same footing as Roman citizens) and *cōnūbium* (the right of inter-marriage with Romans). In 89 BC the Latins were granted Roman citizenship along with all the Italian allies.

Latī'nus, in Roman legend, eponymous hero of the Latins, king of *Latium and, according to Virgil, son of the god *Faunus and the nymph Marīca; thus through Faunus' father *Picus he was descended from Saturn. He was the father of Lavinia whom Aeneas married (see AENEID). A certain Latinos was known to Hesiod, who makes him a son of Odysseus and *Circē (there is a hint in *Aeneid* 12 that Circe was Latinus' mother).

La'tium, originally a small area of land in western Italy around the Alban Mount (about 20 km. or 13 miles south-east of Rome), lying between the Apennines and the Tyrrhenian Sea, whose boundaries were gradually extended north to the river Tiber and south to Sinuessa. In historical times Latium was inhabited by Latini (see LATIN).

Lātō'na, Latin name for the Greek goddess *Leto.

Laus Pisō'nis, see DE LAUDE PISONIS.

Lausus. 1. In Virgil's *Aeneid*, the son of *Mezentius. While trying to save his father he is killed by Aeneas.

2. Name of a son of Numitor, king of *Alba Longa, killed by his uncle Amulius.

Lavi'nia, in Virgil's *Aeneid*, daughter of *Latinus; she is betrothed to *Turnus but is given by her father in marriage to Aeneas.

Laws (*Nomoi*), dialogue by *Plato, his last and longest work (in twelve books), probably left unrevised at his death. It lacks the vigour and charm of the earlier dialogues; the style is tortuous and the sentences very long. The interlocutors are three elderly men, an unnamed Athenian, Cleinias a Cretan, and a Spartan Megillus. The dramatic situation is fully revealed only at the end of book 3. The Cretans have decided to refound a deserted city, and the task has been entrusted to ten commissioners, of whom Cleinias is chief. Cleinias and Megillus have met an Athenian and are walking on a midsummer's day from Cnossus to the cave and temple of Dictē, the traditional birthplace of Zeus. Their conversation turns to the merits of the traditional law-givers of Sparta and Cnossus, Lycurgus and Minos, whom the Athenian criticizes for directing their laws towards superiority in war, whereas peace not war is the business of the legislator. The Athenian stranger seems to have had experience of life in a city under a tyrant, and to represent the views of an organized group of scientific thinkers (such as Plato's Academy at Athens), being knowledgeable about jurisprudence and constitutional theory. The conversation therefore develops into a complete outline of a constitution and code of laws for the new city, and the Athenian lays down for Cleinias the number of its citizens and their distribution, its organization in respect of magistrates, marriage, property (including slaves), and the material conditions of life generally, education, festivals, and other regulations. The three last books are mainly concerned with criminal offences and their expiations. The general purpose of the *Laws* seems to be to provide a model of procedure for those members of the *Academy who at this time were often called upon to assist in drawing up a writ-ten constitution and laws for some newly founded city.

Lea'nder (Leandros), youth of Abȳdus (on the Asiatic side of the *Hellespont) who, according to legend, was in love with Hero, the beautiful priestess of Aphroditē at Sestus on the opposite (Greek) shore. Leander used to swim across to Hero every night, his course guided by a light in a tower. One stormy night the light was extinguished and Leander was drowned. When his body was washed up Hero, in despair, threw herself into the sea. See MUSAEUS 2.

lectiste'rnium, Roman version of the Greek *theoxenia, in which a god or gods were invited to partake of a sacrificial feast, a couch (*lectus*) or couches being prepared for them as for ordinary banqueters. The ceremony was first held in 399 BC, after consultation of the Sibyl-line books, because Rome was struck by plague, and repeated later at times of similar emergency (see Livy 5. 13).

Lēda, in Greek myth, daughter of Thestius, king of Aetōlia, the wife of Tyndareus, king of Sparta, and mother of *Clytemnestra, *Helen of Troy, and of Castor and Polydeucēs (the *Dioscuri). She was loved by Zeus, who approached her in the form of a swan (a favourite subject in ancient art). Stories vary as to which children were fathered by Zeus; usually Helen is so described, and either both the Dioscuri, or Polydeuces alone. Leda is often said to have laid an egg, from which Helen (or Helen and Polydeuces) was hatched. Homer does not mention the egg, and later Greeks disbelieved the story or made fun of it.

legā'ti, during the late Roman republic, senatorial members of a provincial governor's staff, often made military commanders of a detachment or legion.

legend, SEE MYTH.

lemma, see TEXTS, TRANSMISSION OF ANCIENT 2.

Lemnos, large island in the north-east Aegean Sea, where *Hephaestus is said to have fallen when thrown out of heaven; its extinct volcano, which made the island fertile, was said to be the forge of Hephaestus. To its uninhabited shore the hero *Philoctētēs was banished. For the story of the Lemnian women and the Argonauts see HYPSIPYLE. Herodotus relates that when the *Pelasgian (pre-Greek) population was driven out of Attica they occupied Lemnos, and later carried off a number of Athenian women. The Pelasgians afterwards became suspicious of the children of these women (for they banded together and spoke the Attic language), and therefore murdered them and their mothers; so that 'Lemnian deeds' became proverbial in Greece for atrocious acts. Lemnos was seized by *Miltiadēs c.500 BC when he ruled the Thracian Chersonese, subsequently received Athenian colonists, and was under Athenian domination for much of its later history.

le'murēs or **larvae**, in Roman religion, spirits of the dead, ghosts; dead members of the household were believed to haunt the house on 9, 11, and 13 May, the festival of the Lemuria, the most terrifying being those who had died young and were therefore thought to bear a grudge. Ovid gives an account of the ritual which every householder carried out privately at this time. To exorcize the ghosts he rose at midnight and walked barefoot through the house, spitting out (as he went) nine black beans for the ghosts to eat, in order to ransom the living members of the family whom otherwise the ghosts would carry off. (Beans were among the things that the *flamen dialis might not touch.) After performing other rites he succeeded in driving the ghosts away (Ovid, *Fasti* 5. 419 ff.). Contrast the *Parentalia, when the ghosts were of immediate relatives, and regarded as beneficent.

Lēnae'a, at Athens, festival in honour of *Dionysus Lenaios, the epithet meaning either 'of the *lēnos*' ('wine-vat'), or 'of the *lēnai*' ('maenads'); it was celebrated on the twelfth day of the month named Lenaion among the Ionian Greeks, from the festival, but known as Gamelion at Athens, roughly January. There was a procession, but very little is known of the rites. Its chief importance lies in the dramatic competitions held in the Theatre of Dionysus which were inaugurated c.440

BC and in which comedy was particularly important.

Leo'nidas. 1. King of Sparta, who succeeded after the death of his half-brother Cleomenēs, and was commander of the Greeks at the battle of Thermopylae in 480 BC (see PERSIAN WARS).

2. Of Tarentum (first half of the third century BC), Greek writer of *epigrams, one of the best poets of the Greek *Anthology. His verse is highly finished, densely expressed, and often melancholy.

Leō'sthenēs, the Athenian general in the *Lamian War (323–322 BC).

Le'pidus, Marcus Aemi'lius (d. 13 or 12 BC), Roman statesman. As praetor in 49 BC he supported Julius Caesar, and was consul in 46 and Caesar's *magister equitum* in 46–44. After Caesar's death he joined forces with Mark Antony and in 43 planned the triumvirate with Antony and Octavian. His importance to the triumvirate gradually diminished: in 36 his troops left him for Octavian, and he was compelled to retire to an Italian municipality. His wife Junia was a sister of M. Brutus.

Leptinēs, Against, speech in a public prosecution by Demosthenes; see DEMOSTHENES (2) 2.

Lernae'an Hȳdra, see HERACLES, LABOURS OF 2.

Le'sbia, see CATULLUS.

Lesbos, largest of the Greek islands off the coast of Asia Minor. Its chief cities were Mytilēnē and Methymna. The poets Terpander, Arion, Sappho, and Alcaeus were born there. The poet Anacreon (mid-sixth century BC, a generation after Sappho) maliciously alludes to the island in a way that suggests that it was already known for the practice of female homosexuality, to which it has given its name. Lesbos formed part of the *Delian League but (except for Methymna) revolted from Athens in 428 BC during the Peloponnesian War. It was subdued by an Athenian expedition in 427, and under the influence of *Cleon the assembly at Athens voted that the whole population of Mytilene should be put to death or enslaved. On the following day the matter was reopened, and on the proposal of

Diodotus the edict was revoked and a fast trireme sent to overtake the one already sent to carry out the decision. It arrived at Lesbos just in time to prevent the massacre; only the leaders of the revolt were put to death, and the land of the island (except for Methymna) was distributed among Athenian *cleruchs.

Leschēs, see ILIAD, LITTLE.

Lēthē ('forgetfulness'), in the Greek poet Hesiod the personification of forgetfulness, the daughter of Eris (Strife); in later Greek literature a place of oblivion in the Underworld, and in the myth at the end of Plato's *Republic* a plain which contains the 'river of unmindfulness' (*ameles potamos*). In the Latin poets it is one of the five rivers of the Underworld (see HADES); in Virgil's *Aeneid* 6 its water was drunk by souls about to be reincarnated, so that they forgot their previous existence. Ovid, *Metamorphoses* 11, has it as a river flowing around the Cave of Sleep where its murmuring induces drowsiness. The name was borne also by a spring in the oracular cave of the god *Trophonius.

Lēto (Lat. Latōna), in Greek myth, goddess, one of the *Titans, daughter of Coeus and Phoebē. She is one of the few Titans to have had a cult in Greece in historical times. Her chief importance is as the mother of the twin gods Apollo and Artemis, whose father was Zeus. For fear of the anger of Hera, Zeus' wife, no land would receive Leto when the time of their birth approached, until she came to the island of Ortygia (identified later with Delos), then a floating island, but thereafter secured to the seabed. There she gave birth to Artemis and Apollo, after some delay, because Hera would not allow *Eileithyia (goddess of childbirth) to go to her. While giving birth she leaned against Mount Cynthus, or a palm tree (later identified and regarded as sacred).

letters

1. *Greek*. Letters attributed to famous Greeks which have survived from ancient times are almost all spurious. The most important surviving collections are those attributed to *Isocrates, *Plato, and *Demosthenes. It is possible that none is genuine.

2. *Latin*. The Romans were great letter writers and important men in Cicero's time had among their slaves couriers (*tabellarii*) to deliver and collect letters, who might cover 80 km. (50 miles) a day. Cicero's voluminous correspondence seems to have been preserved in various ways. Atticus, Cicero's most intimate friend, to whom Cicero wrote in his own hand, kept the letters he received, as did Cicero's brother Quintus. His secretary Tiro appears to have kept copies of the letters Cicero sent to his various other friends, and these copies were collected and published after Cicero's death (see CICERO (1) 7 and TEXTS, TRANSMISSION OF ANCIENT 8). Nearly a hundred letters received by Cicero have also been preserved, providing an interesting contrast of styles. Most of the letters of the Younger *Pliny, of which we have ten books, are more self-consciously composed for publication. See also SENECA (2).

Leuci'ppē and Clei'tophon, see NOVEL.

Leuci'ppus. 1. Atomist philosopher; see PHILOSOPHY 1.
2. In Greek myth, son of Oenomaus; see DAPHNE.

Leucothe'a, Greek goddess of the sea; see DIONYSUS.

Leuctra, village in the territory of Thespiae in Boeotia, the scene of a battle in 371 BC, in which the Thebans under Epaminondas defeated the Spartans, thus bringing to an end the period of Spartan hegemony in Greece which had followed the Peloponnesian War.

Liba'nius (AD 314–c.393), of Antioch (in Syria), Greek rhetorician. He studied at Athens (336–40), and afterwards taught rhetoric at Constantinople (until 346) and at Nicomedia (in Bithynia, on the shores of the Propontis). Having declined a chair of rhetoric at Athens, in 354 he accepted instead a chair at Antioch, and remained there for the rest of his life. Although he remained a pagan, deeply attached to old ways, he had many distinguished Christian pupils, including John Chrysostom, and perhaps Basil the

Great and Gregory of Nazianzus. Among his voluminous writings, his sixty-four speeches, which include his autobiography (Oration 1) and his funeral oration on the emperor Julian, and some sixteen hundred letters, are of considerable historical importance.

Libation Bearers (*Choephoroe*), see ORESTEIA.

libations (Lat. *libationes*, Gk. *loibai* or *spondai*), offerings to the gods, usually of unmixed wine, but sometimes also of milk, honey, and other fluids, including pure water, poured on the ground. At the beginning of a drinking-party (*symposium*), a little unmixed wine was poured on the floor to the Good *Daimon. The wine was usually mixed in three wine-bowls (*craterĕs*), and in Athens at least a libation was poured from each, to Zeus and the Olympian gods, to the heroes, and to Zeus Sōtēr ('saviour').

Liber, Italian god of fertility, commonly identified with the Greek god Dionysus, although Liber seems not to have had any connection with wine. He had no temple in Rome but an important cult on the Aventine hill with his female counterpart Libera and with Ceres. His festival, the Liberalia, was on 17 March, characterized by crude songs and the use of masks, apparently hung on trees (see Virgil, *Georgics* 2. 385 ff.). This festival was a popular time for boys to assume the *toga virilis* ('man's toga'). The Romans connected his name with *libertas* ('liberty').

liberal arts, see SEVEN LIBERAL ARTS.

Liber spectāculo'rum, see MARTIAL.

Libitī'na, Italian goddess of funerals, in whose temple at Rome registers of the dead were kept.

libraries. The first considerable collection of books of which we are reliably informed is that of Aristotle, although the tyrant Polycrates of Samos was said to have collected books, and the Athenian tyrant Peisistratus is even said to have founded a public library at Athens. Euripides is also credited with a collection of books. It seems to have been the arrangement of Aristotle's library that provided a model for the *Alexandrian Library, founded in the third century BC. The Attalid kings of Pergamum also formed a great library at about this time, said to have contained 200,000 volumes when Mark Antony presented it to Cleopatra. The Seleucid king Antiochus the Great (223–187 BC) had a library at Antioch of which the poet *Euphorion had charge. Perseus of Macedon (king 179–168 BC) also possessed a library. Athens did not have a public library until the second century BC, the gift of a Ptolemy. This Ptolemaion, as it was called, was visited by Cicero and Pausanias.

At Rome we hear of private libraries formed by Aemilius *Paullus, *Sulla, and *Lucullus, all of whom brought to Rome collections of Greek books which they had captured in their wars in the East. Cicero and his friend Atticus both had considerable collections of books. Julius Caesar had the intention of setting up a public library at Rome, and of placing *Varro in charge of it, but the credit for achieving that seems to belong to C. Asinius *Pollio, in the reign of the emperor Augustus. It contained Greek and Latin books, was adorned with portraits of authors, and was housed in the Atrium Libertātis ('hall of liberty'), the site of which is not known with certainty. Augustus founded two other libraries, one in the Campus Martius (the Octavian) and the other on the Palatine. The Bibliotheca Ulpia ('Ulpian library') of the emperor Trajan (AD 98–117) was the most famous of those set up at Rome by the later emperors. Under the empire the gift of a library to a provincial town was a recognized form of public munificence. For an example of a private library see HERCULANEUM.

libri linte'i ('books written on linen'), lists (now lost) of magistrates at Rome from 509 BC, the foundation of the republic, onwards, although they seem upon occasion to have been defective. Supposed to have been of great antiquity, they were probably not compiled before the mid-second century BC. They were stored in the temple of *Juno Moneta, and were consulted by Livy and other Roman historians.

Libya, see AFRICA.

Licinian–Sextian laws (Licinian rogations), in Roman history, according to tradition, proposals originally made in 376 BC by the tribunes of the *plebs* P. Licinius Stolo and L. Sextius Laterānus and after a long struggle passed in 367 BC, enacting that one consul might be a plebeian and reducing in other areas the political inequalities between patricians and plebeians.

lictors (*lictorēs*), attendants who always walked before Roman magistrates having *imperium*, and before certain priests; they proceeded in single file, each carrying the *fasces on his left shoulder, symbolizing the magistrate's right of arrest, summons, and, in early times, execution. The number of lictors varied with the importance of the office: a dictator had twenty-four; consuls had twelve.

Linear A and B, two scripts used in Crete in the second millennium BC. Linear A, which developed from a pictographic form of writing, seems to have been used throughout Crete from c.1750 to c.1450 BC but comparatively few specimens are known and no suggested decipherment has yet won general acceptance. Linear B, which was used on the mainland during the high period of *Mycenaean civilization (c.1400–c.1200 BC) as well as in Crete, is an adaptation of Linear A, many of the signs being identical or nearly so. It was deciphered in 1952 by the British scholar Michael Ventris, who showed it to be an early form of Greek. The script consists of about ninety signs, each of which represents a syllable; this syllabary is not well adapted to show Greek noun inflexions, so that there are ambiguous cases; there are also many words which cannot be matched with words known in later Greek. Nevertheless, the script was adequate for the day-to-day accounts and inventories which are all that the thousands of clay tablets so far discovered seem to record. The tablets are valuable for the light they throw on economic conditions and the nature of the administration; those concerned with temple property have been particularly interesting for the gods they name (see GODS). See also ALPHABET.

Līnus, in Greek literature, an ancient and apparently mournful song containing the refrain *ailinon*, *ailinon* which was interpreted as *ai, Linus* or 'alas for Linus!'. The history of Linus was variously told in different parts of Greece; according to one version, he was a music teacher killed with his own lyre by Heracles, whom he had reprimanded. The 'song of Linus' was sung at harvest and vintage time from Homeric times onward. Compare LITYERSES.

literary criticism, Greek and Roman. See ARS POETICA, DEMETRIUS (3), DIONYSIUS OF HALICARNASSUS, *LONGINUS ON THE SUBLIME*, POETICS, QUINTILIAN, RHETORIC, and ORATORY.

Little Iliad, see ILIAD, LITTLE.

liturgy (*leitourgia*), at Athens in the fifth and fourth centuries BC, a public service involving considerable expense compulsorily required of the richer citizens and *metics. Exempted were *archons and members of the *boulē during their year of office, and descendants of *Harmodius and Aristogeiton. There were some sixty liturgies a year in Athens alone, apart from the rest of Attica. One of the most costly was the *chorēgia (provision of a chorus) for one or other of the various lyric and dramatic contests. Others included the *gymnasiarchiā*, the management (with nine others) of the *gymnasia and everything connected with them, and the *architheōria*, the leadership of a public embassy to one of the panhellenic festivals. In addition to the regular liturgies there was the occasional charge of the *trierarchia*, for the equipment of a trireme (i.e. a warship). This was imposed only or principally in time of war, and only on the wealthiest citizens.

Litye'rsēs, in Greek legend, son of *Midas, king of Phrygia. It is said he used to require all comers to help in the harvest, and if they did not surpass him in activity would kill or beat them, until a mightier hero (some say Heracles) arrived and killed him. It is also said that 'Lityerses' is the Phrygian reapers' song; it would seem therefore to be a traditional song with a story to explain it (compare LINUS).

Li'via. 1. Later known as Julia Augusta
(58 BC–AD 29), wife, first of Tiberius
Claudius Nero (Cicero's first choice as
husband for his daughter Tullia), and
mother by him of the emperor Tiberius
and of Claudius Drusus, father of the
emperor Claudius; and secondly of the
emperor Augustus. In 39 BC when she
was pregnant with her second son, Nero
was obliged to divorce her because
Octavian (later the emperor Augustus)
wished to marry her himself. Although
she had no children by Augustus she
retained his affection and high regard
throughout their long marriage. She was
a woman of intelligence, dignity, great
beauty, and tact, and she ruled over an
orderly, well-regulated household. It is
impossible to tell how much influence she
exerted in matters of state, but Augustus
valued her counsel, and she won the
reverence of the Roman people. Under
Augustus' will she was adopted into the
*Julian *gens* and renamed Julia Augusta;
she was the link between the Julian and
the Claudian houses in the Julio-Claudian
dynasty. After the accession of her son
Tiberius, discord arose between them. At
her death he refused to execute her will
or allow her to be deified (as Julius
Caesar and Augustus were deified after
their deaths); the emperor Caligula later
carried out the former, and her grandson
Claudius, when emperor, the latter.
Some believed her to have acted ruth-
lessly to promote her own wishes (such as
the succession of her son Tiberius) and to
have had a hand in the deaths of *Marcellus and of Augustus' grandsons C. and L.
Caesar (see JULIA), as well as of *Agrippa
(2) and of her grandson *Germanicus
(son of Claudius Drusus).

2. Livia or Livilla, b. *c.*13 BC, the
daughter of Claudius Drusus who was the
son of Livia (1) above, the sister of Germanicus (see above), and wife first of
C. Caesar, Augustus' grandson, and
secondly of Drusus, son of Tiberius. In
league with *Sejanus, Tiberius' prefect of
the praetorian guard, she caused her
husband Drusus to be poisoned. In AD 25
Sejanus proposed to marry her but
Tiberius refused. In 31 she was accused of
misconduct and put to death.

Li'vius Androni'cus, Lucius (*c.*284–

204 BC), Roman writer. He was probably
by origin a Greek of Tarentum, taken as
a prisoner of war, after the fall of that
city, to Rome in 272. (An alternative
chronology in antiquity made him come
to Rome in 209 after the Romans recaptured Tarentum from Hannibal.) He
probably became tutor to the family of
the father of M. Livius Salinātor, from
whom he took his name when he was
freed. It can be claimed that he is the
father of Roman literature. He seems to
have wanted to introduce Greek
literature to the Romans, and translated
Homer's *Odyssey* into the long-
established Italian saturnian metre (see
METRE, LATIN 1). His translation remained
a school text-book for more than two centuries; forty-six lines of it survive. He is
credited by Livy with introducing plot
into the hitherto plotless Roman stage
performances (see COMEDY, ROMAN 1); he
did so for the first time in 240 (according
to the earlier chronology), producing a
tragedy and a comedy, probably based on
a classical Greek tragedy and a play of
New Comedy (see COMEDY, GREEK 6), for
the celebrations to mark the end of the
(First) Punic War. He continued as a
playwright; the titles of at least eight tragedies are known, but very few lines;
even less is known of the comedies. In
207 BC he was commissioned to compose
a 'maiden-song' to Juno (see LYRIC
POETRY 2). This does not survive; Livy
considered the words too 'unpleasing and
graceless' to quote, though good enough
for the time at which they were written.
As reward the temple of *Minerva on the
Aventine was set aside as a place where
writers and actors might meet and make
dedications as a *collegium* ('guild'). His
work was regarded by Cicero as anti-
quated and not worth reading, but his
historical importance is considerable; he
introduced to Roman literature Greek
epic, drama, and lyric. Horace tells us
that he used to learn Livius' *Odyssey* by
heart, under threat of beating by
*Orbilius.

Livy (Titus Livius) (59 BC–AD 17),
Roman historian. He was born at
Patavium (Padua) in north-east Italy,
probably of a well-to-do family, but little
is known of his life. The evidence sug-

gests that he did not come to Rome until his adulthood. There he gave readings of his work, and won and retained the friendship of the emperor Augustus, who respected his republican sympathies, and encouraged the future emperor Claudius in his historical studies. Livy appears never to have held any public office, but to have devoted his life to literature and history. He began his immense 'History of Rome from its Foundation' (*Ab urbe condita libri*) in or shortly before 29 BC, and published it in instalments; it immediately brought him fame. He survived Augustus by three years, and is said to have died at Patavium.

The history consisted of 142 books, of which the last twenty-two dealt with the events of his own day from the death of Cicero in 43 BC. An epitome of it was written as early as the first century AD, and from this were compiled *periochae* or short abstracts of each book, of which there were perhaps two versions. Of the original work there survive books 1–10, 21–45 (41 and 43 incomplete), and a palimpsest fragment of book 91. The epitome is lost except for the parts covering books 37–40 and 48–55, which have been found on an Egyptian papyrus in the twentieth century; the *periochae* survive for all the books except 136 and 137. Books 1–5 describe the legendary founding of the city, the period of the kings, and the early republic down to its conquest by the Gauls in 390 BC. Books 6–15 deal with the subjugation of Italy (the Samnite Wars) before the conflict with Carthage, 16–30 with the first two Punic Wars; 31–45 with the Macedonian and other eastern wars down to 167. Of the subsequent books, now lost, 46–70 covered the succeeding period to the outbreak of the Social War; 71–90 to the death of Sulla; 91–108 to the Gallic War; 109–16 the civil war to the death of Caesar; 117–33 to the death of Antony; 134–42 the rule of Augustus down to 9 BC. The whole survived to late antiquity, but the Middle Ages knew no more books than are known today.

The work opens with an introduction in which Livy explains his purpose, to commemorate the deeds of the leading nation of the world, to describe the men and the mode of life that had raised Rome to greatness, and the decline of morals which brought about the troubles of the first century BC, so that his readers might thereby learn important lessons. His general purpose is thus ethical and didactic. His methods were those of the fourth-century Greek Isocrates (see HISTORIOGRAPHY): it is the duty of the historian to tell the truth and be impartial, but the truth must be elaborated and given literary form. Livy's attitude to the early legends which he relates is that he neither affirms nor denies their truth, but regards it as of no great importance: if the legends are not true, they resemble the truth. They illustrate those aspects of Roman character which led to Rome's imperial greatness, as well as the true traditions to which Livy hoped, in the early Augustan period, that Rome might return from the moral decay, luxury, and indiscipline of the recent past. Livy used as his sources the earlier *annalists, then *Polybius (in books 31–45), and for the latest books *Posidonius, Julius Caesar, and Augustus' own *Memoirs*. He relied on written histories and made comparatively little use of original records, nor does he criticize his source material; he lacked the scientific method and the insight of Thucydides and Polybius. His inexperience of military affairs makes his descriptions of battles unrealistic; he has little understanding of political institutions, and throws little light on economic conditions or social life in Rome. He sometimes confuses his sources or misunderstands them so that his narratives are inconsistent; they are often given an anachronistic or implausible slant because of his ignorance of conditions at different times and in different places, e.g. in early Rome or in the East. But significant events are treated dramatically and memorably: the action is set against what Livy imagines its background to be in time and place; previous deliberations, changes of mind and heart, the characters of the protagonists, all such circumstances are explored and explained, so that the reader is presented with a story fully comprehensible in the way in which Livy wishes it to be comprehended, whatever its relation to actuality. Livy's prose is eloquent, clear, orderly, and full, developed from that cf Cicero. Asinius *Pollio saw in it an ement which he humorously called 'Patavinity', i.e. provincialism.

Livy was much praised by his immediate successors, Tacitus, the Senecas, and Quintilian, and drawn upon by Plutarch and Lucan. He is little heard of in the Middle Ages, but the Renaissance adopted him with enthusiasm. Dante speaks of him as the historian 'who errs not'. Among the many famous narratives found in the extant books are the following.

Book 1. Romulus and Remus (chapters 4–7); the rape of the Sabines (9–13); the fight of the Horatii and Curiatii and the death of Horatia (24–6); the coming of Lucumo (Tarquinius Priscus) to Rome (34); the accession of Lucius Tarquinius and the crimes of Tullia (46–8); the rape of Lucretia by Sextus Tarquinius and the revenge of Brutus (57–60).

Book 2. The execution of the sons of Brutus by their father (5); 'how Horatius kept the bridge' (10); Mucius Scaevola's attempt to kill Porsena (12); Cloelia swimming the Tiber (13); Menenius Agrippa and the parable of the belly and the members (32); the meeting of Coriolanus and his mother outside Rome (40); the 306 Fabii marching out against the Veientes (49).

Book 3. The summoning of Cincinnatus from the fields to be dictator (24); Appius Claudius and Verginia (44–58).

Book 4. The fight between Cossus and the Etruscan king, in which the former won the *spolia opima (19).

Book 5. The siege of Veii, and the Greeks in Rome.

Book 6. The execution of M. Manlius Capitolinus (20).

Book 7. M. Curtius leaping into the abyss (6).

Book 8. T. Manlius Torquatus ordering the execution of his son who, in defiance of orders, had fought and killed an enemy chief (7); P. Decius Mus 'devoting' himself to death (see DEVOTIO) for the victory of his army (9); the anger of Papirius Cursor against his *magister equitum*, Q. Fabius Maximus Rullus (30).

Book 9. The disaster of the Caudine Forks (1); and the unexpected digression on what would have happened had Alexander the Great encountered the Romans (17).

Book 21. The character of Hannibal (4), the siege of Saguntum (12), Hannibal's crossing of the Alps (30), the battle of the Trebia (52).

Book 22. The battle of Lake Trasimene (4); the conflict of Q. Fabius Maximus (grandson of Fabius above) with his impetuous *magister equitum*, Minucius (14); the defeat at Cannae (44); Maharbal's criticism of Hannibal's delay, that he knew how to conquer but not how to use his victory (51).

Book 23. Hannibal at Capua, the debilitating effect of Capuan luxury on his army (45), and the turning point of the war.

Book 24. The siege of Syracuse by Marcellus and the defensive devices of Archimedes (34).

Book 25. The capture of Syracuse (24) and the death of Archimedes (31).

Book 26. Hannibal's approach within three miles of Rome (10; the land on which his camp stands is sold in the city at its full price, 11); Scipio Africanus appointed commander in Spain at the age of 24 (18), and capturing Nova Carthago (46); his generosity and restraint in the treatment of a beautiful Spanish captive (50).

Book 27. The interception and defeat of Hasdrubal.

Book 30. The romantic story of *Sophonisba, Syphax, and Masinissa (15); the battle of Zama (32).

Book 33. The defeat of Philip V of Macedon at Cynoscephalae (7); the notable speech of Flamininus on making peace with a defeated enemy (12); the proclamation of Greek freedom at the Isthmian games (32).

Book 34. The repeal of the Oppian sumptuary law (1).

Book 35. The conversation of Scipio and Hannibal at Ephesus about great military commanders (14).

Book 38. The proud reminder by Scipio Africanus when tried for embezzlement that the day was the anniversary of his victory at Zama (51).

Book 39. The discovery and suppression of the Bacchanalian orgies (8); the character of Cato the Censor (40).

Book 44. The victory of Pydna (40).

logo'graphers (*logographoi*). **1.** Early

Greek prose writers who were forerunners of historians proper (see HISTORIOGRAPHY 1), and who lived mostly in Ionia (Greek Asia Minor) in the sixth and fifth centuries BC. None of their works has survived, but there are numerous references to them and quotations in later authors. The earliest are said to have been Cadmus and Dionysius, both of Miletus, but very little is known of either. *Hecataeus, also of Miletus, was one of the most famous. Pherecȳdēs of Athens, active in the first half of the fifth century BC, wrote *Histories* (i.e. 'inquiries') in ten books, both mythical and genealogical. Charōn of Lampsacus, Xanthus of Lydia, and *Hellanīcus of Lesbos were a little earlier than, or contemporary with, Herodotus. Of these, Hellanicus, who outlived Herodotus, was a prolific author, writing on mythological topics (systematic genealogies of heroic families), on regional history (e.g. *Lesbiaca, Persica*), and on local history and chronology; his *Atthis* was criticized by Thucydides for its inadequate chronology of the fifth century.

2. Name given at Athens to persons who were hired to write speeches for litigants to deliver in a court of law. *Antiphon was said to have been the first of these; *Lysias and *Demosthenes (2) were also very successful at this practice. Since many trials were political, speechwriting sometimes laid the foundation for a later political career.

Longī'nus, Ca'ssius (*c.* AD 213–73, to be distinguished from the supposed author of the treatise 'On the Sublime'; see below), an eminent Greek rhetorician and philosopher. A *Neoplatonist, he taught at Athens, and was the teacher of *Porphyry. In the last few years of his life he became the principal counsellor of Odaenathus and *Zenobia, the rulers of Palmyra. For his loyal support of Zenobia he was executed when the city fell to the Roman emperor Aurelian. Fragments of his works survive.

Longī'nus on the Sublime (*Peri hypsous*), Greek literary treatise (a third of which is lost) of unknown authorship and date. Manuscripts attribute it to 'Dionysius Longinus' or 'Dionysius or Longinus' and until the nineteenth cen-

tury it was generally believed to be by Cassius Longinus (above). This tradition is contradicted on chronological grounds by internal evidence indicating a date in the first century AD. The author says that his work is a reply to a similarly entitled treatise of the first century BC by Caecilius of Calactē, who gave what 'Longinus' considers to be an inadequate account of 'sublimity', failing in particular to attach sufficient importance to the emotional element in this concept. It is addressed to a friend, Postumius Terentianus (of whom nothing is known but who is presumed from his name to be Roman), and is on the subject of what constitutes sublimity in literature. It has greatly appealed to later readers by its enthusiasm, sage criticism, apt illustrations (mostly from Greek literature), and clarity of expression. The author analyses the constituents of sublimity, and finds them in elevated thought ('sublimity is the echo of a noble mind', 9. 2); strong emotion; certain kinds of figures of thought and speech; nobility of diction ('truly beautiful words are the very light of the spirit', 30. 1); and composition, i.e. word-order, rhythm, euphony. He lists the faults to be avoided: turgidity, puerility, false emotion, frigidity; discusses the part played by imagination and various figures of speech; and illustrates his points by a wealth of quotation. There are interesting observations on successful and unsuccessful ways of representing supernatural beings and of exciting awe, and comparisons of Homer's *Iliad* and *Odyssey*, and of Demosthenes and Cicero, which are very rewarding. The author finds the chief examples of sublimity of style in Homer, Plato, and Demosthenes, of whom he speaks with appreciative enthusiasm. At one point (in a section on selection and organization of material) his quotation preserves an ode of *Sappho, translated by the Roman poet Catullus (see poem 51). There is a notable passage (9. 9) in which the author points out, as an instance of grandeur in representing the divine, the first verses of Genesis. No other pagan writer uses the Bible in this way, and one must presume that the author had, unusually, both Roman (in the case of his addressee) and Jewish contacts.

This is a critical work of great importance; the writer is able to transcend the rhetorical tradition within which he worked and contribute to our understanding of true literary greatness.

Longus, see NOVEL.

Long Walls. At Athens, the two Long Walls connecting Athens with her ports to the south-west at Piraeus and Phalerum were built between 461 and 456 BC. Around 445 BC a third wall was built parallel to the Piraeus wall and about 170 m. (190 yds.) south of it, the original Phaleric Wall being allowed to fall into ruin. The two walls to Piraeus were each about 6 km. (4 miles) long. The main road from Athens lay outside these parallel walls, the road between them being primarily military. The effect of the walls during the *Peloponnesian War was to turn the whole territory between Athens and the ports into a fortress, victualled from the sea. After the Spartan victory at the end of the Peloponnesian War (404 BC) the walls were dismantled, to the sound of flute music. They were rebuilt by *Conon after his victory at Cnidus in 394 BC, but were in ruins when Philip V of Macedon attacked Athens in 200 BC. Today there is virtually no trace of them to be seen.

Lotus-eaters (Lōtophagoi), in Homer's *Odyssey* 9, a fabulous people whose land Odysseus visits. They live on the lotus-fruit, whose property is to make those who eat it forget their home and desire to remain for ever in Lotus-land.

Lūcan (Marcus Annaeus Lucānus) (AD 39–65), Silver Latin poet, born at Corduba (Cordoba) in Spain. He was grandson of Seneca the Elder, and his father was the brother of Seneca the Younger (and the brother of Gallio of Acts 18). He was educated at Rome, studying philosophy under the Stoic Cornūtus, whose tuition he is said to have shared with the satirist *Persius. He continued his studies at Athens but was recalled by the emperor Nero, who admitted him to his circle, made him quaestor and augur, and greatly admired him for a time. In AD 60 at the first celebration of the games called Neronia he won a poetic competition. In 62 or 63 he published three books of his epic *Pharsalia* (on the civil war between Caesar and Pompey). However, he incurred the enmity of Nero, for which various reasons are given; it is possible that the emperor was jealous of Lucan's literary success, having himself some claim to being a poet. Lucan was forbidden to write further poetry or to plead in the courts. He took to lampooning the emperor and even joined the conspiracy of *Piso (64–5). When this was discovered Lucan, in spite of confessions and abject pleas, was compelled to commit suicide (as were his father and both uncles). There is a biography of him by *Suetonius.

Lucan was a voluminous and precocious writer, but all his works apart from the *Pharsalia* are lost, among them an address to his much-loved wife Polla Argentaria. The *Pharsalia* is the greatest Latin epic after the *Aeneid*, and Lucan's brilliant style won him the admiration of his contemporaries. One of them, Quintilian, while recognizing its qualities, adds that it is 'a safer model for orators than for poets'.

Lucā'nia, see ITALY.

Lū'cerēs, see RAMNES.

Lu'cian (Lūciānus, Gk. Loukiānos) (*c.* AD 115 to after 180), born at Samosata on the Euphrates in Syria, the author (in Greek) of some eighty prose pieces in various forms, essays, speeches, letters, dialogues, and stories, mainly satirical in tone. His native language was Syriac, but he received a good Greek education in rhetoric and became first an advocate and then, like many of his day, a travelling lecturer, although he was a satirist rather than a sophist (see SOPHISTIC, SECOND). The details of his life are known only from his own writings; no contemporary or near-contemporary mentions him. He travelled through Asia, Greece, Italy, and Gaul, but in middle age he moved to Athens and abandoned rhetoric for philosophy. It may have been after that that he developed the dialogue form (familiar from Plato) which made him famous, although it is impossible to date his works securely. His writings were influenced by Attic Old Comedy (see COMEDY, GREEK 3), the dialogues of Plato, and especially

the satires of the Cynic *Menippus, and
he scathingly, if humorously, indicts the
follies of his day. In later life he was
appointed to a minor post in the Roman
bureaucracy in Egypt.

1. Among his writings on literary and
quasi-philosophical subjects are the following: (i) *The Vision* or the *Life of
Lucian* (*Somnium* or *Vita Luciani*), a
chapter of his early life, telling how he
abandoned sculpture (to which his
parents had apprenticed him) for learning; (ii) *Nigrīnus*, which contains an interesting picture of the simplicity and peace
of contemporary Athens contrasted with
the turbulent and luxurious life of Rome;
(iii) *The Literary Prometheus* (*Ad eum
qui dixerat, 'Prometheus es in verbis'*: 'to
him who said, "you are like Prometheus
in your language" '), in which he describes the basis of his satires, namely a
blend of comedy and Platonic dialogue;
(iv) *The Way to Write History* (*De historia
conscrībenda*), an entertaining criticism
of the eccentricities of contemporary
historians, followed by an acute exposition of the qualities required in a history
and its author; (v) *Dēmōnax*, an account
of the character of that Cynic philosopher, Lucian's teacher, praised for his
austere virtue; (vi) *Imāginēs* (*Eikonĕs*), a
dialogue with interesting references to
the chief works of some of the great
Greek artists, Pheidias, Praxitelēs,
Polygnotus, and Apellēs; and (vii) *True
History* (*Vērae historiae*), a parody of
travellers' tales, including Homer's
Odyssey and *Ctesias' Indica*, which
Lucian begins with the assertion that he
tells the truth only when he says that it is
all lies. The adventures related in this last
work are of the most extravagant and
ingenious kind, involving a voyage to the
moon and to the Isles of the Blest, where
the travellers meet Homer and hear him
condemn his critics, and assert, among
other things, that he began the *Iliad* with
the anger of Achilles merely from
chance, without any settled plan. When
the travellers arrive at the Underworld
they find Herodotus and Ctesias there
paying the penalty for their falsehoods.
Both Rabelais in the sixteenth century
and Jonathan Swift in the eighteenth
found inspiration in this work.

2. Lucian's satirical dialogues are
numerous, and together with his fantastic
tales are his most characteristic works,
showing his wit and inventiveness as well
as his hatred of cant, hypocrisy, and fana-
ticism, especially in religion and philosophy. Among the best-known of these
dialogues are the following. (i) *Dialogues
of the Gods* (*Deorum dialogi*) and *of the
Sea Gods* (*Marīnorum dialogi*), short dialogues making fun of the myths about
e.g. the birth of Athena, Apollo's love
affairs, the Judgement of Paris, and the
story of Polyphemus and Galatea. (ii)
Dialogues of the Dead (*Mortuorum
dialogi*), short dialogues set in the Underworld, the interlocutors being such
characters as Pluto, Hermēs, Charon,
Menippus, Diogenēs, Heraclēs, Alexander the Great, and Achilles. Death
shows up the vanities and pretences of
living men (including the arguments of
philosophers), and defeats the intrigues
of expectant heirs. The irony, at the
expense of all humankind, is grim and
tinged with melancholy and resignation.
(iii) *Menippus* (also called *Necyomantia*);
Menippus, the Cynic philosopher,
exasperated by the contradictions of
philosophy, visits the Underworld to consult Teiresias as to the best life to lead,
and is told merely to do, with smiling face
and taking nothing too seriously, the task
that lies to hand. Similar themes are
treated in the *Charon*, where Charon, the
ferryman from the Underworld, visits the
upper world to see what life is like and
what it is that makes men weep when
they enter his boat (i.e. life seen from the
point of view of death); this is the most
poetic of Lucian's dialogues, with its
comparisons of cities to bee-hives
attacked by wasps, and of human lives to
bubbles. The whole is a picture of the
pettiness of mankind; Charon himself
observes, 'This is all laughable'. (iv) *The
Voyage to the Underworld* (*Kataplous*),
describing a boat-load of the dead and
their attitudes. Only the cobbler Micyllus
eagerly accepts his summons to the
Underworld. (v) *The Dream* or *The
Cock*, concerning Micyllus the cobbler
again, who threatens to kill a cock which
has woken him from a happy dream of
riches. The cock reveals himself to be
Pythagoras, in one of his incarnations (a
previous one had been *Aspasia), and

argues that Micyllus is much happier than many rich men. To prove the point the cock and Micyllus, rendered invisible by the former's magic tail feathers, visit the houses of several rich men and observe their miseries and vices. (vi) *The Sale of Lives* (*Vitarum auctio*), an entertaining piece in which the chief proponents of various philosophic creeds are put up for sale, Hermes being the auctioneer: Diogenēs the *Cynic goes for two obols, useful as a house dog; Heracleitus is unsaleable; Socrates (apparently identified with Platonic philosophy), after considerable ridicule, fetches the enormous sum of two talents, bought by Dion of Syracuse; Pyrrhon the *Sceptic is disposed of last, and even after he is in the hands of the buyer is still in doubt as to whether he has been sold or not. (vii) *Icaromenippus*, very Aristophanic in its fantastic plot: Menippus (see (iii) above), disgusted with the disputes of the philosophers, resolves to visit the heavens himself to find out the truth, cutting off the wings of an eagle and a vulture as a mechanical aid. He finds *Empedoclēs in the moon, carried there by the vapours of Aetna. He is civilly received by the gods, and watches Zeus receive human prayers, through ventholes in the floor of heaven; he attends a banquet and hears the gods decide to destroy all philosophers as useless drones. Returned to earth Menippus hastens with malicious pleasure to the *Stoa Poikilē to announce to the philosophers their impending doom. (viii) *The Cross-examination of Zeus* (*Zeus confutātus*), on the conflict between the doctrine of fate and that of divine omnipotence. (ix) *Meeting of the Gods* (*Deorum concilium*), in which Momus complains of the admission among the genuine deities of a number of foreigners, mortals, and others of doubtful credentials, from Dionysus and his hangers-on to the Egyptians Apis and Anubis. (x) *Dependent Scholars* (*De mercēde conductis*), written to dissuade a Greek philosopher from accepting a place in a Roman household, with its attendant hardships and humiliations, for a pittance; it is an excellent example of Lucian's witty good sense. (xi) *Peregrine* (*De morte Peregrīni*), a satirical narrative of the career of a fanatical Cynic and

apostate Christian (a historical character) who, in pursuit of notoriety, had himself burnt alive on a pyre. (xii) *Lucius or the Ass* (*Lucius sive asinus*), a short novel doubtfully ascribed to Lucian; it is perhaps an abbreviated form of an earlier Greek romance which was also the basis of the Latin novel 'The Golden Ass' of *Apuleius. See also TIMON (1).

Lūcī'lius, Gaius (*c.*180–102 BC), Latin satirical poet, born at Suessa Aurunca in Campania, a member of the literary circle of *Scipio Aemilianus, and famous as the creator of that purely Roman form of literature, (poetical) satire. Lucilius established hexameters as the standard metre for Roman satire and in it wrote thirty books of informal discourses, mainly autobiographical, greatly influenced by Greek literature and Stoic philosophy. The subjects he dealt with included incidents in the lives of himself and his friends, travels, literary subjects, public and private morality, and popular philosophy. Some of his satires included outspoken criticism of authors and men in public life. Of these works some 1,300 lines survive, but no single substantial passage. The satires served as a model for later satirists, especially Horace, whose celebrated 'Journey to Brundisium' (*Satire I. 5) was modelled on one, and they were read until the end of the Roman empire.

Lūcī'na, see JUNO.

Lucius or the Ass, see LUCIAN.

Lucrē'tia, in Roman history, the wife of L. Tarquinius Collatinus, nephew of Tarquinius Priscus. According to legend she was raped by Sextus, son of Tarquinius Superbus, and having revealed this to her husband took her own life. This incident led to the insurrection headed by Junius *Brutus and the expulsion of the Tarquins from Rome. The story is told by Livy and is the subject of Shakespeare's poem *The Rape of Lucrece* (1594).

Lucrē'tius. 1. Titus Lucretius Cārus (*c.*99–*c.*55 BC), Roman poet and philosopher, author of *De rerum natura* ('on nature'), his only known work. Of his life virtually nothing has come down to us. *Jerome, in his translation of the

Chronica of Eusebius, states that he was born in 94 BC, was poisoned by a love-philtre, wrote in the intervals of madness some books which Cicero later 'emended', and took his own life at the age of 44. *Donatus (1) states in an aside that he died in 55. The poem, though in a finished state, was clearly not finally completed, and it must be concluded that it was published as it stood after the author's death. It is dedicated to the aristocrat C. Memmius, the patron of Catullus and Cinna (whom Catullus accompanied to Bithynia during Memmius' propraetorship of 57). The description Lucretius gives of Memmius in the proem to Book 1, as excelling in all graces and helping his country in her hour of need, is likely to antedate his disgrace and banishment in 53 for corrupt practices in the elections of 54.

De rerum natura is a didactic poem in six books of hexameters, and is the fullest exposition we possess of the physical system of *Epicurus, in which Lucretius was a convinced and ardent believer. The purpose of the poem is to free men from a sense of guilt and the fear of death by demonstrating that fear of the intervention of gods in this world and of punishment of the soul after death are groundless: the world and everything in it are material and governed by the mechanical laws of nature, and the soul is mortal and perishes with the body. Thus most of the poem is devoted to an exposition of the atomic theory which Epicurus had adopted from the philosophers *Democritus and Leucippus: that an infinite number of atoms moving about in infinite space collide and combine with each other to bring into existence the world in all its variety, and there is nothing in the world that is not material. However, Lucretius allows that men possess free will, and accounts for it by stating that atoms occasionally swerve from their path out of their own volition. He also touches upon Epicurus' moral theory that pleasure is the aim of life.

Book 1 opens with a superb invocation of Venus, goddess of creative life, to grant to the poet inspiration and to Rome peace. It proceeds to the demonstration that the universe consists of void and small particles of matter, atoms, which are solid, indivisible, and indestructible. In passing Lucretius refutes the physical systems of *Heracleitus, *Empedocles, and *Anaxagoras, and demonstrates that the universe is infinite in extent.

Book 2 starts with a passage on the blessings of philosophy. It then deals with the motion of atoms which, endlessly falling through space by their own nature, may swerve a little from their path (the swerve being Epicurus' rejection of a determinist universe) and, colliding with other atoms, form into masses; from these masses the universe is built up by chance arrangement. The book concludes with a demonstration that the universe contains many other worlds similar to ours.

Book 3 starts with praise of Epicurus and then proceeds to a demonstration that the soul too is made of atoms, of an extremely rarefied nature, and, with a long series of proofs, that it is mortal. The book ends triumphantly with an eloquent exposition of the foolishness of fearing death.

Book 4 deals mainly with the Epicurean theory of vision, sensation, and thought, and with various biological processes, digestion, sleep, and the meaning of dreams, and ends with a vigorous denunciation of the physical passion of love which destroys the Epicurean ideal state, peace of mind.

Book 5 begins with an extravagant eulogy of Epicurus, holding him to be partly divine because of his god-like peace of mind. Lucretius attacks the theological view of the world. He shows how the world had a beginning and will have an end, and discusses some problems of astronomy. He then traces the origin on earth of plant and animal life, including human life, and with remarkable insight describes the development of primitive man and the birth of civilization.

Book 6, whose introduction is one more laudation of Epicurus, is the loosest in composition and shows signs of being unfinished. It deals with unusual meteorological and terrestrial phenomena, earthquakes, volcanoes, the magnet, etc., concluding with pestilence and a horrific account of the plague at Athens in 430 (see PELOPONNESIAN WAR).

There is no specific treatment of the subject of moral conduct, but it is clear from various passages that Lucretius accepted the view of Epicurus. Pleasure and pain are the only guides to conduct, but by pleasure he understands the calm that proceeds from absence of pain and desire, and freedom from care and fear. He is deeply moved at the thought of Epicurus' great contribution to the alleviation of human suffering by banishing superstitious fears, introducing peace of mind, and teaching men how to face all the disasters of life with serenity, and he speaks of the philosopher with religious awe. Although he describes Epicureanism with the fervour of a religious convert, he has at the same time a firm grasp of his intellectual arguments, and writes with intelligent understanding of the issues as well as with emotion. Much of the subject-matter does not lend itself easily to poetic treatment, and there are parts that make for tortuous reading, and others where the versification is heavy and clumsy; but the work as a whole is suffused with an intense awareness of the world about him, especially of the beauty of the countryside, with warm sympathy for all living things and a compassionate, even painful, understanding of humanity. His strong moral sense, lightened by a lively feeling for the ridiculous, often leads naturally to satire, while his close observation of the world makes it easy for him to illustrate his arguments with vivid but homely images and similes which drive them home. His hexameters have weight and dignity, though admitting metrical practices that later poets preferred to avoid. The style shows the influence of the old Latin poets, *Ennius (particularly), *Naevius, *Pacuvius, and *Accius. He freely uses alliteration, assonance, and even rhyme, as well as repetition, and archaic forms and constructions; and he does not hesitate to invent new words including such compound adjectives as *terriloquus* ('uttering frightening words') and *horrisonus* ('making a terrifying noise'), complaining of the poverty of his native tongue. He is aware of his own originality and the difficulty of treating such a subject in poetry at all, let alone in Latin with no tradition of writing philosophy in verse. But poetry is important as the 'honey on the rim' of the cup containing the bitter draught of philosophy.

Lucretius aroused the admiration of Virgil (*felix qui potuit rerum cognoscere causas*, 'happy the man who was able to understand the causes of things'; see *GEORGICS*), of Statius (who speaks of the *docti furor arduus Lucreti*, 'the towering frenzy of the learned Lucretius'), even of Ovid. But in the Middle Ages he appears to have been almost completely forgotten; the text is still based upon only two primary manuscripts. It is through Lucretius that the atomic theories of Epicurus are best known today.

2. Quintus Lucretius Vespi'lio (consul 19 BC), who was concealed by his wife Turia during the proscriptions of 43–42 BC until his pardon was obtained. He has been thought to be the author of the remarkable *Laudatio Turiae* ('eulogy of Turia'), an encomium, preserved in an inscription, describing how faithfully and bravely his wife served him.

Lŭcu'llus, Lucius Lici'nius (*c.*114–57 BC), Roman general and statesman. He was Sulla's most reliable officer, entrusted with the diplomatic side of his dealings in the East, and became his literary executor. He governed Africa as propraetor in 77 with honesty and humanity. Consul in 74, he obtained the command against *Mithridatēs, king of Pontus, and carried out a series of brilliant campaigns in the Third Mithridatic War until his troops, kept under strict discipline, began to mutiny. He settled the taxation of Asia fairly, thereby offending business interests at Rome, and in 66 he was replaced by Pompey under the Manilian law (see *PRO LEGE MANILIA*) and returned to Rome, where he had to wait until 63 for a *triumph. He then led the senate's opposition to the eastern settlement of his rival Pompey, but after unpleasant experiences of Caesar's consulate (59) retired and gave himself up to the indulgence of his hedonist tastes, having acquired great wealth in Asia. His luxury became proverbial: 'Lucullan' has been applied as an epithet to good food. He was an ardent philhellene, a lover of literature and the arts. The books of the Pontic kings, booty from the war, remained his private property, but he was always ready to lend them, and his library became a centre for literary Greeks at Rome (see PRO ARCHIA). He wrote a (lost) history in Greek of the Marsian War (90–89 BC). He lapsed into insanity before his death.

lūdi, the public games at Rome, a term used to describe a variety of theatrical performances, sports, and contests which took place on the occasion of festivals of the gods, and were instituted to win their favour or avert their anger, or to comply with some oracular command. They were usually annual but sometimes were held for a specific occasion. They followed an exact ritual, any deviation from which entailed a repetition (*instaurātio*) of the proceedings. Unlike the Greek games they did not for the most part include an element of athletic contest: this was first introduced in imperial times in what were known as *agōnēs*. The earliest *ludi* appear to have been chariot-races, *ludi circenses*, held in honour of Mars or Consus, under the control of magistrates. Then came gladiatorial and other displays in the forum and in amphitheatres, a survival perhaps from Etruscan funeral games. The first permanent site for the games was constructed in 329 BC. There were also games under the control of the priests, like the dances of the *Salii.

lūdus Trō'iae ('game of Troy'), at Rome, apparently of ancient origin, a kind of sham-fight performed by young men of aristocratic rank on horseback, said to have been invented by *Aeneas, and often exhibited by Augustus and later emperors. The significance of *Troiae* is obscure; Virgil (*Aeneid* 5. 596) describes the event and connects it with the games celebrated at the tomb of Aeneas' father Anchisēs.

Lupercā'lia, very ancient Roman festival of purification held every year on 15 February, originally a shepherd-festival; it was in honour of *Faunus, worshipped under the name Lupercus (and presumably had some connection with driving away wolves, *lupi*, from the flocks). Its primary purpose was to secure fertility for the fields, the flocks, and the people. The worshippers gathered at the Lupercal, a cave on the Palatine hill where Romulus and Remus were supposed to have been suckled by a wolf. After sacrifices were made, the priests cut thongs (*februa*) from the skins of the sacrificed animals, and with some of the magistrates ran through the streets of Rome striking with the thongs all whom they met, especially women, who put themselves in the way of blows in order to be rendered fertile. Mark Antony ran as one of the consuls of 44 BC and in his course mounted the Rostra and offered Julius Caesar a diadem twined with laurel, which Caesar refused. The ceremony survived into Christian times, and was finally suppressed in AD 494. See also LYCAEUS.

Lu'scius Lānuvī'nus, writer of Latin comedies in the early second century BC, whose criticisms of *Terence are rebutted by the latter in several of his prologues. His works have not survived.

Lyae'us, epithet of the Greek god *Dionysus.

Lycae'us, name of a mountain in the west of Arcadia, near Bassae, from where there is a view of a large part of the Peloponnese. It was one of the chief centres of the worship of Zeus, who is sometimes given the epithet Lycaeus as a consequence, and the birthplace of the god *Pan, who had a sanctuary there.

Lycā'on, in Greek myth, son of Pelasgus and king of Arcadia, who founded the cult of Zeus *Lycaeus. He sacrificed a child on the altar and was thereupon turned into a wolf (*lykos*). From that time onwards, every time sacrifice was made at that altar a man turned into a wolf; the creature might revert to human shape in the ninth year if it had not tasted human flesh. Another story said that when Zeus and Hermes visited Arcadia, Lycaon, to test Zeus, served him human flesh. Zeus as punishment blasted all Lycaon's sons except one, turned Lycaon into a wolf, and sent a great flood (see DEUCALION). The story seems to represent a belief that the weather-god (*Zeus) could be moved by human sacrifice.

Lycei'us, epithet of *Apollo.

Lȳcē'um (Lȳkeion), grove and gymnasium near Athens, sacred to Apollo Lyceius, where Aristotle taught. The name is sometimes used to signify the philosophy school of Aristotle. The Lyceum lay to the east of the city near the river Ilissus.

Lȳ'cophron. 1. The younger, talented son of *Periander, tyrant of Corinth, exiled by his father to the west Greek island of Corcyra (then under Corinthian control) on account of his bitter hostility. In his later years Periander proposed to hand over his kingdom to Lycophron, and to go himself to Corcyra. To prevent this the Corcyreans murdered Lycophron, whereupon Periander seized three hundred youths from the leading Corcyrean families and sent them off to be made into eunuchs at Sardis; they were saved from this fate by the Samians. (The story is told in Herodotus 3. 50.)

2. (b. *c*.320 BC), Hellenistic poet from Chalcis in Euboea. When a young man he went to Alexandria and became one of the *Pleiad of tragic poets. The only work of his to survive is the *Alexandra*, a dramatic monologue in 1,474 lines of iambic trimeters (SEE METRE, GREEK 5) in which the slave set to watch Alexandra (i.e. *Cassandra) reports her prophecies to her father Priam, king of Troy. They concern the destruction of Troy and the crime of *Ajax, the return of the Greeks and their fate, Aeneas' arrival in Latium, the eventual struggles between Europe and Asia, and the rise of Roman power. These last passages, which concerned events of Lycophron's own lifetime, raised doubts even in antiquity as to whether he could really be the author. The whole poem is written in an extremely obscure and allusive style. Lycophron was also the author of a prose treatise on comedy (which has not survived).

Lycō'ris, see GALLUS.

Lȳcu'rgus (Lȳkourgos). **1.** Legendary king of the Ēdōnēs, a Thracian people; he persecuted the youthful *Dionysus when he came with his nurses seeking refuge, and was consequently struck blind, or driven mad, so that he killed his own son Dryas; he was then eaten alive by wild horses.

2. Legendary legislator of *Sparta, about whom nothing certain is known, not even when he lived. He is said to be the founder of the Spartan constitution and the social and military systems, and so of the *eunomia*, 'good order', the name generally applied to these.

3. (*c*.390–*c*.325 BC), distinguished Athenian orator and statesman, pupil of Isocrates, and a member of the Eteobutadae *genos* (a noble family, one branch of which held the hereditary priesthood of Poseidon Erechtheus, another the priestesshood of Athena Polias). Lycurgus was in charge of Athens' finances from the time of her defeat by Philip II of Macedon at Chaeronea in 338 BC until 326. The increase in the size of the navy at this time is attributed to him, and he embarked on an extensive building programme, including the reconstruction in marble of the temple of Dionysus. He won the confidence of his fellow-citizens to such a degree that they refused to surrender him to Philip's son Alexander the Great in 335 when the latter demanded the arrest of those hostile to Macedon. Lycurgus had statues erected of the tragic dramatists Aeschylus, Sophocles, and Euripides, and an official copy made of all their works (later borrowed by Ptolemy II Philadelphus, king of Egypt, for the library at Alexandria). Of his fifteen orations known to the ancients one survives, the indictment for treason of a certain Leōcratēs, for having allegedly fled from Athens at the news of the defeat at Chaeronea. It was said that after his death Lycurgus was accused of having left a deficit in the city treasury, and that when his sons were unable to repay the money they were imprisoned, in spite of a defence by *Hypereidēs; after an appeal by Demosthenes they were released.

Lȳcus, see ANTIOPE and *HERACLES, MADNESS OF.*

Lȳ'dia, country occupying the centre of western *Asia Minor, with its capital at Sardis. It contained much natural wealth including gold (see PACTOLUS) and, being traversed by two main routes from the west coast to the interior, it gained wealth from trade and contributed greatly to the material prosperity of western Asia Minor, including the Greek cities. Under the dynasty of the Mermnadae, which was founded by *Gyges early in the seventh century BC and ended with *Croesus in the middle of the sixth, a Lydian empire was formed, extending north to the Troad and west to the territories of the Greek cities on the coast. It is clear from the poems of Alcaeus and Sappho that Lydia was not regarded as *barbarian but enjoyed great esteem as a semi-Hellenic state; it was said to be the first country to use coined money. After Croesus was defeated by the Persian king Cyrus, Lydia became the chief Persian satrapy in the west, and was often a threat to the autonomy of the Greek cities. It was closely connected with Greek history during the classical period. After its conquest by Alexander the Great in 333 BC it was settled by Greek colonists, eventually becoming part of *Attalid territory and passing into Roman control in 133 BC with the rest of the Attalid kingdom. Lydia was influenced by and herself influenced Greece. The Lydian language, which seems to be a branch of Indo-European, is found on some inscriptions. Maeonia was an ancient name of Lydia (whence perhaps '*Maeonidēs', i.e. Homer).

Ly'dia, Latin poem of unknown authorship, probably incomplete, consisting of eighty hexameters, and included in the *Appendix Virgiliana. It is a lament by a lover for the loss of his mistress.

Ly'gdamus, see TIBULLUS.

Ly'nceus. 1. In Greek myth, son of Aphareus, king of Messenia, and the younger brother of Idas. The two brothers were inseparable, and both sailed with the *Argonauts. Lynceus' eyesight was so keen that he could see for great distances and even through the earth. In a fight with Castor and Polydeucēs (see DIOSCURI) both brothers were killed, as also was Castor.

2. In Greek myth, a son of Aegyptus, the only one to be spared by his bride, Hypermnestra, on their wedding night (see DANAUS). He became king of Argos and was succeeded by his son *Abas.

lyric poetry
1. *Greek.* Lyric poetry, meaning poetry 'sung to the lyre', existed in Greece from earliest times. Although it was, strictly speaking, song, the words were of primary importance and are now all that remain, knowledge of the accompanying music having been lost in antiquity. The Alexandrian scholars of the third century BC drew up a *canon of nine great lyric poets: Alcman, Sappho, Alcaeus, Stesichorus, Ibycus, Anacreon, Simonidēs, Pindar, and Bacchylidēs. Some added a tenth, Corinna. Lyric poetry is also found in the Attic drama of the fifth century BC, in the choruses (so-called; see CHORUS), but towards the end of the fifth century the chorus was relegated to a subordinate role (see COMEDY, GREEK 5). In relatively modern times, Greek lyric poetry outside drama has been divided into two kinds, choral lyric (also known as choral odes) and monody (Gk. *monōdia*, 'solo song'). Both kinds of lyric were written in a great variety of metres; for examples of possible kinds see METRE, GREEK 8. Elegy and iambic poetry, written in their own particular (non-lyric) metres, are both occasionally included with lyric poetry (strictly speaking erroneously and despite incompatibility of metre) when the subject-matter seems to suggest this grouping.

Choral lyric was sung (and often danced) by a chorus (or by a leader answered by a chorus) to a musical accompaniment usually played on the lyre, occasionally on the flute (*aulos*, a wind instrument like the oboe). It was composed from earliest times and throughout Greek history for public religious ceremonies. To this fact are attributable the predominantly elevated tone and the inclusion of myth and moralizing. Homer mentions many varieties of choral lyric: *dirges, *hymns, *hyporchemata, maiden-songs (see PARTHENEION), and wedding-songs (see EPITHALAMIUM and HYMENAEUS). The procession-song (*prosodion*) is another very ancient form. Later developments were the *dithyramb (accompanying the worship of Dionysus), the *nome, and the *encomium and *epinikion, the two last written in praise of men, and indicative of the increasing secularization of this form of poetry. The earliest choral ode of which a substantial part survives is a *partheneion* by *Alcman (seventh century BC) which seems to be composed in metrically corresponding stanzas known as *strophēs and antistrophēs. In later choral lyric the form became triadic (see TRIAD), reputedly the innovation of *Stesichorus, and of an increasing metrical complexity which reached its culmination in the odes of *Pindar. The material of a choral ode was relatively standardized and included praise of the gods, mention of the occasion and the personalities involved, moral maxims, and mythical narrative, this last providing the main subject-matter.

The development of choral lyric is associated with the Doric-speaking Peloponnese, especially Sparta, and with the names of *Thaletas, *Eumelus, and *Arion, whose works are all but lost. The association is indicated by the ancient convention that choral lyric was written in the Doric *dialect; Doric elements were retained even in the choral lyric of Attic tragedy. The great poets of choral lyric, some of whose works survive, are Alcman, Stesichorus, *Ibycus, *Simonides, Pindar, and *Bacchylides. For choral lyric as an element in Attic drama see CHORUS, TRAGEDY 1, and COMEDY, GREEK 2.

Of monody relatively little survives. It was sung to the accompaniment of a lyre. The intimate nature of the subject-matter—friendship, love, and hate—suggests that it was performed by a single individual on private occasions, for example after a banquet among friends (see SYMPOSIUM and SCOLIA). The surviving lyric of *Sappho, *Alcaeus, and *Anacreon is mostly monody. The fact that a poem is triadic in form is usually taken as an indication that it is a choral rather than a monodic ode; monody is generally simpler than choral lyric in form, metre, and expression. Attic tragedy contains a small amount of monody in the lyrics occasionally sung by individuals (rather than by the chorus). See also ARCHILOCHUS.

2. *Latin*. Comparatively little lyric poetry was written by the Romans. There exist in Latin some fragments of folksongs, hymns, and religious incantations which indicate the existence in early times of an indigenous lyric poetry, but the earliest Latin lyric deserving of the name was modelled on Greek forms, mostly the simpler forms of monody, and it was entirely a literary product, not rooted in social practice, and intended to be read and not sung. Two notable exceptions are, first, the maiden-song composed for Juno at a time of crisis in 207 BC by *Livius Andronicus, based presumably on Greek models; and secondly, Horace's elegant *Carmen Saeculare (17 BC). *Laevius was another early writer of lyrics (probably at the beginning of the first century BC), but only fragments of his work have survived. The two chief writers of literary lyric were *Catullus and Horace. Catullus experimented with lyric metres in poems of great verve (11, 17, 30, 34, 51, and 61), and wrote other equally lively poems in hendecasyllables and scazons (see METRE, LATIN 3 (iii)) which it is natural to regard as lyrics, even if the metres are not strictly speaking those of song (see 1 above); their style and subject-matter both recall the manner of Greek monody. Horace in the *Odes* uses a fair variety of lyric metres found in Greek monody, frequently combining lines of different metres into couplets or four-line stanzas; he also expresses a range of sentiments, from deep seriousness in Pindaric vein (though not attempting the complexities of Pindar's triadic structure), to love poems and drinking songs in a more subjective style (exquisite, but lacking the spontaneity of Greek monody). The iambic metres of the *Epodes* (see ODES) do not strictly belong to lyric, although the subject-matter in most cases makes them close to it. Horace's technical mastery seems to have deterred later poets from attempting to follow him, and lyrical subjects tended to be treated in the elegiac metre. *Statius' *Silvae* include two lyrics (4. 5 and 4. 7), *Martial occasionally used lyric metres, and *Seneca (2) included choral lyrics in his tragedies. The note of true inspiration is not heard again until the Christian hymns of *Prudentius and *Ambrose (to which should perhaps be added the emperor Hadrian's poem to his soul).

Lȳsan'der (Lȳsandros) (d. 395 BC),

Spartan naval commander towards the end of the *Peloponnesian War (431–404 BC), who won a great victory over the Athenian fleet at Aegospotami in 405. He blockaded Piraeus and after the surrender of Athens in the spring of 404 BC supported the establishment of the Thirty Tyrants. He subsequently became estranged from the Spartan government and lost power and influence. At the outbreak of the Corinthian War (395–386; see CORINTH), in which an alliance of Greek states opposed Sparta's tyrannical rule, he invaded Boeotia but was killed there at the siege of the city of Haliartus in 395. He was among the ablest Spartan leaders, but unpopular because of his arrogance. His Life was written by Nepos and Plutarch.

Ly'sias (c.458–c.380 BC), Attic orator, son of Cephalus, a wealthy Syracusan, whom Periclēs persuaded to settle as a metic (resident alien) in Athens, and brother of Polemarchus and Euthydemus. The family owned a prosperous shield-making business; it is the house of Polemarchus, the eldest son, at Piraeus, that provides the setting for Plato's *Republic*, in which Cephalus and Polemarchus take part in the opening discussion. At some time Lysias went with his brothers to *Thurii in south Italy and is said to have studied rhetoric under *Teisias of Syracuse. The defeat of the *Sicilian Expedition led to the expulsion of Lysias from Thurii in 412 and the brothers returned to Athens, where they lived until the tyranny of the Thirty in 404 BC. These, to procure funds, arrested the wealthy, among them Lysias and Polemarchus; Lysias escaped to Megara but Polemarchus was put to death and their property was seized. While in exile Lysias spent what was left of his fortune in aiding the democracy; as a consequence, on his return in 403 an attempt was made to confer citizenship upon him, but it was defeated by a technicality. Being now rather poor he became a professional speech-writer (see LOGOGRAPHERS (2)) and proved outstandingly successful, reputedly composing over 200 forensic speeches. As a metic he could not appear in court in person. However, the first speech of his career he delivered

on his own behalf, perhaps to a court of inquiry. The speech was 'Against Eratosthenēs' (speech 12), the defendant being allegedly the murderer of Lysias' brother, and it contains a vivid description of the writer's experiences under the Thirty.

Of his speeches thirty-five survive, some spurious and only twenty-three entire. They include a funeral oration (*epitaphios*) on those who died in the Corinthian War (395–386; see CORINTH) and a fragment of an epideictic ('display') speech delivered at the Olympic festival of 388 (*Olympiakos*), in which he urges the Greeks to end internal discord and unite against the two great enemies, the Persian king and Dionysius, tyrant of Syracuse. Lysias' speeches cover a range of cases, from murder and treason to adultery and embezzlement. Among the most interesting are: 'For Mantitheus' (a young man accused of having served in the cavalry under the Thirty); 'For the cripple', a defence of a man charged (perhaps justifiably) with receiving a state pension under false pretences; 'Against Alcibiadēs' (son of the famous Alcibiades), for dereliction of military duty; 'On the murder of Eratosthenes' (speech 1, not to be confused with 12; see above), a speech for a husband who had murdered his wife's seducer, fascinating for its glimpse of the life and conversation of an ordinary Greek household.

Lysias was admired in antiquity for the simplicity and naturalness of his style. His precise use of language, avoidance of all affectation and extravagance, and moderation of tone—he is rarely passionate, and pathos is not his strong point—could lead to monotony, but this is avoided by his gift of putting himself in his client's place and preparing for him a persuasive speech such as only he could have made according to his own circumstances, age, and temperament. Without resort to rhetorical devices, the speeches are clear and vivid, and orderly in arrangement (preface, narrative, proof, conclusion). It is said that he wrote a defence for Socrates to speak at his trial, but that Socrates refused it. The *Phaedrus* of Plato contains what purports to be a speech by Lysias on love. It is probably a Platonic parody.

Lȳsi'ppus, of Sicyon, a famous and prolific sculptor, active in the second half of the fourth century BC. *Pliny the Elder said he made 1,500 works—all in bronze—but nothing is known to survive from his own hand. He made many portraits of Alexander the Great (several copies are extant), whose edict, that no one should paint him but *Apellēs, and no one make his statue but Lysippus, is well known. One statue showed Alexander in characteristic pose, with head inclined and tilted upwards. An epigrammatist suggested that he was saying 'I have subdued the earth; you, Zeus, may keep Olympus'.

Lȳsis, see PLATO 2.

Lȳsi'strata (*Lȳsistratē*), Greek comedy by *Aristophanes, produced in the spring of 411 BC (probably at the *Lenaea rather than the Dionysia; it is not known whether the play won first prize). This was an alarming time for Athens: the *Sicilian Expedition had ended in disaster in 413 BC, a large part of her empire was in revolt, and her enemy Sparta had made an advantageous alliance with the Persian satrap Tissaphernēs. Yet though Athens was seriously weakened there was no immediate danger of collapse; for the time being she could hold on. The play is an expression of a natural desire for peace, so long as it can be achieved by compromise, without putting Athens in real danger. It contains no *parabasis*, and in this represents the beginning of a change in the form of Old Comedy (see COMEDY, GREEK 3 (iv) and 5).

The men having failed to bring the war to an end, it occurs to Lysistrata ('disbander of armies') that the women should take over control of affairs and force a peace, first by refusing sexual relations, and secondly by getting possession of the Acropolis and the state's reserve of money in the Parthenon, without which the Athenian war-effort would collapse. She gets the women together, including Lampito from Sparta and women from other enemy states. After some reluctance they fall in with her scheme and swear to carry it out. The foreigners depart to their own countries and Lysistrata with the Athenian wives occupies the Acropolis, which has already been seized by a band of old women. A chorus of old men tries to recapture it, but is driven off by a second chorus of old women with pails of water. An elderly *proboulos is also routed, together with his band of Scythian archers (the Athenian police force). In place of a *parabasis* the two choruses exchange insults. Then Lysistrata has to encourage the women, who are trying to slip away, to keep to their resolve. An anxious husband Cinesias arrives to recover his wife Myrrhinē, is tantalized by her, and finally cheated as she returns to the Acropolis. A herald from Sparta, similarly distressed, arrives to announce his country's intention to sue for peace, and a conference of both sides follows. Lysistrata scolds them all and urges reconciliation; peace is made, and Athenians and Spartans go to the Acropolis for a banquet.

M

Maca'ria, see HERACLES, CHILDREN OF.

Macedon, Macedonia; in general the former is used to describe the political entity, the latter the geographical area. Geographically, Macedonia occupies a central area of the Balkan Peninsula, a largely mountainous region covering parts of what are now south-west Bulgaria, northern Greece, and Serbia. Politically, the kingdom of Macedon is said to have been founded—probably in the mid-seventh century BC—by Perdiccas I, who came from Argos and claimed descent from the mythical Temenus, king of Argos (and the eldest of the *Heracleidae).

During the reigns of Amyntas (late sixth century) and his son and successor Alexander I, considerable territorial gains were made. Friendly relations were established with *Peisistratus and his sons, tyrants at Athens, and the process of Hellenization began (other Greeks persisted in saying that the Macedonians were *barbarians rather than full *Hellenes). Alexander's successor Perdiccas II (king c.452–413) played a shifty role in international politics, vacillating between Athens and Sparta during the Peloponnesian War. He was succeeded in 413 by Archelaus, memorably portrayed by Plato in the *Gorgias* as a monster of cruelty. Nevertheless, he did most to ensure that his country was part of Greece proper by making his new capital at Pella a centre for Greek artists and poets, entertaining among others Euripides, Agathon, Choerilus of Samos, Timotheus, and Zeuxis. Many Macedonian customs which seemed un-Greek, like tattooing, had lapsed by this time, but one or two lingered; by the time of Aristotle it was no longer traditional for a Macedonian who had not 'killed his man' to wear a cord round his waist, but until a very late date no one was permitted to recline at table (having instead to sit upright) who had not killed a wild boar

without nets. (At the age of 35 *Cassander was still sitting up to the table.) The country was wild, and as late as classical times contained lions and bears.

Macedon assumed a central role in Greek history under *Philip II (reigned 359–336 BC), whose expansionist policy roused Athens and Thebes to war against him. When he defeated them at Chaeronea (338) he became master of Greece. Under Philip's son and successor *Alexander the Great, Macedonian power reached its zenith. At his death in 323 he left an empire stretching from the Adriatic to the Punjab, and from north Afghanistan to Libya. However, there was no competent successor in the family and there followed for nearly half a century a complicated power struggle among Alexander's generals for fragments of his empire. Cassander achieved control of Macedon itself, and other generals founded dynasties in various parts of the empire—the *Attalids in Pergamum, the *Ptolemies in Egypt, the *Seleucids in Syria. With the death of Seleucus, the last survivor of Alexander's generals, in 281 the possibility of the union of the empire under one ruler came to an end.

In 279 Macedonia was invaded by a Celtic people known as Gauls (or Galatians), but they were defeated by Antigonus Gonātas (grandson of one of Alexander's generals), who established the *Antigonid dynasty in Macedon and proved a vigorous, successful, and cultured ruler (277–239). This dynasty maintained a partial control over Greece until 168 BC.

After Gonatas, the most prominent of the Antigonids was his grandson Philip V (221–179), a man of remarkable energy and misplaced ambition, who precipitated two wars with Rome—the First and Second Macedonian Wars (214–205 and 200–197). The first war was inconclusive; in the second Philip was defeated by Q. *Flamininus at Cynoscephalae in Thessaly in 197, and in the following year

Flamininus made his famous announcement at the Isthmian Games that Greece was free of Macedonian dominion. Philip V's son *Perseus was the last Macedonian king. In the Third Macedonian War (172–168/7) his army was practically annihilated at the battle of Pydna (168) by the Roman consul Aemilius *Paullus; this was followed by the dethronement of the Antigonids and the break-up of the Macedonian kingdom into four federal republics. The end came twenty years later, when an attempt by a pretender to reunite Macedon was defeated by Caecilius Metellus, and the country became a Roman province (146). Those cities, like Athens and Sparta, which had taken Rome's side, remained Roman allies; the rest were made subject and tributary. Greece became a Roman protectorate (not a province until the time of Augustus).

Macedonian Wars, of Rome, see MACEDONIA.

Macer. 1. Gaius Lici'nius Macer (d. 66 BC), Roman orator and annalist, the father of the poet *Calvus. His annals have not survived, but they were used by Livy for large parts of his books 4 and 5. Macer claimed to have consulted the *libri lintei* ('linen books'), an ancient list of magistrates.

2. Aemi'lius Macer, Roman poet of Verona, d. 16 BC, the author of Latin didactic poems, *Ornithogonia* on birds, and *Thēriaca* on snake bites. These works have not survived. He was a friend of Virgil and of Ovid.

Machā'on and Podalei'rius, in Homer's *Iliad*, sons of *Asclepius and Epionē and doctors to the Greek army at Troy. Machaon was a surgeon, Podaleirius a physician.

Macrō'bius, Ambro'sius Theodo'sius (flourished around AD 400, known to his contemporaries as Theodosius), Roman writer and philosopher. He was probably African by birth, and is generally identified with the praetorian prefect of 430, but little else is known of his life.

Macrobius wrote the *Saturnalia*, a dialogue in seven books dedicated to his son; it is supposed to represent a conversation at a banquet during the *Saturnalian festival, between a number of eminent Romans, at the house of Vettius Praetextatus, praetorian prefect in 384 and the leading pagan intellectual of his time. In form the work is very similar to that of *Athenaeus and of Aulus *Gellius (who is used as a source, though nowhere mentioned). Among those who are purported to be present are *Avienus, *Symmachus (the orator and administrator), *Servius (the Virgilian commentator), and a certain Euangelus, sceptical and rather bitter, who speaks disparagingly of Virgil and Cicero. The discussion covers a multitude of subjects, but the central topic is criticism of Virgil. Book 1 is occupied with the subject of ancient religion, and Praetextatus expounds the theory of the solar origin of mythology, all the gods being ultimately identified with the sun under one or other of its aspects. Book 2 contains a number of anecdotes on the religious and political changes at Rome, including mention of *Laberius, who after taunting Caesar was compelled by him to suffer the humiliation of acting in his own mime, and books 3–6 are devoted to Virgil. He is discussed from various points of view which cover his knowledge of ritual, his power of expressing emotion, his debt to Homer and other Greek authors, his debt to Ennius and other ancient Romans; and he is gradually built up to be the unique scholar and poet in a way which foreshadows the medieval view of him as a wonder-working magician. This section throws light on the history of Virgilian scholarship at the time. Book 7 proceeds to a discussion of various physical, physiological, and psychological questions, in general on the way the brain influences the workings of the body.

The second work of Macrobius is a *Neoplatonist commentary, also dedicated to his son, on the *Somnium Scipionis* ('dream of Scipio') from the sixth book of Cicero's *De republica* ('on the republic'): the successive passages of Cicero's narrative were set out (and were thus preserved when other parts of the *De republica* now known to us were still undiscovered). Macrobius' commentary was attentively studied in the Middle Ages. It depends largely on *Porphyry's (Greek) commentary on Plato's *Timaeus*, either directly or through a Latin intermediary. In it Macrobius examines the enigma of the soul and its destiny in the light of Neoplatonism and of the astronomical and mathematical sciences of the day. Its tendency is to reinforce the doctrine put forward in the *Somnium* of the immortality and divine quality of the soul, from a pagan rather than a Christian standpoint.

Maecē'nas, Gaius (d. 8 BC), the most famous Roman literary patron, descended from a distinguished Etruscan family, an equestrian by birth. He was the trusted counsellor of the emperor Augustus and the enlightened patron of a literary circle which included Virgil, Horace, Propertius, and Varius. The rewards for these protégés were great: Horace owed his Sabine farm and Virgil his independence to him, and both poets addressed him in terms of admiration and gratitude; they made a substantial return by supporting the imperial regime in their poetry. Maecenas is said to have suggested to Virgil the subject of the *Georgics* (3. 41). Only fragments survive of his own poetry and prose. He wrote a *Prometheus*, perhaps a tragedy, and a *Dialogue*, perhaps in the style of Menippean satire (see MENIPPUS). Seneca regarded him as typical of the adage that the style is the man, perhaps indicating a complex personality. After the conspiracy and execution of his brother-in-law Varro (or Licinius) Murena in 23 BC a coolness developed between Maecenas and Augustus and his political career came effectively to an end. He was a man of luxurious tastes and habits (he is said to have introduced heated swimming-baths at Rome), and spent the closing years of his life in the enjoyment of a cultivated leisure. See also AUGUSTAN AGE.

maenads (*mainadĕs* (also referred to as *bacchae* and *thyiadĕs*), 'mad women'), women inspired with ecstatic frenzy by the god *Dionysus. See BACCHANTS.

Mae'nalus, a mountain in Arcadia sacred to *Pan.

Maeo'nidĕs, name sometimes applied to Homer, either because Maeonia was an ancient name for *Lydia where, according to some, Homer was born, or because he was said to be the son of one Maeon.

magi'ster e'quitum ('master of the horse'), at Rome, the assistant of a *dictator.

magistrates, name given to officers of state in Greece and Rome. For Athens see ARCHON, POLEMARCH, and STRATEGOS. For Rome see AEDILE, CENSOR, CONSUL, CURSUS HONORUM, CURULE MAGISTRACIES, DICTATOR, PRAETOR, and QUAESTOR.

Magna Graecia (Megalē Hellas), collective name for the Greek cities of southern Italy founded by *colonization from the mainland of Greece and from the Greek cities of Asia Minor. They became prosperous through trade and the fertility of their land, and developed a flourishing culture and even their own schools of philosophy (see PYTHAGORAS and ELEA). Mutual hostility brought about the destruction of *Sybaris by *Croton, and decline set in *c*.400 BC. By 300 BC most of the cities needed Roman protection, and the Roman wars against Hannibal and Pyrrhus completed their ruin. See also PAESTUM, THURII, and TARENTUM.

Magna Mater ('great mother'), a mother goddess worshipped in Asia from ancient times and introduced into Greece; see CYBELE.

Maia. 1. In Greek myth, eldest of the *Pleiadĕs, daughters of the Titan *Atlas; she was the mother by Zeus of the god Hermes, and lived in a cave on Mount Cyllenē in Arcadia.

2. Obscure Italian goddess associated with Vulcan; on 1 May the *flamen volcanalis* sacrificed to her. She seems to have been connected with the growth of living things, and the name of the month is probably derived from her name. By confusion with (1) she was associated with Mercury, the Roman equivalent of Hermes.

maiden-song, see PARTHENEION.

Ma'mertines (Māmertīni; 'Mamers' is the name of the Roman god Mars in the *Oscan dialect), Italian mercenaries from Campania, settled in Syracuse by the tyrant Agathoclēs who had hired them to fight for him against Carthage. When he died they seized Messana (between 288 and 283 BC), and terrorized north-east Sicily. After a defeat, in fear of the Syracusans, they requested the Carthaginians to install a protective garrison in Messana, but at the same time they also asked Rome for help. The resulting clash of interest between Rome and Carthage precipitated the First *Punic War.

Māmu'rra, of Formiae, Caesar's chief engineer in Spain and Gaul, where he acquired much wealth. He was the first at Rome to face his mansion with marble. He is prominent in Catullus' invectives against Caesar.

mānēs, in Roman thought, the spirits of the dead, named euphemistically the 'kindly ones' (from the old Latin adjective *mānus,* 'good'). From a sense of their collective divinity they were worshipped as the *di manes* ('the divine dead') at the festivals of the *Feralia, *Parentalia, and Lemuria (see LEMURES). By extension the name *manes* was applied by the poets first to the realm of the dead, the Underworld, and secondly to the gods of the Underworld (*di inferi*), Dis, Orcus, Hecatē, and Persephonē. Later the *di manes* were individualized and identified with the *di parentes,* the dead of the family. The individual tomb led to the conception of each dead person having an individual spirit, and *manes,* although a plural noun, came to be used of a single spirit. Graves were originally dedicated to the dead collectively and were inscribed *dis manibus sacrum* ('sacred to the divine dead'); under the empire it became customary to add the name of the dead person, as if the meaning was 'sacred to the divine spirt of so-and-so'. See MUNDUS.

Ma'netho, priest of Heliopolis in Egypt in the third century BC who wrote in Greek a history of Egypt from mythical times to 323 BC, claiming to have consulted the chronological lists of kings. Portions of his history have been preserved by later writers such as *Eusebius and are of great value in establishing biblical chronology.

Mānī'lius. 1. Gaius Manilius, tribune for 67/6 BC, who carried a law conferring on *Pompey the command against Mith-

ridates, with *imperium* over all the provinces of Asia Minor.

2. Marcus Manilius (flourished at the beginning of the first century AD), author of a Latin didactic poem in hexameters in five books entitled *Astronomica,* dealing with astrology. The work as it stands appears unfinished, the fifth book breaking off abruptly. Unlike Lucretius the author sees design and 'heavenly reason' in the organization of the universe. The subject-matter is not universally appealing, but the non-technical parts of book 1, describing the creation and the arrangement of the stars in the heavens, and of book 5, describing the risings of signs, other than those of the zodiac, and their effect on children born on each occasion, contain interesting and eloquent passages.

maniple, in the Roman army, a sub-division of a legion, containing two centuries.

Ma'nlius Capitōlī'nus, Marcus, according to Roman tradition, a commander who held the Capitol against the Gauls when they sacked Rome *c.*390 BC. It is said that, awakened by the cackling of the sacred geese while sleeping in his house on the Capitol, dogs having failed to give warning, he summoned the guards and repulsed a surprise attack by the Gauls. Thereafter the feeding of the sacred geese was a charge on the state. In an annual commemoration geese were carried on litters with purple and gold cushions, and dogs were crucified on stakes of elder (a ritual which survived into Christian times). In the political crisis that followed the withdrawal of the Gauls, Manlius, though a patrician, is said to have supported the poor who were suffering under the stringent laws of debt. He was accused of attempting to make himself tyrant and was thrown to his death from the Tarpeian rock (see TARPEIA). After his death and disgrace no other member of the family received the *praenomen* Marcus.

Ma'nlius Torquā'tus (Titus Manlius Imperiōsus Torquātus), Roman hero who reputedly, in resisting an invasion of Gauls in 361 BC, killed in single combat an enormous Gaul and earned his *cognomen* (see NAMES) by taking from him an ornamental neck-chain, *torquēs*. He also exemplified Roman *pietas* ('dutifulness') in saving his father from prosecution. In the Latin War of 340 BC the consuls, of whom Torquatus was one, forbade single combats with the enemy. When the son of Torquatus nevertheless engaged and killed a Latin champion his father had him executed for disobedience. In later times the expression *Manliana imperia*, 'Manlian orders', became proverbial for commands of extreme severity.

Mantinē'a, small city-state in the southeast of Arcadia, north of Tegea, created by the unification of five villages *c.*500 BC. It was at first friendly to Sparta, but during the *Peloponnesian War entered into alliance with Athens, Argos, and Elis (*c.*420). It was the scene of a decisive Spartan victory in 418 BC in a battle against Athenians and Argives. In the fourth century BC Mantinea was attacked by Sparta and broken up into villages (387–386). After the battle of *Leuctra (371) the city was restored and took part in the pan-Arcadian confederacy founded at this time. It was the scene of another battle in 362 BC between Sparta and Thebes (in which Thebes was victorious but Epaminondas killed. Gryllus, the son of Xenophon, fighting with the Athenian contingent on the Spartan side, was killed in a cavalry engagement at Mantinea shortly before the main battle.

Manto, see MOPSUS.

Ma'ntua (modern Mantova), on the river Mincius in Cisalpine Gaul, seldom mentioned in ancient literature but famous as the town near which the Roman poet Virgil was born.

Ma'rathon, large Attic *deme on the north-east coast of Attica, commanding a long fertile plain lying along a deep bay, sheltered at its northern end, and connected with Athens by a main road running south of Mount *Pentelicus. It was the scene of a defeat inflicted by the Athenians and Plataeans under Miltiades on the invading Persians in 490 BC. (See PERSIAN WARS and, for the Marathon race so-called, PHEIDIPPIDES.) *Herodes Atticus was a native of Marathon.

Marcelli'nus, Greek author of a valuable biography of Thucydides, perhaps a *rhetor of the fifth century AD.

Marce'llus, Marcus Claudius. 1. Roman general (d. 208 BC). As consul in 222 BC he campaigned successfully against the Gauls, winning the *spolia opima* by killing the Gallic chief in single combat. He fought with distinction in the Second Punic War, showing great determination after the disaster at Cannae in 216 BC, and capturing *Syracuse in 211 after a long siege. He was killed in an ambush by Carthaginian forces when consul for the fifth time.

2. Son of Gaius Claudius Marcellus and of Octavia, sister of the emperor Augustus. He was born in 42 BC. In 25 BC he was married by Augustus' wish to the latter's daughter Julia, and in 24 Augustus showed his favour towards him as possible heir by accelerating his progress through the magistracies (see CURSUS HONORUM). In 23, as aedile, Marcellus celebrated particularly magnificent games, but died later that year. He was a youth of great promise, and was lamented by Virgil in a famous passage of the *Aeneid* (6. 861–87), the reading of which was said to have so affected Octavia that she fainted.

Marcus Aure'lius, see AURELIUS.

Mardo'nius, nephew and son-in-law of the Persian king Darius; see PERSIAN WARS.

Margī'tēs ('madman'), title and hero of a lost Greek epic poem, of unknown date and authorship, but an early work, attributed to Homer in antiquity; it was written in hexameters irregularly interspersed with iambic trimeters (see METRE, GREEK 5 (i)). Margites was an ancient Simple Simon, proverbial for his stupidity. He could not count beyond five, nor did he know whether his father or his mother had given birth to him. A tattered papyrus fragment describing a bedroom scene comes from the poem; otherwise only some five lines survive. Aristotle, who believed the author to be Homer, saw in *Margites* the germ of comedy, as the same poet's *Iliad* and *Odyssey* seemed to him to contain the germ of tragedy.

Mā'rius, Gaius (*c.*157–86 BC), Roman

general and statesman born near Arpinum (Arpino, the birthplace also of Cicero) of an equestrian family. As a soldier he served in Spain, Africa (celebrating a *triumph in 104 for the defeat of *Jugurtha), and Gaul, where in 102 and 101 he overthrew the Teutones and Cimbri, invading German tribes who had inflicted severe defeats on Roman armies. Marius won these victories in Gaul with a reorganized army, remedying the long-standing shortage of manpower by converting the old Roman citizen army recruited on a property basis to a professional army of volunteers recruited from all classes including the *proletarii. Thus, without realizing it, he created a new type of client-army which was dependent on its general for its reward, paving the way for the political domination of successful generals and ultimately for the empire.

From 104 to 100 Marius was consul every year, but an unsuccessful political alliance with *Saturninus led to his influence declining and he played only a minor role in the Social War. In 88 Marius by devious means secured the command of the war in the East against *Mithridates, leading to conflict with *Sulla (his bitter rival since they had served together in the war against Jugurtha), who had already had this command bestowed on him by the senate. Sulla marched on Rome and Marius had to flee, arriving in Africa after many dramatic adventures (later much embroidered). After Sulla's departure for the East early in 87 Marius returned to Italy, joined the popular leader Cinna, marched on Rome and captured in late in 87. Marius was consul for the seventh time in 86, thus fulfilling, it is said, a prediction. He then embarked on indiscriminate massacre of all those who might be considered his enemies, until Cinna intervened. His health failed and he died before he could take up the Eastern command which had been voted to him. Marius had no positive policies, but his enmity with the senate gained him a reputation as a friend of the people. Julius *Caesar (the nephew of Marius' widow) won public favour by restoring to the Capitol Marius' trophies, which Sulla had removed.

Mark Antony, see ANTONY, MARK.

Marmor Pa'rium (the 'Parian Marble'), an inscribed marble slab originally set up in the Greek island of Paros and containing a chronological table of events from the beginning of the reign of Cecrops, the mythical first king of Athens (taken to be 1580 BC), down to 263 BC. Two substantial fragments survive, one in the museum on Paros, the other in the Ashmolean Museum, Oxford. The events selected for inclusion are a mixture of political, military, religious, and literary history. Other inscribed tablets found in the nineteenth and twentieth centuries on Paros, relating events in the life of the local poet *Archilochus, are not included under this name.

Māro, *cognomen* (see NAMES) of the poet *Virgil, by which he is occasionally called.

Marpe'ssa, in Greek myth, daughter of the river-god Evēnus. She was loved by Idas (see LYNCEUS) and carried off by him in a winged chariot given him by the god Poseidon (in some accounts his father). They were pursued by Apollo, who also loved Marpessa, and Idas prepared to fight the god, but Zeus intervened and asked the girl to choose: she chose Idas, since, being mortal, he would grow old with her. Marpessa had a daughter Cleopatra who married *Meleager (in consequence Idas and Lynceus took part in the Calydonian boar-hunt). After Idas died Marpessa killed herself; his father Aphareus, king of Messenia, being left without an heir, bequeathed his kingdom to Nestor of Pylos (or Nestor's father Neleus).

Mars, Italian god of war and the most important god after Jupiter, equated with the Greek god *Arēs and consequently regarded as the son of Juno (the equivalent of the Greek goddess Hera). He was also connected with agriculture; the Elder Cato, in his handbook on agriculture, quotes an elaborate prayer to be addressed to Mars by the farmer at the *lustratio of his fields. Since the month named after the god, March (originally the first month of the Roman year), saw both the rebirth of the agricultural year and the start of the campaigning season, it may be that his combination of functions was natural to an agricultural people often engaged in war. Mars had his own priest at Rome, the **flamen martialis*; his altar was in the Campus Martius, and his sacred animals were the wolf and the woodpecker. A succession of festivals in March was dedicated to Mars the god of war and the protector of growth, including, on 14 March, horse-racing in the Campus Martius, and on 23 March the purification of the sacred trumpets, originally used in war (the Tubilustria). On several days in March the **Salian dancers (see SALII) performed a sort of war-dance wearing ancient armour and bearing his sacred shields (*ancilia*), and sang their traditional hymn. All these occasions suggest preparation for war. There were also festivals in October slightly resembling those of March and marking the fact that this is the time of year when farmers and soldiers lay aside their tools and weapons.

A temple of Mars, probably dedicated during the Gallic War of 390 BC, stood on the Appian Way outside the city. Here was celebrated annually the victory of Lake Regillus. The emperor Augustus promoted the worship of Mars in the god's capacity as father of Romulus, founder of Rome, and under his title of Ultor ('avenger'). As early as 42 BC Augustus vowed a temple to Mars 'in vengeance of his father' (i.e. Julius Caesar), and again in 20 BC he ordered a temple of Mars Ultor to be built in the Forum: here were laid the standards lost by Crassus and by Antony and recovered by Augustus from the Parthians; it was eventually dedicated in 2 BC. Both Horace (*Odes* 1. 2) and Ovid (*Fasti* 5. 561) glorify the new cult. Mars' love for Venus was early established as a favourite subject for artists.

Marsian or **Marsic War**, alternative name for the **Social War, from the central Italian tribe the Marsi who precipitated the war by taking the initiative in demanding Roman citizenship.

Ma'rsyas, in Greek myth, a **satyr or silenus associated with the river of that name (a tributary of the Maeander in Asia Minor), who picked up the flute which the goddess Athena had invented but had thrown away because it distorted the player's face. He became so proficient a player that he challenged Apollo to a musical contest (Apollo playing the lyre), with the Muses as judges. It was agreed that the victor should do what he pleased to the other, and when Apollo was judged victor he tied Marsyas to a tree and flayed him alive. The river sprang from his blood or the tears of his mourners. See also MIDAS.

Ma'rtial (Marcus Valerius Martiālis) (*c.* AD 40–103/4), Roman poet, given his *cognomen* (see NAMES) to commemorate his birth on 1 March. He was a native of Bilbilis in Spain and claimed Iberian and Celtic ancestry. In 64 he went to Rome, where his association with his fellow Spaniards Seneca the Younger and Lucan was cut short by their deaths as a result of the conspiracy of **Piso (2). Little of his early career is known and that mostly depends on what he tells us himself. He was poor and lived in a third-floor lodging, but later had a cottage at Nomentum (in Latium, about 20 km. or 13 miles from Rome) and a small house on the Quirinal hill at Rome. He wrote poetry for his living, depending on the sale of his books and on patrons who did not make very generous return for his complimentary verses. Gradually his reputation, if not his wealth, increased, but he took no part in public affairs. His first known work was a *Liber spectaculorum* ('book of spectacles') to celebrate the opening in AD 80 of the Colosseum; of this work thirty-three poems survive, interesting for what they reveal of the shows given on that occasion. In 84–5 were published the collections of elegiac couplets which later appear as books 13 and 14 of the *Epigrams* (see below): they consist of mottoes to accompany *xenia*, guest-gifts (mostly of food and drink), or *apophorēta*, gifts taken home from banquets at the festival of the **Saturnalia (which are of the most varied kind, stationery, clothing, furniture, toys, works of art, food, pets, even slaves).

Martial's more important work, the first twelve books of the *Epigrams*, began to appear in 86. Between that year and 98 eleven of these books were issued. In 98 he returned to Bilbilis (his travelling expenses paid by the Younger Pliny), to a quiet country life on a farm given him by a patroness. From there he issued his twelfth book of epigrams in the winter of 101. The Younger Pliny in a letter of 104 mentions his death. Among Martial's friends, or addressees at least, besides Pliny (who speaks of him as 'talented, subtle, penetrating, witty, and sincere') were Juvenal, Quintilian, Silius Italicus, and Valerius Flaccus.

The *Epigrams*, which number well over 1,500, are short poems each expressing concisely and pointedly some single idea. By far the most are written in elegiac couplets; about a sixth are in hendecasyllables, some eighty in choliambics, a few in iambics and hexameters (see METRE). Many consist of a single couplet; the rest rarely exceed twenty lines. Several of the books are preceded by an interesting preface in prose defending the author's work against criticism, actual or anticipated. The epigrams are for the most part addressed to some individual, but the name may be imaginary; Martial does not give the real names of those he satirizes: *parcere personis, dicere de vitiis*, 'spare the sinner but denounce the sin', is his aim. He depicts with realistic detail the most diverse characters of contemporary Rome, fortune-hunters, gluttons, drunkards, debauchers, hypocrites of various kinds; he includes a few devoted wives, faithful friends, true poets, and honest critics. Many of the pieces are complaints about the meanness of patrons, or requests for gifts or loans. Some are invitations to a simple hospitality, some take leave of a parting guest or greet his return. Many give vivid glimpses of the Roman scene: the vendor of hot sausages on his round, the Gaul who has sprained his ankle in the street and gets a lift home on a pauper's bier, the far-from-perfect guest who arrives too late for breakfast and too early for lunch. Those addressed to the emperor Domitian are markedly adulatory and often frigidly contrived; adulation was no doubt necessary for survival, and his role as suppliant for patrons' favours does not appear to have struck Martial as humiliating. Many are obscene (Martial defends this in the preface to book 1 and in 1. 35,

appealing to the precedent of Catullus among others), but none of these are in book 5, addressed to *matronae puerique virginesque* ('mothers, youths, and maidens'), or book 8. As a rule he feels amusement rather than indignation at the vices he reveals, a trait which has been better received in some ages than in others.

Against this may be set his pride in his Spanish homeland, his admiration for the heroism of Romans in the days of the republic, his delight in country life, his affection for his friends, his occasional tenderness. His poems include some epigrams in the original sense of the word (i.e. 'inscriptions', see EPIGRAM), some touching epitaphs, including three laments for the poet Lucan, and notably that for the young girl Erōtion on whom he bids the earth press lightly, 'for she pressed light on thee': these lines were parodied by the English divine and poet Abel Evans (1679–1737) in his mock epitaph on Vanbrugh, the architect of Blenheim Palace,

> Lie heavy on him, earth! for he
> Laid many heavy loads on thee.

Martial generally writes straightforwardly and without mythological allusion. By giving his poems wit and pointedness, and especially by putting the sting in the tail, he changed the form of the epigram, giving that term the meaning which it bears in modern times, in marked contrast with the Greek epigram, which did not aim to have a pointed conclusion. But he does not merely aim at wit; his view of life is essentially humorous. Some of his lines have become well known, such as that frequently seen on sundials, *soles . . . qui nobis pereunt et imputantur* ('the days that perish and are charged to our account'). A plea that his epigrams are more serious than some authors' tragedies ends with the line, *laudant illa, sed ista legunt* ('*Those* they praise, *these* they read'). A couplet (1. 32) directed against a certain Sabidius acquired a wide circulation in English translation by the satirist Thomas Brown (1663–1704), 'I do not love you, Dr Fell . . .'.

Martiā'nus Cape'lla, of Carthage, Latin writer, the author, probably between AD 410 and 439, of *De nuptiis*

Mercurii et Philologiae ('on the marriage of Mercury and Philologia'), an elaborate allegory in nine books, in Latin prose interspersed with verse (in the manner of Menippean satire or Petronius' *Satyricon*). Mercury, the god of eloquence, having decided to marry, consults the god Apollo, who commends to him the learned virgin Philologia, who possesses all learning. Two books are devoted to the married couple, and one to each of the *seven liberal arts who, personified as handmaids, are given to the bride as a wedding present; thus Grammar, Rhetoric, Logic (or Dialectic), Arithmetic, Geometry, Music, and Astronomy each expound their discipline. The work therefore forms an encyclopaedia of these, in which pedantry and fantasy are mingled. It owes something to the *Disciplinae* of *Varro. Amongst much trivial information there are passages which preserve ancient and curious learning that is otherwise lost. The Middle Ages accepted this work as an authoritative description of the seven liberal arts, and it was the subject of several commentaries.

Masā'da, ancient mountaintop fortress by the Dead Sea, seized by Jewish Zealots in the revolt against Rome of AD 66; it held out until 73, three years after the fall of Jerusalem. When capture was inevitable, the defenders committed mass suicide rather than surrender to the Romans, an episode movingly described by *Josephus. The fortifications and other buildings of Masada (excavated in the 1960s) were built mainly by *Herod the Great.

Masini'ssa, see SOPHONISBA.

Massi'lia (Gk. Massalia; Marseilles), colony founded *c*.600 BC by *Phocaea, an Ionian Greek city, on the Mediterranean coast of France, east of the river Rhône (see COLONIZATION, GREEK 2). In the civil war between Caesar and Pompey, after a resolute stand in favour of the latter, the city surrendered to Caesar in 49 BC.

master of the horse, *magister equitum,* the assistant of a *dictator.

mathematics. Greek tradition ascribed the invention of geometry to the Egyptians and its introduction into Greece to *Thalēs and *Pythagoras. The first Greek mathematician of whose work there is clear evidence is *Hippocratēs (2) (late fifth century BC). See also APOLLONIUS OF PERGE, ARCHIMEDES, ARCHYTAS, ARISTARCHUS OF SAMOS, CONON (2), ERATOSTHENES, EUCLID, EUDOXUS, HIPPARCHUS (2), HYPATIA, METON, PROCLUS, PTOLEMY, THEON, and NUMBERS.

Mātrā'lia, the matrons' festival at Rome, celebrated on 11 June, centred on the goddess *Matuta.

Mātrōnā'lia, in Roman religion, the festival of *Juno on 1 March (the old New Year's Day), when prayers were offered to her and her son *Mars. It was called by the poet Martial the 'Saturnalia of women', when wives received presents from their husbands, and mistresses feasted their female slaves.

Mātū'ta, in Roman religion, a goddess of the dawn, having some connection apparently with young growth. She developed into a protectress of childbirth, and was worshipped at the Matralia. Later she was identified with the Greek goddess Ino, also called Leucothea.

Mausō'lus (Maussōllos), native of Caria (in south-west Asia Minor) who in 377 BC succeeded his father Hecatomnus as ruler of that country and was recognized as its satrap by the king of Persia. However, he ruled in virtual independence of Persia and extended his rule over the Greek cities of the coast and over Lycia, plotting to get control of the neighbouring islands. For this purpose he fomented the revolt of Rhodes, Cos, and Chios from the Athenian League in 357 BC (the Social War) in order to bring them under his control. In this he was successful; but he died in 353 and was succeeded by his widow (and sister) Artemisia. His tomb, the Mausoleum, regarded as one of the *Seven Wonders of the ancient world, included the over life-size statues of Mausolus and Artemisia, now in the British Museum.

Maxe'ntius, see CONSTANTINE 1.

measures, see WEIGHTS AND MEASURES.

Mēdē'a (Mēdeia), in Greek myth, daughter of Aeētēs, king of Colchis, and like her aunt *Circē an enchantress.

When Jason and the *Argonauts arrived at Colchis in pursuit of the Golden Fleece, Aeetes consented to surrender it to Jason if the latter would perform certain apparently impossible tasks. These included the sowing of a dragon's teeth from which armed men arose whose fury was turned against Jason. With the help of Medea's magic the tasks were successfully accomplished, and Medea finally enabled Jason to take the fleece by killing or drugging the serpent that guarded it. She engineered the Argonauts' escape from Aeetes; in one version of the story she murdered and cut into pieces her young brother Apsyrtus, scattering the fragments so that her father might be delayed in his pursuit of the Argonauts by gathering up the body; in other versions Apsyrtus is grown up and leads the pursuit until Medea contrives his murder. At Iolcus Medea took vengeance on Pelias (Jason's uncle) for the wrong done by him to Jason's family. First she restored Aeson, Jason's father, to youth by boiling him in a cauldron with magic herbs, and then persuaded the daughters of Pelias to submit their father to the same process. But on this occasion she deliberately gave them ineffective herbs, and the daughters were unwittingly the cause of their father's death. Acastus, their brother, then drove Jason and Medea from Iolcus and they took refuge in Corinth. For the rest of the story, see MEDEA below. Medea was the subject of tragedies by Aeschylus, Sophocles, and Euripides, but only that of Euripides survives. Seneca the Younger and Ovid (see (2) and (3) below) also wrote tragedies about her; she receives a more romantic treatment by Apollonius Rhodius, and by Ovid in *Heroides* and *Metamorphoses*.

Mede'a. 1. Greek tragedy by *Euripides, produced in 431 BC. Despite its later fame it won only third prize in the dramatic competition. It deals with the later part of the story of Jason and Medea (see MEDEA above). These two have fled to Corinth after Medea has murdered Pelias for Jason's sake. Jason, ambitious and tired of his barbarian princess, has arranged to marry the daughter of Creon, king of Corinth, for prudential reasons he

alleges. The desertion and ingratitude of her husband arouse savage anger in Medea and she openly declares her feelings. Creon, fearing her vengeance upon himself and his daughter, pronounces instant banishment on Medea and her two children. Medea coaxes him into allowing her one day's respite, and by a poisoned robe and diadem contrives the deaths of Jason's bride and her father. Then she kills her own children, partly to make Jason childless, partly because, since they now must surely die, it is better that it should be by her hand than by that of her enemies, who would thus triumph over her. Finally, taunting Jason in his despair, she escapes to Athens where she has secured asylum from king Aegeus (who appears earlier in the play).

2. Roman tragedy by *Seneca (2), based on that of Euripides, with variations of detail. Medea's children are not sentenced to banishment; she asks for them to be allowed to accompany her into exile, but Jason's love for them prevents it. Medea thus learns where Jason is vulnerable and kills them to revenge herself on him. The play contains a famous passage in which Seneca seems to prophesy the discovery of a New World (374 ff.):

> venient annis
> saecula seris quibus Oceanus
> vincula rerum laxet, et ingens
> pateat tellus Tethysque novos
> detegat orbes, nec sit terris
> ultima Thule.

(In later years a new age will come in which Ocean shall relax its hold over the world, and a vast land shall lie open to view, and Tethys shall reveal a new world, and *Thule will not be the last country on earth.)

3. Roman tragedy by *Ovid, of which only two lines have survived. It was praised by *Quintilian.

Medes. Media, mountainous country south-west of the Caspian Sea, was for a century the heartland of a Median empire whose capital was at Ecbatana (Hamadan). The Medes, who were related to the Persians, were the first Asian people to revolt against the dominant Assyrians. The founder of their empire was Deiocēs in the early seventh

century BC, who was succeeded by his son
Phraortēs and then by Cyaxarēs, his
grandson. Cyaxares (615–585 BC) conquered surrounding territories and in
alliance with (probably) the father of
Nebuchadnezzar, king of Babylon, captured the Assyrian capital Nineveh in
612. During the war between the Medes
and the Lydians, under their king Alyat-
tēs, there occurred the eclipse of the sun
(585 BC) which the Ionian Greek philosopher *Thalēs is said to have predicted
for that year. Cyaxares was succeeded by
his son Astyagēs (585–549), who was
defeated and captured by his vassal
*Cyrus, king of the Persians, and from
549 the Persians became the ruling race.

Me'dia, see MEDES.

Medicā'mina faciē'i fēminē'ae
('cosmetics for the female face'), Latin
poem in elegiacs by *Ovid; only one hundred lines survive.

medicine, see ERASISTRATUS, GALEN,
HEROPHILUS, and HIPPOCRATES.

Medū'sa, in Greek myth, one of the
three *Gorgons, the only one who was
mortal. Anyone who looked at her head,
even after her death, was turned to stone.
She was killed by *Perseus.

Me'gaclēs, name of several prominent
members of the aristocratic *Alcmaeonid
genos at Athens.

  1. Archon, 632/1 BC, responsible for
the murder of *Cylon.

  2. Grandson of (1), married to
Agaristē, daughter of Cleisthenēs, tyrant
of Sicyon.

  3. Nephew of *Cleisthenes (2) who was
the founder of Athenian democracy (and
who was himself the son of (2) above),
ostracized in 486, winner of the chariot-
race at the Pythian games in the same
year, and celebrated in Pindar's seventh
Pythian Ode. He was the uncle of
Periclēs.

Megae'ra, see FURIES.

Megalē'sia or **Megale'nsia,** festival
and games at Rome in honour of Magna
Mater ('great mother'), a Phrygian goddess, also known as *Cybelē, introduced
to Rome in 204 BC; the festival was
celebrated on 4 April.

Megalo'polis (Gk. *hē megalē polis*, 'the

big city'), city in Arcadia founded between 369 and 362 BC by *Epaminondas, the Theban general, after his
victory over the Spartans at Leuctra
(371). It was founded to be the capital
of the Arcadian League and was one
of the largest cities in the Peloponnese;
Plato is said to have been invited by
Epaminondas to draw up the constitution
and code of laws, but to have declined. In
the fourth century BC it always took the
side of Macedon. In 234 it joined the
*Achaean Confederacy, but was subdued
and its inhabitants expelled by Sparta
under Cleomenes III. The city was
restored by Philopoemen, the general of
the Confederacy, after he had defeated
the Spartans at Sellasia (222). It was the
birthplace of Philopoemen and the
historian Polybius.

Megalopo'litans, For the, political
speech by the Greek orator Demosthenes. See DEMOSTHENES (2) 3.

Me'gara (Gk. *ta megara*, 'the temples'),
Dorian city at the eastern end of the
Isthmus of Corinth overlooking Salamis,
originally known as Nisa, according to
one story, from its first king *Nisus; the
name was preserved in that of the harbour, Nisaea. Between 730 and 550 BC it
showed considerable colonizing enterprise, founding Chalcedon and Byzantium on the Bosporus, Heraclea Pontica
in Bithynia, and Megara Hyblaea in
Sicily. In about 600 BC it fell under the
rule of the tyrant Theagenes, and the
tyranny was followed by political struggles reflected, according to some critics,
in the poems of the Megarian poet
*Theognis (but see the discussion of dates
for that poet). It lost its western region to
Corinth and Salamis to Athens. Shortly
before 500 BC it joined the Peloponnesian
League and was active in the Persian
Wars. After these ended, the Megarians,
having become involved in boundary disputes with Corinth, left their Peloponnesian allies and placed themselves under
Athenian protection (460); the Athenians
then sent an occupying garrison. After
the Athenian defeat by the Boeotians at
Coronea in 447, the Megarians revolted
and massacred the garrison. Subsequently the Athenians passed a decree
excluding them from all the harbours and

ports of the Athenian empire, and this 'Megarian decree' (there may have been others) became a contributory cause of the *Peloponnesian War. Megara suffered severely in the war, but escaped capture by Athens through the prompt arrival of the Spartan general Brasidas with a relieving force in 424. In the fourth century it remained relatively detached from operations of war, although it allied itself with Athens against Philip. See also MEGARIAN SCHOOL below.

Mega'rian School of philosophy, founded by Eucleidēs of Megara (flourished c.390 BC), a pupil of Socrates. It adopted the doctrines of the *Eleatic philosophers. Its members developed a reputation for skill in dialectical argument (compare ZENO (1)).

Mei'dias, Against, speech prepared by Demosthenes but not delievered. See DEMOSTHENES (2) 2.

Mēla, Pompō'nius, see POMPONIUS.

Mela'mpus (Melampous), in Greek myth, famous seer, son of Amythāon (a grandson of *Aeolus), and supposed ancestor of the prophetic clan of the Melampodidae, who produced famous seers in historic times. He took care of some young serpents whose parents had been killed by his servants, and these one day licked his ears while he was sleeping. Thereafter he understood the language of all creatures. His brother Bias sought to marry Pēro, daughter of *Neleus, but the latter demanded as bride-price the cattle which *Iphiclus had taken from Neleus' mother. Melampus undertook to get them for Bias but was caught and imprisoned. Hearing from the woodworms that the roof was about to fall in, Melampus warned the gaoler. When Iphiclus heard this he was so impressed he promised to hand over the cattle if Melampus could tell him why he was childless. This Melampus was able to do by questioning a vulture, and Bias was thus enabled to marry Pero. Another feat of Melampus was curing the daughters of *Proetus of their madness. According to Herodotus it was Melampus who introduced the name of the god *Dionysus into Greece. Among his mythical descendants who were also seers were

*Amphiaraus and Theoclymenus (see Homer, *Odyssey* 20).

Melani'ppidēs, see DITHYRAMB.

Meleā'ger (Meleagros). 1. In Greek myth, son of Oeneus, king of Calydon, and his wife Althaia. He married Cleopatra, daughter of Idas and *Marpessa. The *Fates appeared at his birth and declared that he should live as long as a brand that was on the fire was not consumed. Althaia snatched the brand from the fire and carefully preserved it. Later, when Meleager was a young man, Oeneus omitted to sacrifice to Artemis and the goddess in anger sent a great boar to ravage Calydon. Oeneus collected a band of heroes to attack the beast, offering the boar's skin to whoever should kill it. *Atalanta, the virgin huntress, was the first to wound it, and when Meleager finally killed it he gave her the spoils, being in love with her. His mother's brothers tried to take them from her and Meleager killed them. When Althaia heard of her brothers' deaths she took out the brand and burned it, and Meleager died. In the version of the myth told by Homer, he is cited as an example of a valiant but misguided warrior of a past generation who refused to aid his people when they were attacked (by the *Curetēs) because he was angry (having been cursed by his mother for killing one of her brothers). Although he was finally persuaded and drove off the enemy, he received no reward because he changed his mind too late. He was sometimes said to have been one of the *Argonauts. Later writers add that after his death the women who mourned him were turned into guinea-fowl (*meleagrides*). The hunt of the Calydonian boar, Meleager leading, was a favourite subject in art.

2. Of Gadara in Syria, Greek poet who lived c.100 BC. He wrote short elegiac poems on love and death, about a hundred of which survive in the Greek *Anthology. They are technically very accomplished and often moving. He was also the compiler of an early anthology of poetic epigrams (which has not survived intact), calling it his 'Garland' (*stephanos*) and likening each poet to a flower.

Melēsi'genēs, name sometimes applied to Homer in allusion to his alleged birthplace Smyrna, on the river Melēs.

Melē'tus, nominal accuser of Socrates in 399 BC, probably son of the tragic poet of the same name who is mocked by the comic poets; probably not identical with the Meletus who prosecuted *Andocidēs for impiety in 400.

Mēlian dialogue, in *Thucydides 5. 84 ff., the discussion between Athenian envoys and the magistrates of Mēlos, a (Dorian) Greek island, the most southerly of the Sporadēs. During the *Peloponnesian War Melos was friendly to Sparta and refused to surrender to Athens. The dialogue took place in 416 BC when the Athenians proposed to subdue the island, and the speeches of the Athenians are an exposition of their ruthless imperial policy. Melos was taken by the Athenians shortly afterwards and the inhabitants put to death or enslaved.

Melice'rtēs, see DIONYSUS. According to Greek myth, the body of the drowned Melicertes (who was deified and known as Palaemon) was washed up on the Isthmus of Corinth, where the Isthmian games were said to have been founded to commemorate him. There was a temple of Palaemon at Corinth.

Meli'ssus, of Samos, the commander of the Samian fleet which defeated the Athenians in 441 BC, but remembered more as the last important member of the *Eleatic School of philosophy.

Mēlos, Greek island, with Thera the most southerly of the Sporadēs. See MELIAN DIALOGUE.

Melpo'menē, the Muse of tragedy; see MUSES.

Me'mmius, Gaius, dedicatee of *Lucretius' poem *De rerum natura*, minor poet and orator, and patron of poets; nothing of his work survives. Catullus and Helvius *Cinna accompanied him to Bithynia where he was propraetor in 57 BC. In 53 he was banished for dishonesty in the elections of the previous year. He married *Sulla's daughter, who later married Milo, and died before 46 BC.

Memnon, in Greek myth, son of *Tithonus and *Eos (Dawn), king of the Ethiopians and brother of Emathion, king of Egypt; he fought on the Trojan side at the siege of Troy. Memnon killed Antilochus and was later killed by Achilles. His story was related in the *Aethiopis* (by Arctinus), a poem of the *Epic Cycle, according to which Zeus made him immortal. His final battle and his body carried away by his mother are favourite subjects for vase-painters. A tradition arose that a colossal statue of Memnon which stood before a temple in Egyptian Thebes used to sing at dawn when struck by the sun (but the statue is engraved with the name of an Egyptian king).

Memorābi'lia (*Apomnēmoneumata*), reminiscences of Socrates by *Xenophon, in four books, which describe his character and some of his opinions, chiefly by means of more or less imaginary conversations between Socrates and various persons (including Xenophon himself).

The first part is a refutation of the particular charges on which Socrates was tried and sentenced to death (that he did not believe in the gods of the state, but introduced other new deities, and that he corrupted the youth). This part is based on a literary exercise by a certain Polycratēs. Xenophon then proceeds to illustrate the character and opinions of Socrates, his helpfulness to his friends, his piety, and his views on education and various philosophical questions, probably derived in part from Xenophon's own recollections, in part from other sources. The opinions attributed to Socrates, for example on the good and the beautiful, do not always accord with those attributed to him by Plato. The work concludes with a peroration on the virtues of Socrates.

Menae'chmi, Roman comedy by *Plautus. A merchant of Syracuse had twin sons so much alike as to be indistinguishable. One of these, Menaechmus, was stolen when seven years old. The other, Sōsiclēs, had his name changed to Menaechmus in memory of his lost brother. When he is grown up Sosicles-Menaechmus sets out in search of his brother, and finally arrives at Epidaurus where his brother is living. Comic misunderstandings arise when he successively encounters the lost brother's mistress, wife, and father-in-law. Wife and father-in-law conclude that he is insane, but owing to a further confusion it is the original Menaechmus, their real husband and son-in-law, whom they attempt to lock up. Finally the twins confront each other and the puzzle is solved.

This play, directly or indirectly, furnished the main idea for Shakespeare's *The Comedy of Errors*.

Mena'nder (Menandros) (342–c.292 BC), the greatest writer of Attic New Comedy (see COMEDY, GREEK 6). He was said to be related to, perhaps a nephew of, the comic poet Alexis (see COMEDY, GREEK 5), a pupil of the philosopher Theophrastus, and a companion in military service of another philosopher, Epicurus. He was also a friend (and fellow pupil) of *Demetrius of Phalerum, the anti-democratic governor of Athens. He was said to have died by drowning in the harbour of Piraeus. Nearly one hundred titles of his plays are known, although some may be alternatives. The plays themselves were lost in the seventh and eighth centuries AD, but in the twentieth century numerous finds of papyri have brought to light one complete play, *Dyscolus ('bad-tempered man'), and sizeable fragments of *Aspis ('shield'), *Geōrgos ('farmer'), *Dis exapatōn ('twice a swindler'), *Epitrepontes ('arbitrants'), *Cōlax ('flatterer'), *Misumenos ('hated man'), *Perikeiromenē ('shorn hair'), *Samia ('woman from Samos'), and *Sicyonios ('man from Sicyon'). There are shorter fragments of many others including *Heros ('hero'), Theophoroumenē ('woman possessed'), Kitharistēs ('flute girl'), and Phasma ('ghost'). Orgē ('anger'), which has not survived, is said to have been his first play, and some authorities say that it won the dramatic competition; on the whole Menander was unlucky at the competitions, winning only eight victories. Quintilian commented that he enjoyed more fame after his death than in his lifetime, and the Latin poet Martial has the line (5. 10), *rara coronato plausēre theatra Menandro*, 'the theatre applauded Menander but he rarely won the crown'.

The number of papyri found of his works is exceeded only for Homer and Euripides. The loss of his plays is due to their exclusion from the Greek school curriculum of the fifth and subsequent centuries AD, largely because they were written not in classical Attic Greek but rather in the *koinē* (see DIALECTS).

Before the discovery of the papyri Menander was known from a large number of quotations, many of them highly sententious, so that a false impression was given of moral earnestness. Even St Paul quoted him (1 Corinthians 15: 33), 'Evil communications corrupt good manners.' In fact many of these famous lines are now seen to have been spoken ironically: 'Whom the gods love die young', to an old man; 'I am a man, and I think nothing that is human to be outside my interest', by a busybody (quoted by *Terence).

His plays are set in contemporary Greece, usually in Athens or the surrounding countryside. The plots are concerned with the private lives of well-to-do families, with a love-entanglement as an important but not always central feature: thus in *Dyscolus* Cremon and his misanthropy are more important than his son's love-affair. The plays contain many features that were commoner in the theatre of the time than in real life: abandoned or kidnapped children, recognitions by means of trinkets, seductions of well-brought-up girls at night festivals (where it was too dark to see their faces), amazing coincidences. Characters too are often conventional, the talkative, self-important cook, the bragging soldier, the angry father, the cunning but cowardly slave, the kind-hearted prostitute. Yet they are given other traits that conventional portraits lack and consequently seem more lifelike. Their speech, too, is apt and appropriate. The plots are often complicated but always skilfully put together and exciting, and the dialogue is fast moving, often pointed and witty. A frequently cited apostrophe from the Alexandrian scholar Aristophanes of Byzantium, 'O Menander and Life, which of you copied the other!' indicates that for all their contrivance the actions and the characters seem natural, and the underlying sentiments real. Menander's attitude to his creations is one of sympathy and gentle irony; resolution of the difficulties is achieved through the virtues of generosity and understanding.

The plays are written in verse, for the most part in iambic trimeters (see METRE, GREEK 4), which contrive to give the effect of natural speech. The Roman rhetor *Quintilian warmly recommended the study of Menander's plays even to students of rhetoric, regarding him as supreme among the writers of New Comedy. Through the adaptations of the Roman comic writers *Plautus and *Terence he deeply influenced the development of European comedy, notably in Molière, the Restoration dramatists, and Sheridan.

Menelā'us (Menelāos, Meneleōs), in Greek myth, king of Sparta, son of Atreus, younger brother of *Agamemnon, and husband of *Helen, whom Paris carried off to Troy, thus bringing about the expedition of the Greek chiefs to recover her. In Homer's *Iliad* he agrees to settle the war by a duel with Paris and would have killed him but for the latter's rescue by Aphroditē. Menelaus acquits himself well in the fighting over the body of Patroclus, but he is usually overshadowed by Agamemnon, the leader of the Greek army. He reappears in the *Odyssey* living at Sparta, reconciled with Helen, and visited by Odysseus' son Telemachus; he had returned to Sparta when Orestēs killed Clytemnestra and Aegisthus. He appears also in Sophocles' *Ajax* and Euripides' *Helen*, *Andromachē*, and *Trojan Women*.

Mene'xenus, dialogue of *Plato (see 2).

Meni'ppus, of Gadara in Syria (third century BC), a *Cynic philosopher who satirized (in Greek) the follies of men and philosophers in a serio-comic style, using a mixture of prose and verse. He was a slave who later acquired his freedom. His writings are lost, but they were imitated in Latin by *Varro in his *Saturae Menippeae* and by *Lucian in his dialogues. Menippus himself figures frequently in the latter's 'Dialogues of the Dead', and one of Lucian's satires bears his name.

Mēno (*Menōn*), a dialogue by *Plato.

Socrates is represented as conversing with a young Thessalian aristocrat Meno on the question of whether virtue can be taught. When attempts to define virtue meet with no success, the origin of knowledge is discussed; Socrates propounds his theory that knowledge is acquired before birth by the soul, which is immortal, and that knowledge is in fact recollection, which it is the purpose of teaching to bring out. Socrates demonstrates how this can be done by eliciting from Meno's slave, through careful questioning, the solution to a geometrical problem. But there are no teachers of virtue; it is not teachable; virtue is at most 'right opinion' (*orthē doxa*), and it arises from an irrational 'divine possession' (*theia moira*). It cannot be stated with certainty how virtue arises until it is known what exactly virtue is.

The historical Meno was a Thessalian general in the expedition of the Ten Thousand, whose treacherous conduct is related by Xenophon in the *Anabasis*.

Mentor. In Homer's *Odyssey*, an old Ithacan friend of Odysseus, to whom the latter, when he left Ithaca for Troy, gave charge of his house. He acts as an adviser to Telemachus, Odysseus' son; hence the use of his name to describe a trusted counsellor.

Mercā'tor ('merchant'), Roman comedy by *Plautus adapted from a Greek comedy by Philemon (see COMEDY, GREEK 6). A young man, sent abroad on a trading venture by his father, falls in love with a girl at Rhodes and brings her back to Athens, pretending that she is a present for his mother. His father discovers her and himself falls in love, with consequent complications.

Mercury (Mercurius), in Roman religion, son of *Maia and Jupiter, the god of trade (*merx*), particularly of the corn-trade, introduced at an early date from a Greek or Graeco-Etruscan source and identified with the Greek god *Hermēs, whose attributes he shared. His temple was on the Aventine overlooking the Circus Maximus; it was dedicated in 495 BC. Like Hermes he was the god of eloquent speech and was often represented carrying a herald's staff, *caduceus*, with two entwined snakes, and winged hat and shoes. His name was later given to the element mercury (quicksilver) because of his imagined quickness of movement. He was also seen as mediator between divine and human wisdom. The fact that he does not have a **flamen* indicates that he was not a deity worshipped at Rome from earliest times.

Me'ropē, name of several heroines in Greek myth.

1. Wife of Cresphontēs (see HERACLEIDAE). Cresphontes, king of *Messenia, was killed by Polyphontēs (another descendant of Heracles), as were two of his sons. A third son, Aepytus, was saved by Merope and sent out of the country. Merope was then forced to marry Polyphontes, but when Aepytus was grown up he returned, killed Polyphontes, and recovered the throne.

2. One of the *Pleiadĕs, the seven daughters of Atlas and the Oceanid Pleionē.

3. The wife of *Sisyphus.

4. Also known as Polyboea, the wife of Polybus, king of Corinth, who brought up *Oedipus.

Messalī'na, Vale'ria (d. AD 48), great-granddaughter of Octavia (sister of the emperor Augustus). She married at the age of 14 in AD 39 or 40 her second cousin the emperor Claudius, then aged 48, as his third wife, and bore him two children, Octavia (later the wife of the emperor Nero) and Britannicus. She was notorious for her promiscuity (pilloried by Juvenal in Satires 6 and 10) to which Claudius alone was blind. In AD 48, though still apparently married to Claudius, she went through the formalities of a marriage with the consul designate C. Silius. While Claudius was still irresolute his freedman Narcissus had the pair killed.

Messa'lla Corvī'nus, Marcus Vale'rius (64 BC–AD 8), Roman patrician and distinguished orator, soldier, and patron of literature. He fought on the republican side at Philippi (42 BC) and then supported Antony, but disillusioned by the latter's conduct with Cleopatra transferred his allegiance to Octavian, fighting against Sextus Pompeius and taking part in the defeat of Antony at Actium in 31. He was employed in Roman administration, and proposed the title 'Pater Patriae' ('father of the country') for the emperor Augustus (2 BC). He was a great patron of poets, notably of Ovid and Tibullus, and was regarded, with Asinius Pollio, as the greatest orator of his time; he was also famous for his linguistic knowledge. See also AUGUSTAN AGE.

Messā'na (modern Messina), on the north-east tip of Sicily opposite the toe of Italy, founded as Zanclē by Euboean colonists *c*.730 BC (Zancle itself colonizing Himera in 648). Later it received immigrants from Messenia in the Peloponnese who changed its name to Messēnē; the Doric form of this name, Messana, seems to have been used from the first half of the fifth century. See also MAMERTINES. After 241 BC Messana became a prosperous city in alliance with Rome. Compare MESSENE below.

Messē'nē, city founded in 369 BC to be the capital of an independent Messenia in the Peloponnese (see below). See also EPAMINONDAS.

Messē'nia, south-west region of the Peloponnese. In mythology it was the kingdom of Aphareus who gave refuge, and later bequeathed his kingdom, to *Neleus, when the latter was driven from Thessaly. Subsequently it was ruled over by Neleus' son Nestor. After the *Dorian Invasion Messenia was ruled by Cresphontēs, and then by his youngest son Aepytus, who gave his name to the Messenian royal line. After the First and Second Messenian Wars against Sparta in the eighth and seventh centuries BC, the land was seized by the Spartans and the Messenians reduced to the status of helots. Their bid for independence after the earthquake of 464 BC, the Third Messenian War, ended with the surrender of their stronghold at Ithōmē after a long siege. During the Peloponnesian War the Messenians were encouraged by the Athenians to revolt, and the threat increased the anxieties of the Spartans. In 369 BC the Theban general

*Epaminondas achieved independence for Messenia. In the second century BC it came with the rest of Greece under Roman control.

Metamorphō'sēs ('transformations').
1. Latin epic-style poem in fifteen books of hexameters by *Ovid, his longest and his only surviving work in this metre. (It is longer than Virgil's *Aeneid.*) The poem is essentially a collection of stories from classical and Near-Eastern legend and, although it purports to tell of miraculous transformations into another form undergone by characters drawn mostly from Greek and Roman myth and legend, the transformation is sometimes of minor importance in the story. A deeper meaning and more significant unity than the poet's desire to entertain are often looked for in the *Metamorphoses*, but no suggestion has won general agreement. The stories are linked together, often tenuously and in a far-fetched manner, by devices of association and contrast. There is a chronological progression starting with the transformation of Chaos into the ordered universe, and after a succession of stories about gods and heroes drawn from Greek mythology the subject-matter passes to what was thought of as history, Aeneas and Dido, Numa and Egeria, the doctrines of Pythagoras, and to Ovid's own times, ending with the death and deification of Julius Caesar. The Eastern tale of the Babylonian lovers, Pyramus and Thisbe, goes beyond the range of classical legend. The poem is composed with great care, and is the work to which Ovid pinned his hopes of immortal fame. It seems to have been composed from *c.* AD 2 onwards, and had not been finally revised when the poet was banished in AD 8. The model for this kind of composition was to some extent the *Aitia* of *Callimachus, but there the stories are unconnected. It is a work of great inventiveness, charm, and originality. Among the narratives usually thought to be best are (book 2) Phaethon driving the chariot of the sun; (book 3) Echo and Narcissus; (book 4) Pyramus and Thisbe, Perseus and Andromeda; (book 5) the rape of Proserpine; (book 6) Pallas Athena and Arachnē; (book 7) Jason and Medea, Cephalus and Procris; (book 8) the flight

of Daedalus, Philemon and Baucis; (book 10) Orpheus and Eurydicē, Venus and Adonis; (book 11) Midas, Ceyx, and Halcyonē; (book 13) Polyphemus and Galatea.
2. See APULEIUS.

Metanī'ra (Metaneira), see DEMETER.

Metaphysics, see ARISTOTLE 4 (ii).

Mete'lli, name of a noble family at Rome, belonging to the plebeian *gens Caecilia.* The Metelli first came to prominence in the First Punic War and thereafter became one of the most distinguished of the Roman families, always supporting the *optimate cause. Members include the following.

1. **Lucius Caeci'lius Metellus,** consul 251 BC, *pontifex maximus* 243, died 221. In 250 BC, during the First Punic War, he won a notable victory against the Carthaginians in Sicily, capturing many war-elephants, hitherto considered invincible. As a consequence the elephant was the symbol used on coin-issues of later members of the family. In 241 he rescued the *Palladium when the temple of Vesta was on fire, and lost his sight as a result.

2. **Quintus Caecilius Metellus Numi'dicus,** consul in 109 BC at a critical time in the war against *Jugurtha. His immediate success earned him his *cognomen* Numidicus, 'of Numidia', but he failed to bring the war to a conclusion and was superseded in 107 by his former subordinate C. *Marius. In 100 he was the only senator not to swear to observe an agrarian law of Saturninus, and went into exile. His recall (probably in 98) was a victory for the senate. He died *c.*91.

metics (*mĕtoikoi*), in the Greek city-states, voluntary resident aliens who had acquired a recognized status in the community; those at Athens, where very large numbers were resident, are best known. Metics enjoyed full civil rights (as opposed to political rights, which they did not possess) except that they could not own land or contract legal marriages with citizens. As a class they concentrated on commercial and industrial activities, and carried on important businesses as bankers, shipowners, importers, and contractors. Some were physicians, philosophers, sophists, and orators (e.g. Aristotle, Protagoras, Lysias); the comic poets Antiphanēs and Philemon were metics.

Mētis ('counsel'), in Greek myth, daughter of *Tethys and *Oceanus, the first wife of Zeus and the wisest of gods. Zeus was warned by Gaia and Uranus that his children by Metis would be dangerously clever. He therefore swallowed her when she became pregnant, and the goddess *Athena was subsequently born from Zeus' head. By swallowing Metis, Zeus also acquired her practical wisdom.

Mēton, Athenian astronomer of the fifth century BC. He suggested a system of regularly intercalating lunar months (seven in a period of nineteen years, the Metonic cycle) to correlate the lunar month and the solar year, with the purpose of providing a fixed system of reckoning for astronomical observations (the civil calendar, it appears, remained unaffected). Since, by Meton's system, the sun and the moon were out of step by one day after seventy-six years, the nineteen-year cycle was superseded a century later by the corrected seventy-six year system of Callipus (fourth century BC), which was used by *Hipparchus (2) and *Ptolemy. Meton appears in Aristophanes' *Birds* as a comic 'town-planner'.

Metre. 1. Greek

1. In English verse the metre (rhythm) of a poem is determined by the particular arrangement of stressed and unstressed syllables in the line. In Greek verse stress accent played no part; the metre of a poem depended on the number of syllables in a line and on their 'quantity', i.e. whether they were long or short. Hence Greek verse (and also Latin; see LATIN 1 below) is often described as 'quantitative', the quantity of a syllable being determined by a number of factors which governed the length of time it took to pronounce (for the rules of quantity see PROSODY). A line of Greek verse is thus composed of words which fit a pattern of long and short syllables, indicated for the purposes of analysis (scansion) by the signs – and ᴗ respectively. At certain places in the line the pattern might allow a syllable to be either long or short; these places are indicated by the sign × (some metricians prefer ᴗ̆) and the position is said to be *anceps*, Latin for 'ambivalent'. In general, a line of Greek verse is formed by the repetition several times of a short sequence of syllables, each sequence being known as a metron or a foot. A line of verse containing two metra is known as a dimeter, three metra a trimeter, four a tetrameter, and so on. In some metres (e.g. the dactylic hexameter; see 3 below) there is no difference between the foot and the metron and either term may be used; in others (e.g. the iambic trimeter) there are two feet to each metron, and in this case it is sometimes more satisfactory to analyse into metra because there are features which occur in each metron but only in every other foot.

Resolution and contraction. Two short syllables are roughly equivalent in duration to one long syllable, and so in many cases two short syllables may be substituted for a long, a feature known as resolution, or two short syllables contracted into a single long; these possibilities may be indicated by the signs ᴗᴗ or ᴗᴗ.

The principal feet and metra are the following:

(i)	dactyl	– ᴗ ᴗ
(ii)	spondee	– –
(iii)	anapaest	ᴗ ᴗ –
	the anapaestic metron is	ᴗ ᴗ – ᴗ ᴗ –
(iv)	iamb(us)	ᴗ –
	the iambic metron is	× – ᴗ –
(v)	trochee	– ᴗ
	the trochaic metron is	– ᴗ – ×
(vi)	tribrach	ᴗ ᴗ ᴗ
(vii)	crētic	– ᴗ –
(viii)	paeon	– ᴗ ᴗ ᴗ
		or ᴗ ᴗ ᴗ –
(ix)	bacchīus or bacchīac	ᴗ – –
(x)	choriamb	– ᴗ ᴗ –
(xi)	epitrite	– ᴗ – –
(xii)	dochmius or dochmiac	ᴗ ᴗ̆ ᴗ̆ ᴗ ᴗ̆

2. *Caesura and diaeresis.* In some metres it is the practice to have word-end coincide with the end of a particular metron in the line, so that at this point a word never runs over into the next metron. This feature is known as

diaeresis. In other metres it is the practice for word-end to occur regularly within, rather than at the end of, a particular metron. This is known as *caesura*, 'cut'. Both diaeresis and caesura are indicated by a broken line, thus ⁝.

3. *The hexameter*. The hexameter established itself at a very early date as the metre of epic and didactic poetry, besides being used for some hymns, for bucolic poetry, and for satire. It consists of six metra or feet, each of which is a dactyl or, its metrical equivalent, a spondee. The fifth foot was usually a dactyl. The sixth foot was always a spondee, of which the last position was anceps. Thus the hexameter pattern is

$$- \smile\smile \mid - \smile\smile \mid - \smile\smile \mid - \smile\smile \mid - \overline{\smile\smile} \mid - \times$$

As a rule, every line had a caesura, regularly occurring at one of the two alternative places in the third foot, either $- \vdots \smile\smile$, the 'masculine' or penthemimeral ('after the fifth position') caesura, or $- \smile \vdots \smile$, the 'feminine' or 'weak' or 'trochaic' caesura. The latter is commoner. For dactyls in lyric see 8 (ii) below.

4. *The elegiac couplet* or *elegiacs*. This was a very popular metre, widely diffused by the seventh century BC. It was used for epitaphs, verse inscriptions, and epigrams generally. It consists of two lines, a hexameter (see 3 above) followed by a so-called 'pentameter' which in fact does not contain five metra or feet in sequence, as the name suggests, but apparently two and a half followed by two and a half, thus:

$$- \overline{\smile\smile} - \overline{\smile\smile} - \mid - \smile\smile - \smile\smile \times$$

Spondees are excluded from the second half of the line. The position of the caesura is invariable. The sequence $- \smile\smile - \smile\smile -$ is often described as a *hēmiepĕs*, 'half a hexameter'.

5. *Iambic metres*. (i) The principal example is the *iambic trimeter* (or *senarius*). This metre was used for occasional poems, sometimes political, often scurrilous, and also for inscriptions. The earliest surviving iambics may be those of the poem *Margitēs ascribed to Homer; Archilochus in the seventh century BC also employed iambic metres. In particular it was the metre of the spoken parts of

drama, of tragedy and (with more metrical freedom) of comedy. As the name indicates, the iambic trimeter consists of three iambic metra (it is sometimes analysed less satisfactorily into six feet). A caesura regularly occurs after the first or third position of the second metron. Thus the pattern of the iambic line is

$$\times \smile\smile\smile \mid \times \vdots \smile\smile \smile \vdots \smile\smile \mid \times \smile\smile\smile \times$$

in which the broken lines indicate the alternative positions of the caesura. Resolution of the first four long syllables is fairly common. The fifth long syllable is resolved rather rarely, and only when the preceding anceps is short. Occasionally the first anceps is resolved into two short syllables and followed by an (unresolved) long syllable; this feature is often described as an 'anapaest in the first foot'. When the line ended with a word forming a cretic ($- \smile -$), the preceding anceps had to be short (Porson's Law). Prepositives, i.e. words that can stand only before another word or words, such as the article and prepositions, are considered for metrical purposes to be part of the following word. Thus Porson's Law would not be broken if a noun of cretic form was preceded by its article, e.g. *tās sȳmphŏrās*.

(ii) In Attic comedy a much freer form of the iambic trimeter is used. In general, resolution is very common.

(iii) The *'limping' iambic trimeter*, *choliambic*, or *scazon* was invented by, or at any rate frequently used by, Hipponax; it has the form of the tragic iambic trimeter (see (i)) except that the penultimate syllable is always long, and the preceding anceps is often long also.

6. *Trochaic metres*. The principal trochaic metre is the *trochaic tetrameter catalectic*, used like the iambic trimeter for political or scurrilous verse, but also found in tragedy and, most commonly, in Attic comedy. It consists of four trochaic metra of which the last is catalectic, 'stops short', i.e. a syllable in the last metron (usually, as in trochaics, the final syllable) is omitted; catalexis is indicated by a caret mark at the end of the metron. There is normally diaeresis at the end of the second metron. Thus the pattern of the line is

ᴗᴗᴗ × | ᴗᴗᴗᴗ × | ᴗᴗᴗ × | – ᴗ – ∧

(A line that does not lack a final syllable, when a distinction is needed, is known as acatalectic.)

7. *Anapaestic metres.* No doubt because of their marching rhythm these are found in drama, and principally in the *parodos* or entrance song of the chorus, in the form of groups of anapaestic dimeters (i.e. lines containing two anapaestic metra), closing with a catalectic line. In tragedy these entrance songs are chanted rather than sung. Sung (i.e. lyric) anapaests, with greater metrical freedom, also occur in tragedy, in monodies and in dialogues where an actor sings his lines. Aristophanes uses anapaests in the form of the anapaestic tetrameter catalectic, i.e. four anapaestic metra, with the final metron in the form ᴗᴗ – – ∧.

8. *Lyric metres.* These are the metres of poetry that was sung rather than chanted or recited.

(i) *Aeolic metres.* These are the metres in which Sappho and Alcaeus wrote most of their poetry, and they are known as aeolic after the poets' homeland, *Aeolis. They are also found elsewhere in lyric poetry, in Anacreon, Pindar, Bacchylides, and many of the lyrics of Greek tragedy. They are analysed not into feet or metra but into *cola* of various kinds; a *colon* is a metrical sequence of not more than about twelve syllables with a recognizable recurring pattern. Sometimes a line of poetry consists of one colon; at other times two or three cola are put together to form a line or a stanza (*strophē). It is characteristic of aeolic metres that the number of syllables in a given colon is always the same; there is no resolution (– into ᴗᴗ) or contraction ᴗᴗ into –). Some cola begin with two syllables which may be either long or short (× ×), although it is rare for both to be short. This feature is known as the 'aeolic base'. The commonest aeolic cola are:

× × – ᴗᴗ – ᴗ –	glyconic
× × – ᴗᴗ – –	pherecratean
× × – ᴗᴗ – ᴗ – –	hipponactean
× – ᴗᴗ – ᴗ –	telesillean
× – ᴗᴗ – –	reizianum
– ᴗᴗ – ᴗ – –	aristophanean

– ᴗᴗ – –	adonean
– ᴗ – × – ᴗ –	lecythion
– ᴗ – ᴗ – –	ithyphallic
– ᴗᴗ – ᴗ –	dodrans A
– ᴗ – ᴗᴗ –	dodrans B
ᴗᴗ – – ᴗᴗ – –	ionic dimeter
ᴗᴗ – ᴗ – ᴗ – –	anacreontic

In the last two pairs of cola, the one colon differs from the other only in the exchange of middle syllables. Such an exchange within a colon or metron is known as *anaclasis*. It will also be seen that several cola differ from each other by having one syllable more or less at the beginning or the end. Other cola can be produced by the internal addition of – ᴗᴗ or – ᴗᴗ –. The *asclepiad*, for example, is a glyconic extended by – ᴗᴗ –, thus:

× × – ᴗᴗ – – ᴗᴗ – ᴗ –

or even

× × – ᴗᴗ – – ᴗᴗ – – ᴗᴗ – ᴗ –

The *sapphic* stanza or strophe (used by both Sappho and Alcaeus) combines aeolic cola in the following way:

– ᴗ – × – ᴗᴗ – ᴗ – –
– ᴗ – × – ᴗᴗ – ᴗ – –
– ᴗ – × – ᴗᴗ – ᴗ – ×
– ᴗᴗ – –

The *alcaic* stanza or strophe (perhaps not used by Sappho) comibines the following cola:

× – ᴗ – × – ᴗᴗ – ᴗ –
× – ᴗ – × – ᴗᴗ – ᴗ –
× – ᴗ – × – ᴗ – ×
– ᴗᴗ – ᴗᴗ – ᴗ – –

These two stanza forms are also familiar from the *Odes* of Horace (see LATIN 3 (iii) below).

(ii) *Simonides, Bacchylides, and Pindar.* (What follows refers mainly to Pindar and Bacchylides; relatively little of Simonides survives.) The poems of these three were mostly *triadic and the metres of two main kinds, aeolic and dactylo-epitrite. With a few exceptions these two metres were not mixed; a poem was written either in the one or in the other. The aeolic poems employ the cola described in (i) above but in a large variety of abbreviated, headless ('acephalous') and catalectic forms, and in unusual combinations, so that it is difficult to identify the cola.

The dactylo-epitrite poems are composed mainly of the sequences $-\cup\cup-\cup\cup-$ (the *hemiepes*; see 4 above) and $-\cup-$ in various combinations, these two sequences often linked by an anceps syllable, usually long. It has become customary to analyse dactylo-epitrite in the following notation:

D $-\cup\cup-\cup\cup-$ e $-\cup-$
d¹ $-\cup\cup-$ d² $\cup\cup-$
E $-\cup---\cup-$ (that is e – e).

Of these, D, e, and E are very common, d¹ and d² relatively rare forms.

(iii) *Dochmiacs*. This metre occurs in sequences in tragedy, at moments of excitement or high emotion. Although the normal dochmiac metron is described as $\cup--\cup-$, it is not in fact the commonest form, which is $\cup\cup\cup-\cup-$. Analysis is made difficult by the large number of possible variants.

2. Latin

1. Spoken Latin had a stress accent which classical Greek apparently did not have, yet the metres of classical Latin poetry were quantitative, as in Greek (see GREEK 1 above); on the whole, Latin poets avoided conflict between stress accent and quantity. All Latin metres were borrowed from Greek (except perhaps the saturnian metre), with adaptations to make them fit the different sound pattern of Latin or to suit the individual poet's technique.

The *saturnian metre*, the oldest Latin verse form, was so named by later poets to suggest its origin in a remote past (such as the Golden Age, when Saturn was king of the gods). It was the metre used by *Livius Andronicus for his translation or adaptation of the *Odyssey* into Latin, by *Naevius for his original Latin epic poem on the First Punic War, and is also found in the hymn of the *arval priests. Later poets expressed repugnance for it. There is no agreement about its metrical form, except that each line fell into two parts, roughly iambic and trochaic respectively.

2. *The metres of Latin drama*. Livius Andronicus and Naevius, as well as writing in saturnian metre, used Greek metres in drama, but *Ennius is the first Roman dramatist of whose tragedies suf-

ficient fragments remain to show that he certainly adopted the Greek quantitative scansion. Plautus and Terence adopted a wide range of quantitative metres, and show a compromise between stress accent and quantity, the latter being frequently modified to fit the former.

The dialogue of the plays was usually written in *iambic senarii* (i.e. lines of six iambic feet, equivalent to iambic trimeters in Greek drama). The Latin senarius, unlike the Greek trimeter, is best analysed into feet. The various possibilities can be indicated thus:

$$\underset{\cup\cup}{\cup}\;\overset{\cup\cup}{}\;\bigg|\;\underset{\cup\cup}{\cup}\;\overset{\cup\cup}{}\;\bigg|\;\underset{\cup\cup}{\cup}\;\overset{\cdot}{\cdot}\;\bigg|\;\underset{\cup\cup}{\cdot}\;\overset{\cdot}{\cdot}\underset{}{\cup\cup}\;\bigg|\;\underset{\cup\cup}{\cup}\;\overset{\cup\cup}{}\;\bigg|--$$

Caesura (see GREEK 2 above) usually occurs in the third foot but sometimes in the fourth; *hiatus is allowed at the caesura. Porson's Law (see GREEK 5) does not apply. Although resolution is common, a sequence of four short syllables is generally avoided.

The lyric songs (*cantica*), common in Plautus, rare in Terence, include a variety of lyric metres.

3. *Later Latin metres*.

(i) The *(dactylic) hexameter*, introduced by Ennius and perfected by Virgil and Ovid, is similar to the Greek hexameter (see GREEK 2 above). The caesura occurs most commonly after the first long syllable of the third foot, less often after the first short syllable. After Ennius, monosyllables at the end of the line became rare, although in Horace's *Satires* monosyllabic adverbs and particles placed in the final position impart a casual, conversational tone to the verse.

(ii) The *elegiac couplet* or *elegiacs*, also introduced by Ennius, and perfected by Tibullus, Propertius, and Ovid, was based on the Greek (see GREEK 4). A monosyllable immediately before the central caesura of the pentameter was avoided unless it followed another monosyllable or a word consisting of two short syllables. Ovid normally ended the line with a disyllabic word; earlier elegists admitted a word of five syllables.

(iii) *Lyric metres*. Latin lyric poetry is less in quantity and not generally as complex as Greek. The chief writers of Latin lyric were Catullus and Horace, but Martial also used lyric metres (hendecasyllables and choliambics; see (*a*) and (*b*) below), as did Seneca in his tragedies.

Horace used especially the sapphic and alcaic stanza forms (see GREEK 8 (i)), and combinations of asclepiads, glyconics, and pherecrateans, in all of which he bound himself by restrictions unknown in Greek.

(*a*) The *hendecasyllable* metre (having a line 'of eleven syllables') was originally Greek; it has the form:

$$\times \ \times - \cup\cup - \cup - \cup - -$$

(*b*) The *scazon* or *choliambic* metre, also adopted from Greek by Catullus and Martial, was a 'limping' iambic trimeter in which a long syllable appeared in place of the short expected in the penultimate position (see GREEK 5 (iii)).

Mētrŏ'on, at Athens, the sanctuary of the Mother (*mētēr*) of the gods (see CYBELE), in the agora. The original small temple may be dated to the beginning of the fifth century BC. After the destructions of the Persian invasion of 480 BC (see PERSIAN WARS) this temple was not rebuilt, and the cult seems to have been transferred to the neighbouring (old) Bouleutērion, council-chamber of the *boulē*. After the new Bouleuterion was built at the end of the fifth century the old building came to be called the Metroon. The building served also as a public record office. In the precinct stood the large earthenware tub in which Diogenēs the *Cynic philosopher is said to have lived.

Me'vius (or Maevius), see BAVIUS.

Mēze'ntius, in Virgil's *Aeneid,* a cruel atheistical tyrant, of Caerē in Etruria (the name is Etruscan), who has been expelled by his people and joins *Turnus in opposing Aeneas and the Trojan settlement in Italy. In contrast his son Lausus is made an attractive figure. Both are killed by Aeneas, Lausus in defence of his father. Mezentius has a horse called Rhaebus. Mezentius and Turnus both figured in the Aeneas legend as known to Cato the Censor.

Midas, legendary king of Phrygia who, having hospitably entertained *Silenus, the companion of Dionysus, when he had lost his way, was given a wish, and wished that all he touched might turn to gold. On discovering that this applied to his food also he asked to be relieved of the gift. He was told to wash in the river Pactolus, which ever since has had sands containing gold. Midas is also said to have captured Silenus, who used to visit his garden, and curious to learn his wisdom made him drunk by mixing wine with the water of the spring. What he told Midas seems to have been a matter of conjecture among the ancients, but according to one version he said that it was best for a man not to be born at all, or once born to die as soon as possible.

On another occasion, having to judge a musical contest between Apollo and *Pan (or *Marsyas), Midas had the indiscretion to decide against Apollo, who thereupon gave him ass's ears to indicate his stupidity. These Midas concealed with his head-dress but was obliged to tell his barber. The latter, unable to keep the secret but afraid to reveal it publicly, whispered the news into a hole in the ground which he then filled up. But reeds grew over the hole and repeated the story whenever the wind blew.

Middle Platonism, the philosophy deriving from the work of Plato in the period between the time of Antiochus of Ascalon, d. *c.*68 BC, to *Plotinus (b. AD 205). Following Antiochus in rejecting the Scepticism of the New *Academy, it turned towards a positive philosophy that included doctrines from several schools and led eventually to *Neoplatonism.

Mīlēs glōriō'sus ('the boastful soldier'), Roman comedy by *Plautus; there is reason for thinking it was produced *c.*204 BC and is therefore an early work. It is uncertain from what Greek comedy it was adapted; *Menander's *Ephesios* ('the Ephesian') has been suggested, this title being in that case a variant for *Alazon* ('boaster') which Plautus gives as the name of his original.

The boastful captain Pyrgopolynicēs (a name recalling Polyneicēs from the Greek myth of the *Seven against Thebes, with the addition of *pyrgos*, 'tower') carries off the girl Philocōmasium from Athens to Ephesus while her lover Pleusiclēs is absent at Naupactus. Pleusicles' slave sets off to inform his master but is captured by pirates and given as a present to Pyrgopolynices at Ephesus. The slave then writes a letter to Pleusicles, who comes to Ephesus and takes up residence with an old family friend next door to the soldier. By the ingenuity of the slave and the kindness of Pleusicles' host, Pleusicles and Philocomasium meet by passing through a hole in the party wall between the two houses. It is given out that the girl's twin sister has arrived, and this explains Philocomasium's appearance now in one house, now in the other. Pyrgopolynices is fooled into believing that Pleusicles' host has a young wife who is dying for love of him; he is therefore induced to dismiss Philocomasium in order to pursue this new love, and is lured into the neighbouring house, where he is well beaten as an adulterer, while Pleusicles and his mistress sail off to Athens.

The *miles gloriosus* was a stock character in Roman comedy (see the prologue to Plautus' *Captivi*); he is the prototype of Ralph Roister Doister and Bobadill and other swaggering soldiers of the English Elizabethan stage.

Milē'sian Tales (*Milēsiaka*), by Aristeidēs of Miletus, a Greek writer of the second century BC, probably short stories of love and adventure; only one fragment survives, but the type may be seen in the tale of the Ephesian widow in the *Satyricon* of *Petronius Arbiter. They were translated into Latin by L. Cornelius *Sisenna. Their generally erotic and titillating character may be inferred from the fact that the Parthians were greatly shocked by a copy found among the spoils after the Roman defeat at Carrhae in 53 BC. They were forerunners of such medieval collections of tales as the *Gesta Romanorum*, the *Decameron* of Boccaccio, and the *Heptameron* of Marguerite of Navarre. 'Milesian Tales' became the name given to this kind of literature.

Milē'tus, Ionian Greek city with a fine harbour, on the coast of Asia Minor near the mouth of the river Maeander. During the seventh and sixth centuries BC Miletus founded many colonies on the Black Sea and was an important sea-power. It

attained great brilliance at the end of the seventh century, under the tyrant Thrasybulus, and during the sixth century it produced the philosophers *Thalēs, *Anaximander, and *Anaximenēs, and a little later *Hecataeus the logographer and *Phocylidēs the poet. *Histiaeus was tyrant at the time of the first Persian expedition into Europe. Later his son-in-law Aristagoras ruled in his place, and both seem to have promoted from Miletus the Ionian Revolt of 499 against Persia (see PERSIAN WARS). Miletus was captured after a siege and burnt by the Persians in 494; its inhabitants were carried off to the Persian capital Susa (see PHRYNICHUS). It was refounded in 479, joined the *Delian League, and revolted against Athens in 412. Famous Milesians of this period were *Aspasia, the *hetaera of Pericles, *Hippodamus the townplanner of the Piraeus, and the poet *Timotheus. In the fourth century Miletus came under the control of *Mausolus, but in 334 it was captured and liberated by Alexander the Great. It was a manufacturing town and the centre of the wool industry, its wool being regarded in antiquity as the finest in the world.

mīliā'rium au'rĕum (the 'golden milestone'), erected by the emperor Augustus at the head of the Forum at Rome, as the point from which roads radiated to various parts of Italy. It seems to have been a column covered with gilt bronze, inscribed with names of places and their distances from Rome.

Mīlō, Titus A'nnius (d. 48 BC), Roman political agitator, tribune of the people in 57 BC and notorious as the rival of *Clodius. Between 57 and 52 Milo and Clodius organized street violence against one another with rival gangs of hired gladiators, thereby contributing to the general collapse of law and order at this time. In 52 Milo killed Clodius in one of their affrays and was brought to trial by Pompey. He was to be defended by Cicero (whose return from exile Milo had promoted), but Cicero was intimidated and withdrew. Milo was condemned and exiled. In 48 he joined M. *Caelius in an abortive rebellion against Caesar and was killed in south Italy. See CICERO (1) 3 and 4.

Mī'lō(n), of Croton in south Italy, a famous wrestler who lived towards the end of the sixth century BC and was victorious six times at the Olympic and seven times at the Pythian games. Many stories were told of his strength, even by Pausanias (VI. 14. 5), who lived some seven hundred years later. He is said to have carried a heifer on his shoulders into the stadium at Olympia, killed it with one blow of his fist, and eaten it in a day. Milo is said to have died when, in attempting to split asunder a tree trunk, his hand became trapped and he was devoured by wild beasts.

Miltī'adēs, name held by several members of the noble (*Eupatrid) family of the Philaïdae at Athens. A certain Miltiades was *archon in 664/3 BC and again in 659/8, and it was his great-grandson (the elder Miltiades) who took settlers to the Thracian Chersonese, a local tribe having invited him to be their king. His death, c.525 BC, was honoured by funeral games. The younger Miltiades (c.550–489), nephew of the former, was sent out to the Thracian Chersonese c.524 to regain possession of his uncle's dominion when it had fallen again into Thracian hands. He was a vassal of the Persian king Darius and after the suppression in 494 of the Ionian Revolt, which he had supported, he returned to Athens in 493, perhaps fearing the Persians. He survived a prosecution for 'tyranny over Greek subjects' in Thrace and became an influential politician in spite of the opposition of the *Alcmaeonidae. As *strategos ('military commander') under the polemarch Callimachus he persuaded the Athenians to adopt his strategy at Marathon and was therefore the architect of that victory. An unsuccessful attempt to capture Paros in 489, for which the Athenians had entrusted him with seventy ships, led to his being impeached (on the accusation of *Xanthippus) and fined fifty talents. Soon after he died in prison of wounds received in the attack.

Miltiades married Hegesipylē, a Thracian princess, who became the mother of

*Cimon and (probably) other children including *Elpinicē.

Milvian bridge, battle of. See CONSTANTINE I.

mime (Gk. *mīmos*, Lat. *mīmus*). Originally a Greek word meaning 'a mimic', the term came to be applied in Greece to a dramatic sketch presenting a scene from daily life ('the quack doctor') or myth ('Dionysus and Ariadne'). In the fifth century BC Sophron of Syracuse wrote mimes in some kind of rhythmic prose and popular (Doric) language; a papyrus fragment and some quotations survive. Sophron was perhaps the first to give mime a literary form, was admired by Plato, and probably influenced *Herodas and *Theocritus.

At Rome the name was applied to a kind of dramatic performance introduced there before the end of the third century BC, perhaps from Magna Graecia. The actors included both men and women, who acted in bare feet and without masks scenes from everyday life or from romance, spoken in prose. Mime gradually ousted the *Atellan farce as a tail piece or finale (*exodium*) after tragedies. It developed into licentious farce, with stock characters of husband, faithless wife, her lover, and the maid. A popular feature of the *ludi Floralēs was the appearance of actresses, *mimae*, naked. The mime took a literary form in the first century BC. The principal writers then were D. *Laberius and *Publilius Syrus, who included elements of social and political criticism. Under the empire, mimes contributed to the decline in stage performances of comedy, being patronized by the emperors and highly popular with the people, who loved their farcical nature, indecency, and topicality. They were finally suppressed in the Roman world in AD 502.

Mime in the ancient world should not be confused with 'mime' in the modern sense, which signifies a play in which the parts are performed by gesture and action alone, without words, and to the accompaniment of music. For this see PANTOMIME.

Mimne'rmus (second half of the seventh century BC), of Colophōn in

Ionia, Greek poet. He wrote chiefly love poems in elegiacs which were collected in two books, one of which was called *Nanno* after the flute-girl he is said to have loved. His most memorable poems are concerned with the pleasures of youth and love and the horrors of old age, but he seems also to have written a *Smyrnēis* or historical poem on Smyrna, which may have formed part of the *Nanno*. Other fragments suggest that he wrote on a variety of themes: a description of the Sun sailing in his cup over the Ocean through the night to his rising (see HELIOS), an account of the foundation of Colophon, and another of the war between Smyrna and *Gygēs of Lydia. He is admired for the musical qualities of his verse, and for the hedonism, tinged with melancholy, that he expresses.

Mine'rva, Italian goddess of crafts and trade guilds, probably a native deity rather than an early borrowing from Greece. She was one of the great Capitoline triad, together with *Jupiter and Juno. She was worshipped in a shrine on Mons Caelius and also had a temple on the Aventine, outside the city wall. Here the guild of flute-players held a festival on the Ides (13th) of June, in the evening of which they dressed in masks and long robes and roamed the streets (see LIVIUS ANDRONICUS). Minerva's festival was the *Quinquatrus, on 19 March, the date of the dedication of the temple. She was identified with the Greek goddess Athena and seems to have taken over the martial characteristics of Athena Promachos ('champion'). Certainly her worship spread at the expense of that of Mars, the Quinquatrus having originally been his festival. Virgil presents her both as a goddess of handicrafts and as a goddess of war.

Mīnō'an, see CRETE.

Mīnos, in Greek myth, a king of Crete. The stories told about him faintly reflect the historical importance of the Cretan civilization known as Minoan, and 'Minos' may have been a dynastic name, or a title like 'pharaoh'. He is represented in the *Odyssey* (book 11) as a just ruler who became a judge of the dead in the Underworld (together with, in later authors, his brother *Rhadamanthys and the hero *Aeacus). Minos, Rhadamanthys, and *Sarpedon were the sons of Zeus and Europa, whom Zeus carried off by assuming the form of a bull. To settle the question of who should be king of Crete, Minos prayed to the sea god Poseidon to send him a victim he might sacrifice, and the god sent a bull from the sea. Thus Minos took the kingdom, but he could not bring himself to kill the magnificent bull. Poseidon thereupon caused Minos' wife *Pasiphaē to fall in love with it, and the result of their union was the Minotaur ('Minos' bull'), which had the body of a man with a bull's head. *Daedalus constructed the *labyrinth, a maze, in which to hide it (and in which he was himself imprisoned).

Minos is said to have been close to his father Zeus, who received him every nine years on Mount Ida and gave him laws to impose on his Cretan subjects. In the course of his reign he made war on Megara and Athens. For the story of the former conflict see SCYLLA. In Athenian legend he is made the villain of a story in which *Theseus is the hero. Minos laid siege to Athens in the time of king Aegeus because of the city's involvement in the death of his son Androgeos, and for its deliverance the city had to agree to pay an annual or nine-yearly tribute of seven youths and girls, who were shut up with the Minotaur. One year Theseus, king Aegeus' son, contrived to be included, and succeeded in killing the Minotaur. Herodotus (7. 170) relates that Minos met a violent death during his pursuit of Daedalus, who had escaped to Sicily. By Pasiphae Minos was the father of many children, including *Phaedra, *Ariadnē, and *Deucalion (and through Deucalion the grandfather of Idomeneus, who fought at Troy). See also BRITO-MARTIS.

Mī'notaur, see MINOS.

Minū'cius Felix, Marcus (flourished AD 200–40), early Latin Christian apologist of whose life virtually nothing is known. He wrote *Octavius*, a dialogue between Octavius Januarius and Minucius, two Christian converts, and Caecilius Natalis, an educated pagan. The setting is imitated from Cicero: the three interlocutors are walking by the sea at Ostia. Caecilius is reproved for saluting an image of *Serapis, and a discussion on Christianity results. Caecilius criticizes the Christians for (*a*) their dogmatism, on the grounds that the human intelligence is incapable of grasping the mystery of the universe, (*b*) their rejection of the ancient religion of Rome, and (*c*) their immoral life. Octavius replies, establishing the existence of God and Providence by the testimony of the pagan writers themselves (those expressing Stoic views, notably Cicero and Seneca the Younger), attacking the Roman mythology, and repudiating the charges brought against the manner of life of the Christians, of which he depicts the virtue and heroism. Caecilius declares himself converted, and the friends separate. Christ is referred to only indirectly in the dialogue, and the defence is rather of the moral and philosophic side of the Christian religion than of its specific dogma. It is addressed in fact to the cultivated Roman pagan and is intended to dissipate his prejudices, as much perhaps by its cultivated tone—the elegant Latin and ironic wit—as by argument. Its urbanity is in strong contrast with the imperious vehemence of *Tertullian's *Apologeticum*, on which it very probably depends.

minuscule script, see BOOKS AND WRITING 6.

Mi'nyans (Minyai), an ancient people, a legendary race of heroes, living in Greece, whose chief branches appear from the *Iliad* to have lived at Orchomenus in Boeotia and Iolcus in Thessaly. As most of the Argonauts were descended from the Minyans they are often called by that name. See MINYAS.

Mi'nyas, legendary ancestor of the *Minyans and founder of Orchomenus in Boeotia. His reputed 'treasury' seen at Orchomenus by Pausanias is in fact a Mycenaean tomb. He was the father of *Clymenē and other daughters. Of these it is told that they resisted the cult of Dionysus, were driven mad, and tore in pieces Hippasus, the son of Leucippē, one of their number. They were turned into bats.

Misē'nus. According to Virgil, *Aeneid*

6, Cape Misenum in the Bay of Naples was named after the Trojan trumpeter Misenus who had followed Aeneas from Troy but, having aroused the jealousy of the sea-god Triton, was dragged into the sea by him and drowned when the Trojans landed at Cumae.

Misū'menos ('the hated man'), Greek comedy by *Menander; in antiquity it was very popular but only a fragment of it survives from a papyrus, and not sufficient to reconstruct the plot. Thrasonidēs, a professional soldier, holds captive a girl Crateia, with whom he is madly in love, but refuses to force himself upon her because of her hatred for him. Her father Demeas seems to have ransomed her; more than that cannot be ascertained. The chief interest of the play must have lain in the relationship between Thrasonides and Crateia, both of whom are made sympathetic.

Mithras, ancient Indo-Iranian god of light and truth, in the Zoroastrian religion the ally of the good power Ahuramazda. His cult came to Rome in the second half of the first century BC in the form of a mystery religion, confined exclusively to men, which offered a happy life to its devotees, with secret rites and various stages of initiation. It was attractive to merchants and soldiers, and soon spread through the Roman empire, flourishing in the important cities and sea-ports of the western Mediterranean. The cult included a form of baptism and a communal meal. Mithras was depicted with a bull which he was said to have captured and sacrificed; the temples of Mithras were built underground in artificial caves recalling the cave in which Mithras had originally killed the bull. *Taurobolium*, bull-slaying, was part of his ritual, as it was of *Cybelē. Mithras seems to have been identified with the sun.

Mithridā'tēs or **Mithradates VI, Eu'pator** (reigned 120–63 BC), king of Pontus (on the south shore of the Black Sea), during his lifetime Rome's most formidable antagonist in the East and a permanent threat to her control over client kingdoms in Asia Minor. The kings of Pontus were of Persian noble birth, claiming descent from *Darius; the population was Hellenized. Mithridates shared the throne with his brother for about six years under his mother's regency; he then imprisoned his mother, murdered his brother, married his sister Laodicē, and proceeded to extend his power around the Black Sea area. He fought three wars against Rome—the Mithridatic Wars—in 89–85, 83–82, and 74–63. During the first, when he quickly overran Bithynia and most of Asia, on a set date in 88 he had Roman and Italian residents in Asia put to death (the number killed was said to have been 80,000). He captured and sacked Athens in 86, but in the same year his army was twice defeated by *Sulla and he withdrew from Europe. In the second war Mithridates was attacked by Lucius Murena, proconsul of Asia but easily repelled the attacks and again Sulla made peace. Mithridates opened the third war by invading Bithynia, which had been bequeathed to Rome by Nicomedes in 75. He was defeated and driven back from his conquered territory first by Lucullus, then by Pompey, and took refuge eventually in the Crimea. Here he failed to raise a new fleet and army, and a revolt against him was led by his son Pharnacēs. He preferred death to captivity, but found that, having taken so many antidotes, he was immune to poison, and had to get a slave to stab him (63 BC).

Mitylē'nē (or, officially, Mytilēnē), see LESBOS.

Mnēmo'synē, in Greek myth, a *Titan goddess, a personification of Memory, and the mother, by Zeus, of the *Muses.

Moerae, Moirai, see FATES.

Molio'nes, in Greek myth, the twin sons of Actor (or Poseidon) and Molionē, named Eurytus and Cteatus; in some accounts (but not in Homer) Siamese twins. They were enemies of the Pylians, and also took part in the Calydonian boar-hunt (see MELEAGER). They fought against Heracles on behalf of their uncle Augeas (see HERACLES, LABOURS OF 6), killing Heracles' brother Iphiclēs; later they were themselves ambushed and killed by Heracles.

Mōmus ('blame'), in Greek myth, a divine personification, and according to Hesiod a son of Night (*Nyx). He had no cult.

Monē'ta, see JUNO.

money and coins

1. *In Greece.* Coinage in the sense of marked metal pieces of standard weight is now generally agreed to have been first used in Asia Minor, in the second half of the seventh century BC, and by the end of the sixth century BC many Greek states had adopted a coinage, mostly based on silver.

Before coinage proper, the Greeks had a primitive currency based on the iron cooking-spit, *obelos; from this derived the names and equivalences of the Greek silver coinage (see DRACHMA). (In Sparta, spits continued to be the only permitted currency long after all other states had coinage.)

Greek money values may be summarized as follows.

6 obols	= 1 drachma
(1 stater	= 2 or 3 drachmas)
100 drachmas	= 1 mina
60 minas	= 1 talent.

At Athens at the end of the fifth century BC a building worker or a rower on a trireme would receive one drachma a day, but would be unlikely to earn more than 300 drachmas in a year. He could feed himself, on bread and 'relish' (i.e. meat, fish, vegetables, or fruit), for a little over a drachma a week. 50 minas was regarded as a large sum to pay for a house; a mean dwelling could have been bought for three.

The coinage of Philip II of Macedon and, especially, of his son Alexander the Great had world-wide circulation; Alexander and his successors introduced portraits of themselves, some of them very fine, on their coins.

2. *At Rome.* The cities of Magna Graecia in south Italy issued splendid series of silver coins as early as the sixth century BC, and in Etruria, to the north of Rome, coinage began in the fifth century BC. But in the rest of Italy at this time coinage, such as it was, consisted of rough lumps of bronze (*aes rudē*) of irregular weight and without any mark of standard value. The Latin word for money, *pecunia*, is

probably derived from the use of livestock, *pecus*, as units of exchange. Later, bronze was in circulation in the form of rectangular bars, but not until the beginning of the third century BC were these issued in a roughly standard weight, equivalent to about 1.5 kg. (3.3 lb.). The earliest Roman coins proper were issued twenty years later. They were heavy bronze pieces of circular form; each was known as an *aes* or *as* (pl. *asses*) and weighed one Roman pound (twelve Roman ounces or 327 g.).

At the end of the third century BC Rome introduced the silver *denarius*, roughly equivalent in value to the Greek drachma. The common unit of currency, in which the Romans expressed even very large sums of money, was the *sestertius*, a coin worth a quarter of a *denarius*.

The early silver coins (from the late third century BC) sometimes bear the name or other indication of the magistrate who struck them. Julius Caesar was the first to have his own head represented on Roman coins, and we have a series of portraits of the emperors on their coins.

monism, monistic theory, see ELEATIC.

monody, monodic poetry, see LYRIC POETRY 1.

Mons Grau'pius, see BRITAIN and AGRICOLA.

Monume'ntum Ancÿrā'num, inscription in Latin (with Greek translation) found in 1555 at Ancyra (Angora, modern Ankara) in Galatia, engraved on the walls of the temple of Rome and Augustus. It contains the text of one of the four documents written by the emperor Augustus and read in the senate after his death, a 'record of his enterprises', *index rerum a se gestarum*, which, in accordance with his wish, was then engraved on bronze tablets and placed outside his mausoleum. The text is not preserved on manuscript, nor has the original inscription survived, but copies were set up in the provinces, of which this is one. Fragments of two other copies have been found at Apollonia and at Antioch, both in Pisidia.

Mopsus, in Greek myth, a seer, son of Manto, who was herself a prophetess, the daughter of *Teiresias. He encountered *Calchas after the Trojan War, and caused his death by outdoing him in a contest of divination. There was also a seer of this name who accompanied the *Argonauts and is therefore contemporary with the generation before the Trojan War. He died on the journey, bitten by a serpent in Libya. (Mopsus is also the name of a shepherd in Virgil's fifth and eighth Eclogues.)

Mōrā'lia, see PLUTARCH.

Morē'tum ('salad'), see APPENDIX VIRGILIANA.

Mo'rpheus, son of Hypnos (Sleep), the Greek god of *dreams.

Morta, see FATES.

Mortuo'rum dia'logi ('dialogues of the dead'), see LUCIAN.

Moschus (flourished c.150 BC), Greek poet of Syracuse whose extant poems include five hexameter pieces, one of which is *bucolic (comparing the pleasures of the countryman with the hard lot of the fisherman), and an *epigram on Eros as a ploughman; there are also an *epyllion *Europa* in 166 hexameters on the rape of Europa by Zeus, and the *Megara*, a hexameter dialogue between Heracles' wife (who gave her name to the poem) and his mother Alcmena, who bewail their misfortunes caused by Heracles' long absence. Also attributed to Moschus, but improbably since *Bion (2) lived at least a generation after him, is the beautiful (bucolic) *Lament for Bion*.

Mostellā'ria ('ghost'), Roman comedy by *Plautus, probably adapted from a Greek comedy by Philemon (see COMEDY, GREEK 6).

The plot depends on the effrontery and resourceful lying of the slave Trānio. Philolachēs, during his father's absence abroad, purchases from a pimp and then frees a girl whom he loves, borrowing money for the purpose from a moneylender, and brings her to live in his father's house. The father returns unexpectedly. Tranio, to prevent him entering the house and discovering what is going on, pretends that the house is haunted by the ghost of a murdered man and has consequently been vacated. But the moneylender appears and demands his money. Tranio tells the father that Philolaches has borrowed it to buy the house of their neighbour Simō, and Simo is induced by further lies to allow it to be inspected. In the end Tranio's lies are exposed, and the father is appeased.

Mother-goddess, see CYBELE.

Mu'lciber, name of the Roman god *Vulcan meaning 'smelter' of metals.

Mu'mmius Acha'icus, Lucius, consul 146 BC. He succeeded *Metellus as the Roman commander against the *Achaean Confederacy in that year, and was responsible for the sack of *Corinth, and for shipping Corinth's art treasures to Italy. He was censor with *Scipio Aemilianus in 142.

Munda, town in Spain, and scene of a battle won by Julius *Caesar in 45 BC, after a revolt by Pompey's sons and Labienus (Caesar's own former legate in the Gallic War). Caesar is reported to have said it was his hardest victory.

mundus, according to Plutarch, a pit in Rome dug by Romulus (traditionally sited in the *Comitium) in which he put first fruits and earth from each country from which his followers came, afterwards filling it up and putting an altar on it. In other Italian cities it was the name given to a pit dug to give access to the *manēs (of the Underworld). The Roman *mundus* was closed with stone except for three days of ill omen, 24 August, 5 October, and 8 November, when *mundus patet*, 'the pit is open'. This pit seems to have been called *mundus Cereris* or *Cerealis*, 'pit of Cerēs'.

mūnici'pium ('municipality'), term describing originally the towns of Etruria, Latium, and Campania, and indicating their status; the inhabitants had the duties of Roman citizenship, including serving in the army and paying taxes, but only the private rights of Roman citizens, not the public rights: they had *civitas sine suffragio*, 'citizenship without the vote'. After the Social War (90–88 BC) all Italian communities had the right to vote and their inhabitants became full Roman citizens; henceforth *municipium* meant an Italian borough.

Mūny'chia (Mounychia), or Munichia, the acropolis (citadel) of *Piraeus and a small harbour adjoining it.

Mūsae'us (Mousaios). 1. Mythical Greek poet, said to have come from Thrace and to have been a pupil of *Orpheus: a collection of oracles was attributed to him. See also ONOMACRITUS.

2. Greek poet of uncertain date but perhaps late fifth century AD; he wrote an epic poem on the love of Hero and *Leander.

Muses (Mousai, Lat. Musae), in Greek myth, daughters of Zeus and *Mnemosynē (Memory), the goddesses of literature, music, and dance, later of all intellectual pursuits. The early Greek poet Hesiod is the first to name them (and perhaps coined their names himself). According to him they were nine in number, and his famous description at the opening of the *Theogony* of their gift to him of song and knowledge of the past, influenced later poets when they came to give an account of how they were inspired to compose poetry. The original seats of the Muses' worship were Pieria, near Mount Olympus in Thessaly, and Mount Helicon in Boeotia (whence they are often spoken of as Pierian or Heliconian), but smaller cults existed throughout Greece. In late Roman times, each Muse presided over one particular art: Calliopē, epic poetry; Clīo, history; Euterpē, flute-playing (and lyric poetry accompanied by the flute); Melpomenē, tragedy; Terpsichorē, (choral) dancing (and the song that goes with it); Eratō, the lyre (and the lyric poetry, often erotic, accompanied by it); Polyhymnia, hymns to the gods, and later, pantomime; Urania, astronomy; Thalia, comedy and bucolic poetry. Their numbers, names, and attributes vary considerably at different times. A few myths are associated with them: the Thracian poet Thamyris competed against them and lost his sight and power of song; the *Sirens competed against them, but were defeated, lost their wings, and jumped into the sea; in one version of the story describing the contest between Apollo and *Marsyas, the Muses are made the judges. Artists of all kinds felt a personal bond with the Muses, who seemed to them to be the source of their gifts. See MUSEUM below.

musē'um (mouseion), in Greece, originally a place connected with the *Muses, sometimes in a religious sense but more usually as a place where the arts and learning were cultivated. Thus 'museum' came to mean a place of education, connected with the Muses. Euripides describes the places where birds sing as *mouseia*. The most famous museum was that of *Alexandria in Egypt, founded by Ptolemy I Soter (ruled 323–283 BC) possibly on the advice of the Athenian *Demetrius of Phalerum. It was distinct from the Library, and housed scholars who were supported by the Ptolemies and, after Egypt came under Roman control, by the emperors. There is no evidence that there was provision for formal teaching, but lectures were given and there were many discussions which even the kings might attend; Cleopatra, the last independent ruler of Egypt, is reputed to have done so. After the foundation of Constantinople in AD 324 many of the Museum scholars are said to have retreated there to avoid the theological controversies of Alexandria. The last member of the Museum to be mentioned explicitly is Theon the mathematician, father of Hypatia, c. AD 400. Dinners with clever conversation were a characteristic institution of the Museum; a poet of the third century BC described it as the 'hen-coop of the Muses'.

music (Gk. *mousikē*, 'art of the Muses').

1. *In Greece*. Music was an integral feature of Greek life, an essential ingredient of all public religious occasions and of banquets and social gatherings. Nearly every form of Greek poetry was traditionally accompanied by some form of music: the Homeric epics were chanted or recited to the lyre, '*lyric' poetry was sung to the lyre, and choral lyric was sung to the accompaniment of music and dancing. In classical times instruction in singing and playing the lyre (and less often the flute) was part of every well-bred boy's education. Thus the citizen body of a Greek city contained a large number of people capable of participating in civic and religious musical performances.

The principal musical instruments were the lyre, of which there were several forms and names, and the so-called flute, *aulos*. The lyre was used mostly to accompany lyric poetry; Pindar's lyric odes, however, were sometimes accompanied by the flute as well. The flute was the usual instrument for accompanying the *dithyramb and for the choruses of tragedy and comedy. It was also played at banquets, sacrifices, and funerals, and was used to mark time for dancers. The lyre was considered the superior instrument both socially (playing the flute distorted the face) and for education, and it was also important in military music; both were used in religious music.

The lyre had vertical strings of equal length (thereby differing from the harp) which were plucked, bowing being unknown in Greece. Pitch was regulated by the tension, and perhaps the thickness, of the strings. The strings of gut or sinew stretched upwards from a holder, over a bridge, to a cross-bar at the top of the instrument, which joined the two slender, curved, side pieces of horn or wood. At the cross-bar there were pegs for tuning. The sound-box at the bottom of the lyre was originally provided by the shell of a tortoise, often replaced by a similarly shaped wooden frame, with a piece of ox-hide stretched over its concave side. The player rested the instrument against his body as he played, plucking (and perhaps dampening) the strings with his left hand directly, and with his right hand plucking the strings with a device made for that purpose, the *plectrum*. The exact function of each hand is not clear.

The translation 'flute' for Greek *aulos* is misleading since the instrument, having a reed and being blown down, was more akin to the clarinet or oboe. The pipe, made of reed, wood, bone, or ivory, was cylindrical or slightly conical, and pierced with holes, as many as sixteen by the late fifth century BC. Auloi were generally played in pairs, the pipes often being held in position by a cheek-band worn by the player. It is not known whether the two pipes were played separately and provided an extended scale or whether they were played together, a rudimentary harmony thus being achieved; possibly both techniques were used. The *syrinx* (or Pan-pipes; see PAN) consisted of about seven pipes (more and fewer are known) bound together and blown directly without the aid of a mouthpiece. In Greece the pipes were of equal length but were stopped internally; the syrinx with a 'stepped' shape, familiar in art, is the Etruscan and Roman variety.

Ancient Greek music was based on a large number of scales or 'modes' (*harmoniai*). The modes roughly resembled modern octave scales, but they differed from each other in the sequence of musical intervals. Classical writers refer to the different modes by ethnic names, Ionian, Aeolian, Lydian, Dorian, and Phrygian, sometimes with the modifying prefixes 'mixo-' ('mixed') or 'hypo-' ('sub-'). Further names were used to indicate the pitch (*tonos*) of a scale, i.e. how high or low it was. In the case of the lyre, each mode probably required its own tuning.

For the Greeks music had an ethical dimension. Plato thought that music not only aroused the emotions temporarily but permanently influenced a man's character. Aristotle too accepts that music expresses moral qualities and thus has an effect on the soul: for education (though not for relaxation, for which all kinds of music are suitable) he would admit only the Dorian.

A few small fragments of Greek music survive, on papyri, on stone, and in manuscripts. It is apparent that the Greeks used two kinds of alphabetic notation, one for the voice and another for musical instruments. Interpretation of the fragments is very uncertain.

See TIMOTHEUS (1) and CINESIAS.

2. *At Rome*. In contrast with Greece, at Rome music did not figure as an essential part of an aristocratic education, and on the whole music as an art, and musicians, were regarded with mild contempt, the latter organizing themselves into guilds (**collegia*) at an early stage for mutual protection. However, music on the tibia accompanied prayers, sacrifices, triumphal marches to the Capitol, processions to the Circus Maximus, and funeral processions. Music for the sung portions of drama (*cantica*) was also played on the tibia. Etruscan influence probably accounts for the use of horns and trumpets in ritual connected with the dead. The trumpets, *tŭbae*, were 'purified' at the annual festival of the Tubilustria on 23 March (see MARS). Stringed instruments were introduced from Greece, and under the empire music became a feature of dinner-parties.

music of the spheres, see HARMONY OF THE SPHERES.

Mūsō'nius Rūfus, Gaius, Roman *Stoic philosopher of the first century AD who probably taught in Greek. Among his pupils were Pliny the Younger, Epictetus, and Dio Chrysostom. He was banished by the emperor Nero for being involved in the conspiracy of *Piso (AD 65), but subsequently recalled. Some of his sayings have been preserved by a pupil, and these show him to have been a humane and attractive figure. They include the remark that marriage is a very good thing, and even a philosopher should accept it gladly. Musonius believed that girls and boys should receive the same kind of education.

Mu'tina (Modena, near Bologna), prosperous town of Cisalpine Gaul famous for its successful resistance to Pompey in 78 BC and to Antony in 43 BC (the *bellum Mutinense*, 'war of Mutina'). On the latter occasion it was held by the republicans under D. Brutus.

My'calē, mountainous promontory in Asia Minor, opposite the island of Samos, the scene of the last battle of the *Persian Wars (479 BC), where the Greeks destroyed the Persian army and fleet.

Mȳcē'nae (Mȳkēnai, Mykēnē), **Mycenae'an civilization.** Mycenae was a very ancient Greek city situated on a hill in the north-east corner of the plain of Argos in the Peloponnese. According to Greek myth it was founded by *Perseus and was subsequently the kingdom of the Homeric hero *Agamemnon who led the Greek army during the Trojan War: Homer calls it 'rich in gold'. In 468 BC, however, the city was destroyed by Argos and never reinhabited. The very considerable ruins were visited in the second century AD by Pausanias, who commented upon the graves, the massive walls, and the Lion Gate, all still to be seen today. All knowledge of the people who had built this remarkable city had disappeared long before the classical period, and the Mycenaeans were known to later Greeks only in the vaguest outlines through myth and legend. Their late Bronze Age civilization was first revealed to the world by the excavations in 1876 of Heinrich Schliemann, a wealthy German merchant and archaeologist, who wished to prove that Mycenae was indeed the city of Agamemnon. In fact Schliemann discovered the tombs of kings who reigned some four hundred years or more before the popular date for the fall of Troy (1184 BC), and in so doing revealed a splendid civilization, the background and basis of later stories of the heroic age (see HEROES and HOMER 4). The term 'Mycenaean civilization' is now applied to late Bronze Age culture (c.1600–c.1125 BC) in Greece and the Greek islands (with the exception of *Crete). Apart from Mycenae itself, the major cities of the time included Thebes, Orchomenus, Pylos, and Tiryns. Building (notably of fortifications) in these and other places was often on an extremely ambitious scale. The most distinctive building-type was the beehive-shaped tomb (*tholos*), the most famous example of which is the 'Treasury of Atreus' (c.1300 BC) in Mycenae; its dome remained the largest in the world until the Pantheon in Rome was built some 1400 years later. The treasures in gold and other precious materials discovered by Schliemann and later excavators bear witness to the wealth of the civilization. There was considerable influence from the Minoan civilization of Crete, indeed Mycenaean jewellery is often indistinguishable from Minoan work of the same period. The end of Mycenaean civilization poses many problems. It has been suggested that the destruction of Troy c.1250 is the reality behind Homer's *Iliad* and the myth of the Trojan War, and that the siege of Troy by the Greeks under Agamemnon, king of Mycenae, was the last united effort of the Mycenaean Greek world. In about 1200

BC Mycenae, Pylos, and other cities in southern Greece were burned. The period c.1200–1125 is one of upheaval, destruction, and decline. Some attempt at recovery was cut short by the final destruction of the large citadels of Mycenae and Tiryns c.1125, perhaps by a wave of Dorian invaders (see DORIAN INVASION). Some areas, notably Attica, seem not to have suffered at the hands of invaders, and their prosperity received no sudden check; but eventually they too declined into the *Dark Age.

My'rmidons, see AEACUS.

Mȳron, of Eleutherae in Attica, one of the most celebrated early classical sculptors of Greece, active c.480–440 BC and thus an older contemporary of Pheidias and Polycleitus. He is now best known for the Discobolus ('discus-thrower'), preserved in several copies. In antiquity, however, his most famous work was the bronze cow that stood in Athens, probably in the market-place, and is celebrated by no fewer than 36 epigrams in the Greek Anthology. It eventually found its way to Rome, where it was still to be seen in the sixth century.

Myrrha (or Smyrna), see ADONIS and ZMYRNA.

My'rsilus. 1. Name by which Candaulēs, king of Lydia, was known among the Greeks; see GYGES.

2. Tyrant of Mytilenē; see ALCAEUS.

My'rtilus, charioteer of Oenomaus; see PELOPS.

Myrtis, Boeotian poetess, said to have been the teacher of *Corinna and Pindar. In a surviving fragment from one of her poems Corinna reproves her for competing with the far more brilliant Pindar. Apart from the summary Plutarch gives of one of her poems, nothing of her work survives.

mysteries, mystery religions. These were secret forms of worship, in contrast with the very public nature of most Greek and Roman religious observances, and available only to individuals who had been specially initiated (Gk. *myein*, to initiate; *mystēs*, an initiate; *mysteria*, the whole proceedings; Lat. *initia*). Their common element seems to be a guarantee

mythology

360

that the initiate will enjoy a happy existence in another world after death; but if the chance of initiation is let slip in this life it cannot be retrieved in the afterlife. Initiation involved the revelation of secrets; it was often open to all, women and non-citizens included. Many mystery-cults are known to have existed in Greece; the best-known, those of *Demeter and Persephonē at *Eleusis (some 20 km., or 12 miles, from Athens), are more extensively documented throughout their thousand-year history than any other Greek cult, from the earliest testimony in the Homeric Hymn to Demeter to the suppression of the cult by the Roman emperor Theodosius in AD 393. Three years later the sanctuary at Eleusis, which had been a sacred site since Mycenaean times, was destroyed by Alaric and the Visigoths. Most, but not all, Athenians seem to have been initiated.

The Eleusinian mysteries were celebrated in the month Boedromion (September–October), at the time of sowing. The priest opened the festival by declaring that those should keep away who 'are not of pure hands and speak an incomprehensible tongue', i.e. murderers and *barbarians. Those participating, having gathered at Athens, bathed in the sea for purification, and then each sacrificed a piglet. After the initiation ceremony for new initiates in the *Eleusinion above the agora, the sacred and secret objects, which had been brought a few days earlier by *epheboi from Eleusis to Athens and placed in the Eleusinion, were taken back to Eleusis in a great procession of initiates along the *Sacred Way. The ritual re-enacted in part the myth of Demeter and Persephone. The rhythmic shout of *Iakch' o Iakche* (see IACCHUS) was also regularly raised during the procession; it was regarded by many as referring to the god Dionysus. In the Telesterion ('hall of initiation') at Eleusis, built to hold several thousand people, the initiating priest showed the sacred objects to the initiated. The details are not known: it appears that after the hall had been in darkness for some time, a bright light suddenly shone, the birth of a divine child (his identity uncertain) was announced,

and gloom gave way to general rejoicing. Demeter and Korē ('daughter', i.e. Persephone), Iacchus-Dionysus, Pluto, and Triptolemus, the mythical hero of agriculture, all had their role. The Eleusinian mysteries claimed to take away the terror of death by guaranteeing to initiates a happy afterlife.

Bacchic mysteries, *orgia*, associated with *Bacchus (Dionysus) are also very ancient in Greece, although direct evidence is available only for the later periods. They seem not to have been associated with particular cult-sites but appeared wherever adherents might be found, who were mainly but not entirely, it would seem, women (Herodotus has a story of the Scythian king being initiated, and Euripides in the *Bacchae* has the aged king Cadmus and the seer Teiresias joining in the rites). Liberation and surrender to Bacchic frenzy in order to achieve a sense of freedom and well-being seem to have been the aim of the Bacchic mysteries, but initiates were also given promises about the afterlife. Other mysteries were associated with the name of *Orpheus over which Plato in the *Phaedrus* has Dionysus preside, and which were apparently performed according to the writings of Orpheus. They too aimed to free from guilt and give better hopes for the afterlife to those who practised their rites, and were based on the myth of *Dionysus Zagreus.

mythology. The term 'mythology' is used to denote either the study of myths or, loosely, myths themselves. Myths are traditional tales, and they have become so because they possess some significance or enduring quality. When stories of this general kind are based on some great historical or purportedly historical event (the Siege of Troy, the Return of the Children of Heracles) they are often described as saga. On the other hand, when they are short narratives which are fictional but attached to a real person or place and given a fairly realistic setting, as for example the stories of the early kings of Rome, they may be termed legends. Myths of these two kinds constituted all the Greeks knew of their early history, and pervaded all aspects of Greek life. A third variety of myth is folk-tales, simple narratives of adventure, often containing elements of ingenious trickery and of magic, perhaps involving superhuman creatures, e.g. monsters and giants; they are characterized by recurring features of character and plot, lost sons seeking their rightful inheritance, princes slaying monsters to win princesses; the stories of *Perseus contain many such. Myth can include any of the features of saga, legend, or folktale, but its particular characteristic is that it is a serious story about the gods (and in Greece about *heroes too) and their relations with one another and with men and women.

There is no touchstone to enable one kind of myth to be clearly distinguished from another, nor can the characteristics of myth be isolated: the same elements may occur in all types, and a given narrative may be categorized differently by different critics. There are myths which explain the origin of the earth, natural phenomena, human (and animal) behaviour, religious practices (see MYSTERIES, concerning the myth of Demeter and Persephonē), and human institutions in general. Another feature of mythical narrative is its fluidity, admitting of endless variations on its general storyline (see HELEN). But Greek myths in general, as we meet them in poetry from Homer to Attic tragedy and beyond, are stories of some complexity and subtlety, and they are the form in which the poets choose to express their ideas. A striking thing about Greek myth is the importance attached to it by the Greeks up to the end of the fifth century. But in the course of that century, the medium for serious thought came to be prose. Out of the mythical genealogies of gods and heroes arose the concept of history (see HISTORIOGRAPHY 1); similarly, the cosmological myths shaped the speculations that led eventually to the rise of science and philosophy (see PHILOSOPHY 1). Both history and philosophy were written in prose. Myth continued to be of

significance in poetry and art as long as it was of religious importance for cult and ritual, but as Greece moved into the *Hellenistic age it became more of a decorative element and less intellectually and emotionally charged.

It is noteworthy that many of the principal Greek myths are connected with *Mycenaean centres, e.g. the stories of Perseus and Atreus with Mycenae itself, that of Oedipus with Thebes, that of Heracles with Thebes and Tiryns, a fact which suggests that the stories are of great antiquity. The sources of our knowledge of Greek myths are in the first place Homer and Hesiod, then the classical Greek poets, in particular Pindar and the dramatists. Further material is provided by the Hellenistic poets, notably Callimachus, and by compilers such as Diodorus Siculus and the author of the *Bibliothēkē* attributed to Apollodorus; also by the Roman poets, especially Ovid. Finally the scholiasts, in their commentaries on the classical authors, frequently furnish mythological information. Naturally the stories drawn from these various sources do not always agree, local traditions and the fancies of the narrators being freely incorporated.

Roman and Italian myths which antedate contact with Greek literature can hardly be said to exist. That of *Romulus is the best-known (see also CACUS). The old Italian gods are vague personalities, and barely anthropomorphic; they are not actuated by human motives, they do not marry or fight or have love affairs with mortals. The myths that the Roman poets and antiquarians attached to them were borrowed from Greece (e.g. by the process of identifying Roman deities with Greek), or invented, largely under Greek influence. Such native Italian traditions as there were have been lost or, where they survive, lack imaginative richness: imagination comes into play only to explain some old custom, ritual, or name.

Mytilē'nē or Mitylene, see LESBOS.

N

nae'niae or **neniae**, at Rome, funeral poems or songs sung by female relatives of the deceased or by hired singers. They gave place in later times to funeral orations.

Nae'vius, Gnaeus (*c.*270–190s BC), Roman tragic and comic dramatist and epic poet from Campania. He fought in the First Punic War (264–241 BC), and started producing his own plays in 235. As well as writing tragedies on themes taken from Greek originals he wrote on subjects drawn from Roman history, *fabulae *praetextae*, and was the first Roman to do so. Of these, very few fragments or titles survive. However, it seems to have been in comedy that he excelled; again, the surviving fragments are very scanty, but some thirty titles are known. These seem to have been based on models from Greek New Comedy, *fabulae *palliatae*, but it is possible that Naevius also wrote comedies with an Italian setting, *fabulae *togatae*. His outspokenness offended the powerful family of the *Metelli: one line in particular became notorious (written in iambics, the metre of spoken drama, and so presumably delivered in a play), *fato Metelli Romae fiunt consules* ('by fate the Metelli become consuls at Rome') implying lack of ability. Naevius may have gone into exile as a consequence; he is said to have died at Utica in North Africa. He is supposed to have composed his own epitaph, claiming that the Latin language died with him. It is quoted by Aulus Gellius (I. 24. 2.) but may not be authentic. His most important work, written in old age, was the epic *Bellum Punicum* ('Punic War'), written in saturnian metre (see METRE, LATIN I) and later divided into seven books. Only about sixty lines survive; the work seems to have contained mythological digressions, including descriptions of the departure of Aeneas from Troy, the founding of Rome, and perhaps that of Carthage also. In certain respects the poem was an influence on Virgil's *Aeneid*.

nai'ads (naiadēs), *nymphs of springs, rivers, and lakes.

names, personal
1. *Greek.* One personal name only was the rule, given at birth for men and women alike; women did not change their name upon marriage. There was a very wide variety of names, many of which were compounds of two common nouns with a flattering meaning; Megaclēs, for example, means 'of great fame'. Others incorporated the name of a god, e.g. Apollodorus, 'gift of Apollo', or reflected personal characteristics (Plato, 'broad-shouldered'), or circumstances (Didymus, 'a twin'). Choice of name was entirely free, although it was quite customary for the eldest son to be named after his paternal grandfather. In Homer it is common for a hero to be called on occasions not by his own name but by a form of his father's name, his 'patronymic': thus Agamemnon is sometimes called Atreidēs, meaning 'son of Atreus'. By classical times the patronymic had ceased to be used in its original sense; a name in patronymic form, e.g. Miltiadēs, was sometimes chosen as an ordinary personal name; occasionally a patronymic was added to indicate the subject's *genos (clan); for example, someone called additionally 'Philaidēs' would belong to the *genos* of the Philaidae, the descendants of Philaios. If an additional name was necessary to aid identification, the father's name was added in the genitive case: thus 'Cimon, (son) of Miltiades'. In some contexts indication of the person's *deme is added, in adjectival form: thus 'Cimon, (son) of Miltiades, Lakiadēs (from the deme of Lakiadai), or Periclēs, (son) of Xanthippus, Cholargeus (from the deme of Cholargos)'. These additional names were not used as a form of address. It is the practice of the historians Herodotus and Thucydides to identify a

person by adding the father's name; in Aristophanes' comedies, on the other hand, characters introduce themselves by name and deme, and this is usually the practice in the fourth-century orators.

2. *Roman.* Among the Italian peoples, including the Etruscans, every man and woman had two basic names, the *praenōmen*, 'forename' or personal name, of which there were relatively few, and (more importantly) the *nōmen*, the 'name' of the **gens* or clan. In addition they usually had a *cognōmen* (see below). The *praenomen* was commonly written in abbreviated form as follows:

A.	Aulus
Ap(p).	Appius
C.	Gaius (see ALPHABET 2)
Cn.	Gnaeus (see ALPHABET 2)
D.	Decimus
L.	Lūcius
M.	Marcus
M'.	Mānius
N.	Numerius
P.	Publius
Q.	Quintus
Ser.	Servius
Sex.	Sextus
Sp.	Spurius
T.	Tītus
Ti.	Tiberius

For Roman women, at least in the upper classes, the *praenomen* was virtually abandoned, and they were usually known by the feminine form of their *nomen* or clan name, e.g. 'Cornelia', 'Claudia'. A person's *nomen* was of course the same as that of the (legal) father; women did not change their name upon marriage. The *nomen* very often ends in *-ius* (Cornelius, Claudius); the (masculine) endings *-a*, *-as*, *-anus*, and *-enus* are characteristic of names from the north of Italy.

The *cognomen* was an extra personal name added after the *nomen*, and functioned originally rather like a nickname, indicative of the bearer's personal characteristic: Rūfus ('red-head'), Brutus ('idiot'), Nāso ('big-nose'), Pictor ('painter'), Scipio ('stick', originally given to a Cornelius who acted as a 'stick' to his blind father). Often, as in the case of Scipio, the *cognomen* was also handed down from father to son, and thus came to designate a sub-division within the

clan, a family. Some clans, even distinguished ones such as that of the Antonii, admitted *cognomina* only rarely (Mark Antony, for example, had no other name; and compare C. *Marius, whose lack of *cognomen* has sometimes been attributed to alleged humble origins). Further *cognomina* (sometimes called *agnomina*; sing. *agnomen*) could be added: thus the Cornelii Scipiones Nasicae were a subdivision of the Cornelii Scipiones.

An adopted son took his adoptive father's names but might add as *cognomen* the adjectival form of his own original *nomen*: thus the elder son of L. Aemilius *Paullus, when adopted by P. Scipio, became P. Scipio Aemilianus; C. Octavius, when adopted by C. Julius Caesar, became C. Julius Caesar Octavianus (Octavian). Slaves were usually called by their own (single) name. Freedmen took their original owner's *praenomen* and *nomen*, adding their own (slave) name as a *cognomen*: thus Cicero's faithful slave *Tiro became M. Tullius Tiro.

In informal surroundings a man might be addressed intimately by his *praenomen*; by friends he might be called by his *nomen* or his *cognomen* alone. In formal circumstances he was addressed by *praenomen* and *nomen* (and perhaps *cognomen* as well).

Under the empire, with the use of a plurality of names and reversal of the usual order, the system broke down, and there was eventually a reversion to the ancient use of a single name.

Nanno, see MIMNERMUS.

Na'rbonese Gaul, see GAUL.

Narci'ssus. 1. In Greek myth, a beautiful youth, son of the Boeotian river god *Cephisus and the nymph Līriopē. The nymph *Echo fell in love with him, but was rejected. Aphroditē punished him for his cruelty by making him fall in love with his own image reflected in water. His fruitless attempts to approach his beautiful reflection led to his despair and he wasted away until he died. The gods changed him into the flower that bears his name.

2. Freedman and private secretary to

the emperor Claudius (d. AD 54), who exercised great political influence and gained enormous wealth. He did not favour Claudius' marriage to Agrippina (mother of Nero), and after the emperor's death and the succession of Nero he was arrested and compelled to commit suicide. See also MESSALINA.

Nāso, *cognomen* of the Roman poet *Ovid, by which he always refers to himself. It is derived from *nasus*, 'nose', and probably means 'big nose'.

Naturā'lēs Quaestiōnēs, see SENECA (2) 3.

Naturā'lis Histo'ria, see PLINY THE ELDER.

Nau'cratis, Greek town in the Delta of Egypt, about 50 km. (30 miles) from the sea on the Canopic (western) branch of the Nile. Naucratis was the principal port of Egypt until the foundation of Alexandria in 332 BC by Alexander the Great. It was famous for its prostitutes, who included *Rhodopis, Doricha, with whom Sappho's brother Charaxus fell in love when he travelled there on business, and a certain Archedicē, said by Herodotus to be 'known by song the length and breadth of Greece'. It was the birthplace of Athenaeus and Julius Pollux.

nauma'chiae, mimic 'sea-fights', held as a popular spectacle at Rome in the flooded arena of an amphitheatre, or in specially constructed lakes, also known as *naumachiae*. The first display of this kind was given by Julius Caesar on an artificial lake in the Campus Martius in 46 BC, and simulated a sea-battle between Tyrians and Egyptians. The emperor Augustus constructed a lake in 2 BC on the right bank of the Tiber, and performed a re-enactment of the battle of Salamis, cited by Ovid in the *Ars amatoria* as a good occasion for meeting girls. Prisoners of war and condemned criminals did the fighting, often to the death unless spared by the emperor.

Nau'plius, in Greek myth, an Argonaut, and the father of *Palamedēs. The town of Nauplia was named after his ancestor, another Nauplius, son of the god Poseidon and *Amymonē.

Nausi'căa or **Nausică'a,** in Homer's *Odyssey* (book 6) the daughter of the Phaeacian king, Alcinŏus. On the night of Odysseus' shipwreck, the goddess Athena, appearing to her in a dream, tells her to go down to the river-mouth next day and do the household washing. This she does, with her maids, and they all play ball. Odysseus, woken by their cries, emerges from some bushes, frightening away the maids. Nausicaa receives him with dignity and offers to show him the way to the city, requesting him to walk the last part alone, so as to avoid giving rise to gossip. The hero is then entertained and sent on his way by Alcinous, who, like Nausicaa herself, had rather hoped that Odysseus might prove a suitable bridegroom. This is one of the most charming and touching episodes in the *Odyssey*. It was dramatized in the lost *Nausicaa* of Sophocles. The English writer Samuel Butler (1835–1902) believed that Nausicaa was a self-portrait by the authoress, as he supposed, of the *Odyssey*.

Naval Boards (*symmoriai*), **On the** (or, *On the Taxation Groups*), political speech by Demosthenes. See LITURGY and DEMOSTHENES (2) 3.

Nea'rchus, of Crete, friend of *Alexander the Great (see 7 and 8). Nearchus wrote an account of his voyage along the coast from the mouth of the river Indus to the Persian Gulf, of which only fragments survive. See ONESICRITUS.

nectar, see AMBROSIA.

Necyomanti'a (*Nekyomanteia*), see LUCIAN.

Nēleus, in Greek myth, a son of the god Poseidon and *Tyro, and king of Pylos (see MESSENIA). He married Chloris, the only daughter of *Niobē to survive. *Heracles, after he had killed Iphitus, sought purification from Neleus, who refused it. Thereupon Heracles killed him and all his sons except *Nestor.

Nĕ'mĕan games, athletic festival held every two years (probably from 573 BC) in the sanctuary of Zeus at Nemea in Argolis.

Nĕ'mĕan Lion, see HERACLES, LABOURS OF 1.

Nemesiā'nus (Marcus Aurelius Olympius Nemesianus), North African Latin poet of the third century AD, author of four pastoral poems in hexameters, long ascribed to *Calpurnius Siculus, by whom, as well as by Virgil, he was strongly influenced. He also wrote *Cynegetica*, a hunting manual in verse which breaks off after 325 lines, at the beginning of the hunt.

Ne'mesis, in Greek myth, a daughter of *Nyx (Night) and the personification of righteous anger, especially that of the gods at human presumption. According to some versions she and not Leda was loved by Zeus and laid the egg out of which Helen (of Troy) was hatched. She provides one of the rare instances where an apparent personification of an abstract quality is the object of an ancient cult. She was worshipped at Rhamnus in Attica, where a magnificent temple was built for her in the fifth century BC.

nē'niae, see NAENIAE.

Neobu'lē, see ARCHILOCHUS.

Neopla'tonism, the dominant philosophy of the ancient pagan world from the time of *Plotinus, mid-third century AD, to the closing of the schools of philosophy at Athens (because they were pagan) by the Christian emperor Justinian in AD 529. It exerted a strong influence on medieval and Renaissance thought. Plotinus is the greatest philosopher of Neoplatonism and is usually considered to be its founder, but there is much that foreshadows his thought in the philosophy of Antiochus of Ascalon (d. c.68 BC; see ACADEMY), *Posidonius (d. c.50 BC), *Philo the Jew (d. AD 45), and others nearer to Plotinus' own time. They all aimed at a comprehensive Greek philosophy, one that incorporated into Platonism the best of Aristotle, Pythagoras, and the Stoics, so as to make a synthesis of the collected wisdom of the ancient world. But Neoplatonism was not only a philosophy; it also met a religious need by showing how the individual soul might reach God. Thus it presented with traditional Greek rationalism a scheme of salvation comparable with those schemes offered by Christianity and the *mystery religions. No one before Plotinus could either achieve the desired philosophical synthesis or convey as he did the inner mystical experience of the merging of the self into some larger life. After Plotinus and his pupil *Porphyry the next notable Neoplatonist was the early fourth-century Syrian *Iamblichus. He introduced into Neoplatonism the idea that the unity of the soul with the One could be achieved not by a man's own mystical efforts but by acts of magic correctly performed and by the power of symbols comprehensible only to the gods. The intellectual content of Plotinus' brand of mysticism was thus rejected.

During the fourth century Neoplatonism became the favoured pagan creed; Latin Neoplatonists included *Macrobius. It also began to influence Christian thinkers, notably Augustine. It was widely taught, but its intellectual centres were Athens and Alexandria. In the latter school the mathematician *Hypatia and her pupil Synesius of Cyrene (c. AD 370–413) were both Neoplatonists. Synesius was a poet and orator rather than a thinker; he has left a collection of hymns and letters and a discourse entitled *Diōn*, a defence of learning and the cultivated life both against extreme forms of Christian asceticism and against the superstitious theurgy of the pagans. Nevertheless his Neoplatonism took the form also of an interest in the occult. In 410 he became bishop of Ptolemais in Libya somewhat reluctantly, not wishing to relinquish his wife, his country pursuits, and his philosophical beliefs, or to profess doctrines which seemed to him more symbolic than actual. The last important Neoplatonist at Athens was *Proclus (AD 411–85), born at Constantinople. Many of the later Neoplatonists carried metaphysical speculation into the realm of fantasy, mingling magic with eastern superstitions. Demonology in particular was highly developed by them, and a complete hierarchy was devised of good and evil demons who were thought to pervade the universe and were the object of semi-religious, semi-magical rites. The teaching of Neoplatonism, ended at Athens by Justinian in 529, continued at Alexandria until the end of the sixth century.

Proclus' writings survived to influence early medieval thought by virtue of being reworked and Christianized soon after his death by someone unknown, who aimed to achieve a synthesis of Neoplatonism and Christian dogma. They were then promulgated under the name of 'Dionysius the Areopagite', who four centuries earlier had been a convert of the apostle Paul (see Acts 17: 34). Although their authenticity was challenged by some, in general they were accepted as the work of Dionysius and the texts commented upon by a succession of eminent theologians. They were translated into Latin by Erigena in the ninth century and became one of the bases of medieval theology, second only to the writings of St Augustine. Their authenticity was not finally disproved until the nineteenth century.

Neoplatonism itself was revived by the Byzantine scholar Psellus in the eleventh century and taken up by some humanists at the time of the Renaissance.

Neopto'lemus, in Greek myth also named Pyrrhus ('red-haired'), son of *Achilles and Dēidamīa. Odysseus was sent as messenger to summon him to the siege of Troy from Scyros after his father's death because his presence was one of the conditions necessary for taking the city. He went also with Odysseus to bring *Philoctētēs to the siege; he was one of the warriors concealed in the Trojan Horse, and it was he who killed the Trojan king Priam, in some versions incurring the wrath of Apollo thereby (and as a consequence being himself killed later, by attendant priests at Delphi). He also killed the Trojan princess Polyxena at the tomb of his father Achilles. His prizes from the sack of Troy were Andromachē, widow of Hector, and Helenus, the latter's brother. In Homer Neoptolemus returned home safely, and Menelaus sent his own daughter Hermionē to marry him. There was another tradition which said Neoptolemus accompanied by Andromache went to Epirus to rule over the Molossians. The kings of Epirus claimed descent from him and were often named after him (see PYRRHUS). In the *Andromache* of Euripides, Neoptolemus

marries Hermione but is murdered by Orestēs, who carries off his widow.

neoterics (*neoterikos*, 'modern'), Greek term often used to describe the 'modern school' of poets at Rome, in imitation of Cicero, who, writing in 50 BC, called them sarcastically in Greek *hoi neōteroi* ('the young ones'); elsewhere he referred to them as *novi poetae*, 'new poets'. Of their writings only the poems of *Catullus survive. They avoided epic and drama as old-fashioned, and turned for their models to *Callimachus and the Hellenistic Greek poets (see EUPHORION), aiming at perfection in miniature, and experimenting with new metres (see METRE, GREEK 3), different kinds of language, new words (often Greek), new themes (romantic, exotic, some bizarre), and a mannered style. Apart from Catullus the neoterics included *Calvus, *Cinna, Bibaculus, and Cornificius. Virgil felt their influence but their style lived on chiefly in the works of the elegiac poets Cornelius Gallus, Tibullus, Propertius, and Ovid.

Nēpos, Cornēlius (*c.*100–*c.*25 BC), Roman biographer; his *praenomen* is unknown. He was a native of Cisalpine Gaul like Catullus who dedicated his book of poems to Nepos (see CATULLUS, poem 1), with a touch of irony at the expense of the latter's 'laborious and learned' universal history in three books, *Chronica* (which has not survived). Nepos was also a friend of Cicero and, more especially, *Atticus. His writings included love poems, a book of anecdotes and other information (*Exempla*), and a series of 'Lives of Famous Men', *De viris illustribus*, in at least sixteen books, of which one survives on foreign generals (nineteen of them Greek). The Lives include Themistoclēs, Miltiadēs, Epaminondas, Pausanias, Hannibal, Hamilcar, and Datamēs the Persian. They are biographical sketches designed to eulogize their subjects and point a moral rather than relate the historical events of their lives. From a historical point of view they are marked by many inaccuracies and omissions and by lack of proportion (the battle of Leuctra, for example, is barely mentioned in the biography of Epaminondas). Of the Greek

Lives the most interesting character portrayal is that of Alcibiadēs. There also survive a short Life of the elder Cato, and a longer one of Atticus, of whom Nepos can speak with intimate knowledge, and whose stance of political neutrality Nepos understood and shared. Both of these Lives show greater talent.

Neptune (Neptūnus), ancient Italian god of water, of whom in his original form hardly anything is known. He was worshipped at the festival of the Neptunālia on 23 July; of the ritual it is known only that arbours of foliage were erected, and the object may have been to obtain sufficient water at this hot and dry time of year. Under Greek influence he became a sea-god and was identified with *Poseidon. Owing to Poseidon's connection with horses, and because horses were associated with the Roman god *Consus, the latter was identified with Neptune.

Nē'reïds, see NEREUS below.

Nēreus, in Greek myth, a sea-god, represented as very old, son of Pontus, husband of the Oceanid Doris, and father of the Nereids, the sea-maidens. He is praised by Hesiod and Pindar for his benevolent justice, and like other 'old men of the sea' he had great wisdom and the gift of prophecy (see HERACLES, LABOURS OF 11), and could transform himself into various shapes (compare PROTEUS). Two of the Nereids were famous, Thetis (see PELEUS) and *Galatea.

Nēro (AD 37–68), Roman emperor 54–68, son of Cn. Domitius *Ahenobarbus and *Agrippina (3), who was later the fourth wife of the emperor *Claudius; the latter adopted Nero as son and heir. Originally named Lucius Domitius Ahenobarbus, he assumed on his adoption the name of Nero, a *cognomen* in the Claudian *gens* (see NAMES) first held by a son of Appius *Claudius Caecus the Censor, from whom the emperor was descended. It is said to be a Sabine word meaning 'brave and energetic'. He was only 16 when he succeeded in 54 and the first five years of his reign ran smoothly under the guidance of his mother and his old tutor *Seneca the Younger. In 59, however, he had his mother Agrippina murdered, his wife Octavia suffering the

same fate in 62 to facilitate his marriage to his mistress Poppaea Sabina, and his reign swiftly degenerated. In 64 half of Rome was destroyed in a disastrous fire; Nero took advantage of the ruin of his own house to build himself a magnificent palace, the Domus Aurea (*Golden House), and it was rumoured (probably unjustly) that the fire had been started on his orders. Nero made the Christians the scapegoats and they were savagely persecuted (according to tradition St Peter and St Paul suffered martyrdom at this time). Nero's devotion to the arts was another source of extravagance and scandal (his own participation in musical and dramatic competitions outraged the senatorial classes). In 65 a plot against his life was discovered and many distinguished men were executed or forced to commit suicide, among them *Piso (2), the leader of the conspiracy, Seneca, and the poet Lucan. In 68 revolts began in the provinces, and when the praetorian guard deserted, Nero fled Rome and committed suicide. His last words are reputed to have been, *qualis artifex pereo!* ('What an artist dies in me!'). Suetonius describes him as having pleasant features but a spotty complexion, yellow hair, spindly legs, and a prominent belly, and as being careless of his appearance.

Nerva, Marcus Cocce'ius (AD 30?–98), Roman emperor AD 96–8. He had come to the fore while aiding Nero in the suppression of the Pisonian conspiracy in 65 (see PISO). Nero also admired his verse composition. He was chosen by the emperor Vespasian as his colleague in the consulship of 71, and was similarly the colleague of the emperor Domitian in 90. After the latter's assassination in 96 the senate chose Nerva as emperor. In his short reign he avoided serious problems, propitiating the army by the adoption of Trajan as heir.

Nessus, see HERACLES.

Nestor, in Greek myth, son of *Neleus and king of Pylos. He lived to a great age, and in Homer's *Iliad* is represented as having outlived two generations, while retaining considerable mental and physical vigour. He fulfils the role of an elder statesman, full of long-winded advice and inclined to be anecdotal. In the *Odyssey* he is shown as having returned safely from Troy to Pylos, where he entertains Odysseus' son Telemachus. For the death of his son see ANTILOCHUS. The Mycenaean vase of beaten gold known as the 'cup of Nestor' (Nat. Mus. Athens) is so called because it resembles (in simpler form) the great gold cup, brought by Nestor from Pylos, described in *Iliad* 11.

Nica'nder (Nikandros), of Colophōn (an Ionian Greek city in Asia Minor), Hellenistic Greek didactic poet of the second century BC, of whose numerous works there survive only the hexameter poems the *Theriaca* ('on poisonous animals') and the *Alexipharmaca* ('antidotes to poison'). He also wrote the *Georgica*, on farming, which had some influence on Virgil, and a mythological poem which apparently influenced Ovid when the latter composed the *Metamorphosēs*. His poems are not inspired but contain some interesting and out-of-the-way pieces of folklore.

Ni'cias (*c*.470–413 BC), Athenian politician and general admired by his contemporaries, including Thucydides, for his virtuous and upright life. After the death of Periclēs at the beginning of the *Peloponnesian War, he became one of the political leaders at Athens in opposition to Cleon; his opinions were moderate and he aimed for peace with Sparta as soon as possible. He was largely responsible for the Peace of 421 that bears his name, by which the war was for a short time suspended. Despite his disapproval of the ambitious *Sicilian Expedition, he was appointed one of its generals, with Lamachus and Alcibiadēs, in 415. Its disastrous outcome may have been largely the result of his irresolute leadership.

Nīco'machus, son of *Aristotle; according to an ancient source, Aristotle dedicated to him the *Ethics* that bear his name (see 4 (iv)), but the name may be owing to his having edited the work.

Night, see NYX.

Nigrī'nus, see LUCIAN.

Nīkē, in Greek religion, the (female) personification of victory. She became especially popular after the Persian Wars,

the Athenians dedicating a statue to her at Delphi after the victory against the Persians at Salamis (480 BC). She was often depicted with wings.

Nī'obē, in Greek myth, daughter of *Tantalus and wife of Amphion, mother of six (or seven) children. She boasted of her superiority to the goddess *Leto, who had only two children, Apollo and Artemis. Thereupon Apollo and Artemis killed all Niobe's sons and daughters with their arrows. Niobe wept for them until turned into a column of stone on Mount Sipylus in Lydia (visited by the Greek traveller Pausanias in the second century AD, and still to be seen).

Nīsus, in Greek myth, son of Pandion and king of Megara, whose life and his city's safety depended on a lock of red hair on his head. His daughter *Scylla cut it off and Nisus was turned into a osprey. The port of Nisaea was named after him. Megareus, the husband of Nisus' daughter Iphinoē, gave his name to the city.

Nīsus and Eury'alus, in Virgil's *Aeneid*, devoted friends and companions of Aeneas, who figure in the foot-race in book 5. They are killed in a sortie from the Trojan camp in Italy.

nō'bilēs, 'nobles', i.e. the 'well-known'; at Rome, those families, whether *patrician or *plebeian, whose members had held *curule magistracies (later, the consulship only), and were therefore allowed to have images (*imaginēs*) of their ancestors. They enjoyed high status. At all times it was possible, though rare, for a man not of a noble nor even of a senatorial family to achieve the consulship, usually with the backing of noble families; if he succeeded he was known as a *novus homo*, 'new man', 'recruit'.

Noctēs A'tticae, see GELLIUS.

nome (*nomos*), in Greek music, originally 'tune', 'melody'; the word was applied especially to a type of melody invented, it was said, by *Terpander as a setting for texts taken from epic poetry, which could be played on the flute or on the lyre. In the late fifth century BC it was applied to a kind of choral lyric poetry approximating to the *dithyramb, composed astrophically (see STROPHE), like *Timotheus' Persae.

nōmen, cognō'men, etc., see NAMES.

Nōme'ntum (Mentana), in Italy, town on the edge of the Sabine hills 23 km. (14 miles) north-east of Rome, with which it was connected by the Via Nōmentāna, the latter crossing the river Anio by a bridge which still stands. There Atticus had a farm, Seneca a country house, and Martial a cottage. Martial told a friend he went there because the noise in Rome made sleep impossible.

Nōna, see FATES.

Nō'nius Marce'llus, a Numidian of the first half of the fourth century AD who, during the reign of the emperor Constantine, wrote in Latin an encyclopaedia in twenty books for his son, *De compendiosa doctrina* ('handbook of instruction'), of which book 16 is lost. The first twelve books deal with the diction and grammar of the older Latin writers, and the later books with their subject-matter. For many fragments of early writers, Varro and Lucilius especially, Nonius is the main source.

Nonnus (fifth century AD), from Panopolis in Egypt, the author of a Greek epic poem *Dionysiaca*, in forty-eight books, on the adventures of the god Dionysus, of which books 13–48 deal with his expedition against the Indians. Nonnus' metrically strict style is of interest to metricians. The poem contains a large fund of mythological learning.

Nostoi ('returns'), lost poem of the *Epic Cycle dealing with the adventures of various heroes on their return from the Trojan War.

Notus (Gk. Notos, Lat. Auster), the south wind; see WINDS.

novel, romantic narrative in rhetorical prose.

1. *Greek.* Five complete novels survive (together with two summaries and a number of papyrus fragments): *Leucippē and Cleitophon* by Achilles Tatius; *Chaereas and Callirrhoē* by Chariton; *Aethiopica* or *Theagenēs and Chariclea* by Heliodorus; *Daphnis and Chloē* by Longus; and *Habrocomēs and Antheia* by Xenophon of Ephesus. The novel as a literary genre

seems to have developed in the Hellenistic age, but flourished especially from the second century AD onwards. It was poor in characterization but strong in plot, characteristic themes being the separation of two lovers, hair-breadth escapes from a series of appalling perils and adversities, and final reunion and a happy ending. The best known of the novels is *Daphnis and Chloe* (mid-third century AD) by Longus (about whom nothing is known), a charming pastoral romance in which adventures give way to descriptions of sentiment and scenery. The innocent lovers were the inspiration for Bernardin de Saint-Pierre's novel *Paul et Virginie* (1787). The *Aethiopica* of Heliodorus is the story of Chariclea, a priestess of Delphi, with whom Theagenes, a Thessalian, falls in love. He carries her off to Egypt. After a long series of adventures Chariclea is on the point of being sacrificed to the gods in Ethiopia when she is recognized as being the daughter of the king, and the lovers are then happily married.

2. *Latin.* The *Satyricon* of *Petronius is the first Latin work that can properly be called a novel; enough survives to show that it contained a continuous narrative of considerable length. It is itself partly a parody of romantic novels. In about the middle of the second century AD appeared *Apuleius' *Metamorphosēs* (also known as 'The Golden Ass'), a series of tales attached to the hero's adventures in the form of an ass. This novel has a surprising and serious ending in the description of the hero's initiation into the *mysteries. Apart from these two great works very little is known about the Latin novel. The anonymous *History of Apollonius, King of Tyre*, may have been written originally in Greek in the third century AD; in about the sixth century it was translated into Latin and given a Christian slant. It is the ultimate source of Shakespeare's *Pericles*.

novels (*novellae*), see JUSTINIAN.

No'vius, see ATELLAN FARCES.

novus homo ('new man', 'recruit'), term used at Rome to describe the first man in a family to obtain a *curule magistracy, and in particular the consulship. See NOBILES.

Numa'ntia, an important town on the upper Douro in Spain, which resisted Rome with great success throughout much of the second century BC, finally falling after siege to Scipio Aemilianus in 133 BC. This event effectively ended Spanish resistance to Rome.

Numa Pompi'lius, in legendary Roman history, successor of Romulus as second king of Rome. He had, according to tradition, a long and peaceful reign (715-673 BC), regarded in later times as a sort of Golden Age, and to him the Romans attributed many of their religious institutions: festivals, sacrifices and other rites, the *pontifices*, the Vestal Virgins, and the Salii. Later legends say that he received counsel from the nymph *Egeria, and make him a disciple of the Greek philosopher and mystic *Pythagoras (in defiance of chronology) to account for similarities between early Roman religion and Greek cults in south Italy (where Pythagoras lived). Most of the reforms attributed to him were probably the result of a long process of cultural development and religious change.

numbers

1. *Greek.* The Greek names for the numbers 1 to 10 are: *hēis, duo, trēis, tessarēs* (or *tettares*), *pentĕ, hex, hepta, octo, ennĕa, deka.* The system commonly found in papyri and manuscripts for writing numbers is based on the *alphabet and is as follows:

1–5	α–ε
6	ς (the minuscule, i.e. small-letter, version of the digamma)
7–9	ζ–θ
10–80 (by tens)	ι–π
90	ϙ (koppa, not in the Attic Greek alphabet)
100–800 (by hundreds)	ϱ–ω
900	ϡ (sampi. in the Carian alphabet, equivalent to σσ or ττ)

It is customary to add a stroke above the line when writing numbers up to 999, e.g. α′, β′, etc. Higher numbers are written as follows:

1,000–9,000 (by thousands)	͵α–͵θ
10,000	M

Multiples of 10,000 are indicated by writing the multiplier on top. Thus (e.g.):

$$21,527 \qquad \overset{\beta}{M},\alpha\phi\varkappa\zeta$$

(For Archimedes' system of expressing very large numbers see ARCHIMEDES.)

2. *Roman.* The Latin names for the numbers 1 to 10 are: *unus, duo, tres, quattuor, quinque, sex, septem, octo, novem, decem.* Roman numerical signs, originally special characters, gradually developed into letters of the alphabet as follows:
I = 1; V = 5; X = 10; L = 50; C = 100; D = 500; M = 1,000. Horizontal lines were often used to denote thousands; thus $\overline{V}$ = 5,000. A notation was constructed by conventions for adding or subtracting according to the following rule: when two figures stand side by side, if the right-hand figure is the larger, the left-hand figure is to be subtracted from it; if the left-hand figure is the larger, the right-hand figure is to be added: e.g. IX = 9; XI = 11; MCM = 1,900. When, as in this last example, a smaller numeral occurs between two larger, it is subtracted from the numeral on the right.

numen, in ancient Roman religion, divine power, a god; the word is derived from *nuĕrĕ* 'to nod' (a god is thought to nod to indicate his will).

Ny'cteus, see ANTIOPE.

nymphs (*nymphē*, 'maiden'), in Greek myth, female personifications of various natural objects, rivers, trees, mountains; they were vague beings, young and beautiful, fond of music and dancing, long-lived but not immortal, usually gentle, occasionally formidable. They possessed some divine gifts, such as that of prophecy. The nymphs of trees, especially oak trees, were called dryads (*drys*, originally 'tree', but commonly 'oak tree'). Hamadryads were tree-nymphs whose life depended on that of their tree. Nymphs of springs, rivers, and lakes were naiads; those of mountains oreads. Before the battle of Plataea against the

Persians (479 BC), the nymphs of Mount Cithaeron were among the deities to whom the Athenian commander Aristeidēs was told to pray by the Delphic Oracle.

Nyx, Night, in Greek myth, one of the earliest deities to come into existence, the child of *Chaos. Her children included Death (Thanatos), Sleep (*Hypnos), and the three *Fates.

O

o'belos, o'bolos (Lat. *obelus*). 1. At Athens, an obol, an iron spit, used also as currency in early times; from the sixth century BC a small silver coin of equivalent value, one-sixth of a drachma. An obol was also used as a small measure of weight; see MONEY AND COINS 1 and WEIGHTS AND MEASURES 1 (i).

2. Critical sign used in the annotation of texts by Alexandrian scholars of the Hellenistic age, a horizontal stroke in the left-hand margin, originally indicating a spurious line in Homer; see ZENODOTUS. The modern equivalent is the obelus, 'dagger'.

Oce'anus (Ocean), in Greek myth, a *Titan, son of Uranus (Heaven) and Gaia (Earth), husband (and brother) of Tethys; his daughters are the Oceanids and his sons the river-gods. Like Uranus and Gaia he also has a cosmological significance in early Greek thought as the wide river encircling the whole plain of Earth (see MAPS). All the rivers of the earth are thought of as having their origin in Ocean through subterranean connections and his waters are therefore fresh. Everything in the world that is strange and fabulous is situated by the 'stream of Ocean', the Aethiopians, Cimmerians, and Pygmies, Geryon and the Gorgons, and the Gardens of the Hesperides. The sun and stars rise and set in the Ocean; a fragment of a poem by *Mimnermus describes the sun sailing over the stream of Ocean from west to east during the night.

Ocnus ('sloth'; but see below), in Greek myth, a symbolic figure in the Underworld. The story was that Ocnus was an industrious man with an extravagant wife who spent everything he earned, so that he came to symbolize useless effort; in the Underworld he endlessly plaits a rope which a she-ass standing behind him continually eats. His name indicates lack of achievement rather than laziness.

Octa'via. 1. d. 11 BC. Sister of *Octavian, later the emperor Augustus; she was married first to C. Claudius Marcellus by whom she had three children including a son, M. Claudius Marcellus, who married Augustus' daughter Julia (see MARCELLUS (2)). In 40 BC her husband died and she was married at once to Mark Antony to seal the Treaty of Brundisium. She was divorced by him in 32 BC but brought up not only their two daughters but also all his surviving children by Fulvia and Cleopatra, as well as her three children by Marcellus. Her Roman virtues of nobility and loyalty as well as her kindness won her general admiration. One of her daughters by Antony was the mother of the emperor Claudius; the other married Lucius Domitius Ahenobarbus (consul 16 BC) and their son Gnaeus was the father of the emperor Nero.

2. b. AD 40, daughter of the emperor Claudius by his third wife *Messalina, and sister of Britannicus; she married the future emperor *Nero in 53. Nero divorced her in 62, banished her, and had her murdered soon after.

Octa'via, Roman tragedy, the only surviving *fabula *praetexta*, a dramatization of the fate of the emperor Nero's first wife (see (2) above). It has been handed down in the manuscripts of the plays of Seneca the Younger, who is included as a character to protest against Nero's cruelty, but it cannot be by him: the 'prophecy' uttered by the ghost of Nero's mother about her son's fate is so true to fact that it shows the play was written after Nero's suicide (and Seneca's own death) in AD 68. The true author is unknown. The play contains too much lamentation and mythological display to be dramatically successful.

Octa'vian, see AUGUSTUS.

Octa'vius, dialogue by *Minucius Felix.

Odaena'thus, see ZENOBIA.

ode (Gk. *ōdē*, 'song'), in Greek or Latin, a *lyric poem in stanza form (see STROPHE and TRIAD).

Odes and *Epodes,* of Horace, short Latin poems in various lyric metres. For the dates when they were written and published see HORACE. The *Epodes*, which Horace referred to as *iambi*, 'iambics', were professed imitations of *Archilochus. They consist of seventeen poems, eleven in iambic metre (where Horace does not observe Porson's Law; see METRE, GREEK 5 (i)), and six in a combination of iambics and dactyls. Their name denotes the form of the metres: an epode is, metrically speaking, the second, shorter, line of a couplet, and thence is applied to short poems written in this way. Horace tells us himself (*Epistles* 1. 19. 23) that he followed the metres and spirit of Archilochus but not the latter's subject-matter or words. Some of the Epodes are on political themes (notably 16, a lament over the fate of Rome, now apparently about to be destroyed by civil strife), some are lampoons on personal enemies, some on love and miscellaneous subjects. Epodes 1 and 9 are notable poems expressing the poet's feelings at the time of the battle of *Actium (31 BC), when Octavian defeated Antony and Cleopatra. Epode 13 is a fine poem on a theme—drink as a remedy against bad weather, with symbolic undertones—that was to become familiar with the *Odes*.

Horace declares that his models for the four books of *Odes* were the early Greek lyric poets Sappho and Alcaeus. Books 1–3 comprise eighty-eight poems; book 4, published later, comprises another fifteen. Thirty-seven poems are in the alcaic metre (see METRE, GREEK 8 (i)), twenty-five in the sapphic, and the rest in a variety of asclepiads and other forms. The first six odes of book 3 are sometimes referred to as the Roman Odes, written in stately alcaics in elevated style on patriotic themes. These grander odes owed something to the inspiration, if not the form, of the Greek poet Pindar, who also had had to evolve a style in which he could address powerful rulers intimately. There are many odes which touch on political themes, as did the lyrics of Alcaeus. They reflect the transition of

Roman feeling from anxiety for the safety of the state to security and triumph under the guidance of Augustus, whom Horace sincerely admired.

Overall the *Odes* cover a variety of subjects, private as well as public, incidents in the poet's own life or the lives of his friends, their departures on voyages or happy returns, their love affairs and his own, the changing seasons, the joys of the countryside and of wine; the poet sometimes treats these last subjects as symbolic of the brevity of human life with its ephemeral pleasures. Mostly the poems address individuals, as did early Greek lyric poetry, or start out with a personal reference. Many of them show Horace's keen sense of situation and his sharp observation of the human comedy; they are full of wit and charm and cleverness, often with a surprise at the end. The *Odes* are the product not of immediate, intense emotion, but of meditation, not lyric in a modern sense nor yet in the original Greek sense (see LYRIC POETRY). They are characterized by faultless economy of phrasing, perfect control, balance and harmony of thought and expression; their euphony and intricate word order have proved inimitable. The moderation and urbane good sense they express, in an often ironic and self-deprecating tone, have endeared them to readers of all periods.

ōdē'um (Gk. *ōdeion*, Eng. odeon), in Greece, a theatre built for musical performances and, unlike other Greek theatres, provided with a roof. An odeum was built by Periclēs east of and near to the theatre of Dionysus at Athens *c*.444 BC for concerts and the musical contests of the *Panathenaea. The *proagon* also took place here. The Athenians themselves set fire to this odeum before the invasion of Sulla in 86 BC so that the enemy would not find in it a ready supply of wood for the siege of the Acropolis. Another odeum was built in the agora *c*.15 BC by M. Vipsanius *Agrippa, but by AD 150 it had ceased to serve its original purpose and a third was built between 160 and 174 by *Herodēs Atticus.

Odo(v)acer, first barbarian king of Italy, AD 476–93; see FALL OF ROME.

Ody'sseus (or Ulyssēs; Lat. Ulixēs), in Greek myth, the son of Lāertēs, king of Ithaca, and Anticleia, daughter of Autolycus. Odysseus was one of the suitors of *Helen but had no hope of being chosen because he was poor. It was he who advised Helen's father Tyndareus to make the suitors swear to support the chosen bridegroom. He then married Penelope, daughter of Icarius, king of Sparta. When Helen was carried off to Troy, Odysseus, bound by oath like the other suitors, joined in the Greek expedition to recover her, having failed to escape his obligation by pretending to be mad (see PALAMEDES). Odysseus figures prominently in Homer's *Iliad*, notably in the embassy to Achilles (book 9) and the night expedition with Diomedēs (book 10). After the death of Achilles, a quarrel arose between Ajax, son of Telamon, and Odysseus in the contest for Achilles' armour. Since Odysseus was much the better speaker he easily persuaded the army that he had best served the Greek cause, and won their vote. Ajax, mortified, committed suicide. It was Odysseus who with Neoptolemus brought *Philoctētēs to Troy from Lemnos. Homer's *Odyssey* relates his adventures on the way home to Ithaca from Troy. After his safe return to Ithaca, and his killing of the suitors of Penelope who had thought him dead, he appeased his last enemy the god Poseidon, founding a shrine in his honour so far inland that an inhabitant mistook the oar he was carrying for a winnowing fan. There he fixed the oar in the ground, and sacrificed a ram, a bull, and a breeding boar to Poseidon. Odysseus met his death at the hands of Telegonus, his son by *Circē, who had come to Ithaca to make himself known to his father and killed him unwittingly. See also PALLADIUM and TROJAN HORSE.

In the *Iliad* Odysseus is represented as good in counsel no less than in battle, cool, energetic, tactful, and at times cunning. Subsidiary stories lay great emphasis on this last trait. In the *Odyssey* his chief characteristics are his longing for home, his endurance of suffering in order to reach it, and his self-control until the moment is ripe for him to destroy Penelope's suitors. He is less favourably depicted in some of the Attic tragedies; Euripides in particular makes him heartless and unscrupulous.

O'dyssey (*Odysseia*), epic poem by *Homer, divided into twenty-four books (for this division see HOMER 6). It is the story of the return of *Odysseus from the siege of Troy to his home in *Ithaca, and of the vengeance he took on the suitors of his wife *Penelope. Various indications in the text suggest that the *Odyssey* is a later work than the *Iliad* (see also HOMER 2), but that they both belong to the same general period. The gods do not take sides, as in the *Iliad*, though Poseidon and Helios exact punishment for offences committed against them personally; Athena, hostile to the returning Greeks in the early stage of the story, later protects Odysseus and takes an active part in promoting his return. The events of the poem occupy six weeks.

When the story opens, ten years have elapsed since the fall of Troy to the Greeks. All the Greek leaders have returned to their homes, or are dead, except Odysseus, who is in the island of *Ogygia where the goddess *Calypso has detained him for seven years. Odysseus' wife Penelope has had no news of him but, hoping that he is still alive, has put off choosing a second husband from her many suitors among the island princes, by insisting that she must first finish weaving a shroud for Odysseus' father Laertes; but each night she has secretly unravelled what she had woven during the day. The trick has now been discovered and she must come to a decision. Meanwhile the suitors are staying at Odysseus' palace lavishly entertaining themselves at his expense. In the hope of hearing news his son Telemachus goes to visit *Nestor at Pylos and Menelaus and Helen at Sparta; the suitors plot to ambush and kill Telemachus on his way home (books 1–4). Calypso is ordered by Zeus to release Odysseus; the latter builds a raft and sails on it for seventeen days until within sight of *Scheria, the land of the Phaeacians. The god Poseidon, who hates Odysseus because he has blinded Poseidon's son *Polyphemus, raises a storm and destroys the raft. Odysseus, after two days in the sea, buoyed up by a scarf given him by the sea-goddess Ino, is washed up on the shore of Scheria (book 5). He is found by *Nausicaa, daughter of the Phaeacian king Alcinous, and by her help is hospitably received in the palace (books 6 and 7). Here he is entertained by the songs of the bard Demodocus (which include the quarrel of Odysseus and Achilles, book 8, 75–82; the love of Arēs and Aphroditē, 266–366; the Trojan Horse, 499–520) and by the athletic contests of the Phaeacians.

Odysseus reveals his name and tells of his adventures since leaving Troy, first of his piratical raid on the Cicŏnes at Ismarus (on the south coast of Thrace), then of his visit to the land of the Lotus-eaters, and afterwards to that of the Cyclōpĕs, where he encountered Polyphemus (book 9). Next he tells of his entertainment by *Aeolus and the gift of the bag containing the adverse winds (which his companions released), of his adventures with the Laestrŷgonĕs, cannibal giants who destroyed eleven of his twelve ships, and of his coming to the island of Aeaea, where the enchantress Circē turned his companions into swine; he himself was protected by the herb moly, given him by the god Hermēs, and he obtained the restoration of his companions. After a year Circe released him and directed him to consult *Teiresias in the Underworld (book 10). Odysseus recounts his visit there, where he saw the ghosts of many dead heroes, their wives and daughters, and conversed with some of them, including his mother Anticleia; Teiresias then prophesied to him the manner of his return (book 11). Odysseus tells of his sailing past the *Sirens and between *Scylla and Charybdis, and of his coming to *Thrinacia, where, in spite of Teiresias' warning, his company killed the cattle of the sun-god Helios. This sacrilege brought about the destruction by Zeus' thunderbolt of the ship and its crew. Odysseus alone was carried on the wreckage to Ogygia, where Calypso received him kindly but refused to let him go (book 12). This brings him to the situation at the opening of the first book.

After finishing his tale (which became proverbial among later Greeks for a long story) Odysseus is carried in a Phaeacian ship to Ithaca (on its return to Scheria the ship is turned into a rock by the god Poseidon). The goddess Athena disguises Odysseus as an old beggar (book 13). He learns of the insolent and extravagant behaviour of Penelope's suitors from the faithful swineherd Eumaeus. He reveals his true identity to Telemachus, when the latter returns safely from Sparta, having escaped the ambush. Together they plot the destruction of the suitors (books 14–16). Odysseus now goes to his house where he is recognized by the old dog Argus, but in his beggar's disguise is beaten and insulted by the goatherd Melanthius and the suitors Antinŏus and Eurymachus, and fights with the beggar Irus (books 17 and 18). Odysseus is recognized by his former nurse Eurycleia, who is ordered to keep her knowledge secret. Penelope reveals her decision to marry the man who the next day will string the bow of Odysseus and shoot an arrow through a line of twelve axe-heads (book 19). The seer Theoclymenus has a vision of the doom of the suitors (book 20). Odysseus alone is able to bend and string the bow, and he shoots an arrow through the axes. He then shoots Antinŏus, and aided by Telemachus, Eumaeus, and another faithful servant, kills the rest of the suitors. Those women servants who have been their lovers are hanged. Penelope is at last convinced, by the hero's knowledge of the peculiar construction of the bedstead, that he is her husband (books 21–3). Odysseus makes himself known to his father Laertes. The relatives of the suitors attempt revenge, but are repulsed, and the goddess Athena stops the blood-feud (book 24).

Oecono'micus ('household management'), treatise by *Xenophon on the management of a household and estate, in the form of a dialogue between Socrates and Critobulus, in the course of which Socrates recounts an earlier conversation (occupying most of the work) which he had with a certain Ischomachus (who seems to represent Xenophon). Chapter 4 describes the horticultural activities of the younger *Cyrus (the Persian king), and the latter's conversation with the Spartan general Lysander on the subject of gardens (imitated by Cicero in *De senectute ('on old age'), ch. 17). The conversation with Ischomachus is an interesting and humane account of the latter's relations with his very young wife, of the wife's equal but separate role in marriage, and of the running of a house. This is the most charming of Xenophon's treatises and is particularly valuable for the information it gives on the position of women in Athenian society.

Oe'dipus (Oidipous, 'swollen-foot'), in Greek myth, the son of *Laius, king of Thebes. When Amphion and Zethus gained possession of Thebes (see ANTIOPE), Laius had taken refuge with *Pelops, but had carried off his host's son Chrÿsippus. The god Apollo warned him that, as punishment, if he fathered a son that son would kill him. Laius recovered his kingdom after the death of Amphion and Zethus, and married Jocasta (Epicastē in Homer). Accordingly, when a son was born, he was given to a servant to expose on Mount Cithaeron, his feet having been transfixed by a spike. Instead the servant gave him to a shepherd who brought him to Polybus, king of Corinth, and Meropē, his queen. These two, being childless, brought him up as their own son, naming him Oedipus from the deformity of his feet.

When Oedipus was grown up, being taunted with being no true son of Polybus, he went to Delphi to enquire about his parentage. He was told only that he would kill his father and marry his mother. Deciding therefore never to return to Corinth he wandered in the direction of Thebes and by chance encountered Laius (whom he did not know) at a place where three roads met. A quarrel ensued in which Oedipus killed Laius. He went on to Thebes, which was at that time terrorized by the *Sphinx, a monster who destroyed those who could not answer the riddle she posed. Creon, brother of Jocasta and regent of Thebes, offered the kingdom and Jocasta as wife to whoever should overcome this pest. Oedipus guessed the answer to the riddle and the Sphinx killed herself. He married Jocasta and they had two sons, Eteoclēs and Polyneicēs, and two daughters, Antigonē and Ismenē.

According to Homer, when it was discovered that Oedipus had married his mother, the latter hanged herself, but Oedipus continued to rule in Thebes. In Sophocles' tragedy *Oedipus Tyrannus*, discovery was precipitated by plague and famine, and the pronouncement of the Delphic Oracle that these could be averted only if the killer of Laius was expelled from the city. Oedipus' attempts to discover the truth revealed that he himself was Laius' son and killer; Jocasta hanged herself and Oedipus blinded himself. Oedipus was deposed and went into retirement, at first shut up in Thebes; later he went into exile, wandering, attended by Antigone, to Colonus in Attica, where he was protected by *Theseus and where he died (see OEDIPUS AT COLONUS). His sons having quarrelled about who should succeed to the throne, Oedipus before he died put a curse on them that they should each kill the other. When they first took the throne they agreed to divide the inheritance, ruling in alternate years. Eteocles ruled first, but when his year of kingship had elapsed he refused to make way for Polyneices. The latter had spent his year of absence from Thebes at the court of Adrastus, king of Argos, and had married his daughter Argeia. Adrastus supported his son-in-law and gathered an army, headed by seven champions, the *Seven Against Thebes. Their names (as usually given) are: Adrastus, Polyneices, Tÿdeus (the other son-in-law of Adrastus), Capaneus, Hippomedon, Parthenopaeus, and *Amphiaraus. Each champion was stationed at one of the seven gates of Thebes, and Eteocles similarly assigned a Theban defender to each gate, deciding to confront Polyneices himself. The Argive army was routed and all the champions killed except Adrastus. The brothers Eteocles and Polyneices both died.

Creon, now king of Thebes, ordered that the bodies of the enemy, including that of Polyneices, should not be buried (thus preventing their spirits from entering the Underworld, according to traditional belief). What followed is variously told. One version is given by Euripides in the *Suppliants. Sophocles, in *Antigone, tells how Antigone, rebelling against Creon's decree, contrived secretly to perform the burial rite for her brother. For this Creon had her placed alive in a stone tomb, although she was to marry his son Haemon. There she hanged herself, and

Haemon stabbed himself beside her body. The story was related in the lost poem of the *epic cycle *Thebāis*. See also EPIGONOI.

Oe'dipus, Roman tragedy by *Seneca (2), based on Sophocles' play *Oedipus Tyrannus*, but with long descriptions of the plague at Thebes, and of necromantic and sacrificial rites. Jocasta's suicide takes place on stage.

Oe'dipus at Colō'nus (*Oidipous epi Kolōnōi*, Lat. *Oedipus Colōneus*), Greek tragedy by *Sophocles written not long before his death in 406/5 BC, produced in 401 BC by his grandson Sophocles the Younger.

*Oedipus, blind and banished from Thebes, has wandered, attended by his daughter Antigonē, to Colonus, a deme of Attica a little north of Athens. He is warned by the inhabitants to leave, but having learnt that this is the locality foretold in an oracle as the place where he will die, refuses to go. Theseus, king of Athens, is appealed to, and assures Oedipus of his protection and of a burial place on Attic soil; in this way his spirit will be a protection to Athens (see HEROES). Oedipus' second daughter Ismenē arrives and tells him of the quarrel between his sons Eteoclēs and Polyneicēs for the throne of Thebes, arousing his anger against them. Creon, regent of Thebes and brother of Oedipus' dead wife Jocasta, arrives to seize Oedipus so that Thebes and not Athens may have his body; his guards carry off Ismene and Antigone, and Creon himself is about to lay hands on Oedipus when Theseus intervenes and rescues him and his daughters. Meanwhile Polyneices has arrived and with professions of repentance asks for his father's favour in his struggle with Eteocles. Oedipus turns on him with bitter anger and places on his sons a curse that they may die by each other's hand. Peals of thunder warn Oedipus that the time of his death is approaching. He withdraws, and a messenger reports that he blessed his daughters, withdrew to a lonely spot, and in the presence of Theseus alone met his end, the exact form of which remained unknown to the messenger.

Oe'dipus Tyra'nnus (*Oidipous Tyrannos*, Lat. *Oedipus Rex*, 'Oedipus the king'), Greek tragedy by *Sophocles, of unknown date; some tenuous indications suggest it may have been written in the years following 430 BC. The tetralogy (see TRAGEDY 2) of which it was part is reputed to have come only second in the dramatic competition, yet *Oedipus Tyrannus* itself is regarded by many as Sophocles' masterpiece, and was particularly admired by Aristotle (in the *Poetics*). It deals with that portion of the story of *Oedipus in which he is king of Thebes and husband of Jocasta. When the discovery is made that he is the son of the same Jocasta and of the previous king Laius (whom he has murdered), Oedipus blinds himself and Jocasta commits suicide.

Oedipus learns from the Delphic Oracle that a plague which has fallen on the city is due to the presence there of the murderers of king Laius. He calls upon all who have any knowledge of the matter to come forward. Teiresias, the blind seer, is first summoned. He knows the truth but at first refuses to divulge it. Accused by Oedipus of plotting with Creon, Jocasta's brother, against him, he then speaks the truth but it sounds too far-fetched for Oedipus to entertain it as true. Oedipus next turns against Creon whom he charges with trying to oust him from the throne. He is deeply disturbed by Jocasta's description of the scene of Laius' death and of the retinue he then had with him, which matches the circumstances in which Oedipus himself had once killed a man. On one point he seems now to receive enlightenment: a messenger comes from Corinth to announce the death of the king Polybus and the election of Oedipus to succeed him, and Oedipus, still dreading that he may unwittingly marry his mother in fulfilment of the oracle, expresses reluctance about returning to Corinth. But the messenger then reveals that Oedipus is not in fact the son of Polybus; he himself had given Oedipus as a baby to the king and his wife Meropē, having received the baby from a shepherd on Mount Cithaeron (near Thebes). Whose son then is he? Jocasta guesses the truth and retires. An old shepherd who has been sent for as the only surviving member of Laius' retinue at the time of the latter's death now completes the disclosure. It was he who had carried the infant Oedipus, son of Laius and Jocasta, to Cithaeron, and had from pity given him to the Corinthian. Oedipus rushes into the palace, to find that Jocasta has hanged herself, and blinds himself with her brooch. Creon takes over the government and Oedipus, though begging to be sent away from the city, remains in Thebes.

Oeneus, see MELEAGER.

Oeno'mäus, in Greek myth, king of Pisa and father of Hippodamīa; see PELOPS.

Oenō'nē, in Greek myth, nymph of Mount Ida near Troy, who was loved by *Paris before he knew that he was a Trojan prince. Later she tried to persuade him not to sail to Greece, where the beautiful *Helen lived, having prophetic powers and foreseeing the outcome. Failing to persuade him she promised to heal him if he was wounded. When, towards the end of the Trojan War, he was shot by the poisoned arrow of *Philoctētēs, he sought her help but she refused because he had deserted her. Soon after she repented, but he had already died; in her grief she hanged herself.

Ogy'gia, in Homer's Odyssey, the island of Calypso. It is described by Homer as being far away to the west beyond Scheria (generally identified in antiquity with Corcyra), and as the 'navel of the sea'; but it is not clear whether it was thought of as being in the Mediterranean or in the Ocean further west.

Old Comedy, see COMEDY, GREEK 3.

Old Oligarch, see *CONSTITUTION OF THE ATHENIANS* (2).

oligarchy (*oligarchia*, 'rule of the few'), the limitation of political power to a portion of the community, such as a few families or individuals (the oligarchs). It was characteristic of oligarchs that they possessed greater wealth and influence than the rest of the community; high birth was not a necessary condition (compare ARISTOCRACY), but in Greece it commonly happened that the oligarchs were a sec-

tion of the old nobility which had excluded from power the poorer nobles. Even during the second half of the fifth century BC, when Athenian ascendancy promoted democratic forms of government, there were still many oligarchic states in Greece, the most notable perhaps being at Corinth and at Thebes. The government at Rome under the republic is often described as 'oligarchical'; see NOBILES and REPUBLIC.

Oly'mpia, the main sanctuary of Zeus in Greece, in the state of Elis near the west coast of the Peloponnese on the north bank of the river Alpheus. (The location is quite separate from Mount Olympus, which is some 275 km. or 170 miles to the north.) Olympia was on a well-watered site in a fertile region among gentle hills, a fairly unusual landscape for Greece and particularly appealing to Greek sensibility. It was in marked contrast with its rival in religious importance, the main sanctuary of Apollo in the dramatic setting of Delphi. The sacred precinct of Zeus, a walled enclosure, was known as the Altis (the local dialect form of *alsos*, 'precinct'). In the seventh century BC permanent buildings began to be erected, first the famous temple of Hera, built mid-century in the precinct. The temple of Zeus himself was built *c*.470 on a vast scale (covering about twice the area of the *Parthenon in Athens). It housed *Pheidias' great seated statue of the god, one of the *Seven Wonders of the ancient world. Its appearance is now known only through small reproductions on coins and gems, but a good deal of the superb sculptural decoration of the temple survives (Olympia Museum).

As well as the temples, the precinct contained very many statues of athletes and race-horse owners who had been successful at the famous Olympian (or Olympic) games, the most important part of the festival held every four years in honour of Zeus and the major athletic competition of the ancient world. Because of their universal prestige the Olympian programme and rules were accepted as the norm for games everywhere, and the four-year period between festivals, known as an *Olympiad, was used by the Greeks as a dating system. The games were held without a break from 776 BC until at least AD 261, and finally suppressed as a pagan cult by the Christian Roman emperor Theodosius in AD 391 or soon after. In the sixth century the whole site was covered with debris from an earthquake, an event to which is owed the burial and hence preservation of many objects.

Oly'mpiacus, see LYSIAS.

Oly'mpiad (*hē Olympias*), the four-year period between two Olympian festivals (see OLYMPIA). Greek writers of the post-classical era often date an event by ascribing it to a particular Olympiad, each Olympiad being numbered in sequence from the first recorded games of 776 BC. The first list of Olympian victors, which such a dating system presupposes, is thought to have been published by the sophist *Hippias (2) in the late fifth century BC. According to ancient sources the numbering system was introduced either by *Timaeus or by *Eratosthenes. The years within an Olympiad were numbered (by Eratosthenes) one to four. Thus by this reckoning the battle of Marathon (490 BC) occurred in Olympiad 72, 3 (for strict accuracy it must be remembered that the Olympian year, like the Attic year, began in the summer). From Eratosthenes onwards all Greek dating was based on, or synchronized with, Olympiads. There was some difficulty in Roman times in relating Olympiads to the Roman consular year, which from 153 BC began on 1 January and so included parts of two Olympian years.

Olympian festival, games, see OLYMPIA.

Olympian gods, see GODS 1.

Oly'mpias, wife of *Philip II of Macedon and mother of Alexander the Great. In 331 BC she left Macedon for Epirus, which she virtually ruled by herself for a number of years; after Alexander's death in 323 she returned to Macedon, where she made Alexander's posthumous son Alexander IV sole king. Her violence brought back *Cassander, who condemned her to death, and she was finally killed by relatives of those she had murdered.

Olympiē'um (Olympieion), name given to the temple of Zeus Olympius (Olympian Zeus) at Athens, situated south-east of the Acropolis. The first important temple was begun on the site of an earlier temple at the end of the sixth century BC. With the fall of the Peisistratid tyranny in 510 BC, work on the temple was discontinued and was not resumed until 174 BC when Antiochus IV Epiphanēs, the *Seleucid king of Asia (176–165), undertook to rebuild it at his own expense, but it was again left unfinished at Antiochus' death and remained so for three centuries. In 86 BC Sulla removed some of the columns to Rome. It was finally completed by the emperor Hadrian in AD 132, making it one of the largest of Greek temples. Fifteen of the columns are still standing.

Oly'mpus (not to be confused with *Olympia), the highest mountain in Greece, situated at the eastern end of the chain of mountains which forms roughly the northern boundary of Greece proper, overlooking the Vale of Tempē. In Greek myth it was believed to be where the twelve Olympian gods had their houses, built for them by the god Hephaestus, with Zeus' house occupying the summit. (The gods could also be thought of as dwelling in the heavens above Olympus.)

Oly'nthiacs, three political speeches by Demosthenēs. See DEMOSTHENES (2) 5.

Oly'nthus, Greek city north of Potidaea on the mainland of Chalcidicē. It was a city of mixed race, and after 433 BC became the capital of a Chalcidian confederacy (see CHALCIDIC LEAGUE). Sparta, suspicious of its power, captured it in 390 and disbanded the confederacy, which reformed after the Spartan defeat at Leuctra in 371. When Amphipolis fell to *Philip II of Macedon in 357, Olynthus and the confederacy went over to him, but becoming alarmed by his increasing power turned to Athens. Athens, however, failed to save the city. It was betrayed to Philip in 348 and completely destroyed.

O'mphalē, see HERACLES.

O'mphalos, see DELPHI.

Onēsi'critus, Greek historian with

Alexander the Great in India, who with *Nearchus explored the sea-route from India to the Persian Gulf. The longest surviving fragment from his narrative of Alexander's Indian campaign describes an interview between the author and some Indian fakirs. His reputation in antiquity was of being a great liar.

Ōnē'tōr, see DEMOSTHENES (2) 2.

Onoma'critus, an Athenian who lived at the court of the tyrant *Peisistratus and his sons at Athens in the late sixth century BC. He was engaged to collect and edit the oracles of *Musaeus and is said to have been detected by *Lasus of Hermione in inserting a false one (that the island of Lemnos would disappear into the sea). When the Peisistratids had been overthrown, they employed him to give oracles to the Persian king Xerxēs which favoured his planned invasion of Greece. Onomacritus was later believed to have been the author of some of the poems ascribed to *Orpheus, and was also said to have been given the task by Peisistratus of editing Homer's *Iliad* and *Odyssey*.

onomatopoe'ia, the formation and use of words to imitate sounds. A famous example occurs in a line of the early Roman poet Ennius: *at tuba terribili sonitu taratantara dixit* ('the war-trumpet with terrifying sound blew *taratantara*'). The word is used also, in a wider sense, of the formation of whole phrases or sentences which suggest in sound what they describe, such as Virgil's dactylic hexameter, *quadrupedante putrem sonitu quatit ungula campum* ('the horses' hooves with four-fold beat shake the crumbling plain'). For an interesting ancient discussion see Dionysius of Halicarnassus, *De compositione verborum* 14–20.

Opeconsī'va or **Opiconsī'via,** see OPS.

O'ppian (Oppiānos, early third century AD), of Cilicia in south-east Asia Minor, writer of Greek didactic poetry in hexameters. His *Halieutica* ('on fishing') is in five books; the *Cynegetica* ('on hunting'), in three books, is also ascribed to him but seems to be the work of a different poet,

a native of Syria, though perhaps of the same name. Both poems contain passages of power and beauty, despite the unpromising material.

Ops, Roman goddess of abundance. Her festivals, Opalia on 19 August and Opiconsivia on 25 August, were close to festivals of *Consus, the god of the granary. Because her December festival was also close to the *Saturnalia she was usually associated with Saturn, and since he was identified with the Greek *Cronus she was identified with Rhea, the consort of Cronus. Her oldest place of worship was a small shrine in the Regia or ancient royal palace, where her harvest ceremony was performed, attended only by the *pontifex maximus* and the Vestals, symbolizing the storage of the state crops by the king and his daughters.

optimā'tēs ('the best class'). In Roman politics, until the time of the Gracchi (*c*.133 BC) there was no serious challenge to the overwhelming predominance of the noble families in the ruling oligarchy (see NOBILES). In response to the rise of the *popularēs*, political leaders 'on the side of the people', the Roman upper class called themselves *optimates*, understanding the term socially and morally on the model of the Greek *kaloi kagathoi*; thus in the late republic the name was applied to the senatorial party and their supporters, those who acted in the interests of the *optimi*, the 'best men'.

oracles. An oracle (Gk. *manteion, chrēstērion,* Lat. *orāculum*) was an answer given by a god to a question asked him by a worshipper; it usually took the form of a command or a prediction or a statement of fact. An oracle may also mean the shrine itself where the answers were given. In each of the many oracular shrines in the ancient world the god was consulted in his own particular way. The most famous were those of Zeus at Dodona in Epirus, and of Apollo at Delphi. The former dates from very ancient times and is mentioned in Homer's *Iliad* and *Odyssey*; there the oracles seem to have been extracted in some manner from a sacred oak-tree, perhaps by the rustling of its leaves (late legends say by the sound of a sacred spring or brazen gong), and interpreted by priests known as Selloi, 'of unwashed feet and sleeping on the ground'. Zeus had another oracular shrine at Olympia (see IAMUS). At Delphi a priestess, the Pythia, seated on a tripod and under the inspiration of Apollo, answered the question put to her by the enquirer (see DELPHIC ORACLE). Apollo had many oracles of similar type in Greece and Asia Minor. The healing god *Asclepius had a shrine at Epidaurus particularly famed for sending curative visions to the sick through *incubation. The shrine of the hero *Amphiaraus at Oropus was similarly credited with healing properties. One of the most famous hero-oracles was that of *Trophonius in a cave at Lebadea in Boeotia. Among foreign oracles that of Zeus *Ammon at Siwa in the Libyan desert, consulted notably by Alexander the Great, had a high reputation among the Greeks. Very many oracular responses to questions are known, and mostly they direct the questioner to perform some religious act, such as a sacrifice to a particular god. It seems probable that the famous replies said to have been given on notable historical occasions are not in fact genuine. From at latest the sixth century BC (see ONOMACRITUS) collections of oracles were made and peddled.

There were no oracular shrines in Italy comparable in importance with those in Greece. During the Roman republic oracles, apart from the Sibylline books (see SIBYL), were not consulted by the state. However, under the empire, and with the increased worship of Greek and oriental divinities, more attention was paid to oracular predictions. As in Greece, the collection of oracles at Rome must have begun quite early. In 213 BC at a critical time in the Second Punic War the senate made the praetor Acilius seize and suppress several collections in circulation. With the similar purpose of arresting panic the emperor Augustus had 2,000 books of prophecies burnt. The most important oracle in Italy was at Cumae, where the Sibyl's cave was situated under the temple of Apollo. At Praenestē there was an ancient and famous temple of Fortune (see FORTUNA), where oracles known as *sortēs*, 'lots',

were given: tablets, each inscribed with its own oracle, were shuffled by a child who drew one and gave it to the questioner. *Faunus was regarded as a prophetic god, as was the nymph *Carmentis (mother of Evander); both are referred to by Virgil. At the temple of Faunus at Tibur incubation was practised; a sheep was killed and the enquirer slept in its skin. The use of oracles as an aid to decision-making became particularly apparent in the second century AD with the popularization of the *sortes Virgilianae* (see VIRGIL), a practice said to have originated with the emperor Hadrian, by which the enquirer opened Virgil's works and chose a line at random to be a guide to the future. Copies of the *Aeneid* were deposited in temples for that purpose.

oral poetry, poetry composed and transmitted without the aid of writing. The term is usually applied to narrative poetry composed in pre-literate societies, since there is very little evidence for other kinds of poetry. The Greek epic poems of *Homer, the *Iliad* and *Odyssey*, are generally believed to be in origin oral compositions. It is characteristic of oral poetry that it contains '*formulae', repeated words, especially 'stock' epithets and phrases, even whole lines and paragraphs describing typical scenes, which enable the poet who has already committed them to memory to deliver a poem extempore when required. It is generally felt that if a poem is the product of oral composition, disproportionate significance should not be given to, for example, epithets which fit the metre but not the context, or slight discrepancies between one typical scene and another. See EPIC.

Ōrā'tōr, Latin treatise by *Cicero written in 46 BC and dedicated to M. Brutus, which describes the ideal orator and outlines a scheme for his education. He must be a master of the three styles, the plain, the grand, and the middle.

oratory. Although in general usage the two terms oratory and *rhetoric are virtually synonymous, in what follows a distinction is made between them: rhetoric is taken to denote the theoretical art of speaking, oratory its practical application. Both were exhaustively studied in the ancient world, for mastery of the spoken word was the key to success in the fields of politics and law, and successful careers in either field (though both were generally associated) brought power, prestige, and wealth.

1. *Greek.* Attic Greek oratory, in its period of splendour (from *c.*460 BC to the suppression of political freedom at Athens at the end of the fourth century BC), produced a large number of people who professed to be able to teach it, known as *rhetors. The earliest teachers, Corax and Teisias, were active in Sicily in the middle of the fifth century BC when the rule of tyrants gave place to democracy; the lawsuits which followed this change of constitution are said to have given Corax the idea of systematizing and writing down the rules for speaking in a law-court. According to Aristotle, *Empedoclēs too played some part in this development. *Gorgias of Leontini (in Sicily) brought this new style of public speaking to Athens in 427 BC, adopting in particular a poetic style, although it is clear from the earlier plays of Euripidēs that oratory was already a developed art in the city. Gorgias' influence has been detected in the speeches of Thucydidēs and Isocratēs. The teaching of rhetoric was part of the stock-in-trade of many *sophists, some of whom specialized in particular aspects of the subject, such as semantics or figures of speech. The sophists and rhetors laid emphasis on the techniques necessary for winning over an audience. The teaching of this kind of rhetoric aroused the hostility of Socrates and especially of Plato, who thought that persuasive speech should be based on knowledge of the truth, and thus introduced the idea of an opposition between rhetoric which aimed to persuade and philosophy which aimed to know the truth (see *GORGIAS*). The theoretical study of rhetoric was further developed by *Aristotle (see 4 (v)), who was probably the first to divide oratory into three kinds, judicial (or forensic), political (or deliberative), and *epideictic (the oratory of display), each with its own particular style.

No speech by any of the great political figures of the fifth century survives, though the Funeral Speech of Pericles as it is reproduced by *Thucydides (2. 35–46) may possibly give some idea of his lofty style. The earliest and only truly fifth-century Attic orator whose speeches in part survive is *Antiphon (*c.*480–411 BC); he was followed by *Andocides (at the very end of the fifth and beginning of the fourth century), and the great fourth-century orators *Lysias, *Isocrates, *Isaeus, *Demosthenes, and *Aeschines. Of the remaining Attic orators the most important were *Lycurgus, *Hypereides, and *Deinarchus (see CANONS). After the end of the fourth century BC the political situation in Greece did not give much scope for the practice of political oratory; but its importance in education did not decline and the study of oratory was still pursued at Athens and also among the Greeks of Asia Minor, at Rhodes and Pergamum, where oratory of a rich, exuberant, and declamatory kind developed, the so-called Asianic style, in contrast with the simple lucid Attic style modelled on Lysias. The former term arose, according to a grammarian, when the Greek language spread into Asia (from the late fourth century BC) and the Asians used Greek circumlocutions when they did not know the precise words. Quintilian's view is that the style reflected the bombastic and boastful nature of the Asians, compared with Attic speakers who despised vapid and redundant speech.

2. *Roman.* At Rome, as in Greece, oratory was recognized as an art from early times. Even in the fourth century BC Appius *Claudius Caecus the Censor had a high reputation as an orator. In the survey that Cicero gives in his *Brutus* of the great Roman speakers, the principal names are those of *Cato the Censor, the *Gracchi (especially Gaius, described by Cicero as wise, lofty, and weighty, but lacking the final polish), M. *Antonius (grandfather of Mark Antony), L. Licinius *Crassus (consul in 95 BC, whose speeches were deliberately built up in accordance with the rules of Greek oratory), Julius *Caesar, C. Licinius *Calvus, an exponent of the pure Attic style, and *Hortensius, noted, on the contrary, for his luxuriant Asianism.

Cicero found himself under attack as an Asianist by admirers of Calvus who thought his periodic and rhythmical style over-elaborate; he defended himself in the *Brutus* and *Orator*.

From the second century BC onwards Roman orators were a product of Greek schools or of Greek teachers who had migrated to Rome. Handbooks such as the *Rhetorica ad Herennium* were based on Greek models. But Greek theory was subordinate to Roman practice: it was the institutions of the law-courts and above all the senate, where affairs of state were debated before an intelligent, educated, and trained audience, that moulded the dignified Roman oratorical style. Of this wealth of eloquence only the speeches of Cicero survive.

As in Athens in the late fourth century BC, so in Rome under the empire oratory as a living art declined when the political decisions were taken by the emperor and no longer followed public debate. But rhetoric still remained the fundamental element in education, though now it was taught only for the law-courts or display purposes, and exercised in consequence a strong influence on all forms of literature. Professorships of rhetoric were set up in all the large cities of the empire, and for as long as the empire lasted higher education was almost entirely rhetorical. *Quintilian was the first professor of rhetoric at Rome and, like Cicero, saw rhetoric as providing the finest literary discipline. In the second century AD *Dio Chrysostom and Aelius *Aristeides in the eastern empire could draw large audiences to hear performances of their epideictic oratory. Orators or teachers of rhetoric in the West included many of the greatest figures of their time, e.g. St *Augustine, St *Ambrose, and *Ausonius. True understanding of much of classical literature and ancient literary criticism requires appreciation of the large role of rhetoric and oratory in ancient life and culture.

Orbi'lius Pupi'llus, Lucius (c.112–c.17 BC), of Beneventum, a grammarian, famous as the schoolmaster of Horace, who calls him *plagosus*, 'whacker', from beatings inflicted during lessons on *Livius Andronicus' version of Homer's

Odyssey. There is an account of him in Suetonius.

orchestra ('dancing-floor'), see DIONYSUS, THEATRE OF.

Orcho'menus, name of several Greek cities but especially of that in Boeotia on the north of the Copāic plain (known locally as Erchomenus). It became important in the Mycenaean period and was apparently the principal Boeotian city until it was eclipsed by Thebes. Orchomenus was proverbial for its wealth and associated in legend with the *Minyans. It has been suggested that its wealth depended upon the fertility of the Copaic plain after the lake was drained, and that its decline is reflected in the story that Heracles, hero of the rival city of Thebes, broke down the drainage system and flooded the plain. Orchomenus was the site of an ancient and famous cult of the Graces. The city was destroyed by a confederacy of Boeotian towns in 364 BC.

Orcus. In Roman religion Orcus is apparently a synonym of *Dis, the god of the Underworld, or the Underworld itself.

orders, at Rome in the early republic, the two hereditary estates or broad social divisions of the Roman people, namely patricians (the rich) and plebeians (the poor); each had its own privileges and disabilities sanctioned by law, religion, and custom. The practical distinctions between patricians and plebeians largely disappeared after 366 BC. In the first century BC the term 'order' denotes only the senatorial or equestrian order. Cicero's *concordia ordinum*, 'harmony of the orders', was the union of senators and equestrians; see CICERO (1) 3.

orders, of architecture, see ARCHITECTURE and VITRUVIUS.

o'rĕads (Gk. *oreiadĕs*, Lat. *orēades*), *nymphs of the mountains.

Orestei'a, the collective name given to the three Greek tragedies (trilogy) by *Aeschylus on the story of *Agamemnon, Clytemnestra, and Orestēs, produced at Athens in 458 BC when it won the dramatic competition. It is the only trilogy that survives complete. The plays are *Agamemnon, Choēphoroe* ('libation bearers'), and *Eumenidēs* ('kindly ones', a euphemism for the *Furies).

The story is taken from the mythical history of the descendants of *Atreus in which crime led to further crime through several generations. The *Agamemnon* opens in an atmosphere of hope mingled with foreboding, as the watchman on the roof of Agamemnon's palace in Argos looks out for the signal beacon to announce the fall of Troy. After the signal is seen, the news is confirmed by the arrival of a herald. Agamemnon's wife Clytemnestra appears jubilant, but the chorus of Argive elders recall Agamemnon's sacrifice of his daughter Iphigeneia to enable the Greek fleet to set sail, and brood over the possible consequences. Agamemnon arrives, bringing with him the captured Trojan princess Cassandra, his concubine. Clytemnestra treacherously welcomes him and then leads him into the palace. Cassandra, who has not spoken up to this point, is now moved to frenzied prophecy, foresees Agamemnon's murder and her own, as well as having a vision of the past crimes of the house, and utters a lament. She too enters the house, knowingly going to her death. The cries of the dying Agamemnon are heard. The interior of the palace is revealed, with Clytemnestra exulting over the bodies of the two victims. She answers the elders' reproaches by citing as justification Agamemnon's sacrifice of Iphigeneia. Aegisthus, her lover, appears, and subdues the elders with threats of force. The latter can only hope that one day Agamemnon's son Orestes will avenge him.

In the *Choephoroe*, Orestes, the son of Agamemnon, after years of exile, returns to Argos with his friend Pyladēs, to avenge his father on the god Apollo's instructions; he comes to his father's tomb and dedicates on it a lock of his hair. The two draw aside while Electra, Orestes' sister, and a chorus of Argive women approach to pour libations on the tomb by order of Clytemnestra, who has been disturbed by ominous dreams. Electra recognizes the lock of hair and footprints nearby as strikingly similar to her own; her brother reveals himself and a reunion takes place (a scene thought by

some to be mocked by Euripides in his *Electra*, where Electra rejects these proofs of identity). Electra and Orestes join in an impressive invocation of their father's dead spirit, calling upon his aid in their pursuit of vengeance. Orestes and Pylades, disguised as travellers bringing news of the former's death, enter the palace. Aegisthus is summoned and on his arrival is killed by Orestes. Clytemnestra pleads with her son for her life, and for a moment Orestes falters; but Pylades, in his only speech, reminds him of Apollo's command, and Orestes drags her into the palace and kills her. While he is justifying his action he sees avenging Furies arrive to haunt him, and he flees from them.

Eumenides opens to show Orestes as suppliant at the shrine of Apollo in Delphi. The Furies, forming the chorus, are asleep around him. Orestes is promised protection by Apollo, who tells him to go to Athens to seek justice from the goddess Athena. After he leaves, the ghost of Clytemnestra stirs up the Furies to pursue him. The scene changes to the front of Athena's temple on the Acropolis at Athens. Athena, having heard the pleas and justifications of the Furies and of Orestes, refers the judgement to a tribunal of Athenian citizens acting as judges (i.e. the historical Areopagus court for judging cases of homicide, of which this episode was the legendary foundation). The Furies prosecute, and Orestes defends himself. Athena votes with the other judges, and the votes are found to be equally divided. Athena therefore declares that in future, when the votes are equal the defendant is to be acquitted (as was Athenian practice at this time). The Furies are indignant at Orestes' escape, but are conciliated by Athena's promise of a permanent home in her city and honour in their new role as beneficent powers.

For Stesichorus' poem *Oresteia* see STESICHORUS.

Ore'stēs, in Greek myth, son of *Agamemnon and Clytemnestra, and brother of Iphigeneia and Electra. See PELOPS, *ORESTEIA*, and the articles on the tragedies *Orestes* (below), *Electra*, and *Iphigeneia in Tauris*. For his marriage with Hermionē (daughter of Menelaus and Helen) see NEOPTOLEMUS.

Ore'stēs, Greek tragedy by *Euripides produced in 408 BC. For his story see ORESTEIA above.

Orestes, having killed his mother Clytemnestra and her lover Aegisthus, has been driven mad by the Furies and is tenderly nursed by his sister Electra. The citizens of Argos are about to pass judgement on them for their crime, and a sentence of death is expected. At this point Agamemnon's brother *Menelaus appears, on his way home to Sparta from Troy, together with his wife Helen, but is too cowardly to help, although Orestes appeals to him. Sentence of death is passed on Orestes and Electra who now, urged on by *Pyladēs, plan to kill Helen, the source of all their troubles, and to seize Menelaus' daughter Hermionē as a hostage. Helen mysteriously disappears. They then threaten to kill Hermione unless Menelaus intervenes to save their lives. However, in this confused situation Apollo appears and dictates a general pacification, explaining that Helen has been carried off to heaven, and that it is Orestes' destiny to be brought to trial at Athens and, after being freed, to marry Hermione and become ruler of Argos.

O'rganon, see ARISTOTLE 4 (i).

Orientalizing age, name given to one of the five periods of the Greek era (based on the differences in pottery styles), denoting very roughly the period from 720 to 620 BC (compare PROTO-GEOMETRIC, GEOMETRIC, ARCHAIC, and CLASSICAL).

O'rigen (Ōrigenēs) (AD *c*.185–*c*.254), the successor of *Clement as head of the Christian (catechetical) school of Alexandria, the first great scholar among the Greek Fathers of the Church. He was a pioneer in the textual criticism of the Bible, and is chiefly famous for his *Hexapla*, an edition of the Old Testament containing in six parallel columns the Hebrew text, the same transliterated into Greek letters, the *Septuagint, a revision of the Septuagint, and two other Greek translations. Only fragments of the work survive. Many of Origen's voluminous theological writings have also been lost, but we still have *First Principles*, the first

work of Christian dogma to be produced, and *Against Celsus*, a work of Christian apologetic. Origen exerted considerable influence, but his speculations were often considered heretical and were condemned by the Church.

Orīgines ('origins'), of the Italian cities, a work by *Cato the Censor.

Orī'on, in Greek myth, a giant and a hunter of Boeotia, already in Homer identified with the constellation of that name, and the subject of various stories. He pursued the *Pleiades, and both he and they were turned into constellations. He was deprived of sight by the god Dionysus, or killed by Artemis (either because he challenged her to throw the discus against him or from jealousy because he was loved by Eos, Dawn), or stung to death by a scorpion sent by Gaia (Earth), because he boasted that he would kill all wild beasts. Ovid (*Fasti* 5. 495) relates the curious story of how he was created from the urine of three gods (based on the false derivation of his name Orion from *ouron*, 'urine').

Ornī'thes, see BIRDS.

Orō'pus, town on the borders of Attica and Boeotia, near the sea, for a long time a subject of contention between the two states. For the oracular shrine there see AMPHIARAUS.

Oro'sius, Paulus (early fifth century AD), a Christian historian from Spain, who took refuge with St *Augustine in North Africa from the barbarian invaders of his homeland. At Augustine's request he composed in AD 417 a *History against the Pagans* in seven books, a history of the world down to his own day, to counter the pagan view that the conversion of the Roman empire to Christianity was the cause of recent disaster (which he does by citing disasters that occurred before the rise of Christianity). The final part of the last book, covering the events of Orosius' own time, is a valuable historical source. During the Middle Ages his work was the standard history of the ancient world.

Orpheus, in Greek legend, a pre-Homeric poet, dated by the Greeks to a generation before the Trojan War and associated with the expedition of the *Argonauts, by his singing helping them to resist the lure of the *Sirens. He was said to be a Thracian, a follower of the god *Dionysus, the son of a *Muse, perhaps Calliopē, and so marvellous a player on the lyre that he could charm wild beasts and make even trees and rocks move by his music. His story is well known from the Roman poets Virgil and Ovid. He married Eurydicē, a *dryad. While being pursued by *Aristaeus, Eurydice trod on a snake, was bitten and died. Orpheus went down to the Underworld to recover her and by his music induced the goddess Persephone to let her go, but on condition that he should not look back at her as she followed him. When they approached the world of the living, Orpheus forgot the condition and looked back, and Eurydice immediately vanished for ever. Later Orpheus was torn to pieces by women, either Thracians who were jealous of his love for Eurydice, or by *maenads because he did not honour their god Dionysus (this story was the subject of a lost play by Aeschylus). His severed head, floating down the Thracian river Hebrus, and in some versions still singing, reached the island of *Lesbos, the home of lyric poetry, where it was buried.

From perhaps the middle of the sixth century onwards the authorship of several poems that referred to mystery cults (see MYSTERIES) was attributed to Orpheus. These poems dealt with purifications and initiations; secret rites that were supposed to free participants from ancient guilt, and impart to them better hopes for the afterlife, were performed according to the books of Orpheus and *Musaeus (see also ONOMACRITUS). The name of Orphism is sometimes used to describe the beliefs and practices of those who took part in mystery cults based on the poems attributed to Orpheus, or who engaged in ascetic practices. However, it is uncertain to what extent Orphism can be thought of as a unified spiritual movement. Interesting information has come from the *Derveni papyrus, which contains an ancient commentary on the theogony of Orpheus. Orphic myth, now known mostly from references in Plato and the Neoplatonists, explained the mixture of good and evil in human nature by the myth of *Dionysus Zagreus. It departed from normal Greek beliefs in making the guilt and punishment of the individual after death the centre of its doctrine; it would seem that, according to Orphic myth, men bear the guilt for the death of Dionysus Zagreus, and they have to pay the penalty after death to Persephone before she allows them to rise to higher existence. It also taught the transmigration of souls (having much in common with Pythagoreanism); after the soul has been reincarnated three times and has each time lived a virtuous life, it dwells in the Isles of the Blest for ever. But as well as a virtuous life, ritual purity and correct knowledge as prescribed by Orphic doctrine are necessary. Evil doers, and the uninitiated, risk punishment after death. The high ethical tone and ascetic practices of some of the followers of Orpheus became debased into the superstition and charlatanism of others, and although Pindar and Plato were attracted by some of the doctrines, to others of the fifth century BC 'Orphic' was a term of contempt. There was a revival of belief under the Roman empire.

Orth(r)us, in Greek myth, the dog of *Geryon and the offspring of the monsters *Typhon and *Echidna. See HERACLES, LABOURS OF 10 and SPHINX.

Orty'gia, see LETO.

Oscan, Oscans. The Oscans (Gk. Opikoi) were an early Italic people of southern Italy who established themselves principally in Campania. When *Sabelli replaced them in Campania and elsewhere their name survived and in due course was used to describe the newcomers' very similar language: Samnites, Frentani, Campanians, Lucanians, Bruttians, Mamertines, and Apulians all spoke Oscan-type languages. Oscan and *Umbrian form one group of Italic languages, Latin and *Faliscan the other (see LATIN LANGUAGE). After the Social War of 90–88 BC Oscan was gradually replaced by Latin, but it was still being spoken at Pompeii in AD 79. The *Atellan farces were in origin an Oscan literary form.

Oschopho'ria, at Athens, the festival of the vintage, celebrated in October, which had as its central ceremony the carrying of vine-branches with clusters of grapes from a sanctuary of Dionysus in Athens to the shrine of Athena Skiras at Phalerum, by two young men dressed in female robes. They were followed by a choir singing special hymns. The festival was popularly associated with the myths of *Theseus.

Osī'ris, most widely worshipped of the Egyptian gods, representing male fertility in nature and incarnated in the sacred bull Apis. According to myth he had been a pharaoh of Egypt who had civilized and educated his people but had been murdered and his body cut in pieces by his brother Set (identified with the Greek *Typhon). *Isis, his sister and wife, collected and buried his mangled remains, and with her son Horus took revenge on Set, the author of all evil. Thereafter Osiris was regarded as the god of the dead, but the source, through Horus (the Sun), of renewed life. The Greeks identified him with *Dionysus. See also SERAPIS and HARPOCRATES.

Ossa, mountain in Thessaly; see PELION and OTUS.

o'stracism (*ostrakismos*), at Athens in the fifth century BC, an institution traditionally ascribed to *Cleisthenēs in 508/7 BC whereby a prominent but unpopular citizen might be banished without loss of property for ten years. Each year the *ecclesia voted on whether an ostracism should be held that year. If an ostracism was agreed upon, every citizen who wished to vote scratched on a potsherd (*ostrakon*; see OSTRAKA below) the name of the person whose banishment from the state seemed to him necessary for public well-being. Provided there was a total of 6,000 votes cast in all, the person whose name appeared most often was banished. Prominent men known to have been ostracized are *Xanthippus, *Aristeidēs, *Themistoclēs, *Cimon, and *Thucydidēs son of Melesias. Ostracism existed in a few other Greek states. At Syracuse the institution was called 'petalism' because the names were written on olive-leaves (*petala*).

o'straka ('potsherds'), broken fragments of pottery used as writing material, especially in Egypt after the Greek conquest at the end of the fourth century BC. Ostraka were not greatly used for writing in Greece except as voting tablets (see OSTRACISM above). Latin ostraka have been found near Carthage.

O'strogoths, see GOTHS and JUSTINIAN.

Otho, Marcus Sa'lvius (AD 32–69), Roman emperor briefly in AD 69 in the chaos that followed Nero's death. He was a friend of Nero and husband of Poppaea Sabina, whom Nero loved and later married. From 58 to 68 he was governor of Lusitania. He was hailed as emperor after organizing a conspiracy among the praetorian guard, but he was defeated by *Vitellius and committed suicide.

Ōtus and Ephia'ltēs, in Greek myth, giant sons of Alōeus (whence they are called Alōīdae), or of Poseidon and the wife of Aloeus. They attacked the gods and tried to pile Mount Ossa on Olympus, and Mount Pelion on Ossa, in order to reach the heavens themselves and attack the gods there. They were destroyed by Zeus. A passage in Homer's *Iliad* tells how they imprisoned Arēs, the god of war, in a bronze jar for thirteen months, where he would have perished if Hermēs had not released him. A different tradition makes them beneficent heroes who founded cities and the worship of the Muses. Ephialtes was also the name of the demon of nightmare among the Greeks. See also GIANTS.

ovā'tio, see TRIUMPH.

Ovid (Publius Ovidius Nāso, 43 BC–AD 17), Roman poet. He was born at Sulmo, in a valley of the Apennines east of Rome, on 20 March. He tells the story of his life in one of his own poems, *Tristia* IV. 10. His family was of equestrian rank, and he was educated at Rome; by his father's wish he studied rhetoric with a view to practising law, but his taste for poetry asserted itself. According to the Elder Pliny he applied himself to the emotional rather than the argumentative side of rhetoric. He travelled, and visited Athens, Asia Minor, and Sicily. For a time he held some minor official posts in Rome, but soon abandoned public life for poetry. He was one of the group of poets around *Messalla and stood slightly apart from the Augustan circle centred on *Maecenas. Horace and Propertius were among his friends, but his warmest feelings were expressed in his elegy for *Tibullus (*Amores* III. 9), also a member of Messalla's circle. Virgil he only saw. He was three times married and had one daughter, probably by his second wife. His third wife remained devoted to him, and loyal during his exile.

Ovid's poetry had made him a leading figure in the social and literary circles at Rome, when in AD 8 he was suddenly banished by Augustus to Tŏmis on the western shore of the Black Sea and his books removed from the public libraries. (He suffered only *relegatio*, which meant that he retained his property and civic rights at Rome, not the more severe *exsilium*.) According to Ovid himself the grounds for this sentence were two, *carmen* and *error*, that is, a poem and a blunder; the poem was the *Ars amatoria*, published eight years before. The *error*, which Ovid refers to only obliquely, but insists was not *scelus*, 'a crime', was connected with the Julian family to which Augustus belonged; Ovid seems to have been present when something culpable was done, perhaps being involved in one of the adulteries of Augustus' granddaughter Julia, also banished in AD 8. The *error* must have provided the occasion for the emperor to satisfy his resentment at the poem, which ran counter to his moralistic legislation and had been published and won enormous success soon after Augustus discovered his daughter *Julia (see (4)) to be a notorious adulteress (2 BC). Ovid has described in a famous poem (*Tristia* I. 3) his last sad night at Rome and the hardships of his voyage to Tomis, and many of the poems of the *Tristia* and the *Epistulae ex Ponto* (see below) attest the tedious years of boredom, deprivation, and even danger (from barbarian attack) he had to endure, as well as the rigours of the climate, in that bleak land. There he died after ten years of unbroken exile. He eventually became reconciled to its inhabitants: they were kind and considerate and won his esteem. Though the city was a Greek foundation, half the population was Getic and either spoke Greek with Getic accent or used the local language. Ovid not only learned the language but wrote in it a poem (which has not survived) in honour of Augustus and Tiberius.

The order in which Ovid wrote his works is difficult to establish but is roughly as follows (see under each name): *Amores*, of which the first edition may have appeared as early as 20 BC, the second shortly before the *Ars amatoria*; *Heroides*, published between the first and second editions of *Amores*; *Medicamina faciei femineae*, written before the third book of the *Ars amatoria*, i.e. perhaps before 1 BC; the first two books of the *Ars amatoria* (published not before 1 BC, the third book was added later); *Remedia amoris*, AD 1; *Metamorphoses* and *Fasti* contemporaneously, from AD 2 onwards; *Tristia*, AD 9; *Ibis*, *c.* AD 11; *Epistulae ex Ponto* I–III, AD 13 (book IV probably appeared posthumously). A tragedy, *Medea*, was praised by Quintilian and Tacitus, but only two lines survive. The poems *Halieutica*, of which only a fragment survives, *Nux*, and *Consolatio ad Liviam*, all attributed to Ovid, were probably not by him. All Ovid's works are in elegiac couplets except for *Metamorphoses* (and *Halieutica*), in hexameters (see METRE).

Ovid was born in the year after the murder of Julius Caesar, too late to experience the horrors of civil war and so to welcome the policies of the Augustan regime. He was single-mindedly devoted to poetry, and his virtuosity, linguistic as well as metrical, was considerable. He refined even more strictly the rules of composition for the elegiac couplet. His wit and inventiveness make him the most consistently entertaining of the Roman poets, and a brilliant, sometimes over-exuberant, epigrammatist. Frivolous and irresponsible his poetry may sometimes seem, but when, as not infrequently happens, his imaginative sympathy is aroused, he can write movingly and simply, without artificiality or straining for effect. He is a gifted story-teller, skilful at focusing upon the telling scene or significant moment in a narrative, and with a sensitivity to natural beauty rare in the ancient world. The Elder Seneca has preserved a story illustrating Ovid's fondness for verbal extravagance. He was once asked by his friends if they might choose three lines to be excised from his works. He agreed, on condition that he might choose three lines that were on no account to be sacrificed. The lines chosen on each side turned out to be the same. One of them was (of the Minotaur), *semibovemque virum semivirumque bovem*, 'a man half bull and a bull half man'.

As a story-teller and guide to Greek myth and Roman legend Ovid was very influential on later Roman writers and was read, quoted, and adapted during the Middle Ages. He was the favourite Latin poet of the Renaissance. Shakespeare seems to have been well acquainted with Ovid in Latin as well as in Arthur Golding's excellent English translation of the *Metamorphoses* (1565–7).

Oxyrhy'nchus (El Bahnasa), place in Upper Egypt, south of the Faiyum, where many ancient papyri, some of literary importance, have been found from the last decade of the nineteenth century onwards. Very little is known of the history of the town. See PAPYROLOGY.

Oxyrhy'nchus historian, the, Greek historian, unknown by name, fragments of whose work were discovered at *Oxyrhynchus in 1906 on papyri containing about 900 lines of prose. These covered in detail and in a style commanding considerable respect events in the Greek world from 396 to 395 BC. The close agreement between *Diodorus Siculus and the Oxyrhynchus historian, where the two can be compared, shows that the latter was used by Diodorus' source Ephorus himself. This fact has led to the realization that Diodorus is a more reliable source at this point than had hitherto been thought.

P

Pactō'lus, tributary of the river Hermus in Lydia. See MIDAS.

Pacu'vius, Marcus (220–*c*.130 BC), Roman writer of tragedies (and also a painter), nephew of the poet Ennius, born at Brundisium. There exist the titles and fragments of twelve tragedies, based on Greek originals, and of one *fabula* *praetexta* (a drama having its subject in Roman history) on Paullus (probably L. Aemilius *Paullus). Of the titles, only *Antiopa* (Gk. *Antiopē*), his most famous work, indicates an original by Euripides (contrast *Ennius and *Accius); the original of *Niptra* ('the foot-washing', of Odysseus by his old nurse) was probably by Sophocles; other titles suggest post-Euripidean originals. The poets *Lucilius and *Persius ridiculed certain peculiarities of his diction, especially compound adjectives, but his work showed command of pathos and passion, and impressive character drawing. He was known as *doctus*, 'learned', a term of high praise, probably on account of his Grecisms and his familiarity with lesser-known stories of Greek legend. Varro and Cicero looked upon him as the greatest of Roman tragedians; the latter in his *De amicitia* testifies to the popular enthusiasm with which a scene in Pacuvius' *Orestes* was received.

Paean (Paiān or Paiōn). In the *Linear B tablets and in two passages in Homer's *Iliad*, Paian (Paion) appears as the name of a healing god. Also in Homer, and in later Greek literature, the name is given to the Olympian god *Apollo in his aspect of a god of healing who drives out pestilence, averts evil, and brings about victory. The cult hymn of Apollo is called a paean, from the cry *iē, ie Paian*, which came to be used as a refrain. Literary sources say that the paean was introduced to Sparta from Crete as a healing hymn and dance at the beginning of the seventh century BC, and was particularly associated with feasts of Apollo in Sparta.

Later the paean could be addressed to other gods also: Sophocles is said to have composed one to Asclepius, and Xenophon in his *Anabasis* describes the Greeks singing a paean to Zeus. Several paeans by Pindar have been discovered, in a rather fragmentary condition, on papyri. For the metrical term *paeon* see METRE, GREEK I.

paedagō'gus, in Greece, a slave employed to take boys to and from school.

Paeli'gni, central Italian tribe inhabiting the high valleys of the Apennines east of Rome. They were allies of Rome before 300 BC and remained loyal until the Social War (see ROME 6) when their chief town, Corfinium, became the capital of the Italians. They were rapidly Romanized after 90 BC. In their territory lay Sulmo, birthplace of Ovid.

Paestum (Gk. Poseidonia), Roman name for a coastal town of Lucania in south Italy, originally a Greek colony founded by *Sybaris *c*.600 BC. Rome made it a Latin colony in 273 BC. It is famous for its Greek temples, of which the fine ruins still remain. Virgil speaks of its roses flowering twice a year.

Paetus, see ARRIA.

Pāgānā'lia, at Rome, the celebration in the *pagi* (hamlets) of the sowing, a festival associated with the earth-goddesses Ceres and Tellus, who according to Ovid were then invoked to protect the seed. The date for its celebration was not fixed.

pāgā'nus ('pagan'), the inhabitant of a *pagus*, 'hamlet', the smallest division of the community in the Italian countryside. By the first century AD it had acquired the contemptuous sense of 'one who stays at home' (i.e. a civilian, in contrast with a soldier), and hence in Christian writers 'one who is not a soldier of Christ', 'a heathen'. It has also been suggested that its last meaning is derived from the sense of 'rustic', 'uncultured'.

Palae'mon, in Greek myth, a sea-god. See DIONYSUS.

palaeo'graphy. Palaeography is the study of manuscripts or their equivalent (e.g. papyri and wax tablets) in respect of their handwriting, and includes the study of variations in the latter which help to establish date and place of writing. It is also concerned with the layout of the writing on the page and with the form of the book. See also BOOKS AND WRITING.

palae'stra ('wrestling school'), in Greek cities, the place where boys were instructed in wrestling and gymnastics. It was generally in private ownership (in contrast with the municipally owned *gymnasium).

Palamē'dēs, in Greek myth, a proverbially ingenious hero, son of Nauplius, said to have invented some of the letters of the alphabet and the game of draughts. When *Odysseus tried to avoid his obligation to join in the expedition to Troy by pretending to be mad, Palamedes exposed his deceit. In revenge Odysseus forged a letter purporting to come from king Priam of Troy arranging for Palamedes to betray the Greeks in return for gold. Palamedes, in whose tent Odysseus hid the gold, was consequently stoned to death by the army. Nauplius avenged his son by luring the Greek fleet, returning from Troy, on to the rocks of Euboea by false beacons.

Pa'latine (Palātīnus mons), chief of the seven hills of Rome and traditionally the site of the first Roman settlement. Traces of Iron Age occupation have been found. It was here that Aeneas was shown by Evander (*Aeneid*, book 8) the cave of Lupercal (see LUPERCALIA). From 330 BC at the latest many famous Romans chose to build their houses on the hill, including in their day Hortensius, Cicero, Crassus, Milo, and Mark Antony. The house of Hortensius was acquired by the emperor Augustus and became the nucleus of a group of buildings known as *palatia* (pl.), from which the English word 'palace' is derived.

Pa'latine Anthology, see ANTHOLOGY 1.

Pālēs, in Roman religion, a deity of flocks and shepherds, similar to Pan among the Greeks, male according to Varro and others, female according to Virgil and Ovid. The festival of Pales, the Parilia, took place on 21 April, the traditional 'birthday' of Rome (and still regarded as such). It seems to have been a ritual purification of shepherds and flocks, firmly connected (for reasons which remain obscure) with the foundation of Rome. The sheep pens were cleaned and decorated with greenery, and sulphur was burnt on bonfires so that the smoke purified the sheep; offerings of cake and milk were made to Pales. The shepherd washed himself in dew, drank milk, and leaped through the bonfire. At the urban celebration of the festival the ashes of the calves burnt at the *Fordicidia were sprinkled on the fire. Ovid believed that the Parilia were older than Rome itself.

palimpsest (*palimpsēstos*, 'scraped again'), manuscript in which the text has been written over an effaced earlier text. The practice of writing on the renovated surface of an old manuscript was frequent among the monks of the Middle Ages, and since perfect removal of the original writing was seldom achieved, it has proved possible to recover valuable old texts of e.g. the Bible, Cicero, and Plautus.

Palino'dia, see STESICHORUS.

Palinū'rus, in Virgil's *Aeneid* (books 5 and 6), the helmsman of Aeneas, who, overcome by the god of sleep, fell overboard, was washed up on the shore of Italy and there murdered by the inhabitants. Aeneas, visiting the Underworld, met his ghost; it had not crossed the river Styx because his body remained unburied. A tomb was subsequently erected to Palinurus, and a cape (on the west coast of Italy) named after him.

Pa'lladas, Greek writer of *epigrams who lived at Alexandria *c.* AD 400. About 150 of his poems are in the Greek *Anthology. He was a schoolmaster embittered by poverty, and a pagan, or at least agnostic, in an age of expanding Christianity. His bitterness, vigorously expressed, and his cold pessimism recall the manner of classical Greek poetry, but sound a wholly individual note.

Pallā'dium, an image of the Greek goddess *Pallas Athena, identified by the Romans with Minerva, said to have been sent down from heaven by Zeus to *Dardanus, the founder of Troy (or to his son Ilus). Since Troy could not be captured while it contained this image, legend related that the Greek heroes Diomedēs and Odysseus carried it off and thus made it possible for the Greeks to sack Troy. It is variously said to have found its way to Athens, or Argos, or Sparta, or Rome. The Romans believed that an image in the temple of *Vesta, thought to have saved Rome from the attack of the Gauls in 390 BC, was the Palladium, either brought safely to Rome by the Trojan Aeneas after the sack (Diomedes having succeeded in stealing merely a copy) or else surrendered by Diomedes. When the temple of Vesta caught fire in 241 BC the image was rescued by the *pontifex* L. Metellus at the cost of his eyesight. Whatever its origin, it seems clear that such a talismanic object was kept in Rome. For the Palladium at Athens see ERECHTHEUM.

Palla'dius (Palladius Publius Rutilius Taurus Aemilianus), author in the fourth century AD of a Latin treatise on agriculture (*De re rustica*) in fourteen books, with an appendix in elegiacs on grafting trees. The first book contains general directions on the choice of a site, on farm buildings, the management of poultry, and agricultural implements. The next twelve books deal with the work to be done on the farm in each month. The fourteenth book, published for the first time in 1926, is on veterinary medicine. The work was quite well known in later times and a translation was made into Middle English.

Pallăs, title of the Greek goddess *Athena (who is often called Pallas Athena); suggested meanings include 'maiden' and 'brandisher' (of weapons). A late legend says that Pallas was the friend of Athena whom the goddess accidentally killed. See PALLADIUM.

Pallās, in Greek myth, the name of (i) a Titan, (ii) a giant, (iii) an Attic hero;

none is of particular importance. It was also the name of (iv) an Arcadian hero, founder of the city of Pallanteion, the grandfather of Euandros (see EVANDER) who figures in the story of the founding of Rome; and (v) the son of Evander, who accompanies Aeneas to the war against the Italians and is killed by Turnus.

palliā'ta, fā'bula, in Latin literature, term applied to Roman comedies adapted or imitated from Greek comedies, for instance the plays of Plautus and Terence. The name is derived from *pallium*, a Greek cloak. Compare PRAETEXTA.

Palmȳ'ra, oasis-city between Syria and Babylonia, whose trade it organized. In Roman imperial times it was an independent city between the Roman and Parthian empires, and in the early third century AD supported Rome. For its rise to prominence thereafter see ZENOBIA.

Pan, Greek god of shepherds and of flocks, for whose fertility he is responsible. Native to Arcadia, where he was born on Mount *Lycaeus, he has a human torso and arms but the legs, ears, and horns of a goat. He is generally thought to be the son of *Hermēs (the only other Arcadian god of importance), but his mother is variously named; she is generally a nymph, often *Callisto, but some stories say she is Penelopē. Pan has little mythology; a late story tells how he invented the musical pipe of seven reeds which he named *syrinx* in honour of the nymph of that name whom he loved and who was changed into a reed in order to escape from him. Other stories describe how he also loved the nymphs Pitys and Echo, who when they fled from him were changed respectively into a pine tree and a voice that can only repeat the last words spoken to her. Generally he loves mountains, caves, and lonely places; he was reputed to be the cause of sudden groundless fear, 'panic', especially that which may be felt in such remote surroundings. His cult began to spread beyond Arcadia in the early fifth century BC. Herodotus (6. 105) tells how in 490 BC Pan appeared to the Athenian runner *Pheidippidēs and promised help against the Persians, as a consequence of which the Athenians gave him after the battle of Marathon (490 BC) a cave-shrine on the Acropolis, still to be seen on the north slope.

A famous story narrated by Plutarch tells how, in the reign of the Roman emperor Tiberius (AD 14–37), the passengers in a ship sailing along the west coast of Greece heard a great voice shouting from the direction of the islands of Paxi that the god Pan was dead. In Christian legend this story was associated with the death and resurrection of Christ, which entailed the death of the pagan gods. Since his name is also the Greek word 'all', and the classical Greeks themselves sometimes understood the name to have this meaning, in later times speculations concerning a universal god were attached to his name. Sometimes a collection of Pans is found, the god's individuality submerged in a generalized representation of pastoral nature. By the Romans he was identified with *Faunus.

Panae'tius (*c*.185–109 BC), of Rhodes, Greek *Stoic philosopher. In *c*.144 he went to Rome and joined the circle of P. *Scipio Aemilianus, whom he accompanied on a mission to Egypt and Asia. After his return *c*.138 he divided his time between Rome and Athens; in 129 he succeeded Antipater as head of the Stoic school in Athens, and there he died. He adapted Stoic doctrine to fit Roman ideals, dwelling on the active virtues of magnanimity and benevolence rather than the passive virtues of indifference to misfortune and danger and of avoiding wrongdoing; he emphasized the subordination of private ambition to the good of the state, conformity to the same standard of virtue in public and private life, and the suppression of self-indulgence. The most important of his works was *On Duty* (now lost), on which Cicero modelled his own *De officiis*. He was a powerful influence on Roman thought.

Panathēnae'a, ancient Athenian festival supposedly founded in the time of *Theseus in honour of the birth of Athena, the patron goddess of the city, and held every year at the end of July. For three out of four years it was held on 28 and 29 Hekatombaion (July) and

called the Lesser Panathenaea, but starting from the archonship of *Hippocleidēs in 566/5 BC it was celebrated with particular splendour every fourth year, when it lasted from 21 to 28 Hekatombaion and was called the Great Panathenaea. The augmented festival included games, horse-races, and musical contests, to which the Peisistratids added poetical recitations by *rhapsodes. The equestrian events were held on that part of the Panathenaic Way (from the Dipylon Gate to the Acropolis) which crossed the agora. Pericles extended the musical contests and built a special theatre, the Odeum, for them. The prizes at the athletic contests were beautiful vases (some of which still survive, the earliest dated 570–560 BC) filled with olive oil; as many as 140 of them were given as the principal prize. The festival culminated on the last day in a magnificent procession along the Panathenaic Way and up to the Parthenon, in which Athena's new robe, a *peplos*, was carried to her statue (see ERECHTHEUM). This peplos was a costly garment, woven by Athenian girls of good family; it was a signal honour for a girl to be thought 'worthy of the peplos'. It was carried on a great ship on wheels, followed by girls known as *arrēphoroi* bearing baskets with the implements of sacrifice, by groups of boys bearing pitchers and old men with olive branches, by chariots, and finally by a cavalcade of young men on horseback (as depicted on the frieze of the Parthenon). The feast was completed with a *hecatomb of oxen, the flesh distributed among the people. In the fifth century BC the Panathenaea had not only a civic but a political character, being held in honour of the patroness not of the city alone but of the *Delian League also; the part taken by the allies in the sacrifices was regulated by decrees.

Panathēnā'icus, late work by *Isocratēs in praise of Athens.

pancra'tion, an event in Greek athletic *festivals. It was a specialized form of all-in wrestling in which the aim was to get an opponent to admit defeat when he was in danger of strangulation or a broken limb. The only tactics we know to have been forbidden were biting and gouging out an opponent's eye. Success in this event was highly esteemed.

Pa'ndarus, in Homer's *Iliad*, son of *Lycaon and leader, in the Trojan War, of the Trojans who lived about the foot of Mount Ida. He breaks the truce and wounds Menelaus with an arrow, and is eventually killed by Diomedēs. The story of his relations with Troilus and Cressida as told by Chaucer and by Shakespeare is derived ultimately from the work of *Dictys Cretensis and *Darēs Phrygius. His name survives in the English 'pander'.

Pandects (*pandectae*, 'digests'), one of the four parts of the corpus of Roman law drawn up by the emperor *Justinian.

Pandi'on, legendary king of Athens, variously described as grandson or great-grandson of *Erechtheus, or son of Erichthonius. He was father of *Philomela and Procnē.

Pandō'ra, in Greek myth, the first woman; see PROMETHEUS.

panegyric (*panēgyris*), see FESTIVALS.

Panegy'rici. 1. For the panegyric of Isocratēs see ISOCRATES.
2. For the panegyric on Trajan by Pliny see PLINY THE YOUNGER.
3. A collection of eleven complimentary speeches in Latin by rhetoricians, ranging in date from AD 289 to 389, in honour of the emperors of this time, chiefly Maximian, Constantius, Constantine I and II, Julian, and Theodosius. The collection also contains Pliny's panegyric (see 2 above) on which the later speeches were modelled. They were composed in the rhetorical schools of Gaul and have little literary merit, except as examples of pure Pliny-like Latinity, but throw much light on the history of fourth-century Gaul.

panhellē'nic, involving all the Greek states and colonies.

Paniō'nium, see POSEIDON.

Panthe'on or **Pa'ntheon,** at Rome, a magnificent temple consecrated, as the name implies, to all the gods, built by Hadrian (emperor AD 117–38) to replace that of M. Agrippa built 27–25 BC in the Campus Martius. It consists of a huge domed rotunda with a pedimented portico, and the basic structure (although not the decoration) has survived virtually intact. It was dedicated as a Christian church by Pope Boniface IV in AD 609.

pantomime, form of dramatic entertainment among the Romans in which a single actor/dancer (*pantomimus*) mimed a story in dumb show, playing all the parts himself, supported by a chorus of singers and a small orchestra. The stories chosen were almost entirely mythological. Pantomime in this form was introduced to Rome in 22 BC by Pyladēs of Cilicia (in south-east Asia Minor) and Bathyllus of Alexandria; hitherto in Rome dumb shows had been enacted by individuals, but it was Pylades' innovation to introduce chorus and orchestra. Bathyllus was so popular in this form of drama that his name came to be used for any pantomime actor. Performances took place on the public stage and privately. The actor wore a graceful silk costume and a mask with closed lips. The songs of the chorus were of minor importance; surviving fragments are in Greek. Pantomime and *mime, the delicate sophistication of the former contrasting with the coarseness of the latter, came to dominate the Roman stage, and contributed to the decline of serious drama there.

Panya'ssis, of Halicarnassus, older kinsman of Herodotus and the last great epic poet of archaic Greece (i.e. of the period before 480 BC), who lived in the early part of the fifth century and was put to death for his political activities by Lygdamis, tyrant of Halicarnassus, in the 460s or early 450s. He wrote two works: on Heraclēs, the *Heracleia* (9,000 lines in fourteen books), of which a few fragments remain, and on the Ionian colonial settlements, the *Ionica* (7,000 lines, and perhaps written in elegiacs: see METRE), of which poem, as far as is known, nothing survives. Panyassis' language appears to be basically Homeric, but includes some unusual words. The fragments of the *Heracleia*, few as they are, still provide valuable information about Greek myths and legends.

Paphos, city near the south-west coast of Cyprus, where according to tradition Aphroditē was born from the sea-foam, and the site of an ancient and widely famed temple to that goddess. This temple seems to date originally from the twelfth century BC, when the Mycenaean Greeks settled there (traditionally, the Arcadian contingent on their way back from Troy, led by Agapenor). Already in Homer's *Odyssey* Paphos is the home of Aphrodite. See also CYPRUS.

Papi'nian (Aemilius Pāpiniānus), d. AD 212, famous Roman jurist during the late second and early third centuries, the 'classical' period of jurisprudence. His origins are unknown: he may have come from Syria or Africa. He accompanied the emperor Severus to Britain and took part in the imperial tribunals held at York. In 203 he became praetorian prefect (see PRAEFECTUS PRAETORIO), assisted by the equally brilliant jurists *Paulus and *Ulpian. After the death of Severus the latter's son Caracalla succeeded to the throne; it is said that, having murdered his brother Geta, he asked Papinian to defend his action before the senate. Papinian replied that parricide was not so easy to defend as to commit, whereupon Caracalla put him to death. His principal works were thirty-seven books of *Quaestiones* (discussions of hypothetical or actual cases), and nineteen books of *Responsa* (collections of opinions); there are many excerpts from them in the Digest of *Justinian.

papyro'logy, the decipherment and elucidation of anything written on papyrus, and the study of the papyrus roll as a form of book. For the manufacture and uses of papyrus see BOOKS AND WRITING 2. Most papyri discovered in modern times come from Egypt where the rainless climate favours their survival. Serious excavations began in the nineteenth century, and at *Oxyrhynchus in particular. The earliest papyrus book we have, the *Persae* of *Timotheus, dates from the fourth century BC. Since many of the papyri are of school texts, and the education available was the traditional Greek one (Egypt was conquered by Alexander the Great in 332 BC), more than half of the several thousand surviving literary papyri are of Homer. Of the rest, fragments of works hitherto

unknown slightly outnumber the fragments of works already familiar. New texts discovered include several plays of Menander (mostly incomplete), much of Bacchylidēs, some poems of Sappho, Pindar, and other lyric poets, much of Callimachus, the mimes of Herodas, the *Ichneutae* of Sophoclēs, and several other sizeable fragments of tragedy; and, in prose, Aristotle's *Constitution of Athens*, the *Hellenica Oxyrhynchia* (a history continuing that of Thucydides), and several speeches of Hypereidēs. Other papyri contain fragmentary scientific and medical texts, and works on astrology and magic, important as social documents. Discoveries of Christian literary papyri have been equally important, adding further testimony to works already known, most valuably in the case of the New Testament text, and revealing hitherto unknown works, for example the *Sayings of Jesus* (part of the Gnostic *Gospel of Thomas*).

Most of the papyri discovered, however, are not literary but documentary: private letters and accounts, legal and administrative documents. A great deal has been learnt from these about the Greek language at various periods, in its most educated and in its semi-literate forms; in particular, the language of contemporary documents has thrown new light on the syntax, vocabulary, and idiom of the New Testament.

Latin papyri have been found in Egypt and a few other places but are comparatively rare. Most date from after the late third century AD, when the emperor Diocletian opened up Egypt, making it equal in status to the rest of the empire and encouraging all the eastern provinces in the use of Latin. Nearly all papyrus fragments of Latin literary texts belong to prose works, but there are important papyri of Juvenal and of Terence's *Andria*. Some fragments of Christian texts have been found, including one of a trilingual phrase-book in Greek, Coptic, and Latin, presumably of use to those intending to visit the monasteries.

para'basis, see COMEDY, GREEK 3.

pa'raloi or **para'lioi** ('coastmen'), see PEISISTRATUS.

parasang, Persian unit of length, very roughly equivalent to 3 miles.

parasite (*parasītos*), in Greek, originally 'fellow-diner', 'guest'. In the Old Comedy of the fifth century BC it had acquired the pejorative sense of 'sponger', one who earns a meal by flattering and humouring his host. To judge from surviving titles, the parasite often played a leading role in Middle Comedy; in New Comedy he is a stock character, the companion of another of the same, the boastful soldier, whose vanity he flatters in return for being kept. The names of notorious parasites in real life appear in some comedies. See COMEDY, GREEK.

Parcae, see FATES.

Parentā'lia, at Rome, the festival of the dead (13–21 February), on the last day of which was a public ceremony, the *Feralia; the rest of the time was reserved for private commemorations at family graves. Immediately after the Parentalia, on 22 February, the Caristia were celebrated, a family reunion and worship of the *lar familiaris* (see LARES), and an acknowledgement of the relationship existing between the dead and living members of the family.

Parian Chronicle or **Marble,** see MARMOR PARIUM.

Parī'lia, see PALES.

Paris. 1. In Greek myth, a son of *Priam king of Troy and his wife *Hecuba, also called Alexander (Alexandros). He was exposed when he was born because his mother had dreamed that she would bear a firebrand which would destroy the whole city, and a seer foretold that he would bring destruction on Troy. However, he was rescued and brought up by shepherds, and passed his youth pasturing sheep on Mount Ida, wedded to the nymph *Oenōnē. He had a favourite bull which Priam's servants carried off to be the prize at some funeral games. Paris, determined to win back the animal, entered for the games, won every event, and was identified by Priam's daughter Cassandra and restored to the family. Priam sent Paris on an embassy to Menelaus, king of Sparta, whose wife Helen fell in love with him (see PARIS,

JUDGEMENT OF). They fled together to Troy, thus bringing about the Trojan War, in which Paris, a skilful archer, took part. Homer represents him as affectedly bold and self-consciously martial in appearance, but unable to withstand the onslaught of Menelaus. In the single combat between the two, to decide the war, Paris was dragged off by Menelaus and had to be rescued by Aphroditē. It was his arrow, guided by Apollo, which finally killed Achilles. At the fall of the city he was fatally wounded by a poisoned arrow from *Philoctētēs' bow (which had belonged to Heraclēs) and sought, in vain, a cure from the nymph Oenone whom he had deserted.

2. The name of two popular *pantomime dancers, one of whom was executed by order of the emperor Nero (AD 67), the other by Domitian (AD 87). For one of them the poet *Statius wrote his libretto *Agavē*.

Paris, Judgement of. In Greek myth, at the marriage feast of *Peleus and the goddess Thetis, Eris (Discord) threw down a golden apple (the 'apple of Discord') inscribed 'for the most beautiful'. The goddesses Hera, Athena, and Aphroditē all claimed it, and they applied to Paris, the most handsome of mortal men, then a shepherd on Mount Ida near Troy, to settle the dispute. Each goddess offered him a reward in return for the apple: Hera greatness, Athena success in war, and Aphrodite the most beautiful woman in the world as his wife (compare the 'choice of *Heraclēs'). Paris awarded the apple to Aphrodite, and with her help carried off *Helen. It was ultimately this judgement which brought about the Trojan War, but it is not an aspect of the story used by Homer: he retains the hostility of Hera and Athena for Troy, but leaves it unexplained.

Parme'nidēs (*c.*515–after 450 BC), Greek philosopher from Elea (Lat. Velia) in south-west Italy, a Greek colony founded in 540 BC by Phocaea, the most northerly of the Ionian Greek cities in Asia Minor. He is said to have given laws to his city. According to tradition he was a pupil of, but did not follow, the Ionian philosopher *Xenophanēs, preferring to associate with Pythagoreans. He is said to have visited Athens late in his life and to have met Socrates (see PLATO 2 for the dialogue *Parmenides* in which he is one of the chief interlocutors). He was the founder of the so-called *Eleatic school of philosophy, and the first Greek philosopher whose doctrines survive fairly intact; they are found in a coherent series of quotations from the (lost) didactic poem in which he set out his thought. Written in hexameters, the poem consists of a prologue and two sections called the *Way of Truth* and the *Way of Seeming*.

The prologue opens with an allegory describing Parmenides' journey by chariot through the gate that leads from Night to Day, i.e. from false reasoning to true reasoning, the latter represented by a goddess who proceeds, in the *Way of Truth*, to tell the philosopher the truth of things as they really are. She begins by defining the two possible ways of enquiry, each contrary to the other: either a thing 'is, and cannot not-be'; or it 'is not, and must not-be'. The latter way is rejected on the grounds that it is impossible to conceive of the non-existent: one can only think or speak about 'what is'. There is a third way which combines the two others: ordinary mortals, deluded by their sense perceptions, believe that a thing both is and is not ('what is' can become something different, i.e. what it hitherto was not, by means of change). This too is rejected, on the grounds that it is self-contradictory. Once the premiss 'a thing is' is established by elimination as the only possibility, Parmenides (in the person of the goddess) deduces all that follows from it: 'what is' is not subject to birth or decay; it is single and not divisible; it is complete in itself and unchanging. All of these conclusions are reached by reason alone, without appeal to the senses.

This section is followed by the *Way of Seeming*, in which the goddess, starting from an acceptance of the opposites light and darkness, builds up a cosmology which apparently represents the erroneous beliefs of men, based on the senses. Since Parmenides rejects these, believing only in the *Way of Truth*, and since in any case his cosmology had little apparent influence later, it hardly matters that the text of this part is too fragmentary to permit reconstruction. But in describing a self-consistent cosmology Parmenides seems here to be admitting the possibility of structure and pattern in the world of the senses. The mutually exclusive nature of the two Ways may indicate that Parmenides considered the world as explained by the senses and the world as explained by reason to be utterly different and unrelated constructions, only the latter representing reality. The interest of the *Way of Seeming* lies also in the incidental fact that Parmenides here implies, for the first time in Greek thought, the requirements of a scientific theory, that it should account for and correspond with all the observed phenomena, and should be coherent and systematic. The doctrines of Parmenides (and of his formidably brilliant disciple *Zeno) offend against experience and common sense, but he was the most influential of the Presocratic philosophers; he had shown that even what men regard as fundamentally true was open to question. (For the answer of the atomists to Parmenides see DEMOCRITUS.)

Parme'nidēs, dialogue by Plato (see PLATO 2).

Parna'ssus, in Greece, a mountain a few miles north of Delphi, rising to about 2,460 m. (8,070 ft.). The towns of Phocis lie on its eastern flank, and the plain of Crisa with the high valley of Delphi on the south. On it were the *Corycian cave and the Castalian spring (see CASTALIA), and the whole mountain, as well as the spring, was sacred, associated with the worship of Apollo and the Muses. The two peaks between which the Castalia flows were sometimes spoken of as the two peaks of Parnassus, but the summit is in reality hundreds of metres above them.

pa'rodos, see TRAGEDY 3 and COMEDY, GREEK 3.

parody. Burlesquing serious poetry for comic effect was known in Greek literature from very early times. It might have been possible to see the *Margitēs* (perhaps *c*.700 BC) as a parody of Homeric epic had more of it survived. One tradition ascribes the invention of parody to *Hipponax (mid-sixth century BC); Aristotle in the *Poetics* attributes its invention to Hegemon of Thrace, who was later than Hipponax and may have been the first to win a contest for parodies. In surviving Greek literature the most notable parodists are Aristophanes, Plato, and Lucian. The first has a wide range, but mostly parodies tragic style in general and that of Euripides in particular, exploiting the comic possibilities in the latter's idiosyncracies of style and thought. Plato's parodies, of the style and manner of his interlocutors, are more subtle and have more than humorous ends in view; those of the participants in the *Symposium* are the most obviously funny; scholars still debate whether the speech purportedly by *Lysias in *Phaedrus* really is by him or by Plato. Lucian's parodies, often at the expense of the Olympian gods as they are depicted in mythology, are very funny in an obvious way.

In Latin literature parody occurs less often. Roman comedy burlesques in the Aristophanic manner the linguistic pomposities of Ennius and Pacuvius, but to a much lesser degree. The only sustained Latin parody is in the tenth poem of the *Catalepton* (see APPENDIX VIRGILIANA), in which Catullus' address to his yacht (poem 4) is turned into an address to an officious magistrate.

paronoma'sia, in figures of speech, a play on words, a pun.

Parrha'sius, of Ephesus, a famous Greek painter who lived *c*.400 BC and practised mostly at Athens. The story of his contest with the younger painter *Zeuxis in producing illusion is well-known. Zeuxis painted some grapes so naturalistically that birds came to peck at them, and victory seemed to be his. He then asked Parrhasius to draw back the curtain concealing the latter's picture, but the curtain turned out to have been painted by Parrhasius. Zeuxis declared himself defeated; he had succeeded in deceiving the birds, but Parrhasius had succeeded in deceiving him.

parthenei'on ('maiden song'), form of Greek choral *lyric, a processional hymn sung by a choir of girls, upon a religious, but not a solemn, occasion. Partheneia were composed by Alcman, Simonides,

Bacchylides, and Pindar. Fairly substantial fragments of some by Alcman and Pindar have been found on papyri.

Parthe'nius, of Nicaea (first century BC), Greek poet taken as a prisoner-of-war by the Romans and sent to Rome in 73 BC. Freed there, he exerted great influence on the Roman poets of the day (see ALEXANDRIANISM, LATIN). His poetry, mostly in elegiacs, was highly thought of, but very little of it survives. Extant are the prose outlines he made (in Greek) of love stories found in Greek poetry and fictional literature, intended for use by his poet friend *Gallus to ornament either epic or elegy; they provide evidence about the Greek novel.

Pa'rthenon ('temple of the maiden'), the temple of Athena Parthenos built on the highest part of the *Acropolis at Athens under the administration of Pericles, begun in 447 BC and dedicated in 438. A temple had been begun on the site before the Persian invasion of 480 BC, and its foundations were used for the new building. The architect was Ictinus, assisted by Callicrates, and the work was supervised by *Pheidias, who made the great cult statue of the goddess for the interior. The adornment of the temple with sculptures continued, almost certainly under the direction of Pheidias, until 432. These sculptures were more elaborate, more relevant to the cult, and more unified in theme than most temple sculptures. The ninety-two metopes (decorative slabs above the colonnade), represented in high relief on the east the battles of the gods and the giants, on the west the victory of the Greeks over the Amazons, on the south the struggle of the Centaurs and the Lapiths (these now the best preserved), and on the north the Trojan War, the common theme being the triumph of Greek civilization over barbarism—appropriate to a building that was in a sense a victory monument over the Persians. The pediments showed the birth of Athena from the head of Zeus (east end), and the contest of Poseidon and Athena for the possession of Attica (west end). These figures are carved in the round. The frieze, in low relief, 160 m. (524 ft.) long, which ran high around the inner building, is unique in apparently showing a contemporary scene, the procession at the *Panathenaea, although the figures may also make symbolic reference to the Persian Wars.

In the late 6th century the Parthenon was converted into a Christian church (the dedication—to Holy Wisdom—perpetuating an attribute of Athena) and after Athens was captured by the Turks in 1458 it became a mosque. It remained almost intact until 1687 when, in the course of a siege of the Acropolis by a Venetian force, it was partially destroyed by an explosion of gunpowder stored there by the Turkish garrison. Most of the surviving sculpture (together with some other pieces, including a *caryatid from the *Erechtheum) were acquired by the seventh Earl of Elgin when he was envoy to Constantinople (1799–1803) and sold (at a loss) to the British Government in 1816. They are now in the British Museum and known as the Elgin Marbles.

Parthenopae'us, in Greek myth, one of the *Seven against Thebes; his mother was *Atalanta and his father either Meleager or Milanion. His son Promachus, fighting among the Epigonoi (sons of the Seven), avenged his death.

Parthe'nopē, in Greek myth, one of the *Sirens. Parthenope was also the name of a Greek colony from Cumae on the site of modern Naples.

Pa'rthia, originally a small district of western Asia which gave its name to the Parthians, a semi-nomadic military aristocracy, who spoke a north-Iranian dialect but seem to have claimed a Scythian origin. The Parthians occupied this territory in 247 BC, but later they ruled an empire extending from the Euphrates to the Indus. Their king Arsacēs I threw off Seleucid domination and established the Arsacid dynasty. They fought a long series of wars against the advancing Romans (see CRASSUS), who did not succeed in conquering the greater part of the country until the reigns of the emperors Trajan, Antoninus, and Caracalla (second and early third centuries AD). The Arsacid dynasty came to an end c.226. The Parthians were famous for their cavalry; their peculiar skill was the ability to shoot backwards when retreating (the 'Parthian shot').

Partitiō'nēs orato'riae, see CICERO (1) 4.

Pa'sion (c.430–370 BC), in Athens, at the time of his death the richest banker and manufacturer of his day. He began his career as a slave in a banking firm, and later acquired his freedom, becoming an Athenian citizen by decree of the assembly. Several speeches of Demosthenēs and a speech by Isocratēs, *Trapeziticus* ('speech against the banker'), give much information about his business dealings.

Pāsi'phăē, in Greek myth, wife of *Minos king of Crete, daughter of Helios (Sun), mother of Ariadnē and Phaedra. When Minos refused to sacrifice to Poseidon, as he had promised, a fine bull, Poseidon punished him by inflicting on Pasiphae a passion for the bull. Enabled by the help of *Daedalus to gratify her passion she became the mother of the Minotaur, part bull and part man.

pastoral poetry, see BUCOLIC.

paterfami'lias, at Rome, the (male) head of the family; in the early republic he had very large powers (*patria potestas*, 'power of a father') over his family.

pater pa'triae ('father (i.e. saviour) of one's country'), honorific title given at Rome to those who had given outstanding service to the state. Cicero was so addressed in the senate after his consulship of 63 BC, and likewise the emperor Augustus in 2 BC.

patrēs conscri'pti, see SENATE.

patri'cians, at Rome, members of certain families, a privileged class, distinguished fom the *plebeians, the rest of the citizen body. Their name is probably connected with *pater* in the sense of 'member of the *senate'. If, as may be the case, the right to membership of the senate became hereditary in early times, that would have distinguished certain families from the rest of the citizen body. In the patriciate itself a distinction was gradually made between the 'lesser clans' (*gentes minores*, those of later creation) and the 'greater clans' (*gentes maiores*, those longer established). Until 445 BC patricians were not allowed to marry plebeians. Under the early republic they held the magistracies and the important religious offices: only a patrician could become *rex sacrorum*, *interrex*, and perhaps *princeps senatus*. The diminution of their political strength corresponds to some extent with the reduction in their numbers: about fifty patrician clans are known in the fifth century, but only fourteen at the end of the republic. Patricians could renounce their status by a special public act or simple adoption (compare CLODIUS). Julius Caesar and Octavian admitted new members to the patriciate.

Patro'clus (Patroklos or Patroklēs), in Homer's *Iliad*, son of Menoetius and the favourite companion of Achilles. For his story see ILIAD.

patron (Lat. *patrōnus*), at Rome, a powerful man who agreed to protect another by making the latter his *client.

patronage, literary. In Greece, literary patronage was exercised among others by the tyrants of Corinth (see CYPSELUS), Athens (see PEISISTRATUS), Samos (see POLYCRATES), and Sicily (see HIERON), who supported at their courts the poets Alcman, Anacreon, Bacchylidēs, Pindar, and Simonidēs. Archelaus, king of Macedon at the end of the fifth century BC, invited Agathon, Timotheus, and Euripidēs to his court. In the same century the city of Athens itself with its musical festivals and commissions for temple decoration and other works of art offered the advantages of patronage, and there were wealthy Athenian aristocrats giving hospitality to philosophers and teachers (see SOPHISTS). Similarly, in the Hellenistic age the kings of Egypt, the Ptolemies, were great supporters of all the arts, rivalled by the Attalids, kings of Pergamum.

At Rome, literary patronage was an extension of the relationship between *patron and client, and even included Greek writers. Under the empire Augustus and many later emperors were patrons of literature, as were wealthy individuals such as Maecenas and the Younger Pliny. Among those benefiting

were Virgil, Horace, Statius, and Martial.

patrony'mic, see NAMES.

Paullus, Lucius Aemi'lius (*c.*230–160 BC), Roman general and statesman, given the *cognomen* Macedonicus because of his victory at Pydna in 168, which brought the Third Macedonian War (see MACEDON) to an end. When Epirus was sacked on instructions from the senate the enormous proceeds of the booty were scrupulously paid into the Roman treasury. Paullus kept for himself only the books which had belonged to the Macedonian king Perseus, thereby forming the first private library at Rome. The triumph that he celebrated at the end of 167 BC was the most spectacular that Rome had until then seen. Paullus combined the traditional Roman virtues of integrity and devotion to duty with admiration for the culture of ancient Greece, and was a strong influence on his circle of friends as well as on Roman public life (See also PACUVIUS.)

Paul the Silentiary (Paulus Silentiārius, d. *c.* AD 575), an officer of the imperial household of the Roman emperor Justinian, responsible for maintaining peace and quiet in the palace; he wrote an elaborate poetical description of the restored church of St Sophia at Constantinople, which has considerable architectural as well as poetic interest. He is also the author of some hundred epigrams in the Greek *Anthology.

Paulus, Julius (flourished *c.* AD 210), one of the greatest Roman jurists. Together with *Ulpian he assisted *Papinian when the latter was praetorian prefect (see PRAEFECTUS PRAETORIO). Banished by Elagabalus (emperor AD 218–22) he was recalled by the latter's successor Alexander Severus, and may himself have shared the office of praetorian prefect with Ulpian. His voluminous writings survive in short excerpts in the Digest compiled by the emperor *Justinian.

Pausa'nias. 1. d. 467/6 BC, Spartan general in the Persian Wars, son of the king Cleombrotus I and nephew of Leonidas. He commanded the Greek forces that defeated the Persians at

Plataea (479) and captured Byzantium (478), but he was suspected of treasonable negotiations with the Persian king Xerxēs. He was twice acquitted of the charge, but was later suspected of fomenting a revolt by the helots (the Spartan serfs). To escape arrest he took refuge in a sanctuary, where he was walled up and left to starve. At the point of death he was taken out, to die on unconsecrated ground (467/6 BC).

2. (flourished *c.* AD 160), Greek traveller and geographer, the author of an extant 'Description of Greece' (*Periēgēsis Hellados*), who appears from passages in it to have been born in Lydia. The work is in ten books, namely: 1, Attica and Megara; 2, Corinth and Argolis; 3, Laconia; 4, Messenia; 5 and 6, Elis (with Olympia); 7, Achaea; 8, Arcadia; 9, Boeotia; 10, Phocis (with Delphi). Pausanias generally outlines the history and then the topography of important cities, followed by their religious cults and mythology. He is most interested in objects and places of historical and religious interest, and especially in artistic monuments; indeed his work is the most important literary source for the history of Greek art (what he tells us is based on his own travels and his general accuracy is attested by the extant remains of the monuments he describes). Only occasionally does he refer to the scenery and natural products of the regions he describes. He is honest about reputed marvels, such as the spotted fish of the river Aroanius; these he admits did not, as was supposed, sing like thrushes, although he waited by the river till sunset. Of the two stories accounting for the presence of a pickled Triton (perhaps some sea-creature) in a temple at Tanagra, he thinks it more credible that the creature was lured ashore by a bowl of wine and decapitated as it lay drunk on the beach, than that it was killed in single combat by the god Dionysus. His style is simple and unpretentious.

Peace (*Eirēnē*, Lat. *Pax*), Greek comedy by *Aristophanēs, produced at the Great *Dionysia in 421 BC, where it came second in the dramatic competition.

The *Peloponnesian War between Sparta and Athens is in progress; the Athenian demagogue and general *Cleon and the Spartan general *Brasidas have been killed in the summer of 422 at Amphipolis, and Aristophanes anticipates the successful outcome of negotiations for the Peace of Nicias (concluded some ten days after the performance). Trygaios, an Attic vine-grower, who with his family is suffering from the food-shortage, decides to imitate the mythical hero Bellerophon on his winged horse Pegasus, and ride to heaven on a dung-beetle, fattening it up to gigantic size for the purpose. The voyage is successfully accomplished, but Hermēs who answers the door tells him that Zeus and the other gods have moved house so as to be further away from the war down below, and War (Polemos) is in charge; he has cast Peace into a deep cave, from which, perhaps, she will never emerge, and is preparing to pound all the states in a mortar. While War looks for a pestle (failing to borrow one from Athens or Sparta because their 'pestles of war', Cleon and Brasidas, are lost), Trygaios and the Attic farmers (the chorus) whom he has summoned, having bribed Hermes with extravagant promises of festivals and a gold cup, draw Peace out of the cave with her two attendants Opōra ('harvest') and Theōria ('holiday'; literally, 'attendance at festivals'), and return with them to Greece. General jubilation follows (except on the part of arms manufacturers), and preparations are made for the wedding of Trygaios and Opora.

Peace, On the, title of speeches by *Isocrates and Demosthenes (see DEMOSTHENES (2) 4).

Peace of Nicias, see NICIAS and PELOPONNESIAN WAR.

Pe'gasus, in Greek myth, a winged horse who, with his brother Chrysaor, was sprung from the blood of the *Gorgon Medusa, pregnant by Poseidon, when she was killed by Perseus. The fountain Hippocrene on Mount Helicon in Boeotia, sacred to the Muses, was said to have been produced by a stamp of his hoof. With divine aid *Bellerophon was able to catch this horse when it was drinking at the fountain Peirēnē in Corinth, and bridle it. Mounted on it he succeeded in killing the *Chimaera, but was thrown when he attempted to fly to Olympus on its back. Pegasus appears on a handsome series of Corinthian coins, symbolizing the city.

Peirae'us, see PIRAEUS.

Peirē'nē, celebrated fountain at Corinth; see PERIANDER and PEGASUS.

Peiri'thŏus, see CENTAURS and THESEUS.

Peisi'stratus (*c*.600–527 BC) and the **Peisistra'tidai.** Peisistratus was three times tyrant of Athens; the Peisistratidai ('Peisistratids') were his sons and successors, Hippias and Hipparchus. During the struggles for political power that developed following the reforms of Solon in the early sixth century, Peisistratus (a relative of Solon) emerged as leader of the poorer 'hillsmen' (*diakrioi* or *hyperakrioi*). In about 560 he seized the Acropolis and made himself tyrant. The other two parties (the plainsmen and the coastmen) eventually united to drive him out of Athens, but he soon returned (in the mid-550s), accompanied in his chariot by a tall and beautiful woman whom he had dressed up as the goddess Athena. He said she had come to restore him to the city and was received with acclamation. Although he was soon forced into exile again, Peisistratus returned in 546 with a force of mercenaries, defeated his opponents and remained in power for the rest of his life. His eldest son Hippias succeeded him, and associated his brother Hipparchus in the tyranny. Hipparchus was unpopular because of his dissolute arrogance, and in 514 was killed by *Harmodius and Aristogeiton. After this the rule of Hippias became harsher. His fall was brought about chiefly by the Alcmaeonids (see CLEISTHENES (2)), who induced Sparta to invade Attica. Hippias, besieged in the Acropolis, capitulated and retired to Sigeum in 510. Here he negotiated with the Persians in order to secure their help in his restoration. His hopes frustrated, he subsequently died at Lemnos.

Tradition said that Peisistratus was a moderate and benevolent ruler. It is not always possible to distinguish his work from that of his sons. He created a citizens' property tax which provided subsidies to poor farmers, enabling them to avoid debt (which Solon had failed to achieve). Under him the commercial importance of Athens greatly increased; her wine, oil, and pottery reached all the surrounding countries. Under his sons better roads were built between the city and country demes, and lawsuits in the demes were heard by travelling judges, so that country people did not need to travel to the city to have their cases heard. Athens was provided with a good water-supply; the famous spring-house (Enneakrounos, 'nine-jets') was built in the agora, the water channelled in clay pipes from the spring Callirrhoē. The Peisistratids beautified the city with new temples (remains of the buildings have been found on the *Acropolis, as well as many marble statues) and they encouraged art and literature: for instance, *Simonidēs of Ceos and *Anacreon of Teos were invited to Athens. The *Panathenaic festival was celebrated with greater splendour from 566 onwards, with the addition of contests in athletics, music, and poetry; recitals of Homer by rhapsodes were said to have been introduced by the Peisistratids (see HOMER 6). Peisistratus is also credited with the creation of the state festival of the City *Dionysia in 534, and with encouraging the cult of Demeter at *Eleusis.

Pelasgians, apparently a north Aegean people scattered throughout Greece by the migrations of the Bronze Age and preserving a common, non-Greek language. The Greeks used the name to describe the original pre-Greek inhabitants of Greece and the Aegean area, with whom they sometimes included the Tyrrhenians (Etruscans).

Pela'sgus, early king of Argos, father of *Lycaon.

Pēleus, in Greek myth, son of *Aeacus (mythical king of Aegina); he became king of Phthia, in Thessaly. His name may mean 'man of Pelion' (a mountain in Thessaly). When he and his brother *Telamon killed their half-brother Phocus, Aeacus banished them; Peleus went to Phthia, where the then king purified him of his crime and gave him his daughter in marriage and a share of his kingdom. Peleus took part in the Calydonian boar-hunt (see MELEAGER), where he accidentally killed one of the participants and was again banished. He went to Iolcus in Thessaly where Acastus, son of Pelias, purified him, and he took part in Pelias' funeral games where he wrestled with Atalanta. Acastus' wife, Astydameia, fell in love with Peleus. When he rejected her she sent a message to his wife saying that he was about to marry another woman; at that his wife hanged herself. Astydameia told her husband that Peleus had made advances to her; Acastus then took Peleus hunting on Mount Pelion, hid his sword as he slept, and left him to be attacked by the centaurs. The centaur *Chiron, however, restored his sword; Peleus then captured Iolcus and took his vengeance on Astydameia by killing her and marching his army between the pieces of her severed body. He was given as wife the goddess Thetis (see NEREUS). Zeus had previously fallen in love with her, but when told by Prometheus that she was fated to bear a son more powerful than his father, decided to give Thetis to a mortal so that her son should be mortal also. It is said that Peleus had to wrestle with her in order to win her. Thetis' child was Achilles, whom Peleus took to Chiron to be brought up.

Pe'lias, in Greek myth, son of Poseidon and *Tyro, and the usurper king of Iolcus in Thessaly, the rightful king being his half-brother Aeson, father of Jason; see ARGONAUTS.

Pē'lion, high wooded mountain in (Magnesian) Thessaly, famous as the home of the centaur *Chiron. In Greek myth, the Giants *Otus and Ephialtēs, in an attempt to scale the heavens and overthrow the gods, piled Pelion upon Ossa (another Thessalian mountain) and Ossa upon Olympus.

Pella, capital of Macedonia c.400–167 BC (i.e. from the time of king Archelaus until the conquest by Rome). It became the largest Macedonian city until overtaken by Thessalonika in 146 BC. Pella was later a Roman colony.

Pelo'pia, daughter of Thyestēs and mother of Aegisthus. See PELOPS.

Pelo'pidas (c.410–364 BC), Theban general, who with his friend and colleague *Epaminondas brought *Thebes to the zenith of her power. In 379 BC, with six confederates dressed as women, he killed the pro-Spartan generals who, with the support of a Spartan garrison, were tyrannizing Thebes. At the battle of Leuctra in 371 BC Thebes drove the Spartans out of central Greece; Pelopidas won great fame for his leadership of the *Sacred Band both at this battle and the earlier battle at Tegyra (375 BC). He accompanied Epaminondas on his first invasion of the Peloponnese (370/69), but after that looked northwards to Thebes' other enemies, *Alexander of Pherae (in Thessaly), and Macedon. In 364, in an expedition against Alexander of Pherae, Pelopidas, although victorious, was killed at the battle of Cynoscephalae.

Pe'loponnese (Peloponnēsos, 'island of Pelops'), the southern part of Greece, connected with central Greece by the Isthmus of Corinth. Its chief political divisions were Argos, Laconia (Sparta), Messenia, Elis, Achaea, and Arcadia.

Peloponne'sian League, the earliest and longest-lived Greek alliance, dating from the sixth century BC when Sparta negotiated treaties with Peloponnesian states (see above) whereby Sparta could expect the support of all members in war if a majority vote favoured such a course, each state having one vote. *Chilon, one of the Seven Sages, is credited with its creation. The League was dissolved in 366 BC.

Peloponne'sian War (431–404 BC), a war between Athens and Sparta—the two leading Greek city-states—and their respective allies. A number of sources of friction sparked it off, notably Athenian intervention in a quarrel between Corinth (Sparta's ally) and her colony Corcyra, but the real reason for the conflict, according to the Athenian historian *Thucydidēs, was the rise of Athens to greatness, which made the Spartans fear for their own position. Athens was morally the aggressor, but it was Sparta who declared war. Sparta's army was far superior in quality and quantity, but the Athenians had an even bigger advantage at sea. The defences of Athens were strong and the city could not be starved into surrender, as it was connected to the port of Piraeus by the *Long Walls and could import supplies almost with impunity. It had sufficient finances to buy supplies and pay the fleet (and army). This was the assessment of the situation made by *Periclēs, the Athenian leader, and his strategy was based upon it. He persuaded the country population to move themselves and their possessions into the city and into the space between the Long Walls, temporarily sacrificing their farms.

The first ten years of the war, known as the Archidamian War from the name of the Spartan king who led the incursions into Attica, were indecisive. The Peloponnesians who invaded and ravaged Attica in 431 found it deserted, and after about a month returned home; this was to be, in general, the pattern for the next six years. In 430 a devastating plague broke out in Athens and the city lost more than a quarter of her population. Pericles died as a result of it in 429, his death depriving Athens of the only man who could impose a single policy on the Athenians. Nevertheless the Athenians won a number of victories on land and at sea in the next few years, notably the capture of *Pylos in 425, and Sparta gave up her annual invasions of Attica and made overtures for peace. *Cleon, who had succeeded Pericles as the most influential politician in Athens, persuaded the Athenians to reject the Spartan offers, but both he and the outstanding Spartan general *Brasidas were killed at *Amphipolis in 422, and thus the two chief opponents of peace were removed (the 'pestles of war' as they were called in Aristophanes' *Peace*). The Peace of *Nicias was concluded in 421. It was in the main a victory for Athens, especially since she kept her empire intact while her enemies were divided, Corinth and Boeotia refusing to sign the Peace.

The truce was unstable and broke down completely in 415, when Athens, under the influence of *Alcibiades, sent a great fleet to attack Syracuse—the *Sicilian Expedition. The expedition was a disaster, ending in 413 with the defeat of the Athenian fleet and army and the exhaustion of their finances. Sparta, meanwhile, was developing a good fleet of her own, financed by Persia. The war at sea continued to go Athens' way for several years, but in 405 the Spartan commander *Lysander destroyed the Athenian fleet at Aegospotami. Besieged by land and sea, without money or allies, Athens capitulated in April 404 and became virtually the subject-ally of the victor.

The principal literary authority for the Peloponnesian War up to 411 is Thucydides; for 411 to the end, Xenophon in the *Hellenica*; see also DIODORUS SICULUS.

Pelops, in Greek myth, son of the Lydian king *Tantalus; his mother is usually said to be Dionē, daughter of Atlas. He was the founder of the Pelopid family after whom the Peloponnese is named. According to the usual story he was expelled from Sipylus in Lydia by Ilus, an early king of Troy, and brought his great wealth to Pisa in Elis, where he became king. There are two main stories about Pelops. In the first, his father Tantalus killed him when a child and served his flesh to the gods at a banquet, to see if they could tell it from that of some animal. *Demeter, absorbed in her grief for Persephonē, ate part of the shoulder; but the other gods detected the nature of the dish, brought Pelops to life again, and replaced the missing shoulder with one of ivory. Tantalus was punished in Hades. The other story tells how Pelops, grown up, sought to marry Hippodameia, daughter of Oenomaus king of Elis. The condition of winning her was that he should outdistance Oenomaus in a chariot-race. If he was caught, Oenomaus would spear him. Pelops bribed Myrtilus, the king's charioteer, to take out the lynch-pin of a wheel on his master's chariot; the wheel fell off, Oenomaus was thrown and killed, and Pelops carried off his bride. But he refused to give Myrtilus the promised reward and threw him in the sea (hence, perhaps, the name of the Myrtoan Sea, east of the Peloponnese). The dying Myrtilus (or Oenomaus) cursed Pelops, which is the origin of the curse upon his house. For the time being Pelops flourished and fathered six sons. He was supposed to be buried at Olympia, where he was worshipped as a hero and sometimes said to be the founder of the Olympic games.

Two of Pelops' sons were Atreus and Thyestēs, in whom the curse was manifested. Atreus became king of Mycenae, and Thyestes seduced his brother's wife Aëropē; thereupon Atreus banished Thyestes but later recalled him on pretence of being reconciled and prepared a banquet for him consisting of the flesh of his two sons. When Thyestes realized what he had eaten, he fled in horror, calling down a curse on the house of Atreus. He now became, by his own daughter Pelopia, the father of Aegisthus, who was exposed at birth by his mother but brought up by shepherds; when Atreus heard of the boy's existence he sent for him and brought him up as his own child. When Aegisthus was grown up, Atreus sent him to kill Thyestes, but the latter recognized him as his own son and the two contrived the death of Atreus instead. Atreus was the father of *Agamemnon and Menelaus. When Agamemnon led the Greek expedition to Troy and left the kingdom of Mycenae in the care of his wife Clytemnestra, his cousin Aegisthus seduced her and joined with her in murdering Agamemnon on his return. Later, Agamemnon's son Orestēs, with the help of his sister Electra, avenged their father by killing Aegisthus and Clytemnestra. The curse on the house was not finally expunged until the purification of Orestes. (See also ORESTEIA, ORESTES, and ELECTRA.)

This legend (Agamemnon's murder excepted) is not known to Homer, for whom the kingdom of Mycenae passes naturally from Pelops to Atreus, Thyestes, and Agamemnon.

penā'tēs, di, in Roman religion, 'the gods dwelling in the store cupboard' (*penus*, 'provisions'), who had their images in the atrium of every Roman house and were regarded together with the *lares* as protectors of the house. There were also state *penates* (*penates publici*, protectors of Rome); their cult was attached to the temple of Vesta.

According to Virgil, Aeneas had brought these to Italy from Troy. For Virgil, not only Rome and Troy had their *penates* but even Carthage, the city of a hated enemy; similarly in the fourth Georgic the bees, the most human-like of the animal creation, 'have their *penates* and their fixed abode'. The worship of the domestic *penates* and *lares* centred on the family meal: a portion was set aside and thrown on the flames of the hearth for the gods, and the table always held a saltcellar and small offerings of first-fruits for them. A member of the family, returning after an absence, would greet the *penates* as living members of the household, the traveller's stick perhaps hung up beside their images. Generally speaking, every notable event of family life involved a prayer to the *lares* and *penates*.

Pēne'lopē (also Pēnelopeiā), in Homer's *Odyssey*, daughter of Icarius (brother of Tyndareus) of Sparta and wife of *Odysseus. She faithfully awaits her husband's return during his twenty years' absence (ten years at the siege of Troy, ten years in his wanderings afterwards), although wooed by numerous suitors among the local nobles. She pretends she cannot remarry until she has woven a shroud for Odysseus' father, Laērtēs. This she unravels every night, so that the work is never completed, but her deception is revealed by one of the maids and she is compelled to finish it. She then promises to marry the suitor who can bend the bow of her absent husband. Odysseus returns in disguise at this juncture, wields the bow against the suitors and, when he reveals to her his knowledge of the construction of their bed, is finally accepted by Penelope as her husband.

An entirely different tradition makes Penelope the mother of Pan by the god Hermēs.

pene'stae, see THESSALY.

Pēnē'us (Pēneios), principal river of Thessaly in Greece; it flows through the vale of Tempē between Mount Olympus and Mount Ossa.

penta'meter, in Greek and Latin, line of verse containing five metrical units (*metra*); see METRE, GREEK 1 and 2. In practice the term almost always refers to the elegiac pentameter.

pentāthlon, an event in the Greek athletics *festivals. Competitors in this event had to enter five contests: long jump, foot race, throwing the discus, throwing the javelin, and wrestling. It seems that by a process of elimination, only the two best competitors were selected for the final contest, the wrestling.

Pentēkontaē'tia, in Greek history, the 'period of fifty years' (roughly) between the end of the Persian and the beginning of the Peloponnesian Wars (479–431 BC). It was described (but not so called) by the historian Thucydides (1. 89–118), with some omissions and some doubtful chronology. This was the period in which Athens developed her empire (see DELIAN LEAGUE) and produced some of her greatest works of art and literature. It was the age of the statesman Pericles, the tragedians Aeschylus and (for the first half of their productive lives) Sophocles and Euripides, the philosopher Anaxagoras, the sophist Protagoras, and the artists Polygnotus and Pheidias; the Parthenon was built during this time, and Socrates, Thucydides, and Aristophanes grew up. Thucydides represents Pericles as describing the Athens of his day as 'the school of Greece'. In other parts of Greece it was the period of Pindar, Bacchylides, Herodotus, Parmenides, Zeno, Empedocles, and Polycleitus.

Pente'licus, mountain, about 1,100 m. (3,610 ft.) high, which bounds the Athenian plain on its north-east side, 16 km. (10 miles) from Athens. In earlier times it was called Mount Brilessus, its later name deriving from the famous marble quarried in the deme of Pentelē on its side. Pentelic marble is of a pure white colour and it weathers to a beautiful golden brown. It was used freely by the second quarter of the fifth century; 22,000 tons of it were used to build the Parthenon at Athens.

Penthesilē'a (Penthesileia), in Greek myth, queen of the *Amazons who came to the aid of Troy after the death of Hector. She fought with distinction but was eventually killed by Achilles, who grieved over her body.

Pentheus, in Greek myth, son of Echion and of Agavē, daughter of Cadmus king of Thebes. See BACCHAE.

peplos, see PANATHENAEA.

Pe'rdiccas, name of several notable Macedonians. The king Perdiccas II was active in the Peloponnesian War, changing allegiance several times from one side to the other in his own interest. Another Perdiccas was second-in-command to Alexander the Great and became in effect regent of the empire after Alexander's death; soon after that he was killed in a mutiny. See MACEDONIA.

Perdix, see DAEDALUS.

Pe'regrine (*Peregrīnus*), see LUCIAN.

Pe'rgamum (Pergamon). **1.** Name of the citadel of Troy.

2. City of Mysia in the valley of the Cāïcus in the north-west of Asia Minor, originally a hill-fortress founded by Greeks in mythical times, according to local tradition (see ANDROMACHE). In the third century BC, as the capital of the *Attalids, Pergamum became a splendid and beautiful city with a famous school of sculpture and a library second only to that of Alexandria in size. For its importance as a literary centre and place where parchment was first used extensively for books, see BOOKS AND WRITING 3. It was an important cultural centre during the Second *Sophistic.

Peria'nder (Periandros), tyrant of *Corinth from about 625 to 585 BC who succeeded his father *Cypselus and brought Corinth to the height of fame and prosperity. Periander was probably a stern ruler, and is reputed to have killed his wife and quarrelled with his sons; he was certainly a powerful and energetic man, and his practical good sense led to his being included by some among the *Seven Sages of Greece (his court is the scene of Plutarch's dialogue, the *Banquet of the Seven Sages*). He was a patron of the arts (*Arion the dithyrambic poet stayed at his court) and he was probably responsible for the construction of the *diaulos* or portage way across the Isthmus of Corinth (see CORINTH, ISTHMUS OF).

Pe'riclēs (*c.*495–429 BC), Athenian statesman, an *Alcmaeonid, son of

*Xanthippus. In politics he supported the *democracy and came into political prominence as one of the state prosecutors of *Cimon in 463. In 462/1 he and *Ephialtēs joined in reducing the powers of the *Areopagus, and after the latter's murder and Cimon's *ostracism, both in 461, he became the most influential man in Athens. From this time until his death he dominated Athenian politics, and he has given his name to the most brilliant age of Greek history, 'Periclean Athens' standing for one of the high points of world civilization. Under his guidance Athens adopted an imperialistic policy, and the *Delian League, created to keep the Persians out of Greece, was converted into an Athenian empire. This imperialism brought Athens into conflict with Sparta, which was at war with Athens from 460 to 446 (sometimes called the First Peloponnesian War). The peace that followed gave Pericles the opportunity to carry on a great building-campaign, most notably of the *Parthenon. When war broke out again with Sparta in 431 (the *Peloponnesian War), Pericles dictated a policy for Athens calculated to neutralize Spartan superiority on land, but it involved considerable hardship for the population of Attica. Nevertheless his authority was undiminished until the ravages of the plague in 430 broke Athenian morale. He was then removed from office, tried for embezzlement, and fined. Soon after, he was reinstated, but he too had caught the plague, and he died six months later. No other Athenian ever achieved Pericles' unchallenged ascendancy. The historian Thucydides, his great admirer, says that under him Athens, though nominally a democracy, was in fact ruled by its first citizen. He was a man of powerful character, incorruptible, grave and reserved in manner, dignified in speech. He associated with the cultivated men and intellectuals of the day, Pheidias, Anaxagoras, Sophocles, Herodotus. The Funeral Oration which he delivered over the Athenian dead after the first year of the Peloponnesian War (Thucydides 2. 35–46) expresses his high concept of Athens and the Athenian democracy, although his ideals included undisguised imperialism.

Peri hi'ppikēs, see HORSEMANSHIP.

Peri hy'psous, see LONGINUS ON THE SUBLIME.

Perikeiro'menē ('shorn hair'), Greek comedy by *Menander, of which about half has been discovered on papyrus.

A poor merchant Pataecus has exposed his twin children, a boy and a girl. The boy Moschion is adopted by a rich woman who subsequently marries Pataecus, and the latter adopts Moschion, not knowing that he is really his own son. The girl Glycera, now the mistress of a soldier Polemon, is discovered kissing Moschion, whom she knows to be her brother, although he is still ignorant of this fact. In jealousy Polemon cuts off her hair (hence the title of the play), whereupon she takes refuge in the house of the now wealthy Pataecus. Some trinkets left with her when she was exposed reveal her identity, and Moschion also discovers his identity by eavesdropping. Thus all are reconciled and Glycera is able to marry Polemon.

Pe'rillus, see PHALARIS.

Pe'riochae ('summaries'), see LIVY.

perioi'koi ('dwellers around', i.e. around Sparta), in Laconia (the southeast district of the Peloponnese), the free inhabitants of such small towns and villages as were not subjugated to *Sparta. They were, however, under Spartan supervision, served in the army and paid taxes on a par with Spartan citizens although they had no political rights in the Spartan state. They carried on what industry and commerce there was, from which Spartans were excluded.

Peripate'tic School, the Aristotelian school of philosophy in Athens (see ARISTOTLE 1). Aristotle taught in the groves and gymnasium of the *Lyceum; one of the buildings (either in his day or in that of his successor Theophrastus) had a covered walk, *peripatos*, from which the school derived its name. Another explanation given in ancient times for the origin of the name was that Aristotle was accustomed to 'walk about' (*peripatein*) while lecturing.

peripetei'a, in Greek tragedy, a 'surprising turn of events'; see POETICS.

Pe'riplus (*Periplous*, 'voyage of exploration'); see ARRIAN and SCYLAX.

Pe'riplus maris Erythrae'i ('voyage of exploration around the Red Sea'), the work of an anonymous Greek traveller of the first century AD, describing the coasts of the Red Sea and the Arabian Gulf. It shows knowledge of part of India, and of East Africa as far south as Zanzibar.

Pēro, daughter of Neleus; see MELAMPUS.

Persa ('the Persian'), Roman comedy by *Plautus. The subject is the deception of a pimp, to whom a Persian sells a beautiful Arabian captive. But the Persian is in fact the *parasite Saturio and the captive is his daughter; he has agreed to the deceit for the sake of a good meal.

Persae. 1. Greek tragedy by Aeschylus; see PERSIANS. **2.** A nome by *Timotheus (2).

Perse'phonē (Lat. Prōse'rpina), also known as Korē ('daughter'), in Greek myth, the daughter of Zeus and Demeter, snatched away to be queen of the Underworld by *Hadēs while she was picking flowers in the meadows of Enna in central Sicily. For Demeter's search for her daughter see DEMETER. Zeus yielded at length to her lamentations, but Persephone could not be entirely released from the Underworld because she had eaten some pomegranate seeds (as was revealed by Ascalaphus, son of Acheron, river of the Underworld, whom Demeter thereupon turned into an owl). It was arranged that she should spend eight (or six) months of the year on earth and the remainder with Hades. The myth is told in the *Homeric Hymn to Demeter, by Ovid in his *Fasti* and *Metamorphoses*, and by Claudian in *De raptu Proserpinae*. Persephone was understood in ancient times to symbolize the seed corn that must descend into the earth so that from seeming death new life may germinate; she later came to symbolize death. Cicero visited Enna and tells in his Verrine orations (see CICERO (1) 1) how he found the priestess and inhabitants griefstricken because Verres had stolen their statue of Demeter.

Perse'polis, in Persia, the residence and the burial place of the Achaemenid kings (Cyrus, Darius, Xerxēs, etc.). In 331 BC it was sacked by Alexander the Great.

Perseus. 1. In Greek myth, the son of Zeus and Danae. See DANAE for the story of his birth, of the prophecy that he would kill his grandfather Acrisius, and of the casting away of mother and child and their arrival on the island of Seriphos, where Polydectēs was king. Polydectes f   in love with Danae, but his love was not returned. Perseus was now a young man, and Polydectes, finding him an obstacle to his designs on Danae, persuaded him to undertake the dangerous venture of obtaining the head of Medusa (see GORGONS), thinking that he would be destroyed. But the gods favoured him: although accounts vary as to which gods gave him which gifts, they commonly say that Pluto lent him a helmet which would make him invisible, Hermes wings for his feet, Athena a mirror (so that he need not look directly at Medusa, whose gaze turned people to stone), and the nymphs a wallet to put the head in. Directions for finding Medusa were given him by the *Graiae. On his return, having killed Medusa, Perseus rescued *Andromeda from where she was chained to a rock, and married her, after turning Phineus, another suitor, to stone when he attempted to carry her off. It is also said that with the Gorgon's head he turned *Atlas into a mountain, because Atlas had been inhospitable to him on his travels. Perseus then returned to Seriphos, just in time to save Danae from the violence of Polydectes, whom he turned to stone. Leaving his brother Dictys there as king Perseus now went to his native Argos, but found that his grandfather Acrisius had gone to Larisa in Thessaly. There Perseus, taking part in some games, accidentally killed him when throwing a discus and thus fulfilled the prophecy. He refused to take his grandfather's kingdom himself, to which he was heir, but withdrew to Asia, where his son Persēs became ruler of the Persians, supposedly named after him; or, according to another version, took Tiryns in exchange for Argos and founded Mycenae.

2. King of Macedon 179–166 BC, elder son of Philip V. He devoted his energies to consolidating Macedonian power and prestige in Greece at a time when Greece, while nominally independent, was under the protection (and will) of Rome. He was defeated by Aemilius *Paullus in the Third Macedonian War (see MACEDON) and taken to Rome, where he died.

Persians (Gk. *Persai*, Lat. *Persae*), Greek tragedy by *Aeschylus, produced in 472 BC. Pericles was *choregos*.

The chorus of Persian elders express their anxiety for the fate of Xerxēs' expedition of 480 against Greece (see PERSIAN WARS), and Atossa, mother of Xerxes, tells of ominous dreams and portents. A messenger arrives and announces the disaster of Salamis, giving a vivid account of the battle and the destruction of the Persian fleet. The chorus call up the spirit of the dead Darius (father of Xerxes), who sees in the catastrophe the accomplishment of oracles and the punishment by the gods of excessive pride. He foretells the defeat at Plataea. Xerxes himself arrives and the play ends in general lamentations. The author displays a certain compassion for the vanquished, mingled with pride in the great victory of the Greeks.

Persian Wars, a series of conflicts between the Greek states and the Persian empire, beginning in 490 BC, when the Persian king Darius invaded mainland Greece, and ending in 479 BC, when his son Xerxes, having suffered comprehensive defeats on land and at sea, was forced to withdraw from the Aegean (more loosely, the Wars can be said to extend from 499, when the Ionian Greek cities of Asia Minor rebelled against Persian rule, to c.449, when Greece and Persia agreed peace). After the rebellion, Persian rule in Asia Minor was restored in 494, and Darius decided to punish Athens and Eretria for the help they had given the Ionian colonists. In 492 the Persians conquered Thrace and Macedonia, but the Persian fleet was wrecked in a storm, bringing the expedition to an end. Two years later the Persians attacked again; they destroyed Eretria and landed an army in Attica in the Bay of Marathon. The Athenians appealed to Sparta for help (see PHEIDIPPIDES), but

the Spartans arrived too late and the Athenians, numbering some ten thousand, had to face a far stronger enemy with help only from Platea, who sent all her hoplites (heavy infantry), a thousand men. Led by *Miltiades, the Greeks won a great victory, utterly routing the enemy. According to Herodotus, 6,400 Persians were killed, and only 192 Athenians. This was the end of the First Persian War, in reality a minor affair aimed only at Athens and Eretria, but in popular estimation soon acquiring mythical status. For Aristophanes and others sixty years later the 'men who fought at Marathon', *Marathōnomachai*, epitomized the stubborn virtues of the old soldier. The epitaph of Aeschylus the tragedian claimed as his only glory that he had fought in the battle.

Darius at once set about measures for a new invasion. He died in 486, but his son and successor Xerxes carried on the preparations on a huge scale and in 480 attacked by land and sea. The numbers given by Herodotus for the size of the Persian forces are fantastic; modern estimates are 200,000 men for the army and 600 ships for the navy. The route of the Persian army lay through the narrow pass of Thermopylae, which was held by the Spartan king Leonidas. For two days he and his contingent held back the Persians and inflicted heavy losses on them. Then a traitor showed the Persians a mountain path by which they could outflank the Greek position. When Leonidas heard what had happened he dismissed his allies but remained with his 300 Spartans to die heroically in an impossible last stand (for their epitaph see SIMONIDES). The Persians now advanced into Attica, and Athens, which had been evacuated, was captured and burned in September 480. At sea, however, the Athenians remained strong, and within days of the sack of Athens the Greeks won a brilliant and crushing victory over the Persian fleet at Salamis. Xerxes, who had watched the battle from a throne on the mainland shore, returned to Persia, leaving a picked force to winter in Thessaly and continue the campaign by land. In the following year (479) the Greeks won a decisive victory near Plataea, during which the Persian commander Mardonius was killed. Meanwhile the Greek fleet had gone on to the offensive, and on the same day (it is said) as the battle at Plataea won another victory at Mycalē on the Ionian coast. These two victories ended the Persian threat, and until hostilities were formally ended by the Peace of *Callias, the Greeks were on the offensive.

As a result of the Persian Wars, Greeks in general became increasingly conscious of their own nationality and superiority, and the Athenian city-state in particular gained enormously in pride and self-confidence. Our knowledge of these wars is derived mainly from Herodotus. Of contemporary evidence there are inscriptions, some epigrams of Simonides, and Aeschylus' tragedy the *Persians*. The Persian side of the story is unknown.

Pe'rsius Flaccus, Aulus (AD 34–62), known generally as Persius, Latin satirical poet. Born at Volaterrae in Etruria, he belonged to an equestrian family and was a relative of the famous *Arria, wife of Paetus. He was educated at Rome, and became the pupil of the *Stoic Cornutus, who exercised a strong influence on him; a fellow pupil was the Roman epic poet Lucan. He joined the group of Stoics around *Thrasea Paetus, the senator who was married to the younger Arria. He bequeathed his books and a part of his large fortune to Cornutus, who accepted the books but not the money. Persius is said to have been a modest and gentle man. He took no part in public life, died young, and left only a small amount of literary work: six satires (650 hexameter lines) modelled on Lucilius and Horace, and a prologue (in scazons; see METRE, LATIN 3 (iii) *b*). Except for the first satire, these poems are homilies rather than satires in the strict sense, preaching an uncompromising Stoic morality as it could be applied to private life, and only incidentally touching on public life. He uses an incongruous mixture of styles and his language is obscure, but his moral sincerity is unforced and scarcely priggish when considered against the background of Nero's Rome.

Satire 1 is a criticism of the poets at Nero's court and the contemporary fashion for elegant, unrealistic poetry, which Persius finds significant of the corruption of Roman virtue and hardihood. Satire 2 is concerned with the right use of prayer, mocking those who ask for external goods rather than virtue. Satire 3 is a diagnosis of the damage done to sick souls by sloth and vice. Satire 4 urges a young statesman (Nero?) to disregard public admiration and pursue virtue by examining his own character. Satire 5 is a eulogy of Cornutus, describing the simple and studious life the poet leads when in the philosopher's company; its subject is the rarity of true freedom—we are all the slaves of our passions or superstitions. Satire 6 is addressed to Caesius Bassus (a lyric poet commended by Quintilian) who edited Persius' satires after his death and is said to have died in the eruption of Vesuvius in AD 79; it expounds the wisdom of living comfortably, but not covetously.

Perusine War. Campaign by Mark Antony's wife *Fulvia and brother Lucius Antonius against Octavian while Antony was in Egypt. Lucius was besieged in the Etruscan hill-city of Perusia (Perugia) during the winter of 41/40 until starved into surrender. Octavian executed the Perusine senate but forgave Lucius.

Pervigi'lium Ve'neris ('eve of Venus'), a poem preserved in the Latin Anthology (see ANTHOLOGY 2) written in trochaic tetrameters (see METRE, GREEK 2), ninety-three lines long; the author and date are unknown, but it was written after the second century AD, perhaps as late as the fourth century. The setting is Sicily, on the eve of the spring festival of Venus; the poem celebrates the triumph of spring, the resurgence of life in the world, and the next day's festival, its spirit summed up by the passionate refrain, *cras amet qui nunquam amavit, quique amavit cras amet* ('tomorrow he who has never loved and he who has loved, let them both love'). The poem ends on a poignant note: *illa cantat; nos tacemus; quando ver venit meum?* ('[the nightingale] sings; we are silent; when will my own springtime come?'). The poem is unique in Latin for its sensuous beauty here enhanced by the strong beat of the trochaic rhythm and by assonance, both characteristic of later Latin accentual poetry.

Petrō'nius A'rbiter (d. AD 65), Latin satirical writer, author of the *Satyricon* ('tales of satyrs'), usually assumed to be the voluptuary of that name at Nero's court, whose life and death are memorably described by Tacitus (*Annals*, 16. 18). He was at one time governor of Bithynia and later a consul, and was subsequently admitted by the emperor Nero to the inner circle of his intimates and chosen by him, in Tacitus' words, as his 'arbiter of taste', *elegantiae arbiter*, a play on his name. Tigellinus, prefect of the praetorians, whose jealousy he aroused, falsely accused him to the emperor as implicated in the conspiracy of Piso (see ROME 10); he committed suicide, but not before he had smashed a valuable wine-ladle to prevent it falling into the emperor's hands, and written a letter detailing the latter's vices. Tacitus describes Petronius as devoted to the refined pursuit of pleasure, indolent in his ordinary life, but energetic in public affairs.

Of his long picaresque novel, the *Satyricon*, only parts of books 14, 15, and 16 survive. Like the Menippean satires (see MENIPPUS) it is in prose interspersed with verse, and describes the disreputable adventures of two young men Encolpius (the narrator) and his friend Ascyltus, and the boy Giton who plays the others off against each other, as they wander through the low haunts of the semi-Greek cities of southern Italy. The three are completely devoid of morals but have a quick intelligence which sees them through their escapades, narrated with dispassionate realism. The principal episode in the surviving portion of the work is the *Cena Trimalchionis*, 'Trimalchio's dinner-party' (it appears in only one manuscript, not found until the seventeenth century). Trimalchio is a freedman, a vulgar *nouveau-riche* to whose dinner-party the adventurers obtain admission. He and his wife Fortunata present an ostentatious display of wealth in the decoration of the house and in the profusion of fantastic dishes set before the guests; there are grotesque incidents during dinner—a drunken brawl and a dog-fight—and ridiculous conversation;

Trimalchio's absurd conduct as he becomes more and more drunk finally reaches a maudlin stage in which he describes the contents of his will and his future monument. Two good ghost stories round off the episode, one about a werewolf, the other about witches substituting a changeling made of straw for a boy. The whole is told with amazing vitality and panache.

A further character in the remaining incidents is a disreputable old poet named Eumolpus with whom the adventurers travel to Croton in south Italy to advance their fortunes by fraud. The sea-voyage ends in shipwreck, and the extant portion of the work ends with various amorous adventures and misfortunes. In the course of these Eumolpus expounds his views on epic poetry (in chapter 118 he refers, in a phrase that has since become famous, to *Horatii curiosa felicitas*, 'Horace's studied felicity'). As illustration of the kind of inspirational poetry of his own day that he deplores, he recites sixty iambics on the fall of Troy and some 300 hexameters on the civil war of 49 BC. It is Eumolpus who, at an earlier stage (111), relates the story of the widow of Ephesus who, watching inconsolably in the vault where her recently dead husband has been laid, is induced by a kindly soldier to take food, and presently to accept him as her lover. This is a story very similar in type to the *Milesian Tales*. Petronius' characters, while thoroughly disreputable, are not wholly unlikeable. The racy, vivid, colloquial Latin in which the *Satyricon* is written reveals a great deal about the popular speech of the time, as does the Rabelaisian humour about tastes and attitudes. A few lyric and elegiac poems by the same author have also survived.

Phaeā'cians (Phaiākes), in Homer's *Odyssey*, the magical sea-faring people of the island of Scheria on which Odysseus was cast ashore. Their king was Alcinŏus.

Phaedo (Phaidōn), of Elis, in the north-west Peloponnese (b. *c*.418 BC), founder of the philosophical school there. He came to Athens as a young man, perhaps brought as a slave and later set free, and became one of Socrates' most devoted pupils. Plato named after him the dialogue in which Socrates' last hours are described. After the latter's death Phaedo returned to Elis.

Phaedo (see above), dialogue by *Plato in which Phaedo narrates the discussion that took place between Socrates and his friends during the last hours of his life, and the manner of his dying. The dialogue starts from the remark of Socrates that the genuine philosopher is one who is willing to die because it is his affirmation of the principles by which he has lived; the philosopher will be convinced that after his death the soul of the just man will be under the care of good and wise gods no less than before—and perhaps in the company of the best men of the past; moreover, death is the release of the soul from the body, and it has been the philosopher's aim during his lifetime to make the soul independent of bodily vicissitudes. Cebēs' objection that the soul may not survive death leads to the series of arguments which make up the core of the dialogue and which, as they develop, are intended to vindicate Socrates' belief in the immortality of the soul. The reader is presented with the argument that learning is recollection of knowledge possessed in a former existence (an argument prominent in *Meno* also) and therefore the soul must have existed before its present incarnation. The reader also meets the theory of Ideas or Forms by which a particular thing is what it is (e.g. by which a beautiful thing is beautiful) by partaking of the Idea of e.g. beauty. It is also argued that soul, which imparts life to the body, cannot admit death, and is therefore immortal. Socrates introduces this last section by giving an account of his intellectual history, memorably describing his conceptual difficulties with the kind of explanation of the physical world offered in the natural sciences (including the explanation of Anaxagoras; see PHILOSOPHY I) and the evolution of his own method of enquiry based on the formulation of successive hypotheses. The argument is rounded off with a myth which gives a speculative picture of the afterlife and the judgement of departed souls. Belief in 'either this or something like it' is said to be a noble risk. The dialogue ends with the moving description of Socrates' fearless acceptance of the cup of hemlock. This is the work from which *Cato (of Utica) is said to have drawn strength on the night before he committed suicide.

Phaedra, in Greek myth, daughter of *Minos, king of Crete, and Pasiphaē, and sister of Ariadnē; she married Theseus, king of Athens. For her story see HIPPOLYTUS.

Phaedra, Roman tragedy by *Seneca (2), based on the *Hippolytus* of Euripides with certain variations. Here it is Phaedra herself (not the nurse on her behalf) who declares her love to her stepson Hippolytus; she then in person (not in a posthumous letter) slanders him to Theseus; and finally it is she herself who discloses her guilt, before she dies (not the goddess Artemis after her suicide).

Phaedrus, a dialogue by *Plato in direct speech between Socrates and his friend Phaedrus, in a pleasant spot on the banks of the river Ilissus a little outside Athens. Socrates claims (only in this dialogue, and perhaps ironically) to be moved by the beauties of nature, to the extent that he ascribes the exalted tone of his second speech to their influence. The dialogue begins with Phaedrus reading a speech purporting to be by the Attic orator *Lysias (see also PARODY) expounding a paradoxical view of love, that it is better for a boy to accept as a lover a man who is not truly in love with him than to accept one who is, which Socrates counters with a cleverer speech on the same theme. However, Socrates is then prevented from departing by his 'divine sign' (see SOCRATES) which convinces him that he has been blasphemous to associate love only with physical passion: he recants in another speech. The true lover is worthy of respect; he is mad with a madness that comes from the gods. To understand this it is necessary to understand the nature of the soul, and Socrates first establishes that the soul is immortal. He then describes its nature and destiny by the analogy of a charioteer driving a pair of winged horses. These represent the three parts of the soul: reason, in control of man's sensual and spiritual appetites.

The true lover may be at first attracted physically to a like-minded person, and if his love is reciprocated, and the sensual appetites overcome, both lovers may leave behind love of physical beauty for the common pursuit of that beauty which is to be finally found only in the Idea (or Form) of the Good. After this the conversation returns, with an abrupt change from the poetic to the prosaic, to a discussion of rhetoric based on the three speeches just made; rhetoric should have as its foundation knowledge of the truth, which can be obtained only by those passionate in its pursuit. The ancients debated whether the dialogue was concerned primarily with love or with rhetoric.

Phaedrus, Gaius Julius (*c*.15 BC–*c*. AD 50), Thracian slave who came to Rome and became a freedman in the household of Augustus, the author (in Latin) of a collection of fables in five books containing some hundred stories, published probably in the thirties of the first century AD. There is also an appendix of another thirty-two fables, probably also by Phaedrus. The collection includes fables proper, a number of anecdotes (e.g. about Aesop, Socrates, and Menander), and defences of the author against detractors. The fables are based on those of *Aesop and on beast-stories from other sources which had come to be attributed to Aesop. They are written in verse, in iambic senarii (see METRE, LATIN 2), and their object is two-fold, to give advice and to entertain. They are generally serious or satirical, dealing with the injustices of life and social and political evils, but occasionally they are light and amusing. In general they express patient resignation. Phaedrus observed in the prologue to the third book that the fable was invented so that a slave might say obliquely what he dared not speak openly. Their political allusions, intentional or imagined, offended *Sejanus, and Phaedrus suffered some unknown punishment. Many of the stories are well known to us, having been handed down (often through the Greek collection of *Babrius) through medieval times to the present day. They include 'The Wolf and the Lamb', 'The Fox and the Sour Grapes' and 'King Log and King Watersnake'. The fables are inferior to those of the French poet La Fontaine in dramatic sense and poetry, but the style is clear and simple. Phaedrus is the source of the expression 'adding insult to injury', *iniuriae qui addideris contumeliam* (v. 3. 5).

Phaeno'mena, astronomical poem of *Aratus.

Phaestus, ancient city of south Crete, the site of a Minoan palace (see CRETE) destroyed in about 1400 BC. The clay tablet found there in 1908, known as the Phaestus disc, apparently dates from early in the second millennium and is inscribed on both sides with pictographic writing, otherwise unknown but almost certainly syllabic, running from left to right. The script does not seem to relate to *Linear A or B, and it is not known whether the disc originated in Crete or what its purpose was.

Phā'ethon, in Greek myth, son of *Helios (Sun) and Clymenē (2). When he grew up he sought out his father who recognized him and offered him his choice of gift. Phaethon asked to be allowed to drive his father's chariot for one day. In spite of Helios' warning he attempted to do so, but soon proved unequal to controlling the horses. They bolted from their course and the earth was in danger of being burnt up, when Zeus intervened and hurled a thunderbolt at Phaethon, who fell into the river *Eridanus. His sisters wept for him until they were turned into poplars; their tears, oozing from the trees, hardened into amber.

phalanx, generally, Greek heavy infantry (*hoplites) arranged in battle formation, but the name is specifically applied to the Macedonian infantry formation developed by Philip II of Macedon and his son Alexander the Great. It owed part of its great success to the fact that Macedonia could produce as many as 25,000 men to serve in such formations. In contrast with the hoplite battle-line of about eight rows, the phalanx consisted of sixteen ranks of infantry; the soldiers were armed with unusually long pikes (*sarisai*, about 4 m. or 13 ft.

long), so that they presented *en masse* an impenetrable thicket of shafts. The phalanx had comparatively little flexibility but prevailed by sheer weight and perfect drill. Its vulnerable flanks and rear were guarded by cavalry. Under Alexander, Macedonian manpower began to decline, and towards the end of his career Alexander planned a mixed phalanx of Greeks and light-armed Persians with bows and javelins. Weaknesses in the phalanx gradually became apparent; its inferiority in flexibility to the Roman maniple was shown by the Roman defeat of Philip V at the battle of Cynoscephalae in 197 BC and of Perseus at Pydna in 168 BC.

Pha'laris, tyrant of Acragas in Sicily in the mid-sixth century BC, soon after the foundation of that city (*c*.580 BC). He was remembered for his cruelty, supposedly roasting his enemies to death in a brazen bull with a fire underneath, their cries sounding like the roar of the bull. This was the invention of a certain Perillus, who was its first victim. The so-called 'Letters of Phalaris' were proved by the English scholar Richard Bentley (1662–1742) to be a forgery. The real author was a sophist of perhaps the second century AD.

Phalē'rum, modern Phaleron, the principal harbour of Athens until the early fifth century BC, i.e. before the Persian Wars and the development and fortification of *Piraeus, east of which it lies. It is an open roadstead, offering little protection to ships. For the Long Wall connecting it with Athens see LONG WALLS.

phallus, model of the male genital organ, the symbol of fertility carried in procession in many ancient religious ceremonies in order to stimulate the fruitfulness of the earth, the flocks, and the people, and so prevent weakness of the race. In Greece the phallus was especially associated with the worship of Dionysus, the god of fertility (hence its connection with comedy; see COMEDY, GREEK 1 and 2); of Hermēs, the god of pastures, crops, and herds (see also HERMAE); of Pan, the protector of flocks; and of Demeter, the earth-goddess. Occasionally a god Phalēs

was invoked, the personification of the phallus. In the Roman festival of the Liberalia (comparable with the Greek Dionysia) the phallus was similarly carried in procession (see also PRIAPUS).

Phāon, legendary boatman of Mytilenē (in Lesbos), to whom Aphroditē gave youth and beauty because he had carried her (in the guise of an old woman) across the sea without taking payment. See SAPPHO.

Pharos, the white marble lighthouse built probably in the reign of Ptolemy II Philadelphus on the island of Pharos at *Alexandria (hence its name), and one of the *Seven Wonders of the ancient world. The light came from a fire burning in the top, projected by some arrangement of mirrors. The Pharos stood until the fourteenth century.

Pharsā'lia or **Pharsā'lus,** in Thessaly, the scene of the decisive defeat of Pompey by Caesar in the summer of 48 BC. Pharsalus was the name of the town, Pharsalia of its territory.

Pharsā'lia, Latin epic poem by *Lucan (AD 39–65) in ten books of hexameters, on the civil war between Pompey and Julius Caesar (the title in the manuscripts is *De bello civili*, 'on the civil war': the name *Pharsalia* comes from the battle of Pharsalus). The poem was apparently not completed and ends abruptly in the tenth book with Caesar at war in Egypt. Lucan probably intended to continue the narrative to the death of Caesar, if not further. His main source was Livy, but it was not his purpose to give a full, historical account of the war (for which see CAESAR), and apart from omissions there are a few notable departures from historical truth, as when he portrays Cicero haranguing Pompey on the eve of the battle of Pharsalus: in fact Cicero missed the battle because of illness. The poem is written with strong sympathy for the cause of Pompey and the republic.

Book 1 first touches on the sources of the war and gives a vivid sketch of the characters of the two leaders; then proceeds to Caesar's crossing of the river Rubicon into Italy. A striking passage shows Caesar confronted by the spirit of

Rome, which challenges his right to advance. The dismay at Rome is described, and the flight of citizens and senators.

Book 2 continues the relation of events in Italy (with a long digression on the massacres of Marius and Sulla), the resolution of Cato (2) and (Marcus Junius) Brutus to resist Caesar, the episode of the resistance of Corfinium (under the command of the senator Lucius Domitius Ahenobarbus), Pompey's withdrawal to Brundisium and his escape to Epirus.

Book 3 is concerned with the occupation of Rome by Caesar and with the fighting on land and sea about Massilia (Marseilles): there is a notable description of the sacred Druid grove in the neighbourhood of the town which Caesar had felled. The book ends with the horrific description of a sea-battle.

The first part of *book 4* deals with Caesar's campaign in Gaul. The narrative then passes to Illyricum (in the northwest of Greece) and includes the incident of the attempted escape of some Caesarian soldiers on three rafts; one of these is stopped and the soldiers on board, Gauls from Opitergium (Oderzo), kill each other rather than surrender. There follow the expedition of Curio, Caesar's commander, to Africa, and his defeat and death at the hands of Juba. There is a digression on the legend of Hercules and Antaeus.

The most interesting parts of *book 5* describe the Delphic Oracle, which Appius, a Pompeian, goes to consult, receiving an ambiguous reply; and Caesar's attempt to cross the Adriatic Sea in a small boat on a stormy night.

Book 6 is occupied with the fighting around Dyrrhachium (Epidamnus, in Illyria) and Caesar's withdrawal to Thessaly. The fight to the death of Caesar's centurion Scaeva is graphically described. (In reality he survived, with, according to Caesar, 120 holes in his shield.) To Lucan's disgust, Sextus Pompeius (Pompey's younger son) consults the Thessalian witch Erichtho, who employs necromancy to foretell the destiny of the Pompeians.

Book 7 describes Pompey's deceptively happy dream before the battle of Pharsalus, the battle itself, and the ensuing scenes.

Book 8 deals with Pompey's flight first to Lesbos to join his wife and then to Egypt, and his murder there by the order of Pothinus, the pharaoh's chamberlain.

In *book 9*, Pompey's spirit is borne to heaven and Cato pronounces a splendid panegyric on the dead leader. Cato resolves to continue the war and marches with his troops to Mauretania (in North Africa). Confident in his Stoic faith and in the rightness of the course that he has chosen, he refuses to consult the oracle of Ammon. This book is largely praise of Cato. There is a digression on Egyptian serpents, their legendary origin in the blood of Medusa, the Gorgon, and their varieties. The Egyptians present Pompey's head to Caesar, who hypocritically laments his fate.

Book 10 describes Caesar's actions in Egypt, and his affair with Cleopatra. He is besieged by the troops of Pothinus and Achillas. At this point the poem ends abruptly.

Lucan had a difficult task in writing epic about events only a century before his own day. As a Stoic he discarded the epic convention of divine interventions to direct human actions, substituting an impersonal Fate or Fortune. He introduced a number of digressions, often displaying seemingly irrelevant learning (see *book 9* above). In general his work is often absurdly rhetorical and his straining for effect grotesque (e.g. his description of Caesar enjoying his breakfast among the corpses after Pharsalus, and of the wild beasts devouring the dead). But it is carried through with great vigour and brilliance; the sensational scenes are interspersed with passages of considerable power and pathos, such as that describing Pompey's farewell to Italy. The author's gift for incisive epigram is evident, and some lines have achieved fame: *victrix causa deis placuit sed victa Catoni* ('the conquering cause pleased the gods, the losing cause pleased Cato'); of Caesar, *nil actum credens cum quid superesset agendum* ('believing that nothing had been done if anything remained still to do'); and of friendship, *nulla fides unquam miseros elegit amicos* ('nobody ever chooses to be the faithful friend of those already unfortunate'). Lucan's feelings for his subject were sincere: he detested Caesar and all he stood for, while admitting his greatness; he makes Pompey a tragic figure and evokes sympathy for him and his cause. The verse is somewhat monotonous in technique and lacks flexibility, but at its best the rhetoric is vigorous and carries the reader along.

Phēgeus, in Greek myth, father of Arsinoë, wife of *Alcmaeon.

Phei'dias (*c*.490–*c*.432 BC), Athenian sculptor, the most famous artist of the ancient world. He was a friend of *Pericles, who gave him a leading role in his great building-programme in Athens; most notably, he was in charge of the sculptural decoration of the *Parthenon. A good deal of this sculpture survives (mostly in the British Museum), but Pheidias' gold and ivory ('chryselephantine') cult statue of Athena for the temple is not extant; the Greek traveller Pausanias (1. 24. 5) gives a description of it, from which several (much smaller) Roman copies have been identified. Another huge cult statue, considered Pheidias' masterpiece, was made for the temple of Zeus at *Olympia, and is known only from its representation on coins and gems. Pheidias' style was serene and majestic; it is said that when asked what model he was going to use for the likeness of Zeus, he replied that he would model it on Homer's lines in the *Iliad*, 'Cronion [Zeus] spoke, and nodded his dark brow, and the ambrosial locks waved from the king's immortal head; and he made great Olympus quake' (1. 528). In 432 enemies of Pericles, trying to attack him through his friends, accused Pheidias of embezzling gold intended for the statue of Athena, but he was able to prove his innocence. He was then charged with impiety and sent to prison, where Plutarch says he died.

Pheidi'ppidēs (or Philippides), the Athenian runner who, according to Herodotus (6. 105–6), was sent to request help from Sparta before the battle of Marathon in 490 BC (SEE PERSIAN WARS, also PAN). He arrived there the day after he left Athens, covering in that time a distance of 200 km. (125 miles) or more. On his way back he is said to have met the god Pan. The basis of the modern Marathon race (introduced at the first modern Olympic games at Athens in 1896) is a legend, which has no authority, that he ran from Athens to Marathon (a distance of about 40 km., 25 miles) in order to join in the battle against the Persians, then ran back to Athens and, having announced the victory ('Greetings, we win!'), dropped dead. The distance of 26 miles 386 yards (42.195 km.) was not standardized until the 1908 Olympic Games in London; this peculiarly precise figure was the distance between the starting-point at Windsor Castle and the finish at White City Stadium.

Pheidon (perhaps first half of the seventh century BC, possibly nearly a century earlier), king of *Argos; he was a Heraclid, descended from *Temenus. According to Aristotle he exceeded his hereditary powers and made himself tyrant. He was clearly an important figure, but his dates and activities are obscure. He was remembered for three achievements: his recovery of the 'lot of Temenus', i.e. his unification of the Argolid; his standardization of weights and measures; and his seizure of the management of the Olympian games from Elis. Evidence suggests that he was a very successful military leader, perhaps responsible for Argos succeeding Chalcis (in Euboea) as the greatest military power in Greece.

Phere'cratēs, SEE COMEDY, GREEK 4.

Pherecȳ'dēs, of Leros and Athens, a *logographer of the early fifth century BC who is sometimes confused with Pherecydes of Syros (an island in the Cyclades), a philosopher and reputedly the teacher of Pythagoras.

Philē'bus, dialogue of Plato; SEE PLATO 2.

Philē'mōn, one of the chief writers of Greek New Comedy; SEE COMEDY, GREEK 6.

Philē'mōn and Baucis, an old man and his wife, in a story told by Ovid, who entertained Zeus and Hermēs in disguise as hospitably as their poverty would allow, after the gods had been repulsed by the rich. For this Philemon and Baucis were saved from a deluge that overwhelmed the land where they lived, and their dwelling was transformed into a temple of which they were made the first priest and priestess. They were also granted their request to die at the same time, and were then turned into trees whose boughs intertwined.

Philē'tās (or, perhaps more correctly, Philītas) of Cos (born not later than 320 BC), Greek poet and grammarian of the Hellenistic age, tutor of the (subsequent) king of Egypt Ptolemy II Philadelphus. His other distinguished pupils were said to include the scholar Zenodotus and the poet Theocritus. He was a writer of amatory poems, and particularly famed for his elegies, mentioned by Ovid and Propertius as their model. Only fragments of his work survive.

Philip (Philippos). 1. **Philip II** (383/2–336 BC), king of *Macedon 359–336 BC. Philip unified Macedon and made it the strongest power in Greece, laying the foundations for the achievements of his son Alexander the Great. As a boy he had seen his two elder brothers—who reigned for a few years each as Alexander II and Perdiccas III—struggle in vain against insubordinate vassal princes and outside interference. Philip came to power after Perdiccas was killed in battle against invading Illyrians. Initially he was regent for his nephew Amyntas, but he siezed the throne for himself and proved a brilliant and vigorous ruler. He suppressed opposition, strengthened the economy, and forged a professional army with national spirit. Philip was himself a formidable warrior (he lost an eye in battle and was wounded many other times), but he was also a skilful politician, and he expanded his territories by diplomacy as well as conquest. The interests of Athens were gravely threatened, especially when Philip's new fleet began to harass the city's trade, and *Demosthenes ((2) 4) in his speech known as the *First Philippic* (351) called upon the Athenians to prepare to fight. However, a precarious peace was kept until various acts of hostility in 341 developed into open war in 340. Athens and Thebes allied, despite their inveterate hostility, but Philip crushed their joint army at Chaeronea (338). He was now master of Greece and made plans for waging a Greek war against Persia, with himself as general. Preparations were made for the invasion, and his commander Parmenio was sent to secure a footing in Asia Minor; but while walking in procession during the celebration of his daughter's marriage to the king of Epirus Philip was murdered by an assassin, Pausanias. Apparently he was pursuing a private grievance, although it has been alleged that it was the result of a plot by Olympias, Philip's now deposed wife, of which his son *Alexander was aware. Excavations at Aegae (Vergina) in Macedonia have uncovered the tombs of Philip and his family, with magnificent grave goods and wall-paintings. Philip's own body has been identified beyond reasonable doubt.

2. **Philip V** (238–179 BC), king of Macedon; see MACEDON.

Phi'lippi, city in Macedonia east of the river Strymon on the border with Thrace, refounded under this name by Philip II of Macedon in 356 BC, the scene of the defeat in 42 BC of the republican forces of (Marcus Junius) Brutus and (Gaius) Cassius by those of Mark Antony and Octavian, and of the death of the two former.

Phili'ppica, see THEOPOMPUS.

Phili'ppics, four political speeches by *Demosthenes (see (2) 4) attacking Philip II, king of Macedon. The title was adopted by *Cicero ((1) 6) for the fourteen speeches that he delivered against Mark Antony.

Phili'ppides, see PHEIDIPPIDES.

Phili'ppus, title of a discourse by *Isocrates.

Philī'tas, see PHILETAS.

Philo. 1. **Philo of Lari'sa** (159–80 BC), head of the *Academy at Athens in 109 BC, like Carneadēs a moderate Sceptic.

2. **Philo Jūdae'us,** 'Philo the Jew' (c.30 BC–c. AD 45), a member of a prosperous Jewish family in Alexandria, who took part in an embassy sent to Rome in AD 39–40 to seek exemption for Jews from the obligation to worship the emperor (at that time Caligula). Except for this event

nothing is known of his life. He was the most important Hellenistic Jew of his age and a prolific author of philosophical and exegetical writings. His religious outlook was eclectic, but his lasting achievement was the development of the allegorical interpretation of scripture, enabling him to find a great deal of Greek philosophy in the Old Testament. His works were a strong influence on later Greek Christian thought as helping to mediate between philosophy (including *Neoplatonism) and Christianity. A considerable portion survives.

Philo'chorus, of Athens; see ATTHIS.

Philo'cratēs, Peace of, between Greece and Philip II of Macedon, 346 BC; see DEMOSTHENES (2) I and AESCHINES.

Philoctē'tēs, in Greek myth, son of Poeas; the father had been persuaded, by the gift of *Heracles' bow and arrows, to light the pyre on which the latter was burnt alive. These descended to Philoctetes, who led seven ships from Methonē and other towns of that region in the expedition to Troy. On their way to Troy the Greeks sacrificed in Tenedos, and there Philoctetes was bitten in the foot by a serpent. The stench from his wound, which would not heal, and his terrible cries and curses caused the Greeks, persuaded by Odysseus, to abandon him on the solitary coast of the island of Lemnos, where he supported himself by the bow and arrows which never missed their mark. After many years the Trojan seer Helenus, captured by Odysseus, revealed that Troy would never fall unless Philoctetes could be persuaded to come and fight with his bow and arrows. Accordingly Odysseus and Neoptolemus (or Diomedēs) went to Lemnos and brought him back. *Machaon healed his wound and Philoctetes, by shooting Paris, helped to conquer Troy. According to the *Odyssey* Philoctetes returned home safely. He is mentioned in the *Iliad* and is the subject of a play by Sophocles.

Philoctē'tēs, Greek tragedy by *Sophocles, produced in 409 BC.

*Philoctetes is living wretchedly on Lemnos, suffering from his wound, supporting himself by shooting birds with his beloved bow of Heracles. Odysseus and Neoptolemus arrive to carry him off to the siege of Troy. Odysseus reveals his plan to Neoptolemus: the latter is to pretend that he has quarrelled with the leaders of the Greek army and is on his way home; he is to heap abuse on Odysseus, and to try to get possession of the bow. Neoptolemus is at first unwilling to join in this deceit, but eventually agrees. He meets Philoctetes and tells his story. Philoctetes makes a pitiful appeal to be taken to Greece, and Neoptolemus agrees. But Philoctetes is seized with a paroxysm of pain, after which he falls asleep. Before sleeping, however, he entrusts his bow to Neoptolemus. When he wakes up, Neoptolemus, stung with remorse, confesses the plot. He is on the point of returning the bow when Odysseus appears and takes it. He and Neoptolemus depart with it to the ships; Philoctetes is left lamenting his loss, while the chorus of sailors try to persuade him to join them. They are about to leave him when Neoptolemus returns, determined to give back the bow but pursued by Odysseus. Philoctetes, having regained the bow, tries to shoot Odysseus but is prevented by Neoptolemus who again tries to persuade Philoctetes to accompany him to Troy. He fails, and reluctantly decides to abide by his promise and take Philoctetes home to Greece. At this point Heracles appears from the dead; he reveals Zeus' plan for Philoctetes, that he is to go to Troy with Neoptolemus; Philoctetes yields to the voice of one whom he cannot disobey.

Philodē'mus, see HERCULANEUM.

Philomē'la and Procnē, in Greek myth, daughters of Pandīon, a legendary king of Athens. Procne was married to Tereus, king of Thrace. The latter fell in love with Philomela, and after raping her cut out her tongue and hid her in a lonely fortress so that she could not reveal what had happened. But Philomela managed to depict her sufferings on a tapestry which she sent to Procne by a servant. Procne then went to her sister disguised as a *Bacchant during the festival of Dionysus, and smuggled her into the palace similarly disguised. Seeking revenge Procne stabbed her son Itys to death, to deprive Tereus of an heir, and served up his flesh to her husband. When, after the meal, Philomela brought in the boy's head so that Tereus understood what had happened, he drew his sword to kill the sisters, but was changed into a hoopoe; Philomela was changed into a swallow (since, having no tongue, she could merely chatter like one) and Procne into a nightingale (or, according to Latin authors, Philomela into a nightingale and Procne into a swallow).

Philopoe'men (*c*.250–182 BC), of Megalopolis in Arcadia, the bold and vigorous general of the *Achaean Confederacy, in which post he reorganized its army and repeatedly defeated the Spartans. It is recorded that after one of his victories Philopoemen was present at the Nemean games when Pyladēs, the most famous singer of his day, was singing part of the *Persians* of *Timotheus. At the words, 'who gives to Greece the glorious crown of freedom', the people rose and gave an ovation to the general. In 183 BC, when he was about 70, he took part in an expedition against Messenē, which had revolted from the Confederacy. He was captured by the Messenians, thrown into prison, and forced to drink poison. His remains were brought back to Megalopolis, his urn being carried by the young *Polybius.

philosophy (Gk. *philosophia*, 'love of knowledge').

1. *Greek*. For the Greeks, 'philosophy', the pursuit of knowledge by rational enquiry, was an elastic term; it began with scientific speculation but it also included speculation as to the conduct of political and social life, and this last was one of the main concerns of philosophers in the fifth and fourth centuries BC. Later Greek philosophy dealt with moral and religious questions, the concept of virtue and the individual's relations with the divine; it had then become not merely a mental activity but a way of life, to be followed in accordance with philosophical beliefs. Greek philosophy had its origins in the sixth century BC among the Ionian Greeks of Asia Minor. It was then mainly occupied with speculation about the cause of the universe, and associated with the name of *Thales of Miletus,

whose chief successors (also sixth-century Milesians) were *Anaximander and *Anaximenes. These sought the material principle of the universe in some single uncreated and imperishable substance which underwent various modifications to produce the multitude of phenomena in the world: Thales thought that it was water, Anaximander something indeterminate, without specific qualities, and Anaximenes air. *Heracleitus of Ephesus (writing in about 500 BC), standing apart from this school and rejecting the notion of a permanent substance underlying the variations of matter (though he thought the essential stuff of the universe to be pure fire), saw all things in a state of flux, and matter itself constantly changing.

*Pythagoras (last quarter of the sixth century BC), an Ionian Greek from Samos who migrated to Croton, an Achaean colony on the toe of Italy, founded there a second school of philosophy which in some ways resembled a mystical sect, having secret doctrines not to be revealed to the uninitiated. The Pythagoreans saw in numbers and their relations the basis of the universe. The third school was that of Elea (also in Magna Graecia), founded by *Parmenides (early fifth century BC) and continued by *Zeno. This school distinguished between the true stuff of the universe, single, eternal, and unchangeable, and the unreal phenomena of change, diversity, and motion which are apparent to the senses. *Empedocles of Acragas in Sicily, *Anaxagoras of Clazomenae in Ionia, and Leucippus (perhaps Ionian also), all working in the fifth century BC, evolved fresh hypotheses about the physical basis of the universe, assuming not one single basic stuff but plural constituents.

Empedocles was the first to propound the theory of the four elements, earth, air, fire, and water, out of which everything is composed in varying proportions. Anaxagoras believed in an original mixture containing 'seeds' of every substance; more significantly, however, he introduced the important concept of an intelligence (*nous*) as a principle of force and order distinct from matter. Leucippus was said to be the originator of the school of atomist philosophy, which rested on the doctrine that the universe is composed of a vast number of atoms, mechanically combined. This doctrine was developed by *Democritus, and found its most eloquent exponent in a later age at Rome, in Lucretius. During the sixth century the Ionian polymath and philosopher *Xenophanes, relying on logic, constructed a rational theology.

Greek philosophy culminated in *Socrates, in the second half of the fifth century, and *Plato and *Aristotle, in the fourth. The conquests of Alexander the Great, however, towards the end of the fourth century, swept away the context of their moral teaching, the independent city-states, the continued existence of which they had not doubted; and the later philosophies, those in particular of the *Stoics and Epicureans (see EPICURUS), reveal a change of outlook: in them, interest has shifted from the theoretical problems of the nature of reality and the scope of knowledge to the practical problems of everyday behaviour. They are to some extent philosophies of resignation; they seek a road to peace and happiness in the state of mind of the individual, by making him independent of external circumstances. See also SCEPTICS, CYNICS, MEGARIAN SCHOOL, PERIPATETIC SCHOOL, ARISTIPPUS (founder of the Cyrenaic School), THEOPHRASTUS (the successor of Aristotle), ACADEMY, and NEOPLATONISM.

2. *Roman*. Rome came into close contact with Greek civilization, including philosophy, with the conquest of Magna Graecia in the third century BC and the occupation of Sicily, Greece, and part of Asia Minor in the second. At first Rome regarded Greek philosophy with some suspicion, and fears of its possibly subversive effects led to the temporary banishment of Greek philosophers in 173 and again in 161 BC. In 155 *Carneades, Diogenes, and Critolaus, the heads respectively of the Academic, Stoic, and Peripatetic schools of philosophy in Athens, were sent on an embassy to Rome (to appeal against a large fine imposed by the Romans on Athens) and, giving lectures there, made a great impression. A little later *Scipio Aemilianus received into his household the Stoic philosopher *Panaetius of Rhodes; and in the early part of the first century BC a successor of the latter, *Posidonius, became the friend

and teacher of Varro in Rome and of Pompey and Cicero in Rhodes. The Romans were not much interested in theories as to the constitution of the universe, nor in elucidating the processes of thought and knowledge; and they produced no great original speculative philosophers or metaphysicians. *Lucretius alone, in his poem *De rerum natura* ('on nature'), expounded with enthusiasm the atomic theory put forward by Leucippus and Democritus.

The attention of the Romans was chiefly concentrated on ethical principles, and here they were mainly divided between Epicureans and Stoics, the latter prevailing. Stoic notions of duty and fate appealed to Roman severity. Cicero, who did much to make Greek philosophical thought known to his countrymen, was himself a follower of the New Academy (the Platonic school), with leanings towards the Stoics; he was in fact an eclectic, that is, he did not accept wholly the teaching of any one particular school, but picked out from their various doctrines those which commended themselves to him. *Seneca (2) was the principal Roman Stoic author, and his writings had considerable influence on Christian ethics. The most famous of the later Roman Stoics were Marcus *Aurelius (who wrote his *Meditations* in Greek) and *Epictetus (who also wrote in Greek). The satirist Persius, under the influence of his teacher Cornutus, and the poet Lucan were followers of the same school. Under the influence of Seneca and his successors, the general tendency of Stoics was to become more practical and human. The tranquillity which the earlier Greek Stoics thought was the exclusive attainment of the sage who lived in detachment from the world was now seen to be attainable by men living fully in the world, through the exercise of fortitude and self-control. See also BOETHIUS.

Philo'stratus, the name borne by four writers, members of a family belonging, according to Suidas, to Lemnos, who lived in the second and third centuries AD. The most important works (in Greek) which have come down under this name are: (i) (by Flavius Philostratus) *Lives of the Sophists*, that is, of the *sophists and rhetoricians from Protagoras (in the fifth century BC) to the author's own times; (ii) (written for *Julia Domna) a life of Apollonius of Tyana, the wandering Pythagorean mystic and miracle worker of the first century AD (which furnished material for anti-Christians who wanted a pagan narrative to set against the Gospel life of Jesus); (iii) *Eikonĕs* ('images'), two sets of descriptions in prose of pictures which the author purports to have seen (the first set far superior to the second); (iv) *Herōicus*, a dialogue in which the ghosts of heroes of the Trojan War appear; and (v) a collection of *Letters* (sophistical exercises for the most part), chiefly noteworthy as containing in Epistle 33 the source of Ben Jonson's 'Drink to me only with thine eyes'.

Phily'ra, in Greek myth, daughter of *Oceanus and Tethys, loved by *Cronus. When Rhea (his wife) found them both together, Cronus changed himself and Philyra into horses. Philyra's child was the centaur *Chiron; she was so horrified to see the baby's shape that she prayed to the gods to change her shape also, and she was turned into a lime tree (Gk. *philyra*) from which her name is taken.

Phīneus. 1. In Greek myth, a Thracian king, plagued by the *Harpies who stole or defiled all his food. When the *Argonauts arrived at his land he agreed to prophesy to them their future adventures in return for deliverance from the Harpies. The sons of Boreas (Calais and Zetes) drove them away, turning back at the islands afterwards known as Strophadĕs ('islands of turning'). Phineus' original offence is variously described. The best known version says that he married Cleopatra, daughter of Boreas, and had sons, but at her death remarried; their stepmother so slandered his sons that Phineus blinded them (or let their stepmother do so). Thereupon Zeus gave him the choice of death or blindness; he chose the latter, and Helios (Sun), who sees all, angry at Phineus' choice, sent the Harpies.
    2. See PERSEUS.

Phle'gethon (or Pyriphlegethon), one of the rivers of the Underworld; see HADES.

Phōcae'a, most northerly of the Ionian Greek settlements on the coast of Asia Minor, founded by emigrants from Phocis. Because of its two excellent harbours it soon became famous as a maritime city; according to Herodotus the Phocaeans were the first Greeks to sail far west, visiting Tartessus in southern Spain. In about 600 BC it founded the colony of Massilia (Marseilles), giving the Greeks access to southern Gaul. When Ionia was conquered by the Persian king Cyrus in 540 BC, most of the citizens preferred emigration to submission and finally settled at Elea (Velia) in Lucania, south Italy; Phocaea never recovered its former prosperity.

Phō'cion (fourth century BC), Athenian general and statesman during the time of Philip II of Macedon and his son Alexander the Great. He commanded universal respect and was elected *strategos* forty-five times. In politics he was an advocate of peace with Macedon, being convinced that Athens was no longer a match for her in military strength. After Athens' defeat at Chaeronea in 338 he assisted Demades in preserving peace with Philip and Alexander, and sought to prevent Athens from joining in the *Lamian War. When democratic rule was (briefly) restored at Athens in 318, Phocion was put to death on a charge of treason. Plutarch's *Life of Phocion* portrays him as a patriot, with a stern and stoical sense of duty.

Phōcis, small country of central Greece, to the west of Boeotia, important in Greek history as containing Delphi, of which she occasionally lost control, becoming involved in the *Sacred Wars. Her bid for independence in the Third Sacred War ended in her subjugation by Philip II of Macedon (346 BC).

Phocus, see TELAMON.

Phōcy'lidĕs, of Miletus (mid-sixth century BC), Greek poet famous for composing *gnomic couplets in elegiacs and hexameters in which he embodied moral observations and precepts; a few of these survive. In each he introduced his own name.

Phoebē (Phoibē, 'the bright one'), in Greek myth, according to Hesiod, a Titaness (see TITANS), daughter of Uranus

(Heaven) and Gaia (Earth); she became the wife of Coeus and mother of *Leto, and is thus grandmother of Apollo and Artemis. In later mythology her name was frequently used for Selenē (Moon).

Phoebus Apo'llo, see APOLLO.

Phoeni'cia (Phoinīkē, the biblical Canaan), country forming a narrow strip along the coast of Syria and including the towns of Tyre and Sidon (the former not known to Homer, for whom Sidon is the great city of Phoenician craftsmen and traders). Probably before 1000 BC the Phoenicians, a Semitic people, invented their *alphabet (on which the Greek alphabet was based), and at about the same period earned their reputation as a great sea-faring people. *Carthage was founded by the Phoenician queen *Dido in about 814 BC. After the time of Alexander the Great (late fourth century BC) they were incorporated into the Hellenistic world.

Phoeni'ssae (Phoinissai, 'Phoenician women').
1. Greek tragedy (which has not survived) by *Phrynichus.
2. Greek tragedy by *Euripides, produced between 412 and 408 BC. The play derives its name from the chorus of Phoenician maidens dedicated by the citizens of Tyre to the temple of Apollo at Delphi, who happen to be at Thebes on their way to Delphi and witness the events while having no connection with them. The subject is the same as Aeschylus' *Seven against Thebes. It is the longest Greek tragedy in existence and covers the greatest stretch of story.

The drama takes up the legend of *Oedipus at the start of the quarrel between his two sons: Polyneicēs has been refused by his brother Eteoclēs his share of their alternating rule of Thebes, and has come with Adrastus, king of Argos, and the five other leaders of the Argive army, to enforce his rights. Jocasta, wife of Oedipus, endeavours to reconcile their two sons, but her efforts fail and the attack on Thebes becomes inevitable. The seer *Teiresias predicts the victory of Eteocles and Thebes if a son of Creon (brother of Jocasta and friend of Eteocles) is sacrificed. Accord-

ingly Menoeceus, Creon's younger son, gives his life heroically for his city, in spite of his father's resistance. The Argives are driven back in the first onset, and it is arranged that the quarrel shall be settled by a single combat between the brothers. In this each kills the other, and Jocasta in despair takes her own life with one of their swords; their sister Antigonē brings the news to Oedipus. Creon takes over the government and proclaims that Polyneices' body will lie unburied and that the blind Oedipus will be expelled; moreover, Antigone will marry Creon's son Haemon. Antigone refuses, and accompanies her father into exile, announcing that she will return and secretly bury her brother.
3. Roman tragedy by *Seneca (2), which survives in an imperfect condition. It appears to combine material from *Oedipus at Colonus by Sophocles (the blind Oedipus wandering under the guidance of Antigonē), with a situation derived from other sources (Antigone at Thebes with her mother Jocasta, who tries in vain to reconcile her two sons). The surviving portions may be fragments of two distinct plays.

Phoenix. 1. In Greek myth, son of Amyntor, a king in Thessaly. His mother persuaded him to seduce his father's concubine, out of jealousy. When his father found out he cursed him with childlessness; Phoenix left home and went to Phthia, where he was kindly received by Peleus and put in charge of the young *Achilles (Peleus' son). In the Trojan War he was one of the ambassadors sent to bring Agamemnon's offer of reconciliation to Achilles, whom he had accompanied to Troy.
2. The *eponymous ancestor of the *Phoenicians, son of Agenor, king of Tyre, and brother of Cadmus and Europa.

Phoenix, Latin poem in elegiacs, 170 lines long, on this mythical Arabian bird, whose resurrection to life from death appealed to Christians and to pagan believers in mystery religions. The poem is usually ascribed to *Lactantius. The phoenix is described by Herodotus (2. 73), Tacitus (Annals 6. 28), and others with varying details. In general it was thought to resemble an eagle but with red (*phoinix*) and gold plumage; every 500 years it makes a nest and dies; from the nest arises a new phoenix which carries its parent's body to Heliopolis in Egypt for funeral in the temple of Helios (Sun). The version that has become popular in modern times has the new phoenix arising from the funeral pyre which the old phoenix has made for itself.

Phōlus, *centaur by whom Heracles was entertained when in pursuit of the Erymanthian Boar (see HERACLES, LABOURS OF 3). Pholus died after the fight between Heracles and the centaurs; while inspecting one of Heracles' arrows he dropped it on his foot and was killed by the poison.

Phorcys, Greek sea-god, son of Nereus or of Pontus (Sea) and father of the *Graiae, the *Gorgons, and *Scylla.

phorminx, see MUSIC.

Pho'rmio, see DEMOSTHENES (2) 2.

Pho'rmio, Roman comedy by *Terence, based on a Greek play of the third century BC, 'The Claimant', by Apollodorus of Carystus, a writer of Greek New Comedy (see COMEDY, GREEK 6). It was produced at Rome in 161 BC.

Antipho, a young Athenian, while his father Demipho is out of the country, has fallen in love with a girl whom he found weeping for her recently dead mother, whose funeral she must arrange, being now alone in the world. Phormio, a resourceful *parasite, taking advantage of the law that orphan girls must be married to their next-of-kin (within the permitted degree), has pretended, in collusion with Antipho, that the latter is the girl's nearest relative and obtained a court order that he is to marry her, and the marriage has taken place. Meanwhile Antipho's cousin Phaedria is desperately in love with a slave girl, a lute-player, but lacks the money to buy her from the pimp who owns her. His father Chremēs, Demipho's brother, has been away in Lemnos. Both fathers return at this juncture. Demipho is furious at his son's marriage and determined to put an end to it. Phormio offers the father, for a sum of money, to take the bride away and marry her himself. Having obtained the money he hands it over to Phaedria who now

purchases his lute-player. Meanwhile it has been discovered through a nurse that the girl Antipho has married is in fact the daughter of Chremes, who has bigamously kept a wife on Lemnos; daughter, wife, and nurse had come to Athens to look for him, and there the wife had died. Chremes wishes above all else to keep from his legitimate wife in Athens all knowledge of his liaison. To avoid trouble the two fathers decide to recognize Antipho's marriage, but their attempt to recover the money paid to Phormio leads to the exposure of Chremes to his wife. She is mollified, however, and all ends happily. The play is aptly named: Phormio dominates it, and no other character in Roman comedy quite reaches his commanding position. (The proverb, 'to have a wolf by the ears', is first found in this play, l. 506.)

Phō'tius (c. AD 810–c.893), patriarch of Byzantium 858–67 and 878–86 and a very important figure for the survival of Greek studies in the *Byzantine age. Among other works he compiled a lexicon of Attic Greek prose usage, which survives. After his day many manuscripts of ancient Greek literature were destroyed, and he was able to read more than anyone since. His fame rests on the *Bibliothekē* ('library'), also known as the *Myriobiblos* ('vast compendium'), consisting of 280 accounts of books read (usually called codices); the accounts range in size from a couple of lines to seventy or so pages of detailed comment, but most give a synopsis of the text. Slightly more than half the books are theological. The rest are Greek prose authors, ranging from the classical to the early Byzantine; quite a few of these works are known to us only through Photius (some twenty of the thirty-three historians, for example).

phrā'triai ('brotherhoods', phratries), at Athens and other Greek cities, groups of related families (or at least in theory related), in existence from earliest times. In historical times each phratry consisted of a noble family and its dependants who all shared in the family cult and claimed descent from a common ancestor, often calling themselves by a name formed from his. The phratries were a major political force until the end of the sixth century BC, when their power in that sphere was broken by the reforms of *Cleisthenēs (2). After this the phratries seem to have covered the whole citizen body, chiefly as religious and social organizations.

Phrixus, SEE ATHAMAS.

Phry'gia, territory in the west of Asia Minor, including part of the central plateau, conquered towards the end of the second millennium BC by a European people, the Phrygēs. The kingdom was associated in Greek legend with the names of Gordius (SEE GORDIAN KNOT) and *Midas. It was conquered by *Lydia and was never again independent. In the third century BC it was overrun by *Galatians; in 116 BC most of the territory was absorbed into the Roman province of Asia.

Phrȳnē, famous *hetaera of the fourth century BC from Thespiae in Boeotia, whose outstanding beauty gave rise to some notable works of art, including the painting of Aphroditē Anadyomenē by Apellēs and Praxitelēs' Aphrodite of *Cnidus. There was a gilded statue of her at Delphi dedicated by herself (according to Pausanias) or by her admirers (according to other authorities). See also HYPEREIDES (at the end).

Phrȳ'nichus. 1. Of Athens, a tragedian, coupled with *Thespis by some ancient authorities as both being the originators of tragedy; Phrynichus first won a competition for tragedy between 511 and 508 BC. Of his plays only scanty fragments survive. He produced, probably in 492, with Themistoclēs as *choregos, a play dealing with the capture of *Miletus by the Persians in 494 during the Ionian Revolt (SEE PERSIAN WARS), and was fined by the Athenians because, Herodotus said, he had reminded them too vividly of the misfortunes of a kindred people. His *Phoenissae* ('Phoenician women'), celebrating the Greek victories over the Persians in 480–79, with the chorus composed of the wives of the enemy's Phoenician sailors, was also famous. This may have been produced in 476, a year in which Themistocles was again his *choregos*. Aristophanes seems to have admired

his lyrical passages particularly, while mocking his dramas' deficiency in action.
2. One of the extreme oligarchs at Athens at the time of the revolution of the *Four Hundred in 411 BC, towards the end of the Peloponnesian War. After his return from Sparta, where he had gone to negotiate peace, he was assassinated in the agora.

Phrȳnis, SEE NOME.

phylae, in Greek, *tribes.

Phy'sica (*Physikē akroāsis*, 'Physics'), treatise by *Aristotle (see 4 (iii)).

Pīcu'mnus and Pīlu'mnus, in ancient Roman religion, two brothers, perhaps agricultural deities, the beneficent gods of matrimony and the protectors of women in childbirth. Pilumnus was thought to be the inventor of the pestle (*pilum*) for grinding corn; Virgil makes him the ancestor of *Turnus.

Pīcus ('woodpecker'), Italian god of agriculture, sometimes described as a son of *Saturn and as the first king of Italy, possessed of prophetic powers and usually taking the form of Mars' sacred bird, the woodpecker. This bird was of great importance in augury; omens were drawn from the sight of it and from its note. It was said that it helped to feed Romulus and Remus. There was a story that Picus was turned into a woodpecker by Circē ('hawk'), whose love he had spurned. Virgil makes him the father of *Faunus and grandfather of Latinus.

Pīe'ria, in Macedonia, district on the northern slopes of Mount *Olympus, whence, according to tradition, a colony migrated south to Mount *Helicon in Boeotia in prehistoric times. The cult of the *Muses was said to have been brought from Pieria (the birthplace of the Muses and of Orpheus) to Helicon; hence they are sometimes described as Pierian (or Pierides).

Pīe'ridĕs, SEE MUSES and PIERIA.

Pillars of Hercules, SEE HERACLES, LABOURS OF 10.

Pīlu'mnus, SEE PICUMNUS.

Pi'nakĕs, SEE CALLIMACHUS.

Pīnā'rii and Potī'tii, SEE HERCULES.

425 **Pindar**

Pinax, see CEBES.

Pindar (Pindaros) (518–after 446 BC), Greek lyric poet, born near Thebes in Boeotia, famous for his Epinician ('victory') Odes written in honour of the victors at the four great panhellenic Games. These odes are accordingly grouped as Olympian, Pythian, Nemean, and Isthmian, commonly abbreviated to *O.*, *P.*, *N.*, *I.*

Very little is known about Pindar's life. Legend relates that he received instruction in composition from the Boeotian poetess *Corinna, and that he went to Athens for his musical education. His devotion to the god Apollo was rewarded by special privileges at *Delphi. His attitude to the great historical events of his time was panhellenic rather than narrowly bound by local loyalties; thus he saw the Persian invasions as a threat to Greece as a whole and her deliverance as a blessing. His personal feelings about the consequences to Thebes of her pro-Persian policy cannot be ascertained, though he laments the sorrow and loss that war brought her; his admiration for Athens seems to have been unaffected by the mutual animosity of the two cities. It is said that he was fined by his countrymen for his praises of Athens, but that the Athenians paid him the amount of the fine twice over. Some of his greatest odes were for the Sicilian tyrants, particularly Hieron I of *Syracuse. He attained great fame in his lifetime, and was soon quoted as an authority (e.g. by Herodotus and Plato). In the destruction of Thebes in 335 (a punishment for her revolt against Macedonian rule) Alexander the Great ordered Pindar's house to be spared; its ruins were still visible when Pausanias visited Thebes *c.* AD 150.

Pindar's numerous poems, which included all the chief forms of choral *lyric, were grouped by the Alexandrian scholars into seventeen books according to their types. Of these only the four books of Epinician Odes survive, virtually entire, in manuscript. The rest are known mostly from quotations, although discoveries of papyri in the late nineteenth and twentieth centuries have greatly augmented our knowledge.

Pindar wrote in the literary Dorian *dialect but used epic forms as well, particularly for mythical narratives. Close analysis reveals that the odes follow a conventional pattern of praise; but the poet's skill succeeds in intertwining rather disparate elements into an artistic whole, and the reader's attention is distracted from the technical aspects of the composition by the rapid and varied flow of the poetry. The essentially repetitious nature of the subject-matter is not particularly obvious even when the forty-four odes are read in sequence, as their author can hardly have supposed they would be; the reader marvels rather at the variety. Pindar has complete control over his medium, and his technique is distinguished by constant variation, complexity, and vitality. Some of his sentences are long and periodic, others are arrestingly short. Sometimes (especially in the later odes) the language seems almost stark, stripped of ornament, and the word order simple and prosaic; in other odes the language is rich and magnificent, the word order intricate. Myths are narrated economically, allusively, and vividly. The poet is skilful at building up climaxes within the ode. Transitions from one topic to another are sometimes made abruptly for rhetorical effect, sometimes unobtrusively. Metaphors and metonomies (e.g. the variety of words used to express 'victory') abound.

The Epinician Odes are written from an essentially religious standpoint; it is this background that imparts grandeur to Pindar's themes and language. Men are nothing by themselves: success is god-given; but men attain an almost divine happiness at the moment of success. The poet himself has a skill that is god-given and cannot be taught; he is 'the mouthpiece of the Muses'. Zeus and Apollo are the gods most often invoked. The gods favour those who have struggled hard for their victory, but the victors are those whose breeding makes them worthy of it; Pindar admires aristocratic qualities, the beauty and strength fostered in the gymnasium, wealth and standing, courage and preparedness, the aristocratic institution of guest-friendship, traditional worship of the gods, devotion to family and homeland; and he warns against the unjust use of power and the envy from lesser men which success brings in its train. The qualities which he admires he sees exhibited in the heroes of old, and especially Heracles, the hero most often cited in the Odes. Pindar treats myth with freedom and with sensitivity to its appropriateness, always in a way that comports with the dignity of the occasion.

Horace, in the opening stanzas of *Odes* IV. 2, praised Pindar's rushing eloquence, bold originality in metres and diction, and admirable use of myth, and believed that his own odes could never reach such heights. Quintilian shared the general view that Pindar was by far the greatest of the Greek lyric poets. In modern times poets have tried to imitate his free-flowing, vigorous style with varying degrees of success. Of English odes, those of the seventeenth-century poet John Dryden, *Song for St Cecilia's Day* and *Alexander's Feast*, and of the eighteenth-century poet Thomas Gray, *Progress of Poesy* and *The Bard*, capture something of the true feeling.

Pirae'us (Peiraieus or Peirāeus), chief port of Athens, on a promontory 8 km. (5 miles) south-west of the ancient city, fortified by *Themistocles from the time of his archonship (493/2 BC, a little before the first Persian invasion) in order that the growing Athenian fleet might have a safer anchorage than that provided by the open roadstead of *Phalerum. For the Long Walls connecting Piraeus (and Phalerum) with Athens see LONG WALLS. The city was laid out on a grid plan by *Hippodamus in the mid-fifth century. The fortifications were demolished by the Spartan Lysander in 404 BC, at the end of the Peloponnesian War, but replaced by the Athenian admiral Conon in 393. The Roman general Sulla laid siege to Piraeus and subsequently destroyed it in 87–86 BC.

Pīrē'nē, see PEIRENE.

Piri'thŏus (Peirithoos), king of the Lapiths, friend of Theseus; see CENTAURS and THESEUS.

Pisa, name of the small district around Olympia in the western Peloponnese, presumably centred on a city (now disap-

peared); the name was frequently used in Greek poetry to refer to Olympia itself. It was destroyed by *Elis some time before 471 BC, but the date is uncertain; the two were frequently in conflict about the control of the Olympian festival and games (see OLYMPIA). In Greek myth, Oenomaus and Pelops had their home here.

Pīsi'stratus, see PEISISTRATUS.

Piso. 1. Lucius Calpurnius Piso Caesonī'nus, at Rome, consul in 58 BC; his daughter Calpurnia married Julius Caesar. He refused to support Cicero against Clodius, and was rewarded by the latter with the governorship of the province of Macedonia. His administration there (57–55) was attacked by Cicero in two speeches, *De provinciis consularibus* and *In Pisonem* (see CICERO (1) 4). After Caesar's assassination in 44 BC he tried to prevent civil war, but died within a short time. He was an Epicurean and a friend and disciple of the Greek Epicurean philosopher Philodemus, whom he very probably made a resident of his own magnificent villa at *Herculaneum. The villa excavated there which contained charred rolls of Philodemus' writings may be Piso's.

2. Gaius Calpurnius Piso (d. AD 65), the figurehead of the great conspiracy against the emperor Nero. Exiled during the reign of Caligula (AD 37–41), consul under his successor Claudius, Piso was a rich and popular figure at Rome, and a great orator. The conspiracy to assassinate Nero and to put Piso on the throne was betrayed and he was executed.

Pi'ttacus (mid-seventh century–*c.*570 BC) of Mytilenē in Lesbos, statesman, included among the *Seven Sages. He commanded the Mytilenaeans in a war against Athens for the possession of Sigeum at the mouth of the Hellespont, and killed in single combat the Athenian general and great athlete Phrynon. He appears by name in the poetry of his younger contemporary *Alcaeus; the latter savagely attacks him as a former comrade-in-arms in overthrowing tyranny at Mytilene, who has now broken with his old friends. The political struggles of the city remain unclear, but the citizens elected Pittacus *aisymnetēs* ('dictator') for ten years to restore order. He did not alter the constitution, but reformed the laws. After his period of office Pittacus laid down the dictatorship and retired to live quietly. Many sayings were attributed to him. His answer to the question 'What is best?' was 'To do the present thing well'. One of his sayings, 'It is hard to be good', was the starting point of a poem by Simonidēs discussed in Plato's *Protagoras*.

Pitys, see PAN.

Planu'dēs, see ANTHOLOGY and AESOP.

Platae'a, city in Boeotia on the border with Attica. Plataea, alone of the Boeotian cities, became allied to Athens when threatened by her Boeotian rival Thebes in the late sixth century BC. At Marathon in 490 the Plataeans were the Athenians' only allies in the battle (see PERSIAN WARS). Both cities were sacked by the Persians in 480, but in the following year Plataea was the scene of a great Greek victory over the invaders. Plataea was again sacked (427) in the Peloponnesian War, and yet again in 372 by the Thebans. Alexander the Great restored the city as a symbol of Greek bravery in resisting the Persians, and in Roman times Plutarch describes the Persian War memorial festival, the Eleutheria, as still celebrated.

Platā'icus, see ISOCRATES.

Plato (Plătōn) (427–347 BC), Greek philosopher, founder of philosophical idealism and one of the greatest of Greek prose-writers.

1. Plato was born of a noble family which claimed descent from Codrus, an early king of Athens. His life and writings show the enormous influence upon him of *Socrates' life and the manner of his death. At first he wrote poetry (probably none of the epigrams attributed to him is genuine) but meeting Socrates in about 407 BC turned his attention to philosophy. He was ill at the time of Socrates' execution in 399 and was not present during his last moments. Shortly afterwards Plato retired to Megara with other disciples of Socrates; he travelled widely in the next twelve years, visiting Egypt and making

the acquaintance of the Pythagoreans in Magna Graecia, in particular Archytas of Tarentum. In *c.*387 he visited Sicily where he met (and soon fell out with) Dionysius I tyrant of Syracuse and, most importantly, the young Dion, who became Plato's pupil and absorbed his teaching.

After a while Plato returned to Athens and there founded a school, the *Academy. Here Plato and his pupils, who included Aristotle, engaged in mathematics, dialectic, and all studies that seemed relevant for the education of future statesmen and politicians; and in this activity Plato spent the remaining forty years of his life. According to his Seventh Epistle (see 6 below) he had twice made some attempt to enter politics: at the end of the Peloponnesian War in 404, under the Thirty Tyrants (among whom were numbered Critias, his mother's cousin, and Charmidēs, his maternal uncle), and after the restoration of the democracy in 403 (see ATHENS 2 (iii)); but he had been repelled by the criminal acts of the former and by the condemnation of Socrates under the latter. He was driven to the conclusion that there was no hope for cities until philosophers became rulers or rulers philosophers. He made two more visits to Syracuse, one when Dionysius I died in 367 and was succeeded by his son Dionysius II; Dion summoned Plato to try to create in his nephew Dionysius II, then aged about 30, the Platonic philosopher-king. But Dionysius banished Dion, whose motives he suspected, and Plato returned to Athens. Another visit at Dionysius' request in 361 had no better outcome, and many of Plato's Epistles are devoted to explaining his very unsuccessful role in the affairs of Syracuse. Plato died at Athens in 347.

2. *Philosophical writings.* Plato published perhaps twenty-five philosophical dialogues (the authenticity of some is disputed) and the *Apology* (not a dialogue but a reproduction of Socrates' defence at his trial), written over a period of fifty years, and they all survive. There are also thirteen letters (the Epistles) whose genuineness is much debated. Plato himself thought that the spoken word was superior to the written (see *PHAEDRUS* and

the Seventh Epistle), and Aristotle makes reference to doctrines not found in the dialogues; hence it may be that only Plato's lectures would have given the authentic statement of his views. The precise chronological order of the dialogues is not known, but the evidence of style and the evaluation of doctrine allow a rough division into three periods. The early period includes *Apology, Charmides, *Crito, *Euthyphro, Hippias Minor, Ion, Lachēs, and perhaps Lysis (which may be later). In these Socrates is the principal figure, examining and demolishing the views put forward by his interlocutors. The second period includes *Protagoras, *Gorgias, *Meno, *Menexenus, Euthydemus, *Phaedo, *Phaedrus, *Cratylus, Parmenidēs, *Republic, *Symposium, and *Theaetetus. In these Socrates is still the foremost figure, and now puts forward positive doctrines which may be regarded as Plato's own, or at least Plato's interpretation and development of the views of Socrates. The third group, the work of Plato's later years, includes the Critias, Philebus, Politicus, *Sophist and *Timaeus; the *Laws, Plato's longest and last work, was published after his death, probably unrevised.

Of the dialogues, Charmides, Laches, and Lysis are concerned with the nature of, respectively, temperance, courage, and friendship. In the Hippias Minor, a discussion with the Elean *sophist of that name, Socrates shows by a sophistic argument that he who does evil intentionally is less blameworthy than he who does it unintentionally. Ion is the genial mockery of a rhapsodist who is shown to possess no knowledge of his art. Euthydemus is a humorous satire on the sophists. In the Menexenus, which some have hesitated to ascribe to Plato, Socrates recites a funeral oration (after the style of Pericles' Funeral Oration in book 2 of Thucydides' history) which he says was composed by the hetaera Aspasia (see PERICLES) and which is apparently satirical. In Parmenides, the young Socrates meets the older Eleatic philosophers Parmenides and Zeno, defends rather naïvely the theory of Ideas (see below) and receives some telling criticisms; it is a difficult dialogue. The Critias is an unfinished dialogue, a sequel to the *Timaeus. It includes the legend of the Athenian victory over the people of the lost island of Atlantis. The Philebus is a discussion of the relative merits of pleasure and wisdom as ingredients in the good life. In the Politicus ('statesman') the nature of the Platonic ideal of king or statesman is investigated; in the absence of the ideal ruler, the best practical course is for the citizens to frame the laws with care and make them inviolable.

Much of the charm of Plato's dialogues consists in their dramatic setting, the description of the scenes in which they take place, the amusing and interesting characters whom he stages, and the genial irony of Socrates.

3. It is difficult to know in the early dialogues how far Plato is reproducing Socrates' views and to what extent he has moved beyond them, but in the later dialogues it is reasonable to think that Plato is propounding his own doctrines. His primary concern is with moral education. Plato believes that on the one hand it is possible to be a good man without properly knowing what it means to be a good man or what goodness is. This is to have right opinion (orthē doxa); as one might think correctly that a road leads to Larisa (Plato's example in Meno) without having been along it and reached Larisa oneself. But on the other hand only to have right opinion is to be in a precarious state: meeting a new idea about goodness might throw one into confusion so that cne could not judge its value. True knowledge is needed, which is different from right opinion in that with it one is able to define or give an account of what one knows. The early dialogues portray Socrates seeking definitions of particular virtues, of courage in Laches, temperance in Charmides, piety in Euthyphro, or virtue in general in Meno, but without reaching positive conclusions. Virtue is a matter of knowledge. Both Socrates and Plato were attracted by the notion that knowledge of virtue is similar in kind to knowledge of how to practise a craft, such as cobbling shoes. It followed for Socrates and Plato (though not for many others) that wrong-doing is the result of ignorance; if people truly knew the good they were bound to do it. In any case knowledge of what goodness is would enable people both to be good

themselves and to lead others to knowledge of goodness. A man having such knowledge would constitute the ideal ruler. Only philosophical enquiry, that is, the practice of *dialectic, can lead to true knowledge, and it must be preceded by the study of mathematics and of abstract thinking in general, including logic, as well as of the science of government. Only a select few may be capable of gaining this kind of true knowledge; the rest must be content with having the right opinions.

4. For Plato all objects of knowledge, abstractions such as 'beauty' as well as concrete things, were real entities, but like the objects of mathematical knowledge, the ideal triangle or circle, they did not exist in our world of the senses. Plato postulated another world, the world of Ideas or Forms (of things), leaving the relationship between Ideas and the material things of this world somewhat vague; but the things we see now in this world remind us of the Ideas that they imitate and in some sense partake of. Knowledge of the world of Ideas is attainable in this world only by thought (as is true of the objects of mathematical knowledge; see 5 below) and true knowledge can only be of these Ideas, because they are eternal and unvarying whereas the objects of this world are forever changing. (Aristotle's criticism of this doctrine was that ideas only had reality in so far as they were embodied in particular objects.)

5. Plato believed in a dualism of immortal soul and mortal body. The soul before birth (that is, before its incarnation) was acquainted with the world of Ideas; knowledge of the Ideas in this life is achieved through the soul's recollection of what it has previously known, a recollection which is brought about by the practice of philosophy (i.e. dialectic). Life should therefore be devoted to the cultivation of the soul and the suppression of the body (which may hinder the soul's activities). Beyond all other Ideas is that of the Good (which in some way that is never explained is the cause of things), knowledge of which it is the soul's ambition to attain. Love of what is good and beautiful in this world can lead by stages, through philosophy, to the soul's contemplation of the Idea of Goodness in another world, for which it yearns.

Plato once advertised a lecture on the Good. A large audience collected expecting to hear about the good things they valued—health, wealth, and material happiness. When they found themselves listening to a discourse on mathematics in which they were told that the Good is Limit (*peras*), they went away contemptuous and angry. This was a favourite story of Aristotle, who drew from it the moral that a prospective audience should always be told in advance what a lecture is really going to be about.

6. Thirteen Epistles attributed to Plato have come down to us. They were regarded as genuine in antiquity and are quoted by Cicero and Plutarch. They are addressed to correspondents in Sicily, and all relate to Plato's dealings with Dion and Dionysius, which they were intended to defend. Perhaps none of them was written by Plato himself, but it is generally accepted that the Seventh Epistle, which is addressed to the friends of Dion after the murder of the latter in 353 BC, is a reliable record of the events of Plato's life even if not written by him. It contains a defence of Plato's political ideals and is a passionate lament for his friend Dion.

7. In the disciplines and methods of philosophy, and the rigour of their application, Plato's immediate heir was Aristotle, but ultimately his intellectual heirs are all those who have tried to think systematically about morals and politics, science and mathematics. Plato has exerted an enormous influence on subsequent philosophic and religious thought by his theory of Ideas, his sense of an unseen and eternal world behind the changing unrealities of the world of the senses, his conception of God, and his connection of morality with religion. In Judaism his influence is felt in the Book of Wisdom and in the system of *Philo. Among the Romans his philosophy appealed to Cicero in particular, as it did to all who revolted against materialism. In the third century AD Plotinus and others provided systematic exegesis of the dialogues as well as reinterpretations, which together made *Neoplatonism the

dominant pagan philosophy of that time. Christian thought was infused with Platonic notions from the time of (the Greek) Clement of Alexandria and Origen (second century AD), and Latin Christianity too was influenced indirectly by Platonic teaching from a variety of sources including *Boethius and (from the ninth century) translations of (pseudo)-Dionysius the Areopagite. At the beginning of the Renaissance, reaction by humanists against scholasticism took the form of disparagement of Aristotle and enthusiasm for Plato. Latin translations of his works were made in the fifteenth century by the Italian humanist Marsilio Ficino (1433–99). Knowledge of Plato came to England in the sixteenth century and Platonism was embraced enthusiastically by the seventeenth-century Cambridge Platonists, so-called, who were in this as in much else opposed to the thought of their age. Although nowadays a Platonist philosophy is not usually thought to be tenable, Plato remains a source of philosophical inspiration.

Platonism, see ACADEMY, MIDDLE PLATONISM, and NEOPLATONISM.

Plautus, Titus Ma'ccius (or Maccus) (c.250–184 BC), Roman writer of comedies. He was born at Sarsina in Umbria, reputedly in humble circumstances. Twenty of the 130 plays that were attributed to him have survived, all included in the twenty-one named by Varro as authentic. Of the twenty-first, the *Vidularia* ('wallet'), only one hundred or so lines exist in a *palimpsest. The plays are all adaptations from Greek New Comedy (see COMEDY, GREEK 6) of the fourth and third centuries BC, now lost (but see *DIS EXAPATON*); three or four are known to be from Menander, two from Diphilus, two from Philemon, and one apparently from Alexis, and they reproduce Greek life and, with humorous exaggeration, Greek character, as presented by the Greek originals. They were known among the Romans as *fabulae *palliatae*. They contain no satire on public affairs. Plautus' success in winning the approval of his uncultivated audience lay in the freedom and liveliness with which he handled the Greek orig-

inals. In practice he completely recreated these works, simplifying or abridging the plot and making its progress clear, and at the same time introducing other elements, some incongruous and anachronistic, aimed at appealing to his contemporary Roman audience: short stock scenes where characters exchange threats or insults; stock motifs such as that of the 'running slave' entering to deliver a message ostensibly in a hurry but with a great deal of by-play; the slave in the role of popular entertainer, daringly outspoken and insolent in what the Romans may have felt was the Greek fashion, sometimes contrasted with a loyal slave expressing sentiments towards his masters likely to win the approval of slave-owners in the audience; coarse jokes, a great deal of alliteration, puns, and general word-play. As well as this, instead of having plays consisting almost entirely of spoken dialogue (*diverbium*), Plautus greatly increased (to about two-thirds of the play) the element of song and recitative (*cantica*), so that the plays resembled musical comedy. The spoken part was written chiefly in iambic senarii (see METRE, LATIN 2), but the scansion was far less regular than in later authors, and was based in great part not on quantity but on stress accent, probably in accordance with colloquial pronunciation. The sung portion was written in a number of lyric metres.

The plays show variety of manner: sentimental comedy in *Captivi*, domestic in *Trinummus*, romantic in *Rudens*, burlesque in *Amphitruo*, and farcical in *Miles gloriosus*. Most plots centre on the tricks of a resourceful slave to forward the love-affair of his young master who is being thwarted by a rival, a pimp, or a stern father. The girl in question is usually a slave-prostitute who is eventually discovered to be free-born and so able to marry her Athenian lover. Often the heroine was kidnapped in childhood and her recognition forms the climax of the play. Among the stock characters may be included a boastful soldier, a *parasite, and a cook. For descriptions of the plays see the entries under their titles. The best-known are: *Amphitruo, Aulularia, Bacchides, Captivi, Menaechmi, Mostellaria, Miles gloriosus, Pseudolus, Rudens,*

Trinummus. Less popular are: *Asinaria*, *Casina*, *Cistellaria*, *Curculio*, *Epidicus*, *Mercator*, *Persa*, *Poenulus*, *Stichus*, *Truculentus*. (For *Vidularia* see above.)

These plays are almost the only evidence we have for the Latin language at that period. They were greatly admired in the late republic and under the early emperors, but dropped out of favour later because of the difficulty of the language. Plautus was rediscovered and widely translated in the Renaissance, and his influence is traceable in much sixteenth-century English comedy. Henry VIII had two of the comedies performed to entertain the French ambassador in 1526. Shakespeare used the plot of the *Menaechmi* in *The Comedy of Errors* (1594), and Molière's Harpagon in *L'Avare* (1668) is taken from Euclio in *Aulularia*.

plebei'ans, plebs (Lat. sing. noun, 'the common people'), name given to the body of Roman citizens other than the privileged *patricians. In the early republic the plebeians were excluded from religious *collegia*, magistracies, and perhaps from the senate, and from intermarriage with patricians by a law of the *Twelve Tables. The 'conflict of the orders' in the fifth and fourth centuries BC was a successful struggle to have these civil disabilities abolished. See also TRIBUNES OF THE PLEBS.

Pleiad, the, name given to a group of eight or more Greek writers of tragedy who lived in Alexandria in the reign of Ptolemy II Philadelphus (285–246 BC). None of their tragedies survives. Their name, derived from the constellation (see below), was later taken over by a group of seven sixteenth-century French poets. See LYCOPHRON 2.

Plei'ădĕs (Eng. Pleiades), in Greek myth, the seven daughters of the Titan *Atlas and Pleionē. Their names were Maia (the mother of Hermēs by Zeus), Tāygetē, Ēlectra, Alcyonē, Asteropē, Celaeno, and Meropē. They were pursued by *Orion and he and they were turned into constellations (as were their sisters the *Hyadĕs). The Pleiads, a cluster of seven stars, have special significance for marking the seasons, in particular the time for sowing and planting. In Hesiod, the first rising of the Pleiads before sunrise (early May) marks harvest-time, their setting just before sunrise (at the beginning of November) marks the time for ploughing and sowing. The name is very old and of uncertain meaning.

Pliny. 1. Pliny the Elder (Gaius Plinius Secundus) (AD 23/4–79), Roman writer on natural history. He was born at Cōmum (Como) in north Italy of an equestrian family and probably educated at Rome. From the age of about twenty-three to thirty-five he spent his life in military service, mostly with the armies of the Rhine, being at one time the comrade-in-arms of the future emperor Titus. He returned to Italy in 57 or 58 and it was perhaps at this time that he spent a period (mentioned by his nephew Pliny the Younger) as an advocate at the bar. After the accession of the emperor Vespasian in AD 69 his fortunes improved and he held a succession of procuratorships in Gaul, Africa, and Spain which he discharged 'with the utmost scrupulousness' according to Suetonius. He became a counsellor (*amicus*, 'friend') of Vespasian and then of Titus who succeeded in 79, and was appointed commander of the fleet at Misenum (near Naples). It was from there that he sailed on 24 August 79 to observe the eruption of Vesuvius from the neighbourhood of Stabiae (south of Pompeii). His nephew Pliny the Younger (see (2) below) describes in a letter to Tacitus (6. 16) how his uncle had his attention drawn to the column of smoke rising above the nearer mountains and set off in a light vessel to investigate; how he dictated his observations under a hail of stones and the next day went out on the shore despite the darkness and explosions, with a pillow around his head for protection against falling debris, and was suffocated by the fumes.

Pliny was a man of extraordinary industry and thirst for knowledge. He slept little, had books constantly read to him, and took an immense quantity of notes. He wrote works which are now lost on cavalry tactics, oratory, grammar, and history (twenty books on Rome's wars against the Germans, thirty-one books continuing the Roman history of Aufidius Bassus, who lived in the time of the emperors Augustus and Tiberius). His greatest achievement, which has survived, is the *Naturalis Historia* ('natural history') in thirty-seven books, dedicated to Titus in 77 and published posthumously. Pliny tells us in the preface that it consists of 20,000 important facts obtained from 100 authors, but the total of both is much higher. Book 1 consists of a table of contents and list of authorities; book 2 deals with the physics of the universe, and its constituent parts; books 3–6 are on the geography and ethnology of Europe, Asia, and Africa; book 7 on human physiology; books 8–11 on zoology (land animals, sea animals, birds, insects); books 12–19 on botany; books 20–7 on the medicinal properties of plants; books 28–32 on medicines derived from animals; books 33–7 on metals and stones, including the use of minerals in medicine, art, and architecture, with a digression on the history of art, the source of many good anecdotes and much valuable information about Greek artists.

In spite of many errors and much carelessness, credulity, superficiality, unscientific arrangement, and the tedium of dry catalogues, the work is remarkable for the vast labour and the boundless curiosity of the author that it represents; it contains much that is interesting and entertaining, and much unique information about the art, science, and civilization of the author's day. It is full of stories, such as that about the skeleton of the monster by which Andromeda had been menaced, brought from Joppa (Jaffa) and exhibited at Rome (9. 11; Joppa evidently traded on the legend, for the marks of the chains with which Andromeda was fastened were also shown there, 5. 69); the tricks that elephants were taught (8. 4–8); the coracles of the British (7. 206); the introduction of barbers into Italy (7. 211). Roman life is illustrated by passages such as those about the variety of mattresses and woollen cloths in use (8. 190–3); the price of a cook (9. 67); ostrich feathers worn in military helmets (10. 2); wrinkles removed with asses' milk (28. 183).

Like Seneca the Younger, Pliny is a believer in a beneficent deity, a spirit pervading the world. He is an enthusiastic admirer of nature, and a vigorous critic of his times, which he saw as marked by folly, luxury, inhumanity, and ingratitude. He has a sturdy Roman dislike of the Greeks and distrust of their influence.

2. Pliny the Younger (AD 61/62–c.113), Roman administrator known through his letters. He was called Gaius Plinius Caecilius Secundus after being adopted by his maternal uncle Pliny the Elder (see (1) above). He was born at Comum (Como) in north Italy, and studied at Rome under *Quintilian, whose influence may be detected in the simplicity and restraint of his pupil's prose. Another of his teachers was the Stoic philosopher Musonius (who also taught Epictetus). He was three times married, his first two wives dying young; his letters show that his marriage to Calpurnia, the third wife, was a very happy one. He began a career at the bar at the age of 18, specializing in cases of inheritance. He passed through the regular series of magistracies (see CURSUS HONORUM) and succeeded by his discretion in avoiding (though he stood in some danger) Domitian's persecution of the Stoic opposition, in spite of his sympathy with its views. Under Trajan (AD 98–117) he became one of the officials in charge of the state treasury; he was *consul suffectus* in 100, then a curator of the river Tiber at Rome, responsible for keeping its banks in repair to prevent flooding and for maintaining the sewers. He became augur in 103 (succeeding *Frontinus) and finally governor of the disorderly province of Bithynia–Pontus along the south coast of the Black Sea (in about 110), where he apparently died in office.

Pliny was very rich and owned estates in various parts of Italy which he administered with efficiency. He was notably considerate to his slaves, and munificent. He founded a library at Comum and made many large gifts and charitable bequests. He practised in the courts and was proud of his oratory. His only surviving speech is a revised edition of the *Panegyricus* which he delivered to Trajan on entering on his consulship in AD 100, an expression of the relief felt under the new reign after the oppression of Domitian, and a document which throws light on Trajan's reforms. Among other important speeches that Pliny delivered was one on behalf of the Africans, impeaching Marius Priscus, who had been proconsul of Africa. In this he was associated with Tacitus, who, according to Pliny, spoke eloquently and with majesty.

Pliny's fame rests on his ten books of letters. The first nine books of personal letters were carefully selected and published at intervals by Pliny himself before he went out to Bithynia. In general the letters are not dated, and Pliny professes to have arranged them haphazardly. Book 10 was published posthumously; it begins with fourteen short official letters to Trajan, and is followed by correspondence relating to Bithynia. The first three books deal with the events of 97–102, and are closed by a letter on the death of the poet Martial in 103/4; these were published c.107. Books 4–7 refer to the events of 103–7; in the last letter of book 7 Pliny expresses the hope of being included in the *Histories* of his friend Tacitus. Books 8–9 cover the years 108–9, and show Pliny enjoying a leisurely time on the estate of his Tuscan villa at Tifernum (Città di Castello), reading and writing to his friends. Twice he speaks of being recognized and linked with Tacitus as a famous author (see below). His appointment to Bithynia ended this period of cultivated leisure.

The letters resemble short essays on a wide variety of subjects: public affairs (especially the prosecutions of officials, with which he was concerned), descriptions of his villas or of scenery, or of how he spends his day (sometimes in hunting, but he takes his writing materials too), reproof of a friend who fails to come to dinner, literary or rhetorical points, interpretation of a dream, ghost stories, the purchase of a statue or an estate, a murder. He writes movingly of his new marriage, his grief at his wife's miscarriage, and his hopes for further children (not to be fulfilled). Several of his letters are addressed to his friends Tacitus and Suetonius. Among the former is the famous letter (6. 16) describing the eruption of Vesuvius and his uncle's death. Other interesting letters are those containing eulogies of the poets Silius Italicus and Martial (3. 7 and 21), that relating the heroism of *Arria, wife of Paetus (3. 16), and that containing a bibliography of the works of the Elder Pliny (3. 5). The style of the letters is adapted to the subject, serious or light-hearted, and in general strikes a mean between the amplitude of Cicero and the brevity of the Younger Seneca, but the letters are more studied and artificial than those of Cicero to Atticus. Apart from the charm they derive from the agreeable nature of their author, they are interesting for their depiction of the life of a wealthy Roman during a happy period of the empire, and help to correct the unfavourable impression left by the bitter satire of Juvenal and the sombre pessimism which Tacitus retained even when writing under Trajan. The senate is seen, for instance, deliberating on matters of importance within its restricted sphere, punishments are inflicted on dishonest officials, and family life pursues its course with a degree of loyalty and decency.

The correspondence with Trajan in the tenth book throws valuable light on the administration of an imperial province. It displays Pliny as an honest but timid governor, referring to Rome such small matters as the absence of a fire-brigade and water-buckets at Nicomedia. The emperor's replies are precise and clear and show him encouraging an extraordinary degree of centralization. The most famous of these letters are Pliny's submission of the question how the Christians should be treated, and the emperor's answer.

Pliny prided himself not only on his oratory but on his poetry, and published two volumes of verse. Some rather bad specimens are included in his letters. His pleasure in his literary fame appears when he tells (9. 23) how a Roman *eques*, sitting next to Tacitus at the Circus and conversing with him, asked him who he was, and being answered, 'You know me from your reading', enquired, 'Are you Tacitus or Pliny?'

Plōtī'nus (c. AD 205–270) greatest Greek philosopher of late antiquity, the chief exponent of *Neoplatonism, probably born at Lycopolis in Egypt. He settled in

Rome in 244, after having accompanied the expedition of the emperor Gordion to Mesopotamia in order to learn something of eastern thought. He was admired for his extreme spirituality, mysticism, and asceticism. 'He seemed ashamed of being in a body', says his biographer and disciple *Porphyry. Plotinus wrote philosophical essays arising out of discussions and intended for circulation among his pupils. These were collected by Porphyry and arranged in six books of nine essays each, called *Enneads* ('the nines'). Ennead 1 deals with ethics and aesthetics; Enneads 2 and 3 with physics and cosmology; Ennead 4 with psychology; Enneads 5 and 6 with metaphysics, logic, and epistemology. Because of his weak sight Plotinus never read through what he had written; the writings read like oral discourse and are brief, elliptical, and allusive, with abrupt transitions, and are therefore very difficult to understand.

Plotinus' philosophy may be summarized as follows. The universe is to be explained as a hierarchy of realities (or hypostasēs), a great chain of being, in which the higher reality is the cause of and gives existence to whatever is immediately below it; this process Plotinus calls emanation, an 'overflowing' from a higher to a lower level. In this process there is a gradual diminution, so that every existent is slightly inferior to its cause. At the top of the hierarchy are three divine realities, the One (*Hen*), Mind (*Nous*), and Soul *Psȳchē*). At the very summit is the One, supreme goodness, which can to a large extent be identified with Plato's Idea of the Good (see PLATO 5). Mind, which comes immediately below the One, and derives its form from contemplating its source, is a fragmented image of the One, and corresponds to intuitive thought. The Platonic Ideas (see PLATO 4) are to be found in Mind. Soul, which derives from Mind, can only contemplate its objects in succession, moving from one to another, and so it creates time and space. It generates the next reality, Nature (*Physis*), the principle of life and growth. Beyond Nature, at the lowest level of reality, exist material things (matter). Human beings are microcosms, containing within themselves parts of Matter, Nature, Soul, and

Mind. What a human being becomes depends on the level to which he directs his consciousness. By intellectual discipline a person may hope to rise to the level of Mind. It is even possible to rise beyond that and be identified, by ecstasy, with the supreme unity of the One (an experience which Plotinus says came four times to him). In ethics Plotinus enjoined purification by self-discipline, with a view to ascent, impelled by love and enthusiasm, towards the One. His writings are based on personal experience and are a classic of mysticism. He makes no explicit reference to Christianity, and unification with the One is not thought of as attainable by divine grace. Plotinus also makes an important contribution to aesthetics: whereas Plato had argued that art imitates natural objects, Plotinus propounds the view that art and nature alike both impose a form on matter in accordance with an inward vision of archetypal Forms or Ideas.

Plūtarch (Ploutarchos) (*c*. AD 46–*c*. 120), Greek biographer, historian, and moral philosopher.

1. Plutarch was born at *Chaeronēa in Boeotia, of a wealthy and cultivated family, and spent most of his life there. He studied philosophy at Athens under the Platonist *Ammonius, a man of practical as well as philosophical ability. He visited Egypt and Italy, lecturing and teaching at Rome, and had a wide circle of influential and cultivated friends. But the last thirty years of his life were centred on Chaeronea and Delphi; he was a citizen of both, and served them with devotion for many years. Neither Pliny the Younger nor Tacitus (his contemporaries) mentions him. Plutarch is one of the most attractive and readable of ancient prose authors, writing with charm, geniality, and tact. An ancient catalogue of his works exists, ascribed to Lamprias. His surviving writings (half his complete works) consist of (i) a series of fifty biographies known as *Parallel Lives* (*Bioi parallēloi*) in which he relates the life of some eminent Greek (statesman or soldier) followed by the life of some similar Roman offering some points of resemblance, and then adds a short comparison of the two; and (ii) seventy-eight

miscellaneous works now known as the *Mōrālia* (Gk. *Ēthika*).

2. *Parallel Lives*. These consist of twenty-three pairs of lives, nineteen of them with comparisons attached, and also four single lives. They include lives of Solon, Themistocles, Aristeides, Pericles, Alcibiades, Nicias, Demosthenes, Philopoemen, Timoleon, Dion, Alexander, Pyrrhus, Marius, Sulla, Pompey, Mark Antony, Brutus, Julius Caesar, and Cicero. Of the Roman emperors, only the lives of Galba and Otho survive. Plutarch's object is to bring out the moral character in each case, rather than to relate the political events of his time; hence his full treatment of the subject's education and natural disposition, and his relation of anecdotes calculated to reveal the nature of the man, 'a light occasion, a word, or some sport' which 'makes men's natural dispositions more plain than the famous battles won, in which ten thousand men may be killed'. Although Plutarch distorts the truth in order to exemplify virtue or vice, in general he is as reliable as his sources, and sometimes very valuable. He shows no bias or unfairness in his treatment of Greeks and Romans, no flattery of the now dominant power of Rome or vanity in the past glories of his own nation. He believed in the compatibility of Rome the ruler and Greece the educator.

The *Lives* contain, besides interesting anecdotes, many memorable historical passages: the catastrophe in the Peloponnesian War of the Athenian expedition to Syracuse (*Nicias*), Pompey's defeat by Caesar and subsequent murder, the death of the younger Cato, and the suicide of Otho. There are also great battle-pieces: the victory of the Roman general Marius over the German Cimbri, the victory of the Corinthian general Timoleon over the Carthaginians at the river Crimisus, the siege of Syracuse (when Archimedes was there) by the Roman Marcellus; and striking descriptions of a quite different kind, of the happy state of Italy under Numa, of Sicily pacified by Timoleon, and of Cleopatra sailing up the river Cydnus in her barge to visit Antony. The most famous translation of the *Lives* into English was that of Sir Thomas North (1579) made not from Greek but from the French version of Jacques Amyot (1559). It was Shakespeare's major source for *Julius Caesar*, *Antony and Cleopatra*, and *Coriolanus*, and a minor source for *A Midsummer Night's Dream* and *Timon of Athens*.

3. *Moralia*. These treatises are usually referred to by their Latin titles and their subjects are varied. There is one group of rhetorical works and another on moral philosophy (treated in a popular style) on themes such as 'On Busy-bodies' (*de cūriōsitāte*), 'On Garrulity' (*de garrulitāte*), 'On the Restraint of Anger' (*de cohibenda ira*), 'How to Distinguish a Flatterer from a Friend' (*quomodo adūlātōr ab amico internoscatur*). Plutarch's warm and sympathetic personality is apparent in his 'Advice to Married Couples' (*coniugalia praecepta*) and 'Consolation to My Wife' (*consolatio ad uxorem*) on the death of their infant daughter. There is a religious group, in which Plutarch appears as the interpreter and defender of the old beliefs. It includes the treatise 'On Superstition' (*de superstitione*), in which he regards superstition as the opposite extreme to atheism, and piety as the mean between the two. Plutarch was a (not altogether orthodox) Platonist and was opposed to some of the doctrines of the Stoics, and still more to the Epicurean school and its encouragement of withdrawal from the duties of social life: see his treatises on 'The Unnoticed Life' (*an recte dictum sit latenter esse vivendum*), 'Advice on Public Life' (*praecepta gerendae reipublicae*), and 'Not Even a Pleasant Life is Possible on Epicurean Principles' (*non posse suaviter vivi secundum Epicurum*). There is an interesting treatise 'On the Delays of Divine Justice' (*de sera numinis vindicta*) in which he explains the puzzle of the apparent prosperity of the wicked, and another 'On the E at Delphi' (*de E apud Delphos*), i.e. on the letter E inscribed in the temple of Apollo there (for which he offers a Pythagorean explanation, that it is the Greek for 'Thou Art', identifying the one eternal principle of the universe); also interesting is 'On the Cessation of Oracles' (*de defectu oraculorum*), which contains a discussion of demons (see DAIMONES), beings intermediate between gods and

men, and refers to the legend of the genii of the British Isles.

Plutarch used the *dialogue form extensively and often to great effect. The nine books of 'Table Talk' (*quaestiones convivales*) are dinner-party conversations of wise men (rhetoricians, physicians, etc., some of them historical characters) on a multitude of subjects. The treatise 'On Socrates' Sign' (*de genio Socratis*) combines many elements: exciting narrative (the liberation of Thebes), philosophical conversation, and an elaborate myth, in the manner of Plato, on the fate of the soul after death. A different kind of treatise is that 'On the Face in the Moon' (*de facie quae in orbe lunae appāret*), a speculation on the cosmos. Several important antiquarian works have also survived: the 'Greek' and 'Roman Questions' (*quaestiones Graecae, Romanae*) are a mine of information about religious antiquities. Plutarch wrote some literary criticism, including a comparison of Aristophanes and Menander, and an essay 'On the Malignity of Herodotus' (*de malignitate Herodoti*; see HERODOTUS), in which Plutarch's complaint seems to be that Herodotus did not conceal the pro-Persian sympathies of the Boeotians. It is noteworthy that Plutarch, in spite of his familiarity with Roman society, history, archaeology, and religion, almost completely ignores Roman literature (his knowledge of Latin appears to have been limited). In his Life of Lucullus he gives a Greek version of a passage from Horace, but never mentions Virgil or Ovid.

4. Among the *Moralia* have survived several slightly later works not written by Plutarch but of great importance: 'On the Education of Children' (*de liberis educandis*) was very influential in the Renaissance; 'On Fate' (*de fato*) is valuable as a work of Middle Platonist philosophy; 'The Lives of the Ten Orators' (*vitae decem oratorum*) is an important source for ancient knowledge of the Attic orators from Antiphon to Deinarchus; 'The Doctrines of the Philosophers' (*de placitis philosophorum*) is another important source book; and 'On Music' (*de musica*) is one of the principal sources of modern knowledge about the history of Greek music and lyric poetry.

5. Plutarch's *Moralia* were widely read in medieval times and studied by many later authors. They were translated into French by Amyot in 1572, and into English by Philemon Holland in 1603. These and the *Lives*, perhaps more than the work of any other ancient writer, transmitted to Europe knowledge of the moral and historical traditions of the classical world, and influenced immeasurably its ways of thought.

Pluto, Latin form, commonly used in English, of Ploutōn, in Greek myth, a name of *Hades, god of the Underworld, meaning 'the wealth-giver' (Gk. *ploutos*, 'wealth'), because wealth comes from the earth. Compare *Plutus* below. It is also the name of a Titaness, mother of *Tantalus.

Plūtus (*ploutos*, 'wealth'), in Greek myth, the personification of wealth, the son of *Demeter and *Iasion, whom Homer regarded as a mortal. He was originally connected with abundance of crops and became a figure of popular rather than literary mythology. He was worshipped with Demeter at Eleusis. There was a tradition that Zeus blinded him in order to make him indiscriminate in the distribution of riches. See the Greek comedy *Plutus* by Aristophanes, below.

Plūtus (*Ploutos*, 'wealth'), Greek comedy by *Aristophanes produced in 388 BC; at what festival and with what success is not known. It is the last of Aristophanes' extant plays. An earlier play of the same name, now lost, had been produced by him in 408 BC. The lyrics to be sung by the chorus are very scanty in this play, but provision appears to have been made at various places for choral interludes which had no particular connection with the plot (for the diminishing role of the chorus in the latest plays of Aristophanes see COMEDY, GREEK 5).

Chremylus is so indignant at seeing bad men grow rich while honest men like himself remain poor that, accompanied by his slave Carion, he has been to consult the Delphic Oracle as to whether he should bring up his son to be good or bad if the latter is to succeed in life. The god advises Chremylus to accost the first person he meets on leaving the shrine and induce him to enter his house. This is a blind old man; pestered by Chremylus and Carion he reveals that he is Plutus, god of wealth, whom Zeus has blinded out of ill-will to men so that, being unable to distinguish good men from bad, he will reward them indiscriminately, without regard to their virtue. Chremylus decides that the sight of Plutus must be restored so that he may associate only with honest men. Plutus is terrified of the vengeance of Zeus but is persuaded that he himself is more powerful than that god: he can put a stop to Zeus' sacrifices by not providing men with the money to buy them. He therefore consents to be taken to the temple of Asclepius to be cured. The goddess of Poverty intervenes and tries to deter Chremylus, pointing out the disastrous effects of what he proposes to do, for it is Poverty, the source of all virtue and effort, that has made Greece what she is. But Chremylus remains unconvinced, and he and Carion go off to the temple with Plutus. Carion returns to tell Chremylus' wife of the successful cure, with much entertaining detail; presently Plutus returns and enriches Chremylus' house. Then come a series of visitors: an honest man who has long been poor and is now prosperous; an informer, indignant at being impoverished; an old woman who has lost her young lover now he no longer needs her money; the god Hermēs, who is desperately hungry, now no one bothers to sacrifice to the gods, and is looking for a job; and finally the priest of Zeus who is also hungry now he cannot get his share of the sacrifices. Chremylus seems to identify Plutus and Zeus, and suggests that they install Plutus in the Treasury on the Acropolis. A procession for that purpose ensues.

pnigos, see COMEDY, GREEK 3 (iv).

Pnyx, hill at Athens a little way west of the Acropolis, where from the time of *Cleisthenēs (end of the sixth century BC) the assembly of the Athenian citizens (the *ecclesia*) used to meet. In Roman times (i.e. after 146 BC) the Pnyx lost its importance and the assembly met in the Theatre of Dionysus.

Podalei'rius, see MACHAON.

Poe'nulus ('little Carthaginian'), Roman comedy by *Plautus. The two daughters of Hanno, a Carthaginian, who were stolen from him in their childhood, have been bought by a pimp and taken to Sicyon (in Greece). In the same place is living Agorastoclēs, son of Hanno's cousin (and the 'little Carthaginian' of the title); he likewise was stolen in infancy and has been adopted by a wealthy citizen of Sicyon. He has fallen in love with the elder of the sisters, not knowing of their kinship to him. He and his slave devise a plot for ruining the pimp in order to free the girl. Meanwhile Hanno, who has been searching every country for his daughters, arrives at Sicyon; he discovers them and his relative Agorastocles, recovers the girls, and bestows the elder on her lover. Some of Hanno's speeches appear to be in the Carthaginian language.

Poetics (Gk. *Peri poiētikēs*, Lat. *Poetica*), treatise by *Aristotle on poetry, primarily a philosophical work of aesthetic theory. Like all Greeks, Aristotle believed that art is essentially representational. In the *Poetics* his fundamental belief is that imitation is the basis of the pleasure derived from all forms of art, not only poetry but also music, dancing, painting, and sculpture. The artist, by pointing out similarities, gives us the pleasure of understanding things better.

Aristotle divides poetry according to whether it imitates people above or below the average state of humanity (tragedy represents good characters, comedy bad) and according to whether it is narrative (epic) or dramatic. He traces the special origins and development of *tragedy and *comedy. An analysis of tragedy follows: its constituent elements are plot, the imitation of character, verbal expression, the imitation of intellect, spectacle, and song-writing; the plot (the pre-eminent part of tragedy) should represent a single action of a certain magnitude; the poet's aim is to produce pleasure in the spectator by eliciting from the representation the emotions of pity (for others) and fear (for oneself). Plato had attacked tragedy for stimulating the emotions a good man tries to suppress; Aristotle seems to suggest that the *catharsis* (purging) of these emotions may incidentally be beneficial. He discusses the construction of the plot, including the complex (as opposed to the simple) plot which contains 'reversal of fortune' (*peripeteia*) and recognition (*anagnōrisis*). This part includes the notable saying that poetry is more like philosophy and more worthwhile than history, because it tells general truths while history tells particular facts, 'what Alcibiades did and what happened to him'. There follow sections on characterization, poetic imagination, and diction.

Aristotle proceeds to discuss epic poetry, the rules to which it should conform, and its metre. Finally he deals with criticisms of Homer and how they may be met, and ends with a comparison of tragedy and epic.

The *Poetics* became the most influential book on poetry ever written. It has, however, the peculiarity that the genuine views of Aristotle contributed no more to its influence than the misinterpretation of these views arising from the author's compressed and elliptical style. The dramatic unities of time, place, and action, for example, which were so rigidly adhered to by the French classical dramatists, find their origin in Aristotle's observations on the practice of his day (he insisted only on the necessity for unity of action) but took their absolute nature from the elaborations of Italian Renaissance scholars and in particular from the widely read *Poetics* (1561) of Julius Caesar Scaliger.

po'lemarch (*polemarchos*), at Athens, one of the nine *archons appointed annually, originally the commander-in-chief of the army; after 487 BC when the archons were appointed by lot the chief command was transferred to the *strategoi and the polemarch's powers were limited to certain judicial and ceremonial functions.

Po'lemon, head of the *Academy 313–270 BC.

polis, 'city' (pl. *poleîs*), the Greek city-state, the small self-governing community which emerged at the end of the Dark Age and was the characteristic political unit of the Greek world. There were several hundreds in Greece and the colonies. A *polis* consisted of only one city, with its citadel (*acropolis*) and market-place (*agora*), and the surrounding countryside. The citizens lived in city or country, but the government of the state was entirely concentrated in the city, and in the hands of those citizens empowered by the constitution to exercise it (see ARISTOCRACY, OLIGARCHY, DEMOCRACY). The government was carried on by an assembly (see ECCLESIA), council (see BOULE), and magistrates (see ARCHONS). Citizens had certain obligations towards the city: to worship the state gods and take part in their cult, perform military service, pay taxes, and obey the laws. There was also a large non-citizen population of slaves and perhaps of resident foreigners also (see METICS). Political struggles mostly centred on the kind of constitution the city possessed (e.g. between supporters of oligarchy and supporters of democracy) and on social and economic conditions; civil war (*stasis*) was frequent. The large number of independent city-states was the chief reason for the endless internal wars in Greece and the infrequency of any panhellenic action. The *poleis* lost much of their vital life when they lost their independence after the conquests of Alexander the Great and the emergence of the Hellenistic kingdoms in the late fourth century BC, but for Aristotle the *polis* 'belongs to the class of objects which exist by nature, and man is by nature a political animal (*politikon zōon*)', i.e. one whose nature it is to live in a *polis* (*Politics* 123 5a).

Politics, title of a treatise on political science by *Aristotle (see 4 (iv)).

Poli'ticus ('statesman'), dialogue by *Plato (see 2).

Polity of the Athenians (Athenaiōn politeia, 'The Athenian Constitution', treatise by *Aristotle (see 3 (ii)).

Po'llio. 1. Gaius Asi'nius Pollio (76 BC–AD 4), Roman historian, literary patron, statesman, and supporter of the emperor Augustus. In his youth he was an associate of the poet Catullus, and a supporter first of Julius Caesar in the civil war against Pompey and later of Mark

Antony, whose legate he was in Transpadane Gaul. He was consul in 40 BC, when he helped to bring about the treaty of Brundisium between Antony and Octavian. In 39 he obtained a triumph for his victory over an Illyrian tribe. He refused to fight against Antony at Actium, but became a supporter of the Augustan settlement. It was he who first recognized the genius of Virgil, and came to his assistance when Virgil's farm near Mantua was confiscated after the battle of Philippi in 42. The poet celebrated him in his fourth and eighth Eclogues. His history of the civil wars, from the consulship of Metellus in 60 BC (when Caesar and Pompey made their original pact) to the battle of Philippi in 42 BC (and perhaps continued to the end of the 30s), has unfortunately not survived but was used by Appian and Plutarch; it receives high praise from Horace in *Odes* II. I. Pollio also wrote tragedies and erotic poems, and won a reputation as an orator. A sharp critic, he ventured to correct Cicero, Caesar, and Sallust, and to criticize Livy for his provincialism (which he calls *patavinitas*). He founded the first public library in Rome, and is said by the Elder Seneca to have introduced the practice of reciting his own works to an audience.

2. Trebellius Pollio, see *HISTORIA AUGUSTA*.

pollution. The Greeks, in common with many races at all times, believed that people were defiled or polluted by close contact with impurity, by breaking a religious rule, or by committing a crime that had religious overtones. The effect of pollution might be similar to the consequences of divine anger; a polluted city, for example (such as Thebes as described at the opening of Sophocles' *Oedipus Rex*), might be struck by sterility and plague; the source of the pollution had to be found and expelled, and purity restored by religious acts of purification. Impurity was abhorrent to the gods, and a polluted person was excluded from temples and all religious occasions. Like *Oedipus, the unwitting perpetrator of parricide and incest, he was contagious and might infect others with his pollution, and therefore his company was shunned.

Pollution could result from contact with something itself unclean, a corpse for example. (At Athens, trials for murder always took place in the open air.) Birth and death were the two commonest natural pollutions, both shunned by the gods. Households in which either occurred had to be purified.

The most notable cause of pollution was murder, requiring ritual purification of varying degrees of elaboration to get rid of the victim's blood, thought of as clinging to the murderer's hands. Blood shed in battle could be simply washed away, and similarly the blood of a villain could be easily removed by a straightforward ritual. At the other extreme, the *Alcmaeonidae in the fifth century BC were still dogged by accusations of pollution arising from a particularly sacrilegious murder committed in the seventh (see CYLON). Epilepsy and madness were commonly regarded as if they were the result of pollution, and were treated by rites of purification (but see HIPPOCRATES (I)). Occasionally, as if to mark a new beginning, scapegoats carrying a community's impurities were expelled from a city (see THARGELIA). After the final expulsion of the Persian invaders from Athens in 479 BC (see PERSIAN WARS), all the fires in the city 'polluted' by the Persian presence were extinguished and rekindled from the hearth of Apollo's shrine at Delphi (Rome too was purified after the expulsions of the Tarquins and the Gauls).

Pollux, see DIOSCURI.

Pollux, Julius, see JULIUS POLLUX.

Polyae'nus (second century AD), Macedonian, author of *Stratēgēmata* (in eight books), a collection of 'ruses in war', written in Greek and dedicated to the emperors Marcus Aurelius and Verus to aid them in the latter's Parthian war (AD 162).

Poly'bius (*c.*200–after 118 BC), Greek historian of Rome's rise to power, born at Megalopolis in Arcadia, the son of Lycortas, who was a prominent member of the *Achaean Confederacy and friend of its general *Philopoemen. Polybius was given the honour of carrying the ashes of Philopoemen to burial in 182. In

181 he was chosen, with his father, to serve on an embassy to Egypt, but this was cancelled when the king there died suddenly. Nothing more is known of his life until 169, when he was made *hipparchos* (cavalry commander) of the Confederacy. In 168, in a political purge following the Roman conquest of Macedonia, Polybius was among a thousand Achaeans sent to Rome for examination and kept there for sixteen years without accusation or trial. He was fortunate to become tutor to the sons of Aemilius *Paullus (who had commanded the Roman army at Pydna), the younger of whom became by adoption Publius *Scipio. Polybius' enduring friendship with the latter, and his consequent connections with two of the leading philhellenic families in Rome, allowed him on several occasions to intercede between Greece and Rome. The Achaean exiles were permitted to return to Greece in 150, and Polybius went with them, but in 147–146 he accompanied Scipio to the siege of Carthage and witnessed the capture of that city. When war suddenly broke out between Rome and the Achaean Confederacy, leading to a Greek defeat and the sacking of Corinth by Mummius in 146, Polybius acted as intermediary and was entrusted with organizing many details of the new administration. In this difficult task he earned the approval of the Romans and the gratitude of the Greek cities. Little is known of the last twenty years of his life, which must have been largely occupied with his literary work, of which only the *History* survives (in part), written in Greek. According to one source he died as a result of a fall from his horse at the age of 82.

Polybius declares the original aim of his *History* in the introduction: '[to relate] by what means and under what system of government the Romans succeeded in less than fifty-three years [from 220 BC, the start of the Second Punic War, to 168 BC, the end of the Third Macedonian War] in bringing under their rule almost the whole inhabited world'. Subsequently he extended his scheme to cover the preliminary period from the beginning of the First Punic War (264) to the destruction of Carthage and Corinth

in 146 (see above). In this extended form the history consisted of forty books, of which only the first five survive complete. Of the rest we have only excerpts and quotations, some quite substantial. Book 6 includes a sketch of the Roman constitution in Polybius' day and a comparison of this with the constitutions of Athens, Thebes, Crete, Sparta, and finally Carthage.

Polybius attributed the greatness of Rome to the perfection of the Roman constitution, as an even blend of monarchical, aristocratic, and democratic elements. His history was addressed primarily to Greeks but also to the upper-class Romans of his own day who were familiar with the Greek language. His chief aim was to be useful, to give good advice to the politicians, and to teach all his readers, by examples, how to bear the vicissitudes of fortune. He describes his work as *pragmatikē historia*, a factual history of events in war and politics with careful avoidance of the emotional and sensational (unlike the Greek historians of the Hellenistic age; see HISTORIOGRAPHY 1). His history was breaking new ground (only Ephorus had anticipated him) in being a universal history which offered wide scope for exemplifying the various truths that Polybius wanted to communicate, and in particular the significant role that fortune played in the rise of Rome (see TYCHE). Polybius attributed to her intervention the rise of Rome, while at the same time indicating that Rome deserved her good fortune through her own merits, an attitude of mind exemplified by Terence's observation that 'fortune favours the brave'.

Polybius is unusually revealing about the qualities needed by one who would write 'pragmatical history': such a one should have studied the writings of others, must know the countries he is writing about, and have personal experience of political life (which includes warfare). A historian should be first of all a man of action (as Polybius was). Polybius envisages history as being for the most part about events which can be recalled by those still alive; the interrogation of eye-witnesses is regarded as supremely important; most of his own history fell within living memory or within the lifetime of the previous generation. Above all a historian must have a passion for the truth. Polybius systematically seeks the causes of events ('nothing whether probable or improbable can happen without a cause'), tracing the evolution of nations and their decline. He does not shrink from exposing the reasons for the decadence of Greece. His narrative is clear and simple, without rhetorical artifice, written in the *koinē* or 'common dialect' of Greek which prevailed from 300 BC (see DIALECTS), and without the elegance of the Greek prose writers of the classical period. It is somewhat monotonous; Dionysius of Halicarnassus included Polybius' history among the works no one ever managed to finish. Polybius himself is severely critical of the methods of other historians.

Po'lybus, in Greek myth, the childless king of Corinth (or Sicyon), who with his wife adopted the infant *Oedipus to rear him as their own child.

Polyclei'tus (second half of the fifth century BC), of Argos, one of the most celebrated Greek sculptors. His most famous work was the very large statue of Hera in gold and ivory made for her temple (*Heraeum) at Argos. Ancient writers compared it favourably with *Pheidias' statue of Zeus at Olympia; Strabo said the Zeus was more magnificent but the Hera more beautiful in workmanship. Also celebrated was his *Doryphorus* ('youth holding a spear'), which is known through Roman copies. Polycleitus is said to have written a book on proportion and to have embodied his ideal of physical perfection in this statue.

Poly'cratēs, tyrant of Samos from *c.*540 BC. He made the island a strong naval power and dominated the eastern Aegean. In *c.*522 he was lured to the mainland of Asia Minor by the Persian satrap Oroetēs, who pretended to be plotting against the Persian king Darius, and was crucified there. Polycrates was a noted art-lover; he had many beautiful buildings erected and maintained a sumptous court where the poets Anacreon and Ibycus enjoyed his patronage. Herodotus relates that Amasis II, king of Egypt, alarmed by the constant good fortune of Polycrates, advised him to throw away something that he valued highly so as to avert the jealousy of the gods. Polycrates accordingly threw into the sea a beautiful seal-ring, his most prized possession, but a few days later the ring was returned to him in the belly of a fish which a fisherman had presented to him. Amasis, concluding that Polycrates was marked down for destruction, renounced his friendship.

Polydeu'cēs (Lat. Pollux), brother of Castor; see DIOSCURI.

Polydō'rus. 1. In Greek myth, the youngest son of Priam, king of Troy, and his wife Hecuba, murdered by Polymestor, king of the Thracian Chersonese (for the story see HECUBA). In Virgil's narrative (*Aeneid* 3. 22), Aeneas, landing in Thrace, pulls up some cornel bushes and finds the roots dripping with blood. He hears groans and a voice from the mound telling him that the murdered Polydorus is buried there. Aeneas performs funeral rites and the spirit of Polydorus then rests in peace.

2. In Greek myth, one of the *Epigonoi.

Polygnō'tus (active 475–447 BC), of Thasos, later a citizen of Athens, a famous Greek painter. Pausanias describes his celebrated murals in the Cnidian Leschē (public room) at *Delphi, of the 'Capture of Troy' (*Iliupersis*) and the 'Descent of Odysseus to the Underworld' (*Nekyia*), each containing about seventy figures. He represented people as serious and dignified in character, but showed advance on earlier art by the life and expression of the faces; for this he is praised by Aristotle and Lucian.

Polyhy'mnia, see MUSES.

Polynei'cēs, see OEDIPUS.

Polyphē'mus, in Greek myth, a Cyclops (see CYCLOPES), son of *Poseidon. He is represented in Homer's *Odyssey* as one of a race of savage, one-eyed giants, rearing sheep and goats on an island identified in later literature with Sicily. Odysseus with twelve of his men enters Polyphemus' cave. The latter, having returned with his flocks and closed the mouth of the cave with a huge rock, discovers the intruders and kills and eats two of them. The next evening Odysseus, who has been kept imprisoned in the cave during the day and has seen four more of his men devoured, makes Polyphemus drunk with wine and destroys his eye with a pointed stake. He has told the Cyclops that his name is No-man (Outis), and when the other Cyclopēs come on hearing his cry Polyphemus replies to their enquiries that No-man is killing him; they therefore go away. Next morning Odysseus lashes the rams together in threes, and under each three conceals one of his comrades. When the blinded Polyphemus releases his flocks, they thus escape, Odysseus hiding himself under the shaggy belly of the largest ram. He thereafter taunts Polyphemus, who hurls rocks at Odysseus' departing ship and nearly destroys it. See also Euripides' play CYCLOPS.

In the sixth and eleventh Idylls of the Hellenistic poet *Theocritus the boorish Polyphemus is represented as falling in love with the nymph Galatea and being repulsed by her. According to Ovid he crushed Galatea's young lover Acis with a rock; this is the version adopted by John Gay in his libretto to Handel's opera *Acis and Galatea* (c.1718).

Poly'xena (Polyxenē), a daughter of Priam, king of Troy, and his wife Hecuba. See ACHILLES.

Pōmō'na, Roman goddess of fruit (*pōma*), the wife of Vertumnus. For the story of his wooing of her under various shapes see under his name.

Pompe'ii, prosperous port and market town in Italy about 8 km. (5 miles) southeast of Vesuvius, having some 20,000 inhabitants when it was suddenly destroyed by the volcanic eruptions of 24 August AD 79 (described by the Younger Pliny in his Letters 6. 16 and 20). The city was buried in pumice and ash to a depth of more than 5 m. (16 ft.); about 2,000 people are thought to have died. The site was rediscovered in 1748, and most of it has now been excavated. The thriving city life that has been revealed is comparable with that depicted in the *Satyricon* of *Petronius. See also HERCULANEUM.

Pompe'ius. 1. **Gnaeus Pompeius Magnus,** see POMPEY below.

2. **Sextus Pompeius** (c.67–36 BC), younger son of Pompey the Great who spent his life in fighting for his father's cause, on the republican side, against the Caesarians. He was defeated in 36, captured, and put to death by one of Antony's officers whom he had once spared.

3. **Pompeius Trogus,** see TROGUS.

Pompey (Gnaeus Pompeius Magnus, 'the Great', 106–48 BC), Roman general and statesman, famous as the associate and later the opponent of Julius Caesar. He fought so successfully for *Sulla in his civil war against Marius that he was allowed a triumph by Sulla in 81 or 80, although he was technically ineligible by not having held a high magistracy, and was granted the honour of the *cognomen* Magnus. In 77 he was sent to Spain to suppress the revolt of *Sertorius, and after returning to Italy in 71 he cooperated with *Crassus in putting an end to the slave revolt led by *Spartacus. Again he was granted a triumph, and he and Crassus were elected consuls for 70, even though Pompey was technically ineligible. In 67 Pompey was appointed to expel pirates from the Mediterranean, which he successfully accomplished in three months, and in the following year was given command against *Mithridates, king of Pontus, Rome's great enemy in the east. This campaign was Pompey's finest achievement; he utterly defeated Mithridates, made provinces of Bithynia, *Pontus, and Syria (capturing Jerusalem after a siege), and established an eastern frontier for Rome that lasted—with few changes—for 500 years. In 62 he returned to Italy and in 61 celebrated the most spectacular triumph that Rome had yet seen. However, the ingratitude of the Senate led Pompey to form an alliance with Caesar and Crassus (called in modern times 'the first triumvirate') and they became in effect rulers of Rome. In 54 the death of Julia (Caesar's daughter who had married Pompey in 59) broke the strongest bond between Caesar and Pompey, and in 53 Crassus was killed in Parthia; the triumvirate was ended. Pompey was appointed sole consul in 52, and in 49 civil war began between him and Caesar. In 48 Pompey was defeated at Pharsala and fled to Egypt, where he was assassinated (for the events of the civil war see CAESAR). There is a Life of Pompey by Plutarch.

Pompō'nius. 1. **Lucius Pomponius**, of Bonōnia, see ATELLAN FARCES.

2. **Pomponius Secu'ndus**, Roman tragic dramatist of the mid-first century AD who incurred the suspicion of the emperor Tiberius but survived to attain consular rank and military command in Germany after the latter's death. Pliny the Elder served under him against the Germans and wrote his Life, and mentions having seen in his possession papers written by the *Gracchi about 200 years previously. Quintilian regarded him as the best tragic poet of his day. Only the title of one of his plays, *Aeneas*, a *fabula *praetexta*, survives.

3. **Pomponius Mēla**, of Tingentera (in Spain, near Gibraltar), the author *c.* AD 43 of the earliest surviving Latin work on geography, *De chōrographia* (or *De situ orbis*), 'on places', in three books. The work is intended for general readers and is based on earlier accounts. After a summary description of the earth and the three continents Europe, Asia, and Africa, he describes in greater detail the countries around the Mediterranean, starting from Mauretania and working round to Spain; then passing to Gaul, Germany, Scythia, the islands (including the British Isles), India, and the Persian Gulf. He occasionally preserves information not found elsewhere, as, for example, on the Druids. He enlivens his account by descriptions of national characteristics and customs, scenery, and natural phenomena, and by references to birthplaces, battle-fields, and historical and legendary associations. He offers explanations of the tides (the action of the moon is one of them) and of the midnight sun; he writes of the earth as if it were a disc.

Pons Subli'cius ('bridge on wooden piles'), the oldest bridge, and for several centuries the only bridge, at Rome, famously defended by Horatius *Coclēs against the Etruscans. In consequence of the difficulty on that occasion of breaking it down it was rebuilt exclusively of wood (so as to be easily taken apart) by the *pontifices*, 'priests', from which fact they were said by Varro to derive their name; any repairs to it were accompanied by religious rites. See also ARGEI. It was swept away in a flood in AD 69.

Pontic Epistles, see EPISTULAE EX PONTO.

po'ntifex ma'ximus, at Rome, the head of the college of pontiffs (*pontificēs*, 'priests'; see below), exercising disciplinary function over them as well as over the *Vestal Virgins, whom he appointed, together with the *flamens and *rex sacrorum*. He also published the decisions (*decreta*, without the binding force of laws) of the college of pontiffs. He had his official headquarters in the *Regia, and an official residence (Domus Publica). The position was one of great dignity and importance, exercising control over the whole state religion; it was held by Julius Caesar and by all the emperors down to Gratian (who dropped the title after AD 381).

ponti'ficēs, pontiffs, at Rome, the most important college of priests (see COLLEGIUM), who had supreme control in matters of state religion. They seem originally to have numbered three, but were successively increased in number until finally (under Julius Caesar) they reached sixteen. Originally they were all patricians, but after 300 BC half the number was chosen from the plebeians.

Pontus. 1. Sea; in Greek myth, according to Hesiod, son of Gaia (Earth) and father of *Nereus and *Phorcys.

2. (Gk. *pontos*, 'sea'), in particular, in Greek and Latin, the Black Sea, and by extension the region around it. The name was especially applied to the region of Asia Minor south of the Black Sea, between Bithynia and Armenia, the centre of the empire of *Mithridates VI. In 63 BC at the end of the Mithridatic wars Pontus was broken up; Pompey added the western part to the province of Bithynia (now known as Bithynia and Pontus), and in AD 64 Nero incorporated the eastern portion in the province of

Galatia. See also Ovid's EPISTULAE EX PONTO.

Popi'lius Laenas, Gaius, see SELEUCIDS.

Poppae'a Sabī'na, wife of Otho (friend of the emperor Nero and emperor himself briefly in AD 69), and Nero's mistress. At her instigation, it was said, Nero murdered his mother Agrippina in AD 59 and in 62 divorced, banished, and executed his first wife Octavia. Nero now married Poppaea, and she bore a daughter Claudia, who died at four months. Poppaea is said to have died (in 65), when she was pregnant again, from a kick given her by Nero in a fit of temper.

populā'rēs ('on the side of the people'), the name adopted at Rome from the time of the Gracchi (i.e. about 133 BC) by those Roman political leaders who, working through the people (*populus*) rather than the senate, challenged the political predominance of the oligarchic republican government. Some were motivated by concern for the people; others by the belief that they could promote their own career in this way. Their political opponents called themselves *optimātēs*, 'the best men'.

populus ('people'), at Rome, the citizen-body. The 'Roman people', *populus Romanus*, meant the body of those eligible to be soldiers (see below), to participate in public religious rites, and attend meetings of the popular assembly, together with their families. It seems originally to have denoted the citizens as a military body (in contrast to *Quirites*), hence the title *magister populi*, 'master of the infantry' (see DICTATOR). During the struggles of the *orders between patricians and plebeians *populus* continued to denote the whole community and not 'people' in the sense of 'plebeians'; however, at a later period *populus* designated the classes supporting the *populares* in their opposition to the senate. In the phrase, 'The senate and people of Rome', *senatus populusque Romanus*, *populus* denotes the people as the sovereign body.

Porch, the, name for the Stoic school of philosophy, derived from the alternative translation of *stoa* (usually 'colonnade').

Po'rcia (in Shakespeare's *Julius Caesar*, Portia), daughter of *Cato (2) of Utica and wife of, first, Calpurnius Bibulus (consul with Julius Caesar in 59 BC) and secondly Marcus *Brutus. Like her second husband and her father she was an ardent supporter of the republican cause, and is said to have inflicted a wound on herself in order to show that she was worthy to share in the secret of the plot against Caesar's life. After Brutus sailed for the East she became ill and in the early summer of 43 committed suicide, it is said by inhaling fumes from a brazier.

Poroi, treatise by Xenophon; see REVENUES.

Po'rphyry (Porphyrios) (AD 233–c.305), Neoplatonist philosopher originally from Tyre. He is known by the Greek version of his original Phoenician name Malchus, 'king'. He studied philosophy at Athens and was converted to *Neoplatonism by *Plotinus whom he met at Rome in 262. He was particularly hostile to Christianity. His work *Against the Christians* was burnt in the fifth century, and is now known only through quotations. He was the author of numerous philosophical works including a history of philosophy down to Plato, from which a life of Pythagoras survives. His most important work was the editing of the lectures of Plotinus under the title *Enneads*, and the composition of Plotinus' biography. His 'Introduction' (*Īsagōgē*) to the 'Categories' of Aristotle was later translated into Latin by *Boethius and became very influential in the medieval schools.

Po'rsen(n)a, Lars, probably an Etruscan title misinterpreted by the Romans as the name of an Etruscan chieftain, prince of Clūsium at the end of the sixth century BC and head of the united forces of Etruria. According to tradition he was summoned by the exiled king of Rome *Tarquinius Superbus to lay siege to Rome in order to restore him to the throne. In the campaign that followed occurred the feats of Horatius *Coclēs, Mucius *Scaevola, and *Cloelia. Repulsed in his attack, Porsena made peace with Rome. One tradition implied by Tacitus and the Elder Pliny seems to have made Porsena at one time master of Rome.

Portū'nus, originally the Roman deity protecting doors, later the protector of harbours as well. Virgil in *Aeneid* 5. 241 makes Portunus give one of the galleys in the boat-race a shove 'into port'. He was represented with a key in his hand. His festival, the Portūnālia, was on 17 August. He had a special **flamen*, the *flamen portunalis*.

Pōrus, Indian king defeated by Alexander the Great in 326 BC.

Posei'don, in Greek myth, the god of earthquakes and later of the sea, and associated with horses. He was the brother of Zeus and Hades and son of *Cronus and Rhea; his wife was Amphitritē, by whom he had a son, *Triton. The derivation of his name is uncertain; it has been explained as 'lord of the waters' and 'lord of earth' (i.e. husband of Earth). He is an ancient and important god; in the *Linear B tablets he appears as the principal god at Pylos. As god of the sea his cult was widespread throughout Greece, as is attested by the city names Potidaea in Chalcidicē and Poseidonia in south Italy. He was worshipped on all occasions connected with the sea and navigation. The Isthmian games were held in his honour near his sanctuary on the Isthmus of Corinth; no doubt Corinth's strategic position, commanding the seas to east and west, made her cult of Poseidon particularly appropriate. His usual representation is with a trident (probably a fish spear). As the god of earthquakes his common epithet is 'earth-shaker' (Enosichthōn, Ennosigaios). Perhaps he is to be thought of as the embodiment of elemental forces. Bulls were sacrificed to him. The Greeks also thought of him as the tamer of horses: the cult of Poseidon Hippios ('of horses') was widespread and has been seen as connected with the introduction into Greece from Anatolia of horses and (war) chariots early in the second millennium BC. In mythology he is sometimes represented as the father of the first horse or of magical horses (see PEGASUS and ARION (2)); he is also made the father of the monsters Chrysaor and Antaeus. He does not have a large mythology, but important myths connect him with Attica: one relates his contest with Athena for ownership of Attica in which he struck a spring of salt water from the Acropolis; Athena with her offer of the olive was adjudged the victor by the Athenians, or *Cecrops; another makes *Theseus his son, and he was worshipped at Athens as Poseidon Erechtheus (see ERECHTHEUM). In the Trojan War he was the enemy of the Trojans because he was cheated by *Laomedon, king of Troy, when he and Apollo built the city walls, but he persistently sought the destruction of the Greek hero Odysseus because the latter had blinded his son, the Cyclops Polyphemus. The Romans identified Poseidon with the water-god *Neptune.

Posīdō'nius (Poseidonios) (*c*.135–*c*.50 BC), of Apamea in Syria, historian, scientist, and philosopher, who spent most of his life at Rhodes and became head of the *Stoic school there. He was a polymath who epitomized the learning of the Hellenistic age and transmitted some part of it to the Roman world. For several years he studied philosophy under *Panaetius at Athens. His fifty-two books of history were a continuation of the history of Polybius, from 146 BC to the dictatorship of Sulla (81 BC). Very few fragments survive, but Sallust, Caesar, Tacitus, and Plutarch all made use of it in different ways. The wars of Pompey, of whom Posidonius was a great admirer, seem to have been dealt with in an appendix. His history was strongly biased in favour of the *optimatēs* and hence was hostile to the Gracchi. He had great influence on the development of Stoic philosophy: he saw the Roman empire as embodying the Stoic view of the kinship of all humanity, since it was intended to cover all the peoples of the world. It also reflected the divinely ordained after-life to which philosophers and statesmen might belong after death, a Stoic idea expounded by Cicero in his *Somnium Scipionis ('dream of Scipio'). He made considerable modifications to the Stoic doctrines of his day. He did not, for example, think that virtue was sufficient for happiness; it needed to be accompanied by external, bodily good. He also tried to banish contradictions from philosophy and religion, to harmonize the doctrines of Aristotle and Plato and the Stoicism of Zeno, and as far as possible reconcile the Stoic principle of divine reason animating nature with the Graeco-Roman religion of his day. Thus he prefigured and influenced later *Neoplatonism. He was also an eminent geographer, ethnographer, and astronomer, and wrote on tides and volcanoes. Nothing of these works has survived. He visited Rome as an envoy from Rhodes at the end of 87 BC to appease *Marius, for whom he personally felt great dislike. In 78 Cicero was taught by him in Rhodes, and often paid tribute to him in his writings. In different ways Cicero, Lucretius, Virgil, Manilius, Seneca the Younger, and the Elder Pliny, as well as the historians mentioned above, were all indebted to him. He was a most important figure, and the loss of his works a particular misfortune.

Post re'ditum, two speeches probably delivered by *Cicero (see (1) 4) after his return from exile in 57 BC.

Potidae'a, Corinthian colony founded c.600 BC (SEE PERIANDER) on the western prong of Chalcidicē in north-east Greece for the purpose of trade with Macedonia. It joined the (Athenian) *Delian League, but the fact that Corinth supplied its annual chief magistrate meant that it was inevitably involved in any hostility between Athens and Corinth. It revolted from Athens in 432 BC but was retaken in 430 after a siege (see PELOPONNESIAN WAR). Athenian *cleruchs held it until 404 when it passed to the Chalcidians. It was recovered by Athens in 363, but in 356 fell into the hands of *Philip II of Macedon (see also DEMOSTHENES (2) 1). Perhaps destroyed in the Olynthian War (348), it was refounded c.316 by Cassander under the name of Cassandreia.

Potī'tii, SEE HERCULES.

praefe'ctus, at Rome, 'officer in charge' of a military unit or branch of administration, etc., and in particular of the administration of justice in provincial towns; he was appointed by a higher authority. Under the empire *praefecti* were officers of equestrian rank.

praefe'ctus anno'nae ('prefect of the corn-supply'), at Rome under the empire, an officer of equestrian rank in charge of the supply of corn, the regulation of its price, and distributions to the poor.

praefe'ctus praetō'rio ('prefect of praetorians'), at Rome under the empire, an officer of equestrian rank who commanded the emperor's praetorian guard (see PRAETORIANS). First appointed by Augustus in 2 BC, they were usually two in number, occasionally one or three. Their position sometimes gave them great influence over the emperor (see SEJANUS). A few were well-known jurists (see PAPINIAN, PAULUS, and ULPIAN), but for the most part they were soldiers.

praefe'ctus urbi ('prefect of the city'), at Rome under the empire, a magistrate instituted by Augustus; he was an officer of senatorial rank responsible for maintaining order within the city boundaries. He also presided in his own court of justice which by the third century had taken over the courts of the regular magistrates.

praefe'ctus vi'gilum ('prefect of the fire-brigade'), at Rome under the empire, an officer of equestrian rank in command of the cohorts of *vigiles forming the fire-brigade, instituted by Augustus.

Praene'stine fi'bula, SEE EPIGRAPHY 2.

praenō'men, SEE NAMES.

praete'xta, fa'bula, in Roman literature, a drama which derived its subject from Roman history. The name is derived from the *toga praetexta*, the bordered toga which the famous Romans who were presented in the plays were entitled to wear by reason of holding high office. (See also TOGATA.) The invention of the *fabula praetexta* is attributed to *Naevius. Only one complete *praetexta* survives, the tragedy *Octavia, and fragments of or references to eleven others, such as the *Clastidium* of Naevius (on the exploits of M. Claudius Marcellus, winner of the *spolia opima* in single combat against a Gaul in 222 BC), the *Rape of the Sabines* of *Ennius, the *Brutus* of

*Accius, and the *Aeneas* of *Pomponius Secundus.

praetor, at Rome, originally the generic term for the holders of *imperium*, or executive authority, and the name of the two *eponymous magistrates who replaced the king (see ROME 2); later (perhaps as a result of the constitutional reforms of the *decemviri in the mid-fifth century BC) they were called consuls. In 366 BC a third magistrate was introduced, the *praetor urbanus*, 'city praetor', who was not eponymous and who administered justice between Roman citizens. Rome's closer contact with foreign states led to the appointment c.242 BC of a second praetor, *praetor peregrinus*, who administered justice where foreigners were involved. In 227 BC the number of praetors was increased to four for the government of the provinces of Sicily and Sardinia, and to six in 197 BC to include Spain. Sulla increased their number to eight.

praetorians, praetorian guard, the household troops of the Roman emperors, formed as a permanent corps by Augustus in 27 BC with nine cohorts each thought to be about 1,000 strong. These Augustus initially kept under his direct control, not until 2 BC appointing two commanders, the *praefecti praetorio*. Their concentration by *Sejanus in AD 23 into one large barracks on the north side of Rome initiated their political importance and at certain moments the praetorian guard played an important part in the history of the empire; they were responsible, for example, for the accession of Claudius (41) and the murder of Elagabalus (222). Constantine disbanded the guard in 312.

Prati'nas, Greek poet of the early fifth century BC from Phlius (in Arcadia), reputed to have been the first to compose satyr plays (see SATYRIC DRAMA). He also wrote tragedies, *dithyrambs, and *hyporchemata.

Praxi'telēs, one of the most famous Greek sculptors, born at Athens c.390 BC. One surviving marble statue is thought to be his original work (although some would argue that it is a Hellenistic copy); it was discovered in 1877 in the Heraeum at Olympia (where *Pausanias had seen it) and represents the god Hermes with the infant god Dionysus on his arm. His most famous work was the Aphroditē of *Cnidus, now known through copies. Praxiteles exemplified the tendency of the Greek sculptors of the fourth century to move away from the severe dignity of the fifth century to an art more concerned with human feeling. His graceful, sinuous poses were much imitated.

prefect, SEE PRAEFECTUS.

Presocratics, early Greek thinkers with a rational interest in science and philosophy, who lived not later than the time of *Socrates (469–399 BC). Their way of thinking gradually brought into existence the concepts of science and philosophy as fields of study separate from each other and from all other subjects. Their works survive only in fragments. See individual entries on the following (in roughly chronological order): Thalēs, Anaximander, Anaximenēs, Heracleitus, Pythagoras, Anaxagoras, Parmenides, Zeno (1), and Democritus.

Priam (Priamos), in Greek myth, son of *Laomedon, king of Troy at the time of the *Trojan War and husband of *Hecuba. He was the father of fifty sons and many daughters, some by Hecuba, the rest by other wives or concubines. His children include Hector, Paris, Polydorus, Cassandra, and Creusa. In Homer's *Iliad* he is already an old man, and a pathetic figure, lamenting the death of many sons and the sufferings of his people, but loyal and kindly to *Helen, the cause of these misfortunes. After Hector's death he goes to the Greek camp secretly, aided by the god Hermēs, to ransom his son's body with rich treasures for Achilles. The *Iliupersis* told how, at the fall of Troy, he took refuge in the palace at the altar of Zeus Herkeios and was there killed by *Neoptolemus. The best-known version is that of Virgil in *Aeneid* 2. His name became almost proverbial for a man who had known the extremes of good and bad fortune.

Priāpē'a (or *Priapeia*), collection of eighty Latin poems in honour of the god *Priapus written in the time of the emperor Augustus and collected in the first century AD. Two other poems of this kind are attributed to Tibullus, and three others are found in the *Catalepton* (see APPENDIX VIRGILIANA). The poems are mainly written in hendecasyllables and elegiacs (see METRE, LATIN 3 (iii) *a*); they are lively, sometimes witty, and, as befits their subject, of varying degrees of obscenity.

Priā'pus, god of fertility, originally worshipped at Lampsacus on the Hellespont, where asses—thought of as symbolizing lust—were sacrificed to him; he was said to be the son of Dionysus and of either Aphroditē or a local nymph. His cult spread to Greece during the Hellenistic age (after *c*.300 BC) and thence to Italy, but he seems never to have been taken very seriously. In Italy he was adopted as a god of gardens, where statues of him were often placed, showing him as a small misshapen creature with an enormous phallus, scaring off thieves and birds, a combined scarecrow and guardian. It was customary to compose short humorous poems or epigrams purportedly (or in fact) to be inscribed on his statues (see previous entry).

princeps ('chief', 'leader'), title taken by the emperor *Augustus (and adopted by his successors) to indicate his constitutional position. In the late republic the word had been used in the plural, *principes*, to signify 'the chief men in the state', and the singular had been applied to important individuals like Pompey and Julius Caesar. It was not an official title, and was chosen to indicate the civil nature of Augustus' primacy, not carrying connotations of dictatorship or monarchy.

princeps senā'tūs ('the leader of the senate'), at Rome, the senator placed by the censors at the head of the list of members of the senate and ranked as the senior member. When decisions had to be taken by the senate he was the first to be asked his opinion.

principate, at Rome, the term often used in preference to 'empire' to describe the rule of the Roman emperors after 31 BC from *Augustus until (usually) the accession of Diocletian in AD 284. The word designates the period during which the forms at least of republican government were maintained under the *princeps. In the words of the English historian Edward Gibbon it was 'an absolute monarchy disguised by the forms of a commonwealth'. With the accession of Diocletian the senate lost all independent authority and no longer was any attempt made to disguise the monarchical nature of the empire. The period from 284 onwards is often known as the Later Roman Empire.

Pri'scian (Prisciānus Caesariensis), native of Caesarēa in Mauretania and a grammarian at Constantinople under the emperor in the East, Anastasius (AD 491–518). He wrote in Latin an *Institutiōnēs grammaticae* ('grammar') in eighteen books, rich in quotations from the classical Latin authors and also from earlier republican writers, and founded largely on the (Greek) grammatical works of *Apollonius Dyscolus. It became famous in the Middle Ages: more than a thousand manuscripts of it are still in existence.

proa'gōn, at Athens, a day or two before the dramatic competitions at the Great *Dionysia and the *Lenaea, the ceremonial appearance of *choregoi, poets, actors, and choruses, when the names and subjects of the plays were announced. It was at the *proagon* of 406 BC after the death of Euripides that the audience was greatly moved by the appearance of Sophocles in mourning, with his actors and chorus not wearing the usual garlands.

***Pro A'rchia pōē'ta,** speech by *Cicero (2) delivered in 62 BC in defence of the claim of the Greek poet Archias to Roman citizenship.

Archias, a literary figure and known to Cicero, was attached to the household of the general L. Licinius *Lucullus. His claim to Roman citizenship was based on his citizenship of Heraclea in Lucania. Archias' claim had been doubted through lack of documentary evidence of his enrolment. Cicero meets this by producing witnesses of it. He also appeals to the sentiment of the jury by an eloquent panegyric of literature, which later became famous: *Haec studia adulescentiam acuunt, senectutem oblectant, secundas res ornant, adversis perfugium ac solacium praebent, delectant domi, non impediunt foris, pernoctant nobiscum, peregrinantur, rusticantur* (7. 16). 'These studies sharpen youth and delight old age; they enhance prosperity and provide a refuge and relief in adversity; they enrich private life and do not interfere with public life; they are our companions at night, on journeys, and in our country retreats.'

Pro Balbo ('for Balbus'), see CICERO (1) 4.

probou'loi ('commissioners'), in Greece, in particular those appointed at Athens in 413 BC after the failure of the *Sicilian Expedition, to oversee affairs of state. They comprised ten men over the age of 40 (and included the poet Sophocles).

Prŏbus, Marcus Vale'rius (late first century AD), the outstanding Latin grammarian and scholar of his age, from Berytus in Phoenicia, who gathered together a large number of manuscripts and worked on the texts of the classical Latin authors including Virgil, Horace, and Lucretius. He used critical signs in the manner of the Alexandrian scholar Aristarchus (see TEXTS, TRANSMISSION OF ANCIENT 1). Some of his notes survive in the scholia to Terence and Virgil, and there are references to Plautus and Sallust; later grammarians quote him, but it is difficult to establish exactly the scope of his work.

Pro Cae'lio ('for Caelius'), see CICERO (1) 4.

Pro Clue'ntio ('for Cluentius'), see CICERO (1) 1.

Proclus (AD 412–85), Neoplatonist philosopher (see NEOPLATONISM). He was born in Lycia but spent most of his life at Athens, succeeding to the headship of the Academy. He was a prolific writer and a scholar of vast learning, so much so that it has been doubted whether all the works that have come down under his name can be genuinely his. Writing as a Neoplatonist (and influenced by the superstitions of his time), he gives in his *Elements of Theology* a concise summary of Neoplatonist metaphysics; he wrote commentaries on several Platonic dialogues as well as on the works of earlier mathematicians including Euclid. His literary works include a book of hymns, scholia on Hesiod's *Works and Days*, and a *Chrēstomathia* ('summary of useful knowledge'), a handbook of literature, of which only an epitome exists. It has been thought that this last work, important for preserving summaries of six poems of the *Epic Cycle dealing with the Trojan War, may be the work of an earlier Proclus.

Procnē, see PHILOMELA.

proconsul, a *consul whose powers had been prolonged for a further year following his year of office. After 146 BC, when Rome had an increased number of provinces to govern, such prolongation of office (*prorogatio*) became the usual procedure to allow magistrates a further year as governors of provinces.

Procō'pius (*c.* AD 500–after 562), of Caesarea in Palestine, Byzantine Greek historian and secretary to *Belisarius (the famous general of the Roman emperor Justinian) whom he accompanied on his early campaigns in Africa and Italy. He returned to Constantinople (then the capital of the Roman empire) in 542, and was made prefect of the city in 562. His *History of the Wars of Justinian* in eight books, covering the years 527–53, is a clear and reliable account of the events of his own times and is our main source for the first two-thirds of Justinian's reign. His chief praise is reserved for Belisarius; Justinian and his empress Theodora are treated with much less enthusiasm. He also wrote a work on the buildings and works of art in Constantinople and the empire, a panegyric of Justinian clearly commissioned by the latter and a valuable source of information about the art and architecture of the time. Procopius is also the author of a remarkable supplement to his *History*, a *Secret History* (*Anecdota*), covering the same period but making a virulent attack on the whole policy of Justinian. On the basis, apparently, of court gossip he also makes scurrilous comments on the dubious morals of the empress Theodora. It cannot have been published in the author's lifetime, and was perhaps not known until the tenth century; *Photius appears not to have known it, but it is referred to in the *Suda.

Procris, see CEPHALUS.

Procru'stēs (or Damastes), legendary brigand said to be the son of Poseidon, who lived beside the road between Athens and Eleusis. He ensnared strangers with hospitality, then seized them and fastened them to a bed which he then made them fit, cutting short their limbs if they were too long for it, or racking them if they were too short. *Theseus applied the same treatment to Procrustes and cut off his head.

procura'tor, at Rome under the empire, in general, an employee of the emperor in civil administration. In particular, procurators might oversee the revenues in the imperial provinces, and also, independently of the governors, in the senatorial provinces. They could also govern some of the minor provinces.

Pro'dicus, see SOPHIST.

Proetus, in Greek myth, son of Abas and Aglāia and twin brother of Acrisius (father of *Danaē). The two brothers had a life-long feud; when Abas left them his kingdom jointly they fought each other for its possession. Acrisius drove Proetus out, but was himself ousted in turn. See BELLEROPHON and DIONYSUS.

Pro Flacco ('for Flaccus'), see CICERO (1) 3.

Pro legĕ Manī̆lia ('in support of the Manilian law'; also known as *De imperio Cn. Pompeii*, 'on the command of Pompey'), speech by *Cicero in 66 ((1) 1) delivered before the people when Cicero was praetor, in support of the proposal of the tribune Manilius to extend Pompey's command in Asia to Bithynia, Pontus, and Armenia so as to enable him to take over the command in the war against *Mithridates. This was Cicero's first speech on purely public affairs, and was delivered in order to promote the interests of the equestrian order (who, being the businessmen of Rome, were suffering severe financial losses because of the disturbed condition of the rich province

of Asia Minor). Although this command was against the wishes of the senate the proposal was carried.

prolē'psis ('anticipation'), figure of speech in which a person or thing is referred to by name or epithet which will be later, but is not yet, appropriate; e.g. *submersas obrue puppes*, 'overwhelm the sunken ships'. The word is also used to describe, in a speech, the forestalling of objections that an opponent may raise.

prōleta'rii, at Rome, the citizens placed in the lowest property-class who because of their poverty were exempted from compulsory military service and from the *tribūtum* or property-tax, and served the state only with their children (*prōlēs*).

Pro Ligā'rio ('for Ligarius'), see CICERO (1) 4.

prologue (*prologos*), see TRAGEDY 3 and COMEDY, GREEK 3.

Pro Marce'llo ('for Marcellus'), see CICERO (1) 4.

Promē'theus ('forethinker'), in Greek myth, a *Titan, son of Iapetus and Themis (or Clymenē, daughter of Oceanus). He was thought of as the champion of humankind against the hostility of the gods. In some stories he himself created men out of clay (from Panopea, near Chaeronea in Boeotia, visited by Pausanias (x. 4. 3) in the second century AD). When Zeus, having no love for men, deprived them of fire, Prometheus stole a spark from heaven (or from the forge of Hephaestus) and brought it to them in a stalk of fennel (*narthex*). He also taught them all kinds of arts and sciences, thus improving their brutish lives. In the apportionment of sacrificed animals between men and the gods, he induced Zeus by a trick to choose the less desirable portion (bones covered with fat), the meat being left for men. (This story is obviously meant to account for the fact that it was usually the inedible parts of a sacrifice which were allotted to the gods.) To avenge himself Zeus caused Hephaestus to create a woman, Pandora, fashioned out of clay. Athena breathed life into her, and the other gods endowed her with every charm (whence her name, 'all gifts'), but Hermes taught her flattery and guile. This woman was sent not to Prometheus, who was too cunning to accept such a dangerous gift, but to his brother Epimetheus ('he who thinks afterwards'), who gladly received her, although warned by his brother not to take any gifts from Zeus. She brought with her a jar containing all kinds of evils and diseases from which men had hitherto been free; this she opened, and they all flew out, leaving only Hope inside, under the lid, as a consolation for men. Pandora's jar seems to have become a 'box' in post-classical times by a confusion with the box which *Psyche was forbidden to open in the story in Apuleius' *Golden Ass*.

Prometheus also knew the secret concerning the marriage of Thetis (see PELEUS and PROMETHEUS BOUND below), but refused to reveal it to Zeus, who wished to marry Thetis himself. To punish him Zeus had him chained to a lonely rock usually said to be in the Caucasus, where an eagle daily fed on his liver which grew again each succeeding night (being a Titan, Prometheus was immortal). This torture continued for long ages until Prometheus was released either by Heracles shooting the eagle with his bow, or by his submitting and revealing the secret about Thetis. Prometheus was worshipped in Attica as a god of craftsmen; he was the father of *Deucalion by a wife variously named.

Promē'theus Bound (Gk. *P. desmōtēs*, Lat. *P. vinctus*), Greek tragedy attributed to *Aeschylus, though perhaps completed or even written by another after the former's death in 456 BC. No one in antiquity doubted that it was by Aeschylus, but in several respects the style is markedly different from that of his six other surviving plays. It is the only one of his plays for which there is no didascalic information (see DIDASCALIA) about production, date, and trilogy. It is possible that it was the second play of a connected trilogy, followed by *Prometheus lyomenos* ('P. Unbound'), of which a few fragments survive, and preceded by *Prometheus pyrphoros* ('P. Fire-carrier'), of which only one line exists, but the order

of plays, and even the existence of a connected trilogy, are very uncertain.

*Prometheus the Titan, who in the past has aided Zeus to set up his rule over Cronus and the other Titans, has incurred Zeus' anger by becoming the champion of mankind and giving them fire and the arts. In the opening scene of the play, the god Hephaestus, at the order of Zeus, together with Kratos (Power) and Bia (Force), reluctantly nails Prometheus (possibly represented by a huge dummy figure behind which the actor spoke) to a high rock in the Caucasus, to suffer torment for as long as Zeus pleases. The chorus of Oceanidēs, the daughters of the Titan *Oceanus, come to grieve with him and comfort him. Oceanus himself also comes, offering to intercede with Zeus if Prometheus will moderate his attitude. Prometheus scornfully rejects his offers, and then enumerates to the chorus all his benefactions to mankind. Another victim of Zeus' tyranny arrives, *Io, a mortal whom Zeus has loved and whom Hera, out of jealousy, has made partly cow-like in form. She is doomed to long wanderings pursued by a gad-fly and haunted by the myriad-eyed *Argus. Prometheus tells her about her sufferings, about her descendant Heracles who will eventually release Prometheus, and about the fatal marriage which Zeus will one day make unless Prometheus warns him. After Io departs Hermes enters, sent by Zeus to demand from Prometheus the revelation of his secret; although Hermes predicts increased torments for him Prometheus haughtily refuses and is plunged into the abyss with the Oceanides, who decide to share his fate.

If a reconciliation between Prometheus and Zeus took place in a following play, it is impossible to say how the author devised it. From the fragments of *P. lyomenos*, it seems that the play opened with Prometheus restored to the light after thirty thousand years, and that the chorus was composed of Titans.

As a suffering god, the creator of mankind, and also as the champion of the oppressed and an independent thinker, Prometheus has had a wide appeal to people of various religions and political beliefs. The English poet Shelley (1792–1822) in his 'Prometheus Unbound' could not accept Prometheus' apparent defeat at the end of the play: in his poem Prometheus is released and it is Jupiter (i.e. Zeus) who is vanquished.

Pro Milō'nĕ ('for Milo'), see CICERO (1) 4 and MILO, TITUS ANNIUS.

Pro Murē'na ('for Murena'), speech by *Cicero in 63 BC ((1) 2) when he was consul, in defence of Lucius Murena, who had been elected consul for the following year and was accused at the instigation of Cato of bribery in the election. The charge was brought at the height of the crisis due to Catiline's conspiracy; if Cato had succeeded in overturning the election of Murena, a man of proved courage and military ability, it would have been beneficial to the cause of Catiline. The speech is a good example of persuasive pleading; Cicero almost condones electoral corruption provided the best man is elected consul, and jokes at the formalism of Roman lawyers and the rigid creed of Stoics such as Cato.

Prope'rtius, Sextus (*c.*50 BC–after 16 BC), Roman elegiac poet. He was born at Asisium (Assisi) in Umbria, deprived of his estate when young by the confiscations of Octavian in 41–40 BC (after the defeat of the republicans at Philippi), was educated at Rome for the practice of law, but turned to poetry instead. He left four books of elegies, of which the first, published probably in 29 or 28 BC, shows Propertius as a member of a small and intimate group of poets who included Ovid (*Tristia*, IV. 10. 45). The book's great success admitted him to the wider circle around *Maecenas, but he seems to have admired the older poets (e.g. Virgil, in 2. 34) rather than known them well. Horace, whom he does not mention, refers to him with some contempt as aping Callimachus and Mimnermus (*Epistles*, II. 2. 90). His first book of poems, known in antiquity as the *Cynthia monobiblos* ('the single volume called *Cynthia*'), consists almost entirely of elegant and witty love poems to his mistress 'Cynthia' so-called, a Greek pseudonym for, reputedly, a certain Hostia (compare 'Lycoris' of the poet Gallus and 'Delia' of Tibullus). Book 2 is improbably long and may be

a conflation of two books; no poem in it is later than 25 BC. The text is particularly disordered in the manuscripts, which in many cases give no indication of where individual poems begin and end. In style this book is similar to book 1 though now are included some poems on imperial themes pleasing to the new regime (see ROME 9), and the book does not quite have the lyrical freshness of its predecessor. Book 3, published soon after 23 BC, shows a wider range of subject-matter, but also a greater degree of generalization and abstraction. Although the influence of the Hellenistic Greek poets was perceptible in the earlier books, it is with this book that Propertius begins to think of himself as the Roman *Callimachus, writing small-scale poems in a refined style, and no longer confines himself to love poetry; only about a third of the poems in this book are concerned with love, and the final poem is a farewell to Cynthia. Book 4 appeared after a longish interval, not before 16 BC, perhaps constructed around two commissioned and honorific poems, 6 and 11. Some of the poems are antiquarian in subject, in the manner of Callimachus' *Aitia*; the rest are miscellaneous, and include two of his most brilliant on Cynthia (7 and 8). Poem 11, an epicedium (a song sung in mourning over a corpse) for the nobly born Cornelia (daughter of Scribonia, the first wife of Octavian), is written as if spoken by the subject herself, and is a touching expression of the virtues of a Roman matron.

Propertius is perhaps the most fascinating of the Roman poets. He has an intense visual imagination which colours everything he writes: the setting of a poem must first be grasped and its implications understood if the reader is to make sense of the poet's abrupt changes of mood and his train of thought. Corruptions of the original text add to the difficulties of interpretation. No other Roman poet shows such strong personal characteristics, the recurrent melancholy, the passionate but objective, occasionally obsessive, self-observation, as he records his ecstasy, torment, and humiliation. His passion appears in a great variety of moods, inspired by Cynthia's beauty, of her venality, or her dangerous illness, and by the vicissitudes of his relations with her. The self-absorption, the striking imagery, the bold and difficult language, mark a new spirit in Latin literature.

Pro Pla'ncio ('for Plancius'), see CICERO (1) 4.

Propo'ntis, now the Sea of Marmora, an intermediate sea between the Aegean and the Black Sea. Its principal cities were Byzantium and Chalcedon at the mouth of the Bosporus.

Propylae'a, at Athens, the great roofed gateway and entrance to the *Acropolis, on the western side, built of Pentelic marble, designed by Mnesiclēs, and erected as part of Pericles' building programme between 437 and 432 BC, after the completion of the Parthenon. Much of it is still intact.

Pro Qui'nctio ('for Quinctius'), see CICERO (1) 1.

Pro Rabi'rio ('for Rabirius'), see CICERO (1) 2.

Pro Rabi'rio Po'stumo ('for Rabirius Postumus'), see CICERO (1) 4.

Pro Regĕ Dēio'taro ('for king Deiotarus'), see CICERO (1) 4.

Pro Ro'scio Amerī'no ('for Roscius of Ameria'), speech by *Cicero in 80 BC ((1) 1) in defence of Sextus Roscius (not the actor of the same name, for whom see below) on a charge of murdering his father. This, Cicero's first speech in a criminal case, gives the origin of the expression *cui bono* ('who profits?'). If Sextus did not kill his father, says Cicero, who did? He then quotes this expression as being the frequent saying of an illustrious judge, L. Cassius Longīnus, in trials of this kind, and proceeds to show that the accusers of Roscius had themselves profited.

Pro Ro'scio comoe'do ('for Roscius the comic actor'), speech by *Cicero ((1) 1) on behalf of the great actor, of uncertain date, but possibly 77 BC. It concerned a claim involving the profits from a farm that Roscius managed. The outcome is not known.

Pro Scauro ('for Scaurus'), see CICERO (1) 4.

proscriptions. At Rome, a *proscriptio* was a published list of Roman citizens who were declared to be outlaws and whose property was confiscated and auctioned by the state. Those proscribed could be killed by soldiers with impunity; rewards and punishments were used to encourage their friends and families to betray them. This procedure was employed by Sulla in 82–81 BC (more than 4000 people were said to have been named) and by the triumvirs Antony, Lepidus, and Octavian during the civil war in 43–42 BC; it was a means both of getting rid of enemies and of acquiring funds.

prose
1. *Greek*. Prose as a means of literary expression was developed in Greece as in other countries long after poetry. In early times when writing was in its infancy and literary compositions survived by being committed to memory, those written in metrical form were easier to memorize (in Greece, writing was reintroduced at the end of the eighth century; see ALPHABET). The earliest writers of Greek prose appear to have been the chroniclers (see LOGOGRAPHERS (1)) and philosophers (see PHILOSOPHY) of Ionia in the sixth century BC. From this time onward the development of prose was rapid. Heracleitus in about 500 BC was already writing prose of subtlety and style. By the middle of the fifth century BC a technical prose had been developed which was adequate to express all that was needed for a scientific or philosophical treatise. Democritus (*c*.460–*c*.357 BC), to judge from his fragments, was a competent prose writer, and the earliest works in the Hippocratic Corpus (see HIPPOCRATES) show at least the capacity for accurate and concise statement.

The first fully developed prose work that has survived in its entirety is the history of Herodotus (*c*.490–*c*.425 BC). Attic prose reached its height in the dialogues of Plato (*c*.429–347 BC) and the speeches of Demosthenes (384–322 BC). The sophist Gorgias (*c*.483–*c*.385) developed a very mannered oratorical style which did not have a long-lasting influence. Isocrates (436–338) on the other hand exercised through his school a deep influence on later Greek prose, in the direction of greater elaboration and ornament. With the end of the fourth century BC came the close of the classical period of Attic literature, the dialect of Athens then giving place to a common Greek dialect, the *koinē* (see DIALECTS), less subtle, varied, and accurate in expression. Greek prose was influenced by 'Asianism' (see ORATORY I), the florid style favoured by the rhetoricians of the third century BC. There was an energetic reaction against this, and an Attic revival, at Rome in the Augustan age; of this Dionysius of Halicarnassus is the best example. In the second century AD Lucian wrote in a very good imitation of classical Attic prose. See also NOVEL and SOPHISTIC, SECOND.

2. *Latin*. Latin prose was developed, in its characteristic features, out of public speech, though it originated partly in the *Annales* of the pontiffs (their records of traditional ritual and events of religious importance) which were the origin of written history at Rome. Roman law, published and often learnt by heart, was also a formative influence. Latin prose, unlike Latin poetry, owed little to Greek influences, for it already possessed, before the advent of these, the essential qualities of clarity, precision, and conciseness. In a community like Rome where politics played so great a part, these qualities were naturally esteemed in oratory. We hear of Appius Claudius Caecus and Cato the Censor as noted speakers; and oratory was further developed, with a great variety of appeal, by Gaius Gracchus. Latin prose reached its highest point in the speeches and writings of Cicero. Thereafter it tended to become artificial, epigrammatic, and poetical, under the influence of the poets and of the prevailing education in rhetoric and through the practice of declamation (see DECLAMATIONES). Seneca's prose is typically epigrammatic; that of Tacitus is marked by its excessive compactness and its poeticisms. The Younger Pliny also shows the influence of the rhetorical schools. Quintilian opposed the artificiality of his day and wrote in a style free from conceits and studied effects; but although a professed follower of Cicero he did not recapture the amplitude and symmetry of Cicero's prose.

Pro'serpine (Proserpina), perhaps an original Italian goddess of the earth, or perhaps an adaptation of the Greek *Persephonē*, with whom Proserpina in Roman religion was identified. For her cult at Rome see DIS.

Pro Sestio ('for Sestius'), see CICERO (I) 4.

proso'dion, see LYRIC POETRY I.

pro'sody, the study of versification; in Greek and Latin in particular, the study of the rules which govern the quantity (i.e. length) of syllables in verse (see METRE, GREEK I). Syllables are classified according to the length of time they took to pronounce and are called long, short, or anceps ('ambivalent', i.e. either long or short). A syllable is long or short 'by nature' according as it contains either a long vowel or diphthong, or a short vowel. The general rules of Greek and Latin prosody (to which there are exceptions) are the following.

1. *Greek*

(i) By nature the vowels η and ω are long, ε and o short; α, ι, and υ are sometimes long by nature, sometimes short. Diphthongs are long (i.e. αι, αυ, ει, ευ, ην, οι, ου, υι, ᾳ, ῃ, ῳ), except that οι and αι, which appear to have been of shorter duration, are sometimes scanned short.

(ii) A syllable long by nature is sometimes shortened if it comes immediately before another vowel. This happens most often at the end of a word (i.e. before another word beginning with a vowel). The shortening is known as *correption (and see (iii) below).

(iii) A syllable that is short by nature is lengthened in pronunciation, and so becomes long 'by position', if the vowel is immediately followed by two (or more) consonants or by a so-called double consonant, ζ (= sd), ξ (= ks), or ψ (= ps), whether or not the consonants are in the same word. There is an exception to this general rule: in Attic poetry (which includes tragedy and comedy), a naturally short syllable usually remains short if it is followed by one of several combinations of two consonants, the first a so-called 'mute' (for this purpose one of π, β, φ, τ, δ, θ, κ, γ, χ), and the second a 'liquid' (λ, ϱ, μ, ν). This phenomenon is known as Attic correption.

2. *Latin*

(i) The vowels a, e, i, o, u (and y) are sometimes long by nature, sometimes short. Diphthongs (ae, au, ei, ou, oe) are long. A vowel which immediately precedes another vowel in the same word but is not part of a diphthong is generally short.

(ii) Correption of a final long syllable (see I (ii) above) is rare.

(iii) A syllable that is short by nature is lengthened in pronunciation, and so becomes long 'by position', if the vowel is immediately followed by two (or more) consonants, or by a double consonant, x (= ks) or z (= Greek ζ). (When the 'semi-consonants' i and u are equivalent to English j or v they are counted as consonants; h is discounted; qu is counted as a single consonant.)

(iv) An exception to (iii) is that short syllables remain short before certain combinations of so-called 'mute' and 'liquid' consonants (compare I (iii) above), i.e. b, c, d, f, g, p, t followed by l or r. This licence does not occur when the two consonants belong to different words or to different parts of a compound verb (e.g. ābrumpere).

Pro Sulla ('for Sulla'), speech by *Cicero ((I) 3) in defence of P. Cornelius Sulla (elected consul for 65 but convicted of bribery and so disqualified; he was a relation of the famous Sulla, in whose *proscriptions he amassed great wealth). Sulla was acquitted and rewarded Cicero well.

protagonist, see TRAGEDY 2.

Prōta'goras, of Abdēra (in Thrace), born *c*.485 BC, one of the earliest and most famous of the *sophists. His teaching career began *c*.455 and in his lifetime he made a great deal of money. What he professed to teach was *aretē*, 'virtue', by which he meant worldly success achieved through practical good management of public and private affairs. He appears as the opponent of Socrates in the dialogue by Plato named after him (see below), Socrates attaching a somewhat different meaning to 'virtue'. He was a friend of Pericles, and was said to have been prose-

cuted and expelled from Athens for atheism (compare ANAXAGORAS). His best known works (which have not survived) were *On Truth* and *On the Gods*. Sceptical about any claim to absolute and universal truth, he taught the doctrine of the relativity of all knowledge, summed up in the dictum quoted in Plato's *Theaetetus*, 'a person is the measure of all things' (usually rendered, 'man is the measure'). He also adopted an agnostic attitude towards the gods: 'Concerning the gods I have no means of knowing whether they exist or not, or what they are like in form. Many things prevent knowledge: the obscurity of the subject and the brevity of human life.' When *Thurii was founded by the Athenians in 433 BC Protagoras was appointed to draw up a code of laws for the new colony.

Protagoras, dialogue by *Plato in which the interlocutors are, besides Socrates, the sophists Protagoras (see above), Hippias, and Prodicus. It is a dialogue on the nature of 'virtue' (or 'goodness'; see above), what it is and how it is to be acquired. Protagoras argues that virtue (in his sense) is something that can be taught just as well as any other subject. The dialogue reaches the conclusion that all the virtues are essentially one, founded upon knowledge of the good, and that virtue is in fact knowledge. In the course of the dialogue a poem of *Simonides is analysed, an encomium on 'the good man'; this dialogue remains its only source (see PITTACUS).

Protagoras is presented as a reasonable man, sincere in his arguments and of equable temperament, not provoked by Socrates' sometimes biting irony at his expense. His arguments are thoughtful and based on common sense; those of Socrates more searching and also paradoxical. The dialogue contains a noteworthy declaration by Protagoras that under a rational system criminals are punished to deter them from doing wrong again, not as retribution for past misdeeds.

Prōtesilā'us, in Greek myth, Thessalian prince, son of Iphiclus. Soon after his marriage he left to take part in the Greek expedition against Troy. When the Greek fleet reached the Trojan coast he was the first to leap ashore, and was subsequently the first to be killed (some said in conscious fulfilment of an oracle that the first to tread on Trojan soil would be the first to die). His wife Laodamia was plunged into such grief at his death that the gods allowed her husband to return to her for three hours, but when he left her again she killed herself.

Prōteus, in Homer's *Odyssey* (4. 351), a minor sea-god, who herds the seals, knows all things, and has the power of assuming different shapes in order to escape answering questions; this he will do if held until he resumes his true shape. In Herodotus and in Euripides' tragedy *Helen* he is a virtuous king of Egypt who keeps *Helen safe throughout the Trojan War.

proto-geometric, name given to one of the five periods of the Greek era (based on the differences in pottery styles, denoting the early part of the Greek *Iron Age, very roughly 1050–875 BC. (Compare GEOMETRIC, ORIENTALIZING, ARCHAIC, and CLASSICAL.)

province, Roman, a territory outside Italy subject to Rome, governed by a resident Roman magistrate (see PROCONSUL) and obliged to pay tribute (see REPETUNDAE).

pro'xenos, in a Greek state, a local citizen chosen to look after the interests of citizens from another state, a sort of consul (in the modern sense). Pindar at Thebes was *proxenos* of the Athenians staying in that city; Demosthenes at Athens was *proxenos* of the Thebans.

Pro'xenus, Boeotian friend of Xenophon, at whose invitation he took part in the expedition of Cyrus related in the *Anabasis*.

Prude'ntius Clemens, Aurē'lius (AD 348–after 405), Christian Latin poet, native of Spain; some of his hymns composed in classical metres are still sung. Other poems are on Christian dogma or tell of the martyrs. His *Psychomachia* ('battle for the soul'), an allegory of the spiritual struggle in the human soul, set in epic form, was well known in the Middle Ages and was a strong influence on medieval poetry.

prytanē'um, in the chief city of a Greek state, the common 'home' of the whole state, containing the hearth (see HESTIA) where a fire was kept continually burning and from which fire was taken to a new colony. Here also were the offices of the local magistrates; it was the place where ambassadors were entertained and distinguished citizens were rewarded by the provision of meals at the state's expense. The prytaneum at Athens was in the agora. See PRYTANY below.

pry'tany (*prytaneia,* 'presidency'), **prytanēis** ('presidents'). At Athens, after the political reforms of *Cleisthenes (1) in 508/7 BC, each of the newly constituted ten tribes chose by lot every year fifty of its members to serve on the *boulē* ('council'). Each group of fifty served as the executive committee of the *boule* for one-tenth of the year, when they were known as *prytaneis,* and the period as a prytany.

Pseu'dolus, Roman comedy by *Plautus produced in 191 BC. The title is taken from the name of a character in the play.

A Macedonian captain has bought a girl, Phoenicium, from a pimp for 20 minae, paying 15 down. The girl is to be delivered to his messenger when he sends the 5 minae still owing and a certain token. Calidōrus, a young Athenian, is in love with her. The play deals with the trick by which his father's slave, Pseudolus, having intercepted the captain's letter and token, cheats the pimp and carries off Phoenicium for Calidorus. (The part of the pimp Ballio was chosen by *Roscius, the great comic actor of Cicero's day.)

Psȳchē ('soul'), the name of the heroine in a tale, told in books 4–6 of the *Golden Ass* of *Apuleius, the narrator being an old woman who is trying to amuse a girl captured by robbers. Psyche was so beautiful that Venus became jealous of her and sent Cupid to make her fall in love with some unsightly creature; however, Cupid himself became her lover. He placed her in a palace but only visited her in the dark, and forbade her to attempt to see him. Her sisters, out of jealousy, told her he was a monster who would devour her. One night she took a lamp and looked at Cupid while he slept, but a drop of hot oil woke him. Thereupon the god left her, angry at her disobedience. Psyche, solitary and remorseful, sought her lover all over the earth, and various superhuman tasks were required of her by Venus. The first was to sort out before nightfall an enormous heap of various kinds of grain. But the ants took pity on Psyche and arriving in hordes did the task for her. By one means or another all the tasks were completed except the last, which was to descend to the Underworld and fetch a casket of beauty from Persephonē. Curiosity overcame Psyche and she opened the casket, which contained not beauty but a deadly sleep, to which she succumbed. Jupiter, at Cupid's entreaty, at last consented to their marriage, and Psyche was brought to heaven. This fairytale has often been interpreted as an allegory of the soul's journey through life and its final union with the divine after suffering and death.

Pto'lemies (Ptolemaioi), Macedonian Greek dynasty that ruled Egypt from the death of Alexander the Great in 323 BC until the Roman conquest in 30 BC. It is named after the first of the dynasty—Ptolemy I Sōter (b. *c*.367, ruled 323–283 BC), one of Alexander's generals, who received Egypt in the division of his empire after his death (see DIADOCHOI). Other notable members were his son Ptolemy II Philadelphus, b. 308, who ruled 285–246 BC, for the first two years joint ruler with his father; and Ptolemy III Euergetēs, born between 288 and 280, who ruled 246–221 BC and won for a time a large part of Seleucid Asia. *Cleopatra was the sister and wife of Ptolemy XIII (b. 63, ruled 51–47 BC) and ruled with him. The last to bear the name were another brother of Cleopatra, Ptolemy XIV (b. *c*.59, ruled 47–44 BC, jointly with Cleopatra), and Cleopatra's son by Julius Caesar, Ptolemy XV Caesar (b. 47, ruled nominally 44–30 BC, jointly with Cleopatra), better known as *Caesarion. The Ptolemies were immensely enriched by their exploitation of Egypt, and they raised their capital *Alexandria to great wealth and magnificence. By their patronage of art and literature, and

especially by the establishment of the *Museum or literary academy of Alexandria, and the *Alexandrian Library, the first Ptolemies made the city a centre of Hellenistic culture. Ptolemy I himself wrote the best of the histories of Alexander the Great (now lost) based on his own recollections and using much official material. It was used by the historian *Arrian. Greek settlements were planted in many parts of Egypt, most extensively in the reclaimed land of the Faiyum. To these Greek settlers we owe numerous papyri, discovered in modern times in places where physical conditions have been suitable for their preservation, and on these many fragments of Greek literary works have been discovered (see PAPYROLOGY). See also EGYPT.

Pto'lemy (Claudius Ptolemaeus, *c*. AD 100–*c*.178), Greek astronomer, mathematician, and geographer, born at Ptolemais Hermiou in Upper Egypt; later he lived in Alexandria. He summed up the astronomical knowledge of the age in his *Mathēmatikē syntaxis* ('system of mathematics'), translated later into Arabic and, to distinguish it from another *syntaxis*, called by the Arabs 'the Greatest' (*Almagest*, compound of the Arabic article and the Greek adjective *megistē*). The work contains thirteen books. In it Ptolemy developed a theory to explain the relative movements of the sun, moon, and planets around the stationary earth, a system which his predecessors had almost universally believed in (for the exception see ARISTARCHUS). This theory (with modifications) was accepted until the time of Copernicus and Kepler in the sixteenth century. Ptolemy himself constructed the first viable theory of the five planets, and his fixed-star table is based on his own fresh observations. The *Almagest* soon became the standard work on the subject and remained so until the end of the Middle Ages, not only in the Greek but also in the Arab world, passing thence into medieval Europe (see TEXTS, TRANSMISSION OF ANCIENT 7). It is an important source for knowledge of earlier works.

Ptolemy also wrote a number of other scientific treatises, including one on optics surviving only in a Latin translation from the Arabic, and one on the mathematical theory of musical harmony. Regarded as authoritative for as long as the *Almagest* was his 'Outline of *Geography' (*Geōgraphikē hyphēgēsis*) in seven books, followed by an eighth book containing his famous *maps. After a general introduction the first book has a discussion of maps, with instructions on how to make them; the following six books are devoted to lists of some 8,000 places, located by latitude and longitude. The surviving maps in the eighth book are probably not as Ptolemy originally drew them but later reconstructions. Among numerous errors which the work contained was the notion that Asia stretched much further to the east than is in fact the case. It was this that misled Columbus into thinking that he had reached Asia when he was in fact in the Caribbean. Ptolemy's work on astrology, in which he attempts to find a scientific basis for the various astrological practices, also exerted great influence. Chaucer's Wife of Bath in his *Canterbury Tales* quotes a proverb from Ptolemy, calling him 'the wise astrologe'.

Publi'lius Sȳrus (first century BC), writer of Latin *mimes who was brought to Rome as a slave, possibly from Antioch, and manumitted. He is known by a collection of moral maxims made for school use which purport to have been selected from his plays. One of his maxims, *iudex damnatur cum nocens absolvitur* ('When the guilty man is let off the judge stands condemned') was adopted by the *Edinburgh Review* (1802) to express its stern attitude in literary criticism.

punctuation. Punctuation existed in Greek texts from at least the fourth century BC, but its use was sporadic (as it was later in Latin texts). What it consisted of can be inferred from the papyri (see PAPYROLOGY) and early manuscripts, and from explicit statements by Dionysius Thrax. In practice scribes of Greek and Latin texts rarely used more than two marks, the equivalent of the full-stop and the comma. Only for Homer was there a more sophisticated system, invented by Nicanor in the second century AD. See also BOOKS AND WRITING.

Pūnica, see SILIUS ITALICUS.

Punic Wars, three wars (264–241 BC; 218–201 BC; and 149–146 BC) in which Rome successfully fought *Carthage for dominance in the western Mediterranean. The name comes from the Latin word *Poeni* ('Carthaginians', adj. *Punicus*, 'Carthaginian'). Rome, having by 270 BC won control of the Italian peninsula, found herself confronted across the Straits of Messina by a rival power who now ruled not only the north and west of Sicily but also the greater part of North Africa, Sardinia, Corsica, and the cities on the coast of southern Spain. In 264 the Carthaginians occupied Messana (modern Messina) in north-east Sicily, and the Romans felt that trade and security would be threatened if Carthage encroached further. While the senate hesitated, the people decided to accept an alliance with Messana which led directly to war.

The First Punic War was centred on Sicily. The Romans won sea battles at Mylae (260) and Cape Ecnomus (256), overcoming superior Carthaginian seamanship by the innovative use of grappling-irons. Mastery of the sea allowed them to land unopposed in Africa, but after early successes there, they were defeated, and *Regulus, who had commanded the force, was captured. However, another Roman sea-victory off the Aegātēs Insulae (242) caused the Carthaginians to sue for peace. They evacuated Sicily (except for the dominion of Hieron II), which then became the first Roman province, and paid a large indemnity.

When the First Punic War ended, Carthage turned to Spain to recoup wealth and man-power, and between 237 and 219 *Hamilcar Barca, *Hasdrubal, and *Hannibal gradually conquered that country. Hannibal's attack on Rome's Spanish ally Saguntum in 219 deliberately precipitated the Second Punic War. This was one of the great struggles of the ancient world, fought in several theatres. Hannibal anticipated the dispatch of Roman expeditions to Spain and Africa and struck first by invading north Italy. There he defeated one great army after another, that of P. Scipio at the river

Ticinus in 218, that of Scipio and Tib. Sempronius Longus at the river Trebia in the same year (both rivers tributaries of the Po), and that of C. Flaminius at Lake Trasimene in 217, when Flaminius was himself killed. Hannibal then moved to the south to detach the allies from Rome. At this crisis Rome appointed a dictator, Quintus *Fabius Maximus, who acquired the *cognomen* Cunctator, 'delayer', from following the invader and harassing him, while refusing a general engagement. In 216 the new consuls C. Terentius Varro and L. Aemilius Paullus were authorized to risk a decisive battle to protect the territory of Rome's allies, with the result that at Cannae Rome suffered the bloodiest of all her defeats, losing perhaps 50,000 men, half of them Roman. Hannibal remained in Italy for fifteen years and was undefeated in battle, but Fabius continued to wear down his strength and the tide began to turn against Carthage. M. Claudius Marcellus captured Syracuse in 211, despite the weapons of war devised by *Archimedēs, and thus weakened the power of Carthage in Sicily; Hasdrubal, who had gone to aid Hannibal in Italy, was defeated and killed at the river Metaurus (in Umbria, 207); and Scipio Africanus drove the Carthaginians from Spain (206). The scene of war was now transferred to Africa and Hannibal and the Punic army were recalled from Italy. They were beaten by Scipio in a pitched battle at Zama (202) and Carthage accepted harsh peace-terms. It was the end of her position as a great Mediterranean power.

Carthage retained, however, her commercial importance; she continued to compete successfully with Rome in trade, and was a source of uneasiness there. She had undertaken to wage no wars in Africa without the consent of Rome, but in 151 the depredations of Masinissa, the ruler of the adjoining Numidian kingdom and the friend of Rome, goaded her into retaliation (150). In 149 Rome used this pretext to initiate the Third Punic War. *Cato (the Censor), from motives of revenge and fear, urged its destruction, and an army under Manilius landed in Africa. Carthage surrendered, handed over hostages and arms, and then heard the terms that the city must be destroyed.

Unexpectedly she refused to comply and withstood a siege until 146, when *Scipio Aemilianus captured the city and demolished it. With Carthage destroyed her territory was made into the Roman province of Africa.

Pyane'psia or **Pyanopsia,** at Athens, a popular festival held in honour of Apollo, which celebrated the harvest and gave its name to the month Pyanopsion, roughly October. It took its name from the cooked beans (*pyana*) which were offered to the god as first-fruits and partaken of by all the members of the household. An olive-branch (known as *eiresiōnē*) wreathed with wool and hung with various fruits and models of wine cups and bottles of oil was carried about and set before each house and before the temple of the god.

Pydna, in Macedonia on the Thermaic Gulf, the scene of the battle in 168 BC in which the Romans under L. Aemilius Paullus decisively defeated Perseus, king of *Macedonia, and ended the Third Macedonian War.

Pygmā'lion. 1. Legendary king of Tyre, brother of Elissa (*Dido), whose husband Sychaeus he killed in the hope of obtaining his fortune.

2. Legendary king of Cyprus, who fell in love with a beautiful statue (according to Ovid made by himself). He prayed to Aphroditē to give him a wife resembling the statue; and she did more than this, for she gave the statue life, and Pygmalion married the woman so created. Their child was Paphos, the mother of *Cinyras.

pygmies, in Greek myth, a race of dwarfs thought to inhabit Africa (usually, but also India or Scythia), with whom the cranes were supposed to carry on war. This belief is frequently referred to by ancient writers, Homer, Aristotle, Ovid, and the Elder Pliny. The fact that tribes of very small stature exist in equatorial Africa may be the origin of the belief.

Pȳ'ladēs. 1. In Greek myth, the constant friend of *Orestes. He was the son of Strophius, king of Phocis, and his wife Anaxibia, sister of Orestes' father Agamemnon. He accompanied Orestes to the land of the Tauri (see IPHIGENEIA), and later to Mycenae when Orestes took vengeance on Clytemnestra and Aegisthus (see ELECTRA, Sophocles' tragedy). He also killed Neoptolemus at Delphi and married Electra.

2. An actor at Rome; see PANTOMIME.

Pylae, see THERMOPYLAE.

Pȳlos. 1. Legendary kingdom of *Neleus and *Nestor in the Peloponnese.

2. Town on the west coast of the Peloponnese, in Messenia. This and the adjoining bay of Pylos, and the island of Sphacteria which almost closes the mouth of the bay, were the scene of an important defeat of the Spartans by the Athenians in 425 BC (see PELOPONNESIAN WAR). The Athenians held it with a garrison until 409 BC.

Py'ramus and Thisbē, hero and heroine of a love story almost unknown in classical literature except through Ovid. The two lovers, who were next-door neighbours in Babylon, were forbidden by their parents to marry, but they spoke to each other through a chink in the party-wall. Finally they arranged to meet at the tomb of Nisus outside the city walls, under a white mulberry tree. Thisbe arrived first, but being frightened by a lion coming from its kill, fled into a cave, dropping her cloak which the lion mauled. On his arrival Pyramus found the tattered and blood-stained cloak and the animal's prints and, concluding that Thisbe was dead, stabbed himself with his sword. Thisbe. emerging from the cave, distraught at the sight of the dying Pyramus, fell upon his sword. Their blood flowed to the roots of the mulberry tree, which thereafter bore dark red fruit. Their parents buried their ashes in a single urn. The story is acted by Bottom and his fellow tradesmen to entertain the wedding-party in Shakespeare's *A Midsummmer Night's Dream*.

Pyriphle'gethon, see HADES.

Pyropolyni'cēs, the boastful captain of the title in the *Miles gloriosus* of Plautus.

pyrrhic dance (*pyrrhichē*), Spartan mimic war-dance, perhaps a form of the *hyporchema*. It is said to have originated with the Dorians in Crete. It was danced at the Spartan festival of the Gymnopaediae and also at the Athenian festival of the *Panathenaea. The origin of the name is uncertain.

Pyrrhic victory, see PYRRHUS (1).

Pyrrhon, see SCEPTICS.

Pyrrhus. 1. (319–272 BC), king of Epirus in Greece from 307, second cousin of Alexander the Great. Pyrrhus was ousted from his throne in 302, but with the help of Ptolemy I of Egypt was restored in 297. He hoped to revive the empire of Alexander the Great and was at one time (286), after a successful war against *Demetrius Poliorcetēs, the most powerful ruler in the European part of it, having secured Thessaly and a portion of Macedonia. But he was soon driven back to Epirus (283) by Lysimachus (one of the *diadochoi*, Alexander's 'successors'). He then turned to the West and accepted the invitation of the Greek city of Tarentum in Itaiy to lead the Italian Greeks of *Magna Graecia against Rome. He won battles in 280 and 279 with a large army and twenty elephants but was unable to establish himself in Italy. The expression 'Pyrrhic victory' to describe a victory gained at too great a cost alludes to an exclamation attributed to him after the battle of Asculum in 279 where he routed the Romans but lost the flower of his army: 'One more such victory and we are undone.' Pyrrhus then transferred his forces to Sicily, and by 277 had almost succeeded in expelling the Carthaginians from that island. He broke off the war there and returned to Italy. After an indecisive battle against the Romans at Beneventum (275), he withdrew to Epirus. Once again in 274 he attempted to conquer Macedonia, with some success, but was diverted to an attack on Sparta (272). He was killed in the same year in an attempt to seize Argos. A brilliant tactician, Pyrrhus was quick to take advantage of an opportunity but made no lasting gains. See also FABRICIUS.

2. Alternative name of the Greek hero *Neoptolemus.

Pȳtha'goras, Greek polymath, philosopher, and mystic of the sixth century BC. He wrote no books, but so impressive were his doctrines, his learning, and his way of life that by the end of the fifth century he had become a figure of mystery and legend with a reputation as a great sage and a possessor of miraculous powers (as well as of a golden thigh). The traditions concerning his life are contradictory and confused, but it is believed that he was born at Samos *c*.580 BC and emigrated (perhaps through hostility to the tyranny of Polycratēs) to Croton in *Magna Graecia. There he attracted followers, both men and women, who formed a community and lived according to his rule of life. Even after his death, *c*.500 BC, Pythagorean societies continued to flourish in Croton and elsewhere in Magna Graecia. The members seem to have been active in the politics of the time and, presenting a united front, were no doubt a powerful force; they became unpopular and eventually (*c*.450 BC) the societies were broken up and the members killed or exiled.

Part of Pythagoras' teaching was religious and mystical, and it was presumably this aspect which led his contemporary *Heracleitus to regard him as a fraud. Another contemporary, *Xenophanēs, mocked the most celebrated aspect of his teaching, his doctrine of reincarnation or the transmigration of souls (*metempsychōsis*), with the story that Pythagoras once claimed to recognize a friend's voice in the howling of a puppy which was being beaten. Pythagoras also declared that he remembered his own previous incarnations, including that as the Trojan Euphorbus, killed in the siege. Pythagoras taught that the soul (a combination of life-principle, self, and mind) is immortal, a fallen divinity imprisoned in the body as in a tomb. Since the soul is rational and responsible for its actions, the choices it makes determine the kind of body into which it is reincarnated, human or animal (perhaps even plant; *Empedoclēs, who was greatly influenced by Pythagorean ideas, declares that in one of his incarnations he was a bush). By keeping itself pure from the pollutions of the body the soul may eventually win release from it (see also ORPHEUS and compare Orphic beliefs, with which Pythagoras obviously had much in common). Pythagoras and his followers adhered to a rule of life

by which release for the soul might be attained; this was an austere regimen the details of which are not clear but which perhaps entailed silence, self-examination, and abstention from eating flesh and beans (no reason is known for this latter prohibition). The idea of metempsychosis is foreign to Greek tradition and its source uncertain; it may have reached Greece from central Asia or even India. Many precepts of Pythagoras were collected at some time under the name of *acusmata* (Gk. *akousmata*, '(oral) instructions'). Some sound like taboo-prohibitions, e.g. 'Do not poke the fire with a sword' (which *Porphyry interpreted as meaning, 'Do not vex with sharp words a man swollen with anger'). Others sound like traditional wisdom: 'What is the wisest of the things in our power? Medicine. What is the fairest thing? Harmony. What is the most powerful? Knowledge. What is the best? Happiness.'

Pythagoras' name is also linked to the study of numbers and proportions as well as astronomy. It is impossible to ascertain what discoveries should be attributed to him personally, but he is credited with the discovery that the relation between the chief musical intervals produced on a vibrating string can be expressed as ratios between the first four whole numbers: octave, $2:1$; fifth, $3:2$; fourth, $4:3$. From this evolved the idea that the explanation of the universe is to be sought in numbers and their relations, of which the objects of sense are representations. According to Aristotle, even abstracts like 'opinion' or 'opportunity' or 'injustice' were numbers in the Pythagorean system, and had their place in the cosmos. Since the first four whole numbers are important in expressing musical harmonies and since their sum can be represented as an equilateral triangular array of ten dots in rows of one, two, three, and four, it was thought that this pattern, the *tetraktys*, 'foursome', of the decad, was of mystical significance, embracing the whole nature of number: the number one could be identified with the point, two with the line, three with the surface, and four with the solid. Pythagoras is also credited with the theorem that still goes under his name, namely that the square on the hypotenuse of a right-angled triangle is equal to the sum of the squares on the other two sides; on discovering it he is said to have made the important sacrifice of a hecatomb. The Pythagoreans believed that the earth is a sphere; later Pythagoreans had an astronomical system in which the heavenly bodies (the sphere of the fixed stars, the five planets, the sun, moon, earth, and counter-earth, the last included to bring the number of bodies up to ten) revolve around a central fire, a system to which an earlier belief in a '*harmony of the spheres' was accommodated.

Pythagoreanism influenced not only Empedocles but also Plato, whose science and metaphysics are infused with Pythagorean ideas. Later the doctrines were revived at Rome under the early empire, and became confused with Orphic beliefs with which they had affinities.

Py'theas. In the second half of the fourth century BC, a Greek explorer from Massilia (modern Marseilles), who, according to Strabo, Diodorus Siculus, and the Elder Pliny, made a courageous voyage up the west coast of Europe to Britain, Jutland, and the Orkneys and Shetlands. See THULE.

Py'thia, priestess of Apollo at *Delphi.

Py'thian festival, the most important Greek games after the Olympian, held in honour of Apollo Pythius at Delphi. From 582 BC they were held every four years in the third year of each Olympiad.

Py'thias, see DAMON.

Python, see DELPHI.

Q

Quadriga'rius, Claudius, see HIS-TORIOGRAPHY 2.

quadri'vium ('meeting place of four roads'), the four mathematical disciplines of astronomy, geometry, arithmetic, and music which during the Middle Ages constituted the advanced part of the educational curriculum, known as the *seven liberal arts. The *trivium*, the more elementary part, consisted of grammar, rhetoric, and logic. The term *quadrivium* seems to have been invented by *Boethius.

Quaestiō'nēs, see PAPINIAN.

Quaestiō'nēs convīviā'lēs, etc., see PLUTARCH 3.

quaestors, magistrates at Rome; in the early republic they were two officers chosen by the consuls and acting as their deputies in administering criminal justice. Soon after 451 BC the quaestors became properly constituted magistrates elected annually by the people (see DECEMVIRI); in 421 their number was increased to four, of whom two administered the state treasury, *aerarium*, and were called in consequence *quaestores aerarii* or *urbani* ('of the city'). Four more were instituted in 267 and others added later as the number of Roman provinces increased and financial officers were required. Sulla fixed the total at twenty; Julius Caesar doubled it, but the emperor Augustus returned to the former figure. Sulla also made the office compulsory in the *cursus honorum*, entailing automatic entry to the senate for the holders, and declared that 30 was the minimum age for holding it.

quantity, in metric, see METRE, GREEK I and PROSODY.

Quinqua'trus, in Roman religion, a festival celebrated on 19–23 March, starting five (*quinque*) days after the Ides, whence perhaps its name. The first day commemorated the birthday of the god-dess Minerva; the last day was the *Tubilustrium. The festival was celebrated especially by those whose activities were under the care of the goddess, such as spinners, weavers, and dyers.

quinque'nnium Nerō'nis ('Nero's five years'), phrase applied to the early years of the reign of the emperor Nero (AD 54–68), viewed, in retrospect, and in contrast with the horrors of his later years, as a Golden Age.

Quinti'lian (Marcus Fabius Quin-tiliānus) (b. *c.* AD 35; the date of his death is not known, but his *Institutio oratoria* was published about AD 95). Born at Calagurris in Spain, Quintilian was a famous teacher of rhetoric at Rome. He may have received all his education at Rome; at some period he returned to Spain, whence he was brought back by the emperor Galba. He was the first rhetorician to receive an official salary from the state treasury (under the emperor Vespasian), and he acquired great wealth; the Younger Pliny was among his pupils. He also practised advocacy in the courts. The emperor Domitian made him consul and tutor to his great-nephews. He retired, probably in 88, in order to write. Before he retired he married, but his wife died before her nineteenth birthday, and his two sons later, at the ages of 5 and 9; the introduction to the sixth book of his *Institutio* makes clear his grief. His earlier work 'The Decline of Oratory' (*De causis corruptae eloquentiae*) is lost. Two collections of *Declamationēs* ('declamations') are attributed to him, probably falsely, although some may reproduce themes used in his school. These are rhetorical themes on imaginary problems of conduct in various circumstances or on problems arising out of the conflict of laws, etc. The *Institutio oratoria* ('education of an orator'), in twelve books, is his most famous work. It covers the training of an orator from babyhood to the grown man. The poet Martial called Quintilian 'the supreme guide of wayward youth'.

Petrarch (1304–74) had only an imperfect copy of the *Institutio*, but the Florentine humanist Poggio Bracciolini (1380–1459) discovered a complete manuscript at the Abbey of St Gallen (St Gall) in Switzerland in 1416. It was first printed in 1470 and acquired a great reputation in the Renaissance, when Quintilian's conception of the purpose of (rhetorical) education, namely, to produce a man of good character and cultivation and not merely a pedant, was in harmony with that of the humanists. See TEXTS, TRANSMISSION OF ANCIENT 8.

Quinti'lius Vārus, see VARUS.

Quintus Cu'rtius, see CURTIUS.

Quintus Smyrnae'us (Quintus of Smyrna). He lived probably in the fourth century AD and was author of an extant epic poem in Greek in fourteen books known by its Latin title, the *Posthomerica* (Gk. *Ta meth' Homēron*), which filled the gap in events between Homer's *Iliad* and *Odyssey*. The work is mainly of antiquarian interest; its sources probably date from the Hellenistic age.

Quirī'nal, most northerly of the seven hills of Rome, traditionally occupied by Sabines, and one of the four regions (see REGIONES) of republican Rome. On it were many famous temples and houses, including at various periods the temple of Quirinus (see below), the residence of the king Numa and his ancient citadel, the temple of Flora, the temple of Salus, goddess of health (adorned with paintings by Fabius Pictor), the shrine of Dius Fidius, a temple of Venus Erycina, and the houses of the poet Martial and of Cicero's friend Atticus.

Quirī'nus, in Roman religion, originally the local deity (perhaps the war god) of the Sabine community settled on the Quirinal hill before the foundation of Rome. When this community came to be incorporated into Rome, Quirinus was included among the state gods of the city with Jupiter and Mars. His festival, the Quirinalia, was celebrated on 17 February, but nothing is known of his ritual. Quirinus was identified with the deified Romulus by the Romans of the late republic (but not by Livy). He had his own *flamen, the *flamen Quirinalis*.

Quirī'tes, name given to the earliest inhabitants of Rome, Latin and Sabine, which survived later in official phraseology to be applied to the Roman people in their civil capacity. It was superseded by the name *Romani* (Romans) or *populus Romanus (Roman people). The term was not applicable to Romans when serving in the army: Caesar is said to have quelled a mutiny of his soldiers by addressing them as 'Quirites'. The origin of the name is uncertain. The Romans generally believed that it originally signified the inhabitants of the Sabine town of Curēs.

R

Rabi'rius, Gaius, subject of a speech for the defence by *Cicero (see (1) 4).

Ramnēs, one of the three *tribes of which the primitive Roman people is said to have consisted. The other two are Titiēs and Lucerēs. The origin of the names is obscure.

Rānae, Latin title of the *Frogs* of Aristophanes.

Rape of the Sabines, see ROMULUS.

Rave'nna, ancient city of north-east Italy, to the south of the river Po, built in the manner of Venice on the lagoons which existed there at that time. After the *Visigothic invasions of AD 401 and 403 its strong and secluded location caused the emperor in the West, Honorius, son of Theodosius the Great, to move his court there from Rome. His successors for the most part followed his example, and not only the Roman emperors ruled from there until the *fall of the Roman empire in 476, but also the Gothic kings, Odoacer and Theodoric, who followed them.

recension, critical examination of all the surviving manuscripts (or other evidence) for the constitution of a text, or the text based on such an examination. See TEX-TUAL CRITICISM.

Rē'gia, at Rome, the royal palace said to have been built by king *Numa at the foot of the Palatine on the edge of the Forum. The earliest foundations have been dated to the sixth and fifth centuries BC. It adjoined the temple of Vesta and the house of the Vestals. In republican times the Regia was the official head-quarters of the *pontifex maximus*. The building was several times burnt and restored. In 36 BC it was rebuilt of marble and on its walls were inscribed the *fasti consularēs* and *fasti triumphalēs* (records of consuls and of triumphs at Rome).

rēgifu'gium ('flight of the king'), ceremony held at Rome on 24 February, of which all that is known is that the *rex sacrorum*, after the sacrifice, concluded the ritual by running away from the *Comitium. It was thought in ancient times that this symbolized the flight of the last Tarquin king from Rome.

Rēgi'llus, Lake, in Latium, on the shores of which the Romans in the early days of the republic, c.496 BC, defeated the Latins, who were attempting to re-establish the Tarquins at Rome. For the intervention of the gods Castor and Pollux see DIOSCURI.

rēgio'nēs (sing. *regio*), 'regions', at Rome, the four wards into which the city was divided during the republic; these were the Suburana (see SUBURA), which included the Caelian hill, the Esquilina (the *Esquiline hill), the Collina, including the *Quirinal and Viminal hills, and the Palatina (the *Palatine hill). The emperor Augustus divided the city into fourteen new *regiones*.

Re'gulus, Marcus Atī'lius, Roman consul in 265 and 256 BC. As a commander in the First *Punic War he defeated the Carthaginian navy at Cape Ecnomus, but in the following year—leading the Roman expedition to Africa—he was captured. It is said that he was sent on an embassy to Rome to negotiate peace, the Carthaginians making him swear to return if the negotiations failed. He advised the Romans to continue the war, then kept his word and returned to Carthage, where he was tortured to death. The story (as related by Horace in *Odes* III. 5) made him a national hero, but it has been suggested that it was invented to excuse the cruel treatment of Carthaginian prisoners in Rome.

Reme'dia amo'ris ('cures of love'), Latin poem in elegiacs by *Ovid, of some 800 lines. It professes to give instructions for overcoming unfortunate or misplaced love, by hunting, travel, agricultural occupations, avoidance of wine and of the love poets, and other less innocuous precepts.

Rēmus, see ROMULUS.

repetu'ndae ('restitution'; in full, *res repetundae*, 'restitution of property'). When a Roman provincial governor returned to Rome, any accusations made by provincials about extortion were brought before a special court. The penalty was simple restitution.

republic, Roman, see ROMAN REPUBLIC.

Republic (Gk. *Politeia*), dialogue in ten books by *Plato. The traditional English title is derived from the Latin translation, *Respublica*, of the Greek title, and is perhaps misleading. The original meaning is closer to 'society' or 'the state'. The *Republic* was written in the early years of the *Academy, the school which Plato founded to give a philosophical education to those embarking on a political career. It is an exposition of the principles on which an ideal society, in Plato's view, should be based. The rulers ('guardians') are to be philosopher-kings who alone have knowledge of the ideas of Justice and the Good (see PLATO 4 and 5); they will rule in the interests of the majority, who have only limited perception. Book I has the conversational form of an early Socratic dialogue (see PLATO 2), but the rest of the work is a more or less continuous exposition by *Socrates of what one must suppose to be Plato's own views on society at the time of writing (about 375 BC). The interlocutors are Socrates, an old man Cephalus (father of the orator *Lysias) and his son Polemarchus, Thrasymachus a sophist, and Plato's brothers Glaucon and Adeimantus. The discussion takes place at the house of Cephalus.

The dialogue starts with the question 'What is justice?', which at its simplest means 'Why should we be good?' The conventional definition offered by the poet Simonidēs, that it means giving a person his due, is shown to be inadequate. Thrasymachus rejects conventional morality and maintains that human behaviour is, and should be, guided by self-interest. Socrates reduces Thrasymachus to silence, but Glaucon

and Adeimantus remain unsatisfied and restate his case for him. Glaucon argues that justice is a matter of expediency, and that we would all be unjust to our own advantage if we could. Adeimantus argues that justice is pursued only for mercenary reasons. Socrates must show that justice is preferable to injustice for its own sake and not for the rewards it brings. Socrates suggests that justice will best be seen in the macrocosm of a perfect city-state, and if discovered there, can be found by analogy in individuals. Accordingly Socrates proceeds to construct the ideal state. This is seen to consist of three classes, guardians or magistrates (in whose education Plato is particularly interested), auxiliaries or soldiers, and producers. In the first resides the wisdom of the state, in the second its courage. Temperance or restraint must be present in all three classes, while political justice is that which keeps each class to its proper functions. Similarly, individuals have the qualities of the three classes present in their souls, but in varying proportions. They are wise in respect of the rational element in them, courageous and moved by generous impulses in respect of the spiritual element, and they are moved to satisfy their appetites. In a disciplined individual, spirit and appetite are subordinated to reason; justice consists in the harmony of all these elements. The discussion of the ideal state is continued; Socrates' proposal for the community of women and children is explained, and it is shown that for the efficient working of the constitution the supreme power must be in the hands of philosophers. Socrates expounds the proper education of the guardians (from which the misleading tales of the poets must be excluded) and the nature of true knowledge, which is not of the objects and images of the world of the senses, but of the realities of the intellectual world, apprehended by pure intelligence. The theory of Ideas or Forms (see PLATO 4 and 5) is developed; and the liberating nature of right education is illustrated by the simile of men chained in a subterranean cave representing, in Plato's view, the general human condition, who see only the shadows of objects behind them thrown by firelight

467 **Rhesus**

on the wall in front of them, so that they take these shadows for the only realities: the guardians will struggle out of the cave into the world of knowledge and wisdom. Socrates resumes (book 8) the subject of the various types of political organization and personal character, and traces the process of degeneration from the perfect type and the perfect man, namely aristocracy and the aristocratic man, through four stages to the worst, namely tyranny and the tyrannical man. Finally the rewards of virtue are considered, chief among these being the reward that the soul receives in the life after death, the soul being immortal, but rewards are merely a secondary consideration. The nature of this afterlife is indicated in the tale of Er the son of Armenius, who twelve days after his death returned to life and described what he had seen in the other world.

Respo'nsa, see PAPINIAN.

Return of the Heracleidae, see HERACLEIDAE.

Revenues (Gk. *Poroi ē peri prosodōn*, Lat. *De vectigalibus*), one of the minor works of *Xenophon, written not before 355 BC and probably his last work. The ascription to him has been doubted.

Xenophon discusses various means of increasing the revenue of Athens, notably by encouraging the resident aliens (metics), who were engaged in manufacturing and trade generally, and by making ingenious suggestions such as for investment in accommodation that could be rented to visitors, and in slaves to be hired out to operators of the Laurium silver-mines (a transaction from which the author expected a return of 33 per cent on the capital expended). See also ISOCRATES 5.

rex sacrō'rum ('king of the sacred things'), at Rome after the expulsion of the kings (510 BC), a priest whose duty it was to perform some of the king's religious functions. He was a patrician, appointed for life, and unlike the *pontifex maximus* (to whom he was superior in rank and precedence though inferior in religious authority) disqualified from holding any other office. He and his wife

(*rēgīna*, 'queen', who had some religious duties) performed certain state sacrifices.

Rhadama'nthys (Lat. Rhadamanthus), in myth, son of Zeus and *Europa; he did not die but went to *Elysium, where he became a ruler; in some accounts he was made judge of the dead in the Underworld, with *Minos and *Aeacus.

Rhampsinī'tus, Rameses (III?), pharaoh of Egypt, of whom the Greek historian Herodotus (2. 121) tells the following folk-tale. He had a treasury built, in the wall of which the builder secretly left a movable stone. After his death the builder's sons, by means of this, were able to creep in and steal the treasure. The king, finding the seals of the door unbroken but the treasure diminished, set a man-trap, in which one of the brothers was caught. He immediately called to his brother and bade him cut off his head and take it away to avoid detection, which was done. (Compare TROPHONIUS).

rhapsode (or rhapsodist; *rhapsōdos*, 'one who stitches songs together'), in Greece, a professional reciter of poetry, usually of Homer (i.e. epic), but also of other poems. Rhapsodes were a familiar sight at public festivals and games, where they competed for prizes. Plato's dialogue *Ion* is a satire on their pretensions.

Rhēa, in Greek myth, one of the *Titans, daughter of Uranus and Gaia, wife (and sister) of *Cronus, mother of Zeus and other Olympian gods. She was often identified with *Cybelē. The Romans identified her with *Ops.

Rhēa Si'lvia, see ILIA.

Rhēsus, tragedy doubtfully attributed to *Euripides; if it is his work, it would appear to be earlier than any other of his extant plays.

Rhesus is a dramatization of the tenth book of Homer's *Iliad*. The Greeks have been driven back to their ships, and Hector sends the Trojan Dolon by night to spy out their intentions. Rhesus, king of Thrace, arrives with his army to support the Trojans. Hector reproaches him for his delay; Rhesus replies proudly and confidently, and then retires to rest. Odysseus and Diomedēs enter the Trojan camp; they have killed Dolon after learning the password from him. Directed by the goddess Athena they fall upon the sleeping Thracians, kill Rhesus, and lead away his horses. His charioteer relates his death by an unknown hand and accuses Hector of his murder. Hector is exculpated by the Muse Terpsichorē, mother of Rhesus, who descends from heaven to carry off her son's body.

rhētor (Gk. and Lat. *rhētor*), at Athens originally, a public speaker in the *ecclesia*, a politician; later at Athens, and at Rome, a teacher of public speaking, a rhetorician.

rhetoric, the theoretical art of speaking so as to persuade; it is *oratory reduced to a system which can be taught. In the Greek world rhetoric was reputedly first developed in Sicily in the mid-fifth century BC and further refined by the *sophists, most of whom regarded a knowledge and command of it essential for men embarking on a political career. During the first century BC (as a consequence of the spread of Greek culture) the study of rhetoric became an important part of Roman education and exercised an increasing influence on Roman literature during the empire. The elements of rhetoric were treated under five headings: invention, arrangement, diction, memory, delivery. 'Invention' was the discovery (*inventio*) of the relevant material; 'arrangement' entailed putting the materials together in a structured way; 'diction' concerned finding the appropriate style of speech for the occasion, grand, middle, or plain (sometimes known as low). 'Memory' gave guidance on how to memorize speeches; 'delivery' gave guidance on the techniques of public speaking. The following deal with rhetoric: *Aristotle (see 4 (v)); Cicero, *Brutus, *De inventione, *De optimo genere oratorum, *De oratore; *Demetrius (3); *Dionysius of Halicarnassus, *On the Arrangement of Words; *Longinus on the Sublime; Quintilian, *Institutio oratoria; Tacitus, *Dialogus de oratoribus; and the Rhetorica ad Herennium below.

Rhēto'rica ad Here'nnium, Latin treatise on oratory in four books, written between 86 and 82 BC and addressed to C. Herennius by an unknown author; some attribute it to a certain Cornificius, on slight evidence in Quintilian. It is ascribed in the manuscripts to Cicero, and it seems connected in some way with Cicero's early *De inventione. *Rhetoric is treated under its five headings; the section on style is the oldest surviving treatment in Latin. The work is modelled on Greek writers, and is interesting as a relatively early example of Latin prose.

Rhodes (Rhŏdos), most easterly of the Aegean islands, close to the mainland of Caria (in Asia Minor), colonized by Dorian Greeks who founded three city-states, Iālysus, Lindus, and Camīrus. The three Rhodian cities amalgamated in 408 BC into one state with a new federal capital which took its name from the island. During the fifth century BC Rhodes had been a member of the *Delian League, paying tribute to Athens, but in 412 BC Rhodes defected to the Peloponnesians. It joined the Second Athenian League but again revolted in 357 BC. During the third century it was a considerable naval power, standing for freedom of trade and suppressing piracy. In the struggles which followed the death of Alexander the Great in 323 BC it tried to follow a policy of neutrality, but in 304 the capital was besieged by Demetrius Poliorcētēs ('besieger') of Macedonia; the *Colossus of Rhodes was erected to commemorate the successful defence of the city. Rhodes was associated with Pergamum in a policy of friendship to Rome in the early second century BC, but it soon roused the jealousy of Rome by its independent attitude. Its trade was also severely damaged by the Roman free port of *Delos, and sank into relative insignificance. The capital was captured and pillaged by Cassius in 43 BC.

Rhodes was a considerable literary centre; it was the birthplace of *Panaetius and the seat of the school founded by his pupil *Posidonius. *Hipparchus the mathematician probably spent part of his life there. Pindar's seventh Olympian ode was written for the victory of the Rhodian boxer Diagoras. The city was destroyed by an earthquake in 225 BC and again c. AD 155; as rebuilt, it was described by

Aelius *Aristeides as the most beautiful of Greek cities.

Rhodō'pē or **Rhodō'pis,** Greek courtesan, said to have been a Thracian and a fellow-slave of Aesop, and to have been taken to Naucratis in Egypt. *Aelian relates that one day while Rhodope was bathing, an eagle flew away with one of her slippers and dropped it into the lap of the pharaoh of the day, Psammetichus. The king was struck with the beauty of the slipper, had a search made for the owner, and married her. There was a story (rejected by Herodotus) that she built the third pyramid; Herodotus confuses her with the courtesan Doricha (SEE SAPPHO).

rhopa'lic verse, verse of which each word in a line contains one more syllable than that before it; e.g. *lux verbo inducta, peccantibus auxiliatrix* ('Light | revealed | by the Word, | a comforter | of all those in sin'). The name is derived from Greek *rhopalos*, 'club', suggesting the gradual increase. See AUSONIUS.

Rōbī'gus (or Robigo, the female equivalent), in Roman religion, the god of 'blight' who averted red mildew or rust from crops. He was propitiated and the pest averted by the annual sacrifice of a rust-coloured dog at the festival of the Robigalia on 25 April.

Roman age of Greek literature, term used to describe Greek literature written from the time when Rome subjugated the Mediterranean world, i.e. from the second half of the second century BC to AD 529, when the emperor Justinian closed the schools of philosophy at Athens and ended the long history of that city as the focus of Greek intellectual life and culture. See also SOPHISTIC, SECOND.

romance, see NOVEL.

Roman empire, a term that is applied to (i) the government of Rome under Augustus (the first Roman emperor) and his successors, and (ii) the lands governed by the Romans at any time from about the third century BC, when her power began to expand beyond the Italian peninsula. For the division of the empire into two halves, see BYZANTINE AGE and FALL OF ROME. See also PRINCIPATE.

Roman republic, the period in Roman history between the abolition of monarchy in 510 BC and the accession of the first emperor, Augustus, in 27 BC. The Latin words *res publica* mean 'affairs affecting the state', 'the state' itself, or 'the constitution' of the state. The Roman constitution was a republic in the modern sense of the word, in that the supreme power rested with the people; arbitrary rule by an individual (monarchy or tyranny) or by a small group (oligarchy) was renounced, and the right to take part in political life was given to all adult male citizens. Although it was thus nominally a democracy in that all laws had to be approved by an assembly of citizens, the republic was in fact organized as an aristocracy or broad-based oligarchy, governed by a fairly small group of about fifty noble families (see NOBILES) who regularly held all the *magistracies. Magistracies had to be held in a fixed order (see CURSUS HONORUM) before a candidate could hold the highest office of all, the consulship. The two consuls, who had exactly equal authority, were in charge of the state for their year of office, their powers limited by the laws and by each other's potential veto and that of the ten *tribunes.

Citizens exercised their political rights in assemblies and were divided into tribes or centuries according to the nature of the assembly (see COMITIA). In elections and all other matters put to the assemblies, decision was reached by the votes of a majority of these groups; an individual's vote merely helped determine that of his group. The groups of the rich and powerful voted first; those to which the poorest people were alloted voted last. Since the result was declared as soon as a simple majority was reached, the last groups rarely voted at all. Voting took place only at Rome, with the consequence that those living in rural areas were usually unable to vote. The assemblies were not deliberative or debating bodies; they could only approve or reject policy that had been decided elsewhere. The sole deliberating body was the senate, which decided upon all policy, relating to both home and foreign affairs. A citizen was not free to address an assembly without the consent of the magistrates and tribunes, who alone had the right to summon a public meeting and to debate. The members of the assembly could only express an unofficial opinion, by shouting for example.

This organization was reflected in the towns (*municipia*) throughout Italy; their citizens were also (in the later republic) citizens of Rome but the towns retained local autonomy, with their own senate and senators (known as *decuriōnēs*).

See also DICTATOR.

Rome (Rōma)

Ancient Rome stood on the left bank of the river Tiber, about 22 km. (14 miles) from the sea, in the territory of *Latium near its northern boundary, south of Etruria. The site was already inhabited in the second half of the second millennium BC. Rome's history is divided into three main eras: a largely obscure early period ending in (traditionally) 510 BC, when the last king was expelled and a republic was set up; the republic, lasting from then until 27 BC, when Augustus became the first emperor; and the empire, which came to an end when the last emperor, Romulus Augustulus, was deposed in AD 476.

The surviving traditions about the foundation and early history of Rome depend mainly upon historians who were writing more than 500 years after the event (see HISTORIOGRAPHY 2), by which time it was not easy to distinguish between fact and legend. Moreover, a desire that Rome should share in some way in Greek achievements had led the Romans to connect their history with that of Greece: *Romulus, who traditionally founded the city in 753 BC, was given an invented ancestry that made him a descendant of *Aeneas. Reputedly under the kingship of Servius Tullius, but more likely in the fourth century BC, the city was enclosed within a wall (the Servian wall, so called) and now comprised the seven hills of Rome, namely the Palatine, Aventine, Capitoline, Caelian, Esquiline, Viminal, and Quirinal. (In Latin, the first five are termed *montēs*, 'peaks', 'mountains', the last two *collēs*, 'hills', but the distinction bears no apparent relation to their heights.) The four regions were also created at this time

(see REGIONES). Under the kings Rome was a great hill-top fortress, with the Capitoline hill (see CAPITOLIUM) equivalent to the Acropolis at Athens, and with the Aventine as a religious centre. According to tradition Rome was ruled after Romulus by a succession of six kings, Numa Pompilius, Tullus Hostilius, Ancus Marcius, Tarquinius Priscus, Servius Tullius, and Tarquinius Superbus ('Tarquin the Proud'), some at least of whom have a historical basis.

There appear to have been many wars during the early regal period as a result of which Roman territory was enlarged. Rome destroyed Alba, according to legend, when Tullus Hostilius was king (see HORATII AND CURIATII), and under Ancus Marcius founded a colony at Ostia near the mouth of the Tiber. Under Tarquinius Priscus (Tarquin, said to be an adventurer, half Greek and half Etruscan, who came to try his fortune at Rome and won the throne) and his two successors, *Etruscan influence became strong at Rome. The Etruscans, a powerful commercial and industrial people, may have conquered Rome; or the Etruscan cities may have accepted Tarquin as their king.

The Tarquins were expelled in 510 BC, and with their departure the probable domination by Etruscans was ended; despite the efforts at restoration by Lars *Porsen(n)a, monarchy was abolished at Rome. The struggle is reflected in the famous legend of the outrage on *Lucretia.

The constitution which followed the expulsion of the kings in 510 BC was an aristocratic republic. The king was replaced by two magistrates elected annually (*praetors, later called *consuls). Later, in times of national crisis, their powers might be temporarily superseded by the appointment of a *dictator, but the senate was now the real governing force in the state. The history of the republic during the next 250 years consists in the main of two struggles: an internal class struggle between the privileged *patricians and the unprivileged *plebeians, during which the republican constitution was hammered out; and an external struggle with the surrounding peoples, at first mainly defensive but subsequently aggressive, at the end of which Rome emerged supreme as the head of a confederacy embracing all Italy. The class struggle (often known as the conflict of the *orders) saw the plebeians gradually admitted to various offices of state and ended in 287 with the Hortensian Law (passed by the dictator Quintus Hortentius), which made the decrees of the *concilium plebis* binding on all the Roman people, not just the plebeians. The outcome of the struggle was the formation of a mixed patrician and plebeian oligarchy of *nobilēs*, who monopolized office as exclusively as the patricians alone had done hitherto.

In its external relations, in this early period of the republic, Rome had to face assaults from every side (the legends of Lars Porsen(n)a, Horatius *Coclēs, *Cloelia, and Mucius *Scaevola all refer to Rome's struggles with Etruria). In the second half of the fifth century Rome passed from defence to aggression, capturing the Etruscan town of Veii in 396 BC, but in about 390 BC Rome itself was sacked by the Gauls, except for the Capitol (according to the usual legend), which was bravely held by a small force under M. Manlius Capitolinus (see MANLIUS for the story of the geese saving the Capitol). Thereafter the city was rebuilt and refortified, and Rome entered on a long and arduous period of expansion. For seventy years Rome was at odds with the Samnites, a warlike mountain-people of the Abruzzi, east of Rome, before finally subduing them in 290.

Rome was now drawn into southern Italy, where the Greek cities of Magna Graecia were being hard pressed by Lucanian tribes, and by 270 had subjugated the whole region. By successful wars against the Umbrians, Picentēs, and Sallentīni in 270–266 she became supreme in the whole peninsula south of the river Rubicon. Peace was at last substituted for war as the normal condition of life in Italy. Rome did not force her civilization on others, but gradually local languages, cults, and customs gave way to a common culture based on the Latin language and Roman law. When Ptolemaic Egypt entered into a treaty of friendship (*amicitia*) with Rome in 273 it signalized the fact that Rome was now a Mediterranean power. This was the era to which Romans looked back nostalgically as to an ideal time, the formative period of the Roman character when life was simple and austere, and morality uncorrupted.

Rome was now a Mediterranean power, and as such came into contact with Carthaginian interests in Sicily. The conflict with Carthage and Rome's eventual triumph (see PUNIC WARS) gave her control of the western Mediterranean. Rome wished for no further conquests, but she desired security and that meant crushing any rival power; Macedonia, for example, was annexed as a province in 146, and a long series of Spanish campaigns, terminated in 133 by the capture of Numantia, resulted in the subjugation of the greater part of Spain. In the same year Attalus of Pergamum bequeathed his dominions to Rome (see ATTALIDS). They were formed into the Roman province of Asia. In the West the southern part of Gaul, Gallia Narbonensis, was made a province in 120. There was thus an enormous expansion of Roman territory in the second century BC. At the same time economic and social life in Rome and Italy underwent profound changes. In many parts peasant husbandry had given place to capitalist farming of huge estates. Industry and commerce had expanded generally and, although the aristocracy did not take part in these enterprises, the *equitēs* (see EQUESTRIAN ORDER) were considerably enriched. Slavery increased, both on the land and in households. Rome quite suddenly acquired immense wealth from booty and tribute, there was a great increase in luxury of all kinds, and great public building works were undertaken. In all spheres, art and architecture, literature and religion, Greek influence was strong; the earliest Roman historians actually wrote in Greek.

The last century of the Roman republic was a period of acute social and political struggle. There was discontent in the provinces, whose governors were often unscrupulous and ambitious, seeking to enrich themselves and to acquire power. Army commanders were also personally ambitious, and the army increasingly looked to them rather than to the senate to provide bounties and distributions of land, thus introducing a dangerous element into political life. The senate itself had become more oligarchic and less democratic in its attitudes, showing a selfish attitude towards the Italian allies, denying them citizenship and many of the spoils of war which they had helped to win. The first attempt to deal with some of these problems was made by the *Gracchi, who tried to reform agrarian laws in favour of the poorer citizens. Their eventual failure was followed by a conservative reaction, and by the war with Jugurtha (112–105). This war was conducted so ineffectually by the senate that the people and *equitēs* acting together had the command given to *Marius. His dispute with *Sulla for the command against Mithridates of Pontus led to Sulla's march on Rome in 88 at the head of his legions, and ushered in a period of civil war and bloodshed. Sulla was established as dictator and sought to re-establish the power of the senate over the tribunate and over army commanders, but these measures did not long survive his retirement in 79.

The second stage of Rome's civil wars is associated with the names of *Pompey, Julius *Caesar, *Crassus, and *Cicero. In this struggle all thoughts about the good of the republic gave way to the ambitions of individuals who sought power for themselves alone. Their fortune was built on their conquests as military commanders and they enjoyed what amounted to private control over loyal and effective troops, who realized that their own profit depended upon the success of their leaders. In 60 was formed the compact between Caesar, Pompey, and Crassus known (in modern times only) as 'the first triumvirate', by which they secured for themselves a commanding position in the state. It endured, while Caesar was conquering Gaul and Britain, until Crassus was killed after a Roman defeat by the Parthians at Carrhae in 53, after which rivalry between Caesar and Pompey developed into war. Pompey was utterly defeated at Pharsālus (in Thessaly) and was murdered in Egypt in 48. Whether or not Caesar intended to end the republic, his dictatorship introduced the principle of personal autocracy into the constitution. His programme of beneficial legislation was cut short by his assassination at the hands of senatorial conspirators in 44. Instead of the restoration of the republic which the conspirators had hoped for, a third round of civil war followed. Mark *Antony, Caesar's colleague in the consulship of 44 and at first the natural leader of the Caesarian party, found his position threatened by *Octavian, Caesar's heir. Antony's defeat at the battle of Actium in 31 and his death at Alexandria in 30 left Octavian sole master of Rome and all her territories, and in 27—as Augustus—he became the first emperor.

The republic had collapsed through lack of a large bureaucracy capable of managing the very complicated empire Rome now governed, and through the rise of military dictators. Using the framework of the old republic Augustus created a new system which was to some extent a compromise: he retained sole control of the military forces and foreign policy as well as general supervision over the machinery of government, but he left a share in administration to the senators and, especially, to the *equites*. Augustus himself adopted the outward appearance and mode of life of a republican magistrate, but his real position far exceeded that of a magistrate and he was in effect raised to a monarchical position. He made a great effort to restore by legislation the traditional religion and morality of the Roman people and to restrain luxury. The effect of his laws for this purpose was at best only temporary. As regards foreign policy, ambitious plans in the East were abandoned, and the efforts of the empire concentrated on the Romanization of Gaul and the acquisition of a strong frontier in the West. During the subsequent 300 years the centre of gravity of the empire was to shift to the East, the constitution of Augustus was to be radically modified, and in the end the West was to be overrun by barbarians. But none of this was to happen until Augustus' aims of Romanizing western Europe had been achieved in a form that would survive these upheavals.

Augustus died in AD 14. The next four emperors—Tiberius, Caligula, Claudius, and Nero—were related by blood or adoption and are known as the Julio-Claudian emperors. The key events of this period—AD 14–68—included the conquest of Britain in 43 (under Claudius) and the burning of Rome (under Nero). The fire gave Nero the opportunity to begin rebuilding Rome on an imposing scale, and he drew up regulations for broad, orderly streets in place of the twisting alleys of the old city. His own great monument—the *Golden House— was destroyed after his death, but this made available to his successors a large area for building, on which were erected some of Rome's greatest landmarks over the next half century—above all the Colosseum.

When Nero died in 68, the last of Augustus' line, there was no constitutional provision for the succession, and civil war broke out. Galba, Otho, and Vitellius were successively and very briefly made emperor by provincial armies until stability was restored under the wise and efficient rule of Vespasian (69–79) and his sons, Titus and Domitian (although Domitian's final years were despotic). Vespasian restored by prudent economy the finances which had been utterly disorganized by the prodigality of Nero and by the civil war, strengthened the existing frontiers, and admitted more provincials into the senate so that it became more representative of the empire. Vespasian's son Domitian was succeeded by Nerva, who ruled briefly (96–8) and then by Trajan (98–117). Under Trajan, Hadrian (117–38), and the *Antonines (138–92) the Roman empire reached its greatest extent—stretching from Scotland to North Africa and from Spain to the Persian Gulf—and its peak of peace of prosperity. In a famous passage in his *Decline and Fall of the Roman Empire* Edward Gibbon memorably evoked this age: 'If a man were called to fix the period in the history of the world, during which the condition of the human race was most happy and prosperous, he would, without hesitation, name that which elapsed from the death of Domitian [96] to the accession of Commodus [180].'

As the quotation from Gibbon suggests, it is with Commodus (180–92) that

the decline of the empire is usually said to begin. After his murder there was civil war, but Septimius Severus (193–211) established a new dynasty, which ruled until 235. His son Caracalla (211–17) extended Roman citizenship to all freemen throughout the empire. When the last of the dynasty, his cousin Alexander Severus (222–35), was murdered, military anarchy followed, with emperors succeeding one another rapidly and increasingly bad government in the provinces. The frontiers were under pressure from the enemies—particularly the Goths in the north—who would eventually overrun the empire. Diocletian (284–305) divided the empire into four administrative units—two eastern and two western—ruled by joint emperors. Constantine (306–37) restored the unity of the empire and moved his capital to Constantinople. Theodosius I (379–95) was, however, the last ruler of a unified Roman state, the division between east and west becoming permanent at his death. In 402 the capital of the western empire was moved from Rome to Ravenna, and Rome was sacked by Visigoths in 410 and Vandals in 455. The last Roman emperor in the west, Romulus Augustulus, was deposed in 476 by Odoacer, who became the first barbarian king of Italy.

For a period of almost a thousand years after this, Rome degenerated, and—even though it was the seat of the papacy—it was of only marginal or intermittent importance in European affairs. Its history from the fifth to the early fifteenth century is one of extraordinary strife and chaos, and it was sacked by the Arabs in 846 and the Normans in 1084. The population, which at the height of the Roman empire probably reached a million, had dropped by the fourteenth century to about 20,000. Large areas within the ancient walls were densely wooded and inhabited by wild beasts, and sometimes only the tops of ancient buildings projected above piles of debris. It was Pope Martin V (reigned 1417–31) who began the restoration of Rome to a great city.

Ro'mulus, the legendary founder of Rome, his name being a back-formation from that of the city. He and his twin brother Remus were grandchildren of Numitor, king of Alba Longa, who had been deposed by his brother Amulius. To ensure that Numitor's only child, Rhea Silvia, did not marry and produce an heir, Amulius made her a Vestal Virgin, but her twins were fathered by the god Mars. Amulius imprisoned the mother and threw the children into the Tiber. They were washed ashore and suckled by a she-wolf until discovered by the royal herdsman Faustulus, who with his wife Acca Larentia brought them up. They were eventually recognized, overthrew Amulius, and restored Numitor to his kingdom. They then decided to found a new settlement where they had been washed ashore. An omen in the form of a flight of birds settled the kingship in favour of Romulus. He proceeded to build the city named after him on the Palatine Hill; the traditional date for his foundation is 753 BC. Remus showed his contempt for it by jumping over the beginnings of the city wall, and was thereupon killed by Romulus or one of his companions. Romulus expanded his new city by encouraging runaway slaves and even criminals to settle there. To secure wives for his people he invited the neighbouring *Sabines to witness games, and while these were proceeding the Romans carried off the Sabine women ('the Rape of the Sabines'). War followed, but eventually the two peoples settled down together. Romulus ruled for forty years and then disappeared from the earth, enveloped in a cloud during a thunderstorm. His divinity was at once proclaimed by those who witnessed the miracle (see QUIRINUS). The story of Romulus was well known by the beginning of the third century BC, and is retold by, for example, Livy and Plutarch.

Ro'mulus Augu'stulus, last emperor of Rome, AD 475–6; see FALL OF ROME.

Ro'scius Gallus, Quintus (d. 62 BC), the most famous comic actor of his day at Rome, although he also played tragic roles. He amassed great wealth and was on intimate terms with Catullus and Sulla; Cicero defended him in a private suit (see *PRO ROSCIO COMOEDO*). Though handsome he had a squint, and to conceal it is reported to have introduced into Rome the wearing of masks when acting, wigs having been worn previously. The name of Roscius is occasionally used in English literature to denote a great actor.

Rosetta Stone, slab of black basalt now in the British Museum on which is inscribed an Egyptian decree of 197 BC honouring the king Ptolemy V Epiphanēs. The inscription is given in three versions, Greek and two forms of Egyptian: hieroglyphics ('picture-writing') and demotic, the simplified form of hieroglyphic in common use. The discovery of the stone in Egypt in 1799 made possible the eventual decipherment of hieroglyphics by the French scholar Jean-François Champollion (1790–1832).

Rostra, at Rome, the platform in the *Forum from which speakers addressed the people. It took its name from the bronze prows (*rostra*) of the Latin ships captured at Antium in 338 BC during Rome's Latin War, with which it was decorated. On it were placed statues of famous men. Here too was erected Rome's first sundial (see CLOCKS).

Roxa'na (Rōxănē), wife of *Alexander the Great.

Ru'bicon, small Italian river, reddish in colour (hence the name, from *rubicundus*, 'ruddy'), falling into the Adriatic and marking the boundary in republican times between Italy and the province of Cisalpine Gaul. Julius Caesar, by crossing the river into Italy in 49 BC without disbanding his army as the senate had ordered, effectively declared war on Pompey and the senate. Suetonius gives Caesar the words, *iacta alea est*, 'the die is cast'. 'Crossing the Rubicon' is proverbial for taking an irrevocable decision.

Rudens ('rope'), romantic comedy by *Plautus adapted from a Greek comedy by Diphilus (see COMEDY, GREEK 6). This is one of Plautus' best plays, with a well-integrated plot, interesting characterization, and lively dialogue.

The prologue is spoken by the star Arcturus. The scene is the rocky coast of Cyrēnē near a temple of Venus and the country house of an elderly Athenian, Daemonēs, whose daughter Palaestra was stolen from him in her childhood.

She has fallen into the hands of a young pimp, Labrax of Cyrene; a young Athenian, Plesidippus, has fallen in love with her, and made part-payment for her purchase. But Labrax has thought to improve his fortunes by secretly carrying the girl off to Sicily. Thereupon Arcturus has raised a storm and wrecked the ship near the scene of the play. Palaestra and another girl reach land in a boat and are kindly tended by the priestess of Venus. Labrax is also washed ashore; he discovers the girls and tries to carry them off from the temple. They are defended by Daemones and presently rescued by Plesidippus, who marches Labrax off to justice. A box belonging to Labrax is pulled from the sea in the net of a fisher-man, who quarrels over it with a slave of Plesidippus while hauling on the rope (*rudens*) of the net; the quarrel leads to the discovery in the box not only of the gold of Labrax but also of trinkets belonging to Palaestra, which show her to be the lost daughter of Daemones. There is joyful recognition, followed by the betrothal of Palaestra to Plesidippus.

Rufus, Quintus Cu'rtius, see CURTIUS.

Rumī'na, in Roman religion, goddess who protected mothers suckling their children. She had a sanctuary at the foot of the Palatine hill, where the *ficus Ruminalis* stood, the fig-tree under which *Romulus and Remus were supposed to have been suckled by the wolf.

S

Sabā'zios, Phrygian god introduced to Athens in the fifth century BC. He was sometimes identified with the Greek god Dionysus. Aristophanes refers to him, and is said to have written a comedy (now lost) in which Sabazios and other foreign gods are brought to trial and expelled from the state. His worship seems to have had connections with that of the Magna Mater ('great mother'; see CYBELE), and private mysteries were celebrated in his honour. Practically nothing is known of his rites until the time of the Roman empire, when his worship was widely spread in Italy. His chief attribute was the snake.

Sabe'lli, collective name given by the Romans to the tribes of central Italy who spoke the *Oscan-type Italic languages. They include Samnites and Apulians. The Sabelli moved outwards from their original Sabine homeland, imposing their language upon the populations they settled among; these migrations continued into the fourth century BC.

Sabines (Lat. Sabini), an Italian people living north-east of Rome in early times, famous for their bravery, simple morality, and strong religious feelings. Many traditional stories, particularly relating to Roman religious institutions, indicate a Sabine element in the early development of Rome, probably arising rather from amalgamation than from conquest. However, Livy records numerous Roman wars against the Sabines, ending in 449 BC with a resounding Roman victory. In 290 BC M'. Curius Dentatus conquered them, and they were absorbed into the Roman state, receiving full citizenship in 268. For the Rape of the Sabines see ROMULUS. See also TITUS TATIUS.

Sacred Band (*hieros lochos*), at *Thebes, an élite corps of 300 hoplites chosen from noble families and professionally trained, formed in 378 BC by the general Gorgidas to defend Thebes against Sparta's highly trained army. The special character of the Sacred Band derived from its being composed of 150 pairs of lovers, each member bound to the other by strong emotional ties of love and loyalty. The corps had a notable leader in *Pelopidas. It was partly responsible for the Theban victories over Sparta at Leuctra in 371 and Mantinea in 362, but it was too small to carry a battle by itself, as was shown at the battle of Chaeronea in 338 when Athens and Thebes were beaten by Philip II 'of Macedon. The Band did not share in the general flight but fought to the death.

Sacred Wars, name given to wars waged by the *Amphictyony (i.e. league of neighbouring states) of Delphi for the protection of Apollo's shrine there and for the punishment of sacrilege. The First Sacred War in the early sixth century BC arose from a quarrel between Delphi and neighbouring *Crisa concerning Crisa's right to exact tolls from pilgrims. Crisa was destroyed and its fertile plain dedicated to Apollo, with an undertaking that it would never be cultivated.

The Second Sacred War occurred in 448 BC when the Phocians seized control of Delphi, the Spartans intervened to restore the sanctuary to the Delphians, and Athens under Pericles reinstated Phocis. It is not known when Delphi was once again liberated, but under the terms of the Peace of Nicias between Athens and Sparta its independence was guaranteed (421 BC; see PELOPONNESIAN WAR).

The Third Sacred War (355–352 BC) was touched off when Thebes, then in control of the Amphictyony, persuaded it to impose a heavy fine on the Phocians for cultivating the Crisaean plain (see above). The Phocians refused to pay and seized Delphi (356); in 355 the Amphictyony declared war on Phocis. Most of the Greek states became involved and the war was indecisive until Philip II of Macedon intervened, turning the scales against Phocis. In 346, after the Peace of

Philocratēs between Athens and Macedon, Phocis was isolated and surrendered to Philip, who took her place on the Amphictyonic Council.

In 338 an Amphictyonic war was once more a pretext for the invasion of Greece by Philip, this time with momentous results. Philip captured Amphissa, and then turned on Thebes, now allied with Athens, and won the victory at Chaeronea which gave him the hegemony of Greece.

Sacred Way, at Rome, see VIA SACRA; at Athens, the road to Eleusis, leaving the Ceramicus by the Sacred Gate (see MYSTERIES).

saga, see MYTHOLOGY.

Sagu'ntum (Sagunto), city in Spain about 30 km. (19 miles) north of Valencia. Its alliance with Rome, and its later capture by Hannibal, in 219 BC after a siege, were the immediate cause of the Second *Punic War (218–201). It was recaptured by Rome in 212.

Sa'lamis. 1. Island separated by a narrow channel from the south-west coast of Attica, near Piraeus. In Greek myth it was the home of Telamon, father of Ajax. It originally belonged to Aegina, was occupied by Megara c.600 BC but was soon after conquered by Athens as a result of a stirring appeal by *Solon, thereafter sharing her fortunes. It was the scene in September 480 BC of the great naval defeat of Persia by the Greeks (see PERSIAN WARS), and it was the birthplace of Euripides.

2. In Greek times the principal city of Cyprus, on the east coast, said to have been founded by Telamon's son *Teucer.

Sale of Lives, see LUCIAN.

Sa'lii, the Salian priests at Rome, so called from the verb *salire,* 'to dance'. They were an ancient college (see COLLEGIUM) of twelve, later twenty-four, priests of Mars; they were required to be of *patrician birth and have both parents living. They wore a striking costume consisting of the old (perhaps Bronze Age) Italian war-dress, with sword, bronze breast-plate, short military cloak, and the distinctive spiked head-dress, the *apex.* They carried in their right hands a spear or staff, and on their left arms the sacred figure-of-eight shields, *ancilia.* They were prominent during March and October (the months that marked the beginning and end of the campaigning season), on certain days going in procession through the city, halting at certain places and performing elaborate ritual dances, beating their shields with their staves and singing the *carmen saliare* ('salian song') in the saturnian metre (see METRE, LATIN 1), a song so ancient that according to Quintilian in the first century AD it had become almost unintelligible even to the priests themselves. A few fragments of it survive. Compare ARVAL PRIESTS.

Sallust (Gaius Sallustius Crispus) (86–35 BC), Roman historian. He was born at Amiternum in the Sabine country, of a plebeian family. He was tribune of the *plebs* in 52 BC, when he acted against *Cicero ((1) 4) and *Milo. It is said that the hostility he showed to Milo after the murder of Clodius in that year was the result of his being horse-whipped by Milo when caught in the act of adultery with the latter's wife. He was expelled from the senate in 50 BC, perhaps for playing a part in fomenting the riots of 52. He then joined Julius Caesar, commanding a legion in 49. Elected praetor in 47 he became governor of the province of Numidia in 46, where he enriched himself considerably at the provincials' expense and was (unsuccessfully) charged with extortion upon his return to Rome. He became the owner of fine gardens, *horti Sallustiāni,* withdrew from public life, and devoted the rest of his life to writing historical monographs, the *Bellum Catilīnae, Bellum Iugurthīnum* (see CATILINE and JUGURTHA) and the *Historiae* of the period 78–67 BC (the years following the abdication of Sulla). The first two works and fragments of the third have survived.

Sallust's work shows an advance on his annalistic predecessors (see HISTORIOGRAPHY 2) both in narrative powers and in its more scientific method: he endeavours to explain the causes of political events and the motives for men's actions. His weaknesses lie in his vagueness and inaccuracy in chronological and geographical matters, and in his biased attitude to the *populares* and his hostility to the *nobilēs*, natural perhaps for a **novus homo*. Nevertheless he can recognize merit in political adversaries and faults in his own side. His characters, notably those of Jugurtha and Catiline, Marius, and Sulla, are vividly drawn. For his history of Catiline he must have relied heavily on Cicero ((1) 2) as well as his own recollections of events; for Jugurtha he used a variety of sources, including the autobiography of Sulla and the *History* of Sisenna; he had gathered information while in Africa and had had Punic documents translated. In selecting Catiline and Jugurtha as subjects he was influenced, as he says himself, by the striking and potentially dangerous nature of their actions. All his monographs have a common theme, namely the struggle of the *populares*, at successive stages, against the entrenched nobles. His principal models were Thucydides and the Elder Cato, his narrative enlivened by speeches (in the manner of Thucydides), letters, digressions, and character studies. His political thought is not profound but reflects an essentially Roman moralistic outlook, with emphasis on traditional *virtus* ('virtue'), and a pessimistic attitude towards contemporary corruption. He furnishes us with the starting-point of the late republic, dating Rome's moral collapse from the return of Sulla's booty-laden troops from the East and their bloody seizure of Rome.

The ancient critics noted the characteristics of his style: the use of archaisms, brevity to the point of obscurity, innovative vocabulary, Graecisms, epigrams, rapidity. In these respects he influenced the style of later historical writers, notably Tacitus.

Sa'lmacis, SEE HERMAPHRODITUS.

Salmō'neus, in Greek myth, son of *Aeolus (2) and father of *Tyro, and consequently the ancestor of Pelias and Jason (SEE ARGONAUTS). He is placed by Virgil in the lowest depths of Tartarus because of his impious arrogance in claiming to be the equal or even the superior of Zeus, driving about in a chariot of bronze to imitate thunder and throwing firebrands to imitate lightning.

Zeus destroyed him and his city with a thunderbolt.

Sā'mia, Greek comedy by *Menander, produced probably between 317 and 307 BC; a considerable part of it has been recovered in modern times from a papyrus.

While two neighbours, Demeas and Nicēratus, are abroad, the latter's daughter Plangon gives birth to a baby by Demeas' son Moschion. A marriage is arranged, and Demeas' mistress Chrȳsis, who has suffered a miscarriage, agrees to keep the baby and pass it off as her own by Demeas. The neighbours return; Demeas overhears an old woman speak of the baby as Moschion's and concludes that since Moschion wants to marry Plangon he was unwillingly seduced by Chrysis. Demeas drives Chrysis and the baby out of the house whereupon they are taken in by Niceratus; both fathers are bewildered by conflicting evidence as to the identity of the baby's parents. Moschion, in despair, prepares to go abroad as a soldier, but eventually all is sorted out and the marriage takes place. (The happy resolution of the plot is lost.)

Samnium, an *Oscan-speaking region in the southern Apennines, whose inhabitants (Samnites) were particularly warlike. They were finally subdued by the Romans in 290 BC. See also SABELLI.

Sāmos, Ionian island off the south-wêst coast of Asia Minor, between Ephesus and Milētus. Its most flourishing period was in the second half of the sixth century BC under the tyranny of Polycratēs. It was famous for its navy, metalwork, and woollen products. Samos joined the *Delian League, revolted from Athens in 441 BC, and was reduced by Pericles himself. During the oligarchic revolution of the *Four Hundred in 411, the Athenian fleet was stationed at Samos, and the island was the centre of the democratic movement that overthrew the oligarchy. Alone among the subject allies of Athens Samos did not revolt at the end of the *Peloponnesian War for which the Samians were rewarded with Athenian citizenship; but the city was reduced by the Spartan general *Lysander in 404. Subsequently it fell into the power of Persia; it was captured for Athens in 365 by *Timotheus (2), and *cleruchs were settled on the land of exiled Samians. These were ousted by Alexander the Great and the exiles restored. Samos was the birthplace of Pythagoras and the astronomer Conon.

Samo'sata, city on the right bank of the Euphrates, the birthplace of *Lucian, and the capital of the kings of Commagēnē, a territory in north Syria.

sapphic, see METRE, GREEK 8 (i).

Sappho, Greek lyric poetess, born in the late seventh century BC at Eresus in *Lesbos, a contemporary of the Lesbian poet Alcaeus. Her father was Scamandronymus, her mother Clēis. While still young she went into exile in Sicily, presumably because of political troubles in Lesbos. (A statue of her erected in Sicily in the fourth century BC was stolen by the notorious Roman governor Verres.) She returned to spend the rest of her life at Mytilene. She had three brothers, one of whom, Charaxus, a merchant, sailed with a cargo of wine to Naucratis in Egypt and there became expensively entangled with an Egyptian courtesan named Doricha (Herodotus, who refers to the story at 2. 135, confuses Doricha with *Rhodopis). Sappho is said to have expressed strong disapproval of the affair. She married Cercylas and had a daughter Cleis. A famous story, perhaps originating in Greek comedy, related that she fell in love with a certain *Phaon who rejected her and in consequence she threw herself off the cliff of Leucas (an island off the west coast of Greece). The date of her death is unknown.

Sappho's poetry, which was almost entirely monody (see LYRIC POETRY), was divided into nine books according to metre; book 1 consisted of poems in the sapphic metre (see METRE, GREEK 8 (i)), book 2 of poems in dactylic pentameters, and so on. The ninth book contained those *Epithalamia which did not fit into the other books for metrical and other reasons. Her dialect was the Lesbian vernacular, a branch of Aeolic Greek (see DIALECTS). Of her poems only the address to Aphroditē is certainly complete; some passages have been preserved in quotations, but for the most part the poems are known from papyrus fragments discovered in the twentieth century (see PAPYROLOGY). Her subject-matter seems to be almost entirely confined to her personal world of family and female friends.

Sappho was apparently the leading personality among a circle of women and girls who must have comprised her audience. Whether she was in some formal sense their teacher or mentor remains unclear, but it seems unlikely that they were bound by a common cult of Aphrodite and the Muses, as has been suggested. She was on intimate terms with them and wrote with great simplicity but passionate intensity about her love (and occasionally her hate) for individuals. Her two most famous poems are, first, the address to Aphrodite mentioned above in which she summons the goddess in a style reminiscent of a cult-song and asks to be delivered from unrequited love for a girl; and secondly a declaration of love for a girl, the mere sight of whom moves Sappho intensely while a young man sitting beside her seems godlike in his indifference (Catullus translated this in his poem 51). There are no explicit references to physical relations in the surviving fragments, although the poet *Anacreon a generation later seems to be indicating maliciously that the name of the island connotes female homosexuality. The Epithalamia are different in tone, in some ways more formal and less personal, and contain elements from Lesbian folk song; but they too have a deceptive simplicity. Sappho created a form of subjective personal lyric never equalled in the ancient world in its immediacy and intensity.

Sarā'pis, see SERAPIS.

Sarpē'don, in Homer's *Iliad*, son of Zeus and *Laodamia, leader (with *Glaucus (3), his friend and comrade in battle) of the Lycians, and the best warrior among the allies of the Trojans. His death by the spear of Patroclus (*Iliad* 16) is movingly recounted. His father Zeus had wanted to avert his death, but allowed it after being rebuked by Hera. He ordered Apollo to carry Sarpedon's body off the battlefield, and Sleep and Death bore it to Lycia for burial. According to another version Sarpedon was the son of Zeus and Europa, and brother of *Minos and Rhadamanthys.

satire (Lat. *satura*, 'medley', 'farrago', from *satur*, 'full'). Quintilian claimed satire as 'entirely our own', i.e. a Roman creation: *satura quidem tota nostra est* (*Institutio oratoria* x. 1. 93). Although there were satirical elements to be found in Greek literature, notably in Attic Old Comedy (see COMEDY, GREEK 3) with Aristophanes' attacks on personalities of the day, e.g. Cleon, and in the Cynic-Stoic *diatribes of *Bion the Borysthenite and *Menippus, it was the Roman achievement to develop satire as a separate literary genre characterized by variety of subject-matter and occasionally of form (dialogue, fable, anecdote, precept, verse of various metres, combination of verse and prose). Livy (7. 2) describes as *saturae* early dramatic performances (originally put on to placate the gods at a time of plague) combining song, music, and mimetic dancing. On the one hand these contributed to the evolution of Latin comedy, on the other there developed from them the semi-dramatic, mixed literary form of 'satire', a commentary from a personal viewpoint, good-humoured, biting, or moralizing, on current topics, social life, literature, and the faults of individuals. Roman sources say *Ennius (239–169 BC) was the first to write satires in verse (among much else) but apparently without including invective or personalities. *Lucīlius (c.180–c.102 BC) was the first to confine himself entirely to this genre, and it was he who gave it its character as well as establishing the hexameter as the appropriate metre for it. All later Roman satirists regarded him as their founding father. He was followed by M. Terentius *Varro (116–27 BC), who took as a model the satires of Menippus in which prose and verse in a variety of metres were rather oddly intermingled, but who wrote in a less bitter, mildly didactic vein.

The *Satires* of Horace (see below), written in the 30s BC, show the strong influence of Lucilius but are more genial in tone, containing no dangerous invective against powerful individuals or serious vices, and the personal slant is

charmingly autobiographical. *Persius (AD 34–62) also felt Lucilius' influence, but his satires, characterized by earnest Stoic moralizing, contain no direct attacks on individuals. His editor Cornutus toned down a line of verse which the emperor Nero might have resented. Roman satire reached its peak in the *Satires* of Juvenal (published in the first part of the second century AD), whose bitter denunciations of the vice and folly of his own times (safely attached to names of people of the previous generation) embrace most men and all women.

The genre took a different direction in two brilliant Menippean satires which appeared in the reign of the emperor Nero (AD 54–68), Seneca's *Apocolocyntosis*, a caricature of the deification of the late emperor Claudius, and the *Satyricon* of *Petronius. In the fourth century AD the emperor *Julian wrote (in Greek but in the Roman tradition) the *Caesars*. The form of Menippean satire, but not the tone or purpose, was followed by *Martianus Capella in the *Marriage of Mercury and Philology* and by *Boethius in the *Consolation of Philosophy*.

Satires (*Sermōnes*), of *Horace, two books of 'discourses' (in hexameters) written in the 30s BC (the first refers to an event of 37, the second to the events of 31). See also SATIRE. In the first book Horace presents his own personality through his views on a variety of topics, moral and literary criticism, and simple autobiography (including a touching tribute to the author's father). In the second book all the satires except one are written in dialogue form. Painful invective against individuals is almost entirely absent. In this respect Horace differs markedly from his model Lucilius, as he does also in the deliberately casual and easy style of his language and metre, the hexameters conveying an impression of colloquial but urbane Latin.

Among the satires the following are notable: I. 5, 'A Journey to Brundisium' (corresponding to Lucilius' 'Journey to Sicily') describes his travels in the suite of Maecenas with the poet Virgil and the tragedian Varius Rufus; I. 6 is interesting for its autobiographical details, an account of Horace's father and of his own introduction to Maecenas; I. 9, *ibam forte via Sacra* ('I was going by chance along the Sacred Way') is an entertaining description of an encounter with a bore and the author's efforts to get rid of him; I. 8 is the least personal, a story of witches put to flight in the midst of their incantations by the sudden cracking of a wooden statue of Priapus. In the second book, the adoption of dramatic form gives life and humorous variety to the illustrations of Roman life. II. 5 is a parody of epic in which Odysseus, in a continuation of the Underworld episode in *Odyssey* 11, consults Teiresias as to the recovery of his lost fortune and receives advice in the (Roman) art (or vice) of legacy-hunting. II. 6 is the famous satire on town and country life illustrated by the fable of the town mouse and the country mouse. Alexander Pope's imitation (1738) of the last part of this satire is the best known of his *Imitations of Horace*.

Satires (*Saturae*), of *Juvenal.

Satire 1 is an introductory poem in which Juvenal explains that his subject-matter is not taken from outworn mythology but is concerned with *quidquid agunt homines* (85), 'all the activities of people'. The vices of the age provide the stimulus: *facit indignatio versum* (79), 'indignation prompts my verse'. But it is safe to write only of the dead; at the present time *probitas laudatur et alget* (74), 'honesty is praised but left out in the cold'. Satire 2 is an attack on those who give the appearance of being stern moralists but are immoral in their private lives: *nemo repente fuit turpissimus* (83), 'no one becomes vicious all at once'. Satire 3 is a picture of life at Rome and is perhaps Juvenal's best satire, imitated by Samuel Johnson in his *London* (1738). Juvenal approves of his honest friend Umbricius for fleeing to the country from the vices and perils of the city, which include 'poets reciting in the month of August'. Umbricius cannot stand the invasion of Greeks and pillories the versatile 'Greek in search of a meal', *Graeculus esuriens* (78). The honest and poor Roman has no chance in Rome: *nil habet infelix paupertas durius in se / quam quod ridiculos homines facit* (152), 'luckless poverty has no misery harder to

endure than this, that it exposes men to ridicule'. Poverty stands in the way of merit: *haut facile emergunt quorum virtutibus opstat / res angusta domi* (164), 'it is not easy for men to rise when straitened circumstances at home stand in the way of merit'. The city is described: the tall houses with pigeons nesting on the roofs, ready to fall about the ears of the inhabitants; the frequent fires, the impossibility of sleep because of the noise of wagons in the narrow, winding streets and the abuse of drovers, the danger of being crushed by a heavy load or hit by rubbish thrown down from open windows. Then the city at night: a great man passing in his scarlet cloak, with torches and a retinue of clients and slaves, the affray with a bully 'if affray it can be called, when you do all the beating and I get all the blows', *si rixa est, ubi tu pulsas, ego vapulo tantum* (289). When one is finally behind locked doors at home, there is still the danger of being murdered by a burglar.

Satire 4 is a skit on the administration of the emperor Domitian, who had to call a council meeting to consider how to dispose of a mullet too large for any dish. Satire 5 is about the humiliation of poor *clients at the tables of their rich patrons. Satire 6, the longest and most virulent of Juvenal's satires, is a denunciation of women. The poet professes astonishment that a friend should contemplate marriage when there is so much rope to be had, and then depicts, at great length, the vices of women, their insatiable and reckless sexual appetite, their extravagance, tyranny, and quarrelsomeness in the home. The jealous woman, the gossip, the virago, the athlete are among the offenders, worse are the ostentatious pedant and the superstitiously religious. If you chance on a good woman, who is a 'rare bird on earth, as common as a black swan', *rara avis in terris nigroque simillima cygno* (165), she will be haughty. It is useless to set a guard on one's wife, for 'who will guard the guards themselves?', *quis custodiet ipsos custodes*? (O 31).

Satire 7 is on the unprofitability of the literary professions and especially that of teacher (*Quintilian has been lucky). Moreover, the teacher has to endure much monotonous repetition, *crambe *repetita* (154), 'cabbage served up again and again'. Satire 8 attacks pride of ancestry. 'Virtue is the only true nobility', *nobilitas sola est atque unica virtus* (20). It is the greatest sin to prefer life to honour 'and to lose for the sake of living all that makes life worth having', *et propter vitam vivendi perdere causas* (84). Satire 9 is an attack on sexual vice, put in the mouth of a repentant sinner. In Satire 10 (the model for Samuel Johnson's poem *The Vanity of Human Wishes*, 1749) Juvenal writes on the folly of human prayers; wealth exposes a man to dangers, whereas 'the empty-handed traveller will cheerfully sing when confronted by a robber', *cantabit vacuus coram latrone viator* (22); power (consider *Sejanus), long life, and beauty are all sources of trouble. Better leave your fate to the gods, or pray for at most 'a healthy mind in a healthy body', *mens sana in corpore sano* (356), and for courage and endurance. The only things the public cares for are 'bread and circuses', *panem et circenses* (80). Satire 11 contrasts extravagance and simplicity of living; in Satire 12 Juvenal celebrates a friend's escape from shipwreck, and attacks legacy-hunters.

Satire 13 is an eloquent plea to a friend not to seek vengeance against one who has defrauded him; the guilty man will be punished by his own conscience: 'it is always the little, weak, and petty mind that delights in vengeance', *quippe minuti / semper et infirmi est animi exiguique voluptas / ultio* (189). The poet refers approvingly to the *Delphic Oracle's condemnation of a man who had merely thought of committing an offence: 'for he who secretly meditates a crime has all the guilt of having done the deed', *nam scelus intra se tacitum qui cogitat ullum, / facti crimen habet* (209). Satire 14 is about the influence of parental example in education. The parents' faults will be copied by the children: 'if you have any shameful deed in mind, the greatest reverence is owed to the young', *maxime debetur puero reverentia, siquid turpe paras* (47). In Satire 15, after describing a conflict in Egypt, resulting in an act of cannibalism, Juvenal praises tenderness of heart as the quality which distinguishes humans from beasts. Satire 16, on the abusive privileges of the military, is unfinished.

satrap, title given to a Persian provincial governor, in effect a vassal king with very wide powers; the territory he governed was known as a satrapy. *Darius divided the Persian empire into twenty satrapies which remained the basis for later territorial administration.

sa'tura, see SATIRE.

Sa'tura Meni'ppeae, see VARRO.

Saturn (Sāturnus), ancient Italian god whose original function remains obscure. He may have been a blight-god. His name has also been connected with *satus*, 'sowing', and he has been thought of as a seed-god, a supposition supported by the date of his festival (the *Saturnalia) which occurs in the calendar of *Numa on 17 December, between the Consualia for the god of the granary and the Opalia for the god of plenty. Sacrifices to him were made in the Greek manner, with head uncovered; the Romans themselves thought that he had been introduced from Greece, and identified him at an early stage with the Greek god *Cronus, the father of Zeus. Thus he came to symbolize the good old days, the *Golden Age. His temple stood at the foot of the Capitoline hill and served as the treasury (*aerarium*) of the Roman people; there too were kept the Tables of the law and the records of decrees of the senate. He was regarded as the husband of *Ops and father of *Picus.

Saturnā'lia, in Roman religion, festival celebrated from 17 to 19 December, the most cheerful of the year, a time of enjoyment, goodwill, and licence, of present-giving and lighting candles, the prototype of some aspects of the modern Christmas festivities. The holiday began with a sacrifice at the temple of Saturn followed by a public feast open to everyone. Slaves were freed from their duties and might even be waited on by their masters. Each household chose a mock king to preside over the festivities. Not everyone enjoyed it: the Younger Pliny built himself a sound-proof room to which he retired throughout the holiday. By about the fourth century AD many of these customs were transferred to New

Year's Day, and hence were added to the traditional Christmas celebrations.

Saturna'lia, dialogue by *Macrobius.

saturnian, SEE METRE, LATIN 1.

Saturnï'nus, Lucius Appule'ius, Roman statesman. As tribune of the *plebs* in 103 and 100 he co-operated with the consul *Marius to enable the latter to get land-allotments for his landless veterans, and he was able to pass other popular measures against optimate opposition, often by violence, and with the help of the praetor *Glaucia. His personal influence and his ability to act independently of Marius grew considerably. When in 99 he stood again for the tribunate and Glaucia for the consulship, a rival of Glaucia was assassinated. At this Marius dissociated himself from both of them and with the backing of the senate took action to suppress them; Saturninus and Glaucia were both killed.

satyric drama (satyr-plays). At Athens, at the dramatic festivals, each trilogy (consisting of three tragedies) was followed by a semi-comic satyr-play, written by the same author, in which the chorus was always composed of *satyrs, led by Silenus, wearing horses' tails and ears. Aristotle at one point in the *Poetics* expresses the belief that tragedy originated from this type of performance. Others believed that satyr-plays were a later development. Euripides' *Cyclops* is the only complete specimen still surviving, but substantial fragments of the *Dictyulci* ('drawers of nets') of Aeschylus and the *Ichneutae* ('trackers') of Sophocles have been found in recent times on papyrus (see PAPYROLOGY). The subject-matter of satyr-plays was a burlesque of some mythical episode appropriate to the preceding trilogy, with a certain amount of coarse language and gesturing. *Pratinas of Phlius, writing at the beginning of the fifth century in Athens, is said to have turned the satyr-play into a literary form; he is also said to have written thirty-two satyr-plays himself. Satyric drama continued to be written even in Roman times; rules for its composition are given by Horace in the *Ars poetica*.

Saty'ricōn, SEE PETRONIUS ARBITER.

satyrs (*satyroi*), in Greek mythology, attendants of the god *Dionysus, boisterous creatures of the woods and hills, represented as mainly of human form but with some bestial aspect, e.g. a horse's tail or the legs of a goat (but they are not usually represented as goats until the fourth century BC). They are lustful and fond of revelry. The Romans identified them with the Fauni (see FAUNUS). The chorus in Attic satyr-plays was dressed to represent satyrs (see SATYRIC DRAMA). See also SILENUS.

Scaean Gate, see TROY.

Scae'vola. 1. **Gaius Mu'cius Scaevola,** legendary Roman who, when Lars *Porsen(n)a, king of Clusium, was besieging Rome at the end of the sixth century BC, made his way to the enemy camp and attempted to kill Porsena. He was taken prisoner, and to show his indifference to the death with which he was threatened, thrust his right hand into the fire. The king was so impressed that he released Mucius, who thus acquired the *cognomen* Scaevola, 'left-handed'.

2. **Publius Mucius Scaevola,** see ANNALS, ANNALISTS.

3. **Quintus Mucius Scaevola** (*c.*170–87 BC), known as 'the augur', consul in 117 BC, son-in-law of *Laelius and father-in-law of L. Licinius Crassus the orator. He was a distinguished jurist and taught (among others) his son-in-law and Cicero, who greatly admired him. He is one of the interlocutors in Cicero's *De oratore*, *De amicitia*, and *De republica*.

4. **Quintus Mucius Scaevola** (*c.*140–82 BC), *pontifex maximus* in 115, consul with L. Licinius Crassus the orator in 95 BC. He was himself an orator of distinction, noted according to Cicero for the concise accuracy of his language. He published the first systematic treatise on civil law. Cicero in his youth received instruction in the law from him after the death of his relative and namesake, the augur (see 3 above). In his consulship he and Crassus passed the Licinian—Mucian law, instituting proceedings against aliens who had been illegally enrolled as citizens. This brought about the expulsion of many Italians from Rome and was in consequence a contributory cause of the Social War. Cicero remarked on the fact that

such an unfortunate measure was due to such excellent men. Scaevola was assassinated by the Marian party (see MARIUS) in the temple of Vesta.

scansion, metrical analysis of poetry into long and short (or stressed and unstressed) syllables, and metra or feet. See METRE, GREEK 1.

scāzon, see METRE, GREEK 5.

Sceptics (from Gk. *skepsis*, 'speculation'), Greek philosophers who asserted the impossibility of knowledge. As the name of a particular school of philosophy Scepticism began with Pyrrhon of Elis (*c*.365–*c*.270 BC), but sceptical attitudes were expressed by philosophers, notably the *sophists, long before that. Pyrrhon travelled to India in the train of Alexander the Great and there, tradition relates, met some 'magi' who influenced the development of his philosophical views. He returned and lived the rest of his life quietly at Elis. He left no writings, and only fragments survive of the writings of his pupils. Pyrrhon inferred from the deceptions inherent in sense-perceptions and the contradictions in the teachings of 'dogmatic' philosophers that knowledge of the true nature of things is unattainable. Hence the proper attitude is to follow the appearance of things (*phainomena*), to suspend judgement (*epochē*), and to avoid commitment, with the aim of achieving mental quietude (*ataraxia*). His most influential pupils were *Timon (2) of Phlius, Philo of Larisa (head of the *Academy at Athens in the first century BC), and Nausiphanēs of Teos; our chief source of information on the Sceptics is the lengthy account by *Sextus Empiricus (late second century AD). It remains unclear what the relationship was between Pyrrhon's Scepticism and that of the Academy at Athens, introduced by Arcesilaus (head of the Academy *c*.265 BC) and developed a century later by *Carneades. It seems probable that Arcesilaus was influenced by Pyrrhon.

Sche'ria (Scheriē), name of the island of the Phaeacians (see *Odyssey*, book 5), on the coast of which Odysseus was cast ashore. Some have identified it with Corcyra (modern Corfu).

scholasticism, see TEXTS, TRANSMISSION OF ANCIENT 7.

schō'lium, in Greek, name given in antiquity to a short explanatory note written to elucidate a difficulty in a text. The plural, scholia, is often used to describe the commentaries on classical texts written in the margins of manuscripts by ancient scholars, and copied along with the text from manuscript to manuscript. In this form they are a compilation, greatly abbreviated and sometimes garbled, made from earlier, fuller commentaries or excerpted from monographs of various dates. Thus they sometimes contain valuable information about antiquity from reliable sources which has not otherwise come down to us. The scholia to Homer, Hesiod, Pindar, Aristophanes, and the tragedians are particularly useful, and although the manuscripts in which they are found are of the later *Byzantine age, the notes sometimes go back to the great scholars of the *Hellenistic age, Zenodotus, Aristophanes (of Byzantium), and Aristarchus. There are also scholia on Latin authors, e.g. Horace.

Sci'pio. 1. **Publius Corne'lius Scipio Africā'nus Maior** (236–183 BC), Rome's greatest general in the Second *Punic War. He was the son of P. Cornelius Scipio, who was defeated by Hannibal at Tĭcīnus in 218 BC. In 210 when only about 25 his exceptional military ability brought about his appointment by the people to the command in Spain, the first *privatus*, 'private citizen', to be granted the *imperium* of a proconsul. By 206 he had driven the Carthaginians out of Spain. He was elected consul for 205, and, managing to get the better of senatorial opposition, especially that of Fabius who thought Hannibal should be defeated in Italy, crossed over to Africa with his army. He finally defeated Hannibal at the battle of Zama in 202, and earned the *cognomen* Africanus.

In 199 he was elected censor and became *princeps senatus*, 'leader of the senate'; in 194 he was consul for a second time. In 190, although nominally merely the legate of his brother Lucius in the command against Antiochus of Syria, he led the first Roman army into Asia. When the brothers returned to Rome, political attacks, directed by *Cato the Censor, were launched against them both, accusing them of misconduct in public affairs. A series of trials resulted, and although at the last the charges were not pressed home (Scipio is said at one point to have reminded the people that the day of the trial was the anniversary of Zama) the influence of the Scipios was broken, and Africanus retired to his estate at Līternum in Campania, where he died. The Younger Seneca in Epistle 86 vividly evokes the simplicity of his life there. Like many members of his family he was an ardent philhellene; that and his military brilliance and magnetic personality prompted comparisons with Alexander the Great. He married Aemilia, sister of L. Aemilius *Paullus; one of his daughters was *Cornelia, mother of the Gracchi.

2. Publius Cornelius Scipio Aemiliā'nus, known as Africanus Minor (*c*.185–129 BC), Roman general and statesman. He was the second son of L. Aemilius *Paullus, the conqueror of Macedonia, and was adopted by P. Scipio, the son of Scipio Africanus Major (see (1) above). He fought under his father at the battle of Pydna in 168 BC, to end the Third Macedonian War, destroyed Carthage in 146 to end the Third *Punic War, and brought the long and costly war in Spain against the Numantines to a successful conclusion in 133. At his return to Rome in 132 he took the lead amongst those opposed to the radical reforms of the *Gracchi but died suddenly in 129 at the height of the political unrest. It was suspected that he had been murdered, perhaps by his wife Sempronia, sister of the Gracchi. He was a great orator, the leading figure in the philhellenic circle at Rome, and a patron of Greek and Latin literature and learning; his friends included Polybius, Panaetius, Lucilius, Terence, and Laelius. His combination of intellectual and active virtues, of high culture with outstanding military and political success, moved Cicero to unbounded admiration of him as the ideal statesman. Cicero made him the central character in *De republica* and *De senectute*. His *De amicitia* dwells on the friendship of Scipio and Laelius.

3. Publius Cornelius Scipio Nasi'ca Sera'pio, consul in 138 BC, a man of strongly conservative and aristocratic views. In 133 he vigorously opposed his cousin Ti. *Gracchus, and was leader of the group of senators and clients who attacked and killed him. In later times the deed sharply divided the *optimatēs* who approved and the *populārēs* who condemned it.

Scipio's Dream, see SOMNIUM SCIPIONIS.

Scīron, in Greek legend, a brigand who preyed on travellers along the cliff road from Athens to Megara. He made them wash his feet, and as they did so he kicked them over the cliff, where, according to some, they were eaten by a giant tortoise. *Theseus on his way to Athens threw Sciron over the edge, and his bones were turned into the cliffs which bear his name.

Sciropho'ria, Athenian festival, also called Scira, celebrated on the twelfth Scirophorion (midsummer). Many aspects of it were even in late antiquity a matter of dispute, including the meaning of the name, and remain so in modern times. It seems to have been a women's festival, dedicated to Demeter, or perhaps to Athena, in the course of which various offerings, including piglets, were thrown into a pit and recovered three months later at the *Thesmophoria.

sco'lia (from *skolios*, 'crooked'), at a Greek banquet or drinking-party, short songs sung by guests in succession but in random order, 'crookedly'. These songs were accompanied by the lyre. *Athenaeus (book 15) preserves a collection of anonymous Attic scolia of the late sixth and early fifth centuries BC. They either comment on some historical incident (such as the assassination attempt of *Harmodius and Aristogeiton) or contain some personal sentiment or comment on life. The singer held a myrtle branch while he sang, and when he had finished passed the branch to another. Tradition makes *Terpander the originator of the scolion.

Scōpads, Scōpas, see CRANNON and SIMONIDES.

Scopas, of Paros, eminent sculptor of the early fourth century BC, notable for his power of expressing violent emotion. He worked on the Mausoleum at Halicarnassus (see MAUSOLUS), and three relief slabs from it portraying the Battle of Greeks and Amazons (British Museum) are very plausibly attributed to him.

Scribo'nia, wife of *Octavian (later the emperor Augustus). She was married at least three times; by one of her first two husbands she became the mother of that Cornelia whose premature death occasioned an elegy of consolation from Propertius (IV. 11). Octavian married her for political reasons in 40 BC, but divorced her in 39 after the birth of their daughter Julia. She accompanied Julia into exile in 2 BC and remained with her until the latter's death in AD 14. She herself was still alive in 16.

scripts, see BOOKS AND WRITING.

Scȳlax, of Caryanda in Caria, sent by the Persian king Darius (521–486 BC) on a voyage of exploration from the Indus round the coast of Arabia. The voyage has been doubted, but the book Scylax wrote afterwards (*Periplus*, 'voyage') is apparently quoted by *Hecataeus as well as later authors. The surviving *Periplus* attributed to him dates from the fourth century BC.

Scylla. 1. In Greek myth, daughter of *Phorcys and *Hecatē. She was sometimes described as originally human but turned into a monster by a rival in love. She is represented as having six heads, each with a triple row of teeth, and twelve feet; she lived in a cave (traditionally situated in the Straits of Messina between Sicily and Italy) with the whirlpool of Charybdis opposite. Her diet was fish but she devoured sailors if a ship came near. Homer describes the passage of Odysseus' ship past the cave in *Odyssey* 12. To be 'between Scylla and Charybdis' is to be in a situation where the two possible courses of action are equally dangerous.

2. Daughter of Nīsus, king of Megara, which was besieged by *Minos of Crete. Nisus was inviolable and the city safe as long as a red or purple lock among his white hair remained intact. Scylla cut it off and thus killed him in order to deliver the city to the besiegers, either out of love for Minos or because she had been bribed. Minos was horrified at the deed and drowned her (or she drowned herself). Nisus was turned into an osprey and Scylla into a sea-bird (*ciris*), ever pursued with hatred by her father.

The Latin poets Virgil, Ovid, and Propertius sometimes confuse the two Scyllas.

Seasons (Horai), in Greek myth, daughters of Zeus and *Themis, attendants on the gods and generally three in number (spring, summer, winter). The first two are more often invoked since they are thought of as the goddesses of life and growth, and they are often associated with Aphroditē and the Graces.

Second Sophistic, see SOPHISTIC, SECOND.

seisachthei'a, see SOLON.

Sējā'nus, Lucius Ae'lius (d. AD 31), Roman statesman. He was appointed prefect of *praetorians in AD 14 and exercised a steadily increasing influence over the emperor Tiberius. When the latter's son Drusus died suddenly in 23, Sejanus was suspected of poisoning him and of hoping to bring about a dynastic marriage with his widow, Livilla. His background, however, was too humble for the emperor to accede to this request. When at his persuasion Tiberius withdrew to Capri in 27 Sejanus became all-powerful. Tiberius, however, denounced him in a letter to the senate (the poet Juvenal's *verbosa et grandis epistula*, 'long-winded and lengthy letter') and Sejanus was brought before the senate, condemned of plotting to overthrow the emperor, and executed. It is said that after his execution his body was torn to pieces by the people whose hatred he had incurred, and thrown into the Tiber. Ben Jonson's *Sejanus his Fall* was produced in 1603 with Shakespeare in the cast.

Selē'nē, in Greek myth, the moon-goddess (Roman Luna), according to Hesiod the daughter of the *Titans Hyperion and Theia and sister of Helios and Eos (Sun and Dawn); but some authorities give different genealogies. She has little cult and few myths (but see ENDYMION). She is sometimes identified with the goddess Artemis, perhaps because both had been identified with *Hecatē.

Seleu'cids, dynasty which eventually obtained Syria and much of Asia as its share in the empire of Alexander the Great (see DIADOCHOI). The founder of the dynasty was Seleucus I (*c*.358–281 BC), an officer of Alexander, who, after the latter's death, received the governorship of Babylonia (321). After a shaky beginning, by the end of the fourth century he had extended his rule eastwards over all Alexander's provinces as far as India. In 281 Seleucus acquired northern and central Asia Minor by defeating and killing Lysimachus (another of Alexander's generals) at the battle of Corupedium. Now entertaining the hope of winning *Macedonia, the possession of which was still undecided, he invaded Europe, but was assassinated by Ptolemy Ceraunus, a son of Ptolemy I of Egypt. His most remarkable successor was Antiochus III (the Great, 223–187). His expansionist policy in the West (he invaded Europe in 196 to recover Thrace), led him into conflict with Rome, and after losing three battles against the Romans he was forced to evacuate all Asia Minor west of Mount Taurus. Thereafter, despite its Mediterranean seaboard, the Seleucid empire ceased to be a Mediterranean power. It broke up through dynastic wars into a multitude of free cities and small kingdoms and territory was lost to the Parthians in the east. Finally, in 64 BC Syria was annexed to Rome by Pompey. The importance of the Seleucids lies in their Hellenization of Asia, particularly in founding scores of cities, more or less Greek in character; Seleucus I founded Antioch on the Orontēs as his Syrian capital and Seleucia on the Tigris as the capital of his empire.

sella curū'lis, see CURULE MAGISTRACIES.

Se'melē, see DIONYSUS.

Semnai, see FURIES.

Sēmō'nidēs (mid-seventh century BC), Greek iambic and elegiac poet originally of Samos but always connected with Amorgos (an island of the Sporades in the Aegean Sea), in the colonization of which he is said to have joined. Very few fragments of his poetry survive. The longest piece, in iambics (see METRE, GREEK 5), describes various types of women by comparing them with animals. There is also a piece of elegiac verse on the shortness of life. Semonides writes with satirical humour in the Ionic *dialect.

sēnā'rius, see METRE, GREEK 5 and LATIN 2.

senate (*senātus*), the legislative council of Rome, in origin the council of the kings which survived the abolition of the monarchy in 510 BC. The number of members first attested is 300, increased by Sulla to 600, by Julius Caesar to 900, and reduced by Augustus again to 600. It was at first a purely *patrician body and it became in practice an assembly of ex-magistrates. Senators received no payment. Although a property qualification was not stipulated until the time · of Augustus, senators were usually rich men from important families (see OPTIMATES, NOBILES, NOVUS HOMO), and membership of the senate tended to be hereditary. Owing to its functions and permanence the senate was the real head of the state. It prepared legislative proposals to be brought before the people, and its resolutions, called *decreta* or, more commonly, *senatus consulta*, had some measure of effective if not legal authority (they could be vetoed by the tribunes). It administered the finances, assigned magistrates to provinces, and dealt with foreign relations. It also supervised the practice of the state religion. Since it was a body of ex-magistrates, serious clashes were avoided between the *imperium of the magistrates and the authority of the senate, and in general it exercised strong control over holders of office, tending to use them as its tools. The collapse of the republic came about when the authority of the senate was powerless against military leaders backed by their armies. Under the empire, although the senate lost its sovereign power, it was not without important functions, and *Augustus endeavoured to share with it the administration of the state. But in fact, partly owing to its own inefficiency, its power gradually diminished.

The senate met for business either in the Curia (senate house), which stood in the Forum, or within a mile of the city in a consecrated place. The first sitting of the year was in the temple of Jupiter Capitolinus. When a decision had to be reached each senator was asked his opinion according to his rank, censors followed by consuls, praetors, aediles, etc., patricians taking precedence over plebeians in each category. The senator heading the list was known as the *princeps senatus*, 'leader of the senate'.

senā'tūs consu'ltum u'ltimum ('the final resolution of the senate'), issued to the magistrates in a grave emergency, authorizing the consuls to use force for the protection of the state and suspending the right of appeal to the people. It was first used in 122 BC against C. *Gracchus, and, among other occasions, against *Saturninus in 100 and *Catiline in 63. It was last employed (against Salvidienus Rufus) in 40 BC. The senate's legal right to enforce such a measure was always contested by the *populares*, for example in connection with C. Rabirius, who in 63 BC was defended by *Cicero.

Se'neca, Lucius Annae'us. 1. 'The Elder' or the 'Rhetorician', born at Corduba (Cordoba) in Spain *c*.55 BC of Italian stock and educated at Rome. He died between AD 37 and 41, before the exile of his son and namesake (see (2) below). The Elder Seneca devoted himself to the study of rhetoric, and in his old age assembled for his sons a collection of *Controversiae* ('debates') and *Suasoriae* ('speeches of advice'). These were model exercises on rhetorical themes used in the schools of rhetoric: the former covered the oratory of the law-courts and took the form of debates about imaginary problems in criminal or civil cases, e.g. whether a soldier has committed sacrilege by fighting bravely with weapons taken from a hero's tomb after losing his own; the latter were exercises in deliberative (political) oratory and were speeches on such themes as whether 300 Spartans at Thermopylae (see PERSIAN WARS) should fight the Persians or run away. All the examples, dating from the time of Cicero to Seneca's old age, are extracts from rhetoricians whom Seneca had heard dur-

ing his long life, a testimony to his astonishing memory (which he himself tells us was unrivalled) and an invaluable source for literary history. Of particular interest are the prefaces to the *Controversiae* where he discusses various orators, their analyses (*divisiones*) and lines of approach (*colores*) to the debates that follow, with many digressions and anecdotes. Only five of the original ten books of *Controversiae* and one book of *Suasoriae* are extant.

2. 'The Younger' or 'the Philosopher' (*c*.4 BC–AD 65).

1. He was the second son of Seneca the Elder (see above) and was born at Corduba (Cordoba) in Spain. He was brought as a child to Rome and educated there in rhetoric and philosophy. Embarking on a senatorial career he became an advocate, quaestor, and senator, and achieved a considerable reputation as an orator and writer, so much so that he provoked the jealousy of the emperor Caligula and in 39 narrowly escaped being put to death. Under Claudius, Seneca occupied a position at court. In 41 he was banished to Corsica for alleged adultery with Julia (sometimes called Livilla), the youngest daughter of Germanicus and Agrippina the Elder, and sister of Caligula. Julia's sister, also called Agrippina (the Younger), mother of *Nero, had him recalled in 49 and he was made tutor to the young Nero. In 51 Burrus, who was to become Seneca's friend and colleague, was made prefect of praetorians. On the accession of Nero in 54 Seneca became the emperor's political adviser, and for the next few years Rome and the empire enjoyed good government, largely under the direction of Seneca and Burrus. But Nero's behaviour became increasingly wilful, and after the death of Burrus in 62 the willingness of others to condone the emperor's excesses reduced Seneca's influence and he asked permission to retire. He left Rome and devoted the next three years to philosophy and his friends. In 65 he was implicated in the unsuccessful conspiracy of Piso against Nero's life and forced to commit suicide. His courageous death is described by Tacitus (*Annals* 15. 64).

The inconsistencies between Seneca's

moral principles, his political life, and the behaviour of his pupil emperor have provoked much speculation, and he has been severely judged. He would appear to have condoned the murders of Claudius, Britannicus, and Agrippina, and he certainly acquired enormous wealth at a court where his professed moral principles were utterly ignored. He conformed to his principles too late to save his reputation. However, he was a humane and tolerant man, for many years a successful politician and an influence for good, and a writer of considerable and varied talent.

2. Seneca wrote voluminously. Besides the works that survive we have titles or fragments of treatises on geography, natural history, and ethics, among many others. His extant prose works comprise, first, the ten ethical treatises given the name *Dialogi* ('dialogues'): *De providentia, De constantia sapientis, De ira* (in three books), *De consolatione ad Marciam, De vita beata, De otio, De tranquillitate animi, De brevitate vitae, De consolatione ad Polybium, De consolatione ad Helviam matrem*. These seem to have been written between 37 and 43. The 'Consolation to Marcia' is an attempt to console the daughter of Cremutius Cordus (a historian, victim of Sejanus) for the death of her sons. The 'Consolation to Helvia' written to his mother to console her for his own exile in 41, shows fortitude and dignity. The 'Consolation to Polybius' is addressed to a freedman of the emperor Claudius, an unattractive piece written c.43 to obtain recall from exile. (This Polybius appears to have translated Homer into Latin prose and Virgil into Greek). The treatises 'On the constancy of the wise man', 'On tranquillity of the soul', and 'On leisure' (*De otio*) were addressed to Annaeus Serēnus, *praefectus vigilum* under Nero. The theme of the first is that a wise man can suffer neither wrong nor insult. The second is concerned with the pursuit of peace of mind; the third is a defence of leisure and relaxation, and of the value of philosophical speculation and meditation.

Outside this collection of treatises there are further moral essays, *De clementia* and *De beneficiis*, and the *Epi-*

stulae morales, a collection of 124 letters addressed to his friend Lucilius, divided into twenty books. The letters are also in effect moral essays (the fiction of a genuine correspondence is only sporadically aimed at), and are written in the tradition of the philosophical letter (compare PLATO 6) or the *diatribe. The nature of the subject-matter—on happiness, the supreme good, riches, the terrors of death, and so forth—and the charm and informality of style, have made them the most popular of Seneca's works. They are persuasive, not dogmatic, in tone, and furnish interesting personal details about the author himself, as well as being illuminating about contemporary life. They were approved and made use of by early Christian writers. Seneca was thought in the Middle Ages to have been a Christian, and was believed by St Jerome and others to have corresponded with the apostle Paul. His treatises were studied by Petrarch (1304–74) and known to Chaucer (c.1343–1400).

3. Of a different order are the seven books of Seneca's *Naturales quaestiones*, dedicated to Lucilius and written during Seneca's retirement towards the end of his life. This work is an examination of natural phenomena, not from a scientific but from a *Stoic standpoint. It is not a systematic work but a collection of facts about nature. The phenomena are grouped according to their connection with one or other of the four elements, earth, air, fire, and water, with moral observations scattered throughout. The purpose of the work seems to be to find in nature a foundation for Stoic ethic. Though of little scientific value the work was used in the Middle Ages as a textbook of natural science.

The *Apocolocyntosis* is a clever and original piece of satirical burlesque on the death of the emperor Claudius, written in the form of a Menippean satire in a medley of prose and verse.

Most of Seneca's prose work is philosophical, and an important source for the history of Stoicism. His own brand of that philosophy was undogmatic and tempered by experience and common sense, and is often used as the basis for moral exhortation rather than expounded as a system of thought in its own right.

The style is lively and rhetorical; it catches the attention immediately, but its unremitting brilliance, lacking depth of thought, is tiring: 'sand without lime' (i.e. cement that crumbles) is how the emperor Caligula described it.

4. Seneca's most important poetical works are nine tragedies adapted from the Greek: *Hercules furens, Medea, Troades* (*Trojan Women), *Phaedra* (all based at least in part in Euripides), *Agamemnon* (presumably owing a debt to Aeschylus but one not easily traced), *Oedipus, Hercules Oetaeus* (the former very Sophoclean, the latter, which may not be genuinely by Seneca, not very like its presumed source, Sophocles' *Trachiniae*), *Phoenissae* (owing a little to Sophocles' *Oedipus Coloneus*), and *Thyestes* (a gruesome story with no extant source). A tenth tragedy attributed to Seneca, *Octavia*, is obviously not by him. (See individual entries for each of these.) The plays are written on Greek lines, that is, with dramatic episodes (written in iambic senarii; see METRE, LATIN 2) separated by choral odes (in lyric metres, most often anapaestic); it is likely that Seneca intended his tragedies for private recitation rather than for acting. They are exaggerations of the Euripidean style, showing psychological insight but markedly rhetorical and pointed in manner, and Seneca loves to dwell on the horrific and macabre elements of the plot. But the *stichomythia is often more effective than that of the Greek original, and the ending of Seneca's *Medea* is more dramatic than that of Euripides. There are fine passages of description, much moralizing, and some striking epigrams. The plays also convey the Euripidean sense of the individual as victim. They exerted a great influence in the Italian Renaissance and in Tudor and Jacobean times in England; stock characters in the romantic plays of Shakespeare, such as the ghost, the nurse, and the barbarous villain, were transmitted from the Greek through the medium of Seneca.

The *Anthologia Latina* (see ANTHOLOGY 2) includes a number of short poems by Seneca, some containing references to his own life and family.

septenā'rius, see METRE, LATIN 2.

Se'ptuagint (in abbreviation LXX), Greek version of the Hebrew Old Testament which derives its name from a story, now known to be false, contained in an Alexandrian work of the second century BC, the *Letter to Philocratēs*, supposedly by a Greek called Aristeas. The story states that the translation from the Hebrew was made at the request of Ptolemy II Philadelphus (king of Egypt 283–246 BC), who wanted it for the royal library, and that the translators were seventy-two (or seventy, Lat. *septuaginta*) learned Jews, kept in seclusion on the island of Pharos off Alexandria until their task was finished. The translation must in fact have been made by Egyptian Jews working independently of one another and living at different periods in the Hellenistic age. The Septuagint differs from the Old Testament both in the order of the books and in the inclusion of those books which are usually known as the Apocrypha. There are also textual differences. The Christian Fathers down to the late fourth century AD regarded the Septuagint as the standard form of the Old Testament and seldom referred to the Hebrew. *Origen, however, was very interested in its relation to the Hebrew and to other Greek versions. See also VULGATE.

Serā'pis (or Sarapis), new god introduced to Egypt by Ptolemy I Soter (367–283 BC). Serapis retained many aspects of the Egyptian *Osiris, and was identified with several Greek gods in his several roles. As a divine healer, he was identified with Asclepius: *Demetrius of Phalērum (a close adviser of Soter) was cured of his blindness, reputedly by the god, in Alexandria, and in consequence wrote a paean to him. It is thought that Soter may have prompted Serapis' cult to unite his Greek and Egyptian subjects in the worship of a god whom both could appreciate. Ptolemy III Euergetēs (reigned 246–221) built the Serapeum, a vast temple to Serapis, at Alexandria and his cult spread widely in the Graeco-Roman world.

Sermō'nes, see SATIRES of Horace.

Sertō'rius, Quintus, distinguished Roman soldier, supporter of *Marius. He joined Cinna in his march on Rome in 87 BC but opposed Marius' indiscriminate slaughter. He became praetor in 83 and was given Spain as his province. In 80 BC he accepted an invitation by the Lusitanians (in western Spain) to lead them in a revolt against Rome. With the support of some exiles from Rome he was successful against many Roman commanders (including Pompey) and at one time held most of Roman Spain. Gradually losing ground to Metellus and Pompey, and his popularity having waned, he was murdered in 73 or 72 by his lieutenant Perperna.

Se'rvius (Marius Servius Honorātus), Latin grammarian and commentator of the early fifth century AD, whose greatest work was a commentary on Virgil. Since it was intended for school use it dwells mostly upon grammatical, rhetorical, and stylistic points, but some notes on the subject-matter are included which contain very valuable information. The commentary is found in the manuscripts in a shorter (the original Servian) and a longer version, the latter known as *Servius auctus* ('augmented Servius') or *Servius Danielis* (named after its discoverer, P. Daniel, and published in 1600), incorporating much earlier material.

Se'rvius Tu'llius, semi-legendary king of Rome, sixth in succession from Romulus; according to tradition he reigned from 578 to 535 BC. He was the successor of Tarquinius Priscus, in whose house he was brought up as a slave. There was a legend of his miraculous birth to a slave-woman and the fire-god Vulcan. His rule is said to have been mild, and a number of public works and constitutional reforms were attributed to him. Archaeological finds confirm that the temples of Fortuna and Mater *Matuta ascribed to him were founded in the sixth century BC. He was murdered by the order of Lucius Tarquinius, son of Priscus, at the instigation of his own daughter, Tullia, who was Lucius' wife. Lucius succeeded him and was known as Tarquinius Superbus.

seste'rtius (pl. *sestertii*, Eng. sesterces), in Roman currency, a small silver coin; there were 4 sesterces to the denarius. See MONEY AND COINS.

Sestus, in its day the principal Greek town of the Thracian Chersonese, on the Hellespont (Dardanelles) opposite Abydus (see LEANDER). Until eclipsed by *Byzantium it was the usual port of departure for those crossing from Europe to Asia. From 478, after the Persian defeat at Mycalē, it remained in Athenian hands until it fell to Sparta at the end of the *Peloponnesian War. It regained its independence in the early fourth century and retained it against Athenian attack, but in 353 it fell to the Athenian general Charēs, who killed or enslaved the inhabitants.

Seven against Thebes, The (Gk. *Hepta epi Thēbas*, Lat. *Septem contra Thēbas*), tragedy by *Aeschylus, produced in 467 BC, the third play in a trilogy dealing with related events, the first two plays being *Laius* and *Oedipus*; the *satyr-play which followed it was also related in subject-matter, being entitled *Sphinx*; all these plays except the *Seven* are lost.

Polyneicēs, son of Oedipus, has come, aided by the Argive army, to claim the kingdom of Thebes, unjustly retained by his brother Eteoclēs (see OEDIPUS). The scene is the city of Thebes, and the chorus is composed of Theban women. A messenger announces the disposition of the Argive army and describes the seven champions preparing to lead the attack, one at each of the seven gates of Thebes. Eteocles appoints a Theban opponent to withstand each one, finding himself left to oppose Polyneices; Eteocles rushes out to face his brother in spite of the dissuasions of the chorus. Their deaths at each other's hands are announced, and their bodies are borne in, mourned by the chorus. In a scene probably added by an imitator their sisters Ismenē and Antigonē join in the lamentation. A herald announces the decree that the body of Polyneices, who has waged war on his own city, shall lie unburied. Antigone at once declares that she will defy the edict: she will bury him herself.

For the Argive background see ADRASTUS. The seven champions in Aeschylus' play are Adrastus, Tydeus (an exile at Argos from Calydon), Parthenopaeus (an Arcadian, son of Atalanta), Capaneus, Hippomedon, Amphiaraus, and Polyneices. In other versions of the story two alternative champions were sometimes included, Eteocles, son of Iphis, instead of Adrastus, and Mecisteus, Adrastus' brother, instead of Polyneices. The story was told in the *Thebais*, a poem of the *Epic Cycle.

seven hills of Rome, the Capitoline, Palatine, Aventine, Quirinal, Viminal, Esquiline, and Caelian hills.

seven liberal arts, a loose classification of the subjects comprising the educational curriculum in the West during the Middle Ages, from the late fifth century AD onwards. The name 'liberal arts' seems to originate with Aristotle who in the *Politics* talks of *eleutherai epistēmai*, 'branches of knowledge worthy of free men', the basic knowledge needed for a properly educated citizen. They were divided into the *trivium, namely grammar (i.e. literature), rhetoric, and dialectic, and the more advanced *quadrivium, namely arithmetic, geometry, music, and astronomy. For the original nine see VARRO; see also CASSIODORUS and MARTIANUS CAPELLA.

seven kings of Rome, the succession of seven kings who according to tradition ruled Rome before the founding of the republic: Romulus (founder of the city), Numa Pompilius, Tullus Hostilius, Ancus Martius, Tarquinius Priscus, Servius Tullius, and Tarquinius Superbus.

Seven Sages, name given by Greek tradition to seven men of practical wisdom—statesmen, law-givers, and philosophers—of the seventh and sixth centuries BC. The list of sages is variously given in different authorities, but generally it comprises *Solon of Athens, *Thalēs of Miletus, *Pittacus of Mitylēnē, Cleobulus of Rhodes, *Chilon of Sparta, Bias of Priēnē, and *Periander of Corinth. Many pieces of proverbial wisdom were attributed to them, such as those inscribed at *Delphi, 'Know yourself' and 'Nothing in excess'.

Seven Wonders of the Ancient World. Listed in Hellenistic times, these were the Pyramids of Egypt, the Hanging Gardens of Babylon, the Mausoleum at Halicarnassus (see MAUSOLOS), the Temple of Artemis at *Ephesus, the statue of Zeus at Olympia (by *Pheidias), the *Colossus of Rhodes, and the *Pharos of Alexandria.

Seve'rus, Lucius Septi'mius, Roman emperor AD 193–211. See BRITAIN.

Sextus Empi'ricus (flourished *c.* AD 200), Greek physician whose writings are the chief source of information on the *Sceptical school of philosophy. In his 'Outlines of Pyrrhonism' (*Pyrrhōneioi hypotypōseis*) in three books, he states the case for the Sceptics and attacks dogmatic philosophies. In his other work 'Against the Professors' (*Pros tous mathēmatikous,* Lat. *Adversus mathematicos*) he refutes the teachers of the various branches of learning in succession.

Shield of Heracles (*Aspis Herakleous*), Greek narrative poem in 480 hexameters attributed to *Hesiod but written too late to be by him. The first 56 lines tell the story of Alcmena, mother of Heracles, and come from the *Catalogue of Women* or *Eoeae*, also erroneously attributed to Hesiod. The poem goes on to relate briefly the killing by Heracles of Cycnus, son of Arēs. For the encounter Heracles has put on armour given him by Hephaestus, including a shield, the disproportionately long description of which (in imitation of Homer's description of the shield of Achilles in the *Iliad*) gives the poem its title.

Sibyl (Sibylla), general name given by the Greeks and Romans to various prophetesses in the Greek and Roman world, who sometimes had individual names as well. Thus the most ancient Sibyl known in legend was Hērophilē, who prophesied to Hecuba, queen of Troy, before the Trojan War. She was also known as the Erythraean Sibyl from her birthplace Erythrae (perhaps the city of that name on the coast of Asia Minor opposite Chios). The Sibyls prophesied in an ecstatic state, and were believed to be possessed by a god, usually Apollo, who spoke through them (compare the Pythia at Delphi). Their utterances were written down, and cities made official collections of what were believed to be their prophecies; at Athens similar collections of oracles were kept on the Acropolis (see ONOMACRITUS and ORACLES).

The most famous Sibyl in antiquity was that of Cumae in Campania (sometimes identified with the Erythraean) whom Virgil represents as being visited by Aeneas (see AENEID 6). The cave in which she lived still exists. Her prophecies were said to have been inscribed on palmleaves. According to legend she offered nine volumes of oracles to the last king of Rome, Tarquinius Superbus, at a high price. When he refused to buy she burned three volumes and offered the remainder at the same price. When he again refused she burned three more, and finally sold the last three to him at the original price. The king is said to have entrusted these Sibylline books (*libri Sibyllini*) to the care of two patricians.

However acquired, books of oracles certainly existed in Rome at an early date, and were consulted not only for guidance about the future but in order to find out how to placate divine anger in times of great calamity, such as earthquake and plague. They were kept in a chest in a stone vault under the temple of the Capitoline *Jupiter. When the oracles were destroyed in the temple fire of 83 BC, envoys were sent to various places to make a fresh collection of similar oracular sayings, which was subsequently placed by Augustus in the temple of Apollo on the Palatine hill. The last known consultation was in AD 363. The collection was still in existence in the temple when the latter was destroyed by Stilicho, the general of the emperors Theodosius I and Honorius early in the fifth century. Fourteen miscellaneous books of oracles, of Judaeo-Hellenistic and Christian origin, still survive. Because of Christian interpolations in the Sibylline oracles, the Sibyls came to be thought of as on an equality with Old Testament prophets, and frequently figure with them in Christian literature and art.

A famous story told of the Cumaean Sibyl relates that the god Apollo once offered her anything she wished if she would take him as her lover. She asked to live as many years as there were grains of sand in a pile of sweepings, and these numbered a thousand, but she failed to ask for continued youth. Trimalchio, a character in *Petronius' *Satyricon*, had seen her with his own eyes, he said, hanging from the ceiling of her cave in a bottle, and when children asked her what she wanted, she used to reply, 'I want to die.' In the days of the Greek traveller Pausanias (second century AD) a jar was shown at Cumae said to contain her bones.

Sicilian Expedition (415–413 BC), an episode in the *Peloponnesian War when Athens made an ill-fated invasion of Sicily. Athens responded to an appeal for help from Segesta, who was at war with Selinus, her neighbour on the island, but the real reasons for the expedition were to curb the growing power of Syracuse (Sicily's main city), to gain a foothold on Sicily, and to obtain complete control of the sea. The expedition was the greatest naval and military force ever mounted by a Greek city, but it failed disastrously. It was commanded by the incompatible *Alcibiades, *Lamachus, and *Nicias. Alcibiades was soon recalled on a charge of sacrilege, but he escaped and went over to Sparta; Lamachus was killed in a skirmish; and Nicias, who was left in sole command, had opposed the invasion from the beginning and proved an incompetent general. He besieged Syracuse in 414 but was crushingly defeated on land and at sea. Athens lost more than 30,000 men and 200 ships—blows from which she never recovered.

Sicily (Gk. Sikelia, Lat. Sicilia), the largest island of the Mediterranean, separated from Italy by the Straits of Messina. The Thrīnacia mentioned in Homer's *Odyssey* (from Greek *thrīnax*, 'trident') is perhaps to be identified with it. Trīnacria was a Latin poetical name for the island. Its strategic position, fine climate, and fertile soil made it a meetingplace for settlers from east and west, and from Italy and Africa, and gave it great importance in the history of the Mediterranean world. Ancient writers speak of their being three native peoples there, Elymi in the west, Sicani in the westcentral, and Siceli in the east. Thucydides says that the Sicanians and Sicels were

Iberian and Italian respectively; the Elymi he describes as fleeing from the sack of Troy.

From about the eighth century BC it was colonized variously by Greeks, Phoenicians, and Carthaginians, and its history was often one of bloody conflict (for the Athenian invasion of 415–13 BC see SICILIAN EXPEDITION). During the first part of the fifth century BC the courts of the Sicilian tyrants were places of culture and great wealth, as may be seen from odes written for them by *Pindar in celebration of their victories at the Panhellenic games, as well as from the surviving ruins. The main city was Syracuse, and in the fourth century it came to control all Sicily except for the Carthaginian territories in the far west. After Rome's victory over Carthage in the First *Punic War (264–241 BC) almost the whole island came under Roman rule, which was often harsh and corrupt (see VERRES).

Sicily produced many Greeks famous in literary history, among them the poet Stesichorus, the sophist Gorgias, the scientists Empedoclēs and Archimēdēs, the historian Timaeus, the pastoral poet Theocritus, and Herodas the writer of mimes.

Sicyō'nius ('the Sicyonian man'), Greek comedy by *Menander, of which some 470 fragmentary lines from the second half have been recovered from a papyrus used by Egyptian mummifiers when making a papier mâché mummy case (see PAPYROLOGY). The play concerns Stratophanēs (the Sicyonian of the title), a successful captain of mercenaries who on returning to Athens after service in Caria has taken a house at Eleusis, and his discovery of his real father and of the identity and Athenian citizenship of a girl whom he has purchased as a slave in Caria and now wishes to marry.

Sidō'nius (Gaius Sollius Apollināris Sidonius, canonized as St Sidonius Apollinaris, c. AD 430–c.480), a notable Gallo-Roman poet and bishop of Augustonemetum (Clermont-Ferrand), chief town of the Arverni region of Gaul (now the Auvergne). He was born at Lugdunum (Lyons) of a prominent Christian family, and his father and grandfather both held important civic offices. When his wife's

father Avītus was proclaimed Roman emperor in the West in 455, Sidonius pronounced a panegyric in verse, for which he was rewarded by a statue in the Ulpian Library of Trajan at Rome. When Avitus was dethroned in 456, Sidonius was reconciled to the new emperor Majorian for whom also he wrote a panegyric (458). When Majorian was overthrown in 461, Sidonius withdrew to Gaul but wrote a third panegyric for a later emperor Anthemius. He became bishop in 469, and resisted an invasion of Visigoths with courage and devotion, giving up the struggle only when the whole Auvergne was ceded to them in 475. Released from imprisonment in 476 he devoted himself to his diocese and to literature until his death. Sidonius was one of the last major figures of classical culture. His poems (twenty-four survive), addressed to friends, are replete with mythological allusions and show great technical skill if limited originality. He also published nine books of letters, many written with an eye to publication and the rest carefully revised. One of the letters records the classic if rather meaningless example of a palindrome (a phrase which reads the same forwards and backwards): *Roma tibi subito motibus ibit amor*, which may be translated, 'Rome, your love, will suddenly collapse in disturbances'. Both letters and poems are often interesting for the light they throw on life and conditions in Gaul in the fifth century.

siki'nnis, in Greece, violent dance associated with the performance of satyr-plays (see SATYRIC DRAMA), the name sometimes said to have been derived from its Cretan inventor. It may have originated with dances performed by votaries of Bacchus or Dionysus.

Silē'nus (Seilēnos). In Greek myth Silenus represented the spirit of wild life in a creature half-man, half-animal in form (compare SATYRS). He is shown on Attic vases of the early sixth century BC having horse-ears and sometimes horse-legs and a tail. Sometimes a collection of sileni are found, and classical authors frequently confuse them with satyrs, but in general, whereas satyrs are young, sileni are thought of as old men, and being old are thought to be wise. A famous story relates how *Midas made Silenus drunk in order to learn his secrets. In Virgil, Eclogue 6, Silenus is caught by two shepherds and sings them songs of ancient myths. He is sometimes represented as Dionysus' tutor, or depicted in the train of Dionysus, making music or getting drunk. (See also the *Cyclops* of Euripides.) *Socrates was often compared with Silenus, and likenesses of the former are remarkably similar to ancient portrait heads of the latter. But the comparison was meant to include not only physical appearance but a common incongruity between outward appearance and inner wisdom.

Si'lius Ita'licus (Tiberius Catius Ascōnius Silius Italicus; *c*. AD 26–*c*.101), Latin poet. His life is chiefly known to us from a letter of the Younger Pliny (3. 7), and from references in Martial's epigrams. He was probably born at Patavium (Padua) and having won fame as an advocate was consul in 68, the last year of the emperor Nero's reign. Later, *c*.77, he won praise as proconsul for his administration of Asia. Thereafter he lived in retirement on his estates near Naples. He was wealthy man, bought country houses (including a villa once belonging to Cicero, whom he revered), and was a collector of books and works of art. He had a profound admiration for Virgil, whose tomb near Naples, on one of his properties, he restored. Finding that he was suffering from an incurable disease he starved himself to death at the age of 75. He was the author of the longest surviving Latin poem, *Punica*, an epic in seventeen books of hexameters on the Second *Punic War (218–201 BC). It begins with *Hannibal's oath, his appointment to the command, and, except for digressions on the captured Roman general Regulus and Dido's sister Anna, it proceeds in order through the principal episodes of the war, the crossing of the Alps, the battles of the Ticinus, the Trebia, Lake Trasimene, and Cannae, the capture of Syracuse, the battle of the Metaurus, Scipio in Spain and Africa, and the final battle of Zama.

Silius was highly praised as Virgil's poetic heir by Martial, but the Younger Pliny's remark that his epic was written with more diligence than inspiration (*maiore cura quam ingenio*) has been found more apt. The subject-matter came from Livy, the form from study of Virgil and Lucan. Following Virgil's practice (and in contrast with Lucan) Silius retained the intervention of the gods in the conflict, traditional in epic since Homer. However, to mythicize the real world of Hannibal and Scipio so as to mingle gods and men without incongruity required more tact and delicacy than Silius shows; it is, for example, bizarre to find the Carthaginian general Hannibal saved from death by the goddess Juno, just as the legendary Turnus is saved in the *Aeneid*. Almost equally incongruous are the traditional epic ingredients of catalogues (of Hannibal's allies, of the Roman forces at Cannae, for example), funeral games, description of a hero's shield (Hannibal's), Nereids (sea-nymphs) disturbed by a vast fleet (Carthaginian), and altercations of antagonists on the battlefield. The greatness of the theme—Rome's heroic rise from defeat to victory—is lost through lack of proportion and good sense, and some aspects repel the reader, notably the excessively realistic descriptions of slaughter (perhaps due to Lucan's influence). The work as a whole is dull and lifeless and lacks the power of Lucan. But the writing is generally lucid and straightforward, the composition runs easily and pleasantly, and the shorter episodes are well told. There are some memorable phrases: *rarae fumant felicibus arae*, 'rarely do the altars of the fortunate smoke [with sacrifices]', and *explorant adversa viros*, 'adversity is the test of men'.

silloi ('squint-eyed' poems, 'lampoons'), see TIMON (2). The name was applied generally to Greek satirical poems, and appears to have been given to certain poems of *Xenophanēs satirizing the myths of Homer and Hesiod.

silvae. The Latin word *silva* in its sense of 'raw material' (compare Greek *hylē*) was extended in a literary sense to the raw material of a literary work; Quintilian explains it as a quickly produced first draft of a poem. It was used in the plural, *silvae*, of collections of occasional poems, and thus it came to be the title given by the poet *Statius to his collection of (mostly) short poems published in five books. The first four books appeared between AD 91 and 95; the fifth was probably put together after Statius' death in 96. The survival of these poems depended on a manuscript discovered in 1417. Most are written in hexameters, but six are in lyric metres, alcaics, sapphics, and hendecasyllables (see METRE, GREEK 3 and 8). Statius wrote them for his patrons, who included the emperor Domitian, on a variety of subjects suggested by incidents in the patrons' lives as well as in the poet's own; his poem on the death of a friend's parrot is well known (2. 4). He has been accused of servility, and it is true that he wrote what his patrons wanted to hear. But some of the poems are sincere and moving: an invocation to sleep (5. 4), an affectionate address to his wife Claudia (3. 5), and an epithalamium on the marriage of his friend Assuntius Stella (1. 2).

Silva'nus, 'of the wood', in Roman religion, the god of the wild land beyond the boundaries of the cultivated fields. He thus resembled the Greek *satyrs or *Silenus, and was sometimes identified with them, but more often with the god *Pan. His cult was regarded as very ancient, and it was important to propitiate him before violating his territory, e.g. cutting down trees.

Silver Age, of Latin literature, term sometimes applied to the post-Augustan period; see LATIN LANGUAGE 2.

Sīmo'nidēs. 1. Of Ceos (a small Ionian Greek island off the coast of Attica), 556–468 BC, Greek lyric and elegiac poet and famous writer of sepulchral *epigrams. He was uncle of the poet Bacchylides. As a professional poet he travelled widely in the Greek world. He was the guest of *Hipparchus at Athens during the Peisistratid tyranny, and subsequently went to Thessaly, where he was the guest of the Scopads and later wrote a dirge lamenting their deaths (see below). He seems to have been in Athens in 490, when his epitaph on the Athenian dead at the battle of Marathon (see PERSIAN WARS) was preferred to that of Aeschylus who had fought in it. After the Persian Wars he became the ally of *Themistocles, on whose behalf he attacked in his poetry the Rhodian poet Timocreon. When he was 80 he won the dithyrambic competition at Athens 'in the archonship of Adeimantus' (477). In about 476 he was invited to the court of Hieron, tyrant of *Syracuse, with whom he stayed until his death; while there he is said to have settled a quarrel between Hieron and Theron (tyrant of Acragas). He died in Sicily and was buried at Acragas.

Very many stories circulated about him, some concerning his fondness for money, which became proverbial (he is said to have been the first Greek poet to write eulogies for pay). The most famous story concerns his visit to the Scopads of Thessaly where at a banquet he sang a lyric glorifying his patron, but including a lengthy digression in praise of Castor and Polydeuces (see DIOSCURI). Scopas said that he would pay the poet only half the fee, and he might apply for the rest to the two heroes to whom he had devoted an equal share of the praise. A little later a message came to say that two young men were asking for Simonides at the door of the hall. Simonides rose to speak to them but found no one there; while he was outside, the roof of the hall collapsed, killing all the other guests. Although the dead were crushed out of recognition Simonides was able to remember where each guest sat and so identify each body for burial (he is also said to have invented a technique for remembering).

Despite his great reputation in antiquity, most of Simonides' poetry is lost. Comparatively little survives in quotation, and papyrus finds have been very fragmentary. He wrote *hymns, *scolia, *encomia (including the poem to Scopas from which a long passage survives in Plato's *Protagoras, quoted there as the basis for discussion), *epinicians (the few surviving lines suggest that these were more playful than Pindar's), and elegies. He was most famed for *dirges and for *epigrams to be inscribed on dedications and tombstones, particularly for those referring to the dead of the Persian Wars, although it is difficult to be sure which ones were genuinely written by him.

Probably genuine is that on the Spartan dead at Thermopylae:

Tell them in Lacedaemon, passer-by,
That here obedient to their words we lie.

2. Alternative spelling of *Semonides.

Sinis, brigand killed by *Theseus.

Sinon, see TROJAN HORSE.

Sirens (Seirēnēs), in Greek myth, female creatures who had the power of drawing men to destruction by their song. In Homer's *Odyssey* there are two of them who live on an island near *Scylla and Charybdis (in the Straits of Messina). Odysseus, when his ship was about to pass their island, in order to escape them filled the ears of his men with wax but left his own unblocked and had himself lashed to the mast so that he could hear their singing and yet survive. According to later legend the Sirens drowned themselves from vexation at his escape. The body of one of them, Parthenopē, was washed ashore in the bay of Naples, which originally bore her name. The *Argonauts, on their return voyage, passed near the Sirens; Orpheus, by playing on his lyre more beautifully than the Sirens sang, saved the other Argonauts from listening to their song (except for one man, who sprang overboard but was rescued by Aphrodite). In Homer the Sirens are not described, but in art they are represented as half women and half birds; in time they came increasingly to be shown as beautiful women, and also as creators of music; in the Myth of Er at the end of Plato's *Republic* they make the music of the spheres (see HARMONY OF THE SPHERES); thus in Hellenistic art and literature they came to symbolize music. 'What song the Sirens sang' is said by Suetonius to be one of the impossible questions with which the emperor Tiberius used to tease the scholars at his court.

Siro (Siron), see VIRGIL.

Sise'nna, Lucius Corne'lius, Roman historian, praetor in 78 BC, one of the defenders of Verrēs (see CICERO (1) 1) in 70, and legate to Pompey in 67. He was the author of a history of his own times, which has not survived. He also translated into Latin the *Milesian Tales*.

Si'syphus, in Greek myth, son of Aeolus and Enaretē, founder of the city of Corinth (which is called Ephyrē in the *Iliad*), reputedly the most cunning of men. For that reason he was sometimes associated with the master-thief *Autolycus and was perhaps the father of Odysseus. (When Autolycus stole his cattle Sisyphus was able to recognize his own, having marked their hoofs. His revenge was to seduce Autolycus' daughter Anticlea, so that it was suspected that he rather than her husband Laertes was Odysseus' father.) Having observed the seduction of the nymph Aegina by Zeus he revealed the truth to her father, the river-god Asopus, in return for a spring of fresh water on the citadel. Zeus punished Sisyphus by sending Death for him, but Sisyphus chained Death up in a dungeon, so that mortals ceased to die; the gods in alarm sent Arēs to release Death, who came after Sisyphus once again. Sisyphus instructed his wife Meropē to leave his body unburied and make no offerings, with the result that the Underworld gods Hadēs and Persephonē allowed the supposedly indignant Sisyphus to return from the Underworld to earth to punish his wife and make her bury the body. Once in the world again Sisyphus resumed his life and lived to a great age. However, when he eventually died the gods of the Underworld devised for him a famous punishment: to roll up to the top of a hill a rock which always rolled down again just as it was about to reach the summit. Sisyphus was the father of four sons, one of whom was Glaucus, father of *Bellerophon.

Skirophoria, see SCIROPHORIA.

Sleep (Gk. Hypnos, Lat. Somnus), personified in Greek myth as the brother of Death (Thanatos), son of Night (*Nyx). Homer, in the episode of Hera beguiling Zeus with the aid of Sleep (*Iliad* 14. 225), describes his home as a cave on the island of Lemnos; Ovid places it in the dark mists of the far North.

Smyrna or (Myrrha), see ADONIS and ZMYRNA.

soccus, the low-heeled, loose-fitting shoe worn by Roman actors of comedy, of Greek origin. The word is often used to symbolize comedy; the poet Milton speaks of 'Johnson's learned sock'. Compare COTHURNUS.

Social War. 1. In Greek history, name given to the war (357–355 BC) between Athens on the one hand and Chios, Cos, Rhodes, and Byzantium on the other, all of which had revolted from Athens' second confederacy. At the end of the war the independence of the principal members of the League was recognized.
2. In Roman history, an uprising against Rome (90–88 BC) by its Italian allies (*socii*), most of whom were fighting to win Roman citizenship. From a military point of view the fighting was inconclusive, but the Romans conceded the main issue: full citizenship was granted to all Italians south of the Po. See SOCII below.

socii ('allies'), of Rome. Although Rome had allies outside Italy, the term commonly denoted her Italian allies, *socii Italici*, those people, Italian, Greek, and Etruscan (but excluding the Latins, who had a special relationship with Rome and special privileges; see LATIN RIGHTS), living in some 150 communities, who were allied to Rome by formal treaties. They differed from the Romans and Latins in language, laws, and customs. All were obliged to provide military aid when required and to surrender to Rome control of foreign affairs. Their feelings of injustice led to the outbreak of war in 90 BC (see SOCIAL WAR).

So'cratēs (469–399 BC), Greek philosopher, born in the Attic deme of Alōpekē near Athens. His father was Sophroniscus, a sculptor or stonemason, and his mother Phaenaretē, a midwife. He himself was a stonemason. Rather late in life he married the reputedly shrewish Xanthippē, by whom he had three sons, who were still young at the time of his death. He fought in the Peloponnesian War and as a soldier he was distinguished by his courage and physical resilience. Although he generally avoided public affairs, when he

did take part his behaviour accorded with his principles. Under the *Thirty Tyrants, for example, he refused to assist in the arrest of an innocent man whom the Thirty had condemned to death, thus risking his own life. He preferred to follow his own conviction, irrespective of the will of either the people or the oligarchs. His manner of life won him many enemies, and in 399 he was brought to trial by Anytus (a democratic politician), Meletus, and Lycon on the charge of not believing in the gods whom Athens believed in but of introducing new gods, and of corrupting the youth of the city; the death penalty was asked for.

Two versions of Socrates' speech in his own defence exist in the *Apology* (Gk. *apologia*, 'defence') by Plato and (in a less authentic form) in that by Xenophon, but neither makes exactly clear the precise significance of the charges. They were connected, however, with Socrates' well-known association with many of the Thirty Tyrants who overthrew the democracy, notably *Alcibiades and *Critias. The attack on him was not merely because of the political views of his protégés; it was also felt that he had undermined the traditional morality and religion of the city, the practice of which had in former times, it was felt, made Athens great; Alcibiades was suspected of sacrilege and Critias was an atheist. It is unlikely that Socrates' accusers wished or expected the death penalty to be inflicted; it would have been possible for him to follow the usual course of going into voluntary exile before the verdict, or of proposing banishment as an alternative to the death penalty, when it would probably have been accepted. However, his unconditional belief that he had done no harm to the city led to his obviously unacceptable counter-proposal that he should be dined for life at public expense (a privilege afforded to great benefactors of the state) or alternatively that his friends should pay a fine on his behalf; perhaps not surprisingly a greater number of the jury voted for the death penalty than had condemned him in the first place. Execution was postponed, Xenophon says for a month, during the absence of the state ship on a sacred embassy (see DELOS); during this period Socrates was in prison and visited by his friends, their conversations recorded in Plato's dialogues *Crito and *Phaedo. The latter dialogue movingly describes Socrates' unflinching acceptance of the cup of hemlock (by which the death penalty was carried out at Athens).

Socrates himself wrote no books, and we are dependent mainly upon the widely diverging descriptions of Aristophanes, Xenophon, and above all Plato for our knowledge of his beliefs and also for our understanding of his uncompromising adherence to the philosophic life. This had such a profound effect upon his contemporaries and, through Plato, on subsequent philosophy, that all earlier Greek philosophers are referred to as the Presocratics. Xenophon conveys the deep reverence he felt for the man, but was unable to understand his philosophical concerns. Aristophanes' malicious and satirical portrayal in the *Clouds reflected the anti-intellectual prejudices of his audience, depicting Socrates as no different from the other intellectuals of the day, the *sophists. (In Plato's Apology Socrates refers to the influence of 'the comic poets' as a factor in his unpopularity; Plato in the *Symposium is at pains to show that a friendly relationship existed between Socrates and Aristophanes in real life.) Plato's picture of Socrates is also in some measure his own creation, but it is possible to identify from it some features genuinely those of Socrates: his concern with the difference between true knowledge and opinion which may merely happen to be correct; his search for definitions (What is courage? What is justice?) without which true knowledge is unattainable, in the belief that there are such things as courage and virtue; his particular method of inquiry by question and answer (see ELENCHUS) in order to reach these definitions; the question of whether 'goodness' (aretē, 'virtue', 'excellence of character') can be taught, as the sophists said it could; the feeling that goodness is connected with knowledge of the good, and that once one has that knowledge one cannot deliberately act badly ('no one errs deliberately'). And all this intellectual examination was aimed, as Socrates insisted, at the practical end of achieving

happiness in this life by right living: 'the unexamined life is not worth living.'

There is no doubt that this kind of questioning made Socrates highly unpopular with his fellow citizens, if not with the young who enjoyed seeing their elders ridiculed. He compared himself with the gadfly, stinging people out of their complacency. (Alcibiades compared him with a sting-ray, inducing a state of numb helplessness.) Unlike the people he questioned, he himself professed complete ignorance, asking his questions purely for information. When his friend Chaerephon visited the Delphic Oracle to enquire if any man was wiser than Socrates, and returned with the answer that there was none, Socrates concluded that his wisdom consisted of knowing his own ignorance, as others did not know theirs. Some thought his assumption of ignorance was merely a pose and described it as an example of 'Socratic irony'. In a famous passage of Plato's *Theaetetus Socrates is represented as comparing himself with a midwife; he is not a teacher and cannot himself give birth to wisdom, but he can help others to discover and bring to birth the truth within themselves.

Both Plato and Xenophon refer to a less rational aspect of Socrates, his *daimonion* or 'divine sign', which he often called simply 'the customary sign'. Plato has Socrates describe it in the Apology (where Socrates supposes it to be the reason behind his indictment for introducing new gods into the city) as a kind of inner voice which since childhood has turned him back from action but never urged him towards it; it was this divine sign that prevented him from taking part in politics. He believed that the sign was sent by the gods, in whom, unlike most of the sophists, he believed unquestioningly. He differed from his sophist contemporaries in many other respects: for example, he did not teach, in the sense that he did not impart formal knowledge, nor did he ever take fees from the young men who associated with him; far from being sceptical or a moral relativist, he believed that there was such a thing as virtue, that it was knowable, and that the good life had little to do with material success. But the effect on others of his questioning unexamined assumptions had its destructive and demoralizing aspect.

With his broad, flat, turned-up nose, prominent bulging eyes, thick lips, and a paunch, Socrates was famous for his ugliness. Yet his appearance in no way detracted from his magnetic personality. Alicibiades in Plato's *Symposium* contrasted his outward appearance with his inner worth. (See also SILENUS.)

Much of Socrates' later influence was due not so much to his doctrines as to the integrity and consistency of his life and death, and to the memory he left behind of an inspired talker and an outstanding intellect. The scantiness of and uncertainty about his positive doctrines led to schools of the most diverse opinions being founded by his disciples, by *Plato, Antisthenēs the *Cynic, *Eucleidēs of Megara, and *Aristippus, the predecessor of Epicurus.

See also MEMORABILIA and SYMPOSIUM of Xenophon.

Sōlī'nus, Julius, Latin author, probably soon after AD 200, of *Collectanea rerum memorābilium* ('collection of memorable things'), substantially an epitome of the Elder Pliny's *Natural History* and the geography of Pomponius Mela. The title *Polyhistor* is sometimes given to this work. Solinus introduced the name 'Mediterranean Sea'.

Sōlon (*c*.640–after 561 BC), Athenian statesman, celebrated for his humane reform of the city's laws; he was also a poet, and wrote elegiac and iambic poetry to publicize and justify his political policies. For later Greek historians his poetry was the main source of information on the economic and social crisis that he attempted to deal with.

Solon was elected *archon for 594/3 at a time when Athens was on the brink of revolution, largely owing to an agrarian system in which the rich landowners grew richer and the poor were reduced in some cases to slavery and altogether to despair. Selling a debtor as a chattel slave if his possessions failed to cover the debt was an accepted practice and many Athenians had found themselves unable to meet their obligations and had either been sold over the border of Attica as slaves or had

fled into exile to avoid that fate. Solon's two relief measures were first of all the cancellation of all debts for which land or freedom was the security (a reform known as the *seisachtheia*, 'shaking-off of burdens') and secondly the prohibition of all future borrowing on the security of the person himself. Other economic reforms were credited to him (perhaps not reliably): notably the prohibition of the export of any crops except the olive (thus keeping for home consumption the surplus grain of the rich landowners who had been selling it outside Attica), and the granting of citizenship to immigrant craftsmen, to strengthen home industry. He also introduced a more humane legal code, repealing all the laws of *Draco except those concerned with homicide. His great reform of the constitution was to grade eligibility to political office in terms of wealth, not birth, and thus to break the hereditary monopoly of power.

It was said by later writers that after his reforms Solon spent ten years in overseas travel, visiting Egypt and Cyprus among other places (but on chronological evidence almost certainly not meeting Croesus of Lydia, despite the legends). He returned to find Athens distracted by regional strife and lived long enough to see *Peisistratus voted a bodyguard, the first step towards his tyranny.

Solon used verse to express his ideas and explain the motives, indeed the moral philosophy, that lay behind his reforms. His poetic eulogy of 'good order', *Eunomia*, has as much to do with the idea of justice as with its practical application. In a famous reply to the poet Mimnermus, who had said that he wanted to die when he reached 60, Solon declared that the poet should rather say 80. This should probably be taken with another famous line by Solon to the effect that even as he grows old he still continues to learn, *gēraskō d'aiei polla didaskomenos*.

So'mnium, see LUCIAN.

So'mnium Scipiō'nis ('dream of Scipio'), surviving portion of the otherwise lost sixth book of Cicero's *De republica*, preserved in the commentary of *Macrobius. It takes the form of a narrative placed in the mouth of *Scipio

Aemilianus. He relates a visit to the court of Masinissa (see SOPHONISBA), a Numidian ally of Rome during the Second Punic War (218–201 BC), during which there was much talk of the first great Scipio, the hero of that war, who was given the *cognomen* Africanus. When the younger Scipio retired to bed, the ghost of the elder appeared to him in a dream, foretold his future, and exhorted him to virtue, patriotism, and disregard of human fame; for those who have served their country well there will be the reward of a heavenly habitation in the afterlife (see also POSIDONIUS for the Stoic origin of this idea). The narrative incidentally indicates Cicero's concept of the universe, borrowed from Greek philosophers. The 'Dream' is largely modelled on the myth of Er in the tenth book of Plato's *Republic*. A poetical summary of it occurs in Geoffrey Chaucer's *Parliament of Fowls* (perhaps 1382).

sophist (*sophistēs*), originally meaning in Greek a man who had a particular skill and therefore a claim to wisdom. In the fifth century BC it came to be specially, though not exclusively, applied to itinerant teachers who went from city to city giving lectures and private instruction for a fee. The subjects they taught were wide ranging, such as geography, mathematics, science, linguistics, but their overriding purpose was to train rich young men to be successful in public life; in their own words they 'taught virtue' (*aretē*). To this end all of them to some extent included in their curriculum the teaching of rhetoric, the art of public speaking; some, notably *Gorgias, concentrated on this subject exclusively and gave public performances to advertise their rhetorical skill; the ability to argue persuasively was essential for political advancement, and politics was the career above all other in the ancient world that offered power, fame, and fortune. The sophists satisfied a need among the ambitious for a kind of advanced education which was not obtainable elsewhere, attuned to the times, inclusive of new knowledge, practical and sophisticated. It is not surprising that sophists enjoyed great popularity among those for whom they catered, and amassed large fortunes.

Their emphasis upon worldly success as well as their advocacy of the idea, which much impressed the Athenians, that the ability to plead a case and win depends on a skill that can be taught rather than on having a just cause (see the *Clouds* of Aristophanes), were factors in promoting the scepticism and moral relativism that were associated with their name. Famous sophists were Gorgias of Leontini, *Protagoras of Abdera, Prodicus of Ceos, *Hippias of Elis, and *Thrasymachus of Chalcedon (see also ANTIPHON). Most Athenians of the day would have included *Socrates, not aware of the radical differences in his outlook, but seeing that he too was an intellectual who questioned people's unexamined beliefs about the gods, the laws, and traditional values.

The dangerous effect of the sophists was evident in the late fifth-century phenomenon of able, cynical, and recklessly self-seeking politicians, but, on the other side, the intellectual stimulus they provided is manifested in the arguments and educational theories of Plato.

Sophist, The (*Sophistēs*), dialogue by *Plato, a sequel to *Theaetetus*; Plato once more applies himself to problems raised by the *Eleatics. The main speaker is an Eleatic philosopher, left unnamed; Socrates and Theodorus have scarcely anything to say. The dialogue starts with the definition of a *sophist, at the end of which the question arises whether what the sophist produces is false, and whether there can be a 'false' or 'unreal' thing, since the Eleatics believe that 'what is not', and therefore falsehood, cannot exist (see PARMENIDES). The dialogue finds a solution in the doctrine that all things partake of 'difference'; in making a denial we are not making an antithesis between something and nothing, but an opposition between something and something else different from it: 'what is not' is in fact 'what is different'. Plato is thus able to demonstrate the existence of falsehood and error.

Sophistic, Second, in Greek parts of the world under the Roman empire during the second century AD, a revival of the teaching and practice of Greek rhetoric of the late fifth and fourth centuries BC,

associated with a general cultural flowering made possible by the peace and
security of the times. The term Second
Sophistic was coined by Flavius
*Philostratus (second to third century AD)
who wrote in his 'Lives of the Sophists'
the biographies of his predecessors and
contemporaries. He used the term to distinguish the later from the first sophistic
age, the time of the fifth-century *sophist
Gorgias; according to him the Second
Sophistic, with its interest in historical
themes, originated with the orator *Aeschines, but did not emerge as a recognizable movement until the second century
AD. The name 'sophist' has a wide meaning in the later context; it includes professional rhetors and teachers, and may
include others whose profession was
primarily concerned with the written or
spoken word, such as lawyers. On the
whole the sophists distinguished themselves from philosophers.

Despite freedom of speech, the
rhetoric of this period was of an artificial
kind, consisting of declamations (see
DECLAMATIONES) delivered as public
entertainment, and subsequently published as literature. These sophists continued the tradition and imitated the
virtuoso performances of the fifth-century sophists, as well as carefully imitating the language and style of the best
Attic writers, Xenophon, Plato, and
Demosthenes. Most of them moved to
and settled in the great cultural centres of
the time, Athens, Smyrna, Ephesus, and
to a lesser extent Pergamum, but their
lecture tours took them far afield. The
audiences were educated and sophisticated, familiar with the themes (i.e. the
subjects for declamation), appreciative of
variation, allusion, and subtle effect.
Often the audience selected the theme,
which the rhetor would meditate on for a
few minutes before delivering his declamation extempore. Others preferred to
speak on a prepared subject. Although
the practice, which concentrated so much
on form at the expense of content, could
be seen as stultifying, study of the Attic
models infused the rhetoric with something of the philosophy of the originals
and helped create for some a new Platonism (see PLATO), for others a philosophical Hellenism which amalgamated the

central beliefs from different philosophical systems.

Many of the sophists of this period are
described by Philostratus (see above).
For individuals who were sophists or
moved in sophistic circles see ARISTEIDES
(3), APULEIUS, DION CHRYSOSTOM,
FAVORINUS, FRONTO, GALEN, HERODES ATTI-
CUS, LUCIAN, and MAXIMUS OF TYRE; see
also PLUTARCH.

The unsettled conditions of the mid-
third century brought about a decline in
literature, but there was a revival in the
late third and fourth centuries, the last
great peaceful and prosperous classical
period, when sophists once again
flourished; see HIMERIUS, LIBANIUS, and
THEMISTIUS; see also the emperor JULIAN.

Sophists, Against the, see ISOCRATES.

So'phoclēs (*c*.496–406/5 BC), one of the
great Athenian tragedians, born at Col-
ōnus near Athens, the son of Sophilus, a
wealthy manufacturer of armour. The
anonymous ancient biography of the poet
gives a great deal of information about
him, no doubt much of it unreliable. His
beauty and his skill in music and dancing
early attracted attention; as a boy he led
the chorus which sang the paean in
honour of the Greek victory over the Persian invaders at Salamis in 480 BC. His
first victory in the tragic competitions was
at the Great *Dionysia in 468 BC, at his
first attempt it is said, when he defeated
Aeschylus. His early life coincided with
the expansion of the Athenian empire,
and though he took no active part in
politics as far as is known, he was twice
elected *strategos* ('general'). After the
failure of the *Sicilian Expedition in 413
he was made one of the *probouloi* ('commissioners') to deal with the crisis. Ami-
able and popular, he was a good citizen
who lived and died in Athens; he is said
to have refused invitations to visit the
courts of kings (unlike Aeschylus and
Euripides). Aristophanes in the *Frogs*,
writing a year after Sophocles' death,
summed up his character in the line (82),
'contented among the living, contented
among the dead'; only a few months
before his death Sophocles presented his
chorus and actors at the *proagon* in
mourning garb for the death of
Euripides. He left two sons: by

Nicostratē, Iophon the tragedian; and by Theōris of Sicyon, Agathon, father of the younger Sophocles, also a tragedian.

He is said to have composed 130 plays, of which seven were later judged to be spurious, and to have won twenty-four dramatic competitions with his tetralogies (i.e. ninety-six plays were successful); with the rest he came second, never third. Seven tragedies are extant; the suggested dates seem likely but (except for *Philoctētēs* and *Oedipus Coloneus*) by no means certain: *Antigonē* 441; *Trachiniae* and *Ajax* probably earlier; *Oedipus Tyrannus* soon after 430; *Electra* between 418 and 410; *Philoctetes* 409; *Oedipus Coloneus* probably written 406/5, produced posthumously in 401 by the younger Sophocles. For the plots of these plays see their individual titles. A large fragment of his satyr-play *Ichneutae* ('trackers'; see SATYR DRAMA) has been recovered from a papyrus found in modern times. Its plot concerned the theft of Apollo's cattle by Hermes soon after the latter's birth. As well as writing tragedies he was the author of a prose treatise, 'On the Chorus'.

According to Aristotle in the *Poetics*, Sophocles was an innovator in tragedy: he added a third to the previously accepted two actors, introduced 'scene painting', and increased the chorus from twelve to fifteen; he also abandoned the Aeschylean practice of writing trilogies on related events (see TRAGEDY 1), instead giving each play a self-contained plot. Since the actors in Greek tragedy might play more than one part, the introduction of the third actor enabled Sophocles to make plot, dialogue, and the relationship of characters much more complex. His characters were admired by Aristotle for being 'like ourselves only nobler'; Sophocles is said to have remarked that he depicted people as they ought to be, Euripides as they are; nevertheless his characters are not wholly idealized but remain manifestly human. His heroes and heroines are placed in circumstances in which they must act, and by their actions, which often have tragic consequences, they show their heroic stature. More than those of the other tragedians, Sophocles' heroes and heroines give the impression that it is their innate characters that initiate the action, and that they could not have behaved otherwise. When, as in *Ajax*, *Antigone*, and *Trachiniae*, the main character dies well before the end of the play and the plot takes a turn in another direction, some slackening of the tension is inevitably felt; but even so, the concluding part still seems to follow necessarily from what has preceded. In the other plays the unity is complete; in particular, the tight-knit plot of *Oedipus Tyrannus* (which for Aristotle represented Greek tragedy at its greatest) is handled with amazing dexterity and at a rapid pace.

Sophocles rarely introduces into the self-contained world of the play ideas that relate more to contemporary affairs, a factor that makes dating the plays on internal evidence difficult. He was a master of dialogue, both in speeches and in *stichomythia. One feature for which he became famous is dramatic irony, of the kind where the speaker's words have an underlying significance for the audience, already familiar with the outlines of a story drawn from a well-known body of myth (see TRAGEDY 1). The language of Sophocles is dignified, avoiding the grandiose and over-naturalistic, and often dense, rather in aid of economy than at the expense of clarity. Some of the lyric odes are outstanding, moving the action on to a different plane. According to Plutarch, Sophocles distinguished three periods in his own style: the first, when he imitated the 'high-flown' style of Aeschylus; the second, when his style was 'harsh and artificial'; and the third, when it was 'most suitable for expressing characters and best for drama'. All his extant plays seem to belong to the third period.

The plays show a conventional but deeply felt piety: that the gods enforce their justice upon human life, and the wise act as best they may in accordance with divine will. In this connection Matthew Arnold's judgement of Sophocles (in his sonnet, *To a Friend*) as one 'who saw life steadily and saw it whole' is often quoted. The poet Shelley had a volume of Sophocles in his pocket when he was drowned in 1822.

Sophoni'sba, daughter of a Carthaginian general Hasdrubal, son of Gisgo; she married Syphax, king of Numidia, at the time of the Second Punic War (218–201 BC) and drew him away from his alliance with Rome on to the Carthaginian side. When he was defeated in 203 by a Roman army led by Masinissa, a Numidian prince in alliance with Rome, Masinissa fell in love with the captive Sophonisba, and according to the romantic story in Livy sent her poison as the only means of saving her from the disgrace of being sent as a captive to Rome by Scipio, who was afraid of her influence on Masinissa's loyalty. Sophonisba calmly drank the poison. James Thomson's tragedy of 1730 (one among many on the subject) contained the notorious line, 'Oh! Sophonisba! Sophonisba! Oh!'.

Sō'phron, SEE MIME.

sortēs, SEE ORACLES and VIRGIL.

sortition, election by lot, a method of appointing *magistrates in Greek democracies, best known from its use at Athens. This method of appointment, combined with the prohibition of, or severe restriction on, re-election, allowed considerable rotation in office and reinforced the sovereignty of the assembly. The *strategoi and some financial officers, however, in whom technical skill was required, were appointed by vote.

So'sii, famous booksellers at Rome, referred to by Horace (*Epistles* 1. 20. 2).

Sō'tadēs (third century BC), of Marōnea in Thrace, Greek iambic poet, said to have been put to death for writing lampoons against the marriage in 276/5 of Ptolemy II Philadelphus and his sister Arsinoe II (a marriage of a kind traditional in pharaonic Egypt but scandalous to Greeks). He invented a flexible form of metre named after him (sotadean), which was used for several centuries after his time for coarse satires and mythological burlesques. Only a dozen or so lines and a few titles of his works remain.

Spain (Gk. Ibēria, from the name of the river Ibērus, Ebro; Lat. Hispania). From earliest times the races of Spain have been mixed; peoples arriving from Africa in Neolithic times (to exploit the mineral resources) spread throughout the south and east, mixing in the centre and west with Celts invading from the north in the late Bronze and early Iron Ages. According to tradition, Phoenicians from Tyre discovered *Tartessus and colonized *Gades *c.*1100 BC. In the third century BC the Carthaginians under Hamilcar, Hasdrubal, and Hannibal conquered much of Spain, but the Romans, under Scipio Africanus, drove them out of the country (206) during the Second *Punic War. Two Roman provinces were established in Spain in 197. They comprised at first only a relatively small portion of the peninsula, and were known as Hispania Citerior, 'Hither Spain', the eastern seaboard, and Hispania Ulterior, 'Further Spain', roughly modern Andalusia. But the native population had not then been effectively subdued, and unrest continued for many years. An important pacification was brought about in 179 by Ti. Sempronius Gracchus (father of the Gracchi), who by his personal character won the confidence of the Spaniards. But native risings were renewed in 154, and Numantia resisted the Romans for nine years. Its capture by Scipio Aemilianus in 133 brought the Spanish wars to a close, the Romans then occupying about two thirds of the peninsula, failing to hold only the mountainous region in the north and north-west.

In the civil wars of the first century BC Spain was held by the Marian leader *Sertorius against the party of Sulla, and later against Pompey, until Sertorius was murdered in 72. The military talent of Julius Caesar was first revealed when he was propraetor in Spain in 61. He subsequently waged war there in 49 against the Pompeian generals Afranius and Petreius, and in 45 against the sons of Pompey, finally making himself master of the Roman empire by his victory at *Munda. Notable among the colonies that he founded were Hispalis (Seville) and Tarraco (Tarragona). A final pacification of the whole peninsula, including the north and north-west, was achieved by the emperor Augustus.

In literature, Spanish colonies produced the two Senecas and Lucan; Columella, Quintilian, and Martial came from native stock. The emperor Trajan was born in Spain, and Hadrian and Marcus Aurelius belonged to Spanish families. The Frankish invasions of the early third century AD severely disrupted northern Spain, but a strong Christian church emerged in the fourth century, inspiring the works of *Prudentius and *Orosius; it survived the barbarian invasions of the fifth century, and converted the Visigothic kings to Christianity. The seventh-century bishop of Seville, *Isidore, was an important link in continuity between classical culture and the Middle Ages.

Sparta (Spartē, or *Lacedaemon), the capital of Laconia, a state in the southeast of the Peloponnese founded by Dorians (see DORIAN INVASION and HERACLEIDAE). Lacedaemon was the usual name for both the city and the state; the name Sparta was applied only to the city, and then in poetic or patriotic contexts. The city was situated on high ground on the west bank of the river Eurotas, and consisted of little more than a group of villages, without fine buildings, and unfortified until the end of the fourth century BC.

By 700 BC all the territory of the eastern coastal strip of Laconia had been incorporated into the Spartan state, and the population there was either reduced to a condition of limited independence in which they were known as *perioikoi, 'dwellers round about', or had become serfs, known as *helots, bound to the land which they cultivated for their Spartan masters. The creation of this class was the first stage in a way of life that was to distinguish Sparta from every other Greek state. The helot system relieved the Spartans of tending the land themselves and allowed the men to spend an abnormally large amount of time training as soldiers.

After the age of 7 the Spartan boy was devoted to a military regime which produced the finest army in Greece and, gradually, a proverbially famous austerity of life. He was taken from home and enrolled in a group of his contemporaries under the leadership of an older boy, and with this group he lived for the next fourteen years, educated for toughness, endurance, and military discipline.

Spartan girls also underwent physical training. Music and dancing were part of the curriculum because they had military uses, but only the essentials of reading and writing were taught. Other details are obscure. At the end of his education the Spartan joined the eirěněs or young men who had completed their twentieth year, and remained with them living in barracks until he was 30, when he became a full citizen with the right to vote in the assembly. The Spartan political system, associated with the name of *Lycurgus, was a rigid oligarchy in which considerable power was given to the kings, magistrates (*ephors), and council of elders (*gerousia). There were two royal houses (Agiads and Eurypontids), and two kings ruled concurrently. They were the religious representatives of the state and leaders of the army in war, but the ephors had greater power and could even sentence the kings to be fined or imprisoned.

In foreign relations, Sparta at first followed a policy of conquest and expansion, establishing her predominance in the Peloponnese, and defeating and weakening her principal rival Argos. Towards the middle of the sixth century she abandoned this policy and set about consolidating her position. She formed a league of the Peloponnesian states (including Corinth and Megara but neither Argos or Achaea) under her own leadership, with meetings held at Sparta and was now the strongest power in Greece. Her narrow and inward-looking policy was made evident when in 499 she refused assistance to the Ionian Greeks in their revolt against Persia (see PERSIAN WARS). But when Xerxes prepared for war against Greece itself, Sparta combined with Athens in measures of defiance and showed the bravery of her soldiers at the battles of Thermopylae and Plataea. This co-operation ceased after the final defeat of the Persians at Mycalē in 479, and Sparta no longer took the lead in Greek affairs. This was partly as a result of the rise in importance of Athens (see DELIAN LEAGUE) and Sparta also suffered a devastating earthquake in 464 and a war (464–460) caused by a revolt of the helots. Jealousy and fear of Athenian expansion twice brought about war between Athens and Sparta: in 460–446 (sometimes called the First Peloponnesian War); and in 431–404 (the *Peloponnesian War).

The defeat of Athens in 404 left Sparta supreme in Greece, but her falling citizen population (the reasons for which have been much debated), rigid institutions, and the individualist ambitions of her leaders (see LYSANDER and AGESILAUS) did not fit her for an imperial role. She entered on a period of arrogant aggrandisement which aroused the hostility of her neighbours and led to a crushing victory for *Thebes over Sparta at Leuctra in 371. Thereafter Thebes took the role of the aggressor. Sparta was repeatedly invaded by the Theban commander Epaminondas, who dealt her a fatal blow by freeing Messenia (370/69) and refounding it as an independent state after 300 years of servitude to Sparta. The formation of a league of Arcadian cities (see MEGALOPOLIS) after Leuctra also weakened Sparta's influence; this too was the work of Thebes. Sparta was not actually captured by Philip II of Macedon when he invaded the Peloponnese after the battle of Chaeronea in 338, but her territory and power were further diminished, and her important role in Greek history now came to an end. The city became prosperous under the Romans but was sacked by Goths in AD 395.

Sparta differed from other Greek states not only in her peculiar constitution and in the supreme importance she attached to military efficiency, but in certain other respects: she did not use coined money until the third century BC, the currency taking the form of iron 'spits', *oboloi*; and women enjoyed a position in some respects approaching equality with men, with greater independence and authority than at Athens, and were expected to interest themselves in the welfare of their country. The warlike attitude of the Spartan state meant that it offered virtually no encouragement to the arts, but in the seventh century BC, before militarism because a way of life, Sparta was famous for choral *lyric poetry (see ALCMAN, TERPANDER, and THALETAS). At the same period *Tyrtaeus wrote war-songs.

Thereafter, however, the art of poetry seems to have died. The Spartan reputation for terseness has given 'laconic' (from Laconia) to the English language — when Philip of Macedon wrote to them, 'If I invade Laconia I shall turn you out,' they wrote back, 'If'.

Spa'rtacus, Thracian slave-gladiator who in 73 BC escaped from a school of gladiators at Capua with seventy companions and led a revolt, joined by large numbers of other slaves and desperate men. Spartacus' army is said to have numbered 90,000 men, and within the year he had defeated two Roman armies and devastated southern Italy. In 72 he defeated another three armies, and reached Cisalpine Gaul, but his followers refused the chance to escape over the Alps and marched south again to plunder Italy; he was finally defeated and killed in 71 by M. Licinius *Crassus, who subsequently crucified any rebels he captured. Pompey returned from Spain in time to annihilate the remnants, thereby taking credit for ending the war. Spartacus quickly became a legend not only for his daring successes but for personal qualities of bravery, strength, and humanity. His name has often been invoked by revolutionaries, but he was fighting for personal liberty rather than trying to bring down Rome.

Sparti (Spartoi), see CADMUS.

Spartiā'nus, Ae'lius, see *HISTORIA AUGUSTA.*

Speusi'ppus (*c*.407–339 BC), nephew of Plato and his successor as head of the *Academy from 347 to 339. Of his voluminous writings only fragments survive, together with accounts of his work by later writers. He seems to have continued along the lines of Platonic dogmatism; Aristotle speaks of him with respect.

spheres, harmony or **music of the,** SEE HARMONY OF THE SPHERES.

sphinx (from *sphingein*, 'to bind fast'), in Greek myth, a monster usually depicted with the head of a woman on the (winged) body of a lion; bearded male sphinxes are sometimes found in early Greek art. Hesiod made her the child of *Chimaera and *Orthrus; according to others she was the child of *Echidna and *Typhon. In the story of *Oedipus and the Sphinx, the riddle she posed was 'What is it that walks on four legs in the morning, on two at noon, and on three in the evening?' The answer was 'A man', who as an infant crawls on all fours and in old age walks with a stick.

spo'lia opi'ma ('spoils of honour'), the arms taken by a Roman general, in full command of his army, from the body of an enemy leader whom he has killed in single combat. They were reckoned by the Romans to have been won three times: by Romulus from Acron, king of the Caeninenses, in the hostilities that followed the Rape of the Sabines; by Aulus Cornelius Cossus, according to Livy in 437 BC, when he killed Tolumnius the Etruscan king; and by M. Claudius Marcellus who killed the Gaul Viridomarus in 222 BC. The spoils were dedicated to Jupiter Feretrius; lesser spoils, *spolia secunda* and *tertia*, were dedicated to Mars and Janus Quirinus.

spondee, see METRE, GREEK 1 (ii) and 3.

SPQR, in Roman documents, inscriptions, etc., abbreviation for *senatus populusque Romanus*, 'the senate and people of Rome'; see POPULUS.

stade, stā'dium (*stădion*), Greek unit of length, the 'stade', 600 (Greek) feet long, and so in the range 175–200 metres or somewhat less than an English furlong. Because the most famous running-track, that of Olympia, was exactly a stade long, the word came to denote any running-track, 'stadium'. A stadium was generally a piece of level ground a little over 200 m. long and up to about 40 m. wide, with a starting line at each end. In the middle of each line was a turning post round which runners had to make a turn for any race longer than a single length. Since level ground of such a size was not easy to find in mountainous Greece, one end of the stadium was often left curving naturally into the hillside. In this way the stadium came to have what is now considered its characteristic U-shape. The best-preserved ancient stadia may be seen at Olympia, Delphi, Athens, and Epidaurus. The stadium at Athens was

rebuilt by *Herodes Atticus in marble, with seats to hold 50,000 spectators.

Stagei'ra (or Stageiros), Greek town near the east coast of Chalcidicē, famous as the birthplace of Aristotle, who in consequence is sometimes referred to as 'the Stagīrite'. It was destroyed by Philip II of Macedon in 348 BC, but rebuilt by him in honour of Aristotle, whom he appointed as tutor to his son Alexander.

Statei'ra, see ALEXANDER (2) 6.

stater, a Lydian coin which circulated widely in the ancient world, generally having the monetary value and the weight of two drachmas (see MONEY .and WEIGHTS).

Stā'tius. 1. Caeci'lius Statius, see CAECILIUS.

2. **Publius Papi'nius Statius** (*c.* AD 45–*c.*96), Roman poet, born at Naples, the son of a *grammaticus* or schoolmaster and teacher of literature, who was himself a poet and encouraged the literary aptitude of his son. In Rome he recited his poems to large audiences and won a contest held by the emperor Domitian. His (extant) epic in twelve books, the *Thebaid, was published in 90 or 91 after twelve years' toil; it tells the story of the quarrel between Oedipus' sons Eteoclēs and Polyneicēs. Soon afterwards Statius began to issue the *Silvae. In (probably) 94 he failed to win the Capitoline poetry competition and was deeply disappointed. About this time he retired to Naples, where he began the composition of an epic, the *Achilleid, broken off in book 2 by the poet's death, apparently before the murder of Domitian in September 96.

Statius married Claudia, a widow with one daughter, and was deeply attached to her. He had no children of his own; his sorrow at the death of an adopted son is expressed in the last poem of the *Silvae*. He associated with prominent men, including Domitian himself, whom he flattered obsequiously. His lost works include the libretto for a *pantomime *Agavē*, on the story of Pentheus, and an epic *De bello Germanico* ('on the German war') on Domitian's campaigns. His poetry strikes many as generally overworked; it is full of literary and rhetorical devices, allusive, and in a highly artificial language; the *Silvae*, being simpler, more spontaneous, and less polished, have for many readers a greater appeal, but the *Thebaid* has attractions for those with a taste for hyperbole and the macabre, and there are episodes of drama and pathos.

Statius was much admired in the Middle Ages; regarded by Dante as a Christian, he appears in Cantos 21 and 22 of the *Purgatorio* where his spirit meets that of Virgil, appropriately enough in view of Statius' reverence for the earlier poet. Statius is made to explain how he was led to Christianity by certain passages in Virgil. The English poets Alexander Pope and Thomas Gray both translated portions of the *Thebaid*.

Stentor, Greek at the siege of Troy who could shout as loudly as fifty men (*Iliad* 5. 785).

Ste'ropēs, name of one of the three *Cyclopēs.

Stēsi'chorus ('choir-setter'), Greek lyric poet writing in the first half of the sixth century BC whose real name was Teisias. He was said to have been born at Matauros (Metaurum) in the toe of Italy and to have lived at Himera in Sicily. He wrote narrative *lyric poetry (of what type is not certain) classified by the ancients as choral lyric because its structure was *triadic, and is even said to have been the inventor of this particular form. It has seemed to some that the great length of his poems precludes their being sung and danced by a chorus, and that it is more likely that the poet performed them himself, to the accompaniment of a lyre, in the manner of a Homeric bard (see HOMER). Certainly the poems were long: the *Geryonēis* exceeded 1,800 lines (by comparison, not many of Pindar's choral odes are much over a hundred lines long), and the *Oresteia* occupied two books. The Alexandrian scholars collected the poems into twenty-six books. Only fragments survive, and most of these have been recovered from papyrus in the twentieth century.

Existing titles indicate that the subjects were taken from a wide range of epic sources, from the *Epic Cycle as well as Homer. His *Oresteia* differed from the story in Homer in placing the death of Agamemnon at Sparta (not Mycenae or Argos); as Aeschylus did in the *Choephoroe*, Stesichorus included Clytemnestra's dream and gave some part to Orestes' nurse. The *Geryoneis*, which told of Heracles' search for the cattle of Geryon (see HERACLES, LABOURS OF 10) is remarkable for an early mention of the silver mines of Tartessus (see SPAIN); it also has a memorable description of the cup of the Sun (see HELIOS). The *Funeral Games of Pelias* is connected with the legends of the Argonauts, the *Boarhunters* with the Calydonian boar-hunt, the *Eriphylē* with Theban legend. The *Iliupersis*, 'Sack of Troy', drew on the Epic Cycle and included an account of Epeus, who made the Wooden Horse; some believe that it may have been the source for the stories of Aeneas' wanderings to Italy (see TABULA ILIACA). Stesichorus told the story of Helen of Troy twice, first in the usual version as the cause of the Trojan War, 'and secondly in the form familiar from Euripides' play *Helen*, according to which Helen's phantom went to Troy while she herself remained behind in Egypt. Legend relates that he was struck with blindness for 'slandering' Helen in the first poem, and that his sight was restored after he recanted and wrote his famous *Palinode*, blaming Homer for the earlier story. His language and style show the strong influence of epic, but have many features of later choral lyric, e.g. the rich use of epithets. The metre he used was a form of dactylo-epitrite (see METRE, GREEK 8). His influence on contemporary art was considerable, many of his subjects appearing on the vases of the day.

Stheneboe'a, see BELLEROPHON.

Sthenno, see GORGONS.

stichomy'thia, 'talking by the line', in Greek drama, dialogue that is conducted by two characters speaking in alternate lines (though strict regularity is not always maintained). Stichomythia can be very effective in a confrontation, but the difficulty of maintaining such a form can lead to artificiality of expression, nicely illustrated in A. E. Housman's famous parody, 'Fragment of a Greek Tragedy':

Chorus: Might I then hear at what your presence shoots?
Alcmaeon: A shepherd's questioned mouth informed me that—
Chorus: What? For I know not yet what you will say.
Alcmaeon: Nor will you ever if you interrupt.
Chorus: Proceed, and I will hold my speechless tongue.
Alcmaeon:—This house was Eriphyla's, no one's else.

Stichus, Roman comedy by *Plautus. The title is taken from the name of one of the characters, a slave. The comedy has little plot. The two daughters of Antipho are married to two brothers. These have gone abroad on a trading venture to retrieve their fortunes, and at the opening of the play they have been absent for three years and no news has been received. Antipho urges his daughters to marry again, but they insist on remaining faithful to their husbands. The husbands have prospered and now return, and their home-coming is a matter of celebration. Much comedy is derived from the behaviour of a hungry *parasite and from the portrayal of slaves enjoying themselves.

Sti'licho, Flavius (c. AD 365–408), general of the Roman armies and, when the young emperor Honorius (b. 384) succeeded Theodosius I in 395, the effective ruler of the western Roman empire. He successfully repelled the first invasions into Italy of Alaric and the Visigoths in 401 and 403, but was put to death by order of Honorius in 408 (before the sack of Rome by Alaric in 410). See CLAUDIAN.

sto'a, Greek word for a roofed colonnade or portico (English 'porch') with a wall on one side, erected as a separate building near temples or gymnasia or in market-places as a sheltered place in which to walk and talk or hold meetings. The wall was often decorated with paintings or inscriptions. Thus the Stoa Poikilē ('painted colonnade') in the agora at Athens, built c.460 BC, was adorned with frescos by famous artists, including one by *Polygnotus representing the destruction of Troy. It was from this stoa, frequented by the philosopher Zeno and his disciples, that the Stoic school of philosophy derived its name.

Stobae'us, Johannes (i.e. John of Stobi, in Macedonia), compiler in the early fifth century AD of an anthology of excerpts from (pagan) Greek poets and prose-writers, in the first instance for the instruction of his son Septimius. These excerpts were originally arranged in four books whose subjects included philosophy, physics, rhetoric, poetry, ethics, morals, and politics. They were later grouped under the titles *Eklogai* and *Anthologion*. The latter has survived, and preserves quotations from works which have not otherwise come down to modern times.

stoichē'don, see EPIGRAPHY I.

Stoics. The Stoic school of philosophy was founded in Athens c.300 BC by *Zeno of Citium (in Cyprus), taking its name from the *Stoa Poikilē at Athens where Zeno did his teaching. He came to Athens c.311 BC and first attended lectures at the *Academy (the Platonic school) but was converted to Cynicism by Cratēs (see CYNIC PHILOSOPHERS). Study of the works of *Antisthenēs, a devoted follower of Socrates (and regarded by some as the founder of Cynicism), turned him to Socratic philosophy, out of which he developed his own 'Stoic' system, embracing logic, theory of knowledge, physics, and above all ethics. At his death Athens honoured him with a public funeral, as a man who 'had made his life an example to all, for he followed his own teaching'. Although the school seems to have been less strictly organized than the Academy and the Lyceum (the school of Aristotelian philosophy), it nevertheless had a succession of heads to at least AD 260, and probably for some years after. It gradually faded out, however, and was no longer in existence when the emperor Justinian closed the philosophical schools at Athens in AD 529.

The main Stoic doctrines were the following. Nature (the whole universe, that is) is controlled by reason, *logos*, which is identified with God and shows itself as fate (also called necessity or providence); whatever happens is in accordance with divine reason. It is thus the aim of the wise man who knows this truth to accept what happens and to live in harmony with nature (or divine reason); this is virtue and the only good. Whatever happens to us cannot be otherwise; the wise man aims to achieve willing acquiescence. Not to do this is to show moral weakness instead of virtue, and this is the only evil. Everything else—pain, poverty, death (even a cold in the head, as the poet Horace ironically observes at the end of his first Epistle)—is indifferent. It is beyond the power of anyone to deprive the wise man of virtue; always knowing the only true good, he is therefore happy. He is also absolutely brave, since he knows that pain and death are not evils, and self-controlled, since he knows that pleasure is not the good.

Matter breaks down into the four elements, earth, air, fire, and water. Fire, the element most closely related to divine reason, periodically consumes the universe, and out of it in time a new universe arises, and so on for ever. Every man possesses a spark of that divine fire. This belief led, importantly, to the Stoic concept of the universal brotherhood of man, without distinction between Greek and barbarian, freeman and slave, and of the consequent duty of universal benevolence and justice. In spite of this, Stoicism was in the main a doctrine of detachment from and independence of the outer world.

The immediate successor of Zeno was *Cleanthēs, followed in 232 BC by *Chrysippus of Soli (in Cilicia), converted to Stoicism by Cleanthēs, who completed and systematized the Stoic doctrine. Among Zeno's pupils was Sphaerus, who inspired the revolution of Cleomenes III at Sparta (see CLEOMENES (2)). All these philosophers belonged to the Early Stoa. The famous names of the subsequent period, the second and first centuries BC, the so-called Middle Stoa, are those of *Panaetius and Posidonius. The former, who spent much time in Rome, was the first to reject the doctrine of periodic universal conflagrations, and also rejected the belief that only the absolutely wise man can be virtuous,

teaching that those who merely aspired to virtue were making progress. While at Rome he joined the circle of P. *Scipio Aemilianus, and his practical version of Stoic ethics, seemingly adapted for the needs of active statesmen and soldiers, had very great influence on the Scipionic circle. Through his writings Panaetius influenced the Younger *Cato, *Brutus, *Cicero (1), and many others. Posidonius submitted the doctrines of the early Stoics to an even more thoroughgoing revision, and his influence was wide and far-reaching.

During the Roman empire the Late Stoics were almost exclusively concerned with ethical questions. The most important Stoics of the first century AD were *Seneca the Younger, *Cornutus, *Musonius Rufus, and, towards the end of the century, *Epictetus. Stoicism provided the philosophical basis for opposition to the one-man rule of the emperors: Paetus *Thrasea and his son-in-law *Helvidius Priscus, resolute opponents of Nero, were Stoics; the emperors Vespasian and Domitian both banished the philosophers from Italy. But after Epictetus the emperor M. *Aurelius was the most famous Stoic in the second century. During the third century the school gradually died out, but it had an important and long-lasting effect on the life and thought of many, influencing *Neoplatonism and permeating the Christianity of some of the early Fathers of the Church.

Strābo (Strabōn, 64 BC–after AD 24), Greek geographer from Amasia in Pontus, a member of a distinguished local family. He came to Rome in 44 BC to complete his education and subsequently visited the city several times. He travelled 'from Armenia to Etruria, from the Black Sea to the borders of Ethiopia', returning to his home in about 7 BC where he remained until his death. At some time he became a *Stoic; he also developed a profound admiration for the Romans: like *Posidonius, he regarded them as the creators of an earthly world-state comparable with the heavenly one.

He was the author of *Historical Sketches* in forty-seven books, now lost, which comprised an outline of historical

events up to the opening of Polybius'
history, followed by a complete history
from 146 BC (where Polybius ended) up to
at least the death of Julius Caesar. His
surviving great work, the *Geography* in
seventeen books, seems to have been
completed by 7 BC. It has been suggested
that it was originally published at
Amasia, where it was perhaps revised
and republished in about AD 18, in order
to account for the surprising fact that it
was not known to the Romans, not even
to the Elder Pliny, although it seems to
have been known in the East. Strabo
insists that his geography is intended for
political leaders and its aim is to impart
practical wisdom; but it remains unclear
whether it was intended for Romans or
for the Greeks of his native Pontus. He
describes the physical geography of the
chief countries in the Roman world, giving the broad features of their historical
and economic development and an
account of anything remarkable in the
customs of their inhabitants or in their
animal and plant life. The first two books
serve as a general introduction; after a
remarkable preface in which he discusses
geography as a branch of scientific
inquiry, Strabo deals with the dimensions
of the inhabited world and the position of
various places with reference to a simple
grid. Books 3–17 embrace Spain, the Isles
of Scilly, Gaul, Britain (of which he
knows little), Italy, Sicily, north and east
Europe (he knows nothing of northern-
most Europe and Asia), central Europe,
north Balkans, Greece, Asia around the
Black and Caspian Seas, Asia Minor,
India, Persia, Mesopotamia, Palestine,
Arabia, Egypt, Ethiopia, and North
Africa (Strabo takes Africa to be a triangle north of the equator).

Strabo based his geography on
*Eratosthenēs, whom he brought up to
date. He regarded the world as a sphere,
having one land mass, in the northern
hemisphere, entirely surrounded by
ocean. His whole work is invaluable in
informing us about the state of
geographical knowledge in his day, as
well as containing incidentally many
entertaining descriptions: how the
Indians capture elephants and long-tailed
apes, how the Arabians get fresh water
out of the sea, how the Egyptians feed

their sacred crocodiles; the Hanging
Gardens of Babylon, the whales of the
Persian Gulf, the aromatics of the
Sabaeans. The work, in an epitomized
form, was used as a school-book in the
Middle Ages.

Stratēgē'mata, see FRONTINUS and
POLYAENUS.

stratē'gos, in Greece, a military commander. At Athens in the fifth century BC
strategoi were often political as well as
military leaders. The board of *strategoi*
formed an important administrative
council, responsible for all duties relating
to war and the enlistment of soldiers and
sailors. Pericles was *strategos* almost continuously from 443 until his death in 429;
Cleon, Nicias, and Alcibiades all held this
office.

Strife, see ERIS.

strophē ('turn'), in Greek *lyric poetry
(and Latin written in imitation) a stanza.
It was said to have derived its name from
the performance of choral lyric, in which
a stanza or strophe was sung as the chorus
proceeded in its dance in one direction,
followed by a second stanza, the anti-
strophe, corresponding exactly in metre
with the strophe, sung when the chorus
turned and reversed its dance in the
opposite direction. See also TRIAD.
'Astrophic' composition describes
extended lyric passages not written in
stanza form.

Stymphā'lian Birds, see HERACLES,
LABOURS OF 5.

Stymphā'lus, name of a lake in a narrow upland valley under Mount Cyllēnē
in northern Arcadia; the emperor
Hadrian built an aqueduct to take water
to Corinth from one of its springs.

Styx ('the abhorrent'), in Greek myth,
the principal river of the Underworld (see
HADES) over which the souls of the dead
were traditionally said to be ferried by
Charon. According to Hesiod, Styx was
one of the river-spirits who were
daughters of Oceanus and Tethys. Styx
and her children, Zēlos (Glory), Nikē
(Victory), Kratos (Strength), and Bia
(Force), aided Zeus in his quarrel with
the *Titans, in consequence of which she
was greatly honoured, and an oath by

Styx was held inviolable by the gods. According to the Greek historian Herodotus, people swore solemn oaths by a small river of this name in Arcadia which still falls from a tall cliff (the Mavroneri falls), leaving a black stain on the rocks; its water was reputed to be poisonous. Plutarch and Arrian report that Alexander the Great was poisoned by this water, sent to him in a mule's hoof (which withstood its reputedly corrosive nature).

Suāsō'riae, see SENECA (1).

Subli'cian Bridge, see PONS SUBLICIUS.

Sublime, Longinus on the, see LONGINUS.

Successors, the, see DIADOCHOI.

Suda, The (*hē Souda*, 'fortress', formerly referred to as *Suidas*, as if the name of a person), name of a Greek lexicon or literary encyclopaedia compiled at the end of the tenth century AD and containing many valuable articles on Greek literature and history. It is based partly on earlier lexica (see HESYCHIUS), partly on texts, with *scholia, of Homer, Sophocles, Aristophanes, and the Palatine Anthology which the compiler consulted himself, and partly on excerpts made in earlier times from the works of historians, grammarians, and biographers.

Suetō'nius. 1. **Gaius Suetonius Pauli'nus,** see BRITAIN.

2. **Gaius Suetonius Tranqui'llus** (b. *c.* AD 69), Roman biographer. He was the son of the equestrian Suetonius Laetus who as a tribune in the thirteenth legion fought at *Bedriacum in AD 69. The son practised in the law-courts at Rome and was a friend of the Younger Pliny. He became a secretary at the imperial palace, where he would have been able to consult the imperial archives, but in 121/2 he was dismissed by Hadrian, together with the praetorian prefect, allegedly for some indiscretion involving the emperor's wife. After this nothing more is known of his life.

Of his writings, which include works on Roman antiquities, natural sciences, and grammar, much is lost. The surviving works consist of the 'Lives of the Caesars' (*De vita Caesarum*) and part of his 'On Famous Men' (*De viris illustribus*) comprising over half of the sections on the grammarians (*De grammaticis*) and rhetoricians (*De rhetoribus*); in addition his Lives of Terence, Virgil, Horace, and Lucan have been transmitted in manuscripts of these authors' own works; perhaps the Lives of Tibullus and Persius are also by Suetonius. *De grammaticis* sets out what Roman education understands as 'grammar', i.e. broadly the study of literature, and relates its introduction at Rome by *Cratēs (4), as well as giving some account of twenty of the principal grammarians. *De rhetoribus* relates the growth at Rome of the study of rhetoric, which at first was disapproved of by influential Romans, explains the method of teaching it, and illustrates the themes used in the schools. An account of five of the principal teachers of rhetoric follows. The Lives of the poets contain fact, anecdote, and misinformation inextricably confused; passages about the personal appearance of the poets have their own fascination: for instance, that Horace was short and fat.

The 'Lives of the Caesars' include the biographies of Julius Caesar and the eleven subsequent emperors: Augustus, Tiberius, Gaius Caligula, Claudius, Nero, Galba, Otho, Vitellius, Vespasian, Titus, and Domitian. It is clear that Suetonius followed whatever source attracted him, without caring much whether it was reliable or not. It has been thought that he had completed only the Lives of Julius Caesar and Augustus when he was dismissed from the palace, since he makes no direct quotation from correspondence of any emperor later than Augustus. His biographies give an account of the ancestry and career of each emperor, but show little historical grasp or penetration; they consist chiefly of anecdotes, gossipy and salacious, but lively and with interesting detail. The Life of Caesar mentions his dark piercing eyes and his attempts to conceal his baldness. Augustus is said to have been short but well-proportioned, with an aquiline nose and eyebrows that met, careless in dress, frugal, and sparing in diet. Suetonius gives an interesting account of Tiberius' retirement at Rhodes from 6 BC to AD 2, and reproduces the scandalous and perhaps ill-founded stories of a vicious old age at Capri. There is a vivid picture of the grotesque appearance of Caligula, of his waywardness and insane cruelties; of the awkward walk, loud guffaw, and stammer of Claudius, and his blend of culture and good sense with silliness and excessive timidity. The Life of Nero reveals much about his stage displays and his passion for horses (even after he became emperor he used to play with ivory horses and chariots on a table); about his elaborate organization of a claque to applaud his own productions; about his wanderings incognito at night in the streets of Rome; about his *Golden House, and his conduct while Rome burned. The Life of Titus mentions his notable saying at the end of a day when he had done no good to anyone: 'I have lost a day', and his mastery of shorthand and aptitude for imitating the handwriting of others; and that of Domitian records his restoration of the libraries which had been burnt down and his efforts to collect manuscripts.

The pattern Suetonius followed is always the same: the subject's family and early life, public career, physical appearance, private life. The work became a model for biography in the Middle Ages.

Suˉ'idas, see SUDA.

Sulla, Lucius Corne'lius (c.138–78 BC), Roman general and leader of the *optimatēs (aristocratic party) in the civil war against the *popularis *Marius. Born of a patrician but not distinguished family, Sulla had outstanding success as a soldier in the war against *Jugurtha, whose surrender he obtained in 107 BC, in campaigns against German tribes, and in the *Social War (90–88 BC). He gained the consulship in 88 and was designated by the senate for the command against *Mithridates, who had invaded the Roman province of Asia. But the tribune of 88, P. Sulpicius Rufus, a supporter of Marius, transferred the command to the latter, and Sulla was forced to leave Rome. The six legions which Sulla had assembled at Capua marched with him against the (legitimate) government at Rome and for the first time a consul

entered the city at the head of his army. Marius escaped with difficulty (arriving in Africa after many adventures), and Sulla took control of the city by force, killing Sulpicius and shocking even his friends by his violent measures. His vindictive cruelty was long remembered.

After devising a temporary political settlement he proceeded to the East, where he defeated Mithridates and acquired a vast amount of booty. Marius meanwhile had died (in 86), but his party had regained the upper hand in Rome. Sulla invaded in 83 and was joined by *Pompey and *Crassus. A ruthless civil war ensued and Sulla finally seized Rome in 82 after a victory at the *Colline Gate. He was elected dictator and granted complete immunity, taking the *cognomen* Felix ('fortunate'). He now adopted in his turn Marius' policy of exterminating his enemies, adding the device of proscription, the posting-up of the names of victims who might be killed without trial and their property confiscated, while the murderers and informers were rewarded for their efforts. These terrible events marked the advent of a new era, the late republic (see SALLUST), a time when individuals with great personal ambition, made powerful by their leadership of large armies, brought about the ruin of Italy and the collapse of republican government.

After having his eastern settlement ratified, Sulla set about a complete constitutional reform at Rome which aimed to improve administrative efficiency, increase the power of the senate, and restrict that of the people and their tribunes. His most important measure was the full organization of a system of criminal procedure. This was one of the few parts of his work which survived the reaction that followed his death. After completing his reforms he abdicated his power, restored constitutional government, becoming consul in 80, and retired to private life in 79. He died in 78, having devoted his last year to the composition of his memoirs in twenty-two books; these have not survived.

Sulmo, birthplace of the Roman poet Ovid, in a valley of the Apennines, east of Rome.

Sulpi'cia, see TIBULLUS.

Sulpi'cius. 1. **Publius Sulpicius Rufus**, tribune of the *plebs* 88 BC and a supporter of *Marius. He proposed that the newly enfranchised Italians should vote in all the tribes and not be confined to a few (see COMITIA); also that the command against Mithridates should be transferred from *Sulla to Marius. These proposals were carried by force, but when Sulla reacted by marching on Rome Sulpicius had to flee. He was captured and put to death, and his laws annulled.

2. **Servius Sulpicius Rufus** (*c.*106–43 BC), great Roman jurist and orator, contemporary of Cicero, known to us by the latter's praise of him in his **Brutus* and in the *Ninth Philippic* and by his correspondence with Cicero. He was consul in 51. He wrote to Cicero two celebrated letters, one describing the murder of M. Marcellus in May 45, the other a consolation on the death of Cicero's daughter Tullia, which was admired and copied by St Ambrose as worthy of a Christian.

Sū'nium (Sounion), cape forming the southernmost point of Attica. It is mentioned by Homer (*Odyssey* 3. 278) as the point off which Apollo killed the pilot who guided Menelaus on his way to Troy. A temple to Poseidon was built on the promontory in the 440s BC; eleven of its Doric columns still stand.

Suppliants, The (Gk. *Hiketidĕs*, Lat. *Supplicēs*, 'suppliants' or 'suppliant women').

1. Greek tragedy by *Aeschylus, of uncertain date, but in a year, possibly 463, in which Sophocles was also a competitor (the latter's first dramatic production was in 468). It was the first play of its trilogy; the others were *Aegyptii* ('sons of Aegyptus') and *Danaidĕs* ('daughters of Danaus'); the satyr-play was the **Amymōnē*.

The suppliants are the fifty daughters of *Danaus who have fled from Egypt to avoid marriage with their cousins, the fifty sons of the usurping king Aegyptus. They have come with their father Danaus to Argos, with which they claim connection through their descent from *Io, to ask for protection from their pursuers. The king of Argos hesitates and consults

his people. These vote in favour of the suppliants, and the demand of the enemy herald for their surrender is rejected.

The role of the suppliants themselves is taken by the chorus, which thus becomes virtually the protagonist; it is not therefore inappropriate that choral lyrics occupy more than half the play. The reason for the suppliants' flight from marriage, not made unambiguously clear by Aeschylus, has been much debated, but inconclusively; it does not seem to be of importance to the poet or essential to the plot. The trilogy probably ended with the confirmation of marriage as a natural institution, exemplified by *Hypermnestra's sparing of her husband.

2. Greek tragedy by *Euripides produced probably *c.*422 BC; the goddess Athena's words at the end relate to an Argive alliance, actual or in view at the time of writing.

The Thebans have refused to allow the burial of the bodies of the Argive chieftains (the '*Seven against Thebes') who have unsuccessfully attacked the city, thus violating the sacred custom of the Greeks. The mothers of the chieftains (who form the chorus of suppliants from whom the play is named) have come with Adrastus, king of Argos, surviving leader of the expedition, to Eleusis in Attica and made supplication at the shrine of Demeter to Aethra, mother of Theseus, king of Athens. Theseus rejects the arrogant demand of the Theban herald for their surrender; he yields to the prayer of the suppliants and recovers the bodies for burial by force. Evadnē, widow of Capaneus, one of the chieftains, throws herself on his funeral pyre.

supplicā'tio ('supplication'), at Rome and elsewhere in Italy, on the occasion of some great national misfortune or rejoicing, such as a military defeat or victory; it was a solemn adoration of the gods, when public access was granted to their statues or other emblems, often by placing them on platforms.

Su'pplicēs, see SUPPLIANTS.

Sy'baris, Achaean Greek colony founded *c.*720 BC near a similarly named river on the Gulf of Tarentum in Italy. In the sixth century it was an important trading centre, and its wealth and luxury became proverbial (hence English 'sybaritic'). It was destroyed *c.*510 BC by its rival *Croton, and the neighbouring river Crathis was diverted from its course to flow over the site. It was never rebuilt. See also THURII.

sy'cophant (sykophantēs, 'fig-denouncer'), at Athens, a man who prosecuted another maliciously, on a trumped-up charge, for the sake of private gain. For most offences at Athens there was no public prosecutor; that role was left to a public-spirited private individual, but the system was open to abuse. Since there could be financial rewards for bringing successful prosecutions (a share of the fines), or a rich victim could be blackmailed into paying off a would-be prosecutor, those individuals who made a habit of such prosecutions earned this abusive name, the origin of which is obscure. Today 'sycophantic' means 'obsequious'.

syllē'psis ('taking together'), figure of speech in which one word is applied to two others in different senses, e.g. 'he bolted the door and his dinner'; thus in Tacitus *Annals* 2. 29: *manus ac supplices voces ... tendens*, 'raising hands and voices in supplication'. It was sometimes called zeugma.

Sy'mmachus, Quintus Aure'lius (*c.* AD 340–*c.*402), prefect of Rome in 384, a Roman noble, regarded by his contemporaries as an outstanding orator and prose stylist. His eloquence was referred to by *Macrobius as *pingue et floridum*, 'rich and florid'. He was pagan, but of moderate views. His best known work is the *Relatio*, 'report', which, as prefect of Rome, he addressed to the young emperor Valentinian II in 384, defending the ancient religious institutions against Christian inroads. In it he urged the restoration to the senate-house of that symbol of the historic greatness of Rome, the Altar of Victory (probably erected by Augustus in 29 BC), which the emperor Gratian under the influence of St *Ambrose had had removed in 382. Symmachus' Report was preserved as a model of eloquence, but was successfully opposed by St Ambrose. His cor-

respondence (over 900 letters) was published by his son in ten books. The first nine consist of carefully composed letters to his friends, trivial and uninteresting to later readers since mostly they ignore external events; the tenth book contains official correspondence.

Symplē'gadĕs ('the clashing ones'), in Greek myth, the 'clashing rocks' at the north end of the Bosporus through which the *Argonauts had to pass to enter the Black Sea. The rocks were believed to clash together, crushing ships that passed between them. The Planctae ('wandering ones') were similar rocks mentioned in the *Odyssey* (12. 61), in an unspecified place.

Sympo'siaca, see PLUTARCH 3.

sympo'sium ('drinking-party', 'banquet'), the male drinking-party, an important social institution in the life of aristocratic Greek men. It was held in the *andrōn,* 'men's apartment'; the (male) guests, their heads garlanded with flowers, reclined on couches (an Eastern practice introduced into Greece before the sixth century BC), usually two, sometimes more, to a couch (*klinē*), propped on their left arm; low tables to hold food and wine cups were placed in front of the couches. Wine was served from a large mixing-bowl (*krātēr*) where it was blended with water to make it fairly mild, and poured by young slaves of both sexes, often chosen for their good looks. At least as important as the drinking was the entertainment, sometimes provided by slaves specially hired to sing and dance, but often by the guests themselves and of a rather regularized kind; there were riddles and games, and lyric poems and *scolia were sung. Much of the lyric of Alcaeus, Anacreon, and Archilochus, and some of the short elegiac poems of Theognis, for example, were written for this kind of setting. Sometimes guests delivered short speeches on agreed topics (see Plato's SYMPOSIUM below). Homosexuality derived much of its vitality as an institution from the circumstances of the symposium, where freeborn respectable women were absent and male beauty, charm, and wit were highly regarded. In a comic scene in Aristophanes' *Wasps*, an 'aristocratic' son tries to teach acceptable symposiastic behaviour to his embarrassingly boorish father. See also SYMPOSIUM (2) below. Today, a symposium means no more than a discussion-group.

Sympo'sium ('drinking-party', 'banquet'). 1. Dialogue by *Plato written perhaps c.384 BC. The dialogue is supposed to have taken place at a banquet held in Athens at the house of the tragic poet *Agathon who is celebrating his first victory in the competitions for tragedy at the Lenaea of 416 BC. The dialogue is narrated by a friend of Socrates, Apollodorus of Phalerum, who was not present (being too young) but had the story from an eye-witness and admirer of Socrates, Aristodemus. Each of the guests delivers a short speech in honour of love, Phaedrus from a mythical standpoint, Pausanias from that of a sophist, Agathon from that of a poet, and so on; Aristophanes turns the dialogue towards comedy. Each speech is a clever parody by Plato of the style of the purported speaker. Socrates takes the discussion on to a higher plane. He has learnt from Diotīma, the priestess of Mantinea, that love may have a nobler aspect. The need in a human being which is manifested on a lower plane by sexual love can also take an intellectual form, the desire of the soul to create conceptions of wisdom and beauty such as poets and legislators produce. One should proceed from the love of a beautiful form to the perception and love of universal divine beauty, which has no physical aspect. *Alcibiades now joins the party, slightly drunk. He confesses the fascination which Socrates exercises on him and his hope of receiving lessons in wisdom from him. He tells of various incidents in the life of Socrates, including his own failure to seduce him. Socrates is like the statuettes of *Silenus that conceal images of gods inside them, and like *Marsyas the satyr who with his pipe could charm the souls of men.

The term 'Platonic love' refers to the argument for the superiority of non-sexual love.

2. A narrative by *Xenophon of an imaginary banquet supposed to have taken place on the occasion of the Great *Panathenaea of 421 BC at the house of

*Callias, Socrates being among the guests. Those present at the banquet are all well-known historical characters except for a comedian called Philippus and a Syracusan in charge of the dancers. The narrative gives a vivid picture of the conversation and amusements at an Athenian symposium. The conversation is a mixture of humour and seriousness, and Socrates is presented in a relaxed mood. There are a good many jokes about his personal appearance; he is the central figure, and, amid all the jokes, delivers a serious speech on the superiority of spiritual to carnal love.

Syne'sius, see NEOPLATONISM.

synizē'sis ('melting into one'), coalescence of two vowels into one sound without alteration of letters.

Syphax, see SOPHONISBA.

Sȳ'racuse (Gk. Syrakousai, Lat. Syracusae), the chief city of Sicily, founded as a colony by Corinth in 733 BC. It was a flourishing place by the end of the sixth century, and was raised to the position of first city in Sicily by *Gelon, who became tyrant c.490 BC and won great glory by repelling a Carthaginian invasion in 480. Gelon was succeeded by his brother Hieron I (478–67), who added to the cultural splendour of Syracuse and was made famous by the Epinician Odes of Pindar and Bacchylides, and by the fact that Aeschylus and Simonides spent some time at his court. Xenophon wrote an imaginary dialogue between the latter and Hieron.

Soon after Hieron's death a democracy was set up at Syracuse, and internal dissensions were followed by external aggression against other Sicilian cities, a situation which Athens was led to believe she could turn to her own advantage; her hope of controlling some part of the island led to the disastrous *Sicilian Expedition of 415. Its failure was followed by the rise of Dionysius (later Dionysius I), a man of demagogic power, who was sole ruler from 405 to 367. He made himself master of half Sicily and extended his conquests to the mainland of Italy, winning effective control over most of Magna Graecia. His rule brought prosperity to Syracuse, but was generally considered oppressive. Plato visited his court (see PLATO 1) but there is a legend that when Plato was leaving Syracuse Dionysius contrived to have him sold into slavery, from which Plato's friends rescued him. Dionysius had a taste for literature and bought for himself the writing tablets of Aeschylus. Thus inspired he actually won the prize at the *Lenaea in 367 with a tragedy, the *Ransoming of Hector*; his death is said to have been caused by a drinking-bout in celebration of this victory. A surviving line from a play of his, 'Alas, I've lost a useful wife', rather confirms the ancients' poor view of his talent.

Dionysius II succeeded his father, but was expelled by his uncle and brother-in-law Dion, who was himself assassinated in 353. The relations of Plato with these tyrants form the subject of several of his Epistles (see PLATO 6). After Dion's death Syracuse became increasingly anarchic and decline began, though Dionysius II recovered his throne in 346. The Syracusans appealed for assistance against him to their mother-city Corinth, who in 344 sent them *Timoleon. He restored peace to Sicily, introducing at Syracuse a moderately oligarchic government on the Corinthian model, but a further period of unrest followed under Agathoclēs (d. 289), a demagogue, who made himself first tyrant (317) and then

king (305). He attacked other Sicilian cities, and fought against the Carthaginians, who occupied the west of the island. The reign of Hieron II (269–216), mild and just, celebrated by Theocritus in Idyll 16, was the last golden age of Syracuse. He had allied himself with Rome against Carthage in the First Punic War and contributed to her final victory. After his death Syracuse forsook Rome for Carthage, an act which signalled its final downfall. The city was besieged (213–211) and finally sacked by M. Claudius Marcellus; in their defence the Syracusans were substantially aided by *Archimedes, who perished when the city was taken. Under Roman rule Syracuse retained its beauty and to some extent its importance, but it suffered at the hands of the governor *Verrēs.

Sy'ria. The region known as Syria in the ancient world is roughly that of modern Syria, but its boundaries varied and are ill-defined. At its greatest extent it was bounded by the river Euphrates in the east and the Mediterranean in the west, the range of Mt. Taurus in the north and the Arabian desert in the south. It included *Phoenicia, the coastal strip on the west, and the southern part known as Coelē-Syria. See SELEUCIDS.

sȳrinx, see PAN and MUSIC.

T

Ta'bula Ī'liaca, marble relief of *c*.15 BC, found by the Via Appia near Bovillae, about 20 km. (12 miles) south-east of Rome. It represents scenes from the Trojan War, and indicates the sources from which they are taken. An inscription states that the central panel represents the (lost) *Iliupersis* of *Stesichorus (Greek lyric poet of the early sixth century BC), and its details have been believed to be Stesichorean. Among other things the panel shows Aeneas bearing his father Anchisēs on his shoulders from Troy, accompanied by his son Ascanius, with an inscription saying that he is sailing to '*Hesperia' (i.e. Italy). If Stesichorus did indeed include this episode, then he is the first authority for the legend of Aeneas' migration to Italy. Many scholars doubt the authenticity of the attribution to Stesichorus.

Ta'citus, Publius (or Gaius; sources vary) **Corne'lius** (b. AD 56 or 57, d. after 117), Roman historian. He was possibly a native of Narbonese Gaul. Comparatively little is known about his life, but he had a normal senatorial career, begun under the emperor Vespasian (AD 69–79); he married *Agricola's daughter in 77, was praetor in 88, *consul suffectus* in 97, and governor of Asia in 112–13. His experience of the tyranny of Domitian's reign (81–96), to which he owed advancement, as he admits, led him to write in the introduction to his *Life of Agricola* and *Histories* of the pains and the difficulties of surviving in public life under such an emperor. But he won fame during his lifetime: the Younger *Pliny, who was his friend, was proud to be considered his equal in popular estimation.

His *Agricola* was published in 98, early in Trajan's reign. It is essentially a panegyric of his father-in-law, especially of his great achievements in *Britain, on which Tacitus has valuable information; but it is also a defence of the integrity and service of those administrators who,

like Agricola and Tacitus himself, as well as Trajan, had managed to survive Domitian's reign. His *Germania* or 'On the Origin and Country of the Germans' was published in the same year. It is an account of the various tribes north of the Rhine and the Danube, heavily dependent on earlier writers such as Livy and the Elder Pliny. The Germans' love of freedom and their vigour and bravery are implicitly compared with the corruption at Rome. His *Dialogus de oratoribus* ('dialogue on orators') is set in the seventies; four distinguished men of the day discuss the decline of Roman oratory and the reason for it, namely the dependence of oratory on a free political life. It used to be thought an early work but now is agreed to belong to the period 100–5. The fact that its style is very different from that of Tacitus' other works is explained by reference to the requirements of a different literary genre. Tacitus had studied rhetoric as a young man and he became famous as a speaker. In 97 he delivered a funeral oration over the consul Verginius Rufus (a distinguished general whom his soldiers had wanted to become emperor, and whose consulship Tacitus completed), and in 100 he spoke as advocate for the province of Asia against the ex-governor Marius Priscus; the Younger Pliny notes the eloquence and dignity of the latter speech.

His major works were the *Histories* and the *Annals*. A projected work on the happier reigns of Nerva and Trajan 'which I am saving for my old age' did not materialize. The *Histories*, on which Tacitus was working in 106–7, covered the period AD 69–96, the reigns of the emperors Galba, Otho, Vitellius, Vespasian, Titus, and Domitian, and were perhaps written in fourteen books. Only the first four and part of the fifth survive, dealing with the events of 69 and 70, but even those two years justify his description of the period as one 'full of

catastrophe, fearful in its fighting, torn by
mutinies, bloody even in peace'. He gives
a vivid picture of the civil wars of 69 (the
'Year of the Four Emperors') and their
contenders, ending with the one emperor
who 'changed for the better', Vespasian.
The *Annals*, on which Tacitus was working *c*.116, may have consisted of sixteen
books covering AD 14–68, i.e. the reigns
of Tiberius, Caligula, Claudius, and
Nero. Parts of 5 and 6 and the whole of 7–
10 are missing; 16 breaks off in AD 66
before Nero's death. His sources overall
were the works of other historians, public
records, and, where possible, his own
experiences.

The *Annals* in particular show Tacitus
to have been one of the greatest of
historians, with a penetrating insight into
character and a sober grasp of the significant issues of the time. He knew that the
empire was to be a permanent institution;
but he shared the ancient Roman view
that it is individuals who create history,
and he was deeply pessimistic about
Rome's ability to find a good emperor.
The impartiality he claimed in writing the
histories of the emperors was affected by
his preference for the republic at its worst
to the imperial system at its best, and he
was driven to dwell on the evils of the
latter. He saw it as the historian's function to record virtue and ensure that vice
was denounced by posterity (*Annals* 3.
65), and to this end he created a style as
memorable as the events he records, condensed, rapid, and incisive, with a flavour
all of its own and impossible to render in
translation. Edward Gibbon (1737–94)
admired Tacitus more than any other
ancient historian, and his own biting, epigrammatic style comes closest in English
to the Latin of his exemplar.

Tala'ss(i)us, Roman marriage god, the
personification of the ritual cry *Talassio*
(compare *Hymenaeus* in Greek) when
the bride is escorted to the groom's
house.

talent, a standard weight in the ancient
world, representing a man's load; see
WEIGHTS AND MEASURES and MONEY AND
COINS.

Tālos. 1. In Greek myth, the bronze man
of Crete, made by the god Hephaestus
and given by him to king Minos (or by
Zeus to *Europa). He guarded the island
by walking round it three times a day; if
he saw strangers approaching he made
himself red-hot and then embraced them
when they landed. His one vulnerable
spot was a vein of blood which ran
through his body and was closed in his
head by a nail. When he tried to drive the
Argonauts away from Crete, *Medea
used her magic powers on him; according
to one story she removed the nail, causing him to bleed to death.

2. The nephew of *Daedalus.

Ta'ntalus, in Greek myth, son of Zeus
and the Titaness Pluto ('wealth'), king of
the region around Mount Sipylus in
Lydia. He married Dionē, daughter of
Atlas, by whom he became the father of
Niobē and *Pelops, and thus the ancestor
of the Pelopidae. Tantalus offended the
gods and was punished in *Tartarus by
being set, thirsty and hungry, in a pool of
water which always receded when he
tried to drink from it, and under fruit
trees whose branches the wind tossed
aside when he tried to pick the fruit.
Another account of his punishment was
that a great stone was suspended over his
head, threatening to crush him, so that he
was in too much terror to enjoy a banquet
which was set before him. The reason for
these punishments is variously described:
either he invited the gods to dinner and
served them his son's flesh (see PELOPS),
or he stole nectar and ambrosia from the
gods' table, where he had been invited,
and gave them to his friends, or he told
his friends the gods' secrets. From his
name we have the word 'tantalize'.

Tare'ntum (Taranto), important city
and harbour on the 'instep' of south
Italy, on the gulf named after it. It was
founded by Sparta, traditionally in 706
BC. Originally an aristocracy, Tarentum
became a democracy *c*.475 BC, and
flourished especially in the fourth century
BC during the lifetime of the philosopher
*Archytas. The Tarentines quarrelled
with the encroaching Romans in 282,
relying on help from *Pyrrhus, and thus
provoked Rome's Pyrrhic wars. The
Romans conquered Tarentum in 272, but
imposed generous terms. *Livius
Andronicus, probably a Tarentine cap-

tive taken to Rome, was an important figure in early Roman literature. Tarentum played an important part in the Second Punic War: in 213 it was captured by Hannibal, and in 209 recaptured by Fabius Cunctator (and thoroughly plundered). Thereafter it suffered a decline. It lay in very fertile country; its honey, olives, scallops, wool, and purple dye were praised by Horace, its pine-woods by Propertius.

Tarpē'ia, woman in early Roman history whose legend explained the name of the Tarpeian Rock at the south-west corner of the Capitoline hill, from which criminals sentenced to death were hurled. When the Romans were at war against the Sabines (see ROMULUS), Tarpeia, the daughter of a Roman officer, undertook to betray the citadel on the Capitol if, she said, the Sabines would give her 'what they had on their left arms', meaning their gold bracelets. But when the Sabines broke in they rewarded her treachery by crushing her under their shields, also worn on the left arm. (In an alternative version Tarpeia was a heroine, her intention being to gain possession of the Sabine shields in order to help the Romans.)

Tarquin (Tarquinius), name of two of the (semi-legendary) kings of Rome. Although they were probably historical figures, their biographies seem to be pure invention. They were thought to have been Etruscans, and archaeological discoveries have confirmed a strong Etruscan presence at Rome in the supposed era of the Tarquins. Tarquinius Priscus, the elder Tarquin, was the fifth king of Rome and is said to have reigned 616–579 BC; he was murdered at the instigation of his predecessors' sons who felt they had been cheated of their inheritance. Lucius Tarquinius Superbus, 'the Proud', was the last king of Rome, reigning from 534 to 510. The achievements and institutions of the two Tarquins are thoroughly confused in the sources, but the younger Tarquin was depicted in later tradition as having all the objectionable characteristics of a Greek tyrant, thereby justifying his expulsion by L. *Brutus. See also LUCRETIA and SIBYL.

Ta'rtarus, in Greek myth, an elemental deity, son of Aither (Sky) and Gaia (Earth), and by his mother the father of Typhon. The name also describes a part of the Underworld where the wicked suffer punishment for their misdeeds on earth, especially (in the early poets) those such as Ixion and Tantalus who have committed some outrage against the gods. See HADES.

Tarte'ssus, vaguely defined region of southern Spain, 'Tarshish' of the Old Testament; the name was also given to the river Baetis (Guadalquivir), which flows to the south of the Sierra Morena, mountains rich in silver, and to a town at its mouth. It was proverbially rich as a result of trading in tin and silver between Britanny and south-west England on the one hand, and the Phoenicians and Carthaginians on the other. The Phocaean Greeks visited the region in the late seventh century. (For an early reference to Tartessus see STESICHORUS.)

Tauri, the Taurians, the inhabitants of the Tauric Chersonese ('peninsula') in the Black Sea, i.e. the Crimea.

Tāÿ'getē, one of the *Pleiads, the nymph of the high range of mountains named after her in the Peloponnese, west of Sparta. The goddess Artemis turned her into a doe to escape the attentions of Zeus, but by him she became the mother of *Lacedaemon, eponymous ancestor of the Lacedaemonians.

Tecme'ssa, see AJAX.

Te'gea, ancient city in the south-east of Arcadia, mentioned in the *Iliad*; there seems to have been a Mycenaean settlement on the site. In very early times Tegea fought successfully against Sparta; in the first half of the sixth century the Spartans, reputedly trusting an ambiguous oracle from Delphi, advanced into Tegea to seize the land but were defeated, and Spartan prisoners were made to till the land wearing the chains which they had brought with them for use on the Tegeans. In the mid-sixth century, again on advice from Delphi, the Spartans were told to find and bring back to Sparta the bones of the hero Orestes (son of Agamemnon). Having brought the bones from Tegea the Spartans were then victorious over the Tegeans who, after agreeing not to harbour Messenians (see MESSENIA), were taken into alliance with Sparta.

Teire'sias, in Greek myth, the blind Theban seer. Several reasons are given for his blindness: one story is that he saw the goddess Athena bathing and she blinded him, but gave him as compensation, since his mother was her friend, the gift of prophecy and a life seven generations long. In another version, he saw snakes coupling and killed one of them with a stick, whereupon he changed into a woman; later the same thing happened again and he changed back into a man. Since he was now uniquely qualified to answer, Zeus and Hera consulted him as to whether a man or a woman derived more pleasure from the act of love. When Teiresias replied that women received nine times as much pleasure as men, Hera struck him blind, but Zeus gave him the gift of unerring prophecy. Teiresias plays a part in many myths: in Homer's *Odyssey* Odysseus is sent to the Underworld to consult him about his return to Ithaca; he also figures in Sophocles' *Antigonē* and *Oedipus Tyrannus*, in Euripides' *Bacchae* and *Phoenissae*, and in Statius' *Thebaid*.

Tei'sias. 1. Of Syracuse, flourished in the first half of the fifth century BC, an early teacher of *rhetoric, pupil of Corax, with whom he is linked as the founder of forensic oratory.

2. The real name of *Stesichorus.

Te'lamon, in Greek myth, king of the island of Salamis, son of Aeacus (king of Aegina) and Endēis, brother of *Peleus, and father of (the greater) *Ajax and *Teucer. He and Peleus killed their half-brother Phocus (whose mother was the Nereid Psamathē), perhaps at the instigation of Endeis. As a consequence Aeacus exiled them, Telamon going to Salamis. There he married Glaucē, daughter of the king, and inherited the throne. After Glauce's death Telamon married Eriboea (or Periboea) by whom he became the father of (the greater) Ajax. He was one of the Argonauts, and joined in the Calydonian boar-hunt (see MELEAGER). He helped Heracles in an early sack of Troy (see LAOMEDON), and Heracles gave him Laomedon's daughter Hesionē as concubine. Heracles' prayer that Telamon and Eriboea would have a brave son was shown to have been answered by the appearance of an eagle (Gk. *aietos*) sent by Zeus, after which the baby was named Ajax (Gk. Aias). Hesione also bore Telamon a son, Teucer. Telamon's death is variously narrated. He is usually said to have died at Salamis after banishing Teucer for failing to prevent Ajax' death.

Telchi'nēs, in Greek myth, magical and malevolent beings living in Rhodes, perhaps the original inhabitants, who were particularly skilled at metalwork. They were finally destroyed by a god, usually said to be Zeus, by means of a great flood. The poet Callimachus applied the name to his literary critics.

Tele'gonus, according to post-Homeric legend, the son of *Odysseus by Circē, and the unwitting killer of his father. According to Italian legend Telegonus founded the town of *Tusculum in the Alban hills outside Rome.

Tele'machus, in Greek myth, the son of Odysseus and Penelope; for his history see ODYSSEY. Post-Homeric legend made Telemachus marry *Circē. Homer in the *Odyssey* represents him as at first diffident, lacking his father's energy and resource, but at the end of the story astonishing his mother by taking command of the house and fighting resolutely against the suitors.

Tē'lephus, in Greek myth, son of Heracles and Augē (daughter of a king of Arcadia), who gave birth to him secretly in a shrine of Athena; as a consequence the land was struck by plague, and when the king discovered the reason he had the child exposed and Auge sold overseas. She came into the possession of Teuthras, king of Teuthrania in Mysia, who adopted her. The child was rescued by shepherds, and when he grew up went to Mysia. Here he was about to marry Auge when their relationship was revealed. He became king of Mysia; the Greeks on their way to Troy landed in his kingdom, mistaking it for their destination, and in the fighting that ensued Telephus was wounded by Achilles. After the Greeks returned home Telephus' wound was still not healed. To find a cure he went to the Greek camp at Aulis to seek Achilles, having been told by the Delphic Oracle that the wounder would also heal. 'The wounder' was found to mean the spear, rust from which cured the wound. Euripides wrote a (lost) tragedy on the subject containing a scene, twice parodied by Aristophanes, in which Telephus appears disguised as a beggar, dressed in rags, and saves his own life in a melodramatic fashion by seizing Agamemnon's infant son Orestes as hostage. The tetralogy of which it was a part (and which included the still extant *Alcestis*) won second prize in the dramatic competitions of 438 BC.

Telesi'lla, Argive Greek poetess of the fifth century BC, famous for arming the women of Argos after Cleomenēs of Sparta had defeated the Argive men. Only a few fragments of her work survive. The telesillean metre is named after her (SEE METRE, GREEK 8).

Tellus, in Roman religion, the earth-goddess, associated with agricultural festivals such as the *Fordicidia.

Te'menus, among others of this name, one of the *Heracleidae, descendants of Heracles. After these had conquered the Peloponnese, Temenus received Argos as his share.

Ten Thousand, the, see ANABASIS.

Terence (Publius Terentius Āfer) (d. 159 BC?), Roman writer of comedy. The main source for his life is a biography written by Suetonius *c.* AD 100 and preserved in Donatus' commentary to Terence, but that itself is uncertain about many events. The manuscripts are divided between those who say he died at the age of 24 and those who say 34. He was said to have been born at Carthage and to have been a slave at Rome. In composing his plays he was alleged to have been aided by *Scipio Aemilianus, C. *Laelius, and others of that circle, allegations to which he himself refers with some pride (at being thought to have such distinguished friends). He is said to have died at sea while returning from a visit to Greece.

Terence wrote six plays (for details see individual titles): *Andria* ('girl from Andros'), *Hecyra* ('mother-in-law'), *Heauton timorumenos* ('self-tormentor'), *Eunuchus* ('eunuch'), *Phormio*, and *Adelphoe* ('brothers').

His plays are *fabulae *palliatae*, and with two exceptions are adapted from *Menander; he follows his Greek originals more closely than *Plautus did, although sometimes combining portions of two plays. He thus represents scenes of the same Greek life as Plautus depicted, but by keeping the settings and conventions of his Greek sources, and excluding specifically Roman elements, he avoided obvious incongruity. Although the characters and subjects (young men's complicated love affairs) are much the same in both playwrights, the spirit is different. In Terence portraiture takes the place of caricature; conversation is much more natural than in Plautus, lacking the boisterous, farcical element of the latter. In all respects Terence is more refined and sophisticated than Plautus, but less robust. He abandoned the expository kind of prologue, and instead inserted necessary background information into the action; he also avoided the somewhat unnatural monologues of his models, re-scripting them as dialogues. He introduces a more prosaic note by almost entirely avoiding lyric passages (*cantica*) and opera-like scenes; but only half of his lines are in the spoken metre of iambic senarii (see METRE, LATIN 2); the rest are iambic and trochaic septenarii, which were certainly 'sung' in the form of recitative. In general Terence aims at greater realism.

The plays of Terence did not have popular appeal but were greatly admired by discriminating critics like Cicero and Horace. They were widely known and studied in the Middle Ages, and were adapted into Christian form by Hroswitha (tenth century), the abbess of the Benedictine convent of Gandersheim in Saxony, for her nuns to read. Terence was much read in England in the sixteenth century and even acted (*Phormio* was performed by the boys of St Paul's School before Cardinal Wolsey). His influence can be traced in early English comedy and again in the comedy of manners of the Restoration. Several of his lines have become proverbial: *quot homines, tot sententiae* ('as many opinions as there are men'), and *fortis fortuna adiuvat* ('fortune favours the brave'), both from *Phormio*; see also HEAUTON TIMORUMENOS.

Tēreus, see PHILOMELA.

te'rminus, boundary-stone; in Roman religion the **numen* of such stones was the object of an annual ritual (the Terminalia) on 23 February, which included a sacrifice and a feast by the neighbouring land-holders. These rural *termini* had their state counterpart in the god Terminus, whose boundary-stone was located in the temple of Jupiter Optimus Maximus on the Capitol, and according to tradition was there before the temple was built. It was left inside the temple, which had an opening in the roof to ensure that the stone remained under the open sky.

Terpa'nder (Terpandros) (mid-seventh century BC), Greek lyric poet and musician of Lesbos, famous in legend, but of whose life nothing is known for sure. He was said to have won a musical competition during the period 676–673, at the games in honour of Apollo Carneius at Sparta, where he was believed to have founded a music school. The invention of the seven-stringed lyre (*cithara*) was ascribed to him. He composed **nomes* (settings of epic poetry), preludes or introductions to the singing of epic poetry, and **scolia* (drinking songs); it is very doubtful whether the few surviving fragments ascribed to him are authentic; it seems probable that none of his work was known by the Alexandrian scholars of the Hellenistic age.

Tertu'llian (Florens Quintus Septimius Tertulliānus) (*c.* AD 160–*c.*225), the Father of Latin theology. Born at Carthage the son of a centurion and brought up as a pagan, receiving a good literary and rhetorical education, he was converted to Christianity before 197. He was learned in philosophy and science, and especially in law, and was the author of many apologetic, theological, controversial, and ascetic works. He appeals for the toleration of Christians, who are no danger to the state. It seems to him that natural instinct bears witness to the existence of God: *o testimonium animae naturaliter Christianae* ('O witness of the soul naturally Christian!'). He believed that Christians needed to separate themselves from pagan society to avoid contamination from the latter's immorality and idolatry, and since separation might involve disobeying the law of the state, it could prove necessary to accept martyrdom: Tertullian's actual words are traditionally known in the form, 'The blood of the martyrs is the seed of the Church.'

Both of the above quotations come from the *Apologēticum*, written *c.*197 in the form of a speech by an advocate, addressed to the governors of Roman provinces, in which, with a blend of passion and irony, he seeks to secure for Christians protection from attacks by the populace and, when they are brought up for trial, from illegal procedures. Other treatises are directed to regulating in minute detail the life of Christians in a pagan society, and show Tertullian's strong ascetic slant. At some period of his life he was won over to the ascetic and enthusiastic Montanist movement, which brought about a rupture, apparently never healed, between him and the Catholic church. Tertullian wrote with much rhetorical skill, and with a rich and varied vocabulary; he created many new words and helped to develop the form and terminology of theological Latin.

Tethys, according to Hesiod, a **Titan, daughter of Gaia (Earth) and Uranus (Heaven), consort of **Oceanus. Homer in the *Iliad* (14. 201) speaks of Tethys and Oceanus as the parents of the gods, but this was a myth that seems to have been forgotten in classical times.

tetra'logy, in Greek, originally a term used in oratory to describe a group of four speeches (*logoi*) delivered in the same law-suit. For its application to Greek drama see TRAGEDY 2.

tetra'meter, see METRE, GREEK 1.

tetrarchy, see AUGUSTUS, THE.

Teucer (Teukros). **1.** In Greek myth, legendary king ruling in the neighbourhood of **Troy who became the ancestor of the Trojan kings through his daughter who married *Dardanus. From him the Trojans are sometimes called Teucri.

2. In Greek myth, son of *Telamon and Hēsionē, and half-brother of *Ajax. He was called Teucer (i.e. Trojan) because his mother was a daughter of *Laomedon, king of Troy. He was the greatest archer among the Greeks at the siege of Troy. On his return to Salamis from the siege he was banished by his father as responsible for his brother's death, and went to Cyprus where he founded a town also called Salamis. See AJAX.

texts, transmission of ancient

1. In Greece the first literature, Homeric epic, was composed and handed down orally (see HOMER). According to tradition it was the Athenian tyrant *Peisistratus in the middle of the sixth century BC who first ordered an official text of Homer to be written down, and one may guess that the lyric poetry of Archilochus, Alcaeus, and Sappho circulated in written form also. Certainly from the late seventh century onwards the new prose works, which could not have been as easily memorized as poetry, could hardly have survived by oral transmission and must have been written down. Books were not common until well into the fifth century BC, but soon after the middle of that century some sort of book-trade developed, which made it possible for individuals to collect books and form libraries (for books at this time see BOOKS AND WRITING 3).

Aristotle's arrangement of the library at the Lyceum served as a model for the library at Alexandria set up in the third century BC (see ALEXANDRIAN LIBRARY); to the editorial labours of the Alexandrian librarians and scholars, in particular to Callimachus, Zenodotus, Eratosthenēs, Aristophanes of Byzantium, and Aristarchus, we owe the texts of classical Greek literature that we still possess today, and some of the ancient notes (*scholia) which have come down with them. The manuscripts which reached Alexandria had been copied with varying degrees of care, and most contained numerous mistakes and deviations ('corruptions') from what the authors had written. The scholars' task was to restore the original texts, as far as was possible, to classify them according to type (in *lyric poetry, for example, there were many different kinds), and also to write commentaries explaining their linguistic, literary, and antiquarian aspects. Restoring the original posed problems of convention; spelling in early texts differed according to the version of the Greek alphabet used in the author's own city, and these texts had to be transliterated into the Ionic alphabet which was in general use in Greece after 403 BC (see ALPHABET). Some obviously wrong readings found in manuscripts of the Middle Ages go back to errors in transliteration made in the third century BC.

Another problem presented by the manuscripts was that of simple interpretation. Texts were written without word division and continued to be so written long after the Hellenistic age; it was not until the Middle Ages that there was consistent separation of words. *Accents, a Hellenistic invention, were likewise not used consistently until the Middle Ages. *Punctuation was rudimentary and used sporadically; in the texts of plays a change of speaker was indicated by a horizontal stroke at the beginning of a line or by a colon, with inevitable inaccuracy. Lyric poetry was written in continuous lines as if it was prose; *Aristophanes of Byzantium was credited with establishing the colometry of lyric (i.e. of distinguishing the individual metric units or cola), a discovery which enabled it to be written in lines like modern poetry.

The scholars at Alexandria aimed to collect copies of all the known literature of ancient Greece. Out of all known literature they drew up lists of the best authors in each genre (see CANONS), thus facilitating the survival of their works at the expense, it would appear, of the works of lesser authors. The critical signs written in the margins by Alexandrian scholars are in some cases still in use today. Lines thought to be spurious were 'obelized', that is, a horizontal stroke, *obelos*, was placed beside the line in the left-hand margin; the *diplē* > indicated that something in the line was notable; the *asteriskos* ⁂ marked a line incorrectly repeated in another place; the sigma and antisigma (⊂ and ⊃) marking two consecutive lines showed that they might be interchanged. Thus there gradually developed the business of scholarship and in particular of textual criticism and the standardization of texts. For the scholars the priority in textual criticism had been to detect and remove interpolations, i.e. inauthentic additions; and then to a lesser degree, and with increasing caution as knowledge increased, to replace what they thought to be errors with what they conjectured to be the right readings. Their practice was continued by their successors (see DIDYMUS).

2. In the ensuing *Roman age, Greek was a foreign language to many readers of Greek texts and in consequence the demand was not so much for textual and literary criticism as for popular annotated editions, grammars, and commentaries published separately from the text. These preserved the best of Alexandrian scholarship. From the second century AD scholarship declined with the disappearance of readers interested in or capable of understanding the classical Greek authors, although there still were scholars engaged in preserving and continuing the tradition of Alexandrian research: in grammar, *Apollonius Dyscolus and *Herodian, in metric *Hephaestion, in the compilation of lexicons Harpocration and *Hesychius. But interest in the old authors was limited, and selections and anthologies, e.g. that of *Stobaeus, came to be preferred to the complete work of a poet.

The revival of interest in classical Attic Greek in the second century AD (see SOPHISTIC, SECOND), combined with the emphasis on rhetoric in education, ensured the survival of the admired models, Plato, Xenophon, and Demosthenes, and in verse the popular plays of the tragedians and of Aristophanes. A factor which led to losses at this time, however, was the change in the form of books from the papyrus roll to the parchment codex with leaves as in the modern book (see BOOKS AND WRITING 4). It must always have been the case that works were lost simply by the disintegration of papyrus rolls before they had been recopied, but the general change from

roll to codex entailed the complete recopying of ancient literature from one form to another during the second to fourth centuries AD. Inevitably, some works did not seem worth the effort. Also, the absence of a roll or two at the time of copying might mean that a work was thereafter transmitted with part missing.

Classical literature was the basis of the whole educational system for Christian and pagan alike, since there were no alternative Christian texts. However, most Christians had no further interest in reading pagan literature once their education was over. Hence there was less incentive in a Christian society to copy texts apart from those which appeared on the school curriculum, and not enough, it would appear, to ensure their survival through the wars and destructions of the fourth and subsequent centuries. But although the Roman and early *Byzantine periods were a time of loss, it is clear from a comparison of later manuscripts with early papyri, some of the latter not much later than the Alexandrian scholars themselves, that there was no appreciable corruption during this time and that the quality of surviving texts was hardly impaired.

3. By the end of the sixth century a serious decline in learning and literacy had begun in the eastern empire, and for three centuries there is little recorded about classical studies. After the eighth century, the darkest time of this Dark Age of Greek literature, came a period of peace and a revival in the ninth century associated with the names of *Photius and Arethas, who sought out surviving classical books. At the same time there were two important changes in manuscripts, one of material and one of handwriting. First, papyrus became scarce, particularly after the Arab conquest of Egypt (AD 639–42), and was replaced by parchment (made from animal skins) and later by paper (this was not common in the West before about the 13th century, but it was used earlier in Byzantium). Secondly, the old hand, uncial, was replaced by minuscule, which could be written rapidly in half the space (see BOOKS AND WRITING 5)—parchment was expensive, so economical use of it was important.

The translation of the uncial manuscripts into minuscule began in the ninth century and it is obvious that many texts in which there was little interest were not recopied at this time. However, recopying ensured the preservation of many works for posterity: most of the surviving manuscripts of ancient authors descend from one or two minuscule manuscripts written at this period.

After the losses of the ninth and tenth centuries, the survival of most of what was left of the Greek classics was virtually certain. The literary texts were copied regularly and so too were those of the medical and mathematical writers. Nevertheless, losses still occurred; the libraries of Constantinople must have suffered severely when the city was sacked by the Franks in 1204 during the Fourth Crusade. However, serious though this was it did not for long disrupt the progress of learning. It was followed by a flowering of Greek scholarship from the late thirteenth to the fifteenth centuries, when much consolidation of learning took place and resulted in careful editions of the surviving texts.

This period of scholarship is associated particularly with the names of Planudes and Triclinius. The latter sought out manuscripts and was often rewarded by the discovery of different readings, which we now have only in his marginal notes; thus his own manuscripts of an author (or copies of them), although relatively late (fourteenth century), are often no less valuable witnesses to a text than the earliest surviving manuscript perhaps 500 years older. The phrase 'merely late, not worse' (*recentiores non deteriores*), has been used by a modern scholar to describe manuscripts of this kind. Triclinius' searches had a particularly fortunate outcome in the discovery of a hitherto virtually unknown text of nine plays by Euripides, not selected for reading in schools like the other surviving plays but preserved by chance. When Byzantium fell to the Turks in 1453 the only ancient Greek text known to have been lost as a result was a complete copy of the *World History* by *Diodorus Siculus. Even before the flight of Byzantine scholars to the West, the Italian humanists had been collecting Greek manuscripts from the Byzantine empire in large numbers. By the time Byzantium fell the survival of Greek literature in the West was assured.

4. Latin literature began in the third century BC and by the middle of the following century a considerable body of texts was in existence, of poetry, plays, and prose. However, although books must have circulated by that time, very little is known about the way in which texts, presumably written on papyrus rolls as in Greece, were copied and published. The epics of Naevius and Ennius were in a sense a national possession and received some scholarly attention; but dramatic texts, for example, being distributed as acting copies, suffered many alterations and recastings (Plautus' *Poenulus* and Terence's *Andria* both have two different endings preserved in the manuscripts). The influence of *Crates (4), a Pergamene grammarian who visited Rome *c.*168 BC, and scholarship of the Alexandrian school (see HELLENISTIC AGE), gave rise to a desire for authentic texts, and a succession of scholars using the methods of the Alexandrians worked to this end down to the time of the emperor Augustus. (See, for example, the research on Plautus done by *Varro.) On the other hand a revival of interest in the old authors such as Plautus during the early first century BC had a contrary effect. There was a demand for more easily intelligible texts than the original versions with their archaic, obscure, and often recherché vocabulary. Thus popular texts of these authors with considerable variety of readings circulated by the side of the authentic texts. This process was extended to later writers who were more widely read, such as Virgil, and systematic revision of the texts in circulation became necessary; this was carried out with sound scholarship on the basis of the best manuscripts available, at least during the first three centuries AD. *Asconius did important work on Cicero, Virgil, and Sallust, but the outstanding scholar of the later part of the first century AD was M. Valerius *Probus.

In the second century AD there was again a revival of interest in early Roman writers, and it is to this revival that we owe most of our knowledge of Ennius and Cato who, though not surviving in manuscript, are quoted and referred to by compilers of excerpts (such as Aulus *Gellius). During the third and fourth centuries many Latin texts were epitomized, continuing and increasing a tendency that had been apparent in the first century AD when Livy was so treated. This was the great age of commentators, among whom were *Donatus and *Servius. The last pagan revival came at the end of the fourth century, in the face of the triumph of Christianity during the reign of the pious Theodosius (378–95), attested by, among other things, the 'subscriptions' or notes written at the end of a text by whoever originally checked and corrected it, which gave details about when the manuscript was copied and by whom. This subscription was often copied verbatim from manuscript to manuscript, and is valuable as evidence of pedigree. In general, Latin-speaking Christians like their Greek counterparts accepted that the pagan Latin texts were still essential for education and could be used, but with caution. The old Roman educational system prevailed until it came to be replaced much later by that of monastic and episcopal schools.

5. The destructions of the fourth and fifth centuries were exceeded by those of the sixth century and by the final collapse of the western Roman empire under the waves of barbarian invaders (see FALL OF ROME). The cultivated world narrowed with the fall of North Africa to the Vandals; Spain, which survived the Frankish invasions of the third century and the Visigothic in the fifth (even transmitting a residuum of Roman culture through *Isidore, bishop of Seville), succumbed early in the eighth century to the Arabs; and Gaul under the Franks was not in a position to preserve classical learning. Nevertheless, books continued to be produced in the fourth and fifth centuries, including luxury copies of Virgil. Although the Latin Church was predominantly hostile to pagan literature, yet pagan Latin texts were included by this time in the important collections of books being made at the ecclesiastical centres of Rome, Ravenna, and Verona. At the beginning of the sixth century it was still possible to

obtain copies of most of the important Latin classical and post-classical authors except for the very early literature which had disappeared in the course of the previous centuries. (For the copying of books in a sixth-century monastic library see CASSIODORUS).

The period from the mid-sixth to the mid-eighth centuries, a dark age in the Latin West as in the Greek East, brought about a steep decline of interest in classical literature, texts of which seem scarcely to have been copied at all, while a large number of biblical and patristic works was produced. Many Latin works perished when old parchments had their original text removed by washing and were then reused for religious texts (reused manuscripts are called *palimpsests), less from hostility than from complete lack of interest in the classics. The surviving part of Cicero's *De republica* is known only from what has been recovered from underneath the commentary of St Augustine on the Psalms.

But at the same time, from the late sixth century onwards, classical literature was being saved and propagated by missionaries from Ireland; impelled by a zeal for books and learning they spread across Europe founding monasteries to which they passed on their own enthusiasm, e.g. at Luxeuil in Burgundy, Bobbio in northern Italy, and St Gall in Switzerland, and creating a need for books of all kinds. It was the importation of books into England in great quantity which enabled the biblical scholar and historian Bede (673–735), who had never left Northumbria, to acquire his vast learning. Anglo-Saxons in turn became missionaries and scholars. A special variety of Latin handwriting, known as 'insular', is associated with the early scholarship of the British Isles.

At the end of the eighth century came the new interest in learning that was crucial for the preservation of Latin literature, the Carolingian revival, brought about in Charlemagne's reconstituted Roman empire of western Europe, and centred on the monasteries. Of this revival, Alcuin, the perfect exemplar of Anglo-Latin culture, was the chief promoter. Alcuin (735–804), who had been born and educated at York, made the acquaintance of Charlemagne at Parma in 781 and was placed by him at the head of a school attached to his court, where he followed the programme of Cassiodorus in teaching the *seven liberal arts. Later he became Abbot of St Martin's at Tours, where he remained until his death. Among much else he taught his monks to copy manuscripts, and as a result France contributed greatly to the transmission of texts in the ninth and tenth centuries (see BOOKS AND WRITING 6). German monasteries also played an important part, as did the monasteries of Bobbio and Monte Cassino in Italy, and of Cluny and Corbie in Burgundy. A legible script was developed in France, Caroline minuscule, from which evolved eventually a minuscule that became the normal script of western Europe. Our soundest Latin texts, apart from the little that is preserved by manuscripts of greater age, date from this time.

6. By the end of the ninth century the survival of a large number of Latin works was secured by their being part of the educational curriculum or established as works of literature; but there were others which were rarely studied, and some which were represented, as far as can be seen, by one copy only. In the late eleventh and early twelfth centuries there was suddenly a renewed interest in the classics, and books on the verge of extinction began to be copied. Because of this we still possess the texts of Varro's *De lingua Latina* and Frontinus' *De aquis*. During the twelfth century generally the more active intellectual life was no longer being pursued in the monasteries but in the cathedral schools. Although education continued to be based on Latin literature it was becoming more secular, catering for the needs of those who wanted to study law, medicine, and logic, while at the same time there was now a leisured class who wanted from literature a reflection of its own life and desires. It is therefore a matter of regret that when for the first time for many centuries love poetry and satire were in demand for their own sakes, the age was without the poetry of Catullus, Tibullus, and Propertius, who had not yet been rediscovered. As far as classical literature is concerned it was an age of consolida-

tion; its two outstanding scholars were the historian William (librarian) of Malmesbury (d. 1143), and John of Salisbury (c.1110–80).

7. The teaching of the seven liberal arts, under the influence of Alcuin, did much to prepare the way in the eleventh century for the application of philosophical method to the study of theology, an educational pattern which became known as scholasticism. To the scholastics, classical literature was no longer important for its form or style or for other literary reasons, but for its material content, information, or moral anecdote. These aspects could be more readily absorbed in excerpts than by reading complete texts. Ovid and Seneca, who can be easily appreciated in selections, became very popular; Virgil, who could not, languished. But perhaps the most significant aspect of scholasticism for classical literature in the long run was the importance acquired by Aristotle, even if only for his works on logic, and the resulting revival of interest in Greek. Until the end of the twelfth century Aristotle was known in the West only in the Latin translations of, and commentaries on, a few of his logical works, by *Boethius and others (see ARISTOTLE 5). Plato similarly was known only from a Latin version of the *Timaeus*, made in the fourth century, and from Latin quotations. From the mid-eighth century onwards, translations into Arabic and Syriac of Greek philosophical works in which Islamic thinkers were particularly interested, initiated by a desire for the medical works but including Plato, Aristotle, Theophrastus, and the mathematical writers, circulated in the Arab world. Towards the end of the twelfth century, Arabic translations and commentaries on these Greek authors by Avicenna (980–1037) and Averroes (1126–98), Aristotle's greatest Muslim disciple, were themselves translated into Latin at Toledo in Spain and diffused rapidly through Europe. But the great step forward came in the thirteenth century when these Latin translations from the Arabic were superseded by other Latin translations made direct from the original Greek. Robert Grosseteste (c.1168–1253) translated Aristotle's

Ethics and some of the works of Pseudo-Dionysius the Areopagite (see NEO-PLATONISM), and William of Moerbeke (*c*.1215–86) a number of Greek commentaries on Aristotle, many at the request of Thomas Aquinas (1225–74). Roger Bacon (*c*.1214–94), a pupil of Grosseteste, lamenting the general ignorance of Greek, tried to remedy matters by compiling a Greek grammar.

8. Stimulated by the general revival of intellectual interests characteristic of the Renaissance, Italians of the fourteenth century began to demand more and better texts. But manuscripts were scarce and copyists not very efficient; there was a need for scholarship to match enthusiasm. The combination was found above all in Petrarch (1304–74) and (with more enthusiasm than scholarship) Boccaccio (1313–75). Petrarch's greatest reverence was for Cicero, for whose works he searched throughout Europe; by the end of his life he had collected almost all Cicero's philosophical and rhetorical works and a wide range of speeches, but was most moved by his discovery (which others had made before) of Cicero's Letters to Atticus, to his brother Quintus, and to Brutus. His attempts to learn Greek (from the monk Barlaam) were not successful, but his earnest desire to understand the Greek background to Roman literature moved others to achieve this end. To Boccaccio's enthusiasm for collecting classical books we probably owe the rediscovery of, among others, Martial, Ausonius, Ovid's *Ibis*, parts of the *Appendix Virgiliana* and the *Priapea*. He played some part in propagating the texts of Tacitus, Apuleius, and Varro, which only the library at Monte Cassino possessed. Petrarch and Boccaccio both persuaded Barlaam's pupil Leonzio Pilato to translate Homer into Latin and to teach Greek at Florence. Discoveries continued until well into the fifteenth century and beyond: the unique source of the Younger Pliny's letters to Trajan (book 10) was found in Paris in 1500, and the only manuscript of Tacitus *Annals* I–VI at Corvey in 1508.

The declining fortunes of the Byzantine empire in the East led to many Greek-speakers moving into Italy even before the exodus which followed the fall of Byzantium in 1453. Spurred on by their new knowledge of Greek, the Italians were keen to collect Greek manuscripts, which included, of course, as well as classical literature the Greek New Testament. Access to the Greek text of this led Bessarion at least to anticipate the attitude of Erasmus, that the proper basis for the interpretation of the New Testament was the Greek text and not the Latin Vulgate of Jerome, and so there were new beginnings in theology also. The latter part of the fifteenth century saw the arrival of the printing press, and a new step was taken in the preservation of the classics, notably by the Venetian editor and printer Aldus Manutius (1449–1515), whose books were distinguished by accuracy as well as by the beauty of the typography. He was the first printer to produce small books that were convenient for the student to carry around with him. See also PAPYROLOGY and TEXTUAL CRITICISM below.

textual criticism. The manuscripts in which the works of Greek and Latin literature are preserved for the most part date from the ninth to the fifteenth centuries AD (see TEXTS, TRANSMISSION OF ANCIENT, and PAPYROLOGY); they are thus at many removes from the authors' autographs. The aim of textual criticism is to restore the original text as far as possible, from manuscripts which, in the course of being copied by hand through many centuries, have been altered ('corrupted') by accidental miscopying and by deliberate insertions ('interpolations'), and have deteriorated by natural wear and tear. The first stage is to compare the manuscript copies of a text with each other so as to understand their relationships (for example, which manuscripts are copied from others still surviving) and to gain an idea of the state of the text of the nearest common ancestor of them all, the archetype. (The archetype, which is very rarely still in existence, is as far back as the manuscript evidence goes, but is itself usually many centuries later than the author's autograph.) This stage is known as recension (*recensio*, 'review'), and the results are if possible set out in a 'family tree of manuscripts' (*stemma codicum*), in which manuscripts are identified by letters of the alphabet. (Where a scribe has introduced readings from more than one source, his manuscript is said to be 'contaminated', and may not fit easily into a *stemma*.) At this point manuscripts which are found to be direct copies of others still in existence are eliminated as having no independent value.

The next stage is to examine critically the text of the manuscripts selected as significant in the light of the *stemma*. The editor's task is to identify the authentic readings in those places where the manuscripts differ and to detect places where all of them seem to be in error; these last the editor corrects ('emends') if he can; if he cannot, he isolates the error and indicates that the text is not sound by 'obelizing' the corrupt words, i.e. printing a 'dagger' or obelus before and after them. (The dagger thus † is a modern critical sign: the *obelos* of the Alexandrian scholars was a horizontal line; see TEXTS, TRANSMISSION OF ANCIENT I.) In some places in the texts the manuscripts will offer a variety of readings some or all of which have a claim to be considered as authentic; the editor's task is then to decide between them. Nowadays these variant readings, together with the plausible emendations of previous editors, are printed by the editor at the bottom of each page of text. This part of the text, usually written in Latin and with considerable use of abbreviations, is known as the *apparatus criticus*, 'critical apparatus', and enables readers to assess for themselves the evidence for and reliability of the text they are reading.

Thālēs, of Miletus (flourished *c*.600 BC), by tradition the earliest Greek philosopher-scientist, one of the *Seven Sages. He is credited with offering sound advice in many spheres including politics, but he was chiefly famous as an astronomer and geometer. He is said to have predicted an eclipse of the sun within the year 585 BC which actually took place on the day of the battle of the Halys between the Medes and the Lydians. It is, however, impossible for one of his time to have known a system for predicting a solar eclipse at a given geographical latitude. Slightly more plausible is the belief that after visiting Egypt he originated geometry by generalizing from Egyptian land measurement. Aristotle attributed to him the view that all things are modifications of a single eternal (and therefore divine) substance, which Thales held to be water. With this is connected his saying that 'all things are full of gods'. See PHILOSOPHY.

Thalē'tas, poet from Gortyn in Crete who came to Sparta in the first half of the seventh century BC in order, it was said, to rid the Spartans of a plague (by appeasing the god Apollo with his poetry). There he composed *paeans and *hyporchemata for the festivals, using paeonic and cretic metres (see METRE, GREEK I). Nothing of his work survives.

Thalī'a, see MUSES.

Tha'myris or **Thamyras,** legendary Thracian poet and musician. According to Homer (*Iliad* 2. 594) he boasted that he would win a contest even if the Muses opposed him, but they blinded him and made him forget his skill. Later authors attribute various musical inventions to him.

Thanatos (Death), see HYPNOS.

Thapsus, city in North Africa, famous as the site of Julius Caesar's victory over the supporters of Pompey in 46 BC.

Thargē'lia, principal festival of Apollo at Athens and throughout Ionia, celebrated on the 7th Thargelion (May–June), a pre-harvest festival with first-fruit offerings from the still unripe crops of all kinds of corn and vegetables cooked together in a pot (the offering being called *thargelos*). The interesting feature of this festival took place on the day before, namely purification (perhaps for a new beginning) by means of scapegoats. Two men (representing the men and women of the city), chosen for their ugliness, were fed and led around the city (so as to absorb all *pollution), then pelted, flogged with branches of figs, and driven out; in early times they were no doubt killed by being beaten with real rods and stoned.

Thāsos, rocky island off the coast of Thrace, colonized from Paros *c*.680 BC (see ARCHILOCHUS). It became wealthy from its own gold mines and from the mines which its inhabitants worked on the neighbouring mainland. It joined the Delian League but revolted in 465 (and was subdued in 463). It was a permanent member of Athens' second League. In 340 it passed into the control of Philip II of Macedon and remained a Macedonian dependency until freed by the Romans in 196.

Theaetē'tus, dialogue by *Plato, named after an Athenian mathematician (*c.*414–369 BC), friend and pupil of Plato. This dialogue deals with the nature of knowledge. In the introductory scene Theaetetus is reported to have been brought home, mortally wounded in the Corinthian War between Athens and Corinth (in 369) in which he has shown great bravery. A conversation is then recalled that took place between him and Socrates shortly before the latter's death in 399, and since it had been written down (in direct dialogue form), a slave is summoned and reads the manuscript. Various definitions of knowledge are considered, such as 'knowledge is sensible perception', but are all found wanting; the problem is left unresolved and is resumed in the *Sophist*. In the course of the dialogue there occurs Socrates' famous comparison of himself to a midwife who brings to birth the thoughts of others.

Thea'genēs and Chariclē'a, alternative title of the *Aethiopica* of Heliodorus; see NOVEL.

theatre
1. *Greek*. The Greek theatre appears to have originated with the open-air circular dancing floor (*orchēstra*), a level space of hard earth constructed for performances of choral *lyric, of which one variety, the dithyramb, is according to one tradition the progenitor of Attic *tragedy (see 1). All large Greek theatres were open to the sky (but see ODEUM). The arrangement described below, which may be regarded as typical, is based on that of the theatre of Dionysus at Athens (see DIONYSUS, THEATRE OF). In the middle of the *orchestra* was a *thymelē* or altar of Dionysus, on the steps of which the flute-player who accompanied the *chorus probably stood.

For the spectators at Athens there was a *theatron*, 'watching-place', on the slope of the Acropolis above the *orchestra*. Important spectators sat on seats made of stone at the front of the *theatron*; the rest sat on backless wooden benches placed on rising terraces of earth, crossed at intervals by passageways for access. Beyond these bare facts the details of the construction of the theatre are very obscure. At each side of the *orchestra* was a *parodos* or 'way-in', used by the spectators when they entered the theatre and by the chorus and actors on entering and leaving the *orchestra*. In later times a convention grew up that when the scene was Athens, characters purporting to come on the scene from the agora or Piraeus should enter from the audience's right, since these places were situated in fact in that direction; coming from the country they entered from the left. At the back of the *orchestra* was a low platform or stage, perhaps 8 m. (25 ft.) wide and 3 m. (10 ft.) deep, connected by steps with the *orchestra*. Behind it and extending beyond it on each side was a building, the *skēnē* ('tent', 'hut'), containing the dressing rooms, with a wide double door in the façade giving access to the stage. The *skene* provided the backdrop for the stage, and its roof could serve as a stage for action at a higher level, the setting of the solitary watchman on the palace roof in *Agamemnon*, for example.

There were two pieces of stage equipment, perhaps used mainly in tragedy (which would account for their being the object of mockery in comedy), the *mēchanē* ('machine') and the *ekkyklēma* ('the roll-out'). The *mechane* was a kind of crane which could swing a character round and into view, particularly when a god is announced as being above the house or coming through the sky. The appearance in this manner of a god who provided a solution in an intractable situation originated the Latin phrase *deus ex machina*, 'a god on a machine', to describe an unexpected outside intervention which resolves a difficulty. Euripides was thought by some to be over-fond of this expedient for concluding a play. The *ekkyklema* was a device by which off-stage events in the drama could be revealed to the actors on stage and to the audience; a tableau was arranged on a platform which was then wheeled out through the central door of the *skene* (e.g. in *Agamemnon*, Clytemnestra standing over the murdered bodies of Agamemnon and Cassandra). Various other stage-properties might be used in the Greek theatre, e.g. statues, altars, or other prominent features of the play, and scenery might be painted on boards. There was, however, no curtain. For the actors and their dress see COMEDY, GREEK 3 and TRAGEDY 2. For the admission charge see THEORIC FUND.

Glimpses of the lighter side of Greek theatre-going may be found in the *Characters* of *Theophrastus which include the loquacious man who talked so much that his neighbours could not follow the play, the mean man who availed himself of a free day to bring his children, the shameless man who took advantage of his foreign guests to get admitted without paying, and the stupid man who fell asleep during the play and was left alone in the theatre when the audience had gone. Philochorus writing in the third century BC describes how the audience fill their cups with wine when the chorus enter and fill them again when the chorus leave. Aristotle comments that the eating of sweets is commonest when the actors are bad.

The theatre was used for many kinds of ceremonies apart from plays (see DIONYSIA).

2. *Roman*. There was no permanent theatre at Rome until 55 BC, when Pompey built one in stone from the spoils of the Mithridatic War. It was erected in the Campus Martius, next to the Curia (where Julius Caesar was later assassinated). There seem to have been seats for about 10,000 spectators. Two other stone theatres were subsequently built in Rome, both in the Campus Martius, that of L. Cornelius Balbus dedicated in 13 BC, and that known as the theatre of Marcellus, built by the emperor Augustus and named after his adopted son.

In the time of Plautus, Terence, Ennius, and Pacuvius (late third and the second centuries BC), plays were performed on wooden stages in front of a temporary wooden building having three doors opening on to the stage. These stages would be erected in the Forum or Circus Maximus, with circles of wooden seats; an attempt to erect a permanent theatre in 155 BC was thwarted by the consul Scipio Nasica who induced the senate to demolish the building as it constituted a danger to public morality. But in the first century BC even the temporary theatres became quite elaborate, with linen awnings to keep the sun off the spectators in the auditorium (*cavea*), and ornately decorated stage buildings. The theatre had a semicircular *orchestra*; at the back of it was a stage wider and deeper than the Greek stage (as it existed later at least; see 1 above).

The *orchestra* was not used for dancing, as in Greece, but for seating, reserved for senators, priests, and officials. After 68 BC the *equites* had the right to occupy the first fourteen rows of the auditorium behind the *orchestra*. Behind the stage was the stage building which might rise as high as the sloping auditorium. The auditorium was much more enclosed than in a Greek theatre, and could even have the awnings replaced by a roof, as at Pompeii. The uncomfortable nature of the seating is mentioned by Ovid (*Ars amatoria* 1. 141), who refers to the narrow space allotted to each spectator, and to the knees of those behind pressing into the backs of those in front. From the end of the second century BC Roman theatres had a curtain, kept in a slot in the floor of the stage and raised at the end of the play (a convenient way of indicating that the performance was over). Stage scenery was said to have been first introduced in 99 BC. The chorus in the tragedies of Ennius, Pacuvius, and Accius (unlike the chorus of Greek drama) stood on the stage, not in the *orchestra*, and could enter and exit like any other character (whereas with very rare exceptions the Greek chorus did not leave until the end of the play). This was more realistic; the functions of the chorus had changed and there was no longer that important lyrical element in drama for which it had been the mouthpiece.

The players were slaves or freedmen, trained to the profession, and organized in companies (*grex*, *caterva*) under the direction of a manager (*dominus gregis*) paid for by the magistrate who gave the *ludi* ('games') at which the plays were performed. The players' pay gradually increased, and although actors (like musicians) were originally despised, the examples of *Roscius and *Aesopus showed that popular actors might become rich and socially acceptable. Female parts (except in mimes and late comedy) were played by men. It is said that the type of character was indicated at first by wigs (white for old men, red for slaves, etc.) and later by masks (see ROSCIUS), but whether masks were in fact worn in the Roman theatre, and if so, when, is a matter of dispute. Tragic actors wore long flowing robes and high buskins (*cothurni*); comic actors wore ordinary dress and the *soccus* or low-heeled shoe.

Thē'bäid (*Thēbăis*) Latin epic poem in twelve books of hexameters by *Statius. The author, who spent twelve years on the work, published it in AD 90 or 91.

The subject is the expedition of the *Seven against Thebes in support of the attempt by Polyneicēs to recover the throne from his brother Eteoclēs (see OEDIPUS). The first three books deal with the preliminaries of the war—the arrival of Polyneices and Tydeus at Argos, the embassy of Tydeus to Thebes and the subsequent attempt by some Thebans to destroy him in an ambush (he fights single-handed against fifty Thebans, 2. 496), and the prophecy of Amphiaraus. Books 4, 5, and 6 include the consultation of the seer Teiresias, the Argive march on Thebes, the episode of *Hypsipylē, her account of the massacre at Lemnos, 5. 85, and the funeral games for the child Opheltēs, including the exciting chariot-race, 6. 296. With book 7 the fighting begins, after a vain attempt by Jocasta at mediation. The pious Amphiaraus is swallowed up by the earth; the fighting continues through books 8, 9, and 10, with many incidents: the death of Ismenē's lover Atys, the episode of Tydeus and Melanippus, the feats of Hippomedon, the self-sacrifice (*devotio*) of Menoeceus, the death of Capaneus by a thunderbolt. Book 11 contains the fatal combat of Eteocles and Polyneices, Creon's refusal of burial to the latter, and Jocasta's suicide. Book 12 completes the story with the meeting between Polyneices' wife Argia and Antigonē, the funeral pyre of the two sons of Oedipus, with its divided flames, the intervention of Theseus, and the death of Creon. At the end, Statius takes leave of his long task, and with a humble reference to Virgil speculates whether his own work will endure.

Statius follows epic tradition in having the gods interfere in men's affairs, writing a catalogue of the forces fighting, describing funeral games, and so on. Many of his incidents and much of his language are imitated from Virgil. The modern reader finds an excess of mythological lore; the occasional lively narrative hardly relieves the tedium of the rest.

Thēbā'is, see EPIC CYCLE and *THEBAID*.

Thebes (Thēbai). 1. The principal city of Boeotia in Greece and the most important in Greek history after Athens and Sparta. Its fame in myth and legend was unequalled; Sophocles (in a surviving fragment) described it as 'the only city where mortal women are the mothers of gods' (i.e. Dionysus and Heracles). For its early legendary history see CADMUS, ANTIOPE, HERACLES, and OEDIPUS. According to the usual legend (but see ANTIOPE) the city was founded by the leader of a Phoenician colony, Cadmus, whose daughter gave birth to the god Dionysus. It was probably the centre of a large kingdom in the *Mycenaean age, but it was destroyed by the *Epigonoi in the generation before the Trojan War; hence the absence of the name from the catalogue (in *Iliad* 2) of the Greek cities which fought against Troy. After its eclipse in the *Dark Age, Thebes recovered by the sixth century BC to take the lead in a loose confederation of Boeotian cities (see BOEOTIA), but was never strong enough to unite them into a single state with itself at the head. In the fifth century Thebes was hostile to Athens and supported Persia in the *Persian Wars and Sparta in the *Peloponnesian War. After the Peloponnesian War came a period of rivalry between Thebes and Sparta for supremacy in Greece, and, under the leadership of *Pelopidas and *Epaminondas, Thebes attained its zenith. Not only did the city defeat and humiliate Sparta (in the years following the Spartan defeat at Leuctra in 371), it extended its power in the north, bringing parts of Thessaly under its protection and establishing its authority at the court of Macedon. However, under *Philip II, Macedon swiftly rose to be the strongest state in Greece, posing such a threat that Thebes allied itself with the Athenians. Together they were defeated by Philip at Chaeronea (338); Philip then dissolved the Boeotian confederacy and established a Macedonian garrison in the citadel of Thebes. Shortly after the accession of Philip's son Alexander the Great the Thebans revolted (335) and Alexander destroyed the city. The punishment shocked Greece, and when it was rebuilt by Cassander in 317 many Greek cities helped with contributions. The new Thebes continued to exist throughout Roman times.

*Teiresias and *Amphion in myth, and, historically, the poet Pindar were born at Thebes, and the poetess Corinna at Thebes or Tanagra. In the last destruction of the city the house of Pindar was spared by Alexander's order (the subject of John Milton's sonnet, 'When the assault was intended to the city'). See also CADMEA.

2. Greek name of a city of Upper Egypt, on the site of which Luxor now stands. It became the capital of Egypt at the time of the twelfth dynasty (c.2000 BC), supplanting Memphis, the earlier capital, and attained great splendour under the kings of the eighteenth to twentieth dynasties (c.1400–1100 BC). Homer calls it 'hundred-gated' and speaks of 200 warriors with horses and chariots issuing from each gate. It is now famous for the remains of its great temples and royal tombs.

Themis ('just order'), Greek goddess, according to Hesiod a Titan, daughter of Gaia (Earth), and by Zeus the mother of the *Seasons and the *Fates; in some accounts she is the mother of *Prometheus. Later she is a personification of justice.

Themi'stius (c. AD 317–c.388), Greek rhetorician from Paphlagonia; he opened a rhetorical school in Constantinople c.345, where he was appointed prefect (383–4) by the emperor Theodosius I and tutor to the latter's son, the future emperor Arcadius. He was entrusted with many official missions, and was given the name Euphradēs, 'the eloquent'. Thirty-four of his orations survive, many of them panegyrics on the emperors, but including an interesting funeral oration on his father. He wrote paraphrases of Aristotle's works, some of which are extant. A pagan, he advocated toleration of other religious beliefs.

Themi'stoclēs (c.524–c.459 BC), Athenian statesman and naval strategist. After the failure of Darius' invasion in 490 (see PERSIAN WARS), Themistocles foresaw that the Persians would try again and persuaded the Athenians to concentrate on strengthening their fleet. Thus the city was prepared for the second Persian invasion under Xerxes in 480, and Themistocles determined the strategy that won for the Greeks the great sea-battle of Salamis. In spite of this triumph, in 479 the chief Athenian commands went to others, and Themistocles went to Sparta as Athenian envoy. In the following years he lost influence to Cimon and the aristocrats, and in about 471 was ostracized and retired to Argos, where he stirred up feeling against Sparta. In about 468 Sparta claimed to have evidence that he and *Pausanias were plotting with Persia; he was condemned to death at Athens and his property confiscated. He escaped to Asia by way of Corcyra, Epirus, and Macedonia, and was made governor of Magnesia on the Maeander, where he was much honoured and died in 459. His remains were brought home, it is said, and buried outside the walls of Piraeus, Athens' harbour, which he had done so much to develop and strengthen. There is a famous sketch of his character by Thucydides (1. 138).

Napoleon, writing to the Prince Regent after his defeat at Waterloo in 1815, compared his situation with that of Themistocles, throwing himself on the mercy of the Molossian king in Epirus.

Theocly'menus. 1. In Greek myth, a seer, descended from *Melampus; see ODYSSEY, book 20.

2. See HELEN.

Theo'critus (first half of the third century BC), Hellenistic Greek poet, the originator of pastoral or bucolic poetry. He was born probably at Syracuse in Sicily and may have lived in south Italy; later he went to the island of Cos and to Alexandria during the reign of Ptolemy II Philadelphus. His extant poems, generically known as *Idylls, and mostly in the hexameter metre, include court poems, mythological poems, and epigrams, but his fame stems from the seven or so poems which were primarily *bucolic. These were to have a strong influence on Virgil (in the *Eclogues) and through him on later European literature. Since there is no complete agreement on the criteria that define a bucolic poem, not all readers agree on which of Theocritus' poems are most characteristically bucolic: poems 1, 3, 4, 5, 6, and 11 are always included, 7 and 10 sometimes, and 27 (which is in any case spurious) occasionally; 8 and 9, known and imitated by Virgil, are not now considered authentic. Though Theocritus writes in an artificial, literary Doric dialect (see DIALECTS) for a sophisticated urban circle, the poems still convey an impression of the timeless pastoral life in the hills of Sicily and south Italy. The English poet John Dryden considered that his dialect had 'an incomparable sweetness in its clownishness'.

The first Idyll contains the beautiful lament for *Daphnis, a dirge imitated in the *Adonis* and of *Bion and in the *Bion* attributed to *Moschus, and the prototype of later pastoral elegies, Milton's *Lycidas*, Shelley's *Adonais*, and Matthew Arnold's *Thyrsis*. Idylls 14 and 15, which are set in towns, recall the mimes of *Herodas; the second of these, entitled *Adōniazūsae* ('women at the festival of Adonis'), is a sketch of two simple and admiring Syracusan women, now housewives in Alexandria, visiting a festival at the palace there, closing with a hymn which they hear sung in honour of Adonis and Aphroditē. Idyll 2, *Pharmaceutria* ('woman preparing a love charm'), similarly recalls mime: it tells the story of the unhappy love of Simaetha and her magical incantations to regain her lover. Other Idylls deal with mythological subjects: the love of the one-eyed Cyclops Polyphemus for the nymph Galatea (11),

the abduction of Hylas (13), the fight between Pollux and Amycus (24). Two are flattering addresses (in the hope of patronage) to Hieron II, tyrant of Syracuse (17), and Ptolemy II, king of Egypt (16), and one is a poetic epistle accompanying the present of a distaff to the wife of a friend (28). In Idyll 7, entitled *Thalysia* ('harvest festival'), the setting is Cos, the author, calling himself Sīmichidas, sings of the loves of a certain Aratus, in contest with the enigmatic Lycidas; autobiographical details seem to break through the pastoral convention. The end of the poem evokes the feeling of harvest time in an Aegean island. A number of epigrams purportedly written for tombs or statues is also attributed to Theocritus.

Theodo'ric the Great, see BOETHIUS and GOTHS.

Theodo'sius. 1. Theodosius the Elder, Roman general who between AD 368 and 370 restored security in *Britain after invasions by Picts, Scots, and Saxons.

2. Theodosius I, 'the Great' (AD 347–95), Roman emperor 388–95, son of (1) above. He spent the early years of his reign fighting the invading Visigoths and, failing to drive them out of the empire, had to agree to assign them lands in Thrace. He was a devout Christian, and dealt harshly with heretics. In 391, perhaps under the influence of St *Ambrose, he put an end to all forms of pagan religion in the empire, and thus founded the orthodox Christian state. It is for this that he acquired his title. After Theodosius the Roman empire was divided into two halves, eastern and western. See BYZANTINE AGE.

Theo'gnis, of *Megara, Greek elegiac poet, perhaps of the first half of the sixth century BC though his lifetime is put by many half a century later. Nearly 1,400 lines of poetry ascribed to him survive in manuscript, mostly in short poems one to six couplets long, divided into two books; however, it is a matter of dispute how much is authentic, since some of the lines are also found in poems ascribed to Tyrtaeus, Mimnermus, and Solon, and some of the poems were clearly written at a much later date and against a different background. The collection seems to be in the nature of an anthology, based on the authentic poems of Theognis but augmented by other poems of similar theme drawn from various sources. It is usually accepted that poems addressed to the boy Cyrnus, with whom Theognis was in love, were authentic. Theognis' poems seem typical of those sung or recited at *symposia; they express passionate support for the aristocratic belief in the value of good breeding, and deplore the success of new wealth. There are also many poems of moral exhortation and reflection on life which, with the homosexual love poems, are often expressed with great liveliness.

Theo'gony (*Theogonia*), Greek poem in about a thousand hexameter lines by *Hesiod, and unique in surviving Greek literature in being a systematic account of the gods of Greece and their genealogy. The poet begins with a famous description of how, while pasturing sheep on Mount Helicon, he was inspired by the Muses to compose this poem. It begins at the beginning of the world, with the coming into being of primordial Chaos ('chasm', perhaps conceived of as the dark space between Earth and *Tartarus), followed by Gaia (Earth), Tartarus, and Eros (Love). Gaia produced Uranus (Heaven), and these two were the parents of the Titans, Cyclopēs, and other giants. Last-born of the Titans was Cronus, who at his mother's instigation castrated Uranus. The Titans Rhea and Cronus were the parents of the Olympian gods, whom Cronus ate as soon as they were born, except for Zeus. Zeus later overthrew Cronus and made him restore his other children. One of the Titans, *Prometheus, deceived Zeus in the matter of fair division of sacrificed animals between gods and men, and also stole fire from the gods for men. As his punishment Zeus bound him to a rock where an eagle daily ate his liver, and as a punishment for men Zeus created a woman. War broke out between the older gods, the Titans, and the younger (Olympian) gods, the children of Uranus, led by Zeus. The latter were victorious, and the Titans and *Typhoeus, who helped them, were thrown down to

Tartarus by Zeus. The gods then chose Zeus to be their king. He took a series of goddesses to wife, the last of whom was Hera. Their child Hēbē married Zeus' mortal son Heracles, who became after death a god himself. The last part of the poem deals with the offspring of goddesses and mortal men, and ends with two lines added in later times to lead into the *Catalogue of Women*.

Theōn, of Alexandria (fourth century AD), Greek mathematician and astronomer. His reworkings of *Ptolemy's astronomical tables are the only form in which these were known to Arabic astronomers and through them became known to medieval Europe. He was the last known member of the Museum at Alexandria, and father of *Hypatia (see also NEOPLATONISM). Others of the same name include a grammarian and commentator on the Hellenistic Greek poets, of the first century BC.

Theophra'stus (*c*.370–*c*.287 BC), of Eresus in Lesbos, the pupil and friend of Aristotle and his successor (in 322) as head of the *Peripatetic School of philosophy at Athens. He was the teacher of *Deinarchus and of *Demetrius of Phalerum, and was also on friendly terms with *Cassander and Ptolemy I Soter of Egypt. He wrote in Greek on a great variety of subjects, of which output only a tiny fraction survives, including the following: *Historia plantarum* ('inquiry into plants'), nine books; *De causis plantarum* ('on the aetiology of plants'), six books; a short treatise on metaphysics; and numerous fragments from other philosophical and scientific works. He is best known for a minor work, 'Characters' (*Charaktērĕs*), a collection of thirty descriptive sketches of various types of character. Each exemplifies some deviation from the proper norm of behaviour, exhibiting some failing such as tactlessness, followed by a list of the things that the tactless person will do. There are touches of humour (e.g. the children of the loquacious man asking their father to talk to them at bedtime 'so that we may go to sleep'). The 'Characters' delineate in a concise form types similar to those found in the New Comedy of *Menander (who was said to be a pupil of

Theophrastus), an aspect of the work which suggests that it was intended less as moral essays prompted by Aristotle and more as dramatic monologues written to entertain, or even as aids to forensic oratory (in which characterization was important). It was popular in the seventeenth and eighteenth centuries, especially in France, influencing La Fontaine's *Fables* and La Bruyère's *Caractères*, as well as the character-sketches in some *Spectator* essays of Addison and Steele.

Theopo'mpus (*c.*376–after 323 BC), of Chios, Greek historian, pupil of Isocrates, friend of Philip II and Alexander the Great of Macedon. He was exiled from Chios for having Spartan sympathies, restored by Alexander, and fled to Egypt at the latter's death (323). Little remains of his numerous books except for fragments of his two most important works, the *Hellenica* and *Philippica*. The former was a continuation of Thucydides, a history of Greece from 411 to the battle of Cnidus in 394 BC; the latter, a vast work in fifty-eight books, used the life of Philip as the connecting thread in what was virtually a world history composed of extensive digressions. He was a great admirer of Philip and declared that Europe had produced no one to match him.

theo'ric fund (i.e. 'spectators' fund'), at Athens, a state subsidy for the poorer citizens to enable them to pay for admission to the theatre at the Dionysiac festivals, introduced, it was said, by Pericles. Suppressed when Athens was impoverished by the Peloponnesian War, it was revived in 394 BC, but Demosthenes secured the abolition of the system in 339 BC, so that the state should have extra resources available to it in time of war.

Theoxe'nia, in Greek religion, a festival in honour of various gods in which they were regarded as taking part in a banquet with men, couches being set for them to recline upon. The best known festival of this nature was at Delphi in the month Theoxenios (March–April); Pindar's sixth *paean* was written for one such occasion. His third Olympian ode was also written for a Theoxenia at Acragas in Sicily. Compare LECTISTERNIUM.

Thēra (Santorini), Greek island, one of the Sporadĕs, formed of part of the cone of an ancient volcano. The island had been colonized from Minoan Crete before a large part of it disappeared beneath the sea in the Middle Bronze Age following what seems to have been the largest volcanic eruption known (*c.*1400 BC). In the 630s BC on the advice of the oracle at Delphi Thera colonized Cyrēnē (in North Africa), under the leadership of *Battus, after many difficulties and several false starts. The islanders took no part in the Persian Wars; although *Dorian and therefore likely to sympathize with Sparta (also Dorian) they were allies of Athens in the Peloponnesian War.

Thēra'menēs (d. 404/3 BC), Athenian politician, one of those responsible for the setting up of the revolutionary oligarchic council of the *Four Hundred in 411 BC. He was, however, a moderate (although Thucydides' picture is hostile) and instrumental in overthrowing the Four Hundred and setting up a broader based voting assembly of 5,000 citizens. This apparent change of policy gave him an appearance of shiftiness, since it wholly supported neither the extreme oligarchs nor the democrats; his enemy *Critias called him 'Cothurnus' (the loose boot, also worn on stage, that fitted either foot). In 406 he commanded a ship in the Athenian naval victory over Sparta at Arginusae; the blame for failure to pick up survivors was disputed between Theramenes and the generals, and the latter were put to death. After Athens' final defeat in the *Peloponnesian War in 404 he was sent to negotiate with the Spartans; the blame for the three months' delay during which Athens starved is often laid at his door. When peace was made he was appointed one of the *Thirty Tyrants, but his moderate position brought him into conflict with the extreme oligarch Critias who had him put to death. Aristotle regarded him as a statesman genuinely seeking a moderate political position.

Thē'riaca, see NICANDER.

Thermo'pylae (or Pylae), narrow pass linking Greece with the north, between Thessaly and Locris, having in classical times the sea close by on one side (it has now receded) and on the other steep cliffs, the spurs of Mount Oeta. It was an important strategic position and the scene of several battles, most notably the heroic defence by a small force of Spartans, who in 480 BC held at bay a large army of invading Persians before being overwhelmed (see PERSIAN WARS).

Thēron, tyrant of *Acragas in Sicily 488–472 BC, who married his daughter Demaretē to *Gelon, tyrant of Syracuse. In 483 he seized the city of Himera, and after the latter appealed for Carthaginian help, he and Gelon won a crushing victory there over the Carthaginians in 480. He made Acragas one of the most beautiful of Greek cities. Pindar wrote his second and third Olympian odes for him. He claimed descent from Thersander (see below).

Thersa'nder, in Greek myth, son of Polyneicēs (son of Oedipus) and Argeia. He took part in the successful expedition of the *Epigonoi against Thebes, and afterwards became king of Thebes. From there he took part in the Greek expedition to Troy, but was killed by *Telephus in Mysia. Theron (see above) claimed descent from him.

Thersī'tēs, in Homer's *Iliad*, the only low-born character among the Greeks at Troy (though in post-Homeric legend said to be of good family), physically ugly and abusive of the Greek leaders. When he attacked Agamemnon for stealing the girl Briseis from Achilles, and suggested that the army should return to Greece, Odysseus beat him for his insolence. For his death see ACHILLES.

Thēsē'um, see THESEUS.

Thēseus, in Greek myth, the national hero of Athens, son of Aegeus, king of Athens (or the sea-god *Poseidon) and of Aethra, daughter of Pittheus, king of Troezen. He was represented as the friend and contemporary of *Heracles (whose exploits he often emulates) and thus belonged to the generation before the Trojan War. When Aegeus left Aethra at Troezen, he told her that when their son reached manhood he was to lift a certain large rock and bring to Athens the sword and sandals which were hidden underneath it. Theseus, the son, in due course lifted the rock easily and with the tokens set out for Athens by the dangerous land route. On the way he destroyed various bandits and monsters including *Procrustēs, *Sciron, and Sinis, who used to tie his victims to two pine trees which he bent to the ground and then released, tearing the victim in two. (It is obvious that these adventures have been influenced by the similar stories told of Heracles.) On his arrival at Athens, Medea (see ARGONAUTS), who had taken refuge with Aegeus, realized who he was and tried to destroy him by persuading Aegeus to send him against the bull of Marathon, according to some, Pasiphae's bull brought from Crete by Heracles. On the way to Marathon he was hospitably received by an old woman, Hecalē; when he returned after killing the bull he found Hecale dead and ordered that her memory should be honoured (see also CALLIMACHUS). He returned to Athens where Medea then tried to poison him, but Aegeus recognized his son in time; Medea was obliged to return to Colchis, taking with her Medus, her son by Aegeus.

Theseus now heard of the tribute which *Minos of Crete had imposed on Athens, that seven youths and seven girls had to be sent to be eaten by the Minotaur, and volunteered to be one of the youths. On the way to Crete he demonstrated that Poseidon was his father by diving into the sea and recovering a gold ring Minos had contemptuously thrown in to test him. *Ariadnē with her thread enabled him to find his way out of the Labyrinth after killing the Minotaur. Theseus sailed away with the other Greeks but abandoned Ariadne at Naxos. He had arranged with his father that on returning to Athens his ship would carry a white sail if he was safe, but he forgot to change the black sail, seeing which his father, concluding that Theseus had perished, threw himself from the cliffs to his death. According to some, his death-leap is commemorated in the name of the *Aegean Sea.

Theseus was now king of Athens. He is credited with bringing about the union (synoecism) of the various Attic communities into one state with Athens as the capital city. The event is historical, but its date in Attic history is unknown. With Heracles he took part in an expedition against the Amazons and took the Amazon Antiopē (or Hippolyta, the Amazon queen) as his wife. To recover her the Amazons invaded Attica and occupied the Acropolis, but were defeated and withdrew. When *Pirithous, king of the Lapiths, raided Marathon he was met by Theseus, and the two became friends. Theseus was present at his wedding-feast and at the subsequent fight between Lapiths and *Centaurs, and later helped Pirithous to invade the Underworld in an attempt to carry off Persephonē. Theseus was ultimately rescued by Heracles and in gratitude gave asylum to Heracles after the latter, in a fit of madness, had killed his own wife and children. He is also said to have carried off *Helen when she was a child, but she was rescued by her brothers Castor and Polydeuces (see DIOSCURI). When Creon refused burial to the bodies of the *Seven against Thebes, Theseus supported Adrastus and the sons of the Argive leaders, marched with an army against Creon, and buried the dead. Later he gave refuge to *Oedipus. After the death of his first wife, by whom he became the father of *Hippolytus, he married Phaedra, sister of Ariadne. Theseus was finally driven from Athens by rebellions, took refuge in Scyros, and died or was murdered there. He continued to protect his city, however, and was seen in gigantic size fighting for the Greeks at the battle of Marathon (490 BC). In 475 BC after the Persian Wars the Athenian *Cimon, in obedience to an oracle, brought home from Scyros the bones of a huge man which were believed to be those of Theseus, and buried them at Athens in a shrine, the Theseum, where they received the worship due to a hero. The Theseum was near the site of the later gymnasium of Ptolemy on the southern side of the agora, and seems to have been originally open to the sky, but made into a building in the fourth century BC (it is no longer extant and is to be distinguished from the well-preserved fifth-century temple sometimes known by

this name but more correctly called the Hephaesteum). Theseus, though probably purely mythical, was believed by the Athenians to have been one of their early kings. There is a Life of him by Plutarch, who brings together the various stories.

thesis, SEE ARSIS.

Thesmopho'ria, three-day festival held in Athens and in almost every part of the Greek world in honour of *Demeter; it was attended only by women and apparently excluded virgins. Celebrated at Athens during 11–13 Pyanepsion (October/November), its ceremonies were a 'mystery', known only to the participants. Its purpose was evidently to ensure the fertility of the cereal crops sown at this time of year. Aristophanes' comedy Thesmophoriazusae (see below) is imagined as taking place during the festival.

Thesmophoriazū'sae ('women celebrating the Thesmophoria'), comedy by Aristophanes produced in 411 BC, probably at the Dionysia.

The women are about to celebrate their private festival, the *Thesmophoria (from which men are excluded). Euripides has learnt that, since his portrayal of legendary wicked women in his tragedies has given all women a bad name, they intend to plot his death. Taking an elderly kinsman with him he tries to persuade the effeminate tragic poet *Agathon to disguise himself as a woman, attend the rites, and plead the cause of Euripides. Agathon refuses. Thereupon the elderly relative offers to go instead. He is shaved and suitably dressed and goes off to the festival, having made Euripides swear to come to his aid if there is any trouble. The women gather and speeches are made against Euripides; the old man defends him by pointing out how much worse were the charges he might truthfully have made against women. The general indignation he causes is interrupted by the arrival of Cleisthenēs (notorious for his effeminacy) with news that a man has got into the festival in disguise. Search is made and the old man is discovered and put under guard. Imitating the hero of Euripides' tragedy Palamēdēs (now lost) the old man writes a message on a votive tablet of the temple and throws it out. He then assumes the character of Helen from Euripides' extant tragedy of that name, and Euripides appears as Menelaus; there is a recognition scene, the only sustained parody by Aristophanes of which we possess the original, but the guard prevents the reunion of the pair. A Scythian policeman now arrives and ties up the old man. Euripides reappears as Perseus and the old man takes on the character of Andromeda, from Euripides' lost tragedy of that name, tied to her rock. But the Scythian stops the attempted rescue. Euripides now comes to terms with the women: he will never again slander them if they release his relative. They agree. But the Scythian has to be dealt with. He is lured away by the promise of a dancing girl, and the old man and Euripides escape.

The old man is nowhere given a name in the text. The only manuscript to preserve this play calls him Mnesilochus (the name of Euripides' father-in-law) in the *scholia, but this may be a guess on the part of a commentator.

Thespis, from Icaria in Attica, according to one tradition the inventor of Greek tragedy (see TRAGEDY 1). He is said to have won the competition when tragedies were first presented at the *Dionysia at Athens between 536 and 533 BC. Aristotle credits him with taking the vital step of transforming a choral performance into drama by inventing an actor, playing the part of a character, who spoke the prologue and conversed with the chorusleader. He is also said, less credibly, to have invented the mask. Four play titles, drawn from mythology, are known, but they may not be genuine. Nothing can be said about the nature of his plays. 'Thespian' now refers to drama in general.

The'ssaly (Thessalia), district of northeastern Greece, consisting of fertile plains almost completely walled in by mountains, including Mount Olympus. Its chief river was the Pēnēus, flowing into the Aegean through the beautiful Vale of Tempe, and its chief cities were Crannon, Larissa, and Pherae. Thessaly was powerful in the sixth century BC, but

declined because of internal rivalries. In the early fourth century it was briefly united under *Jason of Pherae, but in the late fourth century Thessaly came under Macedonian control; liberated by Rome in 196, it was incorporated into the Roman province of Macedonia in 148 BC.

In mythology Thessaly was the home of the *Centaurs and Lapiths; it was from Thessaly that the *Argonauts set out, Pelias and Aeson being rulers of Iolcus. It was regarded as pre-eminently the country of magicians.

Thetis, see PELEUS and ACHILLES.

Thirty (Tyrants), the, an *oligarchy that governed Athens in 404–403 BC in cooperation with Sparta after Sparta had defeated Athens in the Peloponnesian War. *Critias and *Theramenēs were leading members. The Thirty abolished the law-courts and began exterminating their enemies and confiscating their property. About 1,500 citizens and metics are said to have been put to death also, including the brother of the orator *Lysias, who barely escaped with his life (see his speech *Against Eratosthenēs*). A band of exiles led by *Thrasybūlus captured Piraeus, Critias was killed, and the full democracy restored. Most of the Thirty were eventually put to death.

Thirty Years' Peace, the peace which in 446 BC terminated the state of war which had existed between Athens and the Peloponnesians since 459; it was to be for thirty years but in fact lasted barely fifteen.

Thisbē, see PYRAMUS.

Thrace. The boundaries of Thrace were not clearly defined until Roman times, but it was the most northern area of Greece, bounded by the river Ister in the north, the Black Sea and Bosporus in the east, the Propontis, Hellespont, and north Macedonia in the south, and Illyria in the west. The Romans divided it into two parts separated by Mount Haemus and called the northern part Moesia. The Thracians were considered by the Greeks to be a primitive people, and until classical times they lived in villages; urban civilization was developed only under the Romans. The coast was extensively colonized by other Greek states, but their

influence did not spread inland. Philip II
of Macedon imposed tribute and founded
Philippopolis in his own honour, and
Thrace became a Macedonian protectorate. The Romans incorporated the part
west of the river Hebrus into the province
of Macedonia.

Thracian Chersonese, see CHER-
SONESE.

Thra'sea Paetus, Publius Clo'dius,
prominent Roman senator under the
emperor Nero, leader of the Stoic and
republican opposition. His father-in-law
was A. Caecina Paetus, husband of Arria
(the elder). He modelled himself on
*Cato of Utica, of whom he wrote a Life.
Condemned for disloyalty, he committed
suicide in AD 66. See also HELVIDIUS
PRISCUS.

Thraso, the boastful soldier in Terence's
comedy *Eunuchus.

Thrasybū'lus. 1. Tyrant of *Miletus in
the seventh century BC.
2. Athenian naval commander who
with *Thrasyllus led the democratic reaction in the Athenian fleet at Samos in 411
BC, against the oligarchic rule of the
*Four Hundred, and recalled Alcibiadēs.
With Thrasyllus he defeated the Spartan
fleet in the same year at Cynossēma. At
*Arginusae he was one of the subordi-
nate officers. Banished by the *Thirty
Tyrants, Thrasybulus was once more
leader of the democratic party in 404/3,
and successfully led the exiles to seize
Piraeus and defeat the troops of the
Thirty. He then led his men to Athens
and the democracy was restored. He was
killed in 388.

Thrasy'llus, one of the Athenian naval
commanders executed after the victory of
*Arginusae in 406 BC.

Thrasy'machus, of Chalcēdōn in
Bithynia, a Greek *sophist and rhetorician in the last quarter of the fifth century BC, figuring in Plato's *Republic and
defending the proposition that might is
right. He played a part in the development of Attic oratorical style, emphasiz-
ing the importance of rhythm and of
polished sentence structure.

Thrīna'cia (Thrīnakiē), in the *Odyssey*

(book 12) the island where *Helios kept
his cattle.

Thūcy'didēs (Thoukydidēs).   **1.**
Athenian politician, born *c.*500 BC. He
succeeded *Cimon (a relative by marriage) as leader of the wealthy aristocratic
and oligarchical faction, and was the
political enemy of Pericles, whose use of
tribute money from the *Delian League
for building works in Athens he attacked.
He was ostracized in perhaps 443 BC. In
his old age he was brought to trial in a
manner condemned by Aristophanes. He
is mentioned by Pindar as a famous
trainer of wrestlers.
2. Greek historian, author of the
(incomplete) History of the *Peloponnesian War between Athens and Sparta
(431–404 BC), in eight books. He was
born probably between 460 and 455 BC
and died *c.*399; he caught the plague at
some time between 430 and 427 but
recovered from it. As *strategos in 424 he
was sent to protect the coast of Thrace
from the Spartan general *Brasidas but
failed to save Athens' valuable colony of
Amphipolis from falling into Spartan
hands, and was condemned in his absence
and exiled. He returned to Athens twenty
years later when the war was over, and
died within a few years; there was a tradition that he was assassinated. He seems
to have been related to *Cimon and Thucydides (1) above.
Thucydides had intended to take his
history down to the fall of Athens in 404,
but the narrative breaks off in mid-sen-
tence with the events of the winter 411/
10. Its continuation by Theopompus and
Cratippus is lost, together with the rest of
their works. Thucydides says that at the
beginning of the Peloponnesian War he
realized that it would have a greater
importance in the history of Greece than
any previous wars (including the Persian
Wars) and would be for that reason more
worth writing about. Since he spent most
of the war in exile and removed from the
immediate action, he was in a good position to gain first-hand information from
both sides and to have a clearer perspec-
tive. His object was to provide an accurate record of what happened and to be
instructive, because knowledge of the
past is a useful guide to the future. His

work was to be a 'possession for all time' (*ktēma es aiei*) not something 'written for display, to make an immediate impression'. A feature of the history is the reporting of speeches, for which he does not claim the same degree of accuracy as for events. With regard to these speeches he says that he kept as closely as possible to the sense of what was actually spoken while setting out the arguments which in his opinion the situation required. The speeches serve to reveal the policies or attitudes which lay behind the decisions of the generals and politicians who made them. Often he presents the speeches of two opponents advocating opposite courses of action. Since all the speeches are reported in Thucydides' own idiosyncratic style, some critics have thought that they must be his original compositions, designed to make clear in dramatic form what Thucydides thought to be the fundamental issues, but this is to disbelieve his statement to the contrary. Some critics have also felt that in his search below the surface for underlying causes he resembles the scientists and physicians of his day (see, for example, HIPPOCRATES); in his analysis of the causes of the Peloponnesian War he distinguishes between the immediate causes and pretexts—quarrels about the alliances of lesser city states, Corcyra and Potidaea—and the primary cause, Sparta's fear of Athenian expansion. It is possible that this last was added at a later stage of composition, with the benefit of deeper reflection.

Of the eight books, book 1 comprises an introduction, giving a brief summary of early Greek history (the so-called 'Archaeology', chapters 1–23) and the author's aims in writing the work, a description of events at Corcyra and Potidaea, and the political manœuvrings of 433–432, followed by a history of the growth of Athenian power during the years 479 to 435 (chapters 89–118, the Pentekontaetia). Books 2–5. 24 describe the main events of the first ten years of war, 431–421, known as the Archidamian War; they include Pericles' Funeral Oration at the end of the first year of war (2. 34–46), the plague at Athens (2. 47–54), the revolt at Mitylene in 428/7 (3. 1–50), the destruction of Plataea in 427 (3. 51–

68), civil war in Corcyra in 427 (3. 69–86), the capture of the Spartan garrison on Sphacteria in 425 (4. 1–42), the loss of Amphipolis to Brasidas (4. 102–116), and the deaths of Cleon and Brasidas and the Peace of Nicias (5. 1–24). The rest of book 5 describes the precarious peace, the Mantinea campaign 418–417 (63–83), and ends with the destruction of Melos in 415. Books 6 and 7 are devoted to the Sicilian Expedition. Book 8, which is incomplete and contains no speeches, covers the beginning of the so-called Decelean War (413–404) and describes the revolt of the Athenian allies and the naval warfare off the coast of Asia Minor, before stopping in 411.

Thucydides displayed a passion for accuracy and exactness that no other ancient historian approached and which was probably a product of his own individuality as much as the result of influence from contemporary scientific writers. Moreover, he saw history as explicable entirely in human terms without recourse to the supernatural; omens and oracles earned his contemptuous dismissal. He reported what could be observed, and did not ponder what part if any the gods played in it. He is generally impartial, although it has been felt that his view of Pericles was too favourable and his portrait of a detestable Cleon somewhat prejudiced. His subject is treated with the utmost seriousness and at a high level; there is no room for anecdote or scandal or hearsay, and certainly no room for the romantic. Apart from Thucydides we have no history of the Peloponnesian War; we cannot, except in rare cases, know what he has chosen to omit or test the accuracy of what he includes. His overall attitude is the only justification for our acceptance of his picture of events, both of the facts he gives and his interpretation of them.

His brilliant but difficult style is well-suited to the narration of great events. It has a poetic flavour apparent in, for example, his occasional use of Ionic dialect forms which sound old-fashioned in the context of his normal Attic usage (see DIALECTS 2); other poeticisms include making abstract nouns like 'war' or 'hope' sound like personifications, and using an unnatural word-order, for emphasis. Thucydides' sentences, though not usually short, show remarkable compression, the meaning telescoped into a few words, his rapidity of thought achieved by a plentiful use of abstract nouns. This impression of concentration is particularly apparent in the speeches.

Thulē, northern land never certainly identified, first noticed by *Pytheas in the fourth century BC on his circumnavigation of Britain and thought from his route to be Norway or Iceland; it lay six days' sail north of Britain and the sun did not set there at midsummer. *Eratosthenēs drew the Arctic circle through it; *Ptolemy located it at Shetland (midnight sun notwithstanding); it was probably Shetland that was seen by Agricola's fleet (see BRITAIN) when they claimed to have seen Thule. Virgil's phrase 'ultima Thule' (farthest Thule) (*Georgics* 1.30) has come to mean figuratively the uttermost point attained or attainable.

Thu'rii (Thourioi), Greek colony situated in south Italy on the Gulf of Tarentum very near the site of *Sybaris (destroyed by the neighbouring city of Croton *c.*510 BC). The descendants of the Sybarites who had been driven out asked the assistance of Sparta and Athens to refound their city there. Under the direction of Pericles Athens agreed. Athenian colonists were sent out under Lampon (a celebrated soothsayer, satirized in the comedy of the day) and a certain Xenocritus in 443 BC, and were joined by others from all parts of the Greek world, reputedly including Herodotus and Lysias. *Hippodamus may have laid out the city; *Protagoras wrote its law code.

Thye'stēs, see PELOPS.

Thye'stēs, Roman tragedy by *Seneca (2), dealing with the gruesome revenge of Atreus against his brother (see PELOPS). No Greek drama on this subject is extant, but the theme had already been used by three Roman writers in tragedies now lost: Ennius in his *Thyestes,* Accius in *Atreus,* and *Varius in his *Thyestes* (a famous play).

thyrsus, a wand wreathed in ivy and vine-leaves, with a pine-cone at the top, carried by the worshippers of *Dionysus.

Tiber (Tiberis, also Tibris and Tybris), the chief river of central Italy, rising in the Apennines and flowing in a generally southerly direction between Etruria on the west, Umbria and the country of the Sabines on the east, and Latium on the south. The silt it carries with it on its journey of 400 km. (250 miles) accounts for the yellowish tinge of its water. Ancient Rome stood on its left bank about 25 km. (16 miles) from its mouth at Ostia. See TIBERINUS below.

Tiberī'nus, eponymous hero who gave his name to the river Tiber in Italy. In Roman tradition he is variously described as the son of the god Janus, or as a descendant of Aeneas and king of *Alba Longa (his father then being Capetus); he was drowned in the river then known as Albula, after which the river was renamed.

Tibērius (Tiberius Claudius Nero Caesar), born in 42 BC, Roman emperor AD 14–37, elder son of Tiberius Claudius Nero and *Livia. Livia subsequently married the emperor Augustus, who accepted his stepson Tiberius as his heir. Tiberius ruled moderately and parsimoniously; his drastic cutting of luxury expenditure, notably on public shows, strengthened finances but made him unpopular in Rome. Within his own family there was jealousy and continual intrigue. Embittered and increasingly misanthropic, Tiberius retired to Capri and ruled through *Sejanus. The end of his reign was a time of terror, with spying, prosecutions, vengeance, and suicides. His life has been painted in the darkest colours by Tacitus and Suetonius (he is said to have had a taste for cruelty and perverted vice), but he was enthusiastically praised by Velleius Paterculus.

Tibu'llus, A'lbius (*c.*55–19 BC), Roman elegiac poet of equestrian rank. He was a friend of Horace and Ovid, and belonged to the circle of poets around M. Valerius *Messala Corvinus, whom he may have followed on campaign in Gaul and the Near East between 31 and 27 BC. He wrote two books of elegies, the first published *c.*27 BC; the date of the second is unknown. The first book contains mostly love elegies, five about his love for

Delia (pseudonym for Plania) and three for a boy Marathus; the second contains only six poems, three concerning his love for a girl Nemesis; the opening poem, a dramatization of the *Ambarvalia, is a notable work. The rest of the works that have come down in his corpus are by other poets, notably the elegies of one Lygdamus, rather sentimental compositions by a poet who writes like Ovid, and six elegies (IV. 7–12) by Sulpicia, the niece of Messala, recording her love for Cerinthus (a pseudonym). Tibullus' favourite themes are romantic love and the pleasures of country life. He is a minor poet, a little dull perhaps, but *tersus atque elegans*, 'polished and discriminating' (Quintilian).

Tibur (Tivoli), town about 28 km. (17 miles) north-east of Rome. Many rich Romans had villas there, including Catullus and the emperor Augustus, and perhaps Horace also; the most famous was the great villa of Hadrian (emperor AD 117–38).

Tigelli'nus, d. AD 69, the emperor Nero's notorious commander of the praetorian guard (62–8), who was the cause of many executions at Rome. He was a Sicilian exiled from Rome in 39 for adultery with the emperor Caligula's sisters, but was again at court early in Nero's reign. For his part in discovering the conspiracy of *Piso against the emperor in 65 he was lavishly rewarded. He abandoned Nero at the end and transferred his allegiance to Galba, but when Otho became emperor he was forced to commit suicide.

Timae'us (c.356–260 BC), Greek historian of Tauromenium in Sicily, who migrated to Athens c.317 and spent the next fifty years there, probably returning to Sicily under Hieron II. His most important work was a history of Sicily in thirty-eight books from earliest times to 264 BC (before the Romans attacked the Carthaginians there). He seems to have been the first to establish a chronology based on the *Olympiads, and *Eratosthenes must have taken over the system from him. Polybius praised him for his invention, but also attacked him for deliberate falsification and ignorance.

Timae'us, dialogue by *Plato, usually thought to be a late work, in form a sequel to one of the themes of the *Republic*, in which the author places in the mouth of Timaeus, a Pythagorean philosopher, an exposition of the origin and system of the universe. The creator god or demiurge (see DEMIURGUS), being good, created the material universe from the elements earth, air, fire, and water as a unique copy of the ideal universe which exists only in the realm of (Platonic) Ideas or Forms (see PLATO 4). From these elements in various proportions the demiurge also created the soul of the world, the lower gods, and the stars. The lower gods created men's mortal bodies, though the demiurge created their immortal souls. Men who lived a wicked life would suffer reincarnation first as women, and then if unreformed as animals. The origin of sensations and diseases is then traced; the three-fold division of the soul into reason, emotion, and appetite, and the fate of the individual after death are briefly indicated.

In a preliminary myth *Critias recounts the conquest of the empire of Atlantis (a continent west of the Pillars of Hercules, now sunk beneath the sea) by the ancient Athenians, a legend which is continued in the unfinished dialogue *Critias*.

Cicero translated or adapted *Timaeus* but most of his work is lost. *Timaeus* was an influential dialogue in late antiquity, influencing *Neoplatonism with its anticipation of the latter's elaborate spiritual hierarchy; the demiurge was also easily seen by Christians as the Creator God of Genesis. The idea that the demiurge created the stars and other heavenly bodies with souls gave authority to astrology, which regarded them as divine.

Timo'crates, Against, speech in a public prosecution by *Demosthenes; see (2) 2.

Timo'creon (first half of the fifth century BC), Greek lyric and elegiac poet from Rhodes, who took the Persian side when the Persians occupied that island. Only small fragments of his work survive in quotation. He was a personal enemy of *Themistoclēs and *Simonidēs; the latter pilloried him in a couplet purporting to be his epitaph.

Tīmō'leon (d. *c.*336 BC), Corinthian statesman and general who *c.*365 BC conspired with his friends in killing his brother Timophanēs when the latter attempted to make himself tyrant. Timoleon thereafter lived under a cloud until sent by the Corinthians in 345 with a small force of mercenaries to their daughter-city Syracuse whose aristocrats had appealed for help against their tyrant Dionysius II. He defeated the enemy forces, restored order, and then retired into private life, remaining at Syracuse until his death as the adviser of the people.

Tīmon. 1. Semi-legendary Athenian who, supposedly owing to the ingratitude of his friends, became a notorious misanthrope, refusing to meet anyone except, according to Plutarch, *Alcibiadēs. Aristophanes is the first to refer to him. Shakespeare's *Timon of Athens* is based on his story as told by Plutarch in his Life of Mark Antony, and by Lucian in his dialogue *Timon*.

2. Of Phlius (flourished *c.*250 BC), a Sceptic philosopher, author of a book of lampoons, of which only fragments survive, entitled *Silloi* (i.e. 'squint-eyed' pieces), in mock-Homeric hexameters, in which he ridiculed the dogmatic philosophers.

Timo'theus. 1. Greek poet of Miletus (*c.*450–*c.*360 BC), reputedly a friend of Euripides. He is famous for his *nomes and *dithyrambs. Although most of his eighteen books of poems are lost, some 250 lines of the nome *Persae* have been found on an Egyptian papyrus of the fourth century BC, the oldest surviving Greek literary text. It is an impression of the battle of Salamis written in a bombastic imitation of the elevated style of choral lyric; various metres are used (probably the music was as important as the words), and the composition is astrophic (see STROPHE). Timotheus figures in John Dryden's poem 'Alexander's Feast' (1697).

2. Athenian politician (d. 354 BC), son of *Conon (1) and pupil of Isocrates. He promoted an imperialist policy, capturing Samos from the Persians in 365 and extending the dominion of Athens in the Thracian Chersonese and Chalcidicē. In consequence of his failure to support his fellow-general Charēs in an attack on Chios in 356 he was tried and fined.

Tīre'sias, see TEIRESIAS.

Tīro, Marcus Tu'llius, slave, confidential secretary, and friend of *Cicero ((1) 7), who freed him in 53 BC. He survived his master and was the author of a Life of Cicero (now lost), and editor of some of his speeches and of his letters *Ad familiares* ('to his friends'), which include letters to Tiro himself. He wrote also on grammar, and developed a system of shorthand; a surviving collection of abbreviations is known as *notae Tironiānae*.

Tiryns, ancient Greek city in the southern part of the plain of Argos, inhabited from the early Bronze Age (before 2200 BC). The huge Cyclopean walls, built *c.*1400 BC of roughly hewn blocks of stone, are still standing (see CYCLOPES). The city is associated in myth with *Mycenae, some fifteen kilometres to the north, and with the story of *Heracles.

Tī'sias, see TEISIAS.

Tissaphe'rnēs, the Persian satrap of the coastal provinces of Asia Minor with whom Sparta entered into alliance against Athens in 412 BC, and with whom *Alcibiades intrigued. When in 401 Cyrus the Younger of Persia challenged the army of the Persian king Artaxerxēs, his brother, at the battle of Cunaxa, Tissaphernes with his cavalry played the decisive part in Artaxerxes' victory. Thereafter he harassed Xenophon and the Ten Thousand who had fought for Cyrus (see ANABASIS). He was once more ruler of the Aegean coast when Sparta began war with Persia in 400, and Xenophon relates in his *Hellenica* and *Agesilaus* how Tissaphernes was outwitted and crushingly defeated by the Spartan king *Agesilaus. After this failure he was assassinated by order of Artaxerxes.

Tītans (Tītānēs, of uncertain meaning, perhaps simply 'gods'), in Greek myth the older gods of the generation before the Olympian gods (see GODS I), children of Uranus (Heaven) and Gaia (Earth). The story of the marriage of Heaven and Earth and the birth of gods from the marriage is very widespread in myth from all parts of the world. According to Hesiod the Titans were twelve in number, six sons and six daughters: Oceanus, Coeus (Koios), Crīus (Krios), Hyperion, Īapetus, Cronus, and Theia, Rhea, Themis, Mnēmosynē, Phoebē, Tethys. The names are a mixture of Greek, non-Greek (e.g. Oceanus, Iapetus, Cronus) and abstractions (Themis, 'justice', and Mnemosyne, 'memory'). Some of their children were also regarded as Titans, notably Prometheus and Atlas. When Zeus, aided by his mother Rhea, compelled *Cronus to disgorge his other children, battle ensued (the Titanomachy) between the Titans on the one hand and Zeus and his brothers and sisters on the other (Prometheus fighting on the side of Zeus). The battle lasted for ten years, shaking the universe to its foundations, but eventually the *Cyclopĕs and *Hecatoncheirĕs came to the help of Zeus, and the Titans were overcome and imprisoned in Tartarus, guarded by the Hecatoncheires; Atlas was punished by being made to support the sky on his shoulders. It was sometimes thought that eventually Zeus freed the Titans. In literature the Titanomachy is often confused with the Battle of Gods and *Giants (the Gigantomachy).

Tithō'nus, in Greek myth, son of Laomedon, king of Troy, and brother of Priam. Eos (Dawn) fell in love with him, and by her he was the father of Emathion (killed while trying to prevent Heracles from stealing the Golden Apples of the Hesperidĕs) and of *Memnon (killed at Troy). Eos obtained immortality for him from Zeus but forgot to ask also for eternal youth, so that Tithonus became an old shrivelled creature little more than a voice, and according to some was turned into a cicada, which renews its skin every year. The story is the subject of a dramatic monologue, 'Tithonus' (pub. 1860), by the English poet Tennyson.

Ti'tiĕs, see RAMNES.

Titi'nius, writer of comedies at Rome in the second century BC, a contemporary of Terence, and the earliest known author of *fabulae *togatae,* comedies with Roman plots and characters. Only fifteen titles and some fragments survive.

Tītus (Tītus Flavius Vespasianus), AD 39–81, Roman emperor 79–81, elder son of the emperor Vespasian whose rule he had previously shared. He is famous for the capture of Jerusalem in AD 70 after a long siege. The Arch of Titus commemorating this, erected in the Forum at Rome by his brother Domitian (when the latter succeeded as emperor), is still standing, in part restored. During his campaign in Judaea Titus fell in love with *Berenīcĕ, daughter of the Jewish king Herod Agrippa I (grandson of Herod the Great); in Acts 25: 13 she is mentioned as assisting her brother Agrippa II in the business of government. She accompanied Titus when he returned to Rome but the Romans disapproved of a connection between the emperor's son and colleague and a Jewess; Titus had to dismiss her, to the sorrow of them both. This is the subject of Racine's tragedy *Bérénice.* Titus was universally popular, and his short reign was remembered as a happy one, despite the eruption of Vesuvius in 79 and the plague and fire in Rome the following year. He gave generous help to those who had suffered; his building works included the completion of the Colosseum (begun by Vespasian) and the Baths of Titus. See also SUETONIUS (*Lives of the Caesars*).

Titus, Arch of, see above.

Tītus Andro'nicus, Roman tragedy by Shakespeare, whose hero has no counterpart in Roman history or literature.

Tītus Tā'tius, legendary king of the *Sabines who, after the reconciliation between his people and the Romans which followed the Rape of the Sabines, ruled jointly with *Romulus over the combined peoples.

Ti'tyus, in Greek myth, a *Giant, son of Gaia (Earth), who was killed, for assaulting the goddess Leto, by Zeus or by Apollo and Artemis (Leto's children). Odysseus (in the *Odyssey,* book 11) saw him lying in the Underworld covering 9 *plethra* ('acres') of ground, while two vultures tore at his liver.

tmēsis ('division'), in grammar, the division of a word into two parts with other words interposed; e.g. in Ennius, *saxo cere comminuit brum*, 'he shattered his skull (*cerebrum*) with a rock'; more obvious is Virgil's *talis Hyperboreo septem subjecta trioni*, 'beneath the Hyperborean sky' (*septentrioni*).

tŏgā'ta, fabula ('a play in a toga'). These *fabulae* were Roman comedies of the second century BC about Italian life and characters, set in some small Italian town. Nothing of them has survived except for a few titles and quotations. *Afranius was the chief author; see also ATTA and TITINIUS.

Tolō'sa (Toulouse), town in the Roman province of Gallia Narbonensis, which at the time of the Gallic rebellion in 107 BC fell into the hands of the invaders. It was recaptured in 106 by the consul Q. Servilius Caepio, who sacked the temples and removed the gold from the sacred offerings. This was regarded as an act of impiety, bound to bring misfortune. The gold mysteriously disappeared on its way to Rome; the escort was said to have been overwhelmed; hence the expression 'Toulouse gold', *aurum Tolosanum*, for ill-gotten goods.

Tōmis (Lat. *Tŏmis*, Tomi), colony of Miletus on the west coast of the Black Sea. It was brought under Roman rule in 72 BC, but continued to suffer raids from outlying tribes until that area of northeastern Thrace became the Roman province of Moesia in the early first century AD. It is famous as the place of Ovid's banishment. See *TRISTIA*.

To'pica, see ARISTOTLE 4 (i); for Cicero's abstract of the work see CICERO (1) 5.

torch-race (*lampadēdromia*), form of sacred contest common to many cults throughout Greece. In Athens it formed part of the *Panathenaea and of the festivals of the fire gods Prometheus and Hephaestus. The competitors had to carry lighted torches to the goal, usually the altar of the god or goddess being celebrated. Anyone whose torch went out was disqualified, and the winner

placed his torch on the altar. The race was run by teams from each tribe as a relay race, or by single competitors. At the festival of the Thracian goddess Bendis, referred to at the beginning of Plato's *Republic*, there was the novelty of a torch-race on horseback.

Torquā'tus, see MANLIUS TORQUATUS.

Trachi'niae ('women of Trachis'), Greek tragedy by *Sophocles, of uncertain date but with indications that, with *Ajax* and *Antigonē*, it is early among his surviving works, written in the years after Aeschylus' *Oresteia* (458 BC).

Since his murder of Iphitus, son of Eurytus, *Heracles and his family have been exiled from Tiryns to Trachis (in Malis, a little west of Thermopylae). The chorus is composed of Trachinian women. When the play opens, Heracles has been absent for fifteen months. He had told Dēianeira, his wife, that at the end of this period the crisis of his life would come, and he would either die or have a happy life thereafter. Deianeira sends Hyllus, their son, in search of his father. As she reflects on her anxieties a messenger announces the arrival of Heracles in Euboea nearby. This is presently confirmed by the report of a herald, who brings with him a train of captive women taken by Heracles when he sacked Oechalia in Euboea, the city of his enemy Eurytus. Deianeira discovers that these include Iolē, daughter of Eurytus, with whom Heracles has fallen in love. With a love-charm which she had been given by Nessus, the Centaur, when he was dying at the hands of Heracles, she decides to win back her husband's love, and smears the charm on a robe she is sending him. Too late she discovers that it has shrivelled a piece of wool and is a deadly poison. Hyllus returns, describes the agony of Heracles, his flesh consumed by the robe, and denounces his mother as a murderess. Deianeira goes out in silence, and presently her old nurse enters to say that she has killed herself. The dying Heracles is brought in; he tells Hyllus to carry him to Mount Oeta and there burn him on a pyre before the agony returns, and afterwards to marry Iole. Hyllus reluctantly consents, bitterly reproaching the gods for their pitiless treatment of his father.

tragedy (i.e. tragic drama), from Greek *tragōidia*, 'goat song'. There is no satisfactory explanation of this name. It may have arisen because, it has been suggested, the chorus in tragedy originally wore goat-skins, or in connection with a goat-sacrifice, or even because there was a competition with a goat as prize.

The Monk in Chaucer's *Canterbury Tales* defines the essence of tragedy as he knew it, and as it is in most surviving Greek tragedies:

> Tragedie is to seyn a certeyn storie,
> As olde bookes maken us memorie,
> Of hym that stood in greet prosperitee,
> And is yfallen out of heigh degree
> Into myserie, and endeth wrecchedly.
> And they ben versified communely,
> Of six feet, which men clepen exametron.

(Tragedy is, as old books inform us, a kind of story concerning someone who has enjoyed great prosperity but has fallen from his high position into misfortune and ends in wretchedness. Tragedies are commonly written in verse with six feet, called hexameters.)

There are some Greek tragedies which have a happy ending for the good (see e.g. Euripides' *Helen*). Plays of this type Aristotle (in the *Poetics*) considered to be an inferior form of tragedy.

1. *The origin of Greek tragedy*. The only Greek tragedy we possess is Athenian; for that reason it is known as 'Attic' tragedy (from the state of Attica, of which Athens was the chief city). Tragedy was usually regarded as an Attic invention (but not always; see below). It is very difficult to trace its history back beyond the fifth century BC. There are several different accounts of its origin current in antiquity. Aristotle thought that it originated 'in the improvisations of those who led the *dithyramb'*, but adds that it was said by some to have evolved from choral performances in the (Dorian) Peloponnese. Certainly choral song remained an important constituent of tragedy, and the dialect of the choruses, (literary) Doric, attests the origin of the choral element in a Doric-speaking region (see DIALECTS). Drama, however,

requires actors. A tradition followed by Horace in the *Ars poetica* attributed the invention of the actor to *Thespis, who came to Athens from Icaria in Attica and won the tragedy competition in 533 or a little earlier. Thus Attic tragedy may be thought to have originated no earlier than the mid-sixth century BC.

The tradition which gives tragedy a Peloponnesian origin claims that the decisive step towards drama was taken by *Arion (possibly of the seventh century BC and also credited with the development of the dithyramb into a recognized literary form), who brought on stage '*satyrs speaking verse'. Aristotle also says that tragedy acquired dignity by development from the style of satyr-plays (see SATYRIC DRAMA). Arion may provide a tenuous link between dithyramb, tragedy, and satyr-plays, but it is still not clear whether (and how) Attic dithyramb and tragedy evolved from the same background as satyr-plays, and to what extent the choral performances in the Peloponnese became dramatic; nothing as specific is said of Arion's supposed innovation as is said of the introduction of an actor by Thespis. The Greek word for actor, *hypokritēs*, probably means 'answerer' (rather than the possible meaning 'interpreter'); the actor's answers to the questions of the chorus provided the occasion for their song, and their exchanges (by this account) brought drama into existence (see CHORUS).

By 472 (the date of the earliest surviving play, Aeschylus' *Persians*) tragedy had acquired the dignity and seriousness of which Aristotle spoke (see above), stemming from its concern with the human condition and the latter's relation to divine ordinance. It is impossible to know how much its development was shaped by Aeschylus, since we know so very little of his predecessors and contemporaries (see 4 below). The plot of a Greek tragedy is nearly always based on an episode from myth (for exceptions see PERSIANS, PHRYNICHUS, and AGATHON), and the influence of Homer is marked.

2. *Performances of Greek tragedies*. Performances of tragedies in Attica were part of religious celebrations and, until the Hellenistic age, appear to have been confined to the festivals of Dionysus.

(For the close connection between the god and the performance of drama see DIONYSIA and DIONYSUS, THEATRE OF.) Thus plays were produced on only a few occasions during the year, and for a single performance on each occasion. The most important setting for new tragedies was the Great Dionysia in March, but tragedies were also produced at the *Lenaea in January, and second productions might be staged at the Rural Dionysia. In the fifth century the only second productions at the Great Dionysia (with one exception; see below) were revised versions of plays which had been unsuccessful in their original form, such as Euripides' *Hippolytus*, but it may be that comedies were more often restaged than tragedies. The one notable exception was in the case of Aeschylus: after his death it was decreed that his plays might be produced at the Great Dionysia by anyone who wished. From 386 BC it was permitted to produce an earlier tragedy and from 339 an earlier comedy.

Tragedy was produced under the auspices of the state, supervised by magistrates. Drama at Athens was a matter for competition. Since dramatic competitions at the Dionysia were known to be in existence in the 530s (see I above) it is likely that they were instituted (and the festival itself first organized) by the tyrant *Peisistratus and his sons. Three tragic poets were selected from all those applying and 'granted a chorus' by the archon, i.e. given permission to compete for the prize of best tragic poet. A main actor ('protagonist') was allocated to each poet by lot, from three chosen and paid for by the state. Apart from that the costs of production were borne by the *choregoi. Each poet staged three tragedies (the trilogy) followed by a satyr-play, the set of four being known as the tetralogy. (These terms we owe to the Alexandrian scholars.) The contests were decided by judges, five in number, chosen by lot from lists of names selected by each tribe; no doubt the judges were influenced on occasion by the expressed views of the audience. The successful poet was rewarded with a crown of ivy; from the mid-fifth century the best actor among the protagonists also received a prize. Actors and chorus were all male, and only Athenian citizens were allowed to take part, although *metics were admitted at the Lenaea at a later date.

Greek tragedy contained two elements, choral song in lyric metres, with musical accompaniment, and dramatic spoken exchanges between characters, which were mainly in iambic trimeters (Chaucer's 'hexameters'; see METRE, GREEK 5). Some parts were a blend of the two. The importance of the chorus varied from play to play (in Aeschylus' *Eumenides* it might be considered corporately as one of the main characters); on the whole its role declined in significance towards the end of the fifth century. In general the chorus plays the part of spectators of the action, humble in rank, taking a limited part in but rarely initiating action, sympathizing with one or other of the chief characters, and commenting on or interpreting the dramatic situation. The choral songs were composed in a variety of lyric metres arranged in *strophēs and antistrophēs, occasionally with epodes added (see TRIAD). The chorus comprised twelve performers in the plays of Aeschylus, increased to fifteen by Sophocles. It was drawn up in a rectangular form (in contrast with the circular chorus of the dithyramb) and its movements were based on this arrangement. It was accompanied by the flute. Very little is known about the dances performed by the chorus after the early fifth century when, we are told, Phrynichus and Aeschylus invented many dances. The term *emmeleia* ('gracefulness') was often used to denote the grave and dignified dance of tragedy. At the end of the fifth century BC the dance degenerated. Choruses continued to form a part of tragedies throughout the fifth and for part at least of the fourth century BC, after choruses in comedy had been discontinued; but it is not known precisely how long they survived.

To the single actor of Thespis' invention Aeschylus added a second and Sophocles a third, and three actors seem to have remained the norm. Originally the poet acted in his own plays; this is recorded of Thespis and Aeschylus, and of Sophocles in his earliest plays (not extant). From the time of Sophocles the relative importance of the actors was indicated by the names protagonist ('first actor'), deuteragonist ('second actor'), and tritagonist. To the first was assigned the longest and most difficult part, together with such other parts as could be combined with it. All the actors and the chorus wore masks (according to one tradition introduced by Thespis) appropriate to their parts; this feature was perhaps a relic of Dionysiac cult, for some parts of which the worshippers were masked. Only the flute-player was unmasked. No fifth-century masks have survived, but it is clear from vase-paintings that they covered the whole front half of the head including the ears and had wigs attached. They seem to have been made of linen stiffened with plaster and painted. The wearing of masks facilitated the doubling of parts by a single actor, or even the splitting of a single part between two actors. In Euripides' *Bacchae*, for example, Dionysus and the messenger were probably played by the same actor; in Sophocles' *Oedipus Coloneus* the doubling and splitting of parts has become extremely complicated, with Theseus played by perhaps three actors, and Ismenē by a silent extra (*kōphon prosōpon*, 'dumb mask') unless, exceptionally, a fourth actor was allowed. Nonspeaking extras were used, and known, like their modern equivalents, as 'spear-carriers' (*doryphorēmata*). Aeschylus was said to have given the actors a more dignified costume; by the end of the fifth century they were wearing heavy, long-sleeved, ornamented robes reaching to the ground; Euripides was notorious for clothing his heroes in rags when the plot suggested it. Actors in classical times either went barefooted or wore tall laced boots (**cothurni*). Female characters were played by men.

3. *Construction of Greek tragedy*. A Greek tragedy normally contained the following parts.

(i) The prologue (*prologos*), the part preceding the entrance of the chorus, a monologue or dialogue which sets out the subject of the drama and the situation from which it starts. In the earliest tragedies the play begins with the entrance of the chorus, who set the scene without prologue.

(ii) The *parodos*, the song which the chorus sings as it enters. Once on stage, the chorus does not usually leave before the end of the play.

(iii) The episodes (*epeisodia*), scenes in which one or more actors take part, with the chorus. The word *epeisodion* probably meant originally the entrance of an actor to announce something to the chorus. The episodes might also contain lyrical passages, such as lamentations or incidental songs by the chorus, but they were divided from each other by the songs of the chorus known as *stasima* (see below).

(iv) *Stasima*, songs of the chorus 'standing in one place', i.e. in the *orchestra*, in contrast with the *parodos* which was sung during its entrance. In the earlier extant tragedies the *stasima* are usually connected, if only obliquely, with the events of or emotions aroused by the preceding episode. But this connection became more tenuous, until *Agathon became reputedly the first to introduce choral lyrics which had nothing to do with the plot (and could fit any tragedy), called by Aristotle *embolima*, 'interpolations'.

(v) The *exodos* or final scene, after the last *stasimon*.

For Aristotle's analysis of the nature of tragedy and its qualitative elements see POETICS.

4. *Principal Greek tragedians*. Before Aeschylus the principal tragic poets were *Phrynichus, *Pratinas, and *Choerilus. None of their plays survives. Apart from Aeschylus, Sophocles, and Euripides the most famous was Agathon, and after him perhaps *Ion of Chios and *Critias. There were about a dozen others who won the fifth-century tragedy competitions from time to time. The descendants of Aeschylus and Sophocles included some able tragedians. A younger Euripides produced posthumous plays by the elder Euripides and was himself a dramatist. But inspiration was failing by the end of the fourth century, and although tragedy was still being written in the third century at Athens, Alexandria (on a grand scale), and elsewhere, we know nothing except the (otherwise unknown) names of some of the writers and about forty lines of their work;

nothing more was thought worthy of preservation.

5. *Roman tragedy*. For the origins of Roman drama see COMEDY, ROMAN 1. A new impulse was given when in 240 BC *Livius Andronicus first staged rough adaptations of a Greek tragedy and a Greek comedy, to be followed by other adaptations from Greek. *Naevius, his contemporary, appears to have been the first to compose, besides tragedies on Greek subjects, *fabulae *praetextae*, dramas whose themes were drawn from Roman history or legend. His successors *Ennius, *Pacuvius, and *Accius also wrote occasional *praetextae* as well as tragedies modelled on Greek originals. After them Roman tragedy declined, and there was no important tragedian in the later years of the republic. Under the emperor Augustus, Asinius *Pollio wrote tragedies which have perished, as have also the *Medea* of Ovid and the *Thyestes* of Varius Rufus, both of them popular plays praised by Quintilian. To the age of the emperor Nero belong the highly rhetorical tragedies of *Seneca the Younger; like most of his predecessors he borrowed his subjects from Greek sources, and it is improbable that his tragedies were intended for the stage. The ordinary metre of Roman tragedy was the iambic senarius (see METRE, LATIN 2); this was used in dialogue. The sung portions were in simple lyrical metres adapted from the Greek. The chorus, where there was one, appeared on the stage, not, as in Greek tragedy, in the *orchestra*, and could take a greater part in the action.

Horace in his *Ars poetica* gives critical advice on the writing of tragedy, perhaps because the Pisones to whom the poem is addressed were interested in the genre. But conditions at Rome were unfavourable to the development of tragedy. Performances were not, as at Athens, part of a religious festival with cultic associations and social significance. There was no homogeneous audience in sympathy with the poet's view of things, religious, national, ethical, and social. Greek themes did not greatly interest the Roman spectator, and tragedies on Roman themes were perhaps problematical for political reasons; they were

certainly few. Tragedy at Rome was moral and didactic, inculcating energy and fortitude, valued for its displays of oratory, and occasionally as appealing to national or political sentiment. But it does not appear to have produced any great original conceptions or the subtlety and character-drawing of its Greek prototype, though Quintilian rated the lost *Thyestes* of Varius as equal to any Greek tragedy. Roman tragedy was further inhibited by the extinction of political life under the empire, which made it difficult for the playwright to choose a subject that was not liable to sinister interpretation by a suspicious emperor.

See also THEATRE.

Trajan (Marcus Ulpius Trāiānus), Roman emperor AD 98–117. He was born, probably in AD 53, of an Umbrian family which had settled in Spain, his father being of senatorial rank. He had a highly successful military career which earned him his adoption by the emperor Nerva in 97 when he was governor of Upper Germany. After his accession in the following year he did not go immediately to Rome but preferred to organize the Rhine and Danube frontiers. Later he also conquered a large part of the Parthian empire, reaching the Persian Gulf in the course of his expedition. He strove to be on good terms with the senate, many of whose members he appointed to oversee his schemes such as the system of subsistence allowances (*alimenta*) paid to poor children in Italy, and he showed concern for the well-being of the provinces. He devoted vast sums of money to building projects at Rome, notably his Forum (Forum Traiani), where the Column of Trajan commemorated his campaigns. Pliny the Younger delivered a panegyric on him, and when governor of Bithynia corresponded with him regularly. His decisions and advice on the problems referred to him, notably on the matter of the Christians (Pliny, *Epistles* 10. 97) illustrate his firm humanity and good sense. He died in Cilicia on his way home from the Parthian campaign; his ashes were deposited in the base of his column. Trajan's reign, which saw the Roman empire at its greatest extent, was remembered as a time of peace and prosperity, and set the standard for a good emperor. See ANTONINES.

transmigration of souls, see PYTHAGORAS.

Transpadane Gaul, that part of north-west Italy which is 'beyond the river Padus', i.e. between the Po and the Alps; part of Cisalpine *Gaul.

Trasimene, Lake, battle of; see PUNIC WARS.

Trebe'llius Po'llio, see *HISTORIA AUGUSTA*.

triad, in a Greek lyric poem, a group of three stanzas, of which the first two, called strophē and antistrophē, are symmetrical, i.e. correspond in metre, but the third, called the epode, has a different though related metrical form. If the poem consists of more than one triad the epodes, at least in Pindar, correspond with one another, as do all the strophes and antistrophes. This form of composition, which broke the monotony of a long series of similar stanzas, was thought to have been introduced by *Stesichorus and followed by Simonides and Pindar. It is generally believed that lyric poetry written in triadic form was sung and danced by a chorus, whereas monodic lyric was usually sung by an individual (see LYRIC POETRY 1).

tribes (Gk. phylai)
1. In early times the various Greek peoples were divided into large kinship groups known as tribes, which were further sub-divided into *phratriai*, 'brotherhoods'. Thus the Dorian people was divided into three tribes known as the *Hylleis*, *Pamphyloi*, and *Dymānĕs* which were found in almost all Dorian cities. Tribes were corporate groups, with hereditary membership and their own priests and officials. In early times they were the basis of state administration for military and governmental purposes. At Athens, *Cleisthenes' reforms of the democracy in the late sixth century BC involved the dismantling of the old tribes and the creation of ten new tribes based on the *demes. A similar change was made at Sparta during the Lycurgan reforms, when administration came to be based on the *obai*, the constituent villages, in preference to the tribes.

2. At Rome the people were in the earliest times divided into three tribes based on kinship, Titienses (abbreviated to Tities), Ramnenses (Ramnes), and Luceres. According to tradition, the king *Servius Tullius replaced these with four urban tribes based on locality (compare Cleisthenes' similar reform at Athens), in order to include in the citizen body the large number of aliens who had settled at Rome. These three tribes were known as the Sucusana, Esquilina, Collina, and Palatina. To these were gradually added 'rustic' tribes for the country regions. By 387 BC there were twenty-one tribes in all; by 241 BC the number had reached thirty-five, which was never exceeded. The tribes were the administrative units for the census, taxation, and the military levy, as well as for assemblies of the *plebs* (see COMITIA TRIBUTA).

Tribō'niān (Tribōniānus, d. *c*. AD 545), probably of Sīdē in Pamphylia, a jurist of great learning, particularly in legal history, and 'quaestor of the palace' under the emperor *Justinian; he was the latter's collaborator in the codification of the law.

tribrach, see METRE, GREEK 1 (vi).

tribunes of the plebs or **people** (*tribūni plēbis*), at Rome, magistrates who were themselves *plebeian and of free birth, first created, according to tradition, in 494 BC, and numbering ten by 450. Their role was to protect the lives and property of the plebeians, and they could thwart elections, laws, and decrees of the senate. They were elected annually by the *concilium plebis* and could summon meetings of the plebeians; *patricians could become tribunes only by getting themselves adopted into a plebeian family (see the case of Clodius under CICERO (1) 3). The tribunate became gradually indistinguishable from the other magistracies, but it never wholly lost its revolutionary flavour. Under the empire the emperor was invested with tribunician power (*tribunicia potestas*) and the real tribunes lost all importance.

tribu'ni aerā'rii ('tribunes of the treasury'), at Rome, originally officials of the *tribes who collected the *tribūtum* or war-tax on property, and saw to the payment of soldiers. In the first century BC this name was given to a property class similar to but less wealthy than the *equites* from which certain jurors were drawn.

tribū'ni mī'litum, at Rome in later republican times, senior army officials, six to a legion; they were elected by the people and ranked as magistrates (which meant that they did not command subsections of the legion as subordinate officers). Under Julius Caesar the tribunes declined in importance with the rise of *legati* as legion commanders.

tribū'ni plēbis, see TRIBUNES OF THE PEOPLE.

tribute lists, Athenian, name given to a series of fragmentary inscriptions on stone of the fifth century BC, recovered from the Athenian Acropolis, relating to the finances of the *Delian League. They record the sum of money paid each year by each allied city in the Delian League to (the treasurers of) the goddess Athena. Modern historians have elicited a great deal of political and social information from the lists.

Tricli'nius, Deme'trius, see TEXTS, TRANSMISSION OF ANCIENT 3.

trilogy, see TRAGEDY 2.

Trima'lchio's Banquet, see PETRONIUS ARBITER.

tri'meter, see METRE, GREEK 1.

Trīna'cria, Trinacia, Thrinacia, see SICILY.

Trinu'mmus ('three pieces of silver'), Roman comedy by *Plautus adapted from a Greek Comedy by Philemon (see COMEDY, GREEK 6). The play takes its name from a coin paid as a day's wages to a hired impostor, whose part in the plot is relatively unimportant. The exact value of the coin is disputed.

While Charmidēs, a wealthy Athenian, is out of the country, his dissolute son Lesbonīcus has spent all his father's money and even put the house up for sale. At his departure Charmides had entrusted his son and daughter to the care of his friend Calliclēs, and confided to the

latter that a treasure was concealed in the house. Callicles therefore, anxious about the treasure, has bought the house himself. Lesbonicus' friend, Lysitelēs, wishing to help the financial situation, offers to marry Lesbonicus' sister without a dowry. Lesbonicus, though approving the match, will not accept an arrangement discreditable to his family, and Callicles thinks the sister should have a dowry out of the treasure. The difficulty is how to arrange this without revealing to Lesbonicus the existence of the treasure. Callicles' solution is to hire 'for three pieces of silver' a 'sycophant' (i.e. a man prepared to do anything for money), who is to deliver to Lesbonicus a thousand gold pieces and a letter purporting to come from his father, explaining that the money is to be used for a dowry (while in fact being part of the treasure). Charmides himself now arrives unexpectedly and meets the sycophant knocking at the door. Learning his errand he reveals the imposture, and then discovers that the house is no longer his own but belongs to Callicles. He begins to abuse the latter, but when all is revealed warmly thanks him, gives his daughter, with a dowry, to Lysitelēs, and pardons the now penitent Lesbonicus.

Tripto'lemus, in Greek myth, the young man chosen by the goddess *Demeter to go about the world and teach men the skills of agriculture, in some accounts identified with the child whom Demeter tried to make immortal. His parentage is variously described: he is said to be the son of the hero *Eleusis (after whom the town was named), or, in Orphic literature, of Oceanus and Gaia (Earth). He was the recipient of sacrifice at Eleusis, where the Greek traveller Pausanias reports having seen his temple. Probably because of his Orphic connections Plato made him, with Minos and Rhadamanthys, judge of the dead in the Underworld.

Tri'stia ('sorrows'), Latin elegiac poems by *Ovid in five books, written in AD 8–12, the early years of the poet's exile to Tomis. The metre must have seemed appropriate, since elegiac was commonly thought in ancient times to have been originally the metre of lament (see

ELEGY). Most of the poems are in the form of letters to his wife and friends, written to ensure that he was not forgotten at Rome, in which he laments his fate and prays for some mitigation of his severe punishment. The poems appear to have been sent individually to Rome and then collected in groups for publication.

Book I consists of poems composed on the long journey to Tomis and sent back to Rome on Ovid's arrival. They include descriptions of storms and hardships encountered. The real destination of these poems is Augustus, on whom Ovid brings moral pressure to rescind his banishment; he reminds the emperor of his status as a poet and of his achievement. The third poem of the book is the moving account of the poet's last night at Rome.

Book II is a single poem, written at times in a satirical manner, but still a serious defence of the autonomy of poetry, in the face of which the emperor's attitude to the poet is made to seem beside the point. (The fact that Ovid's first loyalty has always been to poetry is made clear in his autobiographical poem IV. 10, written to show that poetry was not for him a matter of choice but a true vocation; like Alexander Pope he 'lisped in numbers for the numbers came': *et quod temptabam scribere versus erat*, 'all I attempted to write turned out as verse' (IV. 10. 26).)

Books III, IV, and V include glimpses of life at Tomis, a precariously held outpost of civilization: the flat, treeless landscape, the rigorous climate, the attacks of barbarians on the town (when even Ovid is constrained to take up arms for its defence), the poet's loneliness among his Getic hosts. The casual reader may become bored by a certain monotony in Ovid's complaints, but these are by no means abject, and often run the risk of making too clear for safety the poet's view that he was a victim of tyrannical injustice.

Triton, in Greek myth, a merman, son of *Poseidon and Amphitritē, with human head and shoulders and a fish tail from the waist down. The origin of his name (as also of Amphitrite) is obscure and may not be Greek. He is commonly shown blowing on a conch-shell, and Virgil describes how the trumpeter Misenus challenged him to a contest on this instrument and was drowned by him. In some stories there are several Tritons (as in the case of Eros). *Pausanias on his travels saw what he was told was a Triton preserved in brine.

Tritō'nia (or Tritogeneia), epithet sometimes used of the goddess Athena; the origin is unknown, but it was explained that she was born beside a river Triton or a Lake Tritonis, variously found in Boeotia, Libya, and Crete.

trittys, at Athens, 'a third', i.e. of a *tribe. *Cleisthenes (2) in his constitutional reforms created thirty *trittyĕs*, territorial divisions, each containing a number of demes. Each of his (new) ten tribes was composed of three *trittyes*, one each from the city, interior, and coastal regions. See DEME.

triumph, at Rome, the celebratory procession of a victorious Roman general from the Campus Martius outside the city walls to the temple of Jupiter Capitolinus. It was Etruscan in origin, and was regulated by strict rules of a religious nature. To be granted a triumph it was at first necessary for the general to hold a magistracy with *imperium (even Scipio Africanus had been denied a triumph after his victories in Spain through not holding a regular magistracy), to have won a great victory over a foreign enemy, with at least 5,000 of the enemy killed, and to have brought home at least a token army to show that the war was won. Later, holding a regular magistracy was not a prerequisite (see POMPEY), but the other requirements meant that a triumph was a fairly rare event. Under the empire only the emperor could celebrate a triumph; the last to do so was Diocletian in 302. Preceded by his lictors the *triumphator*, richly dressed and wreathed in bay, was carried on a four-horse chariot, a slave murmuring to him words to avert the possible ill consequences of outstanding success such as 'remember you are mortal'. The army shouted '*io triumphe*' and also sang rude songs (see FESCENNINE VERSES). The procession was joined by the magistrates and senators, captives, spoils, and sacrificial animals. At the temple of Jupiter Capitolinus the general made sacrifice and surrendered his bays to the god.

When a triumph was disallowed an *ovatio* was usually granted. This was a less spectacular form of triumph, the general entering Rome on foot or on horseback rather than in a chariot. The last recorded *ovatio* was in AD 47.

triumvirate. The unofficial coalition of Julius Caesar, Pompey, and Crassus in 60 BC is often referred to for convenience, but strictly speaking incorrectly, as the first triumvirate. The (second) officially constituted triumvirate in 43 BC was formed by Antony, Lepidus, and Octavian.

Tri'via, see DIANA.

tri'vium, see SEVEN LIBERAL ARTS.

Troas, the Troad, the territory around *Troy, forming the north-west extremity of Asia Minor, between the Hellespont and the island of Lesbos, including Mount Ida.

Trō'adĕs, see TROJAN WOMEN.

trŏchee, trocha'ic, see METRE, GREEK I (v).

Troezen, in Greece, a city of the Peloponnese in the north-east corner of the promontory of Argolis, opposite and to the south of Athens across the Saronic Gulf. Many of its legends are connected with Athens. It was the home of Aithra, mother of Theseus, and the location of the death of Theseus' son *Hippolytus, who had an important cult there. Many Athenian women and children fled to Troezen at the time of the Persian invasion in 480 BC.

Trogus, Pompē'ius, Roman historian in the time of Augustus (emperor 27 BC–AD 14), a native of Narbonese Gaul, whose father had been a lieutenant of Julius Caesar. He wrote a universal history in forty-four books entitled *Historiae Philippicae* ('Philippic histories'), centred as the name indicates on the history of Macedon, especially under Philip II, and probably based on Greek sources (e.g. the important *Theopompus). We have only an epitome of it by *Justin which is nevertheless very valuable for the history of Macedon and the Hellenistic kingdoms.

Trōilus, in Greek myth, a younger son of Priam king of Troy and Hecuba, mentioned briefly in Homer's *Iliad* as already killed by Achilles. For the post-classical story of Troilus and Cressida (which Chaucer and Shakespeare get from Boccaccio) see PANDARUS. Cressida is the Greek maiden called *Chryseis in · the *Iliad*.

Trojan Horse, also known as the Wooden Horse, a device resorted to by the Greeks, after the death of Achilles, to capture Troy. The story is known to Homer and is referred to in the *Odyssey* as well as being part of the cycle of stories about Troy (see EPIC CYCLE; ILIAD, LITTLE; and ILIUPERSIS), but the *Iliad* ends well before this event. Epēius, a skilful craftsman, constructed a very large wooden horse inside which picked Greek warriors, including Odysseus, were concealed. Then the Greek army sailed out of sight, leaving Sinon, one of their number, behind. He pretended to the Trojans that he was a deserter and that the horse was an offering to Athena; if brought within the city it would render it impregnable. In spite of the warning given to the Trojans by Lāocŏon (a priest of Apollo) not to trust 'Greek gifts', the Trojans dragged the horse into the city, convinced that the destruction of Laocoon and his sons by two serpents after he had given his warning was a punishment for impiety. Cassandra too prophesied disaster but was disbelieved. At night the Greeks came out of the horse and the city was taken. In Homer's *Odyssey* (book 4) Menelaus reminds Helen how, when the horse was inside the walls of Troy, she had walked round it calling out the names of the men she suspected might be inside, and Odysseus had prevented anyone from answering. In book 8 Odysseus at the court of Alcinous asks the bard to sing the story of the Wooden Horse. Virgil tells the story of the horse in *Aeneid* 2.

Trojan War, the subject of the most important and most pervasive of Greek legends; an episode in the war is the subject of Homer's *Iliad*, the war's aftermath that of his *Odyssey*. The ancient city of *Troy stood on the Asian side of the Hellespont; archaeological evidence has revealed that it was destroyed by violence c.1250 BC, and this is possibly the historical basis of the Homeric Trojan War. The archaeological date is not far removed from *Erastosthenes' calculation of 1184 for the fall of Troy. In the Homeric account the war was waged by the *Achaeans (i.e. the Greeks) led by Agamemnon to recover *Helen, the wife of Agamemnon's brother Menelaus and the most beautiful woman in the world, who had been abducted by *Paris, a prince of Troy. The Achaeans laid siege to the city but at the end of nine years had still failed to take it. Then followed the events recounted in the *Iliad*. After this, according to post-Homeric legend, occurred the arrival of the Amazons under Penthesilēa (see ACHILLES) and of the Ethiopians under *Memnon to reinforce the Trojans, the death of Achilles, the summoning of *Neoptolemus and *Philoctētēs, the incident of the *Trojan Horse, and the fall of the city.

Medieval legend relating to the Trojan War is mainly based on Latin works which purported to be translations of the narratives of *Darēs Phrygius and *Dictys Cretensis. In England the most prominent form of the medieval legend was the story which Geoffrey of Monmouth (d. 1155) made popular: that Brutus ('Brut'), great-grandson of Aeneas, collected a remnant of Trojans, settled in Britain, which was uninhabited at the time ('except for a few giants'), and became the progenitor of a line of British kings which included King Arthur; and that he founded 'New Troy', Troynovant, later known as London. (The name was based on that of the British tribe the Trinovantes whose territory was north and east of London.) This legend was taken seriously even beyond medieval times.

Trojan Women (*Trōadĕs*). **1.** Greek tragedy by *Euripides. It was produced in 415 BC, shortly after the capture of *Melos by the Athenians, who slaughtered its male inhabitants and enslaved its women and children. One of the most poignant of Euripidean dramas, it presents not so much a narrative as a tragic situation: the condition of the Trojan women when their men-folk have been killed and they are at the mercy of their captors. Grieving and anxious they await their fate. Talthybius, the herald, announces that they are to be distributed among the victors. The Trojan queen Hecuba is to become the possession of the hated Odysseus; her daughter Cassandra has been allotted to Agamemnon, and it is revealed that her other daughter Polyxena has been slaughtered on the tomb of Achilles. The tragic figure of Cassandra appears; being a prophetess she foretells some of the disasters which will come upon the conquerors. Andromachē enters with her small son Astyanax; she is to be the prize of Neoptolemus. Talthybius returns to carry off Astyanax whose death has been ordered by the Greeks. The meeting of Menelaus and Helen follows; he is determined to destroy her, and Hecuba encourages his anger. But Helen pleads her cause, and when Helen and Menelaus depart their reconciliation has been foreshadowed. Talthybius appears once more with the broken body of Astyanax, and Hecuba prepares the burial. Finally Troy is set on fire and its towers collapse as the women leave for captivity.

2. Roman tragedy by *Seneca (2), based on (1) above and combining with it the sacrifice of Polyxena from Euripides' *Hecuba*. This is one of the best (to modern taste) of the Senecan tragedies, containing passages of great passion and pathos.

Trophō'nius ('nourisher') **and Agamē'dēs,** in Greek myth, sons of Ergīnus of Orchomenus (in Boeotia) who lived in the time of Heracles. Trophonius is sometimes said to be the son of Apollo. They were architects and reputedly built the temple of Apollo at Delphi and a treasury for the Boeotian king Hyrieus (or for Augēas, king of Elis). The story told about them is similar to that told of *Rhampsinitus. The two brothers robbed the treasury by means of a movable stone in the wall; the king set a trap, and when Agamedes was caught Trophonius cut off his head to avoid identification. Trophonius was subsequently swallowed up by the earth at Lebadeia in Boeotia. When the Boeotians were suffering from a drought the oracle at Delphi told them to consult Trophonius' oracle. They did not know how to find it, but one of the envoys, following a swarm of bees into a cave, saw a vision of Trophonius who told him he was now the oracle of the cave.

The oracle was consulted by Croesus, king of Lydia, in the sixth century BC, Epaminondas, and Philip II of Macedon, and was still in existence in Roman times. According to Plutarch it was the only Boeotian oracle that remained active in his day (early second century AD). The method of consulting the oracle was highly unusual, as we know from Pausanias (IX. 39. 4) who consulted it himself. After elaborate preparations, which included drinking from the springs of Forgetfulness and Memory, the enquirer descended into a chasm, at the bottom of which was a small opening. Into this he inserted his legs and was immediately snatched away to another place 'as if a deep fast river was catching a man in a current and sucking him down'. Here the enquirer learned the future from things he saw or heard, before being returned feet first the same way. The priests then took him to the Throne of Memory and asked him what he had learnt; this was written down and the tablet dedicated to the god. The enquirer emerged pale and terrified, so that it became proverbial to say of people looking gloomy that they had consulted the oracle of Trophonius. See also ORACLES.

Trōs, see TROY below.

Troy (Troia), otherwise known as Ilium, an ancient city famous in legend; its siege by the Greeks is the subject of Homer's *Iliad* (see TROJAN WAR and TROJAN HORSE above). Its site in north-west Asia Minor some 6 km. (4 miles) from the Aegean Sea, a little south of the Hellespont, was identified at the modern Hissarlik by the German archaeologist Heinrich Schliemann, who between 1870 and 1890 excavated the occupation mound, composed of the accumulated debris of centuries. He and later archaeologists have established nine principal strata, representing nine successive periods of occupation (called Troy I, Troy II, and so on), dating from the Bronze Age to Roman times.

By 1300 Troy had enjoyed settled prosperity for six centuries. The source of its wealth has been much disputed. It is clear that by its position it could control a large part of east–west trade, and was itself the possessor of rich agricultural lands; it was famous for its horses, according to Homer, and, to judge from the large number of spinning whorls discovered there, was a flourishing producer of textiles. The city was destroyed by a massive earthquake *c*.1300; the population seems to have survived and to have set about the rebuilding at once (Troy VIIa). This phase of Troy's life lasted not much more than a generation. The archaeological evidence shows that by 1250 BC Troy VIIa was once more destroyed, this time by human agency; it was consumed by fire, and traces of human bones in houses and streets suggest violence. If there is any fact at all behind the story of the Trojan War, 1250 or thereabout seems to be·the latest reasonable date for mainland Greece to be making a concerted attack on the city, since after that time Greece herself was involved in the general upheavals of the Mediterranean world which began in the middle of the century. Greek authors gave different dates for the Trojan War, from *c*.1280 to 1184 and even later. The second date was that arrived at by *Eratosthenes, and subsequently favoured. He worked backwards from the established date of the first Olympic games, 776 BC, using the genealogies of the Spartan kings, which gave him 1104 for the *Dorian Invasion. According to tradition this happened two generations, i.e. 80 years, after the Trojan War.

The legendary family tree of the kings of Troy is as follows. *Dardanus son of Zeus 'established Dardania' (as Homer says), a district north-east of Troy, and married the daughter of the local king Teucer (Teukros). He had as descendants Trōs (from whom the Troad and the Trojans were named) and Ilus, who founded the city of Troy, sometimes called after him Ilium (Ilion). Ilus had two sons, *Laomedon father of *Priam, and *Tithonus, and a daughter Hesionē, mother by *Telamon of another Teucer, half-brother of Ajax.

Trucule'ntus ('the boor'), Roman comedy by *Plautus.

The play, which has little plot, is mainly concerned with the doings of a covetous prostitute who shamelessly exploits her three lovers, a dissolute young Athenian, a boastful soldier, and a young man from the country (whose sour and aggressive slave gives the play its title). She palms off on the soldier a child she has acquired, by pretending that it is his. The child turns out to be that of the dissolute Athenian and a free-born girl, whom the penitent seducer agrees to marry. The slave tries to prevent his master wasting his money on the prostitute, but then falls in love himself with her maid.

Tryphiodō'rus (third or fourth century AD), Greek epic poet, a native of Egypt. Only his *Capture of Troy* survives. A short epic of 691 lines, it resembles in style the epic of *Nonnus.

Tubilu'stria, in Roman religion, a festival of the god *Mars on 23 March, when the sacred trumpets (*tubae*), originally used in war and later on ceremonial occasions, were purified. See QUIN-QUATRUS.

Tucca, Plō'tius, see AENEID.

Tu'llia. 1. In Roman legendary history, daughter of king Servius Tullius and wife of Tarquinius Superbus; see TARQUIN. She incited her husband to overthrow her father, and when the latter had been murdered, drove her chariot over his dead body.

2. The much-loved daughter of Cicero (1) and Terentia, born *c.*79 BC. She was three times married, to Calpurnius Piso Frugi, of whom Cicero was fond, but who died during the latter's exile; to Furius Crassipēs, who divorced her; and thirdly to the dissolute P. Cornelius Dolabella who supported alternately Julius Caesar and Brutus in the civil war. Her death in 45 BC threw her father into despair; see CICERO (1) 4 and SULPICIUS RUFUS.

Tulliā'num, at Rome, the underground execution cell of the prison, at the foot of the Capitoline hill, where most state prisoners were executed, including Jugurtha, the Catilinarian conspirators, and the Gaul Vercingetorix.

Tullus Hosti'lius, in Roman legendary history the third king of Rome (673–642 BC). His reign was said to have been occupied by constant warfare (hence his name), which included the capture and destruction of Alba Longa (see HORATII AND CURIATII).

Tully, name by which Marcus Tullius *Cicero was known to English readers down to the early nineteenth century.

Tū'riae laudā'tio, see LUCRETIUS (2).

Turnus, in Virgil's *Aeneid*, Italian hero, son of Daunus and the nymph Venilia, brother of the nymph Juturna. He was the king of the Rutulians and suitor of Lavinia, daughter of king *Latinus. The Latins joined with the Rutulians to fight the Trojans; Turnus killed Pallas, son of Evander, was twice saved by Juno, but was finally killed by Aeneas (see AENEID, books 7–12).

Tu'sculan Disputations (*Tusculānae disputatiōnēs*, 'discussions at Tusculum'), philosophical treatise in five books by Cicero on the conditions for happiness. The work was completed in 44 BC (see CICERO (1) 5) and is addressed to Marcus *Brutus. It takes the form of conversations between two characters indicated as M and A.

After an introduction defending the adoption of philosophy as a subject for treatment in Latin literature, Cicero in book 1 deals with the proposition that death is an evil and an impediment to happiness. His answer is that death is either a change of place for the soul or annihilation; in neither case is it an evil; 'How can what is necessary for all be an evil for one?' In a famous sentence Cicero says that he would rather be wrong with Plato than right with some other philosophers: *errare, mehercule, malo cum Platone* . . .

Tu'sculum, ancient Italian town in the mountains near Frascati about 24 km. (15 miles) south-east of Rome. Under the late republic and early empire it was a fashionable resort. Lucullus, Maecenas, and Cicero all had villas there. For the legendary founder see TELEGONUS.

Twelve gods, see GODS.

Twelve Tables, the earliest Roman code of laws drawn up by a special commission of ten, *decemviri legibus scribundis* ('ten men for writing out the laws'), in 451/0 BC, on the demand of the plebeians. No complete text of the code survives, and it is known only from quotations and references. According to tradition envoys were sent to Athens to study Greek laws before the decemvirs started work. The Twelve Tables embraced all spheres of law, private, criminal, public, and sacred; they were never abolished, but later enactments made them obsolete. As late as Cicero's day, although not for much longer, schoolboys still learned them by heart.

Tychē, 'chance', 'fortune', good or bad, in Greek religious thought the incalculable element in life. In popular belief each person and city had its own *tyche*, much like a *daimon*. Belief in this abstraction strengthened after the fifth century BC as worship of the old gods declined. Pindar calls Tyche one of the Fates, stronger than her sisters, but she never became fully personified or a subject of myth. Compare Latin FORTUNA.

Tȳdeus, in Greek myth, son of Oineus, king of Calydon. Exiled for homicide (his victim is variously given), at Argos he married Dēïpylē, daughter of Adrastus, while Polyneicēs married her sister Argeia. He was one of the leaders in the expedition of the *Seven against Thebes and was father of *Diomedēs.

Tynda'ridae ('the Tyndarids'), name sometimes given to Castor and Polydeucēs (Pollux; see DIOSCURI), whose mother *Leda was wife of Tyndareus, king of Sparta.

Typhō'eus or **Tȳphon,** according to Hesiod, son of *Tartarus and Gaia (Earth), born after Zeus' defeat of the *Titans. He was a monster with a hundred serpent heads, fiery eyes, and a tremendous voice; Zeus at once attacked him with thunderbolts and cast him into Tartarus, setting Aetna on fire on the way. In Pindar and Aeschylus he is the force under that volcano, and he is the source of storm winds which cause shipwreck and devastation. For the identification of Typhon with the Egyptian god Set, see OSIRIS.

tyrant (*tyrannos*, 'king', perhaps a Lydian word), in Greece, name given to an absolute monarch who seized power illegally. There were many such in Greek cities of the seventh and sixth centuries BC, who were often originally members of a ruling oligarchy but who led a popular revolt against oppressive government. In such cases they sometimes paved the way for democratic government. Under the later democracies of classical Greece, when the idea of tyranny became repugnant, the word 'tyrant' acquired its pejorative overtone, but most of the early tyrants made important contributions to the adornment and general cultural standing of their cities. A tyranny rarely lasted for more than two generations.

Tȳro, in Greek myth, daughter of *Salmoneus, a king of Elis, brought up by a cruel stepmother. Tyro was loved by the god Poseidon, who took the form of the Thessalian river Enipeus and made a great wave curl over them. She bore two sons, Pelias (see ARGONAUTS) and Nēleus (father of Nestor), whom she abandoned. She was married to Salmoneus' brother Crētheus and became the mother of Aeson and grandmother of Jason. See also MELAMPUS.

Tyrrhē'nians, see ETRUSCANS.

Tyrtae'us (seventh century BC), Greek elegiac poet who lived at Sparta and was probably of Spartan birth. The story that he was an Athenian schoolmaster who was sent to Sparta as the result of an oracle must be a fabrication. He encouraged the Spartans to capture Messēnē by his war-songs and exhortations in verse. The Alexandrian scholars collected his works in five books, but only fragments survive.

U

Uli'xēs or **Ulyssēs,** see ODYSSEUS.

U'lpian (Domitius Ulpiānus), famous Roman jurist, born of a family long established at Tyre (in Syria). His writings, which numbered nearly 280 books, date mostly from the reign of the emperor Caracalla (AD 212–17). With *Paulus he assisted *Papinian when the latter was praetorian prefect in 203 (see PRAEFECTUS PRAETORIO). He was banished by the emperor Elagabalus (218–22) but became praetorian prefect at the beginning of the reign of the next emperor, Alexander Severus. In 223 he was murdered by the praetorian guard ostensibly over his plans for its reform.

Ulpian's summing-up of earlier legal writings was so thorough and effective that the codifiers of Justinian's reign used him far more than any other writer. Nearly a third of the *Digesta* is taken from his works (see JUSTINIAN).

U'lpian Library, at Rome, built by Trajan, emperor AD 98–117, and so called from his own name, Ulpius. See LIBRARIES.

Uly'ssēs, see ODYSSEUS.

U'mbria, region of central Italy, northeast of Rome. The Umbrian language, an Italic dialect, survives in inscriptions from *c.*400–90 BC. It was written partly in the Latin alphabet and partly in Greek (through the influence of Etruria). See LATIN LANGUAGE.

uncials, in Greek and Latin handwriting, one of the two forms of majuscules or large letters used in papyri and early manuscripts, the other being capitals. Uncials are a curvilinear form of the latter, being easier to write with a pen on soft material than the angular capitals, which are more readily cut on metal or stone. The name first appears in Jerome's preface to the Old Testament book of Job, and is generally taken to mean 'letters an inch long' (Lat. *uncia*, 'inch'), but the derivation is uncertain.

Underworld, see AFTERLIFE and HADES.

Ûra'nia. 1. One of the *Muses.

2. Title of the goddess *Aphroditē, describing her as 'heavenly', i.e. spiritual, to distinguish her from Aphrodite Pandemos, 'vulgar' love, as in Plato's *Symposium*.

Û'ranus (Heaven), in Greek myth, the personification of the heavens. Uranus and *Gaia (Earth), who herself gave birth to Uranus, are the primeval parents in Greek cosmogony. Uranus fathered numerous children but prevented them from being born. Gaia called upon her son *Cronus to help, and he castrated his father with a sickle (an act which seems to represent the separation of Heaven and Earth, a frequent motif of myth all over the world). Uranus' children could then be born (see TITANS, CYCLOPES, and HECATONCHEIRES), after which he himself loses importance and disappears from view. Various divine monsters were born from the drops of his blood which fell on the earth, Erinyes (see FURIES), *Giants, and Meliae (tree-nymphs); his genital organs were flung into the sea by Cronus, and from the foam that bubbled around them Aphrodite was born.

V

Vacū'na, a Sabine goddess whose functions were already forgotten by the time Horace in his *Epistles* (I. 10. 49) puns on her name to make her a goddess of vacation.

Valē'rius Flaccus, Gaius, Latin poet of whose life little is known except that dateable references in his only known work, the *Argonautica*, suggest that he began it in the early 70s AD, that he died prematurely in 92 or 93 before completing it, and that he was one of the *quindecimviri sacris faciundis* (see SIBYL). The *Argonautica*, an epic poem written in hexameters, ends abruptly in the eighth book. Valerius' main source was the similarly entitled Hellenistic Greek epic of *Apollonius Rhodius, but other poets including *Varro Atacinus had treated the same subject and he may have consulted their works; the Underworld scene in book I is indebted to similar scenes in Homer's *Odyssey* and, especially, to Virgil's *Aeneid*, but Valerius also introduces scenes of his own invention. Book 7, and the incomplete book 8, the episode of Jason and Medea, are the best part of the poem, where with some subtlety and in a graver, less playful manner than Apollonius, he develops the character of Medea, torn between her passion for Jason and loyalty to her father, and enlists the reader's sympathy for her. He leaves Jason contemplating the betrayal of the bride on whom his success depends.

Valē'rius Maximus, Latin compiler of an extant collection of anecdotes in the early first century AD. Very little is known of his life; he followed his patron Sextus Pompeius (consul AD 14) to Asia in AD 27, and dedicated his work to the emperor Tiberius after the fall of Sejanus in AD 31. His nine books of *Facta et dicta memorabilia* ('memorable deeds and sayings'), anecdotes and examples for the use of orators, are arranged roughly as follows: book 1, religion, omens, prophecies; book 2, social customs; books 3–6, virtuous conduct (fortitude, moderation, humanity, etc.); books 7–8, a miscellaneous group including good fortune, military stratagems, famous law-suits, eloquence, and many other items; book 9, evil conduct. The examples on each topic are divided into 'Roman' and 'foreign'. The work shows little originality and the style is highly rhetorical, but it proved useful and was very popular in the Middle Ages; two epitomes were made of it, perhaps in the fourth or fifth centuries.

Vandals, a Germanic people who left their original homes in Scandinavia and settled on the south coast of the Baltic Sea, then gradually moved further south until they became the western neighbours of the *Visigoths. They attacked the Roman provinces in the third and fourth centuries AD. On 31 December 406 they crossed the Rhine near Mogontiacum (Mainz), moved on to devastate Gaul, and in 409 invaded Spain. Here too they caused great destruction, but subsequently made apparently permanent settlements. However, in 429 most of them crossed over into Africa under Gaiseric (see CARTHAGE), who built a fleet and controlled the western Mediterranean; in 455 he captured Rome and carried off many works of art. The last Vandal king Gelimer was defeated by a Roman army under *Belisarius in 533 and subsequently captured and taken to Constantinople.

Va'rius Rufus, Lucius, Roman poet of the first century BC, friend of Virgil and Horace, both of whom admired his poetry, and regarded as a leading epic poet in his day. He was the author of a tragedy on the story of *Thyestes, performed in 29 BC at the games in celebration of Octavian's victory at Actium, which earned him a million sesterces from the victor, and which Quintilian thought the equal of any Greek tragedy. He also wrote epics on Julius Caesar and the wars of Augustus. None of his works has survived. After Virgil's death Varius and Plotius Tucca edited the *Aeneid*, upon instructions from Augustus.

Varro. 1. **Marcus Tere'ntius Varro** (116–27 BC), Roman man of letters called 'Reātīnus' because he was born at Reatē in Sabine territory. He was opposed to Julius Caesar in politics and was a Pompeian officer in Spain at the time of the civil war, but was reconciled to Caesar and was to have been the head of the public library whose creation Caesar was contemplating in 47. In 43 he was proscribed by Mark Antony, but escaped with the loss of some property and books. He was a poet, satirist, antiquarian, jurist, geographer, grammarian, and scientist, and wrote on education and philosophy also. Quintilian called him 'the most learned of Romans'. His enormous literary output ran to more than 600 volumes. Of these only his *De re rustica* ('on farming') survives complete; we also have six books out of the twenty-five of his *De lingua Latina* ('on the Latin language'), and some 600 fragments of his *Saturae Menippeae* ('Menippean satires'). He died pen in hand.

De lingua Latina is a systematic treatise on Latin grammar, dealing successively with etymology, inflexion, and syntax, a pioneer work showing occasional penetration, amid many absurd derivations. Books 5–10, which we possess, are dedicated to Cicero.

The *Saturae Menippeae* were satires on the model of *Menippus, in a mixture of prose and verse, some of them in dialogue or semi-dramatic form. They were critical sketches of Roman life with a wide range of characters and scenes including some from myth; the language is vigorous, earthy, and inventive. Many of the sketches were directed, with humour and nostalgia for the decencies of the previous century, against the greed, luxury, and sophisticated pretensions of Varro's day, as exemplified by the contemporary Greek schools of philosophy, for example.

His *Hebdomadēs* ('sevens'), or *Imaginēs* ('portraits'), in fifteen books, now lost, was a collection of character sketches in prose of celebrated Greeks and Romans, accompanied by coloured portraits of the subjects, to each of which an epigram was appended. Much of our knowledge about the lives of eminent Romans derives ultimately from Varro.

Among his other more important works were (i) the antiquarian treatise *Antiquitatēs rerum humanarum et divinarum* ('human and divine antiquities'), a historical encyclopaedia, of which roughly speaking the first part dealt with the history of Rome and the second part with Roman religion (the arrangement of facts followed a simple pattern of people, places, dates, and events); (ii) *De gente populi Romani* ('on the Roman nation'), concerning the prehistory and early chronology of Rome; (iii) *De vita populi Romani* ('on the way of life of the Roman people'), concerning the history and style of Roman society; (iv) *Disciplinae* ('studies'), on the liberal arts (grammar, dialectic, rhetoric, geometry, arithmetic, astronomy, music, medicine, and architecture), all except the last two forming the medieval *trivium* and *quadrivium*, and subsequently utilized by *Martianus Capella; and (v) a treatise on philosophy, *De philosophia*. Many fragments survive of the *Res divinae* ('on religion') preserved by St Augustine when he attacked it in the *City of God*. Varro was highly praised by Cicero (who dedicated to him the second edition of his *Academica*) and by Quintilian. He was influenced by the Platonism of Antiochus of Ascalon (see ACADEMY), as well as by Stoic and Pythagorean ideas, yet he insisted that an ancient city should adhere to its traditional religion, and accepted that the greatness of Rome had depended in part on its religious observances: at the least, religion, even if untrue, was useful.

2. **Publius Terentius Varro**, 'Atacīnus' (i.e. from the valley of the river Atax in Narbonese Gaul), Latin poet, b. 82 BC. Nothing is known of his life, and his work survives only in fragments. He wrote an epic poem on Julius Caesar's exploits in Gaul in 58 BC called *Bellum Sequanicum* ('war against the Sequani'). He also wrote a geographical poem called *Chōrographia* and a free translation of the *Argonautica* of the Greek poet *Apollonius Rhodius.

Vārus. **1.** The *cognomen* of a friend of Horace, given the name Quintilius in some manuscripts. He may be P. Alfenus Varus, a jurist and patron of literature, to whom Catullus may also have written a poem.

2. Quinti'lius Varus, Roman general who in AD 9 was entrusted with the settlement of Germany. He and his three legions were lured by the German chief Arminius, whom he had trusted, into the Teutoburgian forest and ambushed. The legions were annihilated, Varus committed suicide and Roman expansion in north Germany was ended for ever.

Vatican, at Rome in classical times, an outlying district on the west bank of the river Tiber on the Vatican hill, northwest of the ancient city. (The hill was not one of the seven hills of Rome.) The region was noted for its unhealthy air, unproductive soil, and bad wine. Its only claim to fame in republican times was that here *Cincinnatus was cultivating his four acres when he was summoned to be dictator. Its only building of note was the Mausoleum of the emperor Hadrian, now the Castello di S. Angelo. Here was the infamous Circus of Nero, where Christians were enveloped in pitch and burnt to serve as torches for the midnight games, and where the martyrdom of St Peter took place.

Vati'nius, Publius, tribune 59 BC. In 56 Cicero, defending Sestius, delivered an invective against Vatinius, but successfully defended him in 54 (see CICERO (1) 4). He was consul in 46. One of his letters to Cicero (*Ad familiares* 5. 10) survives. He is mentioned by Catullus as the enemy of his friend *Calvus.

vau, see DIGAMMA.

Vē'diovis (Vēiovis, Vendius), in Roman religion, an ancient deity about whom little is known; he was taken by the Romans to be 'the opposite of Jupiter', i.e. harmful. His festival was on 21 May.

Vege'tius (Flāvius Vegetius Renātus), military writer under the emperor Theodosius (AD 379–95). His *Epitoma rei militaris* ('military epitome') is a compilation of material from many periods but aims to describe and advocate the training and organization of the classic Roman legion.

Veii, Etruscan town captured by Rome in 396 BC.

Vellē'ius Pate'rculus, Gaius (*c*.19 BC–after AD 30), Roman historian. He served for several years with the army in Germany, was quaestor in AD 7 and praetor in AD 15. He was the author of a compendium of Roman history from earliest times to AD 29 in two books, the first of which (down to 146 BC) is incomplete. The history shows partiality for the imperial house of the Caesars and enthusiasm reaching adulation for Tiberius. The work is not profound (he admits that he wrote hurriedly), but his interest is in individuals and the work is especially valuable for its biographical sketches, e.g. that of Tiberius (which is in strong contrast with the picture given by Tacitus) and on a small scale those of Caesar, Pompey, and Maecenas. The history is notable also for its chapters on the evolution of Latin literature. He discusses the reasons for its decline and suggests that the perfection reached in the Augustan age had driven later writers in despair to seek minor fields. The style of the history is artificial and rhetorical, but some of his epigrams are acute.

venatiō'nēs ('huntings'), at Rome, fights of men against animals or animals against animals, introduced in 186 BC as entertainment, and frequently occurring in the first century BC as part of the various public games. How long these spectacles continued is uncertain, but they were taking place after the abolition of gladiatorial shows, and still existed at Constantinople as late as the sixth century AD.

Vēnus, originally an Italian goddess of whom virtually nothing is known; her name means 'charm', 'beauty', and she seems to have presided over the fertility of vegetable gardens. In Rome at an early date she became identified with and acquired the mythology of the Greek goddess *Aphroditē, the goddess of love, through the cult of Aphrodite on Mount Eryx in Sicily which, according to tradition, had been founded by Aeneas after the death of his father Anchisēs. Venus of Eryx (Venus Erycina) had a temple on the Capitoline hill in Rome dedicated in 217 BC at a dire moment in the Second Punic War, and another outside the Colline Gate. Aeneas was the son of Aphrodite/Venus; the story of his wanderings and final settlement in Italy was particularly important to the Julian family (of which Julius Caesar and the emperors down to and including Nero were members) because it was claimed that they were descended from Aeneas' son Iulus (Ascanius) and so from Venus. Julius Caesar, in gratitude to her for his success at the battle of Pharsalus, dedicated a temple to Venus Genetrix, 'universal mother', in 46 BC in the Forum Iulium. It is this aspect of Venus that *Lucretius extols at the beginning of his poem, *De rerum natura*, and that is celebrated in the *Pervigilium Veneris* written for the spring festival. Venus was also thought of as concerned in the origin of the Roman people as the consort of *Mars. 'Venus' was the name given to the highest throw at dice.

Venu'sia (Venosa), town on the river Aufidus in Apulia, south Italy, near the border of Lucania, famed as the birthplace of Horace.

Vēra histo'ria, see LUCIAN.

Vercinge'torix, king of the Gallic tribe of the Arverni who in 52 BC raised a revolt in Gaul against Rome and was eventually defeated by Julius Caesar. See COMMENTARIES 1 (book 7). He surrendered and was brought to Rome for Caesar's triumph in 46 BC before being put to death (see TULLIANUM).

Vergil, see VIRGIL.

Verginia, see VIRGINIA.

Verrēs, Gaius, Roman propraetor in Sicily 73–71 BC. He plundered the province for his personal enrichment, in a way that was typical of many Roman governors of the time but perhaps more thoroughgoing than most. He must have expected to survive a prosecution in the *repetundae* (extortion) courts, with the help of bribery, powerful allies, and Q. *Hortensius to defend him, but he was defeated by the oratorical and legal genius of *Cicero (see (1) 1) whose *Ver-*

rine Orations have made Verres' crimes notorious. He retired to Massilia and kept much of his plundered treasures. These later attracted the greed of Mark Antony, and Verres was proscribed and murdered in 43.

ver sacrum ('sacred spring'), in ancient Italy (and apparently in some parts of Greece also), at a time of great emergency, the dedication to a god, often Jupiter, of all that was born in the spring. The animals were sacrificed, and the children born then (*sacrani*), when aged 20, were expelled from the country to go where they pleased and found a new community. The ceremony (without the expulsions) was revived at Rome during the Second Punic War in 217 BC, together with many other religious acts in that desperate year (see VENUS). The progeny of the pigs, sheep, goats, and oxen in the ensuing spring was dedicated to Jupiter (Livy 22. 10).

verse. As well as having the obvious meaning of poetry in general, 'verse' in the context of Latin and Greek poetry usually means 'metrical line', rarely 'stanza'.

Vertu'mnus, see VORTUMNUS.

Vespae, see WASPS.

Vespā'sian (Titus Flavius Sabinus Vespasianus) (AD 9–79), Roman emperor 69–79, the first of the Flavians. He came from a humble background and rose in the army through sheer ability; he was responsible for the pacification of southern Britain in the invasion of AD 43. After the death of Nero in 68, there was a chaotic period in which Galba, Otho, and Vitellius briefly ruled, but Vespasian (who was in Judaea leading the war against the Jews) was declared emperor by his troops, and after defeating and killing Vitellius was recognized by the senate—the first emperor not to come from an aristocratic family. He was a sound and just ruler, though firm (see HELVIDIUS PRISCUS), remarkable for the simplicity of his life and the economy and efficiency of his administration. Among his public works at Rome were the *Colosseum (completed by his son and heir Titus), the reconstruction of the temple of Jupiter Capitolinus, and a temple to

Peace (after his victory over Jerusalem), thought by the Elder Pliny to be one of the most beautiful buildings in the world.

Vesta, in Roman religion, the ancient Roman goddess of the hearth, the etymological and religious equivalent of the Greek goddess Hestia (but unaffected by Greek influence). She was worshipped at the hearth in every Roman household, and since the state cult was based on family cult the sacred fire on the symbolic hearth of the state was kept burning, in a small round temple in the Forum. This fire was rekindled every year on 1 March (the ancient New Year's Day), by rubbing two sticks together, and was looked after for the rest of the year by the *Vestal Virgins. The round temple of Vesta was thought to have represented the original round house and hearth of the king of Rome in ancient times, and the Vestals his daughters. In the temple was the storehouse, *penus*, of the state (see PENATES), where sacred objects were kept including the *Palladium, and generally only the Vestals and the *pontifex maximus* were allowed to enter. On 9 June each year for the festival of Vesta, the Vestālia, it was opened to married women, who walked barefoot to it in procession, bringing simple food-offerings. This festival was also regarded as the bakers' holiday; asses were freed from the treadmill and decked with garlands and little cakes. From 9 to 15 June the temple stood open, a time of ill-omen while the building was cleaned. 15 June was marked in the calendar (*Q(uando) St(ercus) D(elatum) F(as)*, which meant that it was a normal working day 'when the dirt has been lawfully cleaned away'.

Vestal Virgins, in Roman religion, virgins who were considered to represent the daughters of the early Roman kings and whose duty it was to watch in turn, by day and night, the fire in the temple of *Vesta on the state hearth. They also made the salt cake (*mola salsa*) for various festivals and had custody of a number of sacred objects including the *Palladium and the ashes for the Parilia (see PALES). The Vestals, said to have been instituted by the king Numa, and originally drawn from patrician families, were four (later six) in number, chosen by the *pontifex maximus* from suitable girls aged between 6 and 10. Their period of service was for thirty years, but generally the Vestals continued to serve the goddess for the rest of their lives. They lived in a house near the Forum known as the Atrium Vestae ('hall of Vesta') and were maintained at public expense. They were under the control of the *pontifex maximus* and could be scourged for offences such as letting the fire out. Their purity was all-important: any Vestal found guilty of unchastity was entombed alive. A letter of the Younger Pliny (4. 11) describes such an event under the emperor Domitian. Vestals were held in high repute, and great weight was attached to their intervention on behalf of those in trouble. They wore a linen dress of old-fashioned style.

Via A'ppia, see Appian Way.

Via Sacra, the Sacred Way, the street connecting the Forum with Velia (a narrow ridge joining the Palatine and Oppian hills). Its name is derived from the sacred buildings, including the temple of Vesta and the Regia, which it passed. There Horace famously encountered his Bore (*Satires* 1. 9).

Vidula'ria ('wallet'), title of a play by *Plautus surviving in a *palimpsest of which only fragments are legible. The plot appears to have resembled that of the *Rudens.

vi'gilēs, at Rome, the fire-brigade, instituted by the emperor Augustus after a fire of 23 BC. After another fire in AD 6 he created a corps of 7,000 freedmen under the command of a *praefectus vigilum* appointed by the emperor.

Vīnā'lia, two festivals held at Rome in connection with wine-production, the *Vinalia priora* ('first V.') on 23 April and the *Vinalia rustica* ('country V.') on 19–20 August. At the first the wine casks which had been filled the preceding autumn were opened, the first draught being offered as a libation, called *calpar*, to Jupiter. It supposedly had its origins in Aeneas' vowing the vintage to Jupiter if he won the war against Turnus. The second festival inaugurated the grape harvest. Lambs were sacrificed to Jupiter, and the *flamen dialis* broke off the first grapes.

Vi'rbius, see DIANA.

Virgil (Publius Vergilius Maro) (70–19 BC), Roman poet, born at Andēs near Mantua (Mantova) in Cisalpine Gaul. According to ancient sources which may not be altogether reliable his father was quite rich but of humble origins, his mother perhaps well-connected. He was educated at Cremona and Mediolānum (Milan), and later studied philosophy and rhetoric at Rome; at some time he was a pupil of the Epicurean philosopher Sīro at Naples. His family estate suffered loss, it was said, in the confiscations of land for the army veterans of Antony and *Octavian which followed the battle of Philippi in 42 BC, but he was on friendly terms with the commissioners for the redistribution of the confiscated lands (*Gallus, *Varus, and *Pollio), and may have been given a property near Naples in recompense. It was around 42 BC when he began the composition of the *Eclogues*. Pollio was the first to recognize Virgil's talents, but with the publication of the *Eclogues* (perhaps finally in 37) Virgil moved from the circle of Pollio to the patronage of *Maecenas (to whom he introduced Horace) and Octavian. At this time he lived chiefly in Campania, at Naples and Nola. In 37 Horace records their journey together to Brundisium (*Satires* 1. 5). He spent the following seven years in the composition of the *Georgics*, published in 29 BC, and immediately afterwards began on the *Aeneid*, which was to occupy him for the remaining ten years of his life. In his last year he undertook a voyage to the East to visit some of the places he had described; he fell ill at Megara in Greece and returned to Italy, dying at Brundisium. His body was brought to Naples and buried outside the city, where his tomb was soon honoured as a shrine. He is said to have dictated the inscription for it on his death-bed:

*Mantua me genuit, Calabri rapuere, tenet nunc
Parthenope: cecini pascua, rura, duces.*

'Mantua brought me life, Calabria death; now Naples holds me: I sang of flocks and farms and heroes.' (For the name Parthenopē see SIRENS.)

The *Aeneid* was incomplete at the author's death, and Virgil is said to have made Varius promise to burn it if he died before his return, but on the orders of Augustus it was published after the literary executors Varius and Tucca had 'lightly corrected' it.

The *Eclogues*, *Georgics*, and *Aeneid* are described under those titles. A number of minor poems attributed to the poet are collected in the *Appendix Virgiliana*.

Virgil is described by *Donatus as tall and dark, with the appearance of a countryman. His health was weak, he was shy and led a retired life, rarely appearing in Rome. Although he became famous during his lifetime, he was diffident of his own poetic powers. His fame was based primarily on his position as the epic poet who revealed the greatness of the Roman empire, but his poetic eminence rests also on the technical perfection of his verse and its sustained beauty and melodiousness, and on the poet's tenderness and melancholy, and his love of nature. He is the poet not only of the destiny of Rome but of the beauty and fertility of Italy, its morality and its religion.

Virgil's fame grew after his death into superstitious reverence. In the first century AD his birthday (15 October) was celebrated and his works and tomb were almost the object of cult by *Silius Italicus. He came to be regarded as a magician and miraculous powers were attributed to him. The *sortēs Virgiliānae*, 'Virgilian lots', attempts to foretell the future by opening his books and picking a line at random, were widely practised from an early date (reputedly as early as the emperor Hadrian). Memoirs of King Charles I relate that when the king was in the Bodleian Library at Oxford during the Civil War he sought his future by this method and hit upon Dido's curse against Aeneas (*Aeneid* 4. 615), *At bello audacis populi vexatus et armis* . . ., 'harassed by war and the hostility of a bold nation . . .'. Virgil's works soon became one of the most widely used of school books and the subject of commentaries and learned discussion by Donatus, *Servius, *Macrobius, and others. Early Christian writers often reveal a conflict in their minds between admiration for his poetry and distrust of his paganism (see JEROME). The number and high quality of the manuscripts surviving from the third to the fifth centuries AD attest the high estimation in which he was then held. His ideas were made acceptable to Christians by allegory (book 2 signifying the trauma of birth, book 6 the acquisition of enlightenment, for example), this kind of interpretation persisting even in the thirteenth century in Dante (although not in the *Divine Comedy*). The widespread feeling that only mischance prevented Virgil from dying a Christian is expressed in the legend that the apostle Paul wept over his tomb at Naples, described by an anonymous poet at Paris in the twelfth or thirteenth century:

> *'quem te', inquit, 'reddidissem*
> *si te vivum invenissem*
> *poetarum maxime.'*

> 'What would I have made of you, greatest of poets,' he said, 'had I found you alive!'

Dante regarded Virgil not only as *il nostro maggior poeta* ('our greatest poet'), but as a prophet of Christianity, who guided him to the Gates of Paradise but had himself to be excluded. Several translations preceded John Dryden's famous version of the whole of Virgil in 1697. Alfred Lord Tennyson in his lines 'To Virgil' (1882), for the nineteenth centenary of his death, paid a tribute to him as 'Wielder of the stateliest measure / Ever moulded by the lips of man'. In the twentieth century he is perhaps not so much thought of as the composer of melodious lines as the poet who understood that 'at the heart of things there are tears', *sunt lacrimae rerum* (*Aeneid* 1. 462).

Virgi'nia (Verginia), according to Roman tradition, daughter of L. Verginius, a centurion, around 450 BC when the *decemvirs had been appointed at Rome to publish a code of laws (see TWELVE TABLES). Appius Claudius, one of the decemvirs, intended to seduce her and in order to get her into his possession had one of his dependants claim her as a slave belonging to his own household;

Appius Claudius himself pronounced judgement in the case, in favour of his dependant. Before Virginia could be taken away her father stabbed her to death, declaring that her death was better than her dishonour, and made his escape to the army camp. A rising followed in which the decemvirs were overthrown and more democratic procedures instituted. The story is told by Livy (3. 44) and retold by Petrarch and by Chaucer in *The Physician's Tale*.

Visigoths, i.e. west *Goths, a Germanic tribe which in the late third century AD occupied Dacia, north of the Danube. They were driven across that river by the Huns in 376, and in 378 they killed the Roman emperor Valens at the great battle of Adrianople. After devastating Greece they invaded Italy in 401 under their leader *Alaric and again in 403, but were driven back. In 410, however, they sacked Rome itself; it was the first occasion the city had been entered by an enemy since the Gallic invasion of 390 BC. Later they moved to Gaul and Spain. In the sixth century most of those in Gaul were driven out and retreated to Spain. There the Visigothic kingdom survived until it was overrun by the Arabs in 711. In the fourth century the Visigoths were converted to Arian Christianity, and became Catholics in the late sixth century. See FALL OF ROME.

Vision, The, see LUCIAN.

Vita'rum au'ctio, see LUCIAN.

Vite'llius, Aulus (AD 15–69), Roman emperor, the last of three (following Galba and Otho) who ruled briefly in 69 before order was restored by Vespasian. He was notorious for his gluttony.

Vitru'vius Po'llio, Roman engineer and architect of the first century BC, who saw military service under Julius Caesar. He wrote a treatise in ten books, *De architectura* ('on architecture'), dedicated to the emperor Augustus. Compiled partly from his own experience and partly from similar works by earlier architects, mostly Greek, it is the only treatise of its kind to have survived. Although it was fairly well known in manuscript copies in the Middle Ages, it was not until the Renaissance that it assumed great importance, becoming adopted as the supreme architectural authority (in spite of the frequent obscurity of the text). The first printed edition appeared *c*.1486, the first illustrated edition in 1511. The term 'Vitruvian man' refers to his theory of human proportion, in which the human figure is shown to fit into a square circumscribed by a circle (illustrated by Leonardo da Vinci).

Book 1 of *De architectura* deals with town planning, architecture in general, and the qualifications necessary for an architect; 2, building materials; 3 and 4, temples and the 'orders' of *architecture; 5, theatres (and their acoustics), baths, and other public buildings; 6, domestic architecture; 7, interior decoration, *mosaic pavements, decorative plasterwork, and the use of colouring; 8, water supplies; 9 includes geometry, astronomy, mensuration, etc., with interesting remarks about water-clocks; 10, machines, civil and military.

Volcā'tius Gallicā'nus, see HISTORIA AUGUSTA.

Volsci, tribe of central Italy, who spoke an Italic dialect resembling Umbrian. By 500 BC they had moved to an area southeast of Rome; three important Volscian towns were Arpinum (birthplace of Cicero), Antium, and Tarracina (Volscian name, Anxur). They were a threat to the independence of Rome, which Rome met by making alliances with the Latins. The exploits of *Coriolanus relate to this time. By the end of the fourth century BC the Volscians were subject to Rome and they rapidly became Romanized.

Voltu'rnus, see TIBERINUS.

Volu'mnia, wife of *Coriolanus.

Vopi'scus, Flavius, see HISTORIA AUGUSTA.

Vortu'mnus (or Vertumnus), Roman god of orchards and fruit, who presided over the changes of the year. He was regarded as the husband of *Pomona, whom he wooed in a succession of various forms, reaper, ploughman, pruner, etc. His name, connected with *vertere*, 'to turn', was explained variously, as of the god who changes his shape, or who presides over the 'turn' of the year (autumn), or who once turned back a flood of the Tiber.

Voyage to the Lower World, see LUCIAN.

Vulcan (Volcānus), early Roman deity, the god of fire, perhaps a god of the smithy, later identified with the Greek god *Hephaestus. His festival of 23 May coincided with the *Tubilustria, and there was another festival in his honour on 23 August. He was the patron deity of Ostia, where he had an important cult.

Vulgate (Lat. *editio* or *lectio vulgāta*, 'the common text').

1. In textual criticism, the version of an author's text in general circulation (not necessarily the most accurate or authentic; see TEXTS, TRANSMISSION OF ANCIENT 4).

2. The Latin version of the Bible most widely used in the West, largely the work of St *Jerome. Its various books came to be collected into a single Bible (probably in the sixth century), with the following constituent parts: Jerome's translation from the Hebrew of the Old Testament, except for the Psalms (see SEPTUAGINT); the Psalms, translated by Jerome earlier from the text of *Origen (the 'Gallican Psalter'); Jerome's translation of Tobit and Judith, and the rest of the Apocrypha in the Old Latin (unrevised) version; Jerome's revision of the Gospels, for which he used a Greek text; and a revised text of Acts, Epistles, and Revelation, not by Jerome. *Cassiodorus writing in the sixth century is the first to refer unambiguously to a collection of biblical books within one cover. The oldest extant manuscript of the Vulgate is the Codex Amiatinus (Biblioteca Laurenziana, Florence), written at Wearmouth or Jarrow between *c*.690 and 700.

W

Wasps (*Sphēkēs*, Lat. *Vespae*), comedy by *Aristophanes, produced in 422 BC at the *Lenaea, where it won second prize.

The play is a satire on the system of the jury courts at Athens which at that time provided, through payment for jury service, an important means of support for a sizeable number of poor and elderly men who were Athenian citizens. Philocleon ('love-*Cleon') is consumed by a passion for serving on juries. His son Bdelycleon ('loathe-Cleon') has tried to cure him and has finally imprisoned him in his house. Philocleon's friends, the chorus of old jurymen, dressed as wasps to show their readiness to inflict punishment, come along before dawn to take him with them to the courts, and try to effect his escape. There is a scuffle, and Bdelycleon eventually persuades the chorus to listen while he urges his father to change his ways. A debate follows between father and son, the father dwelling upon the pleasures and benefits of exercising power irresponsibly, the son demonstrating that the jurors' power is an illusion; they are really manipulated by the politicians, who divert the city's revenues for their own ends. The chorus are converted, but Philocleon is reluctant, and as consolation Bdelycleon arranges for him to play the juror at home, the first to be tried being Labēs, the house dog, who has stolen a cheese. Tricked by his son, Philocleon unintentionally acquits the prisoner, the first that he has ever let off. Bdelycleon now takes in hand his father's social life, polishing his manners for the more relaxed pleasures of a dinner party (see SYMPOSIUM). Philocleon takes to this with gusto and returns drunk and in high spirits with a kidnapped slave-girl, and followed by threatening tradespeople whom he has assaulted on the way home. Bdelycleon is dismayed, but the play ends in a riotous dance, *cordax, led by Philocleon. Racine imitated the *Wasps* in *Les Plaideurs*.

weights and measures

1. *In Greece*

(i) *Units of weight*. In Greece, units of weight had the same names as units of *money (since these latter denote weights of metal), thus

6 obols	= 1 drachma	(4.31 g.)
100 drachmas	= 1 mina	(431 g.
		454 g. = 1 lb.)
60 minas	= 1 talent	(25.86 kg., about 57 lbs.)

(ii) *Units of length*. These were based primarily on parts of the human body, with the foot as the fundamental unit. Fractions of a foot and a few longer measures were reckoned in fingers (*daktyloi*) as follows:

16 fingers	= 1 *pous* (foot)	
24 ,,	= 1 *pēchys* (cubit, elbow to fingertips)	
27 ,,	= 1 'royal' cubit	
Multiples of feet were:-		
2½ feet	= 1 *bēma* (pace)	
6 ,,	= 1 *orguia* (a stretch of both arms, a fathom)	
100 ,,	= 1 *plethron*	

(An area 100 feet square, the Greek 'acre', representing the amount of land which could be ploughed in one day in Greece, was also known as a *plethron*.) The later Greek unit the *stadion* (*stade) is equivalent to 600 Greek feet; the *parasang (*parasangēs*), consisting of 30 stades, was adopted from Persia.

The Greek foot as used in building measured 294–6 mm. and the Olympic foot (as used in the running track at Olympia) 320 mm. (the modern foot is 305 mm.). The stade may therefore be taken to be 192 m. (210 yards).

2. *At Rome*

(i) *Units of weight*. The Roman units of weight were based on the pound, *libra* (or *as*), their highest weight, equivalent to 327 g. (about ¾ lb). It was subdivided into 12 ounces (*unciae*, 'twelfth parts', each roughly equivalent to the ounce avoirdupois), and the ounce was subdivided down to the *scrīpulum* ('scruple'), its 24th part.

(ii) *Units of length*. The Roman foot, *pes* (pl. *pedēs*), was sometimes divided into 16 fingers (*digiti*), as in the Greek system but more usually into 12 inches (*unciae*, 'twelfth parts'). The other units were:

    5 feet = 1 *passus* (pace)
    126 paces = 1 *stadium* (stade)
    1,000 paces = *mille passus*, 1 (Roman) mile

The Roman foot measured 296 mm. (about ⅓ inch less than the modern) and the mile 1480 m. (about 140 yards less than the modern mile).

winds, wind gods. The winds were thought of as gods by both Greeks and Romans. In Homer the winds are sometimes under the control of *Aeolus, sometimes independent, invoked by men with prayer and sacrifice, or acting under the orders of Zeus. They had well-defined personalities, particularly (in Greece) Boreas, the North Wind, and Zephyrus, the West Wind. Hesiod speaks of three winds, Boreas, Zephyrus, and Notus (the South Wind), the children of Astreaus and Eos. Four, including the East Wind, Eurus, are found in Homer. The 'Tower of the Winds' at Athens, built in the first century BC and still in good condition, depicts eight winds in human form; in compass order they are (in their Greek forms) Boreas, Kaikias, Apēliōtēs, Euros, Notos, Lips, Zephyros, Skīrōn.

In Italy the West Wind, Favonius, was the favourite. The name of the North Wind, Aquilo ('eagle'), suggests the idea of the wind as a mighty bird. Sacrifices were made to the winds where necessary (compare IPHIGENEIA). At Rome there was a temple to the Tempestatēs or weather-goddesses where sacrifices were offered. White animals were sacrificed to the beneficent winds, black animals to the stormy winds. See TYPHOEUS.

Works and Days (*Erga kai hēmerai*), Greek poem in 828 hexameters by *Hesiod; the 'works' are the activities of the farming year, the 'days' (from line 765 onward) are an almanac of days in the month that are favourable or unfavourable for different activities. No reason is given for the category of a particular day except for the implication that Zeus has ordained it so. Lucky or unlucky days are scarcely mentioned again until Hellenistic times.

The chief themes of the poem are justice and the need for hard work. After an invocation to the Muses the poet addresses his brother Persēs, urging him to a reconciliation of their quarrel (see HESIOD). To explain why men have to work hard and act justly he uses myth: *Prometheus and the story of Pandora, the five ages or generations (*Golden, Silver, Bronze, Heroic, and Iron), and the fable of the hawk and the nightingale, illustrating the unjust use of power; the whole is blended with proverbs, moral maxims, and threats of divine anger. In the remaining two thirds of the poem Hesiod gives Perses instructions on how to work as a farmer, which are mostly an enumeration of the tasks of the various seasons with some practical advice, for example on how to construct a plough; there is a fine descriptive passage on the rigours of winter (504–35), balanced by a picture of the farmer enjoying the languorous heat of summer (582–96). There follow some brief advice on sea trading, a collection of proverbial maxims about religious and social conduct, and the almanac of lucky and unlucky days. The poem is a work of exhortation and instruction, for which parallels exist, but in Near Eastern literature rather than in Greek; the poems of *Phocylidēs and *Theognis are comparable in tone, but much more limited in scope. *Works and Days* is given unity chiefly by the personality of the author. Whether the circumstances of its composition are real or imaginary, the poem represents the life-experience of a cautious and conservative farmer, inured to hardship and adversity, suspicious of pleasure, and no lover of women, but one who by reflection had come to believe that the conditions of life were divinely and justly ordained.

writing, writing materials, see ALPHABET and BOOKS AND WRITING 5.

X

Xanthi'ppē, wife of *Socrates.

Xanthi'ppus. 1. Father of *Pericles. In the *Persian Wars he commanded the Athenian fleet after the battle of Salamis and in 479 BC at the battle of Mycalē, where he had a large share in the victory. He had earlier married Agaristē, niece of Cleisthenēs (2) and a member of the *Alcmaeonidae whose political ally he was. He had been ostracized in 484, but recalled at the time of the invasion by Xerxes.

2. A Spartan who, in the course of the First Punic War, reorganized and commanded the Carthaginian defence force in Africa and in 255 BC inflicted a crushing defeat on the Romans under *Regulus.

Xanthus, of Lydia, see LOGOGRAPHERS (1).

Xeno'cratēs, head of the *Academy 339–314 BC.

Xeno'phanēs, of Colophon, in Ionia, an early Greek philosopher who spent most of his long life wandering in Greek lands, chiefly perhaps in Sicily. His own words, written when he was 92, indicate that he was born c.570, and he is said to have lived on to the time of Hieron (tyrant of Syracuse 478–467 BC). According to tradition he was the teacher of *Parmenidēs, and thus in some sense connected with the origins of *Eleatic philosophy. He is said to have written a poem in hexameters on the foundation of Colophon and the colonization of Elea (in *Magna Graecia), but the surviving fragments of his writings are either from his satirical *Silloi or from occasional elegiac poems. He was not an original philosopher, but the fragments, dealing with theological or physical matters, indicate that he thought deeply about religion and the gods. He was well known for his revolutionary attack on the polytheism and anthropomorphism of the traditional Greek religion, and on the immoral stories about the gods found in Homer and Hesiod. His god is single and eternal, in no way resembling men, effecting things by mind alone. This radical monotheism was new in Greek thought. From the presence of sea shells in the mountains and the impression of a fossil fish and of seaweed in the Syracusan quarries, Xenophanes deduced that the land was once covered with water, and infers that it may be so again. In other fragments he shows the same radical approach to accepted opinions, denouncing athletic success in the games as of less value than his own intellectual achievement.

Xe'nophon. 1. (c.428–c.354 BC), Greek historian and disciple of Socrates. He was an Athenian, son of Gryllus, and had two sons Gryllus and Diodorus. As a knight (see HIPPEIS) and an associate of the aristocratic circle of young men around Socrates, he may have found life difficult in Athens during the oligarchic revolution and the democratic restoration (see FOUR HUNDRED and THIRTY TYRANTS), and he left in 401. At the invitation of his Boeotian friend Proxenus he joined the expedition of *Cyrus the Younger, described in his *Anabasis*. After having extricated the Ten Thousand from this failed adventure by his own determination and military skill, he accepted service in 396 with the Spartan king *Agesilaus to whom he became strongly attached, against the Persian Pharnabazus. When Agesilaus was recalled by events in Greece Xenophon accompanied him and was present (perhaps as a non-combatant) on the Spartan side at the battle of Coronea, against Athens and Boeotia, in 394. Already it seems he had been banished from Athens and his property confiscated. The Spartans provided him with an estate at Scillus near Olympia, and elected him the Spartan *proxenos for the entertainment of Spartans visiting Olympia. Here he spent the next twenty years, enjoying the country life and writing his books. In 371 Elis claimed Scillus and Xenophon retired to Corinth. The decree of his banishment from Athens was revoked, probably *c*.368. When the Athenians were expelled from Corinth in 366 he returned to Athens; his two sons fought in the Athenian contingent on the Theban side at the battle of Mantinea in 362 and the elder, Gryllus, was killed.

Xenophon wrote on numerous subjects suggested by his varied experience (see individual titles). Socrates' personality made a profound impression on him and he wrote three books of recollections, *Memorabilia*, *Apology*, and *Symposium*. However, he has no real grasp of philosophy and seems to have misunderstood Socrates as profoundly as he admired him. (It is related that Socrates first met Xenophon, then a boy, in the street, and stopping him asked where various articles could be got. Xenophon told him. Socrates then asked, 'Where can you get brave and virtuous men?' and when Xenophon was puzzled told him to come with him.) *Oeconomicus* was inspired by his home life; *Anabasis* and *Cyropaedia* by his experiences in Persia; his treatises *The Cavalry Commander*, *Horsemanship*, and *Cynegeticus* by his military career and devotion to sport; *Hellenica*, *Agesilaus*, *Constitution of the Lacedaemonians*, *Hieron*, and *Revenues*, by his acquaintance with political affairs in various countries. The *Constitution of the Athenians*, preserved among his works, is certainly not by him. As a historian Xenophon sometimes omits matters of importance and is guilty of taking sides. On military and sporting matters he is an expert and an enthusiast and writes engagingly. He was a pious man, possessed of great common sense, an easy, lucid, and agreeable writer. Quintilian speaks warmly of his unaffected charm.

2. Of Ephesus, see NOVEL.

Xerxēs (*c*.519–465 BC), king of Persia from 486 BC, the son and successor of *Darius the Great. In 480 he launched a huge invasion of Greece (see *Persian Wars), leading his army over the Hellespont on a bridge of boats. (The first attempt was a failure because a storm destroyed the boats, and Xerxes had the sea whipped in punishment.) He also had a canal cut across the promontory of Mount Athos to spare his fleet a dangerous piece of navigation. The Persians sacked Athens, but after his crushing defeat at Salamis Xerxes returned home. He was assassinated by a member of his court.

Xūthus (Xouthos). In Greek myth, the ancestor of the Ionians and Achaeans. He is presented either as the son of Hellen and brother of Dorus and Aeolus (see HELLENES and DEUCALION), or as the son of Aeolus (see ION).

Y

'**year of the four emperors**', AD 69, when, following the death of Nero in 68, three emperors (Galba, Otho, and Vitel-lius) briefly held power before order was restored by Vespasian (ruled 69–79).

Z

Za'greus, see DIONYSUS ZAGREUS.

Zama, Battle of, in Numidia in 202 BC, the final defeat of Hannibal by Scipio Africanus to end the Second *Punic War.

Zēno (Zēnōn). **1.** Of Elea (c.490–after 445 BC), Greek philosopher. Little is known of his life except that he was a disciple of *Parmenidēs and thus belonged to the so-called *Eleatic school of Greek philosophy which believed that the basic matter of the universe is single, indivisible, and unchanging. He seems to have written, in support of this belief and against those who made fun of it, a book of philosophical paradoxes which reduce to absurdity the supposition that plurality and motion exist. (Because of his method he was called by Aristotle the inventor of *dialectic.) Only two of his forty arguments against plurality have survived, and the essence of these can be summarized as follows. If there are many things, they must be both limited and unlimited in number (which is absurd): limited, because they are as many as they are; unlimited, because things are only two in number when they can be distinguished from one another, i.e. when they are separated; but things are only separated where there is something in between; that in turn must be separated by two intervening things from those it originally separated, and so on *ad infinitum*.

Of his four arguments (according to Aristotle) against the possibility of motion, the most famous is the paradox of Achilles and the tortoise. If a tortoise is given a start in a race against Achilles, Achilles will never be able to overtake it because when he arrives at the tortoise's starting point it will have moved ahead to a new position, and when he reaches that position the tortoise will again have moved ahead, and so on indefinitely. On this basis the tortoise must always be ahead, by however small a margin. The simplest and usual explanation of fallacy in the argument is that while it takes Achilles an infinite number of these increments of distance to catch the tortoise, their sum, i.e. the total distance required, is in fact finite. Nevertheless, the argument raises questions about the ideas of infinity and divisibility which are philosophically important, and formal refutation is not a trivial matter. One of Zeno's other arguments against motion similarly divides the distance to be covered by an athlete in the stadium into the geometrical series $\frac{1}{2} + \frac{1}{4} + \frac{1}{8} + \ldots$ and asserts that the distance, having an infinite number of divisions, can never be covered, and therefore motion is impossible. It is an argument of the same nature as that of Achilles and the tortoise.

Zeno appears in the dialogue *Parmenides* of Plato.

2. Greek philosopher of Citium in Cyprus (c.333–262 BC), and founder of the *Stoic school, regarded by his contemporaries as of Phoenician stock.

Zēno'bia, widow, successor, and perhaps murderer in AD 266 or 267 of Odaenathus, ruler of Palmyra, a city state in Syria which from the second century AD had enjoyed the protection of successive Roman emperors. She embarked on wars of expansion; in 269 she conquered Egypt and in 270 overran Asia Minor except Bithynia. When in 271 she proclaimed her son Augustus (for the title see AUGUSTUS, THE) the emperor Aurelian reoccupied Asia Minor and after a series of battles captured Palmyra, the queen herself, and her sons. Palmyra was utterly destroyed, but the queen, having been exhibited in Aurelian's *triumph, was granted a pension and a villa at Tibur. See also LONGINUS, CASSIUS.

Zēno'dotus, of Ephesus, scholar at Alexandria, pupil of Philetas of Cos, who became the first head of the *Alexandrian Library c.285–c.270 BC. He is reputed to have divided Homer's *Iliad* and *Odyssey* into twenty-four books each, and to have worked on the text, perhaps even produced an edition. He seems also to have worked on the lyric poets. Traces of his critical work and views survive in the Homeric *scholia.

Ze'phyrus, in Greek myth, the personification of the west wind, sometimes said to be the husband of Iris, goddess of the rainbow. By the *Harpy Podargē he became the father of Achilles' horses Xanthus and Balius. See WINDS, FLORA, and HYACINTHUS.

Zētēs, see CALAIS.

Zēthus, see ANTIOPE.

zeugma, see SYLLEPSIS.

Zeus, in Greek myth and religion, the supreme god, the youngest (according to Homer the eldest) son of *Cronus whom he overthrew and succeeded. His name indicates an Indo-European origin, being found in the Indic sky-god Dyaus pita, the Roman Jupiter, the German Tuesday, Latin *deus*, 'god', *dies*, 'day', and Greek *eudia*, 'fine weather'. For the Greeks he is the god of weather rather than of the 'bright sky' of day. According to his Homeric epithets he is the cloudgatherer, the thunderer on high, hurler of thunderbolts. He was born in Crete, according to what is probably the oldest myth, or was born in Arcadia and brought to Crete, where he was hidden in a cave on Mount *Dictē or Mount *Ida and fed by the goat *Amalthea. The *Curētēs, in order to conceal him, drowned his cries by their noisy ritual. (The Cretans also had a peculiar myth of Zeus dead and buried.) After the overthrow of Cronus, Zeus and his brothers divided the universe by casting lots, Zeus obtaining the heavens, Poseidon the sea, and Hadēs the underworld. Zeus dwells on the tops of mountains where the storm clouds gather, on Mount *Lycaeus in Arcadia, or Mount Ida near Troy, or on Mount Olympus, the highest mountain in northern Thessaly. The thunderbolt, which only he commands, signifies his irresistible power, over other gods as well as men, and it enabled him to defeat the *Titans, the *Giants, and *Typhoeus. Thus it is Zeus who must be supplicated to grant victory in war. He is the protec-

tor of political freedom, Zeus Eleutherios ('liberator'), or Sōtēr ('saviour'), and festivals were instituted in his honour. After the Greek victory at Plataea in 479 BC (see PERSIAN WARS) a sanctuary for Zeus Eleutherios and the festival of the *Eleutheria were instituted.

Zeus is the only Greek god to have as children other powerful gods, Apollo, Artemis, Hermēs, Dionysus, Athena, and Persephonē. By his wife Hera he was the father only of Arēs, Hebē, and Eileithyia. The mother of *Athena, Mētis (Wisdom), was fated to have a second child more powerful than its father, and so Zeus swallowed her, thereafter combining supreme power and wisdom within himself. His mortal children included Heracles, Helen, Perseus, Epaphos, Minos, and the brothers Amphion and Zethus (see also DIOSCURI). Zeus is called 'the father of gods and men' and had perhaps been so addressed since Indo-European times, although he is not the father of all the gods and did not create men (for stories about the creation of men see DEUCALION and PROMETHEUS). Epithets added to his name indicate his particular roles: he is father in the sense of ruler and protector, defender of the house (Herkeios), of the hearth (Ephestios), of the rights of hospitality (Xenios and Hikēsios), of oaths (Horkios), and the guardian of property (Ktēsios), his image set up in the store room. He is also the protector of law and morals; in that capacity the poet Hesiod invokes him in *Works and Days, and represents the goddess of justice, Dikē, as enthroned beside him. The impartiality of his judgements is represented by Homer in the *Iliad* in the image of Zeus holding golden scales in his hand; as Achilles and Hector fight, the fall of a pan indicates that Hector is doomed. Zeus has the power, if he wishes, to save Hector whom he loves, as he might have saved his own son *Sarpedon, but it is men's 'fate' (*moira*) or 'portion' (*aisa*) to die, and Zeus does not overrule the apportionment (see FATE).

Zeus is also called Chthonios, 'of the Earth'. Sometimes the phrase simply stands for Hades or Pluto, the god of the Underworld; the sky god is not meant.

More often the phrase signifies Zeus whose all-embracing power extends into the earth as well, from whom the growth of crops is expected. Apart, however, from general overseership given by his position of supremacy, Zeus had little to do with the day to day concerns of men, war, agriculture, crafts, etc.; but the wide scope of his functions made him unique in his importance to all Greece. His festival at *Olympia asserted his supreme position and the essential unity of all who worshipped him. To participate in his festival was to be a Hellene; the admission of the Macedonians and later of the Romans were events of great political significance. His universality, of which the beginnings are apparent in Aeschylus, paved the way for the later philosophical pantheism of the *Stoics. He corresponds to, and was identified with, the Roman *Jupiter.

Zeus confūtā' tus, see LUCIAN.

Zeuxis, of Heraclea in *Magna Graecia, one of the most famous painters of ancient Greece, working in the late fifth century BC. One of his most celebrated paintings was a picture of Helen (of Troy) for the temple of Hera at Croton. He is said to have assembled the five most beautiful maidens of the city and combined the best features of each into one figure of ideal beauty. For another famous anecdote about him see PARRHASIUS.

Zmyrna, short Latin epic poem in hexameters on the myth of Myrrha and *Adonis by C. Helvius *Cinna (c.70–44 BC). Only three lines survive. It was worked on by its author for nine years, and seems to have typified the influence of *Alexandrianism on Roman poetry. Catullus predicted immortality for it.

Zō'ilus, of Amphipolis, *Cynic philosopher, rhetorician, and critic of the fourth century BC, also perhaps a sophist, who earned notoriety for the bitterness of his attacks on Isocrates, Plato, and especially Homer, earning himself the name of Homēromastix, 'scourge of Homer', by his nine books of criticism. He found fault with Homer mainly on points of invention (such as the description of the companions of Odysseus 'weeping' when turned into swine), but also on points of grammar. His name became proverbial for a carping critic.

Zo'simus (late fifth century AD), Greek historian, author of an extant history, in Greek in four books, of the Roman empire from Augustus to AD 410 (the sack of Rome by the Visigoths). Book I summarizes the events of the first three centuries, books 2–4 give a fuller account of the fourth century, and particularly of the years 395–410, for which he is the most important source. Being a pagan he attributes the decline of the empire to the rejection of the pagan gods.

OXFORD

MORE OXFORD PAPERBACKS

This book is just one of nearly 1000 Oxford Paperbacks currently in print. If you would like details of other Oxford Paperbacks, including titles in the World's Classics, Oxford Reference, Oxford Books, OPUS, Past Masters, Oxford Authors, and Oxford Shakespeare series, please write to:

UK and Europe: Oxford Paperbacks Publicity Manager, Arts and Reference Publicity Department, Oxford University Press, Walton Street, Oxford OX2 6DP.

Customers in UK and Europe will find Oxford Paperbacks available in all good bookshops. But in case of difficulty please send orders to the Cash-with-Order Department, Oxford University Press Distribution Services, Saxon Way West, Corby, Northants NN18 9ES. Tel: 01536 741519; Fax: 01536 746337. Please send a cheque for the total cost of the books, plus £1.75 postage and packing for orders under £20; £2.75 for orders over £20. Customers outside the UK should add 10% of the cost of the books for postage and packing.

USA: Oxford Paperbacks Marketing Manager, Oxford University Press, Inc., 200 Madison Avenue, New York, N.Y. 10016.

Canada: Trade Department, Oxford University Press, 70 Wynford Drive, Don Mills, Ontario M3C 1J9.

Australia: Trade Marketing Manager, Oxford University Press, G.P.O. Box 2784Y, Melbourne 3001, Victoria.

South Africa: Oxford University Press, P.O. Box 1141, Cape Town 8000.

OXFORD PAPERBACK REFERENCE

From *Art and Artists* to *Zoology*, the Oxford Paperback Reference series offers the very best subject reference books at the most affordable prices.

Authoritative, accessible, and up to date, the series features dictionaries in key student areas, as well as a range of fascinating books for a general readership. Included are such well-established titles as Fowler's *Modern English Usage*, Margaret Drabble's *Concise Companion to English Literature*, and the bestselling science and medical dictionaries.

The series has now been relaunched in handsome new covers. Highlights include new editions of some of the most popular titles, as well as brand new paperback reference books on *Politics*, *Philosophy*, and *Twentieth-Century Poetry*.

With new titles being constantly added, and existing titles regularly updated, Oxford Paperback Reference is unrivalled in its breadth of coverage and expansive publishing programme. New dictionaries of *Film*, *Economics*, *Linguistics*, *Architecture*, *Archaeology*, *Astronomy*, and *The Bible* are just a few of those coming in the future.

THE OXFORD DICTIONARY OF PHILOSOPHY

Edited by Simon Blackburn

* **2,500 entries covering the entire span of the subject including the most recent terms and concepts**

* **Biographical entries for nearly 500 philosophers**

* **Chronology of philosophical events**

From Aristotle to Zen, this is the most comprehensive, authoritative, and up to date dictionary of philosophy available. Ideal for students or a general readership, it provides lively and accessible coverage of not only the Western philosophical tradition but also important themes from Chinese, Indian, Islamic, and Jewish philosophy. The paperback includes a new Chronology.

'an excellent source book and can be strongly recommended . . . there are generous and informative entries on the great philosophers . . . Overall the entries are written in an informed and judicious manner.'
Times Higher Education Supplement

Oxford
Paperback
Reference

THE CONCISE OXFORD DICTIONARY
OF POLITICS

Edited by Iain McLean

Written by an expert team of political scientists from Warwick University, this is the most authoritative and up-to-date dictionary of politics available.

* Over 1,500 entries provide truly international coverage of major political institutions, thinkers and concepts

* From Western to Chinese and Muslim political thought

* Covers new and thriving branches of the subject, including international political economy, voting theory, and feminism

* Appendix of political leaders

* Clear, no-nonsense definitions of terms such as veto and subsidiarity

Oxford
Paperback
Reference

THE CONCISE OXFORD COMPANION
TO ENGLISH LITERATURE

*Edited by Margaret Drabble and
Jenny Stringer*

Derived from the acclaimed *Oxford Companion to
English Literature*, the concise maintains the wide
coverage of its parent volume. It is an indispensable,
compact guide to all aspects of English literature.
For this revised edition, existing entries have been
fully updated and revised with 60 new entries added
on contemporary writers.

* **Over 5,000 entries on the lives and works of
  authors, poets and playwrights**

* **The most comprehensive and authoritative
  paperback guide to English literature**

* **New entries include Peter Ackroyd, Martin
  Amis, Toni Morrison, and Jeanette Winterson**

* **New appendices list major literary prize-
  winners**

From the reviews of its parent volume:

'It earns its place at the head of the best sellers: every
home should have one'
Sunday Times

CONCISE SCIENCE DICTIONARY
New edition

Authoritative and up to date, this bestselling dictionary is ideal reference for both students and non-scientists. Fully revised for this third edition, with over 1,000 new entries, it provides coverage of biology (including human biology), chemistry, physics, the earth sciences, astronomy, maths and computing.

* **8,500 clear and concise entries**

* **Up-to-date coverage of areas such as molecular biology, genetics, particle physics, cosmology, and fullerene chemistry**

* **Appendices include the periodic table, tables of SI units, and classifications of the plant and animal kingdoms**

'handy and readable . . . for scientists aged nine to ninety'
Nature

'The book will appeal not just to scientists and science students but also to the interested layperson. And it passes the most difficult test of any dictionary—it is well worth browsing through.'
New Scientist

Oxford
Paperback
Reference

THE CONCISE OXFORD DICTIONARY
OF MUSIC

New Edition

Edited by Michael Kennedy

Derived from the full *Oxford Dictionary of Music* this is the most authoritative and up-to-date dictionary of music available in paperback. Fully revised and updated for this new edition, it is a rich mine of information for lovers of music of all periods and styles.

* **14,000 entries on musical terms, works, composers, librettists, musicians, singers and orchestras.**

* **Comprehensive work-lists for major composers**

* **Generous coverage of living composers and performers**

'clearly the best around . . . the dictionary that everyone should have'
Literary Review

'indispensable'
Yorkshire Post

Oxford
Paperback
Reference

THE CONCISE OXFORD DICTIONARY
OF OPERA

New Edition

Edited by Ewan West and John Warrack

Derived from the full *Oxford Dictionary of Opera*, this is the most authoritative and up-to-date dictionary of opera available in paperback. Fully revised for this new edition, it is designed to be accessible to all those who enjoy opera, whether at the opera-house or at home.

* **Over 3,500 entries on operas, composers, and performers**

* **Plot summaries and separate entries for well-known roles, arias, and choruses**

* **Leading conductors, producers and designers**

From the reviews of its parent volume:

'the most authoritative single-volume work of its kind'
Independent on Sunday

'an invaluable reference work'
Gramophone